D1614648

Property and Conveyancing Library

SNELL'S EQUITY

AUSTRALIA
The Law Book Company
Sydney

CANADA
The Carswell Company Ltd.
Toronto, Ontario

INDIA
N. M. Tripathi Private Ltd.
Bombay

Eastern Law House (Private) Ltd.
Calcutta

M.P.P. House
Bangalore

Universal Book Traders
Delhi

ISRAEL
Steimatzky's Agency Ltd.
Tel Aviv

PAKISTAN
Pakistan Law House
Karachi

PROPERTY AND CONVEYANCING LIBRARY

SNELL'S EQUITY

TWENTY-NINTH EDITION

BY

P. V. BAKER
Q.C., B.C.L., M.A.
A Bencher of Lincoln's Inn
A Circuit Judge

AND

P. St. J. LANGAN
Q.C., M.A., LL.B., Ph.D.
of Lincoln's Inn
A Recorder of the Crown Court

LONDON
SWEET & MAXWELL
1990

First Edition	(1868)	By Edmund Henry Turner Snell
Second Edition	(1872)	By J. R. Griffith
Third Edition	(1874)	By J. R. Griffith
Fourth Edition	(1878)	By Archibald Brown
Fifth Edition	(1880)	By Archibald Brown
Sixth Edition	(1882)	By Archibald Brown
Seventh Edition	(1884)	By Archibald Brown
Eighth Edition	(1887)	By Archibald Brown
Ninth Edition	(1889)	By Archibald Brown
Tenth Edition	(1892)	By Archibald Brown
Eleventh Edition	(1894)	By Archibald Brown
Twelfth Edition	(1898)	By Archibald Brown
Thirteenth Edition	(1901)	By Archibald Brown
Fourteenth Edition	(1905)	By Archibald Brown
Fifteenth Edition	(1908)	By Archibald Brown
Sixteenth Edition	(1912)	By Archibald Brown
Seventeenth Edition	(1915)	By H. Gibson Rivington and A. Clifford Fountaine
Eighteenth Edition	(1920)	By H. Gibson Rivington and A. Clifford Fountaine
Nineteenth Edition	(1925)	By H. Gibson Rivington and A. Clifford Fountaine
Twentieth Edition	(1929)	By H. Gibson Rivington and A. Clifford Fountaine
Twenty First Edition	(1934)	By H. Gibson Rivington
Twenty Second Edition	(1939)	By H. Gibson Rivington
Twenty Third Edition	(1947)	By R. E. Megarry
Twenty Fourth Edition	(1954)	By R. E. Megarry and P. V. Baker
Twenty Fifth Edition	(1960)	By R. E. Megarry and P. V. Baker
Second impression, revised	(1963)	By R. E. Megarry and P. V. Baker
Twenty Sixth Edition	(1966)	By R. E. Megarry and P. V. Baker
Twenty Seventh Edition	(1973)	By R. E. Megarry and P. V. Baker
Twenty Eighth Edition	(1982)	By P. V. Baker and P. St.J. Langan
Twenty Ninth Edition	(1990)	By P. V. Baker and P. St.J. Langan
Second impression	(1991)	By P. V. Baker and P. St.J. Langan

Published by
Sweet & Maxwell Ltd. of
South Quay Plaza, 183 Marsh Wall, London E14 9FT
Computerset by P. B. Computer Typesetting, Pickering, N. Yorks.
Printed and bound in Great Britain by Hartnolls Ltd., Bodmin

British Library Cataloguing in Publication Data

Baker, P. V. (Paul Vivian)
Snell's equity.—29th ed.
1. England. Law. Equity
I. Title   II. Langan, P. St. J. (Peter St. John)   III.
Snell, Edmund Henry Turner *1841–1969*.
Snell's principles of equity
344.20604

ISBN 0–421–42790–6

©
Sweet & Maxwell Ltd.
1990

PREFACE

THE doctrines of equity continue to show great vitality, none more than those relating to what have long been designated as resulting, implied or constructive trusts. These hallowed labels have long resisted precise definition and in this edition we have attempted a new classification between informal (or non-express) trusts based on intention, and those imposed by law. This has required a substantial rewriting and re-arrangement of the former text. The related subject of equitable estoppel has also been extensively revised, as have the sections on undue influence, equitable accounting and interlocutory injunctions, including *Mareva* orders. All this and much else has been brought about by the unremitting flow of reported decisions. Statutes, too, have had their impact. The Law of Property (Miscellaneous Provisions) Act 1989 has seen off, for the time being at least, the doctrine of part performance. The Charities Act 1985 has improved the administration, though not touching the definition, of charity. Above all the Insolvency Act 1986 has necessitated the complete rewriting of the sections on setting trusts aside and on the order of payment of the debts of insolvent estates. In short, we have endeavoured to take account of all developments to the date of this preface.

We are grateful to Mr. Rhys Jones of the Middle Temple, Barrister, for preparing the Index and to the publishers for preparing the Tables of Cases and Statutes.

P.V.B.
P.St..J.L.

Lincoln's Inn
September 17, 1990

CONTENTS

TABLE OF CASES

TABLE OF STATUTES

TABLE OF STATUTORY INSTRUMENTS

1. General

2. RULES OF COURT

ABBREVIATIONS

A.E.A.	Administration of Estates Act.
Austr.L.J.	Australian Law Journal.
B.S.	Building Society.
C.A.	Conveyancing Act.
C.I.R.	Commissioners of Inland Revenue.
C.L.J.	Cambridge Law Journal.
Can.B.R.	Canadian Bar Review.
Col.L.R.	Columbia Law Review.
Conv.(N.S.)	The Conveyancer and Property Lawyer, New Series (Vol. 1–41).
Conv.	The Conveyancer and Property Lawyer, New Series (1978–date).
E.G.D.	Estates Gazette Digest.
Harv.L.R.	Harvard Law Review.
Holdsworth H.E.L.	Holdsworth's History of English Law.
I.R.C.	Inland Revenue Commissioners.
J.A.	Judicature Act (Supreme Court of Judicature Act).
J.S.P.T.L.	Journal of the Society of Public Teachers of Law.
K. & E.	Key and Elphinstone's Precedents in Conveyancing (15th ed., 1953).
L.C.A.	Land Charges Act.
L.P.A.	Law of Property Act.
L.P.Am.A.	Law of Property Amendment Act.
L.Q.R.	Law Quarterly Review.
L.R.A.	Land Registration Act.
L.T.A.	Land Transfer Act.
Mich.L.R.	Michigan Law Review.
M.L.R.	Modern Law Review.
R.S.C.	Rules of the Supreme Court.
S.C.A.	Supreme Court Act.
S.E.	Settled Estate(s).
S.I.	Statutory Instrument.
S.L.A.	Settled Land Act.
S.R. & O.	Statutory Rule and Order.
S.S.	Selden Society.
S.T.	Settlement Trust(s).
T.A.	Trustee Act.
Toronto L.J.	University of Toronto Law Journal.
W. & T.L.C.	White and Tudor's Leading Cases in Equity (9th ed., 1928).
W.T.	Will Trust(s).
Yale L.J.	Yale Law Journal.

INTRODUCTION

THE arrangement of a book on equity is a matter of some difficulty. The nature of equity, as providing a supplement and a corrective to the common law, makes it necessarily a system which is neither comprehensive nor orderly. Nevertheless, there is a coherence of ideas and approach which is illustrated by the maxims of equity; and it is necessary to examine the basic concepts before turning to the details.

Accordingly, this book has been divided into seven parts. In the first part, the nature and history of equity are briefly considered; the nature of equities is examined; and after the maxims of equity, dealings with equities are discussed. The next three parts cover the three main substantive fields of equity jurisdiction, namely, trusts, the administration of assets, and securities (in particular, mortgages). The five ancient equitable doctrines of conversion, reconversion, election, performance and satisfaction come next; and then there are the cases in which equity has intervened to protect those who, by their status or their circumstances, are in need of protection. Last, there is the wide range of equitable remedies.

It will be observed that this scheme does not include every sphere of equity's activities. For example, the important subject of restrictive covenants is excluded, and so is partnership. Omissions such as these are made not on any ground of principle but merely for convenience. No book on real property or land law could properly exclude restrictive covenants; and with their kinship to easements they are far better examined as an integral part of land law. Again, partnership, much of which is now statutory, is habitually taught as a separate subject, and there are separate books on it. But apart from exceptions such as these, this book surveys the whole field of equity.

Part I

EQUITY AND EQUITIES

CHAPTER 1

THE NATURE, HISTORY AND COURTS OF EQUITY

Section 1. Nature of Equity

1. "Equity." Some attempt must be made to define the subject-matter of this book. In its broad popular sense equity is practically equivalent to natural justice or morality; yet it would be a mistake to suppose that the principles of equity as administered in the courts and described in this book are coextensive with the principles of natural justice. Owing to the difficulty and doubtful wisdom of framing and enforcing any general rules to cover them, many matters of natural justice are not subject to legal sanctions but are left to the dictates of public opinion or to the conscience of each individual. Thus, in dismissing a claim against a company director who had perpetrated a sharp but not illegal practice, Fry L.J. was constrained to say, "If we were sitting in a court of honour, our decision might be different."[1]

2. Enforcement. Nevertheless, by far the greater portion of natural justice is enforced by legal sanctions administered by the courts. Lord Romilly M.R. was hardly exaggerating when he said, "The legal duty, in this instance, as I believe it is in all cases where it is fully understood and examined, is identical with the moral duty."[2] Yet when the rules of natural justice enforced by the courts are examined, it will be seen that many of them are rules of the common law, many others statutory, and some are derived from ecclesiastical and other sources. Only a small fraction of the whole can be said to be rules of equity in the technical sense.

3. Evolution. Equity is thus a body of rules or principles which form an appendage to the general rules of law, or a gloss upon them. In origin at least, it represents the attempt of the English legal system to meet a problem which confronts all legal systems reaching a certain

[1] *Re Cawley & Co.* (1889) Ch.D. 209 at 236.
[2] *Cooper* v. *Jarman* (1866) L.R. 3 Eq. 98 at 102; see *post*, p. 323.

stage of development. In order to ensure the smooth running of society it is necessary to formulate general rules which work well enough in the majority of cases. Sooner or later, however, cases arise in which, in some unforeseen set of facts, the general rules produce substantial unfairness.[3] When this occurs, justice requires either an amendment of the rule or, if (as in England[4] some five or six centuries ago) the rule is not freely changeable, a further rule or body of rules to mitigate the severity of the rules of law. This new body of rules (or "equity") is therefore distinguishable from the general body of law, not because it seeks to achieve a different end (for both aim at justice), nor because it relates necessarily to a different subject-matter, but merely because it appears at a later stage of legal development.

A classic eighteenth century statement is that "Equity is no part of the law, but a moral virtue, which qualifies, moderates, and reforms the rigour, hardness, and edge of the law, and is a universal truth; it does also assist the law where it is defective and weak in the constitution (which is the life of the law) and defends the law from crafty evasions, delusions, and new subtilties, invented and contrived to evade and delude the common law, whereby such as have undoubted right are made remediless; and this is the office of equity, to support and protect the common law from shifts and crafty contrivances against the justice of the law. Equity therefore does not destroy the law, nor create it, but assist it."[5]

4. Dual meanings. "Equity" has therefore come to have a narrow and technical meaning in addition to its broad and popular sense.[6] Sometimes both are found in the same instrument, as in the former Courts Ordinance of the Gold Coast. This enacted that the courts there were to apply "the common law, the doctrines of equity, and the statutes of general application which were in force in England" on a certain date, and also empowered them to give effect to any native law or custom, "such law or custom not being repugnant to natural justice equity and good conscience."[7] Here the first phrase refers to equity in the narrow sense and the second to equity in its wide sense. And in modern English statutes, provisions relating to what is "equitable"[8] will usually be construed as merely referring to what is "fair."[9]

---

[3] On this dilemma, see Paton's *Text Book of Jurisprudence* (4th ed., 1972), pp. 230 *et seq.*; and see *Earl of Oxford's Case* (1615) 1 Rep.Ch. 1. at 6, 7; **1 W. & T.L.C. 615 at 617.**
[4] Roman law experienced a similar but not identical development: Lee's *Elements of Roman Law* (4th ed., 1956), pp. 10, 11; Buckland's *Equity in Roman Law* (1911).
[5] *Lord Dudley and Ward* v. *Lady Dudley* (1705) Prec.Ch. 241 at 244, *per* Sir Nathan Wright L.K.
[6] See *Rayner* v. *Preston* (1881) 18 Ch.D. 1 at 12.
[7] Laws of the Gold Coast (revised ed., 1954), cap. 4, ss.83, 87, re-enacting the Supreme Court Ordinance, 1876; later replaced by the Courts Act 1960, of Ghana: see ss.66, 67.
[8] See, *e.g.* Public Health Act 1875, s.268 (now Highways Act 1980, s.233); Landlord and Tenant (War Damage) Act 1939, s.15(3).
[9] See, *e.g. Westminster Bank Ltd.* v. *Edwards* [1942] A.C. 529 at 535; *Re Fitzhardinge's Lease* [1944] 2 All E.R. 145 at 148; and see *ibid.* [1945] Ch. 48 at 59, 60; *R.* v. *Minister of Housing and Local Government, ex p. Finchley Borough Council* [1955] 1 W.L.R. 29 at 31; *cf.* at p. 35.

5. Intervention by equity. Although in many cases equity intervened to put right an injustice, it must not be thought that every injustice was the subject of an equitable intervention. In truth, there was no certainty when equity would come into play. Sir William Blackstone, writing in the eighteenth century, gives several instances where "equity" failed to abate the rigour of the common law and remedy an obvious injustice. "Hard is the common law still subsisting, that land devised, or descending to the heir, shall not be liable to simple contract debts of the ancestor or devisor, although the money was laid out in purchasing the very land; and that the father shall never immediately succeed as heir to the real estate of the son: but a court of equity can give no relief; though in both these instances the artificial reason of the law, arising from feodal principles, has long ago entirely ceased."[10] Both these defects were subsequently remedied by statute.[11] Thus it is not possible to define equity solely in terms of natural justice: any definition must have regard to form and history as well as to substance or principle. There is much truth in the view that equity is an historical accident.

6. Morals and ethics. Matters of morals and ethics which are not directly enforceable as part of the rules of law or equity may nevertheless play an important part in the courts. Quite apart from the natural tendency of the courts to strain to uphold just claims and reject the unjust, even if the law appears to produce other results,[12] morals and ethics sometimes directly affect the decision of cases. Thus although a bequest will normally lapse if the legatee predeceases the testator, a legacy made in pursuance of a moral duty will not[13]; and in procedural matters, such as an application for leave to adduce fresh evidence, moral and ethical considerations may play a large part.[14]

<h3 style="text-align:center">Section 2. History of Equity[15]</h3>

1. The origins of equity

(a) *Common law.* The period from the Norman Conquest to the reign of Henry III in the thirteenth century witnessed the inception and rapid growth of the common law. This was administered by the King's justices on circuit and in the three common law courts of King's Bench,

---

[10] 3 Bl.Comm. 430.
[11] The former by A.E.A. 1833, *post*, pp. 311–313, the latter by the Inheritance Act 1833, now A.E.A. 1925.
[12] See, *e.g. Heap* v. *Ind, Coope & Allsopp Ltd.* [1940] 2 K.B. 476 at 483; *Strongman (1945) Ltd.* v. *Sincock* [1955] 2 Q.B. 525 at 538; *Powell* v. *Braun* [1954] 1 W.L.R. 401 at 406.
[13] *Stevens* v. *King* [1904] 2 Ch. 30; *Re Leach, Chatterton* v. *Leach* [1948] Ch. 232.
[14] See, *e.g. Sanders* v. *Sanders* (1881) 19 Ch.D. 373 at 381.
[15] The history of equity is dealt with in detail in Holdsworth's *History of English Law* and Kerly's *History of Equity*. Useful summaries are contained in Ashburner's *Principles of Equity*, Maitland's *Lectures on Equity*, and Potter's *Historical Introduction to English Law*.

Common Pleas and Exchequer. "The need of a separate court of equity is not yet felt, for the King's court, which is not yet hampered by many statutes or by accurately formulated 'case law,' can administer equity."[16] Thereafter the common law courts were fettered both by precedent and by the Provisions of Oxford, 1258, which restrained the Chancellor from issuing new types of writ of his own initiative.

(b) *Emergence of equity.* Although the common law still continued to develop, perhaps under the somewhat limited authority of chapter 24 of the Statute of Westminster II, 1285 (*In consimili casu*),[17] these fetters prevented it from developing fast enough to do justice in all cases. Moreover, in the rough days of the thirteenth century, a plaintiff was often unable to obtain a remedy in the common law courts, even when they should have had one for him, owing to the strength of the defendant, who would defy the court or intimidate the jury. Either deficiency of remedy or failure to administer it was a ground for petition to the King in Council to exercise his extraordinary judicial powers. A custom developed of referring certain classes of these petitions to the Chancellor, and this custom was confirmed by an Order of Edward III in 1349. The Chancellor acted at first in the name of the King in Council, but in 1474 a decree was made on his own authority, and this practice continued, so that there came to be a Court of Chancery as an institution independent of the King and his Council.[18]

(c) *Conscience.* In the Middle Ages the Chancellor's jurisdiction was undefined. His powers were wide but vague, and coextensive only with the necessity that evoked them. He exercised his powers on the ground of conscience. This appears to have been an importation from the canon law[19]; almost all the medieval Chancellors were ecclesiastics. "Conscience" was in theory based on universal and natural justice rather than the private opinion or conscience of the Chancellor. The principle seems to have been secularised during the sixteenth century, perhaps by Sir Christopher Hatton (Chancellor 1587–91); "conscience" became the Conscience of the Queen,[20] and the Chancellor was designated the Keeper of the Queen's Conscience. Yet this theoretical basis of the principle did not prevent the cynical gibe voiced by Selden (perhaps more in jest than in earnest) about the standards varying with each Chancellor, even as his foot.[21]

---

[16] Pollock & Maitland's *History of English Law* (2nd ed., 1898), Vol. 1, p. 190. For an account of equity during this period, see Allen's *Law in the Making* (7th ed., 1964), pp. 399–406.

[17] It is controversial how far the statute was responsible for this development: see C. H. S. Fifoot, *History and Sources of the Common Law: Tort and Contract* (1949), pp. 66 *et seq.*; S. F. C. Milsom, *Historical Foundations of the Common Law* (2nd ed., 1981), p. 284, collecting the literature.

[18] See Holdsworth, H.E.L., Vol. 1, pp. 400–404. On the court during the 15th century, see Margaret E. Avery (1970) 86 L.Q.R. 84.

[19] See H. Coing (1955) 71 L.Q.R. 223.

[20] 1 Spence's *Equitable Jurisdiction* (1846), p. 414; D. E. C. Yale (1957) 73 S.S. xl.

[21] See *Table Talk of John Selden* (ed. Pollock, 1927), p. 43.

2. The development of equity

(a) *New rules.* After England had been reduced to order by the Tudors with the aid of the Star Chamber, the Chancellor's power to give common law remedies disappeared. Though this period saw an expansion of the Chancellor's jurisdiction in several important directions,[22] *e.g.* the separate estate of married women,[23] the modern Rule against Perpetuities[24] and the rules of equitable waste,[25] its main feature was the consolidation and development of existing doctrines under the guidance of non-clerical Chancellors.

(b) *Principles.* These Chancellors were, for the most part, drawn from the ranks of the common lawyers, and thus conditions were favourable for the construction of a body of precedent.[26] Lord Ellesmere (1596–1617) began to apply the same principle in all cases, instead of following the inclination of the moment under the name of conscience, while Lord Nottingham (1673–82) was "stiled the Father of Equity,"[27] owing to the systematisation of rules under his Chancellorship.[28] Nevertheless, conscience as a basis of decision was still recognised, though it was becoming attenuated. Thus in 1676 Lord Nottingham remarked in a case where it was sought to establish a trust: "With such a conscience as is only *naturalis et interna*, this court has nothing to do; the conscience by which I am to proceed is merely *civilis et politica*, and tied to certain measures; and it is infinitely better for the public that a trust, security, or agreement, which is wholly secret, should miscarry, than that men should lose their estates by the mere fancy and imagination of a chancellor."[29]

(c) *Systematisation.* The work of systematisation begun by Lord Nottingham was continued by subsequent Chancellors, especially Lord Hardwicke (1737–56) and Lord Eldon (1801–27). The Court of Chancery itself, too, became more highly organised. The Master of the Rolls traditionally had the custody of the public records,[30] and from his close association with the Chancellor he began to assist him in his judicial duties. By the seventeenth century he had come to be the Chancellor's general deputy,[31] and a statute of 1729 established his

---

[22] *Re Hallett's Estate* (1880) 13 Ch.D. 696 at 710.
[23] See *post*, p. 533.
[24] See, *e.g.* Megarry & Wade's *Law of Real Property* (5th ed., 1984), pp. 240, 241.
[25] See *post*, pp. 679, 680.
[26] Though earlier reports exist, the first reliable reports of the decisions of the Chancellor are those by Peere Williams (1695–1736).
[27] *Kemp* v. *Kemp* (1795) 5 Ves. 849 at 858, *per* Arden M.R.
[28] For the general scope of Lord Nottingham's contribution, see *Lord Nottingham's Chancery Cases*, edited with introductions by D. E. C. Yale in two volumes for the Selden Society (1957, 1961).
[29] *Cook* v. *Fountain* (1676) 3 Swans. 585 at 600.
[30] The Public Records Act 1958 curtailed these duties.
[31] See Holdsworth, H.E.L., Vol. 1, pp. 418–421, 443, 444.

authority as an independent judge, subject to appeal to the Chancellor.[32] In 1813 the court was strengthened by the appointment of a Vice-
Chancellor; and two more were appointed in 1841 when the equitable
jurisdiction which had been retained by the Court of Exchequer was
transferred to the Court of Chancery.[33] In 1851 a Court of Appeal in
Chancery was established, consisting of two Lords Justices, or the Lord
Chancellor, or any two or all three of them.[34] What had begun as an
irregular process of petitioning the Crown in extraordinary circumstances had become a regular system of courts with a recognised
jurisdiction.

(d) *Rigidity.*   Systematisation has its price, however. "Gradually the
rules of equity themselves came to suffer the fate of rules of law, and
became stereotyped."[35] By the time Lord Eldon retired, the rules of
equity were as fixed as those of the common law: a *"rigor aequitatis"*[36]
had developed, and he could safely say: "The doctrines of this court
ought to be as well settled, and made as uniform almost as those of the
common law, laying down fixed principles, but taking care that they are
to be applied according to the circumstances of each case. I cannot
agree that the doctrines of this court are to be changed with every
succeeding judge. Nothing would inflict on me greater pain, in quitting
this place, than the recollection that I had done anything to justify the
reproach that the equity of this court varies like the Chancellor's
foot."[37]

Again, in 1948, the Court of Appeal said that if the claim[38] being
made did exist, "it must be shown to have an ancestry founded in
history and in the practice and precedents of the courts administering
equity jurisdiction. It is not sufficient that because we may think that the
'justice' of the present case requires it, we should invent such a
jurisdiction for the first time."[39] In view of this development a great
equity judge in 1878 could justifiably make the paradoxical remark:
"This court is not, as I have often said, a Court of Conscience, but a
Court of Law."[40] It is not for the court to pass judgment upon the
personal integrity, good taste or self-respect of the litigants if that is not
an issue in determining legal or equitable rights or liabilities.[41]

[32] 3 Geo. 2, c. 30, 1729. Yet he was still so much regarded as the Lord Chancellor's deputy that not
until June 22, 1829, did he sit at the same time as that at which the Lord Chancellor was sitting: see
Taml. xiii; C. P. Cooper, *Chancery* (1828), p. 350.
[33] 53 Geo. 3, c. 24, 1813; 5 Vict. c. 5, 1841, s.19. For the office and its holders, see R. E. Megarry
(1982) 98 L.Q.R. 370. On the equity jurisdiction of the Court of Exchequer, see *Tito* v. *Waddell
(No. 2)* [1977] Ch. 106 at 256–260 (Megarry V.-C.).
[34] 14 & 15 Vict. c. 83, 1851, ss.1–14.
[35] A. S. Diamond, *Primitive Law* (2nd ed., 1950), p. 349.
[36] Allen's *Law in the Making* (7th ed., 1964), p. 417.
[37] *Gee* v. *Pritchard* (1818) 2 Swans. 402 at 414.
[38] For the nature of the claim, see *post*, p. 358.
[39] *Re Diplock* [1948] Ch. 465 at 481, *per cur.*; affd. *sub nom. Ministry of Health* v. *Simpson* [1951] A.C.
251.
[40] *Re National Funds Assurance Co.* (1878) 10 Ch.D. 118 at 128, *per* Jessel M.R. Lévy-Ullmann's
English Legal Tradition (1935), p. 368 states that a dictum to the same effect by Buckley J. in *Re
Telescriptor Syndicate Ltd.* [1903] 2 Ch. 174 at 195, 196, "made a great sensation"; yet Buckley J.
was merely echoing words a quarter of a century old. See also *Re McArdle* [1951] Ch. 669 at 676,
per Evershed M.R., "But that is a matter for their conscience and not for this court."
[41] See *Re Telescriptor Syndicate Ltd., supra*, at pp. 195, 196.

(e) *Modern equity.* Even so, equity does not seem to be past the age of childbearing.[42] There has been at least one new invention since Lord Eldon's day, namely, the doctrine whereby the burden of restrictive covenants may run with the land.[43] Another doctrine, the "equity" of a deserted wife, made its appearance in 1952[44] but was ultimately rejected as an equitable interest in 1965.[45] Similarly, an attempt to elevate rights under contractual licences to the status of property rights protected by equity[46] has failed[47] save under the principles of constructive trusts.[48]

This has not prevented the extension of long-established doctrines, notably those of implied, resulting and constructive trusts,[49] of equitable estoppel,[50] and of the scope of injunctions.[51] In this the courts are returning to the principle of unconscionability where the detailed rules as previously refined have proved too restrictive.[52] What the court considers is the conscience of the defendant. It is no part of the role of the court to dissolve or vary contracts thought to be harsh on the basis of so-called equitable principles.[53] Its role is to prevent the defendant from insisting on his strict legal rights when, owing to his behaviour, it would be unconscionable or inequitable to allow him to do so.[54] The circumstances which may call for the intervention of equity cannot be stated precisely and exhaustively.[55] "Equity is not a computer. Equity operates on conscience but is not influenced by sentimentality."[56]

3. Procedural reforms

(a) *Disadvantages of separate courts.* The elaboration and expansion of the Chancellor's jurisdiction during the seventeenth, eighteenth and nineteenth centuries aggravated the inconvenience which flowed from the system of distinct courts of common law on the one hand and equity

---

[42] The phrase is Harman J.'s: see Megarry, *Miscellany-at-Law* (1955), p. 142; *Simpson's Motor Sales (London) Ltd.* v. *Hendon Corporation* [1964] A.C. 1088 at 1127 (one report substituted "child-beating": *The Times*, May 7, 1963); and see *National Provincial Bank Ltd.* v. *Ainsworth* [1965] A.C. 1175 at 1224.

[43] See *Tulk* v. *Moxhay* (1848) 2 Ph. 774. The rule was argued in *Duke of Bedford* v. *Trustees of British Museum* (1822) 2 My. & K. 552, and was established by *Whatman* v. *Gibson* (1838) 9 Sim. 196.

[44] *Bendall* v. *McWhirter* [1952] 2 Q.B. 466. The novelty produced a running debate between the bench and counsel recorded in the report.

[45] *National Provincial Bank Ltd.* v. *Ainsworth* [1965] A.C. 1175. See now Matrimonial Homes Act 1983, replacing Matrimonial Homes Act 1967.

[46] *Errington* v. *Errington and Woods* [1952] 1 K.B. 290.

[47] *Ashburn Anstalt* v. *Arnold* [1989] Ch. 1.

[48] *Ibid.* at pp. 21, 22; and see Megarry & Wade's *Law of Real Property* (5th ed., 1984), pp. 806–808.

[49] See *post*, p. 175.

[50] See *post*, p. 568.

[51] See *post*, p. 645.

[52] *Taylors Fashions Ltd.* v. *Liverpool Victoria Trustees Co. Ltd.* [1982] Q.B. 133n. has led the way: see *post*, p. 569. And see *Solle* v. *Butcher* [1950] 1 K.B. 671 at 695.

[53] *Campbell Discount Co.* v. *Bridge* [1961] 1 Q.B. 445 at 459, reversed on grounds not affecting this dictum: [1962] A.C. 600; see at p. 626.

[54] *Taylors Fashions Ltd.* v. *Liverpool Victoria Trustees Co. Ltd., supra*, at pp. 151, 152, 155; *Ashburn Anstalt* v. *Arnold* [1989] Ch. 1 at 22.

[55] *Amalgamated Investment & Property Co. Ltd.* v. *Texas Commerce International Bank Ltd.* [1982] Q.B. 84 at 103.

[56] *Winkworth* v. *Edward Baron Development Co. Ltd.* [1986] 1 W.L.R. 1512 at 1516, *per* Lord Templeman.

on the other. A Commission appointed in 1850 reported that extensive and deep-rooted mischiefs arose from this system of separate courts proceeding on diverse and sometimes antagonistic principles.[57] Often in the course of the same litigation parties were driven to and fro between courts of common law and courts of equity as no court had full power to grant complete relief.[58] The common law courts had no power to order specific performance and only a very limited power of granting injunctions, while the Court of Chancery usually could not give damages. A plaintiff who had obtained a judgment in his favour in a court of law might be prevented from enforcing it by a "common injunction" granted by the Court of Chancery, because in the opinion of the latter court he had obtained the judgment unfairly. This practice had earlier evoked the bitter hostility of the common law courts, until the dispute had finally been resolved in favour of the Court of Chancery by King James I after the *Earl of Oxford's Case*.[59]

(b) *Mitigation.* Some of these evils came to be mitigated by the courts of law themselves. By the nineteenth century, the courts of law would often themselves apply the rule in equity if that differed from the rule at law, in order to save the parties the expense of separate proceedings in equity; but this would be done only when it was plain in the proceedings at law what equity would do.[60] Other evils were mitigated piecemeal by statute. Thus the Common Law Procedure Act 1854[61] gave the common law courts a limited power of granting injunctions; and the Chancery Amendment Act 1858 (commonly called Lord Cairns' Act),[62] gave the Court of Chancery power to award damages either instead of, or in addition to, an injunction or specific performance.

(c) *Fusion.* These Acts, however, did not go to the root of the problem; that was left to the Judicature Acts 1873 and 1875,[63] which came into force on November 1, 1875.[64] The main purpose of the Acts was to amalgamate the superior courts into one Supreme Court of Judicature. The Courts of Queen's Bench, Exchequer and Common Pleas and the Court of Chancery, together with the Court of Exchequer Chamber and the Court of Appeal in Chancery, were all replaced by the Supreme Court, consisting of the Court of Appeal and the High Court, with five (later three) Divisions; and the Supreme Court was directed to

[57] Three reports were issued in 1851, 1852 and 1860 respectively: for references see Holdsworth H.E.L., Vol. 1, p. 636, n. 4.
[58] See, *e.g. Marquis of Waterford* v. *Knight* (1844) 11 Cl. & F. 653; *Moncton* v. *Att.-Gen.* (1848) 2 Mac. & G. 402 at 409.
[59] (1615) 1 Rep.Ch. 1 & App.; **1 W. & T.L.C. 615**; Holdsworth, H.E.L., Vol. 1, pp. 459–465.
[60] *Phillips* v. *Clagett* (1843) 11 M. & W. 84 at 91.
[61] s.79.
[62] See *post*, pp. 588, 656.
[63] Supreme Court of Judicature Acts 1873 and 1875, hereinafter referred to as the Judicature Acts. They were repealed and replaced by the Supreme Court of Judicature (Consolidation) Act 1925, hereinafter referred to as the Judicature Act 1925 ("J.A. 1925"), which was itself repealed and replaced by the Supreme Court Act 1981 ("S.C.A. 1981").
[64] Supreme Court of Judicature (Commencement) Act 1874, s.2.

administer both law and equity. The rules of equity remained distinct from those of law, but both systems were henceforth to be administered in the same courts. Thus it could be said that—

"The Courts that were manifold dwindle
To divers Divisions of one."[65]

Section 3. Content of Equity

1. Definition of equity. No satisfactory definition of equity in its technical sense can be evolved. It is possible to define equity as a portion of natural justice which, although of a nature suitable for judicial enforcement, was for historical reasons not enforced by the common law courts, an omission which was supplied by the Court of Chancery. Yet this is a lame and unsatisfying definition, which gives no indication either of the topics on which equity intervened or of the nature of that intervention. But the point need not be laboured; all that must be added here is that even where a rule of equity has become embodied in a statute, either unamended or in a revised form, it is usual to regard it as remaining part of the corpus of equity, despite its statutory guise and puissance. A trust is still a trust, even if it is created or imposed by statute. Moreover, where a general equitable jurisdiction has been developed, and Parliament steps in with legislation in a particular area, the general jurisdiction is not to be regarded as cut down or abrogated by implication.[66]

2. Classification before 1875. Prior to the Judicature Acts the main work of equity could be classified as follows.[67]

(a) *The exclusive jurisdiction: new rights.* First, equity enforced rights which the common law courts failed to enforce. Uses and trusts which have been protected since at least the fourteenth century, afford a good example of this jurisdiction, for these were matters which the common law courts could have dealt with, but did not. This was known as the exclusive jurisdiction.

(b) *The concurrent jurisdiction: new remedies.* Secondly, equity developed a wide range of remedies for the enforcement of common law rights which were available in addition to the remedies provided by the common law. These included specific performance of a contract, an injunction to restrain or stay the repetition of an injury, the appointment of a receiver to prevent a defendant from destroying or parting with property during the interval between the institution of

---

[65] Pollock, *Leading Cases Done into English* (1892), p. 57.
[66] *Shiloh Spinners Ltd.* v. *Harding* [1973] A.C. 691 at 724, 725 (relief against forfeiture).
[67] *Story on Equity* (3rd Eng. ed., 1920), p. 39.

proceedings and the trial of the action, or an order for an account. These and other remedies which were often necessary to ensure that complete justice was done to the plaintiff were not wholly unknown to the common law courts, but were mainly developed by equity in what was known as the concurrent jurisdiction. Nor did the common law courts always do justice to the *defendant*. A plaintiff who proved an infringement of his legal right was entitled at law to a general and unqualified judgment against the defendant, regardless of the circumstances of the infringement and his own conduct. But in equity there was no *right* to relief, and the plaintiff's conduct or the other circumstances of the case might lead equity to refuse any equitable remedy, even though the plaintiff had proved his case.

(c) *The auxiliary jurisdiction: new procedure.* In the third place, the procedure in the common law courts was defective. This appeared especially in not compelling or even allowing a defendant to give evidence, and in limiting the inquiry to the parties to the action, however great an interest other persons might have in the result of the action. Such persons could be added as parties to proceedings in the Court of Chancery. Finally, the common law courts could not compel discovery of documents. In all these matters, in its auxiliary jurisdiction, equity took a more liberal view.

This three-fold division of the subject was rendered obsolete by the Judicature Acts, which removed the necessity for one court to supplement the jurisdiction of another. As Lord Cairns put it, "The court is now not a court of law or a court of equity; it is a court of complete jurisdiction."[68]

3. Conflicts between law and equity

(a) *Specific cases.* As has been explained above, equity was basically a gloss or appendage to the common law and not a rival or competing system. The fusion of the administration of the two systems accordingly did not necessitate a wholesale modification of the rules either of law or of equity. Nevertheless certain rules of equity contradicted rather than complemented the rules of law and, where this occurred, the Judicature Act 1873, s.25, provided that equity should prevail. Nine[69] special cases of possible conflict were first dealt with. These were the following:

(i) The order of priority of payment of debts of a person dying insolvent.[70]

[68] *Pugh v. Heath* (1882) 7 App.Cas. 235 at 237; and see *Re Powell* (1888) 86 L.T. News 69, *per* Lord Coleridge C.J., in a scathing condemnation of a county court judge.
[69] The section (in subs.(9)) also resolved a conflict between Admiralty and common law rules, the administration of which was similarly fused by the Act.
[70] Subs. (1), replaced by J.A. 1875, s.10. See now Insolvency Act 1986, s.421 and Administration of Insolvent Estates of Deceased Persons Order 1986 (S.I. 1986 No. 1999), art. 4, replacing A.E.A. 1925, s.34(1), 1st Sched., *post*, pp. 323 *et seq.*

(ii)   The period of limitation applicable to claims against express trustees.[71]

(iii) The extent of the liability for waste committed by the owners of limited interests in land.[72]

(iv)   The rule that merger of estates depends on intent and is not automatic.[73]

(v)   The right of a mortgagor to bring an action for possession against a third person without joining the mortgagee.[74]

(vi)   The refusal of the common law but not of equity to recognise the assignment of debts and choses in action.[75]

(vii) The indulgence with which equity regarded the unpunctual compliance with stipulations not of the essence of contracts.[76]

(viii) The power of granting injunctions and appointing receivers.[77]

(ix)   The rules relating to the custody and education of infants.[78]

(b) *General provision.* In addition to these specific rules, which are dealt with in the appropriate passages of this book, the section ended with a general provision. "Generally in all matters not hereinbefore particularly mentioned, in which there is any conflict or variance between the Rules of Equity and the Rules of the Common Law with reference to the same matter, the Rules of Equity shall prevail."[79] As might be expected, it has not often been necessary to resort to this provision[80] but there have been some important instances. Four examples[81] may be taken.

(1) EQUITABLE LEASE. In *Walsh* v. *Lonsdale*,[82] Lonsdale agreed in writing (but not by deed) to grant a seven years' lease of a mill to Walsh at a rent payable quarterly in arrear, but with a year's rent payable in advance if demanded. Walsh entered into possession without any lease having been granted, and paid his rent quarterly in arrear. Subsequently Lonsdale demanded a year's rent in advance and, on Walsh refusing to pay, put in a distress. Walsh claimed an injunction and damages for illegal distress, on the ground that at law he was tenant from year to year at a rent not payable in advance, and that the legal remedy of distress was therefore not open to Lonsdale. The Court of Appeal

---

[71] Subs. (2). See now the Limitation Act 1980, s.21, *post*, p. 292.
[72] Subs. (3). See now L.P.A. 1925, s.135, *post*, p. 672.
[73] Subs. (4). See now L.P.A. 1925, s.185, *post*, p. 423.
[74] Subs. (5). See now L.P.A. 1925, s.98, *post*, pp. 407, 408.
[75] Subs. (6). See now L.P.A. 1925, s.136, *post*, pp. 72 *et seq.*
[76] Subs. (7) as amended by J.A. 1875, s.10. See now L.P.A. 1925, s.41, *post*, pp. 608 *et seq.*
[77] Subs. (8). See now S.C.A. 1981, s.37, *post*, pp. 646, 694.
[78] Subs. (10). See now *post*, p. 535.
[79] Subs. (11). See now S.C.A. 1981, s.49.
[80] See Evershed L.J. [1948] J.S.P.T.L. 171.
[81] See also *Gibbs* v. *Guild* (1882) 9 Q.B.D. 59; *Vibart* v. *Coles* (1890) 24 Q.B.D. 364.
[82] (1882) 21 Ch.D. 9. See also *Swain* v. *Ayres* (1888) 21 Q.B.D. 289; *Lowther* v. *Heaver* (1889) 41 Ch.D. 248; *Zimbler* v. *Abrahams* [1903] 1 K.B. 577; *Manchester Brewery Co.* v. *Coombs* [1901] 2 Ch. 608; and see *post*, p. 40.

decided, however, that Walsh held on the same terms as if a lease had been granted, since the agreement was one of which the court would order specific performance. "There are not," said Jessel M.R., "two estates as there were formerly, one estate at common law by reason of the payment of the rent from year to year, and an estate in equity under the agreement. There is only one court, and the equity rules prevail in it."[83]

(2) VARIATION OF DEED. In *Berry* v. *Berry*,[84] under a deed of separation a husband covenanted to pay his wife a certain allowance. Afterwards the parties made an agreement in writing not under seal reducing the allowance. An action brought by the wife to enforce the terms of the deed was dismissed on the ground that although at law a contract made by deed could be varied only by another deed, in equity a simple contract varying the terms of a deed was a good defence to an action brought on the deed; and the equity rule now prevailed. Hence only the reduced amount was payable.

(3) EXECUTOR'S LIABILITY FOR ASSETS. At law, an executor was liable for the loss of any assets of his testator when once they had come into his hands.[85] In equity, however, the executor was not liable for such assets if they were accidentally lost without fault on his part.[86] In *Job* v. *Job*[87] it was held that since the Judicature Acts the equitable rule is also the rule at law.

(4) CONTRIBUTION BETWEEN SURETIES. If A, B and C were sureties for the payment of £3,000, and A became insolvent, the rule at law was that the liability of B and C remained at the amount which they would have had to contribute if A had paid his share, namely, £1,000 each. But in equity, those who can pay their shares must also make good the share of those who cannot, and so B and C were liable for £1,500 each. In *Lowe & Sons* v. *Dixon & Sons*[88] it was held that the rule of equity now prevails.

(c) *Limits to the rule.* It is only on matters of principle that the equity rule prevails, and not on matters of practice. Where there was a difference in the practice of the two courts before the Judicature Acts, the more convenient practice is now followed.[89] Nor have the Acts abolished the distinction between legal and equitable rights,[90] or

---

[83] *Walsh* v. *Lonsdale, supra,* at p. 14. Even before J.A. 1873, equity would intervene by granting an injunction to prevent a landlord evicting the tenant in breach of agreement: see, *e.g. Browne* v. *Warner* (1807) 14 Ves. 156, 409. See Megarry & Wade's *Law of Real Property* (5th ed., 1984), pp. 640–645 for a full discussion.

[84] [1929] 2 K.B. 316.

[85] *Crosse* v. *Smith* (1806) 7 East 246.

[86] *Jones* v. *Lewis* (1751) 2 Ves.Sen. 240.

[87] (1877) 6 Ch.D. 562; and see *post*, pp. 354, 355.

[88] (1885) 16 Q.B.D. 455; *post*, p. 476.

[89] *Newbiggin Gas Co.* v. *Armstrong* (1879) 13 Ch.D. 310; *Harrison* v. *Duke of Rutland* [1893] 1 Q.B. 142 at 149; and see *J. Bollinger S.A.* v. *Goldwell Ltd.* [1971] R.P.C. 412 at 424.

[90] See *Gentle* v. *Faulkner* [1900] 2 Q.B. 267 at 274, 275.

between legal and equitable remedies.[91] A legal estate is still a legal estate and an equitable interest is still an equitable interest. It is still of great practical importance whether a right is one which was formerly recognised at law or only in equity. Thus a person who acquires a legal estate in property for value and without notice of another person's equitable interest therein takes free from that equitable interest; but if he acquires merely an equitable interest, he will usually be subject to the prior equitable interest, in spite of the fact that he has no notice of its existence and that he gives value.[92]

It is sometimes said that the Judicature Acts fused law and equity. "But it was not any fusion, or anything of the kind; it was the vesting in one tribunal the administration of Law and Equity in every cause, action, or dispute which should come before that tribunal."[93] It is a fusion of administration rather than of principles. As has been well said,[94] the two streams have met and now run in the same channel; but their waters do not mix.[95]

Section 4. Courts of Equity

The courts exercising equitable jurisdiction today are the Supreme Court of Judicature and the county courts. Formerly in addition to the Court of Chancery, the Court of Exchequer had a limited equity jurisdiction[96] and there were two special ancient courts, the Chancery Courts of Lancaster and of Durham.

1. The Supreme Court of Judicature. As already mentioned, in 1875 the Court of Chancery and the Court of Exchequer[97] and the other common law courts were replaced by the Supreme Court of Judicature. It is divided into the Court of Appeal and the High Court of Justice. The Chancery Courts of Lancaster and Durham survived until 1971 when they became merged in the High Court.[98]

(a) *The Court of Appeal.* The civil division of this court hears appeals from the High Court and the county courts.[99] Its judges are

---

[91] *Joseph* v. *Lyons* (1884) 15 Q.B.D. 280 at 285, 286; *Manchester Brewery Co.* v. *Coombs* [1901] 2 Ch. 608 at 617. *Cf. Re Coghlan* [1948] 2 All E.R. 68 (laches not applicable to probate proceedings). But see *Nelson* v. *Larholt* [1948] 1 K.B. 339 at 343.
[92] See, *e.g. Joseph* v. *Lyons* (1884) 15 Q.B.D. 280, and *Hallas* v. *Robinson* (1885) 15 Q.B.D. 288.
[93] *Salt* v. *Cooper* (1880) 16 Ch.D. 544 at 549, *per* Jessel M.R.; and see *Clements* v. *Matthews* (1883) 11 Q.B.D. 808 at 814, *per* Cotton L.J.
[94] Ashburner's *Principles of Equity* (2nd ed., 1933), p. 18.
[95] The doctrine of continued separation was vigorously attacked by Lord Diplock in the House of Lords in *United Scientific Holdings* v. *Burnley B.C.* [1978] A.C. 904 at 924, 925 (and see at pp. 944, 957). See, however, (1977) 93 L.Q.R. 529 (P.V.B.). And see *post*, pp. 608, 609.
[96] See *Tito* v. *Waddell (No. 2)* [1977] Ch. 106 at 256–260. The jurisdiction had been transferred in 1841: see *ante*, p. 10.
[97] There was a separate Exchequer Division until 1880 when it became merged in the Queen's Bench Division.
[98] Courts Act 1971, s.41.
[99] For accounts of the working of the Court of Appeal by three of its members, see Evershed M.R., *The Court of Appeal in England* (1950), Asquith L.J. [1950] J.S.P.T.L. 350, and Russell L.J., *The Lawyer and Justice* (1978), p.251 (address to the Holdsworth Club in 1969).

normally[1] the Master of the Rolls and the Lords Justices of Appeal, whose number is fixed at not more than 28.[2] The translation of the Master of the Rolls in 1881 from being a Chancery judge sitting at first instance[3] to being the virtual President of the Court of Appeal was due to the difficulty of finding members of the Court of Appeal of sufficient calibre to sit on appeals from the decisions of Jessel M.R.[4]

(b) *The High Court of Justice*

(1) ASSIGNED MATTERS.   For the more convenient dispatch of business the High Court is arranged in three Divisions, Chancery, Queen's Bench, and Family (formerly Probate, Divorce and Admiralty). Most of the equitable matters dealt with by the old Court of Chancery are assigned to the Chancery Division, while the Queen's Bench Division mainly deals with matters which formerly came before the common law courts. Thus the following matters are assigned to the Chancery Division by the Supreme Court Act 1981[5]:

(a)   The sale, exchange or partition of land, or the raising of charges on land;

(b)   The redemption or foreclosure of mortgages;

(c)   The execution of trusts;

(d)   The administration of the estates of deceased persons;

(e)   Bankruptcy;

(f)   The dissolution of partnerships or the taking of partnership or other accounts;

(g)   The rectification, setting aside or cancellation of deeds or other written instruments;

(h)   Probate business,[6] other than non-contentious or common form business;

(i)   Patents, trade marks, registered designs or copyright;

(j)   The appointment of a guardian of a minor's estate[7];

and all causes and matters involving the exercise of the High Court's jurisdiction under the enactments relative to companies.

[1] For the full judicial complement see S.C.A. 1981, s.2.
[2] S.C.A. 1981, s.2(1), as amended by Maximum Number of Judges Order 1987 (S.I. 1987 No. 2059), art. 2.
[3] J.A. 1881, s.2.
[4] Evershed M.R., *The Court of Appeal in England* (1950), p. 12.
[5] s.61, Sched. 1, para. 1, replacing with modifications J.A. 1925, s.56, which in turn replaced J.A. 1873, s.34. A direction of the Lord Chancellor dated April 13, 1973, under J.A., 1925, s.57 (see now S.C.A. 1981, s.61(3)), gives wide powers for a Division to which a matter is assigned to grant any remedy or relief connected with that matter even if proceedings for that remedy or relief are assigned to another Division: Practice Direction [1973] 1 W.L.R. 627. See *Midland Bank Ltd.* v. *Stamps* [1978] 1 W.L.R. 635.
[6] Originally added by Administration of Justice Act 1970, s.1, Sched. 2, para. 8.
[7] The Judicature Acts also assigned the wardship of infants to the Chancery Division, but on October 1, 1971, this work was transferred to the Family Division: Administration of Justice Act 1970, s.1, Sched. 1; S.I. 1971 No. 1244. See now S.C.A. 1981, Sched. 1, para. 3, and *post*, p. 535.

Further, the Rules of the Supreme Court assign to the Chancery Division every action in which there is a claim for payment of moneys secured by a mortgage of real or leasehold property, or a claim by the mortgagee against the mortgagor or any other person for possession of the property, whether before or after foreclosure.[8] And under various statutes, *e.g.* the Insolvency Act 1986 and the legislation relating to companies, the Chancery Division exercises the jurisdiction which these Acts give the High Court.[9] Many causes of action, however, are not expressly assigned to any division, and although in most cases it is plain which Division is the more appropriate, the choice between Chancery and the Queen's Bench (*e.g.* in landlord and tenant matters) sometimes depends upon little more than the plaintiff's counsel's sense of where the tactical advantage lies,[10] or even on the Division in which he usually practises. Further, where an action is brought in the wrong Division, or falls into more than one assigned category, the judge of the Division before whom it comes has a discretion whether to retain it or transfer it.[11]

(2) EFFECT OF DIVISION.   Thirteen judges of the High Court, headed by the Vice-Chancellor, are now normally assigned to the Chancery Division. One of these is mainly occupied with patents and similar matters, and the other twelve do the general work of the Division. In addition, a certain section of the Bar mainly confines itself to practice before that Division, and provides its judges. Moreover, the Division has a separate set of Masters recruited from the ranks of solicitors, unlike the Masters of the Queen's Bench Division who are drawn from the Bar.[12] These factors have had a tendency to retard the complete fusion of the administration of law and equity.[13] In general, however, the separation of the High Court into Divisions is merely a matter of convenience, for all jurisdiction vested in the High Court belongs to all the Divisions alike.[14] Each Division constitutes not a separate court, but merely a part of one court, namely, the High Court.[15] Every judge of every Division must recognise and give effect to all equitable rights, obligations and defences, and (subject to the supremacy of equity) to all legal rights and obligations; and he must grant all such remedies as the parties may be entitled to in respect of any legal or equitable claim, so

[8] R.S.C., Ord. 88, r. 2. But the County Courts Act 1984, ss.21(1), (3), 147(1) confers exclusive jurisdiction on county courts in possession cases for dwelling-houses outside Greater London with an annual value not exceeding £1,000.
[9] In *Re H. W. Baker* [1936] Ch. 61, Farwell J., sitting in bankruptcy, refused to exercise simultaneously his general Chancery jurisdiction.
[10] For a striking instance of a libel action in the Chancery Division, see [1948] J.S.P.T.L. 181.
[11] See S.C.A. 1981, ss.61(6), 65, replacing in an altered form J.A. 1925, s.58, proviso (2), applied in *Midland Bank Ltd.* v. *Stamps* [1978] 1 W.L.R. 635.
[12] For the functions of Master, see A. S. Diamond, "The Queen's Bench Master" (1960) 76 L.Q.R. 504; R. E. Ball, "The Chancery Master" (1961) 77 L.Q.R. 331. From January 1, 1982, when the S.C.A. 1981 came into force, the qualification for both offices is a barrister or solicitor: see s.88, Sched. 2, Pt. II.
[13] See Roxburgh J. (1949) 65 L.Q.R. 542; Evershed L.J. [1948] J.S.P.T.L. 171 at 180; and see generally Evershed M.R. (1954) 70 L.Q.R. 326.
[14] S.C.A. 1981, s.5(5), replacing J.A. 1925, s.4(4), added by Administration of Justice Act 1928, s.6.
[15] *Re Hastings (No. 3)* [1959] Ch. 368; appeal dismissed, [1959] 1 W.L.R. 807.

that as far as possible all matters in controversy between the parties may be completely and finally determined, and all multiplicity of legal proceedings avoided.[16]

(3) COMMON INJUNCTIONS. In view of the recognition of equitable defences by all the Divisions of the High Court, the common injunction[17] became unnecessary and was abolished.[18]

2. The county courts

(a) *The jurisdiction.* By statute, a limited jurisdiction in equity has been conferred on county courts. By the County Courts Act 1984,[19] a county court has all the jurisdiction of the High Court to hear and determine proceedings—

(i)   for the administration of the estate of a deceased person not exceeding £30,000 in amount or value;

(ii)   for the execution of any trust or for a declaration that a trust subsists, or proceedings under the Variation of Trusts Act 1958,[20] where the estate or fund subject or alleged to be subject to the trust does not exceed £30,000 in amount or value;

(iii)   for foreclosure or redemption of any mortgage or for enforcing any charge or lien, where the amount owing in respect of the mortgage, charge or lien does not exceed £30,000[21];

(iv)   for the specific performance, or for the rectification, delivery up or cancellation, of any agreement for sale, purchase or lease of any property, where, in the case of a sale or purchase, the purchase-money, or, in the case of a lease, the value of the property, does not exceed £30,000;

(v)   relating to the maintenance or advancement of a minor, where the property of the minor does not exceed £30,000 in amount or value;

(vi)   for the dissolution or winding up of any partnership (whether or not the existence of the partnership is in dispute), where the whole assets of the partnership do not exceed £30,000 in amount or value;

---

[16] S.C.A. 1981, s.49.
[17] See *ante*, p. 12.
[18] See J.A. 1873, s.24(5), and see *post*, pp. 647, 686.
[19] ss.23, 147(1) and S.I. 1981 No. 1123 which increased the limit fixed by earlier legislation: S.I. 1977 No. 600 (£15,000); Administration of Justice Act 1969, s.5 (£5,000); County Courts Act 1959, s.52(1) (£500).
[20] For this Act, see *post*, p. 241.
[21] And see *post*, p. 406.

(vii)   for relief against fraud or mistake, where the damage sustained
         or the estate or fund in respect of which relief is sought does
         not exceed £30,000 in amount or value.

(b) *Other cases.*   The county court also has a limited jurisdiction
under various enactments, *e.g.* the Law of Property Act 1925.[22]
Moreover, by written agreement the parties may consent to the county
court having unlimited jurisdiction to deal with any of the matters
mentioned above, other than proceedings under the Variation of Trusts
Act 1958.[23] Further, a defendant may plead a counterclaim or set off for
any amount, which the county court can hear unless an application is
granted to transfer the proceedings or the counterclaim alone to the
High Court,[24] and generally there are wide powers of transfer between
the High Court and county court.[25]

(c) *Relief.*   In addition to this substantive jurisdiction, the county
court is also empowered to grant such relief, redress or remedy as ought
to be granted in the like case by the High Court.[26] Thus under this
provision the county court may grant an injunction,[27] or decree specific
performance.[28] Injunctions are ordinarily obtainable in the county court
only by way of relief which is ancillary to a money claim,[29] for the
court's general jurisdiction is defined in terms of money claims in
contract and tort[30] and of annual value in actions for the recovery of
land[31]; yet the court does not have to weigh the relative importance of
the money claim and specific relief, so long as the former is genuine.[32]
But in cases relating to land (which includes incorporeal hereditaments)
within the court's jurisdiction, or the possession, occupation, use or
enjoyment of such land, the court has the same jurisdiction as the High
Court to grant an injunction[33]: in such cases claims may therefore be
made for an injunction without also seeking possession or damages. The
court also has power to grant injunctions under statutes which
specifically confer jurisdiction to do so.[34]

---

[22] County Courts Act 1984, s.148(1) and Sched. 2, Pt. II, paras. 2–10 (making various amendments to
L.P.A. 1925); S.L.A. 1925, s.113(3) (as substituted by County Courts Act 1984, s.148(1) and
Sched. 2, Pt. V, para. 20); T.A. 1925, s.63A (inserted by County Courts Act 1984, s.148(1) and
Sched. 2, Pt. I, para. 1); A.E.A. 1925, ss.17(2), 38(4), 41(1A), 43(4) (inserted by County Courts Act
1984, s.148(1) and Sched. 2, Pt. III, paras. 11–14); L.C.A. 1972, ss.1(6A), 5(11) (inserted by County
Courts Act 1984, s.148(1) and Sched. 2, Pt. IV, paras. 16, 17).
[23] County Courts Act 1984, s.24.
[24] *Ibid.* s.43.
[25] *Ibid.* ss.40–42; see Practice Direction [1988] 1 W.L.R. 741.
[26] *Ibid.* s.38.
[27] *Martin* v. *Bannister* (1879) 4 Q.B.D. 491.
[28] *Bourne* v. *MacDonald* [1950] 2 K.B. 422.
[29] *R.* v. *Cheshire County Court Judge and United Society of Boilermakers* [1921] 2 K.B. 694; *Simpson* v.
Crowle [1921] 3 K.B. 243; and see *De Vries* v. *Smallridge* [1928] 1 K.B. 482; *Kenny* v. *Preen* [1963] 1
Q.B. 499. See also P. H. Pettit [1977] C.L.J. 369 discussing the jurisdiction to grant *quia timet*
injunctions (see *post,* p. 651) in the county court.
[30] See County Courts Act 1984, ss.15(1), 147(1); County Courts Jurisdiction Order 1981 (S.I. 1981
No. 1123).
[31] County Courts Act 1984, ss.21(1), (2), 147(1).
[32] *Hatt & Co. (Bath) Ltd.* v. *Pearce* [1978] 1 W.L.R. 885 (damages of £1 and injunction).
[33] County Courts Act 1984, s.22.
[34] *e.g.* Domestic Violence and Matrimonial Proceedings Act 1976, s.1; Sex Discrimination Act 1975,
s.72; Race Relations Act 1976, s.62.

(d) *Defences.*   The court must give effect to every ground of defence
or counterclaim, equitable or legal, as ought to be given by the High
Court.[35] Thus a tenant can resist an action for possession based on the
determination of a weekly tenancy at common law on the ground that
she has an agreement enforceable in equity to remain for life, even
though the county court could not specifically enforce it.[36]

---

[35] County Courts Act 1984, s.38.

[36] *Kingswood Estate Co. Ltd.* v. *Anderson* [1963] 2 Q.B. 169; and see *Cornish* v. *Brook Green Laundry Ltd.* [1959] 1 Q.B. 394. Contrast *Foster* v. *Reeves* [1892] 2 Q.B. 255 (*post,* p. 40), where an equitable *claim* was made.

CHAPTER 2

EQUITIES

THE term "an equity" may have four different meanings, according
to the context in which it is used. Usually it means an equitable
interest in property, *i.e.* some right of ownership enforced by equity
but not by the common law. Sometimes, however, it means a "mere
equity," which is a procedural right ancillary to some right of property,
as, for example, an equitable right to have a conveyance rectified.
Thirdly, it may mean a "floating equity," a term which may be used to
describe the interest of a beneficiary under a will or intestacy in any
property of the deceased which he hopes to receive if it is not required
for the payment of debts or other liabilities. Fourthly, the right to
obtain an injunction or other equitable remedy is sometimes called an
equity. These meanings must be considered in turn.

Section 1. Equitable Interests

1. Historical development. When it would have been unconscionable
for the legal owner of property to keep the property for himself, the
Court of Chancery acted on his conscience and compelled him to hold
the property for the benefit of another person. In their origin, therefore,
equitable interests were merely rights *in personam*. However, in the
fifteenth and sixteenth centuries the Chancellors began to enforce
equitable interests not only against the person originally bound, but also
against his heir, or a donee, or a purchaser who took with notice.[1]
Finally, equitable rights became enforceable against all except a
purchaser without notice, and so it became possible to treat them as
rights *in rem*, or proprietary rights. If T is trustee for B, B has not
merely a right of action against T to compel him to perform the trust
but a proprietary right available also against all persons in whom the
legal interest in the property may afterwards vest, unless for special
reasons they take free from his right.[2] What began as a mere personal
equity has ended as a right of property.[3]

An alternative view is that because equitable rights will not be
enforced against a purchaser without notice of them, they cannot be

[1] See Maitland, *Equity*, p. 112.
[2] And as to the nature of trusts, see *post*, p. 89.
[3] See *Sinclair* v. *Brougham* [1914] A.C. 398 at 441.

regarded as rights *in rem*, at any rate in the same way as legal rights are rights *in rem*, and that they are accordingly best regarded as hybrids, for they are clearly more than mere rights *in personam*. [4]

2. Similarities to legal estates.   In dealing with the equitable interests thus created, the Court of Chancery adopted most of the legal rules. "It is the maxim of this court that trust estates, which are the creatures of equity, shall be governed by the same rules as legal estates, in order to preserve the uniform rule of property."[5] Thus as regards quantum of interest, the rule before 1926 was that there might be the same interests in equity as at law; for "equity follows the law."[6] However, the Law of Property Act 1925 has reduced the possible legal estates in land to estates in fee simple absolute in possession and terms of years absolute; other estates existing at law at the end of 1925 were converted into corresponding equitable interests.[7] But the Act has not in any way curtailed the kinds of possible equitable interests.[8] The equitable interest may still be held not only for the fee simple absolute in possession, or for a term of years absolute, but also for a fee simple determinable on a certain event, or for an entailed interest, or for life; it may be in possession or in remainder; it may be held by joint tenants or by tenants in common; and it may be vested in a minor. Thus in the matter of possible interests,[9] equity does not now merely follow the law, but remains far beyond it.[10]

3. Differences from legal rules.   Equity did not apply strictly the technical rule of common law that an estate in fee simple could not be conveyed *inter vivos* without the use of the word "heirs," or, after 1881,[11] the alternative words "in fee simple." Thus, words of limitation have never been necessary to create an equitable fee simple in a contract to convey, or in an agreement to make a settlement. And even before 1926, in a deed transferring an existing equitable interest the equitable fee simple would sometimes pass without the use of the word "heirs" or the words "in fee simple." For instance, in *Re Arden*[12] a mother executed a deed in 1901, whereby she exercised a power to

---

[4] See A. W. Scott (1917) 17 Col.L.R. 269; Harlan Stone, *ibid.* 467; H.G. Hanbury (1929) 45 L.Q.R. 199; Hohfeld, *Fundamental Legal Conceptions* (1923), pp. 23 *et seq.* A lucid summary of the conflicting views appears in Winfield, *Province of the Law of Tort* (1931), pp. 108–112, and they are analysed by E. J. Mockler at (1962) 40 Can.B.R. 265 at 270–280. And see *post*, pp. 192, 197, 287.
[5] *Hopkins* v. *Hopkins* (1739) West *t.* Hard. 606 at 618, *per* Lord Hardwicke L.C.
[6] See *post*, p. 29.
[7] L.P.A. 1925, ss.1, 39, Sched. I.
[8] See L.P.A. 1925, s.4(1).
[9] See *post*, pp. 47, 573, for equitable interests which are not readily classifiable.
[10] For the incidents attaching to equitable estates before 1926, and the modification of a number of pre-1926 technical rules attaching to legal estates in their application to equitable estates (*e.g.* the rule in *Shelley's Case*) see the 28th ed. of this work at pp. 24, 25, 120.
[11] C.A. 1881, s.51.
[12] [1935] Ch. 326.

appoint the equitable interests in certain freehold property to her children by appointing the property to her son "absolutely." It was held that the son took an equitable fee simple; the appointment was not framed in strict conveyancing language, and so the court was at liberty to give effect to the mother's obvious intention. However, a conveyance of an existing equitable interest in which strict conveyancing language was used had to be construed strictly.[13]

Statute has now abrogated the common law rule; if freehold land is conveyed after 1925 without words of limitation, the conveyance will pass the whole interest which the grantor had power to convey unless a contrary intention appears.[14] And where the former rule applies, the court may be able to rectify the instrument by inserting the appropriate words.[15]

Section 2. Mere Equities

Equitable interests must be distinguished from "mere equities."[16] It is difficult to define these with clarity.[17] Whereas an equitable interest is an actual right of property, such as an interest under a trust,[18] a mere equity is not a right of property but a right, usually of a procedural nature, which is ancillary to some right of property, and which limits or qualifies it in some way.[19] Thus, mere equities include the right to have a transaction set aside for fraud[20] or undue influence,[21] or to have a document rectified for mistake, as by inserting a repairing covenant.[22] Though often ancillary to some right of property, claims to set aside a transaction do not run with property,[23] nor are they normally assignable.[24] But a claim to rectify a document may be enforced by[25] or against[26] successors in title of the original parties, provided that the claim is not barred by the defence of bona fide purchaser for value without notice.[27] The importance of the distinction between equitable interests and mere equities will appear when considering the doctrine of the purchaser without notice.[28]

---

[13] *Re Bostock's Settlement* [1912] 2 Ch. 469; *Re Whiston* [1894] 1 Ch. 661; *Re Irwin* [1904] 2 Ch. 752.
[14] L.P.A. 1925, s.60(1).
[15] *Banks* v. *Ripley* [1940] Ch. 719; for rectification, see *post*, p. 626.
[16] See *Shiloh Spinners Ltd.* v. *Harding* [1973] A.C. 691 at 721, referring to this passage.
[17] See Ann R. Everton (1976) 40 Conv.(N.S.) 209 for a valiant attempt.
[18] *Cave* v. *Cave* (1880) 15 Ch.D. 639.
[19] See *National Provincial Bank Ltd.*v. *Ainsworth* [1965] A.C. 1175 at 1238, 1254; and see generally (1955) 71 L.Q.R. 480; V. T. H. Delany (1957) 21 Conv.(N.S.) 195.
[20] *Ernest* v. *Vivian* (1863) 33 L.J.Ch. 513; and see *Latec Investments Ltd.*v. *Hotel Terrigal Pty. Ltd.* (1965) 113 C.L.R. 265.
[21] See *Bainbrigge* v. *Browne* (1881) 18 Ch.D. 188.
[22] *Smith* v. *Jones* [1954] 1 W.L.R. 1089.
[23] *Gross* v. *Lewis Hillman Ltd.* [1970] Ch. 445.
[24] See *post*, pp. 75, 85.
[25] *Boots the Chemist Ltd.*v. *Street* (1983) 268 E.G. 817 (relying on L.P.A. 1925 s.63(1)).
[26] *Blacklocks* v. *J.B. Developments (Godalming) Ltd.*[1982] Ch. 183 (treating the claim as an overriding interest under L.R.A. 1925, s.70(1)(g)); and see *post*, p. 635.
[27] *Smith* v. *Jones, supra*, at p. 1093.
[28] See *post*, p. 50.

Section 3. Floating Equities

Although equity usually gives effect to equitable claims to property by recognising and enforcing equitable interests in it, there is a class of case in which equity achieves its object by other means. On the death of a person, all his property vests in his personal representatives; yet apart from those to whom specific items have been given, all others who under the will or intestacy are beneficially entitled to the property do not forthwith obtain equitable interests in it, for any or all of it may be needed by the personal representatives for the payment of debts or other liabilities. Even if the estate is obviously solvent, the person entitled to residue cannot know until the administration is complete which particular assets will constitute the residue on the final distribution.

Accordingly, the whole ownership is held to be vested in the personal representatives; and until an assent is made in respect of any particular asset, the beneficiary prospectively entitled to it has no greater interest in it than what may perhaps be described as a "floating equity," which may or may not crystallise. In such cases equity protects the beneficiaries, not by giving them equitable interests, but by ensuring the due administration of assets by the personal representatives.[29]

Section 4. Equitable Rights and Remedies

Between them, equitable interests, mere equities, floating equities and the great doctrines of equity cover most of the field of equity; and they are all concerned to a greater or lesser degree with the rights of property. Yet although the existence of such rights has long been an important factor in deciding whether equity will intervene, it is not essential. Equitable remedies,[30] though often used in aid of property rights, are also often used in other cases. The underlying principle is the inadequacy of the common law remedy of damages.[31] Thus the equitable remedies of rescission and injunction may be employed in relation to contracts for personal services; and injunctions are sometimes granted in cases of tort which involve no rights of property. In this sense there may be equities unrelated to property.

[29] See generally *Commissioner of Stamp Duties (Queensland)* v. *Livingston* [1965] A.C. 694 at 712, 713; *post*, p. 343.
[30] For these, see *post*, Pt. VII.
[31] See *post*, p. 585 (specific performance), pp. 647, 648 (injunction).

CHAPTER 3

THE MAXIMS OF EQUITY

OWING to its haphazard origin, equity is not a complete system. Nevertheless, there are certain general principles upon which the Court of Chancery exercised its jurisdiction. Many of these have been embodied in the so–called maxims of equity. These are not to be taken as positive laws of equity which will be applied literally and relentlessly in their full width, but rather as trends or principles which can be discerned in many of the detailed rules which equity has established. Further, no logical division of these maxims is possible. The maxims do not cover the whole of the ground and, moreover, they overlap, one maxim containing by implication what belongs to another. Indeed, it would not be difficult to reduce them all under the first and the last, "Equity will not suffer a wrong to be without a remedy," and "Equity acts on the person." For all that, each merits separate consideration, for each embodies some peculiar function of equity. The 12 maxims are as follows[1]:

(1) Equity will not suffer a wrong to be without a remedy.

(2) Equity follows the law.

(3) Where there is equal equity, the law shall prevail.

(4) Where the equities are equal, the first in time shall prevail.

(5) He who seeks equity must do equity.

(6) He who comes into equity must come with clean hands.

(7) Delay defeats equities.

(8) Equality is equity.

(9) Equity looks to the intent rather than to the form.

(10) Equity looks on that as done which ought to be done.

(11) Equity imputes an intention to fulfil an obligation.

(12) Equity acts *in personam*.

[1] On the maxims, see generally Roscoe Pound in *Cambridge Legal Essays* (1926), pp. 259 *et seq*.

1. Equity will not suffer a wrong to be without a remedy.   The idea expressed in this maxim is that no wrong should be allowed to go unredressed if it is capable of being remedied by courts of justice, and this really underlies the whole jurisdiction of equity. As already explained,[2] the common law courts failed to remedy many undoubted wrongs, and this failure led to the establishment of the Court of Chancery. But it must not be supposed that every *moral* wrong was redressed by the Court of Chancery. The maxim must be taken as referring to rights which are suitable for judicial enforcement, but were not enforced at common law owing to some technical defect. Its meaning can be best explained by taking a few examples of the cases in which the court has acted upon it.

(a) *The enforcement of trusts.*   It was on this maxim that the Court of Chancery based its interference to enforce uses and trusts. Where A conveyed land to B to hold to the use of, or on trust for, C, and B claimed to keep the benefit of the land for himself, C had no remedy at law. Yet such an abuse of confidence was most distinctly a wrong, and a wrong capable of easy redress in a court of justice.

(b) *The auxiliary jurisdiction.*   Again, to this maxim may be traced the origin of the auxiliary jurisdiction of the Court of Chancery, by virtue of which suitors at law were aided in the enforcement of their legal rights. Without such aid these rights would often have been "wrongs without remedies." For instance, it was often necessary for a plaintiff in a common law action to obtain discovery of facts resting in the knowledge of the defendant, or of deeds, writings or other things in his possession or power. The common law courts, however, had no power to order such discovery, and recourse was therefore had to the Court of Chancery, which assumed jurisdiction to order the defendant to make discovery on his oath.[3]

Since the Judicature Acts discovery can be obtained in any Division of the High Court. In actions begun by writ it is automatic, and can be readily obtained on application in other proceedings.[4] Formerly a lessor was not entitled to discovery in an action brought to forfeit the lease,[5] as the court leans against penalties and forfeitures.[6] This restriction of the normal rule has now been abrogated,[7] and never applied to claims for relief against forfeiture.[8]

Another illustration of the maxim is to be found in the appointment of a receiver by way of equitable execution.[9]

---

[2] See *ante*, p. 8.
[3] For the pre-Judicature Act history, see *Lyell* v. *Kennedy* (1883) 8 App.Cas. 217 and the notes in **2 W. & T.L.C. 136** to *Basset* v. *Nosworthy* (1673) Rep.*t*.Finch 102.
[4] R.S.C., Ord. 24; S.C.A. 1981, ss.33–35; and see *Norwich Pharmacal Co.* v. *Customs and Excise Commissioners* [1974] A.C. 133.
[5] *Seddon* v. *Commercial Salt Co. Ltd.* [1925] Ch. 187.
[6] See *post*, p. 538.
[7] Civil Evidence Act 1968, s.16(1)(*a*).
[8] *Mascherpa* v. *Direct Ltd.* [1960] 1 W.L.R. 447.
[9] See *post*, p. 697.

2. Equity follows the law[10]

(a) *The principle.* The Court of Chancery never claimed to override the courts of common law. "Where a rule, either of the common or the statute law, is direct, and governs the case with all its circumstances, or the particular point, a court of equity is as much bound by it as a court of law, and can as little justify a departure from it."[11] It is only when there is some important circumstance disregarded by the common law rules that equity interferes. "Equity follows the law, but not slavishly nor always."[12]

(b) *Examples.* Equity followed the law in many ways.[13] In particular, the estates and interests in land in equity corresponded to those at law, so that in equity, as in law, there could be a fee simple, a fee tail, a life interest and a term of years, with all their variants. Equity even allowed equitable entails to be barred in the same clumsy way as at law, and permitted curtesy (though not dower) out of equitable interests. Further, equitable interests devolved on intestacy in the same way as legal estates, so that the eldest son took all the land as heir, to the exclusion of his younger brother and his sisters. This was unfair to them, yet equity granted them no relief.

If, however, the eldest son had induced his father not to make a will by agreeing to divide the estate with his brothers and sisters, equity would have interfered and compelled him to carry out his promise. It would have been against conscience to allow him to keep the benefit of a legal estate which he obtained only by reason of his promise. While recognising the legal rule and giving full effect to it as carrying the land to the son, equity said that he must take it as a trustee for himself and his brothers and sisters.[14] Shortly, therefore, it may be said that equity does not interfere with a man's legal rights unless it would be unconscionable on his part to take advantage of them. Equity acts on the conscience.[15]

(c) *Refusal to follow the law.* There were, however, some cases where quite apart from the circumstances of a particular case equity refused to follow the law; and this was often where the law was based on feudal tenure. Thus equity recognised a wide range of future interests in land which did not comply with rules at law that were founded on the technical doctrine of seisin; and there was no escheat of equitable interests on intestacy, for the concept of escheat at law

[10] *Anon.* (n. d.) Cary 11.
[11] Story, *Equity* (3rd English ed., 1920), p. 34.
[12] *Graf* v. *Hope Building Corporation*, 254 N.Y. 1 at 9 (1930), *per* Cardozo C.J.
[13] See generally Megarry & Wade, *The Law of Real Property* (5th ed., 1984), pp. 119, 120.
[14] *Stickland* v. *Aldridge* (1804) 9 Ves. 516 at 519; *cf. Re Gardner, Huey* v. *Cunnington* [1920] 2 Ch. 523; *post*, p. 110.
[15] See *ante*, p. 11.

depended on tenure. There were other exceptions, too,[16] "but the cases, where the analogy fails, are not numerous; and there scarcely is a rule of law or equity, of a more ancient origin, or which admits of fewer exceptions, than the rule, that equity followeth the law."[17]

3. Where there is equal equity, the law shall prevail.

4. Where the equities are equal, the first in time shall prevail: *qui prior est tempore, potior est jure.*

These two maxims govern questions of the priority of rival claimants to the same property in equity. They will be discussed in the next chapter.

5. He who seeks equity must do equity. To obtain equitable relief the plaintiff must be prepared to do "equity," in its popular sense of what is right and fair to the defendant. This is a rule of "unquestionable justice" which, however, "decides nothing in itself; for you must first inquire what are the equities which the Defendant must do, and what the Plaintiff ought to have."[18] The rule has many applications of which the following are examples.[19]

(a) *Illegal loans.* In *Lodge* v. *National Union Investment Co. Ltd.*,[20] B borrowed money from M, an unregistered moneylender, and mortgaged certain securities to him. The contract was illegal and void under the Moneylenders Act 1900.[21] B sued M for delivery up of the securities. Parker J. refused to make the order except upon the terms that B should repay the money which had been advanced to him; for B was seeking equitable relief, and must therefore do what was right and fair.

This decision, however, has not established any wide general principle,[22] and it has been distinguished. Thus if B had asked merely for a declaration that the mortgage was void, he could have obtained it without repayment, because that is not equitable relief[23]; and it may be that by suing in detinue or trover he could have recovered the securities

[16] Megarry & Wade, *The Law of Real Property* (5th ed., 1984), pp. 120–122; and see *ante*, p. 24.
[17] Co.Litt. 290b, n. 1 (xvi), Butler's note.
[18] *Neesom* v. *Clarkson* (1845) 4 Hare 97 at 101, *per* Wigram V.-C.; and see *Oxford* v. *Provand* (1868) 5 Moo.P.C.(N.S.) 150 at 179.
[19] A former example was the wife's equity to a settlement: see *post*, p. 533. See also *R.* v. *Eastern Counties Ry.* (1842) 10 M. & W. 58 at 61, where the doctrine was applied to deodands; *United States of America* v. *McRae* (1869) L.R. 8 Eq. 69.
[20] [1907] 1 Ch. 300.
[21] The Moneylenders Acts 1900 to 1927 were repealed and replaced with a more extensive system of control of credit businesses by the Consumer Credit Act 1974.
[22] *Kasumu* v. *Baba-Egbe* [1956] A.C. 539 at 549.
[23] *Chapman* v. *Michaelson* [1909] 1 Ch. 238; and see *post*, pp. 583, 584, 625.

without repayment.[24] Further, it has been held that if the contract with the moneylender is not illegal but merely unenforceable, the borrower can recover a security without repayment, for otherwise the money-lender would be indirectly enforcing the contract,[25] against a plaintiff not disabled by any illegality from proceeding at law.[26] It seems odd that a moneylender who commits an offence and makes an illegal contract should receive better treatment than one who has merely made an unenforceable contract,[27] but that is how the decisions stand at present.[28]

It has also been held that if a mortgagee's right is barred by the Statutes of Limitation so that he no longer has any title to the property at law or in equity, a mortgagor who is in possession of the mortgaged property can recover the mortgage and other title deeds from the mortgagee without repaying the loan.[29]

(b) *Election.* Where a donor gives his own property to E and in the same instrument purports to give E's property to X, E will be unable to claim the whole of the gift to him unless he allows the gift to X to take effect. This is known as the doctrine of election.[30]

(c) *Consolidation.* In certain circumstances a person who has become entitled to two mortgages made by the same mortgagor may consolidate the mortgages and refuse to permit the exercise of the equitable right to redeem one mortgage unless the other is redeemed as well.[31]

(d) *Notice to redeem mortgage.* A mortgagor who wishes to exercise his equitable right to redeem his mortgage must give his mortgagee reasonable notice of his intention.[32]

(e) *Equitable estoppel.* Some cases of equitable estoppel[33] may be brought under this maxim; but others seem to be independent of it.

6. He who comes into equity must come with clean hands. This maxim, which seems to be related to the *ex turpi causa non oritur actio* of the common law, is very similar to the previous maxim; but it differs from it in looking to the past rather than the future. The plaintiff not

---

[24] See *Lodge* v. *National Union Investments Co. Ltd.* [1907] 1 Ch. 300 at 310.
[25] Yet what Parker J. did was to restore the parties to their position before the contract was made, and to do this is quite different from enforcing the contract.
[26] *Cohen* v. *J. Lester Ltd.* [1939] 1 K.B. 504, a case on the Moneylenders Act 1927, s.6, now repealed, see *post*, p. 560; *Kasumu* v. *Baba-Egbe* [1956] A.C. 539.
[27] See *Kasumu* v. *Baba-Egbe, supra,* at p. 547.
[28] See also on the distinction *Orakpo* v. *Manson Investments Ltd.* [1978] A.C. 95 at 114, 115, citing (1956) 72 L.Q.R. 480 (R.E.M.).
[29] *Lewis* v. *Plunkett* [1937] Ch. 306; see *post*, p. 441.
[30] *Post*, p. 503.
[31] *Post*, p. 399.
[32] *Post*, p. 397.
[33] *Post*, p. 568.

only must be prepared now to do what is right and fair, but also must show that his past record in the transaction is clean; for "he who has committed Iniquity ... shall not have Equity."[34]

For example, "Infants have no Privilege to cheat Men,"[35] and so if an infant, fraudulently misrepresenting himself to be of age, thereby obtains from his trustees a sum to which he is entitled only on coming of age, neither he nor his assigns can compel the trustees to pay the sum over again when in fact he attains full age.[36] Similarly, a tenant who has entered under an àgreement for a lease cannot obtain specific performance of it if he is in breach of the covenants to be contained in the lease.[37] Again, a tenant whose lease has been forfeited for non-payment of rent cannot expect relief against the forfeiture if he has been using the premises as a disorderly house[38]; nor can an equitable interest in land granted with a fraudulent purpose be enforced by a person tainted with the fraud.[39] Similarly, an occupier may be debarred from setting up an equitable licence if his conduct in relation to the property has been very damaging to the legal owner.[40] Where, however, a transaction is against public policy, the fact that the plaintiff has not a clean record in the matter is no bar to his obtaining equitable relief; thus an action may be maintained for delivery up of an instrument which is void on the ground of public policy, even if the plaintiff was a party to the illegality.[41]

The maxim must not be taken too widely; "Equity does not demand that its suitors shall have led blameless lives."[42] What bars the claim is not a general depravity but one which has "an immediate and necessary relation to the equity sued for,"[43] and is not balanced by any mitigating factors.[44] This limitation was not recognised in the reign of Elizabeth I and her immediate successors,[45] and, it seems, it has been lost sight of in some American jurisdictions.[46]

---

[34] *Jones* v. *Lenthal* (1669) 1 Ch.Cas. 154.

[35] *Evroy* v. *Nicholas* (1733) 2 Eq.Ca.Abr. 488 at 489, *per* Lord King L.C.

[36] *Cory* v. *Gertcken* (1816) 2 Madd. 49; *Overton* v. *Banister* (1844) 3 Hare 503 at 506; and see *Nail* v. *Punter* (1832) 5 Sim. 555; *Re Lush's Trusts* (1869) 4 Ch.App. 591; *post*, pp. 549, 550. Contrast *Nelson* v. *Stocker* (1859) 4 De G. & J. 458 (knowledge of infancy).

[37] *Coatsworth* v. *Johnson* (1886) 54 L.T. 520.

[38] See *Gill* v. *Lewis* [1956] 2 Q.B. 1 at 13, 14, 17. For another example, see *post*, p. 181.

[39] *Mason* v. *Clarke* [1954] 1 Q.B. 460; reversed [1955] A.C. 778 on the ground that there was no taint of fraud. See also *Everet* v. *Williams* (1725) 9 L.Q.R. 197 (partnership action by one highwayman against another: Megarry, *Miscellany-at-Law* (1955), p. 76).

[40] *Williams* v. *Staite* [1979] Ch. 291 (where, however, the conduct was not sufficiently grave). For other examples, see *Hubbard* v. *Vosper* [1972] 2 Q.B. 4, followed in *Church of Scientology of California* v. *Kaufman* [1973] R.P.C. 635; *Roanway Properties Ltd.* v. *Gold* (1973) 228 E.G. 2269.

[41] *Lord St. John* v. *Lady St. John* (1805) 11 Ves. 256 at 535; *Lound* v. *Grimwade* (1888) 39 Ch.D. 605. For another example, see *post*, p. 611.

[42] *Loughran* v. *Loughran*, 292 U.S. 216 at 229 (1934), *per* Brandeis J.

[43] *Dering* v. *Earl of Winchelsea* (1787) 1 Cox Eq. 318 at 319, 320; **2 W. & T.L.C. 488 at 489**, *per* Eyre C.B. (see *post*, p. 475); *Moody* v. *Cox* [1917] 2 Ch. 71 at 87; *Duchess of Argyll* v. *Duke of Argyll* [1967] Ch. 302 at 332; but see *Litvinoff* v. *Kent* (1918) 34 T.L.R. 298.

[44] See *Singh* v. *Singh* (1985) 15 Fam. Law 97.

[45] See 1 Spence, *Equitable Jurisdiction* (1846), p. 423, n. (*a*).

[46] See Z. Chafee (1949) Mich.L.R. 877, 1065, where the maxim is elaborately discussed. See, in particular, *Donovan* v. *Donovan*, 263 N.Y.S. 336 (1933), where the maxim was applied to a state trooper's pre-marital fornication so as to debar him from a decree of nullity.

7. Delay defeats equities, or, **equity aids the vigilant and not the indolent:** *vigilantibus, non dormientibus, jura subveniunt.*[47] In the words of Lord Camden L.C.,[48] a court of equity "has always refused its aid to stale demands, where a party has slept upon his right and acquiesced for a great length of time. Nothing can call forth this court into activity, but conscience, good faith, and reasonable diligence; where these are wanting, the Court is passive, and does nothing." Delay which is sufficient to prevent a party from obtaining an equitable remedy is technically called "laches."[49]

This maxim, however, has no application to cases to which the Statutes of Limitation[50] apply either expressly or, perhaps, by analogy. There are thus three cases to consider—

(a) equitable claims to which the Statute applies expressly;

(b) equitable claims to which the Statute is applied by analogy; and

(c) equitable claims to which no statute applies and which are therefore covered by the ordinary rules of laches.

(a) *Express application of the Statute.*   Originally the Statute applied only to courts of common law. But then several statutory provisions were enacted which were in terms applicable to equitable claims. Thus the Real Property Limitation Act 1833[51] provided that an action to recover land or rent in equity must be brought within the same time as if it were a legal claim, and the Trustee Act 1888[52] limited the time within which an action must be commenced against a trustee for breach of trust. These provisions were replaced by the Limitation Act 1939, which carried further the policy of regulating by statute the limitation of claims in equity, and was in turn replaced by the Limitation Act 1980. The principal equitable claims so regulated are as follows:

(i)   Claims by *cestuis que trust* to recover trust property or in respect of any breach of trust.[53]

(ii) Claims to the personal estate of a deceased person.[54]

---

[47] 2 Co.Inst. 690; and see Wingate's *Maxims* (1658), p. 672; *Fenwicke* v. *Clarke* (1862) 4 De G.F. & J. 240 at 245.

[48] *Smith* v. *Clay* (1767) 3 Bro.C.C. 639n. at 640n.

[49] For a discussion of the technical meaning of the term (pronounced "laitches"), see *Partridge* v. *Partridge* [1894] 1 Ch. 351 at 359, 360; Brunyate, *Limitation of Actions in Equity* (1932), pp. 188 *et seq.*

[50] The expressions "the Statutes of Limitation" or "the Statute of Limitations" or simply "the Statute" are often used to denote collectively the series of statutes, commencing with the Limitation Act 1623, which dealt with the limitation of actions. The present statutes are the Limitation Act 1980 (which repealed and replaced the former statutes) and the Latent Damage Act 1986 (which amended the Act of 1980).

[51] s.24.

[52] s.8.

[53] s.21; *post*, p. 292.

[54] s.22; *post*, p. 353.

(iii)   Claims to redeem mortgaged land.[55]

(iv)   Claims to foreclose mortgages of real or personal property.[56]

(b) *Application of the Statute by analogy.* Where a claim is not expressly covered by any statutory period but is closely analogous to a claim which is expressly covered, equity will act by analogy and apply the same period. Thus, formerly, if one *cestui que trust* brought an action against another *cestui que trust* to recover money wrongly paid by the trustee to the latter, the court acted on the analogy of the Limitation Act 1623, and held the claim barred after six years, the action being in the nature of a common law action for money had and received.[57] Claims to recover trust property now fall directly within the provisions of the Limitation Act 1980,[58] as do actions for an account.[59] Again, an application for relief against forfeiture for non-payment of rent where the landlord has peaceably re-entered would probably be held to be barred after six months, that being the statutory period applicable where the landlord has obtained an order for possession.[60]

The class of cases to which the Statute will be applied by analogy is, however, extremely small. In the first place, the Limitation Act 1980 provides expressly for many more equitable claims than its predecessors, and secondly the Statute will not be applied where the case has been deliberately omitted from its express provisions. For this reason a mortgagor's right to redeem a mortgage of pure personalty is not subject to any statutory period.[61]

It is clear that where the Statutes of Limitation apply expressly, delay short of the statutory period is no bar to a claim, whether legal or equitable[62]; but where the statute applies by analogy, the rule may not be the same.[63] Yet even if a claim to a legal right is not barred, a plaintiff who establishes it will not necessarily be entitled to any and every equitable remedy in aid thereof. If he is entitled as of right to a final injunction, delay within the statutory period will not deprive him of it.[64] But normally the court retains a discretion, governed by the doctrine of laches which is discussed below, to refuse to grant an equitable remedy in aid of a legal right even though the right is subject

---

[55] s.16; *post*, p. 438.
[56] ss.15, 20(4) (realty); s.20(2) (personalty); *post*, p. 439, and see *post*, p. 466 for liens.
[57] *Re Robinson, McLaren* v. *Public Trustee* [1911] 1 Ch. 502; and see *Re Mason* [1928] Ch. 385, affd. [1929] 1 Ch. 1; *Re Blake, re Petition of Right of Minahan* [1932] 1 Ch. 54. These authorities must now be read in the light of *Re Diplock* [1948] Ch. 465 at 498, 501, 502, 515, 516.
[58] See s.21; *post*, p. 292.
[59] See s.23; *post*, p. 643.
[60] See *Howard* v. *Fanshawe* [1895] 2 Ch. 581 at 588, 589. For another example see *Williams* v. *Thomas* [1909] 1 Ch. 713 at 732 (action now obsolete for assignment of dower analogous to action to recover land).
[61] *Weld* v. *Petre* [1929] 1 Ch. 33, *post*, p. 438; and see *Mellersh* v. *Brown* (1890) 45 Ch.D. 225 at 229.
[62] *Knox* v. *Gye* (1872) L.R. 5 H.L. 656; *Re Pauling's S.T. (No. 1)* [1964] Ch. 303.
[63] See Brunyate, *Limitation of Actions in Equity* (1932), pp. 257, 258, and consider *Peek* v. *Gurney* (1873) L.R. 6 H.L. 377.
[64] *Fullwood* v. *Fullwood* (1878) 9 Ch.D. 176; and see *Archbold* v. *Scully* (1861) 9 H.L.C. 360; *Re Baker, Collins* v. *Rhodes* (1881) 20 Ch.D. 230.

to an express statutory period which has not expired; and the application of the statutory periods to equitable remedies by analogy is preserved.[65]

(c) *Claims outside the Statute.* The principles which equity applies to cases not covered by a statutory period have been stated thus: "Now the doctrine of laches in courts of equity is not an arbitrary or a technical doctrine. Where it would be practically unjust to give a remedy, either because the party has, by his conduct, done that which might fairly be regarded as equivalent to a waiver of it, or where by his conduct and neglect he has, though perhaps not waiving that remedy, yet put the other party in a situation in which it would not be reasonable to place him if the remedy were afterwards to be asserted, in either of these cases lapse of time and delay are most material."[66]

Laches essentially consists of a substantial lapse of time coupled with the existence of circumstances which make it inequitable to enforce the claim.[67] Delay will accordingly be fatal to a claim for equitable relief if it is evidence of an agreement by the plaintiff to abandon or release his right,[68] or if it has resulted in the destruction or loss of evidence by which the claim might have been rebutted,[69] or if the claim is to a business (for the plaintiff should not be allowed to wait and see if it prospers[70]), or if the plaintiff has so acted as to induce the defendant to alter his position on the reasonable faith that the claim has been released or abandoned.[71] But apart from such circumstances delay will be immaterial.[72] There can be no abandonment of a right without full knowledge, legal capacity and free will, so that ignorance or disability or undue influence will be a satisfactory explanation of delay.[73] Moreover, unlike estoppel, laches is a personal disqualification and will not bind successors in title.[74]

Despite the enlarged scope of the Limitation Act 1980,[75] there are many equitable claims to which these principles apply. They include a claim to redeem a mortgage of pure personalty,[76] or to set aside a purchase of trust property by a trustee of it.[77] Delay may also bar

---

[65] Limitation Act 1980, s.36; and see *post,* pp. 643, 644 (accounts).

[66] *Lindsay Petroleum Co.* v. *Hurd* (1874) L.R. 5 P.C. 221 at 239, 240, *per* Lord Selborne L.C.; and see *Erlanger* v. *New Sombrero Phosphate Co.* (1878) 3 App.Cas. 1218 at 1279, 1280; *Habib Bank Ltd.* v. *Habib Bank A.G. Zurich* [1981] 1 W.L.R. 1265 at 1284, 1285.

[67] See *Tottenham Hotspur Football & Athletic Co. Ltd.* v. *Princegrove Publishers Ltd.* [1974] 1 W.L.R. 113 at 122, referring to this passage.

[68] *Blake* v. *Gale* (1886) 32 Ch.D. 571; and see *Hepworth* v. *Pickles* [1900] 1 Ch. 108.

[69] *Reimers* v. *Druce* (1857) 23 Beav. 145; *Bourne* v. *Swan & Edgar Ltd.* [1903] 1 Ch. 211 at 219, 220.

[70] *Re Jarvis* [1958] 1 W.L.R. 815.

[71] *Allcard* v. *Skinner* (1887) 36 Ch.D. 145; *Butlin-Sanders* v. *Butlin* (1985) 15 Fam. Law 126. For the relationship between laches and acquiescence, see *post,* p. 655.

[72] *Re Eustace* [1912] 1 Ch. 561; *Weld* v. *Petre* [1929] 1 Ch. 33; *Rochefoucauld* v. *Boustead* [1897] 1 Ch. 19; *Lazard Bros & Co. Ltd.* v. *Fairfield Properties Co. (Mayfair) Ltd. The Times,* October 13, 1977.

[73] See *Rees* v. *De Bernardy* [1896] 2 Ch. 437 at 445; *Allcard* v. *Skinner* (1887) 36 Ch.D. 145; *Beale* v. *Kyte* [1907] 1 Ch. 564.

[74] *Nwakobi* v. *Nzekwu* [1964] 1 W.L.R. 1019, distinguished in *M.E.P.C. Ltd.* v. *Christian-Edwards* [1978] Ch. 281 at 293 (personal representatives of contracting party would be bound).

[75] *Post,* p. 292; but see *Att.-Gen.* v. *Cocke* [1988] Ch. 414.

[76] *Weld* v. *Petre, supra.* See also *Brooks* v. *Muckleston* [1909] 2 Ch. 519 (foreclosure of advowson).

[77] *Baker* v. *Read* (1854) 18 Beav. 398; *Morse* v. *Royal* (1806) 12 Ves. 355.

claims for equitable remedies such as specific performance,[78] rescission,[79] rectification,[80] and injunctions,[81] apart from final injunctions to which a party is entitled as of right.[82] In such cases, fatal delay may occur after as well as before the issue of the writ.[83]

8. Equality is equity. It has long been a principle of equity that in the absence of sufficient reasons for any other basis of division, those who are entitled to property should have the certainty and fairness of equal division; for "equity did delight in equality."[84] The maxim is "equality is equity," and this has been applied in a variety of ways.

(a) *Presumption of tenancy in common.* The maxim has long been illustrated by equity's dislike of a joint tenancy.[85] On the death of one joint tenant, the whole estate belongs to the survivor, and the representatives of the deceased take nothing. There is here no equality except, perhaps, an equality of chance. Equity therefore leans in favour of a tenancy in common. Hence in the absence of an express declaration as to the beneficial interests, equity may treat persons who are joint tenants at law as tenants in common of the beneficial interest, so that although at law the survivor is entitled to the whole estate, he will hold in part as trustee for the representatives of the deceased. The presumption arises in three main classes of case to which, however, it is not restricted.[86] Thus a lease to two persons as joint tenants for their several business purposes will be held by them as tenants in common in equity in shares proportional to the benefits each enjoyed.[87]

(1) PURCHASE IN UNEQUAL SHARES. If A and B purchase property with purchase-money provided in *unequal* shares, and take the conveyance to themselves jointly, on A's death B becomes entitled to the whole of the property at law, but in equity he is treated as a trustee for A's representatives proportionately to the share of the purchase-money advanced by A. Had the purchase-money been advanced equally, B would have been entitled to the whole estate in equity as well as at law; for where two purchasers advance the money equally they may be presumed to have purchased with a view to benefit of survivorship.[88]

---

[78] *Milward* v. *Earl Thanet* (1801) 5 Ves. 720n.; *Mills* v. *Haywood* (1877) 6 Ch.D. 196; *M.E.P.C. Ltd.* v. *Christian-Edwards* [1978] Ch. 281, affirmed on more general grounds: [1981] A.C. 205, see *post*, p. 615; *post*, p. 609.
[79] *Lindsay Petroleum Co.* v. *Hurd* (1874) L.R. 5 P.C. 221.
[80] *Beale* v. *Kyte* [1907] 1 Ch. 564.
[81] *G.W. Ry.* v. *Oxford, etc., Ry.* (1853) 3 De G.M. & G. 341.
[82] See *ante*, p. 34, and *post*, pp. 652, 655.
[83] *Re Jarvis* [1958] 1 W.L.R. 815 at 819.
[84] *Petit* v. *Smith* (1695) 1 P.Wms. 7 at 9, *per* Lord Somers L.C.; and see *Re Bradberry* [1943] Ch. 35 at 40.
[85] But see *Re Cohen, National Provincial Bank Ltd.* v. *Katz (No. 1)* [1953] Ch. 88 at 95.
[86] *Malayan Credit Ltd.* v. *Jack Chia-MPH Ltd.* [1986] A.C. 549 at 560.
[87] *Malayan Credit Ltd.* v. *Jack Chia-MPH Ltd.* [1986] A.C. 549.
[88] *Lake* v. *Gibson* (1729) 1 Eq.Ca.Abr. 290; on appeal *Lake* v. *Craddock* (1732) 3 P.Wms. 158; **2 W. & T.L.C. 876.** And see *post*, pp. 177, 178.

(2) LOAN ON MORTGAGE.   If a mortgage is made to A and B jointly, it is immaterial whether the money is advanced equally or unequally; the mere circumstance of the transaction being a loan is sufficient to repel the presumption of an intention to hold the mortgage on a joint tenancy, and the survivor is therefore a trustee for the representatives of the deceased mortgagee to the extent of his proportion of the loan.[89] As between the mortgagees and the mortgagor the mortgage money is deemed to be money lent on a joint account, so that the survivor can give a good receipt.[90] But this does not affect the rights of the mortgagees *inter se*; the survivor must account to the personal representatives of the deceased mortgagee for his share.[91]

(3) PARTNERSHIP.   Where partners acquire property, they are presumed to hold it as beneficial tenants in common.[92] *Jus accrescendi inter mercatores locum non habet.*[93]

(b) *Severance of joint tenancy.*   Even where the property is vested in the parties as joint tenants in equity as well as at law, as where the parties are expressly declared joint tenants in equity or in the case of a joint purchase where the money is advanced equally, equity will readily treat the joint tenancy as severed so as to exclude the incident of survivorship. Thus, not only will an actual alienation of his share by one tenant sever the joint tenancy in equity as regards that share, but also a mere agreement to alienate the share will have the same effect. Such an agreement need not be specifically enforceable, at all events if it is an agreement between the joint tenants themselves.[94] The agreement must be entered into for value, *e.g.* in consideration of marriage.[95]

Since 1925, no severance of the legal joint tenancy in land so as to create a tenancy in common at law is possible,[96] but where a legal estate (not being settled land) is vested in joint tenants beneficially, it is provided by statute that any tenant desiring to sever the joint tenancy in equity may give the others a written notice of his desire, or do such other acts or things as would in the case of personal estate have been effectual to sever the tenancy in equity.[97] Thereupon, under the trust for sale which now affects all land held beneficially by joint tenants of a legal estate (unless the land is settled land[98]), the net proceeds of sale and the net rents and profits until sale will be held on the trusts which

---

[89] *Morley* v. *Bird* (1798) 3 Ves. 628 at 631.
[90] L.P.A. 1925, s.111, replacing C.A. 1881, s.61. Before 1882 it was usual for mortgages to contain a clause, known as the joint account clause, to the same effect.
[91] See *Re Jackson, Smith* v. *Sibthorpe* (1887) 34 Ch.D. 732.
[92] *Lake* v. *Craddock, supra*; but see *Barton* v. *Morris* [1985] 1 W.L.R. 1257.
[93] *Buckley* v. *Barber* (1851) 6 Exch. 164 at 179 (the right of survivorship has no place among merchants).
[94] *Burgess* v. *Rawnsley* [1975] Ch. 429.
[95] *Brown* v. *Raindle* (1796) 3 Ves. 256 at 257; *Burnaby* v. *Equitable Reversionary Interest Society* (1885) 28 Ch.D. 416; *Re Hewett, Hewett* v. *Hallett* [1894] 1 Ch. 362. For other methods of severance, see *Williams* v. *Hensman* (1861) 1 J. & H. 546 at 557, 558; *Re Denny* [1947] L.J.R. 1029; contrast *Barton* v. *Morris* [1985] 1 W.L.R. 1257.
[96] L.P.A. 1925, ss.1(6), 36.
[97] *Ibid.* s.36(2).
[98] See *Re Gaul and Houlston's Contract* [1928] Ch. 689.

would have been requisite for giving effect to the beneficial interests if there had been an actual severance.[99]

It seems that even apart from the statutory power to give notice, a unilateral declaration by a joint tenant communicated to the other joint tenants[1] will effect a severance.[2] On the other hand, physical division and separate occupation of the parts of the property is not inconsistent with the continuation of the joint tenancy.[3]

(c) *Equal division*

(1) THE PRINCIPLE. In addition to equity's ancient dislike of a joint tenancy, the maxim "equality is equity" may be illustrated by a number of more modern instances. In general, the maxim will be applied whenever property is to be distributed between rival claimants and there is no other basis for division. "I think that the principle which applies here is Plato's definition of equality as a 'sort of justice': if you cannot find any other, equality is the proper basis."[4]

(2) HUSBAND AND WIFE. For example, after a divorce the court has refused to dissect meticulously the joint bank account into which the husband and wife paid their income, and upon which they both drew, and instead divided the balance equally between them.[5] The same principle was applied where a husband, his wife and the wife's mother had all contributed towards the purchase and equipment of a house.[6] But even between husband and wife the principle does not apply while they are still living together, for then their rights in a joint bank account are not meant to be attended by legal consequences,[7] and each will be sole beneficial owner of any property which he or she buys with money drawn from the joint bank account, subject to any contrary intention.[8] The principle, too, has been rejected as between a man and his mistress.[9]

---

[99] L.P.A. 1925, s.36(2).

[1] This is essential: *Burgess* v. *Rawnsley* [1975] Ch. 429 at 444, 448.

[2] *Hawkesley* v. *May* [1956] 1 Q.B. 304 at 313, 314, followed in *Re Draper's Conveyance* [1969] 1 Ch. 486. These cases were not followed in *Nielson-Jones* v. *Fedden* [1975] Ch. 222 where it was pointed out that *Re Wilks, Childs* v. *Bulmer* [1891] 3 Ch. 59 to the contrary had not been cited. The latter two cases were, however, doubted in *Burgess* v. *Rawnsley* [1975] Ch. 429, C.A.

[3] *Greenfield* v. *Greenfield* (1979) 38 P. & C.R. 570.

[4] *Jones* v. *Maynard* [1951] Ch. 572 at 575, *per* Vaisey J. See also Maine's *Ancient Law* (12th ed., 1888), p. 58.

[5] *Jones* v. *Maynard* [1951] Ch. 572; and see *Rimmer* v. *Rimmer* [1953] 1 Q.B. 63 (discussed at (1953) 69 L.Q.R. 11) for a similar example. Contrast *Re Cohen, National Provincial Bank Ltd.* v. *Katz (No. 1)* [1953] Ch. 88, where another basis was found; but the same estates later furnished an occasion for the application of the maxim: *Re Cohen, National Provincial Bank Ltd.* v. *Katz (No. 2)* [1960] Ch. 179; *post*, p. 335. See also *post*, p. 188.

[6] *MacDonald* v. *MacDonald* [1957] 2 All E.R. 690.

[7] *Gage* v. *King* [1961] 1 Q.B. 188.

[8] *Re Young, Trye* v. *Sullivan* (1885) 28 Ch.D. 705; *Re Bishop* [1965] Ch. 450; contrast *Re Warm and Warm* (1969) 8 D.L.R. (3d) 466 (land purchased by husband from joint account held for husband and wife jointly), doubting *Re Bishop. Re Bishop* was followed in *Feaver* v. *Feaver* [1977] 5 W.W.R. 271 in which, however, *Re Warm and Warm* was not cited.

[9] *Diwell* v. *Farnes* [1959] 1 W.L.R. 624, criticised at (1959) 75 L.Q.R. 296; and see now *Cooke* v. *Head* [1972] 1 W.L.R. 518.

(3) OTHER CASES. The rule of equality has been applied in relation to club property as between the members of a club which has ceased to exist[10]; and in relation to commission as between two estate agents who have been instructed in the sale of the same property.[11] Again, when an author bequeaths the manuscript of a work to A and the copyright to B, and publication of the work is made possible only by using the manuscript, prima facie the proceeds of sale of the copyright will be divided equally between A and B.[12] The maxim also appears to be responsible for the decision that where property has been settled in unequal shares with a provision that any share which fails to vest shall accrue to the other shares by way of addition, accruer prima facie takes place in equal shares and not in the proportions laid down by the settlor for the original shares,[13] even though equality is attained only at the price of altering the proportions prescribed by the settlor.[14]

9. Equity looks to the intent rather than to the form. "Courts of Equity make a distinction in all cases between that which is matter of substance and that which is matter of form; and if it find that by insisting on the form, the substance will be defeated, it holds it to be inequitable to allow a person to insist on such form, and thereby defeat the substance."[15] Thus if a party to a contract for the sale of land fails to complete on the day fixed for completion, at law he is in breach of his contract, and will be liable for damages, *e.g.* for delay.[16] Yet in equity it will usually suffice if he is ready to complete within a reasonable period thereafter, and thus the other party will not be able to avoid performance.[17] Again, whether equity will regard an agreement as being negative depends not on the precise language but on the substance of the agreement.[18] This maxim also lies at the root of the equitable doctrines governing precatory words, mortgages, penalties and forfeitures, all of which are fully considered in the later chapters of this book.[19]

Another aspect of the maxim is shown by equity's impatience with mere technicalities. Equity was never much impressed by a deed, and it will refuse to decree specific performance of a voluntary agreement even if it is made by deed and so enforceable at law.[20] Similarly, informal

---

[10] *Re Sick and Funeral Society of St. John's Sunday School, Golcar* [1973] Ch. 51; *Re Bucks Constabulary Widows' and Orphans' Fund Friendly Society (No. 2)* [1979] 1 W.L.R. 936; *Re G.K.N. Bolts & Nuts Ltd. (Automotive Division) Birmingham Works Sports and Social Club* [1982] 1 W.L.R. 774.

[11] *Hampton & Sons* v. *Garrard Smith (Estate Agents) Ltd.* (1985) 274 E.G. 1139.

[12] *Re Dickens* [1935] Ch. 267 (Charles Dickens' *Life of Christ*).

[13] *Re Bower's S.T.* [1942] Ch. 197.

[14] See (1942) 58 L.Q.R. 311. For other examples of the operation of the maxim, see *Re Kavanagh* (1949) 66(1) T.L.R. 65; *Miller* v. *Huddlestone* (1851) 3 Mac. & G. 513 at 523; and *post*, pp. 97, 98, 115, 155.

[15] *Parkin* v. *Thorold* (1852) 16 Beav. 59 at 66, *per* Romilly M.R.

[16] *Raineri* v. *Miles* [1981] A.C. 1050.

[17] *Parkin* v. *Thorold, supra* at p. 67; and see *post*, p. 609.

[18] *Metropolitan Electric Supply Co. Ltd.* v. *Ginder* [1901] 2 Ch. 799; see *post*, p. 677.

[19] See *post*, pp. 113, 392, 538. See also *post*, pp. 283, 488 for other instances.

[20] *Post*, p. 592.

alterations to a prescribed form may be accepted as effectual.[21] It is
also "a principle of equity that the Court does not require unnecessary
formalities to be gone through,"[22] and so equity will avoid circuity of
action by holding valid a transaction which, although unauthorised,
could lawfully have been effected by going through two or more
separate transactions.[23]

10. Equity looks on that as done which ought to be done.[24] This
maxim has its most frequent application in the case of contracts. Equity
treats a contract to do a thing as if the thing were already done, though
only in favour of persons entitled to enforce the contract specifically and
not in favour of volunteers.[25] Agreements for value are thus often
treated as if they had been performed at the time when they ought to
have been performed, with the same consequences as if they had then
been completely performed. For example, a person who enters into
possession of land under a specifically enforceable agreement for a lease
is regarded in any court which has jurisdiction to enforce the
agreement[26] as being in the same position as between himself and the
other party to the agreement as if the lease had actually been granted to
him.[27] The doctrine has been applied to a consent order for the grant of
a new lease.[28]

Other examples of the maxim will be found in the enforcement of an
imperfect trust made for value, the qualified trust for a purchaser
imposed by equity upon the vendor, the rule in *Howe* v. *Earl of
Dartmouth*, and the doctrine of conversion.[29]

11. Equity imputes an intention to fulfil an obligation. Where a man
is under an obligation to do an act, and he does some other act which is
capable of being regarded as a fulfilment of his obligation, the latter act
will prima facie be so regarded; for it is right to put the most favourable
construction on a man's acts, and to presume that he intends to be just
before he affects to be generous. For example, suppose that a husband
covenants with the trustees of his marriage settlement to pay to them
the sum of £50,000, to be laid out by the trustees in the purchase of
lands in the county of Devon which are to be settled upon the trusts of
the settlement. In fact, the husband never pays the money to the
trustees, but after the marriage purchases lands in Devon for £50,000,
and has them conveyed to himself in fee simple; and he then dies

[21] *Re Danish Bacon Co. Ltd. Staff Pension Fund Trusts* [1971] 1 W.L.R. 248.
[22] *Sprange* v. *Lee* [1908] 1 Ch. 424 at 430, *per* Neville J.
[23] *Re Lord Gisborough's S.E.* [1921] 2 Ch. 39; *Re Collard's W.T.* [1961] Ch. 293; see *post*, p. 279.
[24] *Banks* v. *Sutton* (1732) 2 P.Wms. 700 at 715.
[25] *Re Anstis* (1886) 31 Ch.D. 596; *Re Plumptre's Marriage Settlement* [1910] 1 Ch. 609.
[26] *Foster* v. *Reeves* [1892] 2 Q.B. 255.
[27] *Walsh* v. *Lonsdale* (1882) 21 Ch.D. 9; *ante*, p. 15.
[28] *Tottenham Hotspur Football & Athletic Co. Ltd.* v. *Princegrove Publishers Ltd.* [1974] 1 W.L.R. 113,
    where this passage was referred to at p. 121.
[29] *Post*, pp. 120, 195, 225, 485.

without bringing the lands into settlement. The purchased lands are in equity presumed to have been purchased by the husband in pursuance of his covenant, and as being in fact his performance of that covenant, so that they become subject to the trusts of his marriage settlement.[30] It is on this maxim that the doctrines of performance and satisfaction are founded.[31]

12. Equity acts in personam. This maxim which is descriptive of the procedure in equity, is of less significance now than formerly.

(a) *Methods of enforcing judgments.* A judgment of the common law courts was enforced by one of the ordinary writs of execution by means of which the plaintiff was forcibly put into possession of the property to which he was entitled under the judgment. But the Court of Chancery, originally at any rate, did not itself interfere with the defendant's property, but merely made an order against the defendant personally, and if he failed to comply with it, punished him for his disobedience by attachment or committal for contempt, *i.e.* by "execution *in personam* peculiar to the Court of Equity."[32] However, in some cases imprisonment proved ineffectual to compel compliance with its orders, and the Court of Chancery afterwards had recourse to the writ of sequestration, under which sequestrators were appointed to take possession of the property in dispute, and eventually of all the defendant's property, until he did the act which he had been ordered to do.[33] But that was all. A defendant who refused to comply with an order to deliver up a document for cancellation might languish in prison, but in the meantime the document remained valid at law.[34]

This power of enforcing its orders by committal of the person or sequestration of the estate has been supplemented by statute. Thus, the court may make vesting orders in various cases, or instead of making a vesting order, may appoint a person to execute a transfer.[35] Further, by a more general provision,[36] where any person neglects or refuses to comply with a judgment or order directing him to execute any conveyance, contract, or other document, or to indorse any negotiable instrument, the court may nominate some person to do the act for him. Again, since the Judicature Acts, the orders of the Chancery Division can be enforced by any of the legal writs of execution which may be applicable to the particular case. For instance, an order for the payment of a sum of money can be enforced by a writ of *fieri facias*.[37] Further, the court may administer a trust fund to which a possible or certain

---

[30] *Sowden* v. *Sowden* (1785) 1 Bro.C.C. 582.
[31] *Post,* pp. 513 *et seq.*
[32] See *Lever Brothers Ltd.* v. *Kneale* [1937] 2 K.B. 87 at 94, *per* Greene L.J. Attachment has been abolished; committal survives: see *post,* p. 675.
[33] See Ashburner's *Equity* (2nd ed., 1933), pp. 30–34.
[34] See (1459) Y.B. 37 Hen. 6, Hil., pl. 3, fo. 13 at 14, *per* Priscot C.J.
[35] T.A. 1925, ss.44 *et seq.*, re-enacting T.A. 1893, ss.31 *et seq.* See also A.E.A. 1925, s.43(2).
[36] S.C.A. 1981, s.39, replacing J.A. 1925, s.47, which replaced J.A. 1884, s.14.
[37] See R.S.C., Ord. 45; and see *post,* p. 581.

claimant is a foreign sovereign against whom personally no order can be made.[38] Yet the mere fact that an equitable remedy is claimed does not confer jurisdiction: the court "would not grant an injunction against the French Republic marching an army across the Rhine or the Alps."[39]

(b) *Jurisdiction over property abroad*[40]

(1) THE PRINCIPLE.   Although at the present day equity is not confined to acting *in personam*, still its jurisdiction is primarily over the defendant personally. It is therefore immaterial that the property in question is not within the reach of the court, provided that the defendant himself is within the jurisdiction, or is capable of being served with the proceedings outside the jurisdiction,[41] and that there is some equitable right which the plaintiff could have enforced against him had the property been here.[42] The jurisdiction is grounded "not upon any pretension to the exercise of judicial and administrative rights abroad, but on the circumstance of the person of the party on whom this order is being made being within the power of the Court."[43] Accordingly, in the leading case of *Penn* v. *Lord Baltimore*,[44] specific performance was ordered of an agreement relating to the boundaries[45] of land in America, the defendant being in this country.

As Lord Selborne L.C. said in *Ewing* v. *Orr Ewing (No. 1)*[46]: "The courts of Equity in England are, and always have been, courts of conscience, operating *in personam* and not *in rem*; and in the exercise of this personal jurisdiction they have always been accustomed to compel the performance of contracts and trusts as to subjects which were not either locally or *ratione domicilii* within their jurisdiction. They have done so as to land, in Scotland, in Ireland, in the Colonies, in foreign countries." In this case, the House of Lords held that where some of the executors and trustees of a will were in England, the English court had jurisdiction to administer the real and personal assets of a testator who died domiciled in Scotland, even though the greater part of the personalty and all the realty were situate in Scotland. Eventually, however, an administration action was started in Scotland, and the House of Lords stayed the English administration on the ground of

---

[38] *United States of America* v. *Dollfus Mieg et Cie S.A.* [1952] A.C. 582 at 617, 618; *Sultan of Johore* v. *Abubakar Tunku Aris Bendahar* [1952] A.C. 318 at 343, 344.
[39] *Duke of Brunswick* v. *King of Hanover* (1848) 2 H.L.C. 1 at 27, *per* Lord Campbell; and see *post*, p. 669.
[40] See G. W. Keeton (1951) 4 *Current Legal Problems* 107; *Richard West and Partners (Inverness) Ltd.* v. *Dick* [1969] 2 Ch. 424 at 430–432.
[41] *Duder* v. *Amsterdamsch Trustees* [1902] 2 Ch. 132; *Jenney* v. *Mackintosh* (1886) 33 Ch.D. 595; and see *Re Liddell's S.T.* [1936] Ch. 365 (wards of court). Cf. *Eastern Trust Co.* v. *McKenzie, Mann & Co. Ltd.* [1915] A.C. 750 at 760 (defendant restrained from receiving property from the Crown).
[42] See *Deschamps* v. *Miller* [1908] 1 Ch. 856 at 863.
[43] *Lord Portarlington* v. *Soulby* (1834) 3 My. & K. 104 at 108, *per* Lord Brougham L.C.
[44] (1750) 1 Ves.Sen. 444; **1 W. & T.L.C. 638.** See also *Earl of Kildare* v. *Eustace* (1686) 1 Vern. 423 (trust of Irish land).
[45] As to the fixing of boundaries, see *Wake* v. *Conyers* (1759) 1 Eden 331; **1 W. & T.L.C. 167;** Hunt's *Law of Boundaries, Walls and Fences* (6th ed., 1912), pp. 251–262; Powell-Smith's *Law of Boundaries and Fences* (2nd ed., 1975), pp. 31–33.
[46] (1883) 9 App.Cas. 34 at 40.

convenience.[47] In other circumstances a defendant may be restrained from taking proceedings in a foreign country.[48]

(2) APPLICATION.   On this principle the court can give judgment on a variety of matters affecting land outside England, such as for the redemption or foreclosure of a mortgage of it,[49] for specific performance of an agreement to create a mortgage of it[50] or to sell it,[51] or for the rent[52] or an account of the rents and profits of it and, if necessary and effectual, for the appointment of a receiver thereof.[53] The Court has even made an interlocutory order for the inspection of land abroad on the basis of an equity alleged but not yet established in the action.[54] Where there is an English contract for a mortgage of land outside England, the English equitable rule against clogging the equity of redemption will be enforced against a contracting party here.[55]

(3) JURISDICTON EXCLUDED.   On the other hand, if an action involves merely a question of title to land outside the jurisdiction, and the plaintiff has no equity which he could have enforced against the defendant had the land been English, the courts of this country will not entertain the action; the question of title can be better dealt with by the courts of the country in which the land is situate.[56] Such actions are of a class known as "local," being actions where it is essential, if full effect is to be given to the judgment, that they should be laid in the locality in which the land is situate. Before the Judicature Act 1873, such actions could not have been brought in any English court, and that Act did not confer any new jurisdiction on the Supreme Court.[57] Thus no action can be brought here to obtain damages for trespass to land outside England,[58] or for damages for and an injunction to restrain a conspiracy to trespass on land abroad,[59] or to recover a rent charged on such land which the defendant is only liable to pay by reason of his being the owner of the land, and not by reason of any contract.[60] Notwithstanding this general rule, however, where a court of equity is administering an estate or trust which comprises property in England and abroad, the

---

[47] *Ewing* v. *Orr Ewing (No. 2)* (1885) 10 App.Cas. 453. Contrast *Chellaram* v. *Chelleram* [1985] Ch. 409 (Indian settlements: stay of English proceedings refused).
[48] *Re North Carolina Estate Co. Ltd.* (1889) 5 T.L.R. 328.
[49] *Toller* v. *Carteret* (1705) 2 Vern. 494; *Paget* v. *Ede* (1874) L.R. 18 Eq. 118.
[50] *Ex p. Pollard* (1840) 1 Mont. & Ch. 239; *Re Smith, Lawrence* v. *Kitson* [1916] 2 Ch. 206.
[51] *Richard West and Partners (Inverness) Ltd.* v. *Dick* [1969] 2 Ch. 424.
[52] *St. Pierre* v. *South American Stores (Gath & Chaves) Ltd.* [1936] 1 K.B. 382.
[53] *Mercantile Investment and General Trust Co.* v. *River Plate Trust, Loan and Agency Co.* [1892] 2 Ch. 303. And see *Duder* v. *Amsterdamsch Trustees* [1902] 2 Ch. 132.
[54] *Cook Industries Inc.* v. *Galliher* [1979] Ch. 439; but see *Altertext Inc.* v. *Advanced Data Communications Ltd.* [1985] 1 W.L.R. 457.
[55] *British South Africa Co.* v. *De Beers Consolidated Mines* [1910] 2 Ch. 502, reversed on appeal on another point, [1912] A.C. 52. See *post*, p. 394, as to "clogging."
[56] *Re Hawthorne* (1883) 23 Ch.D. 743.
[57] See *Mostyn* v. *Fabrigas* (1775) 1 Cowp. 161; 1 Smith's L.C. 642. Locality of venue for actions *within* the country, however, has in general been abolished: R.S.C., Ord. 33, r. 4.
[58] *British South Africa Co.* v. *Companhia de Moçambique* [1893] A.C. 602; *cf. The Tolten* [1946] P. 135 as to Admiralty jurisdiction.
[59] *Hesperides Hotels Ltd.* v. *Muftizade* [1979] A.C. 508, following *British South Africa Co.* v. *Companhia de Moçambique, supra*, and approving *The Tolten, supra.*
[60] *Whitaker* v. *Forbes* (1875) L.R. 10 C.P. 583.

court will adjudicate on questions of title to the foreign property even if
it consists of immovables and even if no fiduciary relationship or
personal equity is involved.[61]

---

[61] See *Earl Nelson* v. *Lord Bridport* (1846) 8 Beav. 547; *Re Piercy, Whitwam* v. *Piercy (No. 1)* [1895]
1 Ch. 83; *Re Duke of Wellington* [1947] Ch. 506, affirmed [1948] Ch. 118; and see J. H. C. Morris
(1948) 64 L.Q.R. 268.

CHAPTER 4

PRIORITIES

1. Priorities.   Many different questions of priorities may arise. These may concern any interest in property, as when there are rival conveyances of land, or competing assignments of beneficial interests in trust funds; but usually they relate to mortgages. Thus there may be two rival mortgages of property worth enough to satisfy one but not both. The mortgages may both be legal, or the first legal and the second equitable, or vice versa, or both may be equitable. This last category includes two distinct heads, namely, those cases where the estate mortgaged is legal but the mortgages are merely equitable (*e.g.* where a tenant in fee simple creates two informal, and therefore equitable, mortgages of his legal estate), and those cases where the mortgages are necessarily equitable because only an equitable interest has been mortgaged, as where a beneficiary under a settlement makes successive mortgages of his equitable interest.

2. The two categories.   In solving these conflicts, the courts have gradually established various rules, and these have been subjected to substantial modifications by statute. There are two broad categories.

(a) *Order of creation.*   First, there is the basic rule that competing interests will prima facie rank according to the order of their creation. This basic rule may, however, be modified by subsidiary rules relating to—

   (i)   the purchaser without notice;

  (ii)   fraud, estoppel and gross negligence;

 (iii)   registration; and

 (iv)   overreaching.

This category includes all dealings with legal estates in land; and similar rules apply to unregistered dealings with shares.[1] In the case of land,

---

[1] See Gower, *Principles of Modern Company Law* (4th ed., 1979), pp. 455 *et seq.* and see *post*, p. 67.

registration is now the most important head, and the other heads must be read subject to this.

(b) *Order of notice.*   Secondly, there are certain dealings which stand outside these rules and have their relative priorities determined by the quite distinct rule in *Dearle* v. *Hall*,[2] whereunder priority primarily depends upon the order in which notice of the dealings has been received. The dealings within this rule are dealings with equitable interests in any property, real or personal.[3]

3. Classification.   It will be observed that in order to decide which set of rules to apply, what is important is not the nature of the dealing but the nature of what has been dealt with; the question is not whether the competing mortgages are legal or equitable, but whether the property which has been successively mortgaged is legal or equitable. Further, the categories are not exhaustive. They include all interests in land, whether legal or equitable, and equitable interests in pure personalty. But dealings with most[4] legal interests in pure personalty stand outside not only these categories but also the scope of this book; and mortgages and other dealings with chattels under which possession is not transferred are usually regulated by the complex provisions of the Bills of Sale Acts 1878 and 1882.

PART 1

THE GENERAL RULES

Section 1. The Basic Rule: Order of Creation

1. The rule.   At law, as in equity, the basic rule is that estates and interests primarily rank in the order of creation. *Qui prior est tempore potior est jure*[5]: he who is earlier in time is stronger in law. Thus, in the comparatively rare cases before 1926 where there were two or more legal mortgages of a legal estate in land created by the grant of successive leases,[6] the second mortgage would prima facie be postponed to the first, for the second lease would take effect in reversion upon the first, and a legal estate in reversion was postponed to one in possession.[7] Again, where there are two competing equitable interests, the general

---

[2] (1828) 3 Russ. 1.
[3] Before 1925 this rule was confined to equitable interests in pure personalty; after 1925 it was extended to equitable interests in unregistered land; and after 1986 to equitable interests in registered land: *post*, pp. 66, 67.
[4] Not all: see, *e.g.* shares (*supra*) and choses in action (*post*, p. 66).
[5] *Barclays Bank Ltd.* v. *Bird* [1954] Ch. 274 at 280.
[6] See *Aldridge* v. *Duke* (1679) Rept.t.Finch 439; *Jones* v. *Rhind* (1869) 17 W.R. 1091.
[7] See Coote, *Mortgages* (9th ed., 1927), p. 1240; and see *Mason* v. *Rhodes* (1885) 53 L.T. 322.

rule of equity is that the person whose equity attached to the property first will be entitled to priority over the other. Where the equities are equal and neither claimant has the legal estate, the first in time prevails, since "every conveyance of an equitable interest is an innocent conveyance, that is to say, the grant of a person entitled merely in equity passes only that which he is justly entitled to and no more."[8]

2. Operation of the rule. The rule may be illustrated by a case where a company hired machinery from A under a hire-purchase agreement whereby the property in the machinery was not to pass to the company until all instalments had been paid, and a right was given to A to remove the machinery on the company's failure to pay an instalment. The machinery was fixed on the business premises of which the company was the legal owner, and so the legal interest in the machinery vested in the company. Afterwards the company created an equitable mortgage of the premises in favour of B who had no notice of the hire-purchase agreement. It was held that A's right to remove the fixtures was an equitable interest in the land, and that as it had attached before B's equitable mortgage was created, it had priority over B's rights.[9]

Section 2. The Purchaser Without Notice

An important qualification to the basic rule is the doctrine of the purchaser[10] without notice, which demonstrates a fundamental distinction between legal estates and equitable interests.

1. The doctrine. A legal right is enforceable against any person who takes the property, whether or not he has notice of it, except where the right is overreached or is void against him for want of registration. If V sells to P land over which W has a legal right of way, P takes the land subject to W's right even if he was ignorant of it. But it is different as regards equitable rights. Nothing can be clearer than that a purchaser for valuable consideration who obtains a legal estate at the time of his purchase without notice of a prior equitable right is entitled to priority in equity as well as at law.[11] In such a case equity follows the law; the purchaser's conscience is in no way affected by the equitable right. Where there is equal equity the law prevails. The onus of proving the purchase of a legal estate without notice rests on the purchaser.[12]

[8] *Phillips* v. *Phillips* (1862) 4 De G.F. & J. 208 at 215, *per* Lord Westbury L.C.
[9] *Re Samuel Allen & Sons Ltd.* [1907] 1 Ch. 575, followed in *Re Morrison, Jones and Taylor Ltd.* [1914] 1 Ch. 50; and see *Hawks* v. *McArthur* [1951] 1 All E.R. 22. See generally H. A. Hollond (1928) 3 C.L.J. 173; A. G. Guest and J. Lever (1963) 27 Conv.(N.S.) 30. Equities of this kind would not appear to be registrable: see *post*, pp. 59, 61.
[10] For a discussion of the different meanings of "purchaser," see *Powell* v. *Cleland* [1948] 1 K.B. 262.
[11] *Pilcher* v. *Rawlins* (1872) 7 Ch.App. 259.
[12] *Re Nisbet and Potts' Contract* [1906] 1 Ch. 386 at 404, 409, 410; but see *Shears* v. *Wells* [1936] 1 All E.R. 832.

2. Illustrations. Suppose that L, a fraudulent landowner, forges a duplicate set of title deeds and deposits the genuine deeds with A to secure a loan of money, thereby creating an equitable mortgage in his favour. L then sells the land to B and conveys the legal estate to him, handing over to him the forged title deeds; and B has no notice of A's equitable mortgage. B, who has acquired the legal estate bona fide for value without notice, has an equity to retain the estate equal to A's right to enforce his equitable claim to it, and therefore the court will refuse to give A any relief as against B.

Again, *Cave* v. *Cave*[13] illustrates both the basic rule and its modification. The sole trustee of a marriage settlement used the trust funds to purchase lands in breach of trust, and took the conveyance in the name of his brother. The brother then created a legal mortgage in favour of A and an equitable mortgage in favour of B, neither A nor B having notice of the trust. It was held that A's legal mortgage had priority over the equitable interests of the beneficiaries, but that those interests had priority over the equitable mortgage.

3. Registration. The doctrine is quite distinct from the system of registration discussed below.[14] For—

(i)   some of the rights which are void against a purchaser if not registered are legal rights, whereas the doctrine of purchaser without notice has never enabled a purchaser to take free from legal rights, as distinct from equitable interests; and

(ii)   under the old system, a purchaser without notice took free from equities if he gave *value* and acquired a *legal estate*. An unregistered right is sometimes void against a purchaser if he gave *value* and acquired *any interest, legal or equitable*, and sometimes void against a purchaser only if he gave *money or money's worth* and acquired a *legal estate*.

In the application of the doctrine of the purchaser without notice, the following points must be considered.

A. Value

The purchaser must have given value for the property, although it need not be shown that the consideration was adequate.[15] A volunteer always

---

[13] (1880) 15 Ch.D. 639.
[14] See *post*, pp. 58 *et seq.*
[15] *Basset* v. *Nosworthy* (1673) Rep.t.Finch 102; **2 W. & T.L.C. 136**; and see *Midland Bank Trust Co. Ltd.* v. *Green* [1981] A.C. 513.

takes subject to any equitable rights attaching to the property at the time when the legal interest is transferred to him, and so does a squatter.[16] The only point requiring remark in this connection is that the satisfaction of an existing debt is sufficient value to support the defence[17]; yet a volunteer does not become a purchaser for value merely because he undertakes to use in a particular way the property which has been given to him.[18]

B. Legal Estate

1. The rule. The purchaser must have obtained a legal estate.[19] If he has taken a mere equitable interest, he has nothing superior to the equity from which he claims to be free, and as that will be prior in time, it will prevail; the vendor of an equitable interest can convey only what is vested in him, and if part of his equitable interest was already assigned or charged, the purchaser could only take what was left.[20] But if the purchaser takes a legal estate, he will be protected by the doctrine, even if there is some defect in his title.[21]

2. Qualifications. There are three qualifications to the rule that the purchaser must take a legal estate.

(a) *Better right to legal estate.* A purchaser of an equitable interest without notice will take free from a prior equity if his purchase gave him the better right to a legal estate. Thus if the purchaser has the legal estate conveyed to a trustee for him, and neither he nor the trustee has notice of a prior equity, the purchaser will take free from it; for his right to the legal estate is the better.[22] So, too, where trust money is misappropriated by the trustee and paid into court to satisfy a claim against him by a third party, the latter has the better right to the legal title in the money which has been transferred to the Accountant General.[23] It is otherwise where no transfer of the legal estate is made as where it is outstanding in a third party at all material times so that the trustee can transfer an equitable interest only.[24]

---

[16] *Re Nisbet and Potts' Contract* [1906] 1 Ch. 386.
[17] *Thorndike* v. *Hunt* (1859) 3 De G. & J. 563; *Taylor* v. *Blakelock* (1886) 32 Ch.D. 560 at 568, 570.
[18] *Re Diplock* [1947] Ch. 716 at 781–785; [1948] Ch. 465 at 545.
[19] *Wigg* v. *Wigg* (1739) 1 Atk. 382; but see *Sharpe* v. *Foy* (1868) 4 Ch.App. 35.
[20] *Phillips* v. *Phillips* (1862) 4 De G.F. & J. 208.
[21] *Jones* v. *Powles* (1834) 3 My. & K. 581.
[22] *Wilkes* v. *Bodington* (1707) 2 Vern. 599; *Taylor* v. *London and County Banking Co.* [1901] 2 Ch. 231 at 262, 263.
[23] *Thorndike* v. *Hunt* (1859) 3 De G. & J. 563.
[24] *Assaf* v. *Fuwa* [1955] A.C. 215. In *McCarthy & Stone Ltd.* v. *Julian S. Hodge & Co. Ltd.* [1971] 1 W.L.R. 1547 at 1557 it was suggested that a declaration of trust of the legal estate by the vendor for the purchaser may be sufficient, but this seems doubtful.

(b) *Subsequent acquisition of legal estate.* A purchaser without notice who at the time of the purchase fails to obtain either a legal estate or the better right to one will nevertheless prevail over a prior equity if, without being party to a breach of trust,[25] he subsequently gets in a legal estate, even if he then has notice of the equity. Between himself and the owner of the prior equity the equities are equal, and there is no reason why the purchaser should be deprived of the advantage he may obtain at law by superior activity or diligence.[26]

(c) *Mere equities.* Although the purchaser of an equitable interest without notice will not take free of prior equitable interests, he will take free of any "mere equities."[27]

C. No Notice

Subject to important exceptions to be presently mentioned, the purchaser must have had no notice of the equitable interest at the time when he gave his consideration for the conveyance. Thus, where a purchaser who had notice of an equitable charge completed his purchase on the faith of a forged discharge, he was held to be subject to the charge; a purchaser who chooses to complete in reliance upon the assurance of the vendor or of the vendor's solicitor that an equitable interest has been got in or destroyed does so at his own risk.[28]

The degree of notice is summarised by statute.[29] A purchaser (which includes a mortgagee or lessee[30]) is not to be prejudicially affected by notice of any instrument, matter, fact, or thing, unless—

(a) "it is within his own knowledge, or would have come to his knowledge if such inquiries and inspections had been made as ought reasonably to have been made by him"; or

(b) "in the same transaction with respect to which a question of notice to the purchaser arises, it has come to the knowledge of his counsel, as such, or of his solicitor or other agent, as such, or would have come to the knowledge of his solicitor or other agent, as such, if such inquiries and inspections had been made

[25] See *Bailey* v. *Barnes* [1894] 1 Ch. 25 at 37; *Saunders* v. *Dehew* (1692) 2 Vern. 271; *Perham* v. *Kempster* [1907] 1 Ch. 373.

[26] *Bailey* v. *Barnes* [1894] 1 Ch. 25 at 36; and see *Mumford* v. *Stohwasser* (1874) L.R. 18 Eq. 556; *Taylor* v. *Russell* [1892] A.C. 244. This doctrine has not been affected by the abolition of tacking by L.P.A. 1925, s.94 (*post*, p. 436); though it is a form of tacking, the section seems to be confined to mortgages: see *McCarthy & Stone Ltd.* v. *Julian S. Hodge & Co. Ltd.* [1971] 1 W.L.R. 1547 at 1556, where, however, it was held that the second purchaser had notice when he purchased the equitable interest. And see (1977) 93 L.Q.R. 324 (D. T. Donaldson); *ibid.* 487 (R. M. Goode).

[27] *Phillips* v. *Phillips* (1862) 4 De G.F. & J. 208 at 215–218; *Cave* v. *Cave* (1880) 15 Ch.D. 639; *Westminster Bank Ltd.* v. *Lee* [1956] Ch. 7; *National Provincial Bank Ltd.* v. *Ainsworth* [1965] A.C. 1175 at 1238; *Allied Irish Banks Ltd.* v. *Glynn* [1973] I.R. 188. For "mere equities," see *ante*, p. 25.

[28] *Jared* v. *Clements* [1903] 1 Ch. 428; and see *Gibbs* v. *Messer* [1891] A.C. 248.

[29] L.P.A. 1925, s.199, replacing C.A. 1882, s.3.

[30] L.P.A. 1925, s.205(1)(xxi).

as ought reasonably to have been made by the solicitor or other agent."[31]

But this does not absolve a purchaser from any liability under, or any obligation to perform or observe, any covenant, condition, provision, or restriction contained in any instrument under which his title is derived, mediately or immediately.[32]

From this it is clear that a purchaser is affected by notice of an equity in three cases:

(1) actual notice: where the equity is within his own knowledge;

(2) constructive notice: where the equity would have come to his own knowledge if proper inquiries had been made; and

(3) imputed notice: where his agent as such in the course of the transaction has actual or constructive notice of the equity.[33]

1. Actual notice. It has been said of actual notice that to make it binding it must be given by a person interested in the property and in the course of the negotiations, that it must be clear and distinct, and that vague reports from persons not interested in the property will not affect the purchaser's conscience.[34] It seems, however, that a purchaser cannot safely disregard information from any source if it is of such a nature that a reasonable man or a man of business would act upon the information.[35]

Registration of any instrument or matter required or authorised to be registered under the Land Charges Act 1972, or any enactment which it replaces, is deemed to constitute actual notice of such instrument or matter.[36] But notice and knowledge are distinct concepts: if a purchaser of land has by statute notice of a matter of which he is in fact ignorant, the vendor is not exonerated from any duty to disclose the matter.[37]

2. Constructive notice

(a) *The principle.* The general principle is that a purchaser will be treated as having constructive notice of all that a reasonably prudent purchaser, acting on skilled advice,[38] would have discovered.[39]

---

[31] L.P.A. 1925, s.199(1)(ii).
[32] L.P.A. 1925, s.199(2).
[33] Imputed notice is sometimes included under the head of constructive notice, but it is better to use the terms as stated in the text: see *Espin* v. *Pemberton* (1859) 3 De G. & J. 547 at 554.
[34] *Barnhart* v. *Greenshields* (1853) 9 Moo.P.C. 18, explained in *Reeves* v. *Pope* [1914] 2 K.B. 284.
[35] *Lloyd* v. *Banks* (1868) 3 Ch.App. 488.
[36] L.P.A. 1925, s.198; L.C.A. 1972, s.18(6).
[37] *Rignall Developments Ltd.* v. *Halil* [1988] Ch. 180, doubting *Re Forsey and Hollebone's Contract* [1927] 2 Ch. 379.
[38] *Northern Bank Ltd.* v. *Henry* [1981] I.R. 1 at 18.
[39] See, *e.g. Bailey* v. *Barnes* [1894] 1 Ch. 25 at 35. A similar test applies for the purposes of the Matrimonial Causes Act 1973, s.37: *Kemmis* v. *Kemmis* [1988] 1 W.L.R. 1307.

Constructive notice has been said to be "in its nature no more than evidence of notice, the presumptions of which are so violent that the court will not allow even of its being controverted."[40] There are two main heads of constructive notice, namely—

(i) those where the purchaser had actual notice that the property was in some way incumbered, in which case he will be held to have constructive notice of all that he would have discovered if he had investigated the incumbrance[41]; and

(ii) those where the purchaser has, whether deliberately[42] or carelessly,[43] abstained from making those inquiries that a prudent purchaser would have made.

(b) *Failure to investigate the known.* Under the first head, a purchaser with notice of a mortgage will have constructive notice of any other incumbrances referred to in the mortgage deed[44]; and trustees who distributed a beneficiary's share to an assignee of that share (who was in fact their solicitor) without examining the assignment were held to have constructive notice of an incumbrance on the share to which the assignment was expressly made subject.[45] This applies even if the vendor tells the purchaser that the document contains nothing adverse to the title.[46] But this doctrine is confined to documents which in some way necessarily affect the title; mere notice of some other document is not notice of its contents if the purchaser has been told that its provisions do not affect the property in question and he honestly believes this statement.[47]

(c) *Abstention from investigation.* The following illustrates the second head. A mortgagee who lent money on land knowing that the title deeds had been deposited with some other person, but without inquiring why, has been held to have constructive notice of the charge that was in fact secured by the deposit, on the ground that he had deliberately abstained from inquiry.[48] Most cases under the second head, however, are cases of careless rather than deliberate abstention from inquiry. "Generally speaking a purchaser or mortgagee is bound to inquire into the title of his vendor or mortgagor, and will be affected with notice of what appears upon the title if he does not so inquire."[49]

---

[40] *Plumb* v. *Fluitt* (1791) 2 Anstr. 432 at 438, *per* Eyre C.B.
[41] *Jones* v. *Smith* (1841) 1 Hare 43 at 55; affirmed (1843) 1 Ph. 244.
[42] *Jones* v. *Smith, supra.*
[43] *West* v. *Reid* (1843) 2 Hare 249 at 257; *Oliver* v. *Hinton* [1899] 2 Ch. 264; *Hudston* v. *Viney* [1921] 1 Ch. 98.
[44] *Bisco* v. *Earl of Banbury* (1676) 1 Ch.Ca. 287.
[45] *Davis* v. *Hutchings* [1907] 1 Ch. 356.
[46] *Patman* v. *Harland* (1881) 17 Ch.D. 353.
[47] *Jones* v. *Smith* (1841) 1 Hare 43; affirmed (1843) 1 Ph. 244; *English and Scottish Mercantile Investment Co.* v. *Brunton* [1892] 2 Q.B. 700; *Re Valletort Sanitary Steam Laundry Co. Ltd.* [1903] 2 Ch. 654; and see S. J. Bailey (1942) 8 C.L.J. 36. See also *Re Diplock* [1948] Ch. 465 at 477–479 (legatee not necessarily affected with notice of invalidity of will).
[48] *Birch* v. *Ellames* (1794) 2 Anstr. 427; and see *Nelson* v. *Larholt* [1948] 1 K.B. 339.
[49] *Wilson* v. *Hart* (1866) 1 Ch.App. 463 at 467, *per* Turner L.J.

Inasmuch as a purchaser under an open contract is generally entitled to call upon the vendor to show a title for the last 15 years,[50] he is deemed to have notice of any equitable rights appearing on the title during that period, even though under the contract his right of investigation is restricted to a shorter period[51]; and if he takes a title depending upon adverse possession, he is fixed with notice of equitable rights which an investigation of the title during the last 15 years would have revealed.[52] But a purchaser is not affected by notice of any matter or thing of which, if he had investigated the title or made inquiries in regard to matters prior to the period of commencement of title fixed by statute or by any rule of law, he might have had notice, unless he actually makes such investigation or inquiries.[53]

(d) *Title to reversion.* If a freeholder is granting a lease, statute deprives the lessee of any right to investigate the freehold title unless he has contracted for such a right.[54] In *Patman* v. *Harland*[55] it was held that a lessee's failure to stipulate for such a right had the same effect as if prior to the statute he had agreed not to investigate the title, so that he had constructive notice of all that he would have discovered on such an investigation. This rule has been reversed for contracts made after 1925.[56] It is now provided that where an intending lessee or assignee is precluded by the section from calling for the title to the freehold or to a leasehold reversion, he is not to be deemed to be affected with notice of any matter or thing of which, if he had contracted that such title should be furnished, he might have had notice.[57] Nevertheless, this does not prevent the lessee from being bound if he has actual notice, or if the matter in question is registered under the Land Charges Act 1972, or the title to the land leased is registered under the Land Registration Act 1925 and the matter in question is entered on the charges register.[58]

This may cause real hardship, for as a land charge is registered against the name of the person creating it and not against the land, an intending lessee or assign may not know the names against which to search; and in the case of registered land, the register is at present open for inspection only with the authority of the registered proprietor.[59] The legislature has thus taken away with one hand what it has given with the other: the abolition of the doctrine of *Patman* v. *Harland*[60] has been offset by the increase in the number and importance of the interests which, being

---

[50] L.P.A. 1925, s.44(1), as amended by L.P.A. 1969, s.23. The period, originally 60 years, was reduced first to 40 years by the Vendor and Purchaser Act 1874, s.1, and then to 30 years by L.P.A. 1925, s.44(1).
[51] *Re Cox and Neve's Contract* [1891] 2 Ch. 109.
[52] *Re Nisbet and Potts' Contract* [1906] 1 Ch. 386.
[53] L.P.A. 1925, s.44(8).
[54] Vendor and Purchaser Act 1874, s.2, replaced by L.P.A. 1925, s.44(2), (11).
[55] (1881) 17 Ch.D. 353.
[56] L.P.A. 1925, s.44(5).
[57] *Shears* v. *Wells* [1936] 1 All E.R. 832.
[58] *White* v. *Bijou Mansions Ltd.* [1937] Ch. 610, affirmed on other points [1938] Ch. 351.
[59] L.R.A. 1925, s.112; L.R.A. 1988, s.1. From December 3, 1990, the register will be open for public inspection: 1990, S.I. Nos. 1359, 1362.
[60] (1881) 17 Ch.D. 353.

registrable, will bind a person who may have no real opportunity of discovering them.[61] The full benefit of the statutory change is felt only where the land charge is not registrable (*e.g.* because it was made before 1926) and the contract was made after 1925. However, a purchaser who suffers loss from a land charge of which he had no actual knowledge may now be able to claim compensation.[62]

(e) *Title deeds.* A purchaser ought to require not only an abstract of the vendor's title to be delivered, but also production of the title deeds. If he neglects to call for them, or is put off by an excuse for their non-production which would not have been acted upon by a prudent man without an attempt at verification, and it turns out that the deeds are in the possession of an equitable mortgagee, the purchaser will take subject to the mortgage.[63] This rule is not affected by the Law of Property Act 1925.[64] But the mere absence of the title deeds has never been held sufficient of itself to affect a purchaser with notice if he has bona fide inquired for the deeds and a reasonable excuse has been given for their non-production, for the court cannot in such a case impute to the purchaser either fraud or negligence.[65]

(f) *Inspection of land.* Apart from investigating the deeds, a prudent purchaser will inspect the land itself. If any of the land is occupied[66] by any person *other* than the vendor, this occupation is constructive notice of the estate or interest of the occupier,[67] the terms of his lease, tenancy or other right of occupation,[68] and of any other rights of his,[69] except, it seems, a mere equity, *e.g.* to have his tenancy agreement rectified for mistake.[70] But such occupation is no notice of the rights of other persons, so that if the occupier pays his rent to some person other than the vendor, the occupation is no notice of any rights in the land which that other person may have; yet actual knowledge of the rent being so paid is constructive notice of that other person's rights.[71] Despite earlier rulings to the contrary,[72] and subject to the statutory provisions about overreaching,[73] it is now settled that if the land is occupied by a person *jointly* with the vendor, usually his wife or other relative, this occupation

---

[61] See generally, D. W. Logan (1940) 56 L.Q.R. 361.
[62] See *post*, p. 61.
[63] *Peto* v. *Hammond* (1861) 30 Beav. 495; *Spencer* v. *Clarke* (1878) 9 Ch.D. 137; *Oliver* v. *Hinton* [1899] 2 Ch. 264.
[64] See s.13 of that Act.
[65] *Plumb* v. *Fluitt* (1791) 2 Anst. 432; *Hewitt* v. *Loosemore* (1851) 9 Hare 449; *Agra Bank Ltd.* v. *Barry* (1874) L.R. 7 H.L. 135.
[66] See *Lloyds Bank plc* v. *Rosset* [1989] Ch. 350 as to occupation of semi-derelict land undergoing renovation where the C.A. was divided. In H.L. the point was left open; [1990] 2 W.L.R. 867 at 878.
[67] *Daniels* v. *Davison* (1809) 16 Ves. 249; (1811) 17 Ves. 433; *Allen* v. *Anthony* (1816) 1 Mer. 282. ss.1–39 of L.P.A. 1925 do not prejudicially affect the interest to which any person in possession or actual occupation of the land is entitled in right of such possession or occupation: *ibid.* s.14.
[68] *Taylor* v. *Stibbert* (1794) 2 Ves.Jun. 437.
[69] *Barnhart* v. *Greenshields* (1853) 9 Moo.P.C. 18.
[70] *Smith* v. *Jones* [1954] 1 W.L.R. 1089; *Westminster Bank Ltd.* v. *Lee* [1956] Ch. 7 at 21–23.
[71] *Hunt* v. *Luck* [1902] 1 Ch. 428.
[72] *Caunce* v. *Caunce* [1969] 1 W.L.R 286; *Bird* v. *Syme Thomson* [1979] 1 W.L.R. 440.
[73] *City of London B.S.* v. *Flegg* [1988] A.C. 54. For overreaching see *post*, pp. 62–64.

will be constructive notice of any rights stemming from a contribution to the purchase price.[74]

(g) *Limits of doctrine.* The courts will not extend the doctrine of constructive notice.[75] The negative form in which the statute[76] is drawn shows that the legislature intended a restriction rather than an extension of the doctrine.[77] Thus where a vendor is not living with his wife in the property, the purchaser is not affected with notice from the wife's occupancy of any claim the wife has made or might make in matrimonial proceedings.[78]

3. Imputed notice

(a) *Agency.* It has long been settled that any actual or constructive notice which an agent has (*e.g.* a purchaser's solicitor or counsel) will normally be imputed to his principal.[79] Formerly, notice acquired by the agent in a previous transaction might be notice to the principal.[80] But under the present law, the notice must have been obtained by the agent in the same transaction, and it must have come to the agent as such.[81] Notice acquired in a previous transaction, however closely connected with the transaction in which the question of notice to the principal arises, is not sufficient to affect the principal. And even if the notice is acquired by the agent in the same transaction, it affects the principal only if it is so material to the transaction as to make it the duty of the agent to communicate it to the principal. For example, if a solicitor, while acting for a client in connection with a transfer of a first mortgage, acquired knowledge of a second mortgage, the knowledge so acquired would not prevent the client from tacking a further advance, for the knowledge was not material to the business of the transfer for which alone the solicitor was employed.[82]

(b) *Dual agency.* Where the same solicitor acts for both parties to a transaction, any notice he acquires is imputed to each party,[83] except where he enters into a conspiracy with one party to conceal something from the other,[84] or where he is employed generally by one party only,

---

[74] *Kingsnorth Finance Co. Ltd.* v. *Tizard* [1986] 1 W.L.R. 783, applying *Williams & Glyn's Bank Ltd.* v. *Boland* [1981] A.C. 487 at 505 (which disapproved the cases cited in n. 72, *supra*); *Hodgson* v. *Marks* [1971] Ch. 892 at 934.

[75] *English and Scottish Mercantile Investment Co. Ltd.* v. *Brunton* [1892] 2 Q.B. 700 at 708; and see *Wilson* v. *Kelland* [1901] 2 Ch. 306.

[76] L.P.A. 1925, s.199, replacing C.A. 1882, s.3; *ante*, pp. 50, 51.

[77] *Bailey* v. *Barnes* [1894] 1 Ch. 25; *Caunce* v. *Caunce* [1969] 1 W.L.R. 286 at 293.

[78] *Whittingham* v. *Whittingham* [1979] Fam. 9, Balcombe J. (affirmed *ibid.* C.A., on other grounds, *post*, p. 61), considered in *Kemmis* v. *Kemmis* [1988] 1 W.L.R. 1307.

[79] *Le Neve* v. *Le Neve* (1747) Amb. 436; **2 W. & T.L.C. 157.**

[80] *Fuller* v. *Bennett* (1843) 2 Hare 394.

[81] L.P.A. 1925, s.199, replacing C.A. 1882, s.3; see *Re Cousins* (1886) 31 Ch.D. 671.

[82] *Wyllie* v. *Pollen* (1862) 3 De G.J. & S. 596.

[83] *Dryden* v. *Frost* (1838) 3 My. & Cr. 670; *Rolland* v. *Hart* (1871) 6 Ch.App. 678; *Meyer* v. *Charters* (1918) 34 T.L.R. 589; *cf. Bateman* v. *Hunt* [1904] 2 K.B. 530.

[84] *Sharpe* v. *Foy* (1868) 4 Ch.App. 35.

the other employing him merely to draw up the conveyance.[85] And where one person is an officer of two companies, his personal knowledge is not necessarily the knowledge of both companies. The knowledge which he has acquired as officer of the one company will not be imputed to the other company, unless he owes a duty to the first company to communicate his knowledge, and also a duty to the second company to receive the notice.[86] Moreover, a trustee or personal representative acting for the purposes of more than one trust or estate is not, in the absence of fraud, affected by notice of anything in relation to any particular trust or estate if he has obtained notice thereof merely by acting for the purposes of another trust or estate.[87]

(c) *Fraud.* The knowledge of an agent will not be imputed to his principal when the agent is shown to have intended a fraud on the principal which would require the suppression of his knowledge.[88]

(d) *Partners.* These rules apply to partners, being agents for each other: notice to an active partner is notice to the firm, except in the case of a fraud on the firm committed by or with the consent of that partner.[89]

D. Successors in Title

1. The rule. The protection of the doctrine of purchaser without notice extends to any person who claims through such a purchaser, unless that person was himself previously bound by the equity. Thus a purchaser with notice of an equitable interest will nevertheless not be bound by it if he purchases from a person who himself was a purchaser without notice. Here the second purchaser may shelter under the first purchaser, because otherwise a bona fide purchaser might be unable to deal with his property, and the sale of property would be clogged.[90] But a trustee cannot defeat the equities of his beneficiaries by selling the trust property to an innocent purchaser and then buying it back.[91]

2. Illustrations. Thus in *Harrison* v. *Forth*,[92] A purchased an estate with notice of an equitable charge, and then sold the estate to B, who had no notice; and B afterwards sold the estate to C, who had notice. The court held that C was not bound by the equitable charge, because B

---

[85] *Kettlewell* v. *Watson* (1882) 21 Ch.D. 685, reversed on grounds not affecting this point: (1884) 26 Ch.D. 501.
[86] *Re Hampshire Land Co.* [1896] 2 Ch. 743; *Re Fenwick, Stobart & Co. Ltd.* [1902] 1 Ch. 507; *Re David Payne & Co. Ltd.* [1904] 2 Ch. 608.
[87] T.A. 1925, s.28.
[88] *Kennedy* v. *Green* (1834) 3 My. & K. 699; *Cave* v. *Cave* (1880) 15 Ch.D. 639; *Houghton & Co.* v. *Nothard, Lowe and Willis Ltd.* [1928] A.C. 1.
[89] Partnership Act 1890, s.16.
[90] *Barrow's Case* (1880) 14 Ch.D. 432; *Wilkes* v. *Spooner* [1911] 2 K.B. 473.
[91] *Barrow's Case, supra,* at p. 445; *Gordon* v. *Holland* (1913) 82 L.J.P.C. 81.
[92] (1695) Prec.Ch. 51.

had no notice. But if the estate had afterwards got back into A's hands, A would have been bound by the charge.[93] Again, in *Wilkes* v. *Spooner*,[94] V, the lessee of a pork butcher's shop, sold another shop where he carried on a general butcher's business, and covenanted with the purchaser not to carry on a general butcher's business in the shop retained by him. Afterwards V surrendered the lease of that shop to his lessor, who had no notice of the covenant and therefore was not bound by it, and the lessor then executed a new lease to V's son. The court held that the son was not bound by the covenant, although he was fully cognisant of it. But if the lease had instead been granted to V, he would have been bound by the covenant.[95]

Section 3. Fraud, Estoppel and Gross Negligence

A person with a prima facie claim to priority for his interest may lose it through his own misconduct. The owner of a legal interest may be postponed to a subsequent equitable interest owing to his fraud, or by estoppel, or through his gross negligence; and the owner of a prior equitable interest may be postponed if his conduct is inequitable.

1. Fraud. A prior legal interest will be postponed to a subsequent equitable interest if the owner of the prior interest has connived at or assisted in some fraud which has led to the creation of the subsequent equitable interest without notice of the prior interest.[96]

2. Estoppel. If the owner of the prior legal interest either expressly or by implication makes some misrepresentation whereby the owner of the later interest is deceived, the former owner may be estopped from asserting his priority.[97] Thus if the owner of a legal estate entrusts the title deeds to another person with authority to raise a certain sum on them, and that person creates an equitable mortgage for a larger sum, the owner of the legal estate is estopped from denying the validity of the mortgage for that larger sum.[98] Other examples have occurred where vendors of land[99] or holders of mortgage bonds[1] have executed transfers stating the consideration paid without in fact receiving the purchase-money.

---

[93] See note 91, *supra*.
[94] [1911] 2 K.B. 473.
[95] *Piggott* v. *Stratton* (1859) 1 De G.F. & J. 33.
[96] *Peter* v. *Russel* (1716) 1 Eq.Cas.Abr. 321; *Northern Counties of England Fire Insurance Co.* v. *Whipp* (1884) 26 Ch.D. 482 at 494; and see *Midland Bank Trust Co. Ltd.* v. *Green* [1980] Ch. 590 at 624 (Lord Denning M.R.), 629–631 (Sir Stanley Rees, dissenting); in the House of Lords arguments based on fraud were abandoned: [1981] A.C. 513 at 527.
[97] *Dixon* v. *Muckleston* (1872) 8 Ch.App. 155 at 160.
[98] *Perry Herrick* v. *Attwood* (1857) 2 De G. & J. 21; *Brocklesby* v. *Temperance B.S.* [1895] A.C. 173.
[99] *Heid* v. *Reliance Finance Corp. Pty. Ltd.* (1984) 154 C.L.R. 326.
[1] *Rimmer* v. *Webster* [1902] 2 Ch. 163. Contrast *Lloyds Bank Ltd.* v. *Bullock* [1896] 2 Ch. 192, where a receipted mortgage was handed to a solicitor in escrow.

3. Gross negligence. If the legal owner is grossly negligent in failing to obtain the title deeds he will be postponed to a subsequent equitable owner who has exercised due diligence. Failure to ask for the deeds at all postpones the prior owner,[2] but not failure to get them subsequently from some even earlier mortgagee when the earlier mortgage is paid off.[3] Moreover, the legal owner is not grossly negligent if he asks for the deeds and is put off with some reasonable excuse,[4] nor, it seems, if having once got the deeds he is so careless in keeping them in safe custody that the creation of a subsequent equitable interest is facilitated.[5] If the legal owner is postponed, so also will be beneficiaries for whom he is a trustee, as they can be in no better position than their trustee.[6]

4. Successive equitable interests. Similar principles apply where there is a conflict between two equitable interests; the rule that the first in time prevails applies only where the equities are equal. In this instance, however, it is not so much a matter of estoppel or gross negligence as of the positive conduct of the prior owner or his trustee[7] in relation to the equitable interest claimed.[8] For instance, where a vendor conveyed land to a purchaser without receiving the purchase money, yet signed a conveyance containing a receipt for it, his equitable lien[9] for the unpaid purchase-money was postponed to a subsequent equitable mortgagee who obtained the title deeds without notice of the lien.[10] By contrast, where a trustee for sale fraudulently executed a conveyance without receiving the purchase-money, the beneficiaries under the trust for sale did not lose their priority to a later equitable mortgagee.[11] They were not claiming an equitable lien arising out of the sale and conveyance, so that their equitable interests were unaffected by the conduct of their trustee.[12]

Section 4. Registration

The tendency of modern times has been to curtail the equitable doctrine of purchaser without notice and to replace it by provisions for the registration of rights. In general, in such cases the question is no longer

[2] *Walker* v. *Linom* [1907] 2 Ch. 104; and see *Lloyd's Banking Co.* v. *Jones* (1885) 29 Ch.D. 221.
[3] *Grierson* v. *National Provincial Bank of England* [1913] 2 Ch. 18; and see *Coleman* v. *London County and Westminster Bank Ltd.* [1916] 2 Ch. 353.
[4] *Manners* v. *Mew* (1885) 29 Ch.D. 725; *Hewitt* v. *Loosemore* (1851) 9 Hare 449. Contrast *Oliver* v. *Hinton* [1899] 2 Ch. 264, where the excuse was insufficient.
[5] *Northern Counties of England Fire Insurance Co.* v. *Whipp* (1884) 26 Ch.D. 482.
[6] *Walker* v. *Linom, supra*; and see *Lloyd's Banking Co.* v. *Jones, supra; Coleman* v. *London County and Westminster Bank Ltd, supra.*
[7] *Lloyds Bank Ltd.* v. *Bullock* [1896] 2 Ch. 192.
[8] *Capell* v. *Winter* [1907] 2 Ch. 376 at 382.
[9] See *post*, p. 464.
[10] *Rice* v. *Rice* (1854) 2 Drew. 73; and see *Re King's Settlement* [1931] 2 Ch. 294.
[11] *Capell* v. *Winter* [1907] 2 Ch. 376.
[12] See also *Shropshire Union Ry. and Canal Co.* v. *R.* (1875) L.R. 7 H.L. 496; *Coleman* v. *London County and Westminster Bank Ltd.* [1916] 2 Ch. 353; *B.S. Lyle Ltd.* v. *Rosher* [1959] 1 W.L.R. 8; *post*, p. 66.

the state of the purchaser's mind but the state of the register.[13] There are four principal systems of registration[14]:

(1) Land charges;

(2) Charges affecting registered land;

(3) Charges by companies; and

(4) Local land charges.

1. Land Charges.[15] The Land Charges Act 1972[16] provides for the registration of many instruments or matters affecting land. Failure to register some classes of these instruments or matters renders them void against purchasers of a legal estate for money or money's worth; failure to register other classes renders them void against purchasers who for any valuable consideration (whether money, money's worth or marriage) take any interest, legal or equitable, in the land.[17] Actual or constructive notice will not prevent an unregistered instrument or matter from being void for want of registration.[18]

(a) *Void against purchaser of legal estate.* The following are the principal matters which are void only as against a purchaser of a legal estate for money or money's worth if not registered before completion of the purchase.[19] Save in the case of bankruptcy petitions and orders, there is no requirement that the purchaser should be in good faith nor that the consideration be adequate.[20]

(1) ESTATE CONTRACT: any contract, whether written or oral,[21] by an estate owner, or by a person entitled at the date of the contract to have a legal estate conveyed to him, to convey or create a legal estate (even if it is greater than the estate actually vested in the estate owner[22]), including a contract conferring either expressly or by statutory implication a valid option of purchase, a right of pre-emption,[23] or any

---

[13] See [1985] C.L.J. 280 (M. P. Thompson).
[14] There was formerly a fifth, the registration of deeds of land in Yorkshire and Middlesex. The Middlesex registry has been closed since 1940 (see L.R.A. 1936, s.2(2); Middlesex Deeds Act 1940, s.1). The registries in the North and West Ridings of Yorkshire closed in 1972 and that in the East Riding in 1976 (see L.P.A. 1969, Pt. II).
[15] This section gives only an outline, and is intended to show the relationship of registration to notice. For details of all registrable charges, reference should be made to books on the law of land, *e.g.* Megarry and Wade's *Law of Real Property* (5th ed., 1984), pp. 170–193.
[16] Brought into force January 29, 1973: S.I. 1972 No. 2058. It replaced the Land Charges Act 1925.
[17] See *ante*, p. 48. For "purchaser," see L.C.A. 1972, s.17(1); *cf.* L.P.A. 1925, s.205(1)(xxi).
[18] See L.P.A. 1925, s.199; *Hollington Bros. Ltd.* v. *Rhodes* [1951] 2 All E.R. 579n. at 580.
[19] L.C.A. 1972, ss.2, 4(6).
[20] *Midland Bank Trust Co. Ltd.* v. *Green* [1981] A.C. 513 (sale of farm worth £40,000 for £500).
[21] *Universal Permanent B.S.* v. *Cooke* [1952] Ch. 95 at 104.
[22] *Sharp* v. *Coates* [1949] 1 K.B. 285.
[23] See *Greene* v. *Church Commissioners for England* [1974] Ch. 467 (term in lease requiring tenant to offer to surrender before assigning); *First National Securities Ltd.* v. *Chiltern D.C.* [1975] 1 W.L.R. 1075 (right of pre-emption under Housing Act 1957, s.104). It has been held that a right of pre-emption does not confer any interest in land on the grantee but the property legislation may have proceeded on the mistaken assumption that it did: *Pritchard* v. *Briggs* [1980] Ch. 339, *sed quaere*: see H. W. R. Wade (1980) 96 L.Q.R. 488; C. Harpum [1980] C.L.J. 35.

other like right.[24] A contract appointing an agent to sell land is not an estate contract.[25]

(2) RESTRICTIVE COVENANT: a covenant or agreement (not being made between a lessor and lessee) restrictive of the user of land entered into after 1925.

(3) EQUITABLE EASEMENT: any easement right or privilege over or affecting land created or arising after 1925, and being merely an equitable interest. "Right or privilege" have been restrictively construed and do not include a right to take possession after requisitioning,[26] the right of a lessee to remove a building or other fixture,[27] an equitable right of entry attached to an assignment of a lease[28] or an equity in the nature of an easement created by estoppel.[29] The binding nature of all these interests depends on the old rules as to notice which thus still have an extensive role.[30]

(4) PETITIONS IN BANKRUPTCY AND BANKRUPTCY ORDERS. These, if unregistered, will not affect the purchaser of a legal estate in the bankrupt's land, though only if the purchaser is in good faith.[31]

(b) *Void against purchaser of any interest.* The following are the principal matters which are void against a purchaser for value of any interest in the land[32] if not registered before completion of the purchase.

(1) PUISNE MORTGAGE: any legal mortgage not being a mortgage protected by a deposit of documents relating to the legal estate affected.

(2) GENERAL EQUITABLE CHARGE: any equitable charge not secured by a deposit of documents relating to the legal estate affected, which does not arise or affect an interest arising under a trust for sale or a settlement and is not included in any other class of land charge. It does not include a charge given by way of indemnity against rents equitably apportioned or charged exclusively on land in exoneration of other land, and against the breach or non-observance of covenants or conditions[33]; nor does it include a contract for the sharing of the proceeds of sale of land.[34]

---

[24] See *Turley* v. *Mackay* [1944] Ch. 37; *Beesly* v. *Hallwood Estates Ltd.* [1960] 1 W.L.R. 549 (affirmed on grounds not affecting this point: [1961] Ch. 105); *Haslemere Estates Ltd.* v. *Baker* [1982] 1 W.L.R. 1109 at 1118, 1119.
[25] *Thomas* v. *Rose* [1968] 1 W.L.R. 1797.
[26] *Lewisham Borough Council* v. *Maloney* [1948] 1 K.B. 50.
[27] *Poster* v. *Slough Estates Ltd.* [1969] 1 Ch. 495.
[28] *Shiloh Spinners Ltd.* v. *Harding* [1973] A.C. 691.
[29] *E.R. Ives Investments Ltd.* v. *High* [1967] 2 Q.B. 379; see *post*, pp. 578, 579.
[30] See (1972) 88 L.Q.R. 336 (P.V.B.).
[31] See L.C.A. 1972, ss.5(8) and 6(5)(6) (as amended by Insolvency Act 1985, s.235(1), (3); Sched. 8, para. 21(1)–(3); Sched. 10, Pt. III), 17(1).
[32] L.C.A. 1972, ss.2, 4(5).
[33] L.P.(Am.)A. 1926, Sched.
[34] *Thomas* v. *Rose* [1968] 1 W.L.R. 1797.

(3) MATRIMONIAL HOME: a charge affecting any land by virtue of the Matrimonial Homes Act 1983.[35]

(4) PENDING ACTIONS, WRITS AND ORDERS. This head includes any action, information or proceeding pending in court relating to land or any interest in or charge on land; any writ or order affecting land issued or made by any court for the purpose of enforcing a judgment, statute or recognisance; and any order apppointing a receiver or sequestrator of land.[36] It includes applications for anciliary relief in matrimonial proceedings involving the sale or transfer of interests in land,[37] or for leave to commence proceedings for breach of a tenant's repairing covenant, as this involves a claim for forfeiture of the lease.[38] It does not include simple claims for damages for breach of covenants concerning land[39]; and too tenuous are claims for a *Mareva* injunction,[40] or for a charge for repayment of expenditure based on proprietary estoppel.[41]

(c) *Compensation.* Land charges are registered against the name of the estate owner affected. Thus it may happen that a charge was registered against a former estate owner more than 15 years before the sale, and cannot be discovered by the purchaser who is nevertheless bound by it. If in such circumstances a purchaser has no actual knowledge of the charge and suffers loss by reason of it, he may claim compensation out of public funds.[42]

(d) *Damages.* If a purchaser fails to register a charge at all, and thus be unable to claim compensation out of public funds, he may, nevertheless be entitled to claim damages against the creator of the charge, for he does not owe him any duty to register, and the latter is still contractually liable.[43]

2. Registered land. Where the *title* to land is registered (and an ever-increasing number of titles are being registered) the Land Charges Act 1972 is irrelevant. Matters which would be protected by registration against the name of the creator of the charge under that Act if the title were unregistered are instead protected by entries on the register of title to the land itself.[44] Moreover, investigation of the title consists of inspecting the register, and not, as has been seen in the case of unregistered titles, of investigating past transactions over a period of

[35] Replacing Matrimonial Homes Act 1967, which was examined in *Wroth* v. *Tyler* [1974] Ch. 30.
[36] L.C.A. 1972, ss.5, 6.
[37] *Whittingham* v. *Whittingham* [1979] Fam. 9 (see *ante*, p. 55); *Perez-Adamson* v. *Perez-Rivas* [1987] Fam. 89.
[38] *Selim* v. *Bickenhall Engineering Ltd.* [1981] 1 W.L.R. 1318.
[39] *Regan & Blackburn Ltd.* v. *Rogers* [1985] 1 W.L.R. 870.
[40] *Stockler* v. *Fourways Estates Ltd.* [1984] 1 W.L.R. 25.
[41] *Haslemere Estates Ltd.* v. *Baker* [1982] 1 W.L.R. 1109 at 1119, 1120.
[42] L.P.A. 1969, ss.25, 29.
[43] *Wright* v. *Dean* [1948] Ch. 686; *Hollington Bros. Ltd.* v. *Rhodes* [1951] 2 All E.R. 578n.
[44] See Ruoff & Roper's *Registered Conveyancing* (5th ed., 1986), p. 779.

time.[45] If matters which should be protected by an entry on the register
are not, a purchaser acquiring title under a registered disposition is not
concerned with them, whether or not he has express, implied or
constructive notice of them.[46]

3. Charges by companies. Some classes of charges by companies
registered under the Companies Act 1985 are void to the extent of any
security on the company's property, though not as to the debt, unless
the charge is registered with the Registrar of Companies.[47] The classes
include charges on land, charges on book debts and floating charges.[48]
Thus if a mortgage by a company is not registered it is void against a
subsequent registered mortgagee even if he had express notice of it
when he took his own security.[49] A mortgagee whose charge is void
under this provision cannot retain the title deeds of the property
charged.[50] Apart from floating charges, any charge which is registrable
as a land charge under the Land Charges Act 1972,[51] or as a charge on
registered land under the Land Registration Act 1925,[52] must also be
registered under those Acts.

4. Local land charges. These are charges acquired by local
authorities under such statutes as the Housing Acts. They also include a
number of restrictions and prohibitions on the use of land such as the
listing of buildings, or tree preservation orders, made under the Town
and Country Planning Act 1990. They have to be registered locally by
the proper officer of the local authority, whenever they were created. If
not registered they will be void as against a purchaser for money or
money's worth of a legal estate in the land affected.[53]

Section 5. Overreaching

1. Meaning of overreaching. In comparatively modern times, statute
has laid down that, provided certain conditions are satisfied, a purchaser
of land will take free of certain interests in it, whether he has notice of
them or not, and that the owners of those interests will instead have

---

[45] See *ante*, pp. 52, 53.
[46] L.R.A. 1925, s.59(6).
[47] Companies Act 1985, s.395, replacing Companies Act 1948, s.95(1) which itself replaced earlier
   provisions first enacted by Companies Act 1900.
[48] See Companies Act 1985, s.396 for the full list.
[49] *Re Monolithic Building Co.* [1915] 1 Ch. 643.
[50] *Re Molton Finance Ltd.* [1968] Ch. 325.
[51] See L.P.A. 1969, s.26. Land charges created by companies before 1970 did not have to be registered
   in the land charges register: L.C.A. 1925, s.10(5).
[52] See Ruoff & Roper, *supra*, pp. 572–573, for difficult questions of priority where a charge is not
   registered at the Companies Registry until after a later charge is registered at the Land Registry.
[53] Local Land Charges Act 1975, replacing as from August 1, 1977 (S.I. 1977 No. 984) L.C.A. 1925,
   s.15 (amended by L.P.(Am.)A. 1926, Sched.); Local Land Charges Rules 1977 (S.I. 1977 No. 985,
   amended S.I. 1978 No. 1638; S.I. 1987 No. 389); and see *Ministry of Housing and Local Government
   v. Sharp* [1970] 2 Q.B. 223. See generally J. F. Garner, *Local Land Charges* (10th ed., 1987).

corresponding rights in the purchase-money. Overreaching, which is an attempt to marry the free marketability of land with the preservation of proprietary interests,[54] is thus quite distinct from cases where a right is void for want of registration or unenforceable against a purchaser without notice, for rights overreached are merely transferred from the land to the purchase-money and do not become valueless.

2. Overreaching conveyances. Overreaching is dealt with in the Law of Property Act 1925.[55] A conveyance to a purchaser of a legal estate for money or money's worth will overreach *certain legal estates*, and any equitable interest or power affecting the estate, whether or not the purchaser has notice of it, if the conveyance is made—

  (i)   under the Settled Land Act 1925, or

  (ii) by trustees for sale, or

  (iii) by a mortgagee[56] or personal representative[57] in the exercise of his paramount powers, or

  (iv) under an order of the court,

provided that the legal estate or equitable interest or power is one of those which are capable of being overreached by the conveyance, and that any capital money arising from the transaction is paid—

in cases (i) and (ii) to the trustees, who must be at least two in number, or a trust corporation, and

in case (iii) to the mortgagee or personal representative, and

in case (iv) into, or in accordance with the order of, the court.

3. Settled land and trusts for sale. For instance, a conveyance by a tenant for life under the Settled Land Act 1925 will pass the land to the purchaser free from the equitable interests of persons entitled under the settlement, and a conveyance by trustees for sale will pass the land to the purchaser free from the equitable interests of the persons entitled under the trust instrument to the proceeds of sale, whether the purchaser knows of them or not.[58] In addition, it is further provided[59] that, if the trustees for sale are either two or more individuals approved

[54] For a judicial view of the underlying policy, see *City of London B.S.* v. *Flegg* [1988] A.C. 54 at 73, 74 (Lord Templeman).
[55] s.2, and see S.L.A. 1925, s.72. For a fuller account, see Megarry & Wade, *The Law of Real Property* (5th ed., 1984), pp. 398–410.
[56] See *post*, p. 415.
[57] See *post*, pp. 316, 318.
[58] L.P.A. 1925, ss.27, 28.
[59] By L.P.A. 1925, s.2(2) as amended by L.P.(Am.)A. 1926, Sched.

or appointed by the court[60] or their successors in office, or a trust corporation, a conveyance by the trustees will overreach even equitable interests which have priority to the trust for sale, *i.e.* equitable interests which were in existence when the trust for sale was created. But there are so many equitable interests which are excepted from this provision (*e.g.* restrictive covenants and most interests protected by registration under the Land Charges Act 1972) that this overreaching power and the corresponding provision for settled land[61] are of little practical importance.

4. Mortgages. A special overreaching provision relates to trusts affecting mortgage money.[62] A person dealing in good faith with a mortgagee (or with the mortgagor if the mortgage has been discharged, released or postponed as to the whole or any part of the mortgaged property) is not concerned with any trust at any time affecting the mortgage money or the income thereof, whether or not he has notice of the trust, and may assume, unless the contrary is expressly stated in the instruments relating to the mortgage—

(i)   that the mortgagees (if more than one) are or were entitled to the mortgage money on a joint account; and

(ii) that the mortgagee has or had power to give valid receipts and to release or postpone the priority of the mortgage debt, or to deal with the same or the mortgaged property,

without investigating the equitable title to the mortgage debt, or the appointment or discharge of trustees in reference thereto. This provision applies to mortgages whenever made, but only as respects dealings effected after 1925. It does not affect the liability of any person in whom the mortgage debt is vested for the purposes of any trust to give effect to that trust. Its object is merely to prevent purchasers of property from being affected by notice of equitable interests relating to money lent on mortgage of the property; it does not affect the priority of such equitable interests *inter se*.[63]

PART 2

THE RULE IN DEARLE v. HALL

Having thus considered the general body of rules governing priorities, the rule in *Dearle* v. *Hall*[64] must now be discussed. As mentioned

---

[60] See *Re Leigh's S.E. (No. 2)* [1927] 2 Ch. 13.
[61] S.L.A. 1925, s.21.
[62] L.P.A. 1925, s.113.
[63] *Beddoes* v. *Shaw* [1937] Ch. 81.
[64] (1828) 3 Russ. 1.

above,[65] this rule applies to successive dealings with an equitable interest in any property, real or personal, although before 1926 it was confined to dealings with equitable interests in pure personalty. Thus if a beneficiary under a trust has made successive assignments or mortgages of his beneficial interest, priority is governed by notice under the rule in *Dearle* v. *Hall*, whether the trust property consists of stocks and shares, or land held on trust for sale; and if the assignments or mortgages were made after 1925, the same applies to dealings with a beneficial interest in settled land.[66]

Section 1. The Rule

1. The rule. There are two limbs to the rule in *Dearle* v. *Hall*.

(a) *Receipt of notice.* Priority depends upon the order in which notice of the dealings was received by the person by whom the fund is distributable, or, in the case of settled land, by the trustees of the settlement.[67] "Equitable titles have priority according to the priority of notice."[68] If the notices are received substantially simultaneously, the dealings rank in the order in which they were made.[69]

(b) *Limit to gaining priority by notice.* The first limb of the rule is subject to the important qualification that an assignee who had actual or constructive notice of a previous assignment when he advanced his money cannot gain priority over it by being the first to give notice; for he lent his money knowing that there was a prior assignment.[70] Knowledge of that assignment acquired *after* he advanced his money is, however, no bar to his claiming priority under a notice given with this knowledge.[71]

2. Basis of the rule. The idea underlying the rule seems to be that by failing to give notice the first assignee has left the assignor in apparent possession of the beneficial interest in the fund, and has thus enabled him to make the subsequent assignment; as the first assignee has enabled a fraud to be committed on the second assignee, it is only fair that he should be postponed. But he will not be postponed if the second assignee gave no value, and so, though disappointed, would not

[65] See *ante*, p. 46.
[66] L.P.A. 1925, s.137; *post*, pp. 66, 67.
[67] *Ibid.* s.137(2); see *post*, p. 67, as to settled land.
[68] *Stocks* v. *Dobson* (1853) 4 De G.M. & G. 11 at 17, *per* Turner L.J.
[69] *Calisher* v. *Forbes* (1871) 7 Ch.App. 109; *Johnstone* v. *Cox* (1880) 16 Ch.D. 571; on appeal, (1881) 19 Ch.D. 17; and see *Re Dallas* [1904] 2 Ch. 385.
[70] See *Re Holmes* (1885) 29 Ch.D. 786; *Spencer* v. *Clarke* (1878) 9 Ch.D. 137; *Re Weniger's Policy* [1910] 2 Ch. 291; *Ward* v. *Royal Exchange Shipping Co.* (1887) 58 L.T. 174; *Re Ind, Coope & Co. Ltd.* [1911] 2 Ch. 223 at 233.
[71] *Mutual Life Assurance Society* v. *Langley* (1886) 32 Ch.D. 460.

be defrauded; for as a volunteer the second assignee could take no more than the assignor was able to give.[72]

3. Application of the rule. Although the idea underlying the rule may be fair and equitable, the same cannot be said of every application of it by the courts, and the rule will therefore not be extended.[73] The principle has been lost sight of, and at the present day the rule is absolute. The assignee who first gives proper notice will be paid first, whether or not the other assignee has been guilty of carelessness. This is well illustrated by *Re Dallas*.[74] There a testator made a will giving a legacy to X and appointing him executor. After the testator had become incurably insane, X borrowed money on the security of the legacy, first from A and then from B. On the death of the testator, X renounced probate, and Y was appointed administrator with the will annexed. B was the first to give notice to Y of his charge on the legacy, and he was held to be entitled to be paid first, even though A had given notice as soon as he could and the creation of B's charge was not due to A's failure to give notice earlier.

4. Only priorities. The rule in *Dearle* v. *Hall*[75] is only a rule for regulating priorities, and does not create new rights. Thus a mortgagee cannot by giving notice to the legal owner obtain any rights against the true owners of the beneficial interest if the mortgagor in fact has never owned any beneficial interest in the property.[76]

Section 2. Interests Within the Rule

1. Equitable interests in any property. The rule in *Dearle* v. *Hall*[77] has always applied to all equitable interests in pure personalty or in property which will reach the assignor in the shape of pure personalty. Thus it applies to interests in settled funds and in settled freeholds or leaseholds which are subject to a trust for sale,[78] all of which are sometimes called generically equitable things or choses in action.[79] It has also been applied to equitable assignments of legal choses in action.[80] The rule formerly did not apply to dealings with equitable

---

[72] *Justice* v. *Wynne* (1860) 12 Ir.Ch.R. 289; and see *Fraser* v. *Imperial Bank* (1912) 10 D.L.R. 232.
[73] *Hill* v. *Peters* [1918] 2 Ch. 273; *B.S. Lyle Ltd.* v. *Rosher* [1959] 1 W.L.R. 8 at 14, 22, 24. See D. W. McLauchlan (1980) 96 L.Q.R. 90 (priority of tracing rights over rights protected by the rule).
[74] [1904] 2 Ch. 385.
[75] (1828) 3 Russ. 1.
[76] *B.S. Lyle Ltd.* v. *Rosher* [1959] 1 W.L.R. 8, criticised by Sir Lancelot Elphinstone in (1961) 77 L.Q.R. 69.
[77] (1828) 3 Russ. 1.
[78] *Lloyds Bank* v. *Pearson* [1901] 1 Ch. 865; *White* v. *Ellis* [1892] 1 Ch. 188; *Gresham Life Assurance Co.* v. *Crowther* [1915] 1 Ch. 214.
[79] For this expression, see *post*, p. 71.
[80] *Marchant* v. *Morton, Down & Co.* [1901] 2 K.B. 829; *E. Pfeiffer Weinkellerei-Weineinkauf G.m.b.H. & Co.* v. *Arbuthnot Factors Ltd.* [1988] 1 W.L.R. 150.

interests in land not held on trust for sale[81]; but the rule has been extended to "dealings with equitable interests in land, capital money and securities representing capital money" effected after 1925 in the case of unregistered land,[82] and to similar dealings after 1986 where the land is registered.[83] Broadly speaking, the rule now applies to dealing with equitable interests (as distinct from legal estates) in any form of property, whether real or personal.

2. "Dealing." "Dealing" includes a disposition by operation of law,[84] *e.g.* the vesting of a bankrupt's property in his trustee in bankruptcy. But the provision "does not apply until a trust has been created."[85] This appears to mean that it applies only to dealings with equitable interests already created, and not to the creation of a new equitable interest to take effect out of a legal estate.[86] For instance, if the owner of a legal estate in land creates an equitable charge on the land without depositing the title deeds with the chargee, this equitable charge must be protected by registration under the Land Charges Act 1972,[87] and not by notice under this rule.

3. Shares. The rule does not apply to dealings by the owner of shares in a company governed by the Companies Act 1985. An equitable assignee of such shares will obtain no priority over a previous equitable assignee by giving notice to the company; for the company is not the legal owner of the shares, and is not obliged to accept and record notices of equitable interests or trusts affecting shares.[88]

Section 3. The Giving of Notice

1. Land. As regards dealings with equitable interests in land, by statute notice must be given to the following persons.[89]

(i) In the case of settled land or capital money or securities representing capital money, notice must be given to the trustees of the settlement as defined by the Settled Land Act 1925, or, where the equitable interest is created by a derivative or subsidiary settlement, the trustees of that settlement.

---

[81] *Hopkins* v. *Hemsworth* [1898] 2 Ch. 347; *Re Richards, Humber* v. *Richards* (1890) 45 Ch.D. 589.
[82] L.P.A. 1925, s.137(1). The rule applies even if the moneys or securities are in court: *ibid.*
[83] L.R.A. 1986, ss.5(1) (repealing L.R.A. 1925, s.102(2)), 6(2); S.I. 1986 No. 2117.
[84] L.P.A. 1925, s.137(10).
[85] *Ibid.*
[86] But consider the more far-reaching suggestion by F. R. Crane at (1956) 20 Conv.(N.S.) 448.
[87] *Ante*, p. 60.
[88] *Société Générale de Paris* v. *Walker* (1885) 11 App.Cas. 20; and see *ante*, p. 45.
[89] L.P.A. 1925, s.137(2). This subsection does not apply if the moneys or securities are in court: the assignee should obtain a stop order: *Mutual Life Assurance Society* v. *Langley* (1886) 32 Ch.D. 460; *Stephens* v. *Green* [1895] 2 Ch. 148.

    (ii)   If the land is settled on trust for sale, the notice must be served on the trustees for sale.

    (iii)   In any other case, the estate owner of the land affected is the person to be served.

2. Pure personalty.   As regards equitable interests in pure personalty, there is no statutory provision as to the persons to be served with notice; but the following points have been decided, and they also apply to interests in land so far as the express provisions of the section do not otherwise apply.

(a) *Persons to be given notice.*   The notice required by the rule must be given to the debtor, trustee, or other person whose duty it is to pay the money to the assignor[90]; it should not be given to his solicitor, for such a notice will be good only if the solicitor was expressly or impliedly authorised to receive it.[91] If the assignee is a trustee, his knowledge of the transaction without giving himself any formal notice has been held to affect priorities,[92] though it is otherwise if it is the assignor, not the assignee, who is a trustee[93]; for in order to protect his own interest the assignee would readily disclose the assignment to any prospective assignee, whereas the assignor would not. Nor does notice to an executor who subsequently renounces probate appear to suffice.[94] Yet if a trustee receives notice prior to his appointment and as a reasonable man he would continue to act on it, this will suffice to preserve priority for the assignee over a subsequent assignee, but not to obtain priority for him over a prior assignee.[95]

(b) *Several trustees.*   Where there are several trustees, the rules are as follows.

(1) NOTICE TO ALL.   Notice given to all the trustees remains effective indefinitely, even though they all die or retire without communicating the notice to their successors.[96] An assignee cannot reasonably be expected to do more to preserve his priority than give notice to all the existing trustees. Even so, it may be desirable to give a fresh notice when all the trustees have died or retired, for if they have failed to communicate the notice to the new trustees, the new trustees will not be personally liable to the assignee if, without notice of his interest, they distribute the fund to later assignees or the beneficiary.[97]

---

[90] *Stephens* v. *Green* [1895] 2 Ch. 148.
[91] *Saffron Waldon B.S.* v. *Rayner* (1880) 14 Ch.D. 406.
[92] *Browne* v. *Savage* (1859) 4 Drew. 635. *Quaere* after 1925; see *post,* pp. 69, 70 (notice must be in writing).
[93] *Lloyds Bank* v. *Pearson* [1901] 1 Ch. 865.
[94] *Re Dallas* [1904] 2 Ch. 385; and see A.E.A. 1925, s.6.
[95] *Ipswich Permanent Money Club Ltd.* v. *Arthy* [1920] 2 Ch. 257.
[96] *Re Wasdale* [1899] 1 Ch. 163.
[97] *Phipps* v. *Lovegrove* (1873) L.R. 16 Eq. 80; *Hallows* v. *Lloyd* (1888) 39 Ch.D. 686.

(2) EFFECTIVE NOTICE TO ONE. Notice given to one of the trustees remains effective indefinitely, even after his death or retirement, as regards all transactions effected while he was still trustee.[98] Those engaged in such transactions could have discovered the assignment by asking the trustee.

(3) INEFFECTIVE NOTICE TO ONE. Notice given to one of the trustees has no effect in relation to transactions effected after the death or retirement of that trustee, unless he had communicated it to one or more of the trustees in office at the time of those transactions.[99]

(c) *Register of notices.* The difficulties arising from a change of trustees may be obviated by making use of the statutory power for the trust instrument, the trustees or the court to nominate a trust corporation to whom notices of dealings affecting real or personal property may be given, and who are bound to keep a register of notices.[1] However, little use is made of this power, which is purely optional.

3. Indorsement. The Law of Property Act 1925 makes separate provision to meet cases in which a valid notice cannot be served, or cannot be served without unreasonable cost or delay, *e.g.* where there are no trustees.[2] In such a case a purchaser may at his own cost require a memorandum of the dealing with the equitable interest, whether the property is real or personal, to be indorsed on the instrument creating the trust, or, if the trust is created by statute or by operation of law, or in any other case where there is no trust instrument, on the instrument under which the equitable interest is acquired or which is evidence of the devolution thereof.[3] For instance, if the trust arises by reason of an intestacy, the indorsement would be made on the letters of administration or probate in force when the dealing was effected. The purchaser is also entitled at his own cost to have the instrument produced to him to prove the indorsement of the memorandum.[4] For the purpose of preserving priority, the indorsement will be equivalent to notice to trustees.[5]

4. Form. The notice which the assignee should give in order to preserve his priority might formerly have been given by word of mouth; and, before 1926, even notice received by reading a statement in a newspaper was held to suffice.[6] But any notice of an assignment of an

---

[98] *Ward* v. *Duncombe* [1893] A.C. 369.
[99] *Timson* v. *Ramsbottom* (1837) 2 Keen 35; *Re Phillips' Trusts* [1903] 1 Ch. 183.
[1] L.P.A. 1925, s.138.
[2] *Ibid.* s.137.
[3] *Ibid.* s.137(4)–(6).
[4] *Ibid.* s.137(4).
[5] *Ibid.*
[6] *Lloyd* v. *Banks* (1868) 3 Ch.App. 488.

"equitable interest"[7] given after 1925 must be in writing in order to preserve priority, and this is so whatever the property involved may be.[8] Where a written notice has been given, the trustees from time to time of the property affected are entitled to the custody of the notice; and subject to the payment of costs, any person interested in the equitable interest may require production of the notice.[9] The notice need not state in so many words that the thing in action has been assigned; it is sufficient notice if it conveys to the mind of the recipient the fact that there has been an assignment.[10]

PART 3

SUMMARY

1. In determining questions of priority, it is usually best to consider first whether the rule in *Dearle* v. *Hall*[11] applies, *i.e.* whether or not the conflict is between successive dealings with an equitable interest in real or personal property.

2. If the rule in *Dearle* v. *Hall*[12] does not apply, the question will have to be settled according to the basic rule of the order of creation, except so far as the operation of this rule is modified by the rules relating to—

   (i)   the purchaser without notice;

   (ii)   fraud, estoppel and gross negligence;

   (iii)   registration; and

   (iv)   overreaching.

3. If interests in land are concerned, registration and overreaching cover much of the ground and usually make it unnecessary to look further. These two heads have reduced the doctrine of purchaser without notice to a position of relative unimportance.[13]

---

[7] A phrase which seems to exclude a legal chose in action: *ante*, pp. 66, 67.
[8] L.P.A. 1925, s.137(3).
[9] *Ibid.* s.137(8).
[10] *Smith* v. *The Owners of the Steamship "Zigurds"* [1934] A.C. 209.
[11] (1828) 3 Russ. 1.
[12] *Ibid.*
[13] But see *post*, p. 578, as to equitable estoppel.

CHAPTER 5

ASSIGNMENT OF CHOSES IN ACTION

Section 1. Common Law and Equity

1. Definition. " 'Choses in action' is a known legal expression used to describe all personal rights of property which can only be claimed or enforced by action, and not by taking physical possession."[1] A chose may be legal (*i.e.* enforceable in a court of law), such as a debt, bill of exchange, policy of insurance, sweepstake ticket[2] or share in a company; or it may be equitable, such as a legacy,[3] a legatee's rights in an unadministered estate,[4] a share in a trust fund, surplus proceeds of sale in the hands of a mortgagee,[5] or a right to relief against forfeiture of a lease for non-payment of rent.[6]

2. No assignment at law. The old common rule was that no chose (or thing) in action could be assigned, except by or to the King, unless the debtor assented to the assignment; for it was alleged that to allow such an assignment would be "the occasion of multiplying of contentions and suits, of great oppression of the people, ... and the subversion of the due and equal execution of justice."[7]

3. Assignment in equity. Buller J. once said that "the good sense of the rule seems to me to be very questionable ... Courts of Equity from the earliest times thought the doctrine too absurd for them to adopt."[8] Thus equity gave effect to assignments not only of equitable things in action but also of legal things in action. If the thing in action was equitable, the assignee could bring his proceedings to recover it in the Court of Chancery in his own name, whereas if it was legal, the proceedings in the common law court had to be taken in the name of the assignor, since the assignment was not recognised at law. The way in

[1] *Torkington* v. *Magee* [1902] 2 K.B. 427 at 430, *per* Channell J. (reversed on grounds not affecting this dictum: [1903] 1 K.B. 644).
[2] *Jones* v. *Carter* (1845) 8 Q.B. 134.
[3] *Seys* v. *Price* (1740) 9 Mod. 217; *Deeks* v. *Strutt* (1794) 5 T.R. 690.
[4] *Re Leigh's W.T.* [1970] Ch. 277.
[5] *Bucknell* v. *Bucknell* [1969] 1 W.L.R. 1204; see *post*, p. 416.
[6] *Howard* v. *Fanshawe* [1895] 2 Ch. 581.
[7] *Lampet's Case* (1612) 10 Co.Rep. 46b at 48a.
[8] *Master* v. *Miller* (1791) 4 T.R. 320 at 340.

which the Court of Chancery interfered was to restrain the assignor
from objecting to this use of his name, subject to the assignee giving
him a proper indemnity against costs.[9]

4. Statutory power to assign. The old common law rule against the
assignment of things in action has been gradually relaxed. By the law
merchant, negotiable instruments became assignable, and statute created
other exceptions, at first in particular instances, *e.g.* policies of life[10] and
marine[11] insurance.[12] Ultimately, by the Judicature Act 1873, and now
by the Law of Property Act 1925,[13] "any debt or other legal thing in
action" was made assignable at law. This provision has been construed
as extending to equitable as well as legal choses,[14] and so there are four
categories[15]:

   (i)   Statutory assignments of legal choses;

  (ii)   Statutory assignments of equitable choses;

 (iii)   Equitable assignments of legal choses; and

 (iv)   Equitable assignments of equitable choses.

Although there is nothing equitable about statutory assignments, they
are included here because they are so closely linked to equitable
assignments, and provide a useful contrast.

5. Chose assignable. There can be no assignment if the instrument
creating the chose in action contains a term prohibiting assignment.[16]
Further, the assignment of some choses is barred on grounds of public
policy.[17]

Section 2. Statutory Assignment

1. The rule. By section 136 of the Law of Property Act 1925, what is
required is that there should be an "absolute assignment by writing
under the hand of the assignor (not purporting to be by way of charge
only) of any debt or other legal thing in action,[18] of which express

---

[9] See generally as to such assignments, *Row* v. *Dawson* (1749) 1 Ves.Sen. 331; **1 W. & T.L.C. 87,** and
Ryall v. *Rowles* (1750) 1 Ves.Sen. 348; **1 W. & T.L.C. 90.** And see the historical discussion by S. J.
Bailey at (1931) 47 L.Q.R. 516; (1932) 48 L.Q.R. 248, 547.
[10] Policies of Assurance Act 1867.
[11] Marine Insurance Act 1906, s.50, replacing Policies of Marine Insurance Act 1868.
[12] For other examples see 1 W. & T.L.C. 99.
[13] s.136, replacing J.A. 1873, s.25(6). The provisions of the Policies of Assurance Act 1867 are
expressly declared to be unaffected by this section: L.P.A. 1925, s.136(2).
[14] See *post*, p. 74.
[15] See *DiGuilo* v. *Boland* [1958] O.R. 384 at 397.
[16] *Helstan Securities Ltd.* v. *Hertfordshire C.C.* [1978] 3 All E.R. 262.
[17] See *post*, p. 84, and see *post*, p. 75 for choses incapable of statutory assignment.
[18] The Act of 1873 read "legal chose in action" without apparently differing in meaning. Neither Act
defines the expression.

notice in writing has been given to the debtor, trustee or other person from whom the assignor would have been entitled to claim such debt or thing in action."

2. Requirements of statute. For an assignment to take effect under the Act, the following conditions must accordingly be satisfied.

(a) *Assignment.* There must be a document which purports to assign the chose, and not merely to direct the debtor to pay a third person who knows nothing of the transaction.[19] A cheque is no assignment of any money in the drawer's account, for it is "but an order to pay and not an absolute assignment of anything"; and in any case there is no debt to be assigned, for no debt arises until the customer demands payment from the bank.[20]

(b) *Assignment absolute.* The assignment must be absolute and not by way of charge only. It has been held, however, that an assignment by way of mortgage in the ordinary form, whereby the whole debt is assigned to the mortgagee with a proviso for reassignment on repayment of the money lent, is absolute.[21] So, too, an assignment is absolute even if the assignee covenants to pay part of the proceeds of the chose after receipt to the assignor.[22] But an instrument which appears to be intended merely to assign so much of a debt as will provide security for the repayment of a specified sum is not an absolute assignment, being made by way of charge only.[23] Nor is an assignment merely of part of a debt within the section.[24]

(c) *Writing.* The assignment must be in writing signed by the assignor. It need not be by deed, nor need it be for value.[25]

(d) *Notice in writing.* Express notice must be given to the debtor. This need not be in formal language, but it must be sufficiently plain to make it clear to the debtor that the debt has been assigned.[26] It is not invalidated by omitting to specify the date of the assignment or by

---

[19] *Curran* v. *Newpark Cinemas Ltd.* [1951] 1 All E.R. 295; and see *post*, pp. 77, 78.
[20] *Schroeder* v. *Central Bank of London* (1876) 24 W.R. 710, *per* Brett J.; and see *post*, pp. 77, 78.
[21] *Tancred* v. *Delagoa Bay and East Africa Ry.* (1889) 23 Q.B.D. 239, approved in *Durham Bros.* v. *Robertson* [1898] 1 Q.B. 765 at 771, 772; *Hughes* v. *Pump House Hotel Co. Ltd.* [1902] 2 K.B. 190; and see *Bank of Liverpool and Martins Ltd.* v. *Holland* (1926) 43 T.L.R. 29.
[22] *Ramsey* v. *Hartley* [1977] 1 W.L.R. 686; and see *Comfort* v. *Betts* [1891] 1 Q.B. 737.
[23] *Mercantile Bank of London Ltd.* v. *Evans* [1899] 2 Q.B. 613, as explained in *Hughes* v. *Pump House Hotel Co.* [1902] 2 K.B. 190; and see *Durham Bros.* v. *Robertson* [1898] 1 Q.B. 765.
[24] *Jones* v. *Humphreys* [1902] 1 K.B. 10; *Forster* v. *Baker* [1910] 2 K.B. 636; *Re Steel Wing Co. Ltd.* [1921] 1 Ch. 349; *Williams* v. *Atlantic Assurance Co. Ltd.* [1933] 1 K.B. 81.
[25] *Re Westerton* [1919] 2 Ch. 104.
[26] Contrast *Denney, Gasquet & Metcalfe* v. *Conklin* [1913] 3 K.B.177, with *James Talcott Ltd.* v. *John Lewis & Co. Ltd.* [1940] 3 All E.R. 592.

adding inaccurate surplusage, such as an untrue statement that notice had already been given.[27] But a wrong date for the assignment,[28] or possibly a misstatement of the amount of the debt,[29] will invalidate the notice, for it leads away from the true transaction.

The notice must be in writing even though the debtor cannot read.[30] But the section does not state by whom or at what time it must be given, so that notice given by the assignee after the death of the assignor would be effectual,[31] though not a notice after the action has begun.[32] The notice takes effect when it is received by or on behalf of the debtor.[33] Where there are two joint debtors, notice must apparently be given to both; but if one is bankrupt, notice to the solvent debtor alone is sufficient to enable the creditor to sue him.[34] If no notice is given the assignment will not take effect under the statute, although it may take effect as an equitable assignment.[35]

3. Rights within the statute

(a) *Equitable choses.*   Although the statute in terms applies only to any debt or other "legal" thing in action, the provision for giving notice to (*inter alios*) a trustee strongly suggests that equitable things in action are included within the scope of the section.[36] This view is supported by some authority,[37] and "legal" may perhaps be read as merely meaning "enforceable in a court of justice."[38] Yet the words of the statute ought perhaps to be given a restricted rather than an extended interpretation, and it may be suggested that "trustee" should be confined to "trustee in bankruptcy." " 'Choses in action' ... is an expression large enough to include rights which it can hardly have been intended should be assignable by virtue of the subsection in question, as, for instance, shares which can only be transferred as provided by the Companies Acts ... I think the words 'debt or other legal chose in action' means 'debt or right which the common law looks on as not assignable by reason of its being a chose in action, but which a Court of Equity deals with as being assignable.' "[39]

---

[27] *Van Lynn Developments Ltd.* v. *Pelias Construction Co. Ltd.* [1969] 1 Q.B. 607.
[28] *W.F. Harrison & Co. Ltd.* v. *Burke* [1956] 1 W.L.R. 419; but see (1956) 72 L.Q.R. 321.
[29] *W.F. Harrison & Co. Ltd.* v. *Burke, supra*, at p. 421.
[30] *Hockley* v. *Goldstein* (1921) 90 L.J.K.B. 111.
[31] *Walker* v. *The Bradford Old Bank Ltd.* (1884) 12 Q.B.D. 511; *Bateman* v. *Hunt* [1904] 2 K.B. 530.
[32] *Compania Colombiana de Seguros* v. *Pacific Steam Navigation Co.* [1965] 1 Q.B. 101 at 129.
[33] *Holt* v. *Heatherfield Trust Ltd.* [1942] 2 K.B. 1; contrast the making of equitable assignments, *post*, p. 77.
[34] *Josselson* v. *Borst* [1938] 1 K.B. 723; Insolvency Act 1986, s.345(4), replacing Insolvency Act 1985, s.178(3) which replaced Bankruptcy Act 1914, s.118.
[35] *Post*, pp. 79, 80.
[36] See the discussion in Jenks' *English Civil Law* (4th ed., 1947), p. 891; Marshall's *Assignment of Choses in Action* (1950), pp. 162 *et seq.*
[37] See *Re Pain* [1919] 1 Ch. 38 at 44.
[38] Jenks, *supra*, at p. 891.
[39] *Torkington* v. *Magee* [1902] 2 K.B. 427 at 430, 431, *per* Channell J. (reversed on facts: [1903] 1 K.B. 644); and see *Tolhurst* v. *Associated Portland Cement Manufacturers* [1903] A.C. 414.

(b) *Other choses.* The expression has been held to include a debt not yet payable[40] under an existing contract,[41] the benefit of a contract for the sale of a reversionary interest,[42] a claim for compensation in respect of an interest in land injuriously affected by a railway company acting under its statutory powers,[43] and the right to sue for damages for tort or breach of contract, if connected with property or some other interest such as that of an insurer.[44]

(c) *Choses not included.* On the other hand, the expression does not include a mere right of litigation unconnected with any property assigned, such as a right to set aside a deed for fraud, or to recover damages for breach of contract, or damages for an assault or for waste,[45] for such rights were not assignable in equity, owing to the law of maintenance and champerty.[46] Nor does it include choses which by statute must be transferred in some specified way, *e.g.* shares in a company (which are transferable in the manner provided by the articles of the company),[47] copyrights,[48] and policies of life assurance.[49]

4. Effect of assignment. An assignment which complies with the statute as to the notice and otherwise is "effectual in law (subject to equities having priority over the right of the assignee) to pass and transfer from the date of such notice—

(a) the legal right to such debt or thing in action;

(b) all legal and other remedies for the same; and

(c) the power to give a good discharge for the same without the concurrence of the assignor."[50]

Thus the assignee becomes the owner of the chose at law, and can sue the debtor in his own name without joining the original creditor,[51] who

---

[40] *Walker* v. *The Bradford Old Bank Ltd.* (1884) 12 Q.B.D. 511.
[41] *G. & T. Earle (1925) Ltd.* v. *Hemsworth R.D.C.* (1928) 140 L.T. 69.
[42] *Torkington* v. *Magee* [1902] 2 K.B. 427 (reversed on facts: [1903] 1 K.B. 644).
[43] *Dawson* v. *G.N. Ry.* [1905] 1 K.B. 260.
[44] *King* v. *Victoria Insurance Co. Ltd.* [1896] A.C. 250; *Manchester Brewery Co.* v. *Coombs* [1901] 2 Ch. 608 at 619; *Compania Colombiana de Seguros* v. *Pacific Steam Navigation Co.* [1965] 1 Q.B. 101; *cf. DiGuilo* v. *Boland* [1958] O.R. 384 at 399, 400.
[45] *Defries* v. *Milne* [1913] 1 Ch. 98; *May* v. *Lane* (1894) 64 L.J.Q.B. 236; but see *Ellis* v. *Torrington* [1920] 1 K.B. 399. See also *Stephenson Bros. Ltd.* v. *Commissioners of Customs and Excise* [1953] 1 W.L.R. 335 at 338 (one gift coupon of a set entitling the holder to a "free gift" held not a chose in action). Contrast an assignment of the fruits of a pending action: *post*, p. 84.
[46] *Prosser* v. *Edmonds* (1835) 1 Y. & C. Ex. 481; see *post*, pp. 84, 85.
[47] Companies Act 1985, s.182(1)(*b*). For the previous, more restrictive, provision, see Companies Act 1948, s.73, Sched. 1, Table A, art. 22; and see *Torkington* v. *Magee, supra*, at p. 430; *Re Greene, Greene* v. *Greene* [1949] Ch. 333 at 339.
[48] Copyright, Designs and Patents Act 1988, s.90.
[49] L.P.A. 1925, s.136(2), preserving Policies of Assurance Act 1867.
[50] L.P.A. 1925, s.136(1).
[51] See *Re Westerton* [1919] 2 Ch. 104.

has no further right to the chose.[52] The effect of the assignment on equities is considered below.[53]

5. Conflicting claims. If the debtor, trustee or other person liable in respect of the debt or thing in action has notice that the assignment is disputed by the assignor or any person claiming under him, or of any other opposing or conflicting claims to the debt or thing in action, he may call upon the claimants to interplead, or he may pay the debt or thing in action into court under the Trustee Act 1925.[54]

Section 3. Equitable Assignment

1. Relation to legal assignment. An assignment which does not comply with the statutory requirements is not necessarily ineffectual, for it may operate as an equitable assignment. "The statute does not forbid or destroy equitable assignments or impair their efficacy in the slightest degree."[55] In many cases an assignment which fails to satisfy the statute (*e.g.* because only part of the chose is assigned[56]) is nevertheless fully effective in equity. An assignment, too, may at first be merely equitable, and then, when, *e.g.* the necessary notice is given, become statutory.

2. Essentials of equitable assignment. In determining whether there has been a valid equitable assignment, the following points must be considered.

(a) *Intent to assign essential*

(1) INTENTION. No particular form is required for a valid equitable assignment,[57] whether voluntary[58] or for value.[59] Equity has always looked to the intent rather than the form, and all that is needed is a sufficient expression of an intention to assign. An "agreement between a debtor and a creditor that the debt owing shall be paid out of a specific fund coming to the debtor, or an order given by a debtor to his creditor

---

[52] *Compania Colombiana de Seguros* v. *Pacific Steam Navigation Co.* [1965] 1 Q.B. 101 at 121 (insurer who pays loss and takes assignment of insured's rights may keep all proceeds even if they exceed loss).

[53] See *post*, p. 81.

[54] L.P.A. 1925, s. 136(1); and see T.A. 1925, s.63, *post*, p. 272.

[55] *William Brandt's Sons & Co.* v. *Dunlop Rubber Co. Ltd.* [1905] A.C. 454 at 461, *per* Lord Macnaghten.

[56] On assignments of part of a debt, see J. C. Hall [1959] C.L.J. 99; M. C. Cullity and H. A. J. Ford (1966) 30 Conv.(N.S.) 286 (dealing particularly with gifts of future income).

[57] *William Brandt's Sons & Co.* v. *Dunlop Rubber Co. Ltd.*, *supra*, at p. 462; *I.R.C.* v. *Electric and Musical Industries Ltd.* [1949] 1 All E.R. 120 at 126; affirmed [1950] 2 All E.R. 261.

[58] *Re Wale* [1956] 1 W.L.R. 1346; *Letts* v. *I.R.C.* [1957] 1 W.L.R. 201.

[59] See *post*, p. 79, on the need for value.

upon a person owing money or holding funds belonging to the giver of the order, directing such person to pay such funds to the creditor, will create a valid equitable charge upon such fund; in other words, will operate as an equitable assignment of the debts or fund to which the order refers."[60] Whether the assignment is or is not for value,[61] "the language is immaterial if the meaning is plain,"[62] so that it matters not whether the assignment is a command, a request or a permission, nor whether it is addressed to the assignee or the debtor[63]; but a letter to the debtor's solicitors will not suffice.[64]

(2) OPERATION. For example, in *William Brandt's Sons & Co.* v. *Dunlop Rubber Co. Ltd.*,[65] merchants agreed with a bank by whom they were financed that purchasers of goods sold by the merchants should pay the price directly to the bank. When the merchants sold goods, the bank forwarded to the buyers notice in writing that the merchants had made over to the bank the right to receive the purchase-money, and requested the buyers to sign an undertaking to remit the purchase-money to the bank. It was held that there was evidence of an equitable assignment of the debt with notice to the buyers; the assignment was by way of charge, and so could not be statutory. So also, where a man handed some insurance policies on his life to his son with a request to erect a tombstone for him and pay for it out of the policy moneys, it was held that there was a valid equitable assignment of the policies by way of a charge for the cost of the tombstone.[66]

A mere agreement for value to assign future or unascertained property operates as an actual assignment as soon as the property falls into possession or is ascertained.[67] And an assignment made by letter has been held to be complete as soon as the letter was posted.[68]

(3) ASSIGNMENT. Despite the lack of formal requirements, there must be some transaction which sufficiently manifests an intention to assign, *i.e.* assure or transfer; a mere mandate or authority is not enough.[69] Thus if A owes money to B, who gives C authority to receive it and pay it to D, there is no assignment even if C has promised D to pay the money to him.[70] A cheque, too, "is only a revocable mandate,"[71] and not an assignment of any money standing to the credit of the drawer in

---

[60] *Rodick* v. *Gandell* (1852) 1 De G.M. & G. 763 at 777, *per* Lord Truro L.C. See, *e.g. Burn* v. *Carvalho* (1839) 4 My. & Cr. 690; *Diplock* v. *Hammond* (1854) 5 De G.M. & G. 320; *Cotton* v. *Heyl* [1930] 1 Ch. 510; *Re Warren, ex p. Wheeler* v. *The Trustee in Bankruptcy* [1938] Ch. 725.
[61] *Re Wale* [1956] 1 W.L.R. 1346 at 1350.
[62] *William Brandt's Sons & Co.* v. *Dunlop Rubber Co. Ltd.*, *supra*, at p. 462, *per* Lord Macnaghten.
[63] *Ibid.*
[64] *Rodick* v. *Gandell* (1852) 1 De G.M. & G. 763.
[65] [1905] A.C. 454; and see *Re Kent and Sussex Sawmills Ltd.* [1947] Ch. 177.
[66] *Thomas* v. *Harris* [1947] 1 All E.R. 444.
[67] See *post*, p. 83.
[68] *Alexander* v. *Steinhardt, Walker & Co.* [1903] 2 K.B. 208 (where a letter notifying the assignee was posted simultaneously); *sed quaere*: see *Timpson's Executors* v. *Yerbury* [1936] 1 K.B. 645 at 657, 658. Contrast the giving of notice of legal assignments: *ante*, p. 74.
[69] *Re Williams, Williams* v. *Ball* [1917] 1 Ch. 1 at 6–8.
[70] *Rodick* v. *Gandell* (1852) 1 De G.M. & G. 763.
[71] *Re Beaumont* [1902] 1 Ch. 889 at 894, *per* Buckley J.

his bank account.[72] So, too, a revocable nomination of rights in a pension fund which is not to take effect until the death of the nominator is no assignment.[73] But although there is no restriction to any particular form of transaction, it will usually be found that an equitable assignment will fall under one of the following three heads, namely—

(i)   a direct assignment to the assignee or to trustees for him, or a similar contract to assign;

(ii) a declaration of trust by the assignor for the assignee[74]; or

(iii) if the chose is merely equitable, a direction to the trustees to hold it in trust for the assignee.[75]

(b) *Identified chose.* The assignment must sufficiently identify the chose which is being assigned; "in order to constitute an equitable assignment there must be an engagement to pay out of the particular fund."[76] Thus if C merely directs D to pay a specified sum to X, this will not assign any money which D in fact owes C[77]; but it will if payment is directed to be made "out of moneys due ... from you to me."[78]

(c) *Revocability.* An assignment is not binding on the assignor and the assignee unless it either is made by prior arrangement with the assignee or has been communicated to him[79]; otherwise it is revocable.[80] Thus if D owes money to C, an assignment by C to X made between C and X binds them forthwith, even if D has no notice of it[81]; but if the assignment to X is made between C and D, C and D are not bound until X has notice of it.[82]

(d) *Writing sometimes required.* By statute, "a disposition of an equitable interest or trust subsisting at the time of the disposition, must be in writing," duly signed.[83] Writing is accordingly required for any equitable assignment that falls within this provision, as where an interest under a trust is directly assigned to the assignee or to trustees for him, or the trustees are directed to hold on trust for him instead of for the assignor.[84] But equitable assignments which are not subject to this or

---

[72] *Hopkinson* v. *Forster* (1874) L.R. 19 Eq. 74; and see *ante*, p. 73.

[73] *Re Danish Bacon Co. Ltd. Staff Pension Fund Trusts* [1971] 1 W.L.R. 248; and see *Coulls* v. *Bagot's Executor and Trustee Co. Ltd.* (1967) 119 C.L.R. 460.

[74] This may be not an assignment, but the creation of a derivative trust, or sub-trust: see (1958) 74 L.Q.R. 180, 182.

[75] See *Timpson's Executors* v. *Yerbury* [1936] 1 K.B. 645 at 664; J. W. A. Thornely [1960] C.L.J. 31.

[76] *Watson* v. *Duke of Wellington* (1830) 1 Russ. & M. 602 at 605, *per* Leach M.R.

[77] *Percival* v. *Dunn* (1885) 29 Ch.D. 128; and see *Palmer* v. *Carey* [1926] A.C. 703.

[78] *Brice* v. *Bannister* (1878) 3 Q.B.D. 569.

[79] *Re Hamilton, FitzGeorge* v. *FitzGeorge* (1921) 124 L.T. 737 at 739.

[80] *Morrell* v. *Wootten* (1852) 16 Beav. 197.

[81] *Gorringe* v. *Irwell India Rubber and Gutta Percha Works* (1886) 34 Ch.D. 128; *post*, p. 79.

[82] *Morrell* v. *Wootten, supra.*

[83] L.P.A. 1925, s.53(1)(*c*), discussed *post*, p. 107.

[84] *Grey* v. *I.R.C.* [1960] A.C. 1.

some similar statutory requirement[85] may be made in any way, even by word of mouth.[86]

(e) *Value sometimes required.* Value is necessary for an equitable assignment of rights of property not yet in existence,[87] or for the creation of a mere charge (as distinct from a complete transfer),[88] for such assignments are based on there being a contract that the property in question shall be assigned or stand charged.[89] But value does not appear to be required for other equitable assignments, whether the chose is legal or equitable,[90] provided the assignor has done everything required to be done by him in order to transfer the chose in action.[91] There are difficulties in this doctrine of "every effort," as it may be called.[92] It produces the result that a voluntary assignment of a legal chose in action may be a valid equitable assignment if it is in writing, even if no notice of it has been given,[93] but not if it is oral[94]; for an assignor has not done all that he must do to assign the chose at law if he fails to put the assignment in writing, whereas others besides him may give the notice.[95] Value also seems to be unnecessary for an assignment of an equitable thing in action, such as a legacy or an interest in trust funds,[96] provided that the assignment is complete and perfect[97]; for there is no reason why a man should not be able to give away an equitable interest as freely as he can give away a legal interest.[98]

(f) *Notice not essential but desirable.* An equitable assignment made between the assignor and assignee is complete and binding even if no notice is given to the debtor.[99] And as a trustee in bankruptcy takes subject to all equities affecting the property in the hands of the bankrupt, the assignment will prevail against the subsequent title of the assignor's trustee in bankruptcy, even though the notice required to perfect the assignment as against third parties is not given until after the

---

[85] *e.g.* L.P.A. 1925, s.40, on an assignment of future rents: *Re Whitting, ex p. Hall* (1879) 10 Ch.D. 615. See now Law of Property (Miscellaneous Provisions) Act 1989, s.2, *post*, p. 601.

[86] *Tibbits* v. *George* (1836) 5 Ad. & E. 107; *Gurnell* v. *Gardner* (1863) 4 Giff. 626.

[87] *Post*, p. 83.

[88] *Re Earl of Lucan* (1890) 45 Ch.D. 470.

[89] See *Matthews* v. *Goodday* (1861) 31 L.J.Ch. 282.

[90] *Pulley* v. *Public Trustee* [1956] N.Z.L.R. 771.

[91] *Re Patrick* [1891] 1 Ch. 82; *Re Griffin* [1899] 1 Ch. 408; and see *Blakely* v. *Brady* (1839) 2 Dr. & Wal. 311.

[92] See (1943) 59 L.Q.R. 61.

[93] *Holt* v. *Heatherfield Trust Ltd.* [1942] 2 K.B. 1, an unsatisfactory decision, where value in fact seems to have been given: see (1943) 59 L.Q.R. 58, 208; H. A. Hollond, *ibid.* 129. *Holt's* case was followed in *Pulley* v. *Public Trustee* [1956] N.Z.L.R. 771. Consider also *German* v. *Yates* (1915) 32 T.L.R. 52; *Glegg* v. *Bromley* [1912] 3 K.B. 474 at 491; *Norman* v. *Federal Commissioner of Taxation* (1963) 109 C.L.R. 9.

[94] *Olsson* v. *Dyson* (1969) 120 C.L.R. 365.

[95] *Olsson* v. *Dyson, supra,* at pp. 386, 387 (a dissenting judgment but not on this point): *cf. Re Fry* [1946] Ch. 312, *post*, p. 122.

[96] See *Re Wale* [1956] 1 W.L.R. 1346.

[97] *Bentley* v. *Mackey* (1851) 15 Beav. 12; *Voyle* v. *Hughes* (1854) 2 Sm. & G. 18; *Nanney* v. *Morgan* (1887) 37 Ch.D. 346; and see *Re McArdle* [1951] Ch. 669 (a difficult case: see (1951) 67 L.Q.R. 295).

[98] See the full survey by L. A. Sheridan (1955) 33 Can.B.R. 284.

[99] *Donaldson* v. *Donaldson* (1854) Kay 711; *Gorringe* v. *Irwell India Rubber and Gutta Percha Works* (1886) 34 Ch.D. 128.

trustee in bankruptcy has given notice to the debtor of his claim to the debt.[1] The same principle applies to a judgment creditor of the assignor; he can only make the debt available for payment of the judgment subject to all equities affecting it. Accordingly, if he attaches the debt after the assignment has been made, and the debtor pays the money to him despite receiving notice of the assignment, the assignee can compel the debtor to pay again.[2]

Notice of the assignment should, however, always be given to the debtor or trustee for four reasons.

(i)   The debtor or trustee will be under no liability to the assignee if before receiving notice of the assignment he pays or settles with the original creditor[3] or gives him a negotiable instrument, *e.g.* a cheque or promissory note[4]; but if he disregards the notice he must pay again.[5]

(ii) Notice to the debtor or trustee prevents him from setting up against the assignee any new and independent equities which may arise between the debtor and the assignor.[6]

(iii) Notice *in writing* is necessary to preserve the assignee's priority against subsequent assignees under the rule in *Dearle* v. *Hall*.[7]

(iv) Notice, *if in writing*, may convert the assignment into a statutory assignment, giving the assignee the status of a person entitled to the debt at law, and not merely in equity.

3. Effect of equitable assignment. The effect of an equitable assignment depends upon whether or not the whole interest in the chose has been vested in the assignee.

(a) *Whole interest assigned.*   When the chose is merely equitable and the whole interest in it has been vested in the assignee, equity has always permitted him to sue in his own name without joining the original creditor[8]; for the chose existed only in equity, and so equity was free to hold that the assignee was the sole owner and that no interest remained in the original creditor.[9] As has been seen, there is a similar result on a statutory assignment, which is necessarily of the whole chose.[10]

---

[1] *Re Wallis, ex p. Jenks* [1902] 1 K.B. 719; *Re Anderson* [1911] 1 K.B. 896.
[2] *Yates* v. *Terry* [1902] 1 K.B. 527.
[3] *Stocks* v. *Dobson* (1853) 4 De G.M. & G. 11.
[4] *Bence* v. *Shearman* [1898] 2 Ch. 582.
[5] *Brice* v. *Bannister* (1878) 3 Q.B.D. 569 (where the assignment was equitable despite references to the statute: see *Durham Bros.* v. *Robertson* [1898] 1 Q.B. 765); *Yates* v. *Terry, supra*; *Walter & Sullivan Ltd.* v. *J. Murphy & Sons Ltd.* [1955] 2 Q.B. 584 at 588.
[6] See *post* p. 81.
[7] (1828) 3 Russ. 1; *ante*, p. 66.
[8] See, *e.g. Cator* v. *Croydon Canal Co.* (1843) 4 Y. & C.Ex. 593; *Fulham* v. *M'Carthy* (1848) 1 H.L.C. 703.
[9] See *McMurchie* v. *Thompson* (1906) 8 O.L.R. 637 at 639.
[10] *Ante*, pp. 73, 75, 76.

(b) *Some interest outstanding.* The rule is otherwise if the assignment leaves some interest outstanding. This occurs where there is an equitable assignment of part of the chose, or an equitable assignment of a legal chose; for in the latter case, even if the whole chose is assigned, the original creditor still owns the chose in law,[11] holding it in trust for the assignee.[12] In such cases, neither the assignee[13] nor the original creditor[14] can sue for the chose without joining the other, as plaintiff if he consents and as defendant if he does not.[15] The court must have before it all parties interested in the chose so that there may be a final adjudication binding them all.[16] Further, an equitable assignee cannot exercise contractual rights such as an option conferred on the original creditor.[17]

Section 4. Effect of Assignment on Equities

1. Equities binding assignee. Whether the assignment is legal[18] or equitable,[19] the assignee takes subject to equities having priority over the right of the assignee.[20] The assignee of a thing in action cannot acquire a better right than the assignor had, or, in other words, the assignee takes the thing in action subject to all the equities affecting it in the hands of the assignor which are in existence before notice is received by the debtor.[21] It is this date, and not that of the assignment, that is decisive. If, then, the contract under which the debt arose is voidable by reason of the assignor's fraud, the debtor may set up the fraud in answer to an action brought by the assignee, even though the assignee gave value for the assignment.[22] For the same reason, the debtor has the same rights of set-off against the assignee as against the original creditor.[23] Thus in *Re Knapman*[24] certain legatees, who were also the testator's next-of-kin, brought an action in the Probate Division against the executor claiming revocation of the probate, and pending the action assigned their rights under the will or intestacy. When subsequently their action was dismissed with costs, the court held that the executor

[11] *Cator v. Croydon Canal Co.* (1843) 4 Y. & C.Ex. 593 at 594.
[12] *Fulham v. M'Carthy* (1848) 1 H.L.C. 703 at 722; and see *DiGuilo v. Boland* [1958] O.R. 384.
[13] *Performing Right Society Ltd.* v. *London Theatre of Varieties Ltd.* [1924] A.C. 1.
[14] *Walter & Sullivan Ltd.* v. *J. Murphy & Sons Ltd.* [1955] 2 Q.B. 584.
[15] See *Holt v. Heatherfield Trust Ltd.* [1942] 2 K.B. 1 at 5, citing the substance of this with approval.
[16] *Re Steel Wing Co. Ltd.* [1921] 1 Ch. 349.
[17] *Warner Bros. Records Inc.* v. *Rollgreen Ltd.* [1976] Q.B. 430.
[18] L.P.A. 1925, s.136; *E. Pfeiffer Weinkellerei-Weineinkauf G.m.b.H. & Co.* v. *Arbuthnot Factors Ltd.* [1988] 1 W.L.R. 150.
[19] *Roxburghe v. Cox* (1881) 17 Ch.D. 520.
[20] *Quaere* whether this includes equitable tracing rights: see D. W. McLauchlan (1980) 96 L.Q.R. 90. For tracing see *post*, pp. 297 *et seq.*
[21] *Roxburghe v. Cox* (1881) 17 Ch.D. 520.
[22] *Turton v. Benson* (1718) 1 P.Wms. 496; *Lawrence v. Hayes* [1927] 2 K.B. 111; but see *Stoddart v. Union Trust Ltd.* [1912] 1 K.B. 181.
[23] *Biggerstaff v. Rowatt's Wharf Ltd.* [1896] 2 Ch. 93; and see *Rother Iron Works Ltd.* v. *Canterbury Precision Engineering Ltd.* [1974] Q.B. 1.
[24] (1881) 18 Ch.D. 300, followed in *Re Jones, Christmas v. Jones* [1897] 2 Ch. 190, and distinguished in *Re Pain* [1919] 1 Ch. 38.

had a right to set off the costs against the legacies, and that the assignees took subject to this right.

The rule is that the assignee takes subject to equities, not that he is subject to the equities. Thus where the benefit of a contract is assigned, the assignee can enforce his rights only if he discharges any burdens annexed to the rights assigned[25]; but if he chooses not to enforce his rights, he need not discharge the burdens.[26]

2. Equities not binding assignee.   Notice of the assignment thusfixes the rights of the parties; thereafter the assignor cannot alter them. "After notice of an assignment of a chose in action the debtor cannot by payment or otherwise do anything to take away or diminish the rights of the assignee as they stood at the time of the notice."[27] Thus if after the debtor has notice of an assignment a claim arises out of a contract which is independent of that in which the assigned debt arose (as where L is liable to T on a bond, and T owes L arrears of rent[28]), he cannot set off that claim against the assignee, even though the contract was made before notice of the assignment.[29] But if the set-off directly arises out of the same contract or transaction as the subject-matter of the assignment, the defendant may set it up against the assignee even though it did not accrue to him until after notice of the assignment.[30]

By way of exception, any person who takes a negotiable instrument such as a bill of exchange, promissory note, or cheque before maturity, for value, and without notice of any defect in the title of the holder or of previous dishonour, has a perfect title to it free from all equities. Yet an overdue bill of exchange or promissory note is not negotiable, and the transferee of it takes subject to all defects affecting it in the transferor's hands.[31]

Section 5. Assignment of Expectancies

1. Contract as assignment.   Closely connected with assignments of things in action is the subject of assignments of property to be acquired in the future. There may be an assignment of a present right to future income or profits, or of a pure expectancy, such as a legacy hoped for under the will of a living person. The former are to be regarded as assignments of part of a chose,[32] but the latter are subject to more

---

[25] Contrast *Barker* v. *Stickney* [1919] 1 K.B. 121 with *Erskine Macdonald Ltd.* v. *Eyles* [1921] 1 Ch. 631.
[26] See *Bergmann* v. *Macmillan* (1881) 17 Ch.D. 423; *National Carbonising Coal Co. Ltd.* v. *British Coal Distillation Ltd.* (1937) 54 R.P.C. 41 at 57.
[27] *Roxburghe* v. *Cox* (1881) 17 Ch.D. 520 at 526, *per* James L.J.; and see *Re Pain* [1919] 1 Ch. 38.
[28] *Watson* v. *Mid Wales Ry.* (1867) L.R. 2 C.P. 593.
[29] See *Christie* v. *Taunton, Delmard, Lane & Co.* [1893] 2 Ch. 175; *Re Pinto Leite* [1929] 1 Ch. 221.
[30] *Government of Newfoundland* v. *Newfoundland Ry.* (1888) 13 App.Cas. 199.
[31] Bills of Exchange Act 1882, s.36(2).
[32] *Shephard* v. *Federal Commissioner of Taxation* (1965) 113 C.L.R. 385; see *ante*, p. 76.

restricted rules. At common law such assignments were void, for no one could assign what he had not got. But in equity any such assignment made for valuable consideration has always been treated as a contract to assign.[33] Thus if an assignor who had received the valuable consideration became possessed of the property, he would be compelled to perform his contract, and the beneficial interests in the property would pass to the assignee immediately on the property being acquired[34]; and the same applies to a mere covenant for value to transfer such property.[35] The legal interest, however, would vest in the assignor, and if he transferred it for value to a subsequent purchaser who had no notice of the previous assignment, the title of the subsequent purchaser would prevail; and in this respect the Judicature Act 1873 has made no difference.[36]

2. Consideration required. Both at law and in equity an assignment of an expectancy is ineffective, even if it is made by deed, unless it is made for value[37] or in order to obtain some benefit, *e.g.* by complying with a condition in a will.[38] But if under the authority of an ineffective assignment the property is actually transferred to the assignee, the assignor cannot make the assignee refund it; for he has received it under a valid unrevoked authority, and it matters not that he could not have compelled the transfer.[39]

3. Interests assignable. Among other interests, the following have been treated as assignable in equity:

the mere expectancy of an heir-at-law of succeeding to the estate of his ancestor,[40] or of the next-of-kin of succeeding to the personalty of a living person[41];

the interest which a person might take under the will of a living testator,[42] or the wills of any number of living testators[43];

freight not yet earned,[44] future royalties,[45] and future income, whether from a specified source[46] or from all sources[47];

---

[33] See *Warmstrey* v. *Tanfield* (1628) 1 Rep.Ch. 29; **1 W. & T.L.C. 85**; *Horwood* v. *Millar's Timber & Trading Co. Ltd.* [1917] 1 K.B. 305 at 315.
[34] *Holroyd* v. *Marshall* (1862) 10 H.L.C. 191.
[35] *Re Lind* [1915] 2 Ch. 345; *Re Gillott's Settlement* [1934] Ch. 97; *Re Haynes' W.T.* [1949] Ch. 5.
[36] *Joseph* v. *Lyons* (1884) 15 Q.B.D. 280; *Hallas* v. *Robinson* (1885) 15 Q.B.D. 288. See *ante*, pp. 16, 17.
[37] *Meek* v. *Kettlewell* (1842) 1 Hare 464; (1843) 1 Ph. 342; *Re Ellenborough* [1903] 1 Ch. 697; *Re Brooks' S.T.* [1939] Ch. 993. Cf. *Re Mudge* [1914] 1 Ch. 115.
[38] *Re Burton's Settlement* [1955] Ch. 82.
[39] *Re Bowden, Hulbert* v. *Bowden* [1936] Ch. 71; and see *Re Adlard* [1954] Ch. 29.
[40] *Hobson* v. *Trevor* (1723) 2 P.Wms. 191.
[41] *Re Lind* [1915] 2 Ch. 345.
[42] *Bennett* v. *Cooper* (1846) 9 Beav. 252.
[43] *Re Clarke, Coombe* v. *Carter* (1887) 36 Ch.D. 348.
[44] *Lindsay* v. *Gibbs* (1856) 22 Beav. 522.
[45] *Re Trytel* [1952] 2 T.L.R. 32.
[46] *Re Gillott's Settlement* [1934] Ch. 97.
[47] *Syrett* v. *Egerton* [1957] 1 W.L.R. 1130.

copyright in songs yet to be written[48];

future stock-in-trade to be brought on to mortgaged premises[49];

future book debts, even though not limited to debts to become due in any particular business[50]; and

damages hoped to be recovered by the assignor in a pending action.[51]

Section 6. Ineffective Assignments

On the ground of public policy, there are certain assignments to which no effect will be given in equity. Thus equity might refuse to enforce an assignment of the whole of a man's present and future capital and income.[52] The most important heads are as follows.

1. Public pay.   No effectual assignment can be made of the pay or half-pay of public officers payable to them for the purpose of keeping the dignity of their office or to ensure a due discharge of its duties, *e.g.* the full or half-pay of an officer in the army or navy,[53] or of a civil servant.[54] The restriction, however, does not apply where the office is not a public one[55] or where the pay comes out of local and not national funds[56]; nor does it affect a pension payable solely in respect of past services[57] under a statute which does not prohibit its alienation.[58]

2. Alimony.   On similar grounds, alimony or maintenance granted to a wife by the Divorce Court or by the magistrates is not assignable; it is granted for the support of the wife, and the court has full power to alter it or take it away.[59]

3. Maintenance or champerty.[60]   Equity also refuses to give effect to assignments which involve or savour of maintenance (*i.e.* the supply of pecuniary assistance to the plaintiff or the defendant in an action by a stranger without lawful excuse) or champerty (*i.e.* maintenance coupled

---

[48] *Performing Rights Society* v. *London Theatre of Varieties* [1924] A.C. 1; *Campbell Connelly & Co. Ltd.* v. *Noble* [1963] 1 W.L.R. 252 (American copyright). The Copyright, Designs and Patents Act 1988, s.91, provides for statutory assignments of future copyrights.
[49] *Hallas* v. *Robinson* (1885) 15 Q.B.D. 288.
[50] *Tailby* v. *Official Receiver* (1888) 13 App.Cas. 523.
[51] *Glegg* v. *Bromley* [1912] 3 K.B. 474. Contrast assigning the right of action itself: *ante*, p. 75.
[52] See *Syrett* v. *Egerton*, [1957] 1 W.L.R. 1130, leaving the point open.
[53] *Stone* v. *Lidderdale* (1795) 2 Anst. 533.
[54] See *Lucas* v. *Lucas* [1943] P. 68; contrast D. W. Logan (1945) 61 L.Q.R. 240.
[55] *Feistel* v. *King's College, Cambridge* (1847) 10 Beav. 491 (college fellowship).
[56] *Re Mirams* [1891] 1 Q.B. 594 (chaplain to a workhouse).
[57] See *Willcock* v. *Terrell* (1878) 3 Ex.D 323 (county court judge's pension).
[58] *Crowe* v. *Price* (1889) 22 Q.B.D. 429; Army Act 1955, s.203.
[59] *Re Robinson* (1884) 27 Ch.D. 160; *Paquine* v. *Snary* [1909] 1 K.B. 688; Matrimonial Causes Act 1973, ss.22, 23, 31; Domestic Proceedings and Magistrates' Courts Act 1978, ss.2, 20.
[60] See generally P. H. Winfield (1919) 35 L.Q.R. 143.

with an agreement to divide the spoils).[61] There is no maintenance, however, where the stranger and the party assisted are near relations,[62] or master and servant,[63] or where the stranger is actuated by motives of charity,[64] or where the parties have a common interest,[65] even though one or both contemplate that some profit will be made from their arrangement[66]; thus an angling society has a common interest with one of its members,[67] and a creditor with his impecunious debtor[68]; but one party has no interest in supporting another's libel action.[69] Yet what is a good defence to an action for maintenance is no excuse for champerty.[70] Charity may be indiscreet, but it must not be mercenary.[71]

In general, there is nothing illegal in a purchase or mortgage of the subject-matter of a suit *pendente lite*,[72] for example damages to be recovered in a libel action.[73] There is a great difference between the assignment of an interest in property to which a right to sue is incident, and the assignment of a bare right to sue; the former is valid,[74] the latter invalid.[75] But both rules have exceptions. Thus as to the first rule, it is doubtful whether an order for possession is assignable, even with the premises.[76] Again, a solicitor is absolutely incapacitated from purchasing his client's interest in the subject-matter of a pending action,[77] although this rule does not invalidate a purchase effected before the purchaser became the vendor's solicitor,[78] or a mortgage for costs.[79] As to the latter rule, an assignment of a bare right to sue is valid if made by a trustee in bankruptcy,[80] even back to the bankrupt,[81] or by the liquidator of a company,[82] each of whom has a statutory right to make such an assignment.[83]

---

[61] This principle is unaffected by the abolition of criminal and tortious liability for maintenance and champerty: Criminal Law Act, 1967, s.14(2): see *Trendtex Trading Corporation* v. *Credit Suisse* [1982] A.C. 679 at 702.
[62] *Burke* v. *Green* (1814) 2 Ball & B. 521.
[63] *Wallis* v. *Duke of Portland* (1797) 3 Ves. 494 at 503, affd. (1798) 8 Bro.P.C. 161.
[64] *Harris* v. *Briscoe* (1886) 17 Q.B.D. 504.
[65] *Martell* v. *Consett Iron Co. Ltd.* [1955] Ch. 363; *Trendtex Trading Corporation* v. *Credit Suisse* [1982] A.C. 679 at 702, 703.
[66] *Brownton Ltd.* v. *Edward Moore Inbucon Ltd.* [1985] 3 All E.R. 499.
[67] *Martell* v. *Consett Iron Co. Ltd.*, *supra*.
[68] *Trendtex Trading Corporation* v. *Credit Suisse*, *supra* at pp. 694, 703.
[69] *Alabaster* v. *Harness* [1895] 1 Q.B. 339; *Oram* v. *Hutt* [1914] 1 Ch. 98; and see *Bradlaugh* v. *Newdegate* (1883) 11 Q.B.D. 1.
[70] *Hutley* v. *Hutley* (1873) L.R. 8 Q.B. 112; *Trendtex Trading Corporation* v. *Credit Suisse* [1982] A.C. 679; *Laurent* v. *Sale & Co.* [1963] 1 W.L.R. 829.
[71] *Cole* v. *Booker* (1912) 29 T.L.R. 295.
[72] *Knight* v. *Bowyer* (1858) 2 De G. & J. 421; *Cockell* v. *Taylor* (1851) 15 Beav. 103 at 117.
[73] *Glegg* v. *Bromley* [1912] 3 K.B.474; *ante*, p. 84.
[74] *Ellis* v. *Torrington* [1920] 1 K.B. 399.
[75] *Prosser* v. *Edmonds* (1831) 1 Y. & C.Ex. 481; *Trendtex Trading Corporation* v. *Credit Suisse* [1982] A.C. 679 at 702, 703; *ante*, p. 75.
[76] *Chung Kwok Hotel Co. Ltd.* v. *Field* [1960] 1 W.L.R. 1112 at 1115.
[77] *Simpson* v. *Lamb* (1857) 7 E. & B. 84.
[78] *Davis* v. *Freethy* (1890) 24 Q.B.D. 519.
[79] *Anderson* v. *Radcliffe* (1860) E.B. & E. 819.
[80] *Seear* v. *Lawson* (1880) 15 Ch.D. 426; *Guy* v. *Churchill* (1888) 40 Ch.D. 481.
[81] *Ramsey* v. *Hartley* [1977] 1 W.L.R. 686.
[82] *Re Park Gate Waggon Works Co.* (1881) 17 Ch.D. 234.
[83] Insolvency Act 1986, s.311 (bankruptcy); *ibid.* s.167(1)(*b*), Sched. 4, Pt. III, para. 6 (liquidation).

Part II

TRUSTS

CHAPTER 1

DEFINITION AND CLASSIFICATION OF TRUSTS

Section 1. Definition

1. Problems of definition

(a) *"Trust."* No one has yet succeeded in giving an entirely satisfactory definition of a trust.[1] In Underhill's *Law of Trusts* a trust is defined as "an equitable obligation, binding a person (who is called a trustee) to deal with property over which he has control (which is called the trust property), for the benefit of persons (who are called the beneficiaries or *cestuis que trust*[2]), of whom he may himself be one, and any one of whom may enforce the obligation."[3] But this is not altogether satisfactory, for it is not wide enough to cover trusts for purposes rather than persons. Trusts for charitable purposes (*e.g.* for the repair of a church or the prevention of cruelty to animals) may lack human beneficiaries and yet be valid as trusts[4]; and there may also be other trusts which lack beneficiaries who can enforce them.[5]

Perhaps the most satisfactory definition is that of Professors Sheridan and Keeton[6]: "A trust is the relationship which arises wherever a person called the trustee is compelled in equity to hold property, whether real or personal, and whether by legal or equitable title, for the benefit of some persons (of whom he may be one and who are termed beneficiaries) or for some object permitted by law, in such a way that the real benefit of the property accrues, not to the trustee, but to the beneficiaries or other objects of the trust."

---

[1] Cited in *Allen* v. *Distillers Company (Biochemicals) Ltd.* [1974] Q.B. 384 at 394.
[2] This, and not *cestuis que trustent* (which, though sometimes found, is "hopelessly wrong": C. Sweet (1910) 26 L.Q.R. 196), is the correct plural of *cestui que trust*.
[3] (14th ed., 1987), p. 3, adopted in *Re Marshall's W.T.* [1945] Ch. 217 at 219: *Green* v. *Russell* [1959] 2 Q.B. 226 at 241. For other definitions, see Recognition of Trusts Act 1987, Sched., art. 2; Hart's *Digest of the Law of Trusts*, s.1: Sheridan and Keeton, *The Law of Trusts* (11th ed., 1983), pp. 1–4; *Scott on Trusts* (3rd ed., 1967), p. 37.
[4] See *post*, p. 143.
[5] See *post*, p. 102.
[6] *The Law of Trusts* (11th ed., 1983), p. 2.

(b) *Nature*. Difficult, however, though it may be to give a simple yet satisfactory definition of a trust, it is easy enough to grasp the general idea of it, which is that one person in whom property is vested is compelled in equity to hold the property for the benefit of another person, or for some purposes other than his own. Thus it has been said,[7] somewhat broadly,[8] that "all that is necessary to establish the relation of trustee and *cestui que trust* is to prove that the legal title was in the plaintiff and the equitable title in the defendant."[9] It is not, however, always accurate to say that the trustee is the legal owner while the *cestui que trust* is the equitable owner; the interest of the trustee may be (and often is) equitable only, as where a beneficiary under a settlement makes a settlement of his interest while the legal ownership is still in the hands of the trustees of the former settlement, or for some other reason the legal estate is outstanding.[10] It is therefore better to say that the trustee is the nominal owner of the property, while the *cestui que trust* is the beneficial owner.

(c) *Difficulties*. Yet this does not solve all the difficulties. Thus if T holds property on trust for B, it is still not clear whether B is to be regarded as the real owner of each dividend or other sum received on account of the trust property by T (subject only to T's right to deduct expenses),[11] or whether B's right is merely a right to compel T to account to him for the balance found due.[12] In short, the question "Who is the real owner of the actual notes and coins received?" still remains to be answered.[13] Further, contrary to the general rule,[14] there may be trustees of a trust even though no property is vested in them, as is often the case with Settled Land Act trustees.[15]

2. Illegal trusts.[16]   A trust otherwise valid will not be enforced if it offends against morality,[17] public policy or the provisions of any statute.[18] Thus trusts to seal up a house for 20 years,[19] to carry out a fraudulent purpose,[20] or to provide money to pay the fines of persons

---

[7] *Hardoon* v. *Belilios* [1901] A.C. 118 at 123, *per* Lord Lindley.
[8] The dictum does not distinguish other equitable interests, *e.g.* mortgages. See also *Re Deans* [1954] 1 W.L.R. 332 (President of Probate Division not a trustee); and see *post*, p. 193.
[9] See also *Re Cunliffe-Owen* [1953] Ch. 545 at 563.
[10] See, *e.g. Gilbert* v. *Overton* (1864) 2 H. & M. 110. For "sub-trusts," see *Scott on Trusts* (3rd ed., 1967), p. 707; 74 L.Q.R. 182; and see *post*, p. 103.
[11] *Baker* v. *Archer-Shee* [1927] A.C. 844 (B the real owner for income tax purposes); *Corbett* v. *Commissioners of Inland Revenue* [1938] 1 K.B. 567 at 577; *Nelson* v. *Adamson* [1941] 2 K.B. 12.
[12] *Schalit* v. *Joseph Nadler Ltd.* [1933] 2 K.B. 79 (B not entitled to distrain for rent due under lease of trust property granted by T).
[13] See generally V. Latham (1954) 32 Can.B.R. 520; D. W. M. Waters (1967) 45 Can.B.R. 219 (a searching discussion). For the general nature of equitable rights, see *ante* p. 23.
[14] *Re Barney* [1892] 2 Ch. 265 at 272.
[15] See *Re Marshall's W.T.* [1945] Ch. 217 at 219.
[16] See also *post*, pp. 178, 181.
[17] See *Thornton* v. *Howe* (1862) 31 Beav. 14.
[18] See generally *Bowman* v. *Secular Society Ltd.* [1917] A.C. 406.
[19] *Brown* v. *Burdett* (1882) 21 Ch.D. 667.
[20] *Re Great Berlin Steamboat Co.* (1884) 26 Ch.D. 616.

convicted of offences against the game laws,[21] are all void as being contrary to public policy. On the other hand a trust is not void merely because the main object involves a denial of Christianity[22]; and a bequest for the saying of masses for the dead has been held valid.[23]

3. Fiduciary relationships. The relationship of trustee and beneficiary is but one of a number of relationships generally described as fiduciary. It is a mark of such relationships that one person receives an authority or is entrusted with a job which he is bound to exercise or perform in the best interests of another. Failure to do so will lead to accountability in equity for profits and the return of property. Fiduciary relationships may also give rise to the presumption of undue influence. These matters are fully discussed later.[24] In the following section the distinctions between trusts and other, mostly fiduciary, relationships are considered.

Section 2. Trusts Distinguished from Other Relationships

In a number of ways trusts resemble certain other legal conceptions, notably bailments, agency, contracts and powers[25]; and the execution of a trust has a marked affinity with the administration of the estate of a deceased person. Finally there is the special position of the Crown. The first three categories may be distinguished on the ground that they were enforceable in the common law courts while trusts were enforced only in a court of equity; and much of the administration of estates fell within the competence of the ecclesiastical courts. But apart from historical and procedural differences a number of distinctions of substance must be considered.

1. Bailments. No doubt bailments (*e.g.* a deposit of a chattel) may in a sense be described as a species of trust,[26] for the chattel is held by the bailee subject to duties towards the bailor. Yet bailments were recognised at common law, whereas trusts are merely equitable; and only personal chattels can be bailed, whereas any property may be held in trust. Further, the general property in the case of a trust is in the trustee for the benefit of the beneficiary, whereas a bailee has only a special property, the general property remaining in the bailor. An unauthorised sale by a trustee will accordingly confer a good title upon a

---

[21] *Thrupp* v. *Collett* (1858) 26 Beav. 125.

[22] *Bowman* v. *Secular Society Ltd.* [1917] A.C. 406.

[23] *Bourne* v. *Keene* [1919] A.C. 815. The Dissolution of Colleges Act 1547, alleged to have been infringed by this gift, has been repealed: Charities Act 1960, 5th Sched. Such a gift has been held charitable: see *post*, p. 149.

[24] See *post*, pp. 251–253 (accountability); p. 302 (tracing); pp. 551 *et seq.* (undue influence); p. 558 (abuse of confidence).

[25] See, *e.g. Re Nanwa Gold Mines Ltd.* [1955] 1 W.L.R. 1080 (whether debt, bailment, or trust).

[26] They were even defined by the Court of Appeal in terms of trust in *Rosenthal* v. *Alderton & Sons Ltd.* [1946] 1 All E.R. 583 at 584 (omitted from [1946] K.B. 374).

bona fide purchaser who acquires the legal interest without notice of the trust, whereas such a sale by a bailee usually confers no title as against the bailor.[27]

2. Agency.   An agent and a trustee resemble each other in that each is subject to fiduciary obligations towards his principal or beneficiaries, as the case may be. But there are many differences. Trusts are governed by equity, agency by the common law. In most trusts, there is no contractual relationship between the trustees and the beneficiaries, whereas, apart from agents of necessity, agency normally arises by contract between principal and agent. Usually a trustee has property vested in him, whereas an agent does not; and while a trustee usually cannot involve his beneficiaries in liability, an agent can make his principal liable.[28]

3. Contracts.   It is sometimes difficult to determine whether there is a trust or a contract, *e.g.* creating a debt. The difference may be important. If a fund is vested in T, who is insolvent, B will be paid if T was a trustee for him, but can only claim in T's bankruptcy if T was merely his debtor.[29] Contracts and trusts are in essence two distinct legal concepts. The former was developed by the common law courts and merely gives rise to rights *in personam*; the latter was the invention of the courts of equity and today is regarded as conferring almost a right *in rem*.[30] The same transaction may involve both concepts, as where money is lent on the agreed terms that it will be used to pay specific persons in certain events. Such money is impressed with a trust for the purpose of paying them in those events, and, failing payment to them, for the lender.[31] Furthermore, the trust concept has been imported into the field of contract as a fiction[32] to get round the rule that only a party to a contract may sue upon it. Thus the relationship of contracts with trusts, and the rule against a *jus quaesitum tertio*, must be considered in greater detail in order to provide the setting for the exception from that rule borrowed from trusts.

(a) *Agreement.*   Contracts differ from trusts in that broadly speaking, contracts are agreements either supported by valuable consideration or made under seal. But in many trusts there is no element of contract, as where a testator creates a trust by his will, or a settlor declares himself a trustee of certain property for a volunteer. On the other hand, although

---

[27] The distinction is well brought out in Maitland's *Equity*, Lecture IV.
[28] See generally Powell, *Law of Agency* (2nd ed., 1961), pp. 25, 26.
[29] See *Re Nanwa Gold Mines Ltd., supra.*
[30] See *ante*, pp. 23, 24.
[31] *Barclays Bank Ltd.* v. *Quistclose Investments Ltd.* [1970] A.C. 567; *Carreras Rothmans Ltd.* v. *Freeman Mathews Treasure Ltd.* [1985] Ch. 207; *Re EVTR, Gilbert* v. *Barber* [1987] B.C.L.C. 646. And see (1985) 101 L.Q.R. 269 (P. J. Millett).
[32] See F. E. Dowrick (1956) 19 M.L.R. 374 at 386.

the common law courts persistently refused to recognise as actionable any breach of trust, there appears to be no reason in principle why a trustee's breach of a trust which he has agreed with the settlor to undertake should not be treated as a breach of contract remediable by an action for damages brought by the settlor. Again, if S contracted with B under seal or for valuable consideration to settle property on trust for B, S was liable at law for damages if he broke that contract.

(b) *Ambit.* In one respect, indeed, the equitable rights conferred by agreements relating to trusts are narrower than the rights at common law: an agreement to create a trust under seal but unsupported by valuable consideration will not be enforced by a court of equity.[33] In other respects the equitable rights are wider: they afford the more efficacious remedies, especially of specific performance and of account, and they also may be invoked by *cestuis que trust* who are not parties to the trust. Thus a trustee is liable in equity to the *cestuis que trust* for a breach of trust and not merely to the settlor for a breach of contract. Again, an agreement to create a trust in consideration of marriage is enforceable not merely by those providing the consideration but also by the issue of the marriage.[34]

(c) *Third parties.* It has long been settled at common law that normally only a party to a contract can sue on it. "Our law knows nothing of a jus quaesitum tertio arising by way of contract."[35] A contract may, of course, confer benefits on third parties, as where X and Y agree that X will confer some benefit on B.[36] If X is willing to carry out that agreement, Y cannot require X to confer that benefit on Y instead of B on the ground that B has no enforceable right to that benefit[37] unless B is merely the agent or nominee of Y.[38] Nor can Y require B to hand over the benefit to him after receiving it.[39] But X and Y can together vary the agreement without B's concurrence so as to deprive B of the benefit before it has become due,[40] although this would not be possible if B was a *cestui que trust* and not merely the recipient of a contractual benefit.[41]

---

[33] *Post*, p. 121.
[34] *Post*, p. 126.
[35] *Dunlop Pneumatic Tyre Co. Ltd.* v. *Selfridge & Co. Ltd.* [1915] A.C. 847 at 853, *per* Viscount Haldane L.C. See also *Tweddle* v. *Atkinson* (1861) 1 B. & S. 393. The principle was challenged (see *Smith and Snipes Hall Farm Ltd.* v. *River Douglas Catchment Board* [1949] 2 K.B. 500 at 514–516 and *Drive Yourself Hire Car Co. (London) Ltd.* v. *Strutt* [1954] 1 Q.B. 250 at 272–274) but was re-established in *Scruttons Ltd.* v. *Midland Silicones Ltd.* [1962] A.C. 446. But see *post*, pp. 94, 95.
[36] See generally Finlay, *Contracts for the Benefit of Third Persons* (1939). For a critical analysis, see D. Yates (1977) 41 Conv.(N.S.) 49.
[37] *Re Stapleton-Bretherton* [1941] Ch. 482; and see *Re Miller's Agreement* [1947] Ch. 615; Glanville Williams (1944) 7 M.L.R. 123.
[38] *Re Engelbach's Estate* [1924] 2 Ch. 348; *Re Sinclair's Life Policy* [1938] Ch. 799; *Re Foster (No. 1)* [1938] 3 All E.R. 357. The finding in the first two of these cases that B was a nominee for Y was criticised in *Beswick* v. *Beswick* [1968] A.C. 58 at 94, 96.
[39] *Re Schebsman* [1944] Ch. 83.
[40] *Re Schebsman*, *supra*, at pp. 93, 102.
[41] *Re Empress Engineering Co.* (1880) 16 Ch.D. 125 at 129; see *post*, p. 96.

(d) *Enforcement by third parties.*[42]   Apart from the concept of trust already mentioned, statute has made a number of exceptions to the rule that a contract cannot be enforced by a person who is not a party to it, even if it purports to confer a benefit upon him.[43] The two most important statutory exceptions will be discussed before turning to trusts.

(1) LAW OF PROPERTY ACT 1925, s.56.[44]   This section provides that a person may take "the benefit of any condition, right of entry, covenant or agreement over or respecting land or other property, although he may not be named as a party to the conveyance or other instrument." In its previous form,[45] this was designed to abrogate a very technical rule which distinguished between a covenant in a deed poll and one in a deed *inter partes*. Unlike the former, the latter covenant could not be enforced by a covenantee unless he was a party to the deed.[46] "Normally speaking, a deed between parties is contemplated as a contract, or as carrying out a contract made, so to speak, indoors, round the table by the family, as a matter done not in public but in private. On the other hand, a deed poll is clearly addressed to everybody— 'Know all men by these presents'—or is addressed to 'All to whom these presents shall come.' "[47]

Two views of this section have emerged. The first, and dominant,[48] view is that it is "confined to cases where the person seeking to take advantage of it is a person within the benefit of the covenant in question, if I may use that phrase. The mere fact that somebody comes along and says: 'It would be useful to me if I could enforce that covenant,' does not make him a person entitled to enforce it under section 56."[49] In other words, the deed must purport to make a covenant with, or grant to, the person seeking to enforce it[50]; it is not sufficient merely that it confers a benefit on that person.[51] If, in a contract between X and Y, X agrees to pay money to B, the question is whether X's agreement to pay is expressed as an agreement with B or merely as an agreement with Y; for only in the former case can B sue X.[52] The other view is that any person for whose benefit the contract is

---

[42] For a general survey of the exceptions to the rule, see G. Samuels (1968) 8 Univ. of W. Australia L.R. 378.

[43] In addition to those discussed below, see Marine Insurance Act 1906, s.14(2); L.P.A. 1925, s.47(1); Occupiers' Liability Act 1957, s.3; Road Traffic Act 1972, s.148(4).

[44] See the full discussion by D. W. Elliott (1956) 20 Conv.(N.S.) 43, 114; J. A. Andrews (1959) 23 Conv.(N.S.) 179; E. P. Ellinger (1963) 26 M.L.R. 396.

[45] Real Property Act 1845, s.5 (which was confined to realty), replacing Transfer of Property Act 1844, s.11, which was not: see *Beswick* v. *Beswick* [1968] A.C. 58 at 104, 105.

[46] *White* v. *Bijou Mansions Ltd.* [1937] Ch. 610 at 623 (affirmed [1938] Ch. 351); *Chelsea and Walham Green B.S.* v. *Armstrong* [1951] Ch. 853.

[47] *Chelsea and Walham Green B.S.* v. *Armstrong, supra,* at p. 857, *per* Vaisey J.

[48] See *Beswick* v. *Beswick* [1968] A.C. 58, where, however, the party claiming the benefit succeeded on other grounds: see *post,* pp. 587, 588.

[49] *White* v. *Bijou Mansions Ltd.* [1938] Ch. 351 at 365, *per* Greene M.R.

[50] *Stromdale & Ball Ltd.* v. *Burden* [1952] Ch. 223.

[51] *White* v. *Bijou Mansions Ltd.* [1937] Ch. 610 at 624, 625 (on appeal [1938] Ch. 351 at 365); *Lyus* v. *Prowsa Developments Ltd.* [1982] 1 W.L.R. 1044.

[52] See *Re Miller's Agreement* [1947] Ch. 615; and see *Re Ecclesiastical Commissioners for England's Conveyance* [1936] Ch. 430; *Re Sinclair's Life Policy* [1938] Ch. 799; *Re Foster (No. 1)* [1938] 3 All E.R. 357.

made can enforce it, even if no consideration has moved from him.[53] But by its express terms the section is confined to agreements "respecting land or other property," and it is probable that it is confined in its operation to real property.[54] But even if it also applies to personal property,[55] it cannot apply to other contracts, *e.g.* for personal services, or to contracts to pay money, when no property existed before the agreement and independently of it.[56]

(2) MARRIED WOMEN'S PROPERTY ACT 1882, s.11. Under this section a policy of assurance effected by any man on his own life[57] and expressed to be for the benefit of his wife and children[58] or any of them (and similarly by a woman for her husband and children) creates a trust in favour of the named persons. So long as any object of the trust remains unperformed the policy moneys do not form part of the estate of the insured. They are not subject to his or her debts, except where the policy was effected and premiums paid with intent to defraud creditors, in which case the creditors will be entitled to a sum out of the policy moneys equal to the premiums so paid. The section has been liberally construed to include endowment[59] and accident insurance policies.[60]

The vagueness of the phrase "for the benefit of" has created certain difficulties. Thus a policy effected under the section by a man for the benefit of his wife (unnamed[61]) and children enures for the benefit of a second wife and the children of a second marriage[62]; and, unless the policy provides otherwise, the beneficiaries will take jointly.[63] But, subject to any contrary intention, a named wife forthwith takes an absolute vested interest in the policy, so that if she predeceases her husband, it forms part of her estate[64]; her husband, however, has a lien for any premiums which he pays after her death, as being payments made by a trustee to preserve the trust property.[65] If, however, the person for whose sole benefit the policy was effected is guilty of the

---

[53] *Smith and Snipes Hall Farm Ltd.* v. *River Douglas Catchment Board* [1949] 2 K.B. 500 at 517; *Drive Yourself Hire Co. (London) Ltd.* v. *Strutt* [1954] 1 Q.B. 250 at 271–275; *Beswick* v. *Beswick* [1966] Ch. 538 at 556, 557, 563. This view was rejected by the House of Lords, though the decision was upheld on other grounds: [1968] A.C. 58.

[54] *Beswick* v. *Beswick* [1968] A.C. 58 at 77, 81, 87. The view of the majority is founded on the fact that the section was in a consolidation act not presumed to change the law and replaced a section confined to realty (n. 45, *supra*).

[55] As the minority were disposed to think, even if the change were made *per incuriam*: *Beswick* v. *Beswick*, *supra*, at pp. 94, 105.

[56] *Beswick* v. *Beswick*, *supra*, at p. 76; and see at pp. 87, 105.

[57] Husband and wife have insurable interests to any amount in each other's life as well as their own: *Griffiths* v. *Fleming* [1909] 1 K.B. 805. Hence the wife could effect the policy on her husband's life and take the benefit without recourse to the section, but then the premiums would be her liability.

[58] See *Re Clay's Policy of Assurance* [1937] 2 All E.R. 548 (child adopted *de facto*: section inapplicable).

[59] *Re Ioakimidis' Policy Trusts* [1925] Ch. 403; and see *Re Fleetwood's Policy* [1926] Ch. 48.

[60] *Re Gladitz* [1937] Ch. 588.

[61] See generally (1952) 96 S.J. 720.

[62] *Re Browne's Policy* [1903] 1 Ch. 188. See also *Re Parker* [1906] 1 Ch. 526 and contrast *Re Griffiths' Policy* [1903] 1 Ch. 739.

[63] *Re Davies' Policy* [1892] 1 Ch. 90.

[64] *Cousins* v. *Sun Life Assurance Society* [1933] Ch. 126: and see *Re Kilpatrick's Policies Trusts* [1966] Ch. 730.

[65] *Re Smith's Estate* [1937] Ch. 636; *post*, p. 257.

murder or manslaughter of the insured, the policy moneys will form part of the insured's estate, because it would be against public policy to allow the beneficiary to take the moneys.[66]

(3) TRUSTS OF BENEFIT OF CONTRACT.[67] A person entitled to the benefit of a contract may of course subsequently set up a trust of that benefit for third parties either by declaring himself a trustee of it or by assigning it to trustees for them.[68] In addition, a person may contract as trustee for a third party so that in equity the third party is entitled to the benefit of the contract *ab initio*. If the contract is not performed, the trustee can take proceedings in his own name[69] to enforce it for the benefit of the third party and, if he refuses to do so, the third party can sue, joining the trustee as a defendant.[70] The main difficulty in these cases is to discover what test the courts will apply in deciding whether or not the party intended to contract as trustee. The inquiry plainly involves the construction of the contract and the special circumstances in which it is entered into, but on the authorities as they stand there is little more that can usefully be said.[71] The courts do not readily find that a party intends to constitute himself a trustee.[72]

4. Powers.   A trust must be distinguished from a power. A power is an authority vested in a person to deal with or dispose of property not his own.[73] It can take a number of forms. A power of attorney is simply a special type of agency which allows another to act on behalf of the principal in conveying or transferring the legal estate. Administrative powers are powers to dispose of or manage particular items of property. Finally there are powers of appointment authorising the creation or grant of beneficial interests in property.

---

[66] *Cleaver* v. *Mutual Reserve Fund Life Association* [1892] 1 Q.B. 147 and see *Davitt* v. *Titcumb* [1990] Ch. 110; *post*, pp. 196, 197.

[67] See the surveys by A. L. Corbin (1930) 46 L.Q.R. 12 and J. G. Starke (1948) 21 Austr.L.H. 382, 422, 455; 22 *ibid.* 67.

[68] See *ante*, pp. 71 *et seq.*, for assignment of choses in action.

[69] As, *e.g.* in *Gregory and Parker* v. *Williams* (1817) 3 Mer. 582; *Lloyd's* v. *Harper* (1880) 16 Ch.D. 290. In *Les Affréteurs Réunis Société Anonyme* v. *Leopold Walford (London) Ltd.* [1919] A.C. 801 the trustee was not a party but the defendants agreed to treat the case as if he were.

[70] *Vandepitte* v. *Preferred Accident Insurance Corporation of New York* [1933] A.C. 70 at 79. See, *e.g. Harmer* v. *Armstrong* [1934] Ch. 65.

[71] Contrast *Lloyd's*, *Harmer's*, *Walford's*, *Gregory and Parker's* cases, *supra*, *Tomlinson* v. *Gill* (1756) Amb. 330, *Fletcher* v. *Fletcher* (1844) 4 Hare 67, *Re Gordon*, *Lloyds Bank* v. *Lloyd* [1940] Ch. 851, *Royal Exchange Assurance* v. *Hope* [1928] Ch. 179, *Re Webb* [1941] Ch. 225, *Re Foster's Policy* [1966] 1 W.L.R. 222, and *Lyus* v. *Prowsa Developments Ltd.* [1982] 1 W.L.R. 1044 where the court found a trust with *Vandepitte's* case, *supra*, *Colyear* v. *Countess of Mulgrave* (1836) 2 Keen 81, *Re Engelbach's Estate* [1924] 2 Ch. 348, *Re Sinclair's Life Policy* [1938] Ch. 799, *Re Foster (No. 1)* [1938] 3 All E.R. 357, *Green* v. *Russell* [1959] 2 Q.B. 226, *Re Cook's S.T.* [1965] Ch. 902 (appeal compromised: [1964] *The Times*, November 7), *Beswick* v. *Beswick* [1966] Ch. 538 (in the House of Lords the point was abandoned: [1968] A.C. 58 at 95), *Swain* v. *The Law Society* [1983] 1 A.C. 598, and *Southern Water Authority* v. *Carey* [1985] 2 All E.R. 1077 where the court found none. In *L. French & Co. Ltd.* v. *Leeston Shipping Co. Ltd.* [1922] 1 A.C. 451, the existence of the trust was assumed. And see generally A. L. Corbin (1930) 46 L.Q.R. 12.

[72] See *post*, pp. 123, 124. For a helpful analysis of gifts made subject to some provision for a third party, see T. C. Thomas (1952) 11 C.L.J. 240.

[73] See *Freme* v. *Clement* (1881) 18 Ch.D. 499 at 504.

(a) *Legal or equitable.*   Trusts are necessarily equitable, whereas powers may be legal. Thus a power of attorney may authorise the conveyance of a legal estate, and a mortgagee of freehold land has a statutory power to convey the legal fee simple when he exercises his power of sale.[74] After 1925, however, all powers of appointment are necessarily equitable.[75]

(b) *Imperative or discretionary.*   The substantial distinction is that a trust is imperative, a mere power discretionary. Thus if A holds £10,000 upon trust to divide among a certain class of persons, A has no option in the matter, but is bound to carry out the trust, and if he fails to do so, the court will see that the property is duly divided. If, on the other hand, A is given a mere power to appoint the £10,000 among the members of the class, he cannot be compelled to exercise the power, and if he fails to do so, whether from accident or design, the members have, in the absence of fraud, no claim to the money, which will pass to the persons entitled in default of appointment.[76]

(c) *Marginal cases.*   The distinction between trusts and powers tends to become blurred in two classes of case. First, the so-called trusts of imperfect obligation partake more of the nature of powers than trusts. These are discussed elsewhere.[77] Secondly, an instrument which at first sight appears to confer a mere power of appointment may in fact create a trust; for there are powers in the nature of trusts, or trusts in the garb or under the disguise of powers. In such cases, no failure to exercise the apparent power will prejudice the intended objects, for the court will take upon itself the duties of the donee of the power.

For example, in *Burrough* v. *Philcox*[78] a testator gave property to his two children for their lives, and empowered the survivor of them to dispose of the property by will "amongst my nephews and nieces or their children, either all to one of them, or to as many of them as my surviving child shall think proper." It was held that a trust was created in favour of the testator's nephews and nieces, subject to a power of selection and distribution in his surviving child, and that as the surviving child had failed to exercise the power, the property must be divided equally between the objects. "When there appears a general intention in favour of a class, and a particular intention in favour of individuals of a class to be selected by another person, and the particular intention fails, from that selection not being made, the court will carry into effect the general intention in favour of the class."[79] When equity executes an unexercised trust power, it usually applies the maxim that equality is

---

[74] See *post*, p. 416.
[75] L.P.A. 1925, s.1(7).
[76] *Brown* v. *Higgs* (1803) 8 Ves. 561 at 570; *McPhail* v. *Doulton* [1971] A.C. 424 at 456, 457. See also *post*, p. 117.
[77] *Post*, p. 102.
[78] (1840) 5 My. & Cr. 72; and see *Salusbury* v. *Denton* (1857) 3 K. & J. 529.
[79] *Burrough* v. *Philcox* (1840) 5 My. & Cr. 72 at 92, *per* Lord Cottenham L.C.

equity, and divides the property among all members of the class equally as tenants in common,[80] although the donee of the power might have given unequal shares.

(d) *Gift over in default.* In determining whether a power is a mere power or a power in the nature of a trust, the first thing to consider is whether there is a gift over in default of appointment. If there is, the power is a mere power[81]; if there is not, it will probably be a trust power,[82] though not necessarily so, for the absence of a gift over is not conclusive.[83] The question is whether the donor has shown an intention that in any event the property shall go to the objects of the power. If so, it is a trust power; if not, a mere power of appointment.

5. Administration

(a) *Resemblances.* Trusts were the invention of the Chancellor, whereas the administration of the assets of a deceased person was regulated originally by the ecclesiastical courts. From early times, however, the Court of Chancery exercised a supplementary jurisdiction over the personal representatives, and their position has become more and more assimilated to that of trustees. Thus they must exercise the same degree of care as trustees in carrying out their duties. Moreover, in general the provisions of the Trustee Act 1925 extend to them.[84]

(b) *Distinctions.* There are nevertheless a number of distinctions between trusts and the administration of estates. Six may be mentioned here.

(1) OBJECTIVES. In broad terms, the main function of personal representatives as such is to wind up the estate of the deceased, paying all debts and distributing the assets to those entitled to them or to trustees on their behalf. Trustees, on the other hand, are normally intended to hold the trust property and administer it in accordance with the trusts which bind them. In a phrase, the function of personal representatives is to wind up, and the function of trustees is to hold.

(2) PROPERTY. Until they assent, personal representatives usually have the whole ownership of the property of the deceased vested in them; the beneficiaries have no beneficial interest in any particular asset but merely the right to compel the due administration of the estate. Under a

---

[80] *Re Arnold, Wainwright* v. *Howlett* [1947] Ch. 131 (grandchildren taking *per capita* equally with children); but see *post*, p. 236.
[81] See, *e.g. Re Mills* [1930] 1 Ch. 654; and see *Re Gestetner Settlement* [1953] Ch. 672; see (1953) 69 L.Q.R. 309.
[82] *Re Llewellyn's Settlement* [1921] 2 Ch. 281.
[83] *Re Weekes' Settlement* [1897] 1 Ch. 289; *Re Combe* [1925] Ch. 210; *Re Perowne* [1951] Ch. 785.
[84] T.A. 1925, s.68(17); see also A.E.A. 1925, ss.33, 39.

trust, the beneficial interest in the trust property is in the beneficiaries and the trustees usually have only the bare ownership.[85]

(3) LIMITATION. An action by a beneficiary to recover trust property or in respect of any breach of trust is, in general, barred after six years,[86] whereas the period in respect of claims to the personal estate of a deceased person is 12 years.[87] Neither limit applies in the case of fraud or property retained by the trustee or personal representative or converted to his own use.[88]

(4) JOINT AND SEVERAL AUTHORITY. One of several personal representatives may dispose of pure personalty,[89] whereas trustees must act jointly.

(5) RECEIPT OF SOLE PERSONAL REPRESENTATIVE. Unlike a trustee, a sole personal representative acting as such may give a valid receipt for capital money arising on a trust for sale of land, even though he is not a trust corporation.[90]

(6) NEW TRUSTEES. The Trustee Act 1925 gives wide powers of appointing new trustees.[91] These powers do not apply to personal representatives unless and until they are holding as trustees.[92] Personal representatives as such can be appointed only by will or by the court.

(c) *Dual status.* Despite distinctions such as these the dividing line between trustees and personal representatives often tends to become somewhat blurred, so that a person may at the same time be both a trustee and a personal representative.[93] A will may set up certain trusts and appoint the same persons to be both executors and trustees; and once appointed, a personal representative remains a personal representative for the rest of his life[94] unless the grant is limited or is revoked, or unless he is removed from office by the court.[95] Further, on an intestacy the personal representatives are constituted express trustees.[96]

It follows that no general test can be laid down; the distinction can be drawn only *quoad* the particular assets in question. If the personal representatives have no duties to perform beyond the collection of assets, payment of creditors and distribution of the estate, they will

---

[85] See *Corbett* v. *I.R.C.* [1938] 1 K.B. 567 at 577; and see *ante*, p. 26, and *post*, p. 341.
[86] Limitation Act 1980, s.21(3).
[87] *Ibid.* s.22(*a*).
[88] See generally *post*, pp. 292, 354.
[89] *Post*, p. 318.
[90] See L.P.A. 1925, s.27(2); compare *ante*, p. 63.
[91] See *post*, p. 202.
[92] See *Re Ponder* [1921] 2 Ch. 59; *Re Pitt* (1928) 44 T.L.R. 371; *Re Yerburgh* [1928] W.N. 208; *Re Cockburn's W.T.* [1957] Ch. 438.
[93] See *Re Timmis* [1902] 1 Ch. 176 at 182; and see generally B. S. Ker (1955) 19 Conv.(N.S.) 199.
[94] *Attenborough* v. *Solomon* [1913] A.C. 76 at 83; *Re Timmis supra*, at p. 183.
[95] See *post*, pp. 206, 355.
[96] A.E.A. 1925, ss.33(1), 46(1): and see *Toates* v. *Toates* [1926] 2 K.B. 30.

remain personal representatives[97] (even if they have stated that they are trustees[98]) until assenting,[99] or, if the legatees are infants, until availing themselves of the power[1] to appoint trustees of the gifts to the infants.[2] This will be so even where the payment of the legacy is postponed.[3] But where they are directed to hold the estate or some part of it upon certain trusts (*e.g.* for persons in succession[4] or upon trust for sale and division[5]) they will become trustees when the administration is complete,[6] though in the case of land not, it has been held, until they sign a written assent in their own favour.[7] The moment of transition from administration to trusteeship depends on the circumstances,[8] although when the personal representatives bring in their residuary accounts,[9] or exercise a power of appropriation,[10] there is a presumption that the trusteeship has begun. The mere existence of an outstanding mortgage does not prevent the residue from being ascertained.[11]

6. The Crown

(a) *Trustee.* There is nothing to prevent the Crown acting as trustee.[12] But a trust does not arise in every case where money or property is held by the Crown and used for the benefit of others. The Crown may simply be administering the property in exercise of governmental functions.[13] These public duties are sometimes called "trusts in the higher sense" but do not give rise to an equitable relationship enforceable in the courts.[14]

(b) *Cestui que trust.* The Crown can be a beneficiary under a trust but it has been held that where a minister or other public servant acting in his public capacity takes property on behalf of the Crown, there is no trust and the Crown and the minister are considered as one.[15]

---

[97] *Re Richardson, Pole v. Pattenden* [1920] 1 Ch. 423; *Harvell v. Foster* [1954] 2 Q.B. 36, disapproving dicta in *Re Ponder* [1921] 2 Ch. 59.

[98] *Re Mackay, Mackay v. Gould* [1906] 1 Ch. 25; *Re Rowe* (1889) 58 L.J.Ch. 703.

[99] *Attenborough v. Solomon* [1913] A.C. 76 at 83; and see *Re Aldhous* [1955] 1 W.L.R. 459.

[1] *Post*, p. 364.

[2] *Harvell v. Foster, supra; Re Davis, Evans v. Moore* [1891] 3 Ch. 119: *Re Mackay, Mackay v. Gould, supra.*

[3] *Re Barker* [1892] 2 Ch. 491.

[4] *Re Bowden, Andrew v. Cooper* (1890) 45 Ch.D. 444; *Re Swain* [1891] 3 Ch. 233; *Re Timmis* [1902] 1 Ch. 176; *Re Oliver, Theobald v. Oliver* [1927] 2 Ch. 323.

[5] *Re Claremont* [1923] 2 K.B. 718.

[6] See *Re Cockburn's W.T.* [1957] Ch. 438 at 440; and see *Lilley v. Public Trustee of the Dominion of New Zealand* [1981] A.C. 839.

[7] *Re King's W.T.* [1964] Ch. 542. *Sed quaere*: see R. R. A. Walker (1964) 80 L.Q.R. 328; J. F. Garner (1964) 28 Conv.(N.S.) 298.

[8] *Attenborough v. Solomon, supra*, at pp. 82, 83.

[9] *Re Claremont, supra.*

[10] *Phillipo v. Munnings* (1837) 2 My. & Cr. 309.

[11] *I.R.C. v. Smith* [1930] 1 K.B. 713.

[12] *Civilian War Claimants Association Ltd. v. The King* [1932] A.C. 14 at 27; *Nissan v. Att.-Gen.* [1970] A.C. 179 at 223.

[13] *Tito v. Waddell (No. 2)* [1977] Ch. 106.

[14] *Ibid.* at p. 216, *per* Megarry V.-C.

[15] *Town Investments Ltd. v. Department of the Environment* [1978] A.C. 359; see (1977) 93 L.Q.R. 321.

Section 3. Classifications

Trusts may be classified in various ways. The more important classifications are the following.

1. Express, implied and constructive. A trust may arise in the following ways.

(a) *Express trust:* a trust created by express declaration of the person in whom the property is vested, as where A declares himself a trustee of Whiteacre for B, or conveys it to C on trust for B. This is called an express trust.

(b) *Implied trust:* a trust arising from the presumed intention of the owner of the property, as where he conveys it to another to be held on certain trusts which fail, whether wholly or partly, or uses it for the purchase of other property which, by his direction, is transferred to a stranger. This is called an implied or presumptive trust, or where, as in the examples given, the beneficial interest comes back to the person who conveyed the property or provided the money for its purchase in the name of another, a resulting trust.

(c) *Constructive trust:* a trust imposed by equity, irrespective of the intention of the owner of the property, when it would be an abuse of confidence for him to hold the property for his own benefit, as where a trustee obtains a renewal in his own name of a lease held by him as trustee. This is called a constructive trust.

It should be noted, however, that there is no general agreement on the proper classification of trusts,[16] and, in particular, that the term "constructive trust" is sometimes used so as to include the second as well as the third of these classes.[17]

2. Private and public. Trusts may also be divided, according to their end and purpose, into private and public (or charitable). A trust is private if it is for the benefit of an individual or class, irrespective of any benefit which may be conferred thereby on the public at large; it is public or charitable if the object thereof is to promote the public welfare, even if incidentally it confers a benefit on an individual or class.

---

[16] See, *e.g. Cook* v. *Fountain* (1676) 3 Swans. 585; *Soar* v. *Ashwell* [1893] 2 Q.B. 390; *Re Llanover S.E.* [1926] Ch. 626; G. P. Costigan (1914) 27 Harv.L.R. 437.
[17] As in *Hussey* v. *Palmer* [1972] 1 W.L.R. 1286 at 1289, 1290 where the concepts themselves are confused.

A private trust may be enforced by any of the beneficiaries, a public trust by the Attorney-General.

3. Perfect and imperfect obligation. Trusts which are not enforceable by or on behalf of any *cestui que trust* or object are known as trusts of imperfect obligation, or honorary trusts.[18] In general, trusts for mere abstract and impersonal purposes[19] are not recognised as valid.[20] Thus the courts have declared void the trusts of a large fund expressed for purposes such as the maintenance of good understanding between nations and the preservation of the independence and integrity of newspapers,[21] a trust to devote funds to pursuing inquiries into a new alphabet,[22] and a bequest "for the purpose of providing some useful memorial" to the testator.[23]

On the other hand, the courts have upheld testamentary trusts limited in duration to the perpetuity period[24] for the maintenance of individual animals,[25] or a tomb,[26] or to further foxhunting.[27] These cases have been characterised as "anomalous and exceptional" and, perhaps, "concessions to human weakness or sentiment,"[28] or even "merely occasions when Homer has nodded,"[29] and the decisions upholding them must now be regarded as being of doubtful authority.[30] Moreover, an invalid trust of imperfect obligation cannot be construed as creating a mere power to carry out the specified purpose, subject to a resulting trust in favour of the settlor, residuary legatee or next-of-kin[31]; "an invalid trust cannot be tortured into a valid power," even though more careful drafting, creating a power and not a trust, could, it seems, achieve the settlor's or testator's purpose.[32] Yet an apparent trust for a mere purpose may in reality amount to a trust for ascertainable individuals subject to a power for the trustees to apply the trust

---

[18] See *Hunter* v. *Bullock* (1872) L.R. 14 Eq. 45; *Dawson* v. *Small* (1874) L.R. 18 Eq. 114.

[19] See *Re Denley's Trust Deed* [1969] 1 Ch. 373.

[20] See generally N. P. Gravells (1977) 40 M.L.R. 397.

[21] *Re Astor's S.T.* [1952] Ch. 534.

[22] *Re Shaw* [1957] 1 W.L.R. 729 (will of George Bernard Shaw); an appeal was dismissed by consent on terms allowing for a sum of money to be devoted to the inquiries into the new alphabet: [1958] 1 All E.R. 245n. Mrs. Shaw's will was more fortunate: see *post*, p. 147, n. 42.

[23] *Re Endacott* [1960] Ch. 232; and see *Re Wood* [1949] Ch. 498 ("This Week's Good Cause").

[24] See *Re Clifford* (1911) 106 L.T. 14 (omitted from [1912] 1 Ch. 29); *Re Wightwick's W.T.* [1950] Ch. 260.

[25] *Re Dean* (1889) 41 Ch.D. 552; *Pettingall* v. *Pettingall* (1842) 11 L.J.Ch. 176.

[26] *Re Hooper* [1932] 1 Ch. 38; *Mussett* v. *Bingle* [1876] W.N. 170 (£300 to be applied in erecting monument to first husband of testator's wife held good though gift of interest of £200 to maintain it was admittedly bad); and consider *Re Conner* [1960] I.R. 67; see *post*, p. 160.

[27] *Re Thompson, Public Trustee* v. *Lloyd* [1934] Ch. 342.

[28] *Re Astor's S.T., supra*, at p. 547, *per* Roxburgh J.

[29] *Re Endacott, supra*, at p. 250, *per* Harman L.J.

[30] *Ibid.* at pp. 246, 250, 251; and see *Leahy* v. *Att.-Gen. for New South Wales* [1959] A.C. 457 at 478, 479, 484.

[31] *I.R.C.* v. *Broadway Cottages Trust* [1955] Ch. 20 at 36; *Re Endacott, supra*, at p. 246. The overruling of *I.R.C.* v. *Broadway Cottages Trust* by *McPhail* v. *Doulton* [1971] A.C. 424 (*post*, p. 117) does not affect this dictum: purpose trusts were not there under consideration.

[32] See (1960) 76 L.Q.R. 20. See generally L. A. Sheridan (1953) 17 Conv.(N.S.) 46; (1958) 4 U. of West.Austr.Ann.L.R. 235; O. R. Marshall (1953) 6 *Current Legal Problems* 151; L. H. Leigh (1955) 18 M.L.R. 120 (the conclusion at p. 136 that the courts "will not treat, as a misapplication, any application of funds *already* made" under an invalid trust seems unjustified, and is contradicted on p. 132).

property for purposes at least in part beneficial to the individuals, *e.g.* by providing a sports ground for the use of them and others. Such a trust, if sufficiently certain, will be valid.[33]

Charitable trusts are not trusts of imperfect obligation, for they are enforceable by the Attorney-General.[34]

4. Simple and special. A simple (or bare[35]) trust is one in which property is vested in one person on trust for another, the nature of the trust not being prescribed by the settlor but being left to the construction of the law, as where property is transferred to T "on trust for B absolutely." In such a case, T must permit B to enjoy the property, and must obey his instructions as to disposing of it. But if B in turn becomes a bare trustee of his equitable interest for C, T will hold directly in trust for C[36]; whereas if B holds for C on a special trust for which the legal estate is requisite, B can call for the legal estate from T.[37] A custodian trustee[38] is not a bare trustee, as he is not a mere name or "dummy" for the managing trustees or for the beneficiaries.[39]

A special trust, on the other hand, is one where the trust itself imposes duties on the trustees, *e.g.* a trust for sale; the great majority of trusts are thus "special." Such trusts may be either *ministerial* or *discretionary*, the former merely requiring the application of ordinary intelligence and business aptitude by the trustee, the latter calling for a greater element of judgment and discretion, as where it lies with the trustee to determine how much of the income of the trust property should be paid to each beneficiary.[40]

5. Executed and executory, and

6. Completely and incompletely constituted. These classifications are dealt with later.[41]

---

[33] *Re Denley's Trust Deed* [1969] 1 Ch. 373; *Re Lipinski's W.T.* [1976] Ch. 235, critically examined by K. Widdows (1977) 41 Conv.(N.S.) 179; and see *Gott* v. *Nairne* (1876) 3 Ch.D. 278 (trust to purchase an advowson and present to the living). Contrast *Re Grant's W.T.* [1980] 1 W.L.R. 360 (gift to new Chertsey Constituency Labour Party not a gift to individuals); *R.* v. *District Auditor No. 3 Audit District of West Yorkshire Metropolitan County Council, ex p. West Yorkshire Metropolitan County Council* [1986] R.V.R. 24 (trust for all or any of the inhabitants of a county, who numbered about two-and-a-half million, not effective as a trust for individuals); and see *post,* p. 116, n. 2. See P. A. Lovell (1970) 34 Conv.(N.S.) 77 generally, and especially on the relationship between the *Denley* case and *Leahy* v. *Att.-Gen. for New South Wales* [1959] A.C. 457.
[34] *Post,* pp. 169, 170.
[35] See *Re Cunningham and Frayling* [1891] 2 Ch. 567 at 572; *Tomlinson* v. *Glyns Executor and Trustee Co.* [1970] Ch. 112 at 125, 126.
[36] *Head* v. *Lord Teynham* (1783) 1 Cox Eq. 57.
[37] *Angier* v. *Stannard* (1834) 3 My. & K. 566; *Poole* v. *Pass* (1839) 1 Beav. 600; *Onslow* v. *Wallis* (1849) 1 Mac. & G. 506; and see *Grey* v. *I.R.C.* [1958] Ch. 375 at 382 (in C.A. at p. 690; in H.L. [1960] A.C. 1) where this distinction does not appear to have been taken. See also *ante,* p. 90.
[38] See *post,* p. 209.
[39] *I.R.C.* v. *Silverts Ltd.* [1951] Ch. 521.
[40] See *post,* pp. 136, 137.
[41] See *post,* pp. 118, 119.

EXPRESS PRIVATE TRUSTS

Section 1. Creation

1. Before 1535. Before the Statute of Uses 1535, a trust of any property might have been created by a conveyance or assignment of the property to T to the use of (or in trust for) B. T thereby became the legal owner of the property, but was compelled in Chancery to account for the profits to B. The Statute of Uses was repealed by the Law of Property Act 1925, and so a trust of any property may now be created in the same manner as before the Statute of Uses, subject to what is said below[1] as to the methods of settling land. But the repeal of the Statute of Uses does not affect its operation in regard to dealings which took effect before 1926,[2] and it is therefore necessary to consider its effect briefly.[3]

2. The Statute of Uses 1535. In cases to which the Statute of Uses applied, a conveyance to T to the use of or in trust for B did not create a trust, for the statute deprived T of any interest in the property, and converted B's equitable interest into a corresponding legal estate. The statute achieved this by enacting that where any person was seised to the use, confidence or trust of any other person or of any corporation, the person or corporation having such use, confidence or trust in fee simple, fee tail, for term of life or for years, or otherwise, should be deemed in lawful seisin and possession of the land for the same estate as he or they had in the use, trust or confidence.

3. Failure of statute to abolish trusts. The object of the statute was to abolish uses and trusts, and to ensure that the legal owner of land should always be also the beneficial owner. But it failed to put an end to trusts for three reasons.

(a) *Leaseholds and copyholds excluded.* The Statute of Uses applied only where one person was *seised* of land to the use of another. It therefore did not affect personal chattels, leaseholds or copyholds, of which there could be no seisin in the technical sense; it was, in fact, confined to freehold land.

---

[1] *Post*, p. 105.
[2] L.P.A. 1925, s.1(10).
[3] For further details, see Megarry & Wade's *Law of Real Property* (5th ed., 1984), pp. 1164–1175.

(b) *Active uses excluded.* The statute did not apply where the person to whom freeholds were conveyed had some active duty to perform, as where the land was conveyed to T to the use that he should collect the rents and pay them to B, or upon trust to sell and pay the proceeds to B. Here the legal estate was in T in order that he might carry out the duty imposed upon him. But the statute applied if the use or trust was purely passive, as where the land was conveyed to T upon trust to permit B to receive the rents; here T took no estate, since he had no active duty to perform.[4]

(c) *Use upon a use excluded.* In *Tyrrel's Case*[5] the common law judges held that there could not be a use upon a use, so that if freehold land was conveyed to A to the use of B to the use of C, the only use recognised by law was the use in favour of B; B was the legal owner by virtue of the statute, and C took nothing. This gave the Court of Chancery the opportunity of interfering once more, and eventually[6] the use in favour of C was enforced in equity in the same way as the first use had been enforced before the passing of the statute. In spite of the statute, therefore, it was possible to sever the legal and equitable interests in freehold property, and create a trust, by limiting a use upon a use, or a trust following after a use, the second use being, for distinction's sake, commonly called a trust. It was not necessary, however, that there should be three persons named; it was sufficient, and the usual practice, to convey the property "unto and to the use of" T (the trustee) in trust for B (the beneficiary). In such a limitation the use in favour of T was not executed, or turned into a legal estate, by the statute, for the statute had no application where a person was seised to his own use but only where he was seised to the use of another; the presence, however, of the use in favour of T was effectual to make the trust in favour of B a trust following after a use, and to prevent it from being executed by the statute.

4. Creation of settlements of land today

(a) *Bare trust.* Now that the Statute of Uses is repealed, a conveyance of freehold land to T in fee simple to the use of, or in trust for, B in fee simple would vest the legal estate in T, and B's interest would be equitable only. Such a conveyance would create a bare trust. This, however, is rarely met with, for in most cases in which a trust is created there is not one beneficial owner absolutely entitled, but a number of persons entitled concurrently or in succession.

---

[4] See *Baker* v. *White* (1875) L.R. 20 Eq. 166; *Van Grutten* v. *Foxwell (No. 1)* [1897] A.C. 658.
[5] (1557) 2 Dy. 155a.
[6] At latest by 1700: *Symson* v. *Turner* (1700) 1 Eq.Ca.Abr. 383. See J. E. Strathdene (1958) 74 L.Q.R. 550 (on the place of *Sambach* v. *Dalston (or Daston)* (1634) Tot. 188; *sub nom. Morris* v. *Darston* (1635) Nels. 30); *Grubb & Gwillim* (1676) 73 S.S. 347; J. H. Baker (1977) 93 L.Q.R. 33; and see generally D. E. C. Yale [1957] C.L.J. 72; Megarry & Wade's *Law of Real Property* (5th ed., 1984), pp. 1172, 1173.

(b) *Trust for sale.* If it is desired to settle the land so that it shall be enjoyed by B during his life and shall pass on his death to C in fee simple, the land is not now conveyed to T in trust for B for life, with remainder to C in fee simple; under such a conveyance, owing to restrictions contained in the property legislation of 1925, the legal estate would not pass, but would remain in the settlor. A settlement of this kind can be created only in one of two ways. One way is to convey the land to trustees upon trust to sell it with power to postpone the sale. Under this trust the interests of B and C are notionally converted into interests in the proceeds of sale.[7]

(c) *Settled land.* The other way is to invoke the provisions of the Settled Land Act 1925. Under that Act a settlement of a legal estate in land *inter vivos* is created by means of a vesting deed and a trust instrument. By the vesting deed the land is conveyed to the tenant for life[8] to hold upon the trusts which are declared in the trust instrument. In the example given, the legal estate would be vested in B, provided that he were of full age, and he would hold the land on trust for himself for life, with remainder to C in fee simple. Where such a settlement is made by will, the will is the trust instrument, and the place of the vesting deed is taken by a vesting assent made by the testator's personal representatives, whereby they vest the legal estate in fee simple in B, the tenant for life.

Section 2. Formalities

In general, equity permitted great freedom in the creation of trusts and in the disposition of interests arising under trusts. But statute has long required the observance of certain formalities in many cases.

1. Creation of trusts

(a) *Writing.* By the Law of Property Act 1925, s.53(1)(*b*),[9] "a declaration of trust respecting any land or any interest therein must be manifested and proved by some writing signed by some person who is able to declare such trust or by his will." This provision regulates the creation of express trusts of land, whether freehold or leasehold,[10] but does not affect the creation or operation of resulting, implied or constructive trusts,[11] nor does it affect trusts of pure personalty, which may still be declared orally.[12]

---

[7] See *post*, pp. 485 *et seq.*

[8] If there is no tenant for life of full age, the land will be vested in the statutory owner, *i.e.* usually the trustees of the settlement (S.L.A. 1925, ss.4, 117(1)(xxvi)).

[9] Replacing the Statute of Frauds 1677, s.7. See T. G. Youdan [1984] C.L.J. 306.

[10] *Forster* v. *Hale* (1798) 3 Ves. 696; affirmed (1800) 5 Ves. 308. Trusts of copyholds, too, were within the Statute of Frauds 1677: *Withers* v. *Withers* (1752) Amb. 151.

[11] L.P.A. 1925, s.53(2), replacing the Statute of Frauds 1677, s.8. See *Oughtred* v. *I.R.C.* [1960] A.C. 206.

[12] *Benbow* v. *Townsend* (1833) 1 My. & K. 506; *Re Kayford Ltd.* [1975] 1 W.L.R. 279.

(b) *Evidence.* It is not essential that a trust within this provision should be *declared* by writing in the first instance. It is sufficient if it can be *proved* by some writing signed by the proper party; and the date of the writing is immaterial so long as it is in existence when an action is brought to enforce the trust.[13] The rule is, in fact, a rule of evidence, and is therefore applicable even where the trust relates to land in a foreign country.[14] To create a trust the declaration must amount to a present irrevocable declaration of trust,[15] and the writing must contain all the terms of the trust[16]; and where a trust is being declared of land already held in trust, the writing must be signed by the beneficial owner, not by the trustee in whom the legal estate is vested.[17]

(c) *Wills.* Where a trust is intended to take effect only on the death of the owner of the property, and to be revocable until then, it must be created by a will or codicil duly executed by the owner in accordance with the Wills Act 1837.[18] This statute applies to all forms of property.

2. Dispositions of interests under trusts.[19]

By the Law of Property Act 1925, s.53(1)(*c*),[20] "a disposition of an equitable interest or trust subsisting at the time of the disposition, must be in writing signed by the person disposing of the same, or by his agent thereunto lawfully authorised in writing or by will." This provision differs from the preceding provision in many respects. It applies not merely to land but to all property; it applies to the disposition of interests under resulting, implied or constructive trusts[21]; the signature of an agent authorised in writing[22] suffices; and the disposition must actually be *in* writing, and not merely be *evidenced by* writing. The disposition may be in two or more interconnected documents, only one of which is signed.[23]

"Disposition" has a wider meaning than "grants or assignments," the corresponding phrase in the Statute of Frauds 1677, and it embraces a direction given by the beneficial owner of property to the trustees to hold the property upon trust for others.[24] In such a case, however, the details of the trusts need not be in writing, and may be proved by extrinsic evidence.[25] The statute does not apply where instead of a mere

---

[13] *Forster* v. *Hale, supra*; *Randall* v. *Morgan* (1806) 12 Ves. 74.
[14] *Rochefoucauld* v. *Boustead* [1879] 1 Ch. 196 at 207. *Cf. Leroux* v. *Brown* (1852) 12 C.B. 801.
[15] *Re Cozens* [1913] 2 Ch. 478.
[16] *Smith* v. *Matthews* (1861) 3 De G.F. & J. 139.
[17] *Tierney* v. *Wood* (1854) 19 Beav. 330; *Kronheim* v. *Johnson* (1877) 7 Ch.D. 60. And see *Dye* v. *Dye* (1884) 13 Q.B.D. 147.
[18] s.9, as substituted by Administration of Justice Act 1982, s.17.
[19] See G. Battersby [1979] Conv. 16 and B. Green (1984) 47 M.L.R. 383 for useful discussions.
[20] Replacing the Statute of Frauds 1677, s.9.
[21] See *Oughtred* v. *I.R.C.* [1960] A.C. 206.
[22] Contrast contracts for the sale of land, where the signature of an agent orally authorised suffices: see L.P.A. 1925, s.40, replaced by Law of Property (Miscellaneous Provisions) Act 1989, s.2, *post*, p. 601.
[23] *Re Danish Bacon Co. Ltd. Staff Pension Fund Trusts* [1971] 1 W.L.R. 248. Compare contracts for the sale of land and L.P.A. 1925, s.40: see Megarry and Wade's *Law of Real Property* (5th ed., 1984), p. 578; Law of Property (Miscellaneous Provisions) Act 1989, s.2(1)(2).
[24] *Grey* v. *I.R.C.* [1960] A.C. 1.
[25] *Re Tyler, Graves* v. *King* [1967] 1 W.L.R. 1269; but see at pp. 1277, 1278, referring to *Re Rees, Williams* v. *Hopkins* [1950] Ch. 204 at 210.

transfer of the beneficial interest there is a transfer of the legal ownership (which carries the beneficial interest) made by the trustees on the oral direction of the beneficiary,[26] nor, it seems, where there is a mere revocable nomination of a contingent death benefit under a pension fund.[27] Further, the statute does not apply to the exercise of an option given to trustees by the settlor over property held by nominees on a resulting trust for the settlor where the effect is to transfer the beneficial interest from the settlor to the trustees.[28]

3. Fraud. These statutory provisions were intended to prevent fraud, and the court has not allowed them to be used as "an engine of fraud."[29] It is a fraud for a person to whom land is conveyed as a trustee, and who knows it was so conveyed, to deny the trust and claim the land as his own. A person claiming land conveyed to another may therefore prove by parol evidence that it was so conveyed on trust for the claimant, and may obtain a declaration that the grantee is a trustee for him.[30]

Section 3. Secret Trusts

It was on the ground of not allowing the above statutory provisions to be used as an engine of fraud that the doctrine of secret trusts was originally evolved.[31] In the case of wills, these trusts are of two types which may conveniently be called "fully secret" and "half secret." A trust is fully secret if the will does not disclose that any trust exists, and half secret if the will reveals that there is a trust, but not its terms or the beneficiaries.

1. Fully secret trusts

(a) *Creation.* If a testator makes a gift of property to T without stating in the will that he is to hold it on trust, and either before or after making his will[32] tells T, directly or through an authorised agent,[33] that

---

[26] *Vandervell* v. *I.R.C.* [1967] 2 A.C. 291.

[27] *Re Danish Bacon Co. Ltd. Staff Pension Fund Trusts,* [1971] 1 W.L.R. 248 at 255, 256.

[28] *Re Vandervell's Trusts (No. 2)* [1974] Ch. 269.

[29] Other statutes to which this doctrine has been applied are the Statute of Frauds, now Law of Property (Miscellaneous Provisions) Act 1989, s.2, see *post,* p. 601; L.R.A. 1925, ss.20, 34(4), see *Lyus* v. *Prowsa Developments Ltd.* [1982] 1 W.L.R. 1044 at 1054, 1055; and the Matrimonial Causes Act 1973, s.45 (repealed by Family Law Act 1986, s.68(2) and Sched. 2, and replaced by *ibid.* ss.55, 56 (as substituted by Family Law Reform Act 1987, s.22), see *Puttick* v. *Att.-Gen.* [1980] Fam. 1 at 22.

[30] *Bannister* v. *Bannister* [1948] 2 All E.R. 133; *Rochefoucauld* v. *Boustead* [1897] 1 Ch. 196, overruling *Bartlett* v. *Pickersgill* (1759) 1 Eden 515; *Neale* v. *Willis* (1968) 19 P. & C.R. 836; *Gilmurray* v. *Corr* [1978] N.I. 99; and see *Hodgson* v. *Marks* [1971] Ch. 892, reversed in C.A. *(ibid.)* on grounds not affecting this point. See J. D. Feltham [1987] Conv. 246; T. G. Youdan [1988] Conv. 267.

[31] See *Drakeford* v. *Wilks* (1747) 3 Atk. 539; *McCormick* v. *Grogan* (1869) L.R. 4 H.L. 82 at 88, 89, 97. Lord Jeffreys L.C. has some claim to paternity: see *Crook* v. *Brooking* (1688) 2 Vern. 50.

[32] *Moss* v. *Cooper* (1861) 1 J. & H. 352 at 367.

[33] *Moss* v. *Cooper* (1861) 1 J. & H. 352; *quaere* as to an unauthorised agent *(ibid.* at pp. 370, 371).

he wishes him to hold the property on trust for B, or to make a will in B's favour,[34] T (or his personal representatives) will be compelled to carry out the trust if T either expressly promises that he will do so, or by silence implies it; for he has induced the testator to leave him the property, and had T not accepted the trust, the testator would not have made the gift to him, or, if it was already made, would have revoked it.[35] No doubt it would be sufficient to prevent fraud in such case to compel T to hold on trust for the persons who would have taken the property if there had been no gift to T in the will.[36] But the court has not been content merely to prevent T from profiting by his fraud; it has gone further and compelled T to hold upon trust for B.[37] The basis of the doctrine is that "the testator has died, leaving the property by his will in a particular manner on the faith and in the reliance upon an express or implied promise by the legatee to fulfil his wishes."[38]

(b) *Acceptance before death.* The secret trust, however, is not enforced unless, before the death of the testator, the legatee or devisee has expressly or impliedly accepted it. If the will contains no reference to any trust, and he hears of the intended trust only after the testator's death (*e.g.* by finding an unexecuted document setting forth the trust), he is entitled to keep the property for himself. The trust is not contained in any will or codicil, and it would be no fraud on his part to set up the Wills Act 1837 as a bar to the enforcement of the trust.[39]

(c) *Particulars.* The trust communicated must be definite, and must be proved to exist applying the ordinary standard of proof in civil cases,[40] the onus of proof being on those who seek to establish the trust.[41] It is not enough for the legatee or devisee to know that he is to hold upon trust; he must also know in the testator's lifetime for whom or for what purpose he is to hold the property, and must accept that particular trust. If he agrees to hold upon some trust to be afterwards declared to him by the testator, and only discovers the nature of the trust after the testator's death, he will be a trustee for the residuary legatee or devisee, or, if the gift to him is a gift of residue, for the persons entitled under an intestacy. To enforce the trust in such circumstances would enable a testator in effect to alter his will from time to time by means of an unexecuted codicil.[42] The trust must not be

---

[34] *Ottaway* v. *Norman* [1972] Ch. 698. There is some similarity to the doctrine of mutual wills, *post,* pp. 190 *et seq.*; and see R. Burgess (1972) 36 Conv.(N.S.) 113.

[35] *Jones* v. *Badley* (1868) 3 Ch.App. 362; *Re Maddock* [1902] 2 Ch. 220; *Re Falkiner* [1924] 1 Ch. 88.

[36] See Bogert, *Trusts and Trustees* (2nd ed., 1960), § 501.

[37] *McCormick* v. *Grogan* (1869) L.R. 4 H.L. 82.

[38] *French* v. *French* [1902] 1 I.R. 172 at 230, H.L., *per* Lord Davey.

[39] *Wallgrave* v. *Tebbs* (1855) 2 K. & J. 313.

[40] *Re Snowden* [1979] Ch. 528 not following *Ottaway* v. *Norman* [1972] Ch. 698 at 712 where the higher standard applicable to rectification had been suggested. For the burden of proof in rectification, see *post,* p. 632.

[41] *Jones* v. *Badley* (1868) 3 Ch.App. 362.

[42] *Re Boyes* (1884) 26 Ch.D. 531; *Re Hawkesley's Settlement* [1934] Ch. 384.

illegal; if it is, there will be a resulting trust in the same way as where the trust is indefinite.[43]

(d) *Two or more donees.*   Where the property is given by the will to two legatees or devisees, and one only of them accepts a secret trust, sometimes the other is, and sometimes he is not, bound by the trust. In *Re Stead*[44] Farwell J. held that the authorities established the following propositions:

(1) TENANTS IN COMMON.   If A induces X either to make, or to leave unrevoked, a will leaving property to A and B as tenants in common, by expressly promising, or tacitly consenting, that he and B will carry out the testator's wishes, and B knows nothing of the matter until after X's death, A is bound, but B is not; for to hold otherwise would enable one beneficiary to deprive the others of their benefits by setting up a secret trust.

(2) JOINT TENANTS: PRIOR PROMISE.   If the gift is to A and B as joint tenants, and A's promise is made before the will is executed, the trust binds both A and B, on the ground that no person can claim an interest under a fraud committed by another.

(3) JOINT TENANTS: SUBSEQUENT PROMISE.   If the gift is to A and B as joint tenants, but A's promise is made after the execution of the will, A is bound, but B is not; for the gift to B is not tainted with any fraud in procuring the execution of the will.

It is difficult to see any real difference between a gift made on the faith of an antecedent promise and a gift left unrevoked on the faith of a subsequent promise, or to see why the gift to B as tenant in common is inevitably unaffected. It may be that the authorities do not fully support these propositions, and that the true test is whether the gift to B was induced by A's promise.[45]

(e) *Trusts on intestacy.*   The principle upon which secret trusts are enforced is not confined to wills. It applies also where the owner of property has refrained from disposing of it by will (or has revoked a will already made[46]), relying on the promise of T, who takes the property on an intestacy, to dispose of it in favour of B. Here, too, T holds on trust for B.[47] But it is doubtful whether the principle applies to dispositions *inter vivos.*[48]

[43] *Moss* v. *Cooper* (1861) 1 J. & H. 352.
[44] [1900] 1 Ch. 237 at 241.
[45] See B. Perrins (1972) 88 L.Q.R. 225.
[46] See *Tharp* v. *Tharp* [1916] 1 Ch. 142 (appeal settled [1916] 2 Ch. 205).
[47] *Re Gardner, Huey* v. *Cunnington* [1920] 2 Ch. 523.
[48] See *Re Tyler, Graves* v. *King* [1967] 1 W.L.R. 1269 at 1275.

2. Half secret trusts

(a) *Creation.* In a half secret trust, property is given by will to T with an express direction in the will itself that he is to hold upon trust, but the particular trust is not disclosed in any testamentary document. Thus where T has accepted the obligations of a secret trust, the trust will be fully secret if the will simply gives the property "to T," but half secret if the gift is "to T on the trusts I have already told him." In the case of a half secret trust, there is no chance of T committing a fraud by claiming the property for himself.[49] Nevertheless, if the particular trust on which he is to hold the property is communicated to him before or at the time when the will is made and the will states that it has been so communicated, he must carry it out.[50]

(b) *Acceptance before will.* Unlike a full secret trust, it is doubtful whether there can be any effective communication and acceptance of a half secret trust *after* the date of the will. The testator, it has been said, cannot reserve to himself a power of making future unwitnessed dispositions by merely naming a trustee and leaving the purposes of the trust to be supplied afterwards.[51] Yet these doubts rest on somewhat unsatisfactory dicta, due, perhaps, to a flirtation with the rules governing the incorporation of documents in wills[52]; indeed, if the trusts are declared in a document to which the will refers as an existing document, the document may be incorporated in the will and all secrecy destroyed.[53] On principle, there seems to be no real reason why the communication of the trust at any time before the testator's death should not suffice for half secret as well as fully secret trusts.[54]

(c) *Sufficiency of communication.* Probably there is sufficient communication if the testator hands a letter to T, even if it is in a sealed envelope marked "Not to be opened until after my death,"[55] though in such a case the recipient must know that the envelope sets out the terms of a secret trust and agree to carry them out[56]; and the law for fully secret trusts seems to be similar.[57] If there is no proper communication of the trusts, *e.g.* because they are not communicated in time, or

---

[49] See *Re Rees, Williams* v. *Hopkins* [1950] Ch. 204; *Re Karsten* [1953] N.Z.L.R. 456; *Re Pugh's W.T.* [1967] 1 W.L.R. 1262.

[50] *Blackwell* v. *Blackwell* [1929] A.C. 318. And see *Re Williams, Williams* v. *Parochial Church Council of All Souls, Hastings* [1933] Ch. 244. Contrast *Re Stirling* [1954] 1 W.L.R. 763, following *Re Falkiner* [1924] 1 Ch. 88, where the will expressly negatived any trust.

[51] *Blackwell* v. *Blackwell, supra*, at p. 339; *Re Keen* [1937] 2 Ch. 236 at 246; *Re Karsten, supra*, at p. 461; *Re Bateman's W.T.* [1970] 1 W.L.R. 1463 at 1468.

[52] P. Matthews [1979] Conv. 360, argues that the incorporation doctrine is the true basis of the half-secret trust. To the contrary: D. R. Hodge [1980] Conv. 341.

[53] See *Re Jones, Jones* v. *Jones* [1942] Ch. 328; (1943) 59 L.Q.R. 23.

[54] As in Ireland (see L. A. Sheridan (1951) 67 L.Q.R. 314) and in the U.S.A. (see *Restatement of the Law of Trusts* 2d (1959), § 55, p. 143; Scott *The Law of Trusts* (3rd ed., 1967) § 55.8, p. 441). See also Holdsworth (1937) 53 L.Q.R. 501.

[55] See *Re Keen* [1937] Ch. 236 at 242; *Re Browne* [1944] I.R. 90; but see *Re Roberts, Murphy* v. *Eadsforth* (1956) 106 L.J. News. 663.

[56] See *Lomax* v. *Ripley* (1855) 3 Sm. & G. 48.

[57] See *Re Boyes* (1884) 26 Ch.D. 531 at 536.

because the will prescribes a particular mode of communication and the only trusts communicated were not communicated thus, the beneficial interest in the property belongs to the residuary legatee or devisee, or, if it is a residuary gift, to the persons entitled on an intestacy.[58] And where by a subsequent will a testator increases a legacy which is already bound by a half secret trust, but fails to communicate the increase to the trustees, the trusts will be valid as to the amount of the original legacy only.[59]

3. Basis of secret trusts. Although the doctrine of secret trusts originated on a basis of not allowing statute to be used as an engine of fraud,[60] "the moral turpitude of any particular case must vary infinitely according to the circumstances."[61] The doctrine has in fact been applied in many cases where no real fraud is possible,[62] and it now appears to rest on the simple principle of enforcing the equitable obligations binding a man's conscience.[63] This can be done without collision with any statute, for it is now recognised that secret trusts operate outside the will[64]; they merely impose a trust on the benefits received under the will, and do not affect the operation of the will itself. Accordingly, since a beneficiary under a secret trust takes "a title dehors the will,"[65] he does not lose his benefits if he witnesses the will[66] or predeceases the testator.[67] On the other hand if the secret trustee predeceases the testator the secret trust probably fails because there is a failure of the legacy upon which the trust was intended to operate.[68] It is unsettled whether secret trusts are express trusts or constructive trusts: there are difficulties in either view.[69]

4. Evidence of secret trusts. Where a will gave property to T to be disposed of as already directed, it was once held that a memorandum drawn up by T after the testator's death was not admissible in evidence after T's death to prove the terms of the trust, for the memorandum was not against T's pecuniary or proprietary interest.[70] But such a

---

[58] *Johnson* v. *Ball* (1851) 5 De G. & Sm. 85; *Re Keen* [1937] Ch. 236; *Re Spence, Quick* v. *Ackner* [1949] W.N. 237; and see *Re Karsten* [1953] N.Z.L.R. 456.
[59] *Re Colin Cooper* [1939] Ch. 811.
[60] See *ante*, p. 108.
[61] *French* v. *French* [1902] 1 I.R. 172 at 230, H.L., *per* Lord Davey.
[62] See *ante*, p. 111.
[63] See *Blackwell* v. *Blackwell* [1929] A.C. 318 at 334. See generally J. G. Fleming (1947) 12 Conv.(N.S.) 28; L. A. Sheridan (1951) 67 L.Q.R. 314; B. Perrins [1985] Conv. 248.
[64] *Re Young decd., Young* v. *Young* [1951] Ch. 344 at 350; *Cullen* v. *Att.-Gen. for Ireland* (1866) L.R. 1 H.L. 190; and see J. G. Fleming (1947) 12 Conv.(N.S.) 28.
[65] *Cullen* v. *Att.-Gen. for Ireland, supra*, at p. 198, *per* Lord Westbury.
[66] *Re Young, decd., Young* v. *Young, supra*.
[67] *Re Gardner, Huey* v. *Cunnington* [1923] 2 Ch. 230.
[68] *Re Maddock* [1902] 2 Ch. 220 at 231. But see *Blackwell* v. *Blackwell* [1929] A.C. 318 at 328; *Earl of Inchiquin* v. *French* (1745) 1 Cox Eq. 1.
[69] See R. Burgess (1972) 23 N.I.L.Q. 263.
[70] *Re Gardner's W.T.* [1936] 3 All E.R. 938.

memorandum clearly seems to be admissible now under Part I of the Civil Evidence Act 1968. And there is no rule of evidence based on incompetence or privilege which prevents the administration of interrogatories to a widow regarding a secret trust alleged to have been imposed upon her by her husband, for the marriage is at an end.[71]

Section 4. The Three Certainties

It was laid down by Lord Langdale M.R.[72] that for the creation of a trust three things are necessary:

(i) The words must be so used that on the whole they ought to be construed as imperative;

(ii) The subject-matter of the trust must be certain; and

(iii) The objects or persons intended to have the benefit of the trust must be certain.

These are called "the three certainties."[73]

1. Certainty of words

(a) *Intent.* No particular form of expression is necessary for the creation of a trust, if on the whole it can be gathered that a trust was intended. "A trust may well be created, although there may be an absence of any expression in terms importing confidence."[74] A trust may thus be created without using the word "trust," for what the court regards is the substance and effect of the words used.[75] Indeed, the Statute of Uses 1535 repeatedly used the phrase "use, confidence, or trust."

(b) *Precatory words.* Trusts may even be constituted by *precatory* words, as where a person gives property to another and accompanies the gift with words of wish, hope, desire, confidence, or entreaty that the donee will dispose of the property in some particular way. Such cases chiefly arise under wills, and it is often very difficult to determine whether the testator intended an absolute gift, leaving it in the discretion of the donee to comply with his wishes or not, or whether he intended that the donee should be a trustee of the property, and, as

---

[71] *Shenton* v. *Tyler* [1939] Ch. 620; but see the criticisms at (1939) 2 M.L.R. 319; (1939) 55 L.Q.R. 330; (1940) 56 L.Q.R. 137; and see *Rumping* v. *D.P.P.* [1964] A.C. 814.
[72] *Knight* v. *Knight* (1840) 3 Beav. 148 at 173.
[73] See generally, Glanville Williams (1940) 4 M.L.R. 20.
[74] *Page* v. *Cox* (1852) 10 Hare 163 at 169, *per* Turner V.-C.; and see *Re Kayford Ltd.* [1975] 1 W.L.R. 279 at 282; *Re Multi Guarantee Co. Ltd.* [1987] B.C.L.C. 257.
[75] *Page* v. *Cox, supra*, at p. 169; *Dipple* v. *Corles* (1853) 11 Hare 183 at 184.

such, be bound to dispose of it in accordance with the wish or desire expressed. The answer to this question must be sought from an examination of the whole of the instrument.

(c) *Modern attitude.* There never has been any such entity as a precatory *trust*; the question was whether precatory *words* had created an express trust, and at one time the Court of Chancery was very ready to infer a trust from such words.[76] But by the time of *Lambe* v. *Eames*[77] the tide had turned. For over a century the strong tendency has been against construing precatory words as creating a trust, and undoubtedly many of the older cases would not now be followed.[78] As James L.J. observed after hearing many of the older cases cited, "I could not help feeling that the officious kindness of the Court of Chancery in interposing trusts where in many cases the father of the family never meant to create trusts, must have been a very cruel kindness indeed."[79] The leading case is *Re Adams and the Kensington Vestry.*[80] There, a testator gave all his real and personal estate to the absolute use of his wife, her heirs, executors, administrators and assigns, "in full confidence that she will do what is right as to the disposal thereof between my children," and the Court of Appeal held that the wife took the property beneficially.

(d) *Modern decisions.* Since that decision there have been few cases[81] in which precatory words have been held to create a trust, though there have been many in which the court has negatived a trust.[82] Thus in *Re Conolly*[83] a testator gave "to my sisters, Anne and Louisa, equally the rest of my stocks and shares," and added: "I specially desire that the sums herewith bequeathed shall ... be specifically left by the legatees to such charitable institutions of a distinct and undoubted Protestant nature as my sisters may select, and in such proportions as they may determine"; it was held that the sisters were entitled beneficially. Again, in *Re Hill, Public Trustee* v. *O'Donnell,*[84] a residuary bequest to the testator's five named brothers and sisters "for the benefit of themselves and their respective families" was held to be a gift to the legatees absolutely and not as trustees for their children. Yet the whole of the instrument must be considered: a gift which is stated at first to be "absolute" may be modified by subsequent words.[85]

---

[76] See, *e.g. Harding* v. *Glyn* (1739) 1 Atk. 469; 5 Ves. 501; **2 W. & T.L.C. 285**.
[77] (1871) 6 Ch.App. 597.
[78] See Sugden's *Law of Property* (1849), pp. 375, 376.
[79] *Lambe* v. *Eames* (1871) 6 Ch.App. 597 at 599.
[80] (1884) 27 Ch.D. 394.
[81] See, *e.g. Re Burley* [1910] 1 Ch. 215; *Re Jevons* (1911) 56 S.J. 72 (contrast *Re Green, Shears* v. *Lloyds Bank Ltd.* [1935] W.N. 151); *Re Blackwood* [1953] N.I. 32 ("in accordance with my wishes").
[82] See, *e.g. Re Diggles* (1888) 39 Ch.D. 253; *Re Hamilton, Trench* v. *Hamilton* [1895] 2 Ch. 370; *Re Williams, Williams* v. *Williams* [1897] 2 Ch. 12; *Hill* v. *Hill* [1897] 1 Q.B. 483; *Re Oldfield* [1904] 1 Ch. 549; *Re Johnson, Public Trustee* v. *Calvert* [1939] 2 All E.R. 458 ("request"); *Re Stirling* [1954] 1 W.L.R. 763.
[83] [1910] 1 Ch. 219. See also *Dobie* v. *Edwards* (1912) 80 L.J.P. 119.
[84] [1923] 2 Ch. 259.
[85] *Comiskey* v. *Bowring-Hanbury* [1905] A.C. 84.

(e) *Effect of old decisions.* It is impossible to reconcile all the cases on the subject, but the principle is clear. "You must take the will which you have to construe and see what it means, and if you come to the conclusion that no trust was intended, you say so, although previous judges have said the contrary on some wills more or less similar to the one which you have to construe."[86] Yet if the principle of *Re Steele's Will Trusts*[87] is sound, there is a series of inconvenient and irregular exceptions from the modern doctrine. In that case it was held that if there is a reported decision that a particular form of wording creates a trust,[88] the use of identical expressions today will also create a trust, even if the earlier case was decided before the modern view appeared.[89] The draftsman's remedy is simple: he should state expressly in the will that the precatory words are not to create any trust or legally binding obligation.

2. Certainty of subject-matter. Certainty of subject-matter falls under two heads.[90]

(a) *Trust property.* The property to be held on trust must be certain. A declaration of trust as to "the bulk of my said residuary estate" fails to create any trust,[91] but a gift of part to one and the remainder to another will be divided equally.[92]

(b) *Beneficial interest.* The beneficial interests to be taken by the beneficiaries must be certain. Thus, if a testator devises all his houses to trustees but leaves it uncertain which of the houses, or how many, each beneficiary is to have, the trust fails and the property falls into residue if it was the subject of a specific gift, or if it was a residuary gift, it passes as on an intestacy.[93]

Sometimes, however, this uncertainty can be cured. There are three main heads. First, the court may be able to apply the maxim "Equality is equity" and divide the property into equal shares.[94] Secondly, there is no uncertainty where the settlor does not immediately specify the beneficial interests but confers upon the trustees a discretionary power to pay or apply the trust fund among a class of persons as they think fit.[95] Thirdly, if the whole of the beneficial interest is given to one beneficiary, subject to the right of other beneficiaries to an uncertain

[86] *Re Hamilton, Trench* v. *Hamilton* [1895] 2 Ch. 370 at 373, *per* Lindley L.J.
[87] [1948] Ch. 603.
[88] The earlier decision in point was *Shelley* v. *Shelley* (1868) L.R. 6 Eq. 540.
[89] This passage has been left unchanged despite the criticism at (1968) 32 Conv.(N.S.) 361.
[90] See Glanville Williams (1940) 4 M.L.R. 20 at 22–26.
[91] *Palmer* v. *Simmonds* (1854) 2 Drew. 221. Contrast *Bromley* v. *Tryon* [1952] A.C. 265.
[92] *Salusbury* v. *Denton* (1857) 3 K. & J. 529.
[93] See *Boyce* v. *Boyce* (1849) 16 Sim. 476; and see *Re Moore, Prior* v. *Moore* [1901] 1 Ch. 936.
[94] See *Doyley* v. *Att.-Gen.* (1735) 2 Eq.Ca.Abr. 194; and see *post,* p. 155.
[95] See *Re Isaacs* (1948) 92 S.J. 336, and *post,* pp. 136 *et seq.*

part of it, the direction as to the uncertain part fails and leaves the principal beneficiary entitled to the whole.[96] Thus, in *Curtis* v. *Rippon*,[97] the testator, after appointing his wife guardian of his children, gave all his property to her, "trusting that she will, in fear of God and in love to the children committed to her care, make such use of it as shall be for her own and their spiritual and temporal good, remembering always, according to circumstances, the Church of God and the poor." It was held that the wife was absolutely entitled to the property, there being no ascertained part of it provided for the children or for the Church or for the poor.[98] For the same reason, if a testator gives property to A and directs that so much of it as may not be required by A, or may be possessed by A at A's death, shall go over to B, B will take nothing.[99]

3. Certainty of objects.   If the objects are uncertain, the trust will fail. It must be possible to ascertain who are the beneficiaries.[1] "Uncertainty" in this context means uncertainty of concept, or linguistic or semantic uncertainty, and not mere difficulty in ascertaining the existence or whereabouts of the beneficiaries (although if this is so great as to make the trust administratively unworkable it will fail for impossibility).[2] It has even been held that a power for the trustees to add to the class of beneficiaries does not make the trust uncertain.[3] Yet in a trust for "my old friends," both "old" and "friends" are words with so many shades of meaning that in the absence of anything which defines the class, it is impossible to say whom the settlor intended to include: the concept is thus uncertain, and the trust void for uncertainty,[4] though this would not be so if the trust could be construed as a series of individual gifts to persons answering the description.[5] The court, however, will strain against holding a trust or any other provision void for uncertainty,[6] and although a gift to "dependants" was once held to fail on this ground,[7] the result would probably be different today.[8]

---

[96] Consider the principle of *Lassence* v. *Tierney* (1849) 1 Mac. & G. 551, applied in *Hancock* v. *Watson* [1902] A.C. 14.

[97] (1820) 5 Madd. 434. And see *Buggins* v. *Yates* (1724) 9 Mod. 122.

[98] There also appeared to be no certainty of words.

[99] *Sprange* v. *Barnard* (1789) 2 Bro.C.C. 585; *Parnall* v. *Parnall* (1878) 9 Ch.D. 96; *Mussoorie Bank Ltd.* v. *Raynor* (1882) 7 App.Cas. 321 at 331; *Re Jones, Richards* v. *Jones* [1898] 1 Ch. 438.

[1] See J. W. Harris (1971) 87 L.Q.R. 31; C. T. Emery (1982) 98 L.Q.R. 551.

[2] *Whishaw* v. *Stephens* [1970] A.C. 508 at 519 (the *Gulbenkian* case); *McPhail* v. *Doulton* (the *Baden* case) [1971] A.C. 424 at 457 (taking "all the residents of Greater London" as an example); *Brown* v. *Gould* [1972] Ch. 53 at 57 (a summary); *Re Baden's Deed Trusts (No. 2)* [1973] Ch. 9 ("relatives or dependants"); *R.* v. *District Auditor No. 3 Audit District of West Yorkshire Metropolitan County Council, ex p. West Yorkshire Metropolitan County Council* [1986] R.V.R. 24 (for the facts see *ante*, p. 103, n. 33); but see *Blausten* v. *I.R.C.* [1972] Ch. 256 (power to add any person with settlor's consent).

[3] *Re Manisty* [1974] Ch. 17; and see *Re Hay's S.T.* [1982] 1 W.L.R. 202. In *Blausten* v. *I.R.C.*, *supra*, the Court of Appeal (*obiter*) was more restrictive: see *Re Manisty*, at p. 29.

[4] *Brown* v. *Gould*, *supra*, at p. 57; *Whishaw* v. *Stephens*, *supra*, at p. 524. But see L. McKay (1974) 38 Conv.(N.S.) 269.

[5] *Re Barlow's W.T.* [1979] 1 W.L.R. 278.

[6] *Brown* v. *Gould*, *supra*, at p. 57.

[7] *Re Ball, Hand* v. *Ball* [1947] Ch. 228.

[8] See *Re Baden's Deed Trusts (No. 2)*, *supra*, at p. 21.

In the case of a trust to select among a class of beneficiaries, the former rule was that the trust failed unless the whole range of potential beneficiaries was ascertainable with certainty, so that the trustees could consider the claims of all.[9] But this has now been held to be wrong,[10] and the less stringent rule that applies to powers[11] has been extended to trusts.[12] This rule is that neither a trust nor a power will fail merely because it is impossible to ascertain every member of the class.[13] Nevertheless, it must be possible to say with certainty whether any given individual is or is not a member of the class[14]; the relaxation of the rule for the entirety of the class does not permit uncertainty as to particular members. If there is such uncertainty, the limitation is void, even though there may be some who fall within any conceivable meaning of the language, *e.g.* as to being an "old friend" of the settlor; for trustees cannot, by considering only those who are obviously old friends of the settlor, narrow the class of persons whom he intends should be included in the simple (and uncertain) phrase "my old friends."[15] In any event, if there is a trust for division between *all* the members of a class (*e.g.* in equal shares), it will fail unless all the members of the class are ascertainable with certainty.[16]

4. Absence of certainties. The effect of the absence of any of the certainties may be summarised as follows. The paramount certainty is that of subject-matter, in the first sense; if there is no certainty as to the property to be held upon trust, the entire transaction is nugatory. Next, if that certainty is present but there is no certainty of words, the person entitled to the trust property holds free from any trust. Finally, if both these certainties are present but there is uncertainty of objects, there is a resulting trust for the settlor, for "once establish that a trust [of definite property] was intended, and the legatee cannot take beneficially"[17]; the same applies where there is uncertainty of the subject-matter as regards the beneficial interest, unless one of the beneficiaries can establish a claim to the whole.

It will be noticed that the order in which these points should be considered is the natural order of any limitation in trust, *e.g.* where trustees hold "Blackacre in trust for A and B equally."

---

[9] *I.R.C.* v. *Broadway Cottages Trust* [1955] Ch. 20.
[10] *McPhail* v. *Doulton* [1971] A.C. 424, overruling *I.R.C.* v. *Broadway Cottages Trust, supra.* Contrast P. Matthews [1984] Conv. 22. We and other text-writers find his views unpersuasive: *ibid.* 304.
[11] *Whishaw* v. *Stephens* [1970] A.C. 508.
[12] *McPhail* v. *Doulton, supra.*
[13] *Whishaw* v. *Stephens, supra* (power to appoint to a class including anyone employing X and anyone with whom X resides, whether in his house, in his company or under his care and control: valid); *McPhail* v. *Doulton, supra,* and *Re Baden's Deed Trusts (No. 2)* [1973] Ch. 9 (discretionary trust for staff and former staff of a company and their "relatives or dependants": valid); *Re Hay's S.T.* [1982] 1 W.L.R. 202 (power to appoint to anyone except a handful of specified persons: valid).
[14] *McPhail* v. *Doulton, supra,* at p. 456; and see the divergences in *Re Baden's Deed Trusts (No. 2), supra,* as to the meaning of this test.
[15] *Whishaw* v. *Stephens, supra,* at p. 524. *Quaere* as to *Re Gibbard's W.T.* [1967] 1 W.L.R. 42.
[16] *Whishaw* v. *Stephens, supra,* at p. 524.
[17] *Briggs* v. *Penny* (1851) 3 Mac. & G. 546 at 557, *per* Lord Truro L.C.

Section 5. Executed and Executory Trusts

1. Distinction between executed and executory trusts. Although the objects of a trust must be certain, it is not essential that the instrument creating the trust should mark out precisely the interests which the objects are to take in the trust property; that may be left to be done by a formal settlement to be prepared afterwards. For instance, on the marriage of H and W it may be agreed between them that certain property shall be settled on trust for them and their children. Or a testator may direct his executors to lay out a certain sum of money in the purchase of land and to settle it on X and his children. In these cases, although a valid trust is created, a further instrument is necessary to carry into effect the general intention expressed in the first instrument, and the trust is said to be *executory*. On the other hand, a trust is said to be *executed* when no further instrument is necessary but the trust is finally declared in the first instance, as where the trust funds are vested in trustees on trust for A for life, and after his death for B absolutely.

The expressions "executed" and "executory" are often misunderstood. In this connection they refer to the creation of the trust, not to the carrying out of it. In a sense every trust is executory until it is fully performed. The test for determining whether it is executed or executory is, according to Lord St. Leonards,[18] to ask whether the settlor has been his own conveyancer or draftsman, or whether he has left it to the court to make out from general expressions what his intention is.

2. Effect of distinction

(a) *Executed trusts.* The importance of the distinction lies in the fact that in the case of an executed trust equity tends to follow the law, and so in general required the same words of limitation for an equitable interest as a court of law required for a legal estate. Thus before 1926 a general intent to confer an interest in fee simple would not suffice to overcome the absence of any words of limitation.[19] Yet the rule was never applied with the strictness of the common law, and if under an executed trust there were sufficiently clear words of limitation, effect would be given to them even though they were framed in untechnical language,[20] *e.g.* by using "absolutely" instead of "and his heirs" or "in fee simple."[21]

---

[18] *Egerton* v. *Earl Brownlow* (1853) 4 H.L.C. 1 at 210. And see *Sackville-West* v. *Viscount Holmesdale* (1870) L.R. 4 H.L. 543.
[19] *Re Bostock's Settlement* [1921] 2 Ch. 469.
[20] See *Preston on Estates* (1827), Vol. 2, p. 64; Hayes, *Introduction to Conveyancing* (5th ed., 1840), Vol. 1, p. 91.
[21] *Re Arden* [1935] Ch. 326; *ante*, p. 24.

(b) *Executory trusts.* In the case of an executory trust, equity will not construe with legal strictness the technical expressions in the document declaring the trust, but will mould the trusts according to the intention of the settlor, if such intention can be ascertained.[22] "In construing the words creating an executory trust a Court of Equity exercises a large authority in subordinating the language to the intent."[23]

3. Marriage articles and wills. Executory trusts are found mostly, though not exclusively, in marriage articles and wills. The trusts in the former are always executory; in the latter they are usually executed, but may be executory, as where a testator directs a settlement to be made on a beneficiary's marriage[24] or "as counsel should advise."[25] Whatever the instrument, it is construed according to the settlor's intention; but there is this great difference between marriage articles and wills, namely, that in the case of marriage articles the intention of the settlor (to provide for the issue of the marriage) is apparent from the nature of the instrument itself,[26] whereas in the case of wills the intention can be gathered only from the words used by the testator.[27]

4. Present position. The abolition of the necessity for words of limitation in creating an estate in fee simple at law,[28] as well as the decline in the use of marriage settlements in recent times, have much reduced the importance of the distinction between executed and executory trusts. It may still be significant, however, in the case of entails. Strict words of limitation are required in executed trusts[29] but not, it seems, in executory trusts.

Section 6. Completely and Incompletely Constituted Trusts

1. Distinction between completely and incompletely constituted trusts. The distinction just considered between executed and executory trusts arises only if there is an enforceable trust; granted that a trust has been created, how is it to be construed? The distinction between completely and incompletely constituted trusts, on the other hand,

---

[22] *Glenorchy* v. *Bosville* (1733) Ca.*t*.Talb. 3; **2 W. & T.L.C. 720.** See *Re Flavel's W.T.* [1969] 1 W.L.R. 444, where the intention was too vague.
[23] *Sackville-West* v. *Viscount Holmesdale* (1870) L.R. 4 H.L. 543 at 565, *per* Lord Westbury.
[24] *Re Spicer* (1901) 84 L.T. 195.
[25] *Bastard* v. *Proby* (1788) 2 Cox Eq. 6.
[26] *Trevor* v. *Trevor* (1720) 1 P.Wms. 622.
[27] See *Re Spicer, supra; Bastard* v. *Proby, supra; Sweetapple* v. *Bindon* (1706) 2 Vern. 536; *Papillon* v. *Voice* (1728) 2 P.Wms. 471.
[28] L.P.A. 1925, s.60.
[29] *Ibid.* s.130(1).

relates to whether there is an enforceable trust at all. A trust is said to be completely constituted when the trust property is vested in trustees for the benefit of the beneficiaries; until that has been done the trust is incompletely constituted, or *in fieri*, as it is sometimes called.

This distinction is by no means the same as that between executed and executory trusts. A completely constituted trust is not necessarily an executed trust, nor is an executory trust the same as an incompletely constituted trust. For instance, if a testator bequeaths £10,000 to X and Y upon trust to lay it out in the purchase of land and to settle the land on A and his children, the trust is executory, for the testator has not "been his own conveyancer"; but the trust is nevertheless completely constituted, for the trust property is vested in trustees on trust for A and his children. All trusts arising under wills are completely constituted, although they may be either executed or executory.

2. Volunteers

(a) *Enforcement.*   Once a trust is completely constituted, it can be enforced by any beneficiary, whether he has given value or is a mere volunteer. But if the trust is incompletely constituted, the position is different. Beneficiaries who have given value can enforce it, for equity looks on that as done which has been agreed to be done; an imperfect conveyance for value will be treated as a contract to convey, and the court will see that it is perfected. But volunteers cannot enforce the trust, for there is no equity to perfect an imperfect voluntary trust.[30] As was said by Lord Eldon L.C. in *Ellison* v. *Ellison*[31]: "If you want the assistance of the Court to constitute you *cestui que trust*, and the instrument is voluntary, you shall not have that assistance," adding, however, that if there is a complete transfer of the property, "though it is voluntary, yet the legal conveyance being effectually made, the equitable interest will be inforced by this Court."[32]

(b) *Operation of rule.*   This doctrine is well illustrated by *Jefferys* v. *Jefferys*,[33] where a father by voluntary deed conveyed certain freeholds and covenanted to surrender certain copyholds to trustees in trust for his daughters. Afterwards he devised the same freeholds and copyholds to his widow, and died without having surrendered the copyholds in pursuance of his covenant. The daughters then sought to have the trusts of the deed carried into effect and to compel the widow to surrender the copyholds to which she had been admitted. The court enforced the

---

[30] *Quaere* whether there is any equity to rectify an imperfect voluntary trust: *Van der Linde* v. *Van der Linde* [1947] Ch. 306 at 311. For rectification, see *post*, pp. 626 *et seq.*

[31] (1802) 6 Ves. 656 at 662; **2 W. & T.L.C. 782**.

[32] See also *Paul* v. *Paul* (1882) 20 Ch.D. 742; *Re Bowden, Hulbert* v. *Bowden* [1936] Ch. 71; *Re Adlard* [1954] Ch. 29.

[33] (1841) Cr. & Ph. 138.

trusts as to the freeholds, as they had been duly conveyed to the trustees, but refused to order the widow to surrender the copyholds; the deed did not operate to vest them in the trustees, and as the father's covenant was voluntary, the daughters had no equity to compel the widow to part with the legal interest which she had properly acquired.

(c) *Damages.* In such cases, the trustees of the deed could at common law claim substantial[34] damages against the father's executors for breach of his covenant to surrender, the absence of consideration being immaterial at law where a contract is under seal.[35] Equity, however, will not grant specific performance of a voluntary contract, even though it is contained in a deed, and will not authorise the parties named as trustees to sue for damages for breach of the covenant.[36] Trustees have even been directed not to sue,[37] so that volunteers have been prevented from obtaining indirectly what they cannot obtain directly.[38] These decisions have been attacked on the ground that the court should not intervene positively to protect the settlor,[39] or that the trust was of a chose in action and was completely constituted.[40] On the other hand, they have been defended on the ground that the covenant to settle after-acquired property is concerned with a mere expectancy and is not enforceable at law.[41] If, however, the covenant is made directly with a beneficiary who is a party to the deed, he may sue for damages for breach of covenant in his own right.[42]

3. Modes of completely constituting a trust. There are two main ways in which an express[43] trust may be completely constituted. The settlor may either convey the property to trustees, or he may declare himself to be a trustee of it. If the conveyance upon trust for the beneficiary has been actually and effectually made, equity will enforce the trust, even in favour of a volunteer; and the rule is the same where the settlor simply declares himself a trustee of the property in favour of the beneficiary.[44] But a gift will be effective even if the donee does not intend to accept it as such but, *e.g.* as a loan.[45]

---

[34] *Re Parkin* [1892] 3 Ch. 510; *Re Cavendish-Browne's S.T.* [1916] W.N. 341.

[35] See *Fletcher* v. *Fletcher* (1844) 4 Hare 67.

[36] *Re Pryce* [1917] 1 Ch. 234, a new departure: see J. L. Barton (1975) 91 L.Q.R. 236. The trustees had applied for directions, as to which see *post*, pp. 236, 258.

[37] *Re Kay's Settlement* [1939] Ch. 329, following *Re Pryce, supra; Re Ralli's W.T.* [1964] Ch. 288 at 301; *Re Cook's S.T.* [1965] Ch. 902 (appeal compromised: [1964] *The Times*, November 7).

[38] *Re Kay's Settlement, supra*, at p. 342. Contrast *Beswick* v. *Beswick* [1968] A.C. 58 at 89.

[39] See D. W. Elliott (1960) 76 L.Q.R. 100.

[40] J. A. Hornby (1962) 78 L.Q.R. 228; Meagher & Lehane (1976) 92 L.Q.R. 417; M. W. Frend [1982] Conv. 280. For trusts of choses in action, see *ante*, p. 96.

[41] W. A. Lee (1969) 85 L.Q.R. 313. And see [1967] *Annual Survey of Commonwealth Law*, 387–397. For expectancies, see *ante*, p. 82.

[42] *Cannon* v. *Hartley* [1949] Ch. 213.

[43] Contrast constructive trusts, *post*, p. 197.

[44] See *Milroy* v. *Lord* (1862) 4 De G. F. & J. 264 at 274. These two methods do not very aptly cover the case where a contract between A and B is made for the benefit of C, giving C the benefit forthwith: see *ante*, p. 96.

[45] *Dewar* v. *Dewar* [1975] 1 W.L.R. 1532.

(a) *By conveyance*

(1) MODE OF TRANSFER.   Where the settlor is both legal and equitable owner of the property, and is intending to constitute the trust by conveyance, the conveyance to the trustees must be effectual to pass the legal interest. If any act remains to be done by the settlor to make the conveyance effectual, the trust is not completely constituted, unless the instrument contains a declaration of trust. And the same rule applies where the intention is not to create a trust but to make a direct gift to the donee. The gift will fail if anything remains to be done by the donor to divest himself of the legal interest. Thus, freehold property must be conveyed by deed of grant, leaseholds by deed of assignment, personal chattels capable of passing by delivery either by deed or delivery,[46] and registered shares by a proper form of transfer.[47]

(2) INEFFECTUAL ATTEMPTS.   Accordingly, in *Richards* v. *Delbridge*,[48] where an intending donor indorsed and signed on a lease the following note not under seal: "This deed and all thereto belonging I give to Edward Bennetto Richards from this time forth, with all the stock-in-trade," it was held that the gift failed, for the attempted assignment passed no legal interest and was not a declaration of trust. The same result was reached in *Antrobus* v. *Smith*,[49] where the owner of shares in a company indorsed on the share certificate a memorandum to the effect that he assigned it to his daughter, and in *Re Fry*,[50] where a donor, resident abroad, died after executing a transfer of shares, but before obtaining the requisite consent of the Treasury (for which he had applied) under the Exchange Control legislation.[51] Romer J. in the last case suggested that the donor might have had to furnish further information to the Treasury.[52]

(3) ALL IN DONOR'S POWER DONE.   Where, however, the donor has done all in his power, according to the nature of the property given, to vest the legal interest in the property in the donee, the gift will not fail even if something remains to be done by the donee or some third person.[53] Thus in *Re Rose, Midland Bank Executor & Trustee Co. Ltd.*

---

[46] *Cochrane* v. *Moore* (1890) 25 Q.B.D. 57.
[47] In addition to the cases discussed below, see *Jones* v. *Lock* (1865) 1 Ch.App. 25, *Re Swinburne* [1926] Ch. 38, and *Re Owen, Owen* v. *I.R.C.* [1949] 1 All E.R. 901 (unpresented cheques; and see *ante*, p. 73); *Re Williams, Williams* v. *Ball* [1917] 1 Ch. 1 (indorsement on insurance policy); and *Re Wale* [1956] 1 W.L.R. 1346 (shares; and see *ante*, p. 75, *post*, p. 124).
[48] (1874) L.R. 18 Eq. 11.
[49] (1806) 12 Ves. 39.
[50] [1946] Ch. 312.
[51] Defence (Finance) Regulations 1939, later Exchange Control Act 1947, especially s.18. Exchange control was lifted on October 24, 1979 (or as regards Southern Rhodesia on December 13, 1979): S.I. 1979 Nos. 1333, 1336, 1660.
[52] [1946] Ch. 312 at 317, 318. But see *Re Rose, Midland Bank Executor & Trustee Co. Ltd.* v. *Rose* [1949] Ch. 78 at 89 for a somewhat different explanation.
[53] *Re Griffin* [1899] 1 Ch. 408 at 411; *Re Rose, Midland Bank Executor & Trustee Co. Ltd.* v. *Rose* [1949] Ch. 78; *Re Rose, Rose* v. *I.R.C.* [1952] Ch. 499; *Re Paradise Motor Co. Ltd.* [1968] 1 W.L.R. 1125. And see *Re McArdle* [1951] Ch. 669 (criticised at (1951) 67 L.Q.R. 295). See N. Seddon (1974) 48 Aust.L.J. 13 as to the application of these principles to imperfect gifts of Torrens title land.

v. *Rose*,[54] the donor executed a transfer of shares in a private company and handed it with the share certificate to the donee but died before it had been registered. Although the donee's legal title would not be perfected until the company had passed the transfer for registration, or at least until the donee had an unconditional right to be registered,[55] it was held that the gift was good because the donor had done all that was necessary on his part.[56] Likewise, a gift of registered land becomes effective upon execution and delivery of the transfer and cannot be recalled thereafter even though the donee has not yet been registered as proprietor.[57]

(4) EQUITABLE INTERESTS. Where the settlor (or donor, in the case of a direct gift) has only an equitable interest in the property, as where the legal estate is vested in trustees for him, it is not necessary that he should procure a conveyance of the legal interest, even if he can; it is sufficient for him to assign his equitable interest, or to direct the trustees to hold that interest for the benefit of the donee.[58] Thus in *Gilbert* v. *Overton*[59] A, who was holding land under an agreement for a lease, by deed assigned the agreement to trustees upon certain trusts. Afterwards a lease was granted to him in accordance with the agreement. It was held that the trust was perfect. Again in *Kekewich* v. *Manning*[60] certain shares were vested in trustees upon trust for A for life, and then for B. B by deed assigned her equitable reversionary interest in the shares to the trustees of her marriage settlement. This was held to create a perfect trust. In these two cases it will be noticed that a deed was used; but a deed is not necessary for the assignment of an equitable interest in property, whether it be realty or personalty, though writing is essential, whatever the property may be.[61]

(b) *By declaration of trust*

(1) DECLARATION. The second method of completely constituting a trust is for the settlor to declare himself to be a trustee of the property for the *cestui que trust*, and this he may do whether his interest is legal or equitable. Such a declaration must be evidenced by writing signed by him if it relates to land, but if it relates to other property it may be by word of mouth,[62] or may be inferred from conduct.[63] It need not be a

---

[54] [1949] Ch. 78.
[55] *Moore* v. *North Western Bank* [1891] 2 Ch. 599.
[56] If registration were refused in such a case the gift would probably remain good: see *Re Fry* [1946] Ch. 312 at 317; (1949) 93 S.J. 657 at 658.
[57] *Mascall* v. *Mascall* (1984) 50 P. & C.R. 119; and see *Lloyds Bank plc* v. *Rosset* [1990] 2 W.L.R. 867.
[58] *Re Chrimes* [1917] 1 Ch. 30; *Timpson's Exors.* v. *Yerbury* [1936] 1 K.B. 645 at 664. See *ante*, p. 77, as to assignment.
[59] (1864) 2 H. & M. 110.
[60] (1851) 1 De G.M. & G. 176.
[61] L.P.A. 1925, s.53; *ante*, p. 107.
[62] *Paul* v. *Constance* [1977] 1 W.L.R. 527 (payment into settlor's bank account and words of gift sufficient).
[63] See *ante*, p. 106.

formal declaration; the settlor "need not use the words, 'I declare myself a trustee,' but he must do something which is equivalent to it, and use expressions which have that meaning; for however anxious the Court may be to carry out a man's intention, it is not at liberty to construe words otherwise than according to their proper meaning."[64]

(2) ATTEMPTED TRANSFER.   If without making a declaration of trust[65] the settlor or donor attempts to constitute a trust or make the gift by transferring the property to trustees or to the donee, and the transfer is ineffectual, the court will not treat the attempted transfer as being such a declaration; for the two things are very different. By attempting to transfer the property the settlor or donor has shown an intention to divest himself of it, and not to hold it himself as trustee.[66] In the well-known phrase of Turner L.J. in *Milroy* v. *Lord*,[67] "there is no equity in this Court to perfect an imperfect gift."

4. Effective imperfect gifts.   Notwithstanding the rules considered above, there are five cases where an apparently imperfect voluntary transfer of property is not ineffective. The first three of these are rules of equity, the other two are statutory.[68]

(a) *Property vested in donee.*   Under the doctrine of *Strong* v. *Bird*,[69] an apparently imperfect gift of any property, whether personal or real,[70] is effective if two conditions are satisfied. First, the property given must have become lawfully vested in the donee, as where he becomes one of the donor's personal representatives, whether as executor[71] or administrator,[72] or is appointed a trustee of the property.[73] Secondly, the donor must have manifested an intention to make a present gift of definite property (which includes forgiving a debt[74]), and this intention must have continued until the donor's death.[75] It is not enough if he merely promises to give in the future,[76] nor if the continuance of his *animus donandi* is negatived by his subsequently taking security for the debt forgiven[77] or treating the property given as still being his own.[78] Where these conditions are satisfied, the gift is effective; for the vesting

---

[64] *Richards* v. *Delbridge* (1874) L.R. 18 Eq. 11 at 14, *per* Jessel M.R.
[65] Such as there was in *Re Ralli's W.T.* [1964] Ch. 288.
[66] *Richards* v. *Delbridge, supra*; and see *Milroy* v. *Lord* (1862) 4 De G.F. & J. 264.
[67] (1862) 4 De G.F. & J. 264 at 274.
[68] See also Chafee & Re, *Cases and Materials on Equity* (5th ed., 1967), pp. 565 *et seq.*
[69] (1874) L.R. 18 Eq. 315. See G. Kodilinye [1982] Conv. 14.
[70] L.T.A. 1897, s.1; A.E.A. 1925, s.1; *Re Comberbach* (1929) 73 S.J. 403.
[71] *Strong* v. *Bird* (1874) L.R. 18 Eq. 315.
[72] *Re James, James* v. *James* [1935] Ch. 449, doubted in *Re Gonin* [1979] Ch. 16, but maintained here; see 93 L.Q.R. 486.
[73] *Re Ralli's W.T.* [1964] Ch. 288.
[74] *Strong* v. *Bird, supra*; *Re Pink, Pink* v. *Pink* [1912] 2 Ch. 528.
[75] *Re Wale* [1956] 1 W.L.R. 1346; and see *Re Stoneham* [1919] 1 Ch. 149; *Re Gonin* [1979] Ch. 16.
[76] *Re Innes* [1910] 1 Ch. 188; *Re Freeland* [1952] Ch. 110. *Cf. Re Greene, Greene* v. *Greene* [1949] Ch. 333.
[77] *Re Eiser's W.T.* [1937] 1 All E.R. 244.
[78] *Re Wale, supra*; and see *Re Freeland, supra.*

of the property in the donee as personal representative or trustee completes his title at law, and the donor's *animus donandi* overrides the claims of the beneficiaries entitled to the donor's estate and allows the donee to hold beneficially despite his fiduciary position.[79]

(b) *Donatio mortis causa.* The court will perfect an imperfect voluntary transfer of property if the conditions for a *donatio mortis causa* are satisfied; these are considered later.[80]

(c) *Proprietary estoppel.* If after the imperfect gift has been made the donor knowingly stands by while the donee improves the property, thinking it is or will be his, equity will sometimes estop the donor from asserting his rights, and compel him to perfect the gift.[81]

(d) *Conveyance to minor.* Although after 1925 an attempt to convey a legal estate in land to a minor cannot vest the estate in him,[82] the conveyance is not totally ineffective but by statute operates as an agreement for value by the grantor to execute a settlement on the infant in the proper form, and in the meantime to hold the land in trust for him.[83]

(e) *Imperfect settlement.* If an instrument *inter vivos* intended to create a settlement of a legal estate in land fails to pass the legal estate because it does not comply with the requirements of section 4 of the Settled Land Act 1925 (which prescribes the proper form for such a settlement), it is treated as a trust instrument, and the trustees may, and must on the request of the tenant for life, execute a proper vesting deed; and this will perfect the settlement.[84]

5. Meaning of settlement for value. In determining whether a settlement is voluntary or for value, the following points may arise.

(a) *Good consideration insufficient.* Lawful considerations are either—

    (i) meritorious considerations (sometimes called *good* considerations), being considerations of blood and natural affection, or of generosity and moral duty[85]; or

---

[79] *Strong* v. *Bird* (1874) L.R. 18 Eq. 315; *Re Stewart* [1908] 2 Ch. 251; *Re Pink, Pink* v. *Pink* [1912] 2 Ch. 528; *Re Nelson, Nelson* v. *Nelson* (1947) 91 S.J. 533. See also *Carter* v. *Hungerford* [1917] 1 Ch. 260.
[80] See *post*, p. 380.
[81] See *post*, p. 578.
[82] L.P.A. 1925, s.1(6).
[83] L.P.A. 1925, s.19(4); S.L.A. 1925, s.27(1).
[84] S.L.A. 1925, s.9; see *ante*, p. 106.
[85] See *Sharington* v. *Strotton* (1565) 1 Plowd. 298; Cruise's *Digest* (4th ed., 1835), Vol. 4, p. 24; Elphinstone's *Introduction to Conveyancing* (7th ed., 1918), p. 81; and see *post*, p. 546.

(ii) valuable considerations, such as money, money's worth, or marriage which the law esteems an equivalent for money.

A settlement supported only by the former kind of consideration is regarded as voluntary.

(b) *Marriage.* A settlement made before and in consideration of marriage is made for value,[86] and so is a settlement made after marriage if it is executed in pursuance of an ante-nuptial agreement.[87] But a settlement made after marriage without any ante-nuptial agreement to make it is voluntary.

(c) *Scope of marriage consideration*

(1) SPOUSES AND ISSUE. Although marriage is "the most valuable consideration imaginable,"[88] it is not every object of a marriage settlement who can claim to be a purchaser. After considerable conflict of judicial opinion, it is now settled that the only persons within the marriage consideration are the husband, the wife, and the issue of the marriage[89]; and "issue" includes grandchildren as well as children.[90] Any provision made by the settlement in favour of the issue of the settlor by a possible second marriage, or in favour of the children of either party by a former marriage, or of the parties' illegitimate children, or of the settlor's next-of-kin, is purely voluntary. The old cases which seemed to decide that some, at any rate, of such persons might be treated as purchasers[91] can be supported now only on the ground that, in the special circumstances of the cases, the interests of the volunteers were so mixed up with those of the issue of the intended marriage that it was impossible to separate them.

(2) VOLUNTEERS. The position may be illustrated by contrasting the case of *Re Plumptre's Marriage Settlement*[92] with the case of *Pullan* v. *Koe*.[93] In the first case, the husband and wife on marriage in 1878 covenanted with the trustees of their marriage settlement to settle the wife's after-acquired property on the usual trusts for herself and her

---

[86] A settlement made by a father for the benefit of all his children on the occasion of the marriage of one of them was "a gift made in consideration of marriage" for the purposes of the Finance (1909–10) Act, 1910, s.59(2): *I.R.C.* v. *Rennell* [1964] A.C. 173; and see *Re Park (No. 2)* [1972] Ch. 385. But the Finance Act 1963, s.53, reversed this for the purposes of estate duty, and similarly for inheritance tax: Inheritance Tax Act 1984 (formerly cited as Capital Transfer Tax Act 1984), s.22(4), replacing Finance Act 1975, Sched. 6, para. 6.

[87] *Re Holland, Gregg* v. *Holland* [1902] 2 Ch. 360; *Re Gillespie* (1913) 20 Mans. 311. A recital in a settlement of an *oral* ante-nuptial agreement satisfied the former requirements of the Statute of Frauds 1677, s.4, as to agreements in consideration of marriage: *ibid.*. This part of the Statute of Frauds was repealed by the Law Reform (Enforcement of Contracts) Act 1954.

[88] *Att.-Gen.* v. *Jacobs Smith* [1895] 2 Q.B. 341 at 354, *per* Kay L.J.

[89] *De Mestre* v. *West* [1891] A.C. 264; *Att.-Gen.* v. *Jacobs Smith* [1895] 2 Q.B. 341; *Re D'Avigdor-Goldsmid* [1951] Ch. 1038 at 1053 (reversed on other grounds: *D'Avigdor-Goldsmid* v. *I.R.C.* [1953] A.C. 347).

[90] *Macdonald* v. *Scott* [1893] A.C. 642 at 650; *cf. Re Noad* [1951] Ch. 553.

[91] *e.g. Newstead* v. *Searles* (1737) 1 Atk. 265; *Clark* v. *Wright* (1861) 6 H. & N. 849.

[92] [1910] 1 Ch. 609, following *Re D'Angibau* (1880) 15 Ch.D. 228; see also *Re Pryce* [1917] 1 Ch. 234.

[93] [1913] 1 Ch. 9.

husband successively for life, then for the issue of the marriage, with an ultimate trust in favour of her next-of-kin. In 1884 the husband purchased some stock in her name; she afterwards sold this and invested the proceeds of sale in the purchase of other stock. In 1909 the wife died without issue, and the husband obtained administration of her estate. It was held that the wife's covenant to settle the stock could not be enforced against the husband (as her administrator) by the next-of-kin, who were volunteers and strangers to the marriage consideration. Nor could the trustees of the settlement sue for damages for breach of covenant, for the claim was statute-barred, and even if this had not been the case the court might have directed the trustees not to sue.[94]

(3) PURCHASERS.   On the other hand, in *Pullan* v. *Koe*[95] a similar covenant to settle after-acquired property of the wife was entered into on marriage in 1859. In 1879 the wife received £285, which she paid into her husband's banking account; the money was used to buy some bonds which remained in the husband's possession until his death in 1909 and were in his executor's hands at the date of the action. *There were several children of the marriage.* It was held that the money was specifically bound by the covenant the moment it was received, and was subject to a trust enforceable by all the persons within the marriage consideration, unless it had passed to a bona fide purchaser without notice; the trustees were therefore entitled to recover the bonds from the husband's executor, although their right of action on the covenant was long since statute-barred.

(d) *Value provided by others.*   The rule treating the issue of a marriage as being within the marriage consideration will not be extended to other cases. Thus if in consideration of a payment by his father a son covenants with trustees to settle property on trust for his children, the children cannot enforce the covenant against the son; for although it was made for value, they are mere volunteers.[96]

Section 7. Setting Trusts Aside

There are certain cases where a trust, even though completely constituted, may be revoked by the settlor, or set aside by third parties. These cases fall under four heads.

1. Revocation

(a) *Power of revocation.*   In general, a settlor cannot revoke a completely constituted trust unless the settlement reserves a power of revocation. Nor is the mere absence of a power of revocation from a voluntary settlement, or the presence in it of unusual provisions, any

---

[94] See *ante*, p. 121.
[95] [1913] 1 Ch. 9.
[96] *Re Cook's S.T.* [1965] Ch. 902 (appeal compromised: see [1964] *The Times*, November 7).

ground for setting it aside, provided the provisions of the settlement were brought to the settlor's attention and understood by him.[97] "It is not the province of a Court of justice to decide on what terms or conditions a man of competent understanding may choose to dispose of his property. If he thoroughly understands what he is about, it is not the duty of a Court of justice to set aside a settlement which he chooses to execute on the ground that it contains clauses which are not proper."[98]

(b) *Other grounds for revocation.*   A settlor may revoke a settlement if it was obtained from him by fraud or undue influence,[99] or if he executed it under a fundamental mistake or misapprehension as to its effect. Thus voluntary settlements of a reversionary interest under a marriage settlement made at the suggestion of their father by two children just over 21 years old were set aside 16 years later on the ground that they had not understood nor received any explanation of the effect of the settlements.[1] A settlor is also able to revoke certain trusts in favour of creditors, called "illusory trusts"; these will be dealt with later.[2]

(c) *Mode of revocation.*   If a settlor seeks to set a settlement aside, the burden of proving fraud, undue influence, or mistake is on him.[3] It is otherwise where the relationship between him and the beneficiary is such as to raise a presumption of undue influence, for then the settlement will be set aside unless the beneficiary can prove that the settlor was in fact a free agent and thoroughly understood and intended the settlement.[4] A settlement for value can very rarely be set aside, for the valuable consideration usually consists of marriage, and it is a rule that the court will not interfere unless the parties can be restored to their original position, which is obviously impossible when the marriage has taken place.[5]

2. Transactions at an undervalue

(a) *Conveyances to defraud creditors before December 29, 1986*

(1) LAW OF PROPERTY ACT 1925, SECTION 172.   By section 172 of the Law of Property Act 1925,[6] every conveyance of any property, whether real or personal,[7] which was made with intent to defraud creditors was

---

[97] *Toker* v. *Toker* (1863) 3 De. G.J. & S. 487; *Phillips* v. *Mullings* (1871) 7 Ch.App. 244; *Hall* v. *Hall* (1873) 8 Ch.App. 430; *Henry* v. *Armstrong* (1881) 18 Ch.D. 668.
[98] *Dutton* v. *Thompson* (1883) 23 Ch.D. 278 at 281, *per* Jessel M.R.; see also *James* v. *Couchman* (1885) 29 Ch.D. 212.
[99] See generally *post*, pp. 551 *et seq.*, for undue influence.
[1] *Strauss* v. *Sutro* [1948] L.J.R. 33; and see *Bullock* v. *Lloyds Bank Ltd.* [1955] Ch. 317.
[2] See *post*, p. 140.
[3] *Henry* v. *Armstrong* (1881) Ch.D. 668.
[4] *Powell* v. *Powell* [1900] 1 Ch. 243.
[5] *Johnston* v. *Johnston* (1884) 52 L.T. 76.
[6] Replacing 13 Eliz. 1, c. 5, 1571, for all transactions, whether before 1926 or after 1925.
[7] *Re Eichholz* [1959] Ch. 708.

voidable at the instance of any person thereby prejudiced. "Conveyance" was widely defined,[8] and was probably not confined to instruments in writing.[9] Section 172 was repealed on December 29, 1986,[10] and replaced by the provisions of the Insolvency Act 1986 dealing with transactions at an undervalue which are discussed below.[11] But a transaction entered into before December 29, 1986, cannot be set aside under these new provisions except to the extent that it could have been set aside under the law in force immediately before that day,[12] so that the repealed section 172 and the cases decided under it will remain of importance for some time. Accordingly, a summary of the old law is given here: a fuller account will be found in the last edition of this book.[13]

(2) EXCEPTIONS. There were two main exceptions to the operation of section 172. First, it did not affect the law of bankruptcy, nor the operation of a disentailing assurance.[14] Secondly, it did not apply to any conveyance made in good faith for either valuable or good consideration to any person not having, at the time of the conveyance, notice of the intent to defraud creditors.[15] Persons taking for valuable consideration and persons taking for good consideration[16] were thus apparently put on the same footing, although this had not been so under the Act of 1571 which section 172 replaced.[17] The "good faith" required, though grammatically that of the grantor, must be that of the grantee, for *ex hypothesi* the grantor intends to defraud creditors.[18]

(3) SETTLEMENTS FOR VALUE. Although the marginal note to the section referred to "voluntary conveyances," the section itself spoke of "every conveyance," without using the word "voluntary." A settlement for value, therefore, might be voidable under section 172, as it had been under the Act of 1571, but it could be avoided only if the person taking for value knew of the fraud.[19]

(4) VOLUNTARY SETTLEMENTS. Where the settlement was voluntary, the rule established under the Act of 1571 was that it might be set aside even if the beneficiaries were entirely ignorant of the settlor's intention to defeat his creditors. But section 172 appears to have altered this where there was good consideration: for persons taking upon good

---

[8] See L.P.A. 1925, s.205(1)(ii).
[9] See *Re Eichholz, supra*, at p. 728; but see (1959) 75 L.Q.R. 307. *Quaere* whether it included property passing by delivery: *Re T., W. v. Kahn* (1966) 110 S.J. 387.
[10] Insolvency Act 1985, s.235(3), Sched. 10, Pt. IV: in force on December 29, 1986, by virtue of *ibid.* s.236(2); Insolvency Act 1986, s.443; S.I. 1986 No. 1924.
[11] *Post*, p. 130.
[12] Insolvency Act 1986, s.437, Sched. 11, Pt. III, para. 20.
[13] 28th ed., pp. 130–133.
[14] L.P.A. 1925, s.172(2).
[15] L.P.A. 1925, s.172(3). See *Lloyds Bank Ltd. v. Marcan* [1973] 1 W.L.R. 1387.
[16] See *ante*, pp. 125, 126.
[17] See the 28th edition of this book, pp. 130, 131.
[18] See (on the 1571 Act) *Re Johnson, Golden v. Gillam* (1881) 20 Ch.D. 389 at 394 (affirmed 51 L.J.Ch. 503; [1882] W.N. 22).
[19] *Kevan v. Crawford* (1877) 6 Ch.D. 29; *Re Holland, Gregg v. Holland* [1902] 2 Ch. 360.

consideration and in good faith without notice of the intent to defraud creditors were protected.[20]

(5) PROOF OF FRAUD.   The burden of proving the intent to defraud lay on the creditors seeking to set aside the settlement. An intent to deprive creditors sufficed, without actual deceit or dishonesty.[21] Such an intent might be inferred from evidence of the circumstances in which the settlement was made,[22] and would be presumed when the settlor could not pay his debts without the property settled.[23] Mere indebtedness would not raise the presumption of fraudulent intent, but nor was it necessary to prove absolute insolvency.[24]

(6) TIME FOR AVOIDANCE.   So long as his debt was not statute-barred, a creditor could apply at any time to set aside a conveyance as being fraudulent under section 172: this was so even if the debtor had died,[25] and for several years the creditor had known of the conveyance without taking proceedings.[26]

(7) EFFECT OF AVOIDANCE.   The avoidance of a settlement was only for the purpose of paying the creditors, so that the property still belonged to the beneficiaries so far as it was not required for that purpose.[27] And avoidance did not affect the rights of a bona fide purchaser who, without notice of the intent to defraud, acquired from a beneficiary any interest under the settlement.[28]

   (b) *Transactions after December 28, 1986*

(1) INSOLVENCY ACT 1986, SECTIONS 423–425.[29]   Although the new law is contained in a statute which deals with corporate and individual insolvency, it is not restricted to cases of liquidation or bankruptcy. The language of the Act is refreshingly clear, so a detailed exegesis appears to be unnecessary. The main provisions are summarised in the following paragraphs.

(2) DEFINITIONS.   The Act deals with what are called "transactions at an undervalue," and in relation to these it uses the terms "a victim of the transaction" and "the debtor." The former is a person who is, or is capable of being, prejudiced by the transaction; the latter is the person entering into the transaction.[30]

---

[20] *Ante*, p. 129.
[21] *Lloyds Bank Ltd.* v. *Marcan* [1973] 1 W.L.R. 1387.
[22] See *Mackay* v. *Douglas* (1872) L.R. 14 Eq. 106; *Re Butterworth* (1882) 19 Ch.D. 588.
[23] *Freeman* v. *Pope* (1870) 5 Ch.App. 538; *Re Eichholz* [1959] Ch. 708.
[24] See the test formulated by Page Wood V.-C. in *Holmes* v. *Penney* (1856) 3 K. & J. 90 at 99.
[25] *Re Eichholz* [1959] Ch. 708.
[26] *Re Maddever* (1884) 27 Ch.D. 523.
[27] *Ideal Bedding Co. Ltd.* v. *Holland* [1907] 2 Ch. 157.
[28] L.P.A. 1925, s.172(3); *Harrods Ltd.* v. *Stanton* [1923] 1 K.B. 516.
[29] Replacing Insolvency Act 1985, s.212, which came into force for a *scintilla temporis* on December 29, 1986 (*ibid* s.236(2); S.I. 1986 No. 1924) and was at once repealed by the Insolvency Act 1986, s.438, Sched. 12. Sections 423–425 then came into force: s.443 and the provisions just cited in parentheses.
[30] Insolvency Act 1986, s.423(5).

(3) TRANSACTIONS WHICH MAY BE SET ASIDE. A transaction may be set aside if two conditions are fulfilled. The first relates to the nature of the transaction, which must have been entered into at an undervalue.[31] The second relates to the purpose for which the transaction was entered into.[32]

The Act provides that a person enters into a transaction[33] at an undervalue with another "if—

(a) he makes a gift to the other person or he otherwise enters into a transaction with the other on terms that provide for him to receive no consideration;

(b) he enters into a transaction with the other in consideration of marriage; or

(c) he enters into a transaction with the other for a consideration the value of which, in money or money's worth, is significantly less than the value, in money or money's worth, of the consideration provided by himself."[34]

So a transaction for full consideration, which might have been avoided under the old law given the requisite intent on the one side and absence of good faith on the other, is now immune.

As to the purpose for which a person enters into a transaction at an undervalue, the court must be "satisfied that it was entered into by him for the purpose—

(a) of putting assets beyond the reach of a person who is making, or may at some time make, a claim against him, or

(b) of otherwise prejudicing the interests of such a person in relation to the claim which he is making or may make."[35]

This is simply a modern formulation of the old requirement of intent to defraud.

(4) PROCEDURE AND POWERS OF THE COURT. If the debtor has been adjudged bankrupt, an application for an order setting the transaction aside may only be made by the trustee of his estate or (with the leave of the court) by a victim of the transaction. In any other case, the application must be made by a victim of the transaction.[36] In every case, any application which is made is treated as made on behalf of every victim of the transaction.[37] If the court is satisfied that the applicant has established his case, it may make such order as it thinks fit for restoring

---

[31] *Ibid.* s.423(1).
[32] *Ibid.* s.423(3).
[33] Defined in s.436 as including a gift, agreement or arrangement.
[34] Insolvency Act 1986, s.423(1).
[35] *Ibid.* s.423(3).
[36] *Ibid.* s.424(1).
[37] *Ibid.* s.424(2).

the position to what it would have been but for the transaction and for protecting the interests of victims of the transaction.[38] The Act gives the court a wide range of ancillary powers which will enable it (broadly speaking) to reinstate the *status quo ante* and to make orders of a restitutionary kind.[39]

(5) PROTECTION OF PERSONS ACTING IN GOOD FAITH. An order under these provisions may affect a person whether or not he is the person with whom the debtor entered into the transaction. There are, however, two provisions which are designed to protect a person who took an interest in property or a benefit from the transaction in good faith, for value and without notice of the relevant circumstances.[40] First, an order is not to prejudice any interest in property which was so acquired *from a person other than the debtor*, or prejudice any interest deriving from such an interest. This is the equivalent of one of the exceptions to the operation of section 172 of the Law of Property Act 1925.[41] Secondly, an order is not to require a person who, acting as mentioned, received a benefit from the transaction to pay any sum *unless he was a party to the transaction*.[42]

3. Voluntary conveyance to defraud a subsequent purchaser

Every voluntary disposition of land made with intent to defraud a subsequent purchaser is voidable at the instance of that purchaser.[43] An actual intent to defraud must be proved if the conveyance for value was made after June 28, 1893[44]: the intent will not, as formerly, be conclusively inferred from the mere sequence of a voluntary conveyance being followed by a conveyance of the same land for value.[45]

4. Bankruptcy of settlor

(a) *Voluntary settlements before December 29, 1986*

(1) BANKRUPTCY ACT 1914, SECTION 42. Under section 42 of the Bankruptcy Act 1914, a voluntary[46] settlement of any property might, in certain cases, be avoided on the subsequent bankruptcy of the settlor, even if it was not fraudulent. Section 42 was repealed on December 29,

---

[38] *Ibid.* s.423(2).
[39] For the details, see Insolvency Act 1986, s.425(1).
[40] These are defined as those "by virtue of which an order under section 423 may be made in respect of the transaction": Insolvency Act 1986, s.425(3).
[41] See *ante*, p. 129.
[42] Insolvency Act 1986, s.425(2).
[43] L.P.A. 1925, s.173(1), repealing and replacing 27 Eliz. 1, c. 4, 1585.
[44] L.P.A. 1925, s.173(2), replacing the Voluntary Conveyances Act 1893.
[45] See *Re Barker's Estate* (1875) 44 L.J.Ch. 487 at 489; *Doe* d. *Otley* v. *Manning* (1807) 9 East. 59. The presumption was not made against a charity: *Ramsay* v. *Gilchrist* [1892] A.C. 412.
[46] See *Re Macadam, ex p. Guillaume* v. *The Trustee* [1950] 1 All E.R. 303; *Re Densham* [1975] 1 W.L.R. 1519 (joint purchase resulting from unequal contributions is voluntary as to excess).

1986,[47] and replaced by the provisions of the Insolvency Act 1986 which are discussed below.[48] But a transaction entered into before December 29, 1986, cannot be set aside under the Insolvency Act save to the extent that it could have been set aside under the law in force immediately before that day,[49] so that the repealed section 42 and the cases decided under it will remain of importance for some time. What follows is a summary of the old law: a fuller account will be found in the last edition of this book.[50]

(2) TWO YEARS. A voluntary settlement was voidable by the trustee in bankruptcy if the settlor's bankruptcy commenced[51] within two years after the date of the settlement.[52] Proof of the settlor's solvency at the date of the settlement would not save it.

(3) TEN YEARS. If the settlor's bankruptcy commenced[53] between two and ten years after the date of the settlement, it was still voidable by the trustee in bankruptcy unless those claiming under the settlement could prove—

(i) that the settlor was, at the time of making the settlement, able to pay all his debts without the aid of the property comprised in the settlement[54]; and

(ii) that his interest[55] in such property passed to the trustee of such settlement on the execution thereof.[56]

(4) EXCEPTIONS. The section did not apply to settlements made before and in consideration of marriage,[57] or made in favour of a purchaser in good faith and for valuable consideration,[58] or made on or for the wife or children of the settlor of property which had accrued to him after marriage in right of his wife.[59] Further, the section was confined to settlements of the settlor's own property, or property in which he had a beneficial interest, and did not apply to settlements made in exercise of a power of appointment, even if it were a general power.[60]

---

[47] Insolvency Act 1985, s.235(3), Sched. 10, Pt. IV: in force on December 29, 1986, by virtue of *ibid.* s.236(2); Insolvency Act 1986, s.443; S.I. 1986 No. 1924.

[48] *Post*, p. 134.

[49] Insolvency Act 1986, s.437, Sched. 11, Pt. II, para. 17.

[50] 28th ed., pp. 134–137.

[51] *Re Reis* [1904] 1 K.B. 451 at 455, reversed on other grounds [1904] 2 K.B. 769; *sub. nom. Clough* v. *Samuel* [1905] A.C. 442. For when a bankruptcy commenced, see Bankruptcy Act 1914, s.37.

[52] See *Re H.W. Baker* [1936] Ch. 61.

[53] See n. 51, *supra*.

[54] *Re H.W. Baker, supra*; *Re Densham, supra* (contingent liability to pay stolen money a debt).

[55] See *Shrager* v. *March* [1908] A.C. 402 (declaration of trust sufficient despite reservation of ultimate beneficial interest).

[56] Bankruptcy Act 1914, s.42(1).

[57] See *Re Densham, supra* (must be conditioned to take effect only on marriage).

[58] See *Re a Debtor, ex p. Official Receiver* v. *Morrison* [1965] 1 W.L.R. 1498; *Re Densham, supra*; *Re Windle* [1975] 1 W.L.R. 1628 (covenant to indemnify against mortgage payments not a valuable consideration); *Re Abbott* [1983] Ch. 45 (wife taking property in compromise of claim to property adjustment order a purchaser for valuable consideration).

[59] Bankruptcy Act 1914, s.42(1). For the last exception, see *Re Bower Williams* [1927] 1 Ch. 441.

[60] *Re Mathieson* [1927] 1 Ch. 283; and see *Re Schebsman* [1944] Ch. 83 (affirming [1943] Ch. 366).

(5) SETTLEMENTS VOIDABLE. Settlements within the section were merely voidable, not void, even though it was the latter word which appeared in the section.[61] The trustee in bankruptcy therefore had to apply to the court to set it aside, and the order would only be made subject to the rights of third parties bona fide acquired for value from beneficiaries under the settlement.[62] Further, the order would not necessarily transfer the property to the trustee in bankruptcy, for the settlor might have dealt with the property for value after making the settlement, e.g. by creating a charge on it; in such a case the interest of the holder of the charge would be let in by the settlement being set aside.[63] And the avoidance was not absolute, but only to the extent necessary for satisfying the settlor's debts and the bankruptcy costs.[64]

(6) AVOIDANCE OF ANTE-NUPTIAL COVENANTS TO SETTLE. Settlements made before and in consideration of marriage, being made for value, did not fall within the provisions just considered. But a covenant in such a settlement for the future payment of money to, or the future settlement of property[65] on, the settlor's spouse or children was void against the trustee in bankruptcy if the settlor was adjudged bankrupt and the covenant had not been executed at the date of the commencement[66] of the bankruptcy.[67]

(b) *Transactions at an undervalue after December 28, 1986*

(1) INSOLVENCY ACT 1986, SECTIONS 339, 342.[68] By section 339(1), "where an individual is adjudged bankrupt and he has at a relevant time (defined in section 341) entered into a transaction[69] with any person at an undervalue, the trustee of the bankrupt's estate may apply to the court for an order under this section."

(2) TRANSACTIONS WHICH MAY BE SET ASIDE. It will be apparent that a transaction will be caught by section 339 if two conditions are satisfied. First, the transaction must be at an undervalue, a concept which is defined in terms which mirror precisely those which already have been considered in relation to the provisions of sections 423–425 of the Insolvency Act.[70] Secondly, the transaction must have been entered into at "a relevant time": whereas under the general provisions of sections

---

[61] See *Re Carter and Kenderdine's Contract* [1897] 1 Ch. 776.
[62] *Re Carter and Kenderdine's Contract, supra; Re Hart* [1912] 3 K.B. 6. And see *Re Holden, ex p. The Official Receiver* (1888) 20 Q.B.D. 43 (trustees' lien for costs).
[63] *Sanguinetti* v. *Stuckey's Banking Co.* [1895] 1 Ch. 176.
[64] *Re Parry, ex p. Salaman* [1904] 1 K.B. 129.
[65] This applied to property wherein the settlor had not, at the date of the settlement, any interest, and not being property in right of the settlor's spouse.
[66] As to which see Bankruptcy Act 1914, s.37.
[67] Bankruptcy Act 1914, s.42(2). See *Re Bulteel's Settlements* [1917] 1 Ch. 251; *Re Dent* [1923] 1 Ch. 113. For the operation of s.42(2), and the exceptions to it, see the 28th edition of this book, pp. 136, 137.
[68] Replacing Insolvency Act 1985, ss.174, 175. See *ante*, p. 130, n. 29, which applies to these provisions *mutatis mutandis*.
[69] Defined in s.436: *ante*, p. 131, n. 33.
[70] Insolvency Act 1986, s.339(3); see *ante*, p. 131.

423–425 it is the *purpose* of the transaction which is material, here (as under the pre-existing bankruptcy law) the condition is a *temporal* one.

(3) "RELEVANT TIME." As under the old law, two periods are specified. In general the time at which an individual enters into a transaction at an undervalue is a relevant time if it falls within the five years preceding the presentation of the petition on which he is adjudged bankrupt.[71] This provision is, however, qualified where the transaction was entered into between two and five years before the petition was presented. In such a case the time of the transaction is a relevant time only if the individual is then insolvent[72] or becomes so in consequence of the transaction. The requirement of insolvency is presumed to be satisfied, unless the contrary is shown, where the transaction is entered into by an individual with an associate of his.[73] "Associate" is an expression with a wide scope, which covers (among others) the spouse,[74] or a relative,[75] of an individual, and also the spouse of a relative of the individual or of a relative of his spouse.[76] Thus the traditional family settlement will almost always fall within this presumption of insolvency.

(4) PROCEDURE AND POWERS OF THE COURT. An application under section 339 may only be made by the trustee of the bankrupt's estate.[77] If the trustee establishes his case, the court may make such order as it thinks fit for restoring the position to what it would have been if the transaction had not been entered into.[78] Section 342 gives the court ancillary powers which correspond to those mentioned earlier in this chapter,[79] and it is expressly provided that any sums which are required to be paid to the trustee in accordance with an order of the court shall be comprised in the bankrupt's estate.[80]

(5) PROTECTION OF PERSONS ACTING IN GOOD FAITH. The relevant statutory provisions[81] correspond to those which apply in cases brought under sections 423–425 of the Insolvency Act.[82]

Section 8. Protective and Discretionary Trusts

If a person is given an interest under a trust, it is impossible to deprive that interest of the normal incidents of property, such as the owner's

[71] Insolvency Act 1986, s.341(1)(*a*).
[72] For the purposes of this provision "an individual is insolvent if—(*a*) he is unable to pay his debts as they fall due, or (*b*) the value of his assets is less than the amount of his liabilities, taking into account his contingent and prospective liabilities": Insolvency Act 1986, s.341(3).
[73] Insolvency Act 1986, s.341(2).
[74] Including former and reputed spouses: Insolvency Act 1986, s.435(8).
[75] Brother, sister, uncle, aunt, nephew, niece, lineal ancestor or descendant: Insolvency Act 1986, s.435(8).
[76] See Insolvency Act 1986, ss.341(2), 435.
[77] *Ibid.* s.339(1).
[78] *Ibid.* s.339(2).
[79] *Ibid.* s.342(1); *ante*, p. 132.
[80] *Ibid.*, s.343(3).
[81] *Ibid.*, s.342(2), (4).
[82] *Ante*, p. 132.

power of disposition or the rights of his creditors on bankruptcy.[83]
Accordingly, if a settlor wishes to ensure that an interest under a trust is
protected against both the rashness of the beneficiary and the claims of
his creditors, he must adopt indirect means to achieve what cannot be
done directly.[84] Three heads must be considered.

1. Determinable interests.   Although a condition or proviso against
alienation, or for forfeiture on bankruptcy, is void, a limitation *until*
bankruptcy or attempted alienation is valid.[85] The difference is between
giving the beneficiary, *e.g.* a complete life interest with a condition
against alienating that interest, and giving him a limited life interest, *i.e.*
a life interest until attempted alienation; the limitation in the latter case
marks the bounds or compass of the interest, whereas the condition in
the former case attempts to defeat the interest before it attains its
boundary.

A person cannot, however, make use of the rules governing
determinable interests in order to defeat the bankruptcy laws as regards
his own property.[86] If X settles his own property on a determinable trust
for himself, on his bankruptcy his interest will vest in his trustee in
bankruptcy[87] free from any liability to determination by subsequent
events[88]; in other respects, however, the provision for determination will
be effective.[89] Had the settlement been made by X merely joining in the
exercise of a joint general power of appointment in his own favour, his
trustee in bankruptcy would have had no claim; for there would have
been no settlement by X of property which was his own.[90]

2. Discretionary trusts.[91]   A discretionary trust is one which gives a
beneficiary no right to any part of the income of the trust property, but
vests in the trustees a discretionary power to pay him, or apply for his
benefit, such part of the income as they think fit. The trustees must

---

[83] *Brandon* v. *Robinson* (1811) 18 Ves. 429; *Re Dugdale* (1888) 38 Ch.D. 176. See, however, Glanville
     Williams (1943) 59 L.Q.R. 343.
[84] The restraint upon anticipation by a married woman was formerly an exception, but all such
     restraints were abolished by the Married Women (Restraint upon Anticipation) Act 1949. A similar
     doctrine, available for all beneficiaries, whether male or female or married or single, is available in
     the U.S.A., where "spendthrift trusts" can be created, enabling a beneficiary to continue to be
     entitled to the income despite his creditors. See Griswold, *Spendthrift Trusts* (2nd ed., 1947); and see
     post, p. 233.
[85] *Rochford* v. *Hackman* (1852) 9 Hare 475 (life interest); *Re Leach, Leach* v. *Leach* [1912] 2 Ch. 422
     (fee simple).
[86] See the cases collected in *Mackintosh* v. *Pogose* [1895] 1 Ch. 505.
[87] *Re Brewer's Settlement* [1896] 2 Ch. 503; *Re Burroughs-Fowler* [1916] 2 Ch. 251.
[88] *Re Burroughs-Fowler, supra.*
[89] *Brooke* v. *Pearson* (1859) 27 Beav. 181 (voluntary alienation); *Re Detmold* (1889) 40 Ch.D. 585
     (seizure in execution); *Re Johnson Johnson* [1904] 1 K.B. 134.
[90] *Re Ashby* [1892] 1 Q.B. 872.
[91] See generally, L. A. Sheridan (1957) 21 Conv.(N.S.) 55. Before the Finance Act 1969 discretionary
     trusts had considerable popularity for their advantages in mitigating the burden of estate duty. The
     Act of 1969 greatly reduced the advantages. The replacement of estate duty by the original capital
     transfer tax regime in 1975 further eroded their popularity. However recent changes in the
     inheritance tax regime has rendered them more popular again.

exercise their discretion as and when the income becomes available,[92] but if they fail to distribute in due time, the power is not extinguished so that they can distribute later.[93] They have no power to bind themselves for the future.[94] The beneficiary thus has no more than a hope that the discretion will be exercised in his favour,[95] and so, except as to any money which has already been paid to him,[96] there is nothing which his creditors or assigns can claim,[97] even if it is a case where a person has settled property on himself.[98] He may, however, surrender his right to be considered.[99] Nevertheless, if any income not paid to one beneficiary is bound to be paid to other beneficiaries, and all the possible beneficiaries are *sui juris*, they can together effectively dispose of the income, for they are between them absolutely entitled to it.[1]

If there is a discretionary trust for the maintenance and benefit of a number of persons, and one of them is bankrupt or has alienated his interest under the trust, it is not clear whether the trustee in bankruptcy or the assignee is entitled to the whole of any sums in fact paid to the beneficiary,[2] or only to the excess over the amount needed for his maintenance.[3] The former alternative is perhaps preferable, and it may even extend to goods delivered to the beneficiary,[4] although probably not to sums paid by the trustees to third parties for the maintenance of the beneficiary, *e.g.* to an hotel-keeper[5] or tradesman.[6]

3. Protective trusts[7]

(a) *Meaning.* The term "protective trust" is usually applied to trusts which combine the advantages of determinable interests with those of discretionary trusts. Under such a trust, the interest of the principal beneficiary is made determinable on bankruptcy, attempted alienation and the like, and thereupon a discretionary trust arises in favour of himself and certain other persons.[8] Such trusts may, of course, be created by setting out the terms expressly, but since 1925 it has become

---

[92] But see *Re Gulbenkian's Settlements (No. 2)* [1970] Ch. 408 (postponement in special circumstances justified). See generally A. J. Hawkins (1967) 31 Conv.(N.S.) 117.
[93] *Re Locker's S.T.* [1977] 1 W.L.R. 1323.
[94] *Re Vestey's Settlement* [1950] 2 All E.R. 891 at 895 (not reported on this point at [1951] Ch. 209); and see *post*, p. 260. See also *post*, pp. 235, 236.
[95] The preceding words in this paragraph were cited with approval in *Re Munro's S.T.* [1963] 1 W.L.R. 145 at 148, *per* Wilberforce J., and in *Gartside* v. *I.R.C.* [1968] A.C. 553 at 574, *per* Salmon L.J. (the decision in the later case was reversed but not on grounds affecting these principles: see [1968] A.C. 553 at pp. 614 *et seq.*, *per* Lord Wilberforce).
[96] *Re Smith, Public Trustee* v. *Aspinall* [1928] Ch. 915 at 919.
[97] *Twopeny* v. *Peyton* (1840) 10 Sim. 487.
[98] See *Holmes* v. *Penney* (1856) 3 K. & J. 90.
[99] *Re Gulbenkian's Settlements (No. 2)* [1970] Ch. 408.
[1] *Re Smith, Public Trustee* v. *Aspinall* [1928] Ch. 915; and see *post*, p. 233.
[2] *Re Coleman* (1888) 39 Ch.D. 443; and see *Re Bullock* (1891) 64 L.T. 736 at 738.
[3] *Re Ashby* [1892] 1 Q.B. 872 at 877.
[4] *Re Coleman, supra*, at p. 451.
[5] *Ibid.*
[6] *Godden* v. *Crowhurst* (1842) 10 Sim. 642 at 656.
[7] See generally L. A. Sheridan (1957) 21 Conv.(N.S.) 110, 323.
[8] For the possible use of protective trusts in series, see the comment at (1958) 74 L.Q.R. 182 on *Re Richardson's W.T.* [1958] Ch. 504.

increasingly common to take advantage of section 33 of the Trustee Act 1925.

(b) *Trustee Act 1925, s.33.* Under this section, certain terms are implied in any trust coming into operation after 1925[9] if any income is directed to be held "on protective trusts" for the benefit of any person ("the principal beneficiary") for the period of his life[10] or for any less period. "Income" includes an annuity or other periodical income payment,[11] and also uncertain income, such as income paid from time to time under a discretionary trust.[12] In such a case, subject to any modification by the instrument creating the trust,[13] during the above period ("the trust period") the income is (without prejudice to any prior interest) held—

(a) upon trust for the principal beneficiary until he (whether before or after the termination of any prior interest) "does or attempts to do or suffers any act or thing, or until any event happens, other than an advance under any statutory or express power,[14] whereby, if the said income were payable during the trust period to the principal beneficiary absolutely during that period, he would be deprived of the right to receive the same or any part thereof"; and thereafter,

(b) upon trust for the application thereof for the maintenance or support or otherwise for the benefit of all, or any one or more, of the following persons, namely—

(i) the principal beneficiary and his or her spouse and issue; or if there is no spouse or issue,

(ii) the principal beneficiary and the persons who, if he were dead, would be entitled to the trust property or the income,

as the trustees in their absolute discretion[15] think fit.[16] The section does not validate any trust which would otherwise be invalid,[17] but merely avoids the necessity of setting out the trusts *in extenso.* An appointment on protective trusts made under a special power of appointment will normally be invalid, for it not only delegates authority to the trustees[18] but also authorises payment (under the second limb of the protective trusts) to persons who will usually not be objects of the power.[19]

[9] T.A. 1925, s.33(2).
[10] See *Re Wittke* [1944] Ch. 166.
[11] T.A. 1925, s.33(1).
[12] *Re Isaacs* (1948) 92 S.J. 336.
[13] T.A. 1925, s.33(2).
[14] But for these words, such an advance would perhaps work a determination: *Re Stimpson's Trusts* [1931] 2 Ch. 77. *Sed quaere:* see *Re Hodgson, Weston* v. *Hodgson* [1913] 1 Ch. 34; *Re Shaw's Settlement* [1951] Ch. 833; *Re Rees, Lloyds Bank Ltd.* v. *Rees* [1954] Ch. 202. For the statutory power, see *post,* p. 279.
[15] Consider *Re Powles* [1954] 1 W.L.R. 336.
[16] T.A. 1925, s.33(1).
[17] T.A. 1925, s.33(3); consider, *e.g.* a settlement by a man on himself in an attempt to avoid the bankruptcy laws; *ante,* pp. 132, 136.
[18] See *post,* p. 567.
[19] *Re Boulton's S.T.* [1928] Ch. 703; *Re Morris's S.T.* [1951] 2 All E.R. 528; *Re Hunter's W.T.* [1963] Ch. 372.

Further, a direction to hold income "on protective trusts" for a class at the discretion of the trustees does not import section 33 as no one is the principal beneficiary. A simple discretionary trust is created.[20]

(c) *Operative events.* As to the events which suffice to determine the principal beneficiary's interest and bring the discretionary trust into operation, the Trading with the Enemy Act 1939, and orders[21] thereunder, whereby money payable to those resident in enemy territory had to be paid to the Custodian of Enemy Property, had this effect.[22] And decisions on express discretionary trusts (even though these trusts often differ substantially from those set out in section 33) indicate that the following events will also suffice, namely, the execution by the principal beneficiary of a deed of variation giving up his right to part of the income in certain events,[23] the sequestration of the income,[24] the impounding of part of the income by the trustees to make good sums paid to the principal beneficiary in breach of trust,[25] and the bankruptcy of the principal beneficiary, even if this is already existing when the trust first takes effect.[26]

(d) *Inoperative events.* On the other hand, it appears that it will not suffice if there is an assignment merely of income already accrued due in the hands of the trustees,[27] or of income which never materialises,[28] nor if an attorney or agent is appointed merely to receive the income on behalf of the principal beneficiary,[29] nor if an order of the court is made varying the effect of the trusts[30]; but such an order will not prevent subsequent events (*e.g.* some act or omission by the principal beneficiary) from causing a determination.[31] However, an order which extinguishes the rights of the principal beneficiary "as if he were already dead" brings to an end the discretionary trusts as well as the determinable interest.[32] When the discretionary trust arises, there is no apportionment of the income then accruing due, and the trustees cannot withhold any part of the income subsequently received, but are bound

---

[20] See *Re Trafford's Settlement* [1985] Ch. 32.
[21] *e.g.* Trading with the Enemy (Custodian) Order 1939 (S.R. & O. 1939 No. 1198).
[22] *Re Gourju's W.T.* [1943] Ch. 24; *Re Wittke* [1944] Ch. 166; *cf. Re Furness, Wilson* v. *Kenmare (No. 1)* [1944] 1 All E.R. 575; *Re Hall, Public Trustee* v. *Montgomery* [1944] Ch. 46; *Re Harris, Cope* v. *Evans* [1945] Ch. 316; *Re Pozot's S.T.* [1952] Ch. 427. Later orders vesting rights to payment in the Custodian, *e.g.* Trading with the Enemy (Custodian) (No. 2) Order, 1945 (S.R. & O. 1945 No. 887) contained a proviso that vesting should not take place if it would cause a forfeiture.
[23] *Re Dennis's S.T.* [1942] Ch. 283; see (1942) 58 L.Q.R. 312.
[24] *Re Baring's S.T.* [1940] Ch. 737.
[25] *Re Balfour's Settlement* [1938] Ch. 928; and see *Re Richardson's W.T.* [1958] Ch. 504; *Edmonds* v. *Edmonds* [1965] 1 W.L.R. 58 (orders of divorce court).
[26] See *Trappes* v. *Meredith* (1871) 7 Ch.App. 248; *Re Evans, Public Trustee* v. *Evans* [1920] 2 Ch. 304; *Re Walker, Public Trustee* v. *Walker* [1939] Ch. 974; and see *Re Forder* [1927] 2 Ch. 291, on the effect of an annulment of the bankruptcy.
[27] *Re Greenwood, Sutcliffe* v. *Gledhill* [1901] 1 Ch. 887.
[28] *Re Longman* [1955] 1 W.L.R. 197 (dividend passed).
[29] *Re Tancred's Settlement* [1903] 1 Ch. 715; *Re Oppenheim's W.T.* [1950] Ch. 633; and see *Re Westby's Settlement* [1950] Ch. 296.
[30] *Re Mair* [1935] Ch. 562 (under T.A. 1925, s.57; *post,* p. 239); *General Accident Fire and Life Assurance Corporation Ltd.* v. *I.R.C.* [1963] 1 W.L.R. 1207 (under J.A. 1925, s.192, now Matrimonial Causes Act 1973, s.24; *post,* p. 245).
[31] *Re Salting* [1932] 2 Ch. 57.
[32] *Re Allsopp's Marriage S.T.* [1959] Ch. 81.

(within reasonable limits) to apply the whole of it for the purposes named.[33]

Section 9. Trusts in Favour of Creditors[34]

1. Illusory trusts. As already seen, the general rule is that in the absence of a power of revocation a settlor cannot revoke even a voluntary settlement once it is completely constituted. To this rule, one of the exceptions,[35] which was formerly of greater importance than it is now, is a conveyance by a debtor to a trustee upon trust for his creditors. Such a trust may sometimes be revoked by the debtor, and the creditors have not always a right to compel the trustee to carry out the trusts of the deed.[36] A trust of this kind has therefore been called "illusory."

The reason of this exception was well stated by Lord Brougham L.C. in *Garrard* v. *Lord Lauderdale*[37]: "I take the real nature of this deed to be ... not so much a conveyance vesting a trust in A for the benefit of the creditors of the grantor; but rather that it may be likened to an arrangement made by a debtor for his own personal convenience and accommodation,—for the payment of his own debts in an order prescribed by himself,—over which he retains power and control, and with respect to which the creditors can have no right to complain, inasmuch as they are not injured by it, they waive no right of action, and are not executing parties to it." And in *Acton* v. *Woodgate*[38] it was said that the deed "has the same effect as if the debtor had delivered money to an agent to pay his creditors, and, before any payment made by the agent, or communication by him to the creditors, had recalled the money so delivered."

2. Binding trusts. There are, however, four cases in which such a deed does create a true trust in favour of the creditors or some of them.

(a) *As against executing creditors.* If any creditor is a party to the deed, and executes it, the deed will be irrevocable as to him, and enforceable by him.[39]

(b) *As against assenting creditors who act on it.* If the deed is communicated to any creditors and they signify their assent to or acquiescence in the deed, and are "thereby induced to a forbearance in respect of their claims which they would not otherwise have

---

[33] *Re Gourju's W.T.* [1943] Ch. 24.
[34] See generally L. A. Sheridan (1957) 21 Conv.(N.S.) 280; and *ante,* p. 92.
[35] For the others, see *ante,* pp. 127 *et seq.*
[36] *Johns* v. *James* (1878) Ch.D. 744; *Ellis & Co.* v. *Cross* [1915] 2 K.B. 654.
[37] (1831) 2 Russ. & M. 451 at 455.
[38] (1833) 2 My. & K. 492 at 495, *per* Leach M.R.
[39] *Mackinnon* v. *Stewart* (1850) 1 Sim.(N.S.) 76; *Montefiore* v. *Brown* (1858) 7 H.L.C. 241.

exercised,"[40] the deed is irrevocable as to them. Mere communication to the creditors is not sufficient to make the deed irrevocable; they must have either acted under its provisions or forborne to enforce their remedies on the faith of the deed.[41]

(c) *After debtor's death.* If the trust for payment of debts is not to arise until after the debtor's death, and the debtor dies without revoking it, the deed is irrevocable. The right to revoke the trust is personal to the debtor and is not open to the beneficiaries entitled under the debtor's will, for, being merely volunteers, they take subject to the provision made by the testator for the payment of his debts.[42]

(d) *Intention to create trust.* If it clearly appears to have been the debtor's intention to create a trust and not merely to provide a convenient method of paying his debts, the creditors can enforce a trust. Thus in *New, Prance & Garrard's Trustees* v. *Hunting*,[43] X transferred property to Y upon trust to raise a sum of money out of the property, and therewith make good certain breaches of trust committed by X. It was held that even though the trust had not been communicated to the beneficiaries, it could not be revoked by X or X's trustee in bankruptcy, for X's object was to escape the consequences of his breach of trust, so far as it was possible, and this could not be accomplished if the trust was to be revocable.

3. Void assignments. An assignment for the benefit of the assignor's creditors generally, or where he is insolvent, of any three or more of them, is void unless the assignment is registered with the Department of Trade and Industry within seven days after execution.[44] Further, if the assignment is for the benefit of the creditors generally, it is also void unless before or within 21 days after registration it receives the assent of a majority in number and value of the creditors.[45] Consequently, the rule that a trust in favour of creditors can be revoked is of less importance than formerly; for, as already stated, such a trust cannot be revoked as against assenting creditors who have acted on it. An assignment for the benefit of creditors which affects land must also be registered under the Land Charges Act 1972, otherwise it will be void against a purchaser for value.[46]

Before December 29, 1986, an assignment which comprised the whole, or substantially the whole, of the debtor's property and was made for the benefit of his creditors generally was an act of

---

[40] *Acton* v. *Woodgate* (1833) 2 My. & K. 492 at 495, *per* Leach M.R.
[41] *Browne* v. *Cavendish* (1844) 1 Jo. & Lat. 606 at 635, 636; *Biron* v. *Mount* (1857) 24 Beav. 642.
[42] *Synnot* v. *Simpson* (1854) 5 H.L.C. 121; *Re Fitzgerald's Settlement* (1887) 37 Ch.D. 18; *Priestley* v. *Ellis* [1897] 1 Ch. 489.
[43] [1897] 2 Q.B. 19, affirmed *sub nom. Sharp* v. *Jackson* [1899] A.C. 419.
[44] Deeds of Arrangement Act 1914, ss.1, 2 and 4, as amended by Administration of Justice Act 1925, s.22. See *Re Halsted* [1917] 1 K.B. 695.
[45] Deeds of Arrangement Act 1914, s.3. See, *e.g. Re Zakon* [1940] Ch. 253.
[46] L.C.A. 1972, s.7.

bankruptcy,[47] and could thus be used to support a bankruptcy petition.[48] The concept of "an act of bankruptcy" has no place in the new insolvency law,[49] and it is doubtful whether such an assignment could be set aside as a transaction at an undervalue under the provisions discussed earlier in this chapter.[50]

4. Title to surplus assets. If any property remains in the hands of the trustee after payment of the debts in full and all expenses, the surplus will usually result to the debtor (or, if he is dead, to his personal representatives), or will belong to the person to whom it is given by the deed.[51] If, however, the property was assigned by the deed to the trustee for the benefit of the creditors *absolutely*, there will be no resulting trust, and the surplus will belong to the creditors.[52]

---

[47] Bankruptcy Act 1914, s.1(1)(a).
[48] See the 28th edition of this book, p. 143.
[49] See Insolvency Act 1986, ss.267, 268.
[50] Insolvency Act 1986, ss.339, 342; *ante*, pp. 134, 135. See *Muir Hunter on Personal Insolvency*, para. 2–003.
[51] See, *e.g. Re Rissik* [1936] Ch. 68.
[52] *Smith* v. *Cooke* [1891] A.C. 297.

CHAPTER 3

EXPRESS PUBLIC (OR CHARITABLE) TRUSTS

PART 1

INTRODUCTION

1. Nature. The trusts discussed so far have been trusts for the benefit of specific and ascertainable individuals. Equity has also long enforced trusts for the benefit of large and changing groups of people, or to carry out certain purposes which are beneficial to the community at large. These trusts are known as public or charitable trusts, or more shortly "charities." There is, however, no such legal entity as "charity." It is true that some charitable organisations may be incorporated,[1] but many are not.[2] The question, strictly speaking, is not whether a "charity" exists, but whether the trusts on which property is held are trusts for charitable purposes,[3] or, where the organisation is incorporated, whether the objects of the corporation are charitable.

2. Differences between public and private trusts. For the most part public trusts are subject to the same rules as express private trusts[4]; but there are important divergences. Thus the rules against perpetuity are modified; the trusts can be varied if they become obsolete; they are enforced and regulated by certain public authorities; they may be enforced by action notwithstanding the expiry of the ordinary limitation period; and they are exempt from much taxation. These matters are all discussed later.[5] Finally, unlike private trusts, they cannot fail for uncertainty of object. So long as the trust instrument shows a clear intention to devote the property to charity, it is immaterial that the particular mode in which the intention is to be carried into effect is left uncertain. A settlor or testator may simply direct the property to be applied for charitable purposes, or for such charitable purposes as his

---

[1] Incorporated charities do not strictly hold property on trust, but the effect is virtually identical: see *Liverpool and District Hospital for Diseases of the Heart* v. *Att.-Gen.* [1981] Ch. 193; *post*, pp. 164, 165, 171.
[2] But see *post*, p. 170, n. 26, as to a charity suing.
[3] See *Re Pochin* (1943) [1948] Ch. 182n. at 184; *Re Lucas, Sheard* v. *Miller* [1948] Ch. 175 at 179 (reversed *ibid.* p. 424 on grounds not affecting this point).
[4] See *post*, p. 174.
[5] *Post*, pp. 159 (perpetuities), 165 (*cy-près*), 167 (administration), 174 (taxation), and 292 (limitation).

trustees or executors may select[6]; and he may authorise the trustees to alter the trusts if necessary.[7] Where requisite, the specific objects will be supplied by means of a scheme,[8] that is, an order made by the court or the Charity Commissioners.

3. General scope. It is not every trust to carry out general purposes which is charitable.[9] Yet it is not possible to give a satisfactory answer to the question: "What is a charity?"[10] Certainly no comprehensive definition of legal charity has been laid down either by the legislature or in judicial utterance.

There are two main reasons for this. First, "there is no limit to the number and diversity of the ways in which man will seek to benefit his fellow-men,"[11] so that a rigid definition would be too restrictive.[12] Secondly, the courts have adopted a somewhat ambivalent attitude to charities; for the question whether or not valid charitable trusts have been created has usually had to be resolved in two different types of case. The first is where the contest is between the alleged charity and the next-of-kin or others whose interest it is to claim that the trusts are void. Here a liberal interpretation in favour of charity is discernible. The second type is where the alleged charity is claiming relief from taxation. Here a stricter interpretation is to be found in some cases,[13] though latterly in a tax case the House of Lords has endorsed the giving of a benignant construction generally to trust deeds the intention of which is to set up a charitable trust.[14]

4. The three requirements. The general rule is that in order to be charitable a trust must satisfy three requirements.[15]

(a) *Charitable nature.* No trust is charitable unless it is of a charitable character within the spirit and intendment of the preamble to the statute 43 Eliz. 1, c. 4, 1601, as interpreted by the courts and extended by statute.

---

[6] *Mills* v. *Farmer* (1815) 1 Mer. 55; *Moggridge* v. *Thackwell* (1803) 7 Ves. 36, affirmed (1807) 13 Ves. 416; *Re Willis, Shaw* v. *Willis* [1921] 1 Ch. 44.

[7] As in *Re Roberts, Stenton* v. *Hardy* [1963] 1 W.L.R. 406; and see *Re Beesty's W.T.* [1966] Ch. 223 (revocable power of appointment).

[8] *Re White, White* v. *White* [1893] 2 Ch. 41; *Re Pyne* [1903] 1 Ch. 83. For schemes, see *post*, p. 171.

[9] For non-charitable purpose trusts, see *ante*, p. 102.

[10] For a gallant attempt, see J. W. Brunyate (1945) 61 L.Q.R. 268; and see G. Cross (1956) 72 L.Q.R. 187 for a valuable sequel.

[11] *I.R.C.* v. *Baddeley* [1955] A.C. 572 at 583, *per* Viscount Simonds; and see *Re Cole* [1958] Ch. 877 at 891, *per* Lord Evershed M.R., dissenting.

[12] See *post*, pp. 149–151.

[13] See G. Cross (1956) 72 L.Q.R. 187 at 204 (the writer, as Lord Cross of Chelsea, returned to this theme in *Scottish Burial Reform and Cremation Society Ltd.* v. *Glasgow Corporation* [1968] A.C. 138 at 153 and in *Dingle* v. *Turner* [1972] A.C. 601 at 624, 625; but his brethren were unconvinced: see *ibid.* at p. 614). In Scotland this dichotomy is exposed, as Scots law has its own law of charitable trusts (see the comparison in *Wink's Executors* v. *Tallent*, 1947 S.C. 470, esp. at 476, 477), but has to import the English law in questions of taxation (see *I.R.C.* v. *City of Glasgow Police Athletic Association* [1953] A.C. 380), albeit under protest (see T. B. Smith (1953) 69 L.Q.R. 517).

[14] *I.R.C.* v. *McMullen* [1981] A.C. 1 at 14.

[15] See *Re Cole, Westminster Bank Ltd.* v. *Moore* [1958] Ch. 877 at 891 for the first two, and *post*, p. 154, for the third.

(b) *Public benefit.* No trust is charitable unless it promotes a public benefit.

(c) *Exclusively charitable.* No trust is charitable unless it is wholly and exclusively charitable.

These three requirements will be considered in turn in the next part of this chapter.

PART 2

THE ESSENTIALS OF CHARITY

Section 1. Charitable Nature

1. The Statute of Elizabeth. The statute 43 Eliz. 1, c. 4, 1601, was directed to reforming abuses in the application of property devoted to charitable uses, rather than to defining "charity."[16] Nevertheless, the list of charitable objects set out in the preamble has long furnished a guide to the courts in determining the legal meaning of charity, and this continues despite the repeal of the statute in 1888.[17] The list, in modern orthography, is as follows:

> the relief of aged, impotent and poor people;
> the maintenance of sick and maimed soldiers and mariners, schools
> of learning, free schools and scholars in universities;
> the repair of bridges, ports, havens, causeways, churches, sea-banks
> and highways;
> the education and preferment of orphans;
> the relief, stock or maintenance for houses of correction;
> the marriage of poor maids;
> the supportation, aid and help of young tradesmen, handicraftsmen,
> and persons decayed;
> the relief or redemption of prisoners or captives;
> the aid or ease of any poor inhabitants concerning payment of
> fifteens, setting out of soldiers and other taxes.

2. Interpretation. A gift for any of the objects or purposes set out in the statute is clearly charitable, though changes in the meaning of words must be borne in mind. Thus, to Coke "impotent" was an apt description of a man who had lost a hand.[18] Further, at least one

---

[16] *Royal College of Surgeons of England* v. *National Provincial Bank Ltd.* [1952] A.C. 631 at 650, 651.
[17] Mortmain and Charitable Uses Act 1888. The preamble was repeated in s.13(2) of that Act which was itself repealed by the Charities Act 1960, s.48(2), 7th Sched. (though see s.38(4)). The preamble has thus completely disappeared from the statute book, yet it is still the courts' guide: see, *e.g. Incorporated Council of Law Reporting for England and Wales* v. *Att.-Gen.* [1972] Ch. 73 at 87–89.
[18] Co.Litt. 127b.

category ("the relief of aged, impotent and poor people") has been read disjunctively, so that the aged[19] or impotent[20] do not also have to be poor to be proper objects of a charitable trust.[21] But the list is not exhaustive. Various other objects have been held by the court from time to time to be charitable as being within the spirit and intendment of the Act. A reference to "charity" in a statute prima facie means charity as thus interpreted by the courts.[22]

3. Pemsel's case.   The best classification of charitable purposes is to be found in Lord Macnaghten's speech in *Commissioners of Income Tax* v. *Pemsel*[23]: " 'Charity' in its legal sense comprises four principal divisions: trusts for the relief of poverty; trusts for the advancement of education; trusts for the advancement of religion; and trusts for other purposes beneficial to the community, not falling under any of the preceding heads. The trusts last referred to are not the less charitable in the eye of the law, because incidentally they benefit the rich as well as the poor,[24] as indeed, every charity that deserves the name must do either directly or indirectly."

4. Examples of charitable objects.   Some examples may be given under each of the four classes enumerated by Lord Macnaghten. It must, however, be remembered that some charities may qualify under more than one head, and much may depend on factors which cannot be stated in a brief summary of this kind, such as the character of the trustees.[25]

(a) *Poverty.*   "Poverty does not mean destitution; it is a word of wide and somewhat indefinite import; it may not unfairly be paraphrased for present purposes as meaning persons who have to 'go short' in the ordinary acceptation of that term, due regard being had to their status

---

[19] *Re Glyn* (1950) 66 (2) T.L.R. 510; *Re Bradbury* [1951] 1 T.L.R. 130: *Re Robinson, Davis* v. *Robinson* [1951] Ch. 198; *City of Hawthorn* v. *Victorian Welfare Association* [1970] V.R. 205; *Hilder* v. *Church of England Deaconess' Institution Sydney Ltd.* [1973] 1 N.S.W.L.R. 506; *Joseph Rowntree Memorial Trust Housing Association Ltd.* v. *Att.-Gen.* [1983] Ch. 159.
[20] *Re Lewis, Public Trustee* v. *Allen* [1955] Ch. 104.
[21] This construction is not without its anomalies: see (1951) 67 L.Q.R. 164 ("aged peers" and "impotent millionaires"); (1955) 71 L.Q.R. 16. But see *Hilder* v. *Church of England Deaconess' Institution Sydney Ltd., supra,* at p. 511.
[22] *Ashfield Municipal Council* v. *Joyce* [1978] A.C. 122.
[23] [1891] A.C. 531 at 583. It echoed a similar classification by Sir Samuel Romilly, *arguendo,* in *Morice* v. *Bishop of Durham* (1805) 10 Ves. 522 at 532. But see the warning in *Scottish Burial Reform and Cremation Society Ltd.* v. *Glasgow Corporation* [1968] A.C. 138 at 154. The Nathan Committee on the Law and Practice relating to Charitable Trusts recommended the adoption by statute of a flexible definition based on Lord Macnaghten's classification: Report (1952 Cmd. 8710: the "Nathan Report"), para. 140.
[24] See the discussion in *Verge* v. *Somerville* [1924] A.C. 496.
[25] See *Re Dupree's Deed Trusts* [1945] Ch. 16; *Re Town and Country Planning Act 1947, Crystal Palace Trustees* v. *Minister of Town and Country Planning* [1951] Ch. 132.

in life and so forth."[26] Thus charity includes the encouragement of poor emigrants[27]; the provision of a working men's hostel,[28] or of flats at economic rents where the intention is to benefit aged persons of small means[29]; and the assistance of young women having a first baby in a Salvation Army home,[30] or of widows and orphans of the deceased officers of a bank.[31] On the other hand, a person is not necessarily "poor" in the charitable sense merely because he cannot afford to provide for himself the advantages that are provided by the gift.[32] So gifts to encourage emigration generally,[33] or to provide dwellings "for the working classes,"[34] are not charitable, nor is a mutual benefit fund with no test of poverty.[35]

(b) *Education.* The advancement of education is not confined to education given by a master or mistress in class in a formal institution.[36] But some element of instruction and improvement there must be; the mere increase of public knowledge[37] or acquisition of experience[38] is not enough.[39] The following have been held to be charitable: the foundation of lectureships in a university[40]; the encouragement and advancement of choral singing in London,[41] or of "self-control, elocution, oratory, deportment" and "the arts of personal contact" in Ireland[42]; the spread of knowledge and appreciation of the works of an eminent composer[43]; the study and dissemination of ethical principles[44]; the erection and endowment of a Shakespeare Memorial National Theatre with the object of performing Shakespeare's plays, reviving English classical drama, and stimulating the art of acting[45]; the support of the zoo in London[46]; the production of a dictionary[47]; the publication of law

---

[26] *Re Coulthurst* [1951] Ch. 661 at 666, *per* Evershed M.R.; and see *I.R.C.* v. *Baddeley* [1955] A.C. 572 at 585.

[27] *Barclay* v. *Maskelyne* (1858) 4 Jur.(N.S.) 1294; *Re Tree* [1945] Ch. 325 (explained in *Davies* v. *Perpetual Trustee Co. Ltd.* [1959] A.C. 439 at 456, 457).

[28] *Re Niyazi's W.T.* [1978] 1 W.L.R. 910.

[29] *Re Cottam* [1955] 1 W.L.R. 1299; and see *Re Lucas, Rhys* v. *Att.-Gen.* [1922] 2 Ch. 52; *Re Payling's W.T.* [1969] 1 W.L.R. 1595.

[30] *Re Mitchell, Public Trustee* v. *Salvation Army* [1963] N.Z.L.R. 934.

[31] *Re Coulthurst* [1951] Ch. 661; and see *Re Armitage* [1972] Ch. 438; *Re Denison* (1974) 42 D.L.R. (3d) 652 (indigent lawyers and law students).

[32] *I.R.C.* v. *Baddeley, supra,* at p. 604 (a dissenting speech, but on this point all the members of the House were in agreement among themselves and with both the courts below: see at pp. 585, 593, 613).

[33] *Re Sidney* [1908] 1 Ch. 488.

[34] *Re Sanders' W.T.* [1954] Ch. 265 (an appeal was settled: [1954] *The Times,* July 22); and see *Over Seventies Housing Association* v. *City of Westminster* (1974) 230 E.G. 1593.

[35] *Re Hobourn Aero Components Ltd.'s Air Raid Distress Fund* [1946] Ch. 194.

[36] *Re Shaw's W.T.* [1952] Ch. 163, *infra; Royal Choral Society* v. *I.R.C.* (1943) 112 L.J.K.B. 648.

[37] *Re Shaw* [1957] 1 W.L.R. 729 (G. B. Shaw's alphabet; see *ante,* p. 102, n. 22).

[38] *I.R.C.* v. *Baddeley, supra,* at p. 585.

[39] See, however, *Re Hopkins' W.T.* [1965] Ch. 669 at 680.

[40] *Att.-Gen.* v. *Margaret and Regius Professors in Cambridge* (1682) 1 Vern. 55 (divinity).

[41] *Royal Choral Society* v. *I.R.C.* (1943) 112 L.J.K.B. 648; and see *Re Levien* [1955] 1 W.L.R. 964.

[42] *Re Shaw's W.T.* [1952] Ch. 163 (the wife of George Bernard Shaw); and see *Re McDougall* [1957] 1 W.L.R. 81; *Re Webber* [1954] 1 W.L.R. 1500 (the Boy Scouts).

[43] *Re Delius* [1957] Ch. 299 (Frederick Delius).

[44] *Re South Place Ethical Society* [1980] 1 W.L.R. 1565.

[45] *Re Shakespeare Memorial Trust* [1923] 2 Ch. 398. Contrast *Thomson* v. *Shakespeare* (1860) 1 De G.F. & J. 399.

[46] *Re Lopes* [1931] 2 Ch. 130 ("A ride on an elephant may be educational": *per* Farwell J. at p. 136).

[47] See *Re Stanford* [1924] 1 Ch. 73.

reports[48]; "finding the Bacon-Shakespeare manuscripts"[49]; the maintenance of a students' union attached to a medical school[50] or a
polytechnic[51]; the provision of prizes for sport at an educational
establishment,[52] or for an educational game such as chess[53]; and more
generally the provision of facilities to enable pupils at schools and
universities to play football or other games or sports thereby assisting
their "physical education and development."[54]

On the other hand, the following purposes have been held not to be
charitable: founding a college for training spiritualistic mediums[55];
preserving a useless collection of pictures and furniture as a museum[56];
providing prizes for yacht racing or any other sport,[57] and restocking the
waters fished by an angling society.[58] Further, "political propaganda
masquerading—I do not use the word in any sinister sense—as
education is not education within the Statute of Elizabeth"[59]; nor would
"the education of pickpockets in a thieves' kitchen to make them fit for
their profession,"[60] or a public library "devoted entirely to works of
pornography"[61] be of a charitable nature.

(c) *Religion.* The advancement of religion is not restricted to the
Christian religion, but includes the furtherance of any religion (*e.g.*
Jewish[62]), provided it is not subversive of all religion and morality.[63]
The essential attributes of a religion are faith and worship, so that the
study of ethical principles and cultivation of a rational religious
sentiment are not charitable under this head.[64] Trusts for the support of
a religious order or community[65] such as a monastery or a convent are
plainly within this head, though if instead of engaging in good works
(*e.g.* among the sick and the poor[66]) the order has as its object merely
sanctification by prayer and pious contemplation, it will lack the
necessary element of demonstrable public benefit and so not be

[48] *Incorporated Council of Law Reporting for England and Wales* v. *Att.-Gen.* [1972] Ch. 73. *Contra* in
Australia: see (1972) 88 L.Q.R. 171; and see *post*, p. 150. In New Zealand some purposes of a law
library are charitable: *Re Mason* [1971] N.Z.L.R. 714, esp. at pp. 728, 729.
[49] *Re Hopkins' W.T.* [1965] Ch. 669 (this gift also qualified under the fourth head).
[50] *London Hospital Medical College* v. *I.R.C.* [1976] 1 W.L.R. 613.
[51] *Att.-Gen.* v. *Ross* [1986] 1 W.L.R. 252.
[52] *Re Mariette* [1915] 2 Ch. 284.
[53] *Re Dupree's Deed Trusts* [1945] Ch. 16.
[54] *I.R.C.* v. *McMullen* [1981] A.C. 1.
[55] *Re Hummeltenberg* [1923] 1 Ch. 237.
[56] *Re Pinion* [1965] Ch. 85; *Sutherland's Trustee* v. *Verschoyle*, 1968 S.L.T. 43.
[57] *Re Nottage* [1895] 2 Ch. 649.
[58] *Re Clifford* (1911) 106 L.T. 14 (omitted from [1912] 1 Ch. 29).
[59] *Re Hopkinson, Lloyds Bank Ltd.* v. *Baker* [1949] 1 All E.R. 346 at 350, *per* Vaisey J. (Labour); and
see *Bonar Law Memorial Trust* v. *I.R.C.* (1933) 49 T.L.R. 220 (Conservative); *Re Bushnell* [1975] 1
W.L.R. 1596 (furtherance of socialised medicine, gift taking effect in 1941).
[60] *Re Macduff* [1896] 2 Ch. 451 at 474, *per* Rigby L.J.
[61] *Re Pinion, supra*, at p. 106, *per* Harman L.J.
[62] *Straus* v. *Goldsmid* (1837) 8 Sim. 614; *Neville Estates Ltd.* v. *Madden* [1962] Ch. 832. For Buddhism,
see *Re South Place Ethical Society* [1980] 1 W.L.R. 1565 at 1573.
[63] *Thornton* v. *Howe* (1862) 31 Beav. 14 at 20; *Re Watson, Hobbs* v. *Smith* [1973] 1 W.L.R. 1472.
[64] *Re South Place Ethical Society* [1980] 1 W.L.R. 1565. See the comment at [1981] Conv. 150. The gift
was valid under the previous head: *ante* p. 147.
[65] *Re Banfield* [1968] 1 W.L.R. 846; and see *post*, p. 151.
[66] *Re Delany* [1902] 2 Ch. 642.

charitable.[67] And a gift to establish "a Catholic daily newspaper," has been held not to be charitable, for at best it is no more than partly conducive to religion.[68]

The celebration of masses for the dead is charitable if they are to be said in public and if the moneys given are to provide stipends for the priests saying the masses.[69] The improvement of musical services in a church,[70] and a gift simply "for God's work"[71] have also held charitable. Again, while the upkeep of a particular tomb or vault in a churchyard is not charitable,[72] the repair of the whole churchyard or burial ground is charitable,[73] even if it is restricted to members of a particular religious sect.[74] The repair of all the headstones in a churchyard,[75] or of the churchyard and a specified monument,[76] is also charitable, and so is the upkeep of the whole or any part of a church, including a memorial window[77] or a specific monument or vault in it.[78]

(d) *Beneficial to the community.* The expression "other purposes beneficial to the community" is vague, but it must not be taken to include every object of general public utility.[79] The object must come within the spirit and intendment of the statute even though it does not come within its words.[80] A possible test is to ask whether the trust will provide "some of the indispensables of a settled community"[81]; and another view is that if the object cannot be thought otherwise than beneficial to the community and of general public utility "the proper question to ask is whether there are any grounds for holding it to be outside the equity of the statute."[82] A political purpose (including one in a foreign country[83]) would be such a ground.[84] A trust is regarded as

---

[67] *Cocks* v. *Manners* (1871) L.R. 12 Eq. 574; *Gilmour* v. *Coats* [1949] A.C. 426; *post*, p. 152.

[68] *Roman Catholic Archbishop of Melbourne* v. *Lawlor* (1934) 51 C.L.R. 1. (The High Court of Australia was divided 3–3, and so the decision of the lower court stood.)

[69] *Re Caus* [1934] Ch. 162; *Re Hetherington* [1990] Ch. 1. The validity of gifts for the saying of masses was left open in *Gilmour* v. *Coats* [1949] A.C. 426 at 447, 454, 460.

[70] *Re Royce* [1940] Ch. 514 ("for the benefit of the choir"); contrast *Re Woodhams* [1981] 1 W.L.R. 493 at 496 (tea for choirboys).

[71] *Re Barker's W.T.* (1948) 64 T.L.R. 273.

[72] *Hoare* v. *Osborne* (1866) L.R. 1 Eq. 585.

[73] *Re Eighmie* [1935] Ch. 524.

[74] *Re Manser* [1905] 1 Ch. 68 (Society of Friends).

[75] *Re Pardoe* [1906] 2 Ch. 184.

[76] *Re Eighmie, supra.*

[77] *Re King* [1923] 1 Ch. 243; *Re Hooper* [1932] 1 Ch. 38.

[78] *Hoare* v. *Osborne, supra.*

[79] See *Re Jacques* (1967) 63 D.L.R. (2d) 673 (trust for "community project" not charitable).

[80] *Re Macduff* [1896] 2 Ch. 451 at 466, 467; *Williams' Trustees* v. *I.R.C.* [1947] A.C. 447 at 455; *Re Strakosch* [1949] Ch. 529; *I.R.C.* v. *Baddeley* [1955] A.C. 572.

[81] *Incorporated Council of Law Reporting of the State of Queensland* v. *Commissioner of Taxation of the Commonwealth* (1971) 125 C.L.R. 659 at 669, *per* Barwick C.J.

[82] *Incorporated Council of Law Reporting for England and Wales* v. *Att.-Gen.* [1972] Ch. 73 at 88, *per* Russell L.J., doubted in *Royal National Agricultural and Industrial Corporation* v. *Chester* (1974) 48 A.L.J.R. 304 at 305, 306, and see the qualification in *I.R.C.* v. *McMullen* [1979] 1 W.L.R. 130 at 136, (but see n. 4, *infra*) and see further criticism in *Re South Place Ethical Society* [1980] 1 W.L.R. 1565 at 1574.

[83] *McGovern* v. *Att.-Gen.* [1982] Ch. 321 (Amnesty International).

[84] *National Anti-Vivisection Society* v. *I.R.C.* [1948] A.C. 31; and see *Baldry* v. *Feintuck* [1972] 1 W.L.R. 552 (school milk campaign); *D'Aguiar* v. *Guyana Commissioner of Inland Revenue* [1970] T.R. 31 (citizens' advice service).

having a political purpose[85] if any of its main objects is of a political
nature.[86] But the fact that trustees may have power to use political
means in furthering the non-political purposes of a trust will not
necessarily render the trust non-charitable[87]; and a trust may be upheld
as a good educational charity notwithstanding that it has some political
aspects.[88] The subsequent adoption by Parliament of a political
programme cannot validate a gift to further it.[89]

Public works and the relief of taxation are prominent in this class. It
includes the provision of a fire brigade[90] or crematorium,[91] but perhaps
not of a town hall[92]; the provision of hospitals, whether voluntary[93] or
for paying patients,[94] though not nursing homes run for private profit[95];
the provision of land for "showground, park and recreation purposes"[96];
the publication of law reports[97]; the promotion of the defence of the
country from air attack[98]; the provision of a library and plate for an
officers' mess,[99] or prizes for sport in a regiment[1] (as increasing the
army's efficiency and aiding taxation)[2]; and the provision of self-
contained dwellings for the elderly, even though the beneficiaries might
profit by an increase in the value of their homes.[3] Yet neither the
provision of sports facilities generally for the young,[4] nor that of houses
for ex-officers[5] fall within this class and accordingly they are not
charitable.

This head also includes the encouragement of good domestic
servants,[6] the provision of prizes for the best-kept cottages and gardens
(which promotes horticulture and good housewifery),[7] the planting of a
grove of trees in Israel (as improving agriculture),[8] a war memorial, at

---

[85] For a useful categorisation, see *McGovern* v. *Att.-Gen.* [1982] Ch. 321 at p. 340.
[86] *McGovern* v. *Att.-Gen., supra,* at pp. 341–343.
[87] *Ibid.* at pp. 340, 343.
[88] *Re Koeppler W.T., Barclays Bank Trust Co. Ltd.* v. *Slack* [1986] Ch. 423 (formation of informed international opinion). And see *Att.-Gen.* v. *Ross* [1986] 1 W.L.R. 252 at 263 (encouragement of political awareness among students). *Contra, McGovern* v. *Att.-Gen.* [1982] Ch. 321 (research into human rights a mere adjunct to main political purpose of Amnesty).
[89] *Re Bushnell* [1975] 1 W.L.R. 1596 (socialised medicine).
[90] *Re Wokingham Fire Brigade Trusts* [1951] Ch. 373.
[91] *Scottish Burial Reform and Cremation Society Ltd.* v. *Glasgow Corporation* [1968] A.C. 138.
[92] See *Richmond-upon-Thames L.B.C.* v. *Att.-Gen.* (1983) 81 L.G.R. 156 at 164, 168.
[93] *Re Smith, Barclays Bank Ltd.* v. *Mercantile Bank Ltd.* [1962] 1 W.L.R. 763.
[94] *Re Resch's W.T.* [1969] 1 A.C. 514; and see *Re Adams* [1967] 1 W.L.R. 162.
[95] See *Re Smith, Barclays Bank Ltd.* v. *Mercantile Bank Ltd., supra,* at p. 766.
[96] *Brisbane City Council* v. *Att.-Gen. for Queensland* [1979] A.C. 411.
[97] *Incorporated Council of Law Reporting for England and Wales* v. *Att.-Gen.* [1972] Ch. 73; *Incorporated Council of Law Reporting of the State of Queensland* v. *Commissioner of Taxation of the Commonwealth* (1971) 125 C.L.R. 659; and see *ante,* pp. 147, 148.
[98] *Re Driffill* [1950] Ch. 92.
[99] *Re Good* [1905] 2 Ch. 60.
[1] *Re Gray, Todd* v. *Taylor* [1925] Ch. 362.
[2] Both *Re Good, supra,* and *Re Gray, supra,* were doubted in *I.R.C.* v. *City of Glasgow Police Athletic Association* [1953] A.C. 380 at 391, 401.
[3] *Joseph Rowntree Memorial Trust Housing Association Ltd.* v. *Att.-Gen.* [1983] Ch. 159.
[4] *I.R.C.* v. *McMullen* [1979] 1 W.L.R. 130, C.A., reversed on other grounds: [1981] A.C. 1, H.L. The House pointedly declined to endorse the decision on this ground: [1981] A.C. 1 at 10, 11, 19, 21, 22.
[5] *Re Good, supra; Re Meyers* [1951] Ch. 534.
[6] *Loscombe* v. *Wintringham* (1850) 13 Beav. 87 (a note to the report collects many previous decisions).
[7] *Re Pleasants* (1923) 39 T.L.R. 675; and see *I.R.C.* v. *White* (1980) 55 T.C. 651 (encouragement of crafts and craftsmanship).
[8] *Re Jacobs, Westminster Bank Ltd.* v. *Chinn* (1970) 114 S.J. 515.

least if useful,[9] and the support of a religious community house tending members of the public who need help.[10] But, rather surprisingly, the general benefit and welfare of the inmates of a home maintained by a local authority under statutory powers for delinquent or deprived children has been held to be outside it.[11] So also, in Australia, is the improvement of the breeding and racing of homer pigeons.[12] Yet a trust for the protection and benefit of animals generally (rather than specific creatures) is charitable, provided that the execution of the trust necessarily involves a benefit to the community.[13] A gift for the total suppression of vivisection, which was once held charitable on the ground that it promoted humanitarian views,[14] is now established as not being charitable, for it tends to the disadvantage of mankind.[15]

(e) *Recreational charities.* One class of charities requires separate mention, that of village halls, recreation grounds and the like. The maintenance of a village club and reading room "to be used for the furtherance of conservative principles and religious and mental improvement, and to be kept free from intoxicants and dancing" has been held to be charitable.[16] But the promotion of the moral, social and physical well-being of members of the Methodist church in a particular area, and for their social and physical training and recreation, was held by the House of Lords not to be charitable.[17] Though this decision was based on the vagueness of the particular expressions used, their lordships made general observations on recreational and welfare organisations[18] which led Parliament to amend the law.

The Recreational Charities Act 1958 extends the definition of charity without restricting the purposes which are charitable independently of the Act.[19] Under the Act it is "charitable to provide, or assist in the provision of, facilities for recreation or other leisure-time occupation, if the facilities are provided in the interests of social welfare."[20] For such a trust or institution to be charitable, it must not only be for the public

---

[9] *Murray* v. *Thomas* [1937] 4 All E.R. 545.

[10] *Re Banfield* [1968] 1 W.L.R. 846 (also held charitable under religion: *ante*, p. 148).

[11] *Re Cole, Westminster Bank Ltd.* v. *Moore* [1958] Ch. 877, criticised at (1958) 74 L.Q.R. 481, but reluctantly followed in *Re Sahal's W.T.* [1958] 1 W.L.R. 1243.

[12] *Royal National Agricultural and Industrial Association* v. *Chester* (1974) 48 A.L.J.R. 304.

[13] *Re Wedgwood* [1915] 1 Ch. 113; *Re Grove-Grady* [1929] 1 Ch. 557, compromised on appeal *sub nom. Att.-Gen.* v. *Plowden* [1931] W.N. 89; *Re Moss, Holbrough* v. *Harvey* [1949] 1 All E.R. 495; and see the guarded decision of *Re Murawski's W.T.* [1971] 1 W.L.R. 707. *cf. Re Dean* (1889) 41 Ch.D. 552 and other cases cited, *ante*, p. 102.

[14] *Re Foveaux* [1895] 2 Ch. 501.

[15] *National Anti-Vivisection Society* v. *I.R.C.* [1948] A.C. 31.

[16] *Re Scowcroft* [1898] 2 Ch. 638; and see *Re South Place Ethical Society* [1980] 1 W.L.R. 1565 (Conway Hall).

[17] *I.R.C.* v. *Baddeley* [1955] A.C. 572; *Commissioner of Valuation for Northern Ireland* v. *Lurgan B.C.* [1968] N.I. 104. Contrast *Belfast Y.M.C.A.* v. *Commissioner of Valuation for Northern Ireland* [1969] N.I. 3.

[18] *I.R.C.* v. *Baddeley, supra*, at p. 589; and see *S.C.* in C.A., [1953] Ch. 504 at 536.

[19] The Act is retrospective, but there are savings and other provisions as to past transactions (s.3). Miners' welfare trusts receive special treatment (s.2). For pre-Act examples, see *Re Mann* [1903] 1 Ch. 232; *Re Jones, Williams* v. *Rowlands* [1948] Ch. 67; *Re Spence, Barclays Bank Ltd.* v. *Mayor, etc., of Stockton-on-Tees* [1938] Ch. 96.

[20] Recreational Charities Act 1958, s.1(1).

benefit[21] but also be provided in the interests of social welfare; and this must be shown by satisfying certain conditions.[22] These are as follows.

(1) IMPROVING CONDITIONS: that the facilities are provided with the object of improving the conditions of life for the persons for whom the facilities are primarily intended; and

(2) NEED OR PUBLIC AVAILABILITY: that either—

    (i) those persons have need of such facilities as aforesaid by reason of their youth, age, infirmity or disablement, poverty or social and economic circumstances; or

    (ii) the facilities are to be available to the members or female members of the public at large.[23]

Subject to the facilities being provided in the interests of social welfare, the Act is specifically applied "to the provision of facilities at village halls, community centres and women's institutes, and to the provision and maintenance of grounds and buildings to be used for purposes of recreation and leisure-time occupation," e.g. a public indoor swimming bath[24]; and it extends "to the provision of those facilities by the organising of any activity."[25] But trusts for objects which are neither wholly charitable nor wholly in the interests of social welfare are not protected by the Act even as to those objects which are in the interests of social welfare.[26]

Section 2. Public Benefit

1. The requirement. The second requirement of a valid charitable trust is that it must promote a public benefit[27]; and to this rule there is but one exception.[28] A trust for private purposes, or for purposes which cannot be demonstrated to confer a public benefit, is not charitable. For instance, in *Gilmour* v. *Coats*[29] it was held that the purposes of a community of cloistered and contemplative nuns were not legally

---

[21] *Ibid.* s.1(1), proviso. For this requirement, see *infra*.

[22] For another statutory example of "social welfare," see Rating and Valuation (Miscellaneous Provisions) Act 1955, s.8 (repealed by Rating and Valuation Act 1961), as construed in *National Deposit Friendly Society Trustees* v. *Skegness U.D.C.* [1959] A.C. 293; *General Nursing Council for England and Wales* v. *St. Marylebone Borough Council* [1959] A.C. 540; *Skegness U.D.C.* v. *Derbyshire Miners' Welfare Committee* [1959] A.C. 807. See generally D. W. M. Waters (1959) 23 Conv.(N.S.). 365.

[23] Recreational Charities Act 1958, s.1(2).

[24] *Commissioner of Valuation for Northern Ireland* v. *Lurgan B.C.* [1968] N.I. 104 (on the Recreational Charities (Northern Ireland) Act 1958).

[25] Recreational Charities Act 1958, s.1(3).

[26] *I.R.C.* v. *McMullen* [1979] 1 W.L.R. 130, C.A., criticised J. Warburton [1980] Conv. 173. The House of Lords left the point open: see *ante*, p. 150, n. 4.

[27] For surveys, see G. H. L. Fridman (1953) 31 Can.B.R. 537; P. S. Atiyah (1958) 21 M.L.R. 138; G. Susan Plowright (1975) 39 Conv.(N.S.) 183.

[28] See *post*, p. 154.

[29] [1949] A.C. 426. And see *Re Warre's W.T.* [1953] 1 W.L.R. 725.

charitable, for the benefit to mankind of intercessory prayer and edifying example was too vague, and incapable of proof.[30] The element of public benefit is similarly lacking in a trust for the protection of private investors,[31] or for the education of relations or the descendants of named persons[32] or of the children of employees of a particular employer,[33] or for the provision of a convalescent home for members of a trade union and their wives.[34]

2. Section of the public. A charitable trust may confer a public benefit even though its nature (*e.g.* the provision of sea walls or child welfare) is such that only limited numbers of people are likely to avail themselves of its benefits, or are capable of doing so.[35] There is a distinction "between a form of relief extended to the whole community yet by its very nature advantageous only to the few and a form of relief accorded to a selected few out of a larger number equally willing and able to take advantage of it."[36] The former type does not lack the necessary element of public benefit,[37] even though confined to persons living in a specified area,[38] whereas the latter type does.[39] Moreover, a mere expression of preference for relations or employers will not necessarily vitiate the gift.[40] Whether a gift is charitable as being for the public benefit is a question to be decided by the court on the evidence; the opinion of the donor that his gift will benefit the public is not material.[41]

3. Colour. A provision which provides for conferring benefits on persons of a class defined by reference to colour now[42] takes effect as if the reference to colour is disregarded.[43]

---

[30] Contrast *Holmes* v. *Att.-Gen.* [1981] *The Times*, February 12 (exclusive brethren).

[31] *Corporation of Foreign Bondholders* v. *I.R.C.* [1944] K.B. 403.

[32] *Re Compton, Powell* v. *Compton* [1945] Ch. 123; *Caffoor Trustees* v. *Commissioner of Income Tax, Colombo* [1961] A.C. 584.

[33] *Oppenheim* v. *Tobacco Securities Trust Co. Ltd.* [1951] A.C. 297; and see *Re Cox, Baker* v. *National Trust Co. Ltd.* [1955] A.C. 627.

[34] *Re Mead's Trust Deed* [1961] 1 W.L.R. 1244.

[35] *I.R.C.* v. *Baddeley* [1955] A.C. 572 at 590, 592; *Neville Estates Ltd.* v. *Madden* [1962] Ch. 832 (Jewish synagogue); *Re Dunlop, Northern Bank Executor and Trustee Co. Ltd.* v. *Att.-Gen. for Northern Ireland* [1984] N.I. 408 (home for "Old Presbyterian persons").

[36] *I.R.C.* v. *Baddeley, supra,* at p. 592, *per* Viscount Simonds: see *Re Wedge* (1968) 67 D.L.R. (2d) 433 (trust to help "some needy displaced family" to make a new start held good).

[37] See, *e.g. Verge* v. *Somerville* [1924] A.C. 496.

[38] See *post,* p. 157.

[39] See, *e.g. I.R.C.* v. *Baddeley* [1955] A.C. 572; *Davies* v. *Perpetual Trustee Co. (Ltd.)* [1959] A.C. 439; *Thompson* v. *Federal Commissioner of Taxation* (1959) 102 C.L.R. 315; but see the gloss in *City of Hawthorn* v. *Victorian Welfare Association* [1970] V.R. 205 (class is sufficiently public if anyone can adhere to its beliefs).

[40] *Re Koettgen's W.T.* [1954] Ch. 252; *Caffoor Trustees* v. *Commissioner of Income Tax, Colombo, supra,* at p. 604 (doubting the construction adopted in *Re Koettgen's W.T., supra*); contrast *George Drexler Ofrex Foundation Trustees* v. *I.R.C.* [1966] Ch. 675; *I.R.C.* v. *Educational Grants Association Ltd.* [1967] Ch. 993, affirming *ibid.* at p. 123, where at p. 143 *Re Koettgen's W.T.* is criticised.

[41] *Re Hummeltenberg* [1923] 1 Ch. 237; *Trustees of the Tribune Press, Lahore* v. *Income Tax Commissioner, Punjab, Lahore* (1939) L.R. 66 Ind.App. 241; *National Anti-Vivisection Society* v. *I.R.C.* [1948] A.C. 31.

[42] *i.e.* since June 13, 1977, when Race Relations Act 1976, s.34, came into operation: S.I. 1977 No. 840.

[43] Race Relations Act 1976, s.34. See T. G. Watkin [1981] Conv. 131 for a full discussion.

4. Poor relations, etc. The one exception to the principle that the trust must be for the public benefit consists of trusts for the relief of poverty. These may be charitable even though confined to relations of the donor[44] or employees of a particular employer and their families,[45] or members of a club,[46] and even if the funds are directed to be distributed immediately.[47] The exception is well established,[48] but it is anomalous,[49] and it will not be extended by analogy, *e.g.* to trusts for the education of relations.[50]

Section 3. Exclusively Charitable

1. The rule. Even if a trust satisfies the two foregoing requirements, there is still a third. Charitable trusts are often framed in a somewhat general manner, or as a list of a number of specific purposes, so that the gift authorises the application of the trust funds for many different purposes. In such cases, the gift does not create a valid charitable trust unless every object or purpose is wholly charitable.[51] For instance, if a settlor or testator gives property to be used for such "charitable or deserving,"[52] "charitable or philanthropic,"[53] "charitable or benevolent,"[54] "charitable or public,"[55] "charitable or patriotic"[56] or "charitable or other"[57] objects or "worthy causes"[58] as his executor may select, the gift cannot be charitable. Not every deserving, philanthropic, benevolent, public, patriotic, worthy or other object is charitable, and it would therefore be open to the executor, without committing any breach of his duty, to apply the whole of the property to a non-charitable object. The trusts cannot in such cases be said to be charitable, or, at any rate, exclusively charitable; and there is no escape from this draftsman's trap in a will by asking the court to omit the "or" from probate.[59] A gift to organisations having "in the opinion of my

---

[44] *Re Scarisbrick* [1951] Ch. 622; *Isaac* v. *Defriez* (1754) Amb. 595; 17 Ves. 373n.; *White* v. *White* (1802) 7 Ves. 423; *Att.-Gen.* v. *Price* (1810) 17 Ves. 371; *Re Cohen, Cowan* v. *Cohen* [1973] 1 W.L.R. 415 (relatives "in special need").
[45] *Gibson* v. *South American Stores (Gath & Chaves) Ltd.* [1950] Ch. 177; *Re Coulthurst* [1951] Ch. 661.
[46] *Re Young, Westminster Bank Ltd.* v. *Sterling* [1955] 1 W.L.R. 1269 (the Savage Club).
[47] *Re Scarisbrick, supra.*
[48] *Dingle* v. *Turner* [1972] A.C. 601.
[49] See, *e.g. Re Scarisbrick, supra,* at p. 649; *Re Compton, Powell* v. *Compton* [1945] Ch. 123 at 139; *Dingle* v. *Turner, supra,* at p. 622.
[50] *Ante,* p. 153.
[51] *Morice* v. *Bishop of Durham* (1805) 10 Ves. 522; *Hunter* v. *Att.-Gen.* [1899] A.C. 309; A. W. Scott (1945) 38 Harv.L.R. 548.
[52] Contrast *Re Sutton* (1885) 28 Ch.D. 464 ("charitable *and* deserving").
[53] See *Re Eades* [1920] 2 Ch. 353.
[54] See *Att.-Gen. for New Zealand* v. *Brown* [1917] A.C. 393; *Houston* v. *Burns* [1918] A.C. 337; *Att.-Gen. for New Zealand* v. *New Zealand Insurance Co.* [1936] 3 All E.R. 888; *Chichester Diocesan Fund and Board of Finance (Inc.)* v. *Simpson* [1944] A.C. 341; see the sequel: *Re Diplock* [1948] Ch. 465 (affirmed *sub nom. Ministry of Health* v. *Simpson* [1951] A.C. 251; *post,* pp. 298, 358.
[55] *Blair* v. *Duncan* [1902] A.C. 37; and see *Re Da Costa* [1912] 1 Ch. 337; *Houston* v. *Burns, supra*; *Re Davis, Thomas* v. *Davis* [1923] 1 Ch. 225.
[56] See *Att.-Gen.* v. *National Provincial and Union Bank of England Ltd.* [1924] A.C. 262.
[57] *Re Davidson* [1909] 1 Ch. 567; and see *Re Chapman, Hales* v. *Att.-Gen.* [1922] 2 Ch. 479.
[58] *Re Atkinson's W.T.* [1978] 1 W.L.R. 586.
[59] *Re Horrocks* [1939] P. 198.

trustees" charitable objects is similarly not charitable, for not only may the trustees be mistaken but also the objects of the organisation could be non-charitable as well as charitable.[60]

2. Compound purposes. Where, however, a gift is for certain "educational or charitable or religious purposes," it is valid, for each of these heads is exclusively charitable.[61] And objects described as "charitable *and* deserving," or as "charitable *and* benevolent," will sometimes be construed simply as charitable objects, the added words being treated as merely restrictive of the class of charities to which the property can be devoted.[62] In each case there is a question of construction, namely, whether the "and" or the "or" has been used disjunctively, contrasting two dissimilar conceptions (*e.g.* "acid or alkali"), or conjunctively, coupling together two similar conceptions (*e.g.* "sodium chloride or common salt")[63] and so confining the authorised purposes to, *e.g.* those charitable purposes which are also benevolent.

3. Qualifications to the rule. The rule that all objects must be charitable is subject to a number of qualifications.

(a) *Apportionment.* If an executor or trustee is directed to apportion the property between undefined charitable and non-charitable objects, so that he cannot, without breach of duty, appropriate all of it to the non-charitable objects, the trust will not wholly fail. For in default of apportionment by the executor, the court will apportion the property equally between the two classes of objects (equality being equity) and the trust will fail only as regards the part apportioned to the undefined non-charitable objects.[64]

(b) *Power of variation.* If under a charitable trust the trustees are given power to revoke the trusts and declare new non-charitable trusts, the mere existence of this unexercised power does not make the original trusts non-charitable.[65]

(c) *Ancillary purposes.*[66] A gift will still be charitable notwithstanding that the achievement of the objects which are charitable incidentally promotes other objects which are not. Thus in *Re Coxen*[67] the testator

---

[60] *Re Wootton* [1968] 1 W.L.R. 681; contrast *Gibson* v. *South American Stores (Gath & Chaves) Ltd.* [1950] Ch. 177 at 185.
[61] *Re Ward, Public Trustee* v. *Ward* [1941] Ch. 308.
[62] *Re Sutton* (1885) 28 Ch.D. 464; *Re Best, Jarvis* v. *Birmingham Corpn.* [1904] 2 Ch. 354. *Cf. Williams* v. *Kershaw* (1835) 5 Cl. & F. 111n.; *Re Eades* [1920] 2 Ch. 353; *Att.-Gen. of the Bahamas* v. *Royal Trust Co.* [1986] 1 W.L.R. 1001.
[63] See the cases prior to *Chichester Diocesan Fund and Board of Finance (Inc.)* v. *Simpson* [1944] A.C. 341, collected at (1940) 56 L.Q.R. 452.
[64] *Salusbury* v. *Denton* (1857) 3 K. & J. 529; *Re Clarke, Bracey* v. *Royal National Lifeboat Institution* [1923] 2 Ch. 407.
[65] *Gibson* v. *South American Stores (Gath & Chaves) Ltd.* [1950] Ch. 177; contrast *George Drexler Ofrex Foundation Trustees* v. *I.R.C.* [1966] Ch. 675.
[66] See generally N. P. Gravells [1978] Conv. 92.
[67] [1948] Ch. 747.

entrusted to the Court of Aldermen of the City of London the management of a large fund for the benefit of orthopaedic hospitals and directed that an annual sum not exceeding £100 out of the fund should be applied for a dinner for the Court upon their meeting for the business of the trust. Jenkins J. held that both this direction and also provisions for the payment of certain fees to the trustees were valid as conducing to the attainment of the charitable purposes.[68]

An institution for the promotion of the study and practice of surgery will similarly be charitable, even though an incidental consequence of pursuing that object may be the promotion of the professional interests of practising surgeons,[69] and so will a trust under which a hall is used for social functions ancillary to an adjacent synagogue.[70] Similarly if the main objects of a trust are exclusively charitable, the mere fact that the trustees have incidental powers to further them by non-charitable (*e.g.* political) means will not deprive them of their charitable status.[71] But it is essential that the non-charitable purpose should be merely incidental; an otherwise wholly charitable institution will not be charitable if it can engage in subsidiary non-charitable purposes which are independent of its main purpose and not incidental to it.[72]

(d) *Validation by statute.* The somewhat unexpected decision that the addition of subsidiary but independent non-charitable purposes would make non-charitable an otherwise wholly charitable gift was thought to affect large numbers of existing trusts which had long been accepted as charitable.[73] The situation was alleviated by retrospective but closely circumscribed legislation, namely the Charitable Trusts (Validation) Act 1954.[74]

(1) APPLICATION. For the Act to apply, the following conditions must be satisfied.

  (i)   The terms of the trust (known as "an imperfect trust provision") are such that the property could be used exclusively for charitable purposes but nevertheless could be used for non-charitable purposes,[75] whether the two sets of purposes are

---

[68] See also *Aldous* v. *Southwark London Borough Council* [1968] 1 W.L.R. 1671 (estate offices occupied for purposes of the charity).

[69] *Royal College of Surgeons of England* v. *National Provincial Bank Ltd.* [1952] A.C. 631.

[70] *Neville Estates Ltd.* v. *Madden* [1962] Ch. 832; and see *Glasgow Corporation* v. *Johnstone* [1965] A.C. 609; *Wynn* v. *Skegness U.D.C.* [1967] 1 W.L.R. 52 (convalescent home occupied by paying guests when insufficient patients).

[71] *McGovern* v. *Att.-Gen.* [1982] Ch. 321.

[72] *Oxford Group* v. *I.R.C.* [1949] 2 All E.R. 537; *Ellis* v. *I.R.C.* (1949) 31 T.C. 178; and see *Associated Artists Ltd.* v. *I.R.C.* [1956] 1 W.L.R. 752; *Re Harpur's W.T.* [1962] Ch. 78.

[73] See Nathan Report (1952 Cmd. 8710), Chap. 12.

[74] See also Finance Act 1950, s.37, affecting income tax and stamp duty, and repealed as to the former by Income Tax Act 1952, 25th Sched., as being spent. New Zealand and the Australian States of Victoria and New South Wales have for some time had legislation enabling courts to strike out the non-charitable excess (see Nathan Report, paras. 530, 531; (1946) 62 L.Q.R. 23, 339), though this legislation is not without its problems (see E. H. Coghill (1950) 24 Austr.L.J. 239; and see *Leahy* v. *Att.-Gen. for New South Wales* [1959] A.C. 457).

[75] ss.1(1), 2(3); see *Vernon* v. *I.R.C.* [1956] 1 W.L.R. 1169; *Re Gillingham Bus Disaster Fund* [1959] Ch. 62; P. S. Atiyah (1958) 74 L.Q.R. 190, 489.

expressed separately[76] or compositely.[77] But a gift to institutions carrying on both charitable and non-charitable objects is not a "trust provision" and so cannot be validated,[78] and the same applies to what in substance is a private discretionary trust,[79] even if the objects include provisions for the relief of poverty.[80]

(ii)   The instrument containing the imperfect trust provision took effect before December 16, 1952.[81]

(iii) The trust provision is invalid, but would be valid if the objects had been exclusively charitable.[82]

(iv)   Property or income therefrom had not, prior to December 16, 1952, been paid or distributed on the footing that the imperfect trust provision was void.[83]

(2) OPERATION.   Where the Act applies, the imperfect trust provision has effect—

(i)   as regards the period before the Act came into force on July 30, 1954, as if all the declared objects were charitable, and

(ii) as regards the period after the Act came into force, as if the provision had required the property to be held or applied for the declared objects only so far as they authorise use for charitable purposes.[84]

(e) *Implication.*   In two classes of case the courts have implied into a vague or indefinite gift a limitation confining it to charitable purposes only.

(1) BENEFIT OF LOCALITY.   Trusts for the general benefit of a particular locality,[85] and even for "my country England,"[86] have been held charitable: where no purpose is specified in a gift for the benefit of a locality, the courts will imply a limitation to charitable purposes in that

[76] *Re Mead's Trust Deed* [1961] 1 W.L.R. 1244.
[77] *Re Gillingham Bus Disaster Fund, supra,* at p. 80 (a dissenting judgment, the majority expressing no opinion on this point: pp. 75, 77); and see *Leahy* v. *Att.-Gen. for New South Wales* [1959] A.C. 457 (a decision on a similar statute of New South Wales); *Re Wykes* [1961] Ch. 229; *Re South Place Ethical Society* [1980] 1 W.L.R. 1579.
[78] *Re Harpur's W.T.* [1962] Ch. 78.
[79] See *ante,* p. 117.
[80] *Re Saxone Shoe Co. Ltd.'s Trust Deed* [1962] 1 W.L.R. 943.
[81] s.1(2); the date is that of the publication of the Nathan Report.
[82] s.2(1); see *Vernon* v. *I.R.C., supra,* at p. 1181.
[83] s.2(2).
[84] s.1(2). Under s.3, those with future interests in the property can still attack the validity of the trusts within a year of their interests falling into possession; and time may be extended for disabilities, written acknowledgments and the like: see *Re Chitty's W.T.* [1970] Ch. 254.
[85] *Re Allen, Hargreaves* v. *Taylor* [1905] 2 Ch. 400; *Re Norton's W.T.* [1948] 2 All E.R. 842; and see *Goodman* v. *Saltash Corpn.* (1882) 7 App.Cas. 633.
[86] *Re Smith, Public Trustee* v. *Smith* [1932] 1 Ch. 153.

district,[87] But no such implication is possible if the draftsman has expressed the specific purposes for which the gift is to be used, and these purposes are not confined to charity. It follows that a gift which may by its express terms be used for some non-charitable object is not made charitable by confining it to a particular locality.[88] Thus a trust to provide boys residing in certain districts with knickers bearing an engaging legend on the waistband is not a charitable trust, for there is nothing to exclude the affluent.[89] Similarly trusts for "public, benevolent or charitable purposes" in a district,[90] or for "patriotic purposes in the British Empire,"[91] are not charitable.[92]

(2) GIFTS TO OFFICIALS. A gift *virtute officii* to persons who discharge charitable functions may be a good charitable gift even if made without any definite statement of the purposes to which it is to be applied, for the implication is that it can be used only for his official (and so charitable) purposes.[93] Thus a gift to the Archbishop of Westminster Cathedral for the time being has been held charitable,[94] and so has a gift to the editors of a missionary periodical, who were also trustees of a missionary church.[95]

Added words may or may not drive out that implication. Thus a gift to the vicar and churchwardens of a parish to be applied as in their sole discretion they thought fit,[96] or to a bishop of a diocese to be used by him as he thought fit in his diocese,[97] is charitable, and so is a gift to a vicar "for such objects connected with the church as he shall think fit,"[98] or "for his work in the parish"[99]; for what such persons, in their official capacities, think fitting, or require for their official work, is in no way inconsistent with an exclusively charitable use. But a gift which may, by its express terms, be used for some non-charitable object is not rendered charitable by being given to a charitable corporation or trustees, *e.g.* a bishop.[1] Accordingly, a gift "for parish work"[2] or for "parochial institutions or purposes"[3] is not made charitable merely by being made to the vicar; for much that can be done, whether in a parish

---

[87] See *Williams' Trustees* v. *I.R.C.* [1947] A.C. 447 at 459; *Re Strakosch* [1949] Ch. 529 at 539–541; and consider the gifts "for parish work," *infra*. Contrast M. J. Albery (1940) 56 L.Q.R. 49.
[88] *Re Gwyon* [1930] 1 Ch. 255 at 261; *Re King* [1931] W.N. 232 at 233; *Re Sanders' W.T.* [1954] Ch. 265 at 272.
[89] *Re Gwyon* [1930] 1 Ch. 255. *Cf. Re Pleasants* (1923) 39 T.L.R. 675 (pennyworth of sweets for parish children on bank holiday).
[90] *Houston* v. *Burns* [1918] A.C. 337; see also *ante*, p. 154.
[91] *Att.-Gen.* v. *National Provincial and Union Bank of England Ltd.* [1924] A.C. 262.
[92] See *Re Strakosch* [1949] Ch. 529.
[93] See *Re Spensley's W.T.* [1954] Ch. 233; *Re Rumball* [1956] Ch. 105. See generally V. T. H. Delany (1960) 24 Conv.(N.S.) 306.
[94] *Re Flinn* [1948] Ch. 241; and see *Re Rumball, supra.* Contrast *Re Meehan* [1960] I.R. 82 (to the Bishop of W. "absolutely").
[95] *Re Norman* [1947] Ch. 349.
[96] *Re Garrard* [1907] 1 Ch. 382.
[97] *Re Rumball, supra.*
[98] *Re Bain* [1930] 1 Ch. 224, followed in *Re Eastes* [1948] Ch. 257.
[99] *Re Simson, Fowler* v. *Tinley* [1946] Ch. 299.
[1] *Dunne* v. *Byrne* [1912] A.C. 407; *Re Spensley's W.T.* [1954] Ch. 233 (*a fortiori* if only one out of two or more trustees is a charitable corporation); *Re Endacott* [1960] Ch. 232.
[2] *Farley* v. *Westminster Bank* [1939] A.C. 430.
[3] *Re Stratton* [1931] 1 Ch. 197.

or elsewhere, is not charitable, and an express authority to engage in work that may not be charitable leaves no room for an implied restriction to charity.[4]

PART 3

PERPETUITY

Gifts to charities are exempt from the rule against inalienability. The rule against remoteness of vesting or rule against perpetuities applies to charities in a modified form.[5]

1. The rule against perpetuities. This rule which renders void any gift which may vest outside the traditional period of lives in being and a further twenty-one years, or a specified fixed period not exceeding 80 years,[6] does not apply to charitable trusts in the following circumstances. Property may be given so as to pass from one charity to another at any distance of time,[7] as where there is a bequest to Charity A with a gift over to Charity B if the testator's tomb is permitted to fall out of repair.[8] In all other respects the rule applies. Thus a gift to a charity which does not follow after a gift to another charity is void if it is not to take effect until the happening of a contingency which infringes the rule[9]; and the same applies to a gift over from a charity to individuals[10] or non-charitable purposes,[11] or a gift over to a charity following a gift to individuals[12] or non-charitable purposes.[13]

2. The rule against inalienability. In general a gift is void if its terms preclude the alienation of the capital of the fund for a period which may last longer than the perpetuity period. Gifts to unincorporated societies provide the best illustration of the operation of this rule against

---

[4] Consider *Re Rumball, supra*, at p. 115; and see *Re Davies, Lloyds Bank Ltd.* v. *Mostyn* (1932) 49 T.L.R. 5; *Ellis* v. *I.R.C.* (1949) 31 T.C. 178.

[5] For a general discussion of the rule, which was modified by the Perpetuities and Accumulations Act 1964, see Megarry & Wade's *Law of Real Property* (5th ed., 1984), pp. 240 *et seq.*

[6] Introduced by the Act of 1964 as an alternative period which may be adopted by instruments coming into effect after July 15, 1964.

[7] *Royal College of Surgeons of England* v. *National Provincial Bank Ltd.* [1952] A.C. 631 at 649, 650; *Re Tyler, Tyler* v. *Tyler* [1891] 3 Ch. 252; *Christ's Hospital* v. *Grainger* (1849) 1 Mac. & G. 460.

[8] See *post*, p. 160.

[9] *Re Lord Stratheden and Campbell* [1894] 3 Ch. 265; *Re Mander* [1950] Ch. 547.

[10] *Re Bowen* [1893] 2 Ch. 491. Contrast *Re Randell* (1888) 38 Ch.D. 213.

[11] *Re Davies, Lloyd* v. *Cardigan County Council* [1915] 1 Ch. 543.

[12] *Re Bowen, supra*, at p. 494; *Re Peel's Release* [1921] 2 Ch. 218.

[13] *Re Wightwick's W.T.* [1950] Ch. 260; *Re Spensley's W.T.* [1954] Ch. 233; *Re Bushnell* [1975] 1 W.L.R. 1596.

inalienability (or "rule against perpetual trusts"). If the gift can be construed as an immediate gift, either to the present members of the society individually or to the funds of the society,[14] and there is nothing in the rules to prevent the present members from disposing of the property as they think fit,[15] the gift will be valid,[16] provided that the society has not ceased to exist before the gift takes effect. The gift will, however, fail if the society has ceased to exist before the instrument conferring it comes into operation,[17] or if the rules are not merely contractual but create trusts.[18] Again, if the gift is intended for both the present and future members, so that the present members have no power to appropriate the property for their personal benefit, or to dispose of it for the purposes of the society, the gift will fail unless it is confined to the perpetuity period.[19]

Gifts for charitable purposes are completely exempt from this rule; no charitable gift is void merely because the property will become inalienable in perpetuity.[20]

3. Trusts for the maintenance of tombs.[21]

A trust for the maintenance of a tomb forming no part of a church[22] is not charitable,[23] and so will be void if it is of perpetual duration. If the capital is at all times expendable on the tomb, the trust escapes the rules against perpetuity,[24] but may fail as an ineffective trust of imperfect obligation.[25] However, the rules relating to charitable trusts may be used to some extent to achieve this or any other non-charitable object of this nature. There are two methods.

(i) By a gift to one charity, with a gift over to another if the tomb is not kept in repair.[26] The testator must neither impose on the charity a trust to effect the repairs, nor provide that the trust property is to be used for this purpose, for otherwise he may subject the trust property to a legally binding obligation in

---

[14] *Re Recher's W.T.* [1972] Ch. 526.
[15] *Re Clarke, Clarke* v. *Clarke* [1901] 2 Ch. 110; contrast *Carne* v. *Long* (1860) 2 De G.F. & J. 75.
[16] *Cocks* v. *Manners* (1871) L.R. 12 Eq. 574; *Re Clarke, Clarke* v. *Clarke, supra*; *Re Smith, Johnson* v. *Bright-Smith* [1914] 1 Ch. 937. In *Re Drummond* [1914] 2 Ch. 90, *Re Prevost* [1930] 2 Ch. 383 and *Re Price, Midland Bank Executor and Trustee Co. Ltd.* v. *Harwood* [1943] Ch. 422, it appears that gifts not confined to present members were upheld, but these cases must be considered as of doubtful authority: see *Leahy* v. *Att.-Gen. for New South Wales* [1959] A.C. 457 at 479–481, 484.
[17] *Re Recher's W.T.* [1972] Ch. 526 (society dissolved between making of will and death of testatrix).
[18] *Ibid.* at pp. 538, 539.
[19] *Carne* v. *Long* (1860) 2 De G.F. & J. 75; *Macaulay* v. *O'Donnell* (1933) [1943] Ch. 435n.; *Leahy* v. *Att.-Gen. for New South Wales* [1959] A.C. 457; *Neville Estates Ltd.* v. *Madden* [1962] Ch. 832; *Re Grant's W.T.* [1980] 1 W.L.R. 360.
[20] *Chamberlayne* v. *Brockett* (1872) 8 Ch.App. 206.
[21] See the discussion in [1951] Ir.Jur.News. 17.
[22] See *Re Endacott* [1960] Ch. 232 at 251.
[23] *Ante*, p. 149.
[24] *Re Conner* [1960] I.R. 67.
[25] See *ante*, pp. 102, 103 and consider *Re Endacott* [1960] Ch. 232. This point was not mentioned in *Re Conner, supra.*
[26] *Re Tyler, Tyler* v. *Tyler* [1891] 3 Ch. 252; *ante*, p. 159, *Re Martin, Barclays Bank Ltd.* v. *St. Bartholomew's Hospital Governors* [1952] W.N. 339.

perpetuity (as distinct from a merely moral obligation[27]), and so invalidate the trust[28];

(ii) by a gift for the upkeep as a whole of the churchyard containing the tomb; for this is a charitable gift.[29]

Formerly, it was possible to secure the perpetual maintenance of a tomb by a trust to pay the income of a fund to some corporation as long as it maintained the tomb, with a provision that if the corporation failed to maintain the tomb, the income should be paid to the person entitled to the residue under the will creating the trust.[30] This method depended upon there being no rule to limit the remoteness of time at which a determinable interest might come to an end. However, the Perpetuities and Accumulations Act 1964 made the rule against perpetuities apply to all possibilities of reverter and corresponding resulting trusts under limitations taking effect after July 15, 1964,[31] so that such a provision can no longer be used to maintain a tomb for longer than the perpetuity period.

PART 4

THE CY-PRÈS DOCTRINE

1. The doctrine. If a private trust is initially ineffective or subsequently fails, there is a resulting trust for the settlor.[32] But if a charitable trust[33] is initially impossible or impracticable, or subsequently becomes so, in many cases the trust will not fail, and the court will apply the property *cy-près*, *i.e.* apply it to some other charitable purpose "as nearly as possible" resembling the original trusts[34]; and this will be achieved by means of a scheme.[35]

In the application of this doctrine, two conditions have to be considered: first, whether the trusts are, or have become, impracticable or unenforceable; and secondly, in some (but not all) cases, whether the

[27] See *Re Rogerson* [1901] 1 Ch. 715.
[28] *Re Dalziel* [1943] Ch. 277; *Re Woodhams* [1981] 1 W.L.R. 493 at 496; and see *Re Porter* [1925] Ch. 746 (gift good in part).
[29] *Ante*, p. 149.
[30] *Re Chardon* [1928] Ch. 464. And see the 28th edition of this work, p. 163.
[31] Perpetuities and Accumulations Act 1964, ss.12(1), 15(5).
[32] See *post*, p. 175.
[33] See *National Anti-Vivisection Society* v. *I.R.C.* [1948] A.C. 31 at 64, 65. *Da Costa* v. *De Pas* (1754) Amb. 228 (corrected at 7 Ves. 76) would not, it seems, be followed as to a *cy-près* application on failure of a non-charitable object. Contrast *post*, p. 166, as to a charity ceasing to be such. For Canadian cases, see E. C. E. Todd (1954) 32 Can.B.R. 1100; Waters, *Law of Trusts in Canada* (2nd ed., 1984), pp. 611–632. The *cy-près* application of public legacies was known to Roman law: D.33.2.16.
[34] *Ironmongers' Co.* v. *Att.-Gen.* (1844) 10 Cl. & F. 908; *Re Cunningham* [1914] 1 Ch. 427.
[35] See *Biscoe* v. *Jackson* (1887) 35 Ch.D. 460. On the doctrine generally, see Sheridan and Delany, *The Cy-Près Doctrine* (1959).

donor has manifested a paramount intention of charity. These will be considered in turn; the Charities Act 1960 has to some extent affected both these conditions.[36]

2. Impossibility

(a) *The former law.* Before the Charities Act 1960, the *cy-près* doctrine would be applied only if it was impossible or impracticable to carry out the trust. Such a doctrine was necessary, for charitable trusts may endure for ever,[37] and times change. Thus, seventeenth-century trusts for Harvard College to teach Christianity to the natives in or near the college, and for the propagation of Christianity among the infidels in Virginia had become impossible of performance a century later[38]; and after a century, a trust of 1723 for the redemption of British slaves in Turkey or Barbary had become impracticable.[39] Again, the objects of the trust may cease to be charitable,[40] or the property may be (or become) more than is needed to carry out the selected objects[41]; and a *cy-près* application is not excluded merely because the property consists of surplus income which has been directed to be accumulated beyond the statutory[42] limits.[43]

"Impossible" was generously construed, and extended to cases where the consequences of carrying out the trust would be highly undesirable, so that the court was able to remove a "colour bar" from a hostel for British overseas students when the charity's main object was to promote community of interest in the Empire.[44] However, there were many difficulties in the application of these principles. In particular, they did not permit property to be applied *cy-près* where there was no impossibility, even if other objects would be far more beneficial; in order to encourage charitable gifts, it was held important to disregard the donor's wishes only in cases of necessity.[45] Accordingly, the Charities Act 1960 somewhat relaxed the requirement of impossibility.

---

[36] Charities Act 1960, ss.13, 14; but see s.13(2).

[37] See *ante*, p. 159. The trust in *Att.-Gen.* v. *Webster* (1875) L.R. 20 Eq. 483 was founded in 1585.

[38] *Att.-Gen.* v. *City of London* (1790) 3 Bro.C.C. 171.

[39] *Ironmongers' Co.* v. *Att.-Gen.* (1844) 10 Cl. & F. 908. It may seem strange that the support of Church of England schools was held to be *cy-près* with this: but another part of the property was subject to trusts for this purpose.

[40] See *National Anti-Vivisection Society* v. *I.R.C.* [1948] A.C. 31 at 74.

[41] *Re Campden Charities* (1881) 18 Ch.D. 310; *Re King, Kerr* v. *Bradley* [1923] 1 Ch. 243; *Re Robertson* [1930] 2 Ch. 71.

[42] L.P.A. 1925, s.164, replacing Accumulations Act 1800, s.1; and see Perpetuities and Accumulations Act 1964, ss.13, 14.

[43] *Re Monk* [1927] 2 Ch. 197; *Re Bradwell* [1952] Ch. 575. Yet this seems inconsistent with the statute: see *Re Bradwell* at p. 578.

[44] *Re Dominion Students' Hall Trust* [1947] Ch. 183. See also *Re Robinson, Wright* v. *Tugwell* [1923] 2 Ch. 332 (wearing of black gown by preacher dispensed with); *Re Lysaght, Hill* v. *Royal College of Surgeons* [1966] Ch. 191 (religious discrimination in scholarships dispensed with; see *post*, p. 166); *Re J.W. Laing Trust, Stewards' Co. Ltd.* v. *Att.-Gen.* [1984] Ch. 143 (requirement that trust capital be distributed within 10 years of settlor's death dispensed with); *Re Stewart's W.T.* [1983] N.I. 283 (requirement that hymns used in church be unaltered and unabridged dispensed with).

[45] *Re Weir Hospital* [1910] 2 Ch. 124.

(b) *Charities Act 1960.* The Charities Act 1960[46] makes it unnecessary to decide whether or not there is impossibility in the old sense. Instead, it suffices if the case can be brought under one of the following five heads—

(1) IMPOSSIBILITY: the original purposes, in whole or in part,

  (i)   have been fulfilled "as far as may be," or

  (ii) cannot be carried out, either at all or "according to the directions given and to the spirit of the gift."

(2) SURPLUS FUNDS: the original purposes "provide a use for part only of the property available by virtue of the gift."

(3) BLENDING: the property available by virtue of the gift and other property applicable for similar purposes can be "more effectively used in conjunction, and to that end can suitably, regard being had to the spirit of the gift, be made applicable to common purposes."

(4) CHANGES IN AREA OR CLASS: "the original purposes were laid down by reference to an area which then was but has since ceased to be a unit for some other purpose, or by reference to a class of persons or to an area which has for any reason since ceased to be suitable, regard being had to the spirit of the gift, or to be practical in administering the gift."

(5) INEFFECTIVENESS: "the original purposes, in whole or in part, have, since they were laid down,—

  (i)   been adequately provided for by other means;

  (ii) ceased, as being useless or harmful to the community or for other reasons, to be in law charitable; or

  (iii) ceased in any other way to provide a suitable and effective method of using the property available by virtue of the gift, regard being had to the spirit of the gift."

The "original purposes" means the objects for which the charity was established, and not accompanying administrative provisions.[47] Further,

---

[46] s.13(1).
[47] *Re J.W. Laing Trust, Stewards' Co. Ltd.* v. *Att.-Gen.* [1984] Ch. 143. But the provision in question was deleted under the inherent jurisdiction: *ante,* p. 162, n. 44.

it means the whole of the purposes, so that where a fixed part of the income was given to one purpose and the residue to another, and changes in the value of money have distorted the proportions, the court can adjust them.[48]

(c) *Time for determination.* Whether or not a charitable gift is initially impossible must be determined on the facts existing at the time when the gift is made, *e.g.* as at the death of the testator.[49] If at that moment the trust was impracticable and there was no reasonable prospect of its becoming practicable at some future time, the property should be distributed forthwith, either *cy-près* or, if there was no general charitable intent, to those entitled to residue or on intestacy; for they ought not to be kept in suspense indefinitely on a mere possibility that the trust might one day become practicable.[50] But for this purpose the court will ignore the possibility of a defeasible future charitable trust never taking effect, as where the trust is made liable to be defeated by the birth of issue to a beneficiary; what must be determined is the practicability of the trust if it does take effect.[51] Although laid down on the former law of impossibility, these principles appear to apply under the Charirites Act 1960.

3. Paramount intention of charity

(a) *The requirement.* A distinction must be made between a charitable trust which is impossible *ab initio*, and one which, though initially practicable, subsequently becomes impossible.

(1) INITIAL IMPOSSIBILITY. If the trust is impossible from the outset, the *cy-près* doctrine cannot apply unless the donor has manifested a paramount intention of charity.[52] The property is never subject to any effective charitable trust, and so it will be applied charitably only if the donor has shown a sufficient general intention of charity to support a *cy-près* application to charity against the competing claims of those who would otherwise take the property. But under the Charities Act 1960,[53] no such intention need be shown if the donor has disclaimed, or cannot be identified or found, *e.g.* where money has been raised by collecting boxes or sales.

Where a corporation with charitable objects is dissolved, a subsequent gift made to it is not necessarily impossible from the outset. If the gift is really a gift to the corporation in trust for its objects, it creates an

[48] *Re Lepton's Charity* [1972] Ch. 276 (1715: £3 p.a. to dissenting minister, residue to poor).
[49] *Re Wright* [1954] Ch. 347.
[50] *Re White's W.T.* [1955] Ch. 188.
[51] *Re Tacon* [1958] Ch. 447.
[52] *Re University of London Medical Sciences Institute Fund* [1909] 2 Ch. 1; *Re Wilson, Twentyman* v. *Simpson* [1913] 1 Ch. 314; *Re Packe* [1918] 1 Ch. 437; *Re Ulverston & District New Hospital Building Trusts* [1956] Ch. 622.
[53] s.14. See D. Wilson [1983] Conv. 40.

effective trust for those objects,[54] unless the gift shows that the continued existence of the particular corporate trustee is essential.[55] But if the gift is merely a gift to the corporation, it fails[56] unless the donor has manifested a paramount intention of charity.[57] Where the gift is to an unincorporated association established for charitable purposes, the question is whether those purposes, rather than the association, continue to exist,[58] and, if they do not, whether there is a general charitable intent.[59]

(2) SUPERVENING IMPOSSIBILITY. If a trust is possible at first, but later becomes impossible, the *cy-près* doctrine is not excluded by the absence of any paramount intention of charity.[60] This is so even if the impossibility occurs before the property is available for the charity, *e.g.* during the subsistence of a prior life interest.[61] Where the property has initially been held on charitable trusts, those who would otherwise take the property have already been excluded from it for some period[62]; and if the charitable trusts have continued for a long while, it would often be difficult to ascertain the donor's successors.

(b) *Charity ceasing to exist.* There is no lapse if a simple gift is made to a charitable institution which is in existence at the testator's death, but which subsequently ceases to exist before receiving the legacy. In this case the legacy belongs to the institution, and on its dissolution passes with the rest of its property to the Crown, which will, of its clemency, allow the legacy to be applied *cy-près*, irrespective of any question of general charitable intention[63]: the absence of any trust excludes the jurisdiction of the court to direct a scheme.[64]

(c) *Contrary intention.* These rules are subject to a contrary intention; if the testator intended a gift for only a limited time, with a gift over on failure of the charitable purpose, either the gift over will take effect,[65] or if it is too remote there will be a resulting trust for the testator's estate.[66] Similarly if property is handed over contingently on other property being given, there will be a resulting trust if the latter property is not given.[67]

---

[54] *Re Meyers* [1951] Ch. 534; *Re Vernon's W.T.* (1962) [1972] Ch. 300n.
[55] See *Re Finger's W.T.* [1972] Ch. 286 at 295; and see *post*, p. 200.
[56] *Re Stemson's W.T.* [1970] Ch. 16; *Re Finger's W.T.* [1972] Ch. 286.
[57] See *Re Stemson's W.T., supra* (no paramount intention); *Re Finger's W.T., supra* (paramount intention).
[58] *Re Roberts* [1963] 1 W.L.R. 406; *Re Morrison, Wakefield* v. *Falmouth* (1967) 111 S.J. 758; *Re Finger's W.T., supra.*
[59] See generally J. B. E. Hutton (1969) 32 M.L.R. 283.
[60] *Re Moon's W.T.* [1948] 1 All E.R. 300; *Re Wokingham Fire Brigade Trusts* [1951] Ch. 373; *Re Wright* [1954] Ch. 347; and see *Re British School of Egyptian Archaeology* [1954] 1 W.L.R. 546.
[61] *Re Moon's W.T., supra*; *Re Wright, supra.*
[62] See *Re Wright, supra,* at p. 362.
[63] *Re Slevin* [1891] 2 Ch. 236.
[64] See *post*, p. 171.
[65] See *Re Hanbey's W.T.* [1956] Ch. 264.
[66] *Re Cooper's Conveyance Trusts* [1956] 1 W.L.R. 1096.
[67] *McCormick* v. *Queen's University of Belfast* [1958] N.I. 1.

(d). *The intention required.* What must be shown is "an overriding intention to devote [the property] to charity in general."[68] Yet it is impossible to lay down any satisfactory test to determine what suffices to show this; the reported cases show surprising instances of both liberal[69] and conservative[70] views upon it.[71]

(1) INDICATIONS OF THE INTENTION. The inclusion of the gift in question among other gifts to undoubted charities with kindred objects is some indication of such an intention.[72] So, too, is the fact that the funds were contributed by numerous small anonymous donations,[73] though this is stronger where there is a surplus after the immediate purposes have been fulfilled than when the project has failed *ab initio*.[74] Again, a gift to a charitable institution that has never in fact existed indicates a general charitable intention[75] yet it is by no means conclusive,[76] especially where the result of the gift failing will be that the property will fall into a residuary gift to charity.[77] The court has even extracted a general charitable intention by dissecting a gift into its essential and non-essential parts. If the latter are impracticable, the former may provide a general charitable intention to which effect can be given by means of a scheme which omits the latter.[78]

(2) CONTRARY INDICATIONS. It is very difficult to find a general charitable intention where there is a gift to a particular charity which the testator has taken some care to describe accurately and before the testator's death the charity has ceased to exist[79] (whether through lack of funds[80] or lack of work[81] or for purely administrative reasons[82]), as

---

[68] *Re Sanders' W.T.* [1954] Ch. 265 at 273, *per* Harman J.
[69] *e.g. Re Lysaght, Hill* v. *Royal College of Surgeons* [1966] Ch. 191.
[70] *e.g. Re Stanford* [1924] 1 Ch. 73.
[71] See *Re Wilson, Twentyman* v. *Simpson* [1913] 1 Ch. 314 at 320, 321, for the correct approach to this question (cited in *Re Good's W.T.* [1950] 2 All E.R. 653 at 654); *Att.-Gen. for New South Wales* v. *Perpetual Trustee Co. (Ltd.)* (1940) 63 C.L.R. 209 at 226–228. In *Re Raine* [1956] Ch. 417, two distinct forms of general charitable intention were propounded for specific and residuary gifts, though this seems to be untenable: see (1956) 72 L.Q.R. 170. See generally, Sheridan and Delany, *The Cy-Près Doctrine* (1959), pp. 33–36.
[72] See *Re Davis, Hannen* v. *Hillyer* [1902] 1 Ch. 876; *Re Knox* [1937] Ch. 109; *cf. Re Tharp* (1942) 112 L.J.Ch. 3 (on appeal [1943] 1 All E.R. 257); (1943) 59 L.Q.R. 22; *Re Satterthwaite's W.T.* [1966] 1 W.L.R. 277; *Re Finger's W.T.* [1972] Ch. 286; contrast *Re Jenkins's W.T.* [1966] Ch. 249.
[73] *Re Welsh Hospital (Netley) Fund* [1921] 1 Ch. 655; *Re North Devon and West Somerset Relief Fund Trusts* [1953] 1 W.L.R. 1260.
[74] See *Re Ulverston & District New Hospital Building Trusts* [1956] Ch. 622 at 635, 636. See the critical comment of G. H. Jones (1957) 20 M.L.R. 61; L. A. Sheridan (1956) 34 Can.B.R. 1066; J. C. Hall [1957] C.L.J. 87.
[75] See *Re Davis, Hannen* v. *Hillyer* [1902] 1 Ch. 876; *Re Harwood* [1936] Ch. 285; *Re Knox* [1937] Ch. 109.
[76] See *Re Maynard* (1973) 21 W.I.R. 31, Barbados H.C.
[77] *Re Goldschmidt* [1957] 1 W.L.R. 524. See V. T. H. Delany (1957) 73 L.Q.R. 166.
[78] *Re Lysaght, Hill* v. *Royal College of Surgeons* [1966] Ch. 191 (excluding undesirable religious tests); *Re Woodhams* [1981] 1 W.L.R. 493 (omitting requirement of scholars to be absolute orphans from specified homes).
[79] *Re Rymer* [1895] 1 Ch. 19; *Re Harwood* [1936] Ch. 285; *Re Goldney* (1946) 115 L.J.Ch. 337; *Re Slatter's W.T.* [1964] Ch. 512; *Re Stemson's W.T.* [1970] Ch. 16; *cf. Re Withall* [1932] 2 Ch. 236; *Re Tharp* (1942) 112 L.J.Ch. 3 (on appeal [1943] 1 All E.R. 257); *Re Spence, Ogden* v. *Shackleton* [1979] Ch. 783.
[80] *Re Withall, supra,* at p. 241.
[81] *Re Slatter's W.T., supra; Re Mackenzie* [1962] 1 W.L.R. 880.
[82] *Re Spence, Ogden* v. *Shackleton, supra* (old people's home closed by local authority; same work carried on in other homes).

distinct from being merely altered under a scheme.[83] Similarly, where the testator has only one particular purpose in mind, such as to build almshouses[84] or a hospital[85] or found a school[86] at a particular place and that purpose cannot be carried out, it is difficult to infer any general charitable intention, and so the gift will fall into residue or pass as on intestacy. Nor will even an express assertion of a "general charitable intention" suffice if the context shows it not to be truly charitable.[87]

PART 5

ADMINISTRATION AND SUPERVISION

As with private trusts, the general management of charitable trusts is in the hands of trustees. However, owing to the special circumstances of charitable trusts, especially the usual absence of any beneficiary who can enforce the trusts and the perpetual duration of most charities, a number of official bodies are charged with the supervision of charities and a number of special rules have been established. The law on these topics is now[88] largely to be found in the Charities Acts 1960 and 1985.[89]

Section 1. Persons and Bodies Controlling Charities

1. The Charity Commissioners. Three Charity Commissioners with their staff form a department of state responsible to the Home Secretary.[90]

(a) *General function.* The general function of the Commissioners is to promote "the effective use of charitable resources by encouraging the development of better methods of administration, by giving charity trustees information or advice on any matter affecting the charity and by investigating and checking abuses."[91] Their powers are those of

---

[83] *Re Faraker* [1912] 2 Ch. 488; *Re Lucas, Sheard* v. *Mellor* [1948] Ch. 424; and see *Re Hutchinson's W.T.* [1953] Ch. 387; *Re Roberts* [1963] 1 W.L.R. 406.
[84] *Re White's Trusts* (1886) 33 Ch.D. 449; and see *Re Packe* [1918] 1 Ch. 437 (retreat for clergy and wives).
[85] *Re Ulverston & District New Hospital Building Trusts* [1956] Ch. 622; *Beggs* v. *Kirkpatrick* [1961] V.R. 764 (effect reversed by Ripon Peace Memorial Trust Act 1961 (Vict. Stat. No. 6747)); and see *Re Hillier's Trusts* [1954] 1 W.L.R. 700; *Re Pochin's W.T.* (1943) [1948] Ch. 182n.
[86] *Re Wilson, Twentyman* v. *Simpson* [1913] 1 Ch. 314.
[87] *Re Sanders' W.T.* [1954] Ch. 265 (appeal settled: [1954] *The Times*, July 22).
[88] From January 1, 1961: Charities Act 1960, s.49(3). The Charities Act 1985 came into force on January 1, 1986: *ibid.* s.7(2); S.I. 1985 No. 1583.
[89] The 1960 Act replaced with many amendments the Charitable Trusts Acts 1853 to 1939, and adopted a number of recommendations of the Nathan Report. It was supplemented by the Act of 1985.
[90] Charities Act 1960, s.1(1), (2), 1st Sched.
[91] *Ibid.* s.1(3).

overseers and advisers; they have no power "to act in the administration of a charity."[92]

(b) *Specific functions.*   Their specific powers and functions include the following.

(i)   The duty to maintain a register of charities.[93]

(ii)   The power to institute inquiries with regard to charities or a particular charity or class of charities,[94] to call for documents relating to a charity, to inspect records,[95] and to take steps to remedy misconduct or mismanagement.[96]

(iii)   The power to call for and audit the accounts of any charity and to receive without request the accounts of any charity with a permanent endowment,[97] *i.e.* property held subject to a restriction on the expenditure of capital.[98]

(iv)   The power to establish a scheme, to appoint, discharge or remove trustees, officers or servants of a charity and to make vesting orders.[99]

(v)   The power to authorise transactions which may be expedient in the interests of the charity,[1] and to authorise dealings with property forming part of the permanent endowment of a charity.[2]

(vi)   The power to give advice to trustees.[3]

(vii)   The power to enrol and preserve charity documents.[4]

(viii)   The power to sanction legal proceedings concerning charities.[5] This does not include proceedings in which there is a bona fide dispute as to the existence of the charity.[6]

2. The trustees.   The powers and duties of the trustees of a charity are similar to those of other trustees.[7] Thus the Limitation Act 1980[8]

---

[92] *Ibid.* s.1(4). The Secretary of State for Education and Science (and Secretary of State for Wales) formerly had concurrent powers in respect of educational charities: Charities Act 1960, s.2. These powers were abrogated by the Education Act 1973, s.1, as from February 1, 1974 (S.I. 1973 No. 1661).

[93] Charities Act 1960, ss.4, 5. See *post*, p. 170.

[94] *Ibid.* s.6.

[95] *Ibid.* s.7.

[96] *Ibid.* s.20. For the right of appeal to the court following the exercise of these powers, see *Jones* v. *Att.-Gen.* [1974] Ch. 148 (further proceedings: *The Times*, November 10, 1976).

[97] *Ibid.* s.8. See also Charities Act 1985, s.1.

[98] *Ibid.* s.45(3).

[99] *Ibid.* s.18. As to schemes, see *post*, p. 170.

[1] *Ibid.* s.23. *Cf.* T.A. 1925, s.57, *post*, p. 239.

[2] Charities Act 1960, s.29. See *post*, p. 173.

[3] *Ibid.* s.24. See *Mills* v. *Winchester Diocesan Board of Finance* [1989] Ch. 428 (no duty of care at common law when advising under s.24).

[4] *Ibid.* s.25.

[5] *Ibid.* s.28.

[6] *Hauxwell* v. *Barton-upon-Humber U.D.C.* [1974] Ch. 432.

[7] For the personal liability of charity trustees and their right to be indemnified out of the capital of the trust fund, see A. J. Hawkins (1979) 95 L.Q.R. 99.

[8] See *post*, p. 292.

applies to charitable trustees as it does to others.[9] However, in contrast with the trustees of a private trust,[10] their numbers are not limited by statute,[11] and they need not be unanimous in exercising their powers; a majority may generally[12] bind the minority.[13] Their wide discretionary powers of spending are often more controversial than the powers of most ordinary trustees to conserve the trust property and distribute it in accordance with the terms of the trust instrument. Charitable trustees are under a statutory obligation to keep proper books of account,[14] to apply for registration of the charity,[15] and, where appropriate, to take steps to enable the trust property to be applied *cy-près*.[16] They are also authorised to delegate the execution of instruments,[17] and there are special provisions as to the mode of appointment and discharge of trustees and the vesting of property.[18] Moreover, they have all the powers conferred by the Settled Land Act 1925 on a tenant for life and on the trustees of a settlement, subject to obtaining any consents or orders required apart from the Act.[19] Yet they do not necessarily have to comply with the conditions of the Act; a sole trustee may receive capital money if the scheme governing the charity allows him to do so.[20]

3. The Official Custodian for Charities. The Official Custodian for Charities[21] is a public official in whom the property of a charity may be vested as a custodian trustee,[22] thereby obviating the necessity for transfers of property upon the appointment of new managing trustees. Personal property (including real securities) may be transferred to him with his agreement, and any property may be vested in him by or under an order of the court.[23]

4. Attorney-General. "It is the province of the Crown as *parens patriae* to enforce the execution of charitable trusts, and it has always been recognised as the duty of the law officers of the Crown to intervene for the purpose of protecting charities and affording advice

---

[9] See *Re Robert Gwynne's Charity* (1894) 10 T.L.R. 428; *Edwards* v. *Warden* (1876) 1 App.Cas. 281; and see *Smith* v. *Kerr* [1902] 1 Ch. 774; contrast *St. Mary Magdalen, Oxford* v. *Att.-Gen.* (1857) 6 H.L.C. 189.
[10] See *post*, p. 237.
[11] See *post*, p. 200.
[12] For statutory exceptions, see *post*, pp. 172, 173.
[13] *Re Whiteley* [1910] 1 Ch. 600.
[14] Charities Act 1960, s.32. For the general obligation, see *post*, p. 231.
[15] *Ibid.* s.4(6). For registration, see *post*, p. 170.
[16] Charities Act 1960, s.13(5). See *ante*, p. 161.
[17] *Ibid.* s.34.
[18] *Ibid.* s.35.
[19] S.L.A. 1925, s.29, as amended by Charities Act 1960, 7th Sched. For consents and orders, see *post*, p. 173.
[20] *Re Booth and Southend-on-Sea Company's Contract* [1927] 1 Ch. 579.
[21] Combining the former offices of the Official Trustee of Charity Lands and the Official Trustees of Charitable Funds: see Charities Act 1960, s.48(6).
[22] Charities Act 1960, ss.3, 17(1). For custodian trustees, see *post*, p. 209 and for the position and powers of the Official Custodian, see Charities Act 1960, s.17.
[23] Charities Act 1960, s.16.

and assistance to the court in the administration of charitable trusts."[24] This duty is recognised by the Charities Act 1960, which in addition allows proceedings with reference to a charity (but not as to whether a charitable trust exists[25]) to be taken by "the charity, or by any of the charity trustees, or by any person interested in the charity, or by any two or more inhabitants of the area of the charity, if it is a local charity."[26] Such persons, other than the Attorney-General,[27] must usually obtain an order of the Charity Commissioners (or, if refused, the court) before the proceedings may be entertained or proceeded with[28] in any court.[29] To qualify as a "person interested" in a charity, one must have an interest in securing the due administration of the charity materially greater than, or different from, that possessed by ordinary members of the public (whether they are subscribers or potential beneficiaries or neither).[30] In appropriate circumstances, a local authority may be a "person interested."[31] But the phrase does not extend to persons contracting with the trustees of the charity, for they are claiming against the charity,[32] nor does it include the personal representatives of the founder,[33] although it may well include the founder himself.[34]

The Attorney-General, it seems, has power to enter into bargains with third parties as to the rights of the charity.[35] Further, if there is a strong case for making *ex gratia* payments out of charitable funds, the Attorney-General may authorise the trustees to make them.[36]

Section 2. Special Rules in Administration

1. Registration. The Charity Commissioners maintain a register of charities,[37] which is open to public inspection.[38] "Charity" means any institution, corporate or not, which is established for charitable purposes and is subject to the control of the High Court in the exercise of the court's jurisdiction with respect to charities.[39] The control may be

---

[24] *Wallis* v. *Sol.-Gen. for New Zealand* [1903] A.C. 173 at 181, *per* Lord Macnaghten. See also *Re Royal Society's Charitable Trusts* [1956] Ch. 87 at 92, 93; *Hauxwell* v. *Barton-upon-Humber U.D.C.* [1974] Ch. 432.
[25] *Re Belling* [1967] Ch. 425, followed in *Hauxwell* v. *Barton-upon-Humber U.D.C.* [1974] Ch. 432.
[26] s.28(1); and see ss.45(1), 46, which when read together appear to allow a charitable trust, as distinct from its trustees, to sue; *sed quaere*.
[27] s.28(6); and see s.28(7); and see *Hauxwell* v. *Barton-upon-Humber U.D.C.*, *supra*.
[28] See *Rendall* v. *Blair* (1890) 45 Ch.D. 139.
[29] Charities Act 1960, ss.2(1), 28(2), (3), (5); and see *Rooke* v. *Dawson* [1895] 1 Ch. 480; *Brooks* v. *Richardson* [1986] 1 W.L.R. 385.
[30] *Re Hampton Fuel Allotment Charity* [1989] Ch. 484 at 494.
[31] *Re Hampton Fuel Allotment Charity* [1989] Ch. 484.
[32] *Haslemere Estates Ltd.* v. *Baker* [1982] 1 W.L.R. 1109.
[33] *Bradshaw* v. *University College of Wales* [1988] 1 W.L.R. 190.
[34] *Re Hampton Fuel Allotment Charity*, *supra*, at p. 493.
[35] *Re Freeston's Charity* [1978] 1 W.L.R. 120 at 129 (on appeal, *ibid.*, 741 at 755).
[36] *Re Snowden, Shackleton* v. *Eddy* [1970] Ch. 700 (part of ten-fold increase in value given up to testator's relations).
[37] Charities Act 1960, s.4(1).
[38] *Ibid.* s.4(7).
[39] *Ibid.* s.45(1).

tenuous and residual, as where a statutory body is subject to wide control from outside the body.[40] Registration is compulsory except for—

(i)   exempt charities: these comprise important national institutions such as the British Museum and some universities and colleges[41];

(ii) charities excepted by order or regulations[42]; and

(iii) charities not having permanent endowments nor any income from property amounting to more than £15 a year, nor the use and occupation of any land.[43]

Institutions ceasing to be charities or ceasing to exist or operate must be removed from the register.[44] Subject to certain rights to procure rectification of the register, registration raises a conclusive presumption that an institution is a charity at any time when it is on the register,[45] and also that it was a charity at all times prior to registration while its purposes were the same.[46]

2. Schemes

(a) *Purpose.* A scheme for the administration of charitable trusts may be made in a variety of cases, *e.g.* for the better management of the charity, or when the *cy-près* doctrine is applied,[47] or when land which has been devoted to charitable purposes under certain statutes[48] has ceased to be used for those purposes,[49] or when property has been given to charity without sufficiently specifying the objects or providing for the way in which the trust is to operate.[50] The jurisdiction depends upon the existence of a trust, or a corporate body obliged under its constitution to apply its assets exclusively for charitable purposes.[51] Hence there is no power to direct a scheme if there is a direct gift to a non-existent body and no trust; the gift in such a case is applied in

---

[40] *Construction Industry Training Board* v. *Att.-Gen.* [1973] Ch. 173.
[41] See Charities Act 1960, 2nd Sched. A variety of universities, colleges and institutes have been added, including technological establishments and the Open University: see S.I. 1965 No. 1715; 1966 No. 1460; 1967 No. 821; 1969 No. 1496; 1978 No. 453; 1984 No. 1976; 1987 No. 1823.
[42] A number of orders have been made: see S.I. 1963 No. 2074 and 1964 No. 1825 (religious charities), 1961 No. 1044 (boy scouts), 1965 No. 1056 (armed forces) and 1966 No. 965 (non-exempt universities).
[43] Charities Act 1960, s.4(2), (4). Charities existing at the date of the Act became registrable on the making of orders by the Home Secretary or Minister of Education: *ibid.* s.4(10). For examples, see S.I. 1961 Nos. 987 and 1867 (local charities).
[44] Charities Act 1960, s.4(3).
[45] *Ibid.* s.5: see *Finch* v. *Poplar B.C.* (1967) 66 L.G.R. 324 (seamen's mission).
[46] *Re Murawski's W.T.* [1971] 1 W.L.R. 707.
[47] See *ante,* p. 161.
[48] School Sites Acts 1841, 1844, 1849, 1851 and 1852; Literary and Scientific Institutions Act 1854; Places of Worship Sites Act 1873: see Reverter of Sites Act 1987, ss.1(1), 7(1).
[49] Reverter of Sites Act 1987, ss.2–4. See also Education Act 1973, s.2 and Reverter of Sites Act 1987, s.5.
[50] See *Re Robinson, Besant* v. *The German Reich* [1931] 2 Ch. 122 at 128; *ante,* pp. 143, 144; contrast *ante,* p. 154.
[51] *Liverpool and District Hospital for Diseases of the Heart* v. *Att.-Gen.* [1981] Ch. 193.

accordance with the directions of the Crown under the royal prerogative.[52]

(b) *Jurisdiction.* The court and the Charity Commissioners have in general[53] a concurrent jurisdiction in the making of schemes,[54] except that especially contentious and difficult questions[55] and schemes for charities established by Royal Charter[56] are reserved to the court.[57] The court will not interfere with the details of a scheme unless the Commissioners have exceeded their authority or the scheme contains something wrong in principle.[58] Schemes for altering charities established by statute may be made by the Commissioners and given effect to by statutory instrument.[59]

(c) *Details.* The details of schemes vary infinitely. Thus one scheme may consist of an elaborate constitution and rules for establishing and running a children's home or school, while another scheme may merely direct the division of the property among a number of existing charities. The establishment of common investment funds for a number of charities is expressly authorised.[60] The court is not bound to make a scheme, and has refused to do so where the trustees had acted in breach for many years, where it would have been difficult to settle a useful scheme, and where the result would be to defeat a gift over to another charity.[61]

3. Alteration of objects by resolution. Under section 2 of the Charities Act 1985 the trustees of a local charity for the relief of poverty[62] which is at least 50 years old may unanimously[63] pass a resolution that the objects of the charity be replaced by new, charitable objects.[64] The trustees must be of the opinion that the existing objects are obsolete or lacking in usefulness, or impossible of achievement, having regard to the period that has elapsed since the charity was founded, social and economic changes and other relevant circumstances; and that an alteration of objects is required in order that the charity's

---

[52] *Re Bennett, Sucker* v. *Att.-Gen.* [1960] Ch. 18.
[53] Jurisdiction under the Reverter of Sites Act 1987, *supra*, is vested in the Commissioners, subject to an appeal to the court.
[54] See Charities Act 1960, s.18; and see *London Parochial Charities Trustees* v. *Att.-Gen.* [1955] 1 W.L.R. 42 at 46; *Re Berkhamsted Grammar School* [1908] 2 Ch. 25.
[55] Charities Act 1960, s.18(9).
[56] *Ibid.* s.15. See also *Re Whitworth Art Gallery Trusts* [1958] Ch. 461.
[57] For scheme-making procedure, see Charities Act 1960, ss.18, 21; and see *Re Hyde Park Place Charity* [1911] 1 Ch. 678; *Childs* v. *Att.-Gen.* [1973] 1 W.L.R. 497.
[58] *Re Campden Charities* (1881) 18 Ch.D. 310; *Re Weir Hospital* [1910] 2 Ch. 124.
[59] Charities Act 1960, s.19. The court has very limited powers to alter statutory charities: see *London Parochial Charities Trustees* v. *Att.-Gen.* [1955] 1 W.L.R. 42; *Re Shipwrecked Fishermen and Mariners' Royal Benevolent Society* [1959] Ch. 220.
[60] Charities Act 1960, s.22. See *Re Royal Society's Charitable Trusts* [1956] Ch. 87; *Re University of London Charitable Trusts* [1964] Ch. 282.
[61] *Re Hanbey's W.T.* [1956] Ch. 264.
[62] Defined in Charities Act 1985, s.6(1).
[63] Charities Act 1985, s.2(5).
[64] *Ibid.* s.2(1), (2).

resources may be applied to better effect, consistently with the spirit of the original gift.[65] And the new objects must not, in the trustees' opinion, involve an unjustifiable departure from the intentions of the founder or a violation of the spirit of the gift.[66] The resolution takes effect only if the Charity Commissioners concur with it.[67]

4. Transfer of property to another charity. The trustees of a registered charity or of one which is not required to be registered[68] may, under section 3 of the Charities Act 1985, unanimously[69] resolve that the whole of the charity's property be transferred to another such charity, to be held and applied as property of that charity.[70] The main requirements are that the gross income of the transferor charity in the preceding accounting period was £200 or less[71]; that the transferee charity gives written consent prior to the passing of the resolution; and that the trustees of the transferor charity are of opinion that the transfer would not involve an unjustifiable departure from the founder's intentions or violate the spirit of the gift.[72] Again, the Commissioners must concur.[73]

5. Restrictions on dealings. No property forming part of the permanent endowment[74] of a charity can be mortgaged[75] or charged, or, if it is land, sold,[76] leased or otherwise disposed of without an order of the court[77] or the Charity Commissioners.[78] A similar restriction applies to land not forming part of the permanent endowment but occupied for the purposes of the charity; but in this case a transaction effected without the requisite order is valid in favour of a person who in good faith acquires an interest in or charge on the land for money or money's worth.[79] Consent is not required for transactions authorised by statute or by a scheme, nor for the grant of a lease for not more than 22 years, not being granted for a fine.[80] Exempt charities and charities excepted by order or regulations are not subject to these restrictions,[81] and

---

[65] *Ibid.* s.2(2).
[66] *Ibid.* s.2(3).
[67] *Ibid.* s.2(9).
[68] See *ante,* pp., 170, 171.
[69] Charities Act 1985, s.3(4).
[70] *Ibid.* s.3(1).
[71] This sum may be altered by statutory instrument: Charities Act 1985, s.5(1).
[72] Charities Act 1985, s.3(2).
[73] *Ibid.* s.3(8).
[74] For permanent endowment, see *ante,* p. 168.
[75] See *Fell* v. *Official Trustee of Charity Lands* [1898] 2 Ch. 44.
[76] See *Milner* v. *Staffordshire Congregational Union (Incorporated)* [1956] Ch. 275, on an earlier Act (there is a "sale" of land as soon as the contract is made).
[77] Not an ecclesiastical court: *Re St. Swithin's, Norwich* [1960] P. 77; and see now Charities Act 1960, s.46.
[78] Charities Act 1960, s.29(1). See *Haslemere Estates Ltd.* v. *Baker* [1982] 1 W.L.R. 1109 at 1116, 1117. A number of other restrictions were swept away by the Act.
[79] *Ibid.* s.29(2).
[80] *Ibid.* s.29(3).
[81] *Ibid.* s.29(4). See S.I. 1961 Nos. 225 and 1282, and S.I. 1963 No. 1062, excepting certain land of religious charities of various denominations. For exempt charities, see *ante* p. 171.

special provision has been made for certain charities with an endowment worth £25 or less.[82]

The former restrictions on the acquisition of land by charities, whether *inter vivos* or by will, have now been repealed.[83]

6. Exemption from taxation. The income of a body of persons or a trust established in the United Kingdom[84] for charitable purposes only, which is in fact applied solely,[85] even if indirectly,[86] for those purposes, is exempt from income tax.[87] In some circumstances charities are exempt from inheritance tax,[88] capital gains tax[89] and rates.[90]

7. Similarity to private trusts. Apart from any special provisions, charitable trusts are treated in the same way as private trusts. Thus the trustees may exercise the statutory powers conferred on trustees by the Trustee Act 1925 and the Trustee Investments Act 1961, including any additional powers conferred on them by the court.[91] Further, the rule in *Saunders* v. *Vautier*[92] can be resorted to by a charity as by a private beneficiary.[93]

---

[82] Charities Act 1985, s.4.
[83] Charities Act 1960, s.38. For the restrictions, see 24th ed. of this book, pp. 144, 145.
[84] *Camille and Henry Dreyfus Foundation Inc.* v. *I.R.C.* [1956] A.C. 39.
[85] *I.R.C.* v. *Educational Grants Association Ltd.* [1967] Ch. 993.
[86] *I.R.C.* v. *Helen Slater Charitable Trust Ltd.* [1982] Ch. 49.
[87] Income and Corporation Taxes Act 1988, s.505.
[88] Inheritance Tax Act 1984 (formerly cited as Capital Transfer Tax 1984), s.23.
[89] Capital Gains Tax Act 1979, s.145.
[90] See *Ryde on Rating* (13th ed., 1976), pp. 335–354; Rating (Charity Shops) Act 1976, reversing *Oxfam* v. *Birmingham City District Council* [1976] A.C. 126.
[91] *e.g.* under T.A. 1925, s.57; see *Re Shipwrecked Fishermen and Mariners' Royal Benevolent Society* [1959] Ch. 220. For s.57, see *post*, p. 239.
[92] (1841) 4 Beav. 115, affirmed Cr. & Ph. 240; see *post*, p. 233.
[93] See, *e.g. Wharton* v. *Masterman* [1895] A.C. 186; *Re Knapp* [1929] 1 Ch. 341; but see *Re Levy* [1960] Ch. 346 (indefinite gift of income not a gift of *corpus*, for a charity (unlike an individual) has perpetual existence).

CHAPTER 4

RESULTING, IMPLIED OR CONSTRUCTIVE TRUSTS

This important group of trusts have express statutory recognition,
being exempt from the formalities which are required for the
creation and disposition of express trusts.[1] So their hallmark is
informality. They fall into two broad categories: those which depend
upon the intention of the grantor or settlor, whether presumed or
informally expressed, and those which are imposed by law regardless of
intention. Resulting trusts are firmly based on presumed intention; trusts
imposed by law are invariably known as constructive trusts. The area
between is variously described as comprising implied or constructive
trusts[2] and their development is continuous.

PART I

INFORMAL TRUSTS BASED ON INTENTION

These trusts may arise from the unexpressed but presumed intention of
the settlor,[3] or upon his informally expressed intention. Where the
beneficial interest remains in or reverts to the settlor they are known as
resulting trusts. For the purposes of exposition informal trusts based on
intention can be divided into five categories, namely: failure to exhaust
the beneficial interest; purchase in the name of another; resulting trust
on a voluntary conveyance; acquisition for joint use; and mutual wills.

Section 1. Failure to Exhaust Beneficial Interest

1. Resulting trust to settlor

(a) *Trusts not in fact exhaustive.* A common case of an implied or
resulting trust arises where a settlor conveys property upon trusts which
in the event do not exhaust the whole of the beneficial interest in the
property,[4] as where the trust is for A for life and then equally among

---

[1] L.P.A. 1925, s.53(2). See *ante*, pp. 106, 107 for the formalities.
[2] See, *e.g. Gissing* v. *Gissing* [1971] A.C. 886 at 906.
[3] This concept at times appears to elude the common law mind: see, *e.g. Smith* v. *Cooke* [1891] A.C.
297 at 299, where Lord Halsbury L.C. is reported as saying: "If it is intended to have a resulting
trust, the ordinary and familiar mode of doing that is by saying so on the face of the instrument; and
I cannot get, out of the language of this instrument, a resulting trust except by putting in words
which are not there."
[4] Called "automatic resulting trusts" by Megarry J. in *Re Vandervell's Trusts (No. 2)* [1974] Ch. 269 at
294.

his children, and A dies childless. Here the beneficial interest, so far as
it is not effectually disposed of, results to the settlor, or, if he is dead,
to his residuary devisee or legatee, or the persons entitled under his
intestacy.[5] What a man does not effectually dispose of remains vested in
him.[6] Thus, if a voidable marriage is annulled, there is a resulting trust
to the settlor of the property comprised in the marriage settlement.[7]
Similarly where a trust fund was subscribed for the maintenance and
support of two distressed ladies, the surplus remaining after their death
was held on a resulting trust for the subscribers.[8] Such a surplus is held
rateably for the subscribers according to their subscriptions[9]; and this
rule seems to apply despite the existence of many small gifts from
anonymous donors,[10] even though it might well be more reasonable that
they should pass to the Crown as *bona vacantia*.[11] There can be no
resulting trust under this head if property is purchased in joint names,
each purchaser having a different purpose only one of which fails.[12]

(b) *Trusts partially expressed.* Sometimes the trusts are only partially
expressed. Thus, if a testator bequeaths the residue of his property to T
upon trust to pay the income to B for life without saying what is to be
done with the property on B's death, when B dies T holds as trustee for
the persons entitled as on an intestacy of the testator. And the same
result would follow if, and so far as, the trusts declared offended against
any rule of law, such as the perpetuity rule. By giving the property to T
expressly upon trust the testator has shown that he does not wish T to
take beneficially, and it would not be open to T to produce external
evidence to contradict the intention expressed in the will.[13]

If on a consideration of the whole will, however, it appears that the
testator meant to give the property to T for his own benefit, subject
merely to his carrying out the expressed trusts, T will take the
unexhausted residue beneficially. Thus, where a testator gave all his
property to his sister absolutely on trust to pay his wife an annuity, and
the income was more than enough to pay the annuity, the sister was
held to be beneficially entitled to the balance.[14] Similarly, in a trust for

---

[5] *Re West, George* v. *Grose* [1900] 1 Ch. 84.
[6] See *Vandervell* v. *I.R.C.* [1967] 2 A.C. 291 at 313–315, considering the position of a grantee of an
option; *Re Vandervell's Trusts (No. 2)* [1974] Ch. 269 (C.A.).
[7] *Re Ames' Settlement* [1946] Ch. 217. But see *post*, p. 245, for the power of the court to vary
settlements on granting a decree of nullity of marriage.
[8] *Re the Trusts of the Abbott Fund* [1900] 2 Ch. 326; *Re Hobourn Aero Components Ltd.'s Air Raid
Distress Fund* [1946] Ch. 194; *Re West Sussex Constabulary's Widows, Children and Benevolent
(1930) Fund Trusts* [1971] Ch. 1.
[9] *Re British Red Cross Balkan Fund* [1914] 2 Ch. 419; and see *post*, p. 305.
[10] *Re Gillingham Bus Disaster Fund* [1958] Ch. 300 (affirmed on grounds not affecting this point: [1959]
Ch. 62), criticised by P. S. Atiyah (1958) 74 L.Q.R. 190.
[11] *Re West Sussex Constabulary's Widows, Children and Benevolent (1930) Fund Trusts, supra*, criticised
by M. Albery (1971) 87 L.Q.R. 464; and see *Re Hillier's Trusts* [1954] 1 W.L.R. 9 at 22 (reversed on
grounds not affecting this point: [1954] 1 W.L.R. 700); *Re Ulverston and District New Hospital
Building Trusts* [1956] Ch. 622 at 633, 634; P. S. Atiyah (1958) 74 L.Q.R. 190 at 193; M. A.
Hickling (1966) 30 Conv.(N.S.) 117. Charitable funds are applicable *cy-près*: Charities Act 1960, ss.13,
14, *ante*, p. 161.
[12] *Burgess* v. *Rawnsley* [1975] Ch. 429; see *ante*, p. 36, for joint purchases.
[13] For another example, see *ante*, p. 111.
[14] *Re Foord* [1922] 2 Ch. 519. See also *King* v. *Denison* (1813) 1 V. & B. 260; *Croome* v. *Croome*
(1889) 61 L.T. 814.

the education of certain children, any surplus will be divided between the children when they become adults, the intention being to provide for the children in the manner most useful having regard to their age.[15] Furthermore, there will of course be no resulting trust where the super-added directions are mere motives for the gift not intended as express trusts.[16]

2. Failure of beneficiary's interest

(a) *Trustees.* If trustees hold property absolutely for a person living when the trust is created, and he then dies intestate leaving nobody entitled under his intestacy, there will be no resulting trust, for the settlor has parted with his whole beneficial interest. The equitable interest accordingly passes as *bona vacantia*, usually[17] to the Crown, subject to the payment of debts. This has always been the rule for personalty,[18] and for deaths occurring after 1925 is also the rule for realty.[19]

(b) *Executors.* For deaths occurring after 1925,[20] executors have lost any right they formerly had to take beneficially. The present rule is that if a testator fails to dispose of any part of his estate by will, that part will pass to the surviving spouse (if any) and other relatives entitled on intestacy, or failing them as *bona vacantia* unless the will shows that the executors are to take beneficially.

Section 2. Purchase in the Name of Another

1. Presumption of resulting trust to real purchaser

(a) *The principle.* Another common case of an implied or resulting trust is where on a purchase property is conveyed into the name of someone other than the purchaser.[21] "The clear result of all the cases, without a single exception, is, that the trust of a legal estate, whether freehold, copyhold, or leasehold; whether taken in the names of the purchasers and others jointly, or in the names of others without that of the purchaser; whether in one name or several; whether jointly or *successivè*, results to the man who advances the purchase-money. This is a general proposition supported by all the cases, and there is nothing to

---

[15] *Re Andrew's Trust* [1905] 2 Ch. 48.
[16] *Re Osoba* [1979] 1 W.L.R. 247.
[17] The Duchies of Lancaster and Cornwall are entitled to *bona vacantia* in their respective areas.
[18] See, *e.g. Re Bond* [1901] 1 Ch. 15, where the rule was applied to capital money in the hands of trustees under the Settled Land Acts 1882–90.
[19] A.E.A. 1925, ss.45, 46. For the position before 1926 see the 28th ed. of this work, p. 178.
[20] For the position before 1926, see the 28th ed. of this work, pp. 178–179.
[21] *Anon.* (1683) 2 Ventr. 361. Called "presumed resulting trusts" by Megarry J. in *Re Vandervell's Trusts (No. 2)* [1974] Ch. 269 at 294.

contradict it; and it goes on a strict analogy to the rule of common law, that where a feoffment is made without consideration, the use results to the feoffor."[22] The doctrine applies to pure personalty as well as land.[23]

(b) *Evidence.* If the advance of the purchase-money by the real purchaser does not appear on the face of the deed, and even if it is stated to have been made by the nominal purchaser (*e.g.* in the ordinary receipt in a conveyance on sale), parol evidence is admissible to prove by whom it was actually made, for such evidence in effect shows that the nominal purchaser was really the agent of the true purchaser, a purpose for which parol evidence is always admissible.[24] Even in the case of land, such evidence is admissible, for the statutory rule which requires a declaration of trust respecting the land to be manifested and proved by writing[25] does not affect the creation or operation of resulting, implied or constructive trusts.[26]

(c) *Several purchasers.* The doctrine is not confined to purchases with money provided by one person only. It also applies where two or more persons advance purchase-money jointly and the purchase is taken in the name of one only, in which case there is a resulting trust in favour of the other or others as to so much of the money as he or they advanced.[27]

(d) *Improper purposes.*[28] There is no resulting trust where it would be against public policy to permit the presumption, as where one person purchased an estate in the name of another in order to give him a vote at a parliamentary election.[29] In such a case the person in whom the property is vested holds beneficially.

2. Presumption of advancement. As the doctrine of resulting trusts is based upon the unexpressed but presumed intention of the true purchaser, it will not arise where the relation existing between the true and the nominal purchaser is such as to raise a presumption that a gift was intended.[30] This presumption of advancement, as it is called, applies to all cases in which the person providing the purchase-money is under, or expects to be under, an equitable obligation to support, or make provision for, the person to whom the property is conveyed, *i.e.* where the former is the husband or father of, or stands *in loco parentis* to, the latter.

[22] *Dyer* v. *Dyer* (1788) 2 Cox Eq. 92 at 93, *per* Eyre C.B.; **2 W. & T.L.C. 749 at 750.**
[23] *Re Scottish Equitable Life Assurance Society* [1902] 1 Ch. 282; *The Venture* [1908] P. 218.
[24] *Heard* v. *Pilley* (1869) 4 Ch.App. 548.
[25] L.P.A. 1925, s.53(1); *ante,* p. 106.
[26] L.P.A. 1925, s.53(2).
[27] *Wray* v. *Steele* (1814) 2 V. & B. 388. The sentence in the text was cited with approval in *Gissing* v. *Gissing* [1971] A.C. 886 at 902.
[28] See *ante,* p. 90 and *post,* p. 181.
[29] *Groves* v. *Groves* (1829) 3 Y. & J. 163 at 175; and see *post,* p. 181.
[30] See *Wirth* v. *Wirth* (1956) 98 C.L.R. 228 at 237; and see *Re Pauling's S.T. (No. 1)* [1964] Ch. 303 at 336.

(a) *Wife or fiancée.* Accordingly, if a man buys property and has it conveyed to his wife (or intended wife[31]), prima facie this is a gift to her; *a fortiori* if he contributes to the mortgage payments on a property owned or purchased by the wife.[32] The presumption of advancement existing at the date of the conveyance is not destroyed by the fact that the marriage does not take place,[33] or is afterwards dissolved or is declared null on some ground which made the marriage voidable only, and not void *ab initio*.[34]

On the other hand, no such presumption arises when a wife buys property and puts it in her husband's name; prima facie he holds as trustee for her.[35] Nor does it arise when the purchaser makes the purchase in the name of a woman with whom he has contracted an illegal marriage,[36] or with whom he is cohabiting without any marriage at all.[37] And where a wife mortgages her property for her own purposes and the husband joins as surety,[38] or where the husband guarantees the wife's bank account,[39] no presumption of advancement normally[40] arises if he is afterwards obliged to pay under his guarantee; he can therefore require her to repay him.

(b) *Legitimate child.* Similarly, if a father buys property and has it put in the name of his son or daughter, prima facie it is a gift to the child.[41] Again, where a father pays the premiums of an insurance policy which he holds on trust for his son, the payments will prima facie be taken as advancements and not as payments made *qua* trustee in order to maintain the trust property for which he could claim indemnity.[42] But there is no presumption of advancement where a father-in-law transfers property to his son-in-law,[43] nor where an uncle purchases land in the name of a nephew[44]; and the result has been held to be the same where a mother made a purchase in the name of her child, on the ground that, whether the father was alive or not, she was under no equitable obligation which would raise the presumption.[45] If this is so, the question does not appear to be affected by the fact that statute[46] has now imposed upon a married woman who has property an obligation to

---

[31] *Moate* v. *Moate* [1948] 2 All E.R. 486; *Wirth* v. *Wirth* (1956) 98 C.L.R. 228.
[32] *Silver* v. *Silver* [1958] 1 W.L.R. 259; *Richards* v. *Richards* [1958] 1 W.L.R. 1116.
[33] Law Reform (Miscellaneous Provisions) Act 1970, s.2(1), as explained in *Mossop* v. *Mossop* [1989] Fam. 77, where at p. 84 this passage was cited.
[34] *Thornley* v. *Thornley* [1893] 2 Ch. 229; *Dunbar* v. *Dunbar* [1909] 2 Ch. 639; and see *Silver* v. *Silver* [1958] 1 W.L.R. 259.
[35] *Mercier* v. *Mercier* [1903] 2 Ch. 98.
[36] *Soar* v. *Foster* (1858) 4 K. & J. 152 (deceased wife's sister).
[37] *Rider* v. *Kidder* (1805) 10 Ves. 360.
[38] *Re Salisbury-Jones* [1938] 3 All E.R. 459.
[39] *Anson* v. *Anson* [1953] 1 Q.B. 636.
[40] See *Anson* v. *Anson, supra*, at pp. 641, 645.
[41] *Dyer* v. *Dyer* (1788) 2 Cox Eq. 92; **2 W. & T.L.C. 749**; and see *Shephard* v. *Cartwright* [1955] A.C. 431.
[42] *Re Roberts, Public Trustee* v. *Roberts* [1946] Ch. 1; and see *post*, pp. 248, 257.
[43] *Knight* v. *Biss* [1954] N.Z.L.R. 55.
[44] *Drury* v. *Drury* (1675) 73 S.S. 205.
[45] *Bennet* v. *Bennet* (1879) 10 Ch.D. 474; *Re De Visme* (1864) 2 De G.J. & S. 17. But see *contra, Sayre* v. *Hughes* (1868) L.R. 5 Eq. 376; *Garrett* v. *Wilkinson* (1848) 2 De G. & Sm. 244; and see *Edwards* v. *Bradley* [1956] O.R. 225.
[46] National Assistance Act 1948, s.42(1), replacing the Poor Law Act 1930, s.14(4).

maintain her husband and children, for the matter is merely one of equitable obligation. Yet doubtless very little evidence would suffice to rebut the presumption (if it exists) of a resulting trust in favour of a mother, whether widowed or not; and on slender evidence a widowed mother has been held to be *in loco parentis* to a son of hers.[47]

(c) *Quasi-child.* Lastly, there is a presumption of a gift if the true purchaser stands *in loco parentis* to the nominal purchaser, *i.e* if he has taken upon himself the duty of providing for the child in life.[48] Thus the facts of the case may show that a man is *in loco parentis* to an illegitimate son,[49] to a stepson,[50] or to a grandchild whose father is dead.[51]

An advancement may be effective and beyond recall by the settlor even before there has been any transfer of the property concerned, as where H makes an irrevocable contract with X that X will make certain payments at future dates to H's wife.[52]

3. Rebutting the presumptions

(a) *Evidence of intention.* Both the presumption of a resulting trust and the presumption of advancement can be rebutted by evidence of the actual intention of the purchaser. Indeed, in the case of an asset purchased for the joint use of husband and wife, the presumption of advancement is readily rebutted.[53] The clearest evidence is an express declaration of trust on the face of the conveyance of the legal estate,[54] but even where this is absent the court puts itself in the position of a a jury, and considers all the circumstances of the case, so as to arrive at the purchaser's real intention; it is only where there is no evidence to contradict it that the presumption of a resulting trust, or of advancement, as the case may be, will prevail.[55]

(b) *Acts and declarations admissible.* The acts and declarations of the parties before or at the time of the purchase, or so immediately after it as to constitute a part of the transaction, are admissible in evidence either for or against the party who did the act or made the declaration; subsequent acts and declarations are only admissible as evidence against the party who made them, and not in his favour.[56] Thus, if a father buys

---

[47] *Re Orme* (1883) 50 L.T. 51.
[48] See *Bennet* v. *Bennet, supra; post,* p. 522.
[49] *Beckford* v. *Beckford* (1774) Lofft 490. See also *Currant* v. *Jago* (1844) 1 Coll.C.C. 261; *Soar* v. *Foster* (1858) 4 K. & J. 152 at 160.
[50] *Re Paradise Motor Co. Ltd.* [1968] 1 W.L.R. 1125, where at p. 1139 the discussion in this subsection of the text was referred to with approval.
[51] *Ebrand* v. *Dancer* (1680) 2 Ch.Ca. 26.
[52] *Re Schebsman* [1944] Ch. 83 at 93.
[53] See *post,* p. 185.
[54] See *post,* p. 185.
[55] *Fowkes* v. *Pascoe* (1875) 10 Ch.App. 343.
[56] *Shephard* v. *Cartwright* [1955] A.C. 431, where this passage was cited by Viscount Simonds with approval at p. 445.

property, and has it conveyed into the name of his son, the father's declaration at the time of the purchase that he wished the son to hold as trustee for him would be admissible to rebut the presumption of advancement; but although the father's subsequent declarations could be used by the son to support the presumption of advancement, they could not be used in evidence by the father to rebut it.[57] On the other hand, the subsequent acts and declarations of the son may be used against him by the father, and may rebut the presumption of advancement if there is insufficient evidence of the intention of the father at the time of the purchase to counteract the effect of those acts or declarations.[58] The fact that the son permits the father to receive the profits of the property has been said to be no evidence against him, for it is an "act of reverence and good manners"[59]; but it is otherwise if the father retains the title deeds.[60]

(c) *Improper purposes.*[61] The presumptions are not rebuttable by evidence of an improper purpose. Thus where a husband puts property into his wife's name, he cannot be heard to say that he did so to defeat his creditors,[62] or to evade government restrictions[63] or taxes, whether British[64] or foreign,[65] and that his wife knew this.[66] The rules of equity cannot be used to aid iniquity, and the presumptions will apply unless a proper ground for rebutting them is both pleaded[67] and proved.[68] If the illegal purpose has not been carried out, it seems that the husband can rebut the presumption and recover the property.[69] It is otherwise if the property has been purchased to allow the grantee to effect an illegal purpose, for it no longer rests with the grantor to abandon the intended purpose.[70]

(d) *Rebutting circumstances.* It used to be considered that if a child had already been fully advanced and provided for, that was a strong circumstance against the presumption of a further advance in his favour; but little weight is now given to this, for the father is the sole judge of

[57] *Stock* v. *McAvoy* (1872) L.R. 15 Eq. 55; *Reddington* v. *Reddington* (1794) 3 Ridg.P.C. 106 at 182, 195; *Sidmouth* v. *Sidmouth* (1840) 2 Beav. 447.
[58] *Scawin* v. *Scawin* (1841) 1 Y. & C.C.C. 65.
[59] *Lord Grey* v. *Lady Grey* (1677) 2 Swans. 594 at 600, *per* Lord Finch L.C. (later Earl of Nottingham); and see *Batstone* v. *Salter* (1875) 10 Ch.App. 431; *Commissioner of Stamp Duties* v. *Byrnes* [1911] A.C. 386.
[60] *Warren* v. *Gurney* [1944] 2 All E.R. 472.
[61] See also *ante,* pp. 90, 178.
[62] *Gascoigne* v. *Gascoigne* [1918] 1 K.B. 223; *Tinker* v. *Tinker* [1970] P. 136; *Cantor* v. *Cox* (1975) 239 E.G. 121 (mistress).
[63] *Chettiar* v. *Chettiar* [1962] A.C. 294 (father and son).
[64] *Re Emery's Investment Trusts* [1959] Ch. 410 at 419, 420.
[65] *Re Emery's Investment Trusts* [1959] Ch. 410 (United States withholding tax).
[66] *Gascoigne* v. *Gascoigne, supra.* Contrast *Heseltine* v. *Heseltine* [1971] 1 W.L.R. 342 (no gift where wife innocently allowed herself to be persuaded to transfer funds to her husband "for estate duty purposes").
[67] *Haigh* v. *Kaye* (1872) 7 Ch.App. 469.
[68] *Chettiar* v. *Chettiar, supra*; and see (1962) 78 L.Q.R. 171.
[69] *Perpetual Executors and Trustees Association of Australia Ltd.* v. *Wright* (1917) 23 C.L.R. 185; *Birch* v. *Blagrave* (1755) Ambl. 264.
[70] *Groves* v. *Groves* (1829) 4 Y. & J. 163 at 174, 175, *ante,* p. 178.

the amount of a child's provision.[71] The fact that a son is acting as his father's solicitor would be sufficient to rebut the presumption of advancement, unless the rest of the evidence shows an intention to make a gift[72]; and the circumstances may show that the property was put in another's name merely for convenience,[73] as where a husband in failing health opened a bank account in the joint names of himself and his wife shortly before his death.[74]

Section 3. Resulting Trust on a Voluntary Conveyance

A third head of implied trusts consists of cases where the existing owner of property makes a voluntary transfer of it to another. In most ways this resembles the previous head, *i.e.* that of a purchaser of property having it put into the name of another; but the law is less clear, and there are some special difficulties. Where the transfer is made by a husband, father or person *in loco parentis*, there is in any case a presumption of advancement.[75] What is less clear is how far in other cases there is any presumption of a resulting trust. Subject to statute, prima facie there is[76]; but land and pure personalty must be considered separately.

1. Land

(a) *Before 1926.* Before 1926, if A conveyed freehold land to B without consideration and without expressing a use in favour of B, a resulting use was implied in favour of A. This use was executed (*i.e.* turned into a legal estate) by the Statute of Uses 1535, so that the conveyance passed no interest to B. It was therefore the practice of conveyancers before 1926 to make A convey "unto and to the use of" B. The expression of a use in favour of B prevented any resulting use being implied in favour of A; B took the legal estate, and the equitable interest also unless a trust was engrafted on the use.[77]

(b) *After 1925.* As the Statute of Uses 1535 was repealed as from January 1, 1926, a legal estate in freehold land can now be conveyed by a voluntary conveyance without stating that the land is conveyed to the use of the grantee. Nor need a use be expressed in order to prevent a resulting trust from arising, for it is now provided[78] that in a voluntary

---

[71] *Hepworth* v. *Hepworth* (1870) L.R. 11 Eq. 10.
[72] *Garrett* v. *Wilkinson* (1848) 2 De G. & Sm. 244.
[73] *Hoddinott* v. *Hoddinott* [1949] 2 K.B. 406.
[74] *Marshall* v. *Crutwell* (1875) L.R. 20 Eq. 328. Contrast *Re Figgis* [1969] 1 Ch. 123, where the initial ground of convenience had long ended.
[75] See, *e.g.* *Crabb* v. *Crabb* (1834) 1 My. & K. 511; *Batstone* v. *Salter* (1875) 10 Ch.App. 431.
[76] See, *e.g.* *Coultwas* v. *Swan* (1871) 19 W.R. 485, affirming (1870) 18 W.R. 746; *Rudkin* v. *Dolman* (1876) 35 L.T. 791.
[77] But see Maitland's *Lectures on Equity* (2nd. ed., 1936), p. 77, to the contrary.
[78] L.P.A. 1925, s.60(3).

conveyance a resulting trust for the grantor is not to be implied "merely by reason that the property is not expressed to be conveyed for the use or benefit of the grantee." It thus appears that on a voluntary conveyance of freeholds, no resulting trust in favour of the grantor arises unless the property is expressly given on trusts which do not exhaust the whole beneficial interest.[79] And this seems to be so as regards leaseholds also, for the section appears to apply to them.

(c) *Joint transfer.*   Where land is transferred by A to A and B jointly for no consideration, there is even less occasion for a resulting trust to A alone. Subject to any express declaration of trust, the land will be held on trust for sale, and the proceeds of sale and the income until sale will be held for A and B as joint tenants.[80]

2. Pure personalty

(a) *General.*   As regards property other than land, the law appears to be otherwise. On a voluntary transfer of pure personalty, the better opinion is that the transferee is presumed to hold on a resulting trust for the transferor unless the transferor is the husband or the father of the transferee, or *in loco parentis* to him; this presumption is, however, rebuttable.[81]

(b) *Joint transfer.*   There is certainly a presumption of a resulting trust if A transfers stocks and shares voluntarily to himself and B.[82] Thus in *Re Vinogradoff*,[83] A transferred some War Loan into the joint names of herself and her granddaughter who was four years old and to whom A was not *in loco parentis*.[84] Farwell J. held that there was a presumption that A intended the stock to be held on trust for herself, but surprisingly held that this was not rebutted by the circumstances; and in a later case this principle made a boy of six and a girl of two trustees for their aunt.[85] The unsatisfactory nature of these decisions is best expressed in the language of James L.J. in a similar case which was not cited. He asked whether it was "possible to reconcile with mental sanity" the theory that the donor put the property "into the names of herself and [the child] as trustees upon trust for herself? .What trust— what object is there conceivable in doing this?"[86] And Mellish L.J.

---

[79] In *Hodgson* v. *Marks* [1971] Ch. 892 at 933 the question was described, *obiter*, as "debatable," but L.P.A. 1925, s.60(3) was not there under consideration.

[80] L.P.A. 1925, s.36(1).

[81] See *Fowkes* v. *Pascoe* (1875) 10 Ch.App. 343 at 345, 348; *Lloyd* v. *Spillit* (1740) Barn.C. 384; *George* v. *Howard* (1819) 7 Price 646 at 651; *Re Howes* (1905) 21 T.L.R. 501; *Re Muller* [1953] N.Z.L.R. 879.

[82] *Standing* v. *Bowring* (1885) 31 Ch.D. 282 at 287.

[83] [1935] W.N. 68.

[84] Although after 1925 a minor cannot be *appointed* a trustee, he or she may hold, *e.g.* on a resulting trust; see *post*, p. 199.

[85] *Re Muller* [1953] N.Z.L.R. 879.

[86] *Fowkes* v. *Pascoe* (1875) 10 Ch.App. 343 at 348.

asked whether anything could "be more absurd" than to suppose such a trust.[87]

(c) *Presumption rebutted.*   Where in the case of a joint transfer from A to A and B the presumption of resulting trust is rebutted, an issue arises as to be interest taken by B. There are three main possibilities. First, there may be an immediate gift to A and B jointly. Secondly, and more usually,[88] there may be a gift of the capital to B if he survives A, with A having the right to the income for the rest of his life. Thirdly, there may be merely a gift to B of such part of the capital as remains on A's death, A retaining the power to withdraw some or all of it during his life. It is a question of intention to be inferred from the circumstances and the nature of the property. If it is stock that is given, A may retain the right to the dividends but lose the power to dispose of the capital.[89] If it is money paid into a joint bank account. A will probably retain power to withdraw some or all of it during his life[90]; the gift to B may be explicable as being "an immediate gift of a fluctuating and defeasible asset consisting of the chose in action for the time being constituting the balance in the bank account."[91]

Section 4. Acquisition for Joint Use

1. Introduction.   A development from the trust which frequently results from a purchase in the name of another is the implied (or constructive)[92] trust which may arise where a house is purchased for the joint *use* of two or more persons. They are often husband and wife or cohabiting partners. There is, however, no special category of "family assets" or "family property."[93] Hence unless a property transfer order or similar relief is being sought in matrimonial proceedings,[94] a remedy only available to those who are or have been married,[95] the interests of such joint occupiers fall to be determined by the same principles whatever the relationship (if any) between them.[96] The principles most generally applicable are of trusts rather than of contracts,[97] though the latter are not without relevance.[98] Even so, cases under this head cannot be justly resolved by a simple application of the presumptions. In the

---

[87] *Fowkes* v. *Pascoe* (1873) 10 Ch.App. 343 at 353.
[88] See *ibid.*, at p. 351.
[89] *Fowkes* v. *Pascoe* (1875) 10 Ch.App. 343; *Standing* v. *Bowring* (1885) 31 Ch.D. 282.
[90] *Re Harrison, Day* v. *Harrison* (1920) 90 L.J.Ch. 186; *Russell* v. *Scott* (1936) 55 C.L.R. 440; *Re Figgis* [1969] 1 Ch. 123; and see *Young* v. *Sealey* [1949] Ch. 278 (no conflict with the Wills Act 1837).
[91] *Re Figgis, supra,* at p. 149, *per* Megarry J.; see generally M. C. Cullity (1969) 85 L.Q.R. 530.
[92] See *Gissing* v. *Gissing* [1971] A.C. 886 at 905.
[93] See *Pettitt* v. *Pettitt* [1970] A.C. 777 at 809, 810, 817; *Gissing* v. *Gissing* [1971] A.C. 886 at 899, 904; *Cowcher* v. *Cowcher* [1972] 1 W.L.R. 425 at 429; *Grant* v. *Edwards* [1986] Ch. 638 at 651.
[94] See Matrimonial Causes Act 1973, ss.21–40; *Wachtel* v. *Wachtel* [1973] Fam. 72.
[95] *Mossop* v. *Mossop* [1989] Fam. 77.
[96] See *Pettit* v. *Pettitt, supra,* at pp. 803, 813; *Gissing* v. *Gissing, supra,* at p. 899. See generally A. A. S. Zuckerman (1978) 94 L.Q.R. 26; (1980) 96 L.Q.R. 248, esp. at 251–260.
[97] See *Gissing* v. *Gissing, supra,* at pp. 896, 900, 902, 904, 905.
[98] See *Grant* v. *Edwards, supra,* at pp. 651, 652.

first place; as will be seen, contributions to the purchase price, though important, are not essential to qualify for an interest. Secondly, under modern conditions, with the reduction of the wife's economic dependence on her husband,[99] the force of the presumption of advancement is much weakened.[1]

2. Express trusts. If the party or parties providing the purchase moneys have expressly declared trusts on which the property is to be held, in the conveyance or elsewhere, then in the absence of fraud or mistake the declaration will be decisive, and any implied or resulting trust excluded.[2] Further, a declaration that the parties are to hold beneficially as joint tenants will, on severance, lead automatically to their holding as tenants in common in equal shares and not in some other shares based, *e.g.* on contributions.[3] Even if the declaration of trust is contained in an instrument not executed by the beneficiaries, as commonly occurs in a transfer of registered land executed only by the vendor, it may nonetheless be evidence of an agreement as to how the property is to be held,[4] and, moreover, if it appears that the declaration was inserted with the consent or on the instructions of the purchasers it will probably be conclusive.[5] The mere imposition of the trusts for sale imported by statute[6] does not preclude the setting up of an implied or resulting trust.[7]

3. Conditions for acquisition of interest. In the absence of an express trust, or the absence of any direct contribution to the purchase price so as to give rise to a resulting trust, a claimant may nevertheless acquire an interest if she can establish "a common intention between her and the defendant, acted on by her, that she should have a beneficial interest in the property."[8] Three related questions arise: first, whether there is an intention that each party is to have an interest in the property; secondly, whether the party not having the legal title has acted to his or her detriment; and thirdly, what is the size of the interest each party is to have. In all these questions the making of contributions to the purchase price is relevant though not essential. The principles which

---

[99] Yet even today, in the words of Simon P. quoted by Lord Hodson in *Pettitt* v. *Pettitt* [1970] A.C. 777 at 811, "The cock can feather the nest because he does not have to spend most of his time sitting on it."

[1] See *Pettitt* v. *Pettitt* [1970] A.C. 777 at 793, 811, 815 ("in the absence of all evidence": *per* Lord Upjohn), 824; *Silver* v. *Silver* [1958] 1 W.L.R. 259 at 261, 265; *Fish* v. *Fish* (1965) 110 S.J. 228; *Falconer* v. *Falconer* [1970] 1 W.L.R. 1333; *Gissing* v. *Gissing* [1971] A.C. 886 at 907; and see S. Cretney (1971) 115 S.J. 614 at 616.

[2] *Pettitt* v. *Pettitt* [1970] A.C. 777 at 813; *Goodman* v. *Gallant* [1986] Fam. 106, reviewing earlier authority and disapproving dicta in *Bedson* v. *Bedson* [1965] 2 Q.B. 666 at 681, 682, 685. For rectification, see *post*, p. 626; *Wilson* v. *Wilson* [1969] 1 W.L.R. 1470.

[3] *Goodman* v. *Gallant* [1986] Fam. 106, esp. at 118, 119.

[4] *Re Gorman (a bankrupt)* [1990] 1 W.L.R. 616, not following *Robinson* v. *Robinson* (1976) 241 E.G. 153.

[5] *Pink* v. *Lawrence* (1977) 36 P. & C.R. 98 at 101.

[6] L.P.A. 1925, ss.34–36.

[7] *Goodman* v. *Gallant, supra*, at pp. 110, 111.

[8] *Grant* v. *Edwards* [1986] Ch. 638 at 646, 647, *per* Nourse L.J. (H.L. refused leave to appeal: [1988] 1 W.L.R. 629).

apply are closely akin to those underlying the doctrine of proprietary estoppel.[9] In both the claimant must have acted to his detriment in reliance on the belief that he would obtain an interest.[10] In both equity acts on the conscience of the legal owner to prevent him from defeating the common intention.[11]

(a) *Intention.* The actual or presumed intention of the parties at the time of acquisition is of critical importance.[12]

(1) AGREEMENT "The first and fundamental question" is whether "there has at any time prior to acquisition, or exceptionally at some later date, been any agreement, arrangement or understanding" reached between the parties sharing the house as their home "that the property is to be shared beneficially."[12a] Accordingly, an express agreement at that time that the party is to have an interest[13] will be conclusive,[14] as will normally[15] an oral declaration by the party having the legal title. Such a declaration may be direct,[16] or may be inferred from a reason or excuse for not putting the other party's name on the title.[17] The finding of an agreement or arrangement to share the beneficial interest in the house can only "be based on evidence of express discussions between the partners, however imperfectly remembered and however imprecise their terms may have been."[18]

(2) CONDUCT. Where there is no evidence to support a finding of an agreement or arrangement, as happens in the majority of cases,[19] the intention to share the beneficial interest may be inferred from the parties' conduct "almost always from the expenditure incurred by them respectively" being "expenditure referable to the acquisition of the house."[20] Thus for this purpose[21] expenditure on furniture and household expenses cannot be taken into account,[22] much less

---

[9] For proprietary estoppel, see *post*, pp. 573 *et seq.*

[10] *Grant* v. *Edwards* [1986] Ch. 638 at 656, 657; *Lloyds Bank plc.* v. *Rosset* [1990] 2 W.L.R. 867 at 877.

[11] *Grant* v. *Edwards, supra,* at p. 656; and see *Maharaj* v. *Chand* [1986] A.C. 898 at 907, 908; *Re Basham* [1986] 1 W.L.R. 1498 at 1504.

[12] See *Pettitt* v. *Pettitt* [1970] A.C. 777 at 800, 813; *Re Rogers' Question* [1948] 1 All E.R. 328; *Rimmer* v. *Rimmer* [1953] 1 Q.B. 63; *Bristol and West B.S.* v. *Henning* [1985] 1 W.L.R. 778.

[12a] *Lloyds Bank plc* v. *Rosset* [1990] 2 W.L.R. 867 at 877, *per* Lord Bridge.

[13] As in *Eves* v. *Eves* [1975] 1 W.L.R. 1338; contrast *Tanner* v. *Tanner* [1975] 1 W.L.R. 1346 where the agreement was for a licence only.

[14] The distinction taken in *Cowcher* v. *Cowcher* [1972] 1 W.L.R. 425 at 436 (and approved in *Re Nicholson, Nicholson* v. *Perks* [1974] 1 W.L.R. 476 at 480) between an agreement as to contributions (money consensus) and as to interest (interest consensus) appears to be unsound: *Re Densham* [1975] 1 W.L.R. 1519 at 1525. Though *Cowcher* v. *Cowcher* was apparently not cited in *Grant* v. *Edwards* [1986] Ch. 638, the reasoning is inconsistent with any such distinction.

[15] Contrast *Midland Bank plc* v. *Dobson* [1986] 1 F.L.R. 171 where the declaration was rejected as self-serving recollection.

[16] See *Grant* v. *Edwards* [1986] Ch. 638 at 651, 652.

[17] As in *Eves* v. *Eves* [1975] 1 W.L.R. 1338 (too young); *Grant* v. *Edwards* [1986] Ch. 638 (would prejudice ancillary divorce proceedings).

[18] *Lloyds Bank plc* v. *Rosset, supra,* at p. 877, *per* Lord Bridge.

[19] See *Gissing* v. *Gissing* [1971] A.C. 886 at 906; *Grant* v. *Edwards* [1986] Ch. 638 at 647.

[20] *Grant* v. *Edwards* [1986] Ch. 638 at 647, *per* Nourse L.J.

[21] See below for possible relevance.

[22] *Burns* v. *Burns* [1984] Ch. 317; *Richards* v. *Dove* [1974] 1 All E.R. 888.

decorating the house and supervising the carrying out of repairs in it,[23] doing housework and bringing up a family.[24] Indeed, it seems that such expenditure cannot be taken into account even though it thereby assists the other party in paying the costs of acquisition. "Direct contributions to the purchase price by the partner who is not the legal owner, whether initially or by payment of mortgage payments, will readily justify the inference necessary to the creation of a constructive trust." But it is "extremely doubtful whether anything less will do."[25] Further, a payment made after a house has been acquired and paid for is not referable to its acquisition, albeit the payment was derived from the proceeds of sale of a former matrimonial home.[26] If the common intention is or includes an intention that the price should be raised on mortgage, the mortgagee will take free of the respective interests of both parties.[27]

(b) *Detriment.* An oral declaration of the parties' common intention would not suffice without more, as such a declaration could only take effect as an express trust and would need to be in writing.[28] Yet if the other party has acted on the declaration, even before completion of the purchase,[29] equity will not allow the legal owner to deny the interest so declared.[30] Frequently such acting takes the form of making contributions to the acquisition of the house, and thus the expenditure may perform "the twofold functions of establishing the common intention and showing how the claimant has acted upon it."[31] But expenditure which suffices to raise the equity following a voluntary oral declaration need not necessarily be referable to the acquisition of the house.[32] Indeed, conduct other than expenditure of money may suffice, such as the carrying out of works of improvement.[33] The sort of conduct required is that on which a claimant "could not reasonably have been expected to embark unless she was to have an interest in the house."[34] Thus even if she was not to have an interest, she could normally be expected to go and live in the house and fulfil the role of a wife, but not carry out substantial works of repair and improvement.[35]

Where there is no common intention at the time of the accquisition that the claimant is to have an interest, then in the absence of subsequent agreement or estoppel[36] a person who does work on the

---

[23] *Lloyds Bank plc* v. *Rosset* [1990] 2 W.L.R. 867; and see *Thomas* v. *Fuller-Brown* [1988] 1 F.L.R. 237.

[24] *Burns* v. *Burns, supra; Pettitt* v. *Pettitt* [1970] A.C. 777 at 811; *Button* v. *Button* [1968] 1 W.L.R. 457 (H.L. refused leave to appeal: *ibid.* p. 1961); *Coombes* v. *Smith* [1986] 1 W.L.R. 808.

[25] *Lloyds Bank plc* v. *Rosset, supra,* at p. 877, *per* Lord Bridge.

[26] *Winkworth* v. *Edward Baron Development Co. Ltd.* [1986] 1 W.L.R. 1512.

[27] *Bristol and West B.S.* v. *Henning* [1985] 1 W.L.R. 778.

[28] *Midland Bank plc* v. *Dobson* [1986] 1 F.L.R. 171.

[29] *Lloyds Bank plc* v. *Rosset* [1989] Ch. 350, reversed on grounds not affecting this point: [1990] 2 W.L.R. 867.

[30] *Grant* v. *Edwards* [1986] Ch. 638 at 647, 651, 656.

[31] *Ibid.* at p. 647, *per* Nourse L.J.

[32] *Ibid.* at pp. 647, 648.

[33] As in *Eves* v. *Eves* [1975] 1 W.L.R. 1338.

[34] *Grant* v. *Edwards, supra,* at p. 648, *per* Nourse L.J.

[35] See *Grant* v. *Edwards, supra,* at p. 657.

[36] For estoppel, see *post,* p. 573.

property, of another, or expends money on improving it, has no claim upon the property.[37] However, as between husband and wife statute has now confirmed one line[38] of previous authority[39] that where one of them contributes in money or money's worth to the improvement of real or personal property in which the other is beneficially interested, or both are, then if the contribution "is of a substantial nature"[40] the party contributing is to be treated (subject to any express or implied agreement to the contrary) as having thereby acquired a share or enlarged share in the property.[41] In default of agreement, the amount of the share will be such as in all the circumstances seems just to the court which deals with the question.[42]

(c) *Nature and size of interest.* Occasionally the proper inference from the facts proved may be that the common intention of the parties was that they should have successive interests in the property.[43] Usually, however, both take immediate beneficial interests in the proceeds of sale, the respective shares to be taken being those which the parties intended.[44] This intention may be clear from the outset as where there is an agreement or declaration as to the shares,[45] or may be inferred from subsequent conduct, as where the proceeds of sale or insurance money are divided.[46] In such situations the amount of the respective contributions, much less the amount of any work done,[46a] is irrelevant.[47] But where the common intention is to be inferred from the making of the contributions (including later contributions)[48] the respective interests, as in resulting trusts, will be in proportion to the contributions.[49] Where the contributions take the form of labour or are indirect this can present very difficult questions of fact.[50] In the last resort, and where each party has made a substantial but unascertainable contribution, the maxim "equality is equity"[51] will be applied.[52] The shares once ascertained are absolute and indefeasible,[53] whether they arise under express[54] or implied trusts.[55] They are not liable to be

[37] *Pettitt* v. *Pettitt* [1970] A.C. 777; *post,* p. 467.
[38] Represented by *Jansen* v. *Jansen* [1965] P. 478.
[39] *Davis* v. *Vale* [1971] 1 W.L.R. 1022.
[40] As in *Re Nicholson, Nicholson* v. *Perks* [1974] 1 W.L.R. 476 (central heating).
[41] Matrimonial Proceedings and Property Act 1970, s.37. For the computation of the enlarged share, see *Re Nicholson, Nicholson* v. *Perks, supra,* at pp. 482, 483.
[42] *Ibid.* The court should not make a separate order under this provision when it is dealing with a general claim for ancillary relief consequent on divorce proceedings; *Griffiths* v. *Griffiths* [1974] 1 W.L.R. 1350.
[43] *Ungurian* v. *Lesnoff* [1990] Ch. 206.
[44] *Grant* v. *Edwards* [1986] Ch. 638 at 657.
[45] As in *Goodman* v. *Gallant* [1986] Fam. 106.
[46] *Grant* v. *Edwards* [1986] Ch. 638.
[46a] *Lloyds Bank plc.* v. *Rosset* [1990] 2 W.L.R. 867 at 878.
[47] See *Goodman* v. *Gallant, supra,* at pp. 110, 111.
[48] *Bernard* v. *Josephs* [1982] Ch. 391.
[49] See *ante,* p. 178.
[50] As in *Eves* v. *Eves* [1975] 1 W.L.R. 1338.
[51] See *ante,* pp. 36 *et seq.* (esp. at p. 38).
[52] *Rimmer* v. *Rimmer* [1953] 1 Q.B. 63; *Fribance* v. *Fribance (No. 2)* [1957] 1 W.L.R. 384; see *Gissing* v. *Gissing* [1971] A.C. 886 at 897, 903, 908.
[53] *Turton* v. *Turton* [1988] Ch. 542 at 552, following *Walker* v. *Hall* [1984] F.L.R. 126.
[54] As in *Turton* v. *Turton* [1988] Ch. 542.
[55] *Turton* v. *Turton, supra,* at p. 554.

diminished or defeated by some subsequent event, such as separation of the couple. Consequently the full value of the share is payable when the property is sold or otherwise realised,[56] subject only to such credits as may by allowed by way of equitable accounting, *e.g.* in respect of mortgage payments made after one party has ceased to live in the house.[57]

(d) *Contributions.* From the foregoing discussion it will be seen that contributions made by the claimant may be relevant for four different purposes[58]: (1) in the absence of direct evidence of intention, as evidence from which intention can be inferred; (2) as corroboration of direct evidence of intention; (3) as evidence of the acting by the claimant in reliance on the intention; (4) to quantify the size of the beneficial interest. Save in some cases under the third head,[59] the contributions must be contributions to the purchase price or other costs of acquisition.[60] They include mortgage payments agreed to be made.[61] Also a contribution may consist of a discount allowed to a sitting tenant.[62] But contributing to rent gives no right to share in a long lease for which a premium has been paid.[63] Further, the payment must have been intended as a contribution and not, *e.g.* as a loan which has been applied towards the purchase price.[64] The contribution may, however, at least for some purposes, be future or indirect or both.

(1) FUTURE CONTRIBUTIONS. Payment of the mortgage instalments as they fall due by one or other of the parties while they are still living together in the house[65] normally[66] suffices to give the party paying them an interest in proportion to the contributions.[67] In such cases the contributions are made pursuant to an obligation undertaken at the time of acquisition.[68] Similarly, works of improvement to the property which were contemplated at the time of acquisition and which are subsequently carried out or paid for by the non-owning party may give him an interest.[69] Where there are more than two occupants, one of whom dies, payments by the survivor may continue to be taken into account.[70]

---

[56] *Turton* v. *Turton* [1988] Ch. 542, disapproving *Hall* v. *Hall* (1982) 3 F.L.R. 379; and see *Gordon* v. *Douce* [1983] 1 W.L.R. 563. In so far as this last case suggests the court has a discretion to order valuation at an earlier date, it would not be followed.
[57] See *post*, p.640.
[58] *Grant* v. *Edwards* [1986] Ch. 638 at 655.
[59] See *ante*, p. 187.
[60] Costs as well as price are taken into account: see, *e.g. Re Densham* [1975] 1 W.L.R. 1519 at 1524, 1531.
[61] *Bernard* v. *Josephs* [1982] Ch. 391 at 403, 404; *Marsh* v. *Von Sternberg* (1986) 16 Fam. Law 160.
[62] *Marsh* v. *Von Sternberg* (1986) 16 Fam. Law 160.
[63] *Savage* v. *Dunningham* [1974] Ch. 181.
[64] See *Re Sharpe* [1980] 1 W.L.R. 219; *Hoare* v. *Hoare* (1983) 13 Fam. Law 142. But see *Hussey* v. *Palmer* [1972] 1 W.L.R. 1286.
[65] *Finch* v. *Finch* (1975) 119 S.J. 793. See *post*, p. 640 for the effect of repayments after separation.
[66] See the survey in *Gissing* v. *Gissing* [1971] A.C. 886 at 907–909.
[67] *Re Rogers' Question* [1948] 1 All E.R. 328; *Heseltine* v. *Heseltine* [1971] 1 W.L.R. 342; *Cowcher* v. *Cowcher* [1972] 1 W.L.R. 425.
[68] See *Cowcher* v. *Cowcher* [1972] 1 W.L.R. 425 at 432.
[69] *Smith* v. *Baker* [1970] 1 W.L.R. 1160; *Eves* v. *Eves* [1975] 1 W.L.R. 1338.
[70] *Passee* v. *Passee* (1988) 18 Fam. Law 132.

(2) INDIRECT CONTRIBUTIONS. Contributions are indirect where one party pays or bears expenses which the other would otherwise have to pay, and which enable him the better to pay for the property.[71] Thus where a wife helps her husband regularly and continuously in his business for small wages or none, she will be regarded as having an interest in the business and hence in any house or other property purchased out of profits.[72] In the more usual case, where one spouse has paid the mortgage instalments for the house but the other has borne the joint living expenses the courts have sometimes, but not inevitably,[73] found an intention that the other is to be treated as having made a contribution, albeit indirect, to the purchase of the house.[74] But for the future it is most unlikely that an intention will be inferred from this form of contribution.[75] It may, however, be evidence of acting in reliance on an intention established directly.[76]

Section 5. Mutual Wills

1. Mutuality. Where two persons make an arrangement as to the disposal of their property and execute mutual wills[77] in pursuance thereof, the one who predeceases the other without having departed from the arrangement has performed his part of the bargain, and dies with the implied promise of the survivor that it shall hold good.[78] Usually the parties give each other a life interest with remainders over to the same person[79] but they may give each other an absolute interest with a substitutional gift in the event of the other's prior death.[80] The arrangement will not be presumed from the simultaneous execution of virtually identical wills[81] but must be proved by independent evidence of

---

[71] See *Gissing* v. *Gissing* [1970] A.C. 886 at 896, 903, 908.

[72] *Nixon* v. *Nixon* [1969] 1 W.L.R. 1676; *Muetzel* v. *Muetzel* [1970] 1 W.L.R. 188; *Re Cummins* [1972] Ch. 62.

[73] See *Gissing* v. *Gissing* [1971] A.C. 886; *Burns* v. *Burns* [1984] Ch. 317; *Howard* v. *Jones* (1989) 19 Fam. Law 231; *ante*, p. 189.

[74] *Chapman* v. *Chapman* [1969] 1 W.L.R. 1367; *Gissing* v. *Gissing, supra*, at pp. 896, 897, 903, 908, 909; and see *Fribance* v. *Fribance (No. 2)* [1957] 1 W.L.R. 384 at 387; *Allen* v. *Allen* [1961] 1 W.L.R. 1186 (further proceedings: (1962) 106 S.J. 174); *Hargrave* v. *Newton* [1971] 1 W.L.R. 1611, where some of the expenditure preceded the purchase: see *Cowcher* v. *Cowcher* [1972] 1 W.L.R. 425 at 439; *Hazell* v. *Hazell* [1972] 1 W.L.R. 301.

[75] See *Lloyds Bank plc.* v. *Rosset* [1990] 2 W.L.R. 867 at 877, *ante*, p. 187.

[76] As in *Grant* v. *Edwards* [1986] Ch. 638. See *ante*, pp. 186, 187.

[77] See generally, R. Burgess (1970) 34 Conv.(N.S.) 230; T. G. Youdan (1979) 24 U.Tor.L.J. 390.

[78] *Dufour* v. *Pereira* (1769) 1 Dick. 419; 2 Harg.Jur.Arg. 304. This sentence was cited in *Re Gillespie* [1969] 1 O.R. 585 at 593; 69 D.L.R. (2d) 368 at 372. An instructive exposition of the basic principles of this equitable obligation is to be found in *Birmingham* v. *Renfrew* (1937) 57 C.L.R. 666; and *cf. ante*, pp. 108, 109.

[79] *Re Hagger* [1930] 2 Ch. 190. Probably remainders to different, but agreed, persons would suffice; for the essence is the agreement.

[80] *Re Green, Lindner* v. *Green* [1951] Ch. 148; but consider *Re Oldham* [1925] Ch. 75 at 84, 88. See also *Re Fox* [1951] O.R. 378 (agreement providing for limited changes in wills).

[81] Contrast a joint will: *Re Gillespie* [1969] 1 O.R. 585; 69 D.L.R. (2d) 368, Ont.C.A., Kelly & McLennan JJ.A., Laskin J.A. dissenting.

an agreement not merely to make identical wills but to dispose of the property in a particular way.[82]

2. Revocability. Once one of the parties dies, the arrangement becomes irrevocable, at least if the survivor accepts the benefits conferred on him by the other's will.[83] Until the first death, either may withdraw from the arrangement.[84] Yet the mere making of the arrangement may have some immediate effect as where joint tenants make mutual wills inconsistent with the joint tenancy and thereby sever it.[85]

3. Effect

(a) *Implied trust.* The effect of the arrangement is that the survivor will hold the property concerned on an implied trust for the beneficiaries named in the wills. If he alters his will (as he may do, for no will can be made irrevocable[86]) his personal representative will take the property subject to the trust.[87]

(b) *Lapse.* As the trust arises as soon as one testator has died, the interest of a beneficiary who dies before the survivor will not lapse.[88]

(c) *Property bound.* It is primarily a question of construction to determine what property is bound by the trusts; a well-drawn will should define it.[89] Thus the trusts may bind merely the property left by the first testator to die, or such fraction of the survivor's estate as the wills state to be the notional equivalent thereof.[90] On the other hand, the trusts may bind the interests owned by each party in certain identified property, so that when the first dies, the survivor cannot disregard the trusts even as regards his own interest in the property.[91] But if the trusts extend to the whole of the property of each party, or the residue, it is not clear how far (if at all) the survivor would be free to deal with his own property *inter vivos*, or whether after-acquired property would be caught by the trusts; no view is free from difficulties.[92]

---

[82] *Re Oldham* [1925] Ch. 75; *Gray* v. *Perpetual Trustee Co. Ltd.* [1928] A.C. 391 (no agreement); *Re Cleaver* [1981] 1 W.L.R. 939 (agreement found).

[83] It is doubtful whether acceptance is necessary: see *Stone* v. *Hoskins* [1905] P. 194 at 197; *Re Hagger* [1930] 2 Ch. 190 at 195; J. D. B. Mitchell (1951) 14 M.L.R. 136 at 138.

[84] *Stone* v. *Hoskins* [1905] P. 194.

[85] *Re Wilford's Estate* (1879) 11 Ch.D. 267; *In b. Heys* [1914] P. 192; *Szabo* v. *Boros* (1967) 64 D.L.R. (2d) 48.

[86] *Vynior's Case* (1609) 8 Co.Rep. 81b; *In b. Heys, supra.*

[87] *Re Green, Lindner* v. *Green* [1951] Ch. 148.

[88] *Re Hagger* [1930] 2 Ch. 190 (a joint will).

[89] See, *e.g. Re Kerr* [1948] O.R. 543 (affd.: [1949] O.W.N. 71; [1949] 1 D.L.R. 736) (defined assets pooled).

[90] *Re Green, supra.*

[91] *Re Hagger, supra.*

[92] Contrast *Birmingham* v. *Renfrew* (1937) 57 C.L.R. 666 at 689 with J. D. B. Mitchell (1951) 14 M.L.R. 136 at 139, 140; see *Re Cleaver* [1981] 1 W.L.R. 939 at 946, 947.

(d) *Double gifts.*   If the mutual will of the survivor is revoked by a will which gives similar benefits to the beneficiaries, they may take the benefits under both wills, the first by virtue of the trust and the second under the later will.[93] This is not possible, of course, if the trusts extend to all the property of the survivor, and it may not apply where the legacies given by the two wills are precisely identical.[94]

PART 2

TRUSTS IMPOSED BY LAW

The constructive trust imposed by law is not capable of precise definition and is continually developing. For the present it is sufficient to say that a constructive trust is a trust which is imposed by equity in order to satisfy the demands of justice and good conscience.[95] While this shows that intention is not a necessary ingredient, it is of such generality that it does not provide an acceptable test for decision-making.[96] To see whether it is possible to formulate such a test we may examine the main categories of constructive trusts and the particular principles underlying them and then attempt to extract a more general principle. Whatever the definition, a claim founded on a breach of a constructive trust cannot be equated with a claim in damages for tort.[97]

Section 1. Extensions of Existing Trusts

The main and unquestioned type of constructive trust consists of trusts which arise out of an existing trust or other fiduciary relationship.[98] Thus a constructive trust will be imposed if a trustee makes a profit out of his trust, or if a person not a trustee intermeddles with the trust property.

1. Profit from trust.   With certain exceptions, it is a strict rule of equity that a trustee or other person in a fiduciary position may not profit from his trust. Any such profit is held on a constructive trust. Significantly this trust has been called "a remedial device through which preference of self is made subordinate to loyalty to others."[99] It is fully dealt with below.[1]

---

[93] *Re Green, Lindner* v. *Green* [1950] 2 All E.R. 913 (omitted from [1951] Ch. 148).
[94] *Re Green, Lindner* v. *Green* [1950] 2 All E.R. 913 at 919; and note the comparable doctrine of satisfaction of legacies by legacies, *post,* p. 520.
[95] This formulation was cited approvingly by Edmund Davies L.J. in *Carl Zeiss Stiftung* v. *Herbert Smith & Co. (No. 2)* [1969] 2 Ch. 276 at 301.
[96] This phrase is taken from *Baumgartner* v. *Baumgartner* (1987) 164 C.L.R. 137 at 147.
[97] *Metall und Rohstoff A.G.* v. *Donaldson Lufkin & Jenrette Inc.* [1990] Q.B. 391, esp. at pp. 473, 474, 479, 480 (citing this work).
[98] See *Soar* v. *Ashwell* [1893] 2 Q.B. 390 at 396.
[99] *Meinhard* v. *Salmon*, 249 N.Y. 458 at 467 (1928), *per* Cardozo C.J.
[1] *Post,* pp. 245 *et seq.*

2. Intermeddling. The responsibility of an express trustee may be extended to those who, not being appointed trustees, receive the trust property or assist others to do so.[2] It is, however, not everyone receiving trust property who will become liable as a trustee. The bona fide purchaser without notice of the trust takes free of it.[3] And even a mere donee of the trust property who receives it without notice of the trust cannot be made personally liable as a trustee.[4] Such an innocent volunteer will, however, be liable to return the property if he still retains it, or he has property into which it can be traced.[5] Liability as a constructive trustee depends upon knowledge of the trust and may arise under either of two heads.

(a) *Knowing receipt or dealing.* A recipient of trust property, not being an express trustee, becomes liable as a constructive trustee if he falls within one of three cases. First, he received the trust property knowing that it was trust property and that the transfer to him was in breach of trust.[6] Secondly, although he received the property without knowing it was trust property, he, not being a bona fide purchaser, subsequently acquired knowledge and thereafter dealt with the property in a manner inconsistent with the trust. Thirdly, he received the property as solicitor, banker or other agent of the trustees, and hence knew it to be trust property, and thereafter dealt with it in a manner inconsistent with the trust.[7] The knowledge of the trust required to affix liability in cases of receipt is not confined to actual knowledge. It certainly includes knowledge that would be acquired but for the wilful shutting of one's eyes to the obvious.[8] It probably also includes knowledge which would have been acquired by inquiries which a reasonable man would have made but which the recipient carelessly failed to make.[9] It is, however, doubtful whether knowledge which his solicitor may have had is to be imputed to the recipient.[10] Further, mere knowledge that a claim is being made to the property in question is not enough.[11]

(b) *Knowing assistance.* A person who does not actually himself receive the trust property may also incur liability to the beneficiaries if he knowingly assists in a fraudulent design on the part of the trustee.[12] But "strangers are not to be made constructive trustees merely because

---

[2] This subject is exhaustively treated by C. Harpum (1986) 102 L.Q.R. 114, 267.

[3] See *ante*, pp. 50 *et seq.*

[4] *Re Montagu's S.T.* [1987] Ch. 264 at 271; *Re Diplock* [1948] Ch. 465 at 478, 524, 539. See *post*, pp. 297 *et seq.* p. 305. There is a personal liability in respect of over-payments under a will or intestacy: see *post*, p. 358.

[5] See *post*, pp. 297 *et seq.*

[6] *Re Blundell, Blundell* v. *Blundell* (1888) 40 Ch.D. 370 at 381.

[7] *Lee* v. *Sankey* (1872) L.R. 15 Eq. 204 at 211; *Baden, Delvaux and Lecuit* v. *Société Générale* [1983] B.C.L.C. 325 at 403; *Soar* v. *Ashwell* [1893] 2 Q.B. 390.

[8] *Re Montagu's S.T.* [1987] Ch. 264 at 285.

[9] *Baden Delvaux and Lecuit* v. *Société Générale* [1983] B.C.L.C. 325 at 403; *Nelson* v. *Larholt* [1948] 1 K.B. 339; but see *Re Montagu's S.T.* [1987] Ch. 264 at 285.

[10] *Re Montagu's S.T.* [1987] Ch. 264 at 271.

[11] *Carl Zeiss Stiftung* v. *Herbert Smith & Co. (No. 2)* [1969] 2 Ch. 276, criticised D. M. Gordon (1970) 44 Aust.L.J. 261; C. Harpum (1986) 102 L.Q.R. 267 at 285–287.

[12] *Barnes* v. *Addy* (1874) 9 Ch.App. 244 at 251; *Selangor United Rubber Estates Ltd.* v. *Cradock (No. 3)* [1968] 1 W.L.R. 1555; *Karak Rubber Co. Ltd.* v. *Burden (No. 2)* [1972] 1 W.L.R. 602.

they act as the agents of trustees in transactions within their legal powers, transactions, perhaps of which a Court of Equity may disapprove, unless those agents receive and become chargeable with some part of the trust property, or unless they assist with knowledge in a dishonest and fraudulent design on the part of the trustees."[13] Thus liability will not be imposed on a person who merely acted as an agent for the trustees and did not intermeddle by doing acts characteristic of a trustee.[14] The knowledge which is required to make a person liable under this head has been described as "knowledge of circumstances which would indicate to an honest, reasonable man that such a design was being committed or would put him on inquiry, which the stranger failed to make, whether it was being committed."[15] If this is intended to import the ordinary doctrine of constructive notice to those who have merely given assistance without actually receiving the property it goes too far,[16] for a person who is merely negligent is not to be stigmatised as fraudulent and dishonest.[17] The true distinction is between honesty and dishonesty. One who, however foolishly, does not suspect wrongdoing is not to be stigmatised as dishonest. But one who suspects it yet fails to make inquiries cannot complain if he is treated as having actual knowledge of the fraudulent design.[18]

(c) *Partners.*   As regards a trustee's partners, statute[19] provides that if a partner, being a trustee, improperly employs trust property in the partnership business, no other partner is liable for the trust property to the beneficiaries. Further, where a solicitor becomes liable as a constructive trustee for the misapplication of trust moneys, his partner will not be liable, for there is no implied authority in a solicitor, in the ordinary course of business, to act as a trustee and so make his partners liable.[20] Nor is a partner liable merely because the moneys had passed through the firm's client account.[21] But this does not affect any liability incurred by any partner by reason of his having notice of a breach of trust, nor does it prevent trust money from being followed and recovered from the firm if still in its possession or under its control.

---

[13] *Barnes* v. *Addy, supra,* at p. 251, *per* Lord Selborne L.C., approved in *Mara* v. *Browne* [1896] 1 Ch. 199 at 209. See also *Re Barney* [1892] 2 Ch. 265; *Coleman* v. *Bucks and Oxon Union Bank* [1897] 2 Ch. 243; and *Stokes* v. *Prance* [1898] 1 Ch. 212 at 224.

[14] *Williams-Ashman* v. *Price* [1942] Ch. 219. Contrast *Blyth* v. *Fladgate* [1891] 1 Ch. 337 where the solicitors had acted as trustees and not merely as agents.

[15] *Selangor United Rubber Estates Ltd.* v. *Cradock (No. 3), supra,* at p. 1590, *per* Ungoed-Thomas J.; and see *Karak Rubber Co. Ltd.* v. *Burden (No. 2), supra,* at p. 633, approving the classification in this section of the text. This test was applied in *Rowlandson* v. *National Westminster Bank Ltd.* [1978] 1 W.L.R. 798. It was elaborated in *Baden, Delvaux and Lecuit* v. *Société Général* [1983] B.C.L.C. 325 at 407, 408; but see *Re Montagu's S.T.* [1987] Ch. 264 at 277.

[16] *Competitive Insurance Co. Ltd.* v. *Davies Investments Ltd.* [1975] 1 W.L.R. 1240; *Consul Development Pty. Ltd.* v. *D.P.C. Estates Pty. Ltd.* (1975) 132 C.L.R. 373; *Belmont Finance Corporation Ltd.* v. *Williams Furniture Ltd.* [1979] Ch. 250 (see [1980] 1 All E.R. 393 for further proceedings: no dishonesty under this head, but knowing receipt of trust property); *Lipkin Gorman* v. *Karpnale Ltd.* [1989] 1 W.L.R. 1340. See J. D. Heydon (1977) 51 A.L.J. 635.

[17] See *Carl Zeiss Stiftung* v. *Herbert Smith & Co. (No. 2)* [1969] 2 Ch. 276 at 298, 301.

[18] *Agip (Africa) Ltd.* v. *Jackson* [1990] Ch. 265, and see *Consul Development Pty. Ltd.* v. *D.P.C. Estates Pty. Ltd., supra,* at pp. 410, 411.

[19] Partnership Act 1890, s.13.

[20] *Re Bell's Indenture* [1980] 1 W.L.R. 1217; see Partnership Act 1890, ss.10, 11.

[21] *Re Bell's Indenture, supra.*

Section 2. Fraud

1. General. A constructive trust may be imposed as a result of personal fraud. "It is a jurisdiction by which a Court of Equity, proceeding on the ground of fraud, converts the party who has committed it into a trustee for the party who is injured by that fraud."[22]

2. Statute. A well-established example is the use of a statute as an engine of fraud. The doctrine of secret trusts was originally founded on this principle though its scope was later widened.[23] So too it may be fraudulent to take one's stand on the statutory provisions regulating the creation of express trusts, and dispositions of interests under them.[24]

3. Conveyances and other dispositions. A constructive trust will be raised against one who insists upon the absolute terms of a conveyance to him to renege on an informal undertaking to permit the grantor some right to remain in occupation.[25] Further, one who purchases a property at a reduced price on account of a similar undertaking previously given will be bound by a constructive trust.[26] But the mere grant of a licence to occupy property will not raise a trust,[27] nor will a conveyance simply expressed to be made "subject to" such a licence.[28]

Section 3. Other Cases

Some cases of constructive trusts have been long established but do not fall within the general classifications so far mentioned.

1. Specifically enforceable contract. As soon as a specifically enforceable contract for the sale of land is made, the purchaser becomes the owner of the land in equity, and the vendor becomes a constructive trustee of the land for the purchaser, subject in each case to their respective rights and duties under the contract.[29] Such a trust might be based upon the intention of the parties and so classified as an implied trust; but it has been said to be constructive.[30] On similar grounds a

---

[22] *McCormick* v. *Grogan* (1869) L.R. 4 H.L. 82 at 97, *per* Lord Westbury.
[23] See *ante*, pp. 108 *et seq.*
[24] See *ante*, p. 108.
[25] *Bannister* v. *Bannister* [1948] 2 All E.R. 133; and see *Lyus* v. *Prowsa Developments Ltd.* [1982] 1 W.L.R. 1044.
[26] *Binions* v. *Evans* [1972] Ch. 359, as explained in *Ashburn Anstalt* v. *Arnold* [1989] Ch. 1 at 23.
[27] *Ashburn Anstalt* v. *Arnold* [1989] Ch. 1, not following *D.H.N. Food Distributors Ltd.*v. *Tower Hamlets L.B.C.* [1976] 1 W.L.R. 852 at 859 and explaining *Re Sharpe* [1980] 1 W.L.R. 219.
[28] *Ashburn Anstalt* v. *Arnold, supra,* at pp. 25, 26.
[29] *Lysaght* v. *Edwards* (1876) 2 Ch.D. 499; *Rayner* v. *Preston* (1881) 18 Ch.D. 1; *post,* p. 463.
[30] See, *e.g. Shaw* v. *Foster* (1872) L.R. 5 H.L. 321 at 349, 356. *Quaere* in what sense the term was used.

specifically enforceable covenant for value to settle land makes the covenantor a trustee for the beneficiaries.[31]

2. Surplus proceeds of mortgagee's sale.   A clearer instance of a constructive trust formerly arose when a mortgagee held a surplus in his hands after selling the property under his power of sale. In such a case equity regarded the relationship between the parties as having been sufficiently fiduciary to make the mortgagee a constructive trustee of the surplus proceeds of sale for any subsequent mortgagees and the mortgagor.[32] However, since 1881 statute has replaced the constructive trust in such cases by an express trust.[33]

Section 4. Constructive Trust as a Remedy

1. Development abroad.   In some jurisdictions the constructive trust has come to be treated as a remedy for many cases of unjust enrichment.[34] Broad expressions are found: "a constructive trust is the formula through which the conscience of equity finds expression. When property has been acquired in such circumstances that the holder of the legal title may not in good conscience retain the beneficial interest, equity converts him into a trustee."[35] As examples we may note the following.

(a) *Homicide.*   There is a rule of public policy that one who kills another is not entitled to any property he would have acquired as a result of the death.[36] The English courts have generally considered that in such cases a legal title which would otherwise have devolved on the killer does not so devolve.[37] Such a solution overrides statutory provisions regulating descent on death.[38] Other jurisdictions have shrunk from this and hence hold that the legal estate devolves according to law, but in the hands of the killer it is impressed with a constructive trust for others.[39] Thus where one of two joint tenants murdered the other it was held that the murderer took by survivorship but subject to a constructive trust as to one-half in favour of the victim's next-of-kin.[40] Equity interferes to prevent the benefit of enlargement by survivorship

---

[31] See *Central Trust & Safe Deposit Co.* v. *Snider* [1916] 1 A.C. 266 at 272.
[32] *Banner* v. *Berridge* (1881) 18 Ch.D. 254 at 269; and see *post*, p. 416.
[33] C.A. 1881, s.21(3); L.P.A. 1925, s.105.
[34] See generally *Scott on Trusts*, Vol. 5 (3rd ed., 1967), pp. 3405–3765; A. W. Scott (1955) 71 L.Q.R. 39.
[35] *Beatty* v. *Guggenheim Exploration Co.*, 225 N.Y. 380 at 386 (1919), *per* Cardozo J.
[36] *Cleaver* v. *Mutual Reserve Fund Life Association* [1892] 1 Q.B. 147; *Davitt* v. *Titcumb* [1990] Ch. 110. See generally T. G. Youdan (1973) 89 L.Q.R. 235.
[37] *Re Sigsworth* [1935] Ch. 89.
[38] See the discussion by T. G. Youdan, *op. cit.*, at pp. 251–253.
[39] See *Rosenfeldt* v. *Olson* [1985] 2 W.W.R. 502 (payment of money by police for information earmarked for murderer's family impressed with trust for victim).
[40] *Schobelt* v. *Barber* [1967] 1 O.R. 519; 60.D.L.R. (2d) 519; *Re Pechar* [1969] N.Z.L.R. 574; *Rasmanis* v. *Jurewitsch* (1969) 70 S.R.(N.S.W.) 407, (C.A.).

accruing to the wrongdoer. Where there are only two joint tenants the result is a severance because the estate of the victim is the only alternative repository of the enlargement. But where there are three (or more) joint tenants, the innocent survivor is the repository of the benefit, and severance does not occur more than is necessary to prevent benefit accruing to the wrongdoer. To ensure this, one-third is severed and held for the innocent survivor, and he with the guilty survivor will remain as joint tenants of the other two-thirds.[41]

b) *Acquisition for joint use.* It has been seen that an implied trust based on intention will frequently arise in connection with the acquisition of a house for joint use.[42] In Australia, even where a common intention is not established, a constructive trust has been imposed in connection with such an acquisition in circumstances where it was unconscionable for the owner to maintain an exclusive claim to the house.[43] This approach avoids the necessity of inferring intention from an excuse for not putting the claimant's name on the title[44] but does not define the circumstances in which such a trust will be imposed.[45]

2. Development in England. In England the constructive trust has in general remained essentially a substantive institution; ownership must not be confused with obligation, nor must the relationship of debtor and creditor be converted into one of trustee and *cestui que trust*.[46] Further, it has been said that "there is no general doctrine of unjust enrichment recognised in English law."[47] Thus it has been held that an employee is not a constructive trustee of tax which ought to have been deducted from his salary.[48] Yet the attitude of the courts may be changing. A son who added an extra bedroom to his house to be occupied by his mother who had paid the builder and who later left, was held to be a constructive trustee of the house to the extent necessary to reimburse his mother.[49] The trust "is a trust imposed by law whenever justice and good conscience require it."[50] For the present, however, constructive trusts fall for the most part in well-established categories, and it is only occasionally and in unusual circumstances that it would be necessary to take refuge in such a broad and fundamental principle.

---

[41] *Rasmanis* v. *Jurewitsch, supra.* The actual order was guilty survivor one-third, innocent two-thirds as tenants in common, but this was because only the victim's personal representative and not the guilty survivor appealed from the declaration made in the court below.
[42] *Ante,* p. 184.
[43] *Baumgartner* v. *Baumgartner* (1987) 164 C.L.R. 137. See D. Hayton [1988] Conv. 259.
[44] See *ante,* p. 186.
[45] See *Baumgartner* v. *Baumgartner, supra,* at pp. 35, 36.
[46] See *Lister & Co.* v. *Stubbs* (1890) 45 Ch.D. 1 at 15.
[47] *Orakpo* v. *Manson Investments Ltd.* [1978] A.C. 95 at 104, *per* Lord Diplock.
[48] *Bernard & Shaw Ltd.* v. *Shaw* [1951] 2 All E.R. 267.
[49] *Hussey* v. *Palmer* [1972] 1 W.L.R. 1286.
[50] *Ibid.* at pp. 1289, 1290, *per* Lord Denning M.R.

CHAPTER 5

APPOINTMENT, RETIREMENT AND REMOVAL OF TRUSTEES

Section 1. Capacity to be a Trustee

In general, the ability to be a trustee is coextensive with the capacity to hold property. Thus an alien may hold real and personal property of every description except a British ship, and so, with that exception, may be a trustee of any property.[1] A woman, too, may be a trustee of any property,[2] and since the Married Women's Property Act 1882 a married woman has not needed her husband's assent to the acceptance of a trust or to any disposition of the trust property.[3] If she is guilty of a breach of trust, her husband is not liable unless he has acted or intermeddled in the trust or administration.[4]

Two cases, however, require special mention.

1. Corporations

(a) *In general.*   A corporation may be a trustee of pure personalty,[5] and of land also[6]; the former requirement[7] of either statutory authority to hold land[8] or else a licence in mortmain has now gone.[9] A corporation may in general be a trustee for any purpose (*e.g.* a trustee of a Friendly Society)[10]; and may be a co-trustee with an individual or another corporation, for the Bodies Corporate (Joint Tenancy) Act 1899

---

[1] Status of Aliens Act 1914, s.17, as amended by British Nationality Act 1948.
[2] See *Re Dickinson's Trust* [1902] W.N. 104 (equality with men).
[3] Married Women's Property Act 1882, ss.1(2), 18, 24; L.P.A. 1925, s.170, replacing Married Women's Property Act 1907, s.1, which overruled *Re Harkness and Allsopp's Contract* [1896] 2 Ch. 358. Sections 1(2) and 18 of the Act of 1882 were repealed by, respectively, Law Reform (Married Women and Tortfeasors) Act 1935, s.5(2) and Sched. 2 and Statute Law (Repeals) Act 1969, s.1 and Sched., Pt. III.
[4] Married Women's Property Act 1882, s.24 (partially repealed by Statute Law (Repeals) Act 1969, s.1 and Sched., Pt. III); Law Reform (Married Women and Tortfeasors) Act 1935, s.1.
[5] See *Att.-Gen.* v. *St. John's Hospital, Bedford* (1865) 2 De G.J. & S. 621 at 635.
[6] See *Re Thompson's S.T.* [1905] 1 Ch. 229; *Bankes* v. *Salisbury Diocesan Council of Education Incorporated* [1960] Ch. 631 (corporation sole).
[7] Mortmain and Charitable Uses Act 1888, s.1.
[8] *e.g.* Companies Act 1948, s.14.
[9] Charities Act 1960, s.38.
[10] *Re Pilkington Bros. Ltd. Workmen's Pension Fund* [1953] 1 W.L.R. 1084.

removed the former inability of a corporation to hold property in joint tenancy.[11]

(b) *Trust corporations.* The appointment of certain corporations to be trustees is much encouraged by the Trustee Act 1925 and other Acts of 1925.[12] These corporations, known as "trust corporations," include the Public Trustee, the Treasury Solicitor, the Official Solicitor, certain charitable corporations, and corporations either appointed by the court in any particular case or entitled to act as custodian trustee under rules made under the Public Trustee Act 1906.[13] The corporations which are entitled to act as custodian trustee[14] include any corporation which (i) is constituted under the law of the United Kingdom or of any part thereof or under the law of any other Member State of the EEC or of any part thereof[15] and has a place of business in the United Kingdom, (ii) is empowered by its constitution to undertake trust business, and (iii) is either a company incorporated by special Act[16] or Royal Charter, or else a registered company with an issued capital of at least £250,000, of which at least £100,000 has been paid up in cash.[17] A company which still exists as a legal entity and continues to satisfy this test as to its capital does not cease to be a trust corporation merely because it transfers its assets to another company on amalgamation.[18] The term "trust corporation" also includes a number of other corporations of a public or charitable nature such as Regional and Area Health Authorities.[19]

2. Minors. A minor cannot be appointed a trustee,[20] nor can a legal estate in land be held by a minor.[21] A purported conveyance of a legal estate to a minor on trust will operate only as a declaration of trust and will not pass any legal estate to him; but if the conveyance is made to him and another person of full age, the legal estate will vest in the other person alone.[22] There is nothing, however, to prevent a minor from holding property on an implied, resulting or constructive trust.[23]

[11] See *Re Thompson's S.T., supra.*
[12] See, *e.g. post,* p. 263.
[13] T.A. 1925, s.68(18); L.P.A. 1925, s.205(1)(xxviii); S.L.A. 1925, s.117(1)(xxx); A.E.A. 1925, s.55(1)(xxvii); L.P.(Am.)A. 1926, s.3 (extending the definitions in the former Acts). Certain individuals such as trustees in bankruptcy and trustees under deeds of arrangement are also comprised in the term "trust corporation."
[14] For the functions of a custodian trustee, see *post,* p. 209.
[15] See *Re Bigger* [1977] Fam. 203 (Bank of Ireland).
[16] See, *e.g.* Methodist Church Act 1939, s.10.
[17] Public Trustee Act 1906, ss.4(3), 14; Public Trustee Rules 1912, r. 30. S.I. 1975 No. 1189 with S.I. 1976 No. 836, S.I. 1981 No. 358, S.I. 1984 No. 109, S.I. 1985 No. 132, and S.I. 1987 No. 1891, contains the current form of rule 30 of the Public Trustee Rules 1912.
[18] *In b. Skinner* [1958] 1 W.L.R. 1043.
[19] See note 17, *supra.*
[20] L.P.A. 1925, s.20.
[21] *Ibid.* s.1(6).
[22] *Ibid.* s.19(4), (5); *ante,* p. 125.
[23] See, *e.g. Re Vinogradoff* [1935] W.N. 68; *ante,* p. 183.

Section 2. Number of Trustees

1. Land. Where a settlement of land or a trust for sale of land is created after 1925, the number of trustees must not exceed four; and if more than four trustees are named, the first four named who are able and willing to act will alone be the trustees.[24] There is no minimum number of trustees; but except in the case of a trust corporation a sole trustee of settled land or of land held on trust for sale cannot give a valid receipt for capital money.[25]

2. Exceptions. As the limit of four trustees is confined to settled land and trusts for sale, it does not apply to trusts of pure personalty. There are also three statutory exceptions to the rule[26]: it does not apply to—

(i) land, or the proceeds of sale of land, which is held in trust for charitable, ecclesiastical or public purposes;

(ii) a term of years limited by a settlement on trusts for raising money, *e.g.* portions; or

(iii) a term of years created under the statutory remedies for enforcing rentcharges.[27]

Section 3. Appointment of Trustees

1. Equity does not want for a trustee. The general rule is that a trust will not fail if the settlor or testator has failed to appoint trustees, or if the trustees appointed refuse or are unable to act,[28] or have ceased to exist.[29] A trust may, however, be so framed that its operation is conditional upon a specific trustee undertaking the trust, as where there was a charitable trust for medical students who were to be selected and closely supervised by the Royal College of Surgeons as trustees.[30]

---

[24] T.A. 1925, s.34(1). *Cf.* S.C.A. 1981, s.114, replacing J.A. 1925, s.160, considered in *In b. Holland* (1936) 105 L.J.P. 113 as to the number of personal representatives. Before 1926 there was no such restriction; for the relevant transitional provisions, see T.A. 1925, s.34(2).

[25] See L.P.A. 1925, s.27(2); S.L.A. 1925, ss.18(1), 94; T.A. 1925, ss.14, 37. *Cf.* S.C.A. 1981, s.114 as to personal representatives (*post*, p. 317).

[26] T.A. 1925, s.34(3).

[27] *Ibid.* The Rentcharges Act 1977 prohibits the creation of new rentcharges.

[28] *Moggridge* v. *Thackwell* (1803) 7 Ves. 36 (affirmed, 13 Ves. 416); *Re Willis, Shaw* v. *Willis* [1921] 1 Ch. 44; *Re Armitage, Ellam* v. *Norwich Corporation* [1972] Ch. 438.

[29] *Re Morrison, Wakefield* v. *Falmouth* (1967) 111 S.J. 758.

[30] *Re Lysaght, Hill* v. *Royal College of Surgeons* [1966] Ch. 191; *ante*, p. 166.

2. Initial trustees.   Normally the first trustees are appointed by the will or settlement. If, however, this fails to nominate them, or they disclaim,[31] or, being appointed by will, predecease the testator, the property will revert to the settlor, or remain in the personal representatives of the testator, as the case may be, to be held upon the trusts of the settlement or will.[32]

3. Subsequent trustees.   Unless and until new trustees are appointed, the property remains vested in the first trustees (or such of them as do not retire and are not removed[33]), and when one dies, the trust property devolves upon the survivors. On the death of a sole or sole surviving trustee, the trust property, whether real or personal, vests in his personal representatives, still subject to the trust.[34] Until new trustees are appointed, the personal representatives, though they are not bound to accept the position and duties of trustees,[35] are capable of exercising or performing any power or trust which the deceased trustee could have exercised or performed, unless the trust instrument (if any) contains a contrary direction.[36]

4. Appointment of new trustees.   Once the trust is duly constituted, the settlor has no power to appoint trustees unless he has reserved such a power. Nor, it seems, can the beneficiaries appoint new trustees, even if they are *sui juris* and entitled to the whole beneficial interest,[37] for their collective power to deal with the trust property as they wish is a power to determine the trust[38] and not to appoint trustees under it while it is still afoot.[39] Those who can appoint new trustees fall into three categories.

(a) *Express power.*   The trust may confer an express power of appointing new trustees. The donee of such a power can appoint himself,[40] but should do so only in special circumstances, for the power is fiduciary.[41] Express powers are now unusual, for the statutory power set out below usually suffices, and the trust merely nominates the persons who may exercise that power.

---

[31] For disclaimer, see *post*, p. 210.
[32] *Mallot* v. *Wilson* [1903] 2 Ch. 494.
[33] See *post*, p. 211.
[34] A.E.A. 1925, ss.1 and 3, replacing C.A. 1881, s.30.
[35] *Re Benett* [1906] 1 Ch. 216.
[36] T.A. 1925, s.18(2), replacing C.A. 1911, s.8(1). See P. W. Smith (1977) 41 Conv.(N.S.) 423 for position where personal representatives die without appointing new trustees.
[37] For a limited exception in the case of trustees of settled land, see S.L.A. 1925, s.30(1)(v).
[38] See *post*, p. 233.
[39] Consider *Re Brockbank* [1948] Ch. 206; contrast *Re Spearman S.E.* [1906] 2 Ch. 502.
[40] *Montefiore* v. *Guedalla* [1903] 2 Ch. 723.
[41] *Re Skeats' Settlement* (1889) 42 Ch.D. 522; *Re Newen* [1894] 2 Ch. 297; for self-appointments under the statutory powers, see *post*, pp. 204, 205.

(b) *Statutory power*

(1) THE POWER. The Trustee Act 1925, s.36,[42] confers wide powers to appoint new trustees (including Settled Land Act trustees[43]) whenever the trust was created, subject to any contrary provision in the trust instrument, if any.[44] A new trustee or trustees may be appointed in place of a trustee who falls within any of the following categories.[45]

(i)   He is dead; and this includes a person nominated trustee in a will but dying before the testator.[46]

(ii) He remains outside the United Kingdom for a continuous[47] period exceeding 12 months.

(iii) He desires to be discharged from all or any of his trusts or powers.

(iv) He refuses to act; and this includes disclaimer.[48]

(v)   He is unfit to act, *e.g.* because he is bankrupt.[49]

(vi) He is incapable of acting; this includes lunacy,[50] age and infirmity,[51] or, in the case of a corporation, dissolution,[52] but not absence in an enemy country.[53]

(vii) He is an infant (*e.g.* where the trust is implied, resulting or constructive).[54]

(viii) He is removed under a power in the trust instrument.[55]

(2) THE APPOINTMENT. The appointment must be made in writing,[56] though it may not be made by the will of the last surviving trustee.[57] It may be made by the following persons[58]:

(i)   By the person or persons nominated by the trust instrument for the purpose of appointing new trustees. This means the person or persons nominated generally[59] and not merely in certain specified events.[60] If several persons are nominated, the power

[42] Replacing T.A. 1893, s.10.
[43] See *Re Dark* [1954] Ch. 291.
[44] T.A. 1925, s.69(2).
[45] *Ibid.* s.36(1).
[46] *Ibid.* s.36(8).
[47] See *Re Walker* [1901] 1 Ch. 259 (return for a week breaks continuity).
[48] *Re Birchall* (1889) 40 Ch.D. 436.
[49] *Re Roche* (1842) 2 Dr. & War. 287 at 289; *Re Hopkins, Dowd v. Hawtin* (1881) 19 Ch.D. 61 at 69.
[50] *Re East, Re Bellwood's W.T.* (1873) 8 Ch.App. 735; *Re Blake* [1887] W.N. 173.
[51] *Re Lemann's Trust* (1883) 22 Ch.D. 633.
[52] T.A. 1925, s.36(3), a retrospective provision.
[53] *Re May's W.T.* [1941] Ch. 109.
[54] See *ante*, p. 199.
[55] T.A. 1925, s.36(2).
[56] *Ibid.* s.36(1).
[57] *Re Parker's Trusts* [1894] 1 Ch. 707.
[58] T.A. 1925, s.36(1).
[59] *Re Walker & Hughes' Contract* (1883) 24 Ch.D. 698.
[60] *Re Wheeler & De Rochow's Contract* [1896] 1 Ch. 315; *Re Sichel's Settlements* [1916] 1 Ch. 358.

cannot be exercised by the survivor or survivors[61] unless a contrary intention is shown,[62] or the property is vested in them[63] or they are trustees and hold the power as such[64] or the power was given to a class (*e.g.* "my sons") of whom at least two still exist.[65] If there is no person able and willing to act under this head (as where the persons nominated cannot be found,[66] or they disagree[67]), the appointment may be made under the next head, namely—

(ii)   By the surviving or continuing trustees or trustee. This includes a refusing or retiring trustee, if willing to make the appointment,[68] but not a trustee removed against his will.[69] If there is no such trustee, the appointment may be made—

(iii) By the personal representative of the last surviving or continuing trustee, including the personal representatives of a sole trustee,[70] unless he is appointed by will and predeceases the testator.[71]

(iv)   If (and probably only if[72]) there is no person able to act, or it is doubtful whether he can act,[73] the court may appoint.[74]

When the appointment is made by the personal representatives, the concurrence of any executor who has renounced or who has not proved is not required[75]; but the appointment may be made by a sole or last surviving executor intending to renounce, or all the executors where they all intend to renounce, without thereby accepting the office of executor.[76] Yet although the appointment may be made before probate, the new trustee's title to act will not be complete before the grant of probate (or letters of administration with will annexed if all renounce).[77] No appointment of a new trustee to take the place of a mentally defective trustee who is also entitled in possession to some beneficial interest in the trust property can be made by the continuing trustee or

---

[61] Farwell, *Powers* (3rd ed., 1916), p. 514; and see *Bersel Manufacturing Co. Ltd.* v. *Berry* [1968] 2 All E.R. 552 at 554, 557.
[62] *Re Harding* [1923] 1 Ch. 182.
[63] See *Re Bacon* [1907] 1 Ch. 475.
[64] T.A. 1925, s.18(1); and see *Re Smith, Eastick* v. *Smith* [1904] 1 Ch. 139.
[65] *Jefferys* v. *Marshall* (1870) 19 W.R. 94; but see *Sykes* v. *Sheard* (1863) 2 De G.J. & S. 6.
[66] *Cradock* v. *Witham* [1895] W.N. 75.
[67] *Re Sheppard's S.T.* [1888] W.N. 234.
[68] T.A. 1925, s.36(8).
[69] *Re Stoneham's S.T.* [1953] Ch. 59.
[70] *Re Shafto's Trusts* (1885) 29 Ch.D. 247.
[71] *Nicholson* v. *Field* [1893] 2 Ch. 511.
[72] *Re Gibbon's Trusts* (1882) 30 W.R. 287 (undesirable); *Re Hodson's Settlement* (1851) 9 Hare 118; *Re Higginbottom* [1892] 3 Ch. 132 (probably no jurisdiction).
[73] *Re May's W.T.* [1941] Ch. 109 (absence in enemy territory).
[74] T.A. 1925, s.41; *post*, p. 205.
[75] T.A. 1925, s.36(4).
[76] *Ibid.* s.36(5).
[77] *Re Crowhurst Park* [1974] 1 W.L.R. 583.

trustees without the leave of the appropriate authority under the Mental Health Act 1983.[78]

(3) THE PERSON APPOINTED. It is expressly provided that the person making the appointment may appoint himself.[79] He should not, however, appoint anyone whom the court would not appoint,[80] although the appointment is not necessarily invalid if he does,[81] nor, if he is a trustee, is such an appointment itself a breach of trust.[82] But if the appointor is a minor, the appointment will be closely scrutinised, and may be set aside.[83] There is no legal bar to the appointment of a person living abroad, but such an appointment is improper in the absence of special circumstances, as where the beneficiaries are themselves resident in a foreign country.[84]

(4) NUMBER OF TRUSTEES. On an appointment of new trustees the number of trustees may be increased, subject to the statutory restrictions on the number of trustees,[85] and a separate set of trustees, not exceeding four, may be appointed for any part of the trust property held on distinct trusts.[86] It is not obligatory (except as mentioned below) to appoint more than one trustee where only one was originally appointed, or to fill up the original number where more than two were originally appointed.[87] But (except where only one trustee was originally appointed and a sole trustee when appointed will be able to give valid receipts for all capital money) a trustee is not to be discharged unless there will be either a trust corporation or at least two individuals to perform the trust.[88]

The exception placed in brackets in the last sentence will normally[89] only apply where the trust property consists entirely of pure personalty, for a sole individual trustee cannot give a receipt for capital money arising under a trust for sale of land or a settlement of land.[90] Nothing in the Act authorises the appointment of a sole trustee (not being a trust corporation) where the trustee, when appointed, would not be able to give valid receipts for all capital money arising under the trust.[91] Where

[78] T.A. 1925, s.36(9), as amended by Mental Health Act 1959, s.149(1) and Sched. 7 and further amended by Mental Health Act 1983, s.148(1) and Sched. 4, para. 4(a).
[79] T.A. 1925, s.36(1), altering on this point T.A. 1893, s.10; see *Re Sampson* [1906] 1 Ch. 435. Compare the position under express powers (*ante*, p. 201) and contrast the power of appointing additional trustees (*post*, p. 205).
[80] See *post*, p. 206.
[81] *Forster* v. *Abraham* (1874) L.R. 17 Eq. 351 (tenant for life); *Re Earl of Stamford* [1896] 1 Ch. 288 (solicitor to tenant for life); *Re Coode* (1913) 108 L.T. 94 (husband of tenant for life); and see *Re Cotter* [1915] 1 Ch. 307.
[82] *Briggs* v. *Parsloe* [1937] 3 All E.R. 831.
[83] *Re Parsons, Barnsdale* v. *Parsons* [1940] Ch. 973; *quaere* what this case decided: see (1941) 57 L.Q.R. 25.
[84] *Re Whitehead's W.T., Burke* v. *Burke* [1971] 1 W.L.R. 833.
[85] See *ante*, p. 200.
[86] T.A. 1925, s.37(1).
[87] *Ibid.*
[88] *Ibid.*
[89] Consider, *e.g.* land held on a bare trust.
[90] T.A. 1925, s.14; *post*, p. 263.
[91] T.A. 1925, s.37(2).

new trustees of a conveyance on trust for sale are being appointed, the same persons must be appointed as are for the time being trustees of the settlement of the proceeds of sale.[92]

(5) ADDITIONAL TRUSTEES. Even if no occasion has arisen for the appointment of new trustees, and so long as there are not more than three trustees and none of them is a trust corporation, an additional trustee or trustees may be appointed, provided the number of trustees is not thereby increased above four.[93] There is no obligation to make such an appointment unless the trust instrument (if any) or statute[94] so requires.[95] The appointment must be made by the person nominated by the trust instrument (if any) for the purpose of appointing new trustees, or, if there is no such person, or no such person able and willing to act, by the trustee or trustees for the time being. Unlike the power of filling vacancies[96] this power, by an accident of drafting, does not enable the appointor to appoint himself.[97]

(c) *The court*

(1) TRUSTEE ACT 1925. Under the Trustee Act 1925[98] the court has a wide power of appointing a new trustee or new trustees either in substitution for or in addition to any existing trustee or trustees, or although there is no existing trustee. The appointment can be made whenever it is expedient to appoint a new trustee and it is found "inexpedient, difficult or impracticable so to do without the assistance of the court," *e.g.* when a trustee is imprisoned, or is mentally defective, or is bankrupt, or is a corporation which is in liquidation or has been dissolved. The section authorises the displacement of a trustee against his will.[99] The court also has very extensive powers of making vesting orders with regard to trust land, and orders vesting the right to transfer trust stock or sue for trust things in action.[1] Applications for the appointment of a new trustee and for such vesting orders may be made by any beneficiary or trustee[2]; and in the High Court they are made by originating summons in the Chancery Division.[3]

(2) THE PERSON APPOINTED. In making an appointment, the court considers the wishes of the settlor and the beneficiaries,[4] whether the interests of the proposed trustee conflict with those of the settlor or any of the beneficiaries, and whether the appointment will promote or

---

[92] L.P.A. 1925, s.24; T.A. 1925, s.35(1).
[93] T.A. 1925, s.36(6).
[94] See, *e.g.* L.P.A. 1925, s.27(2); S.L.A. 1925, ss.30(3), 94; T.A. 1925, s.14(2).
[95] T.A. 1925, s.36(6).
[96] *Ante*, p. 204.
[97] *Re Power's S.T.* [1951] Ch. 1074.
[98] s.41, replacing T.A. 1893, s.25.
[99] *Re Henderson, Henderson v. Henderson* [1940] Ch. 764.
[1] T.A. 1925, ss.44–56, replacing T.A. 1893, ss.26–41.
[2] T.A. 1925, s.58.
[3] R.S.C., Ord. 5, r. 3.
[4] *Re Dickinson's Trusts* [1902] W.N. 104 (differing views of beneficiaries: majority prevails).

impede the execution of the trust.[5] The court will not appoint a person under disability, nor a person living abroad (unless the trust property or all the beneficiaries are also abroad),[6] nor as a rule a beneficiary or a beneficiary's solicitor or husband or wife, owing to the fact that the trustee may be placed in a position in which his duty and his interest, or two inconsistent duties, conflict[7]; but where there are advantages to be gained from such an appointment, and no disadvantages, the court may make it,[8] though it will be slow to do so.[9]

(3) JUDICIAL TRUSTEES ACT 1896. The Judicial Trustees Act 1896[10] gives the court a further power of appointing a trustee. On an application by summons[11] by the settlor or a trustee or a beneficiary, the court may appoint any fit and proper person nominated in the application,[12] or an official of the court (usually the Official Solicitor), to be a judicial trustee to act alone or jointly[13] with any other person and, if sufficient cause is shown, in place of all or any existing trustees. The Act allows the court to appoint a judicial trustee to be a Settled Land Act trustee,[14] or to administer the estate of a testator or intestate instead of the executor or administrator,[15] though not to administer part of the estate, since an executorship is indivisible.[16] In all cases the appointment of a judicial trustee is absolutely discretionary.[17] The object of the Act "was to provide a middle course in cases where the administration of the estate by the ordinary trustees had broken down and it was not desired to put the estate to the expense of a full administration" by the court.[18] Until recently the Act offered the only way of replacing a personal representative once a grant had been made and he had begun the administration.[19] The jurisdiction is commonly resorted to where, for reasons not necessarily involving fault on the part of the representative (e.g. illness or conflicting interest), it is expedient to replace him.

A judicial trustee differs from an ordinary trustee in a number of respects. He is an officer of the court, and as such is subject to its control and supervision; he can at any time obtain the court's directions as to the way in which he is to act, without the necessity of a formal

[5] Re Tempest (1866) 1 Ch.App. 485.
[6] Re Freeman's S.T. (1887) 37 Ch.D. 148; Re Liddiard (1880) 14 Ch.D. 310.
[7] Ex p. Clutton (1853) 17 Jur. 988; Re Orde (1883) 24 Ch.D. 271 at 272; Re Kemp's S.E. (1883) 24 Ch.D. 485; Re Coode (1913) 108 L.T. 94.
[8] e.g. Re Marquis of Ailesbury and Lord Iveagh [1893] 2 Ch. 345 at 360.
[9] See Re Earl of Stamford [1896] 1 Ch. 288 at 299; and see Re Spencer's S.E. [1903] 1 Ch. 75.
[10] s.1; and see Judicial Trustee Rules 1983 (S.I. No. 370), replacing with amendments Judicial Trustee Rules 1972 (S.I. No. 1096).
[11] An originating summons if there are no existing proceedings: Judicial Trustee Rules 1983, r. 3(1).
[12] See Douglas v. Bolam [1900] 2 Ch. 749.
[13] It is not, however, desirable for a judicial trustee and a private trustee to hold office jointly: Re Martin [1900] W.N. 129.
[14] Re Marshall's W.T. [1945] Ch. 217.
[15] Re Ratcliff [1898] 2 Ch. 352.
[16] Re Wells, Loggie v. Wells [1968] 1 W.L.R. 44.
[17] Re Ratcliff, supra.
[18] Re Ridsdel [1947] Ch. 597 at 605, per Jenkins J.
[19] See now Administration of Justice Act 1985, s.50 (power of court to appoint substitute for, or remove, personal representative), post, p. 355.

application by summons; he is entitled to such remuneration as the court allows him; every year he must prepare accounts for examination by the court,[20] although a corporate trustee[21] need only submit such accounts to such persons as the court directs[22]; and he cannot appoint a successor under the statutory power[23] for this would usurp the function of the court.[24] In other respects he is in the position of any other trustee, and so, for example, he can compromise claims.[25]

(4) PUBLIC TRUSTEE ACT 1906. Lastly, by the Public Trustee Act 1906,[26] on the application by originating summons of any trustee or beneficiary, the court has power to appoint the Public Trustee to be a new or additional trustee, even though the trust instrument contains a direction that he is not to be appointed.[27]

Section 4. Vesting of Trust Property

1. Vesting declarations. The mere appointment of a person as trustee does not by itself vest the trust property in him; the office of trustee is one thing, the trust property another. On every appointment of a trustee it is accordingly necessary to provide for the vesting of the trust property in the new trustee, either alone (if he is the sole trustee) or jointly with his co-trustees. By virtue of the Trustee Act 1925, s.40,[28] this can often be done without any express conveyance or assignment. The section applies to all trusts, whenever created, unless negatived by the trust instrument, if any[29]; but it does not apply to property held by personal representatives in the course of administration.[30] If the appointment is made by deed, a mere vesting declaration in it suffices to vest the property in those who have become the trustees[31]; and where the deed is made after 1925, then, subject to any express provision to the contrary, it operates as if it contained such a declaration even if none is actually inserted.[32] The section applies to registered land, though the legal estate will not pass until the registrar gives effect to the vesting declaration on the register.[33]

[20] Judicial Trustee Rules 1983, rr. 9, 10, 12. A yearly audit was formerly required: Judicial Trustees Act 1896, s.1(6), partially repealed by Administration of Justice Act 1982, s.75(1) and Sched. 9, Pt. I.
[21] Judicial Trustee Rules 1983, r. 2(1).
[22] *Ibid.* r. 13.
[23] T.A. 1925, s.36, *ante*, p. 202.
[24] *Re Johnston* (1911) 105 L.T. 701.
[25] *Re Ridsdel* [1947] Ch. 597; for the power of compromise, see *post*, p. 270.
[26] s.5.
[27] See further as to the Public Trustee, *post*, p. 208.
[28] Replacing T.A. 1893, s.12.
[29] T.A. 1925, s.69(2).
[30] *Re King's W.T.* [1964] Ch. 542; *sed quaere*; see *ante*, p. 100.
[31] T.A. 1925, s.40(1), (3).
[32] *Ibid.* s.40(1).
[33] L.R.A. 1925, s.47.

2. Exceptions. There are three classes of property to which the section does not apply. They are as follows.[34]

(i) Land held by the trustees by way of mortgage for securing money subject to the trust, except land conveyed on trust for securing debentures or debenture stock.

(ii) Land held under a lease which contains a covenant not to assign without consent, unless before the execution of the deed the requisite consent has been obtained, or unless by virtue of any statute or rule of law the vesting declaration, express or implied, would not operate as a breach of covenant or give rise to a forfeiture.

(iii) Any share, stock, annuity, or property which is only transferable in books kept by a company or other body, or in manner directed by or under Act of Parliament.

These forms of property must be vested in the trustee by the appropriate form of conveyance or transfer. The reason for the first exception is to avoid bringing the trusts on to the title; for otherwise on redemption the mortgagor would have to investigate the title to the mortgage, including, *e.g.* appointments of new trustees, in order to see that he is paying the right persons. The second exception is to avoid accidental breaches of the terms of the lease; and the third exception is made necessary by the normal mode of transferring such property.

3. Vesting orders. If it is difficult or impossible to procure the transfer of the trust property to the trustees, the court has power to make a vesting order.[35]

Section 5. The Public Trustee

1. Appointment and powers. The difficulty frequently experienced in times past of finding a person willing to act as trustee was met by the Public Trustee Act 1906, which established a Public Trustee. The chief advantages derived from appointing him to act as a trustee are as follows. First, being a corporation sole,[36] the office has perpetual existence, despite the death or retirement of the individual from time to time holding it; secondly, the State is responsible for any loss to the trust estate caused by his breaches of trust[37]; and thirdly, he has a wide

---

[34] T.A. 1925, s.40(4).
[35] See *ante*, p. 205.
[36] Public Trustee Act 1906, s.1.
[37] *Ibid.* s.7.

experience in trust matters, and yet his fees are moderate. He may act as a custodian trustee, as an ordinary trustee, or as a judicial trustee, and may act alone or jointly with another person or other persons; and he may hold land.[38]

2. Limits to powers.   There are certain limits to the functions of the Public Trustee.[39] He may decline to accept any trust, except that he must not decline solely on the ground of the smallness of the trust property. Further, he cannot accept any trust exclusively for religious or charitable purposes,[40] nor any except an English trust,[41] nor any trust under a deed of arrangement for the benefit of creditors; nor can he undertake the administration of any estate known or believed by him to be insolvent. He also, as ordinary trustee, cannot carry on a business without the leave of the Treasury, unless he is satisfied that it can be carried on without risk of loss, and he carries it on—

(i)   for not more than 18 months, and

(ii)   with a view to sale, disposition, or winding up.[42]

3. As custodian trustee.[43]   The appointment of the Public Trustee to act as custodian trustee may be made by the court, or by the settlor, or by the person who has power to appoint new trustees. When appointed, the trust property must be transferred to him as if he were sole trustee, and all the securities and documents of title relating to the trust property are to be in his sole custody. Further, all sums payable to or out of the income of the trust property are to be paid to or by him, except that he may allow the dividends and other income to be paid to the other trustees (called the "managing trustees"), or as they may direct. The management of the trust property and the exercise of any power or discretion exercisable by the trustees under the trust remain vested in the managing trustees.[44] Instead of the Public Trustee, certain other corporations may be appointed as custodian trustee,[45] even if the trust is religious or charitable.[46] The court has power to determine a custodian trusteeship if it is expedient,[47] e.g. when it is desirable for the trustee to become an ordinary trustee.[48]

---

[38] *Re Leslie's Hassop Estates* [1911] 1 Ch. 611.
[39] Public Trustee Act 1906, s.2; Public Trustee Rules 1912, r. 7. As to the rules, see *ante*, p. 199, n. 17.
[40] See *Re Hampton* (1919) 88 L.J.Ch. 103. See *ante*, p. 169 for the Official Custodian for Charities.
[41] *Re Hewitt* [1915] 1 Ch. 228.
[42] *Cf.* the powers of personal representatives to carry on a business: *post*, p. 319.
[43] See generally S. G. Maurice (1960) 24 Conv.(N.S.) 196.
[44] Public Trustee Act 1906, s.4.
[45] *Ante*, p. 199.
[46] *Re Cherry's Trusts* [1914] 1 Ch. 83.
[47] Public Trustee Act 1906, s.4.
[48] *Re Squire's Settlement* (1945) 115 L.J.Ch. 90.

4. As ordinary trustee. The Public Trustee may be appointed to be an ordinary trustee, either as an original or a new trustee or as an additional trustee, in the same cases and in the same manner and by the same persons or court as if he were a private trustee; and even if the trustees originally appointed were two or more, the Public Trustee may be appointed sole trustee.[49] This is so despite a direction in the trust instrument that on appointment of new trustees the number shall not be reduced below three.[50] But if the trust instrument prohibits his appointment he may not be appointed a new or additional trustee unless the court otherwise orders.[51] Further, if it is proposed to appoint him as a new or additional trustee, notice must be given to the beneficiaries; and on the application of any beneficiary, the court may prohibit the appointment if it considers it expedient to do so having regard to the interests of all the beneficiaries.[52]

5. As personal representative. The Public Trustee is also given power to obtain probate of a will or letters of administration.[53] Further, with the leave of the court an executor who has obtained probate, or an administrator who has obtained letters of administration, may transfer to the Public Trustee the whole future administration of the estate, and in that way escape all liability in respect of the further administration.[54]

Section 6. Determination of Trusteeship

1. Disclaimer

(a) *Mode of disclaimer.* A person appointed trustee is not bound to act, but may disclaim the trust at any time before he has done anything showing his acceptance of it.[55] Further, he may disclaim even though he had previously agreed to accept the office.[56] The disclaimer is usually effected by deed, though a deed is not essential. It may even be by word of mouth or inferred from conduct,[57] or from the fact that a long time has elapsed since the appointment and the trustee has done nothing,[58] but if informal it must be unequivocal,[59] and may be withdrawn before another party has acted on it.[60]

---

[49] Public Trustee Act 1906, s.5(1).
[50] *Re Moxon* [1916] 2 Ch. 595.
[51] Public Trustee Act 1906, s.5(3).
[52] *Ibid.* s.5(4); see *Re Firth, Firth* v. *Loveridge* [1912] 1 Ch. 806.
[53] Public Trustee Act 1906, s.6(1); Public Trustee Rules, 1912, r. 6.
[54] Public Trustee Act 1906, s.6(2).
[55] See *Re Sharman's W.T.* [1942] Ch. 311 at 314; and see generally on disclaimer *Re Stratton's Deed of Disclaimer* [1958] Ch. 42 (beneficial gift by will).
[56] See *Doyle* v. *Blake* (1804) 2 Sch. & Lef. 231 at 239 (executor).
[57] *Stacey* v. *Elph* (1833) 1 My. & K. 195; and see *Re Paradise Motor Co. Ltd.* [1968] 1 W.L.R. 1125 (gift of shares).
[58] *Re Clout and Frewer's Contract* [1924] 2 Ch. 230; but see *Re Birchall* (1889) 40 Ch.D. 436.
[59] *Re Boyd* [1966] N.Z.L.R. 1109.
[60] See *Re Cranstoun's W.T.* [1949] Ch. 523; *Re Boyd, supra* (benefits under will); *Re Duke of Norfolk's S.T.* [1979] Ch. 37 at 60 (unaffected by the reversal of the decision by C.A.: [1982] Ch. 61).

(b) *Limits to disclaimer.*   A trustee who has accepted the trust cannot afterwards disclaim it; and if a person appointed both executor and trustee proves the will, he is deemed to have accepted the trusts of the will,[61] whereas if he renounces probate, he does not necessarily disclaim the trust, although the renunciation is some evidence of disclaimer.[62] Further, a disclaimer must be of the whole of the trusts; a disclaimer of part, even though distinct and separate from the rest, is ineffectual.[63]

(c) *Effect on property.*   A disclaimer of the trust operates also as a disclaimer of the property, which thereupon reverts to the settlor or his representatives, if the person disclaiming is a sole trustee, or, if there are other trustees, remains in them.[64]

2. Retirement

(a) *Mode of retiring.*   A trustee may obtain a release from his trusteeship in various ways. He may by deed retire from the trust, provided that after his discharge there will be either a trust corporation or at least two individuals to perform the trust, and provided that his co-trustees and the person, if any, entitled to appoint new trustees consent by deed to his retirement.[65] This power applies to all trusts, whenever created, unless negatived by the trust instrument, if any.[66] However, where the Public Trustee has been appointed a trustee, a co-trustee may retire without leaving two trustees and without the consents mentioned above[67]; and a judicial trustee may retire on giving notice to the court stating what proposals he makes as to the appointment of a successor.[68]

(b) *Vesting of property.*   Where a trustee retires under the statutory provision, everything requisite for vesting the trust property in the continuing trustees alone must be done.[69] If the deed of retirement contains a vesting declaration by the retiring and continuing trustees, and by the other person (if any) empowered to appoint new trustees, it will vest the trust property in the continuing trustees alone,[70] except in the case of those properties which cannot be made to vest in this way on the appointment of a new trustee.[71] Where the deed is made after 1925, a vesting declaration is implied unless the contrary is stated.[72]

---

[61] *Mucklow* v. *Fuller* (1821) Jac. 198.
[62] See *Re Gordon, Roberts* v. *Gordon* (1877) 6 Ch.D. 531.
[63] *Re Lord and Fullerton's Contract* [1896] 1 Ch. 228.
[64] *Re Birchall* (1889) 40 Ch.D. 436; *Mallet* v. *Wilson* [1903] 2 Ch. 494.
[65] T.A. 1925, s.39, replacing T.A. 1893, s.11. Before 1893 he could not retire in the absence of an express power, consent of the beneficiaries, or an order of the court: *Manson* v. *Baillie* (1855) 2 Macq. 80.
[66] T.A. 1925, s.69(2).
[67] Public Trustee Act 1906, s.5(2).
[68] Judicial Trustees Act 1896, s.4.
[69] T.A. 1925, s.39(2).
[70] *Ibid.* s.40(2), (3).
[71] *Ibid.* s.40(4); see *ante*, p. 208.
[72] *Ibid.* s.40(2).

3. Replacement. A trustee may be released from his trust by being replaced on the appointment of a new trustee.[73]

4. Removal. Apart from statute, the court has an inherent jurisdiction to remove a trustee (including a trustee of a foreign trust[74]) and to appoint a new one in his place. As the interests of the trust are of paramount importance to the court, this jurisdiction will be exercised whenever the welfare of the beneficiaries requires it,[75] even if the trustees have been guilty of no misconduct.[76] The welfare of the beneficiaries is also the court's guide in exercising its statutory powers of removal, *e.g.* on bankruptcy.[77] A bankrupt trustee ought to be removed from his trusteeship whenever the nature of the trust is such that he has to receive and deal with trust funds so that he can misappropriate them; but if there is no danger to the trust property, bankruptcy by itself will not necessarily induce the court to remove him.[78]

---

[73] See *ante*, p. 202.
[74] *Chellaram* v. *Chellaram* [1985] Ch. 409.
[75] *Re Wrightson* [1908] 1 Ch. 789.
[76] *Letterstedt* v. *Broers* (1884) 9 App.Cas. 371.
[77] T.A. 1925, s.41.
[78] *Re Barker's Trusts* (1875) 1 Ch.D. 43; *Re Adam's Trusts* (1879) 12 Ch.D. 634.

CHAPTER 6

THE DUTIES AND DISCRETIONS OF TRUSTEES

1. The cares of office. The office of trustee is onerous. "A trust is an office necessary in the concerns between man and man, and ... , if faithfully discharged, attended with no small degree of trouble and anxiety," so that "it is an act of great kindness in any one to accept it."[1]

2. Duties and discretions. A trustee has to perform a number of duties and exercise a number of discretions. In discharging his *duties* he must observe the utmost diligence, or *exacta diligentia*, in order to escape liability for any loss sustained by the trust estate. He must obey the trust instrument and the rules of equity unless the court otherwise orders.[2]

In exercising his *discretions*, a trustee must act honestly[3] and must use as much diligence as a prudent man of business would exercise in dealing with his own private affairs; in selecting an investment he must take as much care as a prudent man would take in making an investment for the benefit of persons for whom he felt morally bound to provide.[4] If he is a majority shareholder, he will not, as a prudent businessman, be content with only such information on the company's activities as a minority shareholder would expect to receive.[5] If he takes the same care of the trust property as a man of ordinary prudence would take of his own,[6] he will not be liable for *accidental* loss, such as a theft of the property while in his possession[7] or in the possession of others to whom it has been entrusted in the ordinary course of business,[8] or a depreciation in the value of the securities upon which the trust funds have been rightfully invested.[9]

3. Duties. The duties of trustees are many. Those who are asked to become trustees "are bound to inquire of what the property consists that is proposed to be handed over to them, and what are the trusts. They ought also to look into the trust documents and papers to ascertain what

---

[1] *Knight* v. *Earl of Plymouth* (1747) Dick. 120 at 126, *per* Lord Hardwicke L.C.
[2] *e.g.* under T.A. 1925, s.57, *post*, p. 239.
[3] *Re Smith, Smith* v. *Thompson* [1896] 1 Ch. 71.
[4] *Learoyd* v. *Whiteley* (1887) 12 App.Cas. 727.
[5] *Bartlett* v. *Barclays Bank Trust Co. Ltd.* [1980] Ch. 515.
[6] See *Re Lucking's W.T.* [1968] 1 W.L.R. 866 at 874.
[7] *Morley* v. *Morley* (1678) 2 Ch.Cas. 2.
[8] *Speight* v. *Gaunt* (1883) 9 App.Cas. 1; and see T.A. 1925, s.23, *post*, p. 266.
[9] *Re Chapman, Cocks* v. *Chapman* [1896] 2 Ch. 763.

notices appear among them of incumbrances and other matters affecting the trust."[10] In carrying out the trusts they must take due care of the trust property by investing it prudently and in the manner directed[11]; they must give information to the beneficiaries when required,[12] and in some cases submit to their directions[13]; they must comply with any directions of the court and when in difficulty seek its aid[14]; and, finally, they must make no profit out of the trust unless authorised.[15]

These duties must now be examined in some detail. Yet not all trustees are subject to the same rules. Thus the duties of a trustee in bankruptcy to the bankrupt are not those of an ordinary trustee towards a beneficiary, even though the bankrupt is entitled to any surplus assets; for a trustee in bankruptcy is primarily not a trustee for the bankrupt, but an assignee of his assets for the benefit of his creditors.[16]

Section 1. The Trust Property

A. State of Security

1. Reduction into possession. The primary duty of a trustee is to carry out the directions of the person creating the trust. The directions may be mandatory or permissive, as where a trustee is empowered to retain an asset in the interest of persons not beneficiaries.[17] Subject to any such direction, the overriding duty of a trustee is to place the trust property in a state of security. Thus, if the trust fund be an equitable interest, of which the legal interest cannot for the moment be got in, it is the trustee's duty to lose no time in giving notice to the person in whom the legal interest is vested. Again, if the trust fund be a thing in action which may be reduced into possession, it is the trustee's duty to get it in; and if he neglects to do so for so long that the debt becomes statute-barred or otherwise irrecoverable, he will be liable unless he can show a well-founded belief that an action would have been fruitless.[18]

The same rule applies to an executor. He ought not to allow the assets of the testator to remain outstanding on personal security, even if the debt was a loan by the testator himself on what he deemed an eligible investment; and without good reason he ought not to leave money on loan to bankers for too long a period after the debts and expenses have been paid and more than a year after the testator's death has elapsed.[19] So also a trustee may be in breach of duty if he fails to

---

[10] *Hallows* v. *Lloyd* (1888) 39 Ch.D. 686 at 691, *per* Kekewich J.
[11] *Infra. Quaere* whether he is bound to reside in leasehold property which is subject to a covenant that the tenant should personally inhabit it: see *Lloyds Bank Ltd.* v. *Jones* [1955] 2 Q.B. 298 at 323, 324.
[12] *Post*, p. 231.
[13] *Post*, p. 233.
[14] *Post*, p. 235.
[15] *Post*, p. 245.
[16] See *Re A Debtor, ex p. the Debtor* v. *Dodwell* [1949] Ch. 236 at 240–243: *Re Leadbitter* (1878) 10 Ch.D. 388.
[17] *Hayim* v. *Citibank N.A.* [1987] A.C. 730.
[18] *Re Brogden* (1888) 38 Ch.D. 546. But see T.A. 1925, s.22(2), *post*, p. 271.
[19] See, *e.g. Darke* v. *Martyn* (1839) 1 Beav. 525; and see *post*, pp. 223, 314.

exercise an option to purchase the reversion contained in a lease held by him as trustee.[20] Similarly, where a wife covenanted to settle after-acquired property, the trustee of the settlement was bound to act upon notice or reasonable suspicion that such property had come to her.[21]

There is, however, no positive rule that executors or trustees must, without exercising their own judgment in the matter, call in their testator's mortgages within 12 calendar months from the death, even if the security is risky; nor is there any rule that trustees who retain a security authorised by their trust are liable to make good a loss sustained through any fall in the value of the security.[22] The question in every case is whether the trustees have acted honestly and prudently and in the belief that they were doing what was best for all parties.[23]

2. Joint control by all trustees. Where there are two or more trustees, the trust property should be reduced into the joint control of all the trustees, and it will be a breach of trust for the trustees to leave one of their number in sole control of it. Trustees must not be too trusting, even of their fellow trustees. For instance, if the trust funds were invested in bearer bonds, and A and B, the two trustees, agreed each to hold half of the bonds, B would be liable for the loss if A made away with the bonds in his custody.[24] The proper course to pursue in the case of securities payable to bearer is to deposit them at a bank in the joint names of the trustees.[25] One trustee may, however, safely be left in possession of non-negotiable securities and title deeds; indeed, save in special circumstances, the others have no right to interfere with his possession.[26]

Trustees are now authorised by statute[27] to deposit any document relating to the trust or to the trust property with any banker or banking company, or any other company whose business includes the undertaking of the safe custody of documents; and any sum payable in respect of such deposit is to be paid out of the income.

B. Investment

It is the duty of a trustee to invest the trust property in proper securities so as to obtain the best return by way of income and capital appreciation, judged in relation to the risks involved.[28] The trustee's own social and political views must be disregarded.[29] Originally the only

---

[20] *Elder's Trustee and Executor Co. Ltd.* v. *Higgins* (1963) 113 C.L.R. 426.
[21] *Re Strahan* (1856) 8 De G.M. & G. 291.
[22] *Quaere* whether they are obliged to act on "insider" information which may come their way: see B.A.K. Rider [1978] Conv. 114.
[23] *Re Chapman, Cocks* v. *Chapman* [1896] 2 Ch. 763; *Rawsthorne* v. *Rowley* (1907) [1909] 1 Ch. 409n.; contrast *Re Brookes* [1914] 1 Ch. 558.
[24] *Lewis* v. *Nobbs* (1878) 8 Ch.D. 591.
[25] *Re De Pothonier* [1900] 2 Ch. 529, now made statutory by T.A. 1925, s.7; *post*, p. 224.
[26] *Re Sisson's Settlement* [1903] 1 Ch. 262.
[27] T.A. 1925, s.21.
[28] *Cowan* v. *Scargill* [1985] Ch. 270 at 286, 287.
[29] *Cowan* v. *Scargill* [1985] Ch. 270.

proper investments were mortgages, Government Funds ("Consols") and any other investments authorised by the settlement. The range of authorised investments was substantially extended by a series of statutes, beginning with the Law of Property Amendment Act 1859,[30] and including the Trustee Act 1893,[31] and the Trustee Act 1925, s.1. These permitted trust funds to be invested in a substantial number of securities issued by the Government and various public bodies.

In the years which followed the war of 1939–45, however, this range of securities proved increasingly inadequate, and criticism grew. In particular, in the absence of special powers of investment, trustee could not invest trust funds in good ordinary shares (or "equities") which, by increasing in capital value, could offset the progressive fall in the purchasing power of the pound. The Trustee Investments Act 1961, which was passed and came into force on August 3, 1961, did much to meet these criticisms. It repealed and replaced the Trustee Act 1925, s.1, and established the current list of authorised investments for trustees and personal representatives in the absence of any contrary intention in the trust instrument.[32] It applied to existing trusts.[33] The main provisions of the Act may be stated as follows.

1. Three categories of investments. The First Schedule to the Act establishes three categories of investments. There is power, which has been extensively exercised, to add further investments to any of these categories by Order in Council, subject to disapproval by either House of Parliament.[34]

(a) *Part I: narrower-range without advice.* Defence Bonds, National Savings Certificates, National Development Bonds,[35] British Savings Bonds,[36] National Savings Indexed-Income Bonds,[37] deposits in the National Savings Bank[38] and ordinary deposits in trustee savings banks are the main examples of narrower-range investments which trustees may make without first obtaining advice.

(b) *Part II: narrower-range with advice.* There is a long list of investments which trustees can make subject to obtaining proper advice. Very generally, these investments correspond to the "gilt-edged" securities, bearing interest at fixed rates, which were formerly authorised by the Trustee Act 1925, s.1. They may be divided into six broad categories.

---

[30] See s.32.
[31] See s.1.
[32] See *post*, p. 219.
[33] s.1 and Sched. 1.
[34] s.12.
[35] Added by S.I. 1964 No. 703; and see S.I. 1962 No. 2611 (Ulster Development Bonds).
[36] Added by S.I. 1968 No. 470.
[37] Added by S.I. 1985 No. 1780. And see S.I. 1982 No. 1086 (National Savings Income Bonds); S.I. 1983 No. 1525 (National Savings Deposit Bonds); S.I. 1988 No. 2254 (National Savings Capital Bonds).
[38] See Post Office Act 1969, s.94, Sched. 6, Pt. III.

(1) GOVERNMENT OR PUBLIC SECURITIES: fixed or variable[39] interest securities registered in the United Kingdom and issued by the Government of the United Kingdom,[40] public authorities, nationalised industries,[41] Commonwealth governments and authorities,[42] the International Bank of Reconstruction and Development,[43] or the Inter-American Development Bank,[44] the European Economic Community, the International Monetary Fund and certain other international banking organisations.[45] Certificates of tax deposit,[46] stock of the Bank of Ireland,[47] and securities whose interest is guaranteed by the Government of the United Kingdom[48] are also included.

(2) DEBENTURES: the debentures of large and well-established companies,[49] the Agricultural Mortgage Corporation Ltd. or the Scottish Agricultural Securities Corporation Ltd.,[50] or the debentures or guaranteed or preference stock of certain water undertakings.[51]

(3) LOCAL AUTHORITY LOANS: loans to and deposits with certain local authorities charged on their revenues.[52]

(4) DEPOSITS: deposits in building societies.[53]

(5) MORTGAGES: certain mortgages which are discussed below.[54]

(6) RENTCHARGES: perpetual rentcharges charged on land in England, Wales or Northern Ireland, and feu farm rents, and feu-duties or ground annuals in Scotland.[55]

(c) *Part III: wider-range.* This head includes the shares[56] of building societies within the meaning of the Building Societies Act 1986[57] and units of authorised unit trusts.[58] But the main category consists of

[39] As to variable interest, see S.I. 1977 Nos. 831 (U.K. Government stocks) and 1878 (others).
[40] Trustee Investments Act 1961, 1st Sched., Pt. II, para. 1. The Governments of Northern Ireland and the Isle of Man are also included, and so are Treasury Bills and Tax Reserve Certificates. S.I. 1972 No. 1818 adds certain European fixed interest securities.
[41] para. 3.
[42] para. 4.
[43] para. 5.
[44] Added by S.I. 1964 No. 1404.
[45] Added by S.I. 1983 No. 772 (fixed-interest only).
[46] para. 15, added by S.I. 1975 No. 1710.
[47] para. 7. And see S.I. 1966 No. 401.
[48] para. 2.
[49] para. 6. For the conditions the companies have to satisfy, see under "wider-range," *infra.*
[50] para. 8.
[51] para. 10, varied by S.I. 1973 No. 1393.
[52] para. 9; S.I. 1962 No. 658 (Great Ouse Water Authority): S.I. 1973 No. 1332 (district councils in Northern Ireland); S.I. 1986 No.601 (Inner London Education Authority; residuary bodies under Local Government Act 1985). The interest may be variable: S.I. 1977 No. 1878.
[53] para. 12 (as substituted by Building Societies Act 1986, s.120(1), Sched. 18, Pt. I, para. 4(2)). Loans to designated societies were added by 1981 S.I. No. 1547.
[54] para. 13: see *post,* p. 220.
[55] para. 14. The creation of rentcharges is now prohibited: Rentcharges Act 1977.
[56] Deposits are in Pt. II: see para. 12 thereof, *supra.*
[57] Pt. III, para. 2 (as substituted by Building Societies Act 1986, s.120(1), Sched. 18, Pt. I, para. 4(3)).
[58] para. 3 (as substituted by Financial Services Act 1986, s.212(2), Sched. 16, para. 2(b)).

securities which are not within the narrower range but satisfy five conditions[59]:

  (i)   They are issued in the United Kingdom by a company incorporated in the United Kingdom;

 (ii)   The company has a total issued and paid-up share capital of not less than one million pounds;

(iii)   In each of the five years preceding the calendar year in which the investment is made the company has paid a dividend on all its shares which ranked for dividend for that year;

 (iv)   The price of the securities is quoted on a recognised investment exchange[60]; and

  (v)   The securities are fully paid up, or by the terms of issue are required to be fully paid up within nine months of the date of issue.

2. Division of fund

(a) *Initial division.*   No wider-range investment may be made unless the trust fund has been divided into two parts of equal value at the time of division, called the narrower-range part and the wider-range part.[61] A valuation in writing made by a person reasonably believed by the trustees to be qualified to make it is conclusive in determining whether the division was duly made.[62]

(b) *Subsequent changes.*   If subsequently any property is transferred from one part to the other, a compensating transfer must be made in the opposite direction.[63] Subsequent additions to the trust fund (including any dividends or interest added to it) must be equally divided between the two parts, or else a corresponding equality must be achieved by making a compensating transfer.[64] However, if the addition accrues in respect of property in one part of the fund (as where there is a bonus issue of shares), it is treated as belonging to that part, unless the trustees have to pay for the addition, whether or not at its full value (*e.g.* where there is a "rights" issue of shares), in which case it is treated as a new investment belonging to the fund which provided the money.[65] Further, if in exercising any power or duty the trustees take property out of the trust fund, the Act does not restrict their discretion as to the choice of property to be taken out.[66] The initial equality in the funds is

---

[59] s.1(2), 1st Sched., Pt. IV.
[60] See Financial Services Act 1986, s.212(2), Sched. 16, para. 2(c).
[61] s.2(1).
[62] s.5.
[63] s.2(1).
[64] s.2(3).
[65] *Ibid.*
[66] s.2(4).

thus likely to disappear in time. It is also possible for the principle of equal division to be modified by statutory instrument approved by each House of Parliament, though such a change is limited to producing a maximum proportion of three to one for the wider-range part.[67]

3. Powers of investment. Subject to obtaining proper advice,[68] the Act gives a general authority to trustees to invest funds in any of the three categories of investment; but it subjects wider-range investments to important restrictions.[69] Before any wider-range investments may be made, the fund must be divided in accordance with the previous paragraph[70] and only the wider-range part may be used for making wider-range investments.[71] These provisions as to investment apply not only to trustees but also to persons with statutory powers of making trustee investments[72]; and the Act allows local authorities to pool their funds for the purposes of investment.[73]

4. Express provisions as to investments

(a) *Contrary intention.* The Act takes effect subject to any "contrary intention" expressed in any instrument made after the Act was passed or in any Act or instrument made under an enactment, whenever it was passed or made; but it is not affected by the provisions of any other instrument made before the Act was passed.[74] The Act accordingly enlarged the powers of investment under most pre-existing trusts; and even in trust instruments made after the Act was passed, probably nothing short of an express prohibition will forbid investment in a security authorised by the Act.[75]

(b) *"Special-range property."* The powers conferred by the Act are in addition to all other powers of investment or postponing conversion,[76] *e.g.* a power under an express investment clause or a private Act (called a "special power"). If the trustees wish to invest under the Act, they must first set aside as "special-range property" any investments (except narrower-range investments) which they are authorised to hold

---

[67] s.13.
[68] See *post*, p. 223.
[69] s.1(1).
[70] s.2(1).
[71] s.2(2).
[72] s.7.
[73] s.11.
[74] s.1(3).
[75] See *Re Warren, Public Trustee* v. *Fletcher* [1939] Ch. 684, so construing "contrary intention" in the corresponding T.A. 1925, s.69(2); and see *Re Rider's W.T.* [1958] 1 W.L.R. 974, criticised (1958) 74 L.Q.R. 483; *Re Burke* [1908] 2 Ch. 248. In *Re Havill* [1968] N.Z.L.R. 1116 at 1126, North P. considered that in view of *I.R.C.* v. *Bernstein* [1961] Ch. 399 (cited *post*, p. 279), *Re Warren* should not be followed; but Turner and Richmond JJ. thought otherwise: see at pp. 1131, 1134. Statute sometimes authorises investment in certain securities despite any express prohibition in the trust instrument: see, *e.g.* Finance Act 1918, s.39 (War Loan: see *Re Head* (1919) 88 L.J.Ch. 236); National Loans Act 1939, s.4.
[76] s.3(1).

under a special power, even if they are wider-range investments[77]; and the provisions for division of the fund into the narrower-range part and wider-range part operate only as to the remainder of the fund. In such cases the fund will thus be divided into three parts.

(c) *Special powers.* If since August 3, 1951,[78] either Parliament or the court (*e.g.* under the Variation of Trusts Act 1958[79]) has conferred or varied a special power under the particular trusts in question, the trustees cannot make or retain any wider-range investments under the Act[80]; they must rely on the terms of the special power which Parliament or the court has so recently considered. Although the Act of 1961 did not curtail the powers of the court to authorise the variation of express investment clauses, *e.g.* under the Variation of Trusts Act 1958, or the Trustee Act 1925, s.57,[81] for some years after 1961 the court required evidence of special circumstances[82] before it would extend powers of investment beyond those given by the Act.[83] But with the passage of time, and given the significant changes which have taken place in investment conditions, a more flexible approach is now adopted and each application for extension will be considered on its merits.[84] And it may be that the court will no longer cut down a wide special power so as to bring it into line with the Act.[85] Further, the court may allow a delegation of the power of investment.[86]

5. Mortgages

(a) *Authorised mortgages*

(1) REAL SECURITIES. Before the Trustee Investments Act 1961, trustees had a power to invest in "real securities" in the United Kingdom,[87] and this included mortgages of freeholds and certain unusual types of leasehold with at least 200 years unexpired.[88] The cases established that such mortgages must be first legal mortgages, and not second mortgages[89] or equitable mortgages.[90] Contributory mortgages were also excluded, for under these the trustee would be parting with

---

[77] s.3(3), 2nd Sched.
[78] *i.e.* 10 years before the Act was passed.
[79] See *post*, p. 241.
[80] s.3(4), 3rd Sched.
[81] s.15; and see *post*, pp. 239, 243.
[82] See *Re University of London Charitable Trusts* [1964] Ch. 282; *Mason* v. *Farbrother* [1983] 2 All E.R. 1078; *British Museum (Trustees of the)* v. *Att.-Gen.* [1984] 1 W.L.R. 418 at 425, 426.
[83] *Re Kolb's W.T.* [1962] Ch. 531 (appeal compromised: (1962) 106 S.J. 669); *Re Cooper's Settlement* [1962] Ch. 826.
[84] *British Museum (Trustees of the)* v. *Att.-Gen.* [1984] 1 W.L.R. 418; *Steel* v. *Wellcome Custodian Trustees Ltd.* [1988] 1 W.L.R. 167.
[85] See *Re Clarke's W.T.* [1961] 1 W.L.R. 1471; for the restrictions under the Act, see *ante*, pp. 217, 218.
[86] *Steel* v. *Wellcome Custodian Trustees Ltd., supra.* For delegation see *post*, p. 265.
[87] T.A. 1925, s.1(1)(*a*).
[88] *Ibid.* s.5(1); and see *Re Chennell* (1878) 8 Ch.D. 492.
[89] *Chapman* v. *Browne* [1902] 1 Ch. 785 at 800; *Re Newland* [1904] W.N. 181.
[90] *Swaffield* v. *Nelson* [1876] W.N. 255.

his exclusive control over the trust property[91]; but there was nothing to prohibit sub-mortgages.[92]

(2) MORTGAGES. The Act of 1961 has repealed this power to invest in "real securities" as such, but instead it has included in the list of Part II investments (*i.e.* narrower-range with advice) "mortgages of freehold property" in England, Wales or Northern Ireland, or of "leasehold property in those countries" if the lease has at least 60 years to run, and loans on heritable security in Scotland. The Act, however, gives no indication whether the former restrictions still apply to investing in the inferior types of mortgage mentioned above. Probably they do; for the Act displays no intention of changing the type of mortgage required, as distinct from the property mortgaged. In any case, a trustee would be ill-advised to assume the contrary.

(3) CHARGES. The Act has left unchanged certain other provisions in the Trustee Act 1925, relating to the former power to invest in "real securities." These enable a trustee with such a power to invest on a charge, or a mortgage of a charge, made under the Improvement of Land Act 1864[93] and to accept a security in the form of a charge by way of legal mortgage.[94] Probably these provisions will be treated as extending to the new power to invest in "mortgages."

(b) *Discretion.* Even when a proposed mortgage is authorised, a trustee must exercise a proper discretion. He is not justified in lending upon a mortgage merely because it satisfies the statutory requirements. He should not, for instance, lend on the security of a freehold brickfield[95]; and "if the security is really a business plus the premises upon which it is carried on, trustees are well advised to have nothing to do with it."[96] Yet the circumstances may make a loan of nearly two-thirds the value of business premises a proper transaction[97]; and there is no rule that trustees cannot lend on the security of property let on weekly tenancies.[98]

(c) *Amount of loan on mortgage.* A trustee who is lending trust funds on mortgage must be careful to leave sufficient margin for depreciation. Under the Trustee Act 1925,[99] a trustee may lend not more than two-thirds of the value of any suitable property, provided he complies with the statutory procedure; the margin of one-third allows for fluctuations in value.[1] If a proper mortgage in fact provides insufficient security, the sum realised (or any assets received in lieu of

[91] *Webb* v. *Jonas* (1888) 39 Ch.D. 660.
[92] *Smethurst* v. *Hastings* (1885) 30 Ch.D. 490.
[93] T.A. 1925, s.5(1)(*b*).
[94] *Ibid.* s.5(2). For this form of mortgage, see L.P.A. 1925, s.87; *post*, p. 392.
[95] *Learoyd* v. *Whiteley* (1887) 12 App.Cas. 727.
[96] *Palmer* v. *Emerson* [1911] 1 Ch. 758 at 766, *per* Eve J.
[97] *Palmer* v. *Emerson* [1911] 1 Ch. 758.
[98] *Re Solomon, Nore* v. *Meyer* [1912] 1 Ch. 261 (appeal compromised [1913] 1 Ch. 200).
[99] s.8; see *post*, p. 267.
[1] See *Re Medland* (1889) 41 Ch.D. 476 at 481.

the mortgage debt and interest[2]) will be apportioned between the tenant
for life and the remainderman in the proportions which the arrears of
interest bear to the capital debt.[3]

(d) *Leaving part of price on mortgage.* On a sale of land for an
estate in fee simple or for a term having at least 500 years to run,
trustees[4] may, with the consent of any person whose consent to a
change of investments is requisite,[5] agree to leave not more than two-
thirds of the purchase price on mortgage, though the mortgagor must
covenant to keep any buildings insured against fire to their full value.
No report as to value or advice as to making the loan is required in this
case,[6] and the trustees are not liable if the security proves insufficient.[7]

(e) *Postponed repayment.* With the consent of any person whose
consent to a change of investment is requisite,[8] trustees lending on
mortgage may contract not to call in the mortgage money for a fixed
period not exceeding seven years, provided interest is paid within a
specified time not exceeding 30 days after it becomes due, and provided
that the mortgagor commits no breach of any covenant for the
maintenance or protection of the property.[9]

(f) *Purchase of land.* The former power under the Trustee Act 1925,
to invest in "real securities," and the present power under the Trustee
Investments Act 1961, to invest in "mortgages," do not authorise the
trustee to *purchase* land, because that is an alienation out and out of the
trust property. To justify the purchase of land trustees must accordingly
be able to rely either on some other statutory power or on an express
power.[10] Thus capital money under the Settled Land Act 1925 may be
used in the purchase of land,[11] and under the Law of Property Act
1925[12] trustees for sale of land may buy land either with the proceeds of
sale or with traceable investments of such proceeds,[13] provided they
have not, by parting with all their land, ceased to be trustees for sale
within the statutory definition.[14] Although an express power to "invest"
in land may be wide enough to authorise the purchase of land yielding
an income,[15] it does not authorise the purchase of land for some other
purpose, such as use as a residence for the tenant for life.[16]

---

[2] *Re Morris's W.T.* [1960] 1 W.L.R. 1210.
[3] *Re Atkinson, Barbers' Co.* v. *Grose-Smith* [1904] 2 Ch. 160.
[4] Including a tenant for life or statutory owner.
[5] T.A. 1925, s.10(5).
[6] See *post*, p. 267.
[7] T.A. 1925, s.10(2).
[8] *Ibid.* s.10(5).
[9] *Ibid.* s.10(2).
[10] See *Re Mordan* [1905] 1 Ch. 515; *Re Wragg* [1919] 2 Ch. 58.
[11] S.L.A. 1925, s.73(1)(xi) (freeholds, or leaseholds with at least 60 years unexpired).
[12] s.28(1).
[13] *Re Wellsted's W.T.* [1949] Ch. 296.
[14] L.P.A. 1925, s.205(1)(xxix); *Re Wakeman, National Provincial Bank Ltd.* v. *Wakeman* [1945] Ch.
177. In *Re Wellsted's W.T., supra*, at p. 319, Cohen L.J. expressly left this point open.
[15] See *Re Wragg, supra.*
[16] *Re Power* [1947] Ch. 572 (the court in fact authorised purchase under T.A. 1925, s.57 (see *post*,
p. 239; (1947) 91 S.J. 541).

6. Advice

(a) *Investment.* In exercising his powers of investment, a trustee is under a general duty to have regard to the need for diversification of investments, so far as is appropriate, and to the suitability to the trust of the investments proposed, both as to type and as to the particular investments.[17] Further, except in the case of Part I investments (narrower-range without advice), before investing under the Act of 1961, or under a special power conferred before the passing of the Act or by a statute passed before then, the trustee must obtain and consider proper advice on whether the investment is satisfactory having regard to the need for diversification and (except in the case of mortgages[18]) suitability.[19]

(b) *Retention.* A trustee who retains any such investment must "determine at what intervals the circumstances, and in particular the nature of the investment," make it desirable to obtain proper advice; and he must obtain and consider such advice accordingly.[20]

(c) *"Proper advice."* For these purposes, "proper advice" means the advice of a person whom the trustee reasonably believes to be "qualified by his ability in and practical experience of financial matters"[21]; and the advice must be given or subsequently confirmed in writing.[22] A person may give such advice even if he does so in the course of his employment as an officer or servant,[23] *e.g.* of the trustee itself. However, the requirement of obtaining advice before investing and the obligations relating to advice in the retention of investments do not apply where an officer or servant competent to give advice is himself exercising the powers of a trustee, nor do they apply to one of two or more trustees where he is the person giving the requisite advice,[24] though they seem to apply to his fellow trustees.

7. Extent of powers. A number of supplementary provisions relating to a trustee's powers of investment must be mentioned.

(a) *Deposit pending investment.* Pending the negotiation and preparation of a mortgage, or while an investment is being sought, a trustee may pay trust money into a deposit or other account at a bank; and any interest it earns is applicable as income.[25]

---

[17] Trustee Investments Act 1961, s.6(1).
[18] *Ibid.* s.6(7). For mortgages, see *post,* p. 267.
[19] *Ibid.* s.6(2)., For special powers, see *ante,* p. 219.
[20] *Ibid.* s.6(3).
[21] *Ibid.* s.6(4).
[22] *Ibid.* s.6(5).
[23] *Ibid.* s.6(4).
[24] *Ibid.* s.6(6).
[25] T.A. 1925, s.11(1).

(b) *Redeemable stock.* A trustee may invest in authorised securities even if they are redeemable and the price exceeds their redemption value.[26] A trustee may also retain until redemption any redeemable stock properly purchased.[27]

(c) *Bearer securities.* Unless expressly prohibited by the trust instrument, a trustee may purchase or retain authorised securities even if they are payable to bearer; but any trustee other than a trust corporation must deposit them at a bank for safe custody and collection of income.[28] The trustee is not responsible for any loss occasioned by reason of such a deposit; and any sums payable in respect of such deposit and collection must be paid out of the income of the trust property.[29]

(d) *Securities becoming unauthorised.* If after an authorised investment has been made the security becomes unauthorised, a trustee is not liable for breach of trust merely because he retains it.[30]

(e) *Variation of investments.* The statutory powers of investment are not confined to uninvested money. They apply to all trust property, whether or not already invested; and there is an express power to vary investments.[31] These powers authorise the sale even of securities specifically bequeathed in trust for persons in succession.[32]

8. Companies. In relation to securities in a company, trustees have certain additional powers.

(a) *Calls.* A trustee may apply capital money subject to a trust in payment of the calls on any shares subject to the same trust.[33]

(b) *Reconstruction.* With the consent of any person whose consent is requisite to a change of investment,[34] trustees who hold securities in a company may concur in any scheme or arrangement for the reconstruction of the company, or its amalgamation with another company, or for selling to another company its property and undertaking, or for another company to acquire its securities, or control

---

[26] T.A. 1925, s.2(1). The repeal of part of this subsection by the Trustee Investments Act 1961, s.16, 5th Sched., presumably indicates that the rest applies to investments under the Act of 1961, despite the unpromising wording.
[27] *Ibid.*, s.2(2), presumably applying to the Act of 1961.
[28] *Ibid.*, s.7(1); see, *e.g. Re De Pothonier* [1900] 2 Ch. 529. For trust corporations, see *ante*, p. 198.
[29] *Ibid.*, s.7(2).
[30] *Ibid.* s.4.
[31] Trustee Investments Act 1961, s.1(1), replacing T.A. 1925, s.1(1); and see *Hume* v. *Lopes* [1892] A.C. 112.
[32] *Re Pratt's W.T.* [1943] Ch. 326.
[33] T.A. 1925, s.11(2).
[34] *Ibid.* s.10(5).

of it, or for the release, modification or variation of any rights, privileges or liabilities attached to the securities; and the trustees may exchange their existing shares for any new shares.[35] Provided that the trustees act in good faith, they are not responsible for any consequent loss.[36]

(c) *Preferential rights.* If any conditional or preferential right to subscribe for any securities in a company is offered to trustees in respect of any holding in the company, they may, with the like consent,[37] either exercise such right and apply capital money subject to the trust in payment of the consideration, retaining the securities as if they were the original holding,[38] or else renounce such right, or sell it to any person (including a beneficiary), without being responsible for loss if they act in good faith. If they sell the right, the purchase-money will be capital money.[39]

9. Express investment clauses

(a) *Use of clauses.* There is nothing to prevent a trust instrument containing a clause which allows trustees a wider range of permitted investments than those authorised by the Trustee Investments Act 1961. In the 15 years before the Act was passed, such clauses became increasingly common as under modern conditions the defects of the Trustee Act 1925, s.1, became more apparent; and although the Act of 1961 has reduced the need for such clauses, they are still often employed. The modern tendency is to construe such clauses more liberally than was formerly the case.[40] A trustee may even be (and sometimes is) authorised to invest in such stocks, shares and securities as in his absolute discretion he shall think fit.[41] Yet even words such as these do not authorise loans merely on personal credit,[42] or retaining the settlor's assets in a business which the trustees have no power to carry on.[43]

(b) *Discretion.* However wide the language of such clauses, they give the trustee an absolute discretion in appearance only; as in the case of all discretionary powers, he must act honestly and with ordinary prudence.[44] If, therefore, he selects an investment for the purpose of

---

[35] *Ibid.* s.10(3); Trustee Investments Act 1961, s.9(1), overruling *Re Walker's Settlement* [1935] Ch. 567.
[36] T.A. 1925, s.10(3).
[37] *Ibid.* s.10(5), *supra.*
[38] Trustee Investments Act 1961, s.9(2).
[39] T.A. 1925, s.10(4).
[40] Contrast *Re Maryon-Wilson Estate* [1912] 1 Ch. 55 with *Re Harari's S.T.* [1949] 1 All E.R. 430; *Re Hart's W.T.* [1943] 2 All E.R. 557; and *Re Douglas's W.T.* [1959] 1 W.L.R. 744 (affirmed on another point [1959] 1 W.L.R. 1212). And see *Re Kolb's W.T.* [1962] Ch. 531 ("blue chip category" void for uncertainty).
[41] *e.g. Re Harari's S.T.* [1949] 1 All E.R. 430.
[42] *Re Peczenik's S.T.* [1964] 1 W.L.R. 720.
[43] See *Re Berry* [1962] Ch. 97.
[44] See *ante,* p. 213.

making a private gain,[45] or if at the request of an importunate *cestui que trust* he invests the trust funds on a notoriously doubtful security, even though it may be expressly authorised, he will be liable for any resulting loss.[46] The same rule applies to a power to lend money on personal security, or to continue a loan made by the settlor, so that authority to continue a loan made to a partnership will not, as a matter of course, survive a change in the firm.[47]

Section 2. Howe v. Earl of Dartmouth

A. Duty to Convert

1. Statement of the rule. As has already been mentioned, it is the duty of a trustee to preserve the trust property. It is also his duty to hold the scales evenly between the beneficiaries, and not to favour one at the expense of another.[48] Accordingly, under the rule in *Howe* v. *Earl of Dartmouth*,[49] where there is a residuary bequest of personal estate to be enjoyed by persons in succession, the trustees must, unless the will shows a contrary intention, realise such parts of the estate as are of a wasting character (*e.g.* copyrights) or of a reversionary nature (*e.g.* interests subject to subsisting life interests), or are otherwise not investments authorised by the general law or by the will, and invest the proceeds in some authorised security.

The trustees must do this despite the absence of any express direction to convert in the will; for in the absence of a contrary intention, the court assumes that the testator intended his legatees to enjoy the same thing in succession, and so requires the property to be converted into permanent investments of a recognised character.[50] Wasting and hazardous securities are to be converted in the interest of the remaindermen, reversionary interests for the benefit of the tenant for life. But this duty to convert does not arise where the property is settled by deed,[51] nor where the bequest is not residuary but specific; nor does the duty apply to realty[52] or to property passing on intestacy. In this case, however, statute[53] imposes a trust for sale with power to postpone

---

[45] *Re Smith, Smith* v. *Thompson* [1896] 1 Ch. 71.
[46] *Knox* v. *Mackinnon* (1888) 13 App.Cas. 753.
[47] *Re Tucker* [1894] 3 Ch. 429 at 432.
[48] *Lloyds Bank plc* v. *Duker* [1987] 1 W.L.R. 1324 at 1330, 1331, citing this passage.
[49] (1802) 7 Ves. 137; **1 W. & T.L.C. 60**; *Macdonald* v. *Irvine* (1878) 8 Ch.D. 101. For a general survey of the rule, see S. J. Bailey (1943) 7 Conv.(N.S.) 128, 191; and for an examination of the actual decision, see L. A. Sheridan (1952) 16 Conv.(N.S.) 349.
[50] See *Hinves* v. *Hinves* (1844) 3 Hare 609 at 611.
[51] *Re Van Straubenzee* [1901] 2 Ch. 779.
[52] See *Re Woodhouse* [1941] Ch. 332.
[53] A.E.A. 1925, s.33(1).

sale.[54] Where the duty exists, the conversion must, in general, be effected within a year from the testator's death.[55]

2. Exclusion of the rule. The duty to convert may be excluded either by an express direction to the contrary in the will, or by a sufficient indication in the will of the testator's intention to exclude[56] it, the burden of proof resting on the person who says it is not to arise.[57] For example, the duty to convert does not arise where the testator expressly authorises the retention of unauthorised investments,[58] or where he gives the trustees a discretionary power to sell when and as they shall deem expedient.[59] Nor does it apply where he gives the income of the residue to be enjoyed *in specie* either expressly[60] or impliedly, as by directing his estate to be divided into certain portions at the death of the life tenant,[61] or (if the estate comprises leaseholds but no freeholds) by directing the trustees to pay the *rents* to the tenant for life. In the last-mentioned case the trustees would have to retain the leaseholds[62]; but if the testator left freeholds as well as leaseholds, there would be no implied gift of the leaseholds *in specie*, since the word "rents" could be satisfied by being applied to the freeholds.[63]

The rule does not apply to foreign leaseholds if the foreign law allows the tenant for life to enjoy them *in specie*.[64]

3. Express trust to convert. Sometimes a will imposes an express trust for sale. In such cases, there is no room for the duty to convert implied by *Howe* v. *Earl of Dartmouth*, and the scope and effect of the trust for sale depends on the terms of the will.[65]

B. *Apportionment between Capital and Income*

Where residuary personalty is given to persons in succession, and the trustees do not at once convert the property, questions often arise as to the respective rights of the tenant for life and remaindermen until conversion. If the testator has expressly or impliedly given the tenant for life the whole of any income arising before conversion, neither more nor

[54] See *post,* p. 314.
[55] See *Grayburn* v. *Clarkson* (1868) 3 Ch.App. 605. On the impact of the Trustee Investments Act 1961, see (1961) 80 L.N. 274.
[56] In *Re Gough* [1957] Ch. 323 the indications were very tenuous.
[57] *Macdonald* v. *Irvine* (1878) 8 Ch.D. 101; *Re Evans' W.T., Pickering* v. *Evans* [1921] 2 Ch. 309.
[58] *Brown* v. *Gellatly* (1867) 2 Ch.App. 751.
[59] *Re Pitcairn* [1896] 2 Ch. 199.
[60] *Re Wilson, Moore* v. *Wilson* [1907] 1 Ch. 394.
[61] *Re Barratt* [1925] Ch. 550; and see *Alcock* v. *Sloper* (1833) 2 My. & K. 699.
[62] *Goodenough* v. *Tremamondo* (1840) 2 Beav. 512.
[63] *Re Wareham* [1912] 2 Ch. 312, approving *Re Game* [1897] 1 Ch. 881.
[64] *Re Moses* [1908] 2 Ch. 235.
[65] See *Re Berry* [1962] Ch. 97 at 110, 111.

less, no question arises.[66] But where he has not done so the following rules apply except so far as the will excludes them.[67]

1. Authorised investments.   The tenant for life is entitled as from the death to the actual income of so much of the residue as is at the testator's death invested in authorised securities. Where there is no express direction to convert, any investment which the trustees retain under a power to retain is treated as an authorised investment, even if it is wasting or hazardous.[68] This is so even if there is an express trust for conversion with an independent power to retain,[69] although it is otherwise if the power to retain investments is only ancillary or subsidiary to the trust for conversion.[70]

2. Leaseholds.   Since 1925, in the case of settled land and land held on trust for sale, long leaseholds (*i.e.* leases having more than 60 years unexpired) have been authorised investments[71] and so outside the rule in *Howe* v. *Earl of Dartmouth*.[72] But in any event the tenant for life is entitled to the whole net income of all leaseholds, both authorised and unauthorised, for statute[73] provides that the net rents and profits of land held upon trust for sale, after keeping down costs of repairs and insurance and other outgoings, are to be applied in like manner as the income of investments representing the purchase-money would be applicable if a sale had been made and the proceeds had been duly invested. This applies whether the trust for sale is express,[74] or statutory,[75] or, it seems, arises under *Howe* v. *Earl of Dartmouth* itself.[76]

The same rule also applies where trust money is invested in leasehold securities which have become vested in the trustees free of the equity of redemption, whether by limitation, foreclosure or otherwise. Until sale under the consequent trust for sale,[77] the tenant for life is entitled to the rents in full even if they exceed the interest payable under the mortgage; on the other hand if the rents are less than the interest, the tenant for life has no claim on the capital for the deficiency.[78] This

---

[66] *Re Chancellor* (1884) 26 Ch.D. 42; *Rowlls* v. *Bebb* [1900] 2 Ch. 107; *Re Godfree* [1914] 2 Ch. 110.
[67] See, *e.g. Re Hey's S.T.* [1945] Ch. 294.
[68] *Re Bates, Hodgson* v. *Bates* [1907] 1 Ch. 22; *Re Nicholson, Eade* v. *Nicholson* [1909] 2 Ch. 111.
[69] *Re Inman* [1915] 1 Ch. 187.
[70] *Re Chaytor* [1905] 1 Ch. 233; *Re Berry* [1962] Ch. 97 (it is arguable that the business held unauthorised was in fact authorised: see *Re Crowther* [1895] 2 Ch. 56, *post*, p. 320, not cited in *Re Berry*). See also *Re Rudd's W.T.* [1952] 1 All E.R. 254.
[71] S.L.A. 1925, s.73(1)(xi); L.P.A. 1925, s.28(1), *ante*, p. 222.
[72] *Re Gough* [1957] Ch. 323 (long leasehold as part of settled residue, thus constituting settled land, though still personalty).
[73] L.P.A. 1925, s.28(2).
[74] *Re Brooker, Brooker* v. *Brooker* [1926] W.N. 93.
[75] *Re Berton* [1939] Ch. 200.
[76] See S. J. Bailey (1932) 4 C.L.J. 357.
[77] See L.P.A. 1925, s.31; *post*, p. 261.
[78] *Re Horn's Estate* [1924] 2 Ch. 222.

provision[79] is confined to land, and the other rules stated here are not affected by the legislation of 1925.[80]

3. Unauthorised pure personalty

(a) *Apportionment of income.* Where the securities are not authorised and there is a duty to sell, whether under the rule in *Howe* v. *Earl of Dartmouth*,[81] or under an express direction to sell,[82] the income is adjusted so that the tenant for life receives a fair yield.[83] If the actual income exceeds the fair yield, as is often the case with wasting or speculative shares, the surplus income is treated as capital, although the tenant for life is entitled to any income which it subsequently produces.[84] If, on the other hand, the actual income is less than the fair yield, the tenant for life is entitled to have his income made up to this yield out of any excess income in future (but not past) years, and, if necessary, out of any capital when it is realised.[85]

(b) *The "four per cent." rule.* Originally the "fair yield" was taken as being the income which would have been produced had the securities been realised and the proceeds invested in Consols.[86] Later, when the range of authorised investments had become greatly extended,[87] 4 per cent. on the value of the securities was taken instead,[88] and after this had for a period been reduced to 3 per cent.,[89] it was again raised to 4 per cent.,[90] a figure which was held to be still applicable where the testator died in 1936.[91] A higher figure would probably now be fixed.[92]

(c) *Date of valuation.* Where there is no power to postpone sale, then whether the duty to sell is express[93] or implied under *Howe* v. *Earl of Dartmouth*,[94] the interest must be calculated on the value of the property one year after the testator's death[95] for, having regard to the "executor's year,"[96] this is when the conversion should have been made.[97] If, however, the securities are in fact sold within the year, the net proceeds of sale must be taken instead[98]; and if sale is properly[99]

---

[79] *i.e.* L.P.A. 1925, s.28(2).
[80] *Re Trollope's W.T.* [1927] 1 Ch. 596.
[81] *Meyer* v. *Simonsen* (1852) 5 De G. & Sm. 723; *Brown* v. *Gellatly* (1867) 2 Ch.App. 751.
[82] *Gibson* v. *Bott* (1802) 7 Ves. 89; *Dimes* v. *Scott* (1827) 4 Russ. 195.
[83] See *Re Fisher* [1943] Ch. 377; *Re Eaton* (1894) 70 L.T. 761; and cases in preceding note.
[84] *Re Woods* [1904] 2 Ch. 4.
[85] *Re Fawcett* [1940] Ch. 402.
[86] *Howe* v. *Earl of Dartmouth* (1802) 7 Ves. 137.
[87] *Re Fawcett, supra*, at p. 407.
[88] *Meyer* v. *Simonsen, supra.*
[89] *Re Woods, supra.*
[90] *Re Owen, Slater* v. *Owen* [1912] 1 Ch. 519; *Re Beech* [1920] 1 Ch. 40.
[91] *Re Parry, Brown* v. *Parry* [1947] Ch. 23; and perhaps even in 1947: see *Re Lucas, Bethune* v. *Lucas* [1947] Ch. 558 at 563, 564.
[92] See *post*, p. 289.
[93] *Re Parry, supra.*
[94] *Brown* v. *Gellatly* (1867) 2 Ch.App. 751.
[95] *Dimes* v. *Scott* (1827) 4 Russ. 195.
[96] See *post*, p. 310.
[97] See *Re Parry, supra*, at p. 40.
[98] *Re Fawcett* [1940] Ch. 402.
[99] See *Wentworth* v. *Wentworth* [1900] A.C. 163.

postponed under a power to postpone sale, the valuation must be made as at the testator's death, for lack of any other appropriate moment.[1]

4. Re Earl of Chesterfield's Trusts

(a) *Duty to apportion.* The duty of apportionment under the rule in *Howe* v. *Earl of Dartmouth*, which prevents injustice to the reversioner, is complemented by the rule in *Re Earl of Chesterfield's Trusts*,[2] which prevents injustice to the tenant for life.[3] For if a reversion or other interest which is producing no income[4] is retained, the rule requires that when eventually it falls in or is realised, the sum received should be apportioned between capital and income; and this is so even if part of the sum received consists of interest or other income.[5] The rule has been applied to a mortgage debt with arrears of interest,[6] arrears of an annuity with interest,[7] compensation and interest for loss of the development value of land,[8] moneys payable on a life policy,[9] the price on a sale payable by instalments,[10] and other similar interests,[11] but an income-producing asset in possession is not brought within the rule merely because it is subject to a charge for a fluctuating amount of income.[12]

(b) *Mode of apportionment.* The apportionment is made by ascertaining the sum which, put out at 4 per cent. interest on the day of the testator's death and accumulating at compound interest calculated at that rate, with yearly rests and deducting income tax, would, with the accumulations of income, have produced the amount actually received. The sum so ascertained is treated as capital and the rest as income.[13] At one time the rate of interest was reduced to 3 per cent.[14] though later 4 per cent. was restored,[15] and it may be that a higher figure should now be taken.[16] But this rule does not apply if the will shows an intention that the tenant for life is to have the actual income produced by the residue, in which case he gets no income in respect of property which is yielding none.[17] The rule does, however, apply on an intestacy.[18]

---

[1] *Re Parry, supra; cf. Wentworth* v. *Wentworth, supra.*
[2] (1883) 24 Ch.D. 643.
[3] See *Re Woodhouse* [1941] Ch. 332 at 335.
[4] *Re Chance's W.T.* [1962] Ch. 593 at 613.
[5] *Re Chance's W.T.* [1962] Ch. 593.
[6] *Re Hubbuck* [1896] 1 Ch. 754; *Beavan* v. *Beavan* (1869) 24 Ch.D. 649n.
[7] *Beavan* v. *Beavan, supra.*
[8] *Re Chance's W.T., supra.*
[9] *Re Fisher* [1943] Ch. 377.
[10] *Re Hollebone* [1919] 2 Ch. 93.
[11] See, *e.g. Re Payne* (1943) 113 L.J.Ch. 46; *Re Guinness's Settlement* [1966] 1 W.L.R. 1355 (payments resulting to the testator's estate after a disclaimer of a life interest under a settlement made by him).
[12] *Re Holliday, Houghton* v. *Adlard* [1947] Ch. 402.
[13] *Re Earl of Chesterfield's Trusts* (1883) 24 Ch.D. 643; and see *Re Fisher, supra.*
[14] *Rowlls* v. *Bebb* [1900] 2 Ch. 107.
[15] *Re Baker, Baker* v. *Public Trustee* [1924] 2 Ch. 271.
[16] See *post,* p. 289.
[17] *Mackie* v. *Mackie* (1845) 5 Hare 70; *Rowlls* v. *Bebb* [1900] 2 Ch. 107.
[18] *Re Fisher* [1943] Ch. 377.

5. Realty. These rules as to apportionment apply only to personalty and not to realty.[19] Even where there is an express direction to convert realty, the tenant for life is entitled to the whole net income produced by it until sale,[20] after keeping down costs of repairs, insurance and other outgoings.[21] On the other hand, if the realty is not actually producing income he will have no other claim to any part of the proceeds when it is sold.[22]

6. Exclusion of the rules. In order to avoid complicated accounting, wills often contain a provision excluding the rule in *Howe* v. *Earl of Dartmouth* in all its branches.[23] Such a provision will exclude both the duty to convert and the rules for apportionment, including *Re Earl of Chesterfield's Trusts.* An express power to postpone conversion will not by itself exclude the rules for apportionment[24]; but a power to postpone conversion coupled with a direction that the tenant for life is to receive the income *in specie* pending conversion will, if the power is duly exercised, exclude both branches of the rule.[25] It is otherwise if the trustees merely fail to exercise the power of postponement, whether through supineness or ignorance of the existence of the asset to be converted.[26]

Where *Howe* v. *Earl of Dartmouth* does not apply, a tenant for life can retain the whole of the income which he receives from any unauthorised investments, provided the capital fund is not diminished by reason of such investments; this principle holds good even if the tenant for life happens also to be the sole trustee, or one of the trustees.[27]

Section 3. Duty to Keep Accounts and Records

1. The duty. Another duty of a trustee[28] is to keep accounts and produce them to any beneficiary when required.[29] Trustees must also when required give any beneficiary all reasonable information as to the manner in which the trust estate has been dealt with and as to the investments representing it.[30] When a beneficiary comes of age they

---

[19] *Re Woodhouse* [1941] Ch. 332.
[20] *Re Searle, Searle* v. *Baker* [1900] 2 Ch. 829; *Re Oliver, Wilson* v. *Oliver* [1908] 2 Ch. 74.
[21] L.P.A. 1925, s.28(2).
[22] *Yates* v. *Yates* (1860) 28 Beav. 637.
[23] See, *e.g.* E. F. and J. H. George (1946) 10 Conv.(N.S.) 125 at 129; and even without such a provision, often in practice no apportionment is made.
[24] *Re Berry* [1962] Ch. 97, not following *Re Fisher* [1943] Ch. 377 at 385, 386.
[25] *Rowlls* v. *Bebb* [1900] 2 Ch. 107; *ante*, pp. 227, 228; and see *post*, p. 314 for the statutory trust for sale, power to postpone, and directions as to income pending sale on intestacy.
[26] *Re Fisher, supra; Re Hey's S.T.* [1945] Ch. 294; *Re Guinness's Settlement* [1966] 1 W.L.R. 1355.
[27] *Slade* v. *Chaine* [1908] 1 Ch. 522; *Re Hoyles* [1912] 1 Ch. 67.
[28] For the position of judicial trustees as regards accounts, see *ante*, p. 207. For personal representatives, see A.E.A. 1925, s.25, as substituted by A.E.A. 1971, s.9.
[29] See *Pearse* v. *Green* (1819) 1 Jac. & W. 135 at 140.
[30] *Re Dartnall* [1895] 1 Ch. 474.

must inform him of his interest under the trust.[31] Further, in the absence of special circumstances, they must allow a beneficiary to inspect all title deeds and other documents relating to the trust estate.[32] In this context a beneficiary includes a contingent beneficiary or an object of a discretionary trust,[33] save that trustees who exercise discretionary powers (*e.g.* under a discretionary trust) need not disclose why they have exercised their discretion in a particular way,[34] and so they may refuse to allow a beneficiary to inspect documents which will reveal such information, such as minutes of their meetings.[35] A trustee must, however, produce to his successor documents relating to the administration of the trust[36]; and subject to the payment of costs, statute requires him to produce to any person interested any notice of any dealing with the beneficiary's interest which he has received.[37]

A trustee who fails to deliver accounts may be ordered to pay the costs of any application to the court rendered necessary by his default.[38] It is, however, no part of a trustee's duty to give legal advice to the beneficiary,[39] or, apart from the above-mentioned statutory obligation, to give to him or to any person proposing to take an assignment of his interest, information as to the way in which the beneficiary himself has dealt with that interest; for it is not his duty to assist the beneficiary in squandering or anticipating his fortune.[40]

2. Audit

(a) *Accountant.*   Trustees may, in their absolute discretion, from time to time cause the accounts to be examined or audited by an independent accountant.[41] They may not do this, however, more often than once in every three years unless the nature of the trust or any special dealings with the trust property make a more frequent exercise of the right reasonable.[42] The costs are to be paid out of the capital or income, or partly in one way and partly in the other, as the trustees think fit; but unless they otherwise direct in any special case, costs attributable to capital must be borne by capital, and those attributable to income by income.[43]

---

[31] *Hawkesley* v. *May* [1956] 1 Q.B. 304. Contrast personal representatives: *Re Lewis, Lewis* v. *Lewis* [1904] 2 Ch. 656; *Re Mackay, Mackay* v. *Gould* [1906] 1 Ch. 25 at 32.
[32] *Re Cowin* (1886) 33 Ch.D. 179; *O'Rourke* v. *Darbishire* [1920] A.C. 581 at 626; *cf. Butt* v. *Kelson* [1952] Ch. 197.
[33] *Chaine-Nickson* v. *Bank of Ireland* [1976] I.R. 393.
[34] *Re Beloved Wilkes's Charity* (1851) 3 Mac. & G. 440.
[35] *Re Londonderry's Settlement* [1965] Ch. 918; see (1965) 81 L.Q.R. 192.
[36] *Tiger* v. *Barclays Bank Ltd.* [1952] 1 All E.R. 85.
[37] L.P.A. 1925, s.137(8).
[38] *Re Skinner* [1904] 1 Ch. 289.
[39] *Hawkesley* v. *May* [1956] 1 Q.B. 304. See A. Samuels (1970) 34 Conv.(N.S.) 29.
[40] *Low* v. *Bouverie* [1891] 3 Ch. 82, explained in *Mutual Life and Citizens' Assurance Co. Ltd.* v. *Evatt* [1971] A.C. 793 at 805, 813.
[41] T.A. 1925, s.22(4).
[42] *Ibid.*
[43] *Ibid.*

(b) *Public Trustee.* Under the Public Trustee Act 1906,[44] an application can be made by any trustee or beneficiary to the Public Trustee for an investigation and audit of the trust accounts; but such an investigation and audit cannot be made more than once a year, unless the court otherwise orders. The costs must be borne by the estate unless the Public Trustee orders them to be borne by the applicant or by the trustee personally. An appeal from such an order lies to a judge of the Chancery Division[45]; but where the funds are properly invested and all reasonable information has been given to the applicant, the judge will not set aside an order that the applicant should pay the costs of the audit.[46]

Section 4. Control by Beneficiaries

1. Powers of beneficiaries.[47] In carrying out his duties, a trustee must be guided by the trust instrument and the rules of equity. In the exercise of any power or discretion which is confided to him, he is bound and entitled to use his own judgment, and ordinarily he is not obliged to consult the wishes or accede to the importunities of the *cestuis que trust.* Thus in *Re Brockbank*[48] the court refused to compel one of two trustees of a will, in whom the power of appointing new trustees resided, to concur in the appointment of a new trustee which was demanded by the other trustee and all the beneficiaries, even though the latter were all *sui juris* and together entitled to the whole beneficial interest. And a trustee can bring an action even if the *cestui que trust* to whom he will have to account directs him not to sue.[49]

2. Rule in Saunders v. Vautier. Although the beneficiaries cannot, in general, control the trustees while the trust remains in being, or commit them to a particular dealing with the trust property,[50] they can, if *sui juris* and together entitled to the whole beneficial interest, put an end to the trust and direct the trustees to hand over the trust property as they direct[51]; and this is so even if the trust deed contains express provisions for the determination of the trust.[52] This principle also applies where there is an absolute vested gift made payable on a future event, with a direction to accumulate the income in the meantime and pay it with the principal; for in *Saunders* v. *Vautier*[53] the court declined to enforce a

---

[44] s.13; and see Public Trustee Rules 1912, rr. 31–37. For these rules, see *ante,* p. 199, n. 17.
[45] Public Trustee Act 1906, s.10; *Re Oddy* [1911] 1 Ch. 532.
[46] *Re Utley* (1912) 106 L.T. 858.
[47] See the summary in *Stephenson* v. *Barclays Bank Trust Co. Ltd.* [1975] 1 W.L.R. 882 at 889.
[48] [1948] Ch. 206. Contrast *Butt* v. *Kelson* [1952] Ch. 197 at 207, suggesting that trustee-shareholders can be compelled to vote as the beneficiaries direct; *sed quaere*: see *Re George Whichelow Ltd.* [1954] 1 W.L.R. 5 at 8.
[49] *Morley* v. *Moore* [1936] 2 K.B. 359.
[50] *Napier* v. *Light* (1974) 119 S.J. 166; 236 E.G. 273 (see esp. at 278).
[51] *Anson* v. *Potter* (1879) 13 Ch.D. 141.
[52] *Re A.E.G. Unit Trust (Managers) Ltd.'s Deed* [1957] Ch. 415.
[53] (1841) 4 Beav. 115, affd. Cr. & Ph. 240; approved in *Gosling* v. *Gosling* (1859) Johns. 265.

trust for accumulation in which no person but the beneficiary had any interest. In other words, if an accumulation is directed exclusively for the benefit of a beneficiary, the moment he is *sui juris* he may put an end to it and demand the property. A man who is *sui juris* may do what he likes with his own property.[54]

Again, where trustees are directed at their absolute discretion to pay or apply the whole or any part of the income of a fund to or for the benefit of A, and are told to pay or apply to or for the benefit of B any part of the income not applied for A's benefit, A and B, if both *sui juris*, can together compel the trustees to pay the whole income as they direct, for they are the sole owners of each slice of income.[55] But the rule does not apply if other persons have possible interests in the income,[56] so that A and B alone could not control the trustees' application of the income.

3. Share of property. The general rule is that a person who is indefeasibly entitled to a share in divisible personalty is entitled to have his share transferred to him,[57] unless there is some good reason to the contrary, as where division *in specie* of trust property would give one beneficiary a disproportionate advantage.[58] The general rule applies even if the property is held on trust for sale with power to postpone sale[59] and the transfer would diminish the value of the other shares.[60] It is otherwise if it is land which is thus held.[61] Various reasons have been given for the distinction,[62] but the true basis seems to be that of easy and fair divisibility.

4. Statutory trusts for sale of land. As regards trusts for sale of land which arise by statute (*e.g.* the trust for sale on intestacy[63]), statute[64] directs the trustees, so far as practicable, to consult the persons of full age for the time being beneficially interested in possession in the rents and profits of the land until sale, and so far as consistent with the general interests of the trust to give effect to the wishes of such persons, or in the case of dispute, of the majority of such persons, according to the value of their combined interests. This provision applies whether the

---

[54] *Secus* in the U.S.A. if the continuance of the trust is necessary to carry out a material purpose of the settlor: see *Claflin* v. *Claflin*, 149 Mass. 19, 20 N.E. 454 (1889) (*cf.* J. C. Gray, *Restraints on Alienation* (2nd ed., 1895)); A. W. Scott (1945) 59 Harv.L.R. 157 at 202; and see *ante*, p. 136.

[55] *Re Smith, Public Trustee* v. *Aspinall* [1928] Ch. 915; *cf. Re Nelson, Norris* v. *Nelson* (1918) [1928] Ch. 920n.

[56] *Berry* v. *Geen* [1938] A.C. 575.

[57] *Re Sandeman's W.T.* [1937] 1 All E.R. 368.

[58] *Lloyds Bank plc* v. *Duker* [1987] 1 W.L.R. 1324 (company shares: sale ordered).

[59] *Re Marshall* [1914] 1 Ch. 192.

[60] *Re Marshall, supra; Re Weiner* [1956] 1 W.L.R. 579.

[61] *Re Horsnaill* [1909] 1 Ch. 631; *Re Kipping* [1914] 1 Ch. 62; *Re Marshall, supra.* See *Stephenson* v. *Barclays Bank Trust Co. Ltd.* [1975] 1 W.L.R. 882 at 889, 890.

[62] See, *e.g. Re Kipping, supra,* at p. 67 (effect of trust): *Re Marshall, supra,* at p. 199 (detriment); and see *post,* p. 500.

[63] A.E.A. 1925, s.33, *post,* p. 314.

[64] L.P.A. 1925 s.26(3), as amended by L.P.(Am.)A. 1926, Sched.

trust was created before 1926 or after 1925, but does not apply to a trust for sale created by an instrument unless the instrument shows an intention that it shall apply. Where it applies, it requires the trustees to regard the wishes of the beneficiaries not only as to the exercise of the trust for sale, but also as to the exercise of all other trusts and powers conferred on the trustees by statute or by the trust instrument.[65] The provision regulates trustees and hence does not apply to the court in exercising its jurisdiction under the Law of Property Act 1925, s.30.[66]

Section 5. Control by Court

1. Administration by the court. A trust may be administered or executed by the Chancery Division of the High Court, or by a county court if the total value of the fund does not exceed £30,000.[67] When an order has been made for the administration of the trust by the court, the trustees cannot exercise any of their powers without the sanction of the court.[68]

2. Supervision of trustees

(a) *The power.* It is not usual for trusts to be administered in court; for the court exercises a general controlling influence over all trustees, and has power to give directions and determine questions affecting the trustees and beneficiaries without making an order for administration.[69] Thus, in a proper case the court may order an inquiry whether a particular investment ought to be continued, notwithstanding that the trustees claim to exercise their discretion without the interference of the court.[70] This general advisory jurisdiction is frequently invoked. Further, if a question of construction arises on the terms of a trust the Chancery Division may without hearing argument authorise the trustees to act in accordance with the opinion of counsel of at least 10 years' standing.[71]

(b) *Principles of interference.* Normally, however, if trustees have an absolute discretion as to the mode of executing the trust the court will not interfere with their discretion, provided they exercise it in good faith.[72] For instance, if a testator gives property to A, B and C to hold

---

[65] *Re Jones, Jones* v. *Cusack-Smith* [1931] 1 Ch. 375.
[66] *Smith* v. *Smith* (1975) 120 S.J. 100. See *post*, p. 236, for L.P.A. 1925, s.30.
[67] *Ante*, p. 20.
[68] *Minors* v. *Battison* (1876) 1 App.Cas. 428.
[69] R.S.C., Ord. 85, r. 2.
[70] *Re D'Epinoix's Settlement* [1914] 1 Ch. 890.
[71] Administration of Justice Act 1985, s.48; R.S.C., Ord. 93, r. 21.
[72] *Gisborne* v. *Gisborne* (1877) 2 App.Cas. 300; *Re Blake* (1885) 29 Ch.D. 913; *Re Charteris* [1917] 2 Ch. 379; *Re Steed's W.T.* [1960] Ch. 407; *Re Hayes's W.T.* [1971] 1 W.L.R. 758; and see *post*, p. 260.

upon certain trusts, with power to sell it if they think fit, and A and B and some of the beneficiaries desire a sale but C, in the bona fide exercise of his discretion, refuses to sell, the court will not interfere, and the property cannot be sold.[73] The court will, however, interfere if the trustees refuse to exercise their discretion,[74] or exercise it improperly[75]; and the trustees may, if they wish, surrender their discretion to the court and ask the court to exercise it for them in particular matters[76] though not indefinitely, e.g. under discretionary trusts.[77] The court will not compel trustees to take action, however advantageous to the beneficiaries, which will expose them to a breach of the currency regulations of a state whose law is the proper law of the trust.[78] These principles apply equally to express trusts and to statutory trusts for the sale of land.[79]

(c) *Mode of interference.* Where the court has decided to interfere, it will do so in a manner best calculated to carry out the intention of the settlor.[80] An equal division of the funds between the beneficiaries[81] is a possible way of exercising a discretionary power of division, but it is not inevitable, for other modes of carrying out the trust may be appropriate to the circumstances. Thus the court may draw up a scheme for the distribution of the funds among the potential beneficiaries, e.g. according to their needs and qualifications.[82]

(d) *Statutory provision.* In the case of trusts for sale of land (whether express or statutory) the court's powers have been given statutory expression. If trustees for sale refuse to sell[83] or to exercise certain statutory powers,[84] any person interested[85] may apply for a vesting or other order to give effect to the transaction, and the court may make such order as it thinks fit.[86] The same provision also enables the court to dispense with the consent of any person which is requisite for the execution of the trust for sale or the exercise of the trustee's powers,[87] this being an authority which the court does not possess apart from statute.[88] However, the purpose of the provision is to empower the court to make orders ancillary to an order for sale. Thus no order can

---

[73] See *Tempest* v. *Lord Camoys* (1882) 21 Ch.D. 571; and see *Re 90 Thornhill Road, Tolworth, Surrey* [1970] Ch. 261.
[74] *Prendergast* v. *Prendergast* (1850) 3 H.L.C. 195; *Klug* v. *Klug* [1918] 2 Ch. 67.
[75] *Tempest* v. *Lord Camoys, supra,* at p. 578.
[76] See, *e.g. Re Ezekiel's S.T.* [1942] Ch. 230.
[77] *Re Allen-Meyrick's W.T.* [1966] 1 W.L.R. 499; see *ante,* p. 136.
[78] *Re Lord Cable* [1977] 1 W.L.R. 7.
[79] *Re Mayo* [1943] Ch. 302.
[80] See *McPhail* v. *Doulton* [1971] A.C. 424 at 451, 452, 457; and see generally A. J. Hawkins (1967) 31 Conv.(N.S.) 117.
[81] As in *Longmore* v. *Broom* (1802) 7 Ves. 124. And see *ante,* pp. 97, 98.
[82] See *Re G. (Infants)* [1899] 1 Ch. 719; and see *McPhail* v. *Doulton, supra,* at p. 451.
[83] *Re Mayo, supra.*
[84] viz., the powers conferred by L.P.A. 1925, ss.28, 29.
[85] See *Stevens* v. *Hutchinson* [1953] Ch. 299 (receiver of proceeds of sale not a person interested).
[86] L.P.A. 1925, s.30.
[87] *Re Beale's S.T.* [1932] 2 Ch. 15; and see *Bull* v. *Bull* [1955] 1 Q.B. 234.
[88] *Re Forster's Settlement* [1942] Ch. 199.

be made unless an order for sale is made.[89] Further, the provision does not enable the court to authorise the trustees to carry out a transaction which they could not properly carry out themselves, *e.g.* to grant a lease of trust property to one of themselves.[90]

(e) *Unanimity.* In the case of a private[91] trust, no majority of trustees can bind a minority,[92] and the court will, in general, observe this rule when asked to interfere. Thus, as has been seen, the court will not compel one trustee to exercise a *power* of sale at the wish of the majority.[93] But if there is a *trust* for sale with power to postpone conversion the trust for sale will prevail[94] unless all the trustees concur in exercising the discretionary power of postponement. Accordingly, if B and C refuse to join A in selling, the court will usually at A's request compel their concurrence.[95] But this will not be done if A is also a beneficiary who has by contract disabled himself from requiring a sale.[96] So, too, a sale will not be ordered which would defeat the purpose for which the property was acquired, as where it was bought as a family home and is still required for that purpose,[97] or simply as a matrimonial home and the marriage is still subsisting.[98] If the marriage has ended, and there are no young children, a sale will often be ordered under the ordinary principles.[99] In appropriate cases the application should be made or remitted to the Family Division to allow the jurisdiction over matrimonial property to be exercised.[1] This cannot be done where the husband is bankrupt as the trustee in bankruptcy is not subject to the matrimonial jurisdiction.[2] Normally a sale would be ordered where a joint tenant is bankrupt, whether the parties are still living together in the property[3] or not,[4] but may be refused where the interests of the other party outweigh those of the creditors, *e.g.* where a husband has deserted his wife and children and presented his own bankruptcy petition when no creditors were pressing.[5] If the court does not order an

---

[89] *Bernard* v. *Josephs* [1982] Ch. 391 at 410.
[90] See *Re Johns' Assignment Trusts* [1970] 1 W.L.R. 955 at 960. But there is a separate power for the court to sanction such a transaction: *ibid.; see post,* p. 250.
[91] Contrast *ante,* p. 169, for charitable trusts.
[92] See *post,* p. 260.
[93] See *ante,* pp. 235, 236.
[94] See *Barclay* v. *Barclay* [1970] 2 Q.B. 677; but see *Irani Finance Ltd.* v. *Singh* [1971] Ch. 59 at 80; and *post,* p. 316.
[95] *Re Roth* (1896) 74 L.T. 50; *Re Hilton* [1909] 2 Ch. 548; *Re Mayo* [1943] Ch. 302. See also *Luke* v. *South Kensington Hotel Co.* (1879) 11 Ch.D. 121; *Jones* v. *Challenger* [1961] 1 Q.B. 176; *Rawlings* v. *Rawlings* [1964] P. 398. And see *Harris* v. *Black* (1983) 46 P. & C.R. 366 (on application for new tenancy of premises held on trust).
[96] *Re Buchanan-Wollaston's Conveyance* [1939] Ch. 738. See also *Re Hyde's Conveyance* (1952) 102 L.J. News, 58; (1952) 16 Conv.(N.S.) 132.
[97] *Re Evers' Trust* [1980] 1 W.L.R. 1327.
[98] See *Jones* v. *Challenger, supra,* at pp. 181, 183; but see *Re Turner, a bankrupt* [1974] 1 W.L.R. 1556 (husband bankrupt, sale ordered).
[99] *Re Solomon* [1967] Ch. 573; *Jackson* v. *Jackson* [1971] 1 W.L.R. 1539.
[1] *Williams (J.W.)* v. *Williams (M.A.)* [1976] Ch. 278; see *Brown* v. *Pritchard* [1975] 1 W.L.R. 1366; *Bernard* v. *Josephs* [1982] Ch. 391 at 401 (homes of unmarried couples better dealt with in Family Division).
[2] *Re Holliday (a bankrupt)* [1981] Ch. 405.
[3] *Re Lowrie (a bankrupt)* [1981] 3 All E.R. 353.
[4] *Re Solomon, supra* (parties separated).
[5] *Re Holliday (a bankrupt), supra.*

immediate sale the application should be dismissed leaving the parties to make another application if and when circumstances change.[6]

(f) *Alteration of court's jurisdiction.* The jurisdiction of the court cannot be enlarged by provisions in the trust instrument, *e.g.* by purporting to authorise the settlor to revoke the settlement with the consent of a Chancery judge.[7] Equally the jurisdiction of the court cannot be ousted by provisions in the trust instrument giving power to the trustees generally to decide questions, *e.g.* as to the identity of a beneficiary[8] or any apportionment between capital and income.[9] It is, however, a matter of degree; the jurisdiction is not ousted where specific questions are submitted to an appropriate authority, *e.g.* questions of Jewish blood and faith to a chief rabbi.[10]

3. Departure from the terms of the trust. In general, the court has no power to sanction a departure from the terms of the trust, however advantageous it might appear to the beneficiaries.[11] "I decline," said Farwell J., "to accept any suggestion that the Court has an inherent jurisdiction to alter a man's will because it thinks it beneficial. It seems to me that is quite impossible."[12] Nevertheless, in six cases[13] either by statute or under its inherent jurisdiction, the court may confer additional powers on trustees or vary or allow the variation of the terms of the trust.[14] These circumstances are as follows.

(a) *Management and administration*

(1) EMERGENCIES. Prior to 1926 the court had power to sanction departures from the trust instrument where an emergency, *i.e.* an unforeseen situation, arose in the management or administration of the trust property,[15] or for the purposes of salvage, *e.g.* in effecting essential repairs to buildings.[16] This power did not permit the remoulding of the beneficial interests as distinct from rearrangements of the trust property.[17]

---

[6] *Re Evers' Trust* [1980] 1 W.L.R. 1327.
[7] *Re Hooker's Settlement* [1955] Ch. 55.
[8] *Re Raven* [1915] 1 Ch. 673.
[9] *Re Wynn* [1952] Ch. 271. But see *Dundee General Hospitals Board of Management* v. *Walker* [1952] 1 All E.R. 896; *Re Coxen* [1948] Ch. 747, esp. at 761, 762. *Cf. Re Vaux* [1939] Ch. 465.
[10] *Re Tuck's S.T.* [1976] Ch. 99, Whitford J., affirmed on other grounds, [1978] Ch. 49, C.A., when Lord Denning M.R. agreed with Whitford J., Lord Russell of Killowen and Eveleigh L.J. expressing no opinion.
[11] *Chapman* v. *Chapman* [1954] A.C. 429; *Re Heyworth's Contingent Reversionary Interest* [1956] Ch. 364; and see *Re Earl of Strafford* [1980] Ch. 28, *post*, p. 270.
[12] *Re Walker, Walker* v. *Duncombe* [1901] 1 Ch. 879 at 885, cited with approval in *Chapman* v. *Chapman, supra*, at pp. 445, 456.
[13] See generally O. R. Marshall (1954) 17 M.L.R. 420.
[14] *Re Downshire S.E.* [1953] Ch. 218.
[15] *Re New* [1901] 2 Ch. 534; *Re Tollemache* [1903] 1 Ch. 955.
[16] *Re Jackson, Jackson* v. *Talbot* (1882) 21 Ch.D. 786; contrast *Re Montagu* [1897] 2 Ch. 8.
[17] *Chapman* v. *Chapman* [1954] A.C. 429 at 454, 455.

(2) AFTER 1925. Since 1925 the court has been empowered by the Trustee Act 1925, s.57, to exercise a jurisdiction of this kind even though no emergency exists.[18] The section provides that "where in the management or administration of any property vested in trustees"[19] (other than Settled Land Act trustees[20]) any transaction is expedient[21] for the trust as a whole[22] but the trustees have no power to effect it,[23] the court may confer the necessary power upon the trustees.[24] "The object of section 57 was to secure that trust property should be managed as advantageously as possible in the interests of the beneficiaries and, with that object in view, to authorize specific dealings with the property which the court might have felt itself unable to sanction under the inherent jurisdiction, either because no actual 'emergency' had arisen or because of inability to show that the position which called for intervention was one which the creator of the trust could not reasonably have foreseen; but it was no part of the legislative aim to disturb the rule that the court will not rewrite a trust ... "[25] The section accordingly gives no power to vary the beneficial interests under a trust.

(3) OPERATION OF SECTION. This is an overriding section, the provisions of which are to be read into every settlement.[26] The statutory power has been used to authorise the sale of chattels settled on trusts, which prevent sale,[27] the sale of land where a consent requisite to sale has been refused,[28] the sale of a reversionary interest,[29] the purchase of a residence for the tenant for life,[30] the partitioning of land where there was no power to partition it,[31] the blending of two charitable funds into one,[32] and the enlarging of the range of permissible investments.[33] But where a fund is settled on A for life on protective trusts, the statutory power cannot be used to enable the trustees to release the fund from

---

[18] For previous "benevolent" orders, see *Re Morrison, Morrison* v. *Morrison* [1901] 1 Ch. 701 at 704.

[19] See *Re Downshire S.E.* [1953] Ch. 218 at 247.

[20] T.A. 1925, s.57(4).

[21] See *Riddle* v. *Riddle* (1952) 85 C.L.R. 202.

[22] *Re Craven's Estate (No. 2)* [1937] Ch. 431; and see *Re Earl of Strafford* [1980] Ch. 28 at 32, 33.

[23] See *Re Pratt's W.T.* [1943] Ch. 326; *Municipal and General Securities Co. Ltd.* v. *Lloyds Bank Ltd.* [1950] Ch. 212.

[24] And see Settled Land and Trustee Acts (Court's General Powers) Act 1943, s.1, for an extension of these powers in the case of trusts for sale of land. (The original limit of time for the exercise of the extended powers was removed by the Emergency Laws (Miscellaneous Provisions) Act 1953, s.9 (repealed by Statute Law (Repeals) Act 1974, Sched., Pt. X and again by Statute Law (Repeals) Act 1976, 1st Sched., Pt. XX)).

[25] *Re Downshire S.E.* [1953] Ch. 218 at 248, *per* Evershed M.R. and Romer L.J.

[26] *Re Mair* [1935] Ch. 562. For Canadian alarm, see (1943) 59 L.Q.R. 111.

[27] *Re Hope's W.T.* [1929] 2 Ch. 136; *post*, p. 261.

[28] *Re Beale's S.T.* [1932] 2 Ch. 15.

[29] *Re Cockerell's S.T.* [1956] Ch. 372. Contrast *Re Heyworth's Contingent Reversionary Interest* [1956] Ch. 364.

[30] *Ante*, p. 222, n. 16.

[31] *Re Thomas, Thomas* v. *Thompson* [1930] 1 Ch. 194.

[32] *Re Harvey, Westminster Bank Ltd.* v. *Askwith* [1941] 3 All E.R. 284; *Re Shipwrecked Fishermen and Mariners' Royal Benevolent Society* [1959] Ch. 220, not following dicta in *Re Royal Society's Charitable Trusts* [1956] Ch. 87 at 91.

[33] *Re Shipwrecked Fishermen and Mariners' Royal Benevolent Society, supra*; *Re Brassey's Settlement* [1955] 1 W.L.R. 192 at 196; *Mason* v. *Farbrother* [1983] 2 All E.R. 1078 at 1086, 1087 (but see *British Museum (Trustees of the)* v. *Att.-Gen.* [1984] 1 W.L.R. 418 at 425, 426). See *ante*, p. 220, for the effect of the Trustee Investments Act 1961 on the court's discretion.

the discretionary trusts which would arise if A surrendered his life interest.[34]

(b) *Settled land and trusts for sale.* In the case of settled land and land held upon trust for sale[35] there is a similar though rather wider statutory provision. "Any transaction" concerning such land which is for the benefit of any of the land or of the beneficiaries and could have been effected by an absolute owner may be effected under an order of the court.[36] "Transaction" is widely defined,[37] and is not confined by any reference to "management or administration"; accordingly, in contrast with the previous head, it includes alterations of the beneficial interests.[38]

(c) *Maintenance of beneficiaries.* "Where a testator or settlor has so provided, particularly by way of a trust for accumulation, that the immediate beneficiaries have no fund for their present maintenance, the court—which has shown dislike for trusts for accumulation—will assume that the intention to provide, sensibly, for the family is so paramount that it will order maintenance in disregard of the trusts for accumulation."[39] By providing maintenance the court has saved the beneficiary from "starving while the harvest designed for him was in the course of ripening."[40]

For instance, where a testator directed accumulation of the income of his real and personal estate for 21 years, and gave the accumulated property to his sister for life, with successive remainders to her three sons and their respective children, the court directed a present annual sum to be paid to the sister out of the income of the personal estate for the maintenance and education of her three sons.[41] But only in special circumstances will the court thus virtually set aside *pro tanto* the trust for accumulation; normally it will not interfere with such a trust even if it is hurtful and capricious.[42]

---

[34] *Re Blackwell's S.T.* [1953] Ch. 218. And see *Re Basden's S.T.* [1943] 2 All E.R. 11; *Municipal and General Securities Co. Ltd.* v. *Lloyds Bank Ltd.* [1950] Ch. 212.

[35] *Re Simmons* [1956] Ch. 125.

[36] S.L.A. 1925, s.64(1); and see the extension of these powers by Settled Land and Trustee Acts (Court's General Powers) Act 1943, s.1, as amended by Emergency Laws (Miscellaneous Provisions) Act 1953, s.9, *ante*, p. 239, n. 24.

[37] S.L.A. 1925, s.64(2), as amended by Settled Land and Trustee Acts (Court's General Powers) Act 1943, s.2, and Statute Law (Repeals) Act 1969, Sched., Pt. III. See *Raikes* v. *Lygon* [1988] 1 W.L.R. 281.

[38] *Re Simmons, supra.*

[39] *Re Downshire S.E.* [1953] Ch. 218 at 238, *per* Evershed M.R. and Romer L.J. This head was recognised and discussed in *Chapman* v. *Chapman* [1954] A.C. 429 at 445, 455–457, 469, 471; and see *post*, p. 281. The statutory powers of maintenance and advancement are now usually available: see *post*, pp. 276 *et seq.*

[40] *Chapman* v. *Chapman, supra*, at p. 469, *per* Lord Asquith of Bishopstone.

[41] *Re Collins, Collins* v. *Collins* (1886) 32 Ch.D. 229; and see *Re Allan* (1881) 17 Ch.D. 807; *Re Walker, Walker* v. *Duncombe* [1901] 1 Ch. 879; *Re Spurrell* (1967) 65 D.L.R. (2d) 64 (car for children aged 18 and 13 to go to school).

[42] *Re Alford* (1886) 32 Ch.D. 383.

(d) *Compromises and arrangements.* The court has power to approve, on behalf of minors and unascertained beneficiaries, compromises proposed by or between beneficiaries who are *sui juris*. "Compromise" here is confined to compromises of real (and not simulated[43]) differences, although they need not have reached the stage of a contested dispute.[44] Mere family arrangements whereby a beneficiary gives up his present right in return for some different right are not compromises.[45] Yet where a beneficiary had a right of residing rent-free in a certain house which was on land which it was advantageous to develop, the court approved on behalf of infants a scheme whereby the beneficiary abandoned her rights in the house in return for an annual payment of less than the estimated value of the right of residence.[46]

(e) *Variation of Trusts Act 1958.* The Variation of Trusts Act 1958 was passed as a result of the recommendations of the Sixth Report of the Law Reform Committee,[47] made in consequence of the decision in *Chapman* v. *Chapman*.[48]

(1) THE JURISDICTION. The Act gives the court an extensive jurisdiction to approve variations of trusts (including beneficial interests thereunder) on behalf of infants, unborn persons and others; and the jurisdiction is additional to other statutory powers.[49] Under the Act the court[50] may if it thinks fit[51] approve on behalf of certain persons "any arrangement ... varying or revoking all or any of the trusts, or enlarging the powers of the trustees of managing or administering any of the property subject to the trusts."[52] "Arrangement" has been construed very widely, and is not confined to an agreement between two or more persons.[53] Anyone, even though not a beneficiary,[54] may propose an arrangement, and it matters not whether "there is any other person beneficially interested who is capable of assenting thereto."[55] "Varying" is also construed very widely, and includes the complete replacement of one set of trusts by another,[56] at all events if the substratum of the original trusts remains.[57]

[43] See *Re Powell Cotton's Resettlement* [1956] 1 W.L.R. 23.
[44] *Mason* v. *Farbrother* [1983] 2 All E.R. 1078.
[45] *Chapman* v. *Chapman* [1954] A.C. 429; see (1954) 70 L.Q.R. 473. Contrast *Re Earl of Strafford* [1980] Ch. 28, *post*, p. 270.
[46] *Re Trenchard* [1902] 1 Ch. 378, a case carrying "compromise" to its limit: see *Chapman* v. *Chapman, supra*, at pp. 441, 463. For another example, see *Re Lord Hylton's Settlement* [1954] 1 W.L.R. 1055; and see *Re Wells, Boyer* v. *Maclean* [1903] 1 Ch. 848; *Re Cockerell's S.T.* [1956] Ch. 372.
[47] 1957, Cmnd. 310.
[48] [1954] A.C. 429; *ante*, p. 238, and *supra*. For a full survey of the first decade of the Act's operation, see J. W. Harris (1969) 33 Conv.(N.S.) 113, 183.
[49] Variation of Trusts Act 1958, s.1(6).
[50] See s.1(2), (3).
[51] See *Re Steed's W.T.* [1959] Ch. 354 at 362; [1960] Ch. 407; *Re Van Gruisen's W.T.* [1964] 1 W.L.R. 449.
[52] s.1(1).
[53] *Re Steed's W.T.* [1960] Ch. 407 at 419.
[54] See *Re T.'s S.T.* [1964] Ch. 158 (mother of beneficiary).
[55] s.1(1).
[56] *Re Holt's Settlement* [1969] 1 Ch. 100.
[57] *Re Ball's S.T.* [1968] 1 W.L.R. 899; but see (1968) 84 L.Q.R. 458 at 459, 460.

The trusts may affect both real and personal property, and may arise under any will, settlement or other disposition[58] and in suitable cases[59] the jurisdiction may be exercised over trusts which have a foreign proper law.[60] But the Act does not apply to property settled by Act of Parliament,[61] nor in respect of contingencies which cannot happen, *e.g.* a variation in favour of issue to be born to a woman over 70 years old.[62] In general, it is desirable that the application should be made by one or more beneficiaries and not by the trustees, unless no beneficiary is willing to make it and the trustees are satisfied that it is beneficial; for their proper function is that of watch-dog for the unborn and unascertained.[63]

(2) PERSONS WITHIN THE JURISDICTION. There are four classes of person on whose behalf the court may approve an arrangement.[64]

(i)   Incapacity: "any person having, directly or indirectly," a vested or contingent interest "who by reason of infancy or other incapacity is incapable of assenting."

(ii) Contingency: "any person (whether ascertained or not) who may become entitled, directly or indirectly, to an interest under the trusts as being at a future date or on the happening of a future event a person of any specified description or a member of any specified class of persons." The words "may become entitled" do not cover a person who has an actual interest under a settlement, albeit a very remote one.[65] Further, this head expressly excludes any person who would satisfy the description or be a member of the class if the date had arrived or the event had happened when the application was made to the court. Thus if there is a gift to the next-of-kin of X, who is alive, the court has no jurisdiction on behalf of those who would be X's next-of-kin if he were then dead, and so their consent must be obtained.[66]

(iii) Unborn: "any person unborn."

(iv) Protective trusts: "any person" (whether or not unborn or unascertained[67]) "in respect of any discretionary interest of his" under the statutory[68] or similar[69] protective trusts[70] "where the

---

[58] Variation of Trusts Act 1958, s.1(1).
[59] *Re Paget's Settlement* [1965] 1 W.L.R. 1046 (New York).
[60] *Re Ker's S.T.* [1963] Ch. 553 (Northern Ireland).
[61] s.1(6).
[62] *Re Pettifor's W.T.* [1966] Ch. 257; the court made an order in its administrative jurisdiction: see *ante*, p. 235 and *Re White, White* v. *Edmond* [1901] 1 Ch. 570.
[63] *Re Druce's S.T.* [1962] 1 W.L.R. 363.
[64] s.1(1).
[65] *Knocker* v. *Youle* [1986] 1 W.L.R. 934 at 937.
[66] *Re Suffert's Settlement* [1961] Ch. 1; and see *Knocker* v. *Youle* [1986] 1 W.L.R. 934.
[67] *Re Turner's W.T., Bridgman* v. *Turner* [1960] Ch. 122.
[68] *i.e.* under T.A. 1925, s.33; see *ante*, p. 137.
[69] See *Re Bristol's S.E.* [1965] 1 W.L.R. 469; *Re Wallace's Settlements* [1968] 1 W.L.R. 711.
[70] s.1(2).

interest of the principal beneficiary has not failed or determined."

(3) BENEFIT. The court cannot approve an arrangement on behalf of any person "unless the carrying out thereof would be for the benefit of that person",[71] *i.e.* in all reasonable circumstances, though not necessarily in every remote contingency.[72] The court may "have to take a broad view, but not a galloping, gambling view."[73] This, however, does not apply to those mentioned in paragraph (iv) above, so that the court has a discretionary power[74] to approve an arrangement that is not for their benefit[75]; and they need not be joined as parties.[76]

"Benefit" is not confined to financial benefit,[77] *e.g.* where the beneficiary is an irresponsible minor.[78] Thus a provision forfeiting benefits on "practising Roman Catholicism" has been removed.[79] It may also be a benefit to a mentally incapable person to give away his property where the gift is one which he would have made if of sound mind.[80] But it is not for A's benefit to take from him property mistakenly given to him and give it to B, even if B is a member of the same family.[81]

(4) EXTENT OF JURISDICTION. The Act does no more than empower the court to approve arrangements on behalf of certain persons; if any other beneficiary refuses his consent, the arrangement will not bind him.[82] Thus if one or more adult beneficiaries will not concur, some other jurisdiction to make the change must be invoked. While it is the duty of a guardian *ad litem* for a minor beneficiary to consider the arrangement and inform the court of the course which he thinks should be taken, the court has jurisdiction to approve the arrangement even if this is not done.[83] Thus, with the adult beneficiaries consenting, the jurisdiction is very wide, and has been exercised for a great variety of purposes. These include the revision of administrative provisions, such as the alteration of investment clauses[84] or the termination of an

---

[71] s.1(1), proviso; see *Re Tinker's Settlement* [1960] 1 W.L.R. 1011; *Re Cohen's S.T.* [1965] 1 W.L.R. 1229.
[72] *Re Cohen's W.T.* [1959] 1 W.L.R. 865 (but see (1960) 76 L.Q.R. 22); *Re Holt's Settlement* [1969] 1 Ch. 100.
[73] *Re Robinson's S.T.* [1976] 1 W.L.R. 806 at 810, *per* Templeman J.
[74] See *Re Poole's S.T.* [1959] 1 W.L.R. 651; *Re Steed's W.T.* [1960] Ch. 407; *Re Burney's S.T.* [1961] 1 W.L.R. 545.
[75] s.1(1), proviso.
[76] *Re Munro's S.T.* [1963] 1 W.L.R. 145.
[77] *Re Weston's Settlements* [1969] 1 Ch. 223 at 245; *Re Holt's Settlement* [1969] 1 Ch. 100 at 121.
[78] See *Re T.'s S.T.* [1964] Ch. 158; and see *post*, p. 244.
[79] *Re Remnant's S.T.* [1970] Ch. 560.
[80] *Re C.L.* [1969] 1 Ch. 587.
[81] *Re Tinker's Settlement* [1960] 1 W.L.R. 1011.
[82] *Re Suffert's Settlement* [1961] Ch. 1 (potential next-of-kin); *Knocker* v. *Youle* [1986] 1 W.L.R. 934 (numerous issue with very remote interest).
[83] *Re Whittall* [1973] 1 W.L.R. 1027.
[84] *Re Coates' Trusts* [1959] 1 W.L.R. 375; *Re Clarke's W.T.* [1961] 1 W.L.R. 1471 (bringing an express clause into line with the Trustee Investments Act 1961). For the effect of the Act of 1961 on the jurisdiction under the Act of 1958, see *ante*, p. 220.

accumulation,[85] but the most widespread use has been the variation of beneficial interests,[86] principally to mitigate potential tax burdens.[87]

In a proper case the court may accordingly approve the replacement of fixed beneficial interests by discretionary trusts in a larger sum,[88] the addition of a power of advancement,[89] and the substitution of a foreign trust for an English trust[90] where the beneficiaries are genuinely and permanently settled abroad.[91] But before the Act the court had no power to direct a settlement of a minor's property,[92] and so it has refused to construe the Act as conferring such a jurisdiction.[93] Thus if an irresponsible infant is prospectively entitled to an absolute interest at majority, the court cannot approve a resettlement of her interest on protective trusts for her life with remainder to her issue, though it can approve the postponement of the age at which her absolute interest will vest and the creation of interim protective trusts.[94] Also the court will not approve an arrangement involving an appointment under a special power which is or may fairly be suspected of being a fraud on the power.[95] But jurisdiction is not excluded merely because the proposed arrangement will discourage the marriage of beneficiaries who are unlikely to marry[96]; and a purely future variation may be permitted.[97]

(5) EFFECT OF ORDER. The Act merely empowers the court to give a binding consent to the arrangement on behalf of those unable to give it themselves, so that the variation is effected not by the court but by the consent of all parties.[98] New trusts replace the old,[99] and thus the perpetuity period begins to run anew.[1] The variation takes effect as soon as the order of the court is made, without any further instrument,[2] and the order may be liable to stamp duty.[3] As the court is solely concerned to give its consent to the arrangement, and not to try any specific issue, no estoppel *per rem judicatam* arises.[4]

---

[85] *Re Tinker's Settlement* [1960] 1 W.L.R. 1011.
[86] *Re Poole's S.T.* [1959] 1 W.L.R. 651; *Re Turner's W.T.*, *Bridgman* v. *Turner* [1960] Ch. 122; and see the examples *infra*.
[87] *Re Clitheroe's S.T.* [1959] 1 W.L.R. 1159 (surtax); *Re Sainsbury's Settlement* [1967] 1 W.L.R. 476 (capital gains tax); and see *Re Drewe's Settlement* [1966] 1 W.L.R. 1518 (court's insistence on provision that power to appoint be exercised with consent of trustees after advice of counsel as to estate duty). But see *Re Weston's Settlements* [1969] 1 Ch. 223; (1969) 85 L.Q.R. 15.
[88] *Re Druce's S.T.* [1962] 1 W.L.R. 363.
[89] *Re Lister's W.T.* [1962] 1 W.L.R. 1441.
[90] *Re Seale's Marriage Settlement* [1961] Ch. 574; *Re Windeatt's W.T.* [1969] 1 W.L.R. 692.
[91] See *Re Weston's Settlement* [1969] 1 Ch. 223.
[92] *Re Leigh* (1888) 40 Ch.D. 290.
[93] *Re T.'s S.T.* [1964] Ch. 158; *Allen* v. *Distillers Company (Biochemicals) Ltd.* [1974] Q.B. 384.
[94] *Re T.'s S.T., supra.*
[95] See *Robertson's W.T.* [1960] 1 W.L.R. 1050 and *Re Wallace's Settlements* [1968] 1 W.L.R. 711 (arrangements approved); *Re Brook's Settlement* [1968] 1 W.L.R. 1661 (approval withheld); S. M. Cretney (1969) 32 M.L.R. 317. For fraud on a power, see *post*, p. 562.
[96] *Re Michelham's W.T.* [1964] Ch. 550 (males aged 59 and 62).
[97] *Re Joseph's W.T.* [1959] 1 W.L.R. 1019.
[98] *Re Holt's Settlement* [1969] 1 Ch. 100; *I.R.C.* v. *Holmden* [1968] A.C. 685 at 701, 702, 710, 713; and see *Spens* v. *I.R.C.* [1970] 1 W.L.R. 1173 at 1183, 1184.
[99] See *I.R.C.* v. *Holmden, supra*, at pp. 701, 702, 713; but see at pp. 705, 710.
[1] *Re Holt's Settlement, supra.*
[2] *Re Hambleden's W.T.* [1960] 1 W.L.R. 82; *Re Holt's Settlement, supra.*
[3] See Practice Note [1966] 1 W.L.R. 345.
[4] *Spens* v. *I.R.C.* [1970] 1 W.L.R. 1173.

(f) *Variation by Divorce Court.* A further statutory power of modifying settlements has since 1857 been exercisable, at first by the Divorce Court and later by the Divorce Division of the High Court, now the Family Division. After pronouncing a decree of divorce or of nullity of marriage, the court may vary ante-nuptial and post-nuptial settlements under which property was settled for the benefit of parties to or children of the marriage.[5] The manner in which this jurisdiction is exercised is outside the scope of this book.[6]

Section 6. Trustee Profiting from Trust

With certain exceptions, neither directly nor indirectly may a trustee make a profit from his trust.[7] This rule is part of the wider principle[8] that in order to protect a trustee against "the fallibility of human nature"[9] he may not put himself in a position where his duty and his interest may conflict,[10] or where he may be able to take advantage of knowledge of the property (*e.g.* as to valuable minerals under the land) which he acquired while trustee.[11] "There are canons of the Court of equity which have their foundation, not in the actual commission of fraud, but in that hallowed orison, 'lead us not into temptation'."[12]

The rule depends not on fraud or mala fides, but on the mere fact of a profit made.[13] It applies to all types of trustee, including custodian trustees,[14] and to other persons in fiduciary positions.[15] But the rule is for the protection of the person to whom the duty is owed, and he alone can, in proper cases, relax it; it cannot be used by the trustee as a shield.[16]

The leading case on the subject is *Keech* v. *Sandford*,[17] which concerned the renewal of a lease. This will be considered first, and the wider applications of the rule subsequently.[18]

[5] Matrimonial Causes Act 1973, s.24(1)(*a*) replacing earlier legislation.
[6] See, *e.g. Rayden & Jackson on Divorce* (15th ed., 1988), Chap. 20, sect. xiii, p. 962.
[7] See, *e.g. Vyse* v. *Foster* (1874) L.R. 7 H.L. 318. For a general survey, see G. H. Jones (1968) 84 L.Q.R. 472.
[8] *Broughton* v. *Broughton* (1855) 5 De G.M. & G. 160 at 164.
[9] *Costa Rica Ry.* v. *Forwood* [1901] 1 Ch. 746 at 761, *per* Vaughan Williams L.J.
[10] *Bray* v. *Ford* [1896] A.C. 44 at 51; *Williams* v. *Barton* [1972] 2 Ch. 9; *Re Thomson* [1930] 1 Ch. 203. By enforcing this "great principle," Cardozo suggests that courts of equity "have raised the level of business honor"; *Growth of the Law* (1924), p. 96. On fiduciary obligations generally, see L. S. Sealy [1963] C.L.J. 119; J. C. Shepherd (1981) 97 L.Q.R. 51.
[11] See *Ex p. Lacey* (1802) 6 Ves. 625 at 626, 627.
[12] *Wormley* v. *Wormley*, 21 U.S. 421 at 463 (1823), *per* Johnson J.
[13] *Regal (Hastings) Ltd.* v. *Gulliver* [1942] 1 All E.R. 378, esp. at p. 386; [1967] 2 A.C. 134n., especially at pp. 144, 145. This passage was cited in *Guinness plc* v. *Saunders* [1990] 2 W.L.R. 324 at 332.
[14] *Re Brooke Bond & Co. Ltd.'s Trust Deed* [1963] Ch. 357. For custodian trustees, see *ante*, pp. 199, 209.
[15] See *post*, p. 251.
[16] *Boulting* v. *Association of Cinematograph, Television and Allied Technicians* [1963] 2 Q.B. 606 (unsuccessful attempt by company directors to escape having to join employees' trade union).
[17] (1726) Sel.Cas. *t.* King 61; **2 W. & T.L.C. 648**; see *Ex p. Grace* (1799) 1 Bos. & P. 376; *Re Knowles' W.T.* [1948] 1 All E.R. 866.
[18] For an excellent historical survey and valiant attempt at stating the modern rationale of the rule, see S. Cretney (1969) 33 Conv.(N.S.) 161.

A. The Rule in Keech v. Sandford

1. The rule. In *Keech* v. *Sandford*[19] the trustee of a lease of Romford Market applied for a renewal of the lease for the benefit of the infant beneficiary, and on this being refused, the trustee obtained a renewal of it for himself. It was held that he must hold the lease on trust for the infant, Lord King L.C. cynically[20] remarking: "I very well see, if a trustee, on the refusal to renew, might have a lease to himself, few trust-estates would be renewed to *cestui que* use; though I do not say there is a fraud in this case, yet he should rather have let it run out, than to have had the lease to himself."[21]

2. Extensions of the rule. The rule in *Keech* v. *Sandford*[22] has been extended in a modified form to persons who, though not in any definite fiduciary relationship to the other persons interested, have a partial interest in a lease. The renewed lease is looked upon as a continuation of the original lease,[23] and so if there is any ground for the intervention of equity, the grantee of the renewed lease will be treated as holding it for the benefit of the same persons as were interested in the original lease. Thus if a renewal is obtained by a partner,[24] (or former partner with regard to undistributed assets),[25] a mortgagor or a mortgagee,[26] a joint tenant or a tenant in common,[27] or a tenant for life,[28] there is a rebuttable presumption that the renewed lease is held on a constructive trust. If the lessee can show that he did not in any way abuse his position or intercept an advantage coming to the estate, and is guilty of no breach of faith, he may retain the lease for his own benefit; but it is very difficult for a partner, or, in less degree, for a mortgagor or mortgagee to rebut the presumption.[29]

2. Limits to the rule. In *Re Biss, Biss* v. *Biss*[30] there was a full discussion of the rule in the Court of Appeal. The yearly tenant of a shop died intestate. His widow obtained letters of administration and with the two children who were adults, but who were not themselves co-administrators with the widow, continued to carry on the business. The

---

[19] (1726) Sel.Cas. *t.* King 61. The pleadings are given by D. R. Paling at (1972) 36 Conv.(N.S.) 159.
[20] D. E. C. Yale considers that the dictum was not a cynicism but the result of bitter experience from the South Sea Bubble: *Lord Nottingham's Chancery Cases*, Vol. 2 (1961: S.S. Vol. 79), p. 144.
[21] *Keech* v. *Sandford*, *supra*, at p. 62.
[22] *Supra.*
[23] See, *e.g. Re Biss, Biss* v. *Biss* [1903] 2 Ch. 40 at 56, 61; *Griffith* v. *Owen* [1907] 1 Ch. 195 at 204.
[24] *Featherstonhaugh* v. *Fenwick* (1810) 17 Ves. 298 at 311; *Clegg* v. *Fishwick* (1849) 1 Mac. & G. 294; *Clegg* v. *Edmondson* (1857) 8 De G.M. & G. 787 at 807.
[25] *Thompson's Trustee* v. *Heaton* [1974] 1 W.L.R. 605 (purchase of reversion).
[26] *Rakestraw* v. *Brewer* (1728) 2 P.Wms. 511; *Leigh* v. *Burnett* (1885) 29 Ch.D. 231.
[27] *Palmer* v. *Young* (1684) [1903] 2 Ch. 65n.; *Hunter* v. *Allen* [1907] 1 I.R. 212.
[28] *Randall* v. *Russell* (1817) 3 Mer. 190; *Lloyd-Jones* v. *Clark-Lloyd* [1919] 1 Ch. 424. In the case of land, tenants for life and co-owners will often be in a fiduciary position under the property legislation of 1925.
[29] *Re Biss, Biss* v. *Biss* [1903] 2 Ch. 40 at 62–64.
[30] [1903] 2 Ch. 40.

landlord refused the widow a renewal of the tenancy, but later one of
the two children obtained a new lease. The Court of Appeal held that
the child could keep the lease for himself; for any hope of renewal to
the estate had been extinguished by the refusal of the widow's
application, and the child thus neither had deprived the estate of any
hope of renewal nor had been guilty of any breach of duty or abuse of
position. In short, the rule applies only where the renewal is obtained
either by a person in a fiduciary position or by a person who held a
special position in relation to the old lease and by virtue thereof owed a
duty towards the other persons interested.[31] There is no such special
position between a lessee of a flat and those who share it, contributing
to the rent, and hence the rule does not apply to a renewal of the
lease.[32]

4. Purchase of reversion. Where instead of a renewal of the lease
there is a purchase of the reversion, the principle of *Keech* v. *Sandford*[33]
and its extension have been very restricted in their application. They
apply in cases of fraud, or where the lease was renewable by custom or
contract, so that the purchase cuts off the right of renewal,[34] or where
the trustee obtained the reversion by virtue of his position as
leaseholder, as where the landlord offered enfranchisement to all his
tenants.[35] The same applies when the trustee of an equity of redemption
destroys it by purchasing the property from the mortgagee at a price
equal to the sum due under the mortgage.[36] But in other cases, from the
time of Lord Hardwicke L.C.[37] until 1968, neither the rule nor its
extension has been applied.[38] The reason given for this is that "whereas
in the case of a renewal the trustee is in effect buying a part of the trust
property,[39] in the case of a reversion this is not so; it is a separate item
altogether, and therefore the trustee may purchase it unless, in so doing,
he is in effect destroying part of the trust property."[40] In 1968 the Court
of Appeal gave an unrestricted application to the rule,[41] asserting that it
was "a long established rule of equity from *Keech* v. *Sandford*,
downwards that if a trustee, who owns the leasehold, gets in the
freehold, that freehold belongs to the trust".[42] This decision has been

[31] *Re Biss, Biss* v. *Biss* [1903] Ch. 40 at 61; and see *Thompson's Trustee* v. *Heaton* [1974] 1 W.L.R. 605 at 614.
[32] *Savage* v. *Dunningham* [1974] Ch. 181.
[33] *Supra.*
[34] *Phillips* v. *Phillips* (1885) 29 Ch.D. 673.
[35] *Griffith* v. *Owen* [1907] 1 Ch. 195 at 204.
[36] *Griffith* v. *Owen* [1907] 1 Ch. 195.
[37] See *Norris* v. *Le Neve* (1743) 3 Atk. 26 at 38; affirmed H.L. (1744) 2 Bro.P.C. 73.
[38] *Randall* v. *Russell* (1817) 3 Mer. 190; *Longton* v. *Wilsby* (1887) 76 L.T. 770; *Bevan* v. *Webb* [1905] 1 Ch. 620.
[39] See *post*, p. 249.
[40] *Phipps* v. *Boardman* [1964] 1 W.L.R. 993 at 1009, *per* Wilberforce J.
[41] *Protheroe* v. *Protheroe* [1968] 1 W.L.R. 519, followed in *Thompson's Trustee* v. *Heaton* [1974] 1 W.L.R. 605.
[42] *Protheroe* v. *Protheroe, supra*, at p. 521, *per* Lord Denning M.R., Danckwerts and Widgery L.JJ. concurring. No authorities were cited in argument, and none referred to other than *Keech* v. *Sandford* itself.

described as "in modern terms an application of the broad principle that a trustee must not make a profit out of the trust estate."[43]

5. Lien. A person who is liable as a trustee under these rules has a lien on the property for the costs incurred by him, including the cost of any permanent improvements that he has effected, with interest.[44]

B. No Profit from a Trust

Apart from the somewhat special case of renewing a lease, the principle that a trustee may not profit from his trust has been applied in a wide variety of other cases. The following are among many illustrations of the rule.

1. Speculations. If a trustee lays out the trust fund in a commercial adventure or business of his own or uses it to speculate in land or stock, he will be liable for all the losses and the *cestui que trust* will be entitled to all the gains.[45] Again, if a trustee buys a debt or incumbrance binding the trust property for less than its nominal value, he must account to the *cestui que trust* for the profit.[46]

2. Remunerative employment. A trustee must disgorge any salary or profit he gains by using his position to procure for himself remunerative employment, as, for instance, where a stockbroker trustee procured the employment of his firm to value the trust securities,[47] or where a trustee appointed himself the director of a company by using the voting rights of shares which were part of the trust property.[48] But the *cestuis que trust* cannot claim the remuneration merely because the shares which qualify the trustee for the directorship are trust property,[49] or where he would have been appointed even if he had used the trust shares to vote against his appointment,[50] or otherwise where the remuneration came to him without his volition.[51] The will or settlement, too, may authorise the trustee to retain the remuneration,[52] and this is frequently done.[53]

[43] *Thompson's Trustee* v. *Heaton* [1974] 1 W.L.R. 605 at 612, *per* Pennycuick V.-C.
[44] See *Bradford* v. *Brownjohn* (1868) 3 Ch.App. 711; *Re Lord Ranelagh's Will* (1884) 26 Ch.D. 590; *Rowley* v. *Ginnever* [1897] 2 Ch. 503; and see *post*, p. 257.
[45] *Docker* v. *Somes* (1834) 2 My. & K. 655; *Aberdeen Town Council* v. *Aberdeen University* (1877) 2 App.Cas. 544 (grant of salmon fishings obtained by trustees of land); and see *Re Jarvis* [1958] 1 W.L.R. 815, where the claim failed owing to laches: see *ante*, p. 35. See also *post*, p. 287.
[46] *Pooley* v. *Quilter* (1858) 2 De G. & J. 327.
[47] *Williams* v. *Barton* [1927] 2 Ch. 9.
[48] *Re Macadam, Dallow* v. *Codd* [1946] Ch. 73.
[49] *Re Dover Coalfield Extension Ltd.* [1908] 1 Ch. 65.
[50] *Re Gee* [1948] Ch. 284.
[51] *Re Northcote's W.T.* [1949] 1 All E.R. 442.
[52] *Re Llewellin's W.T.* [1949] Ch. 255.
[53] See *post*, p. 256.

3. Purchase of the trust estate

(a) *The rule.* It is often said that a trustee may not purchase the trust property.[54] This, however, has never been the true rule,[55] which is that a purchase of trust property by a trustee is voidable at the instance of any beneficiary.[56] However honest and fair the sale may be,[57] and even if it was made at a public auction[58] or for a price higher than that obtainable on the open market,[59] or on terms which are generous to the trust estate,[60] any *cestui que trust* has an absolute right to have the conveyance set aside within a reasonable time after he discovers the circumstances[61]; and it matters not whether the purchase by the trustee was from himself alone, as sole trustee, or from his co-trustees.[62] The trustee takes a voidable title, though if it is avoided he is entitled to be recouped his expenditure, with interest.[63] If some of the beneficiaries do not agree to the property reverting to the trust, the court will order a resale.[64] The rule is an application of a wider principle, that a man must not put himself into a situation where his duty and interest conflict, and so it extends to transactions other than sales, *e.g.* the grant of a lease,[65] or the vesting of property in a partnership of which a trustee is a member or a company of which he is managing director.[66] But it does not apply to a merely nominal trustee (such as a person named as executor who has not acted as such) who acquired no special knowledge as trustee and took no part in preparing for sale.[67]

(b) *Third parties.* If instead of selling to himself the trustee sells to a third person he cannot repurchase the property so long as the contract for sale remains executory[68]; but he may do so after completion, provided that the original sale was bona fide and there was no understanding to repurchase.[69] A sale by a trustee to his wife is probably not within the rule,[70] though it would certainly be set aside on

---

[54] See, *e.g. Re Boles and British Land Co.'s Contract* [1902] 1 Ch. 244 at 246.
[55] *Campbell* v. *Walker* (1800) 5 Ves. 678 at 681.
[56] *Campbell* v. *Walker, supra,* at p. 680; *Fox* v. *Mackreth* (1788) 2 Cox Eq. 320; **2 W. & T.L.C. 663**; affirmed *sub nom. Mackreth* v. *Fox* (1791) 4 Bro.C.C. 258; *Holder* v. *Holder* [1968] Ch. 353 at 398, citing this passage.
[57] *Ex p. James* (1803) 8 Ves. 337 at 345; *Re Bulmer* [1937] Ch. 499.
[58] *Ex p. Lacey* (1802) 6 Ves. 625 at 629.
[59] *Aberdeen Ry.* v. *Blaikie* (1854) 1 Macq. 461.
[60] *Re Thompson's Settlement, Thompson* v. *Thompson* [1986] Ch. 99.
[61] *Beningfield* v. *Baxter* (1886) 12 App.Cas. 167; *Randall* v. *Errington* (1805) 10 Ves. 423; and see *Charter* v. *Trevelyan* (1844) 11 Cl. & F. 714 (37 years' ignorance).
[62] *Re Harvey, Harvey* v. *Lambert* (1888) 58 L.T. 449; *Wright* v. *Morgan* [1926] A.C. 788.
[63] See *Re Sherman* [1954] Ch. 653.
[64] See *Holder* v. *Holder* [1968] Ch. 353.
[65] *Ex p. Hughes* (1802) 6 Ves. 617 at 622; *Att.-Gen.* v. *Earl of Clarendon* (1810) 17 Ves. 491 at 500.
[66] *Re Thompson's Settlement, Thompson* v. *Thompson, supra.*
[67] *Holder* v. *Holder, supra.*
[68] *Delves* v. *Gray* [1902] 2 Ch. 606 (purchaser cannot enforce sub-contract).
[69] *Re Postlethwaite* (1888) 60 L.T. 514. *Cf. Christoforides* v. *Terry* [1924] A.C. 566.
[70] But see *Re McNally* [1967] N.Z.L.R. 521 (leave to sell to trustee's wife subject to same standards as leave to sell to trustee).

the slightest suspicion[71]; and a bona fide sale by a trustee to a company which he helps to promote and in which he takes shares cannot be set aside on the ground that it is a sale to himself.[72] Again, the rule does not apply to a trustee who has retired from the trust for a long time, e.g. 12 years,[73] or to an executor who has never proved the will or acted in the administration of the estate,[74] or to a trustee who acquired an option to purchase before assuming the trusteeship.[75]

(c) *Exceptions.* The rule has few exceptions. The trust instrument may expressly authorise such a purchase, and the court also has power to sanction it,[76] or alternatively may give the trustee leave to bid at an auction.[77] Furthermore, the Settled Land Act 1925[78] makes special provision to enable a tenant for life of settled land to purchase and otherwise deal with the settled property which he holds on trust.

4. Purchase from cestui que trust. Purchases of trust property by a trustee from himself must be distinguished from purchases by a trustee of his beneficiary's beneficial interest.[79] Unlike the former, where the trustee is both buyer and seller, the latter are not always voidable. Certainly they are watched by the court "with the utmost diligence,"[80] and are liable to be set aside if there is any hint of an abuse of the trustee's position or of undue influence exercised by him over the *cestui que trust*,[81] and notwithstanding a subsequent sale of the trust property.[82] But they are unimpeachable if "there is a distinct and clear contract, ascertained to be such after a jealous and scrupulous examination of all the circumstances, proving, that the *cestui que trust* intended, the trustee should buy; and there is no fraud, no concealment, no advantage taken, by the trustee of information, acquired by him in the character of trustee."[83] He who alleges that what is in form a

---

[71] *Burrell* v. *Burrell's Trustees*, 1915 S.C. 333 (upheld); *Tanti* v. *Carlson* [1948] V.L.R. 401 (set aside); *Re King's W.T., Newman* v. *Andrews* (1959) 173 E.G. 627 (upheld); and see *Ferraby* v. *Hobson* (1847) 2 Ph. 255 at 261 (sister); *cf. Gilbey* v. *Rush* [1906] 1 Ch. 11. See generally J. G. Fleming (1949) 13 Conv.(N.S.) 248.
[72] Consider *Farrar* v. *Farrars Ltd.* (1888) 40 Ch.D. 395 (one-tenth of shares).
[73] *Re Boles and British Land Co.'s Contract* [1902] 1 Ch. 244. Contrast *Spring* v. *Pride* (1864) 4 De G.J. & S. 395 and *Wright* v. *Morgan* [1926] A.C. 788, where the trustee retired immediately before the transaction. And see *Ex p. James* (1803) 8 Ves. 337 at 352, 353; and *post*, p. 287.
[74] *Clark* v. *Clark* (1884) 9 App.Cas. 733; and see *Stacey* v. *Elph* (1833) 1 My. & K. 195.
[75] *Re Mulholland's W.T.* [1949] 1 All E.R. 460; (1949) 65 L.Q.R. 163; and see *Wright* v. *Morgan, supra.*
[76] *Farmer* v. *Dean* (1863) 32 Beav. 327; and see *Coaks* v. *Boswell* (1886) 11 App.Cas. 232 as to non-disclosure to the court; see also *ante*, p. 235.
[77] *Holder* v. *Holder* [1968] Ch. 353 at 398, 402.
[78] s.68. See *Re Pennant's W.T.* [1970] Ch. 75 (sale held validly made under this power despite parties' ignorance of it).
[79] See *Tito* v. *Waddell (No. 2)* [1977] Ch. 106 at 240, 241 ("self-dealing" and "fair-dealing" distinguished).
[80] *Coles* v. *Trecothick* (1804) 9 Ves. 234 at 244, *per* Lord Eldon L.C.
[81] For undue influence, see *post*, pp. 551, 558.
[82] *Hill* v. *Langley, The Times*, January 28, 1988.
[83] *Coles* v. *Trecothick* (1804) 9 Ves. 234 at 247, *per* Lord Eldon L.C. And see *Morse* v. *Royal* (1806) 12 Ves. 355; *Wright* v. *Carter* [1903] 1 Ch. 27; and see *Dougan* v. *Macpherson* [1902] A.C. 197 (non-disclosure by trustee of valuation obtained *qua* beneficiary).

purchase by a trustee from himself is in substance a purchase from the beneficiaries must prove this clearly.[84]

5. Application to persons in fiduciary position. Principles similar to these are applicable to all other persons who, even though they are not trustees holding property in trust, nevertheless occupy a fiduciary position.[85] All these persons must refund with interest[86] all profits which they have made by means of their position or by means of property held by them,[87] unless they made the profits with the full knowledge and approval of the persons to whom they owe a duty.[88] But any agreement under which such profits are made is voidable only, not void;[89] and it may be set aside on terms[90] which include reasonable remuneration for work done by the fiduciary.[91]

(a) *Agents.* Agents cannot deal with their principals without a full disclosure.[92] Thus neither by themselves nor through a nominee[93] may they become either secret vendors or secret purchasers of property with which they are entrusted on behalf of their principals.[94] The rule is not confined to property in the ordinary sense, so that where X obtained confidential information about a company by acting as a self-appointed agent for trustees who held shares in it, he was held accountable to the trust for all the profits which he gained for himself out of a take-over bid made with the aid of that information,[95] subject to being made a liberal allowance for his work and skill.[96] Further, an agent who takes a secret profit must account for it to his principal,[97] or alternatively, the principal may claim compensation for the actual loss sustained.[98] The agent also forfeits his right to his remuneration.[99]

---

[84] *Williams* v. *Scott* [1900] A.C. 499.

[85] *Tate* v. *Williamson* (1866) 2 Ch.App. 55. For a useful classification of fiduciary relationships, see L. S. Sealy [1962] C.L.J. 69; and for a possible unifying concept, see J. C. Shepherd (1981) 97 L.Q.R. 51; and see *post*, p. 540.

[86] See *O'Sullivan* v. *Management Agency and Music Ltd.* [1985] Q.B. 428.

[87] *Imperial Mercantile Credit Association* v. *Coleman* (1873) L.R. 6 H.L. 189; *Parker* v. *McKenna* (1874) 10 Ch.App. 96 at 124. Contrast *Nordisk Insulinlaboratorium* v. *Gorgate Products Ltd.* [1953] Ch. 430.

[88] *Costa Rica Ry.* v. *Forwood* [1901] 1 Ch 746; and see *Stubbs* v. *Slater* [1910] 1 Ch. 632.

[89] It may be void on other grounds: *Guinness plc* v. *Saunders* [1990] 2 W.L.R. 324, *post*, p. 252.

[90] *O'Sullivan* v. *Management Agency and Music Ltd.*, *supra*.

[91] *Ibid.* And see *Guinness plc* v. *Saunders*, *supra*, at p. 342.

[92] *De Bussche* v. *Alt* (1877) 8 Ch.D. 286.

[93] See, *e.g. Regier* v. *Campbell-Stuart* [1939] Ch. 766.

[94] *Charter* v. *Trevelyan* (1844) 11 Cl. & F. 714; *Lees* v. *Nuttall* (1829) 1 Russ. & M. 53, affirmed (1834) 2 My. & K. 819.

[95] *Boardman* v. *Phipps* [1967] 2 A.C. 46, a 3–2 decision of the House of Lords, criticised as harsh by G. Jones (1968) 84 L.Q.R. 467, but applied in *Industrial Development Consultants Ltd.* v. *Cooley* [1972] 1 W.L.R. 443.

[96] *Phipps* v. *Boardman* [1964] 1 W.L.R. 993, affirmed *sub nom. Boardman* v. *Phipps* [1967] 2 A.C. 46. See *Mida Construction* v. *Imperial Developments* [1978] 5 W.W.R. 577, Man. C.A. (fiduciary allowed remuneration on a *quantum meruit* where contract avoided for non-disclosure. Contrast *Guinness plc* v. *Saunders* [1990] 2 W.L.R. 324 (no *quantum meruit* under a void contract: see *infra*).

[97] *Fawcett* v. *Whitehouse* (1829) 2 Russ. & My. 132; and see *Grant* v. *Gold Exploration and Development Syndicate Ltd.* [1900] 1 Q.B. 233.

[98] *Mahesan* v. *Malaysia Government Officers' Co-operative Housing Society Ltd.* [1979] A.C. 374, criticised A. M. Tettenborn (1979) 95 L.Q.R. 68, but accepted by C. A. Needham, *ibid.* 536 where the remedies against the agent and the briber are discussed.

[99] *Andrews* v. *Ramsay* [1903] 2 K.B. 635; *Hippisley* v. *Knee* [1905] 1 K.B. 1; *Ian Scott & Co.* v. *Medical Installations Co. Ltd.* (1981) 258 E.G. 556.

(b) *Solicitors.* A solicitor who purchases property from his client, or from his client's trustee in bankruptcy,[1] must show that the client was paid a fair price, and that he either was fully informed or had competent independent advice.[2] And the same principles apply to a sale by him to the client, whether the solicitor is himself the beneficial owner or merely a trustee of the property that he is selling.[3] Further, he must account for the interest earned by money which he holds for his clients, despite the difficulty of allocating it to individual clients.[4] These obligations of the solicitor continue after the relationship of solicitor and client has ended if the confidence which arises from the relationship still persists.[5]

(c) *Company directors.* Directors of a company[6] are not under any paramount duty to preserve the *corpus* of the company's property, being free to deal with it for the purposes of the company[7] as commercial men in the exercise of a just discretion.[8] Nevertheless, a resolution of a company which is controlled by their votes is nugatory if it purports to sanction their making a profit[9]; and a company director cannot on behalf of the company effectually deal with himself or a firm in which he is a partner.[10] For a director to fail to disclose to his co-directors his interest in a contract or proposed contract with the company is a breach of statutory duty,[11] and the contract is voidable at the suit of the company.[12] Further, an agreement for remuneration or other reward between a director and the company is void unless made in strict conformity with the articles.[13] Nor can such remuneration be recovered by way of *quantum meruit* or an equitable allowance.[14] But although the directors stand in a fiduciary position to the company,[15] they are not trustees for the individual shareholders, so that they may retain any profit made by buying shares offered to them by a shareholder even if they have not made full disclosure of material facts[16]; nor do they stand

---

[1] *Luddy's Trustee* v. *Peard* (1886) 33 Ch.D. 500; and see *Carter* v. *Palmer* (1842) 8 Cl. & F. 657 (counsel purchasing charges on client's estate).
[2] *Wright* v. *Carter* [1903] 1 Ch. 27; *Demerara Bauxite Co. Ltd.* v. *Hubbard* [1923] A.C. 673. And see *Re Haslam & Hier-Evans* [1902] 1 Ch. 765.
[3] *Moody* v. *Cox and Hatt* [1917] 2 Ch. 71.
[4] *Brown* v. *I.R.C.* [1965] A.C. 244. Yet at one time solicitors were bankers; see (1964) 80 L.Q.R. 480. In many cases statute now requires him to put the money into a clients' deposit account or pay interest in lieu thereof: Solicitors Act 1974, s.33, replacing Solicitors Act 1965, s.8; Solicitors' Accounts (Deposit Interest) Rules 1987.
[5] *Demerara Bauxite Co. Ltd.* v. *Hubbard, supra.*
[6] See generally L. S. Sealy [1967] C.L.J. 83.
[7] See *Selangor United Rubber Estates Ltd.* v. *Cradock (No. 3)* [1968] 1 W.L.R. 1555.
[8] *Sheffield and South Yorkshire Permanent B.S.* v. *Aizlewood* (1889) 44 Ch.D. 412.
[9] *Cook* v. *Deeks* [1916] 1 A.C. 554; *Re The French Protestant Hospital* [1951] Ch. 567. And see *Transvaal Lands Co.* v. *New Belgium (Transvaal) Land and Development Co.* [1914] 2 Ch. 488.
[10] *Aberdeen Ry.* v. *Blaikie* (1854) 1 Macq. 461.
[11] Companies Act 1985, s.317(1).
[12] *Hely-Hutchinson* v. *Brayhead Ltd.* [1968] 1 Q.B. 549; *Guinness plc* v. *Saunders* [1990] 2 W.L.R. 324 at 336, 339.
[13] *Guinness plc* v. *Saunders* [1990] 2 W.L.R. 324.
[14] *Ibid.* esp. at pp. 335, 336, 342. Contrast agents, *ante*, p. 251.
[15] *Regal (Hastings) Ltd.* v. *Gulliver* [1942] 1 All E.R. 378; [1967] 2 A.C. 134n.; *Re The French Protestant Hospital, supra,* at p. 570; *Parker* v. *McKenna* (1874) 10 Ch.App. 96. See also *post,* p. 287, n. 44.
[16] *Percival* v. *Wright* [1902] 2 Ch. 421; contrast *Allen* v. *Hyatt* (1914) 30 T.L.R. 444, where the directors had put themselves in a fiduciary position.

in a fiduciary relation to a person who employs the company to manage his land, so as to be precluded from keeping remuneration paid to them by the company for professional assistance in the management.[17] A director of a parent company does not stand in a fiduciary relation to a subsidiary company with an independent board of directors, and a director-elect owes no duty to the company the board of which he proposes to join.[18]

(d) *Other persons.*[19] Similar restrictions on the making of profits have been imposed on servants,[20] guardians,[21] partners,[22] promoters of companies,[23] managing owners of ships,[24] receivers,[25] managers of young artistes,[26] borough treasurers,[27] and members of a committee of inspection in bankruptcy.[28] Indeed, there is authority for saying that in this context there is a fiduciary relationship "whenever the plaintiff entrusts to the defendant a job to be performed,"[29] so that a servant of the Crown who accepts bribes for misusing his position is accountable to the Crown for the bribes.[30] Similarly, a prospective purchaser who, unbeknown to the prospective vendor, applies for planning permission in the latter's name is accountable for the profits accruing from the permission. He is a self-appointed agent whose acts can be ratified and adopted.[31] But the Law Society is not a trustee of commission received on solicitors' premiums under the compulsory insurance scheme, for the scheme is established, not in performance of a private duty owed to solicitors, but of a public duty under statute.[32]

6. Remuneration of trustees. As a result of the rule that a trustee cannot make a profit from his trust, trustees and executors are generally entitled to no allowance for their care and trouble.[33] This rule is so strict that even if a trustee or executor has sacrificed much time to carrying on a business as directed by the trust, he will usually be

---

[17] *Bath* v. *Standard Land Co. Ltd.* [1911] 1 Ch. 618.
[18] *Lindgren* v. *L. & P. Estates Ltd.* [1968] Ch. 572.
[19] In addition to the examples below, see *Prescott* v. *Birmingham Corporation* [1955] Ch. 210 and *Bromley London Borough Council* v. *Greater London Council* [1983] 1 A.C. 768 (local authorities and ratepayers).
[20] *Reading* v. *Att.-Gen.* [1951] A.C. 507.
[21] *Hatch* v. *Hatch* (1804) 9 Ves. 292; and see *post*, p. 554.
[22] *Aas* v. *Benham* [1891] 2 Ch. 244; *Thompson's Trustee in Bankruptcy* v. *Heaton* [1974] 1 W.L.R. 605; *Chan (Kak Loui)* v. *Zacharia* (1984) 154 C.L.R. 178.
[23] *Erlanger* v. *New Sombrero Phosphate Co.* (1878) 3 App.Cas. 1218; *Gluckstein* v. *Barnes* [1900] A.C. 240; *Jubilee Cotton Mills Ltd.* v. *Lewis* [1924] A.C. 958. See J. Gold (1943) 5 Toronto L.J. 21; and see J. H. Gross (1970) 86 L.Q.R. 493 on who is a promoter.
[24] *Williamson* v. *Hine* [1891] 1 Ch. 390.
[25] *Nugent* v. *Nugent* [1908] 1 Ch. 546.
[26] *O'Sullivan* v. *Management Agency and Music Ltd.* [1985] Q.B. 428.
[27] *Att.-Gen.* v. *De Winton* [1906] 2 Ch. 106.
[28] *Re Bulmer* [1937] Ch. 499.
[29] *Reading* v. *R.* [1949] 2 K.B. 232 at 236, *per* Asquith L.J.; affirmed [1951] A.C. 507.
[30] *Reading* v. *Att.-Gen.* [1951] A.C. 507. See generally J. C. Shepherd (1981) 97 L.Q.R. 51.
[31] *English* v. *Dedham Vale Properties Ltd.* [1978] 1 W.L.R. 93.
[32] *Swain* v. *The Law Society* [1983] 1 A.C. 598.
[33] *Robinson* v. *Pett* (1734) 3 P.Wms. 132; **2 W. & T.L.C. 555**; *Re Thorpe* [1891] 2 Ch. 360; *Re White, Pennell* v. *Franklin* [1898] 2 Ch. 217.

allowed nothing as compensation for his personal trouble or loss of time.[34] And a solicitor-trustee is not entitled to charge anything except his out-of-pocket expenses for any business he does in relation to the trust, whether contentious or non-contentious.[35]

There are, however, important exceptions to this rule.

(a) *Agreement with beneficiaries.* There is nothing to prevent a trustee from contracting with his *cestuis que trust* (being all *sui juris*) for compensation for the performance of the duties of the trust; but such a contract is regarded jealously by the court, and must be free from pressure.[36]

(b) *Order of court.* Where the court appoints a corporation (other than the Public Trustee) to be a trustee or administrator,[37] the corporation may charge such remuneration as the court authorises.[38] Again, a judicial trustee, whether an official of the court or not, may be paid out of the trust property such remuneration as the court may assign him.[39] Apart from the foregoing statutory jurisdiction, there is an inherent jurisdiction to allow a prospective or an existing trustee to retain remuneration where none was provided by the trust instrument.[40] Further, the court can increase or vary the remuneration provided by the trust instrument in respect of both past and future services.[41] When the court authorises payment of remuneration, it is not giving effect to any supposed contract between the trustees and the settlor[42] but is "exercising its ancient jurisdiction to secure the competent administration of the trust property."[43] Although for some purposes the remuneration is a beneficial interest, the court in awarding remuneration is not inhibited by the rule that there is no inherent jurisdiction to vary the beneficial provisions of the trust.[44] In exercising the jurisdiction the court has to balance two conflicting influences. On the one hand the office is generally gratuitous; on the other, the trust should be well administered.[45] Remuneration has been awarded where the services of a particular trustee are of special value and he refuses to act without payment,[46] where there is an implied promise by the beneficiaries to

---

[34] *Brocksopp* v. *Barnes* (1820) 5 Madd. 90; *Barrett* v. *Hartley* (1866) L.R. 2 Eq. 739. This passage was cited in *Guinness plc* v. *Saunders* [1990] 2 W.L.R. 324 at 332.
[35] *Re Barber (No. 2)* (1886) 34 Ch.D. 77; *Re Pooley* (1888) 40 Ch.D. 1.
[36] See *Ayliffe* v. *Murray* (1740) 2 Atk. 58; *Barrett* v. *Hartley* (1866) L.R. 2 Eq. 789.
[37] *Re Masters* [1953] 1 W.L.R. 81.
[38] T.A. 1925, s.42.
[39] Judicial Trustees Act 1896, s.1(5).
[40] *Re Masters, supra,* at p. 83; *Re Worthington, Leighton* v. *MacLeod* [1954] 1 W.L.R. 526 at 528; *Re Duke of Norfolk's S.T.* [1982] Ch. 61 at 75, 76, 80. See also *Re Berkeley Applegate (Investment Consultants) Ltd.* [1989] Ch. 32 (liquidator); and the colonial cases cited at (1982) 98 L.Q.R. 181.
[41] *Re Duke of Norfolk's S.T.* [1982] Ch. 61; *Re Codd's W.T.* [1975] 1 W.L.R. 1139.
[42] *Re Duke of Norfolk's S.T., supra.*
[43] *Ibid.* at p. 78, *per* Fox L.J.
[44] *Ibid.* at pp. 78, 81; see *ante,* p. 238. Contrast *Re Spedding* [1966] N.Z.L.R. 447 at 461, 466.
[45] *Ibid.* at p. 79. See and compare *Guinness plc* v. *Saunders* [1990] 2 W.L.R. 324 at 342.
[46] *Marshall* v. *Holloway* (1820) 2 Swans. 432; *Bainbrigge* v. *Blair* (1845) 8 Beav. 588 at 596; *Re Freeman's S.T.* (1887) 37 Ch.D. 148.

pay,[47] and where the duties have proved unexpectedly onerous.[48] Remuneration will, however, be awarded only on a substantive application; it is not proper to include a provision for increased remuneration as one of the terms of compromise of a dispute between beneficiaries concerning other matters.[49]

(c) *Authorised by Treasury.* The Public Trustee is allowed to charge such fees as may be fixed by the Treasury[50]; and a custodian trustee[51] may charge such fees as the Public Trustee may charge when acting as custodian trustee.[52]

(d) *Solicitor-trustee's costs in litigation.* Under the rule in *Cradock* v. *Piper*,[53] a solicitor-trustee is entitled to his profit costs when he acts as solicitor in an action or other legal proceedings on behalf of himself and his co-trustee jointly (and not himself alone[54]), except so far as the costs have been increased by his being one of the parties. This rule applies not only to hostile proceedings against the trustees but also to friendly proceedings such as an application in chambers for maintenance of an infant[55]; and it is immaterial whether the trustees are plaintiffs or defendants, or applicants or respondents. But the rule does not extend to the administration of the estate out of court[56]; and a solicitor who is liquidator of a company cannot claim profit costs for acting on behalf of the company, unless this is authorised by the liquidation committee, the creditors or the court.[57]

There is nothing, however, to prevent a solicitor-trustee from employing his partner to do any legal work, whether contentious or not, and paying his proper charges in any case in which he could have employed another solicitor, provided the partner will be exclusively entitled to the profit costs for his own benefit.[58] But if he employs his firm to do the work, he cannot recover the firm's charges for doing it, even if he will receive nothing himself[59] or is merely a salaried partner.[60]

[47] *Re Salmen* (1912) 107 L.T. 108.
[48] *Bainbrigge* v. *Blair* (1845) 8 Beav. 588 at 596; *Re Duke of Norfolk's S.T.* [1979] Ch. 37, reversed as to extent of jurisdiction but not affecting this point: see [1982] Ch. at p. 71.
[49] *Re Barbour's S.T.* [1974] 1 W.L.R. 1198.
[50] Public Trustee Act 1906, s.9, as amended by Public Trustee (Fees) Act 1957, and modified by Administration of Justice Act 1965, s.2, as to common investment funds; S.I. 1980 No. 370; S.I. 1981 No. 324. As to the incidence of his fees among the beneficiaries, see Act of 1957, s.1: *Re Riddell* [1936] Ch. 747; *Re Evans's W.T., Public Trustee* v. *Gausby* [1948] Ch. 185. Section 2 of the Act of 1965 is to be repealed by Administration of Justice Act 1982, s.76 and Sched. 8, Pt.I from a date to be appointed.
[51] See *ante*, pp. 199, 209 for custodian trustees.
[52] Public Trustee Act 1906, s.4(3).
[53] (1850) 1 Mac. & G. 664; and see *Re Barber (No. 2)* (1886) 34 Ch.D. 77.
[54] *Lyon* v. *Baker* (1852) 5 De G. & Sm. 622.
[55] *Re Corsellis* (1887) 34 Ch.D. 675.
[56] *Ibid.*
[57] Insolvency Rules 1986 (S.I. No. 1925), r. 4.128(3).
[58] *Clack* v. *Carlon* (1861) 30 L.J.Ch. 639.
[59] *Re Gates* [1933] Ch. 913.
[60] *Re Hill, Claremont* v. *Hill* [1934] Ch. 623.

(e) *Authority in trust instrument*

(1) PROFESSIONAL SERVICES. The trust instrument may expressly authorise the trustee to receive compensation for his care and trouble; and it is common to allow a trustee who is a solicitor, a literary executor (or a company of which he is a director),[61] or other professional man to charge for his professional services. Such a clause in a will is treated as a legacy to the executor or trustee equivalent to the profit he will make under it.[62] Accordingly, he cannot charge profit costs if the estate is insufficient to pay the debts[63]; and if the estate, though sufficient to pay the debts, is insufficient to pay the legacies in full, the costs must abate with the legacies unless the clause gives the costs priority over the other legacies.[64] Again, if a trustee or his wife attested the will, he cannot charge his profit costs,[65] unless he became trustee only by some subsequent appointment or event.[66]

(2) OTHER SERVICES. Unless a charging clause is sufficiently widely drawn, a solicitor-trustee or executor can charge only for strictly professional services, and not for matters which a layman ought to do personally without the intervention of a solicitor.[67] The clause is therefore often drawn so as to extend both to professional business and to business not strictly professional, though it has been said that such a provision should be made only under express instructions given by the client himself, with full knowledge of the effect.[68] And as such a provision will be construed as extending only to costs and charges properly incurred, it may be advisable to authorise the co-trustees to settle the amount of such charges without having them taxed, the co-trustees exercising the discretion of ordinary business men.[69] Such a provision, however, will not enable a trust corporation to charge its fees[70]; but a bank's charging clause may be wide enough to allow it to retain the profit arising from keeping trust moneys on deposit with itself at a mere half per cent. interest.[71]

(f) *Other cases.* Apart from the cases set out above, the rule that a trustee is entitled to no remuneration is rigorously applied. In particular, trust corporations cannot charge unless they can bring themselves under one of the foregoing heads, *e.g.* authority by all the beneficiaries or

---

[61] *Re Orwell's W.T., Dixon* v. *Blair* [1982] 1 W.L.R. 1337.
[62] It may nevertheless be "earned income" for the purposes of income tax: see *Dale* v. *I.R.C.* [1954] A.C. 11; and see *White* v. *Franklin* [1965] 1 W.L.R. 492.
[63] *Re White, Pennell* v. *Franklin* [1898] 2 Ch. 217; *Re Salmen* (1912) 107 L.T. 108.
[64] *Re Brown* (1918) 62 S.J. 487; *Commissioner of Stamp Duties of New South Wales* v. *Pearse* [1954] A.C. 91.
[65] *Re Barber (No. 1)* (1886) 31 Ch.D. 665; *Re Pooley* (1888) 40 Ch.D. 1.
[66] *Re Royce's W.T.* [1959] Ch. 626.
[67] *Re Chapple* (1884) 27 Ch.D. 584; *Clarkson* v. *Robinson* [1900] 2 Ch. 722.
[68] *Re Chapple, supra,* at p. 587; *Re Sykes* [1909] 2 Ch. 241 at 247, 250. See *Re Gee* [1948] Ch. 284. *Cf. Re Llewellin's W.T.* [1949] Ch. 225. For precedents of such a clause, see *Re Ames* (1883) 25 Ch.D. 72; *Re Fish* [1893] 2 Ch. 413.
[69] *Re Fish, supra* and see *Re Wells, Wells* v. *Wells* [1962] 1 W.L.R. 874.
[70] *Re Cooper* (1939) 160 L.T. 453 (in C.A. on another point [1939] Ch. 811, *ante*, p. 112).
[71] *Re Waterman's W.T., Lloyds Bank Ltd.* v. *Sutton* [1952] 2 All E.R. 1054.

(more usually) authority in the trust instrument. This difficulty cannot be surmounted by appointing a corporation to be managing trustee and also custodian trustee, so that it could charge in the latter capacity[72]; such an appointment is inoperative.[73] Where a corporation is entitled to charge, the general rule is that as between the beneficiaries its income fees must be borne by income and its capital fees by capital.[74]

Section 7. Indemnification of Trustee

Although a trustee is in general not entitled to any remuneration for his services, he is normally entitled to be indemnified against his out-of-pocket expenses.[75]

1. Scope of indemnity

(a) *Lien on trust property*

(1) THE RIGHT.   A trustee is entitled to be indemnified out of the trust property against all costs, expenses and liabilities properly incurred in administering the trust,[76] *e.g.* insurance premiums,[77] costs of renewing leases,[78] improvements,[79] and torts committed in managing the trust property.[80] This has always been the rule of equity, and it is now statutory.[80a] "A trustee may reimburse himself or pay or discharge out of the trust premises all expenses incurred in or about the execution of the trusts or powers."[81] Although the reimbursement is usually made out of the *corpus* of the trust estate,[82] it is a first charge on all the trust property, both *corpus* and income, and the trustee has a right to retain the expenses out of income until provision can be made for raising them out of the *corpus*.[83]

(2) BENEFIT OF LIEN.   The lien exists in favour of both express and constructive[84] trustees acting properly, notwithstanding that they are or one of them is beneficially entitled to a life interest,[85] or that one of them is a defaulter and indebted to the estate.[86] Further, any person

---

[72] *Forster* v. *Williams Deacon's Bank Ltd.* [1935] Ch. 359; *Arning* v. *James* [1936] Ch. 158.
[73] *Arning* v. *James, supra.*
[74] *Re Hulton* [1936] Ch. 536; *Re Roberts' W.T.* [1937] Ch. 274; *Re Godwin* [1938] Ch. 341.
[75] See *post*, p. 320 as to liability under contracts.
[76] See *Re Beddoe* [1893] 1 Ch. 547 at 558.
[77] *Re Smith's Estate* [1937] Ch. 636. *Cf. Re Roberts, Public Trustee* v. *Roberts* [1946] Ch. 1.
[78] *Ex p. Grace* (1799) 1 Bos. & P. 376 at 377.
[79] *Rowley* v. *Ginnever* [1897] 2 Ch. 503.
[80] *Re Raybould* [1900] 1 Ch. 199 (mining: letting down the surface).
[80a] *i.e.* properly incurred: *Holding and Management Ltd.* v. *Property Holding and Investment Trust plc* [1989] 1 W.L.R. 1313.
[81] T.A. 1925, s.30(2), replacing part of T.A. 1893, s.24. It is unclear how far this applies to the trustees of charities: see A. J. Hawkins (1979) 95 L.Q.R. 99.
[82] See *Carver* v. *Duncan* [1985] A.C. 1082 at 1120, 1121, as to the incidence between capital and income.
[83] *Stott* v. *Milne* (1884) 25 Ch.D. 710.
[84] *Rowley* v. *Ginnever* [1897] 2 Ch. 503.
[85] *Ibid.*
[86] *Re Frith* [1902] 1 Ch. 342.

advancing money or giving credit to the trustees for the purposes of the trust, or having otherwise a claim against them in their character of trustees, will be subrogated to their right and obtain the benefit of their lien.[87]

(b) *Indemnity by beneficiary.* A trustee normally has no right of indemnity against any beneficiary personally; but there are three cases in which he has such a right.

(1) BARE TRUST. If the trustee is holding property for a person who is *sui juris* and entitled to the whole beneficial interest, the latter is under a personal obligation to indemnify him against any liability incurred through the holding of such property, unless the nature of the transaction excludes such duty. Thus if T is holding shares upon trust for B (who is *sui juris*), B must indemnify T against all liability in respect of calls on the shares[88] and this duty will not be terminated by B assigning his beneficial interest to C, even if T concurs in the assignment and takes an indemnity from C.[89]

(2) CONTRACT. Even if a beneficiary has only a limited interest in the trust property, he may become liable to indemnify the trustee if he expressly or impliedly contracts to do so, *e.g.* where the beneficiary is also the settlor and the trustee accepted office at his request.[90]

(3) CLUB. Members of a club may be liable under the rules to indemnify trustees in whom club property (*e.g.* the lease of the club premises) is vested, though apart from any such rule there will be no liability; for an ordinary club is founded on the basis of a member's liability being limited to his subscription.[91]

2. Costs of litigation. When litigation appears to be prima facie proper and in the interests of the trust, the court will grant trustees leave to sue or defend; however the litigation results, this leave, known as a *Beddoe* order[92] will protect them against the *cestuis que trust* and entitle them to be reimbursed their costs out of the trust estate.[93] Leave will not be given where the litigation is between rival claimants to the trust fund in which the existence of the relationship between trustee and beneficiary is in issue.[94] If trustees omit the precaution of obtaining

---

[87] See *post,* p. 321. For liens generally, see *post,* pp. 467 *et seq.*

[88] *Hardoon* v. *Belilios* [1901] A.C. 118. This principle does not apply as between mortgagee and mortgagor: *Sinfield* v. *Sweet* [1967] 1 W.L.R. 1489, *post,* p. 429.

[89] *Matthews* v. *Ruggles-Brise* [1911] 1 Ch. 194.

[90] *Ex p. Chippendale* (1854) 4 De G.M. & G. 19 at 54; *Jervis* v. *Wolferstan* (1874) L.R. 18 Eq. 18, distinguished in *Robinson* v. *Murdoch* (1881) 6 App.Cas. 855.

[91] *Wise* v. *Perpetual Trustee Co. Ltd.* [1903] A.C. 139.

[92] *Re Beddoe* [1893] 1 Ch. 547; see at pp. 558, 562. See further, *post,* p. 357.

[93] As to settled land, see S.L.A. 1925, s.92. As to actions in which one beneficiary under a will claims the whole estate, see *Re Dallaway, decd.* [1982] 1 W.L.R. 756 (reimbursement allowed); *Re Evans, decd.* [1986] 1 W.L.R. 101 (reimbursement of future costs refused).

[94] *National Anti-Vivisection Society Ltd.* v. *Duddington* [1989] *The Times,* November 23.

leave, they are still entitled to be reimbursed their costs[95] if the action was properly brought or defended for the benefit of the trust estate[96] even though incidentally they were defending their own character against a charge of personal fraud in respect of something connected with their administration of the trust estate.[97] But if litigation is speculative and, in the ultimate result, unsuccessful, a trustee will usually not be allowed his costs, even though he acted in good faith and under the advice of counsel.[98] And a trustee who unreasonably withholds trust property from a beneficiary will be ordered to pay the costs of proceedings to establish the beneficiary's claim.[99]

---

[95] For the basis of taxation, see R.S.C., Ord. 62, r. 12. For cases on the former Ord. 62, r. 31, see *Re Grimthorpe* [1958] Ch. 615; *Re Whitley* [1962] 1 W.L.R. 922; *Re Gibson's S.T.* [1981] Ch. 179 (reviewing taxation), and compare *Re Dargie* [1954] Ch. 16 (hostile litigation).
[96] *Stott* v. *Milne* (1884) 25 Ch.D. 710.
[97] *Walters* v. *Woodbridge* (1878) 7 Ch.D. 504; *Re Dunn* [1904] 1 Ch. 648.
[98] *Re Beddoe* [1893] 1 Ch. 547; *Re Yorke* [1911] Ch. 370; *Re England's S.T.* [1918] 1 Ch. 24.
[99] *Re Chapman, Freeman* v. *Parker* (1895) 72 L.T. 66.

CHAPTER 7

THE POWERS OF TRUSTEES

1. The powers. In order to enable a trustee or personal representative to carry out his duties, various powers have been conferred upon him by statute; and most of these are now contained in the Trustee Act 1925. Some of them have been already mentioned; it remains now to refer to some of the others. Except where otherwise stated, the powers apply whenever the trust was created, but only so far as a contrary intention is not expressed in the trust instrument, if any.[1]

2. Exercise of powers. In general, any power or trust must be exercised by all the trustees. A majority has no power to bind the minority,[2] unless the settlement expressly so provides.[3] But if a trustee dies, any power or trust given to the trustees jointly may be exercised or performed by the survivors or survivor of them for the time being,[4] even in the case of discretionary powers.[5] Further, trustees must exercise their powers in the light of the circumstances existing at the time[6]; they cannot bind themselves or their successors,[7] either directly or indirectly,[8] as to how they will[9] or will not[10] exercise a power at any future date.[11] In exercising powers concerned with the administration of the trust estate, their duty is to consider the estate as a whole; they are under no duty to consider the effect of the exercise as between some beneficiaries and others.[12]

Section 1. Sale

1. Power of sale

(a) *Land.* In addition to land subject to an express trust or power of sale, land bought under an express power by trustees of a personalty settlement, or by trustees of land held upon trust for sale, is held upon

---

[1] T.A. 1925, s.69(1), (2).
[2] *Luke* v. *South Kensington Hotel Co.* (1879) 11 Ch.D. 121 at 125; and see *ante*, pp. 169, 237.
[3] See *Re Butlin's S.T.* (1974) 118 S.J. 757 (further proceedings, see *post*, p. 634).
[4] T.A. 1925, s.18(1), replacing T.A. 1893, s.22(1), which replaced C.A. 1881, s.38.
[5] *Re Smith, Eastick* v. *Smith* [1904] 1 Ch. 139; *cf. Re Harding, Harding* v. *Paterson* [1923] 1 Ch. 182.
[6] *Weller* v. *Ker* (1866) L.R. 1 Sc. & D. 11.
[7] *Re Hirst* [1954] Q.S.R. 344 (see (1955) 71 L.Q.R. 464).
[8] *Oceanic Steam Navigation Co.* v. *Sutherberry* (1880) 16 Ch.D. 236 (grant of future option held bad).
[9] *Moore* v. *Clench* (1875) 1 Ch.D. 447.
[10] *Chambers* v. *Smith* (1878) 3 App.Cas. 795 at 815; *Saul* v. *Pattinson* (1886) 54 L.T. 670.
[11] See also *ante*, p. 137.
[12] *Re Charteris* [1917] 1 Ch. 377; *Re Hayes' W.T.* [1971] 1 W.L.R. 758.

trust for sale, unless the settlement otherwise provides,[13] *e.g.* by directing a house to be bought as a residence.[14] Similarly, if land vested in trustees by way of security becomes discharged from the right of redemption by limitation, foreclosure or otherwise, they hold it on trust for sale.[15] Again, a trustee is under a duty to sell land purchased in breach of trust,[16] unless all the beneficiaries are *sui juris* and direct him to retain the land.[17] Further, a trust for sale is deemed to subsist, so far as concerns a purchaser,[18] until the land has been conveyed to or at the direction of the beneficiaries.[19]

(b) *Chattels.* The general rule is that if chattels are settled upon persons in succession, the duty of the trustees is to hold the chattels; they cannot sell them. But in certain cases statute has conferred powers of sale.

(1) CHATTELS DEVOLVING WITH SETTLED LAND. If chattels are settled to devolve with settled land, the tenant for life may sell them with the leave of the court. The purchase-money is payable to the trustees as capital money arising under the Settled Land Act 1925, and must be dealt with as such, or by purchasing other chattels.[20]

(2) CHATTELS NOT SETTLED WITH LAND.

(i) If chattels are settled for an entailed interest, the trustees may sell them with the consent of the usufructuary for the time being if of full age.[21] The purchase-money must be held on the same trusts as the chattels.[22]

(ii) If the chattels are not settled for an entailed interest, but, *e.g.* on A for life with remainder to B, the trustees have no power to sell them unless—

(a) they are authorised to apply capital money for some specific purpose, when they may raise the money by selling any part of the trust estate, *e.g.* the chattels,[23] or

(b) they are authorised by the court under the Trustee Act 1925, s.57, to sell the chattels.[24]

---

[13] L.P.A. 1925, s.32. And see *Re Gent and Eason's Contract* [1905] 1 Ch. 386.
[14] *Re Hanson* [1928] Ch. 96. But see *Re Pope's Contract* [1911] 2 Ch. 442.
[15] L.P.A. 1925, s.31. See also *ante*, p. 228.
[16] *Re Patten and Edmonton Union* (1883) 52 L.J.Ch. 787.
[17] *Wright* v. *Morgan* [1926] A.C. 788 at 799. See *ante*, p. 233 and *post*, p. 294.
[18] This is of importance for the purposes of overreaching: see *ante*, p. 62.
[19] L.P.A. 1925, s.23, replacing C.A. 1911, s.10(3), (4). Prior to the Act of 1911 the trustee could make title by proving that not all the beneficiaries were *sui juris* or by obtaining the concurrence of one of them: *Re Patten and Edmonton Union* (1883) 52 L.J.Ch. 787; *Re Jenkins and H.E. Randall & Co.'s Contract* [1903] 2 Ch. 362.
[20] S.L.A. 1925, s.67. See *Re Hope* [1899] 2 Ch. 679 ("the Hope diamond"); *Re Waldegrave* (1899) 81 L.T. 632 (proceeds directed to be applied in renovation of other chattels). *Cf. Re Earl of Mount Edgcumbe* [1950] Ch. 615.
[21] L.P.A. 1925, s.130(5). The power is not available where a testator who died before 1926 attempted to settle chattels for an entailed interest, as entailed interests in personal estate could not be created before 1926: *Re Hope's W.T.* [1929] 2 Ch. 136.
[22] *Ibid.*
[23] See T.A. 1925, s.16(1), *infra.*
[24] See *ante*, p. 239.

(c) *General.*   Where trustees are authorised by the trust instrument
or by law to apply capital money for any purpose or in any manner,
they have, and are deemed always to have had, power to raise the
money required by sale, conversion, calling in or mortgage of all or any
part of the trust property for the time being in possession.[25] This applies
notwithstanding a contrary direction in the trust instrument (if any), but
does not apply to trustees of a charity or to Settled Land Act trustees.[26]
This power cannot be used to raise money by mortgaging existing assets
in order to acquire additional assets.[27]

2. Mode of sale.   A trustee exercising a trust for sale or power of
sale of property may sell or concur with any other person in selling all
or any part of the property, either subject to prior charges or not,
together or in lots, by public auction or by private contract, and subject
to such conditions of sale as he thinks fit.[28] A trust or power to sell or
dispose of land includes a trust or power to sell or dispose of part
thereof, whether the division is horizontal, vertical, or made in any
other way,[29] so that a trustee can since 1925 sell surface and minerals
separately.[30] An express power to sell settled land can be exercised only
by the tenant for life or statutory owner, for such a power of sale is
taken away from the trustee and added to the powers of the tenant for
life or statutory owner under the Settled Land Act 1925.[31]

In the case of a trust for sale of land, a power to postpone sale is
always implied unless a contrary intention appears.[32] And trustees for
sale of land have all the powers of a tenant for life and of the trustees of
a settlement under the Settled Land Act 1925.[33]

3. The price.   Trustees are bound to sell at the best price reasonably
obtainable, so that even if negotiations for a sale are so nearly complete
that ordinary commercial morality precludes them from honourably
withdrawing, they still must not reject a better[34] offer without first
probing it.[35] Nevertheless they have a discretion and are not bound
automatically to reject the lower offer; they may "pray in aid the
common-sense rule underlying the old proverb: 'A bird in the hand is

---

[25] T.A. 1925, s.16(1).
[26] *Ibid.* s.16(2).
[27] *Re Suenson-Taylor's S.T.* [1974] 1 W.L.R. 1280 (note possible exception at pp. 1283, 1284,
acquisition of small piece of land to protect existing land).
[28] T.A. 1925, s.12(1).
[29] *Ibid.* s.12(2).
[30] For the position before 1926, see T.A. 1893, s.44; and as to personal representatives, see *Re Chaplin
and Staffordshire Potteries Waterworks Co. Ltd.'s Contract* [1922] 2 Ch. 824.
[31] See T.A. 1925, s.12(3); S.L.A. 1925, ss.108, 109. See *Re Ball, Jones* v. *Jones* [1930] W.N. 111, 120.
[32] L.P.A. 1925, s.25. See *Re Rooke, Rooke* v. *Rooke* [1953] Ch. 716.
[33] L.P.A. 1925, s.28(1). See *post,* p. 268 as to their power to delegate their powers.
[34] The suggestion that a trustee was bound to probe a *lower* offer to see if it would be raised was
rejected in *Davis* v. *Administrator-General* (1965) 9 W.I.R. 100 at 114 (Sup. Ct. Jamaica).
[35] *Buttle* v. *Saunders* [1950] 2 All E.R. 193: there may thus be a fiduciary duty to "gazump."

worth two in the bush.' "[36] There is authority suggesting that trustees cannot sell at a price to be fixed by a valuer,[37] for that would be an unauthorised delegation.[38] With the advance of the science of valuation, it is doubtful whether that strict view would be imposed today.[39]

4. Conditions of sale. Trustees must be careful not to sell under unnecessarily depreciatory conditions,[40] for if the purchase price is thereby rendered inadequate, the beneficiaries can interfere to stop the sale at any time before completion. After completion, the beneficiaries can hold the trustees personally liable for the loss, but the title of the purchaser will be indefeasible unless he acted in collusion with the trustees.[41]

5. Receipt for purchase-money. A purchaser from a trustee is not bound to see to the application of the purchase-money; the trustee's receipt in writing for any money, securities, or other personal property or effects payable, transferable, or deliverable to him under any trust or power is a sufficient discharge for the same.[42] But except where the trustee is a trust corporation, this provision does not enable a sole trustee to give a valid receipt for the proceeds of sale or other capital money arising under a trust for sale of land, or for capital money arising under the Settled Land Act 1925. The section applies notwithstanding anything to the contrary in the instrument, if any, creating the trust. Further, no purchaser or mortgagee paying or advancing money on a sale or mortgage purporting to be made under any trust or power vested in trustees is concerned to see that such money is wanted, or that no more is raised than is wanted.[43]

Section 2. Partition

1. Land. Apart from a joint tenancy of settled land, since 1925[44] land held for persons as joint tenants or tenants in common is subject to

---

[36] *Buttle* v. *Saunders, supra,* at p. 195, *per* Wynn-Parry J.
[37] *Peters* v. *Lewes and East Grinstead Ry.* (1881) 18 Ch.D. 429 at 436, 437; *Re Earl of Wilton's S.E.* [1907] 1 Ch. 50 at 55.
[38] For delegation, see *post,* p. 265.
[39] See [1985] Conv. 44 (G. Lightman).
[40] See *Dunn* v. *Flood* (1885) 28 Ch.D. 586.
[41] T.A. 1925, s.13, replacing T.A. 1893, s.14.
[42] T.A. 1925, s.14, replacing T.A. 1893, s.20; slightly amended by L.P.(Am.)A. 1926, Sched. See also *Elliot* v. *Merryman* (1740) Barn.Ch. 78; **2 W. & T.L.C. 832**.
[43] T.A. 1925, s.17.
[44] Prior to 1926 a partition action could be brought by coparceners, joint tenants or tenants in common, though not during the continuance of a trust for sale; *Biggs* v. *Peacock* (1882) 22 Ch.D. 284. This action is now obsolete.

a trust for sale.[45] The Law of Property Act 1925[46] provides that "where the net proceeds of sale have under the trusts affecting the same become absolutely vested in persons of full age in undivided shares (whether or not such shares may be subject to a derivative trust) the trustees for sale may, with the consent of the persons, if any, of full age, not being annuitants, interested in possession in the net rents and profits of the land until sale—

(a)   partition the land remaining unsold or any part thereof; and

(b)   provide (by way of mortgage or otherwise) for the payment of any equality money."

If a mental patient is entitled to a share, the consent of his receiver will be sufficient to protect the trustees.[47] Similarly, if a minor is absolutely entitled to a share, the trustees may act on his behalf and retain land (to be held on trust for sale) or other property to represent his share.[48] For this power of partitioning to apply, the persons in whom the proceeds of the sale are absolutely vested need not be beneficially interested; they may be trustees or personal representatives.[49] And the court may intervene if the trustees refuse to exercise their powers.[50]

2. Chattels.   "Where any chattels belong to persons in undivided shares, the persons interested in a moiety or upwards may apply to the court for an order for division of the chattels or any of them, according to a valuation or otherwise, and the court may make such order and give any consequential directions as it thinks fit."[51]

Section 3. Insurance

1. Power to insure.   Trustees are not bound to insure the trust property against loss or damage by fire unless the trust instrument imposes such an obligation upon them.[51a] However, under the Trustee Act 1925[52] they may insure any building or other insurable property unless the trust instrument forbids it, or unless they are bound forthwith to convey the property absolutely to any beneficiary upon being

---

[45] L.P.A. 1925, ss.34, 36, 1st Sched., Pt. IV; A.E.A. 1925, s.33.
[46] s.28(3).
[47] See *post*, p. 537, for mental patients.
[48] L.P.A. 1925, s.28(4).
[49] *Re Brooker, Public Trustee* v. *Young* [1934] Ch. 610.
[50] See *ante*, p. 236.
[51] L.P.A. 1925, s.188.
[51a] *Bailey* v. *Gould* (1840) 4 Y. & C. 221.
[52] s.19, replacing T.A. 1893, s.18.

requested to do. The amount of insurance must not exceed three-fourths of the value of the property insured. The premiums may be paid out of the income of the property insured or of any other property subject to the same trusts. Chattels settled to go along with land settled in strict settlement (or "heirlooms," as they are popularly called) are insurable under the statutory provision.[53]

2. Application of insurance money. The Trustee Act 1925[54] provides that money received after 1925 by trustees or any beneficiary under a policy of insurance[55] against the loss or damage of any property subject to a trust or to a settlement within the Settled Land Act 1925, whether by fire or otherwise, is to be capital money if the policy has been kept up under any trust in that behalf, or under any power (statutory or otherwise) or in performance of any covenant or of any obligation (statutory or otherwise) or by a tenant for life impeachable for waste.[56] If the money is receivable in respect of settled land or any building or works thereon, it must be applied like other capital money arising under the Settled Land Act; if receivable in respect of personal chattels settled as heirlooms within the meaning of the Settled Land Act 1925, the money is to be treated as money arising from a sale of the chattels[57]; if receivable in respect of property held on trust for sale, it must be treated like the proceeds of sale; and in any other case the money must be held upon trusts corresponding as nearly as may be with the trusts affecting the property in respect of which it is payable.[58]

The money may also be applied in rebuilding, reinstating, replacing and repairing the property lost or damaged, but only with the consent of any person whose consent is required to the investment of money subject to the trust.[59] The section does not prejudice the right of any person to require the money to be applied in rebuilding, or the rights of any mortgagee, lessor or lessee, whether under any statute or otherwise.[60]

Section 4. Delegation

The office of trustee is one of personal confidence, and so, in general, cannot be delegated; for trustees who take upon themselves the

---

[53] *Re Earl of Egmont's Trusts* [1908] 1 Ch. 821.
[54] s.20, apparently suggested by *Re Quicke's Trusts* [1908] 1 Ch. 887.
[55] This phrase excludes value payments under the War Damage Act 1943 from the section: *Re Scholfield's W.T.* [1949] Ch. 341.
[56] T.A. 1925, s.20(1); and see s.20(2) for the duties of a person other than the trustees by whom the money is receivable.
[57] See S.L.A. 1925, s.67; see *ante*, p. 261.
[58] T.A. 1925, s.20(3).
[59] *Ibid.* s.20(4).
[60] *Ibid.* s.20(5).

management[61] of the trust property have no right to shift their duty on to other persons. For example a trustee of a trust estate which incudes a controlling block of shares in a private company will be liable if he fails properly to supervise the directors.[62] *Delegatus non potest delegare.* But this rule is subject to important qualifications.[63]

1. Employment of agents

(a) *Before 1926.* Trustees have always been entitled to employ agents (at the cost of the trust funds) to act for them when there was any moral or legal necessity for this,[64] *e.g.* a solicitor to do conveyancing work, or a stockbroker to buy and sell stocks and shares. But in the original selection of the agent and in the subsequent supervision of his acts the trustees were bound to act as reasonable men, and so would be liable if they employed him in work outside his usual business.[65]

(b) *After 1925.* The Trustee Act 1925, s.23, has now extended and modified this rule. Subject to any contrary provision in the trust instrument,[66] "trustees or personal representatives may, instead of acting personally, employ and pay an agent, whether a solicitor, banker, stockbroker, or other person, to transact any business or do any act required to be transacted or done in the execution of the trust, or the administration of the testator's or intestate's estate, including the receipt and payment of money, and shall be entitled to be allowed and paid all charges and expenses so incurred, and shall not be responsible for the default of any such agent if employed in good faith."[67]

(c) *Changes in the law.* This provision seems to have made two changes in the law. First, the trustees need no longer establish that there was any moral or legal necessity for the employment of the agent; for the section contains no such restriction. Secondly, the liability of the trustees for any loss no longer depends on reasonableness but merely on good faith; and many an act that is unreasonable may yet be perfectly honest. Another provision, which exempts a trustee from liability for

---

[61] For delegation of powers, see *post*, p. 567.
[62] *Re Lucking's W.T.* [1968] 1 W.L.R. 866; *Bartlett* v. *Barclays Bank Trust Co. Ltd.* [1980] Ch. 515.
[63] The court may confer a wider power of delegation than the statutory powers following: see *Steel* v. *Wellcome Custodian Trustees Ltd.* [1988] 1 W.L.R. 167 at 174; *ante*, p. 220.
[64] *Ex p. Belchier* (1754) Amb. 218; *Speight* v. *Gaunt* (1883) 9 App.Cas. 1; *Re De Pothonier* [1900] 2 Ch. 529; *Field* v. *Field* [1894] 1 Ch. 425.
[65] *Speight* v. *Gaunt, supra*; *Learoyd* v. *Whiteley* (1887) 12 App.Cas. 727; *Fry* v. *Tapson* (1884) 28 Ch.D. 268; *Re Weall* (1889) 42 Ch.D. 674.
[66] T.A. 1925, s.69(2).
[67] *Ibid.* s.23(1).

any loss "unless the same happens through his own wilful default,"[68] supports this conclusion.[69]

(d) *Extent of power.* The section does not confer any power to delegate the duties of a trustee generally, *e.g.* by a power of attorney[70]; power to employ agents to do specified acts is not power to authorise agents to decide what acts to do. But in relation to real and personal property outside the United Kingdom, the section gives wide powers of appointing an agent or attorney with such authority.[71] The section also provides[72] that, without prejudice to his general power of appointing agents, a trustee may appoint a solicitor to receive money or valuable consideration or property receivable by the trustee, by permitting him to produce a deed containing a receipt; and a trustee may depute a banker or solicitor to receive money payable under a policy of assurance by producing the policy with a receipt signed by the trustee. But where the trustee permits property to remain under the control of the banker or solicitor for longer than is reasonably necessary to enable him to transfer it to the trustee, this provision does not exempt the trustee from any liability that he would have been under if the Act had not been passed.[73]

If a testator directs the executors and trustees of his will to employ X as their solicitor in the administration of the estate, this direction is not binding on them; they have a right to select their own agents.[74]

2. Valuation of securities

(a) *Valuation and advice.* When a trustee lends money on the security of any property on which he can properly make a loan, he may in effect delegate the duty of valuing the proposed security. In such a case, the Trustee Act 1925, s.8,[75] provides that the trustee is not to be chargeable with breach of trust by reason only of the proportion borne by the amount of the loan to the value of the property, provided the court is satisfied—

   (i)   that the trustee in making the loan was acting upon a report as to the value of the property made by a person (whether or not a local man) whom he reasonably believed to be an able practical surveyor or valuer, instructed and employed independently of any owner of the property[76];

---

[68] *Ibid.* s.30(1); see *post*, p. 285.
[69] *Re Vickery* [1931] 1 Ch. 572; and see generally (1948) 92 S.J. 81, 92; G. H. Jones (1959) 22 M.L.R. 381 (a critical consideration). Consider also *Hutton* v. *West Cork Ry.* (1883) 23 Ch.D. 654 at 671.
[70] *Green* v. *Whitehead* [1930] 1 Ch. 38, affirmed on different grounds, 46 T.L.R. 11.
[71] T.A. 1925, s.23(2).
[72] *Ibid.* s.23(3).
[73] *Ibid.* s.23(3), proviso; and see *Robinson* v. *Harkin* [1896] 2 Ch. 415; *Wyman* v. *Paterson* [1900] A.C. 276; *Re Sheppard* [1911] 1 Ch. 50.
[74] *Foster* v. *Elsley* (1881) 19 Ch.D. 518.
[75] Repeating T.A. 1893, s.8.
[76] *Shaw* v. *Cates* [1909] 1 Ch. 389.

(ii) that the amount of the loan does not exceed two third[77] parts of the value of the property as stated in the report; and

(iii) that the loan was made under the advice of the surveyor or valuer expressed in the report.

(b) *The principle.* The principle underlying this provision is that the trustee may safely be taken to have done all that his duty requires in this respect if an independent valuer of repute, sufficiently instructed to make a just valuation, represents the value as sufficient, and expressly[78] advises the acceptance of the security, knowing the consequent liability which he will thereby personally incur if his representation and advice are erroneous.[79] If the trustee has given proper instructions to the valuer, he need not himself make inquiries as to the personality of the mortgagor or the details concerning the property, nor need he inquire whether the valuer has at any time acted for the mortgagor.[80]

(c) *Extent of liability.* If the investment is wholly unauthorised, the section does not apply, and the trustee is liable for the whole deficiency, though on replacing the moneys lost he can take over the security.[81] If, however, the investment is in all respects a proper investment for a smaller advance but it exceeds the amount authorised by the section, then whether or not the trustee acted on the advice of a valuer, he is liable only to make good the excess, with interest.[82] In this case, however, the trustee has no right to take over the security.[83]

3. Temporary delegation

(a) *The power.* There is a wide statutory power of temporary delegation. This formerly applied only to trustees intending to remain outside the United Kingdom for over a month, but since October 1, 1971, this restriction has been removed.[84] The power applies to all trustees,[85] including tenants for life, statutory owners and personal representatives,[86] and to all trusts, whenever created.[87] Notwithstanding any rule of law or equity to the contrary, a trustee may, by power of attorney, delegate for a period not exceeding 12 months the execution or exercise of all or any of the trusts, powers or discretions vested in

---

[77] Formerly the maximum was two-thirds for freehold land and half for houses; generally even half was excessive for buildings used in trade: see *Re Olive* (1886) 34 Ch.D. 70.
[78] But see *Re Solomon, Nore* v. *Meyer* [1912] 1 Ch. 261 at 283.
[79] Consider *Re Somerset* [1894] 1 Ch. 231.
[80] *Re Solomon, Nore* v. *Meyer* [1912] 1 Ch. 261 (appeal compromised: [1913] 1 Ch. 200).
[81] *Re Salmon, Priest* v. *Uppleby* (1889) 42 Ch.D. 351; *Re Lake, Ex p. Howe Trustees* [1903] 1 K.B. 439; *Head* v. *Gould* [1898] 2 Ch. 250.
[82] T.A. 1925, s.9; *Re Walker, Walker* v. *Walker* (1890) 59 L.J.Ch. 386.
[83] *Re Salmon, Priest* v. *Uppleby, supra.*
[84] See Powers of Attorney Act 1971, ss.9, 11(4).
[85] T.A. 1925, s.25, as amended by Powers of Attorney Act 1971, s.9.
[86] T.A. 1925, s.25(8).
[87] Powers of Attorney Act 1971, s.9(4).

him as trustee either alone or jointly with any other person or persons.[88]
Delegation may only be effected pursuant to this provision and not by a
power of attorney in general form, even where a trustee is also a
beneficial owner of the relevant property[89]; nor may the delegation take
the form of an "enduring power of attorney,"[90] *i.e.* one which survives
the mental incapacity of the donor of the power.[91] A trustee may
delegate to a trust corporation, but not to a sole co-trustee of his unless
that co-trustee is a trust corporation.[92]

(b) *Exercise.* The instrument must be attested by at least one
witness.[93] Before, or within seven days after, giving the power of
attorney, the trustee must give written notice of its date of operation, its
duration, the reason for it, and, where only some trusts, powers or
discretions are delegated, details of those delegated, to the other
trustees and to any person having power to appoint a new trustee.[94]
Failure to give notice does not invalidate acts done or instruments
executed by the delegate.[95]

(c) *Effect.* The trustee exercising the power remains liable for the
acts and defaults of the delegate as if they were his own.[96] The delegate
may exercise any of the powers conferred on the trustee by statute or by
the trust instrument, including power to delegate to an attorney the
power to transfer any inscribed stock.[97] He may not, however, himself
delegate this general power of delegation.[98] A delegate who acts after
the power has been revoked will not on that account, if he is unaware of
the revocation, incur any liability to the trustee or any other person.[99]
Similarly, where a power has been revoked and a person unaware of the
revocation deals with the delegate, the transaction will be as valid as if
the power were still in existence.[1]

4. **Powers of management of land.**   Under the Law of Property Act
1925, s.29, trustees for sale of land may, until sale, revocably by writing
delegate their powers of leasing, accepting surrenders of leases and
management to any person of full age (not being merely an annuitant)

---

[88] T.A. 1925, s.25(1).
[89] *Walia* v. *Michael Naughton Ltd.* [1985] 1 W.L.R. 1115.
[90] Enduring Powers of Attorney Act 1985, s.2(8).
[91] *Ibid.* s.1.
[92] T.A. 1925, s.25(2).
[93] *Ibid.* s.25(3).
[94] *Ibid.* s.25(4). And see s.25(8) for notices to be given by personal representatives, tenants for life and
statutory owners.
[95] *Ibid.* s.25(4).
[96] *Ibid.* s.25(5). Contrast the power of employing agents under s.23: see *ante*, p. 266.
[97] *Ibid.* s.25(6). And see *ibid.* s.25(7), authorising banks and companies to ignore the notice of the trust
contained in the power of attorney.
[98] *Ibid.* s.25(6).
[99] Powers of Attorney Act 1971, s.5(1).
[1] *Ibid.* s.5(2).

for the time being beneficially entitled in possession to the net rents and profits during his life, or for any less period; and the trustees will not be liable for the acts or defaults of the person to whom such powers are delegated. The court has power to compel such a delegation to be made.[2]

Section 5. Compromise and Valuation

1. Compromise of claims. The Trustee Act 1925[3] gives wide powers of compromise and valuation to a personal representative, to two or more trustees acting together, to a judicial trustee,[4] or (subject to the restrictions imposed in regard to receipts by a sole trustee not being a trust corporation) to a sole acting trustee where by the instrument (if any) creating the trust or by statute[5] a sole trustee is authorised to execute the trusts and powers imposed in him. These persons may, without being responsible for any act or thing done by them in good faith—

   (i) accept any property before the time at which it is made transferable or payable; or

  (ii) sever and apportion any blended trust funds or property; or

 (iii) pay or allow any debt or claim on any evidence that he or they think sufficient; or

 (iv) accept any composition or security for any debt or for any property claimed; or

  (v) allow any time of payment of any debt; or

 (vi) compromise, compound, abandon, submit to arbitration or otherwise settle any debt or claim.

These powers are to be given a wide construction.[6] In compromising a claim to property in the hands of a beneficiary the trustees may accept a surrender of his interest in satisfaction of the claim, if satisfied that such a course is expedient for the trust as a whole.[7] A composition of this kind does not amount to a variation or rearrangement of the trusts of the settlement.[8]

---

[2] L.P.A. 1925, s.30; see *ante*, p. 236.
[3] s.15, replacing T.A. 1893, s.21.
[4] *Re Ridsdel* [1947] Ch. 597.
[5] *e.g.* a trustee of a deed of arrangement: see *Re Shenton* [1935] Ch. 651.
[6] *Re Earl of Strafford* [1980] Ch. 28 at 47, 51.
[7] *Re Earl of Strafford* [1980] Ch. 28.
[8] *Re Earl of Strafford*, *supra*, at pp. 47, 48, 51. See *ante*, p. 241.

Due attention should be paid to the views of the beneficiaries, but the decision rests with the trustees upon a view of all the circumstances.[9] Yet they must exercise an active discretion, and not just passively fail to take proper steps, *e.g.* to collect debts.[10] These powers enable an executor to compromise a claim by his co-executor against the estate.[11] They also allow a trustee under a deed of arrangement to treat a debt as preferential.[12]

2. Reversionary interests

(a) *Powers.* Where trust property includes any share or interest in property not vested in the trustees, or the proceeds of sale of any such property, or any other thing in action, the trustees, on the same falling into possession or becoming payable or transferable, may—

(i) agree or ascertain the amount or value thereof in such manner as they may think fit; or

(ii) accept any authorised investments in or towards satisfaction thereof; or

(iii) allow any deductions for duties, costs, charges and expenses which they may think proper or reasonable; or

(iv) execute any release,

without being responsible in any such case for any loss occasioned by any act or thing so done by them in good faith.[13]

(b) *Protection.* In such cases the trustees are under no obligation—

(i) to place any *distringas* notice or apply for any stop or other like order[14] upon any securities or other property out of or on which such share or interest or other thing in action is derived, payable or charged; or

(ii) to take any proceedings on account of any act, default or neglect on the part of the persons in whom such securities or other property is or has been vested,

unless required in writing so to do by any beneficiary, and unless satisfactory provision is made for payment of the costs of proceedings.[15]

[9] *Re Ezekiel's S.T.* [1942] Ch. 230; *Re Earl of Strafford* [1980] Ch. 28.
[10] *Re Greenwood, Greenwood* v. *Firth* (1911) 105 L.T. 509.
[11] *Re Houghton* [1904] 1 Ch. 622. But see *Re Boyle* [1947] I.R. 61.
[12] *Re Shenton* [1935] Ch. 651.
[13] T.A. 1925, s.22(1).
[14] For stop orders and *distringas* (or stop) notices, see R.S.C., Ord. 50, rr. 10–15.
[15] T.A. 1925, s.22(2).

3. Valuation of trust property. For the purpose of giving effect to the trust or any of the provisions of the instrument (if any) creating the trust or of any statute, trustees may from time to time (by duly qualified agents) ascertain and fix the value of any trust property in such manner as they think proper, and any valuation so made in good faith will be binding upon all persons interested under the trust.[16]

Section 6. Protection Against Claims

1. Payment into court. In case of difficulty, trustees or personal representatives may obtain a discharge by paying into court any trust money or securities in their hands or under their control[17]; and the receipt or certificate of the proper officer is a sufficient discharge.[18] If they are unanimous, they may make the payment into court merely on affidavit[19]; but if only a majority wish to make payment in, they can do so by obtaining an order of the court.[20] Trustees should make a payment in only when there is no other way of obtaining a discharge, as where they cannot obtain a valid receipt[21]; thus a doubt as to which of several persons are entitled to the trust fund should be resolved by instituting proceedings in which those persons are named as defendants.[22] Life assurance companies have a somewhat similar power of paying policy moneys into court in cases of difficulty.[23]

2. Advertisement for claimants

(a) *Advertisement.* With a view to the conveyance to or distribution among the persons entitled to any real or personal property, the Trustee Act 1925, s.27,[24] authorises the trustees of a settlement or of a disposition on trust for sale, or personal representatives, to advertise for claimants, stating their intention to make the conveyance or distribution, and requiring any person interested to send in particulars of his claim within a stated time, not being less that two months. The advertisement must be inserted in the *London Gazette* and in a newspaper circulating in the district in which the land is situated[25]; and such other like notices,

---

[16] T.A. 1925, s.22(3).
[17] *Ibid.*, ss.63(1), 68(17), replacing T.A. 1893, ss.42, 50, which replaced earlier legislation. T.A. 1925, s.63(1) was slightly amended by the Administration of Justice Act 1965, s.36(4). Sched. 3.
[18] T.A. 1925, s.63(2).
[19] R.S.C., Ord. 92, r. 2; Court Funds Rules 1987, r. 14(1)(ii)(*b*). A personal representative may make a written request for payment in: *ibid.* r. 15(1)(ii)(*b*).
[20] T.A. 1925, s.63(3). See *ibid.*, s.63(4) for ancillary powers.
[21] See, *e.g. Re Parker's Will* (1888) 39 Ch.D. 303.
[22] See *Re Birkett* (1878) 9 Ch.D. 576; *Re Giles* (1886) 55 L.J.Ch. 695.
[23] Life Assurance Companies (Payment into Court) Act 1896.
[24] As slightly amended by L.P.(Am.)A. 1926, Sched. The section takes the place of L.P.Am.A. 1859, s.29, which applied only to personal representatives.
[25] If no land is concerned, the practice is to advertise in a newspaper circulating in the district most likely to be affected, *e.g.* that in which the deceased lived.

including notices elsewhere than in England or Wales,[26] must be given as would in any special case have been directed by the court in an administration action. If the trustees or personal representatives are in doubt as to what notices should be given, they should apply to the court for directions.[27]

(b) *Effect of advertisement.* After the expiration of the time fixed by the notice, the trustees or personal representatives may convey or distribute the property to or among the persons entitled of whose claims (whether formal or not) they have notice, without being liable to other persons.[28] The section offers protection against belated claims not only from creditors but also from next-of-kin or beneficiaries under a will.[29] But it does not prejudice the right of the claimants to follow the property, or any property representing it, into the hands of any person except a purchaser, nor does it free the trustees or personal representatives from any obligation to make searches which an intending purchaser would be advised to make.[30] The section applies notwithstanding anything to the contrary in the will or trust instrument, if any.

3. Future liabilities

(a) *Need for protection.* Where a trust estate or the estate of a deceased person included a lease, or land held subject to a rentcharge, the trustees or personal representatives were formerly often in the difficulty that they could not safely distribute the remainder of the estate to those entitled without first setting aside a fund to meet any future liability that might accrue under the lease or rentcharge. This might result in large sums being withheld from the beneficiaries for a long period, especially as the estate of an original lessee remains liable under the covenants in the lease throughout its term. This difficulty can be avoided either by distributing the estate under an order of the court or by taking advantage of the Trustee Act 1925, s.26,[31] a provision which cannot be excluded by anything to the contrary in the will or trust instrument.[32]

(b) *The protection.* Section 26 of the Trustee Act 1925 is of limited benefit, for it applies only to the liabilities of personal representatives "as such." This refers, for example, to the representative liability of personal representatives, and not to the personal liability as assignees

[26] See *Re Achillopoulos* [1928] Ch. 433; and see *post,* p. 343.
[27] *Re Letherbrow* [1935] W.N. 34, 48; *Re Holden, Isaacson* v. *Holden* [1935] W.N. 52.
[28] T.A. 1925, s.27(2). See *Guardian Trust and Executors Co. of New Zealand Ltd.* v. *Public Trustee of New Zealand* [1942] A.C. 115.
[29] *Re Aldhous* [1955] 1 W.L.R. 459 at 462.
[30] T.A. 1925, s.27(2).
[31] Replacing and extending L.P.Am.A. 1859, ss.27, 28; slightly amended by L.P.(Am.)A. 1926, Sched.
[32] T.A. 1925, s.26(2).

that they incur if, as is usual, they take possession of the property.[33] The personal representative or trustee must—

- (i) satisfy all liabilities under the lease or grant which have accrued and have been claimed; and

- (ii) where necessary, set apart a sufficient sum to answer any future claim that may be made in respect of any fixed and ascertained sum which the lessee or grantee agreed to lay out on the property; and

- iii) convey the property to a purchaser, legatee, devisee, or other person entitled to call for a conveyance thereof. For this purpose, a person who is paid to take an assignment is probably not a "purchaser."[34]

On doing this, the personal representative or trustee may distribute the estate to those entitled without setting aside any further fund, and he will not be personally liable in respect of any subsequent claim under the lease or grant.[35] But this does not prejudice the right of the lessor or grantor to pursue his claim by following the assets into the hands of those who have received them.[36]

4. Authority of court. In certain cases the courts may authorise trustees to do what would otherwise be a breach of trust. This has already been discussed.[37]

Section 7. Maintenance and Advancement

Settlements frequently contained powers authorising trustees to apply the income or capital of the trust funds towards the maintenance or advancement of a beneficiary who was still a minor or whose interest was still contingent. Express powers are still to be found, but they have been largely supplanted by statutory powers.

1. Express powers

(a) *Maintenance.* Provisions for maintenance may take the form of a mere discretionary power for the trustees to apply the income of a fund for the maintenance and education of children, or they may amount to an express trust for such purposes. Moreover, without being contrary to

---

[33] *Re Owers, Public Trustee* v. *Death (No. 2)* [1941] Ch. 389; *Re Bennett, Midland Bank Executor and Trustee Co. Ltd.* v. *Fletcher* [1943] 1 All E.R. 467; and see *post*, pp. 335, 336. In practice, trustees sometimes insure against such risks.
[34] So held in *Re Lawley* [1911] 2 Ch. 530, on the Act of 1859; and this may still apply under the Act of 1925: see Hood & Challis, *Property Acts* (8th ed., 1938), p. 626.
[35] T.A. 1925, s.26(1).
[36] *Ibid.* s.26(2).
[37] *Ante*, p. 238.

public policy, such provisions may prohibit any payments being made while the child is in the father's custody or control or while the father has "anything to do with his education or bringing up."[38]

Under a power to apply income for maintenance, the trustees must honestly exercise their discretion; if they do the court will not interfere.[39] But if the trustees pay over the whole fund to the father without exercising their discretion at all, he may be called upon to refund all that he has received.[40] Moreover, they cannot delegate to others a discretionary power of maintenance which is given to them personally.[41] On the other hand, under a trust in a marriage settlement to apply income for the maintenance and education of the children, the father is entitled to have the income so applied without reference to his ability or inability to maintain and educate them, for this is a matter of contract.[42]

(b) *Advancement.* Powers to apply capital are sometimes limited to the "advancement" of a minor or contingent beneficiary, or they may extend to the "advancement or benefit" of such a beneficiary. "Advancement" has been said to be "a word appropriate to an early period of life,"[43] and thus suggests the establishing of a beneficiary in life.[44] This is too restrictive, for it is better regarded as making some permanent provision for a child or other beneficiary.[45] It extends to advances for the purchase of a house for a general medical practitioner,[46] or for a settlement on marriage,[47] but not for the payment of debts of the husband of the beneficiary.[48] "Benefit" is a word of wider import than "advancement"[49]; it authorises payments for the maintenance[50] of a beneficiary,[51] the discharge of his debts,[52] a loan for setting up the beneficiary's husband in business,[53] the making of settlements on beneficiaries in no immediate need, with a view to saving estate duty[54] or avoiding other risks of depleting the trust funds,[55] and even the making of charitable donations in discharge of moral obligations felt by a wealthy beneficiary.[56] Yet however wide the power is, and even if it authorises out-and-out payments to the person

[38] *Re Borwick's Settlement* [1916] 2 Ch. 304.
[39] *Bryant* v. *Hickley* [1894] 1 Ch. 324.
[40] *Wilson* v. *Turner* (1883) 22 Ch.D. 521.
[41] *Re Greenslade* [1915] 1 Ch. 155, distinguished in *Re Mewburn's Settlement* [1934] Ch. 112.
[42] *Murdy* v. *Earl Howe* (1793) 4 Bro.C.C. 223; and see *Re Peel* [1936] Ch. 161.
[43] *Re Kershaw's Trusts* (1868) L.R. 6 Eq. 322 at 323, *per* Malins V.-C.
[44] Similar questions arise as to the meaning of "portions": see *post,* pp. 522, 523.
[45] *Hardy* v. *Shaw* [1976] Ch. 82 (on the meaning of advancement in A.E.A. 1925, s.47).
[46] *Re Williams' W.T.* [1953] Ch. 138.
[47] *Roper-Curzon* v. *Roper-Curzon* (1871) L.R. 11 Eq. 452.
[48] *Molyneux* v. *Fletcher and Clark* [1898] 1 Q.B. 648. See also *Talbot* v. *Marshfield* (1868) 3 Ch.App. 622.
[49] *Lowther* v. *Bentinck* (1874) L.R. 19 Eq. 166 at 169, 170; and see *post,* pp. 280, 281. Compare *Re Livesey* [1953] 1 W.L.R. 1114 ("advancement or preferment").
[50] *Re Breeds' Will* (1875) 1 Ch.D. 226.
[51] Cf. *Re Peel* [1936] Ch. 161 at 164, 165.
[52] *Lowther* v. *Bentinck* (1874) L.R. 19 Eq. 166.
[53] *Re Kershaw's Trusts* (1868) L.R. 6 Eq. 322.
[54] *Re Ropner's S.T.* [1956] 1 W.L.R. 902.
[55] *Re Wills' W.T.* [1959] Ch. 1; and see *post,* pp. 280, 281.
[56] *Re Clore's S.T.* [1966] 1 W.L.R. 955.

advanced, the trustees must have a good reason for making the advance, and see that its purpose is carried out.[57]

2. Statutory power of maintenance. A statutory power of maintenance was conferred by the Conveyancing Act 1881,[58] and this power, in an amended form, is now contained in the Trustee Act 1925, s.31.[59] The power under the Act of 1881 still applies to instruments coming into operation after 1881 but before 1926, whereas the power under the Act of 1925 applies only to instruments which came into operation after 1925.[60] An appointment made after 1925 under a power of appointment created before 1926 is subject to the Act of 1925.[61]

(a) *The power.* Section 31 of the Act of 1925 provides that where any property is held by trustees (including personal representatives[62]) in trust for any person for any interest whatsoever, whether vested or contingent, during the infancy of the beneficiary (if his interest so long continues), the trustees may, at their sole discretion, pay to his parent or guardian or otherwise apply for or towards his "maintenance, education or benefit" the whole or such part of the income of the property as may in all the circumstances be reasonable. If on attaining full age, namely, 18,[63] or 21 if the interest arises under an instrument made before 1970,[64] the beneficiary still has no vested interest[65] in the income, the trustees "shall thenceforth" pay the whole of the income to him until he either attains a vested interest in it or dies, or until failure of his interest.[66] The section applies to all types of property, including settled land.[67]

(b) *Contrary intention.* These provisions apply only so far as no contrary intention is expressed.[68] This is so both as to the discretionary power and as to the apparently imperative direction to pay the income to any beneficiary of full age.[69] An express direction to accumulate income until the attaining of a certain age, whether the age of majority[70] or a greater age,[71] will usually,[72] but perhaps not

---

[57] *Re Pauling's S.T. (No. 1)* [1964] Ch. 303.
[58] s.43.
[59] See generally B. S. Ker (1953) 17 Conv. (N.S.) 273.
[60] T.A. 1925, s.31(5).
[61] See *Re Dickinson's Settlements* [1939] Ch. 27 (special power). Contrast the statutory power of advancement; *post,* p. 279.
[62] T.A. 1925, s.68(17).
[63] The age of 18 was substituted for 21 by the Family Law Reform Act 1969, s.1(3), 1st Sched. The Act came into force on January 1, 1970: see s.28(3); S.I. 1969 No. 1140.
[64] T.A. 1925, s.31(1)(ii); Family Law Reform Act, 1969, s.1(4), 3rd Sched., para. 5(1), preserving the age of 21 years in such cases.
[65] As distinct from having a vested interest liable to defeasance: *Re McGeorge* [1963] Ch. 544.
[66] T.A. 1925, s.31(1); see *Re Jones' W.T.* [1947] Ch. 48.
[67] See T.A. 1925, s.31(2)(ii); contrast *post,* p. 280.
[68] T.A. 1925, s.69(2), replacing C.A. 1881, s.43(3).
[69] *Re Turner's W.T., District Bank Ltd.* v. *Turner* [1937] Ch. 15.
[70] See *Re Reade-Revell* [1930] 1 Ch. 52.
[71] *Re Turner's W.T., supra.*
[72] *Re Turner's W.T., supra; Re Reade-Revell, supra; Re Stapleton* [1946] 1 All E.R. 323.

necessarily,[73] show a contrary intention sufficient to prevent payments being made under the statutory power. This is so even if the direction is void[74]; and such an intention is also shown by deferring a gift, *e.g.* by giving property to X "after the death of Y."[75]

(c) *Right to income.* Before the power of maintenance can apply there must be income available for the purpose under the section. There must accordingly be "property ... held by trustees in trust" for the minor[76]; and although a vested annuity is for this purpose to be treated as the income of such property,[77] a share of income allocated to a minor under a discretionary trust is not.[78] Further, the power takes effect subject to any prior interests or charges affecting the property,[79] so that even if the minor has a vested interest in capital, there may be no income available for his maintenance, *e.g.* because there is a prior life interest in the capital. Where the minor's interest is contingent, it is also necessary to ascertain that the limitation or trust is of a type which carries the intermediate income of the property.[80] This question is considered later, but in general it may be said that all testamentary gifts carry the intermediate income (unless it is otherwise disposed of), with the exception of deferred residuary gifts and contingent pecuniary legacies; and even these latter carry the intermediate income in some important classes of case.[81]

(d) *Gifts to a class.* Where *personalty* is given to a class of persons contingently on their attaining the age of majority, the fact that one of the class has acquired a vested interest by attaining full age does not prevent the trustees from applying the income derived from the shares of those who are still under full age for their maintenance.[82] Each member of the class is maintainable only out of the portion of income attributable to the time when he is living.[83] But in the case of *realty* it was held before 1926 that unless the gift expressly referred to income as well as *corpus*,[84] the whole interest vested in the first member of the class who acquired a vested interest, so that he took the whole income until another share vested.[85] If, however, the gift of realty is contained

---

[73] *Re Thatcher's Trusts* (1884) 26 Ch.D. 426; and see *Re Leng, Dodsworth* v. *Leng* [1938] Ch. 821.
[74] *Re Ransome* [1957] Ch. 348; *Re Erskine's S.T.* [1971] 1 W.L.R. 162. See the critical comment of J. G. Riddall [1979] Conv. 423.
[75] *Re McGeorge* [1963] Ch. 544.
[76] T.A. 1925, s.31(1).
[77] *Ibid.* s.31(4).
[78] *Re Baron Vestey's Settlement* [1951] Ch. 209.
[79] T.A. 1925, s.31(1).
[80] *Ibid.* s.31(3), adopting the rule as established under C.A. 1881 by *Re George* (1877) 5 Ch.D. 837; *Re Dickson* (1885) 29 Ch.D. 331; *Re Eyre, Johnson* v. *Williams* [1917] 1 Ch. 351; *Re Boulter, Capital & Counties Bank* v. *Boulter* [1918] 2 Ch. 40. See also *Re Raine, Tyerman* v. *Stansfield* [1929] 1 Ch. 716; *Re Reade-Revell* [1930] 1 Ch. 52.
[81] See *post,* pp. 370–375.
[82] *Re Holford* [1894] 3 Ch. 30; *Re King, Public Trustee* v. *Aldridge* [1928] Ch. 330.
[83] *Re Joel's W.T.* [1967] Ch. 14, applying Apportionment Act 1870. For the Act, see *post,* p. 375.
[84] *Re Stevens, Stevens* v. *Stevens* [1915] 1 Ch. 429; *Re Bird, Watson* v. *Nunes* [1927] 1 Ch. 210.
[85] *Re Averill* [1898] 1 Ch. 23.

in the will of a person dying after 1925, this decision appears to be overruled by the statutory provision whereby a contingent specific or residuary devise carries the intermediate income from the death of the testator.[86]

(e) *Extent of trustees' discretion.* All payments are made at the trustees' sole discretion; and they may be made whether or not there is another fund available for the same purposes or there is any other person bound by law to provide for the maintenance or education of the beneficiary.[87] The trustees are, however, limited to making payments which in all the circumstances are reasonable; and they are directed to have regard to the age of the minor and his requirements, and generally to the circumstances of the case and in particular to what other income is available. Moreover, where they have notice that the income of more than one fund is available, as far as practicable only a proportionate part of the income of each fund should be applied.[88]

(f) *Accumulation of surplus income.* So far as the income arising during infancy is not expended by the trustees under their statutory power, it must be accumulated in the way of compound interest, although the accumulations may be applied for maintenance as if they were current income.[89] Where the minor's interest in the income is vested, he is absolutely entitled to the accumulations on attaining full age[90] or marrying under that age, and in that latter case he can give a valid receipt for them despite his minority.[91] He is also absolutely entitled to the accumulations if at full age[92] or marriage he is entitled to the property in fee simple (whether absolute or determinable), or absolutely, or for an entailed interest.[93] But in other cases, *e.g.* if the minor has a contingent life interest, or a vested life interest but he dies unmarried under full age, or an absolute interest in personalty that is liable to defeasance (as by the exercise of a power of appointment), the accumulations are an accretion to the capital of the property or share whence they are derived and are subject to the same trusts and powers.[94] When a minor with a vested interest in income dies unmarried, his title to the accumulated income is gone, so that his interest was in substance merely contingent, rather than being vested subject to defeasance.[95] But such a result will not follow if the settlement discloses an intention that the income as and when it falls

---

[86] L.P.A. 1925, s.175; *post*, p. 372.
[87] T.A. 1925, s.31(1).
[88] T.A. 1925, s.31(1) proviso. These limits are often expressly removed.
[89] *Ibid.* s.31(2).
[90] See *ante*, p. 276.
[91] T.A. 1925, s.31(2).
[92] See *ante*, p. 276.
[93] T.A. 1925, s.31(2).
[94] *Ibid.; Re Joel's W.T.* [1967] Ch. 14; *Re Sharp's S.T.* [1973] Ch. 331. Under the Conveyancing Act 1881, s.43, the accumulations were simply directed to be held for the person who ultimately became entitled: see *Re Bowlby* [1904] 2 Ch. 685; *Re King, Public Trustee v. Aldridge* [1928] Ch. 330.
[95] *Stanley* v. *I.R.C.* [1944] K.B. 255.

due shall be held indefeasibly for the beneficiaries.[96] And in the case of a vested annuity, accumulations made during the minority of the annuitant are in any case to be held in trust for the annuitant or his personal representatives absolutely.[97]

3. Statutory power of advancement. Trustees and personal representatives formerly had no power to use *capital* (as opposed to income) for the benefit of either a minor or an adult, except under the authority of an express provision in the settlement or will or under an order of the court. But by the Trustee Act 1925, s.32, a statutory power of advancement is incorporated in trusts created or constituted after 1925.[98] This includes trusts under a will made before 1926 by a testator who dies after 1925,[99] and trusts declared by an appointment made after 1925 under a general[1] (though not a special[2]) power created before 1926. The power may be excluded by an expressed[3] contrary intention,[4] as where there is a trust for accumulation,[5] or a power to raise sums not exceeding a specified amount for the benefit of the beneficiaries.[6]

(a) *The power.* Under the section any capital money subject to a trust may at any time or times be paid or applied by trustees or personal representatives[7] for "the advancement or benefit" of any person entitled to the capital of the trust property or of any share thereof. Although the section refers to "capital money," assets can be conveyed *in specie* to avoid the circuitous course of advancing money to the beneficiary and then selling the assets to him.[8] Further, capital is "applied" even if the beneficiary is merely given a life interest in the income of the capital fund.[9] The power applies[10] whether the beneficiary is entitled absolutely or contingently on his attaining any specified age or on the occurrence of any other event, including a double contingency, such as attaining the age of 21 years and surviving a life tenant.[11] It also applies where his interest is subject to a gift over on his death under any specified age or on the occurrence of any other event, and whether it is in possession or in remainder or reversion, and even if it is liable to be defeated by the exercise of a power of appointment or revocation, or to be diminished

---

[96] *Re Delamere's S.T., Kenny* v. *Cunningham-Reid* [1984] 1 W.L.R. 813 (revocation of trusts appointed in exercise of power).
[97] T.A. 1925, s.31(4).
[98] *Ibid.* s.32(3).
[99] *Re Darby, Farrell* v. *Fargus* (1943) 59 T.L.R. 418; *Re Taylor's W.T.* (1950) 66 (2) T.L.R. 507.
[1] *Re Bransbury* [1954] 1 W.L.R. 496.
[2] *Re Batty* [1952] Ch. 280, criticised by J. H. C. Morris at (1952) 68 L.Q.R. 319. Contrast the statutory power of maintenance, *ante*, p. 276.
[3] See *Re Rees, Lloyds Bank Ltd.* v. *Rees* [1954] Ch. 202.
[4] T.A. 1925, s.69(2).
[5] *I.R.C.* v. *Bernstein* [1961] Ch. 399; and see *ante*, p. 240.
[6] *Re Evans's Settlement* [1967] 1 W.L.R. 1294.
[7] See T.A. 1925, s.68(17).
[8] *Re Collard's W.T.* [1961] Ch. 293 (see (1961) 77 L.Q.R. 161); *Pilkington* v. *I.R.C.* [1964] A.C. 612 at 639; and see *ante*, p. 40.
[9] *Re Hastings-Bass* [1975] Ch. 25.
[10] T.A. 1925, s.32(1).
[11] *Re Garrett* [1934] Ch. 477.

by the increase of the class to which he belongs.[12] But it applies only where the trust property consists of money or securities, or property held upon trust for sale,[13] and is not capital money for the purposes of the Settled Land Act 1925.[14]

(b) *Limitations on the power.*   There are some important limitations on the power,[15] though these can be and frequently are removed or modified by express provisions in the settlement.[16]

(1) LIMIT OF ONE-HALF.   Not more than half of the beneficiary's vested or presumptive share may be advanced. Once the limit is reached, no further advance can be made even if the retained half increases in value.[17]

(2) BRINGING INTO ACCOUNT.   If the beneficiary is or becomes absolutely and indefeasibly entitled to a share in the trust property, the advance must be brought into account as part of the share. However, apart from this provision, a payment under the section appears to take the money out of the settlement altogether,[18] so that the recipient is under no liability to repay it or bring it into account,[19] *e.g.* if he is entitled only contingently and dies before the contingency occurs.

(3) PRIOR INTERESTS.   No advance can be made to the prejudice of a person entitled to a prior life or other interest, whether vested or contingent, unless he is in existence[20] and of full age and gives a written consent. The section does not require the consent of a person who is merely one of an indefinite number of objects of a discretionary trust,[21] even if the trust has come into operation[22]; but the court has no power to dispense with the consent of a person with whom it is impossible to communicate.[23]

(c) *The trustees' discretion.*   The trustees may pay or apply the money for the "advancement or benefit" of the beneficiary "in such manner as they may, in their absolute discretion, think fit."[24] In construing the term "advancement or benefit" the courts are guided by the decisions on express powers.[25] "Benefit" is "the widest possible word one could

---

[12] T.A. 1925, s.32(1).
[13] *Re Stimpson's Trusts* [1931] 2 Ch. 77.
[14] T.A. 1925, s.32(2). Contrast *ante*, p. 276. Settlements of land usually contain provisions for portions.
[15] *Ibid.* s.32(1), proviso.
[16] See *ibid.* s.69(2).
[17] *Re Marquess of Abergavenny's Estate Act Trusts* [1981] 1 W.L.R. 843. See *post*, p. 363, for computation where power partially exercised.
[18] *Re Pilkington's W.T.* [1959] Ch. 699 at 705; and see S.C. on appeal, *sub nom. Pilkington* v. *I.R.C.* [1964] A.C. 612 at 638. *Cf. Hart* v. *Briscoe* [1979] Ch. 1; *Hoare Trustees* v. *Gardner* [1979] Ch. 10 (charge to capital gains tax).
[19] See *Re Fox, Wodehouse* v. *Fox* [1904] 1 Ch. 480 (express power of advancement).
[20] See *I.R.C.* v. *Bernstein* [1961] Ch. 399 at 411.
[21] *Re Harris' Settlement* (1940) 162 L.T. 358.
[22] *Re Beckett's Settlement* [1940] Ch. 279.
[23] See *Re Forster's Settlement* [1942] Ch. 199 (express power of advancement).
[24] T.A. 1925, s.32(1).
[25] *Pilkington* v. *I.R.C., supra*, at p. 634; see *ante*, p. 275.

have,"[26] and so in a proper exercise of their discretion trustees may not only provide for the education of the beneficiary[27] but also make a payment directly to him[28] or make a settlement on him and his family, either for their immediate or their future benefit.[29] This is so even where the members of the family are not objects of the original trust; for it can be a benefit to a person that his family is provided for.[30]

The rule against perpetuities applies to exercises of the statutory power as if it were a special power of appointment contained in the settlement.[31] Yet if parts of such a sub-settlement are void for perpetuity, the advance will be valid if what remains is within the scope of the power, if the trustees have directed their minds to the right considerations and if the result can be regarded as beneficial to the person intended to be advanced.[32]

4. The court

(a) *Inherent jurisdiction.* The court has power to allow a minor's property to be used for his maintenance. Usually only income will be used for this purpose,[33] but there are exceptions. Thus "in order to provide bread for the infant"[34] the court may break into the capital of a legacy if it is small[35] or there is no other source of maintenance,[36] or if payment has to be made for past maintenance.[37] The court will normally make no allowance to the father for this purpose, since a father is bound to maintain his children.[38] An allowance has been made to the mother, however, on the ground that the court does not recognise her as being under a similar obligation[39]; and even the father will have an allowance made to him if he is not able to give the child an upbringing suitable to the child's expectant fortune.[40] The court may order maintenance despite an express direction to accumulate.[41]

A father may be ordered to refund any payments made out of his child's property for its maintenance if they are made in circumstances in which he would not have been allowed anything for maintenance; on the other hand, where he has applied his own property for the child's maintenance in circumstances in which he would have been allowed

---

[26] *Re Moxon's W.T.* [1958] 1 W.L.R. 165 at 168, *per* Danckwerts J.
[27] Assumed in *Re Garrett* [1934] Ch. 477.
[28] *Re Moxon's W.T.* [1958] 1 W.L.R. 165. See generally D. W. M. Waters (1958) 22 Conv.(N.S.) 413.
[29] *Pilkington* v. *I.R.C.* [1964] A.C. 612.
[30] *Re Hastings-Bass* [1975] Ch. 25 at 39.
[31] *Pilkington* v. *I.R.C., supra.*
[32] *Re Hastings-Bass* [1975] Ch. 25 (advancement upheld); contrast *Re Abrahams' W.T.* [1969] 1 Ch. 463 (whole advancement bad).
[33] See *Re Swanston* (1887) 31 S.J. 427; *Re De Teissier's S.E.* [1893] 1 Ch. 153.
[34] *Harvey* v. *Harvey* (1722) 2 P.Wms. 21 at 23, *per* Jekyll M.R.
[35] *Barlow* v. *Grant* (1684) 1 Vern. 255.
[36] *Harvey* v. *Harvey* (1722) 2 P.Wms. 21. See generally *Simpson on Infants* (4th ed., 1926), pp. 206–208.
[37] *Re Howarth* (1873) 8 Ch.App. 415.
[38] *Fawkner* v. *Watts* (1741) 1 Atk. 408.
[39] *Douglas* v. *Andrews* (1849) 12 Beav. 310.
[40] *Buckworth* v. *Buckworth* (1784) 1 Cox Eq. 80.
[41] See *ante*, p. 240.

something for that purpose, he will receive a sum in respect of such past maintenance.[42]

(b) *Extent of maintenance.* In allowing maintenance for a minor, regard will be had to the state and condition of his family. Thus, where one of several children is entitled to property, the court will make a liberal allowance to him out of his property in order that he may be the better able to maintain his brothers and sisters and so derive indirectly a greater benefit from their society.[43] A liberal allowance will also sometimes be made for minors in order to relieve or assist their parents where the latter are in comparatively distressed circumstances.[44] In all these cases it is the minor's benefit which is considered, although the benefit he derives may sometimes seem somewhat remote.[45]

(c) *Statutory jurisdiction.* The court has a special statutory power to dispose of the property of a minor in order to provide funds for his maintenance.[46] "Where an infant is beneficially entitled to any property the court may, with a view to the application of the capital or income thereof for the maintenance, education, or benefit of the infant, make an order—

(*a*)   appointing a person to convey such property; or

(*b*)   in the case of stock, or a thing in action, vesting in any person the right to transfer or call for a transfer of such stock, or to receive the dividends or income thereof, or to sue for and recover such thing in action, upon such terms as the court may think fit."[47]

Thus even if a minor is entitled only in remainder the court can authorise a mortgage of his entailed interest in order to raise money for his maintenance, just as if he had barred the entail.[48] Similarly, the court may appoint a person to convey a minor's entailed interest on sale with a view to resettling the proceeds, for this is a single transaction and is an "application" of the proceeds, for the minor's benefit.[49] Yet although "maintenance, education, or benefit" are words of the widest import, there must be an intention to apply the money for these purposes before the court can authorise a sale of the minor's interest for cash.[50]

---

[42] See *Re Evans, Welch* v. *Channell* (1884) 26 Ch.D. 58.

[43] *Bradshaw* v. *Bradshaw* (1820) 1 Jac. & W. 647.

[44] *Heysham* v. *Heysham* (1785) 1 Cox Eq. 179.

[45] See *Brown* v. *Smith* (1878) 10 Ch.D. 377; *Re Walker, Walker* v. *Duncombe* [1901] 1 Ch. 879.

[46] See generally O. R. Marshall (1957) 21 Conv.(N.S.) 448.

[47] T.A. 1925, s.53.

[48] *Re Gower's Settlement* [1934] Ch. 365.

[49] *Re Meux* [1958] Ch. 154; *Re Bristol's S.E.* [1965] 1 W.L.R. 469; *Re Lansdowne's W.T.* [1967] Ch. 603. In the last two cases, the order was a prelude to a variation of trusts under the Variation of Trusts Act 1958; for the Act, see *ante*, p. 241.

[50] *Re Heyworth's Contingent Reversionary Interest* [1956] Ch. 364.

CHAPTER 8

BREACH OF TRUST

A trustee is guilty of a breach of trust if he fails to do what his
duty requires, or if he does what he is not entitled to do. Breaches
of trust are almost infinitely various. They range from the
fraudulent conversion of trust funds to purely technical failures
of duty which harm nobody, and transactions (such as some
investments in unauthorised securities) which result in a substantial profit for the trust. Indeed, Lindley M.R. once quoted
Selwyn L.J. as saying that "the main duty of a trustee is to commit
judicious breaches of trust,"[1] though he afterwards observed that the
words "main duty" were a mistake and ought to be "great use."[2] A
trustee who rigidly performs all his duties and never exceeds his powers
will be free from liability; but there are occasions when to commit some
technical breach of trust may be in the best interests of all the
beneficiaries. A trustee will not be held liable for an unauthorised act if
it is one which the court would have authorised,[3] although if there is
time it is obviously prudent for the trustee to seek the court's prior
approval of the act.[4]

Where there is a threatened or actual breach of trust, there are four
possible remedies to be considered, namely:

(i)   an injunction to restrain the breach;

(ii) a personal remedy against the trustees;

(iii) a proprietary remedy against the trust property; and

(iv) (probably) a personal remedy against those who have received
      the trust property.

These will be considered in turn.

Section 1. Injunction

If a beneficiary has reason to suppose that the trustee is about to do an
act not authorised by the trust, he need not wait until a breach has been

---

[1] *Perrins* v. *Bellamy* [1899] 1 Ch. 797 at 798.
[2] *National Trustees Co. of Australasia Ltd.* v. *General Finance Co. of Australasia Ltd.* [1905] A.C. 373
    at 376.
[3] *Lee* v. *Brown* (1798) 4 Ves. 362 at 369; *Brown* v. *Smith* (1878) 10 Ch.D. 377.
[4] See *ante*, pp. 235 *et seq.*

committed, but may obtain an injunction to restrain the trustee.[5] The courts have thus restrained the election by the trustees of a church of an unqualified person as minister,[6] an improvident sale of trust property,[7] and the grant of an unauthorised mortgage.[8] Injunctions have also been granted to secure the due conduct of the trust business, *e.g.* to prevent a minority of trustees of a charity from disturbing the management of the trust by the majority.[9]

Section 2. Personal Remedy against Trustees

1. Account.   "The obligation of a defaulting trustee is essentially that of effecting restitution to the trust estate."[10] Thus the liability is to account, not to pay damages.[11]

(a) *Active breaches.*   If the beneficiary has alleged and proved one or more active breaches of trust, an account of the loss occasioned by them will be ordered. The court will not direct a roving inquiry to see whether there are any other breaches.[12]

(b) *Omissions.*   If the complaint is that the trustee has omitted to do something which a prudent trustee ought to have done,[13] an account on the footing of wilful default will be ordered, that is an account of what he might have received but for his wilful default. Formerly the action had to be started by writ,[14] but while that is still possible, the allegation of wilful default may be made in an action commenced by originating summons.[15] In this context wilful default is simply a failure to carry out the duty of a trustee and does not necessarily involve conscious wrongdoing.[16] Yet a mere failure to act is not wilful default; there must be a breach of duty.[17] At least one instance of wilful default must be alleged and proved or admitted.[18] The court may limit the account to that instance,[19] or, if the conduct of the trustees is such as to give rise to the inference that other defaults have occurred,[20] the account may be

---

[5] *Balls* v. *Strutt* (1841) 1 Hare 146; and see *post*, p. 676.

[6] *Milligan* v. *Mitchell* (1833) 1 My. & K. 446.

[7] *Dance* v. *Goldingham* (1873) 8 Ch.App. 902; *Wheelwright* v. *Walker (No. 2)* (1883) 31 W.R. 912.

[8] *Rigall* v. *Foster* (1853) 18 Jur. 39.

[9] *Perry* v. *Shipway* (1859) 4 De G. & J. 353. For the power of a majority to act, see *ante*, p. 169.

[10] *Bartlett* v. *Barclays Bank Trust Co. Ltd.* [1980] Ch. 515 at 543, *per* Brightman J.; and see *post*, p. 287.

[11] See *Re Lake, ex p. Dyer* [1901] 1 K.B. 710 at 715; *Metall und Rohstoff A.G.* v. *Donaldson Lufkin & Jenrette Inc.* [1990] Q.B. 391 at 473, 474.

[12] *Re Wrightson* [1908] 1 Ch. 789.

[13] For the standard of liability, see *ante*, p. 213.

[14] *Dowse* v. *Gorton* [1891] A.C. 190 at 202.

[15] R.S.C., Ord. 5, r. 4; Ord. 85, r. 4.

[16] *Bartlett* v. *Barclays Bank Trust Co. Ltd., supra*, at p. 543. For other examples, see *post*, pp. 356, (personal representatives), 409 (mortgages). Contrast "wilful default" in exemption clauses, *post*, p. 286. See J. E. Stannard [1979] Conv. 345 for the various meanings of wilful default.

[17] *Re Stevens, Cooke* v. *Stevens* [1898] 1 Ch. 162.

[18] *Sleight* v. *Lawson* (1857) 3 K. & J. 292; *Re Youngs* (1885) 30 Ch.D. 421 at 431, 432.

[19] *Re Tebbs* [1976] 1 W.L.R. 924.

[20] See *Re Tebbs, supra*, at p. 930. But see the explanation in *Re Wrightson, supra*, at pp. 799, 800.

ordered in regard to the whole estate.[21] The account may be ordered either at the hearing or any time afterwards.[22]

2. Personal liability. The liability of a trustee has always been essentially a liability for his own acts and defaults and not for those of others; and this rule is now statutory. "A trustee shall be chargeable only for money and securities actually received by him notwithstanding his signing any receipt for the sake of conformity, and shall be answerable and accountable only for his own acts, receipts, neglects, or defaults, and not for those of any other trustee, nor for any banker, broker, or other person with whom any trust money or securities may be deposited, nor for the insufficiency or deficiency of any securities, nor for any other loss, unless the same happens through his own wilful default."[23] This provision must now be examined.

(a) *Liability personal and not vicarious.* The rule has always been that although a trustee is personally liable for any breaches of trust that he has committed, he is not liable for breaches committed by fellow trustees unless he himself is at fault. If A and B are trustees, and A makes away with trust funds, B is not liable for A's acts merely because they are co-trustees; one trustee is not vicariously liable for another. But B may be liable for his own default, *e.g.* in improperly allowing A to receive the funds or have sole control over them; and similarly if a trustee improperly allows trust property to remain in the control of an agent.[24] However, the burden of proof lies not on the trustee but on him who alleges that the loss was attributable to the trustee's default.[25]

The old case of *Townley* v. *Sherborne*[26] illustrates the rule. A trustee who had joined with his co-trustees in signing receipts was liable, though he had received nothing, because the liability of the non-receiving trustee arose, not from his mere signing of the receipts, but from his subsequently leaving in the hands of his co-trustees the money that had been received, which was an "evil-dealing." A trustee may similarly be liable if he conceals a breach which he discovers that his fellow trustees have committed,[27] or if he stands by, knowing that his fellow trustees are committing[28] or even meditating[29] a breach of trust, or if he leaves trust matters in their hands without inquiry[30]; for in so doing he is neglecting his duty to watch over his fellow trustees.[31]

---

[21] *Re Tebbs, supra,* at p. 928.

[22] *Re Symons* (1882) 21 Ch.D. 757; *Smith* v. *Armitage* (1883) 24 Ch.D. 727.

[23] T.A. 1925, s.30(1), replacing part of T.A. 1893, s.24, which replaced L.P.Am.A. 1859, s.31. The section does not apply to the liquidator of a company: *Re Windsor Steam Coal Co. (1901) Ltd.* [1928] Ch. 609; affirmed on another ground [1929] 1 Ch. 151.

[24] See *ante*, pp. 214, 215.

[25] *Re Brier* (1884) 26 Ch.D. 238.

[26] (1634) Bridg.J. 35 at 37, 38; **2 W. & T.L.C. 577**; and see *Brice* v. *Stokes* (1805) 11 Ves. 319; **2 W. & T.L.C. 581.**

[27] *Boardman* v. *Mosman* (1779) 1 Bro.C.C. 68.

[28] *Booth* v. *Booth* (1838) 1 Beav. 125.

[29] *Wilkins* v. *Hogg,* (1861) 5 L.T. 467 at 470.

[30] *Lord Shipbrook* v. *Lord Hinchinbrook* (1810) 16 Ves. 477; *Wynne* v. *Tempest* (1897) 13 T.L.R. 360; contrast *Shepherd* v. *Harris* [1905] 2 Ch. 310.

[31] *Styles* v. *Guy* (1849) 1 Mac. & G. 422 at 433 (executors).

(b) *Signature for conformity.* The statute expressly exonerates a trustee who signs for conformity only, *i.e.* because a receipt must be signed by all the trustees to operate as a discharge; he is thus not liable if in fact he did not receive the money. But even so, the fact of his having joined in the receipt gives him notice that trust money has been received, so that he will not be justified thereafter in allowing the money to remain in the hands of the receiving co-trustee for a period longer than the circumstances of the case may reasonably require.

(c) *Wilful default.* The statutory standard of liability in respect of the acts of another[32] is now one of "wilful default." "An act, or an omission to do an act, is wilful when the person of whom we are speaking knows what he is doing and intends to do what he is doing. But if that act or omission amounts to a breach of his duty," he is not guilty of wilful default "unless he knows that he is committing, and intends to commit, a breach of his duty, or is recklessly careless in the sense of not caring whether his act or omission is or is not a breach of his duty."[33] Thus a trustee was not liable for the fraudulent misappropriation of some proceeds of sale of trust property by her co-trustee, a solicitor, whom she knew to be a dilatory and incompetent muddler but did not know to be dishonest.[34]

Although the words "nor for any other loss, unless the same happens through his own wilful default" are very wide, they must be read in their context. They therefore do not apply generally to all breaches of trust, but only where it is sought to make the trustee liable for losses of the type contemplated by the statute, *e.g.* those caused by the wrongful acts or defaults of another trustee.[35]

(d) *Exemption clauses.* With increasing frequency, trust instruments contain clauses which either negative the duties to which the trustee would otherwise be subject,[36] or which remove or qualify his liability for breaches of trust.[37] Such clauses are construed strictly,[38] and their efficacy is not beyond doubt in so far as they exempt for wilful default,[39] and some may infringe the Unfair Contract Terms Act 1977.[40]

(e) *Breaches by former trustees.* A new trustee is not liable in respect of breaches of trust committed by his predecessors; unless he has reason to believe otherwise, he is entitled to assume that they have performed their duties and got in all the trust property.[41] If, however, he discovers

---

[32] See *Re Lucking's W.T.* [1968] 1 W.L.R. 866 at 874.
[33] *Re City Equitable Fire Insurance Co. Ltd.* [1925] Ch. 407 at 434, *per* Romer J., approved by the majority of the Court of Appeal at pp. 525, 528; and see *Re Vickery* [1931] 1 Ch. 572.
[34] *Re Munton* [1927] 1 Ch. 262; and see *Re Vickery, supra.*
[35] *Re Vickery, supra,* at p. 582.
[36] *Wilkins* v. *Hogg* (1861) 5 L.T. 467; *Bartlett* v. *Barclays Bank Trust Co. Ltd.* [1980] Ch. 515.
[37] *Bartlett* v. *Barclays Bank Trust Co. Ltd, supra,* at pp. 536, 537, points the distinction.
[38] As in *Bartlett* v. *Barclays Bank Trust Co. Ltd., supra,* at pp. 536, 537.
[39] See P. Matthews [1989] Conv. 42.
[40] See W. Goodhart [1980] Conv. 333.
[41] *Re Strahan* (1856) 8 De G.M. & G. 291.

that breaches of trust have been committed, he must obtain satisfaction for them from the old trustees, just in the same way as an original trustee must get in any part of the trust estate which is outstanding[42]; and the only excuse for not doing so is that it would be useless to take proceedings against the old trustees.[43]

(f) *Breaches by subsequent trustees.* A trustee who has retired is prima facie not liable for breaches of trust committed by his successors. But he may be liable if he retired in order to enable the breach to be committed; for in so doing he may not only make the new trustees his agents for the purpose, but also be guilty of a breach of his duty to protect the trust property.[44] However, he is not liable merely because by retiring he facilitated the commission of some breach, or because he knew that some breach was likely: it must be shown that he retired in contemplation of the particular breach committed.[45] Even an analogous breach is not enough.[46]

(g) *Executors.* In general, an executor is answerable for his own acts only, and not for the acts of his co-executors; for each executor has a full and absolute control over the pure personalty of the testator and is competent to give a valid discharge therefor by his own separate act, independently of the others. If, therefore, an executor joins with his co-executor in signing a receipt, this is stronger evidence of his having actually received the money than in the case of trustees; and even if he can show that he did not in fact receive it, he will be liable if he allowed the money unnecessarily to get into the hands of his co-executor, or remain there.[47]

3. Measure of liability

(a) *Capital liability.* The measure of the trustee's liability for breach of trust is the loss caused thereby to the trust estate.[48] Thus if he makes an unauthorised investment he is liable for the loss incurred on realising it.[49] If he wrongfully retains an unauthorised investment, he is liable for the difference between the price for which it is sold and the price which would have been obtained on a sale at the correct time.[50] If he advances

---

[42] See *Re Forest of Dean Coal Mining Co.* (1878) 10 Ch.D. 450 at 451, 452.
[43] *Hobday* v. *Peters* (1860) 28 Beav. 603.
[44] *Head* v. *Gould* [1898] 2 Ch. 250 at 268. This rule probably applies to directors of companies: *Curtis's Furnishing Stores Ltd.* v. *Freedman* [1966] 1 W.L.R. 1219 at 1224.
[45] *Webster* v. *Le Hunt* (1861) 4 L.T. 723; *Head* v. *Gould* [1898] 2 Ch. 250; and see *ante*, p. 250, n. 73.
[46] *Clark* v. *Hoskins* (1868) 19 L.T. 331.
[47] *Clough* v. *Bond* (1838) 3 My. & Cr. 490 at 496; *Joy* v. *Campbell* (1804) 1 Sch. & Lef. 328 at 341; affirmed 2 *ibid.* 740; *Re Gasquoine* [1894] 1 Ch. 470. Probably the same rule applies to administrators; see *post*, p. 318.
[48] *Knott* v. *Cottee* (1852) 16 Beav. 77.
[49] *Ibid.*
[50] *Fry* v. *Fry* (1859) 27 Beav. 144. And see *Robinson* v. *Robinson* (1851) 1 De G.M. & G. 247.

too much money on an authorised security, he is liable for the excessive advance.[51] If he improperly realises a proper investment, he must replace it or pay the difference between the price obtained and the cost of purchasing the investment again[52]; if the investment was in fact resold by those to whom it was improperly sold, the resale price is the measure of the trustee's liability, because this would in fact have been the cost of replacement.[53] Where the court has to assess the cost of replacing the investment the appropriate date for assessing the compensation is probably that of the judgment.[54] The trustee, unlike contract breakers and tortfeasors, is not entitled to any allowance for the tax which the beneficiaries would have suffered if they had received the full amount of capital and income to which they were entitled; his obligation is to effect restitution of assets rather than pay damages.[55]

These examples assume a loss; if in fact a profit accrues from the breach of trust, the beneficiaries may claim it[56]; and a profit made in one unauthorised transaction cannot be set off against a loss incurred in another unauthorised transaction.[57] Yet profits and losses arising from the same transaction[58] or stemming from the same wrongful course of conduct[59] can be set off against each other and a balance struck.

(b) *Interest.* If a trustee makes an unauthorised investment whereby the trust estate is wholly or partly lost, or if he has paid over the estate to the wrong persons, he must replace the money with interest; and if he is guilty of undue delay in investing the trust funds he will be answerable to the *cestui que trust* for interest during the period of his laches.[60] The rate of interest is in the discretion of the court. For decades the rate was 4 per cent.[61]; but more than 4 per cent. was charged in the following cases.

(i) Where the trustee had actually received more than 4 per cent. Here he is accountable for the interest actually received.[62]

(ii) Where he ought to have received more, as where he has improperly called in a mortgage carrying interest at a higher rate. In this case he is charged with the interest he ought to have received.

---

[51] T.A. 1925, s.9; *ante,* p. 221.
[52] *Phillipson* v. *Gatty* (1848) 7 Hare 516, affirmed (1850) 2 H. & Tw. 459; applied in *Re Massingberd's Settlement* (1890) 63 L.T. 296.
[53] *Re Bell's Indenture* [1980] 1 W.L.R. 1217.
[54] *Re Bell's Indenture, supra,* at p. 1233, doubting *Re Massingberd's Settlement, supra,* taking the date of writ.
[55] *Re Bell's Indenture* [1980] 1 W.L.R. 1217; *Bartlett* v. *Barclays Bank Trust Co. Ltd.* [1980] Ch. 515, distinguishing *British Transport Commission* v. *Gourley* [1956] A.C. 185.
[56] *Docker* v. *Somes* (1834) 2 My. & K. 655.
[57] *Dimes* v. *Scott* (1827) 4 Russ. 195; *Wiles* v. *Gresham* (1854) 2 Drew. 258; affirmed 5 De G.M. & G. 770.
[58] *Fletcher* v. *Green* (1864) 33 Beav. 426.
[59] *Bartlett* v. *Barclays Bank Trust Co. Ltd.* [1980] Ch. 515.
[60] *Stafford* v. *Fiddon* (1857) 23 Beav. 386; *Re Jones, Jones* v. *Searle* (1883) 49 L.T. 91; and see *Re Waterman's W.T.* [1952] 2 All E.R. 1054.
[61] *Re Davy* [1908] 1 Ch. 61.
[62] *Re Emmet's Estate* (1881) 17 Ch.D. 142.

(iii)   Where he must be presumed to have received more, as where he has traded with the money. Here the *cestui que trust* could claim either 5 per cent. interest or else, at his option, the profits actually made by the trustee[63]; but the *cestui que trust* has no right to claim such profits from a trader to whom the money has been improperly lent, even though the borrower knew that the money lent was trust money.[64] Normally compound interest is awarded[65] unless the trading has been for the benefit or partly for the benefit of the *cestui que trust*,[66] or the money, while employed in a business or profession, has not been used in the normal course of trading[67]; in such cases simple interest only is awarded.

(iv)   Where the trustee is guilty of fraud or serious misconduct. In this case the court might charge him with 5 per cent. compound interest with yearly[68] or even half-yearly rests,[69] though half-yearly rests are rarely directed.[70]

Recently, with huge and constantly changing interest rates, the court has recognised that it would be unrealistic to abide by these modest rates. Hence, awards of simple interest have been fixed at the rate allowed from time the time on money in court on special (formerly short term investment) account[71]; and awards of compound interest with yearly rests at 1 per cent. above the minimum lending rate.[72]

(c) *Costs.*   A trustee against whom an action for breach of trust succeeds will be ordered to pay costs on the standard (formerly party and party) basis.[73] Costs on the higher indemnity (formerly common fund) basis will not be awarded save in exceptional circumstances.[74] Interest on costs runs from the date of judgment even though it is not until taxation that the trustee knows what he has to pay.[75]

4. Impounding trustee's beneficial interest.   If a trustee who has been guilty of a breach of trust has any beneficial interest under the trust instrument, he will not be allowed to receive any part of the trust fund in which he is equitably interested until he has made good the breach of

[63] *Vyse* v. *Foster* (1872) 8 Ch.App. 309 at 329 (affirmed L.R. 7 H.L. 318); *Re Davis, Davis* v. *Davis* [1902] 2 Ch. 314; *Gordon* v. *Gonda* [1955] 1 W.L.R. 885.
[64] *Stroud* v. *Gwyer* (1860) 28 Beav. 130.
[65] *Jones* v. *Foxall* (1852) 15 Beav. 388; *Williams* v. *Powell* (1852) 15 Beav. 461; *Wallersteiner* v. *Moir (No. 2)* [1975] Q.B. 373.
[66] *O'Sullivan* v. *Management Agency and Music Ltd.* [1985] Q.B. 428.
[67] *Burdick* v. *Garrick* (1870) 5 Ch.App. 233.
[68] See *Re Barclay* [1899] 1 Ch. 674.
[69] *Re Emmet's Estate* (1881) 17 Ch.D. 142.
[70] See *Burdick* v. *Garrick* (1870) 5 Ch.App. 233.
[71] *Bartlett* v. *Barclays Bank Trust Co. Ltd.* [1980] Ch. 515. See Court Funds Rules 1987, r. 26, for special account. The rate of interest is prescribed from time to time by a direction made by the Lord Chancellor with the concurrence of the Treasury: *ibid.* r. 27(1).
[72] *Wallersteiner* v. *Moir (No. 2)* [1975] Q.B. 373.
[73] See *ante*, p. 258, for costs of other litigation by or against trustees.
[74] *Bartlett* v. *Barclays Bank Trust Co. Ltd.* [1980] Ch. 515; *Bowen-Jones* v. *Bowen-Jones* [1986] 3 All E.R. 163.
[75] *Hunt* v. *R. M. Douglas (Roofing) Ltd.* [1990] A.C. 398, overruling *K.* v. *K.* [1977] Fam. 39 applied in *Bartlett* v. *Barclays Bank Trust Co. Ltd., supra.*

trust.[76] The principle is that to the extent to which he is in default[77] he is regarded as having already received his share.[78] The rule applies not only to beneficial interests given to him directly by the trust instrument, but also to interests acquired derivatively, *e.g.* by purchase from another beneficiary or as his next-of-kin.[79] The beneficial interest which he claims under the instrument imposing the trust is treated as being subject to an implied condition of the proper performance of his duties as trustee.[80] His assignee is accordingly in no better position than he would be, even where the default was committed by the trustee after assigning his beneficial interest.[81] But there can be no impounding if the assignor does not become trustee until after the assignment[82]; and if the trustee holds two distinct funds on distinct trusts, and has a beneficial interest in the first but not in the second, the court has no power to impound his beneficial interest in the first to make good his default in the second.[83]

5. Imprisonment. In addition to ordinary methods of execution, a trustee may be imprisoned for not more than a year if he fails to pay any sum in his possession or under his control as ordered by a court of equity.[84] This rule applies to others in a fiduciary capacity, *e.g.* executors[85] and auctioneers.[86]

6. Defences. There are five ways in which a trustee who has caused a loss to the trust estate by committing a breach of trust may escape liability.

(a) *Relief by court*

(1) THE JURISDICTION. By the Trustee Act 1925, s.61,[87] the court may relieve a trustee either wholly or partly from personal liability for a

---

[76] *Re Dacre* [1916] 1 Ch. 344. Contrast impounding orders under T.A. 1925, s.62; *post*, p. 295.
[77] For adjustments to be made in respect of costs, see *Selangor United Rubber Estates Ltd.* v. *Cradock (No. 4)* [1969] 1 W.L.R. 1773.
[78] *Re Dacre, supra.* The principle is also applied as between shareholder directors and companies in liquidation: see *Selangor United Rubber Estates Ltd.* v. *Cradock (No. 4), supra,* discussing *Re V.G.M. Holdings Ltd.* [1942] Ch. 235.
[79] *Jacubs* v. *Rylance* (1874) L.R. 17 Eq. 341; *Doering* v. *Doering* (1889) 42 Ch.D. 203; *Re Dacre, supra.*
[80] *Morris* v. *Livie* (1842) 1 Y. & C.C.C. 380; *Re Pain* [1919] 1 Ch. 38 at 47.
[81] *Doering* v. *Doering, supra.*
[82] *Irby* v. *Irby (No. 3)* (1858) 25 Beav. 632; *Re Pain, supra,* at p. 47.
[83] *Re Towndrow* [1911] 1 Ch. 662.
[84] Debtors Act 1869, s.4; *Re Lord Berwick* (1900) 81 L.T. 797.
[85] *Re Bourne* [1906] 1 Ch. 697.
[86] *Crowther* v. *Elgood* (1887) 34 Ch.D. 691.
[87] Replacing Judicial Trustees Act 1896, s.3. See generally L. A. Sheridan (1955) 19 Conv.(N.S.) 420. For the events leading to the enactment of the Judicial Trustees Act 1896, s.3, see D. R. Paling (1973) 37 Conv.(N.S.) 48 at 53, n. 22.

breach of trust if he "acted honestly and reasonably, and ought fairly[88] to be excused for the breach of trust and for omitting to obtain the directions of the court in the matter in which he committed such breach." The Companies Act 1985[89] gives the court a similar power to relieve a director, officer, or auditor from liability for negligence or breach of trust.[90] The power to grant relief extends to executors as well as trustees.[91] It even enables the court to relieve a trustee where he has transferred the trust property to the wrong person,[92] but not where, though transferring the property to the right person, he has merely failed to protect himself against his personal liability to pay estate duty on it, for to do this is imprudent but no breach of trust.[93]

(2) GRANT OF RELIEF.   The burden lies on the trustee to establish that he acted honestly and reasonably[94]; he must at least show that he was as prudent as he would have been in relation to his own affairs.[95] The statutory procedure for obtaining a proper valuation and report before lending on mortgage[96] provides a standard by which such loans may be judged.[97] But a failure to obtain such a valuation and report does not preclude the grant of relief[98]; and an omission to seek the directions of the court may be excused by the smallness of the sum involved.[99] In general, however, no rules can be laid down as to the circumstances in which the court will or will not grant relief; each case depends on its own circumstances.[1]

(3) PAID TRUSTEES.   "A paid trustee is expected to exercise a higher standard of diligence and knowledge than an unpaid trustee."[2] Thus the court is less ready to grant relief to a trustee who is paid for his services than to one who is not.[3] The court is very slow to relieve a bank which has put itself into a position where its interest as a banker conflicts with its duty as a paid trustee.[4]

---

[88] See *Marsden* v. *Regan* [1954] 1 W.L.R. 423 at 434, 435; *Bartlett* v. *Barclays Bank Trust Co. Ltd.* [1980] Ch. 515 at 537, 538.

[89] s.727, replacing Companies Act 1949, s.448. The section was unsuccessfully invoked in *Guinness plc* v. *Saunders* [1990] 2 W.L.R. 324 at 337, 343.

[90] And see Local Government Finance Act 1982, s.19(3), and Reserve and Auxiliary Forces (Protection of Civil Interests) Act 1951, s.13(3), for a similar formula.

[91] T.A. 1925, s.68(17); and see *Re Kay* [1897] 2 Ch. 518.

[92] *Re Allsop* [1914] 1 Ch. 1; *Holland* v. *German Property Administrator* [1937] 2 All E.R. 807; *Re Wightwick's W.T.* [1950] Ch. 260.

[93] *Re Rosenthal* [1972] 1 W.L.R. 1273.

[94] *Re Stuart* [1897] 2 Ch. 583.

[95] See *Re Turner, Barker* v. *Ivimey* [1897] 1 Ch. 536.

[96] See *ante*, p. 267.

[97] *Re Stuart, supra.*

[98] *Palmer* v. *Emerson* [1911] 1 Ch. 758.

[99] *Re Grindey* [1898] 2 Ch. 593; contrast *Re Gee* [1948] Ch. 284 at 297; *Partridge* v. *Equity Trustees Executors and Agency Co. Ltd.* (1947) 75 C.L.R. 149 at 165.

[1] *Re Kay* [1897] 2 Ch. 518 at 524. For examples, see the cases cited above, and *Perrins* v. *Bellamy* [1899] 1 Ch. 797; *Re Mackay, Griessemann* v. *Carr* [1911] 1 Ch. 300. For the effect of a claim for relief on the right to sever defences, see *Re Spurling's W.T.* [1966] 1 W.L.R 920 at 928.

[2] *Re Waterman's W.T., Lloyds Bank Ltd.* v. *Sutton* [1952] 2 All E.R. 1054 at 1055, *per* Harman J.

[3] See *National Trustees Co. of Australasia Ltd.* v. *General Finance Co. of Australasia Ltd.* [1905] A.C. 373; *Re Windsor Steam Coal Co. (1901) Ltd.* [1929] 1 Ch. 151; *Bartlett* v. *Barclays Bank Trust Co. Ltd.* [1980] Ch. 515; *cf. Jobson* v. *Palmer* [1893] 1 Ch. 71.

[4] *Re Pauling's S.T. (No.1)* [1964] Ch. 303.

(b) *Lapse of time*

(1) THE PERIOD. Formerly, a claim against an express trustee for breach of trust could not be barred by mere lapse of time.[5] "Express trustee" was generously construed, and included many[6] but not all[7] constructive trustees.[8] The present law is laid down by the Limitation Act 1980.[9] The general rule is that except when the Act prescribes some other period, an action by a beneficiary to recover trust property or in respect of any breach of trust may not be brought after six years from the date upon which the right of action accrued.[10] No period of limitation applies to an action by the Attorney-General[11] to enforce charitable trusts; such an action does not involve allegations of breach of trust nor is there any beneficiary in whom the cause of action is vested.[12]

(2) PERSONS PROTECTED. The expression "trustee" here includes a personal representative,[13] and an implied or constructive trustee as well as an express trustee; and it is immaterial whether the trustee has a beneficial interest in the property.[14] The expression also includes a director of a company,[15] and a mortgagee with respect to any balance of the proceeds of sale of the mortgaged property,[16] but not a trustee in bankruptcy,[17] nor, apparently, the liquidator of a company in a voluntary liquidation.[18]

(3) EXCEPTIONS. These rules are subject to the important qualification that no period of limitation applies to an action by a beneficiary:

(a) "in respect of any fraud or fraudulent breach of trust to which the trustee was a party or privy,"[19] or

(b) "to recover from the trustee trust property" (whether capital or income[20]) "or the proceeds thereof in the possession of the trustee,[21] or previously received by the trustee and converted to his use."

---

[5] J.A. 1873, s.25(2), recognising and declaring the rule.
[6] *Soar* v. *Ashwell* [1893] 2 Q.B. 390.
[7] *Knox* v. *Gye* (1872) L.R. 5 H.L. 656; and see *Toft* v. *Stephenson* (1848) 7 Hare 1 (on appeal, 1 De G.M. & G. 28).
[8] See *Re Eyre-Williams* [1923] 2 Ch. 533.
[9] s.21, replacing Limitation Act 1939, s.19, which replaced Trustee Act 1888, s.8, on which see *How* v. *Earl Winterton* [1896] 2 Ch. 626 at 639.
[10] Limitation Act 1980, s.21(3); as to settled land and land held on trust for sale, see s.18.
[11] For this function of the Attorney-General, see *ante*, p. 169.
[12] *Att.-Gen.* v. *Cocke* [1988] Ch. 414.
[13] See *ante*, p. 98.
[14] Limitation Act 1980, s.38(1), T.A. 1925, s.68(17).
[15] *Re Lands Allotment Co.* [1894] 1 Ch. 616. *Cf. Tintin Exploration Syndicate Ltd.* v. *Sandys* (1947) 177 L.T. 412.
[16] *Thorne* v. *Heard* [1895] A.C. 495.
[17] *Re Cornish* [1896] 1 Q.B. 99.
[18] *Re Windsor Steam Coal Co. (1901) Ltd.* [1928] Ch. 609, affirmed on a different ground [1929] 1 Ch. 151.
[19] See *Thorne* v. *Heard, supra.*
[20] *Re Howlett* [1949] Ch. 767; and see A. K. R. Kiralfy (1949) 13 Conv.(N.S.) 276.
[21] See *Thorne* v. *Heard, supra*; *Re Page* [1893] 1 Ch. 304.

In these excepted cases, the trustee, and it seems recipients from the trustee other than bona fide purchasers,[22] remain liable indefinitely.[23] No delay will bar the claim unless it is doubtful whether any trust exists and the delay may have led to a loss of evidence of the alleged trust,[24] or for some other reason the defendant can invoke the doctrine of laches.[25] But trust property is not "converted" to the use of a trustee merely because it is properly[26] paid to a trustee who is entitled to it *qua* beneficiary,[27] nor because it is properly lent on mortgage to enable the mortgagor to repay a debt owed to a firm in which a trustee is a partner.[28] In such cases, time runs in the usual way.

(4) RELIEF. Where a trustee who is also a beneficiary receives or retains trust property as his share in a distribution, his liability in an action to recover trust property after the period of limitation is limited to the excess over his proper share.[29] Thus if the property is divided between three including the trustee, and a further beneficiary claims so that the property is divisible in quarters, the trustee is liable only for the difference between one-third and one-quarter, and not for a whole quarter. This relief is only available if the trustee acted honestly and reasonably in making the distribution.[30]

(5) THE RUNNING OF TIME. In general, time begins to run under the Act in favour of a trustee from the time when the breach of trust was committed, whether the beneficiary knew of it or not.[31] But where the beneficiary is under disability (that is, while a minor or of unsound mind[32]) time runs from the cessation of the disability.[33] Where the beneficiary's interest is reversionary, time begins to run only when his interest falls into possession[34]; but sums do not fall into possession merely because, under a power of advancement, they are invalidly advanced out of a future interest.[35] Time is also postponed if the right of action is concealed by fraud,[36] but fraud in this context means

---

[22] *G.L. Baker Ltd.* v. *Medway Building & Supplies Ltd.* [1958] 1 W.L.R. 1216 (reversed on other grounds: *ibid.*); and see *post*, pp. 302, 303.
[23] Limitation Act 1980, s.21(1). See, *e.g. Mills* v. *Drewitt* (1855) 20 Beav. 632 (33 years); *Re Ashwell's Will* (1859) Johns. 112 (37 years). Compare *McDonnel* v. *White* (1865) 11 H.L.C. 570.
[24] *Att.-Gen.* v. *Fishmongers' Co.* (1841) 5 My. & Cr. 16.
[25] See *ante*, p. 35.
[26] *Re Sharp* [1906] 1 Ch. 793.
[27] *Re Timmis* [1902] 1 Ch. 176. Contrast *Re Landi* [1939] Ch. 828; and see *Re Milking Pail Farm Trusts* [1940] Ch. 996, criticised (1941) 57 L.Q.R. 26.
[28] *Re Gurney* [1893] 1 Ch. 590.
[29] Limitation Act 1980, s.21(2), a new provision introduced by the Limitation Amendment Act 1980.
[30] *Ibid.*
[31] *Re Somerset* [1894] 1 Ch. 231.
[32] Limitation Act 1980, s.38(2).
[33] *Ibid.* s.28.
[34] *Ibid.* s.21(3).
[35] *Re Pauling's S.T. (No. 1)* [1964] Ch. 303 (see at p. 353), affirming S.C. [1962] 1 W.L.R. 86 (see at p. 115).
[36] Limitation Act 1980, s.32.

unconscionable conduct. A trustee who is unaware that he is acting in breach of trust does not conceal the right of action by fraud.[37]

(6) EFFECT. A beneficiary who is barred cannot benefit from proceedings brought by one who is not.[38] Thus if a trustee commits an innocent breach of trust, *e.g.* advances too much on a mortgage, and after the right of the tenant for life has become barred, the remainderman compels the trustee to replace the money lost, the interest on the money until the death of the tenant for life belongs to the trustee himself.[39]

(c) *Discharge in bankruptcy.* A trustee will be freed from further liability for a breach of trust by becoming bankrupt and obtaining his discharge, unless the breach was fraudulent and he was a party to the fraud.[40]

(d) *Beneficiary's acquiescence.* A beneficiary's acquiescence in a breach of trust may have two consequences.

(1) NO ACTION. No beneficiary can proceed against a trustee for the breach if the beneficiary was *sui juris* and with full knowledge of all the facts (and, it may be, their legal consequences[41]) concurred or acquiesced in the breach.[42] Such a beneficiary cannot be heard in a court of equity to complain of acts of the trustee which he has himself knowingly authorised.[43] Thus if trustees made an unauthorised investment, and all the beneficiaries being *sui juris* elect to adopt it as part of the trust fund, the trustee will be absolved from liability.[44] They must, however, positively adopt it: it is not sufficient merely that a beneficiary has become absolutely entitled to a share in the trust fund.[45] Further, concurrence implies capacity, and so, unless guilty of fraud,[46] a beneficiary who concurred in the breach can successfully proceed against the trustees if at the time of the breach he was a minor,[47] or even though of full age, he was under the undue influence of his parents and they were profiting from the breach.[48]

---

[37] *Bartlett* v. *Barclays Bank Trust Co. Ltd.* [1980] Ch. 515.

[38] Limitation Act 1980, s.21(4).

[39] See *Re Somerset* [1894] 1 Ch. 231; *Re Fountaine* [1909] 2 Ch. 382; *Bartlett* v. *Barclays Bank Trust Co. Ltd.* [1980] Ch. 515 at 537.

[40] Insolvency Act 1986, s.281, replacing Insolvency Act 1985, s.128, which itself replaced Bankruptcy Act 1914, s.28.

[41] *Cockerell* v. *Cholmeley* (1830) 1 Russ. & M. 418; *Re Howlett* [1949] Ch. 767 at 775; contrast *Stafford* v. *Stafford* (1857) 1 De G. & J. 193 at 202; *Holder* v. *Holder* [1968] Ch. 353, approving *Re Pauling's S.T. (No. 1)* [1962] 1 W.L.R. 86 at 108 (affirmed: [1964] Ch. 303).

[42] *Fletcher* v. *Collis* [1905] 2 Ch. 24; *Life Association of Scotland* v. *Siddal* (1861) 3 De G.F. & J. 58. See generally *Re Pauling's S.T. (No. 1)* [1964] Ch. 303.

[43] *Brice* v. *Stokes* (1805) 11 Ves. 319; **2 W. & T.L.C. 581;** *Re Deane* (1888) 42 Ch.D. 9.

[44] *Re Jenkins and H.E. Randall & Co.'s Contract* [1903] 2 Ch. 362; *Wright* v. *Morgan* [1926] A.C. 788 at 799. And see *ante*, pp. 233, 261.

[45] Consider *Bartlett* v. *Barclays Bank Trust Co. Ltd.* [1980] Ch. 515 at 543.

[46] See *Overton* v. *Bannister* (1844) 3 Hare 503; *ante*, p. 32.

[47] *Wilkinson* v. *Parry* (1828) 4 Russ. 272 at 276.

[48] *Re Pauling's S.T. (No. 1)* [1964] Ch. 303; for undue influence, see *post*, p. 554.

(2) INDEMNITY.   If some other beneficiary proceeds against the trustee, equity has always had jurisdiction to order the trustee to be indemnified out of the interest of the beneficiary who instigated[49] the breach of trust to the extent to which the beneficiary benefited by the breach.[50] This jurisdiction was considerably enlarged by statute.[51] It is provided that where a trustee commits a breach of trust at the instigation or request of a beneficiary (whether oral or written[52]), or with his consent in writing, "the court may, if it thinks fit, make such order as to the court seems just, for impounding all or any part of the interest of the beneficiary in the trust estate by way of indemnity to the trustee or persons claiming though him."

The court, it will be noticed, has a full discretion under this section; it will not grant an impounding order unless the beneficiary clearly knew the facts which constituted the breach of trust, although it need not be shown that he knew that these facts amounted to a breach of trust.[53] If the order is made, it takes priority over the right of an assignee of the beneficiary's interest under an assignment made after the breach of trust was committed.[54] Moreover, neither the equitable nor the statutory right depends upon possession of the trust fund, so that the order can be made in favour of a former trustee.[55]

(e) *Release or confirmation by beneficiary.*   A beneficiary may, by subsequent confirmation or release, prevent himself from taking proceedings against his trustee for breach of trust. But the confirmation or release will not be binding on him unless he was *sui juris* and had full knowledge of the facts.[56] Whether a trustee or executor is entitled to demand a release on the completion of his duties is not clearly settled. It would seem that an executor is entitled to a release on handing over the residue to the residuary legatee, but that a trustee usually cannot claim to have a release under seal when he has completed the trust, though he often gets it.[57] It is clear, however, that the trustee is entitled to have his accounts examined and settled, for beneficiaries who are *sui juris* ought not to keep a Chancery suit hanging indefinitely over his head. But retirement from his trusteeship does not relieve him from liability for breaches of trust which he has committed; and he is not entitled to a release from an incoming trustee or executor.[58]

---

[49] See *Sawyer* v. *Sawyer* (1885) 28 Ch.D. 595 at 598. In so far as this case appears to apply the rule more favourably towards a married woman beneficiary (even where she was not restrained from anticipation), it would probably not now be followed.

[50] *Raby* v. *Ridehalgh* (1855) 7 De G.M. & G. 104; and see *Re Balfour's Settlement* [1938] Ch. 928, *ante*, p. 139.

[51] T.A., 1925, s.62, replacing T.A. 1893, s.45 (which replaced T.A. 1888, s.6); amended by Married Women (Restraint upon Anticipation) Act 1949, 2nd Sched. Contrast the automatic impounding of the interest of a trustee-beneficiary: *ante*, p. 289.

[52] *Griffith* v. *Hughes* [1892] 3 Ch. 105; *Re Somerset* [1894] 1 Ch. 231 at 266.

[53] *Re Somerset, supra*, at pp. 270, 274.

[54] *Bolton* v. *Curre* [1895] 1 Ch. 544.

[55] *Re Pauling's S.T. (No. 2)* [1963] Ch. 576.

[56] *Burrows* v. *Walls* (1855) 5 De G.M. & G. 233; *Walker* v. *Symonds* (1818) 3 Swans. 1.

[57] *King* v. *Mullins* (1852) 1 Drew. 308; *Re Cater's Trusts (No. 2)* (1858) 25 Beav. 366; but see *Re Wright's Trusts* (1857) 3 K. & J. 419 at 421, 422.

[58] *Tiger* v. *Barclays Bank Ltd.* [1951] 2 K.B. 556 (affirmed on other grounds, [1952] 1 All E.R. 85; *ante*, p. 232).

7. Contribution and indemnity

(a) *Joint and several liability.*   Where two or more trustees are liable for a breach of trust, each of them may be sued for the whole amount of the loss. If they are all sued, the judgment may be executed against any one of them singly; and when the judgment against two co-trustees is partly satisfied by one of them and the other goes bankrupt, the judgment creditor may prove in the bankruptcy for the whole original judgment debt and not merely for the balance of it which remains unsatisfied.[59]

(b) *Contribution.*   The general rule in equity was that, as between themselves, the trustees liable to make good a breach of trust had to bear the burden equally: if one paid more than his share he could claim contribution from the others.[60] In exceptional cases,[61] the rule of equal contribution was replaced by a right on the part of one trustee to obtain an indemnity from the others, but there was no intermediate position between these extremes. These rules have now been superseded by statute.[62] Where the loss occasioned by the breach of trust occurs after 1978,[63] the court has power to award in favour of one trustee against another contribution of such amount as is found to be just and equitable having regard to the extent of the responsibility of the latter trustee for the loss.[64] There is accordingly a degree of flexibility which was lacking under the old law.

(c) *Indemnity.*   In proceedings in which contribution is claimed, the court has power to exempt any person from liability to make contribution, or to direct that the contribution to be recovered from any person shall amount to a complete indemnity.[65] The cases in which it will be thought appropriate to exercise this power are likely to be those in which, under the former rules of equity, a right of indemnity replaced the rule of equal contribution. These were:

(i)   Where one trustee received and misappropriated the trust money, or was otherwise alone morally guilty[66];

(ii)   Where one of the trustees acted as solicitor to the trust, and the breach of trust was committed on his advice,[67] and not independently of it[68];

[59] *Edwards* v. *Hood-Barrs* [1905] 1 Ch. 20.
[60] *Lingard* v. *Bromley* (1812) 1 V. & B. 114; *Bahin* v. *Hughes* (1886) 31 Ch.D. 390; *Jackson* v. *Dickinson* [1903] 1 Ch. 947.
[61] *Infra.*
[62] Civil Liability (Contribution) Act 1978, ss.1(1), 6(1), 7(3).
[63] *Ibid.* ss.7(1), 10(2).
[64] *Ibid.* ss.1(1), 2(1).
[65] *Ibid.* s.2(2).
[66] *Bahin* v. *Hughes* (1886) 31 Ch.D. 390 at 395.
[67] *Lockhart* v. *Reilly* (1856) 25 L.J.Ch. 697; *Re Partington* (1887) 57 L.T. 654; *Re Turner, Barker* v. *Ivimey* [1897] 1 Ch. 536; *Re Linsley* [1904] 2 Ch. 785.
[68] *Head* v. *Gould* [1898] 2 Ch. 250.

(iii)   Where one of the trustees was a beneficiary, to the extent of his beneficial interest: the breach of trust was made good as far as possible out of the beneficial interest before applying the normal rule as to contribution.[69]

(d) *Limitation.*   Special rules govern contribution (and indemnity) claims with regard both to the date on which the right to claim contribution accrues and to the period of limitation.[70] If a beneficiary obtains judgment against a trustee for breach of trust, the trustee's right to claim contribution accrues on the date of the judgment[71]; while, if the trustee compromises the beneficiary's claim (whether or not he admits liability), his right of action for contribution accrues on the date on which he and the beneficiary reach agreement as to the amount to be paid by him.[72] The right of action for contribution becomes statute-barred two years after it has accrued.[73]

(e) *Adjustment.*   A trustee who overpays some beneficiary can adjust accounts by retaining the overpayments out of other interests of the beneficiary, *e.g.* future income.[74] Thus payments out of capital for legacy duty which should have been made out of income,[75] or the amount of tax on payments made gross but which should have suffered deduction of tax,[76] have been recouped in this way.[77] Where, however, the trustee being also a beneficiary underpays himself while overpaying the other beneficiaries, equity will not allow him to adjust accounts in his own favour if this would cause inconvenience and hardship to the beneficiaries.[78]

Section 3. Tracing Trust Property

1. Following or tracing.[79]   Where A's property is in the hands of B in an identifiable form, both common law and equity recognise the right of A to follow or trace the property, and claim it or its value from B. Following at common law merely provides evidence for the purpose of an action for money had and received, *i.e.* by identifying the recipient of the plaintiff's property.[79a] The claim in equity is more potent. In the case of a disposition of trust property in breach of trust, such a claim may have two advantages over a mere personal claim for breach of trust. First, it may be available in cases where there is no effective

---

[69] *Chillingworth* v. *Chambers* [1896] 1 Ch. 685. Consider also the court's powers of impounding: *ante*, pp. 285, 295.
[70] Contrast the position with regard to contribution claims between sureties: *post*, p. 476.
[71] Limitation Act 1980, s.10(3).
[72] *Ibid.* s.10(4).
[73] *Ibid.* s.10(1).
[74] *Livesey* v. *Livesey* (1827) 3 Russ. 287; and see *Re Robinson* [1911] 1 Ch. 502 at 508.
[75] *Re Ainsworth* [1915] 2 Ch. 96.
[76] *Re Musgrave* [1916] 2 Ch. 417.
[77] See also *Re Reading* [1916] W.N. 262.
[78] *Re Horne* [1905] 1 Ch. 76, as explained in *Re Ainsworth, supra.*
[79] For a full discussion of this remedy as applied to commercial transactions, see R. M. Goode (1976) 92 L.Q.R. 360.
[79a] *Agip (Africa) Ltd.* v. *Jackson* [1990] Ch. 265 at 285.

trust. First, it may be available in cases where there is no effective personal claim, as where the trustee is insolvent and B is an innocent volunteer. Secondly, if B is insolvent the claim will give A priority over B's creditors; for it is a proprietary claim which is attached to the property, and so A is a secured creditor. The circumstances in which property is identifiable for these purposes were fully reviewed in *Re Diplock*,[80] where, on a mistaken view of the law,[81] executors had distributed to charities over £200,000 to which the testator's next-of-kin were in fact entitled. Following at common law and tracing in equity will be discussed separately.[82]

A. Following at Common Law

1. Following. The common law[83] treated property as identifiable so long as it had not become mixed with other property. The property might be tangible, *e.g.* "sovereigns in a bag,"[84] or it might be a chose in action, *e.g.* a bank balance.[85] Property purchased with the claimant's money could also be identified provided that there was no admixture of other money. In this latter case the common law "proceeded on the basis that the unauthorised act of purchasing was one capable of ratification by the owner of the money."[86]

2. Limitations. There were, however, serious limitations to the common law remedy.[87] In the first place, as the common law did not recognise equitable rights, a beneficiary under a trust could not at law follow his property into the hands of the trustee, though by joining the trustee he could follow it into the hands of a stranger. More important, the paucity of common law remedies made it impossible to trace property into a mixed fund. Equity, on the other hand, had available the "far-reaching remedy of a declaration of charge"[88]; it could declare the mixed fund or any property bought with it to be subject to a charge which could, if necessary, be enforced by a sale of the property. Equity accordingly developed its own remedy of tracing. "If in 1815[89] the common law halted outside the bankers' door, by 1879[90] equity had had the courage to lift the latch, walk in and examine the books."[91]

---

[80] [1948] Ch. 465 (affirmed on the remedy *in personam* (*post*, p. 358), *sub nom. Ministry of Health* v. *Simpson* [1951] A.C. 251). See generally P. F. P. Higgins (1964) 6 Univ. of W.Austr.L.R. 428.
[81] *Ante*, p. 154, n. 54.
[82] But see *Nelson* v. *Larholt* [1948] 1 K.B. 339 at 343; *cf.* Sir A. T. Denning (1949) 65 L.Q.R. 37.
[83] On the right to trace at common law, see generally R. M. Goode (1976) 92 L.Q.R. 360; S. Khurshid & P. Matthews (1979) 95 L.Q.R. 78.
[84] *Re Diplock, supra*, at p. 521.
[85] *Banque Belge* v. *Hambrouck* [1921] 1 K.B. 321. On the meaning of money, see *Re Diplock, supra*, at pp. 521–523.
[86] *Re Diplock* [1948] Ch. 465 at 518, *per cur.*, citing *Sinclair* v. *Brougham* [1914] A.C. 398 at 441; and see *Taylor* v. *Plumer* (1815) 3 M. & S. 562.
[87] *Re Diplock* [1948] Ch. 465 at 519, 520.
[88] *Re Diplock, supra*, at p. 520, *per cur.*
[89] *Taylor* v. *Plumer, supra*.
[90] *Re Hallett's Estate* (1880) 13 Ch.D. 696.
[91] *Banque Belge* v. *Hambrouck, supra*, at p. 335, *per* Atkin L.J.

B. Tracing in Equity

For property to be traced in equity,[92] there are three conditions, namely:

(i)   the property must be traceable;

(ii) there must be an equity to trace; and

(iii) tracing must not produce an inequitable result.

If these conditions are satisfied, the claimant will be entitled either to the assets into which his property has been traced or else, if there are also other persons who have a claim upon them, to a charge upon them. These points will be considered in turn.

1. Traceable property. Property can be traced only if it is traceable. Sometimes there is little difficulty. Thus if shares are sold, tracing is clearly possible if the money is used to buy a house, and clearly impossible if it is dissipated on living expenses. But many cases are less plain, particularly when money is mixed with other moneys in a bank account or other blended fund. It is for a trustee to prove what is trust property and what is his own; if he cannot distinguish between them the whole will be treated as trust property.[93] Assistance in making the distinction is to be found in the rules relating to the appropriation of payments.

These rules are not confined to tracing, but have a wider application. Thus if X owes Y two separate sums of £100 each, and the earlier debt is statute-barred, it is important to know which debt is discharged when X pays Y £100; for only if it is paid in respect of the earlier debt can Y sue X for a further £100. Again, if S is a surety for one debt and not for the other, his liability will cease only if the debt paid is that for which he stands surety[94]; and if Y owns one debt beneficially and the other as trustee, the rights of the beneficiaries depend upon which debt has been paid.

(a) *First right to debtor.* A debtor has the right to appropriate any payment he makes to whatever debt he chooses, provided he does this at the time of making the payment.[95] The appropriation need not be express, and may be inferred from circumstances known to both parties[96]; but a mere inward intention not communicated to the creditor is not enough.[97]

---

[92] See generally D. M. Schuyler (1952) 65 Harv.L.R. 593; R. H. Maudsley (1959) 75 L.Q.R. 234; R. M. Goode (1976) 92 L.Q.R. 487.

[93] *Re Tilley's W.T.* [1967] Ch. 1179.

[94] See, *e.g. Re Sherry* (1884) 25 Ch.D. 692.

[95] *Anon.* (1587) Cro.Eliz. 68; *The Mecca* [1897] A.C. 286 at 293.

[96] See *Nash* v. *Hodgson* (1855) 6 De G.M. & G. 474 (debtor assumed to pay in respect of promissory note not statute-barred).

[97] *Parker* v. *Guinness* (1910) 27 T.L.R. 129; *Leeson* v. *Leeson* [1936] 2 K.B. 156.

(b) *Second right to creditor.* If the debtor makes no appropriation, the creditor may do so at any time, even in the course of an action, *e.g.* in the witness-box.[98] He may appropriate the payment to a statute-barred debt,[99] but he cannot appropriate the payment to an illegal item if a legal item remains unpaid.[1]

(c) *Rule in Clayton's Case*

(1) THE RULE. When there has been no express appropriation, the rule of convenience[2] known as the rule in *Clayton's Case*[3] is sometimes applied. This is confined to cases where there is an unbroken account between the parties,[4] or "one blended fund,"[5] as in the case of a current account at a bank or between traders[6]; it does not apply where there is no such account or fund, but merely distinct and separate debts.[7] The effect of the rule is that in the absence of any express appropriation, each payment is impliedly appropriated to the earliest debt that is not statute-barred.[8] "It is the first item of the debit side of the account, that is discharged, or reduced, by the first item on the credit side. The appropriation is made by the very act of setting the two items against each other."[9] In short, "first in, first out"; the first payment out is set against the first payment in, and vice versa.

(2) SEPARATE ACCOUNTS. Sometimes a bank will break an account and open a new and distinct account. In this case entries before the break will not be affected by entries after the break.[10] Thus if a bank takes a mortgage from X to secure his overdraft, and later the bank receives notice that X has granted Y a second mortgage on the property, it should at once break X's account and open a new account with him; for otherwise all subsequent payments into the account will be appropriated under the rule towards reducing the existing overdraft, and the bank will be unable to claim priority over Y for subsequent overdrawings by X, since they will be made with notice of Y's mortgage.[11] But where there are two or more concurrent and interdependent accounts of the same nature at a bank (and not, *e.g.* one a loan account and the other a current account), the bank may treat the

[98] *The Mecca* [1897] A.C. 286 at p. 294; *Smith* v. *Betty* [1903] K.B. 317 at 323; *Seymour* v. *Pickett* [1905] 1 K.B. 715. The right is restricted in cases of regulated agreements under the Consumer Credit Act 1974: see section 81.
[99] *Mills* v. *Fowkes* (1839) 5 Bing.N.C. 455. For the effect of such payment on the revival of that and other statute-barred debts, see *Re Footman Bower & Co. Ltd.* [1961] Ch. 443 at 448, 449; *Friend* v. *Young* [1897] 2 Ch. 421; and see *Nash* v. *Hodgson, supra,* at pp. 480, 481.
[1] *Wright* v. *Laing* (1824) 3 B. & C. 165.
[2] *Re Diplock* [1948] Ch. 465 at 554.
[3] *Devaynes* v. *Noble: Clayton's Case* (1816) 1 Mer. 572.
[4] See *Re Sherry* (1884) 25 Ch.D. 692 at 702.
[5] *Devaynes* v. *Noble: Clayton's Case, supra,* at p. 608, *per* Grant M.R.
[6] See, *e.g. Re Footman Bower & Co. Ltd.* [1961] Ch. 443, where *Re Diplock, supra,* at p. 555 was not cited.
[7] *The Mecca* [1897] A.C. 286.
[8] *Re Sherry, supra,* at p. 702; *Nash* v. *Hodgson* (1855) 6 De G.M. & G. 474.
[9] *Devaynes* v. *Noble: Clayton's Case, supra,* at p. 608, *per* Grant M.R.
[10] *Re Sherry, supra,* at p. 702.
[11] *Deeley* v. *Lloyds Bank Ltd.* [1912] A.C. 756.

rule as applying to the accounts as if they were combined[12]; otherwise the rule will be applied to each account separately.[13]

(3) CONTRARY INTENTION. The rule is excluded if the parties otherwise agree, or a contrary intention appears from the circumstances.[14] It is not enough, however, merely to show that the bank refused to allow cheques to be drawn on an overdrawn account unless credits of an equivalent amount were paid in; such credits thus go in reduction of the oldest debts and not in offsetting the newly-drawn cheques.[15]

(d) *The Rule in Re Hallett's Estate.*   The rule in *Clayton's Case*[16] is sometimes excluded by the rule in *Re Hallett's Estate.*[17] Where a trustee draws on a bank account which contains both his own money and trust funds, he is deemed to draw on his own money first, even if it was the most recently paid in, and to draw on the trust funds only after all his own money has gone; for the presumption is against a breach of trust.[18] For example, if he opens a bank account with £500 trust funds, later adds £500 of his own, and then draws and dissipates[19] £500, the £500 left in the account is trust money. But if he then withdraws a further £350, and afterwards pays in £250 of his own, only £150 of the balance of £400 in the account is trust money; for the beneficiaries cannot claim any of the £250 unless they can show that it was intended to replace trust money. In short, the beneficiaries can usually claim no more than the lowest balance in the account during the period in question.[20] The rule is not confined to bank accounts, but applies to other property, *e.g.* shares in a company.[21] In the case of a bank trustee, trust money wrongfully deposited by the bank with itself may be traced so that, on the insolvency of the bank, it will be repaid in priority to other creditors[22]; but trust money properly so deposited may not be traced, because on deposit it ceased to be impressed with any trust.[23]

(e) *Overdrafts.*   If the trust money is paid into the trustee's overdrawn account so as to reduce the overdraft, the account will be charged with the repayment of the money paid in. This charge will extend to any properties purchased with the assistance of the overdraft, but the beneficiaries will not be able to claim the properties themselves

---

[12] *Re E. J. Morel (1934) Ltd.* [1962] Ch. 21; and see *Re Yeovil Glove Co. Ltd.* [1965] Ch. 148.
[13] *Re James R. Rutherford & Sons Ltd.* [1964] 1 W.L.R. 1211.
[14] *The Mecca, supra; Mutton* v. *Peat* [1899] 2 Ch. 556 (reversed on the facts: [1900] 2 Ch. 79); *Re Hodgson's Trusts* [1919] 2 Ch. 189.
[15] *Re Primrose (Builders) Ltd.* [1950] Ch. 561.
[16] *Supra.*
[17] (1880) 13 Ch.D. 696.
[18] *Re Hallett's Estate* (1880) 13 Ch.D. 696; *Re Oatway* [1903] 2 Ch. 356.
[19] See *Re Tilley's W.T.* [1967] Ch. 1179 at 1185; and see *post,* pp. 301, 302.
[20] *James Roscoe (Bolton) Ltd.* v. *Winder* [1915] 1 Ch. 62.
[21] *Brady* v. *Stapleton* (1952) 88 C.L.R. 322.
[22] *Space Investments Ltd.* v. *Canadian Imperial Bank of Commerce Trust Co. (Bahamas) Ltd.* [1986] 1 W.L.R. 1072 at 1074.
[23] *Space Investments Ltd.* v. *Canadian Imperial Bank of Commerce Trust Co. (Bahamas) Ltd.* [1986] 1 W.L.R. 1072.

or a share in them, as they will be regarded as having been purchased with the sums advanced.[24]

(f) *Dissipation.* Often tracing is impossible because the property has been dissipated. "The equitable remedies presuppose the continued existence of the money either as a separate fund or as part of a mixed fund or as latent in property acquired by means of such a fund. If ... such continued existence is not established, equity is as helpless as the common law itself. If the fund, mixed or unmixed, is spent upon a dinner, equity, which dealt only in specific relief and not in damages, could do nothing."[25] Even if the recipient has used the trust money to pay off secured or unsecured loans or other identifiable debts, there can be no tracing; for the payment purchases no asset but merely extinguishes the debt, and there is no equity to revive it or create a new debt in its place.[26]

2. Equity to trace. Even if property is traceable, there is no equitable right to trace and claim it unless some initial fiduciary relationship[27] exists. The right to trace is founded upon the existence of a beneficial owner with an equitable proprietary interest in property in the hands of a trustee or other fiduciary agent. This initial fiduciary relationship is essential. It is not enough to show that one person has acquired some benefit by using the property of another or, in other words, merely to prove a case of unjust enrichment.[28] Yet apart from the usual relationships, *e.g.* trustee and beneficiary, it may arise from the transaction itself as where money is paid under a mistake of fact: the payer retains in the money a continuing equitable proprietary interest.[29]

3. Inequitable results

(a) *Equitable bars.* Even where there is an initial equity and the property is traceable, the right to trace cannot be exercised where it would be contrary to equitable principles to allow it. Thus although property can be traced into the hands of a person who took with notice of the equity, or even without notice if he was merely a volunteer,[30] the

---

[24] *Re Tilley's W.T.* [1967] Ch. 1179.

[25] *Re Diplock* [1948] Ch. 465 at 521, *per cur.* See *Borden (U.K.) Ltd.* v. *Scottish Timber Products Ltd.* [1981] Ch. 25 (resin made into chipboard); *Hendy Lennox (Industrial Engines) Ltd.* v. *Grahame Puttick Ltd.* [1984] 1 W.L.R. 485 (engines incorporated in generating sets); *Clough Mill Ltd.* v. *Martin* [1985] 1 W.L.R. 111.

[26] *Re Diplock, supra,* at pp. 548–550. But possibly there would be a claim by subrogation if an identifiable asset had been purchased with the money lent.

[27] For these, see *ante,* pp. 91, 251 and *post,* p. 553.

[28] *Re Diplock, supra,* at pp. 520, 530, 543, criticised by R. H. Maudsley (1959) 75 L.Q.R. 234 at 241 *et seq.,* and by R. A. Pearce (1976) 40 Conv.(N.S.) 277 at 286 *et seq.* See also Goff and Jones, *Law of Restitution* (4th ed. 1986), pp. 70, 71.

[29] *Chase Manhattan N.A.* v. *Israel-British Bank (London) Ltd.* [1981] Ch. 105, referring to this passage (see *ibid.* p. 118). See the comments at [1980] C.L.J. 272–276.

[30] *Sinclair* v. *Brougham* [1914] A.C. 398 at 443–447, discussing *Re Guardian Permanent Benefit B.S. (Crace-Calvert's Case)* (1882) 23 Ch.D. 440; *Re Diplock* [1948] Ch. 465.

right to trace cannot be exercised against a bona fide purchaser for value without notice of the equity.[31] Again, although mere delay is no bar,[32] there can be no tracing by claimants who have acquiesced in the wrongful mixing or distribution.[33]

(b) *Injustice.* Even where there is no other equitable bar against tracing, equity will not permit the right to be exercised where the effect would be to work an injustice. Thus if an innocent volunteer has spent the trust money on altering or improving his own land or buildings, it would be inequitable to allow the beneficiaries to trace the trust moneys. For their charge on the land or buildings would be enforceable by a sale which would compel the volunteer to exchange his land or buildings for money; and sometimes their market value will not have been increased by the alterations. There would also be practical problems where, for example, part of a building in the middle of a hospital has been improved; for it might not be easy to determine just what entity is subject to the charge, nor how the charge could properly be enforced by a sale. Such cases are quite distinct from those where the volunteer has purchased an asset with a mixture of trust moneys and his own, for then a sale would give him and the beneficiaries alike what each contributed, namely, money.[34] Nor is there anything inequitable in tracing property into the hands of even the most deserving charity, for there is no "different standard of conscientiousness for charitable or other corporations from that appropriate to an individual."[35]

4. Effect of right to trace. When a right to trace has been established, the effect depends upon the property and the claims against it. The simplest case is when it is established that the asset is wholly the property of one claimant or group of claimants, as where a trustee has mixed the funds of a trust with his own and then, after withdrawing his own money, has bought shares with the remainder. But often the circumstances are more complex, as where a trustee has mixed his own moneys with the funds of two or more trusts.[36] The two main categories must be considered; and the right to claim interest must be mentioned.

(a) *First charge.* Where the trustee mixes trust money with his own, the equities are clearly unequal. Accordingly, the beneficiaries are entitled to a first charge on the mixed fund,[37] or on any land, securities or other assets purchased with it.[38] Thus if the trustee purchases shares

---

[31] *Re Diplock, supra,* at p. 539; *Thorndike* v. *Hunt* (1859) 3 De G. & J. 563; *Taylor* v. *Blakelock* (1886) 32 Ch.D. 560; and see *ante,* p. 49.
[32] *Re Eustace* [1912] 1 Ch. 561.
[33] *Blake* v. *Gale* (1886) 32 Ch.D. 571. For laches and acquiescence, see *ante,* p. 35, and *post,* p. 655.
[34] See *Re Diplock, supra,* at pp. 546–548. Contrast the criticisms of the rule in *Clayton's Case, supra,* by Z. Chafee (1950) 36 Cornell L.Q. 176.
[35] *Re Diplock, supra,* at p. 476, *per cur.*
[36] See [1983] Conv. 135 (G. Hodkinson), dealing particularly with changes in value of an item bought with mixed funds.
[37] *Re Hallett's Estate* (1880) 13 Ch.D. 696.
[38] *Re Pumfrey* (1882) 22 Ch.D. 255; *Re Oatway* [1903] 2 Ch. 356.

with part of the mixed fund, leaving enough of it to repay the trust moneys, and then dissipates the balance, the beneficiaries' charge binds the shares; for although under the rule in *Re Hallett's Estate*[39] the trustee is presumed to have bought the shares out of his own money, the charge attached to the entire fund, and could be discharged only by restoring the trust moneys.[40] Where the property purchased has increased in value, the charge will be not merely for the amount of the trust moneys but for a proportionate part of the increased value. Thus if the trustee purchases land with £500 of his own money and £1,000 of trust moneys, and the land doubles in value, he would be profiting from his breach of trust[41] if he were entitled to all except £1,000; the beneficiaries are accordingly entitled to a charge on the land for £2,000.[42]

(b) *Equal equities.* In other cases, there will usually be no ground for according one party priority over the other. Thus a trustee may mix the funds of two separate trusts,[43] or he may give trust money to a volunteer who mixes it with his own[44]; in such cases the claimants will be equally innocent.

(1) IDENTIFICATION. The first step is, if possible, to identify the moneys so mixed. If the mixing has taken place in a current account, ownership is determined in accordance with the rule in *Clayton's Case*,[45] or "first in, first out."[46] This rule, however, may be excluded by the circumstances.[47] Thus subscribers to a fund for a particular purpose are usually treated as giving only so much as, treating all subscribers alike, is in fact needed for that purpose,[48] so that if there is ultimately a surplus the later subscribers cannot claim it to the exclusion of the earlier.[49] Again, a volunteer who withdraws money from a mixed fund may preclude himself from relying upon the rule, as where he earmarks the money as trust funds by putting it in a separate account and recording its origin; for he who mixes may unmix.[50]

(2) PARI PASSU. Where *Clayton's Case*[51] does not apply, the rule is that the parties are entitled to the mixed fund *pari passu*. One set of beneficiaries will share it rateably with the other set[52] or with the

---

[39] (1880) 13 Ch.D. 696; *ante*, p. 301.

[40] *Re Oatway* [1903] 2 Ch. 356.

[41] See *ante*, p. 245.

[42] *Scott* v. *Scott* (1963) 109 C.L.R. 649. (This paragraph was cited with approval in *Re Tilley's W.T.* [1967] Ch. 1179 at 1189.)

[43] *Hancock* v. *Smith* (1889) 41 Ch.D. 456; *Re Stenning* [1895] 2 Ch. 433; *Re Hallett's Estate, supra.*

[44] *Re Diplock* [1948] Ch. 465 at 552–554.

[45] (1816) 1 Mer. 572; *ante*, p. 300.

[46] See authorities in nn. 43, 44, *supra*. For criticism, see D. A. McConville (1963) 79 L.Q.R. 388.

[47] *Re British Red Cross Balkan Fund* [1914] 2 Ch. 419.

[48] See *Re Hobourn Aero Components Ltd.'s Air Raid Distress Fund* [1946] Ch. 86 at 97; affirmed [1946] Ch. 194.

[49] *Re British Red Cross Balkan Fund, supra.*

[50] *Re Diplock, supra,* at pp. 551, 552 (rescinded at p. 559 on the facts, but not affected on the principles).

[51] *Supra.*

[52] *Sinclair* v. *Brougham* [1914] A.C. 398 at 442; *Re Diplock, supra,* at pp. 533, 534, 539.

volunteer,[53] or they will hold a charge *pari passu* on any land, securities or other assets purchased with it,[54] including any increase in value therein.[55] Similarly any surplus of a fund subscribed for a particular purpose will go rateably to the subscribers.[56]

(c) *Interest.*   There is no general right to interest on any property that has been traced. But if the assets into which the property has been traced have earned any interest, the claimants are entitled to it, or to so much of it as is proportionate to the property which has been traced.[57]

Section 4. Personal Remedy against Recipient

Where the proprietary remedy of tracing fails, *e.g.* because the property has been dissipated or is not identifiable,[58] equity has in some cases given the beneficiaries a personal remedy against the person who has wrongly received the property. Such a claim applies in many cases of payment to the wrong persons under a will or intestacy; but it is not so well established in the case of trusts. These claims are dealt with later.[59]

---

[53] *Sinclair* v. *Brougham, supra,* at pp. 442, 443; *Re Diplock, supra,* at pp. 534, 539.
[54] *Re Diplock, supra,* at pp. 524, 539, 546.
[55] See *Lord Provost, etc., of Edinburgh* v. *Lord Advocate* (1879) 4 App.Cas. 823.
[56] *Re British Red Cross Balkan Fund, supra; ante,* p. 176.
[57] *Re Diplock, supra,* at pp. 517, 557.
[58] See *ante,* p. 302.
[59] See *post,* p. 358.

Part III

ADMINISTRATION OF ASSETS

CHAPTER 1

INTRODUCTION

1. Assets. When a person dies, whether testate or intestate, the property vested in him which is available to meet his debts and other liabilities is called his "assets."[1] These assets must be collected and realised; his debts must be paid; and any surplus must be distributed to the persons beneficially entitled under the will or intestacy. These three tasks, known as the "administration of assets," are the duty of his personal representatives, *i.e.* his executors if he has appointed any, and otherwise his administrators. Despite the name "personal representatives" an executor (and doubtless an administrator also) "does not act for a dead man or in his name, but for the estate of the dead man."[2] The administration is normally conducted by the personal representatives out of court; but difficult or complex administrations may take place in court.

2. Jurisdiction. The law relating to the administration of the assets of a testator or intestate has been complicated by the diversity of jurisdiction formerly exercised by three sets of courts. The ecclesiastical courts made grants of probate to executors and letters of administration to administrators; and this continued until the jurisdiction was vested in the Court of Probate in 1858[3] and then in the High Court in 1875.[4] The courts of common law exercised jurisdiction over real property, which until the Land Transfer Act 1897 did not vest in the personal representatives but passed directly to the devisee or heir. But apart from these relatively clear-cut cases, there were various heads of jurisdiction which the Court of Chancery gradually assumed. By the end of the seventeenth century the Chancery had practically taken over the jurisdiction of the ecclesiastical courts over legacies and actions for the distribution of the residue. It has also acquired a jurisdiction concurrent with the common law courts over the construction of devises, and over actions by and against the personal representatives for the collection of assets and the payment of debts.

---

[1] "Assets," from the French "*assez*" (enough) and Latin "*ad satis*" (to sufficiency).
[2] *Stanhope* v. *Stanhope* (1886) 11 P.D. 103 at 110, *per* Bowen L.J.
[3] Court of Probate Act 1857, ss.3, 4.
[4] J.A. 1873, s.16.

309

3. Chancery. At first, the Court of Chancery mainly supplemented and followed the law of the other courts; but in time it not only modified some of this law but also developed other rules of its own. Its success in acquiring jurisdiction was in large part due to its superior administrative machinery, and not least its ability to take complicated accounts. A common law court would merely resolve the particular dispute brought before it by the parties, whereas the Court of Chancery looked at the estate as a whole; if it interfered at all, it would administer the entire estate for the benefit of all the creditors and beneficiaries alike. The result is that the law of the administration of assets, though based in part on the principles of ecclesiastical and common law, is largely equitable.[5]

4. The executor's year. A personal representative owes a duty to creditors and beneficiaries alike to carry out his obligations with due diligence.[6] Usually this requires the completion of his administration of the assets within the "executor's year," *i.e.* the period of one year from the death of the deceased; in general, until then "he is not bound to distribute the estate of the deceased."[7] Thus a legatee cannot require his legacy to be paid before the year has elapsed, even if the will directed payment within a shorter period[8]; but the executor may pay it sooner if he chooses.[9] The circumstances may justify a longer period than a year. Thus an executor will not be liable for failing to call in an insecure mortgage within the year if he honestly and prudently refrained from doing so in the belief that it was for the benefit of the estate[10]; the onus of proof lies on him.[11] Further, the will may vary these requirements, though any such variation will bind only the beneficiaries, who claim under the will, and not the creditors, whose rights are independent of the will.[12] In some cases due diligence may even require that creditors should be paid before the year has run; but in other cases the executor may be able to justify delay beyond the year.[13]

5. Main heads. In addition to the collection and realisation of assets, the payment of debts and the distribution of surplus, some consideration must be given to the remedies available to those concerned in cases of default or difficulty, to legacies, and to *donationes mortis causa*. These will be discussed in turn.

---

[5] See generally Holdsworth, H.E.L., Vol. 6, pp. 652 *et seq.*; *Ministry of Health* v. *Simpson* [1951] A.C. 251 at 266, 267.
[6] See *Re Tankard* [1942] Ch. 69.
[7] A.E.A. 1925, s.44, replacing Statute of Distributions 1670, s.8; L.T.A. 1897, s.3(2).
[8] See *Brooke* v. *Lewis* (1822) 6 Madd. 358.
[9] *Re Palmer* [1916] 2 Ch. 391; and see A.E.A. 1925, s.36(10).
[10] See *Re Medland* (1889) 41 Ch.D. 476; *Re Chapman, Cocks* v. *Chapman* [1896] 2 Ch. 763.
[11] *Re Tankard* [1942] Ch. 69.
[12] *Ibid.*
[13] *Ibid.* at p. 73.

CHAPTER 2

COLLECTION AND REALISATION OF ASSETS

Section 1. What are Assets

Before 1926 realty was usually not available for the deceased's creditors. It therefore did not form part of his assets, as the following account shows.

1. Personalty. At common law, the only property available for payment of all creditors was the personalty (including leaseholds) to which the deceased was entitled in possession or in action,[1] and in which his interest did not cease at his death. Whatever dispositions the deceased had made by his will, this property vested in his personal representatives and was known as legal assets, because it was available at law for the payment of debts; any creditor might sue the personal representatives and recover judgment for payment of his debt out of the legal assets.

2. Realty

(a) *"Assets by descent."* At common law, the deceased's realty did not vest in his personal representatives but passed directly to his heir or the devisee under his will, free from the claims of ordinary creditors. Freehold estates held in fee simple were, however, "assets by descent" in the hands of the heir, and liable for the payment of those specialty debts for the payment of which the deceased had bound his heirs. Although the class of assets by descent was expanded by statute during the seventeenth century,[2] the general rule remained that realty was not liable at law for the debts of the deceased.

(b) *Equitable assets.* The position in equity was different. If the deceased had either devised realty to trustees upon trust to pay his debts or had charged it with payment of the debts, in equity it could be made available for the payment of all debts by means of a suit for

---

[1] For things in actions, see *ante,* p. 71.
[2] Statute of Frauds 1677, ss.10 and 12; Statute of Fraudulent Devises 1691. For the details, see the 28th ed. of this work, p. 308.

311

administration. In these two cases, the realty was called *equitable assets*, because the ordinary creditor's remedy was in equity only.[3]

(c) *Marshalling.* Even where there was no devise or charge to pay debts, the doctrine of marshalling might come to the aid of the ordinary creditors.[4] If the personalty was insufficient to pay both ordinary and specialty creditors, the Court of Chancery, in administering the estate, compelled the specialty creditors to resort in the first place to the realty; and if they had already exhausted the personalty, the ordinary creditors were put in their place as against the realty so far as the specialty creditors had exhausted the personalty.[5]

(d) *Creditor's remedy.* Successive nineteenth-century statutes[6] made the deceased's realty assets in equity for the payment of all his debts, even though he had not charged it for the purpose, and placed all his unsecured creditors, whether specialty or simple contract, on an equal footing. But the realty still did not vest in the proper persons to pay the debts, namely, the personal representatives, unless it was devised to them. Except where it was assets by descent, the creditor's remedy against the realty was to take proceedings in Chancery to have the estate administered by the court. But by Part I of the Land Transfer Act 1897, the realty of a person dying after 1897 was made to vest in his personal representative, who thus became a "real representative" also. The Act of 1897, however, did not apply to legal estates in copyhold or customary freehold, though it applied to equitable interests therein[7]; and it did not apply to trust and mortgage estates, which had been dealt with by an earlier Act[8] nor, apparently, to estates tail.

3. Deaths after 1925

(a) *Property vesting in personal representatives.* Where death occurs after 1925, the foregoing rules have been superseded by the Administration of Estates Act 1925. By section 1 of that Act, real estate to which a deceased person was entitled for an interest not ceasing on his death devolves from time to time on his personal representative, notwithstanding any testamentary disposition; and the personal representative represents the deceased in regard to his real estate as well as

---

[3] As to the distinction between legal and equitable assets (which is of no practical importance for deaths occurring after 1925) see *Cook* v. *Gregson* (1856) 3 Drew. 547, and *O'Grady* v. *Wilmot* [1916] 2 A.C. 231.
[4] For other examples of marshalling, see *post*, pp. 336, 366, 421.
[5] *Aldrich* v. *Cooper* (1803) 8 Ves. 382; **1 W. & T.L.C. 29.**
[6] Debts of Traders Act 1807; Debts Recovery Act 1830, s.9; A.E.A. 1833; A.E.A. 1869 (commonly known as Hinde Palmer's Act). See the 28th ed. of this work, p. 309.
[7] *Re Somerville and Turner's Contract* [1903] 2 Ch. 583.
[8] C.A. 1881, s.30.

in regard to his personal estate. In the Act, unless the context otherwise requires, "personal representative" means "the executor, original or by representation, or administrator for the time being of a deceased person, and as regards any liability for the payment of death duties includes any person who takes possession of or intermeddles with the property of a deceased person without the authority of the personal representatives or the court,"[9] *i.e.* an executor *de son tort*.[10]

"Real estate" includes chattels real (*i.e.* leaseholds), and land in possession, remainder or reversion, and every interest in or over land to which the deceased was entitled at his death.[11] It also includes real estate held on trust (including settled land), realty appointed by the deceased's will under a general power of appointment, and an entailed interest disposed of by the will.[12] But the following interests vested in the deceased do not vest in his personal representatives.[13]

    (i)   an entailed interest not thus disposed of;

   (ii)   his interest under a joint tenancy; and

  (iii)   his interest as a corporator sole in the corporation's real and personal estate.

Thus, either at common law or by statute, all the realty and personalty of a deceased person, with few exceptions, now vest in his personal representatives.

(b) *All beneficial interests are assets.* All the real and personal estate of a deceased person, whether legal or equitable, to the extent of his beneficial interest therein, are assets for payment of his debts and liabilities, whether by specialty or simple contract; and so is any real or personal estate appointed by his will under a general power, including the statutory power to dispose of entails.[14] Any disposition by will inconsistent with this enactment is void against the creditors, and the court must, if necessary, administer the property for the purpose of the payment of the debts and liabilities; but the foregoing provision does not prejudice the rights of incumbrancers.[15] If any beneficiary disposes of his beneficial interest in good faith before an action is brought or process is sued out against him, he will be personally liable for the value of the interest so disposed of by him, so that to this extent the debts of

---

[9] A.E.A. 1925, s.55(1)(xi).
[10] See *New York Breweries Co. Ltd.* v. *Att.-Gen.* [1899] A.C. 62; *I.R.C.* v. *Stype Investments (Jersey) Ltd., Re Clore* [1982] Ch. 456.
[11] A.E.A. 1925, s.3(1).
[12] *Ibid.* s.3(1), (2). See L.P.A. 1925, s.176; and *cf. Acheson* v. *Russell* [1951] Ch. 67 (*sub nom. Re Manor Farm* [1950] 2 All E.R. 572).
[13] A.E.A. 1925, s.3(3)–(5).
[14] A.E.A. 1925, s.32(1).
[15] *Ibid.*

the deceased become his debts[16]; but that interest will not be liable to be taken in execution in the action or under the process.[17]

Section 2. Collection of Assets

The first duty of a personal representative is to take possession of the assets of the deceased, or assume control over them, as soon as he properly can. In particular, he must get in debts owed to the deceased, e.g. arrears of rent,[18] a sum due on a promissory note,[19] or a loan upon a bond.[20] But he may leave a reasonable sum of money in the deceased's bank account[21]; and he need not call in money secured on mortgage unless the security has become inadequate, and even then he has a discretion.[22] Occasionally a beneficiary has been permitted to sue a debtor to the estate in order to make him pay the debt to the personal representatives, but only in special circumstances[23] which embrace a failure by the personal representatives in the performance of their duty to protect the estate or the interests of the beneficiaries in it.[24]

Section 3. The Trust for Sale on Intestacy

1. The trust for sale.   One of the main objects of the Administration of Estates Act 1925 is to assimilate the law relating to realty to the law relating to personalty. In pursuance of this object, section 33[25] creates a trust for sale as regards any realty not disposed of by the will (if any) of the deceased. The section provides that on the death after 1925 of a person intestate as to any real or personal estate the personal representatives shall hold the real estate upon trust for sale and the personal estate on trust to call in, sell and convert into money such part of it as does not consist of money, with power to postpone such sale and conversion.[26]

This statutory trust for sale applies only where the deceased died intestate as to the whole interest in the estate or some part of it, and not where the deceased died intestate as to a partial interest, as where he disposed by will of a life interest in property but not the reversion[27] or vice versa.[28] And unless there is some special reason, reversionary

---

[16] *Re Hedgely* (1886) 34 Ch.D. 379.
[17] A.E.A. 1925, s.32(2), reproducing the law laid down in *Re Moon* [1907] 2 Ch. 304; *Price* v. *Price* (1887) 35 Ch.D. 297; *British Mutual Investment Co.* v. *Smart* (1875) 10 Ch.App. 567; *Re Atkinson, Proctor* v. *Atkinson* [1908] 2 Ch. 307. See also A.E.A. 1925, s.38, and *post*, pp. 358, 359.
[18] *Tebbs* v. *Carpenter* (1816) 1 Madd. 290.
[19] *Caney* v. *Bond* (1843) 6 Beav. 486.
[20] *Powell* v. *Evans* (1801) 5 Ves. 839.
[21] *Johnson* v. *Newton* (1853) 11 Hare 160.
[22] See *ante*, p. 310.
[23] *Re Field* [1971] 1 W.L.R. 555.
[24] *Hayim* v. *Citibank N.A.* [1987] A.C. 730 at 747–749.
[25] For a discussion of the scope of this section, see *Re Yerburgh* [1928] W.N. 208.
[26] See *Re Wilks, Keefer* v. *Wilks* [1935] Ch. 645.
[27] *Re McKee* [1931] 2 Ch. 145.
[28] *Re Plowman* [1943] Ch. 269.

interests[29] must not be sold until they fall into possession, and personal chattels must not be sold unless required for purposes of administration. The expression "personal chattels" means "carriages, horses,[30] stable furniture and effects (not used for business purposes[31]), motor cars and accessories (not used for business purposes), garden effects, domestic animals, plate, plated articles, linen, china, glass, books, pictures, prints, furniture,[32] jewellery,[33] articles of household or personal use[34] or ornament, musical and scientific instruments and apparatus, wines, liquors and consumable stores," but does not include "any chattels used at the death of the intestate for business purposes nor money or securities for money."[35] The value of the chattels relative to the rest of the estate is irrelevant.[36]

2. Application of proceeds of sale. Out of the net money arising from the sale and conversion (after payment of costs) and out of the deceased's ready money (so far as not disposed of by his will, if any) the personal representatives must first pay all such funeral, testamentary and administration expenses, debts, and other liabilities as are properly payable thereout having regard to the rules of administration contained in the Act.[37] Out of the residue they must then set aside a sufficient fund to provide for any pecuniary legacies bequeathed by the will, if any.[38] During the minority of any beneficiary or the subsistence of any life interest, and pending distribution of the estate, the personal representatives may invest the residue in trust investments.[39]

3. Distribution of residue. The residue of the money and any investments for the time being representing it, including any part of the estate retained unsold and not required for administration purposes,[40] is to be distributed in the manner or held on the beneficial trusts mentioned in the Act[41]; there is thus no difference in the devolution of real and personal property. Where the personal representatives exercise

[29] See *Re Fisher* [1943] Ch. 377.
[30] See *Re Hutchinson* [1955] Ch. 255 (racehorses).
[31] See *Re Ogilby* [1942] Ch. 288 (not cattle on a farm).
[32] *Re Crispin's W.T.* [1975] Ch. 245 (clocks).
[33] See *Re Whitby* [1944] Ch. 210 (unmounted diamonds).
[34] See *Re Chaplin* [1950] Ch. 507 (motor yacht); *Re Reynolds' W.T.* [1966] 1 W.L.R. 19 (stamp collection); see (1966) 82 L.Q.R. 18;; *Re Crispin's W.T., supra* (watches).
[35] A.E.A. 1925, s.55(1)(x).
[36] *Re Crispin's W.T., supra.*
[37] *Ibid.* s.33(2): and see *post*, p. 323.
[38] *Ibid.* s.33(2).
[39] *Ibid.* s.33(3).
[40] *Ibid.* s.33(4).
[41] *Ibid.* s.46, as amended for deaths after 1952 by the Intestates' Estates Act 1952, for deaths after 1966 by the Family Provision Act 1966, s.1, for deaths after 1969 by the Family Law Reform Act 1969, for deaths after June 1972 by S.I. 1972 No. 916, for deaths after March 14, 1977, by S.I. 1977 No. 415, for deaths after February 28, 1981, by S.I. 1981 No. 255, and for deaths after May 31, 1987, by S.I. 1987 No. 799. These amendments improved the position of the spouse *vis-à-vis* the issue and other relatives of the deceased, and also improved the position of the illegitimate children.

their power to postpone conversion, the income (including the net rents and profits of real estate and chattels real) of so much of the real and personal estate of the deceased as is not disposed of by his will, if any, or is not required for administration purposes, may be applied as income as from the death, however such estate is invested.[42]

4. Exceptions. The provisions discussed in this section do not affect the rights of creditors or of the Crown in respect of death duties, and take effect subject to any provisions contained in any will left by the deceased.[43]

Section 4. Powers of Personal Representatives

1. Title to act. An executor derives title from the will, so that even before that title is confirmed by the grant of probate wide powers are vested in him.[44] He may commence an action, but cannot obtain judgment before obtaining the grant even if the defendant does not object.[45] An administrator, on the other hand, derives his title solely from the grant of letters of administration, and has no powers before the grant is made.[46]

2. Powers of disposition. A personal representative has always had very wide powers of disposing of personalty (including leaseholds) vested in him.[47] He can sell, mortgage, pledge, or lease it,[48] and, in fact, make any disposition which is necessary in a due course of administration, and for that purpose recover possession from a beneficiary.[49] Both the Land Transfer Act 1897 and the Administration of Estates Act 1925 conferred upon the personal representative the same powers, duties, rights and liabilities with respect to real estate as were in force with respect to chattels real before the Acts came into operation.[50]

The latter Act also contains a wide provision as to both real and personal property, applicable whenever the deceased died. Under this

---

[42] A.E.A. 1925, s.33(5); see *Re Sullivan* [1930] 1 Ch. 84, approved in *Re Thornber* [1937] Ch. 29 and explained in *Re Fisher* [1943] Ch. 377 at 385; and see *ante*, p. 231 for the result where the personal representatives fail to exercise their power to postpone conversion.
[43] A.E.A. 1925, s.33(6), (7); see *Re McKee* [1931] 2 Ch. 145; *Re Thornber, supra*.
[44] *Chetty* v. *Chetty* [1916] 1 A.C. 603. See, *e.g. Whitmore* v. *Lambert* [1955] 1 W.L.R. 495; *Biles* v. *Caesar* [1957] 1 W.L.R. 156.
[45] *Re Crowhurst Park* [1974] 1 W.L.R. 583.
[46] *Chetty* v. *Chetty, supra*, at p. 609.
[47] See, *e.g. Nugent* v. *Gifford* (1738) 1 Atk. 463; *Corser* v. *Cartwright* (1875) L.R. 7 H.L. 731 at 736.
[48] *Oceanic Steam Navigation Co.* v. *Sutherberry* (1880) 16 Ch.D. 236.
[49] *Williams* v. *Holland* [1965] 1 W.L.R. 739, also discussing the beneficiary's liability for mesne profits.
[50] L.T.A. 1897, s.2(2); A.E.A. 1925, s.2(1).

provision[51] the personal representatives, for purposes of administration, or during the minority of any beneficiary or the subsistence of any life interest, or until the period of distribution arrives, have—

(i) the same powers and discretions, including power to raise money by mortgage or charge, as a personal representative had before the Act in respect of personal estate; and

(ii) "all the powers, discretions and duties conferred or imposed by law on trustees holding land upon an effectual trust for sale (including power to overreach equitable interests and powers as if the same affected the proceeds of sale)"; and

(iii) "all the powers conferred by statute on trustees for sale."[52]

These powers authorise personal representatives to sell separately the surface of land and the minerals.[53]

3. Powers of sole personal representative. A sole personal representative has the same powers as two or more representatives.[54] The provision of the Acts of 1925, which requires that capital money arising under a trust for sale or under the Settled Land Act 1925 shall always be paid to two trustees or a trust corporation, does not apply to a personal representative *acting as such.*[55] But if under a will or intestacy any beneficiary is a minor, or a life interest arises, the court cannot grant *letters of administration* to one person only (other than to a trust corporation[56]), unless it appears to the court to be expedient in all the circumstances to appoint an individual as sole administrator.[57] This provision does not prevent a sole executor from obtaining probate, though the court has power whenever there is only one individual executor or administrator to appoint one or more additional personal representatives during the minority of a beneficiary or the subsistence of a life interest and until the estate is fully administered.[58] On the other hand, probate or letters of administration cannot be granted to more than four persons in respect of the same property.[59]

---

[51] A.E.A. 1925, s.39, discussed in *Re Trollope's W.T.* [1927] 1 Ch. 596.
[52] For these, see L.P.A. 1925, s.28.
[53] A.E.A. 1925, s.39, as read with T.A. 1925, s.12. Personal representatives had a similar power under L.T.A. 1897: *Re Chaplin and Staffordshire Potteries Waterworks Co. Ltd.'s Contract* [1922] 2 Ch. 824.
[54] A.E.A. 1925, s.2(1).
[55] S.L.A. 1925, s.18(1); L.P.A. 1925, s.27(2), as amended by the L.P.(Am.)A. 1926, Sched.
[56] For trust corporations, see *ante*, p. 199.
[57] S.C.A. 1981, s.114(2), replacing in a wider form J.A. 1925, s.160, and reversing *Re Hall* [1950] P. 156.
[58] S.C.A. 1981, s.114(4).
[59] S.C.A. 1981, s.114(1), replacing J.A. 1925, s.160. This is strictly construed: see *In b. Holland* (1936) 105 L.J.P. 113 (literary executor counted in total).

4. Joint and several powers

(a) *Pure personalty.*   Where there are two or more executors, their authority over pure personalty is several as well as joint, so that one of them can dispose of pure personalty without the concurrence of the others[60]; and this rule probably applies also to joint administrators.[61] Where, however, one personal representative, believing that he has the authority of his colleague, purports to act on behalf of both, the transaction will be invalid if such authority is lacking.[62]

(b) *Land.*   Although one of several executors can enter into a contract to sell freehold or leasehold land,[63] all must concur in the completion of the contract, for no conveyance, assent, mortgage, lease or other assurance[64] can be made without the concurrence of all the personal representatives or under an order of the court.[65] This rule applies to freeholds and, where the deceased died after 1925, to leaseholds.[66] But the concurrence of executors who have not proved the will is not required even if power has been reserved to them to prove[67]; and special personal representatives appointed to act for the purposes of settled land may dispose of the settled land without the concurrence of the general personal representatives, who may likewise dispose of the other property and assets without the concurrence of the special personal representatives.[68]

5. Protection of purchasers.
The Administration of Estates Act 1925 contains useful provisions which confer protection upon purchasers for money or money's worth from the personal representatives.

(a) *Propriety of disposition.*   As regards personalty (including leaseholds) the rule has always been that a person dealing for value with an executor or administrator is not concerned to inquire whether the disposition is a proper one, even if a long time has elapsed since the death[69]; and when the Land Transfer Act 1897 vested the realty in the executor or administrator, this rule became applicable to realty also. But before the Administration of Estates Act 1925 a purchaser who knew

---

[60] *Jacomb* v. *Harwood* (1751) 2 Ves.Sen. 265; *Attenborough* v. *Solomon* [1913] A.C. 76. For the origin of this rule, see 1 Spence's *Equitable Jurisdiction* (1846), p. 578, note (a). For its application to pleadings, see *Warner* v. *Sampson* [1958] 1 Q.B. 404 at 418–421 (reversed on other grounds: [1959] 1 Q.B. 297).
[61] *Fountain Forestry Ltd.* v. *Edwards* [1975] Ch. 1 at 14, reviewing earlier authorities.
[62] *Fountain Forestry Ltd.* v. *Edwards* [1975] Ch. 1.
[63] *Fountain Forestry Ltd.* v. *Edwards, supra,* at p. 12.
[64] See A.E.A. 1925, s.55(1)(iii).
[65] *Ibid.* s.2(2).
[66] See *ibid.* ss.3(1), 54.
[67] *Ibid.* ss.2(2), 8.
[68] *Ibid.* s.24.
[69] *Re Venn and Furze's Contract* [1894] 2 Ch. 101.

that there was no valid reason for the executor selling did not obtain a good title.[70] This has now been altered,[71] so that a conveyance of a legal estate in land[72] by a personal representative will not be invalidated merely because the purchaser had notice that all the debts, liabilities, funeral and testamentary or administration expenses, duties and legacies have been discharged or provided for.

(b) *Previous assent.* Before the Act of 1925, a purchaser did not get a good title if he bought after the executor had assented to a devise or bequest of the property; for on making the assent the executor divested himself of the legal estate.[73] Now, however, a statement in writing by a personal representative that he has not given an assent in respect of a legal estate will protect a purchaser of that legal estate unless there has been a previous disposition made in favour of another purchaser deriving title mediately or immediately under the personal representative, or unless notice of a previous assent or conveyance affecting that estate has been placed on or annexed to the probate or letters of administration.[74] These provisions apply only to conveyances made after 1925, though it is immaterial when the deceased died.

(c) *Revocation of grant.* A purchaser of realty or personalty from a personal representative is not affected by the subsequent revocation of the grant of administration or probate. This is so even if the grant is revoked by reason of the discovery of a will or later will, as the case may be, appointing executors or different executors in whom the property accordingly vested at the death of the deceased. It is immaterial when the deceased died or when the conveyance was made.[75] The principle is that "the person for the time being clothed by the Court of Probate with the character of legal personal representative is the legal personal representative, and enjoys all the powers of a legal personal representative unless and until the grant of [probate or] administration is revoked or has determined."[76]

6. Carrying on business. The general rule is that personal representatives have no authority, merely *virtute officii*, to carry on the business of their testator and to use his estate therein.[77] This proposition, however, requires some amplification.

---

[70] *Re Verrell's Contract* [1903] 1 Ch. 65.
[71] A.E.A. 1925, s.36(8).
[72] See *ibid.* s.55(1)(vii).
[73] *Attenborough* v. *Solomon* [1913] A.C. 76; *Wise* v. *Whitburn* [1924] 1 Ch. 460.
[74] A.E.A. 1925, s.36(6). See, generally, *Williams on Assents* (1947) App. V. See also *post*, p. 346 and *Re Spencer and Hauser's Contract* [1928] Ch. 598.
[75] A.E.A. 1925, s.37, enacting law laid down by *Hewson* v. *Shelley* [1914] 2 Ch. 13; and see *Re Bridgett and Hayes' Contract* [1928] Ch. 163.
[76] *Hewson* v. *Shelley, supra,* at p. 29, *per* Cozens-Hardy M.R.
[77] *Kirkman* v. *Booth* (1848) 11 Beav. 273. For the powers of the Public Trustee to carry on business, see *ante*, p. 209.

(a) *Realisation.* The business may be carried on for the purpose of selling it as a going concern; and as against beneficiaries and creditors alike the personal representatives may indemnify themselves out of the assets of the deceased.[78] It has even been held that a personal representative may contract with himself for his continued employment in the business.[79]

(b) *Power in will.* A testator may either expressly or by implication authorise his personal representatives to carry on his business, as by authorising them to postpone the sale of any part of his estate. Under such a power of postponement, the carrying on of the business may by implication be authorised indefinitely,[80] or merely for a reasonable time.[81] Where a testator gives his personal representatives power to carry on his business, they are entitled to employ in it only such part of the estate as he has expressly made available for the purposes of the business; if he has not expressly stated what part they may use, apparently they can continue to use only the property which was in the business at the date of his death.[82] Personal representatives disregarding these rules are liable to make good any loss incurred thereby.

(c) *Personal liability of personal representatives.* A personal representative is not personally liable on a mere promise by him to carry out a contract which his testator had made.[83] But subject to cases such as that, a personal representative is personally liable on any contracts which he makes: "no contract can be made with an executor which will not charge him personally."[84] A personal representative is accordingly always personally liable for any debts or liabilities incurred in the course of carrying on a business owned by the deceased, and the creditors may obtain judgment against him personally.[85] Two further questions may then arise, namely, whether he has any right of indemnity out of any assets of the deceased, and whether the creditors have any such right, *e.g.* if the personal representative becomes bankrupt.

(1) INDEMNITY. If the will authorised the personal representative to carry on the business, he is entitled to be indemnified out of those assets which the will authorised to be used in the business[86] (*e.g.* those already employed in the business[87]), or, if no limit has been placed on

---

[78] *Dowse* v. *Gorton* [1891] A.C. 190 at 199; and see *Marshall* v. *Broadhurst* (1831) 1 Cr. & J. 403.
[79] *Rowley, Holmes & Co.* v. *Barber* [1977] 1 W.L.R. 371; see (1977) 93 L.Q.R. 323 (qualifying service for redundancy payment).
[80] *Re Crowther* [1895] 2 Ch. 56; but see *Re Smith, Arnold* v. *Smith* [1896] 1 Ch. 171 at 174.
[81] *Re Smith, Arnold* v. *Smith* [1896] 1 Ch. 171; and see *Re Chancellor* (1884) 26 Ch.D. 42.
[82] *McNeillie* v. *Acton* (1853) 4 De G.M. & G. 744; and see *Re White, McCann* v. *Hull* [1958] Ch. 762.
[83] *Powell* v. *Graham* (1817) 7 Taunt. 580.
[84] *Farhall* v. *Farhall* (1871) 7 Ch.App. 123 at 128, *per* Mellish L.J. But the contract may in terms restrict their liability to the assets: see *Muir* v. *City of Glasgow Bank* (1879) 4 App.Cas. 337 at 355, 361, 368, 377, 386, 388; *Re Robinson's Settlement* [1912] 1 Ch. 717 at 721, 728.
[85] *Owen* v. *Delamere* (1872) L.R. 15 Eq. 134.
[86] *Ex p. Garland* (1804) 10 Ves. 110.
[87] *Cutbush* v. *Cutbush* (1839) 1 Beav. 184.

the assets authorised to be employed, out of the whole estate.[88] But otherwise, unless he has carried on the business merely in order to sell it, he has no right of indemnity.[89]

(2) SUBROGATION. If the personal representative has a right of indemnity out of the assets of the deceased, then by subrogation to him his creditors will have a similar right against these assets.[90] This right applies not only to debts but also to any liability for a tort committed by the personal representative in the due carrying on of the business, e.g. by letting down the surface in working a mine.[91] But as the right extends only to the assets against which the personal representative has a right of indemnity, i.e. those which he is authorised to employ in the business, it cannot affect assets which have been transferred to beneficiaries.[92] If the personal representative is himself in default as regards those assets, the creditors, who are only entitled to enforce his right of indemnity, have no claim against the estate.[93] However, where there were three executors and one only of them was in default, the creditors were held entitled to proceed against the estate by reason of the right of indemnity possessed by the two other executors.[94] If an administration order has been made, the creditors can claim interest on their debts, but only from the date of the Master's certificate certifying them.[95]

(d) *Priorities between creditors.* Where a personal representative carries on his testator's business, a question sometimes arises as to the priority of the creditors of the testator and the creditors of the business.

(1) CREDITORS' ASSENT. If the testator's creditors have assented to the carrying on of the business, the personal representative is entitled to be indemnified out of the assets in priority to the testator's creditors; and this right of indemnity is not limited to the portion of the estate which has come into existence or changed its form after the testator's death.[96] In such a case, the business creditors are accordingly by subrogation entitled to priority over the testator's creditors.

(2) NO CREDITORS' ASSENT. If, on the other hand, the testator's creditors have not assented to the business being carried on, they are entitled to be paid first out of the assets which existed at the death, in spite of the testator having empowered his executor to carry on his business; for the testator cannot, by any direction in his will, deprive his

[88] *Dowse* v. *Gorton* [1891] A.C. 190. See also *post,* pp. 691, 692 (receivers).
[89] *Owen* v. *Delamere, supra*; *Strickland* v. *Symons* (1884) 26 Ch.D. 245 (marriage settlement of a lunatic asylum).
[90] *Ex p. Garland, supra.*
[91] *Re Raybould* [1900] 1 Ch. 199.
[92] *Ex p. Garland, supra.*
[93] *Re Johnson, Shearman* v. *Robinson* (1880) 15 Ch.D. 548.
[94] *Re Frith* [1902] 1 Ch. 342.
[95] *Re Bracey* [1936] Ch. 690. For the rate, see *post,* p. 323.
[96] *Dowse* v. *Gorton* [1891] A.C. 190.

creditors of their right to be paid.[97] The testator's creditors will not be postponed merely because they know that the business is being carried on by the executor and do not interfere to stop it[98]; what is required is an "active affirmative assent."[99]

---

[97] *Re Oxley* [1914] 1 Ch. 604; *Re East, London County and Westminster Banking Co. Ltd.* v. *East* (1914) 111 L.T. 101.

[98] *Re Oxley, supra.*

[99] *Vacuum Oil Co. Pty. Ltd.* v. *Wiltshire* (1945) 72 C.L.R. 319 at 330, *per* Latham C.J.; and see at p. 325.

CHAPTER 3

PAYMENT OF DEBTS

Section 1. Duty to Pay

The second duty of the personal representative is to pay the debts of the deceased. He must do this with due diligence, *i.e.* usually within the executor's year.[1] If any debt carries interest, he must also pay that; in other cases, if a judgment or order has directed an account of debts, or the creditor has established his debt in proceedings under a judgment or order, the debt will carry interest at the rate applicable to judgment debts[2] from the date of the judgment or order.[3] It is also the duty of the personal representative to perform all enforceable contracts of the deceased, even if it would be more beneficial to the estate to break them and pay damages for breach.[4]

Section 2. Order of Payment

1. Insolvent estates. If the estate is solvent, the personal representative must pay all the debts. But if it is insolvent he should take care to observe the prescribed order; for if he pays a debt of lower degree knowing that a debt of higher degree is unpaid, the payment will amount to an admission of assets and he will be personally liable to pay the debt of higher degree.[5] An estate is insolvent if, when realised, it

---

[1] See *ante*, p. 310.

[2] Before April 20, 1971, the rate was 4 per cent.: Judgments Act 1838, s.17. It is now regulated by orders under Administration of Justice 1970, s.44, and is currently (since April 16, 1985) 15 per cent. (S.I. 1985 No. 437). From April 20, 1971, the rate was 7½ per cent., from March 1, 1977, 10 per cent., from December 3, 1979, 12½ per cent., from June 9, 1980, 15 per cent., from June 8, 1982, 14 per cent., and from November 10, 1982, 12 per cent.: S.I. 1971 No. 491; S.I. 1977 No. 141; S.I. 1979 No. 1382; S.I. 1980 No. 672; S.I. 1982 Nos. 696, 1427.

[3] R.S.C., Ord. 44, r. 9.

[4] *Ahmed Angullia Bin Hadjee Mohamed Salleh Angullia* v. *Estate and Trust Agencies (1927) Ltd.* [1938] A.C. 624. And see *Cooper* v. *Jarman* (1866) L.R. 3 Eq. 98; *Re Rushbrook's W.T.* [1948] Ch. 421.

[5] 2 Bl.Comm. 511; and see *Britton* v. *Batthurst* (1683) 3 Lev. 113; *Rock* v. *Layton* (1700) 1 Ld.Raym. 589.

will be unable to meet all the debts and liabilities to which it is subject,[6] including the costs of administration.[7]

2. Types of administration. An insolvent estate may be administered in bankruptcy or otherwise than in bankruptcy. It is administered in bankruptcy if insolvency proceedings which were on foot at the date of death are continued thereafter[8] or if a creditor or the personal representative obtains an insolvency administration order.[9] If, however, the estate is administered out of court or in the Chancery Division or the county court, it is said to be administered otherwise than in bankruptcy even though it is insolvent.

3. Differences. Before 1926 there was considerable complication as to the order in which the debts of an insolvent estate had to be paid.[10] In 1925, however, a uniform set of rules was laid down for this aspect of the administration for all cases in which the debtor died after that year, however and wherever the administration was taking place.[11] Yet there are some minor differences noted below.[12]

4. Statutory provisions. The provisions now in force are contained in the Insolvency Act 1986 and statutory instruments made thereunder. Where the estate is being administered otherwise than in bankruptcy it is expressly provided that, subject to the funeral, testamentary and administration expenses having priority "the same provisions as may be in force for the time being under the law of bankruptcy with respect to the assets of individuals adjudged bankrupt shall apply to the administration of the estate with respect to the respective rights of secured and unsecured creditors, to debts and liabilities provable, to the valuation of future and contingent liabilities and to the priority of debts and other payments."[13] If the administration of the insolvent estate is taking place in bankruptcy, the relevant provisions of the Insolvency Act

---

[6] Insolvency Act 1986, s.421(4).
[7] See *Re Leng, Tarn* v. *Emmerson* [1895] 1 Ch. 652.
[8] See Administration of Insolvent Estates of Deceased Persons Order 1986 (S.I. 1986 No. 1999), art. 5(1).
[9] See *post*, p. 352.
[10] See *e.g. Re Heywood* [1897] 2 Ch. 593 at 598.
[11] A.E.A. 1925, s.34; 1st Sched., Pt. I, essentially reproducing J.A. 1875, s.10, and extending it from administrations in bankruptcy to administrations in all courts and out of court. See *post*, p. 351. These provisions of A.E.A. 1925 were repealed by the Insolvency Act 1985, s.235(3), Sched. 10, Pt. III.
[12] *Post*, p. 329.
[13] S.I. 1986 No. 1999, art. 3(1), Sched. 1, Pt. I, Table and Pt. II, paras. 24, 34 as to priorities; the other matters mentioned in the text are for the most part dealt with in the Insolvency Rules 1986 (S.I. No. 1925) applied by S.I. 1986 No. 199, art. 3.

apply with such modifications as are necessitated by the fact of the insolvent person being dead.[14]

A. The Bankruptcy Rules of Priority

The general rule in bankruptcy is that all creditors must be paid *pari passu*. A judgment creditor has no priority as such, and so cannot keep the fruits of a garnishee order.[15] But there are certain debts which are preferred and others which are deferred.[16] As a result, the order for payment is as follows.

1. Administration expenses: reasonable funeral,[17] testamentary and administration expenses.[18] "Testamentary expenses" are the "expenses incident to the proper performance of the duty of an executor."[19]

2. Specially preferred debts: debts preferred by special statutes, namely, money due to a friendly society,[20] or to a savings bank,[21] from their officers.

3. Preferential debts: debts preferred by the Insolvency Act[22] itself, namely,

(a) *Debts due to Inland Revenue*: "P.A.Y.E." deductions which the deceased should have made from emoluments paid during the period of 12 months before his death[23]; also, deductions which he should have made during that period from payments to sub-contractors in the construction industry.

(b) *Debts due to Customs and Excise*: V.A.T. referable to the period of six months before the death; car tax which became due during the 12 months before death; also, certain betting, gaming and bingo duties which became due during the 12-month period.

---

[14] *Ibid.*, art. 3(1).
[15] *Pritchard* v. *Westminster Bank Ltd.* [1969] 1 W.L.R. 547. In cases of doubt the court will order an inquiry as to the insolvency of the estate and order the garnishee to pay the debt into court: *George Lee & Sons (Builders) Ltd.* v. *Olink* [1972] 1 W.L.R. 214.
[16] Insolvency Act 1986, ss.328, 329, 386, Sched. 6.
[17] "Those which are reasonable, having regard to the positions of the deceased": *Re Walter* [1929] 1 Ch. 647 at 655, *per* Tomlin J.
[18] S.I. 1986 No. 1999, art. 4(2).
[19] *Sharp* v. *Lush* (1879) 10 Ch.D. 468 at 470, *per* Jessel M.R.
[20] Friendly Societies Act 1974, s.59.
[21] Trustee Savings Bank Act 1981, s.45, replacing earlier Acts.
[22] ss.328(1), (2), 386, Sched. 6. The list differs in several respects from that which was applicable under the Bankruptcy Act 1914, s.33, as amended: see the 28th edition of this work, pp. 321, 322.
[23] The date of death is "the relevant date" for the purposes of the Insolvency Act 1986, Sched. 6, in its application to the estates of deceased persons: see *ibid.* s.387(6); S.I. 1986, No. 1999, art. 3(1), Sched. 1, Part II, para. 35.

(c) *Social Security contributions*: sums which became due on account of Class 1 or Class 2 contributions under the Social Security Act 1975 during the 12-month period; and Class 4 contributions assessed on the deceased up to April 5 next before his death, but not exceeding one year's assessment.

(d) *Contributions to occupational pension schemes*: debts to which Schedule 3 of the Social Security Pensions Act 1975 applies.

(e) *Remuneration of employees:* wages, salary or commission (including holiday remuneration and sick pay) of any employee of the deceased in respect of the whole or part of the period of four months before the death, not exceeding £800.[24]

These five classes rank equally between themselves.[25] If a landlord has distrained on any goods or effects of the deceased within three months before his death, these preferential debts are a first charge on the goods or effects so distrained on, or the proceeds of sale thereof[26]; but in respect of any goods or effects surrendered or money paid under any such charge, the landlord is a preferential creditor as against ordinary and deferred creditors.[27]

4. Ordinary debts: all other debts *pari passu.*[28]

5. Deferred debts: debts deferred by particular statutes, namely,

(a) *Credit provided to spouse*: debts owed in respect of credit provided by a person who (whether or not the deceased's spouse at the time the credit was provided) was his or her spouse at the date of death.[29] By contrast with the law in force prior to the Insolvency Act[30] the loan does not have to be made for the purpose of the borrower's trade or business.

(b) *Loan varying with profits*: money lent to the deceased on a contract that the lender should receive a rate of interest varying with the profits of the deceased's business or a share of the profits of the business.[31]

---

[24] The sum fixed by S.I. 1986 No. 1996, art. 4, pursuant to Insolvency Act 1986, s.418.
[25] Insolvency Act 1986, s.328(2).
[26] *Ibid.* s.347(2), (3); S.I. 1986 No. 1999, art. 3(1), Sched. 1, Pt. II, para. 28.
[27] *Ibid.* s.347(4).
[28] *Ibid.*, s.328(3).
[29] *Ibid.* s.329. On a wife's "equity of exoneration," see *Re Pittortou (A Bankrupt)* [1985] 1 W.L.R. 58.
[30] Bankruptcy Act 1914, s.36(1), (2).
[31] Partnership Act 1890, s.3. *Cf. Re Meade* [1951] Ch. 774.

(c) *Vendor's share of profits*: money due to the seller of the good-will of a business in respect of a share of the profits which the deceased when buying the business contracted to pay.[32]

All these three claims are postponed until all other debts for valuable consideration have been satisfied.

B. Other Bankruptcy Rules: All Administrations

1. Secured creditors. As regards secured creditors, the old rule in Chancery was that a secured creditor might both exercise his rights under his security and also prove against the general estate for the *whole* amount of his debt, provided he did not receive more than the full amount of his debt.[33] Now, however, he must elect between—

(i) resting on his security and waiting to be redeemed;

(ii) realising his security and proving for the deficiency, if any;

(iii) valuing his security and proving for the deficiency, if any; and

(iv) surrendering his security and proving for the whole amount of his debt.[34]

2. Claims provable. The general rule is that all debts and liabilities are provable, whether present or future, certain or contingent, ascertained or sounding only in damages.[35] Thus a proof can be lodged for the deceased's liability under a covenant to pay an annuity,[36] even if it is payable only during life or widowhood[37] or *dum casta fuerit*[38]; and the same applies to a contingent liability in respect of possible future calls on shares in a company held by the deceased.[39] The value of any debt which, by reason of its being subject to any contingency, or for any other reason, does not bear a certain value is estimated by the trustee of the insolvent estate,[40] subject to an appeal to the court by any person dissatisfied with his valuation.[41]

---

[32] Partnership Act 1890, s.3.
[33] *Mason* v. *Bogg* (1837) 2 My. & Cr. 443.
[34] *Re Hopkins, Williams* v. *Hopkins* (1881) 18 Ch.D. 370, applying J.A. 1873, s.10; Insolvency Rules 1986 (S.I. No. 1925), rr. 6.109, 6.115–119, applied by S.I. 1986 No. 1999, art. 3(1).
[35] S.I. 1986 No. 1925, r. 12.3(1).
[36] *Re Bridges* (1881) 17 Ch.D. 342; *Re Hargreaves* (1890) 44 Ch.D. 236; *Re Pink, Elvin* v. *Nightingale* [1927] 1 Ch. 237.
[37] *Re Blakemore* (1877) 5 Ch.D. 372; contrast *Dunbar* v. *Dunbar*, 190 U.S. 340 (1903).
[38] *Ex p. Neal, Re Batey* (1880) 14 Ch.D. 579, an embarrassing jurisdiction.
[39] *Re McMahon* [1900] 1 Ch. 173.
[40] Insolvency Act 1986, s.322(3).
[41] *Ibid.* s.303(1).

Before the Law Reform (Miscellaneous Provisions) Act 1934, no claim could be made against the estate in respect of unliquidated damages arising otherwise than by reason of a contract, promise or breach of trust.[42] But by section 1[43] of that Act (the details of which are outside the scope of this book) all causes of action survive against the estate, except for defamation, and thus are debts deemed to be provable in the administration.[44] The ordinary rules as to limitation of actions now apply to such actions.[45]

Certain debts are not provable. These are: any fine imposed for an offence; any obligation under an order made in family or domestic proceedings; and any obligation under a confiscation order made under section 1 of the Drug Trafficking Offences Act 1986.[46]

3. Interest on debts. The bankruptcy rules apply to interest on debts, so that where a debt carries interest, that interest is payable as part of the debt at the contractual rate[47]; and in certain exceptional cases interest at the rate applicable to judgment debts[48] may be proved for even though the debt did not carry interest by contract.[49] This applies to interest up to the date of an insolvency administration order.[50] In the distribution of the estate, interest from the death is allowed only if there is a surplus after payment of the preferential and ordinary debts. Such a surplus is applied in payment of interest on those debts, which for this purpose rank equally with each other, before the deferred debts are paid[51]; and the rate of interest allowed is whichever is the greater of the contractual rate (if any) and the judgment debt rate in force at the date of death.[52]

4. Set-off. The bankruptcy rule as to set-off applies in the administration of the insolvent estate of a deceased person. Accordingly, where there have been mutual credits, mutual debts or other mutual dealings between the debtor and any creditor proving, the sum due from

---

[42] Bankruptcy Act 1914, s.30(1).

[43] As amended by Law Reform (Miscellaneous Provisions) Act 1970, Sched.

[44] Formerly actions for damages for seduction or adultery were also secluded, but such actions were abolished on January 1, 1971: Law Reform (Miscellaneous Provisions) Act 1970, ss.4, 5.

[45] See Proceedings against Estates Act 1970, s.1, which came into force on January 1, 1971, but was repealed as obsolete by Statute Law (Repeals) Act 1986, s.1(1), Sched. 1, Pt. I. For the law prior to 1971 see the 28th edition of this work, p. 324, especially at n. 44.

[46] S.I. 1986, No. 1925, r. 12.3(2). For other debts made provable only when all other creditors have been paid in full, see *ibid.* r. 12.3(2A), inserted by S.I. 1987 No. 1919, art. 3, Sched., para. 143.

[47] Insolvency Act 1986, s.322(2).

[48] *Ante*, p. 323, n. 2.

[49] S.I. 1986 No. 1925, r. 6.113, with amendments and additions made by S.I. 1987 No. 1919, art. 3, Sched., para. 112: debts due under a written instrument and payable at a certain time; debts for which a written demand has been made.

[50] Insolvency Act 1986, s.322(2); S.I. 1986 No. 1999, art. 3(1), Sched. 1, Pt. I, Table, Pt. II, para. 23.

[51] Insolvency Act 1986, s.328(4); S.I. 1986 No. 1999, art. 3(1), Sched. 1, Pt. II, para. 24.

[52] Insolvency Act 1986, s.328(5); S.I. 1986 No. 1999, art. 3(1), Sched. 1, Pt. II, para. 24.

the one party is to be set off against any sum due from the other party, and only the balance of the account is to be claimed or paid on either side respectively.[53]

C. Administrations in Bankruptcy

The four bankruptcy rules which have just been discussed apply to an insolvent estate whether or not it is being administered in bankruptcy. Other bankruptcy rules are of more restricted application.

1. Rules swelling assets. Before the Insolvency Act 1986 certain rules which went merely to swell the assets to be administered did not apply to the administration of a deceased person's estate: the only property to be administered was that which was his at the date of his death, and property vested in another person could not be brought into the estate.[54] Now, however, the bankruptcy rules relating to transactions at an undervalue,[55] preferences,[56] executions and attachments not completed before an insolvency administration order,[57] and transactions defrauding creditors[58] have all been made applicable where an insolvent estate is being administered in bankruptcy,[59] but not otherwise.

2. Limitation of landlord's distress. In bankruptcy, a landlord who distrains after the commencement of the bankruptcy is not allowed to keep more than six months' rent accrued due before such commencement.[60] Where the tenant is dead, this rule applies only if his estate is being administered in bankruptcy[61]; in other cases, the landlord is entitled to distrain and to recover in this way any rent which accrued due within the preceding six years,[62] or, if the holding is an agricultural one, within the preceding year.[63] But if he distrains within the three months next before the tenant's death, he will have to pay out the debts preferred by the Insolvency Act 1986.[64]

---

[53] Insolvency Act 1986, s.323; S.I. 1986 No. 1999, art. 3(1), Sched. 1, Pt. II, para. 23. See further *National Westminster Bank Ltd.* v. *Halesowen Presswork & Assemblies Ltd.* [1972] A.C. 785 (rule cannot be excluded by agreement).
[54] See the 28th edition of this work, pp. 324, 325.
[55] Insolvency Act 1986, ss.339, 341, 342; *ante*, pp. 134, 135.
[56] *Ibid.* ss.340–342.
[57] *Ibid.* s.346.
[58] *Ibid.* ss.423–425, *ante*, pp. 130–132.
[59] S.I. 1986 No. 1999, art. 3(1), Sched. 1, Pt. II, paras. 26, 28, 36.
[60] Insolvency Act 1986, s.347(1).
[61] S.I. 1986 No. 1999, art. 3(1), Sched. 1, Pt. II, para. 28.
[62] Limitation Act 1980, s.19.
[63] Agricultural Holdings Act 1986, s.16, replacing Agricultural Holdings Act 1948, s.18.
[64] s.347(2), (3); for preferential debts, see *ante*, p. 325.

3. Discharge of irrecoverable claims. In bankruptcy an order to pay an irrecoverable claim may be made against the trustee in bankruptcy, for he is an officer of the court and "the Court of Bankruptcy ought to be as honest as other people."[65] This is known as the rule in *Ex p. James*, where money demanded by the trustee and paid to him under a mistake of law was ordered to be repaid.[66] The rule does not apply to a personal representative for, unlike a trustee in bankruptcy, he is not an officer of the court. Thus, where a solicitor died insolvent after receiving money from a client for payment of counsel's fees, the court refused to order his executor to pay the fees to counsel.[67]

Section 3. Payment of Statute-barred Debts

1. Right to pay. A personal representative cannot be required to plead the Statutes of Limitation against a claim which is otherwise well founded,[68] for this might "be doing an unrighteous and improper thing."[69] Accordingly, if he thinks fit[70] he may pay a statute-barred debt, provided that (as is now the case with all ordinary debts[71]) the statute has only barred the remedy and has not extinguished the debt itself. He may pay such a debt even if this will throw a burden on to part of the estate which otherwise would have escaped.[72] But he may not pay a debt for which no action could ever have been maintained, as, for instance, money due under an oral contract requiring to be made or evidenced in writing[73]; nor may he pay a statute-barred debt after the court has declared that it is statute-barred, for this would be disregarding *res judicata*.[74]

2. Effect of order for administration. After an order or judgment for administration, the executor may no longer voluntarily pay a statute-barred debt unless it is owed to the plaintiff in the administration action; for with this exception the other creditors or anyone interested in the estate may object to its payment.[75] Further, even if no order for administration has been pronounced, anyone interested in the estate

---

[65] *Ex p. James* (1874) 9 Ch.App. 609 at 614, *per* James L.J.
[66] *Ex p. James* (1874) 9 Ch.App. 609.
[67] *Re Sandiford (No. 2)* [1935] Ch. 681.
[68] *Norton* v. *Frecker* (1737) 1 Atk. 524 at 526.
[69] *Stahlschmidt* v. *Lett* (1853) 1 Sm. & G. 415 at 419, *per* Stuart V.-C.
[70] *Quaere* whether one executor can pay such a debt over the dissent of his co-executors: see *Midgley* v. *Midgley* [1893] 3 Ch. 282.
[71] Limitation Act 1980, ss.6, 20 (compare s.17); but see *C. & M. Matthews Ltd.* v. *Marsden B.S.* [1951] Ch. 758 at 768, 769. Formerly a debt charged on land (but not any other debt) was extinguished altogether by the lapse of time.
[72] *Lowis* v. *Rumney* (1867) L.R. 4 Eq. 451.
[73] *Re Rownson* (1885) 29 Ch.D. 358 (on which see now Law Reform (Enforcement of Contracts) Act 1954, s.1).
[74] *Midgley* v. *Midgley* [1893] 3 Ch. 282.
[75] *Briggs* v. *Wilson* (1854) 5 De G.M. & G. 12 at 21; *Moodie* v. *Bannister* (1859) 4 Drew. 432.

may object to the payment if proceedings for the court's directions are pending.[76] The court may, however, allow a personal representative to pay a statute-barred debt if no person interested in the estate objects. Moreover, if a foreign judgment is obtained against the executors on a debt that is statute-barred here, the creditor may claim in the administration here upon an implied obligation to satisfy the judgment.[77]

Section 4. Preference and Retainer by Personal Representatives

1. Preference. Formerly, as among creditors in equal degree, an executor had a right to prefer one creditor to another, paying one in full even if it left nothing for the other. This right of preference came to an end if an order was made for the administration of the estate or a receiver was appointed.[78]

2. Retainer. Retainer is the name for the executor's former right to pay his own debt in full in preference to other creditors of equal degree with himself.[79] It was not lost by an order for administration or the appointment of a receiver, for the right was based on the collection and possession of assets by the executor, and his inability to sue himself.[80]

3. Abolition. The rights of preference and retainer were abolished as from January 1, 1972.[81] Nevertheless, if in good faith and with no reason for believing the estate to be insolvent a personal representative pays a debt to any creditor (including himself, unless he is a creditor-administrator), he is not liable to account for the sum so paid to creditors of the same degree as the creditor who has been paid.[82]

Section 5. Order of Application of Assets

If the estate of the deceased is more than sufficient to pay the debts in full the estate is solvent, but what is left may be insufficient to provide for all the gifts in the will. The personal representatives need to know in

[76] *Re Wenham* [1892] 3 Ch. 59. See *post*, p. 356 for such proceedings.
[77] *Re Flynn (No. 2)* [1969] 2 Ch. 403.
[78] For preference, see the 26th edition (1966) of this book, pp. 344, 345.
[79] For a different right of retainer, see *post*, p. 348.
[80] For retainer, see the 26th edition (1966) of this book, pp. 345–349.
[81] A.E.A. 1971, ss.10(1), 14(2).
[82] *Ibid.* s.10(2).

what order they are to resort to the items in the estate for the payment of debts, and thus which of the beneficiaries are to suffer.[83]

A. *Before* 1926

If the deceased died before 1926, the general rule established by case law was that the personalty had to be resorted to before the realty. The general personal estate was primarily liable, unless exempted by express words or necessary implication.[84]

B. *After* 1925

1. The statutory order. Where the death occurs after 1925, the order of administration is governed by the Administration of Estates Act 1925. This provides[85] that "where the estate of a deceased person is solvent his real and personal estate shall, subject to rules of court and the provisions hereinafter contained as to charges on property of the deceased,[86] and to the provisions, if any, contained in his will,[87] be applicable towards the discharge of the funeral, testamentary and administration expenses, debts and liabilities payable thereout" in the following order.[88]

(1) *Property undisposed of*: "property of the deceased undisposed of by will, subject to the retention thereout of a fund sufficient to meet any pecuniary legacies."[89]

(2) *Residuary gift*: "property of the deceased not specifically devised or bequeathed but included (either by a specific or general description) in a residuary gift, subject to the retention out of such property of a fund sufficient to meet any pecuniary legacies, so far as not provided for as aforesaid." For this purpose a gift of "all my real estate" is a residuary gift, even if there is no other gift of realty.[90] Yet the will may make the legacies payable out of the personalty rather than the realty, as where a gift of legacies is followed by a gift of "all my" realty and "the residue of my" personalty.[91]

---

[83] For a similar question as to the properties out of which legacies are to be paid, see *post*, p. 365.

[84] *Duke of Ancaster* v. *Mayer* (1785) 1 Bro.C.C. 454; **1 W. & T.L.C. 1**; *Trott* v. *Buchannan* (1884) 28 Ch.D. 446. For details, see 19th edition of this work (1925), pp. 249–253, and notes to 1 W. & T.L.C. 1.

[85] s.34(3); 1st Sched., Pt. II.

[86] See *post*, p. 337.

[87] As in *Re Martin, Midland Bank Executor and Trustee Co. Ltd.* v. *Marfleet* [1955] Ch. 698 and *Re Feis* [1964] Ch. 106.

[88] A.E.A. 1925, 1st Sched., Pt. II.

[89] See, however, *post*, p. 365.

[90] *Re Wilson, Wilson* v. *Mackay* [1967] Ch. 53, not following *Re Ridley* [1950] Ch. 415.

[91] *Re Wilson, Wilson* v. *Mackay, supra.*

(3) *Property given for payment of debts*: "property of the deceased specifically appropriated or devised or bequeathed (either by a specific or general description) for the payment of debts."

(4) *Property charged with debts*: "property of the deceased charged with, or devised or bequeathed (either by a specific or general description) subject to a charge for the payment of debts."

(5) *Pecuniary legacy fund*: "the fund, if any, retained to meet pecuniary legacies."

(6) *Specific gifts*: "property specifically devised or bequeathed, rateably according to value."

(7) *Property appointed under general power*: "property appointed by will under a general power, including the statutory power to dispose of entailed interests, rateably according to value."

It is also provided that "the order of application may be varied by the will of the deceased," and that these provisions do not "affect the liability of land to answer the death duty imposed thereon in exoneration of other assets."[92]

2. Features of the new order

(a) *No distinction between realty and personalty.* The outstanding feature of the new order is that no distinction is drawn between realty and personalty. This is in accordance with the general principle of the Acts of 1925 to assimilate the law of real and personal property.[93]

(b) *Property undisposed of placed first.* Another noticeable feature is that property undisposed of (including undisposed-of income[94]) is resorted to before property comprised in a residuary gift. Thus a testator may have bequeathed his residuary personalty without devising his realty. Moreover, property undisposed of is not confined to property which the will has omitted to mention but also includes property with which the will has dealt ineffectively, *e.g.* where part of a residuary gift has lapsed. Thus if a testator gave the residue equally to be divided between his two nephews, A and B, and A died before the testator, the gift of A's share of residue lapsed; the will has therefore not effectively disposed of that share, and so, unless the will showed a contrary intention, that share will be resorted to for the payment of debts before B's share.

A mere direction to pay debts is not a sufficient contrary intention.[95] It is otherwise, however, if by the terms of the will the amount of the

---

[92] A.E.A. 1925, 1st Sched., Pt. II, para. 8.

[93] See, however, *post*, p. 366.

[94] *Re Tong* [1931] 1 Ch. 202; and see *Re Gillett's W.T.* [1950] Ch. 102.

[95] *Re Lamb* [1929] 1 Ch. 722. See the criticism in *Re Kempthorne* [1930] 1 Ch. 268 at 298; but see *Re Sanger* [1939] Ch. 238 at 249.

property undisposed of is to be ascertained only after payment of debts,[96] *e.g.* where residue is given "subject to and after" payment of debts,[97] or "subject to" payment of debts,[98] or "after all my debts, and funeral, and expenses are paid,"[99] and there is a lapse of a share of the residue thus ascertained; in such cases the statutory order is displaced by a clear contrary intention. In the latter class of case "there is an express charge of the specified items upon the subject-matter of the gift, while in the other class there is merely a direction to pay the specified items unsupported by any charge express or to be implied."[1] In this context a direction to pay one class of liabilities (*e.g.* testamentary expenses) will readily be construed as including other classes (*e.g.* administration expenses).[2]

(c) *Property specifically appropriated placed third.* It seems curious that property specifically appropriated for payment of debts is placed third and not first on the list. The order of application may be varied by the testator, and if he specifically appropriates property for payment of debts, it might have been supposed that such property would be liable before the residue. Before the Act of 1925, when the general *personalty* was the primary fund, the rule was that a specific appropriation of *personalty* for payment of debts made the appropriated personalty the first fund, but that an appropriation of *realty* for payment of debts made the realty only a secondary fund.[3] The reason was that at common law realty was not available for the payment of ordinary debts, and so if the will made the realty liable for them, this was construed as making the realty liable only if the personalty did not suffice.

Now that the general personalty and the general realty are placed together as the primary fund, it might be thought that a specific appropriation of any property would make it the primary fund. However, such property appears third on the list, and the words which appropriate the property for payment of debts will not by themselves show a contrary intention sufficient to displace the statutory order, for otherwise such property would never occupy the third place assigned to it by the Act.[4] What is required to vary the order here is some additional indication, such as an intention to exonerate some other fund.[5] Thus where there is a residuary gift, the appropriation of property for the payment of debts will readily be held to have ousted the statutory order and made that property liable before property which passes under the residuary gift[6] or is undisposed of by reason of the gift

---

Re Petty [1929] 1 Ch. 726; and see *Re Cruse* [1930] W.N. 206.
[97] *Re Kempthorne* [1930] 1 Ch. 268.
[98] *Re Harland-Peck* [1941] Ch. 182.
[99] *Re Berrey's W.T.* [1959] 1 W.L.R. 30.
[1] *Re Harland-Peck, supra,* at p. 190, *per curiam* (Luxmoore L.J.).
[2] *Re Taylor's Estate and W.T.* [1969] 2 Ch. 245.
[3] *Re Banks* [1905] 1 Ch. 547; *Kilford* v. *Blaney* (1885) 31 Ch.D. 56; *Dacre* v. *Patrickson* (1860) 1 Dr. & Sm. 186.
[4] See *Re Kempthorne* [1930] 1 Ch. 268 at 278.
[5] *Re James, Lloyds Bank Ltd.* v. *Atkins* [1947] Ch. 256. *Cf. Re Ridley* [1950] Ch. 415 (competition between two residuary gifts). Contrast *post*, p. 340.
[6] *Re Littlewood* [1931] 1 Ch. 443; *Re James, supra*; *Re Meldrum* [1952] Ch. 208.

lapsing.[7] But where there is no residuary gift, the statutory order will apply, and property not disposed of will be resorted to before property appropriated for the payment of debts.[8]

(d) *Specific gifts.* The position of property specifically bequeathed or devised depends on whether or not it is charged with debts. If it is, it is resorted to before the pecuniary legacy fund; otherwise it comes sixth on the list.

(1) "CHARGED." A charge may be express or implied. Thus before 1926 it was held that a mere general direction in the will that the debts should be paid had the effect of charging them on the realty, and that the Land Transfer Act 1897, which vested the realty in the executors, made no difference in this respect[9]; if the will contained such a direction to pay debts, realty devised had to be resorted to for payment of debts before the fund available for payment of pecuniary legacies.[10] On the other hand, a mere direction that debts should be paid did not charge them on a specific legacy so as to make the specific legacy liable for debts before pecuniary legacies. The reason was that in its anxiety to secure payment of a testator's debts the court seized hold of the slightest indication of an intention on his part that his realty should be used to pay his debts. How the order is affected by a general direction to pay debts remains to be decided.

(2) "RATEABLY ACCORDING TO VALUE." Where there are two or more specific gifts, they are liable to be resorted to "rateably according to value."[11] This means according to "the value to the testator,"[12] so that, *e.g.* the probate values will be taken, and not the prices at which the properties are later sold.[13] Similarly, if Blackacre, which is subject to a mortgage, is devised to A, and Whiteacre is given to B subject to the payment of certain legacies thereout, in deciding what proportion of the debts each property must bear the mortgage must be deducted from the value of Blackacre but not the legacies from the value of Whiteacre.[14]

(e) *Property appointed under general power.* To the extent to which it is appointed by the will,[15] property subject to a general testamentary power of appointment vests in the testator's personal representatives[16] as part of his assets so as to be subject to the demands of all his creditors in preference to the claim of the appointee. Even if the

---

[7] *Re Atkinson, Webster* v. *Walter* [1930] 1 Ch. 47; and see *Re Petty* [1929] 1 Ch. 726.
[8] *Re Gordon, Watts* v. *Rationalist Press Association Ltd.* [1940] Ch. 769.
[9] *Re Kempster* [1906] 1 Ch. 446.
[10] *Re Roberts, Roberts* v. *Roberts* [1902] 2 Ch. 834.
[11] A.E.A. 1925, 1st Sched., Pt. II, para. 6; and see *Tombs* v. *Roch* (1846) 2 Coll.C.C. 490; *Re Cohen, National Provincial Bank Ltd.* v. *Katz (No. 2)* [1960] Ch. 179.
[12] *Re John* [1933] Ch. 370 at 372, *per* Farwell J.
[13] *Re Cohen, National Provincial Bank Ltd.* v. *Katz (No. 2), supra.*
[14] *Re John* [1933] Ch. 370; and see *Re Saunders-Davies* (1887) 34 Ch.D. 482; *Re Bawden* [1894] 1 Ch. 693.
[15] *Re Hodgson, Darley* v. *Hodgson* [1899] 1 Ch. 666.
[16] See *O'Grady* v. *Wilmot* [1916] 2 A.C. 231.

appointee is a creditor who lent money to the testator upon the faith of a covenant by the testator to exercise the power of appointment by will in his favour, he has no priority over the other creditors.[17] If the appointment fails, the property appointed will still be assets for payment of the appointor's debts, provided that he has shown an intention to take the property out of the power and make it his own to all intents. If he has done so, any lapsed part of it will go as part of his estate and not to the person entitled in default of appointment.[18] The mere appointment of an executor will not amount to the exercise of a general power of appointment[19]; yet if the testator gives legacies, and his own estate is insufficient for the payment of such legacies in full after all his debts are paid, the simple appointment of an executor will operate to exercise the general power of appointment to the extent required for the payment of the debts and legacies.[20]

If a general power is exercised merely by a general residuary gift[21] of the testator's property, whether realty or personalty or both, the appointed property will, it seems, come second on the list,[22] whereas if there is an express appointment it will come last.

(f) *Property not mentioned.* The statutory list does not mention property appointed by *deed* under a general power. Such property, however, is equitable assets for the payment of the appointor's debts, at any rate if the deed operates to transfer the property to the appointee only on the appointor's death and not immediately.[23] For this purpose a power is "general" notwithstanding that an appointment can be made only with the consent of certain persons.[24] Again, the list does not mention the benefit of an option given to a beneficiary to purchase property for less than its true value. Neither the option nor the difference between the option price and the true value is a specific gift for the purpose of the list, and so the property subject to the option is the last to be available for payment of debts.[25]

3. Marshalling

(a) *Need to marshal.* The order in which the various assets of a deceased person are to be applied for the payment of his debts[26] regulates the administration of these assets only as between the various persons beneficially entitled to the deceased's estate; it does not affect the rights of the creditors themselves, who may resort indiscriminately

---

[17] *Beyfus* v. *Lawley* [1903] A.C. 411.
[18] *Shaw* v. *Marten* [1902] 1 Ch. 314; *Re Vander Byl* [1931] 1 Ch. 216.
[19] *Re Thurston* (1886) 32 Ch.D. 508; *Re Lambert's Estate* (1888) 39 Ch.D. 626.
[20] *Re Seabrook* [1911] 1 Ch. 151.
[21] *e.g.* under the Wills Act 1837, s.27.
[22] See *Re Hartley* [1900] 1 Ch. 152 (rule as stated applied to personalty before 1926).
[23] *Re Phillips* [1931] 1 Ch. 347.
[24] *Re Phillips, supra,* distinguished in *Re Watts* [1931] 2 Ch. 302.
[25] *Re Eve* [1956] Ch. 479. And see *post,* p. 385 (*donatio mortis causa*).
[26] See *post,* p. 421, for marshalling as between mortgagees.

to all or any of the assets. It may therefore happen that the assets are not applied in their proper order for payment of the debts. The disturbing action of creditors will give rise to a case for marshalling.

(b) *The principle.*   The general principle of marshalling is that if any beneficiary is disappointed of his benefit under the will through a creditor being paid out of the property intended for that beneficiary, then to the extent of the disappointment the beneficiary may recoup or compensate himself by going against any property which ought to have been used to pay the debts before resort was had to his property.[27] And if the property out of which he recoups himself is not the primary fund for payment of the debts, the person to whom that property was given may in his turn claim recoupment out of any other property which ought to have borne the burden before his. The debts are thus ultimately borne by the different properties in the right order. This doctrine has not been affected by the Administration of Estates Act 1925.[28]

(c) *Illustration.*   For example, if the pecuniary legacy fund (the fifth category) is exhausted in paying debts, the legatees may, to the extent of those debts, resort to the third category (property given for the payment of debts), or the fourth category (property charged with debts), but not the sixth category (specific gifts).[29] The amount of compensation to which they are entitled is the value of the interest of which they are disappointed; so that in the case of a legacy of shares given to a minor contingently on his attaining 21, if the shares are sold to pay debts, the compensation will be the value of the shares when the minor attains 21.[30]

C. Charges on Property

1. Original right to take free.   Until statute intervened, a person who became entitled under a will or intestacy to land[31] or other property[32] that was subject to a mortgage or charge could call on the personal representatives to pay it off out of the deceased's estate in the same way as other debts owed by the deceased.[33] This right was subject to any contrary intention expressed in any will of the deceased.[34] The right applied only if the deceased was the original mortgagor and so was personally liable on a covenant to pay the debt[35]; it did not apply where

[27] This passage was quoted and applied in *Re Matthews' W.T.* [1961] 1 W.L.R. 1415 at 1419.
[28] See s.2(3).
[29] See *Re Wilson, Wilson* v. *Mackay* [1967] Ch. 53 at 72; for the order, see *ante*, pp. 332, 333.
[30] *Re Broadwood* [1911] 1 Ch. 277.
[31] *Bartholomew* v. *May* (1737) 1 Atk. 487.
[32] *Bothamley* v. *Sherson* (1875) L.R. 20 Eq. 304.
[33] But see *Re Butler* [1894] 3 Ch. 250 as to debts charged on realty.
[34] *Hancox* v. *Abbey* (1805) 11 Ves. 179.
[35] *Lawson* v. *Hudson* (1779) 1 Bro.C.C. 58; *Duke of Ancaster* v. *Mayer* (1785) 1 Bro.C.C. 454; **1 W. & T.L.C. 1.**

the charge existed before the deceased acquired the property.[36] Nor did the rule free the beneficiary from liabilities that accrued after the death of the deceased, so that a legatee of shares in a company would be liable for any calls made after the testator's death.[37]

2. Property now subject to charge

(a) *All property.*   By a series of statutes known as Locke King's Acts (or, more properly, the Real Estates Charges Acts) 1854, 1867 and 1877, and now by the Administration of Estates Act 1925, the former rule has been progressively revised. The new rule now extends to all forms of property, whether real or personal (instead of merely to realty and, after the Act of 1877, leaseholds), and it applies to property appointed under a general power, including the statutory power to dispose of entailed property[38]; and all types of mortgage and charge are within the rule.[39]

(b) *The rule.*   The rule is that as between those claiming under the deceased, any interest in property which at the time of his death is subject to a charge is to be primarily liable for the payment of the charge unless the deceased has signified a contrary or other intention by will, deed or other document; and every part of such an interest, according to its value, is to bear a proportionate part of the charge.[40] The beneficiary accordingly now prima facie takes the property subject to the charge, and cannot call for it to be discharged out of the assets of the estate; but this rule applies only as between the beneficiaries, and does not affect the right of the mortgagee or other person entitled to the charge to obtain payment or satisfaction out of the other assets of the deceased or otherwise.[41] Nor does the statute impose any personal liability on the beneficiary, *e.g.* if the charge exceeds the value of the property; he is merely prevented from calling on the estate to pay off the charge.[42]

A number of details in the operation of the rule must now be considered.[43]

3. Options, and gifts of two properties.

3. Options, and gifts of two properties.   Where the will gives an option to a certain person to purchase certain land at a fixed price, he is entitled to have any mortgage or charge on the land cleared off out of the rest of the estate; for on exercising the option he claims as a

---

[36] *Butler* v. *Butler* (1800) 5 Ves. 534; *Scott* v. *Beecher* (1820) 5 Madd. 96; *Earl of Ilchester* v. *Earl of Carnarvon* (1839) 1 Beav. 209.
[37] *Armstrong* v. *Burnet* (1855) 20 Beav. 424; *Addams* v. *Ferick* (1859) 26 Beav. 384; and see *Re Pearce, Crutchley* v. *Wells* [1909] 1 Ch. 819.
[38] Formerly entails were excluded: *Re Anthony, Anthony* v. *Anthony (No. 2)* [1893] 3 Ch. 498.
[39] A.E.A. 1925, s.35(1).
[40] *Ibid.*
[41] *Ibid.* s.35(3).
[42] *Syer* v. *Gladstone* (1885) 30 Ch.D. 614.
[43] The decisions on the former Acts appear, in general, to apply to the Act of 1925.

purchaser and not as devisee,[44] even though the price payable under the option is less than the value of the property.[45] And if two properties are given by separate and distinct gifts to the same person and one is mortgaged for more than it is worth, the balance of the mortgage money is payable out of the rest of the estate, and not out of the other property[46]; but if there is a single undivided gift of the two properties the legatee or devisee takes both subject to the whole burden.[47]

4. Charges within the rule. The obligation of property to bear its own burden extends to equitable as well as legal mortgages,[48] to judgment debts on which execution has been issued and registered before the debtor's death,[49] and to a charge for estate duty,[50] or inheritance tax.[51] The statute expressly includes a vendor's lien for unpaid purchase-money[52]; and a lien given to a company by its articles in respect of debts owed to it by a shareholder has been held to be an "equitable charge" within the section.[53] But where a partner mortgages his own property for a partnership debt, the person to whom he leaves the property is entitled to have it freed from the mortgage unless the partnership assets are insufficient to answer all the partnership debts; for the debt is regarded as a debt of the partnership, not of the testator.[54]

5. Contrary intention. It will be noticed that the contrary intention required to exclude the general rule may be shown by any document. Thus a letter by a testator stating that a devisee is intended to take property free from a mortgage on it may be a valuable document. The statute, however, provides that a mere general direction to pay debts out of personalty or residue, or a mere charge of debts on such property, is not enough, unless such an intention is further shown by words expressly or by necessary implication referring to part or all of the charge.[55]

(a) *Insufficient intention.* It has accordingly been held that a contrary intention is not shown merely by making a specific devise of part of the property charged (leaving the remainder to fall into residue) and charging the residue with the payment of debts; in such a case the property specifically devised must bear a rateable proportion of the

[44] *Re Wilson, Wilson* v. *Wilson* [1908] 1 Ch. 839.
[45] *Re Fison's W.T.* [1950] Ch. 394.
[46] *Re Holt* (1916) 85 L.J.Ch. 779.
[47] *Re Baron Kensington* [1902] 1 Ch. 203.
[48] *Pembroke* v. *Friend* (1860) 1 J. & H. 132.
[49] *Re Anthony, Anthony* v. *Anthony (No. 1)* [1892] 1 Ch. 450; L.C.A. 1972, s.6; L.P.A. 1925, s.195.
[50] *Re Bowerman* [1908] 2 Ch. 340.
[51] See Inheritance Tax Act 1984, s.237, for the present charging provision.
[52] See *Re Kidd* [1894] 3 Ch. 558; *Re Fraser* [1904] 1 Ch. 726; *Re Birmingham* [1959] Ch. 523.
[53] *Re Turner, Tennant* v. *Turner* [1938] Ch. 593.
[54] *Re Ritson* [1899] 1 Ch. 128; *Brettell* v. *Holland* [1907] 2 Ch. 88.
[55] A.E.A. 1925, s.35(2).

charge.[56] Again, a contrary intention is not shown by devising property subject to a right of pre-emption.[57] Further, a direction to pay "mortgage" debts does not extend to a vendor's lien for unpaid purchase-money[58]; and a purchaser's direction to his solicitors to complete the purchase is insufficient, for it relates to the discharge of the vendor's lien in the purchaser's lifetime, and not to what is to happen after his death.[59]

(b) *Sufficient intention.* On the other hand, it is not necessary that the debts should be expressly referred to as mortgage debts; all that is required is that they should be sufficiently identified.[60] Thus a direction to pay "debts (except mortgage debts, if any, on Blackacre)" out of residue shows an intention to exonerate properties other than Blackacre from any mortgages on them.[61] Nor is there any need to show an intention both to discharge the property charged and to charge the rest of the estate.[62] It is enough to show either a discharge of the property charged,[63] or else a charge of debts on some special fund which is not merely the personalty or the residue.[64] Thus a direction to pay debts out of *specific* personalty or *specific* realty suffices,[65] and so does a direction to repay the mortgage out of the rents of all the testator's properties.[66] But if the special fund is insufficient to pay the whole debt, the property charged devolves subject to the balance.[67]

---

[56] *Re Neeld* [1962] Ch. 643, overruling *Re Biss, Heasman* v. *Biss* [1956] Ch. 243.
[57] *Re Biss, Heasman* v. *Biss, supra,* not affected on this point by *Re Neeld, supra.*
[58] *Re Beirnstein* [1925] Ch. 12.
[59] *Re Wakefield* [1943] 2 All E.R. 29; and see *Re Birmingham* [1959] Ch. 523.
[60] *Re Fleck* (1888) 37 Ch.D. 677.
[61] *Re Valpy* [1906] 1 Ch. 531.
[62] Contrast *ante,* p. 334.
[63] *Eno* v. *Tatham* (1863) 3 De G.J. & S. 443.
[64] *Re Fegan* [1928] Ch. 45.
[65] *Ibid.*
[66] *Allie* v. *Katah* [1963] 1 W.L.R. 202.
[67] *Re Birch* [1909] 1 Ch. 787; *Re Fegan, supra* and see *Re Biss, Heasman* v. *Biss* [1956] Ch. 243.

CHAPTER 4

DISTRIBUTION OF ASSETS

Section 1. Transfer of Property

1. Distribution. When the personal representative has paid the debts and provided for the liabilities of the deceased,[1] he will proceed to hand over the assets to the persons beneficially entitled,[2] unless proceedings are pending under the Inheritance (Provision for Family and Dependants) Act 1975.[3] Yet even if there are no such proceedings, or they have been disposed of, he cannot be compelled to distribute until the expiration of the executor's year.[4] A personal representative who has cleared the estate by paying all debts, expenses and legacies holds the residue on trust for the residuary legatees, or next-of-kin, without thereby ceasing to be a personal representative.[5]

2. Ownership of property

(a) *Property in personal representatives.* The ownership of the property of a deceased person between the death and the distribution sometimes gives rise to problems. Although personal representatives are in a fiduciary position, it is wrong to regard them as holding only the legal estate, with the beneficial interests in the beneficiaries. Not until there has been an assent can it be said with certainty whether or not a particular asset will be needed for the payment of debts or other liabilities; and until these have been discharged, it cannot be said what assets there will be in the residuary estate.[6] Accordingly, the general rule is that no beneficiary can assert that he has any legal or equitable interest in any of the assets which are still unadministered[7]; for the

---

[1] See, *e.g. Re Arnold, Calvert* v. *Whelen* [1942] Ch. 272.
[2] For the position where the beneficiary is bankrupt, see B. S. Ker (1954) 18 Conv.(N.S.) 176; and see *post*, p. 355.
[3] *Re Simson, Simson* v. *National Provincial Bank Ltd.* [1950] Ch. 38. The Act replaced and widened the Inheritance (Family Provision) Act 1938 as amended. Applications under the Act of 1975 must be made within six months from the date on which representation for general purposes is first taken out: ss.4, 23. The court may permit a late application, but the possibility of this does not make the personal representatives liable for any distribution of the estate made after the six months has run: s.20: see *Re Salmon, Coard* v. *National Westminster Bank Ltd.* [1981] Ch. 167.
[4] See *ante*, p. 310.
[5] For this, see *ante*, pp. 99, 100.
[6] *Corbett* v.*C.I.R.* [1938] 1 K.B. 567.
[7] See *Lord Sudeley* v. *Att.-Gen.* [1897] A.C. 11 at 18, 21; *Re Cunliffe-Owen* [1953] Ch. 545.

whole right of property in them is vested in the personal representatives.[8] The beneficiary has merely a right to require the deceased's
estate to be duly administered, though this is a chose in action
transmissible by his will.[9]

(b) *Limits of rule.* This rule is clearly established in the case of a
person entitled to residue[10] or a share of residue[11] under a will, or to
some or all of the estate of an intestate.[12] But it does not apply to a
specific bequest or devise. In this case the property is vested in law in
the personal representatives, and they can resort to it for the payment
of debts; but subject to this, in equity the property is in the legatee as
soon as the testator dies.[13]

(c) *Protection of beneficiaries.* Apart from specific gifts, the rights of
the beneficiaries are accordingly protected not by conferring equitable
interests upon them but by the control exercised by the court, whether
under a will[14] or an intestacy,[15] to secure the due administration of the
assets in the interests of the beneficiaries and all other persons
concerned.[16] Any such beneficiary who is prospectively entitled to any
particular asset thus has no more than what may be called a "floating
equity" in it, which may or may not crystallise.[17] Thus for the purpose
of statutory rights of compensation even a beneficiary who is solely
entitled under an intestacy is not "entitled to an interest" in a house
which forms part of the unadministered assets[18]; and in such
circumstances a surviving spouse who has a right to call for the
matrimonial home to be appropriated to her under an intestacy[19] has no
locus standi to defend an action for possession of it.[20]

3. Possession before assent. Before making an assent or conveyance,
a personal representative may permit the person entitled to land to take
possession of it without prejudice to the right of the personal
representative to take or resume possession, or his power to convey the
land as if he were in possession, but subject to the interest of any lessee,
tenant or occupier in possession or actual occupation.[21] Any person

---

[8] *Commissioner of Stamp Duties (Queensland)* v. *Livingston* [1965] A.C. 694 at 712; and see *Re Hayes'
W.T.* [1971] 1 W.L.R. 758 at 764.
[9] *Re Leigh's W.T.* [1970] Ch. 277.
[10] *Dr. Barnardo's Homes National Incorporated Association* v. *Commissioners for Special Purposes of
the Income Tax Acts* [1921] 2 A.C. 1.
[11] *Lord Sudeley* v. *Att.-Gen.* [1897] A.C. 11.
[12] *Eastbourne Mutual B.S.* v. *Hastings Corporation* [1965] 1 W.L.R. 861.
[13] *I.R.C.* v. *Hawley* [1928] 1 K.B. 578 at 583; *Re Neeld* [1962] Ch. 643 at 688; and see *Re Parsons,
Parsons* v. *Att.-Gen.* [1943] Ch. 12 ("competent to dispose"); *post*, p. 343. But see *Kavanagh* v. *Best*
[1971] N.I. 89 at 93, 94.
[14] *Commissioner of Stamp Duties (Queensland)* v. *Livingston* [1965] A.C. 694.
[15] *Eastbourne Mutual B.S.* v. *Hastings Corporation, supra.*
[16] See *Commissioner of Stamp Duties (Queensland)* v. *Livingston, supra,* at pp. 712, 713.
[17] See *ante*, p. 26.
[18] *Eastbourne Mutual B.S.* v. *Hastings Corporation, supra.*
[19] Under Intestates' Estates Act 1952, s.5, 2nd Sched.
[20] *Lall* v. *Lall* [1965] 1 W.L.R. 1249.
[21] A.E.A. 1925, s.43(1).

who, as against the personal representative, claims possession or a conveyance or an assent, may apply to the court, which may make the necessary vesting or other order.[22]

4. Ascertainment of persons entitled. Normally there is no difficulty in ascertaining who is entitled to the property. If there is difficulty, however, the court will have to be asked to administer the estate or conduct an inquiry to ascertain the beneficiaries.[23] If the difficulty arises simply because it is not known whether a missing beneficiary is alive or dead, the court may make a "Benjamin Order."[24] This avoids undue delay in winding up the estate by authorising the personal representatives to distribute the estate on the footing that a missing claimant is dead, or that all the claimants have been ascertained, or on some other stated footing; and a similar order may be made where there is difficulty in ascertaining creditors, *e.g.* owing to war conditions.[25] Such an order protects the personal representatives without preventing any missing beneficiaries or creditors who subsequently appear from following the assets.

5. Transfer to persons entitled. The personal representatives must ensure that the property of the deceased is properly vested in the persons entitled. This is usually done by means of an assent, though in some cases some further act is required. Thus where there is a bequest of shares, the personal representatives hold them in trust for the beneficiary as soon as they have assented to the bequest; but the legal title cannot pass until a transfer of the shares has been duly registered.[26] In such cases, the assent may be an act prior to and distinct from the transfer of the legal title. In considering assents, the law before 1926 must be considered first, for it still governs pure personalty.

(a) *Assents before 1926.* Before 1926, an assent was merely an act which perfected the title of a beneficiary under a will by showing that the personal representatives did not require the property for the purposes of administration,[27] and divesting them of their title as personal representatives.[28] The beneficiary derived his title not from the assent but from the will; the assent, which might be informal and inferred from conduct, merely made the gift operative.[29] This doctrine was "an exception from the general law that a man requires, in order to

---

[22] A.E.A. 1925, s.43(2).
[23] See *post,* pp. 351, 356.
[24] *Re Benjamin* [1902] 1 Ch. 723; and see *Re Beattie* (1926) 81 L.J.News. 163; *Hansell* v. *Spink* [1943] Ch. 396; *Re Newson-Smith's Settlement* [1962] 1 W.L.R. 1478 (marriage settlement).
[25] *Re Gess* [1942] Ch. 37.
[26] *Re Grosvenor* [1916] 2 Ch. 375.
[27] See *Kemp* v. *I.R.C.* [1905] 1 K.B. 581 at 585.
[28] *Wise* v. *Whitburn* [1924] 1 Ch. 460.
[29] See *Attenborough* v. *Solomon* [1913] A.C. 76 at 82, 83.

complete his title, something in the nature of a conveyance."[30] Thus if by reason of an undiscovered codicil an assent to a specific bequest was made in favour of the wrong person, it nevertheless perfected the title of the right person; for assents were to legacies, not to legatees.[31]

When the Land Transfer Act 1897 made all realty vest in the personal representatives instead of passing to the devisee or heir direct, the power to make an assent was applied to devises, though not to devolution on intestacy; alternatively, whether there was a will or an intestacy, the land could be vested in the heir, devisee or other person entitled by means of a conveyance.[32] An assent could still be inferred from conduct, e.g. where the person entitled was permitted to occupy the land for many years[33]; and an assent to a gift of a life interest operated also as an assent to any interests in remainder.[34]

(b) *Assents after 1925.* So far as land is concerned, the Administration of Estates Act 1925 has greatly changed the nature of an assent. It is no longer a mere relinquishment or confirmation by the personal representatives, but is instead an assurance or conveyance which transfers property; it is no longer confined to wills, but can also be made in favour of persons entitled under an intestacy; and it cannot now be made informally. The new rules apply to all assents and conveyances made after 1925, even if the deceased died before 1926[35]; but they do not affect the law governing assents of pure personalty, which continues as before 1926.

6. Power to assent. The Administration of Estates Act 1925 provides that "a personal representative may assent to the vesting, in any person who (whether by devise, bequest, devolution, appropriation or otherwise) may be entitled thereto, either beneficially or as a trustee or personal representative, of any estate or interest in real estate,"[36] which includes leaseholds.[37] This applies to all real estate devolving on the personal representatives to which the deceased was entitled, or over which his will exercised a general power of appointment, including dispositions of entails.[38]

7. Form of assent. An assent to the vesting of a legal estate in land must now be "in writing, signed by the personal representative"; and it must "name the person in whose favour it is given." Such an assent "shall operate to vest in that person the legal estate to which it relates;

[30] *Re Culverhouse* [1896] 2 Ch. 251 at 253, *per* Kekewich J.
[31] *Re West, West* v. *Roberts* [1909] Ch. 180.
[32] L.T.A. 1897, s.3(1).
[33] *Wise* v. *Whitburn* [1924] 1 Ch. 460.
[34] *Ibid.*; *Re Swan* [1915] 1 Ch. 829.
[35] A.E.A. 1925, s.36(12).
[36] *Ibid.* s.36(1).
[37] *Ibid.* s.55(1)(xix).
[38] *Ibid.* s.36(1). For real estate which devolves on the personal representative, see *ante*, pp. 312, 313.

and an assent not in writing or not in favour of a named person shall not be effectual to pass a legal estate."[39]

This provision has given rise to difficulties in cases where no legal estate passes, as where a sole personal representative, X, is also entitled beneficially or as a trustee. Clearly it does not apply to equitable interests, so that, for example, the absence of a written assent does not prevent acts done by X from constituting an acceptance of the beneficial gift sufficient to prevent him afterwards disclaiming it.[40] As regards the legal estate, such an assent is clearly desirable to mark any change of capacity, *e.g.* when X begins to hold as a trustee instead of as personal representative[41]; and if X seeks to sell in his new capacity, a purchaser can require this change to be proved by the production of a written assent.[42]

A written assent is essential before X can begin to hold the legal estate in his new capacity instead of his old.[43] Without such an assent, therefore, X cannot, as trustee, make an appointment of a new trustee which will vest the property in him.[44] This view seems to treat the word "vest" in the statute as including "vest in one capacity instead of another," and "pass" as having a corresponding meaning.[45]

8. Operation of assent. An assent of land operates to vest in the person named the estate or interest to which the assent relates; and unless a contrary intention appears, it relates back to the death of the deceased.[46] As the assent may be to the person entitled "whether by devise, bequest, devolution, appropriation[47] or otherwise," an assent may apparently be made to a purchaser, at any rate if it merely completes a transaction begun by the deceased in his lifetime.[48] An assent or conveyance must be stamped *ad valorem* if made for value,[49] *e.g.* an appropriation of property in satisfaction of a pecuniary legacy.[50] In other cases, an assent made under hand only requires no stamp,[51] whereas a conveyance requires at least a 50p deed stamp.

The usual limited covenant by the personal representative that he has not incumbered may be implied either in an assent or in a conveyance by the use of the expression "as personal representative."[52] The person

---

[39] *Ibid.*, s.36(4), 55(1)(vii).
[40] *Re Hodge* [1940] Ch. 260.
[41] *Re Yerburgh* [1928] W.N. 208.
[42] *Re Hodge, supra*, at p. 264.
[43] *Re King's W.T.* [1964] Ch. 542, a controversial decision, see R. R. A. Walker (1964) 80 L.Q.R. 328.
[44] *Ibid.*
[45] *Re King's W.T., supra*, at p. 548.
[46] A.E.A. 1925, s.36(2), applying to land the rule formerly confined to specific bequests: see *Dr. Barnardo's Homes National Incorporated Association* v. *Commissioners for Special Purposes of the Income Tax Acts* [1921] 2 A.C. 1 at 11.
[47] For appropriation, see *post*, p. 363.
[48] See *G.H.R. Co. Ltd.* v. *I.R.C.* [1943] K.B. 303.
[49] *Jopling* v. *I.R.C.* [1940] 2 K.B. 282; *G.H.R. Co. Ltd.* v. *I.R.C., supra.*
[50] *Jopling* v. *I.R.C., supra.*
[51] *Kemp* v. *I.R.C.* [1905] 1 K.B. 581; A.E.A. 1925, s.36(11).
[52] L.P.A. 1925, s.76(1)(F).

in whose favour an assent or conveyance of a legal estate is made may require that notice of the assent be placed on, or permanently annexed to, the probate or letters of administration at the cost of the estate.[53] If this is done, a statement in writing by a personal representative that he has not given or made an assent or conveyance will not have its usual operation in favour of a purchaser.[54]

9. Effect of assent. An assent or conveyance after 1925 by a personal representative in respect of a legal estate is, in favour of a purchaser for money or money's worth, to be taken as "sufficient evidence" that the person in whose favour the assent or conveyance is given or made is the person entitled to have the legal estate conveyed to him, and upon the proper trusts, if any, but is not otherwise to affect prejudicially the claim of any person rightfully entitled to the estate; but this does not apply if notice of a previous assent or conveyance affecting that legal estate has been placed on or annexed to the probate or administration.[55] "Sufficient evidence" is not the same as "conclusive evidence"; a purchaser accordingly cannot rely on an assent if, on a proper investigation of title, facts come to his knowledge which indicate that the assent was not made in favour of the person rightfully entitled.[56]

10. Protection of personal representatives. An assent or conveyance will not, except in favour of a purchaser of a legal estate for money or money's worth, prejudice the right of the personal representative or any other person to recover the property[57] or to be indemnified out of it against any duties, debt or liability to which it would have been subject if there had not been any assent or conveyance.[58] Moreover, a personal representative may, as a condition of giving an assent or making a conveyance, require security for the discharge of any such duties, debt or liability, though he is not, merely by reason of the subsistence thereof, entitled to postpone the giving of an assent if reasonable arrangements have been made for discharging them.[59] A personal representative also has the power (which he cannot be made to exercise[60]) to give an assent subject to any legal estate or charge by way of legal mortgage.[61]

---

[53] A.E.A. 1925, s.36(5).
[54] *Ibid.* s.36(6), *ante*, p. 319.
[55] *Ibid.* s.36(7), (11).
[56] *Re Duce and Boots Cash Chemists (Southern) Ltd.'s Contract* [1937] Ch. 642.
[57] See also A.E.A. 1925, s.38.
[58] A.E.A. 1925, s.36(9).
[59] *Ibid.* s.36(10). See *Re Rosenthal* [1972] 1 W.L.R. 1273, where the failure to take security proved expensive for the executors.
[60] See *Williams* v. *Holland* [1965] 1 W.L.R. 739 at 743.
[61] A.E.A. 1925, s.36(10).

11. Expenses of transfer. The beneficiary must bear any expenses incurred in completing his title, or in putting him in possession of the property, such as the expense of packing and delivering articles specifically bequeathed; for after the executors have assented to his having the property they hold it as trustees for him, and not in their capacity of executors.[62] But executors who pay the reasonable expenses of packing and transfer out of the testator's assets are probably not surchargeable for so doing.[63]

Section 2. Ascertainment of Settled Residue

1. Rule in Allhusen v. Whittell. Where the residue of an estate is given absolutely, the personal representatives will distribute it in the usual way. Where, however, it is settled on persons in succession, it is sometimes necessary to adjust the accounts; for, as already explained, a tenant for life is not always entitled to the whole of the income.[64] The true residue can be ascertained only by treating the debts, funeral and testamentary expenses and legacies as having been paid partly out of income and partly out of capital. Under the rule in *Allhusen* v. *Whittell*[65] these payments are regarded as having been made with such part of the capital as, together with the interest on that part for one year (less income tax[66]), is sufficient for the purpose. "The tenant for life ought not to have the income arising from what is wanted for the payment of debts, because that never becomes residue in any way whatever"[67]; "it is excluded by the very definition of the term residue."[68]

2. Liabilities within the rule. Contingent legacies are outside the rule, for the assets to pay them remain part of the residue until they are needed, and it may be inconveniently long before the contingency is resolved.[69] But the rule applies to contingent debts, such as an annuity payable under a covenant made by the testator[70] in his lifetime[71]; and it applies to a payment made by the executors to an assignee to take onerous leaseholds.[72]

---

[62] *Re Grosvenor* [1916] 2 Ch. 375; *Re Sivewright* (1922) 128 L.T. 416; *Re Leach, Milne* v. *Daubeny* [1923] 1 Ch. 161; *Re Fitzpatrick* [1952] Ch. 86. Contrast *Re Hewett, Eldridge* v. *Hewett* (1920) 90 L.J.Ch. 126.

[63] See *Re Scott, Scott* v. *Scott* [1915] 1 Ch. 592 at 610.

[64] *Ante*, p. 228.

[65] (1867) L.R. 4 Eq. 295; and see *Corbett* v. *C.I.R.* [1938] 1 K.B. 567 at 584, 585. See generally W. Strachan (1914) 30 L.Q.R. 481; (1916) 32 L.Q.R. 208.

[66] *Re Oldham, Oldham* v. *Myles* [1927] W.N. 113.

[67] *Allhusen* v. *Whittell, supra,* at p. 303, *per* Page Wood V.-C.

[68] *Re Wills* [1915] 1 Ch. 769 at 778, *per* Sargant J.

[69] *Allhusen* v. *Whittell, supra,* at p. 304; *Re Fenwick's W.T.* [1936] Ch. 720.

[70] Contrast *Re Darby, Russell* v. *MacGregor* [1939] Ch. 905, where the testator had made no covenant but merely held property on which the annuities had been charged.

[71] *Re Perkins, Brown* v. *Perkins* [1907] 2 Ch. 596; *Re Poyser* [1910] 2 Ch. 444; *Re Fenwick's W.T., supra,* at p. 724.

[72] *Re Shee* [1934] Ch. 345.

3. Period of operation. The "year" stated in the rule is the executor's year,[73] and applies in normal cases. But the rule will not be "slavishly followed"[74] where it would work an injustice, and accordingly it is modified where the debts and other liabilities are discharged a considerable time before[75] or after[76] the end of the first year. In such cases, instead of the year the period taken is the period from the testator's death until the date upon which each particular liability is in fact discharged. Thus where an annuity is payable under a covenant made by the testator in his lifetime, each instalment "is to be paid by means of a piece of capital together with the income on that piece of capital as from the date of the testator's death down to the date of payment."[77]

4. Limits to rule. The rule "was founded on the broad equitable principle that where residue was limited to persons in succession, their successive enjoyment should be an enjoyment of the same fund."[78] Thus, "extremely elaborate and minute calculations"[79] need not be gone through in every case; and although the strict rule is to take the average rate of interest in each year, in most cases more rough and ready calculations will suffice.[80] The rule is displaced, too, if the will shows a sufficient intention to exclude it,[81] or the nature of the property or the circumstances make it inapplicable.[82] In practice, many wills exclude the rule,[83] and even where this is not done, the rule is often ignored where it would make no great difference.[84]

Section 3. Retainer of Debt Due to the Estate

1. The right to retain. A personal representative is entitled to retain out of a pecuniary legacy or a share of residue a debt (including, it seems, a claim for damages[85]) due from the beneficiary to the estate. This right, though sometimes called a right of set-off, is quite distinct from the ordinary right of set-off in an action. It exists even though the debt is statute-barred, for it rests on the principle that the beneficiary must be regarded as having in his hands an asset of the estate for which he must account, and that he cannot claim any part of the assets without

[73] Re Darby, Russell v. MacGregor [1939] Ch. 905 at 914.
[74] Re McEuen [1913] 2 Ch. 704 at 715, per Sargant J.
[75] Re McEuen [1913] 2 Ch. 704.
[76] Re Wills [1915] 1 Ch. 769.
[77] Re Darby, Russell v. MacGregor, supra, at p. 914, per Greene M.R. See, e.g. Re Perkins, Brown v. Perkins [1907] 2 Ch. 596; Re Poyser [1910] 2 Ch. 444; Re Berkeley [1968] Ch. 744.
[78] Re McEuen, supra, at p. 713, per Sargant J.
[79] Ibid. at p. 716.
[80] Re Wills, supra, at p. 779.
[81] See Re Ullswater [1952] Ch. 105.
[82] Re Darby, Russell v. MacGregor [1939] Ch. 905.
[83] See, e.g. The Statutory Will Forms, 1925, Form 8(7)(c); Re Wynn [1952] Ch. 271 at 273, 276.
[84] See also ante, p. 231, n. 23.
[85] Re Jewell's Settlement [1919] 2 Ch. 161.

bringing into the estate the portion already in his hands.[86] It is also quite distinct from the "personal representative's right of retainer," which was the former right of a personal representative to pay a debt due to himself in preference to other creditors of an equal degree.[87]

2. Conditions to be satisfied

(a) *Beneficiary personally liable.* This right of retainer is exercisable only against the person who owes the debt, and not against any others, *e.g.* those upon whom that person's property has devolved. Thus if X's aunt owes money to X's father, and both die, the father's executors cannot retain the debt out of the share of residue which the father has left to X even though X is his aunt's executor and sole residuary legatee; for he was never indebted to his father in any way.[88] Similarly, if a testator gives his residue to his children living at his death, and provides that the children of any deceased child shall take "such share as [their parent] would have taken if living," his executors cannot retain as against the children of a deceased child a debt which their father owed the testator; for the grandchildren were given the whole share, and not merely the balance which would have been left after it had been used to pay their father's debt.[89] Such a case is quite distinct from a case where the father has had an advancement[90] from the testator; for this is a payment on account of his share and so diminishes it as against both him and his children.[91]

(b) *Sole debt.* The beneficiary's liability must be a sole and not a joint liability; a partnership debt cannot be retained out of a legacy given to one of the partners.[92]

(c) *Debt due.* If the legatee's debt is payable by instalments, the executor cannot retain any instalments of the debt which are not yet due out of a legacy presently payable; for to do so would be to alter the contract between the testator and the debtor, and make the latter pay his debt before it was due.[93]

(d) *Not a specific legacy.* The right to retain applies only to pecuniary gifts, and not to a legacy of something other than money, *e.g.* a specific legacy of stock.[94]

---

[86] *Courtnay* v. *Williams* (1846) 15 L.J.Ch. 204 (affirming (1844) 3 Hare 539); *Re Akerman* [1891] 3 Ch. 212.
[87] See *ante,* p. 331.
[88] *Re Bruce* [1908] 2 Ch. 682.
[89] *Re Binns* [1929] 1 Ch. 677.
[90] See *post,* p. 522.
[91] *Re Scott, Langton* v. *Scott* [1903] 1 Ch. 1 at 9.
[92] *Turner* v. *Turner* [1911] 1 Ch. 716, followed in *Re Pennington and Owen Ltd.* [1925] Ch. 825, a case of attempted set-off in winding up.
[93] *Re Abrahams, Abrahams* v. *Abrahams* [1908] 2 Ch. 69.
[94] *Re Savage* [1918] 2 Ch. 146; *Re Taylor, Taylor* v. *Wade* [1894] 1 Ch. 671; and see *Re Eiser's W.T.* [1937] 1 All E.R. 244 (income payable under discretionary trust need not be retained).

(e) *No release in bankruptcy.*   If a legatee becomes bankrupt after his right to the legacy has accrued, the executor may still retain a debt out of the legacy, unless he has proved for the debt in the legatee's bankruptcy; for the trustee in the bankruptcy is in no better position than the bankrupt.[95] But under the rule in *Cherry* v. *Boultbee*,[96] where the legatee is already bankrupt at the date of the testator's death, the executor may not retain his debt; he can only prove and receive a dividend on the debt *pari passu* with the other creditors, for at no time were there cross-obligations to pay in full. If in such a case the insolvent legatee has meanwhile been released from the debt by obtaining a discharge or under a voluntary arrangement, he is entitled to receive his legacy in full.[97]

Section 4. Future Liabilities

1. Liability of personal representatives.   The personal representatives should retain sufficient assets to meet any future or contingent liabilities from which they are not protected by the Trustee Act 1925, sections 26[98] (future liabilities) or 27[99] (advertisements), or by a sufficient indemnity from the beneficiaries; or they should distribute the estate only under the direction of the court in an administration action. It is not the practice of the court nowadays to order the retention of any assets to meet such liabilities; such an order is unnecessary to protect the personal representative, for he may obtain full protection by distributing under the court's direction in an administration action, and the contingent claimant has no right to require an appropriation of assets to meet his claim.[1]

2. Indemnity by beneficiaries.   When a personal representative is compelled to discharge a debt or liability of the estate after he has distributed the assets, he may call upon the beneficiaries to refund the amount of the assets received by them, or enough to indemnify him. But he cannot claim indemnity if he had notice of the liability at the time of distribution, unless it was merely contingent; and the right extends only to the recovery of the amount received by the beneficiaries, and not to interest on it.[2]

---

[95] *Re Watson, Turner* v. *Watson* [1896] 1 Ch. 925; *Stammers* v. *Elliott* (1868) 3 Ch.App. 195; *Re Melton* [1918] 1 Ch. 37; *Re Lennard* [1934] Ch. 235.
[96] (1839) 4 My. & Cr. 442; and see *Re Hodgson, Hodgson* v. *Fox* (1878) 9 Ch.D. 673.
[97] *Re Sewell* [1909] 1 Ch. 806.
[98] *Ante*, p. 273.
[99] *Ante*, p. 272.
[1] *Re King, Mellor* v. *South Australian Land Mortgage and Agency Co.* [1907] 1 Ch. 72; *Re Nixon* [1904] 1 Ch. 638; *Re Lewis, Jennings* v. *Hemsley* [1939] Ch. 232. For form of order, see *Re Johnson, Johnson* v. *King Edward Hospital Fund for London* [1940] W.N. 195 (not followed in *Re Arnold, Calvert* v. *Whelen* [1942] Ch. 272 on the point of substance).
[2] *Jervis* v. *Wolferstan* (1874) L.R. 18 Eq. 18; *Whittaker* v. *Kershaw* (1890) 45 Ch.D. 320.

CHAPTER 5

REMEDIES

Personal representatives who encounter difficulties may invoke the assistance of the court in various ways. So also may creditors, beneficiaries and next-of-kin who have not received property of the deceased to which they consider they are entitled. First, the court may itself assume the whole or some part of the administration, though this is now rarely necessary. Secondly, the personal representatives or any person interested may apply to the court for guidance on specific difficulties. Thirdly, creditors of the deceased have a right of action against the personal representatives. Lastly, unpaid and under-paid creditors, beneficiaries and next-of-kin may be able to sue the wrongful recipients of the assets. Each of these subjects will be considered in turn.

Section 1. Administration by the Court

1. Courts

(a) *Chancery Division.* Administration of the estates of deceased persons is a matter assigned by the Supreme Court Act 1981 to the Chancery Division of the High Court.[1] Proceedings may be begun either by writ or by originating summons[2] issued by a creditor or any person interested in the estate as legatee, devisee or next-of-kin, or by the personal representative himself. A creditor may bring the action on behalf of himself and all other creditors of the deceased, though he is not obliged to do so.[3] A person who is not a creditor at the date of the issue of the writ or summons, such as an annuitant whose annuity is not in arrear, cannot bring the action,[4] nor can a person who is entitled not to a debt of the deceased himself but to a debt which has only subsequently arisen against the personal representative.[5]

---

[1] *Ante*, p. 18.
[2] R.S.C. Ord. 5, r. 1; Ord. 85.
[3] *Re James, James* v. *Jones* [1911] 2 Ch. 348; see *Re Tottenham* [1896] 1 Ch. 628.
[4] *Re Hargreaves* (1890) 44 Ch.D. 236.
[5] *Owen* v. *Delamere* (1872) L.R. 15 Eq. 134; *Re Kitson* [1911] 2 K.B. 109.

(b) *County court.* A county court may administer the estate of a deceased person if the total value does not exceed £30,000.[6]

(c) *Public Trustee.* The Public Trustee may administer an estate if the gross capital value is less than £1,000.[7]

(d) *Bankruptcy Court.* If the deceased died insolvent, the personal representative may present a petition for an insolvency administration order, *i.e.* to have the estate administered in bankruptcy.[8] So also may a creditor to whom the deceased owed a debt upon which a bankruptcy petition might have been founded, had the debtor been alive.[9] But a petition cannot be presented if proceedings for administration have already been begun in some other court, although that court may transfer the proceedings to a Bankruptcy Court if satisfied that the estate is insolvent.[10]

2. Need for personal representative. No order for administration can be made until a personal representative has been constituted.[11] Where the grant of probate or administration is delayed owing to a dispute as to the validity of a will or the right to administer, and an administrator *pendente lite* has been appointed, a creditor may obtain a decree for administration against him.[12] Further, if proceedings for administration are commenced by a creditor,[13] the court may appoint a receiver to protect the estate pending the constitution of the personal representative,[14] and may require the creditor to undertake, if need be, to take steps to procure a grant of letters of administration to himself.[15] An executor *de son tort* (*i.e.* a person who, not being appointed executor or administrator, has wrongfully intermeddled with the estate) cannot be sued for administration, but he may be made to account for the assets of which he has wrongly taken possession.[16]

3. Refusal to make order. The court (*i.e.* the Chancery Division or the county court) is not bound to make an order for the administration of the estate unless the questions between the parties cannot properly be determined otherwise than under such an order.[17] An order may be

---

[6] County Courts Act 1984, ss.23(*a*), 147(1); S.I. 1981 No. 1123, art. 2; and see *ante,* p. 20, n. 19.

[7] Public Trustee Act 1906, s.3. When administering the estate, the Public Trustee has all the powers of a Master of the Chancery Division: Public Trustee Rules 1912, r. 14.

[8] Insolvency Act 1986, s.272; S.I. 1986 No. 1999, art. 3(1), Sched. 1, Pt. I, Table, Pt. II, para. 6. Bankruptcy proceedings commenced before death may be continued against the estate: *ante,* p. 324.

[9] Insolvency Act 1986, ss.264(1)(*a*), 267; S.I. 1986 No. 1999, art. 3(1), Sched. 1, Pt. I, Table, Pt. II, paras. 1, 3.

[10] Insolvency Act 1986, s.271(2), (3), as substituted by S.I. 1986 No. 1999, art. 3(1), Sched. 1, Pt. II, para. 5. As to the exercise of this discretionary power of transfer, see *Re York* (1887) 36 Ch.D. 233; *Re Hay* [1915] 2 Ch. 198.

[11] *Rowsell* v. *Morris* (1873) L.R. 17 Eq. 20.

[12] *Re Toleman* [1897] 1 Ch. 866.

[13] This had formerly to be by writ and not originating summons: *Re Sutcliffe* [1942] Ch. 453. The rule has now changed: R.S.C. Ord. 5, rr. 1, 2; Ord. 85, r. 4.

[14] See *post,* p. 695.

[15] *Re Sutcliffe* [1942] Ch. 453.

[16] *Coote* v. *Whittington* (1873) L.R. 16 Eq. 534; and see A.E.A., 1925, s.28.

[17] R.S.C., Ord. 85, r. 5; and see *Re Blake, Jones* v. *Blake* (1885) 29 Ch.D. 913.

refused even if the testator has directed his executors to take proceedings to have his estate administered by the court.[18] Further, where no accounts or insufficient accounts have been rendered and a creditor or beneficiary seeks an administration order, the court may order that the application shall stand over for a certain time, and that the personal representatives shall in the meantime render proper accounts to the applicant, with an intimation that if this is not done they may be made to pay the costs of the proceedings; and to prevent proceedings by other creditors or other beneficiaries, the court may make the usual administration order, with a proviso that no proceedings are to be taken under it without the leave of the judge in person.[19] But even an order in this limited form suffices to prevent the personal representatives from exercising their powers of sale and management without the leave of the court.[20]

4. Lapse of time. An action for administration can, of course, be instituted only by persons whose claims are not barred by any statute of limitation.

(a) *Creditors*

(1) DEBT. A simple contract creditor must commence the action within six years,[21] and a specialty creditor[22] or a judgment creditor[23] within 12 years. Time runs from the date on which the cause of action accrued or, in the case of a judgment debt, the judgment became enforceable.[24]

(2) CHARGE. If a debt is charged on property, whether real or personal, the period is 12 years from the date when the right to receive the money accrued.[25] This period applies to the charge even if the debt is a simple contract debt for which, despite the charge, the personal obligation in debt will be barred after six years.[26] It is doubtful whether a direction in a will to pay debts any longer creates a charge on the testator's property. A testamentary direction to pay debts out of realty was construed as creating a charge[27] in days when realty was otherwise not liable for the payment of debts,[28] or where the charge would alter the order for resorting to the assets for paying debts.[29] In such cases the realty was liable for the whole debt even where the charge was on a

[18] *Re Stocken* (1888) 38 Ch.D. 319.
[19] R.S.C., Ord. 85, r. 5.
[20] *Re Viscount Furness, Wilson v. Kenmare (No. 2)* [1943] Ch. 415.
[21] Limitation Act 1980, s.5; a more generous time limit applies to actions in respect of certain loans: s.6.
[22] *Ibid.* s.8.
[23] *Ibid.* s.24; and see *Jay v. Johnstone* [1893] 1 Q.B. 189.
[24] Limitation Act 1980, ss.5, 8(1), 24(1).
[25] *Ibid.* s.20(1).
[26] *Barnes v. Glenton* [1899] 1 Q.B. 885.
[27] *Re Stephens* (1889) 43 Ch.D. 39.
[28] *i.e.* before 1898 when L.T.A. 1897 came into force: see *ante,* pp. 311, 312.
[29] *Re Balls* [1909] 1 Ch. /91.

mixed fund.[30] Since 1925, there has been no distinction between realty and personalty in relation to liability for debts,[31] so that in the absence of more specific language a mere direction to pay debts (and so do what in any case would be done) will probably create no charge.[32]

(3) EXTENSION OF TIME.   In addition to disability, fraud and mistake,[33] the liability of the estate may in any case be kept alive by a part payment or written acknowledgment on the part of the executors, and as regards the personal estate[34] (but not, it seems, as regards the real estate[35]) by the written acknowledgment of even one of the executors.[36]

(b) *Beneficiaries.*   A claim by legatees and those entitled on intestacy to any interest in the personal estate of a deceased person, whether under a will or intestacy, must be brought within 12 years from the date when the right to receive the interest accrued.[37] Further, any action for arrears of interest in respect of any legacy must be brought within six years of the interest becoming due.[38] But where the administration has ended, and the personal representatives are holding as trustees, they may rely on the six-year period applicable to trustees.[39] In either case, no period of limitation applies where the personal representative has been a party or privy to any fraud or fraudulent breach of trust or has in his possession property of the deceased, or has converted such property to his use.[40] Even where the period does apply, it can be extended by disability, fraud, mistake, part payment or written acknowledgment.[41]

5. The order.   An order for administration may be general, or limited to some specific part of the administration, *e.g.* the distribution among the beneficiaries. The order directs such accounts[42] and inquiries as the circumstances may require, *e.g.* accounts of sums due to creditors, of the funeral expenses and of the assets of the deceased which have come to the hands of the personal representatives, or inquiries into what assets are outstanding or undisposed of, or who are the deceased's next-of-kin. Ultimately an order for payment or distribution is made. An action for an account is barred at the same time as the limitation period applicable to the claim which is the basis of the duty to account expires.[43]

---

[30] *Re Raggi* [1913] 2 Ch. 206.
[31] See *ante*, p. 332.
[32] See *Scott* v. *Jones* (1838) 4 Cl. & F. 382; *Freake* v. *Cranefeldt* (1838) 3 My. & Cr. 499.
[33] Limitation Act 1980, ss.28, 32.
[34] *Re Macdonald* [1897] 2 Ch. 181.
[35] *Astbury* v. *Astbury* [1898] 2 Ch. 111.
[36] Limitation Act 1980, ss.29–31.
[37] *Ibid.* s.22(*a*).
[38] *Ibid.* s.22(*b*).
[39] See *ante*, pp. 99, 292.
[40] Limitation Act 1980, ss.21(1), 22, 38(1); see *ante*, p. 292.
[41] *Ibid.* ss.28–32.
[42] See *post*, p. 637.
[43] Limitation Act 1980, s.23; see *Re Blow* [1914] 1 Ch. 233; *Re Lewis, Jennings* v. *Hemsley* [1939] Ch. 232.

6. Substitution or removal of personal representatives. Under section 50 of the Administration of Justice Act 1985 the High Court has power, on the application of a personal representative or a beneficiary of the estate, to appoint a substituted personal representative in place of a sole personal representative or of all or some of several personal representatives. The court may also, where there are several personal representatives and no substitute is to be appointed, terminate the appointment of one or more (but not all) of the existing representatives. The exercise of this jurisdiction will save the expense and complexity attending either a full administration by the court or the appointment of a judicial trustee.[44] An application under section 50 may be treated by the court as though it were one for the appointment of a judicial trustee[45] and *vice versa.*[46]

7. Liability of personal representative

(a) *Assets in his hands.* In general, the liability of a personal representative is limited to the assets which have come to his hands or to the hands of another on his behalf. He can discharge himself from liability for these assets only by showing that he has duly administered them, or by proving that they have been accidentally lost without his fault.[47] Thus a personal representative is not liable if without his fault the goods of the deceased are stolen[48] or, being of a perishable nature, depreciate.[49] Again, he is not liable if he distributes the estate under the direction of the court, or if stock belonging to the estate is reduced in value by Act of Parliament[50]; and probably he is not liable to the trustee in bankruptcy of a legatee if in ignorance of the bankruptcy he pays the legacy to the legatee instead of the trustee.[51]

(b) *Devastavit.* It is otherwise if the loss is attributable to some neglect or mistake of law on the part of the representative. Where this happens he is said to have committed a *devastavit.* Thus he will be answerable if he distributes the residuary estate on a wrong principle of law[52] or if he pays legacies without retaining enough assets to meet debts, or if by his neglect he causes or facilitates a depreciation of the assets. Yet for the most part a personal representative is in the same position as a trustee, whose duties, powers and liabilities have already been considered.[53] Thus, for example, he can avail himself of the

---

[44] For judicial trustees see, *ante,* p. 207.
[45] Administration of Justice Act 1985, s.50(4).
[46] Judicial Trustees Act 1896, s.1(7), inserted by Administration of Justice Act 1985, s.50(6).
[47] *Job* v. *Job* (1877) 6 Ch.D. 562. At common law he was absolutely liable: see *ante,* p. 16.
[48] *Jones* v. *Lewis* (1750) 2 Ves.Sen. 240.
[49] *Clough* v. *Bond* (1837) 3 My. & Cr. 490.
[50] *Davies* v. *Wattier* (1823) 1 Sim. & St. 463.
[51] See *Re Ball* [1899] 2 I.R. 313; *cf. Re Bennett, ex p. The Official Receiver* [1907] 1 K.B. 149; *Re Patrick Fox* [1940] N.I. 42. See generally B. S. Ker (1954) 18 Conv.(N.S.) 176.
[52] *Hilliard* v. *Fulford* (1876) 4 Ch.D. 389.
[53] *Ante,* pp. 213, 260, *Re Marsden* (1884) 26 Ch.D. 783 at 789; *Commissioner of Stamp Duties (Queensland)* v. *Livingston* [1965] A.C. 694.

protection of the Trustee Act 1925, sections 26[54] (future liabilities), 27[55] (advertisements) and 61[56] (relief by the court).

(c) *Assets not in his hands.*   The rule that a representative's liability is limited to assets which have come to his hands has two qualifications.

(1) DEBTS OWED BY THE REPRESENTATIVE.   A debt which he himself owes to the estate will be treated as assets in his hands, not only for payment of debts but also for distribution among the beneficiaries. At law the appointment of a debtor to be executor extinguished the debt, but this is not so in equity[57] unless the testator in his lifetime forgave the debt.[58] Since the debt is thus either discharged or deemed to have been received by the executor, there can be no question of it becoming barred by lapse of time. In the case of an administrator, whose office was cast upon him by the law and not by the deceased, equity did not presume that he had paid himself, but the running of time in favour of the estate was suspended.[59] This rule has been abrogated by statute: now where a debtor becomes his deceased creditor's administrator, the debt is thereupon extinguished but he is accountable for the debt as part of the estate in the same way as an executor.[60] However, there has never been suspension of the running of time where it is the *creditor* who becomes executor or administrator of his debtor.[61]

(2) WILFUL DEFAULT.   A personal representative may sometimes be made to account not only for what he has in fact received, but also for what he might have received but for his wilful default.[62]

Section 2. Guidance by the Court

Administration by the court is complex and expensive, involving the taking of accounts and inquiries and the direction by the court of every stage of the winding-up of the estate. In many cases, however, the personal representatives can manage the administration generally without the court's assistance, but require its guidance on some specific point, *e.g.* the meaning of a clause in the will[63] or the validity of the claim of a creditor. Accordingly, the personal representatives may bring an action, normally by originating summons, for the determination of

---

[54] *Ante,* p. 273.

[55] *Ante,* p. 272.

[56] *Ante,* p. 290.

[57] *Ingle* v. *Richards (No. 2)* (1860) 28 Beav. 366; *Re Bourne* [1906] 1 Ch. 697; *Commissioner of Stamp Duties* v. *Bone* [1977] A.C. 511. And see *Jenkins* v. *Jenkins* [1928] 2 K.B. 501.

[58] *Ante,* p. 124.

[59] *Seagram* v. *Knight* (1867) 2 Ch.App. 628. The distinction between a debtor executor and debtor administrator was not entirely convincing: see the discussion at (1943) 59 L.Q.R. 117.

[60] A.E.A. 1925, s.21A, inserted by Limitation Amendment Act 1980, s.10.

[61] *Bowring-Hanbury's Trustee* v. *Bowring-Hanbury* [1943] Ch. 104. This rule has been justified on the ground that the creditor could retain his own debt (59 L.Q.R. 117, 118). This right has now been abolished (*ante,* p. 331), but the rule would appear to be unaffected.

[62] See *ante,* p. 284 for details.

[63] As to which see Administration of Justice Act 1985, s.48; *ante,* p. 235.

any question arising in the administration, without seeking an order for adminstration by the court.[64] Those who claim to be interested as creditors, beneficiaries or next-of-kin may also bring such an action, though the personal representatives are necessary parties to it.[65] It is not essential that all who have a beneficial interest in the estate or a claim against it should be made parties, but the plaintiff must join those whom, having regard to the nature of the relief or remedy claimed, he thinks fit.[66] The court may order further parties to be joined.[67] Where directions are being sought whether to proceed against a beneficiary,[68] that beneficiary will usually not be entitled to see the evidence or take part in the proceedings for directions, even if he is a party.[69] Yet in the subsequent action the beneficiary can rely on the evidence as to fact given in such proceedings.[70]

Section 3. Actions against Personal Representatives

1. Right to bring action

(a) *Creditors.* Creditors may recover their debts by an action at law against the personal representatives without commencing an administration action.[71] Such an action may now be brought even if no grant of probate or administration has been made.[72] It is brought against "the estate" or "the personal representatives of the deceased,"[73] but cannot be continued until some person is joined to represent the estate.[74]

(b) *Beneficiaries.* Similarly, specific legatees and devisees may sue the representatives after they have assented to the gifts.[75] But a claim to a general legacy[76] or a share of residue, or rights under an intestacy, cannot be enforced in this way.

2. Defences. In addition to any defence which the deceased might have pleaded, a person sued as personal representative may deny that he is an executor or administrator, or allege that his grant has been revoked. He may also plead that he has duly administered all the assets

[64] R.S.C., Ord. 85, r. 2. For the personal representatives' duty to lay full information before the court, see *Re Herwin* [1953] Ch. 701 at 708, 709, 714, 715.
[65] R.S.C., Ord. 85, r. 3(1).
[66] *Ibid.* r. 3(2).
[67] See R.S.C., Ord. 15.
[68] A "Beddoe's" application: see *ante*, p. 258.
[69] See *Re Moritz* [1960] Ch. 251; *Re Eaton* [1964] 1 W.L.R. 1269.
[70] *Midland Bank Trust Co. Ltd.* v. *Green* [1980] Ch. 590 at 604–610 (Oliver J.). In the appellate courts, this point was not in issue: [1980] Ch. 590, C.A.; [1981] A.C. 513, H.L., *ante*, p. 59.
[71] See Law Reform (Miscellaneous Provisions) Act 1934, s.1, as amended by Law Reform (Miscellaneous Provisions) Act 1970, s.7, Sched.
[72] R.S.C., Ord. 15, r. 6A. The power to make this rule was introduced by Proceedings Against Estates Act 1970, s.2, repealed by S.C.A. 1981, 7th Sched.; see *ibid.* s.84(1), (2).
[73] R.S.C., Ord. 15, r. 6A(1), (2).
[74] *Re Amirteymour* [1979] 1 W.L.R. 63.
[75] *Doe* d. *Lord Saye and Sele* v. *Guy* (1802) 3 East 120. *Cf. Re West* [1909] 2 Ch. 180.
[76] *Deeks* v. *Strutt* (1794) 5 T.R. 690; *Holland* v. *Clark* (1842) 1 Y. & C.C.C. 151 at 167.

of the deceased, or all the assets except some earmarked for prior claims. These last pleas, known as *plene administravit* and *plene administravit praeter*, respectively, may be countered by alleging a *devastavit*[77] which, if established, will render the representative personally liable.

Failure to plead *plene administravit* raises a presumption of admission of assets[78] sufficient to cover the claim but not the costs,[79] though this presumption is rebutted if a receiver is appointed between judgment and execution.[80] Further, "an admission of assets to one is an admission to all,"[81] so that the payment of one legacy, unless explained, is an admission of assets to another legatee[82] or a creditor.[83] Claims alleging a *devastavit* are barred by the lapse of six years from the act complained of.[84]

Section 4. Liability of Recipients of Assets

1. Personal claim

(a) *The claim.* An unpaid or underpaid creditor,[85] legatee or next-of-kin has a direct claim against those (including the Crown[86]) who have received assets of the deceased to the extent to which the latter have been paid or overpaid in excess of their right.[87] It matters not that they have spent the assets,[88] or that they were paid or overpaid through a mistake of law on the part of the personal representatives.[89] The claim is available whether or not the estate has been administered in court.[90] It was developed by the Court of Chancery as part of its endeavours to wrest from the spiritual courts jurisdiction over the administration of assets.[91] It is thus not necessarily available to an unpaid or underpaid beneficiary under a trust.[92]

---

[77] See *ante*, p. 355.
[78] *Re Marvin* [1905] 2 Ch. 490; and see *Midland Bank Trust Co. Ltd.* v. *Green (No. 2)* [1979] 1 W.L.R. 460 as to raising the pleas by amendment after judgment.
[79] *Marsden* v. *Regan* [1954] 1 W.L.R. 423.
[80] *Batchelar* v. *Evans* [1939] Ch. 1007; and see *Marsden* v. *Regan, supra.*
[81] *Barnard* v. *Pumfrett* (1841) 5 My. & Cr. 63 at 70, *per* Lord Cottenham L.C.
[82] *Cadbury* v. *Smith* (1869) L.R. 9 Eq. 37.
[83] *Savage* v. *Lane* (1847) 6 Hare 32.
[84] Limitation Act 1980, s.5; *Lacons* v. *Warmoll* [1907] 2 K.B. 350.
[85] A.E.A. 1925, s.32(2) (*ante*, pp. 313, 314); *Hunter* v. *Young* (1879) 4 Ex.D. 256.
[86] *Re Lowe's W.T.* [1973] 1 W.L.R. 882 at 887.
[87] *Ministry of Health* v. *Simpson* [1951] A.C. 251, affirming *Re Diplock* [1948] Ch. 465; see especially [1948] Ch. at p. 502. See *ante*, p. 298, for the facts.
[88] *Ministry of Health* v. *Simpson, supra*, at p. 276. But see G. H. Jones (1957) 73 L.Q.R. 48 at 61 *et seq.*
[89] *Ministry of Health* v. *Simpson, supra*, at pp. 269–273.
[90] *Re Diplock* [1948] Ch. 465 at 502.
[91] *Ministry of Health* v. *Simpson, supra*, at p. 266.
[92] *Ministry of Health* v. *Simpson, supra*, at p. 266; but see *ibid.* at pp. 272–276. Note the more limited right, based on mistake of fact, in *Re Robinson, McLaren* v. *Public Trustee* [1911] 1 Ch. 502; *G.L. Baker Ltd.* v. *Medway Building and Supplies Ltd.* [1958] 1 W.L.R. 1216 at 1227.

(b) *Limits of claim.* The claim is available only if, and to the extent that, the claimant is without remedy against the wrongdoing personal representatives.[93] Moreover, the claim does not exist if, at the time of payment, there was a sufficiency of assets to pay all the beneficiaries in full and the deficiency arose through some subsequent accident[94] or *devastavit*[95] committed by the personal representatives. The claim does not carry interest.[96]

(c) *Limitation.* The claim is liable to be defeated by the Limitation Act 1980.[97] Where the claimant is a beneficiary under the will or intestacy of the deceased, he will be barred 12 years after his right to receive his share or interest accrued,[98] *i.e.* normally one year from the death.[99] A creditor, on the other hand, must bring his action within six years from the accrual of his cause of action, or 12 years if he is a specialty or judgment creditor.[1]

2. Tracing assets. Creditors, legatees, devisees and next-of-kin may trace the assets of the deceased into the hands of recipients other than bona fide purchasers without notice,[2] notwithstanding an assent or conveyance by the personal representative.[3] This process has already been discussed.[4]

---

[93] *Re Diplock, supra,* at pp. 503, 504.
[94] *Fenwicke* v. *Clarke* (1862) 4 De G.F. & J. 240; and see *Re Winslow* (1890) 45 Ch.D. 249.
[95] *Peterson* v. *Peterson* (1866) L.R. 3 Eq. 111; and see *Re Lepine* [1892] 1 Ch. 210.
[96] *Re Diplock* [1948] Ch. 465 at 505, 506.
[97] *Ibid.* at pp. 507–516; affirmed [1951] A.C. 251 at 276, 277.
[98] Limitation Act 1980, s.22.
[99] See *ante,* p. 310.
[1] Limitation Act 1980, ss.5, 8, 24.
[2] *Re Diplock* [1948] Ch. 465 (affirmed on other grounds: *Ministry of Health* v. *Simpson* [1951] A.C. 251).
[3] A.E.A. 1925, ss.36(9), 38; *ante,* p. 346.
[4] *Ante,* pp. 297 *et seq.*

CHAPTER 6

LEGACIES

Section 1. Classification

Bequests or legacies may be classed under the three heads of general, specific and demonstrative.

1. General. A legacy is *general* where it does not amount to a bequest of a particular thing, as distinguished from all others of the same kind. Thus, if a testator gives A a diamond ring, or £1,000 of a named stock, or a horse, not referring to any particular diamond ring, holding of stock, or horse, these legacies are general.[1] The terms "pecuniary legacy" and "general legacy" are sometimes used synonymously[2]; but the former words only mean a legacy of money, and this may be specific, general or demonstrative.

2. Specific. "The court leans against specific legacies and is inclined, if it can, to construe a legacy as general rather than specific."[3] For a legacy to be specific, the thing given must be an identified part of the testator's existing property, severed or distinguished from the general mass of his estate.[4] Thus a legacy of "my £1,000 East India Stock" is specific,[5] and so is a legacy of "all my shares or stock in the Midland Railway Company"[6] or a legacy of "the" securities opposite the name of the legatee in a schedule, the securities answering in every respect to investments held by the testator at the date of the will.[7] But a legacy of

---
[1] *Re Gray, Dresser* v. *Gray* (1887) 36 Ch.D. 205; *Re Gillins* [1909] 1 Ch. 345.
[2] See A.E.A. 1925, s.55(1)(ix). Contrast *Re O'Connor* [1948] Ch. 628.
[3] *Re Rose, Midland Bank Executor and Trustee Co. Ltd.* v. *Rose* [1949] Ch. 78 at 82, *per* Jenkins J.; and see *Re O'Connor, supra,* at p. 632. In *Re Rose, supra,* at pp. 82–85, Jenkins J. succinctly summarised the authorities and principles on the distinction.
[4] See *Bothamley* v. *Sherson* (1875) L.R. 20 Eq. 304 at 308, 309; *Robertson* v. *Broadbent* (1883) 8 App.Cas. 812.
[5] *Ashburner* v. *Macguire* (1786) 2 Bro.C.C. 108; **1 W. & T.L.C. 656.**
[6] *Bothamley* v. *Sherson* (1875) L.R. 20 Eq. 304.
[7] *Re Hawkins, Public Trustee* v. *Shaw* [1922] 2 Ch. 569.

"fifty shares of the York Banking Co." is a general legacy,[8] and so is a legacy of "£948 3s. 11d. Queensland 3½ per cent. Inscribed Stock," even if the testator has that exact amount of stock at the date of his will.[9] A gift of £1,000 "of my stock" is specific if the testator appears to have intended to give an aliquot part of his stock, but demonstrative if his intention appears to have been to give £1,000 payable out of his stock.[10] The forgiveness of a debt is treated as a specific legacy of the sum owed.[11]

3. Demonstrative. A legacy is *demonstrative* where it is "in its nature a general legacy, but where a particular fund is pointed out to satisfy it."[12] Thus in the absence of a context to the contrary, if a testator bequeaths £1,000 out of his Consols the legacy is demonstrative.

Section 2. Ademption and Abatement

The main differences between these three kinds of legacies relate to ademption and abatement. They are as follows.

1. General legacies abate before specific legacies. The fund available for payment of general pecuniary legacies will be resorted to for payment of debts before the specific legacies are touched, unless they are charged wth debts[13]; for this will give effect to the testator's intention to give the entirety of anything which he has specifically bequeathed.[14] Where the pecuniary legacy fund has thus to be resorted to, the legacies are said to "abate."

2. No ademption of general legacies. Unlike a specific legacy, a general legacy is not within the principle of ademption. Under this, a specific legacy fails if the chattel or fund given has ceased to exist as part of the testator's property in his lifetime; and the legatee is not entitled to any compensation out of the general assets, because nothing but the specific thing was given to him.[15] A legacy is also adeemed if the property is changed into something different, even if the thing into which it is changed is in the testator's possession at his death. It is

---

[8] *Re Gray, Dresser* v. *Gray* (1887) 36 Ch.D. 205; *Re Gillins* [1909] 1 Ch. 345.
[9] *Re Willcocks* [1921] 2 Ch. 327; and see *Re Gage* [1934] Ch. 536.
[10] *Kirby* v. *Potter* (1799) 4 Ves. 748; *Davies* v. *Fowler* (1873) L.R. 16 Eq. 308; *Re Pratt, Pratt* v. *Pratt* [1894] 1 Ch. 491.
[11] *Re Wedmore* [1907] 2 Ch. 277.
[12] *Ashburner* v. *Macguire* (1786) 2 Bro.C.C. 108 at 109, *per* Lord Thurlow L.C.; **1 W. & T.L.C. 656 at 657.**
[13] *Re Compton, Vaughan* v. *Smith* [1914] 2 Ch. 119; A.E.A. 1925, 1st Sched., Pt. II, *ante*, pp. 332, 333.
[14] See *Robertson* v. *Broadbent* (1883) 8 App.Cas. 812 at 815.
[15] *Ashburner* v. *Macguire, supra.*

immaterial whether the change is effected by the testator himself or by external authority, for adememption is not dependent upon the intention of the testator[16]; but an unauthorised change will work no ademption.[17] And a legacy may be adeemed *pro tanto*, as where the testator sells part of the property specifically bequeathed.[18]

There is no ademption if the subject-matter of the legacy has been changed only in name and form. For instance, a gift of shares in a company is not affected if the company is merely reconstructed and the testator receives shares in the new company in place of his shares in the old.[19] "The question is whether a testator has at the time of his death the same thing existing—it may be in a different shape—yet substantially the same thing."[20] Further, statute usually prevents ademption on the conversion of government stock,[21] and on public amalgamation and nationalisation schemes.[22]

3. Demonstrative legacies immune from ademption and preferred on abatement.   A demonstrative legacy has the best of both worlds. It is so far of the nature of a specific legacy that, if there is a deficiency of assets, it will not abate with the general legacies so long as the fund out of which it is payable is not exhausted. Yet it is so far of the nature of a general legacy that it will not be liable to ademption by the alienation or non-existence of the specific fund primarily designated for its payment, but will be payable out of other assets.[23]

Section 3. Payment of Legacies

1. Assent.   Whatever the legacy may be, whether general, specific or demonstrative, the executor's assent is necessary to give the legatee the right to its possession.[24] No action can be brought at law to recover a legacy unless it is a specific legacy to which the executor has assented.[25] In other cases, the remedy of a legatee is to start proceedings for the administration of the estate.

---

[16] *Frewen* v. *Frewen* (1875) 10 Ch.App. 610; *Harrison* v. *Jackson* (1877) 7 Ch.D. 339; *Re Slater* [1907] 1 Ch. 665. Contrast *Re Jameson* [1908] 2 Ch. 111, where the change took place before the date of the will, so that there was a mere misdescription. See also, *post*, p. 490.

[17] *Jenkins* v. *Jones* (1866) L.R. 2 Eq. 323.

[18] *Humphreys* v. *Humphreys* (1789) 2 Cox Eq. 184.

[19] *Re Clifford* [1912] 1 Ch. 29; *Re Leeming* [1912] 1 Ch. 828; *Re O'Brien* (1946) 115 L.J.Ch. 340; *McBride* v. *Hudson* (1962) 107 C.L.R. 604 (shares redivided).

[20] *Oakes* v. *Oakes* (1852) 9 Hare 666 at 672, *per* Turner V.-C.; see *Re Kuypers* [1925] Ch. 244.

[21] See, *e.g.* National Debt (Conversion) Act 1888, s.25.

[22] See, *e.g.* Railway Act 1921 (*Re Anderson, Public Trustee* v. *Bielby* [1928] W.N. 46); Transport Act 1947, 5th Sched., Pt. I(5); Pt. II(6); Electricity Act 1947, 3rd Sched., Pt. I(5); Pt. II(6); Gas Act 1948, 2nd Sched., Pt. I(5); Pt. II(6); *Re Jenkins* [1931] 2 Ch. 218.

[23] *Mullins* v. *Smith* (1860) 1 Dr. & Sm. 204 at 210; *Vickers* v. *Pound* (1858) 6 H.L.C. 885; *Walford* v. *Walford* [1912] A.C. 658 at 662, 663; *Re Webster* (1936) 156 L.T. 128.

[24] For assents, see *ante*, p. 343.

[25] *Ante*, p. 357.

2. Appropriation

(a) *Nature*. The personal representative's assent to a general pecuniary legacy is usually shown by his paying the legacy. However, instead of paying it in cash, he may agree with the legatee that the legatee shall take some specific asset, which is available for its payment, in full or partial satisfaction of the legacy.[26] Without prejudice to[27] any other power of appropriation conferred by law[28] or by will, wide powers of appropriation are contained in the Administration of Estates Act 1925, s.41,[29] whenever the deceased died, and whether he died testate or intestate.[30] These powers, however, do not affect the basis of an appropriation, which, unless the will dispenses with the consent of the beneficiary, is a contractual transaction whereby the beneficiary gives up his claim in return for the property appropriated to him[31]; and a partial appropriation is treated as a payment of the cash equivalent of the assets transferred, rather than as a transfer of a fraction of the share or legacy to be satisfied.[32]

(b) *The statutory power*. Section 41 provides that the personal representative may appropriate any part of the real or personal estate in its actual condition in or towards satisfaction of any legacy or any other interest or share in the deceased's property, whether settled or not.[33] But there are certain provisos. Thus an appropriation is not to be made so as to affect prejudicially any specific devise or bequest.[34] Further, certain consents are required, *e.g.* of the person (if any) of full age and capacity absolutely and beneficially entitled, or in the case of a settled share, either of the trustee thereof, if any (not being the personal representative), or the person for the time being entitled to the income, or his parent, guardian or receiver[35]; and although in some cases consent is dispensed with,[36] the personal representative must have regard to the rights of such persons, and of those who then are unborn or cannot be found or ascertained.[37] An appropriation will bind all persons interested whose consent is not made requisite; but unless all

---

[26] *Re Lepine* [1892] 1 Ch. 210; *Re Richardson, Morgan* v. *Richardson* [1896] 1 Ch. 512; *Re Beverly* [1901] 1 Ch. 681; *Re Craven* [1914] 1 Ch. 358; *Re Wragg* [1919] 2 Ch. 58; *Re Cooke, Tarry* v. *Cooke* [1913] 2 Ch. 661.

[27] A.E.A. 1925, s.41(6).

[28] In addition to the cases cited in note 26, see L.P.A. 1925, s.28(3), (4); T.A. 1925, s.15(*b*); *Re Nickels* [1898] 1 Ch. 630.

[29] Replacing L.T.A. 1897, s.4, which gave a power of appropriation that became practically a dead letter, as the power to prescribe provisions for valuation was never implemented. See also the Intestates' Estates Act 1952, s.5, 2nd Sched., and *Re Phelps* [1980] Ch. 275 for the right of a surviving spouse on intestacy to require the appropriation of the matrimonial home.

[30] A.E.A. 1925, s.41(9).

[31] *Jopling* v. *I.R.C.* [1940] 2 K.B. 282.

[32] *Re Gollin's Declaration of Trust* [1969] 1 W.L.R. 1858; but see *Re Leigh's S.T.* [1981] C.L.Y. 2453. Contrast *Re Marquess of Abergavenny's Estate Act Trusts* [1981] 1 W.L.R. 843 where the share had been fully satisfied.

[33] A.E.A. 1925, s.41(1).

[34] *Ibid.* proviso (i).

[35] *Ibid.* provisos (ii)–(iv); Mental Health Act 1959, s.149(1), 7th Sched.; Mental Health Act 1983, s.148(1), Sched. 4, para. 7.

[36] A.E.A. 1925, s.41(4).

[37] *Ibid.* s.41(5).

the conditions are satisfied, there can be no appropriation even if it was the trustee's duty to make one.[38]

(c) *Operation of power*. Property may be appropriated to satisfy a settled legacy or share even if the property appropriated is not an investment authorised by law or by the will, if any, of the deceased; when duly appropriated the property will be treated as an authorised investment and may be retained or dealt with accordingly.[39] Further, in favour of a purchaser for money or money's worth from the beneficiary, an appropriation of land is deemed to be properly made if made in purported exercise of the powers given by the section.[40] The personal representative may value the respective parts of the estate as he may think fit as at the date of appropriation,[41] and should employ a qualified valuer where necessary.[42]

(d) *Extent of power*. The section extends to property over which a testator exercised a general power of appointment, including the statutory power to dispose of entailed interests; and it authorises the setting apart of a fund to answer an annuity by means of the income of that fund or otherwise.[43] The personal representative may appropriate in satisfaction of his own beneficial interest,[44] unless the property consists of securities having no market value.[45]

3. Minors

(a) *Payment*. A will may expressly provide for payment of a legacy to the legatee even if he is a minor; in this case the executors have a discretionary power to make the payment but cannot be required to do so.[46] Apart from such a provision, neither the minor nor his parents, guardian or spouse can give a valid receipt for a legacy.[47] Formerly, the only safe course was to pay the money into court, for it was held that an executor could not free himself from personal liability by appropriating the amount of the legacy and investing it in some trust security.[48]

(b) *Trust or appropriation*. After 1925, however, where there is no gift to trustees for the minor, the Administration of Estates Act 1925, s.42, allows a personal representative to discharge himself by appointing a trust corporation or two or more individuals not exceeding four[49]

---

[38] *Re Matthews' W.T.* [1961] 1 W.L.R. 1415.
[39] A.E.A. 1925, s.41(2).
[40] *Ibid.* s.41(7), (8).
[41] *Re Charteris* [1917] 2 Ch. 379 at 386; *cf. Re Hillas-Drake* [1944] Ch. 235 (valuations for hotchpot made at date of distribution not death).
[42] A.E.A. 1925, s.41(3).
[43] *Ibid.* s.41(9).
[44] See *Re Richardson, Morgan v. Richardson* [1892] 1 Ch. 512.
[45] *Re Bythway* (1911) 104 L.T. 411.
[46] *Re Somech* [1957] Ch. 165.
[47] *Dagley v. Tolferry* (1715) 1 P.Wms. 285; *Rotheram v. Fanshaw* (1748) 3 Atk. 628 at 629; *Roper on Legacies* (4th ed., 1847), p. 879; *Harvell v. Foster* [1954] 2 Q.B. 367.
[48] *Re Salomons* [1920] 1 Ch. 290.
[49] The limit of four applies to realty and personalty alike: contrast *ante*, p. 200.

(whether or not including himself) to be trustees of any devise, legacy, residue or share of residue to which a minor is absolutely entitled under a will or intestacy, and empowers him to vest the property in the trustees so appointed. Where the minor is not absolutely entitled, section 42 does not apply, but an appropriation can be made under section 41 with the consent of the minor's parent or guardian.[50] While the power is useful with regard to gifts by will, it is of small application to intestacy, as on an intestacy after 1925 a minor can be absolutely entitled only if he has married.[51]

4. Property liable for payment

(a) *Before 1926.* Where the testator died before 1926, general legacies were payable only out of his personalty not specifically bequeathed by the will, unless the testator had shown an intention that they should be paid out of other property.[52] The legatees had no right to claim payment out of the testator's realty unless their legacies were charged on the realty.[53]

(b) *After 1925*

(1) INTESTACY.   For deaths occurring after 1925 the position has been modified by the Administration of Estates Act 1925, s.33. Where there is a partial intestacy, section 33 imposes a trust for sale on the undisposed-of property and directs the discharge of pecuniary legacies thereout. Thus property undisposed of by will, whether real or personal, is primarily liable for the payment of legacies.[54]

(2) POSSIBLE APPLICATION OF OLD RULES.   It is controversial whether this rule applies where the undisposed-of property is held on an express trust for sale, thereby excluding the statutory trust for sale. One view is that in such cases the old rules still apply; for section 34, which regulates the order of application of assets in discharging the "funeral, testamentary and administration expenses, debts and liabilities,"[55] does not mention legacies. Thus if a testator gives his residue on an express trust for sale and division, and a share lapses, the express trust excludes the statutory trust,[56] and so the legacies will be paid primarily out of the

---

[50] *Ante*, p. 363.
[51] A.E.A. 1925, s.47; *Re Yerburgh* [1928] W.N. 208; *Re Wilks, Keefer* v. *Wilks* [1935] Ch. 645 at 650. *Cf. Re Kehr* [1952] Ch. 26.
[52] *Robertson* v. *Broadbent* (1883) 8 App.Cas. 812.
[53] *Re Rowe, Bennetts* v. *Eddy* [1941] Ch. 343 at 346.
[54] *Re Worthington, Nichols* v. *Hart* [1933] Ch. 771, followed in *Re Berrey's W.T.* [1959] 1 W.L.R. 30 (lapsed shares of residue); and see *Re Martin, Midland Bank Executor and Trustee Co. Ltd.* v. *Marfleet* [1955] Ch. 698 (undisposed-of realty), though this case was expressed to be decided under s.34.
[55] See *ante*, pp. 332 *et seq.*
[56] *Re McKee* [1931] 2 Ch. 145; and see *Re Beaumont's W.T.* [1950] Ch. 462.

general personalty before it is divided, and not out of the lapsed share under the trust.[57] The other view, which appears to be preferable, looks to the provision in Part 2 of the First Schedule that the primary fund for payment of debts is "property of the deceased undisposed of by will, subject to the retention thereout of a fund sufficient to meet any pecuniary legacies."[58] The retention of the fund to pay legacies implies an obligation to pay them out of it.[59]

(3) EXEMPTION OF REALTY. Apart from the section, realty is not liable for the payment of legacies[60] unless the testator has shown an intention to the contrary, either expressly or impliedly, as by making a gift of legacies generally and then giving the *residue* of his realty and personalty in one mass.[61] Even if the realty does thus become available for the payment of legacies, it is still immune until all the personalty is exhausted, unless the will shows a contrary intention, *e.g.* by directing payment of the legacies out of a mixed fund, in which case they will be paid *pari passu* out of the realty and personalty.[62] This point is obviously important when the residuary personalty and the residuary realty are given to different persons; but even if they are given to the same person, the point is material with regard to the incidence of inheritance tax; for legacies bear their own tax so far as they are paid out of realty.[63]

(c) *Marshalling.* If certain legacies are payable only out of the personal estate and others are charged on the realty in aid of the personalty, the doctrine of marshalling operates to ensure that all the legacies will be paid if possible.[64] This doctrine has already been discussed.[65]

5. Priority of payments

(a) *General rule.* A pecuniary legatee is entitled to be paid his legacy in priority to the residuary legatee[66]; *a fortiori* a specific or demonstrative legatee. But if, for example, a testator gives a sum of £1,000 to A for life, with remainder as to £300 to B, as to £400 to C,

---

[57] *Re Beaumont's W.T.* [1950] Ch. 462; *Re Taylor's Estate and W.T.* [1969] 2 Ch. 245, trenchantly criticised by M. Albery (1969) 85 L.Q.R. 464.

[58] See *ante*, p. 332.

[59] *Re Gillett's W.T.* [1950] Ch. 102; *Re Midgley* [1955] Ch. 698; and see *Re Sanger* [1939] Ch. 238; *Re Martin, Midland Bank Executor and Trustee Co. Ltd.* v. *Marfleet* [1955] Ch. 576. See generally E. C. Ryder [1956] C.L.J. 80 (an illuminating discussion).

[60] *Re Rowe, Bennetts* v. *Eddy* [1941] Ch. 343.

[61] "The rule in *Greville* v. *Browne*" (1857) 7 H.L.C. 689: see *Re Timson* [1953] 1 W.L.R. 1361.

[62] *Re Boards* [1895] 1 Ch. 499; *Re Thompson, Public Trustee* v. *Husband* [1936] Ch. 676; and see *Re Anstead* [1943] Ch. 161 at 164 for an exposition of the method of administering a solvent estate.

[63] See *Re Anstead, supra* (estate duty); and see *Re Owers, Public Trustee* v. *Death (No. 1)* [1941] Ch. 17; and see generally *Dymond's Capital Taxes*, Vol. 1, para. 27.302.

[64] *Hanby* v. *Roberts* (1751) Amb. 127; *Scales* v. *Collins* (1852) 9 Hare 656.

[65] *Ante*, p. 336, and see *post*, p. 421.

[66] *Baker* v. *Farmer* (1868) 3 Ch.App. 537.

and as to the residue or surplus to D, the result will be that B, C and D will 'all have to abate rateably if the £1,000 diminishes;[67] for the gift to D is not truly residuary.

(b) *Special priorities.* *Inter se*, general pecuniary legacies are payable *pari passu.* But if the testator has given some of them priority over the others and the estate proves insufficient, those having priority will be paid first (but without interest[68]), and will not abate with the others. Thus he may expressly provide that in case of insufficiency, some are to be paid before others, or he may give some only on the supposition that the estate will be sufficient to pay for others.[69] On the other hand, near relationship to the testator does not of itself give a legatee any priority, nor does a direction that any particular legacy is to be paid immediately, or within a month or three months after the testator's death,[70] or that it is to be paid first and the others afterwards.[71] It has also been held that a legacy given to a creditor in satisfaction of his debt has no priority,[72] though this is doubtful.[73] But it is clear that there is no priority for a legacy given on condition that the legatee releases a claim against the property of a third person, rather than the testator's estate.[74]

Section 4. Annuities

1. Nature. Annuities given by will are merely pecuniary legacies payable by instalments; unless a contrary intention is shown, they begin to run from the testator's death, although the first instalment is not payable until the end of the first year.[75] If instead of an annuity a legacy is given to A for life with remainder to B, no interest is due until the end of two years from the testator's death; for the legacy is not payable until the end of the first year,[76] and until then there is no fund to produce any income for A.[77]

2. Duration. An annuity given to A simply is for the life of A only; and an annuity given to A expressly for his life, and afterwards to B simply, is an annuity to A for his life, and then to B for his life.[78] An

---

[67] *Page* v. *Leapingwell* (1812) 18 Ves. 463; *Haslewood* v. *Green* (1860) 28 Beav. 1; *Baker* v. *Farmer, supra,* at p. 540.
[68] *Re Wyles* [1938] Ch. 313.
[69] *Stammers* v. *Halliley* (1841) 12 Sim. 42.
[70] *Re Schweder* [1891] 3 Ch. 44, dissenting from *Re Hardy* (1881) 17 Ch.D. 798.
[71] *Beeston* v. *Booth* (1819) 4 Madd. 161: *Re Harris, Harris* v. *Harris* [1912] 2 Ch. 241; *Re Leach, Milne* v. *Daubeny* [1923] 1 Ch. 161.
[72] *Re Wedmore* [1907] 2 Ch. 277.
[73] *Re Whitehead* [1913] 2 Ch. 56; *Davies* v. *Bush* (1831) You. 341.
[74] *Re Whitehead, supra.*
[75] *Gibson* v. *Bott* (1802) 7 Ves. 89 at 96.
[76] See *ante,* p. 341.
[77] *Gibson* v. *Bott, supra,* at p. 96.
[78] *Blight* v. *Hartnoll* (1881) 19 Ch.D. 294; *Mansergh* v. *Campbell* (1858) 25 Beav. 544 at 547; *Kirkby* v. *Phillips* [1948] Ch. 109; and see *Reid* v. *Reid* [1944] A.C. 91.

annuity may, however, be so given as to be a perpetual annuity or (if it is charged on land) a rentcharge in fee simple,[79] as where it is given to a corporation or unincorporated body.[80]

3. No right to capital value. If a will directs the payment of an annuity, prima facie it is payable out of capital if the income is insufficient[81]; and although short-term "borrowings" from capital for temporary necessity during the course of a normal year's administration may be repaid, the income of later years cannot be used to recoup capital thus paid to annuitants.[82] But although the annuitant is entitled to have his annuity secured by the setting aside of a fund producing income sufficient to answer it, he has no right to require the capitalised value of the annuity to be paid to him.[83] However, even when the annuity is not charged on capital, it will prima facie be cumulative, either indefinitely, requiring surplus income to be retained against any possible future deficiencies in the annuity, or (more usually) partially, allowing the surplus income to be distributed after satisfying any past deficiencies in the annuity.[84]

4. Right to capital value. Despite the general rule, in three cases an annuitant can call for a capital sum.

(a) *Insufficient estate*

(1) ACTUARIAL VALUE. The testator's estate, though solvent, may be insufficient to pay the pecuniary legacies in full and also to enable a sufficient sum to be set aside and invested in trustee securities to secure the annuity. Here the rule is to put an actuarial valuation on the annuity, then if necessary abate this value and the legacies rateably, and then pay the annuitant the capital value in full or duly abated, as the case may be.[85] This rule applies both as between pecuniary legatees and annuitants and also as between annuitants *inter se*,[86] but not where there is a single annuity and no other annuity or legacy payable *pari passu* with it.[87] The valuation will normally be made at the end of the due course of administration,[88] which is therefore the moment to determine such matters as the appropriate rates of income tax[89]; and if an

---

[79] *Townsend* v. *Ascroft* [1917] 2 Ch. 14.
[80] *Re Jones, Midland Bank Executor and Trustee Co. Ltd.* v. *League of Welldoers* [1950] 2 All E.R. 239.
[81] See *Wroughton* v. *Colquhoun* (1846) 1 De G. & Sm. 36; *Re Coller's Deed Trusts* [1939] Ch. 277 at 280 (general survey of rules of construction of gifts of annuities).
[82] *Re Croxon* [1915] 2 Ch. 290; *Re Earl of Berkeley* [1968] Ch. 744.
[83] *Re Parry, Scott* v. *Leak* (1889) 42 Ch.D. 570; *Harbin* v. *Masterman* [1896] 1 Ch. 351.
[84] *Re Chance's W.T.* [1962] Ch. 593.
[85] *Re Cottrell* [1910] 1 Ch. 402; *Re Ellis* [1935] Ch. 193; *Re Vardon* [1938] 4 All E.R. 306.
[86] *Re Cox, Public Trustee* v. *Eve* [1938] Ch. 556.
[87] *Wright* v. *Callender* (1852) 2 De G.M. & G. 652.
[88] *Re Bradberry* [1943] Ch. 35; see D. R. Boult (1944) 60 L.Q.R. 383.
[89] *Re Ball, Lucas* v. *Ball* [1940] 4 All E.R. 245; *Re Twiss* [1941] Ch. 141.

annuitant dies in the meantime, the sum which his representatives will receive is based on the actual (and not actuarial) expectation of life which he had at the death of the testator.[90]

(2) EFFECT. Such a payment of a capital sum produces equality of treatment where there is disparity of age between the annuitants. Otherwise, if A is 90 years old and B 19, and the annuity were to be paid by drawing on capital to supplement the deficient income, A might receive the full income for all his life and B for only part of his.[91]

(3) EXCEPTIONS. The rule is a rule of convenience, however, and not a rule of law.[92] It does not apply in the following cases:

(i)   Where the testator has excluded the rule, e.g. by showing that in making his will he had envisaged a possible insufficiency.[93]

(ii)   Where "there is no commercial risk of insufficiency," as where there is no real risk of the capital of the estate being exhausted before the death of the last annuitant.[94]

(iii) Where the will authorises the setting aside of a fund to provide the annuity, and disposes of this fund after the annuitant's death otherwise than by directing it to fall into residue.[95] In this case, the rights of the parties are best effectuated by abating the fund and paying the annuitant his annuity in full for as long as the fund can provide it, thus leaving the persons entitled to the fund on the annuitant's death with some hope of receiving at least part of the fund.[96]

(iv)   Where instead of giving an annuity the testator has settled a legacy on persons in succession. Here the legacy abates and the tenant for life merely receives the income of the abated sum.[97]

(b) *Direction to purchase annuity.*   If a will directs the purchase of an annuity for A for life, A is entitled to take the purchase-money instead of the annuity; "it would be an idle form to direct an annuity to be purchased, which the annuitants might sell immediately afterwards."[98] A gift of the money required to purchase an annuity of £x is treated as a

[90] *Re Bradberry, supra.*
[91] See *Re Cox, Public Trustee* v. *Eve, supra,* at p. 563.
[92] *Re De Chassiron* [1939] Ch. 934.
[93] *Ibid.*
[94] *Re Hill, Westminster Bank Ltd.* v. *Wilson* [1944] Ch. 270.
[95] *Re Nicholson, Chadwyck-Healey* v. *Crawford* [1938] 3 All E.R. 270; *Re Thomas, Public Trustee* v. *Falconer* [1946] Ch. 36, not following *Re Farmer* [1939] Ch. 573 and *Re Wilson, Hartley* v. *Marie Curie Hospital* [1940] Ch. 966; *cf. Re Cottrell, supra,* where the fund was merely to fall into residue.
[96] See *Re Thomas, supra.*
[97] *Re Carew* [1939] Ch. 794; but see *Re Ellis, supra.*
[98] *Stokes* v. *Cheek* (1860) 28 Beav. 620 at 621, *per* Romilly M.R.

vested legacy of the money, so that if the annuitant survives the testator but dies before receiving the money his estate is entitled to it,[99] with interest at 4 per cent. from the testator's death or, if payments on account of the annuity have been made, from the last of these.[1] In the absence of a gift over, a direction that the annuitant shall not receive the capital value of the annuity, or shall not alienate it, is ineffective as being a mere naked prohibition; and it may also be repugnant to the annuitant's absolute interest in the capital value.[2]

(c) *Covenant inter vivos.* Where the deceased has covenanted in his lifetime to pay an annuity, and after taking the capital value of the annuity into account it appears that the estate is insolvent, the annuitant may prove in the insolvency on the basis of that capital value.[3]

5. Arrears. Payments of an annuity which are delayed by an insufficiency in the assets normally carry no interest.[4]

Section 5. Income from Legacies and Devises

If a legacy or devise is immediate, prima facie the legatee or devisee is entitled to any income which the property produces after the testator's death. On the other hand, if the gift is future or contingent, it sometimes does not carry any intermediate income. These two cases must be considered in turn. In each case the rules take effect subject to any provision to the contrary in the will.

A. Immediate Gifts

1. Residuary and specific gifts. An immediate gift of residue, whether realty or personalty, carries with it all the income which the property produces after the testator's death. The same rule applies to an immediate specific devise or specific bequest.[5] Correspondingly, all expenses connected with the property (*e.g.* of upkeep, maintenance and insurance) must be borne by such a devisee or legatee, either from the

[99] *Re Robbins* [1907] 2 Ch. 8.
[1] *Re Brunning* [1909] 1 Ch. 276.
[2] *Woodmeston* v. *Walker* (1831) 2 Russ. & M. 197; and see *Re Mabbett* [1891] 1 Ch. 707. *Secus* if statute forbids alienation of the annuity (*Re Boxall Estate* [1946] 3 W.W.R. 413); *sed quaere*: see (1946) 24 Can.B.R. 818; (1947) 25 *ibid.* 117.
[3] *Re Pink, Elvin* v. *Nightingale* [1927] 1 Ch. 237; *Re Viscount Rothermere* [1945] Ch. 72.
[4] *Torre* v. *Browne* (1855) 5 H.L.C. 555; *Re Earl of Berkeley* [1968] Ch. 744.
[5] *Barrington* v. *Tristram* (1801) 6 Ves. 345 at 349; *Re West, West* v. *Roberts* [1909] 2 Ch. 180; and see *Re Buxton* [1930] 1 Ch. 648.

testator's death,[6] or, where the gift is of property to be selected by the devisee or legatee, from the date of selection.[7] These expenses include matters such as the cost of repairing the premises under a lease on which they have been let to a tenant, unless before his death the testator had contracted (*e.g.* with a builder) to do the specific repairs required, or the obligation was an initial obligation to make the premises fit for occupation, and not merely an ordinary continuing liability to repair.[8]

2. Legacies

(a) *Six per cent.* A general legacy carries interest at the rate of 6 per cent.[9] from the time at which it is payable. This is so even if the subject-matter of the legacy is shares upon which dividends in excess of 6 per cent. have been declared.[10] But normally no interest is payable on arrears of an annuity given by will.[11]

(b) *Interest starts one year after death.* If no time for payment is mentioned in the will, an immediate legacy is payable at the end of the executor's year, and so interest runs only from the end of the year. This applies even where the legacy is given to the widow,[12] or where it is given on a series of limitations,[13] or where it is given to a person on his attaining a certain age, and he attains that age in the testator's lifetime.[14] But if the will directs that the legacy is to be paid at a specified time earlier than the end of the first year, interest runs from the specified time.[15]

(c) *Interest running from death.* In certain cases interest on a general pecuniary legacy is payable from the date of the testator's death. These cases are as follows.

(1) CHARGED ON LAND: the legacy is charged on land only and is vested.[16] The rules settled by the ecclesiastical courts relating to the executor's year do not apply here.[17]

---

[6] *Re Pearce* [1909] 1 Ch. 819; *Re Rooke, Jeans* v. *Gatehouse* [1933] Ch. 970.
[7] *Re Collins' W.T.* [1971] 1 W.L.R. 37.
[8] *Re Day's W.T.* [1962] 1 W.L.R. 1419; and see *Re Smyth* [1965] I.R. 595.
[9] R.S.C., Ord. 44, r. 10, as amended by S.I. 1983 No. 1181, r. 25. Until 1973 the rate was 4 per cent.; and from 1973 to September 30, 1983, 5 per cent: see S.I. 1972 No. 1898, r. 6. And see *post*, p. 372.
[10] *Re Hall, Barclays Bank Ltd.* v. *Hall* [1951] 1 All E.R. 1073. After appropriation, the legatee is of course entitled to the actual income.
[11] *Re Hiscoe* (1902) 71 L.J.Ch. 347. Contrast *Re Salvin* [1912] 1 Ch. 332 (annuity covenanted to be paid by testator).
[12] *Re Bignold* (1890) 45 Ch.D. 496.
[13] *Re Whittaker* (1882) 21 Ch.D. 657.
[14] *Re Palfreeman* [1914] 1 Ch. 877.
[15] *Re Riddell* (1936) 155 L.T. 247 (not reported on this point at [1936] Ch. 747); *Re Pollock, Pugsley* v. *Pollock* [1943] Ch. 338.
[16] *Maxwell* v. *Wettenhall* (1722) 2 P.Wms. 26.
[17] See *Pearson* v. *Pearson* (1802) 1 Sch. & Lef. 10 at 11.

(2) SATISFACTION OF DEBT: the legacy is given to satisfy a debt.[18]

(3) TESTATOR'S MINOR CHILD: the legacy is given to a minor child of the testator or to a minor to whom he stands *in loco parentis* (and not merely to a trustee for such a minor[19]), and no other fund is designated for the minor's maintenance.[20] In such cases the court infers that the testator intends to provide maintenance for his child; and this applies notwithstanding that the child is entitled only contingently upon attaining full age or previously marrying,[21] or even on other contingencies, such as attaining the age of 25 years, if they do not preclude such an inference.[22] It is not clear in these cases whether what is given is interest out of which maintenance is allowed, or maintenance which is treated as interest[23]; but any surplus interest not used for maintenance is added to capital, and does not pass to the child or his estate if he fails to satisfy the contingency.[24] Under this head, the rate of interest has long been 5 per cent. if the income available is sufficient.[25]

(4) INTENT TO MAINTAIN MINOR: the legatee is a minor and the will shows an intention that the income shall be used for his maintenance[26] or education.[27] In this case the legatee (who may be only contingently entitled) need not be a child or quasi-child of the testator.

(d) *Payments on account.*   Where a legacy cannot be paid for some time after the death and payments on account of the legacy are made from time to time, the general rule is that each payment must be appropriated first to the interest due on the unpaid portion of the legacy and then to principal.[28]

B. Future Gifts

1. Right to income.   A future or contingent gift may or may not carry the intermediate income. Before 1926, the decisions established rules of some complexity. Some of these rules have now been superseded by the Law of Property Act 1925, s.175, which provides for many types of gift to carry the intermediate income. Unfortunately, the section does not lay down a comprehensive code, but omits a number of categories, some, it seems, because the gifts already carried the

---

[18] *Clark* v. *Sewell* (1744) 3 Atk. 99; *Re Rattenbury* [1906] 1 Ch. 667; *post*, p. 519.
[19] *Re Pollock, Pugsley* v. *Pollock* [1943] Ch. 338.
[20] *Re Moody* [1895] 1 Ch. 101; *Re West, Westhead* v. *Aspland* [1913] 2 Ch. 345; *Re Ramsey* [1917] 2 Ch. 64.
[21] *Re Bowlby* [1904] 2 Ch. 685.
[22] *Re Jones, Meacock* v. *Jones* [1932] 1 Ch. 642; contrast *Re Abrahams, Abrahams* v. *Bendon* [1911] 1 Ch. 108.
[23] *Re Abrahams, Abrahams* v. *Bendon, supra*, at p. 115.
[24] *Re Bowlby, supra.*
[25] T.A. 1925, s.31(3). The increases in 1973 and 1983 of the rates of interest on other legacies (*ante*, p. 371, n. 9) do not seem to have affected this rate.
[26] *Re Churchill, Hiscock* v. *Lodder* [1909] 2 Ch. 431; *Re Stokes, Bowen* v. *Davidson* [1928] Ch. 716.
[27] *Re Selby-Walker* [1949] 2 All E.R. 178.
[28] *Re Prince* (1935) 51 T.L.R. 526; *Re Morley's Estate* [1937] Ch. 491.

intermediate income, and others because they did not do so and ought not to.[29] There are still some problems, but in broad terms it may be assumed that every future or contingent gift now carries any intermediate income not otherwise disposed of unless it falls within one of the exceptions stated below. Nevertheless, the section must first be considered.

2. Section 175. The Law of Property Act 1925, s.175, applies only to wills coming into operation after 1925.[30] It provides that gifts of property within the section "shall, subject to the statutory provisions relating to accumulations,[31] carry the intermediate income of that property from the death of the testator, except so far as such income, or any part thereof, may be otherwise expressly disposed of"[32]; and for these purposes, income is "expressly disposed of" if the testator makes a complete disposition of it, even if the beneficiary then disclaims.[33] The categories of gift within the section are as follows:

(i) "A contingent or future specific devise or bequest of property, whether real or personal."

(ii) "A contingent residuary devise of freehold land."

(iii) "A specific or residuary devise of freehold land to trustees upon trust for persons whose interests are contingent or executory."

3. Gifts not carrying income

(a) *Deferred or contingent pecuniary legacies.* A testamentary gift may be future or deferred, as where property is given to A "on the death of B," or when certain litigation ends,[34] or when a reversion falls in.[35] A pecuniary legacy which is future or deferred in this way carries no interest until the event occurs[36]; but for these purposes a legacy is not future or deferred merely because it is made payable out of a fund in which the testator had only a future interest.[37] A contingent pecuniary legacy similarly will usually carry no interest until the contingency occurs.[38] But it is otherwise if the will directs the legacy to be set apart for the benefit of the legatee[39]; and, as has been seen, certain contingent legacies to minors bear interest.[40]

---

[29] See generally (1963) 79 L.Q.R. 184.
[30] L.P.A. 1925, s.175(2).
[31] See L.P.A. 1925, ss.164–166, as amended by Perpetuities and Accumulations Act 1964, s.13.
[32] L.P.A. 1925, s.175(1).
[33] *Re Hatfeild's W.T.* [1958] Ch. 469.
[34] *Lord* v. *Lord* (1867) 2 Ch.App. 782.
[35] *Earl* v. *Bellingham (No. 2)* (1857) 24 Beav. 448.
[36] *Lord* v. *Lord, supra*; *Earl* v. *Bellingham (No. 2), supra.*
[37] *Walford* v. *Walford* [1912] A.C. 658.
[38] *Re George* (1877) 5 Ch.D. 837; *Re Raine, Tyerman* v. *Stansfield* [1929] 1 Ch. 716.
[39] *Re Medlock* (1886) 55 L.J.Ch. 738; and see *Re Woodin* [1895] 2 Ch. 309.
[40] *Ante,* p. 372.

(b) *Deferred residuary gifts.* Section 175 applies to future (or deferred) *specific* devises and bequests, but does not mention future *residuary* devises or bequests. There is, therefore, no change in the rule that a deferred bequest of residuary personalty does not carry any intermediate income not disposed of, whether the gift is vested[41] or contingent,[42] and whether or not the gift is liable to defeasance before the time for payment arrives.[43] Such bequests are, however, very different from those which are not deferred but merely contingent. Under a contingent bequest (as distinct from a mere pecuniary legacy) the property given stands immediately appropriated to the legatee, and the testator's probable intention is that the intermediate income should, so far as the law allows, be accumulated so that it may abide the event[44]; whereas the very language that defers a bequest until some event occurs negatives any intention to give the income accruing before that time.[45]

Deferred residuary *devises* have been oddly treated; for the second limb of section 175 makes them carry the intermediate income if they are also contingent but not if they are vested.[46]

4. Gifts carrying income. The combined effect of the decided cases and of section 175 is that, in general, with the exceptions mentioned above, all future and contingent gifts carry the intermediate income. Thus contingent residuary gifts of personalty[47] or of blended realty and personalty[48] have always carried the intermediate income, which is accumulated and added to the capital for as long as the law permits,[49] and thereafter passes as on an intestacy. Where such a gift was of realty, a suspension of vesting of this kind was not permitted, and so the heir-at-law was held forthwith entitled to the intermediate rents and profits[50]; but section 175 now makes the gift carry them.

The section sometimes produces strange results, and it seems to have been drafted under some misapprehension of the law.[51] Thus the section now makes a deferred (or "future") specific devise or bequest carry the intermediate income,[52] despite the principle to the contrary established by the cases. Accordingly, where a will making a specific gift to A absolutely "upon the death of B" contains no express disposition of the intermediate income, the section carries it to A, and so he, being solely entitled, can apparently demand the property forthwith, even though B is still alive.[53] However, if the gift is not absolute but defeasible, *e.g.*

---

[41] *Re Oliver, Watkins v. Fitton* [1947] 2 All E.R. 162 at 166.
[42] *Re Geering* [1964] Ch. 136.
[43] *Re Gillett's W.T.* [1950] Ch. 102; contrast *Re Nash's W.T.* [1965] 1 W.L.R. 221.
[44] See *Re Geering, supra,* at p. 144.
[45] See *Re Gillett's W.T., supra,* at p. 110.
[46] See *Re McGeorge* [1963] Ch. 544 at 551, 552.
[47] *Countess of Bective v. Hodgson* (1864) 10 H.L.C. 656; *Re Taylor, Smart v. Taylor* [1901] 2 Ch. 134.
[48] *Genery v. Fitzgerald* (1822) Jac. 468; *Re Burton's Will* [1892] 2 Ch. 38.
[49] See L.P.A. 1925, ss.164–166, as amended by Perpetuities and Accumulations Act 1964, s.13.
[50] See *Countess of Bective v. Hodgson, supra,* at p. 665; *Wade-Gery v. Handley* (1876) 3 Ch.D. 374.
[51] See *Re McGeorge* [1963] Ch. 544 at 551.
[52] *Re McGeorge* [1963] Ch. 544.
[53] *Re McGeorge, supra,* at p. 550.

under a substitutional gift, the income will be accumulated to await the event.[54]

Section 6. Accretions to Legacies

Accretions to a legacy or bequest sometimes raise problems, as where a bonus issue is made in respect of shares given in trust for persons in succession, or where there is a legacy of shares in a company and soon after the testator's death a dividend is paid. Such cases fall under two main heads, apportionment as to time and apportionment as to subject-matter.

A. Apportionment as to Time

1. Specific legatee and residuary legatee

(a) *Apportionment.*   Where shares are given to A and the residue to B, questions often arise whether any accretion to the shares, whether as a dividend, a bonus, or otherwise, belongs to A or forms part of the residuary estate so as to pass to B. The Apportionment Act 1870 usually provides the answer. Under that Act,[55] "all rents, annuities, dividends, and other periodical payments in the nature of income ... shall, like interest on money lent, be considered as accruing from day to day, and shall be apportionable in respect of time accordingly." The Act applies (*inter alia*) to the dividends of all companies registered under the Companies Acts,[56] even though they are private companies[57]; but it applies only where the dividend is declared in respect of a definite, though not necessarily regularly recurring, period,[58] and it may be excluded by the will.[59]

(b) *Date of declaration.*   If the dividend is declared in the testator's lifetime, it forms part of his residuary estate, even though it may not be payable until after his death.[60] But if it is not declared until after his death, it will go to the legatee, unless it was declared in respect of a particular period which occurred wholly or partly in the testator's lifetime and the Apportionment Act 1870 applies, in which case the dividend will go wholly or partly to the residuary estate.[61] If the Act is inapplicable, the legatee takes all dividends declared after the death. Thus where at T's death the dividends on cumulative preference shares

---

[54] *Re McGeorge* [1963] Ch. 544.
[55] s.2.
[56] *Re Lysaght, Lysaght* v. *Lysaght* [1898] 1 Ch. 115; *Re Oppenheimer* [1907] 1 Ch. 399.
[57] *Re White, Theobald* v. *White* [1913] 1 Ch. 231.
[58] *Re Jowitt* [1922] 2 Ch. 442.
[59] Apportionment Act 1870, s.7; see, *e.g. Re Lysaght, Lysaght* v. *Lysaght, supra.*
[60] *Lock* v. *Venables* (1859) 27 Beav. 598.
[61] *Bates* v. *Mackinley* (1862) 31 Beav. 280; *Jones* v. *Ogle* (1872) 8 Ch.App. 192; *Re Cox's Trust* (1878) 9 Ch.D. 159; *Re Edwards, Newbery* v. *Edwards* [1918] 1 Ch. 142.

which he had bequeathed to A were in arrear because of a lack of profits, A was held entitled to the whole of a dividend which was declared in respect of a year subsequent to T's death, and which included all arrears, for it was a dividend for that year alone, even though its amount was fixed by reference to the arrears.[62]

2. Tenant for life and remainderman. Similar questions arise when shares are given to one person for life and then to another.[63]

(a) *Before death of testator.* Dividends and other accretions declared due in the testator's lifetime must be regarded as part of the testator's property and hence as capital, even if they are not actually distributed until after the testator's death.[64]

(b) *Before death of life tenant.* If the accretions do not form part of the testator's estate, the tenant for life will take as income all dividends and bonuses in the nature of dividends declared before his death, or declared afterwards in respect of a period covered by his life, even if they are declared out of accumulated profits.[65] He will similarly take the proceeds of produce gathered after the testator's death even if it was growing before, *e.g.* wool shorn shortly after the testator's death.[66] The tenant for life of preference shares is also entitled to take as income any ordinary shares which by arrangement are transferred to preference shareholders in satisfaction of their claim for arrears of dividend.[67] But when securities are sold, he is not entitled to part of the price as representing expectations of a future payment of any arrears of interest.[68]

(c) *After death of life tenant.* If no dividend is declared or paid for the financial years included in the life tenancy, the life tenant's executors are not entitled to have the arrears made good out of future dividends, even though the shares are preference shares carrying a fixed cumulative preferential dividend[69]; and they are not entitled to share in the income of a business for the financial year which included his death.[70] Further, where statute provides for a single payment of compensation which includes interest for several years upon the capital element in it, and makes no provision for apportionment, the whole of

---

[62] *Re Wakley* [1920] 2 Ch. 205; *Re Sandbach* [1933] Ch. 505; and see *Re Marjoribanks* [1923] 2 Ch. 307.
[63] For another instance of these questions, see *Re Aspinall* [1961] Ch. 526 (death on quarter day: some rents payable in advance, others in arrears).
[64] *Re Winder's W.T.* [1951] Ch. 916; and see *Re Holder* [1953] Ch. 468 (accrued interest on savings certificates: held capital).
[65] *Lawrence* v. *Lawrence* (1884) 26 Ch.D. 795; *Re Piercy, Whitwham* v. *Piercy (No. 2)* [1907] 1 Ch. 289; *Re Muirhead* [1916] 2 Ch. 181.
[66] *Hassell* v. *Perpetual Executors Trustees & Agency Co. (W.A.) Ltd.* (1952) 86 C.L.R. 513.
[67] *Re MacIver's Settlement* [1936] Ch. 198; *Re Smith's W.T., Smith* v. *Melville* [1936] 2 All E.R. 1210.
[68] *Re Taylor's Trusts* [1905] 1 Ch. 734.
[69] *Re Sale* [1913] 2 Ch. 697. *Cf. McBride* v. *Hudson* (1962) 107 C.L.R. 604 (life tenant of farming business not entitled to natural increase of sheep retained to build up flock).
[70] *Re Moore, Moore* v. *Moore* [1956] V.L.R. 133.

the interest ranks as income of the year of payment and the executors of the tenant for life cannot claim any in respect of the period before his death; for the interest is not within the words "other periodical payments in the nature of income" in the Apportionment Act 1870.[71]

B. *Apportionment of Subject Matter*

1. Mixed payments. Sometimes it is not clear whether a payment is capital or income, as where a company distributes profits in an apparently capital form, or where the payment contains elements both of capital and of income. Thus when a company is wound up the payments to shareholders may include both capital and accrued profits. In such cases it may be necessary to determine whether the payment is to be treated as capital or as income, or whether it is to be apportioned. Prima facie this depends upon the nature of the payment and the language of the will or settlement[72]; but in the case of companies there are also the important restrictions upon the power of a company to make a return of its capital to its shareholders.[73] Such a return can in general be made only on a liquidation,[74] on an authorised reduction of capital,[75] or on an authorised distribution of the share premium account[76]; and although any payment so made is capital in the hands of the recipient, other payments will not be.

2. Capitalised profits

(a) *The rule in Bouch* v. *Sproule.* A company which has made profits may decide either to distribute them as dividends or to retain them and convert them into additional capital. Under the rule in *Bouch* v. *Sproule*[77] the decision of the company is binding on all who are interested in shares in the company under any will, intestacy or trust.

(b) *Capital.* The constitution of a company may permit it to capitalise its profits by retaining them in payment for new shares to be issued to its shareholders. If it does this, the decision binds the beneficiaries interested in any shares, and the new shares rank as capital.[78] This is so whether the capitalisation takes the form of issuing

---

[71] *Re Sneyd, Robertson-Macdonald* v. *Sneyd* [1961] 1 W.L.R. 575. For the Act of 1870, see *ante*, p. 375.
[72] See, *e.g. Re Thompson, Westminster Bank Ltd.* v. *Thompson* [1949] Ch. 1 ("annual produce").
[73] See *Hill* v. *Permanent Trustee Co. of New South Wales Ltd.* [1930] A.C. 720 at 731.
[74] *Re Armitage, Armitage* v. *Garnett* [1893] 3 Ch. 337.
[75] See *Rae* v. *Lazard Investment Co. Ltd.* [1963] 1 W.L.R. 555 at 572.
[76] *Re Duff's Settlements* [1951] Ch. 923.
[77] (1887) 12 App.Cas. 385. See generally S.J. Bailey (1951) 67 L.Q.R. 195; O. M. Stone (1952) 15 M.L.R. 180. The rule applies in deciding whether the distribution is income for the purposes of income tax: *C.I.R.* v. *Blott* [1921] 2 A.C. 171 (super-tax).
[78] *Bouch* v. *Sproule* (1887) 12 App.Cas. 385.

bonus shares,[79] debentures[80] or redeemable loan stock.[81] Even if the company lacks any such power of capitalisation, its decision may make the shares capital; for in all cases the question is whether or not the company intends to capitalise the profits and has in fact capitalised them.[82] Thus, if it gives its shareholders an apparent choice of taking a dividend either in cash or in the form of new shares, the shares may be offered on terms so attractive as to show that the company intended all shareholders to take shares in lieu of cash[83]; but in other cases (and especially where the company has funds readily available to pay the whole dividend in cash) the shares will be treated as income, up to the value of the dividend.[84]

(c) *Income.* If the company decides to distribute the profits as dividends, they rank as income.[85] This is so even if the company describes them as "bonus dividends"[86] or "special bonus"[87]; for not even an express declaration by the company that they are capital can affect their true nature, or alter the rights of the beneficiaries.[88] Again, the distribution of sums as capital profits so as not to attract income tax will not make them capital as between the beneficiaries[89]; and the tenant for life is entitled to them if the profits have not been effectually capitalised.[90] Where, too, a company distributed among its shareholders some government stock which it received as compensation for the nationalisation of its undertaking, the stock was held to be income.[91] The court has power to apportion such payments between capital and income, though this is, perhaps, confined to cases where the trustees have committed a breach of trust in retaining the investment whence the payment is derived.[92]

3. Transfer of securities cum div. Where stocks and shares are comprised in a settlement, and the tenant for life dies, there will normally be dividends accruing due on the investments in respect of a definite period partly before and partly after the death. If the

---

[79] *Bouch* v. *Sproule, supra*; *Re Speir* [1924] 1 Ch. 359 (will giving "dividends, bonuses and income" to tenant for life: held capital); *Re Wright's S.T.* [1945] Ch. 211.
[80] See *C.I.R.* v. *Fisher's Executors* [1926] A.C. 395; *Commissioner of Income Tax, Bengal* v. *Mercantile Bank of India Ltd.* [1936] A.C. 478 (tax cases).
[81] *Re Outen's W.T.* [1963] Ch. 291.
[82] *Re Evans, Jones* v. *Evans* [1913] 1 Ch. 23; *Re Thomas, Andrew* v. *Thomas* [1916] 2 Ch. 331; *Re Taylor, Waters* v. *Taylor* [1926] Ch. 923; *Re Bates, Mountain* v. *Bates* [1928] Ch. 682; *Hill* v. *Permanent Trustee Co. of New South Wales Ltd.* [1930] A.C. 720.
[83] *Re Evans, Jones* v. *Evans, supra*; contrast *Re Northage* (1891) 64 L.T. 625.
[84] *Re Malam* [1894] 3 Ch. 578.
[85] *Bouch* v. *Sproule, supra.*
[86] *Re Northage, supra.*
[87] *Re Alsbury* (1890) 45 Ch.D. 237.
[88] See *Hill* v. *Permanent Trustee Co. of New South Wales Ltd., supra,* at p. 731.
[89] *Re Doughty* [1947] Ch. 263 (disapproving *Re Ward's W.T.* [1936] Ch. 704); *Re Harrison's W.T.* [1949] Ch. 678; and see *Re Whitehead's W.T., Public Trustee* v. *White* [1959] Ch. 579.
[90] *Re Piercy, Whitwham* v. *Piercy (No. 2)* [1907] 1 Ch. 289.
[91] *Re Sechiari* [1950] 1 All E.R. 417; *Re Kleinwort's Settlements* [1951] Ch. 860; *Re Rudd's W.T.* [1952] 1 All E.R. 254. But see *Re Maclaren's S.T.* [1951] 2 All E.R. 414.
[92] *Re Kleinwort's Settlements, supra,* at p. 863; *Re Maclaren's S.T., supra,* at p. 420; *Re Rudd's W.T., supra,* at pp. 258, 259, 261. See A. J. Bland (1953) 17 Conv.(N.S.) 22.

investments are retained,[93] or before the dividends are paid they are transferred to persons absolutely entitled,[94] the Apportionment Act 1870 applies in the normal way, and a proportionate part of the dividends will belong to the estate of the deceased tenant for life. But if the investments are sold *cum div.* (*i.e.* including the right to the whole of the partly accrued dividends) there is no apportionment of the purchase price[95] in the absence of special circumstances[96]; for it will rarely be possible to ascertain with accuracy what portion of the purchase price represents the dividends which are accruing.[97] Trustees will usually try to postpone the sale until the investments are quoted *ex div.* on the Stock Exchange, but they are not bound to wait if an earlier sale is required in the due performance of the trust.[98]

4. Other payments. Apart from shares, there are many cases where some payment is made in respect of trust property, usually under some statutory provision. There is no one rule for determining the rights of beneficiaries, though in general the court endeavours to give them rights corresponding to those which they enjoyed in the property concerned. Sometimes statute provides for apportionment between income and capital on this basis, as in the case of compensation for the compulsory acquisition of coal mines[99]; and even where statute is silent the court may order such an apportionment, as by directing that compensation for war damage to leaseholds should be invested in annuities for periods corresponding to the unexpired periods of the leases.[1] Sometimes, too, a payment will be apportionable under the rule in *Re Earl of Chesterfield's Trusts*,[2] as with payments of compensation for loss of development value and accrued interest under the planning legislation.[3] In other cases, the payment may be wholly capital in nature, as with payments under the Compensation (Defence) Act 1939[4] for damage to requisitioned land,[5] although in the case of settled land it has been held that such a payment may rank as a "casual profit"[6] to which the tenant for life is entitled.[7]

---

[93] *Re Henderson, Public Trustee* v. *Reddie* [1940] Ch. 368 at 377.
[94] *Bulkeley* v. *Stephens* [1896] 2 Ch. 241; *Re Henderson, supra*, at pp. 380, 381.
[95] *Bulkeley* v. *Stephens, supra*; *Re Walker, Walker* v. *Patterson* [1934] W.N. 104; *Re Firth, Sykes* v. *Ball* [1938] Ch. 517; *Re Henderson, supra*.
[96] *Re Winterstoke's W.T.* [1938] Ch. 158 may be explained on this ground; see *Re Henderson, supra*, at p. 382.
[97] *Re Henderson, supra*, at p. 383.
[98] See *Re Winterstoke's W.T., supra*, at p. 161.
[99] Coal Act 1938, 3rd Sched., para. 21(2); *Re Duke of Leeds* [1947] Ch. 525; *Re Blandy-Jenkins* [1948] Ch. 322; *Williams* v. *Sharpe* [1949] Ch. 595.
[1] *Re Scholfield's W.T.* [1949] Ch. 341.
[2] (1883) 24 Ch.D. 643; *ante*, p. 229.
[3] *Re Chance's W.T.* [1962] Ch. 593. The current provisions are in Pt. VII of the Town and Country Planning Act 1990.
[4] s.2(1)(*b*).
[5] *Re Thompson, Westminster Bank Ltd.* v. *Thompson* [1949] Ch. 1.
[6] See *Re Williams' Settlement* [1922] 2 Ch. 750.
[7] See the reluctant decision in *Re Pomfret's Settlement* [1952] Ch. 48, in which *Re Thompson, Westminster Bank Ltd.* v. *Thompson, supra*, was not cited.

CHAPTER 7

DONATIONES MORTIS CAUSA

In *Re Beaumont*,[1] Buckley J. described a *donatio mortis causa* as a gift of an amphibious nature. It is not exactly a gift *inter vivos*, nor exactly a legacy. It is the delivery of property in contemplation of the donor's death upon the express or implied condition that the gift is not to be absolute and complete until the donor dies. Such cases fall within the sphere of equity partly because of the general equitable jurisdiction exercised over personal representatives and the estates of deceased persons, and partly because the assistance of equity is sometimes (though by no means always) required to perfect what would otherwise be an imperfect gift. There are a number of uncertainties in the rules governing such gifts, and the courts will not extend their bounds.[2]

Section 1. Requisites of a Donatio Mortis Causa

There are four requisites for an effective *donatio mortis causa*.[3] These will be considered in turn.

1. Contemplation of death. The gift must have been made "in contemplation of the conceived approach of death,"[4] *i.e.* not merely death at some time or other, but "death within the near future," or "death for some reason believed to be impending."[5] Usually, but probably not necessarily, it is made when the donor is very ill and expecting to die. A mere contemplation of the ordinary risks of imminent air travel is not enough[6]; but there seems to be no need for the donor to be *in extremis*,[7] nor need he be in his "last illness,"[8] so that probably a contemplation of the risks of a surgical operation or active service in war would suffice.[9] It is immaterial that the death

---

[1] [1902] 1 Ch. 889 at 892.
[2] See *Duckworth* v. *Lee* [1899] 1 I.R. 405; *Re Andrews, Andrews* v. *Andrews* [1902] 2 Ch. 394 at 398.
[3] See generally *Roper on Legacies* (4th ed., 1847), Vol. I, pp. 1–24.
[4] *Duffield* v. *Elwes* (1827) 1 Bli.(N.S.) 497 at 530, *per* Lord Eldon.
[5] *Re Craven's Estate (No. 1)* [1937] Ch. 423 at 426, *per* Farwell J.
[6] *Thompson* v. *Mechan* [1958] O.R. 357.
[7] Dicta to the contrary in *Thompson* v. *Mechan, supra*, and *Canada Trust Co.* v. *Labadie* [1962] O.R. 151 seem to be unsound: see (1965) 81 L.Q.R. 21.
[8] *Walter* v. *Hodge* (1818) 2 Swans. 92 at 100, *per* Plumer M.R.
[9] See *Agnew* v. *Belfast Banking Co.* [1896] 2 I.R. 204 at 221.

occurs from a cause different from that contemplated, *e.g.* from a different disease,[10] or by suicide[11]; but before suicide ceased to be a crime[12] it was held that this requirement was not satisfied by a contemplation of suicide.[13]

2. Conditional on death

(a) *The condition.* The gift must have been made upon the condition that it is to be absolute and complete only on the donor's death, and is therefore to be revocable during his life. In the absence of such a condition, the gift either takes effect as an ordinary gift *inter vivos* or fails altogether as being an imperfect gift.[14] The condition need not be express, and will normally be implied from the fact that the gift was made when the donor was ill.[15] But although this condition looks to the future, the gift itself must be a present gift and not merely a future gift or attempted nuncupative will.[16] A *donatio mortis causa* is "a gift *in praesenti*, to take effect *in futuro*,"[17] and until the death the gift is inchoate[18] and the donee's title incomplete.[19]

(b) *Operation of condition.* The operation of the condition depends upon how the gift is made. If it effectually transfers the title to the donee, on revocation he will hold the property in trust for the donor.[20] But if there is no such transfer, the gift "leaves the whole title in the donor"[21] until by his death he perfects the gift, whereupon the donee's title becomes complete without any assent by the donor's personal representatives[22]; for they hold the property for the donee upon a trust raised by operation of law.[23]

(c) *Revocation.* Revocation may be either automatic or express. It is automatic when the contemplated risk ends, as where the donor recovers from his illness.[24] Revocation is express if the donor resumes dominion over the property,[25] or, perhaps, informs the donee of the revocation.[26] But a mere resumption of possession and not dominion, *e.g.* for purposes of safe custody for the donee, will work no

---

[10] *Wilkes* v. *Allington* [1931] 2 Ch. 104 (contemplation of cancer, death from pneumonia).
[11] *Mills* v. *Shields (No. 1)* [1948] I.R. 367.
[12] See Suicide Act 1961, s.1. Yet the objections may not rest on criminality alone.
[13] *Re Dudman* [1925] Ch. 553; *Agnew* v. *Belfast Banking Co.* [1896] 2 I.R. 204.
[14] See *Edwards* v. *Jones* (1836) 1 My. & Cr. 226; *Tate* v. *Hilbert* (1793) 2 Ves.Jun. 111.
[15] *Gardner* v. *Parker* (1818) 3 Madd. 184; *Re Lillingston* [1952] 2 All E.R. 184.
[16] *Treasury Solicitor* v. *Lewis* [1900] 2 Ch. 812; *Re Ward, Ward* v. *Warwick* [1946] 2 All E.R. 206.
[17] *Jones* v. *Selby* (1710) Prec.Ch. 300 at 303, *per* Lord Cowper L.C.
[18] *Agnew* v. *Belfast Banking Co., supra,* at p. 213.
[19] *Duffield* v. *Elwes* (1827) 1 Bli.(N.S.) 497 at 530.
[20] See *Staniland* v. *Willott* (1852) 3 Mac. & G. 664.
[21] *Edwards* v. *Jones, supra,* at p. 235, *per* Lord Cottenham L.C.
[22] See *Tate* v. *Hilbert* (1793) 2 Ves.Jun. 111 at 120.
[23] *Duffield* v. *Elwes, supra,* at p. 543; *Re Dillon* (1890) 44 Ch.D. 76 at 82.
[24] *Staniland* v. *Willott* (1852) 3 Mac. & G. 664.
[25] *Bunn* v. *Markham* (1816) 7 Taunt. 224 at 231. See *Re Mulroy* [1924] 1 I.R. 98.
[26] See *Jones* v. *Selby, supra,* at p. 303.

revocation.[27] Nor can a *donatio mortis causa* be revoked by will,[28] for the donee's title is complete before the will takes effect.

3. Delivery

(a) *Delivery essential.*[29] There must have been delivery of the subject-matter of the gift, or of something representing it, which the donee accepts.[30] In the absence of delivery, it is not enough that there are oral or written words of gift,[31] or that the deceased told his servant to deliver the property to the donee after death[32] or asked his wife to move the property into a particular place,[33] or that his son, by his direction, set the property aside in packets on which were written the names of the intended donees.[34] Nor is it sufficient to put the gift into the post, if it does not arrive until after death.[35] But if there is delivery, it is immaterial that it is accompanied by an unattested writing,[36] or by no writing at all.[37] The delivery may be made either before or after the donor's words of gift; thus an existing bailment may be converted into a *donatio mortis causa* by the bailor uttering appropriate words of gift,[38] and a delivery made, *e.g.* two days after the words of gift, will suffice.[39]

(b) *Intent to part with dominion.* The donor must deliver the property with intent to part with dominion over it and not mere physical possession.[40] Thus delivery with intent merely to ensure the safe custody of the property will not suffice even if the property is labelled in such a way as to suggest that a gift is intended.[41] But an express condition or trust annexed to the gift, *e.g.* that the donee shall pay the donor's funeral expenses, does not invalidate it.[42]

(c) *Parties to the delivery.* The delivery must be made to the donee himself or to someone on his behalf.[43] Where a joint gift is intended, delivery may be made to one donee for himself and as agent for the other donee[44]; delivery to an agent for the donor is not enough,[45] unless

---

[27] *Re Hawkins, Watts* v. *Nash* [1924] 2 Ch. 47.
[28] *Jones* v. *Selby* (1710) Prec.Ch. 300.
[29] See, generally, W. H. D. Winder (1940) 4 Conv.(N.S.) 382.
[30] *Cant* v. *Gregory* (1894) 10 T.L.R. 584.
[31] *Miller* v. *Miller* (1735) 3 P.Wms. 356; *Ward* v. *Turner* (1725) 2 Ves.Sen. 431; **1 W. & T.L.C. 341**; but see *Tate* v. *Hilbert* (1793) 2 Ves.Jun. 111 at 120.
[32] *Hardy* v. *Baker* (1738) West *t.*Hard. 519.
[33] *Bryson* v. *Brownrigg* (1803) 9 Ves. 1.
[34] *Bunn* v. *Markham* (1816) 7 Taunt. 224.
[35] *Re Miller* (1961) 105 S.J. 207.
[36] *Moore* v. *Darton* (1851) 4 De G. & Sm. 517.
[37] *Tate* v. *Hilbert, supra,* at p. 120.
[38] *Cain* v. *Moon* [1896] 2 Q.B. 283.
[39] *Re Weston* [1902] 1 Ch. 680.
[40] *Hawkins* v. *Blewitt* (1798) 2 Esp. 663; *Birch* v. *Treasury Solicitor* [1951] Ch. 298.
[41] *Trimmer* v. *Danby* (1856) 25 L.J.Ch. 424; and see *Wildish* v. *Fowler* (1892) 8 T.L.R. 457 ("Take care of this").
[42] *Hills* v. *Hills* (1841) 8 M. & W. 401.
[43] *Moore* v. *Darton* (1851) 4 De G. & Sm. 517.
[44] *Birch* v. *Treasury Solicitor* [1951] Ch. 298.
[45] *Farquharson* v. *Cave* (1846) 2 Coll.C.C. 356 at 367; *Re Kirkley* (1909) 5 T.L.R. 522; *Re Thompson's Estate* [1928] I.R. 606.

it is made to the agent as trustee for the donee.[46] But there is no need for the donor to make the delivery with his own hands if possession is obtained by the donee acting on the donor's instructions, *e.g.* on his oral request[47] or under a power of attorney given by him.[48]

(d) *What must be delivered.* In the case of a chattel, there must be delivery either of the chattel itself or of something which not only puts it out of the donor's power to interfere with the chattel,[49] but also provides the donee with some effective means of obtaining it.[50] Thus there may be delivery of the keys of a wardrobe containing the key of a safe in which the chattel lies,[51] or delivery of the keys of a safe deposit, even though some further authority from the donor must be produced before the donee will be allowed to gain access to the safe.[52] But it is not sufficient merely to deliver one of two keys[53] or the receptacle containing the chattel without any delivery of the key.[54]

Where the subject-matter of the gift is a chose in action transferable by delivery, similar rules apply to the document representing the chose,[55] as where there is delivery of the key of a box containing bearer bonds.[56] If the chose is not transferable by delivery, there must be delivery of a document which would have to be produced in an action on the chose,[57] though that document need not contain all the essential terms of the contract between the parties.[58] In such a case, the delivery of the document does not pass the legal ownership, but the court will compel the donor's personal representatives to perfect the imperfect gift,[59] contrary to the general rule.[60] Delivery of a mere symbol of ownership, such as a broker's contract note for shares, is not enough.[61]

4. Property capable of passing by donatio mortis causa

(a) *Property capable of passing.* The property must be of a nature capable of passing by *donatio mortis causa.* Anything which is transferable by mere delivery can be given thus, as also can certain other property if there is delivery of a suitable document. The property

---

[46] *Mills* v. *Shields (No. 1)* [1948] I.R. 367.
[47] *Re Weston* [1902] 1 Ch. 680.
[48] *Re Craven's Estate (No. 1)* [1937] Ch. 423.
[49] See *Re Craven's Estate (No. 1), supra,* at p. 427.
[50] *Jones* v. *Selby* (1710) Prec.Ch. 300; *Re Wasserberg* [1915] 1 Ch. 195.
[51] *Re Mustapha* (1891) 8 T.L.R. 160.
[52] *Re Lillingston* [1952] 2 All E.R. 184. See (1952) 96 S.J. 471.
[53] See *Re Craven's Estate (No. 1), supra,* at p. 428.
[54] See *Reddel* v. *Dobree* (1839) 10 Sim. 244; *Re Johnson, Sandy* v. *Reilly* (1905) 92 L.T. 357. See generally, A. C. H. Barlow (1956) 19 M.L.R. 394 (on delivery by key, as related to gifts *inter vivos,* but discussing the cases on gifts *mortis causa*).
[55] See *Re Wasserberg* [1915] 1 Ch. 195.
[56] *Re Wasserberg, supra; cf. Re Harrison, Public Trustee* v. *Best* [1934] W.N. 25.
[57] *Moore* v. *Darton* (1851) 4 De G. & Sm. 517; *Re Dillon* (1890) 44 Ch.D. 76; *Birch* v. *Treasury Solicitor* [1951] Ch. 298.
[58] *Birch* v. *Treasury Solicitor* [1951] Ch. 298, disapproving dicta in *Re Weston* [1902] 1 Ch. 680 and *Delgoffe* v. *Fader* [1939] Ch. 922.
[59] *Re Dillon, supra* at pp. 82, 83.
[60] See *ante,* p. 125.
[61] See *Ward* v. *Turner* (1725) 2 Ves.Sen. 431; **1 W. & T.L.C. 341;** *Re M'Wey* [1928] I.R. 486.

represented by the following document has been held to be capable of being the subject of a *donatio mortis causa*: a bond[62]; a mortgage of land[63]; a banker's deposit-note[64]; a bank deposit book or pass-book[65] (unless withdrawals may regularly be made without producing the book[66]); a cheque or promissory note drawn by a third person, or a bill of exchange, whether payable to bearer or order (and, if payable to the donor's order, even though unindorsed by him)[67]; a Post Office[68] or Trustee[69] Savings Bank book[70]; War Savings Certificates and National Savings Certificates[71]; an "Exchequer Bond Deposit Book" issued by the Post Office[72]; a Victory Bond[73]; and an insurance policy.[74]

(b) *Property not capable of passing.* On the other hand, there cannot be a *donatio mortis causa* of realty or leaseholds,[75] nor of property represented by a railway stock certificate,[76] a certificate of building society shares[77] or an IOU.[78] Nor can there be an effective gift of a promissory note drawn by the donor himself,[79] or of a cheque drawn by him on his banker, for such a promissory note or cheque is not the property of the donor at all; the promissory note is only a gratuitous promise to pay, and the cheque only a revocable authority given to the banker to pay money, so that in neither case is the delivery a delivery of property or of a document of title to property.[80] There might, however, be a good gift of the money to which the cheque relates if the cheque was presented and paid in the donor's lifetime, or even after his death, if the banker had no notice of the death,[81] or if the cheque was negotiated in the donor's lifetime.[82]

---

[62] *Snellgrove* v. *Baily* (1744) 3 Atk. 214; *Gardner* v. *Parker* (1818) 3 Madd. 184.
[63] *Duffield* v. *Elwes* (1827) 1 Bli.(N.S.) 497; *Wilkes* v. *Allington* [1931] 2 Ch. 104.
[64] *Re Dillon* (1890) 44 Ch.D. 76; *cf. Re Mead* (1880) 15 Ch.D. 651. For Scottish cases, see D. G. Antonio, 1954 S.L.T. News. 121.
[65] *Birch* v. *Treasury Solicitor* [1951] Ch. 298.
[66] *Delgoffe* v. *Fader* [1939] Ch. 922.
[67] *Veal* v. *Veal* (1859) 27 Beav. 303; *Clement* v. *Cheesman* (1885) 27 Ch.D. 631; *Re Mead* (1880) 15 Ch.D. 651.
[68] *Re Weston* [1902] 1 Ch. 680.
[69] *Birch* v. *Treasury Solicitor* [1951] Ch. 298.
[70] See generally Watt's *Law of Savings Banks* (3rd ed., 1948), pp. 222–226; Lawton's *Guide to the Law of Trustee Savings Banks* (3rd ed., 1962), pp. 360–365. In Scotland, money in a current account in the joint names of the donor and donee is capable of being given *mortis causa*: *Forrest-Hamilton's Trustee* v. *Forrest-Hamilton*, 1970 S.L.T. 338 at 339, 340.
[71] *Darlow* v. *Sparks* [1938] 2 All E.R. 235.
[72] *Re Lee* [1918] 2 Ch. 320, distinguishing *Re Andrews, Andrews* v. *Andrews* [1902] 2 Ch. 394.
[73] *Re Richards, Jones* v. *Rebbeck* [1921] 1 Ch. 513; also a premium bond: see *Re Finch* (1958) Lawton, *op. cit.*, p. 1026.
[74] *Witt* v. *Amis* (1861) 1 B. & S. 109; *Amis* v. *Witt* (1863) 33 Beav. 619.
[75] *Sen* v. *Headley* [1990] 2 W.L.R. 620, containing a comprehensive review of the law.
[76] *Moore* v. *Moore* (1874) L.R. 18 Eq. 474.
[77] *Re Weston* [1902] 1 Ch. 680. But where, instead of a certificate, building societies have issued a pass-book relating to building society shares, the Registrar of Friendly Societies has held that such a book may be the subject of a *donatio mortis causa*: *Griffiths* v. *The Abbey National B.S.* (1947) [1938–1949] Reg.Rep. 14; 204 L.T.News. 142; and see *Tyler* v. *Tyler* [1935] L.J.N.C.C.R. 137.
[78] *Duckworth* v. *Lee* [1899] 1 I.R. 405; but see *Hewitt* v. *Kaye* (1868) L.R. 6 Eq. 198 at 200.
[79] *Re Leaper* [1916] 1 Ch. 579.
[80] *Re Beaumont* [1902] 1 Ch. 889, approved in *Re Swinburne* [1926] Ch. 38 (a case on a gift *inter vivos*, where *Bromley* v. *Brunton* (1868) L.R. 6 Eq. 275 was disapproved). And see *Re Owen, Owen* v. *I.R.C.* [1949] 1 All E.R. 901, *ante*, pp. 73, 122.
[81] *Tate* v. *Hilbert* (1793) 2 Ves.Jun. 111 at 118. And see *Re While* [1928] W.N. 182.
[82] *Rolls* v. *Pearce* (1877) 5 Ch.D. 730.

Section 2. Comparison with Legacies

1. Differences. A *donatio mortis causa* differs from a legacy in four respects.

(a) *Effective before death*: a *donatio mortis causa* takes effect conditionally from the date of the delivery, and therefore need not be proved as a testamentary act.

(b) *No assent*: it often requires no assent or other act on the part of the personal representatives to perfect the title of the donee.

(c) *Validity depends on situs not domicile*: its validity, if made here, depends upon English law, not on the law of the donor's foreign domicile. Thus a person domiciled in Russia can make a valid *donatio mortis causa* in this country of property situate here, even if such a gift would be ineffective by the law of Russia.[83] However, it has been held that a person domiciled here can make a valid *donatio mortis causa* of property situate abroad even though the foreign law does not recognise such a gift, provided his acts constitute a parting with dominion according to the foreign law.[84]

(d) *Mode of revocation*: it is revocable either automatically by the recovery of the donor, or expressly by his resuming possession and dominion over the property, but not by will.

2. Similarities. A *donatio mortis causa* resembles a legacy in four respects.

(a) *Satisfaction and ademption*: a *donatio mortis causa* is subject, in general, to the rules relating to satisfaction and ademption. But although it may be satisfied by a legacy subsequently given, yet the mere fact that the legacy is of an amount equal to that of the *donatio mortis causa* does not raise a presumption of satisfaction.[85]

(b) *Liability for debts*: it is liable for the debts of the donor on a deficiency of assets.[86]

(c) *Subject to legacy duty*: it was formerly subject to legacy duty in all cases where a legacy would have been so subject.

(d) *Subject to inheritance tax*: it was formerly subject to estate duty[87] and is now subject to inheritance tax. Although it is probable that the

---

[83] *Re Korvine's Trust* [1921] 1 Ch. 343.
[84] *Re Craven's Estate (No. 1)* [1937] Ch. 423, criticised in Dicey & Morris's *Conflict of Laws* (11th ed., 1987), Vol. 2, p. 546, n. 25. For further facts, omitted from the Law Reports, see *Mills* v. *Shields (No. 2)* [1950] I.R. 21 at 28.
[85] *Hudson* v. *Spencer* [1910] 2 Ch. 285; and see *post*, p. 525.
[86] *Smith* v. *Casen* (1718) 1 P.Wms. 406; *Re Korvine's Trust* [1921] 1 Ch. 343 at 348. The contrary proposition is argued by S. Warnock-Smith [1978] Conv. 130.
[87] Finance Act 1894, s.2(1)(c).

executor or administrator is responsible for the payment of this tax,[88] the donee must ultimately bear the burden of it, unless the donor has given a contrary direction in his will. A direction to pay "testamentary expenses" out of the residue would not include the inheritance tax on a *donatio mortis causa*.[89]

---

[88] See *Dymond's Capital Taxes*, Vol. 1, paras. 13.110–119, 27.700.
[89] *Re Hudson* [1911] 1 Ch. 206 (estate duty).

Part IV

SECURITIES

IF one person lends money to another, he may be content to rely upon the personal obligation of the debtor to repay him, which is enforceable by an action for the money. But often the lender will require some security for the loan, so that he will not be left to rely upon the debtor's personal obligation, and will have a claim superior to that of the ordinary creditors if the debtor becomes insolvent. The most important forms of security are mortgages and charges, which give the lender the security of preferential rights over specified property. In addition, there are liens, which in some respects are closely similar to charges; and there are also guarantees or suretyships, which give the lender the security of the personal liability of the surety in addition to that of the debtor. Equity has played a large part under each of thee heads; and they must now be considered in some detail.

CHAPTER 1

NATURE OF MORTGAGES

Section 1. Creation of Mortgages

1. Definition of mortgage. A mortgage is a conveyance of some interest in land or other property "as a security for the payment of a debt or the discharge of some other obligation for which it is given."[1] It should be distinguished from a charge, though for most practical purposes a charge can be regarded as a species of mortgage; for whereas a mortgage is a conveyance of property, a charge merely gives the chargee certain rights over the property as security for the loan.[2] Where a legal estate is transferred, the mortgage is a legal mortgage. Where only an equitable interest is transferred, whether because the borrower (or mortgagor) has merely an equitable interest, or because he uses a form insufficient for the transfer of a legal interest, the mortgage is called an equitable mortgage.

2. Property which can be mortgaged. As a rule, any kind of property may be mortgaged. Thus there may be a mortgage of hereditaments, whether corporeal or incorporeal, or personal property, whether in possession or in action. It is immaterial whether the estate or interest in the property be a legal estate or an equitable interest, or be for life or for an absolute interest, or whether it be a vested, expectant, or contingent interest.[3] A mortgage may itself be mortgaged, the transaction being known as a sub-mortgage. But there are certain kinds of property which, for special reasons, cannot be mortgaged, for example a right of patronage of a benefice,[4] or the pay of public officers.[5] Glebe lands are now vested in the Diocesan Boards of Finance, which have a general power to mortgage such land on terms approved by the Church Commissioners,[6] and most of the statutory

---

[1] *Santley* v. *Wilde* [1899] 2 Ch. 474, *per* Lindley M.R.; *London County and Westminster Bank Ltd.* v. *Tompkins* [1918] 1 K.B. 515.

[2] See *London County and Westminster Bank Ltd.* v. *Tompkins, supra*; *post*, p.443.

[3] See *Property Discount Corporation Ltd.* v. *Lyon Group Ltd.* [1981] 1 W.L.R. 300 (contract to grant lease to developer on completion of development may be mortgaged before development is completed).

[4] Benefices Act 1898, s.1(1)(*b*), (7); Benefices Act 1898 (Amendment) Measure 1923, s.4.

[5] See *ante*, p. 84.

[6] Endowments and Glebe Measure 1976, s.20(1).

restrictions on mortgages of ecclesiastical property have been repealed.[7] Again, in general the estates of a charity cannot be mortgaged without the consent of the Charity Commissioners.[8] And property given for an interest expressly made defeasible on an attempt to mortgage it cannot, of course, be mortgaged.

3. Persons who cannot mortgage. Even as regards freely alienable property, the owner may be under some personal incapacity, such as minority, which prevents him from mortgaging it. And, if property is jointly owned, the legal estate can be mortgaged only if all the joint tenants are parties to the mortgage.[9] Again, if a company has no power to borrow, any mortgage will be void as being *ultra vires*; and similarly as to any mortgage in excess of any limited power to mortgage which the company may have. This rule is equally applicable whether the company is incorporated under the provisions of the Companies Acts,[10] or under any special Act.[11] An ordinary trading company has, however, an implied power to borrow for the purposes of its business.[12] And, since the modification by statute of the *ultra vires* rule, a lender need no longer consider the documents governing the constitution of the company in order to see whether borrowing powers are conferred thereby: he need only be satisfied that the transaction has been decided upon by the directors.[13]

4. Building Societies. Building societies are subject to statutory restrictions as to the kinds of mortgages on which they may advance money. The scheme of the legislation is to divide the assets of the society into three classes, fixed assets, *i.e.* assets used for its business, liquid assets and commercial assets. The last represent the loans made by the society and other investments which the society is allowed to make. They are sub-divided into three classes: broadly, class one are the conventional first mortgages of residential property; class two, other mortgages of land; and class three, other loans and investments.[14] Assets of classes two and three may not constitute more than a prescribed percentage of the whole of the commercial assets.[15] A breach of the restrictions will not affect the validity of the security, since they are enacted for the benefit of the members and creditors of the society and not for that of borrowers.[16]

---

[7] *Ibid.* s.47(4), Sched. 8.
[8] *Ante*, p. 173; and see *ante*, p. 167 for the Charity Commissioners, and p. 168, n. 92 as to the former role of the Secretary of State for Education and Science in relation to educational charities.
[9] See *First National Securities Ltd.* v. *Hegerty* [1985] Q.B. 850. As to the effect on the beneficial interests of a mortgage executed by only one joint tenant, see *post*, p. 486.
[10] *Ashbury Railway Carriage and Iron Co. Ltd.* v. *Riche* (1875) L.R. 7 H.L. 653.
[11] *Baroness Wenlock* v. *River Dee Co.* (1885) 10 App.Cas. 354; and see Palmer's *Company Law* (24th ed., 1987), Vol. 1, paras. 9–07–9–22.
[12] *General Auction Estate and Monetary Co.* v. *Smith* [1891] 3 Ch. 432.
[13] European Communities Act 1972, s.9(1).
[14] Building Societies Act 1986, Pt. III.
[15] *Ibid.* s.20(1)–(4).
[16] *Nash* v. *Halifax B.S.* [1979] Ch. 584 (on Building Societies Act 1962, s.32(1)).

Section 2. The Equity of Redemption

A. Creation of the Equity of Redemption

1. Nature of mortgage at common law. By the old common law, the ordinary mortgage was strictly an estate upon condition. There was a feoffment of the land, with a condition (either in the deed of feoffment itself or in a deed of defeasance executed at the same time) providing that, on payment by the feoffor of a given sum at a time and place certain, it should be lawful for him to re-enter. Immediately on livery of seisin being made, the feoffee became the legal owner of the land, subject to the condition. If the condition was performed, the feoffor re-entered; but if the condition was not performed, the feoffee's estate became absolute and indefeasible as from the time of the feoffment, the legal right of redemption being then lost for ever.

2. The equitable right to redeem. Happily, however, a jurisdiction arose under which the harshness of the old law in this respect was softened without any actual interference with its principles. The courts of equity left the legal effect of the transaction unaltered but declared it to be unreasonable and against conscience that the mortgagee should retain as owner for his own benefit what was intended as a mere security. They accordingly adjudged that relief against the breach of the condition should be granted. Thus although the mortgagor lost his legal right to redeem, he nevertheless had an equitable right to redeem on payment within a reasonable time of the principal, interest, and costs. At first, the common law judges strenuously resisted the introduction of this new principle, but they were ultimately defeated by the increasing power of equity. In their own courts, however, they still adhered to the rigid doctrine of forfeiture, with the result that the law relating to mortgages fell almost entirely within the jurisdiction of equity.

3. Form of modern mortgages. In modern times the form of a legal mortgage has been altered. Instead of giving the mortgagee an estate upon condition, conveyancers adopted the form of an absolute conveyance, with a proviso for reconveyance on payment of the principal with interest at the expiration of (usually) six months. This form simplified proof of title, for whether the estate was vested in the mortgagor or not depended, not on whether the money had been paid within a fixed time, but on whether a reconveyance had been executed. Since 1925, however, a legal mortgage of land can no longer be created by a conveyance of the fee simple, but must take the form of a demise or sub-demise for a term of years absolute, subject to a provision for cesser on redemption.[17] Yet these are only changes of form. After the expiration of the time specified, the mortgage is still irredeemable at law, but redeemable in equity. The substance of the transaction is a security for a loan, and even if there is no express provision for the payment of interest, in the absence of a contrary agreement or special circumstances, the court will imply an agreement for interest. The traditional rate has been five per cent.,[18] but it may well be that a much higher rate would be allowed today.[19]

4. Charge by way of legal mortgage. In 1925 a new form of security was introduced, and this is now almost always used owing to its greater simplicity. Instead of demising land subject to a proviso for cesser on redemption, a borrower may execute a deed charging the land which is "expressed to be by way of legal mortgage." Under such an instrument the creditor has no legal term,[20] but has the same protection, powers and remedies as if he held a mortgage by demise.[21] These include, where the mortgaged property is leasehold, the right as an underlessee to apply for relief against forfeiture of the mortgaged lease.[22] The same result may be achieved in the case of registered land without using the formula "by way of legal mortgage" in the instrument of charge.[23]

5. Court looks to substance of transaction

(a) *Substance.* In determining whether any given transaction is in the nature of a mortgage, equity looks at the substance of the transaction and not merely at the form.[24] Thus, while a mortgage is quite distinct from a sale with a collateral agreement for a repurchase by the vendor within a stipulated time, it depends on the circumstances of each case whether any particular transaction is a mortgage properly so called, or a sale with an option to repurchase.[25]

(b) *Evidence.* Parol evidence is admissible to show that what on the face of it appears to be an absolute conveyance was, in fact, intended by the parties to be by way of security only.[26] A conveyance which is absolute in form may be shown to be in fact in the nature of a mortgage by such circumstances as that the purchase-money so-called would be

---

[17] L.P.A. 1925, ss.85, 86.
[18] *Mendl* v. *Smith* (1943) 112 L.J.Ch. 279.
[19] See *ante,* p. 289. In *Cityland and Property (Holdings) Ltd.* v. *Dabrah* [1968] Ch. 166 at 182, 183, the court fixed a rate of 7 per cent.
[20] *Weg Motors Ltd.* v. *Hales* [1962] Ch. 49 at 74, 77.
[21] L.P.A. 1925, s.87.
[22] *Grand Junction Co. Ltd.* v. *Bates* [1954] 2 Q.B. 160.
[23] *Cityland and Property (Holdings) Ltd.* v. *Dabrah* [1968] Ch. 166. It has been held in the county court that equivalent words will suffice even for unregistered land: *Sopher* v. *Mercer* [1967] C.L.Y. 2543.
[24] See *Re Watson, ex p. Official Receiver in Bankruptcy* (1890) 25 Q.B.D. 27; *Re Lovegrove* [1935] Ch. 464; *Grangeside Properties Ltd.* v. *Collingwoods Securities Ltd.* [1964] 1 W.L.R. 140.
[25] *England* v. *Codrington* (1758) 1 Eden 169; *Re Watson, supra; Maas* v. *Pepper* [1905] A.C. 102.
[26] *Lincoln* v. *Wright* (1859) 4 De G. & J. 16; *Re Duke of Marlborough* [1984] 2 Ch. 133; *Barton* v. *Bank of New South Wales* (1890) 15 App.Cas. 379.

grossly inadequate as the price of an absolute transfer,[27] or that the so-called purchaser either was not let into immediate possession, or was let into possession but accounted for the rents to the grantor and only retained an amount equivalent to his interest.[28] "In all these cases the question is what was the real intention of the parties?"[29] If the transaction was really an out and out sale the time limited for the exercise of the right of repurchase must be exactly observed.[30] If the option of repurchase is in substance a proviso for redemption, it is exercisable in equity even after the stipulated time has elapsed.[31]

6. Nature of equity of redemption

(a) *Nature.* The mortgagor's equitable right to redeem, coupled with his other rights in the property, constitute his "equity of redemption." At first this was regarded as a mere right, but later it was held to be an equitable estate in the land,[32] which amounts to ownership of the property subject to the mortgage.[33] Thus, subject to the mortgagee's rights the mortgagor might exercise all rights of ownership over the land and settle, devise, or again mortgage it; and on his death intestate the mortgagor's equitable estate descended to his heir (if the property mortgaged was freehold) just as if it were a legal estate. The equitable right to redeem and the equity of redemption were thus distinct; the former did not exist until the legal date for redemption had passed,[34] whereas the latter existed as soon as the mortgage was made[35]; and the former was merely one of the elements comprised in the latter.

(b) *After 1925.* Since 1925, a mortgagor of a legal estate in land retains his legal estate, for a legal mortgage of freeholds can now be effected only by the grant of a term of years to the mortgagee, leaving the legal fee simple vested in the mortgagor, and a legal mortgage of leaseholds can be made only by a sub-demise, leaving the lease vested in the mortgagor[36]; in each case there is the alternative of a charge by way of legal mortgage, but this has the same effect.[37] Mortgages created before 1926 by conveyance of the fee simple, or by assignment of the whole lease, were automatically converted into mortgages by demise or sub-demise.[38] The equity of redemption now appears to be annexed to

---

[27] *Douglas* v. *Culverwell* (1862) 4 De G.F. & J. 20; and see *Barnhart* v. *Greenshields* (1853) 9 Moo.P.C. 18.
[28] *Re Walden* (1878) 10 Ch.D. 76.
[29] See *Manchester, Sheffield and Lincs. Ry.* v. *North Central Wagon Co.* (1888) 13 App.Cas. 554 at 568, *per* Lord Macnaghten; and see *Williams* v. *Owen* (1840) 5 My. & Cr. 303 at 306.
[30] It seems that the rule whereby time is of the essence of an option survives *United Scientific Holdings Ltd.* v. *Burnley B.C.* [1978] A.C. 906, see esp. at 945.
[31] See, *e.g. Danby* v. *Read* (1675) Rep.*t.*Finch 226; *Croft* v. *Powel* (1738) 2 Com. 603.
[32] *Casborne* v. *Scarfe* (1737) 1 Atk. 603.
[33] *Re Wells, Swinburne-Hanham* v. *Howard* [1933] Ch. 29 at 52.
[34] *Brown* v. *Cole* (1845) 14 Sim. 427.
[35] *Kreglinger* v. *New Patagonia Meat and Cold Storage Co. Ltd.* [1914] A.C. 25 at 48.
[36] L.P.A. 1925, ss.85, 86, 87.
[37] *Ante*, p. 392.
[38] L.P.A. 1925, 1st Sched., Pts. VII and VIII.

the mortgagor's legal estate and inseparable from it.[39] The term "equity of redemption" is, however, still frequently used to include the mortgagor's legal estate.

B. Clogging the Equity of Redemption

1. The rule

(a) *Clogs.* It is a settled rule of equity that any agreement which directly bars the mortgagor's right to redeem is ineffectual.[40] Stipulations which even indirectly tend to have the effect of making the mortgage irredeemable are equally bad and unenforceable, and so are stipulations which would result in the property being still subject to incumbrances after redemption. Such stipulations are said to be void as clogging the equity of redemption, a doctrine which applies to all types of mortgages, whether legal or equitable, or by way of floating charge or otherwise.[41] Indeed, at one period the courts inclined to go even further, and to lay down the rule that a stipulation in a mortgage for any advantage beyond repayment of the principal with interest was invalid.[42] This was probably due to the fact that the rate of interest permissible was then limited by statute, and any additional (or "collateral") advantage in addition to interest at the permissible rate was in effect an evasion of the usury laws.

(b) *Limits to the rule.* The modern authorities have tended to restrict the rule as to clogging the equity.[43] They also establish that there is no general rule against collateral advantages, but merely a rule against certain objectionable collateral advantages.[44] The House of Lords has laid it down that "there is now no rule in equity which precludes a mortgagee, whether the mortgage be made upon the occasion of a loan or otherwise, from stipulating for any collateral advantage, provided such advantage is not either (1) unfair and unconscionable, or (2) in the nature of a penalty clogging the equity of redemption, or (3) inconsistent with or repugnant to the contractual and equitable right to redeem.[45]

---

[39] See *British General Insurance Co. Ltd.* v. *Att.-Gen.* [1945] L.J.N.C.C.R. 113 at 122, 123.

[40] *Howard* v. *Harris* (1683) 1 Vern. 190; **2 W. & T.L.C. 1**; *Salt* v. *Marquis of Northampton* [1892] A.C. 1.

[41] *Kreglinger* v. *New Patagonia Meat and Cold Storage Co. Ltd.* [1914] A.C. 25; and see *De Beers Consolidated Mines Ltd.* v. *British South Africa Co.* [1912] A.C. 52.

[42] See *Kreglinger* v. *New Patagonia Meat and Cold Storage Co. Ltd.*, *supra*, at p.54.

[43] The doctrine itself "seems to me to be like an unruly dog, which, if not securely chained to its own kennel, is prone to wander into places where it ought not to be": *Kreglinger* v. *New Patagonia Meat and Cold Storage Co. Ltd.* [1914] A.C. 25 at 46, *per* Lord Mersey.

[44] See *Santley* v. *Wilde* [1899] 2 Ch. 474. For criticism of the actual decision, adverse and favourable, see *Noakes & Co. Ltd.* v. *Rice* [1902] A.C. 24; *Kreglinger* v. *New Patagonia Meat and Cold Storage Co. Ltd.* [1914] A.C. 25.

[45] *Kreglinger* v. *New Patagonia Meat and Cold Storage Co. Ltd.*, *supra* (see at p. 61, *per* Lord Parker of Waddington); and see *De Beers Consolidated Mines Ltd.* v. *British South Africa Co.* [1912] A.C. 52; *Re Cuban Land and Development Co. (1911) Ltd.* [1921] 2 Ch. 147.

2. Operation of the rule

(a) *Valid restrictions.* There are many illustrations of the operation of the rule, and its limits. In *Kreglinger* v. *New Patagonia Meat and Cold Storage Co. Ltd.*,[46] money was lent to a limited company, secured by a floating charge on the company's business, and it was agreed that the company should not for a term of five years sell sheep skins to any person other than the lenders, if the lenders were willing to pay as good a price as was obtainable elsewhere. It was held that the lenders could exercise their right of pre-emption, notwithstanding the repayment of the loan before the expiration of five years; the right formed no part of the mortgage transaction, but was a collateral contract entered into as a condition of the company obtaining the loan, and was neither a clog on the equity nor repugnant to the right to redeem.[47] And where a mortgage of a public-house contained a covenant whereby the mortgagor agreed that during the continuance of the security he would take his beer from the mortgagees and not from any other firm of brewers, such a covenant was upheld and an injunction was granted.[48]

(b) *Invalid clogs.* On the other hand, if the covenant in such a case is framed so that the obligation to buy beer exclusively from the mortgagees continues even after repayment of the loan, this is a clog on the equity, and after redemption the public-house is free from the tie.[49] Again, in *Bradley* v. *Carritt*,[50] the owner of shares in a tea company mortgaged them to the company's broker, and agreed to use his best endeavours to secure that "always thereafter" the broker should retain his employment with the company. The owner also agreed that if at any time the company employed another broker, the owner would pay the broker the commission which he otherwise would have earned. It was held that no action lay on this agreement after the mortgage was redeemed, for otherwise the owner could only get back his shares fettered with a practical difficulty as to dealing with them, lest by selling he should lose his voting power in the company and his ability to avoid the employment of another broker.

If a lease containing an option to purchase the freehold is mortgaged and the mortgagee exercises the option, on redemption the mortgagor is entitled to claim the freehold (subject to paying the cost of purchasing it); for the mortgagee of an option cannot keep for himself the fruit of what was mortgaged.[51]

---

[46] [1914] A.C. 25.
[47] See *Re Petrol Filling Station, Vauxhall Bridge Road, London* (1968) 20 P. & C.R. 1 for an analysis of Lord Haldane's speech in the *Kreglinger* case. *Cf.* Glanville Williams (1944) 60 L.Q.R. 190.
[48] *Biggs* v. *Hoddinott* [1898] 2 Ch. 307.
[49] *Noakes & Co. Ltd.* v. *Rice* [1902] A.C. 24.
[50] [1903] A.C. 253.
[51] *Nelson* v. *Hannam* [1943] Ch. 59; and see *Chelsea Estates Investment Trust Co. Ltd.* v. *Marche* [1955] Ch. 328 (relief against forfeiture: new lease held subject to mortgage which bound old lease).

(c) *Other grounds of invalidity*.   A provision which is not invalid as
being a clog may yet be void on other grounds. Thus it may be unfair or
unconscionable, as where a landlord sells a house to the tenant on
mortgage, and by the mortgage requires a premium of over half the
amount of the loan.[52] Again, a provision may be invalid under the
ordinary law[53] as being in unreasonable restraint of trade.[54] But there is
nothing unfair or oppressive in a provision which "index-links" the
amount of principal and interest to be repaid whether to the United
Kingdom index of retail prices[55] or to the value against sterling of a
specified foreign currency.[56]

3. Purchase of the mortgaged property by the mortgagee.   An option
to purchase given to the mortgagee at the time of the loan is a clog on
the equity and therefore void, for otherwise by exercising the option the
mortgagee could put it out of the mortgagor's power to redeem.[57] The
same applies to an option required by a transferee of the mortgage as a
condition of taking it over.[58] On the other hand, there is no objection to
the mortgagee having a mere right of pre-emption (*i.e.* a right to
purchase if the mortgagor chooses to sell).[59] So, too, the mortgagee may
buy the equity of redemption from the mortgagor *after* the mortgage has
been made, even though the only consideration is a release of the
mortgagor from the amount then owing under the mortgage.[60]

4. Postponement of the right of redemption

(a) *General rule*

(1) VALID.   Although the law will not allow a mortgagor to be
precluded altogether from redeeming, yet there is nothing to prevent a
remoter date than the customary six months after the date of the
mortgage being fixed as the date for redemption. It used to be thought
that the right to redeem could be postponed for only a reasonable
period, *e.g.* five or seven years[61]; but in *Knightsbridge Estates Trust Ltd.*
v. *Byrne*[62] the Court of Appeal held that the contractual date for
redemption may be postponed for any period which the parties agree

[52] *Cityland and Property (Holdings) Ltd.* v. *Dabrah* [1968] Ch. 166.
[53] See, *e.g. Chitty on Contracts* (26th ed., 1989), paras. 1133 *et seq.*
[54] *Esso Petroleum Co. Ltd.* v. *Harper's Garage (Stourport) Ltd.* [1968] A.C. 269; and see *Texaco Ltd.*
    v. *Mulberry Filling Station* [1972] 1 W.L.R. 814; *Alec Lobb (Garages) Ltd.* v. *Total Oil (Great
    Britain) Ltd.* [1985] 1 W.L.R. 173 (lease; reasonable restraint).
[55] *Nationwide B.S.* v. *Registry of Friendly Societies* [1983] 1 W.L.R. 1226. For an express statutory
    power to advance money on these and similar terms, see now Building Societies Act 1986, s.10(10).
[56] *Multiservice Bookbinding Ltd.* v. *Marden* [1979] Ch. 84 (Swiss franc); and see on index-linked
    mortgages generally [1978] Conv. 346 (Wilkinson).
[57] *Samuel* v. *Jarrah Timber and Wood-Paving Corporation Ltd.* [1904] A.C. 323.
[58] *Lewis* v. *Frank Love Ltd.* [1961] 1 W.L.R. 261.
[59] *Orby* v. *Trigg* (1722) 9 Mod. 2.
[60] *Reeve* v. *Lisle* [1902] A.C. 461.
[61] *Teevan* v. *Smith* (1882) 20 Ch.D. 724 at 729; *Biggs* v. *Hoddinott* [1898] 2 Ch. 307.
[62] [1939] Ch. 441; affirmed on other grounds [1940] A.C. 613; *infra.*

upon (at any rate if the mortgagee is precluded from calling in the loan for the same period[63]), and that in the absence of circumstances of oppression or undue influence the court will not allow the mortgagor to redeem before the contractual date.[64] In that case a company agreed to pay back the borrowed money by instalments spread over 40 years and was held to its bargain. The perpetuity rule has no application.[65]

(2) INVALID. The limitation on the mortgagor's right to redeem must not, however, result in making the possibility of redemption a mere pretence. Thus if a lease with some 17 years to run is mortgaged, a clause preventing redemption before the last six weeks of the term will be void as a clog on the equity.[66] And when the mortgage fixes a contractual date for redemption and then provides that the right shall not be exercised by the mortgagor for a substantial period thereafter, this is void as a fetter on the equitable right to redeem.[67]

(b) *Debentures.* By statute, a condition contained in debentures or a deed for securing debentures is not invalid by reason only that the debentures are thereby made irredeemable, or redeemable only on the happening of a contingency, however remote, or on the expiration of a period, however long, any rule of equity to the contrary notwithstanding.[68] An ordinary mortgage by a company is a debenture for this purpose.[69]

C. Redemption on Equitable Terms

The right of redemption possessed by a mortgagor who is in default is a purely equitable right, which can accordingly be exercised only on equitable terms; after the time named for redemption, the mortgagor can redeem only if he himself does equity.

1. Notice of redemption

(a) *Six months' notice.* A mortgagor must either give the mortgagee reasonable notice of his intention to pay off the mortgage, or pay interest in lieu of notice; for it is but fair that the mortgagee should have a reasonable time for finding some other investment before he is repaid. Thus in the normal case where the just inference from the transaction is that the loan is intended to be of a permanent character,

---

[63] See *Morgan* v. *Jeffreys* [1910] 1 Ch. 620.
[64] See *West Derby Union* v. *Metropolitan Life Assurance Society* [1897] A.C. 647.
[65] *Knightsbridge Estates Trust Ltd.* v. *Byrne* [1940] A.C. 613.
[66] *Fairclough* v. *Swan Brewery Co. Ltd.* [1912] A.C. 565.
[67] *Morgan* v. *Jeffreys* [1910] 1 Ch. 620 and *Davis* v. *Symons* [1934] Ch. 442, as explained in *Knightsbridge Estates Trust Ltd.* v. *Byrne* [1939] Ch. 441 at 460–462.
[68] Companies Act 1985, s.193; see also Agricultural Credits Act 1932, s.2.
[69] *Knightsbridge Estates Trust Ltd.* v. *Byrne* [1940] A.C. 613.

six months' notice or six months' interest in lieu of notice[70] is required.[71]

(b) *Less than six months' notice.* Where the mortgage is only temporary (as it is in the case of a mere equitable mortgage by deposit) no notice need be given; the mortgagor need only act reasonably, and allow the mortgagee a reasonable time to look up the deeds.[72] Further, even where six months' notice is required and has been given, if the mortgagor fails to pay the money by the day for which he has given notice he must give a new notice or pay interest in lieu thereof; such a notice must be of a reasonable length, so that the facts may thus justify a three months' notice.[73]

(c) *No notice.* No notice is required where the mortgagee has shown that he wants the money, as by giving notice requiring repayment,[74] or commencing proceedings to recover the money,[75] or taking any other steps for enforcing his security, including taking possession of the property, whether before or after the legal date for redemption.[76] If in such a case the mortgagor nevertheless gives six months' notice, he may still repay the money before his notice has expired.[77]

(d) *Mortgagor's rights on expiration of notice.* At the expiration of proper notice of repayment, or on the tender of interest in lieu thereof, a mortgagor who tenders to the mortgagee the mortgage debt, interest and costs is entitled to have his title deeds handed back to him together with the necessary document to discharge the mortgage, *e.g.* a receipt indorsed on the mortgage.[78] As from the date of the tender, interest ceases to run in the mortgagee's favour, even if he refuses to execute the necessary document; but to secure this result the mortgagor must cease to have the use of the money and must either pay it into court (if there be proceedings pending in which this can be done) or set it aside, as by paying it into a bank on deposit and accounting to the mortgagee for any interest obtained from the bank.[79] The tender need not be such as would afford a defence to an action at law, but if it is conditional on the execution of a document of discharge a reasonable time must be allowed for the execution.[80] If after tender the mortgagee improperly refuses to hand over the title deeds and discharge the mortgage, he will be ordered to pay the costs of proceedings for redemption taken by the mortgagor,[81] and may be liable in damages.[82]

[70] *Johnson* v. *Evans* (1889) 61 L.T. 18.
[71] *Browne* v. *Lockhart* (1840) 10 Sim. 420; *Smith* v. *Smith* [1891] 3 Ch. 550.
[72] *Fitzgerald's Trustee* v. *Mellersh* [1892] 1 Ch. 385.
[73] *Cromwell Property Investment Co. Ltd.* v. *Western* [1934] Ch. 322.
[74] *Edmondson* v. *Copland* [1911] 2 Ch. 301.
[75] *Re Alcock* (1883) 23 Ch.D. 372.
[76] *Bovill* v. *Endle* [1896] 1 Ch. 648.
[77] *Ibid.*
[78] L.P.A. 1925, s.115; see *post*, pp. 425, 426.
[79] *Edmondson* v. *Copland, supra*; *Barratt* v. *Gough-Thomas (No. 3)* [1951] 2 All E.R. 48.
[80] *Webb* v. *Crosse* [1912] 1 Ch. 323.
[81] *Edmondson* v. *Copland, supra*; *Rourke* v. *Robinson* [1911] 1 Ch. 480; *Graham* v. *Seal* (1918) 88 L.J.Ch. 31.
[82] *Fletcher* v. *City Marine Finance Ltd.* [1968] 2 Lloyds Rep. 520 (mortgage of ship).

2. Consolidation

(a) *The doctrine.* Another example of redemption being allowed only upon equitable terms is the doctrine of consolidation. The general rule in equity is that a person who is entitled to two mortgages made by the same mortgagor can consolidate those mortgages against the mortgagor, and refuse to allow him to redeem one mortgage without redeeming the other. The doctrine applies whether the property mortgaged is real or personal[83] and whether the mortgages are legal or equitable[84]; and it has been applied to a mortgage and a sub-mortgage,[85] and even to two mortgages on the same property.[86] But there can be no consolidation of a mortgage if the property mortgaged has ceased to exist, *e.g.* because it was a lease which has been determined by forfeiture.[87]

(b) *Conditions.* Four conditions must be satisfied before a mortgagee can consolidate.

(1) REDEMPTION DATES PASSED: there is no question of equitable terms if the mortgagor is not in default, and so no mortgage can be consolidated before the legal date for redemption has passed.[88]

(2) SAME MORTGAGOR: both mortgages must be made by the same mortgagor. It is not enough if one mortgage is made by A and the other by A and B jointly,[89] or if one is made by A and the other by B in trust for A.[90]

(3) RESERVATION OF RIGHT: a mortgagee may consolidate only if an intention to permit consolidation is expressed in the mortgage deeds, or one of them.[91]

(4) SIMULTANEOUS UNIONS OF MORTGAGES AND EQUITIES: there must have been a time when both the mortgages were vested in one person and simultaneously both the equities of redemption were vested in another.[92]

---

[83] See *Watts v. Symes* (1851) 1 De G.M. & G. 240; *Tassell v. Smith* (1858) 2 De G. & J. 713.
[84] See *Tweedale v. Tweedale* (1857) 23 Beav. 341; *Cracknall v. Janson* (1879) 11 Ch.D. 1 at 18.
[85] *Silverthorn v. Glazebrook* (1899) 30 O.R. 408.
[86] *Re Salmon, ex p. The Trustee* [1903] 1 K.B. 147. Waldock, *Mortgages* (2nd ed., 1950), p. 285, note 1, states that "several mortgages on the *same* property raise questions of tacking, not consolidation." But this confuses the nature of the two doctrines: tacking concerns the priority of competing mortgages (*post*, p. 435), while consolidation governs whether a mortgagor may redeem one mortgage without another, and this question clearly may arise where there are several mortgages on the same property. *Cf.* Fisher & Lightwood's *Law of Mortgages* (10th ed., 1988), p. 534, n. (*b*).
[87] *Re Raggett* (1880) 16 Ch.D. 117.
[88] *Cummins v. Fletcher* (1879) 14 Ch.D. 699.
[89] *Cummins v. Fletcher, supra.*
[90] *Sharp v. Rickards* [1909] 1 Ch. 109.
[91] L.P.A. 1925, s.93, replacing C.A. 1881, s.17, which introduced the condition in the case of mortgages made after 1881.
[92] See *Pledge v. White* [1896] A.C. 187 at 198.

(c) *Third parties*

(1) EXTENSION TO ASSIGNS.   The most complex of the four heads mentioned above is the fourth. In its basic form, the doctrine allowed consolidation against the mortgagor himself; but it has been extended to assigns of the equity of redemption, such as a purchaser of the property or a second mortgagee.[93] In general, however, this extension applies only where the right to consolidate arose before the date of the assignment. Thus if A mortgages first Whiteacre and then Blackacre to X, and subsequently conveys or mortgages Whiteacre to B, Whiteacre can be redeemed by B only on terms of taking a transfer of the mortgage on Blackacre, if X so desires. But if A mortgages Whiteacre to X, and then conveys or mortgages Whiteacre to B, B's right to redeem will not be affected by A subsequently mortgaging Blackacre to X; for once A has disposed of Whiteacre he cannot later increase the burdens which bind it.[94] Again, if A mortgages Whiteacre to X and Blackacre to Y, and B then acquires Whiteacre, the fact that Z subsequently takes a transfer of the mortgages on both Whiteacre and Blackacre gives Z no right to consolidate against B.[95] The guiding principle is that the assignee of property which is subject to a mortgage takes the property subject to only such equities as have come into existence before the time of the assignment.[96]

(2) CONSOLIDATION BY CONTRACT.   The only exception to this rule is where there is an express contractual right to consolidate. If there is, a purchaser of the equity of redemption takes subject to the risk of the mortgagee consolidating mortgages subsequently created by the mortgagor,[97] unless, it has been held, the mortgagee had notice of the purchase before making the subsequent loan.[98]

(3) ASSIGNS OF TWO PROPERTIES.   An assignee of two or more properties from one mortgagor stands in a very different position from the assignee of one property only. If A mortgages Blackacre and Whiteacre to X and Y, respectively, and then sells both properties to B, no case for consolidation exists; yet if the two mortgages then become united in the same hand (as by X transferring the mortgage of Blackacre to Y), a right to consolidate will arise.[99] The case of the assignee of two properties from the same mortgagor is a special one; it is anomalous, and constitutes an exception recognised by the House of Lords as being unsound in principle but too firmly established by authority to be disturbed.[1]

[93] *Hughes* v. *Britannia Permanent Benefit B.S.* [1906] 2 Ch. 607.
[94] *Jennings* v. *Jordan* (1881) 6 App.Cas. 698.
[95] *Minter* v. *Carr* [1894] 3 Ch. 498; *Harter* v. *Colman* (1882) 19 Ch.D. 630.
[96] *Harter* v. *Colman, supra.*
[97] *Andrews* v. *City Permanent Benefit B.S.* (1881) 44 L.T. 641.
[98] *Hughes* v. *Britannia Permanent Benefit B.S.* [1906] 2 Ch. 607. *Sed quaere*: Kekewich J. seems to equate consolidation with tacking.
[99] *Pledge* v. *White* [1896] A.C. 187.
[1] See *Sharp* v. *Rickards* [1909] 1 Ch. 109 at 113.

RIGHTS UNDER A MORTGAGE

Section 1. Title Deeds

1. Custody. The first mortgagee has long been entitled to the custody of the title deeds of the mortgaged land; and this right has not been affected by the fact that after 1925 his security does not include the whole fee simple, or the whole lease in the case of a mortgage of leaseholds.[1] Moreover, the mortgagee becomes owner of the deeds and, so long as the mortgage continues,[1a] is not liable to the mortgagor for failure to take reasonable care of the deeds.[2] But possession of the deeds is merely ancillary to the mortgage; the mortgagee has no independent lien on them, and so must return them if the mortgage is void.[3]

2. Inspection. So long as the mortgagor's right to redeem subsists, he is entitled to inspect and make copies or abstracts of or extracts from the deeds at his own cost, and on paying the mortgagee's costs; and this right cannot be excluded by agreement.[4]

3. Redemption. Upon redemption, the mortgagee must hand over the title deeds to the mortgagor or to the next mortgagee; he will be liable in any case to give a suitable indemnity in respect of any title deed that is then missing, and, by analogy with the common law rules as to the liability of bailees,[5] to pay compensation in equity unless the deeds were lost without fault on his part.[6] If on redemption the mortgagee delivers the deeds to a person not having the best right thereto, he is not liable unless he has notice of the right or claim of a person having a better right.[7] "Notice" here does not include notice

---

[1] L.P.A. 1925, ss.85(1), 86(1).
[1a] Contrast the position on redemption, *infra.*
[2] *Browning* v. *Handiland Group Ltd.* (1976) 35 P. & C.R. 345.
[3] *Re Molton Finance Ltd.* [1968] Ch. 325; see J. H. G. Sunnucks (1970) 33 M.L.R. 131. For mortgages by deposit of documents, see *post,* p. 444.
[4] L.P.A. 1925, s.96(1).
[5] See *Gilligan* v. *National Bank Ltd.* [1901] 2 I.R. 513 at 541–547 for a full historical survey.
[6] *Hornby* v. *Matcham* (1848) 16 Sim. 325 (deeds burnt); *Brown* v. *Sewell* (1853) 11 Hare 49 (deeds lost: negligence not disproved). Contrast *James* v. *Rumsey* (1879) 11 Ch.D. 398.
[7] L.P.A. 1925, s.96(2).

implied by reason of registration under the Land Charges Act 1972[8]; there is thus no need for the mortgagee to search before handing over the title deeds.

Section 2. Leases of the Mortgaged Property

1. Grant of leases

(a) *Right to grant.* Formerly a mortgagor could not grant a lease which would be binding on the mortgagee without his consent, unless the mortgage deed authorised him to do so.[9] Now, however, by statute[10] a mortgagor in possession or a mortgagee in possession may grant certain leases which will be effective against both the mortgagee and the mortgagor and not merely against the party making them. The statutory power is exhaustive, and there is no residual common law power of granting leases binding on the other party in circumstances outside the statute.[11] After a receiver has been appointed, and so long as he still acts, the statutory power of leasing is exercisable by the mortgagee and not by the mortgagor; but the mortgagee may by writing delegate the power to the receiver in whole or in part.[12]

(b) *Terms that can be granted.* The lease must be granted for the purpose of agriculture, occupation, or building, but not mining. The term must not exceed 50 years in the case of an agricultural or occupation lease, or 999 years in the case of a building lease.[13] A lease granted by the mortgagor will be valid even if it includes furniture and sporting rights not included in the mortgage[14]; but it will not bind the mortgagee if it includes other land, at an inclusive, unapportioned rent.[15]

(c) *Conditions of grant.* The lease must reserve the best rent that can reasonably be obtained, regard being had to the circumstances of the case,[16] but without any fine being taken.[17] The lease must contain a covenant for payment of rent and a proviso for re-entry on non-payment of rent within a specified period not exceeding 30 days. A counterpart lease must be executed by the lessee and (where the lease is made by the mortgagor) delivered to the mortgagee; but failure so to deliver the

---

[8] L.P.(Am.)A. 1926, Sched.; L.C.A. 1972, s.18(6).
[9] *Keech* v. *Hall* (1779) 1 Doug.K.B. 22; *Iron Trades Employers Insurance Association Ltd.* v. *Union Land and House Investors Ltd.* [1937] Ch. 313.
[10] L.P.A. 1925, s.99, replacing, with amendments, C.A. 1881, s.18, as extended by C.A. 1911, s.3, and applying to mortgages made after 1881: L.P.A. 1925, s.99(16).
[11] *Australia and New Zealand Bank Ltd.* v. *Sinclair* [1968] 2 N.S.W.R. 26.
[12] L.P.A. 1925, s.99(19).
[13] 21 and 99 years respectively if the mortgage was made before 1926.
[14] *Brown* v. *Peto* [1900] 1 Q.B. 346 at 354 (affirmed [1900] 2 Q.B. 653).
[15] *King* v. *Bird* [1909] 1 K.B. 837.
[16] *Coutts & Co.* v. *Somerville* [1935] Ch. 438.
[17] See *Hughes* v. *Waite* [1957] 1 W.L.R. 713 (rent in advance a fine).

counterpart will not invalidate the lease, although as it is a breach of the provisions required to be observed by the mortgagor, it will make the power of sale exercisable forthwith.[18] An oral tenancy may, however, be granted without complying with the foregoing provisions as to covenants, provisos and counterparts.[19]

(d) *Restrictions.* Except in the case of a mortgage of agricultural land made after March 1, 1948,[20] the power may be excluded by the parties in the mortgage deed or otherwise in writing. Alternatively it may be made exercisable only with the mortgagee's consent; the onus of proving the mortgagee's consent to a lease made by the mortgagor lies on the tenant claiming under such a lease.[21] But a covenant by the mortgagor not to exercise the statutory power does not prevent him granting leases or tenancies not binding on the mortgagee.[22]

2. Surrender of leases. Subject to any contrary intention either in the mortgage or otherwise in writing, statute[23] authorises the mortgagor in possession or the mortgagee in possession (or who has appointed a receiver) to accept a surrender of a lease for the purpose of replacing it by another authorised lease. The new lease must take effect in possession within one month of the surrender, and grant a term no shorter than the residue of the surrendered lease at a rent at least as great. Apart from these powers, a surrender to the mortgagor will not be binding on the mortgagee without his consent, even if it is made while the mortgagor is in possession[24]; but a mortgagee who refuses to treat a new tenancy granted to an existing tenant as binding on him cannot also treat the grant as having effected a surrender of the existing tenancy.[25]

Section 3. Possession

1. The right to possession. Upon the execution of a legal mortgage by demise, a first or only mortgagee becomes entitled to an estate in possession. He may therefore take possession of his property, peaceably if he can, and if not, by means of an action for possession[26] against the

---

[18] See *Public Trustee* v. *Lawrence* [1912] 1 Ch. 739; *post*, p. 413.
[19] See *Rhodes* v. *Dalby* [1971] 1 W.L.R. 1325.
[20] Agricultural Holdings Act 1986, s.100, Sched. 14, para. 12, replacing Agricultural Holdings Act 1948, Sched. 7, para. 2.
[21] *Taylor* v. *Ellis* [1960] Ch. 368.
[22] *Iron Trades Employers Insurance Association Ltd.* v. *Union Land and House Investors Ltd.* [1937] Ch. 313; and see *Bolton B.S.* v. *Cobb* [1966] 1 W.L.R. 1.
[23] L.P.A. 1925, s.100, replacing C.A. 1911, s.3, and applying to mortgages made after 1911.
[24] *Robbins* v. *Whyte* [1906] 1 K.B. 125.
[25] *Barclays Bank Ltd.* v. *Stasek* [1957] Ch. 28; and see (1957) 73 L.Q.R. 14.
[26] For the parties to the proceedings, see *Barclays Bank Ltd.* v. *Kiley* [1961] 1 W.L.R. 1050; *Brighton and Shoreham B.S.* v. *Hollingdale* [1965] 1 W.L.R. 376; *Esso Petroleum Co. Ltd.* v. *Alstonbridge Properties Ltd.* [1975] 1 W.L.R. 1474.

mortgagor; and he may retain possession until the mortgagor redeems his security.[27] His right is not affected by his having granted a sub-mortgage.[28] A legal chargee has a corresponding statutory right to possession.[29] This is a right which the legal mortgagee or chargee has as part of his estate, and it is not in the nature of a remedy for enforcing the mortgage. It is therefore exercisable irrespective of whether or not the mortgagor is in default, except in those cases in which it is modified or excluded by statute or contract.[30] The right is not excluded by the existence of a counterclaim on the part of the mortgagor.[31] It must, however, be exercised bona fide, not (for example) as a cloak for the eviction by the mortgagor of tenants who are protected by the Rent Acts.[32] Equitable mortgagees, on the other hand, are generally said to have no right to possession.[33]

2. Restrictions on right to possession

(a) *Generally.* Where the mortgagee has a right to possession and applies to the court for an order for possession, the court has no general jurisdiction to adjourn the application indefinitely while the mortgagor is paying off arrears of interest; but it may grant a short adjournment to a mortgagor who is seeking to redeem the entire mortgage.[34]

(b) *Dwelling-houses.* Where the mortgaged property consists of or includes a dwelling-house the court has additional powers where possession is claimed.[35] For this purpose a dwelling-house includes any building or part of a building which is used as a dwelling, and the fact that part of the premises comprised in a dwelling-house is used as a shop or office or for business, trade or professional purposes does not affect the position.[36] In the case of such mortgaged dwelling-houses the court may adjourn the proceedings, or stay or suspend execution of any judgment for possession, or postpone the date for delivery of possession, for such period or periods as it thinks reasonable.[37] It is

---

[27] *Four-Maids Ltd.* v. *Dudley Marshall (Properties) Ltd.* [1957] Ch. 317. *Cf. R.* v. *Judge Dutton Briant, ex p. Abbey National B.S.* [1957] 2 Q.B. 497.
[28] *Owen* v. *Cornell* [1967] E.G.D. 423.
[29] L.P.A. 1925, s.87.
[30] *Western Bank Ltd.* v. *Schindler* [1977] Ch. 1.
[31] *Mobil Oil Co. Ltd.* v. *Rawlinson* (1981) 43 P. & C.R. 221; *Citibank Trust Ltd.* v. *Ayivor* [1987] 1 W.L.R. 1157.
[32] *Quennell* v. *Maltby* [1979] 1 W.L.R. 318 (collusion between wife-mortgagee and husband-mortgagor with a view to gaining possession from the latter's tenants). And see *ibid.* at p. 322 for a suggestion by Lord Denning M.R. of a wide equitable jurisdiction to prevent a mortgagee from getting possession so long as the interest is paid: for a criticism see [1979] C.L.J. 257 (R. A. Pearce).
[33] See *post*, p. 448.
[34] *Birmingham Citizens Permanent B.S.* v. *Caunt* [1962] Ch. 883, reviewing the authorities; and see *Braithwaite* v. *Winwood* [1960] 1 W.L.R. 1257, where even this indulgence was refused. For the power of the court to stay execution after an order for possession has been made, see *London Permanent Benefit B.S.* v. *de Baer* [1969] 1 Ch. 321. Contrast *Alnwick R.D.C.* v. *Taylor* [1966] Ch. 355 (mortgage under Small Dwellings Acquisition Act 1899).
[35] See generally R. J. Smith [1979] Conv. 266 at 270–281; A. Clarke [1983] Conv. 293.
[36] Administration of Justice Act 1970, s.39.
[37] *Ibid.* s.36(1)(2).

unsettled whether the court is restricted to suspending the order for a specified period[38] or whether it may do so indefinitely.[39] This power may be exercised whether or not the mortgagor is in default,[40] and either unconditionally or subject to conditions, particularly with regard to payment of sums due under the mortgage.[41] The court is, however, confined to exercising the power in two classes of case, being those in which (in the words of the statute) "the mortgagor is likely to be able within a reasonable period to pay any sums due under the mortgage or to remedy a default consisting of a breach of any other obligation arising under or by virtue of the mortgage."[42]

(1) PAYMENT. Instalment mortgages commonly provide that the whole amount secured shall become due in the event of any default by the mortgagor or upon demand by the mortgagee: in such cases the court, for the purposes of exercising its powers to delay giving possession, may treat as due only such amounts as the mortgagor would have been expected to pay in the absence of a provision for earlier payment.[43] The court may treat similarly mortgages for a fixed period secured by an endowment policy where the principal is not due within the period so long as interest is punctually paid.[44] The court may, however, exercise this power only if the mortgagor is likely to be able within a reasonable period to pay off both the arrears (with interest) and any further instalments falling due within that period.[45] The existence of a counterclaim against the mortgagee is not a matter to be taken into account in assessing the mortgagor's ability to pay.[46]

(2) REMEDYING OTHER BREACHES. A common breach is the granting by the mortgagor of a tenancy not authorised by the mortgage.[47] Such a breach can normally only be remedied by the tenant going out of possession.[48] Hence, though the tenant may be a person deriving title under the mortgagor,[49] it is improbable that he can avoid an order for possession merely by paying the outstanding instalments.[50] In any event, a statutory tenant, having no estate, is not a person deriving title under the mortgagor and, accordingly, cannot invoke these provisions.[51]

[38] *Royal Trust Co. of Canada* v. *Markham* [1975] 1 W.L.R. 1416.
[39] *Western Bank Ltd.* v. *Schindler, supra*, at p. 14.
[40] *Western Bank Ltd.* v. *Schindler* [1977] Ch. 1.
[41] Administration of Justice Act 1970, s.36(3), (4).
[42] Ibid.
[43] Administration of Justice Act 1973, s.8, reversing *Halifax B.S.* v. *Clark* [1973] Ch. 307. See S. Tromans [1984] Conv. 9.
[44] *Bank of Scotland* v. *Grimes* [1985] Q.B. 1179, distinguishing *Habib Bank Ltd.* v. *Tailor* [1982] 1 W.L.R. 1218 (mortgage securing bank overdraft payable on demand).
[45] *Western Bank Ltd.* v. *Schindler* [1977] Ch. 1; *Peckham Mutual B.S.* v. *Registe* (1981) 42 P. & C.R. 186; *Citibank Trust Ltd.* v. *Ayivor*, [1987] 1 W.L.R. 1157.
[46] *Citibank Trust Ltd.* v. *Ayivor, supra.*
[47] See *post*, pp. 408, 409.
[48] *Britannia B.S.* v. *Earl* [1990] 1 W.L.R. 422.
[49] Administration of Justice Act 1970, s.39(1).
[50] *Britannia B.S.* v. *Earl* [1990] 1 W.L.R. 422 at 430.
[51] *Britannia B.S.* v. *Earl* [1990] 1 W.L.R. 422.

3. County court jurisdiction

(a) *Concurrent.* If the rateable value of the land is within the county court limit for actions for the recovery of land, the county court has jurisdiction concurrently with the High Court even if there is also a claim for payment (including a claim against a guarantor) and the amount is outside the county court limit for money claims.[52]

(b) *Exclusive.* If the mortgaged property consists of or includes a dwelling-house[53] which is situated outside Greater London and has a rateable value within the county court limits for the recovery of land,[54] the county court has exclusive jurisdiction to hear a mortgagee's action for possession.[55] Where land is not rated, jurisdiction for these purposes is tested by reference to its letting value.[56] The jurisdiction of the High Court is not excluded if, in addition to possession, sale or foreclosure is also claimed,[57] so long as such claims are genuine and not added merely in an attempt to confer jurisdiction on the High Court.[58]

4. Exclusion of the right. A mortgagee normally has no wish to take possession, partly because his sole interest in the property is as a security and partly because he has to account strictly for the fruits of his possession.[59] Indeed, he may covenant not to take possession before the lapse of a certain period or until default is made; an injunction will be granted to restrain the mortgagee from taking possession in breach of such a covenant.[60] A clause which abrogates or restricts the mortgagee's right to possession is common in mortgages repayable by instalments,[61] and may be implied.[62] The inference is never lightly made, and, while the fact that a mortgage is an instalment mortgage may make the inference easier to draw, it is not in itself a sufficient ground.[63]

5. The attornment clause. The right to possession will not pass immediately to the mortgagee if the mortgage contains an attornment clause whereby the mortgagor attorns tenant to the mortgagee,[64] for the

---

[52] County Courts Act 1984, s.21(5).
[53] For definition, see *ibid.* s.21(7), (8). It is identical with that in Administration of Justice Act 1970, s.39, see *ante.*, p. 404, text to n.36.
[54] Net annual value for rating not exceeding £1,000: County Courts Act 1984, ss.21(1)(2), 147(1).
[55] *Ibid.* s.21(3).
[56] *P.B. Frost Ltd.* v. *Green* [1978] 1 W.L.R. 949.
[57] County Courts Act 1984, s.21(4).
[58] *Trustees of Manchester Unity Life Insurance Collecting Society* v. *Sadler* [1974] 1 W.L.R. 770.
[59] See *post*, p. 409. See R. W. Turner's *Equity of Redemption* (1931), p. 90, on the growth of the custom of leaving the mortgagor in possession.
[60] *Doe* d. *Parsley* v. *Day* (1842) 2 Q.B. 147.
[61] See *Hinckley and South Leicestershire Permanent B.S.* v. *Freeman* [1941] Ch. 32; *Robertson* v. *Cilia* [1956] 1 W.L.R. 1502; and see (1957) 73 L.Q.R. 300.
[62] As in *Birmingham Citizens Permanent B.S.* v. *Caunt* [1962] Ch. 883 at 890.
[63] *Western Bank Ltd.* v. *Schindler* [1977] Ch. 1 at 10.
[64] See *Mumford* v. *Collier* (1890) 25 Q.B.D. 279. *Quaere* whether an attornment clause is effective if contained in a charge by way of legal mortgage: see H. R. Gray (1948) 13 Conv.(N.S.) 31; *contra* (1949) 93 S.J. 142.

mortgagee must determine the resulting tenancy before entry.[65] Attornment clauses at a rent equal to the interest were originally inserted in mortgages so as to give the mortgagee power to distrain for the interest *qua* landlord; but the Bills of Sale Act 1878 rendered such a clause void as a security.[66] Attornment clauses at a nominal rent nevertheless survived as enabling the mortgagee to obtain summary judgment for possession against the mortgagor *qua* tenant. Although changes in the Rules of Court in 1933, 1936 and 1937 gave this remedy to mortgagees as such, the clause was still often retained because under the Small Tenements Recovery Act 1838[67] it enabled the mortgagee to recover possession speedily and cheaply by justices' warrant.[68] This Act has now been repealed[69]; yet the clause has been reprieved by a decision that a tenancy by attornment enables the mortgagee as landlord to sue assignees of the mortgagor upon the covenants in the mortgage,[70] although it is doubtful whether the clause is essential for this purpose.[71]

6. Position of mortgagor in possession

(a) *Enjoyment of the property.* In general, a mortgagor who remains in possession is entitled to enjoy the mortgaged premises in the ordinary way. He remains in control of the property and is thus bound by obligations imposed by statute on the "owner."[72] He may cut and sever the crops and cut or sell the underwood,[73] and he is not bound to account to the mortgagee for the rents and profits arising or accruing during his possession, even though the security should afterwards prove insufficient. But where the security is already insufficient, a mortgagor in possession may be prevented by the court from felling timber[74] or cutting and removing the crops and underwood.[75]

(b) *Right to bring actions.* "A mortgagor for the time being entitled to the possession or receipt of the rents and profits of any land, as to which the mortgagee has not given notice of his intention to take possession or to enter into the receipt of the rents and profits thereof, may sue for such possession, or for the recovery of such rents or profits,

---

[65] *Hinckley and Country B.S.* v. *Henny* [1953] 1 W.L.R. 352; see *Alliance B.S.* v. *Pinwill* [1958] Ch. 788 and *Peckham Mutual B.S.* v. *Registe* (1981) 42 P. & C.R. 186 (mortgagee need not give statutory four weeks' notice to quit a dwelling-house).
[66] *Re Willis, ex p. Kennedy* (1888) 21 Q.B.D. 384.
[67] The Act applied to tenancies at will or for not over seven years at a rent not exceeding £20 per annum without a fine.
[68] *Dudley and District Benefit B.S.* v. *Gordon* [1929] 2 K.B. 105. See H. R. Gray (1948) 13 Conv.(N.S.) 31.
[69] See Rent Act 1965, ss.35(5), 52(1), 7th Sched., Pt. II; S.I. 1972 No. 1161.
[70] *Regent Oil Co. Ltd.* v. *J.A. Gregory (Hatch End) Ltd.* [1966] Ch. 402.
[71] See (1965) 81 L.Q.R. 341; (1966) 82 L.Q.R. 21; and see *Portman B.S.* v. *Young* [1951] 1 All E.R. 191; *Steyning and Littlehampton B.S.* v. *Wilson* [1951] Ch. 1018; *Norwich Benefit B.S.* v. *Gregory* [1939] L.J.N.C.C.R. 392 (mortgagee not bound *qua* landlord under Housing Act 1936, s.2, to keep premises fit for habitation).
[72] See *Westminster City Council* v. *Haymarket Publishing Ltd.* [1981] 1 W.L.R. 677 (rating surcharge).
[73] *Trent* v. *Hunt* (1853) 9 Exch. 14.
[74] *King* v. *Smith* (1843) 2 Hare 239.
[75] *Bagnall* v. *Villar* (1879) 12 Ch.D. 812.

or to prevent or recover damages in respect of any trespass or other wrong relative thereto, in his own name only, unless the cause of action arises upon a lease or other contract made by him jointly with any other person."[76] Moreover, as long as the mortgagor remains in possession and no receiver is acting for the mortgagee, the mortgagor can enforce the covenants and the right of re-entry contained in a lease.[77]

7. Position of mortgagee in possession

(a) *The fruits of possession.* A mortgagee in possession may be either in actual occupation of the property or in receipt of the rents and profits, thus depriving the mortgagor of control.[78] So far as these rents are payable under leases already existing at the date of the mortgage, or made subsequently thereto by the mortgagee's authority, the mortgagee is entitled to the benefit of the leases, and on taking possession can enforce payment of all future rent and all arrears due at the time.[79] The same applies to leases made by the mortgagor in possession by virtue of his statutory powers,[80] for such leases have the same effect as if the mortgagee had concurred therein.[81]

(b) *Leases not binding on mortgagee*

(1) GRANTED BEFORE MORTGAGE. Where a purchaser who has been let into possession before completion purports to grant tenancies, those tenancies are good by estoppel as between the purchaser and the tenants. It was formerly held that, when the purchase is subsequently completed with the assistance of a loan secured by a mortgage, the tenancies would bind the mortgagee, upon the theory that there must have been a *scintilla temporis* between the purchaser's acquisition of the legal estate and the creation of the mortgage, during which the estoppel could be fed.[82] But it has now been held that such tenancies are not binding on the mortgagee, upon the more realistic theory that the conveyance or transfer and the mortgage are a single transaction so that the purchaser never had a legal estate free from the mortgage and available to feed the estoppel.[83]

(2) GRANTED AFTER MORTGAGE. If after creating a mortgage the mortgagor grants a lease which is authorised neither by the statute nor by the mortgagee, it does not bind the mortgagee notwithstanding any

---

[76] L.P.A. 1925, s.98, replacing J.A. 1873, s.25(5).
[77] L.P.A. 1925, s.141, replacing C.A. 1881, s.10; see *Turner* v. *Walsh* [1909] 2 K.B. 484.
[78] See *Noyes* v. *Pollock* (1886) 32 Ch.D. 53; *Mexborough U.D.C.* v. *Harrison* [1964] 1 W.L.R. 733.
[79] *Re Ind Coope & Co. Ltd.* [1911] 2 Ch. 223.
[80] See *ante*, p. 402, for the statutory power of leasing.
[81] *Municipal Permanent Investment B.S.* v. *Smith* (1888) 22 Q.B.D. 70.
[82] *Church of England B.S.* v. *Piskor* [1954] Ch. 553.
[83] *Abbey National B.S.* v. *Cann* [1990] 2 W.L.R. 832, H.L., overruling *Church of England B.S.* v. *Piskor, supra.*

statutory protection enjoyed by the tenant against the mortgagor.[84] The mortgagee may thus eject the tenant,[85] even though he knows of the lease some time before commencing proceedings,[86] and has received no interest for some years.[87] He is not, however, entitled to collect arrears of rent due at the date of his taking possession, for there is no relationship of landlord and tenant between him and the tenant.[88] Such a relationship will exist only where there is evidence of a fresh agreement between the tenant and the mortgagee: the creation of a tenancy, even after the appointment of a receiver,[89] may be inferred from the payment of rent to the mortgagee by the tenant.[90] Such a new tenancy will normally be a yearly or other periodic tenancy, not necessarily subject to the terms of the old lease so far as applicable to a periodic tenancy.[91]

(c) Mortgagee's liability to account strictly

(1) LIABILITY. A mortgagee in possession is liable to account to the mortgagor for the rents and profits[92]; and this liability to account does not cease because he in fact abandons possession, for he has no right to give up possession whenever he likes.[93] He also continues accountable even after transferring the mortgage, and is still liable for any default made by the transferee, unless the transfer is made by order of the court, or with the mortgagor's concurrence.[94] But he will be relieved from liability to account if the court appoints a receiver, as in special cases it will do,[95] or if he himself appoints a receiver under the statutory power.[96]

(2) "WILFUL DEFAULT." A mortgagee in possession is liable to account on the footing of "wilful default," that is, he must account not only for sums actually received by him but also for sums which, but for his own default, he might have received.[97] Thus a mortgagee of a public-house who takes possession of his security and lets it as a tied house (e.g. subject to a covenant to take only the mortgagee's own beers) will be accountable for the rent he might have obtained had he let the house as a free house (i.e. without restriction as to the purchase of beer), and not

[84] Britannia B.S. v. Earl [1990] 1 W.L.R. 422.
[85] Dudley and District Benefit B.S. v. Emerson [1949] Ch. 707. Contrast Barclays Bank Ltd. v. Stasek [1957] Ch. 28, ante, p. 403, where the unauthorised lease replaced a lease current at the time of the mortgage.
[86] Parker v. Braithwaite [1952] 2 All E.R. 837.
[87] Taylor v. Ellis [1960] Ch. 368.
[88] Corbett v. Plowden (1884) 25 Ch.D. 678; Kitchen's Trustee v. Madders [1950] Ch. 134.
[89] Stroud B.S. v. Delamont [1960] 1 W.L.R. 431; Chatsworth Properties Ltd. v. Effiom [1971] 1 W.L.R. 144.
[90] Keith v. R. Gancia & Co. Ltd. [1904] 1 Ch. 774; Stroud B.S. v. Delamont, supra.
[91] Keith v. R. Gancia & Co. Ltd., supra, at p. 783.
[92] For accounting, see post, p. 637.
[93] Re Prytherch (1889) 42 Ch.D. 590.
[94] Hall v. Heward (1886) 32 Ch.D. 430.
[95] County of Gloucester Bank v. Rudry Merthyr Steam and House Coal Colliery Co. [1895] 1 Ch. 629.
[96] Refuge Assurance Co. Ltd. v. Pearlberg [1938] Ch. 687.
[97] For wilful default in the context of breach of trust, see ante, p. 284.

merely for the rent he actually obtains.[98] He is also liable to account for rent if he could have let the property but did not, or if he fails to recover the rent in full from tenants able to pay it.[99] And if the mortgagee himself occupies the mortgaged premises, he will be liable for an occupation rent based on the highest possible rental value of the premises.[1] But the mortgagee is not accountable for purely collateral advantages which do not affect the mortgagor, such as the profits made by him in supplying beer to a public-house of which he has taken possession under the mortgage.[2]

(3) WASTE. In addition to his liability for bad management, a mortgagee in possession is liable for waste, *e.g.* opening mines, unless the property is an insufficient security for the purpose of paying the interest.[3] But the mortgagee may work mines already opened,[4] and has power by statute[5] to cut and sell timber and other trees ripe and fit for cutting and not planted or left standing for shelter or ornament, and to contract for any such cutting and sale to be completed within 12 months of such contract.

(d) *Application of rents and profits*

(1) ACCOUNTS AS A WHOLE. After deducting the costs of manage-ment,[6] the rents and profits received by the mortgagee must be applied in satisfaction of his claim for principal and interest. In the absence of special circumstances, the accounts are taken as a whole, setting the total liabilities in respect of the mortgage against the total receipts by the mortgagee, and not on the footing of annual rests, *i.e.* with an annual balancing of accounts.[7] Thus if at any particular date the mortgagee has collected more than enough to meet the interest then due, he need not treat the surplus in hand as a payment *pro tanto* in extinction of the capital debt, but may retain it without paying interest on it[8]; for he is "not bound to accept payment by driblets, but is entitled to have the account taken as a whole."[9] On the other hand, if the rents and profits are less than the interest due, the mortgagor need pay no interest on the deficiency.[10] Further, if a mortgagee in possession sells part of his security there will be no rest in the account of rents and profits, striking a balance to ascertain what still remains due, but merely a rest as regards the proceeds of sale.[11]

---

[98] *White* v. *City of London Brewery Co.* (1889) 42 Ch.D. 237.
[99] *Noyes* v. *Pollock* (1886) 32 Ch.D. 53 at 61.
[1] *Marriott* v. *Anchor Reversionary Co.* (1861) 3 De G.F. & J. 177.
[2] *White* v. *City of London Brewery Co., supra.*
[3] *Millett* v. *Davey* (1863) 31 Beav. 470.
[4] *Elias* v. *Snowdon Slate Quarries Co.* (1879) 4 App.Cas. 454.
[5] L.P.A. 1925, s.18, replacing C.A. 1881, s.19.
[6] For these, see *post*, p. 428.
[7] See, *e.g. Union Bank of London* v. *Ingram* (1880) 16 Ch.D. 53 at 56.
[8] *Ibid.*
[9] *Wrigley* v. *Gill* [1905] 1 Ch. 241 at 254, *per* Warrington J.; affirmed [1906] 1 Ch. 165.
[10] *Union Bank of London* v. *Ingram, supra*, at p. 56.
[11] *Ainsworth* v. *Wilding* [1905] 1 Ch. 435.

(2) ANNUAL RESTS.   If a mortgagee takes possession when no interest is in arrear and there is no peril to his security which he is attempting to forestall,[12] he will be treated as having shown an intention to accept payment by driblets,[13] and so annual rests will be directed; and the same will apply if he remains in possession when no arrears of interest remain because he has agreed to convert them all into principal,[14] or if the rents and profits greatly exceed the interest.[15] Further, if the mortgagee remains in possession after being paid his debt he will be accountable for the rents and profits to the mortgagor with compound interest at 4 per cent. as from the date of payment.[16]

(e) *Mortgagor barred.*   If the mortgagor's right to redeem becomes barred under the Limitation Act 1980,[17] the mortgagee may by deed vest in himself the fee simple, or the whole lease in the case of a mortgage of leaseholds.[18]

---

[12] *Horlock* v. *Smith* (1844) 1 Coll.C.C. 287; *Patch* v. *Wild* (1861) 30 Beav. 99.
[13] *Nelson* v. *Booth* (1858) 3 De G. & J. 119 at 122.
[14] *Wilson* v. *Cluer* (1840) 3 Beav. 136.
[15] *Uttermare* v. *Stevens* (1851) 17 L.T.(o.s.) 115; *Carter* v. *James* (1881) 29 W.R. 437; and see *Thorneycroft* v. *Crockett* (1848) 2 H.L.C. 239.
[16] *Ashworth* v. *Lord* (1887) 36 Ch.D. 545. It is probable that a higher rate would now be allowed: see *ante*, p. 289.
[17] See *post*, p. 438.
[18] L.P.A. 1925, ss.88(3), 89(3).

CHAPTER 3

REMEDIES OF THE MORTGAGEE

A mortgagee normally has five means of enforcing payment: an action
on the covenant for payment; sale; foreclosure; taking possession;
and appointing a receiver. The first three remedies secure repayment
of the loan, and so put an end to the transaction; the other two are
interim measures that leave the mortgage on foot, although in most
cases a mortgagee who takes possession does so only in order to be
able to exercise his power of sale effectually. The rights to sell
and to appoint a receiver are conferred by statute, in place of
express powers formerly inserted in most mortgages, whereas the
other powers arise from the nature of the transaction.

The right to take possession has already been discussed[1]; the other
powers are to be considered here.

Section 1. Action on the Covenant

A mortgage usually contains a covenant to repay the loan, and the
mortgagee can, of course, sue on that covenant on or after the date for
repayment, though not before.[2] This personal liability does not pass to a
person to whom the mortgagor transfers the property,[3] even though the
transfer is made subject to the mortgage[4]; but the transferee is, in the
absence of an express covenant of indemnity, by implication liable to
indemnify the mortgagor.[5]

Section 2. Sale

1. The power of sale. Formerly a mortgagee's power of sale
depended upon an express power being inserted in the mortgage. But,
subject to any contrary intention in the mortgage, a statutory power of
sale is now implied in all mortgages made after 1881 by deed, though
this takes effect subject to the terms of the mortgage deed and with such

---

[1] *Ante*, p. 403.
[2] See, *e.g. Bolton* v. *Buckenham* [1891] 1 Q.B. 278.
[3] *Re Errington* [1894] 1 Q.B. 11.
[4] *Woods* v. *Huntingford* (1796) 3 Ves. 128 at 132.
[5] *Waring* v. *Ward* (1802) 7 Ves. 332.

variations and extensions as the deed provides.[6] This power arises when the mortgage money has become due, and it enables the mortgagee "to sell, or to concur with any other person in selling, the mortgaged property, or any part thereof."[7]

2. When the power is exercisable. Although the power of sale *arises* when the mortgage money has become due, it does not become *exercisable* until:

(i) notice requiring payment of the mortgage money has been served on the mortgagor, or one of two or more mortgagors, and default has been made in payment of the mortgage money or of part thereof for three months after such service[8]; or

(ii) some interest is in arrear and unpaid for two months after becoming due; or

(iii) a breach has been committed of some provision in the mortgage deed or in the Law of Property Act 1925[9] and on the part of the mortgagor or of some person concurring in the mortgage to be observed or performed, other than the covenant to repay principal and interest.[10]

3. Improper sale. It will be noticed that the power of sale does not arise until the date fixed for redemption; until then, the mortgagee has no power to sell. But once the power has arisen, the mortgagee can make title, although if he sells before the power has become exercisable, or otherwise improperly or irregularly, he is liable in damages to the mortgagor.[11] Usually, however, a bona fide purchaser from the mortgagee is not affected by the conduct of the mortgagee; and although he must see that the power has arisen, he is not, either before or on conveyance, concerned to see or inquire whether a case has arisen to authorise the sale, or due notice has been given, or the power is otherwise properly and regularly exercised.[12] But the purchaser cannot safely complete if he has express notice that the mortgagee has not given due notice.[13]

4. Mode of sale. The sale may be made either subject to prior charges or not, and either together or in lots, by public auction or private contract, and subject to such conditions of sale as the mortgagee thinks fit, with power to buy in and rescind or vary any contract of sale,

---

[6] L.P.A. 1925, s.101(1), (3), (4), (5), replacing C.A. 1881, s.19, as amended by C.A. 1911, s.4. A less satisfactory power was formerly given by Lord Cranworth's Act 1860.
[7] L.P.A. 1925, s.101(1).
[8] See *Barker* v. *Illingworth* [1908] 2 Ch. 20.
[9] See, *e.g. Public Trustee* v. *Lawrence* [1912] 1 Ch. 793 (or C.A. 1881), *ante*, pp. 402, 403.
[10] L.P.A. 1925, s.103, replacing C.A. 1881, s.20.
[11] L.P.A. 1925, s.104(2), replacing C.A. 1881, s.21(2). A similar right is available to a mortgagor of a ship: *Fletcher* v. *City Marine Finance Ltd.* [1968] 2 Lloyd's Rep. 520.
[12] L.P.A. 1925, s.104(2), replacing C.A. 1881, s.21(2).
[13] *Selwyn* v. *Garfit* (1888) 38 Ch.D. 273.

and to resell without being answerable for any loss occasioned thereby.[14] On selling, the mortgagee may impose on the property sold, or the property retained by him, restrictions as to building on or other user of the land, and he may sell the mines and minerals apart from the surface, with appropriate conditions.[15]

5. Position of mortgagee on sale

(a) *Validity of sale.* The sale must be a true sale. A "sale" by a mortgagee to himself, whether directly[16] or through an agent,[17] or through a purported exercise of a right of pre-emption vested in him,[18] is no sale at all, and may be disregarded.[19] But a mortgagee may lawfully sell to a second mortgagee[20] or to one of several co-mortgagors.[21] He may sell to a company in which he has an interest but, if the sale is attacked, he will have to establish that he acted in good faith and took reasonable precautions to obtain the best price reasonably obtainable.[22] And although a mortgagee cannot validly sell to himself, if he purports to do so and then resells to a purchaser, the latter sale will be treated as a valid exercise of the mortgagee's power of sale.[23] Further, a sale by a mortgagee is not invalidated by reason of the purchaser being given a right to call upon the mortgagee to repurchase the property within a limited period at the price given for it.[24] Where the sale would have been set aside but for inexcusable delay by the borrower in bringing proceedings, the court may award damages in lieu.[25]

(b) *No trust of power.* A mortgagee is not a trustee of the power of sale; the power is given to him for his own benefit, and if he exercises it bona fide, without corruption or collusion with the purchaser,[26] the court will not interfere even though the timing of the sale be very disadvantageous to the mortgagor.[27] Indeed, there is no duty actually to exercise the power of sale before the mortgaged property becomes worthless.[27a] Yet the mortgagee owes some duty to the mortgagor with

---

[14] L.P.A. 1925, s.101(1).

[15] *Ibid.* s.101(2), applying to mortgages made after 1911. For other mortgages, the mortgagee may sell the surface and minerals apart only if authorised by the mortgage or the court: L.P.A. 1925, s.92.

[16] *Farrar v. Farrars Ltd.* (1888) 40 Ch.D. 395 at 409; and see *ante*, p. 249.

[17] *Downes v. Grazebrook* (1817) 3 Mer. 200.

[18] *Williams v. Wellingborough B.C.* [1975] 1 W.L.R. 1327.

[19] *Henderson v. Astwood* [1894] A.C. 150.

[20] *Shaw v. Bunny* (1865) 2 De G.J. & Sm. 468.

[21] *Kennedy v. De Trafford* [1897] A.C. 180. *Quaere* whether since 1925 the purchaser, who held the equity of redemption on trust for sale, would hold the property on trust for himself and his co-mortgagors.

[22] *Tse Kwong Lam v. Wong Chit Sen* [1983] 1 W.L.R. 1349.

[23] *Henderson v. Astwood, supra.*

[24] *Belton v. Bass, Ratcliffe & Gretton Ltd.* [1922] 2 Ch. 449.

[25] *Tse Kwong Lam v. Wong Chit Sen, supra.*

[26] As occurred in *Latec Investments Ltd. v. Hotel Terrigal Pty. Ltd.* (1965) 113 C.L.R. 265, where the sale was set aside five years later but without prejudice to the rights of those claiming through the purchaser.

[27] *Warner v. Jacob* (1882) 20 Ch.D. 220; *Lord Waring v. London and Manchester Assurance Co. Ltd.* [1935] Ch. 310; and see *Haddington Island Quarry Co. Ltd. v. Huson* [1911] A.C. 722.

[27a] *China and South Sea Bank Ltd. v. Tan Soon Gin* [1990] A.C. 536 (surety).

regard to the manner in which a sale which does take place is conducted[28]; and this duty is also owed to a surety for the mortgagor,[29] but not to a beneficiary under a trust of the mortgaged property.[29a] Although the mortgagee is entitled to act primarily in his own interests,[30] and is not (for example) expected to keep the mortgagor's business in operation until the market in property rises,[31] he must take reasonable care to obtain the true market value of the property at the time when he chooses to sell it.[32] A clause which empowers the mortgagee to sell for such consideration and on such terms as he may think fit does not relieve him of this obligation.[33] Moreover, a building society has a statutory duty to ensure that the price at which the property is sold is the best which can be reasonably obtained,[34] though it, too, is at perfect liberty to sell when it thinks proper.[35] In any event, the court will interfere only at the instance of those who have an interest in the proceeds of sale. Thus neither tenants at will of the mortgagor nor persons jointly liable for the mortgage debt can complain of a sale at an undervalue.[36]

(c) *Involuntary loss.* A mortgagee is protected from liability for involuntary loss happening in or about the exercise of his statutory power of sale, or of any trust connected therewith, or, if the mortgage was executed after 1911, of any power or provision contained in the mortgage deed.[37] But the mortgagee will be liable in damages if by reason of his improper treatment the property is depreciated and the purchase price is therefore less than it should have been.[38]

6. Effect of sale by mortgagee

(a) *Contract.* A contract for sale by the mortgagee puts an end to the mortgagor's right to redeem. This is so even if the contract is subject to a condition which is not performed until after the mortgagor has given notice of his intention to redeem.[39] The mortgagee's power of sale is unaffected by the mortgagor selling his equity of redemption.[40]

[28] *Cuckmere Brick Co. Ltd.* v. *Mutual Finance Ltd.* [1971] Ch. 949, rejecting dicta in *Kennedy* v. *De Trafford* [1897] A.C. 180; and see *Colson* v. *Williams* (1889) 61 L.T. 71 at 72.
[29] See *Standard Chartered Bank Ltd.* v. *Walker* [1982] 1 W.L.R. 1410 (sale by receiver appointed under debenture), disapproving *Barclays Bank Ltd.* v. *Thienel* (1978) 247 E.G. 385 and *Latchford* v. *Beirne* [1981] 3 All E.R. 705.
[29a] *Parker-Tweedale* v. *Dunbar Bank plc* [1990] 2 All E.R. 577.
[30] *Palmer* v. *Barclays Bank Ltd.* (1971) 23 P. & C.R. 30.
[31] *Bank of Cyprus (London) Ltd.* v. *Gill* [1980] 2 Lloyd's Rep. 51.
[32] *Cuckmere Brick Co. Ltd.* v. *Mutual Finance Ltd., supra*; *Tomlin* v. *Luce* (1889) 43 Ch.D. 191; *Holohan* v. *Friends Provident and Century Life Office* [1966] I.R. 1. See generally P. Butt, *The Mortgagee's Duty on Sale*, (1979) 53 A.L.J. 172.
[33] *Bishop* v. *Bonham* [1988] 1 W.L.R. 742.
[34] Building Societies Act 1986, s.13(7), Sched. 4, para. 1.
[35] *Reliance Permanent B.S.* v. *Harwood-Stamper* [1944] Ch. 362.
[36] *Jarrett* v. *Barclays Bank Ltd.* [1947] Ch. 187.
[37] L.P.A. 1925, s.106, replacing C.A. 1881, s.21, as extended by C.A. 1911, s.5.
[38] *Tomlin* v. *Luce* (1889) 43 Ch.D. 191; *McHugh* v. *Union Bank of Canada* [1913] A.C. 299.
[39] *Property and Bloodstock Ltd.* v. *Emerton* [1968] Ch. 94.
[40] *Duke* v. *Robson* [1973] 1 W.L.R. 267.

(b) *Conveyance.*   Although since 1925 the mortgagee has only a term of years, on a sale he can convey not merely the mortgage term but also the whole fee simple estate (if the fee simple is mortgaged) or (if the property mortgaged is leasehold) the leasehold reversion affected by the mortgage. In either case, the conveyance will be free from any subsequent charge (even one held by the purchaser himself[41]) but will be subject to any legal mortgage having priority to the mortgage in right of which the sale is made, although the mortgage term and any subsequent mortgage terms will merge or be extinguished.[42]

(c) *Surplus proceeds of sale.*   Subject to statute,[43] the mortgagee holds any surplus proceeds of sale on trust for any subsequent mortgagees and the mortgagor. Although the mortgagee is not a trustee of the power of sale,[44] he has always been a constructive trustee of the surplus proceeds of sale,[45] for as soon as his mortgage is discharged he has no further right to the land or the proceeds of sale[46]; and on receiving these proceeds his solicitor similarly held them on trust.[47] Statute now seems to make the mortgagee an express trustee of the surplus[48]; and he must account for it to a subsequent mortgagee despite any claim that the mortgagor may have against that mortgagee.[49] However, if all rights to redeem have been barred by lapse of time, the mortgagee is entitled to the surplus beneficially.[50]

Section 3. Appointment of a Receiver

1. The right of appointment.   The power to appoint a receiver is governed by the same statutory provisions as govern the power of sale, so that the power arises, becomes exercisable and is generally subject to the same restrictions and extensions as that power.[51] The fact that the mortgagee has taken possession does not prevent him from appointing a receiver[52] but in the case of a mortgage of registered land the power cannot be exercised before the mortgagee has been registered as

---

[41] *Rust* v. *Goodale* [1957] Ch. 33 at 47. Contrast *Re White Rose Cottage* [1965] Ch. 940, where a transfer by the mortgagor with the concurrence of the mortgagees was held not to be a conveyance by mortgagees free from subsequent charges.
[42] L.P.A. 1925, ss.88(1), 89(1), 104(1).
[43] See, *e.g.* Small Dwellings Acquisition Act 1899, s.6(2), as construed in *Re Brown's Mortgage* [1945] Ch. 166; contrast *Re Caunter's Charge* [1960] Ch. 491. The 1899 Act was repealed by the Housing (Consequential Provisions) Act 1985, s.3(1), Sched. 1, Pt. I: but see Housing Act 1985, s.456, Sched. 18, para. 7.
[44] *Ante*, p. 414.
[45] *Banner* v. *Berridge* (1881) 18 Ch.D. 254; and see *Weld-Blundell* v. *Synott* [1940] 2 K.B. 107. Contrast the position with regard to marshalling, *post*, p. 421.
[46] *Charles* v. *Jones* (1887) 35 Ch.D. 544 at 549.
[47] *Re Bell, Lake* v. *Bell* (1886) 34 Ch.D. 462.
[48] L.P.A. 1925, s.105, replacing C.A. 1881, s.21(3).
[49] *Samuel Keller (Holdings) Ltd.* v. *Martins Bank Ltd.* [1971] 1 W.L.R. 43.
[50] *Re Moat House Farm, Thurlby* [1948] Ch. 191; and see *post*, p. 438.
[51] L.P.A. 1925, ss.101, 109, replacing C.A. 1881, ss.19, 24. For receivers, see *post*, p. 689.
[52] *Refuge Assurance Co. Ltd.* v. *Pearlberg* [1938] Ch. 687.

proprietor of the charge.[53] The appointment is made by writing under the mortgagee's hand.[54]

2. Position of receiver. The receiver, although appointed by the mortgagee, is deemed to be the agent of the mortgagor, who is solely responsible for the receiver's acts and defaults unless the mortgage deed otherwise provides,[55] or unless the mortgagee gives directions to the receiver or interferes with his conduct.[56] The receiver is entitled to recover the income of the property by action, distress, or otherwise, and to give effectual receipts accordingly, and to exercise any powers of leasing or accepting surrenders of leases which the mortgagee may have delegated to him.[57] Persons making payments to him are not concerned to inquire whether any case has happened to authorise him to act.[58] The mortgagee may from time to time by writing under his hand remove a receiver, or appoint a new receiver in his place.[59]

3. Application of money. Although a receiver is nominally an agent of the mortgagor, he must account to the mortgagee.[60] He must apply moneys received by him[61]:

   (i)   in discharge of all rents, rates, taxes and outgoings;

   (ii) in keeping down the interest on prior incumbrances;

   (iii) in payment of his own commission,[62] and the premiums on fire, life, or other insurances, if any, properly payable, and the cost of executing necessary or proper repairs directed in writing by the mortgagee[63];

   (iv) in payment of interest accruing due in respect of any principal money due under the mortgage; and

   (v)   in or towards discharge of the principal money, if so directed in writing by the mortgagee.

The residue, if any, of the money received must be paid to the person who, but for the possession of the receiver, would have been entitled to

---

[53] *Lever Finance Ltd.* v. *L.N. and H.M. Needleman's Trustee* [1956] Ch. 375 at 382.
[54] L.P.A. 1925, s.109(1); and consider *Windsor Refrigerator Co. Ltd.* v. *Branch Nominees Ltd.* [1961] Ch. 375.
[55] L.P.A. 1925, s.109(2). For the origin of this rule, see *Gaskell* v. *Gosling* [1896] 1 Q.B. 669 at 691, 692.
[56] *Standard Chartered Bank Ltd.* v. *Walker* [1982] 1 W.L.R. 1410 at 1416.
[57] L.P.A. 1925, s.109(3).
[58] *Ibid.* s.109(4).
[59] *Ibid.* s.109(5); and see *post*, pp. 692, 693.
[60] *Leicester Permanent B.S.* v. *Butt* [1943] Ch. 308.
[61] L.P.A. 1925, s.109(8).
[62] See *post*, p. 692.
[63] *White* v. *Metcalf* [1903] 2 Ch. 567.

receive the income of which he is appointed receiver, or who is otherwise entitled to the mortgaged property.[64] If so directed in writing by the mortgagee, the receiver must "insure to the extent, if any, to which the mortgagee might have insured and keep insured against loss or damage by fire" all buildings, effects, or property of an insurable nature comprised in the mortgage.[65]

Section 4. Foreclosure

1. Right to foreclose. Subject to statute,[66] foreclosure can be effected only by an order of the court.[67] In foreclosure proceedings the court is asked to set limits to its own indulgence, and to decree that a mortgagor who is already too late to redeem at law shall be deprived even of his equitable right. A foreclosure action is therefore possible the moment the property is forfeited at law. If there is a proviso for redemption on payment of instalments of principal and interest punctually, foreclosure will lie if interest is unpaid, even though the principal is not due.[68] The same result will follow where, although there is no express proviso of this kind, the court concludes that a breach of covenant by the mortgagor is of a nature which bars him at law from recovering his property.[69] Foreclosure may thus be available where the statutory power of sale has not yet arisen.[70] Further, the dismissal of a redemption action[71] on the mortgagor's failure to redeem operates to foreclose his right of redemption[72]; he will not be allowed "to harass the mortgagee" by suing for redemption again later.[73]

2. Parties to proceedings. Where a claim is made to foreclosure, all incumbrancers subsequent to the plaintiff as well as all other persons interested in the equity of redemption must be made parties, or they will not be bound by the foreclosure decree.[74]

---

[64] L.P.A. 1925, s.109(8).

[65] *Ibid.* s.109(7).

[66] See, *e.g.* Small Dwellings Acquisition Act 1899, s.5(1), under which taking possession by the mortgagee operated as a form of summary foreclosure: see *Mexborough U.D.C.* v. *Harrison* [1964] 1 W.L.R. 733. See, as to repeal of 1899 Act, *ante*, p. 416, n. 43; but see Housing Act 1985, s.456, Sched. 18, para. 6(1).

[67] See *Ness* v. *O'Neil* [1916] 1 K.B. 706 at 709.

[68] *Williams* v. *Morgan* [1906] 1 Ch. 804 at 808, 809; *Kidderminster Mutual Benefit B.S.* v. *Haddock* [1936] W.N. 158.

[69] *Twentieth Century Banking Corporation Ltd.* v. *Wilkinson* [1977] Ch. 99 (breach of interest covenant in mortgage where principal not due for 15 years).

[70] *Twentieth Century Banking Corporation Ltd.* v. *Wilkinson, supra.*

[71] See *post*, pp. 424 *et seq.*

[72] See, *e.g. Inman* v. *Wearing* (1850) 3 De G. & Sm. 729 at 734, and the exchange in *Biggs* v. *Hoddinott* [1898] 2 Ch. 307 at 312.

[73] *Marshall* v. *Shrewsbury* (1875) 10 Ch.App. 250 at 254, *per* James L.J.

[74] *Gee* v. *Liddell* [1913] 2 Ch. 62. See *post*, p. 430.

3. Procedure. Unless all parties concerned consent to foreclosure absolute, the first stage in a foreclosure suit is to obtain a foreclosure order nisi. This gives the mortgagor and subsequent mortgagees an opportunity of redeeming the mortgage. The current practice is to give only one period for redemption to all parties, including subsequent mortgagees, and not, as formerly, successive periods to each.[75] At any rate, without prejudice to the right of the incumbrancers as between themselves, only one period will be given for redemption if the subsequent mortgagees do not appear and ask for successive periods, or if questions of priority arise; for the court will not allow the foreclosure action to be unduly prolonged simply because there are numerous incumbrancers.[76] The usual time given for redemption is six months, but the time may be enlarged if the mortgagor shows special circumstances, and pays the interest and costs certified as due.[77] If the property is not redeemed on the date fixed a foreclosure order absolute is made, thus destroying the equity of redemption.

4. Effect of foreclosure absolute. Where an estate in fee simple has been mortgaged by the creation of a term of years or by a charge by way of legal mortgage, and the mortgagee obtains an order for foreclosure absolute, the order will operate to vest the fee simple in him, subject to any prior legal mortgage; the mortgage term will be merged in the fee simple, and any subsequent mortgage term or charge by way of legal mortgage bound by the order will be extinguished.[78] Similar provision is made in the case of leaseholds mortgaged by sub-demise, so as to give the mortgagee the whole lease on foreclosure.[79] If the mortgagee sells the property after foreclosure, he cannot later sue the mortgagor on any express or implied covenant in the mortgage.[80]

5. Opening a foreclosure. Although the order of foreclosure absolute appears to be final, the courts will sometimes open a foreclosure even if the property has been sold by the mortgagee. Circumstances which will induce the court to do this are an accident at the last moment preventing the mortgagor from raising the money, any special value of the property to the mortgagor (*e.g.* if it was an old family estate), a marked disparity between the value of the property and the amount lent, and the promptness of the application.[81] The foreclosure will also be opened if the mortgagee pursues another remedy after obtaining an order of foreclosure absolute.[82]

---

[75] See *Smith* v. *Olding* (1884) 25 Ch.D. 462 as marking the change.
[76] *Platt* v. *Mendel* (1884) 27 Ch.D. 246; *Smithett* v. *Hesketh* (1890) 44 Ch.D. 161.
[77] *Coombe* v. *Stewart* (1851) 13 Beav. 111; *Nanny* v. *Edwards* (1837) 4 Russ. 125.
[78] L.P.A. 1925, s.88(2).
[79] *Ibid.* s.89(2).
[80] *Lloyds and Scottish Trust Ltd.* v. *Britten* (1982) 44 P. & C.R. 249.
[81] *Campbell* v. *Holyland* (1877) 7 Ch.D. 166 at 172–174.
[82] See *post,* p. 420.

6. Sale in lieu of foreclosure. In any action of foreclosure the court may order a sale of the mortgaged property on the application of any person interested in the mortgage money or the right of redemption, without previously allowing any time for redemption, and without first determining the conflicting priorities of incumbrancers.[83] The order is discretionary,[84] and may be made on such terms as the court thinks fit.

Section 5. Exercise of Several Remedies

1. Remedies are concurrent. A mortgagee's remedies are exercisable concurrently so far as they are not inconsistent with one another. Thus the mortgagee can in a single action claim foreclosure and judgment on the mortgagor's covenant to repay. Again, if he is still not fully paid after the property has been sold under his power of sale or under an order of the court, he may sue the mortgagor on the covenant in respect of the balance.[85] And if the mortgagee obtains only part payment on the covenant, he may go on with his foreclosure action, and (giving credit for what he has received) foreclose for the remainder, or he may exercise his power of sale to secure payment of the balance due to him. Further, although a mortgagee who exercises his statutory power of sale after a foreclosure order nisi but before a foreclosure order absolute should first obtain the consent of the court, he may without this consent make title to a bona fide purchaser of the legal estate without notice.[86]

2. Opening the foreclosure. If the mortgagee obtains a foreclosure first, and then the value of the estate proves insufficient to satisfy the mortgage debt, he may still sue on the covenant; yet by doing so he opens the foreclosure and so gives the mortgagor a renewed right to redeem.[87] But if the mortgagee has so dealt with the estate after foreclosure as to be unable to give to the mortgagor the reconveyance to which he is entitled on redemption (as where the mortgagee has sold the estate), no action can be brought on the covenant.[88] However, a second or third mortgagee who consents to a foreclosure order absolute in favour of the first mortgagee does not thereby prevent himself from suing the mortgagor on the covenant.[89]

---

[83] L.P.A. 1925, s.91, replacing C.A. 1881, s.25.
[84] See *Silsby* v. *Holliman* [1955] Ch. 552.
[85] *Rudge* v. *Richens* (1873) L.R. 8 C.P. 358; *Gordon Grant & Co. Ltd.* v. *Boos* [1926] A.C. 781.
[86] *Stevens* v. *Theatres Ltd.* [1903] 1 Ch. 857; and see L.P.A. 1925, s.104(2)(c).
[87] *Palmer* v. *Hendrie* (1859) 27 Beav. 349. This passage was cited with approval in *Mexborough U.D.C.* v. *Harrison* [1964] 1 W.L.R. 733 at 738, and applied to a summary foreclosure under the Small Dwellings Acquisition Act 1899, as to which see, *ante*, p. 418, n. 66.
[88] *Lockhart* v. *Hardy* (1846) 9 Beav. 349; *Lloyds and Scottish Trust Ltd.* v. *Britten* (1982) 44 P. & C.R. 249; contrast *Gordon Grant & Co. Ltd.* v. *Boos* [1926] A.C. 781.
[89] *Worthington* v. *Abbott* [1910] 1 Ch. 588.

Section 6. Marshalling

1. The doctrine. Where there are two creditors of the same debtor,[90] one creditor having a right to resort to two funds of the debtor for payment of his debt, and the other a right to resort to one fund only,[91] the court will so "marshal" or arrange the funds that both creditors are paid as far as possible. "A person having resort to two funds shall not by his choice disappoint another, having one only."[92] Though the doctrine has several applications,[93] marshalling as between mortgagees is perhaps the most usual. If, for instance, a person having two estates, Blackacre and Whiteacre, mortgages both estates to A, and afterwards mortgages only Blackacre to B, either with or without notice of A's mortgage, the proper course is for A to realise his debt first out of Whiteacre and to take only the balance out of Blackacre, in order to leave as much as possible of Blackacre to satisfy B.[94] The doctrine of marshalling is not allowed to prejudice the first mortgagee, however, and A can therefore realise his securities as he pleases,[95] for A is not a trustee for B.[96] The effect of the doctrine is that if A chooses to pay himself out of Blackacre, B is allowed to resort to Whiteacre to the extent to which Blackacre has been exhausted by A, and to have the same priority against Whiteacre as A had.

2. No marshalling to the prejudice of purchasers. In the above example, B's right to marshal will be enforced not only against the original mortgagor but also against all persons claiming through him as volunteers, as where the mortgagor dies and Blackacre and Whiteacre pass to different persons.[97] But it is not allowed to prejudice purchasers or mortgagees of one of the estates. Thus if in the above example the mortgagor had created another mortgage of Whiteacre in favour of C, B would have no equity to throw the whole of A's mortgage on Whiteacre, and so destroy C's security. As between B and C, A is bound to satisfy himself out of the two estates rateably according to their respective values, and thus to leave the surplus proceeds of each estate to be applied in payment of the respective incumbrances thereon.[98] The position would be the same if C were a mortgagee of both Blackacre and Whiteacre, unless C took his mortgage expressly subject to the payment of the two prior mortgages.[99]

[90] *Ex p. Kendall* (1811) 17 Ves. 514 at 520.
[91] See *Webb* v. *Smith* (1885) 30 Ch.D. 192.
[92] *Trimmer* v. *Bayne (No. 2)* (1803) 9 Ves. 209 at 211, *per* Grant M.R., approved in *Webb* v. *Smith, supra*, at p. 202.
[93] See *ante*, pp. 312, 336, 366.
[94] *Lanoy* v. *Duke of Athol* (1742) 2 Atk. 444 at 446; *South* v. *Bloxam* (1865) 2 H. & M. 457.
[95] *Wallis* v. *Woodyear* (1855) 2 Jur.(N.S.) 179.
[96] *Commonwealth Trading Bank* v. *Colonial Mutual Life Assurance Society Ltd.* (1970) 26 F.L.R. 338, Tas.S.C.
[97] *Lanoy* v. *Duke of Athol, supra*, at p. 446.
[98] *Gibson* v. *Seagrim* (1855) 20 Beav. 614 at 619; *Flint* v. *Howard* [1893] 2 Ch. 54 at 72.
[99] *Barnes* v. *Racster* (1842) 1 Y. & C.C.C. 401; *Re Mower's Trusts* (1869) L.R. 8 Eq. 110.

3. Apportionment of mortgage on two properties. If a mortgage debt is secured on two different properties, and the equities of redemption become vested in different persons by reason of death or otherwise, prima facie the debt must be borne rateably by the two properties in proportion to their respective values. But this does not apply if one of the properties was made the primary fund for payment of the debt, or if an intention to exclude the ordinary rule of contribution was shown when the two properties separated.[1] Thus if B mortgages Blackacre and a policy of insurance to L and then conveys Blackacre to P expressly subject to the mortgage, on paying off the entire mortgage B is entitled to recover from P a proportionate part of the amount paid by B.[2] But B could claim no contribution from P if the conveyance to P contained no reference to the mortgage.[3]

[1] *De Rochefort* v. *Dawes* (1871) L.R. 12 Eq. 540; and see *Lipscomb* v. *Lipscomb* (1869) L.R. 7 Eq. 501.
[2] *Re Mainwaring* [1937] Ch. 96.
[3] *Re Darby's Estate* [1907] 2 Ch. 465; *Re Best, Parker* v. *Best* [1924] 1 Ch. 42.

CHAPTER 4

DISCHARGE AND TRANSFER OF MORTGAGES

A mortgage may be discharged in a number of ways. The equity of redemption may be extinguished by foreclosure, by sale under the mortgagee's power of sale, or by the operation of the Limitation Act 1980; these heads are considered elsewhere.[1] The mortgage may also be extinguished by merger or by redemption; or it may be transferred to another. These subjects are now to be discussed.

Section 1. Merger

1. Law and equity. Questions of merger will arise if a mortgage and the equity of redemption come into the same hands, as where the owner of one purchases the other, or both are acquired by one person. The rule at law, whether for mortgages or other interests, was that merger was automatic where two estates or interests in the same property, separated by no intervening vested estate or interest, vested in the same person in the same right.[2] In equity, however, merger depended upon the intention of the person in whom the two estates or interests vested[3]; and if this intention had not been expressed, equity presumed against merger where merger would be against his interests.[4]

2. Equity prevails. The Judicature Act 1873 made the rule of equity prevail, so that now there will be "no merger by operation of law only of any estate the beneficial interest in which would not be deemed to be merged or extinguished in equity."[5] Both at law and in equity merger accordingly now depends on intention.

---

[1] See *ante*, pp. 412, 418 and *post*, p. 438.
[2] See, *e.g. Re Bellville's S.T.* [1964] Ch. 163.
[3] See *Capital and Counties Bank Ltd.* v. *Rhodes* [1903] 1 Ch. 631; *Re Fletcher, Reading* v. *Fletcher* [1917] 1 Ch. 339.
[4] *Ingle* v. *Vaughan Jenkins* [1900] 2 Ch. 368.
[5] L.P.A. 1925, s.185, replacing J.A. 1873, s.25(4).

Section 2. Redemption

1. Repayment of mortgage

(a) *Intention.* The principles of merger may apply when a mortgage is paid off. In such cases, the payment may discharge the mortgage, or it may keep the mortgage alive but transfer it to the person making the payment, depending on the intention of that person.[6] This intention may appear from the documents,[7] the surrounding circumstances,[8] or the evidence of the person himself,[9] or it may be presumed from considering which result will be to the advantage of the person making the payment.[10] Thus if the absolute owner of an equity of redemption pays off the only mortgage on the property, or the mortgage lowest in priority, the general rule is that the mortgage will be discharged[11]; this will simplify the title, and it is "no sort of use" for a man "to have a charge on his own estate."[12]

(b) *Intervening incumbrances.* If, however, there are other in-cumbrances over which the mortgage has priority, an intention to keep it alive will be presumed for the sake of that priority; a man who pays off a first mortgage will be presumed to intend to keep it alive for his own benefit rather than discharge it and so elevate the second mortgagee into first place.[13] A first mortgagee who buys the equity of redemption when second mortgages exist will similarly be presumed to intend to keep his mortgage alive.[14] Again, if an incumbrance is paid off by a tenant for life, whether in possession or in remainder,[15] or by any other limited owner (except a tenant in tail in possession free to bar the entail[16]), he will be presumed to have kept it alive for his own benefit[17] rather than to have discharged it and so to have increased the capital value of the property to which the remainderman will be entitled. A similar rule applies where the payment is made by a tenant in common[18] or a person with no interest in the property.[19]

[6] See, *e.g. Liquidation Estates Purchase Co. Ltd.* v. *Willoughby* [1898] A.C. 321; *Whiteley* v. *Delaney* [1914] A.C. 132.
[7] See, *e.g. Re Gibbon* [1909] 1 Ch. 367 (express declaration).
[8] See, *e.g. Adams* v. *Angell* (1877) 5 Ch.D. 634 (correspondence).
[9] *Lord Gifford* v. *Lord Fitzhardinge* [1899] 2 Ch. 32.
[10] *Thorne* v. *Cann* [1895] A.C. 11 at 19.
[11] *Price* v. *Gibson* (1762) 2 Eden 115.
[12] *Forbes* v. *Moffatt* (1811) 18 Ves. 384 at 390, *per* Grant M.R.
[13] See, *e.g. Whiteley* v. *Delaney* [1914] A.C. 132.
[14] *Adams* v. *Angell* (1877) 5 Ch.D. 634.
[15] *Re Chesters* [1935] Ch. 77.
[16] *Countess of Shrewsbury* v. *Earl of Shrewsbury* (1790) 1 Ves.Jun. 227; *Wigsell* v. *Wigsell* (1825) 2 Sim. & St. 364.
[17] *Burrell* v. *Earl of Egremont* (1844) 7 Beav. 205; *Re Warwick's S.T.* [1938] Ch. 530 at 535 (jointure and interest on portions).
[18] *Re Pride* [1891] 2 Ch. 135.
[19] *Butler* v. *Rice* [1910] 2 Ch. 277; *Ghana Commercial Bank* v. *Chandiram* [1960] A.C. 732.

2. Original mortgagor

(a) *The rule in Otter* v. *Lord Vaux.*   There is one exception to the doctrine that the effect of paying off a mortgage depends upon intention. Under the rule in *Otter* v. *Lord Vaux,*[20] an original mortgagor who pays off a mortgage cannot, even by express provision, keep it alive against any other incumbrance which he has created, whether that incumbrance is subsequent to the charge paid off, or ranks *pari passu* with it.[21] Thus if X has mortgaged Blackacre first to A and then to B, when he pays off A he necessarily makes B the first mortgagee.[22] The reason is that when X mortgaged the property to B he was already bound by covenant to pay the money due under A's mortgage[23]; his mortgage to B was a mortgage of his entire interest,[24] and he "cannot derogate from his own bargain"[25] by setting up "against his own incumbrancer any other incumbrance created by himself."[26] X cannot complain that the improvement in B's position is unmerited, for B is treated as having agreed to hold subject to A's mortgage only so long as A remained unpaid.[27]

(b) *Limits to the rule.*   The rule applies only to the original mortgagor and not, *e.g.* to a purchaser of the equity of redemption who is under no personal liability to make the payment.[28] Such a purchaser can thus keep the prior mortgage alive, although possibly in this case evidence of an intention against merger is required, and a mere presumption derived from the advantage of keeping the charge alive will not be enough.[29]

3. Mode of discharge

(a) *Discharge*

(1) PAYMENT.   When a mortgage is redeemed, no reconveyance is now necessary, both because the mortgagee no longer takes the estate of the mortgagor and because of the statutory provisions relating to receipts. The only estate a mortgagee has after 1925 is a term of years, and on

---

[20] (1856) 6 De G.M. & G. 638. L.P.A. 1925, s.115(3), expressly recognises the rule.
[21] *Re W. Tasker & Sons Ltd.* [1905] 2 Ch. 587; *Parkash* v. *Irani Finance Ltd.* [1970] Ch. 101, where at p. 112 this passage was cited.
[22] See *Platt* v. *Mendel* (1884) 27 Ch.D. 246 at 251.
[23] See *Otter* v. *Lord Vaux* (1856) 2 K. & J. 650 at 656, 657; affirmed, 6 De G.M. & G. 638.
[24] *Frazer* v. *Jones* (1846) 5 Hare 475 at 481.
[25] *Whiteley* v. *Delaney* [1914] A.C. 132 at 145, *per* Lord Haldane L.C.
[26] *Otter* v. *Lord Vaux* (1856) 6 De G.M. & G. 638 at 642, *per* Lord Cranworth L.C.
[27] See *Adams* v. *Angell* (1877) 5 Ch.D. 634 at 642.
[28] See *Thorne* v. *Cann* [1895] A.C. 11 at 18.
[29] *Toulmin* v. *Steere* (1817) 3 Mer. 210, as explained in *Adams* v. *Angell* (1877) 5 Ch.D. 634 at 646. But *Toulmin* v. *Steere* has been criticised almost out of existence: see, *e.g. Thorne* v. *Cann, supra*; *Whiteley* v. *Delaney, supra.*

redemption this becomes a satisfied term and ceases, whether the property mortgaged is freehold or leasehold.[30] Further, a receipt for the mortgage money written on or annexed to the mortgage, stating the name of the person who pays the money, and executed by the chargee by way of legal mortgage, or the person in whom the mortgaged property is vested and who is legally entitled to give a receipt, will operate, without any reconveyance, surrender or release, to merge the term in the immediate reversion and discharge the mortgage.[31] Despite the language of these provisions, a receipt may be effective although it is not executed under seal[32] and although the name of the person who pays the money is not stated.[33] In the absence of fraud, the receipt releases the mortgagor from all liability even where the mortgagee has wrongly calculated the amount of the redemption figure.[34]

(2) RECEIPT. The receipt may be in the statutory form,[35] with or without variations[36]; and the same covenants are implied in it as if the person executing it had by deed expressed to convey the property as mortgagee.[37] These provisions apply to the discharge of a legal charge as well as a mortgage,[38] but not to the discharge of a charge or incumbrance registered under the Land Registration Act 1925.[39] They do not affect the right of any person to require a reassignment, surrender, release or transfer in lieu of a receipt.[40]

(b) *Transfer.* A receipt does not, however, always discharge the mortgage. If by the receipt the money appears to have been paid by a person who is not entitled to the immediate equity of redemption,[41] the receipt will operate as a transfer of the mortgage to him.[42] But this does not apply where it is otherwise expressly provided,[43] or where the mortgage is paid off out of capital money applicable for the discharge thereof and it is not expressly provided that the receipt is to operate as a transfer.[44] Nor do these provisions affect the rule in *Otter* v. *Lord Vaux*.[45]

---

[30] L.P.A. 1925, s.116.
[31] L.P.A. 1925, s.115(1).
[32] *Simpson* v. *Geoghegan* [1934] W.N. 232.
[33] *Edwards* v. *Marshall-Lee* (1975) 235 E.G. 901.
[34] *Erewash B.C.* v. *Taylor* [1979] C.L.Y. 1831 (county court: £1,000 too little).
[35] L.P.A. 1925, 3rd Sched.
[36] *Ibid.* s.115(5), as amended by Finance Act 1971, s.64, Sched. 14, Pt. VI, consequential on the abolition of stamp duty on receipts and discharges of mortgages: *ibid.* s.64.
[37] *Ibid.* s.115(6).
[38] *Ibid.* s.115(8).
[39] *Ibid.* s.115(10).
[40] *Ibid.* s.115(4).
[41] See *Simpson* v. *Geoghegan* [1934] W.N. 232.
[42] L.P.A. 1925, s.115(2).
[43] See *Pyke* v. *Peters* [1943] K.B. 242.
[44] L.P.A. 1925, s.115(2); and see *Cumberland Court (Brighton) Ltd.* v. *Taylor* [1964] Ch. 29 (mortgagor pays off mortgage after conveying property free from incumbrances).
[45] L.P.A. 1925, s.115(3), for the rule, see *ante*, p. 425.

(c) *Building society mortgages*.   Special statutory provisions relate to the discharge of a mortgage made to a building, friendly, industrial or provident society[46]: receipts given under these statutes operate in accordance with the foregoing provisions relating to the discharge of mortgages.[47]

(d) *Discharge after mortgagee's death*.   If the mortgagee dies before the mortgage has been discharged, both the legal right to give a receipt for the mortgage money and whatever estate or interest in the mortgaged property was vested in him pass to his personal representatives.[48] Where a discharge is difficult or impossible to procure, an application to the court to exercise its powers to make a vesting order will sometimes be necessary.[49]

Section 3. Price of Redemption

1. Principal.   On redemption, the redeeming party must pay to the mortgagee the principal of the mortgage debt together with the interest thereon, and the costs reasonably incurred in relation to the mortgage debt, including costs properly incurred in ascertaining or defending his rights.[50] The aggregate amount so to be paid is usually known as the "price of redemption." The mortgage remains in being until there has been actual payment and acceptance of the price of redemption; the mere unilateral appropriation by the mortgagor of a cross-claim against the mortgagee for more than that price works no discharge.[51]

2. Interest

(a) *Agreement as to rate*.   The rate of interest will be that stated in the mortgage. A clause providing that in default of punctual payment the agreed rate of interest shall be increased is treated as penal, however, and cannot be enforced; yet a covenant to pay the higher rate, with a proviso for reduction of that rate on punctual payment, is perfectly valid.[52] "Punctual payment" in such cases is taken literally as meaning payment on the exact date named[53]; and the higher rate will be

---

[46] Building Societies Act 1986, s.13(7), Sched. 4, para. 2; Friendly Societies Act 1974, s.57; Industrial and Provident Societies Act 1965, s.33. The relationship between these provisions and L.P.A. 1925, s.115, is a matter of some difficulty: see Wurtzburg and Mills' *Building Society Law* (15th ed., 1989), paras. 6.45, 6.46.
[47] L.P.A. 1925, s.115(9).
[48] A.E.A. 1925, ss.1–3, replacing (*inter alia*) C.A. 1881, s.30.
[49] T.A. 1925, ss.44 *et seq.*; and see *Re Albert Road, Norwood (Nos. 56 and 58)* [1916] 1 Ch. 289.
[50] *Dryden* v. *Frost* (1838) 3 My. & Cr. 670.
[51] *Samuel Keller (Holdings) Ltd.* v. *Martins Bank Ltd.* [1971] 1 W.L.R. 43; and see *Inglis* v. *Commonwealth Trading Bank of Australia* (1972) 126 C.L.R. 1.
[52] *Bright* v. *Campbell* (1889) 41 Ch.D. 388.
[53] *Leeds and Hanley Theatre of Varieties* v. *Broadbent* [1898] 1 Ch. 348; *Maclaine* v. *Gatty* [1921] 1 A.C. 376.

payable if the mortgagor has not paid on the due date, even though the mortgagee is in possession of the rents and profits, and could satisfy his claim for interest thereout.[54] A provision for capitalisation of interest in arrear is also perfectly valid. But under such a provision compound interest cannot be exacted by a mortgagee in possession who has sufficient rents and profits in hand to meet the interest due; in such circumstances the interest cannot be said to be "in arrear," even if the mortgagor fails to pay it.[55] The mortgagor continues to be liable for interest until either he tenders repayment and, if it is not accepted, also sets the money aside so as to be ready for repayment,[56] or else the mortgagee unequivocally refuses a proposed repayment and so waives tender.[57] The extent to which interest in lieu of notice is payable has already been dealt with.[58]

(b) *Effect of judgment.* Where the mortgagee obtains judgment for the principal due under the covenant for payment, the covenant merges in the judgment, which carries interest at the rate of 15 per cent.[59] If the covenant for interest is to pay interest at the rate of 18 per cent. on any principal due *under the covenant*, the mortgagor's personal liability is for only 15 per cent. after judgment, for the principal is then due not under the covenant but under the judgment.[60] It is otherwise if the covenant is to pay interest on any principal due *on the security*[61]; and in any case interest at the higher rate is due if instead of the personal covenant it is the security which is being enforced, *e.g.* on foreclosure or redemption.[62]

3. Costs

(a) *Mortgagee's right to costs.* A mortgagor who wishes to redeem must pay:

(i) all proper costs, charges and expenses incurred by the mortgagee in relation to the mortgage debt or the security;

(ii) the cost of litigation properly undertaken by the mortgagee in reference to the mortgage debt or security, such as foreclosure proceedings, or more commonly proceedings for possession preliminary to the exercise of the statutory power of sale;

[54] *Union Bank of London* v. *Ingram* (1880) 16 Ch.D. 53.
[55] *Wrigley* v. *Gill* [1906] 1 Ch. 165.
[56] *Barratt* v. *Gough-Thomas (No. 3)* [1951] 2 All E.R. 48.
[57] *Chalikani Venkatarayanim* v. *Zamindar of Tuni* (1922) L.R. 50 Ind.App. 41.
[58] *Ante,* pp. 397, 398.
[59] Administration of Justice Act 1970, s.44; S.I. 1985 No. 437.
[60] *Re Sneyd, ex p. Fewings* (1883) 25 Ch.D. 338.
[61] *Popple* v. *Sylvester* (1882) 22 Ch.D. 98.
[62] *Economic Life Assurance Society* v. *Usborne* [1902] A.C. 147.

(iii) the mortgagee's costs (if any) of the redemption action;

(iv) the costs of defending the title to the mortgaged property against a third party, which he does for the benefit of the mortgagor as well as for himself[63]; but he is not entitled to charge the mortgagor with the costs of defending the mortgage itself against a third party.[64]

An obvious example of reasonable costs is the expense of revesting the property in the mortgagor, even if this has been increased by reason of the mortgagee having settled the security, or by reason of a vesting order being necessary to deal with the legal estate vested in an absconding trustee-mortgagee.[65] Such costs also include the costs of preparing a legal mortgage under a provision in an equitable mortgage giving the mortgagee the right to demand a legal mortgage, and thereby to complete his security.[66] But although the mortgagor must pay such costs as a condition of redemption, he is not personally liable for them.[67]

(b) *Charges for services of mortgagee.* A mortgagee in possession is entitled to his reasonable costs of management, and may charge a commission paid to a receiver appointed for the purpose of receiving rents. But a mortgagee is in a fiduciary position, and is not entitled to make a profit out of his security. Hence a mortgagee in possession who does the work of management himself is not entitled to charge for his services, but is allowed only his actual out-of-pocket expenses.[68] By statute,[69] however, a solicitor lending money on mortgage, either alone or jointly with another, is entitled to recover his profit costs for professional services both preparatory and subsequent to the making of the mortgage. The solicitor can resist redemption unless such charges are paid.

(c) *Preliminary expenses.* The costs of negotiating a loan, investigating the title and preparing the mortgage deed are not costs incurred under or by virtue of the mortgage, and form no charge on the property; but a mortgagee who has to pay these costs to his own solicitor can recover them from the mortgagor as a simple contract debt.[70] By the provision mentioned above, a solicitor-mortgagee can

[63] *Re Wallis, ex p. Lickorish* (1890) 25 Q.B.D. 176 at 181; *Re Leighton's Conveyance* [1937] Ch. 149.
[64] *Parker-Tweedale* v. *Dunbar Bank plc (No. 2)* [1990] 2 All E.R. 588, where the authorities are comprehensively reviewed.
[65] *Webb* v. *Crosse* [1912] 1 Ch. 323, and cases there cited.
[66] *National Provincial Bank of England* v. *Games* (1886) 31 Ch.D. 582.
[67] *Sinfield* v. *Sweet* [1967] 1 W.L.R. 1489.
[68] *Re Wallis, ex p. Lickorish* (1890) 25 Q.B.D. 176.
[69] Solicitors Act 1974, s.58, replacing earlier provisions (commencing with Mortgagee's Legal Costs Act 1895, s.3, replaced by Solicitors Act 1932, s.58 and Solicitors Act 1957, s.58) which overruled *Re Wallis, ex p. Lickorish, supra,* so far as it related to solicitors.
[70] *Wales* v. *Carr* [1902] 1 Ch. 860.

recover such expenses,[71] including a negotiation fee.[72] Yet where a mortgage is not completed, but goes off through the default of the mortgagor, the costs of negotiation and investigation of title are neither a charge on the property, nor (in the absence of express agreement) recoverable as a debt from the proposed mortgagor.[73]

(d) *Misconduct of the mortgagee.* The mortgagee is entitled to the costs of redemption proceedings, and as this right rests substantially on contract, he can be deprived of them only by reason of vexatious or unreasonable conduct amounting to a violation or culpable neglect of duty under the contract.[74] If by misconduct the mortgagee forfeits his right to costs, they are then in the discretion of the court.[75] And, in general, the court can in suitable cases take into account misconduct of the mortgagee as a reason for not requiring the mortgagor to pay interest or costs for which he is not legally liable but which (save for the misconduct) he might be required to pay as a condition of relief.[76]

Section 4. Parties to Proceedings for Redemption

1. Who may redeem. All persons entitled to any interest in the equity of redemption are entitled to come into a court of equity to redeem the property. Those who have a right to redeem thus include not only the mortgagor himself but also the following.

(i)   The personal representatives of the mortgagor.

(ii)   A devisee of the mortgagor.

(iii) A person succeeding to the property on the mortgagor's intestacy.

(iv)   A tenant for life, a remainderman, a reversioner, or other limited owner.

(v)   A subsequent purchaser or lessee, including a lessee whose lease is bad as against the mortgagee.[77]

(vi)   A subsequent mortgagee.[78]

(vii) The Crown on a forfeiture.

[71] Solicitors Act 1974, s.58.
[72] *Re Norris* [1902] 1 Ch. 741.
[73] *Wilkinson* v. *Grant* (1856) 18 C.B. 319.
[74] *Cotterell* v. *Stratton* (1872) 8 Ch.App. 295; *Bank of New South Wales* v. *O'Connor* (1889) 14 App.Cas. 273; *Squire* v. *Pardoe* (1892) 66 L.T. 243.
[75] *Heath* v. *Chinn* (1908) 98 L.T. 855 at 858.
[76] See *Webb* v. *Crosse* [1912] 1 Ch. 323 at 330.
[77] *Tarn* v. *Turner* (1888) 39 Ch.D. 456.
[78] *Fell* v. *Brown* (1787) 2 Bro.C.C. 276.

(viii) A trustee in bankruptcy, or even a bankrupt after annulment of his bankruptcy.[79]

(ix) A mere volunteer claiming under the mortgagor.[80]

(x) A judgment creditor of the mortgagor,[81] provided, at any rate, he has completed his title by execution.

(xi) The mortgagor's husband or wife, if he or she has rights of occupation of the mortgaged property under the Matrimonial Homes Act 1983.[82]

A person interested in any part of the mortgaged property may redeem the whole, subject to the rights of the other persons interested in the property being preserved.[83]

2. "Redeem up, foreclose down"

(a) *Right to redeem.* Where there are successive mortgages, any subsequent mortgagee may redeem a prior mortgage. Every redeeming party is also liable to be redeemed in his turn by those below him, and all are liable to be redeemed by the mortgagor. But if a redemption action has to be brought, there is a special rule as to parties which sometimes prevents a third or subsequent mortgagee or the mortgagor from redeeming one mortgage without also redeeming another.

(b) *Redemption.* The maxim is "Redeem up, foreclose down." In an action of redemption or foreclosure all persons must be made parties who will be affected by the accounts taken in the action. Hence, if a fourth mortgagee wishes to redeem the second mortgagee and has to bring a redemption action for this purpose, he must join as parties to the action not only the second mortgagee, but also the third, and offer to redeem him also; for the third mortgagee will be affected by the account of what is due to the second mortgagee. For the same reason, the mortgagor and all incumbrancers subsequent to the plaintiff are necessary parties, and the plaintiff must ask to have them foreclosed.[84] The court will not allow parties to be joined merely to be bound by the accounts, and requires that, when joined, they should have their rights all finally settled by redemption or foreclosure[85]; equity "in all cases

---

[79] *Re Pearce* [1909] 2 Ch. 492.
[80] *Rand* v. *Cartwright* (1640) 1 Ch.Ca. 59.
[81] *Re Parbola Ltd.* [1909] 2 Ch. 437.
[82] See Matrimonial Homes Act 1983, s.1(5), (7).
[83] *Hall* v. *Heward* (1886) 32 Ch.D. 430.
[84] *Fell* v. *Brown* (1787) 2 Bro.C.C. 276.
[85] See *Ramsbottom* v. *Wallis* (1835) 5 L.J.Ch. 92.

delights to do compleat justice, and not by halves."[86] In such cases, however, the first mortgagee need not be joined,[87] for it does not matter to him how much is due to the second mortgagee.

(c) *Foreclosure.* Similar principles apply in a foreclosure action brought by a second or subsequent mortgagee. Prior mortgagees need not be joined, though all inferior mortgagees, as well as the mortgagor, are necessary parties; here the rule is simply "Foreclose down."[88]

3. Sale in lieu of redemption. Any person entitled to redeem mortgaged property may obtain an order for sale instead of redemption[89] apparently as of right,[90] though the court may direct the plaintiff to give security for the costs of a sale and entrust the sale to the defendant.[91] Moreover, in a redemption action the court may in its discretion order a sale at the instance of the mortgagee, or of any person interested in the mortgage money or in the right of redemption,[92] even though he has no right to redeem.

Section 5. Transfer of Mortgage

1. Power and mode. A mortgagee may transfer his mortgage at any time. A deed executed by a mortgagee purporting to transfer his mortgage or the benefit of it operates to transfer the estate and interest of the mortgagee in the land together with the right to demand and give receipts for the mortgage money and interest then due and unpaid or to become due, and the benefit of all securities, covenants and powers, subject to any contrary intention.[93] Moreover, a mere receipt for the mortgage money may operate as a transfer. This has already been discussed.[94]

2. Concurrence of mortgagor. In general the transfer can be made without the concurrence of the mortgagor. However, a local authority cannot dispose of its interest as mortgagee without the prior written consent of the mortgagor (or all of them if more than one).[95] A purported disposal without consent is void.[96]

---

[86] See *Knight* v. *Knight* (1734) 3 P.Wms. 331 at 334, *per* Lord Talbot L.C. (on another subject).
[87] *Rose* v. *Page* (1829) 2 Sim. 471.
[88] See *ante*, p. 418.
[89] L.P.A. 1925, s.91(1), replacing C.A. 1881, s.25.
[90] *Clarke* v. *Pannell* (1884) 29 S.J. 147.
[91] L.P.A. 1925, s.91(3).
[92] *Ibid.* s.91(2).
[93] *Ibid.* s.114.
[94] *Ante*, p. 426.
[95] Local Government Act 1986, s.7(1), applying to disposals on or after April 1, 1986 (*ibid.* s.7(8)).
[96] *Ibid.* s.7(3).

3. Transfer in lieu of discharge

(a) *The right.* Formerly, on redemption a mortgagee could be compelled only to reconvey the property to the mortgagor and not to transfer the mortgage to a nominee of the mortgagor.[97] Now, however, by statute the mortgagor may instead require the mortgagee to transfer the mortgage as the mortgagor directs.[98] This is so whenever the mortgage was made, and notwithstanding any stipulation to the contrary[99]; but the right is exercisable only on the same terms as those upon which the mortgagor could require a reconveyance.[1] It may be exercised by any incumbrancer, as well as by the mortgagor, and notwithstanding any intermediate incumbrance; but a requisition of an incumbrancer prevails over a requisition of a subsequent incumbrancer or of the mortgagor.[2] Accordingly, a mortgagee cannot safely transfer the mortgage to the mortgagor's nominee without the consent of every intervening incumbrancer of whom he has notice.[3]

(b) *Limits to right.* The right does not apply when the mortgagee is or has been in possession.[4] For unless protected by an order of the court, such a mortgagee is liable for the acts of any transferee[5]; and the mortgagor's request to make the transfer could protect the mortgagee only against the mortgagor, and not against mesne incumbrancers.

---

[97] *Colyer* v. *Colyer* (1863) 3 De G.J. & S. 676.
[98] L.P.A. 1925, s.95(1). The section replaces C.A. 1881, s.15, as amended by C.A. 1882, s.12.
[99] *Ibid.* s.95(5).
[1] *Ibid.* s.95(1); and see *Alderson* v. *Elgey* (1884) 26 Ch.D. 567.
[2] *Ibid.* s.95(2).
[3] *Re Magneta Time Co. Ltd.* (1915) 113 L.T. 986.
[4] L.P.A. 1925, s.95(3).
[5] See *Hall* v. *Heward* (1886) 32 Ch.D. 430 at 435; *ante,* p. 409.

CHAPTER 5

PRIORITIES OF MORTGAGES

THE general rules as to equitable priorities have already been discussed,[1] but there are some special points to be observed in their application to the conflicting rights of incumbrancers.[2] The 1925 legislation made important alterations in the law of priority of mortgages, and it is necessary to consider separately the position before 1926 and after 1925.

Section 1. General Principles

1. Before 1926. Before 1926 in the case of freehold land, there would usually be only one legal mortgage, for a mortgage of freehold land was created by the conveyance of the legal fee simple to the mortgagee, and consequently a second, third or subsequent mortgagee could take only an equitable interest. The legal mortgagee was entitled to priority unless he had been guilty of such conduct as to render it inequitable for him to take advantage of the possession of the legal estate.[3] As between equitable mortgagees of land, the rule was that, if their moral claims were equal, the first in time was entitled to priority unless some later mortgagee prevailed by reason of his acquiring the legal estate or the better right to call for a conveyance of it.

2. After 1925

(a) *The statutory provisions.* The two principal statutory provisions are the Law of Property Act 1925, s.97, and the Land Charges Act 1972, s.4(5).[4] Section 97 governs the priority of mortgages made after 1925, not being mortgages or charges of registered land. It provides that "Every mortgage affecting a legal estate in land made after [1925], whether legal or equitable (not being a mortgage protected by the

---

[1] *Ante*, pp. 45 *et seq.*
[2] See the general survey in Megarry & Wade's *Law of Real Property*. (5th ed., 1984), pp. 986–1012.
[3] See *ante*, p. 57.
[4] Replacing L.C.A. 1925, s.13(2).

434

deposit of documents relating to the legal estate affected) shall rank according to its date of registration as a land charge pursuant to the Land Charges Act 1925," or 1972.[5] Section 4(5) provides in effect that any puisne mortgage or general equitable charge[6] created or arising after 1925 shall "be void as against a purchaser of the land charged with it, or of any interest in such land, unless the land charge is registered in the appropriate register before the completion of the purchase." And in the Act, unless the context otherwise requires, "purchaser" includes a mortgagee.[7]

(b) *Scope of the provisions.* The terms of section 97 and the definitions of puisne mortgages and general equitable charges have the effect of confining these provisions to mortgages of a legal estate in land which are not protected by a deposit of documents relating to the legal estate affected. But provided the estate mortgaged is legal, it is immaterial whether the mortgage itself is legal or equitable. Mortgages of equitable interests (*e.g.* mortgages of the interest of a tenant for life or remainderman under a settlement) thus do not fall into this category at all, but depend upon the rule in *Dearle* v. *Hall.*[8] Further a mortgage of a legal estate which is protected by such a deposit of documents appears to rank for priority according to the time of its creation.

(c) *Operation of the provisions.* Where the two sections both apply, they often produce the same results; but sometimes they conflict. Thus if a legal estate is successively mortgaged to A and B (neither receiving the title deeds) and, after the mortgage to B, the mortgagees register in the order A, B, then according to section 97 they rank for priority in that order, while according to section 4(5) A's mortgage is void as against B's mortgage for want of registration. It is uncertain how this apparent conflict will be resolved. There may be even more complex problems. Thus if registrable mortgages are granted to A and B, A then registers, and then a further registrable mortgage is granted to C, A has priority over C, who has priority over B, who has priority over A. Such problems may perhaps be soluble on principles of subrogation,[9] though there is no easy solution.

Section 2. Tacking

Tacking is a means by which the rules relating to priorities may be modified. It applies to realty and personalty.[10] There are two heads, the *tabula in naufragio* and the tacking of further advances.

---

[5] See L.C.A. 1972, s.18(6).
[6] For the meaning of these expressions, see *ante*, p. 60.
[7] L.C.A. 1972, s.17(1).
[8] (1828) 3 Russ. 1; *ante*, p. 64.
[9] See *Re Weniger's Policy* [1910] 2 Ch. 291; G. Gilmore (1961) 71 Yale L.J. 53; Megarry and Wade's *Law of Real Property* (5th ed., 1984, pp. 1001, 1002); W. A. Lee (1968) 32 Conv.(N.S.) 325.
[10] Coote, *Mortgages* (9th ed., 1927), p. 1245.

A. *The Tabula in Naufragio*

Formerly, a third mortgagee who bought up the first mortgage and obtained a conveyance of the legal estate could insist upon being paid the aggregate amount of the first and third mortgage debts before the second mortgagee received anything at all. This was known as the doctrine of the *tabula in naufragio*, for the legal estate was the plank on which the third mortgagee could save himself in the shipwreck while the second mortgagee was drowned.[11] This curious doctrine was abolished at the end of 1925.[12] Priority acquired by a third or subsequent mortgagee before 1926 by tacking is preserved, but no priority can be acquired in this way after 1925.

B. *Tacking of Further Advances*[13]

1. Before 1926. There is another kind of tacking which was possible before 1926 and is still allowed; indeed, in some ways it has been enlarged. A *legal* mortgagee who makes a further advance without notice of a subsequent mortgage has always been allowed to tack the further advance to his security and refuse to be redeemed by the subsequent mortgagee except on payment not only of the money originally advanced but also of the further advance.[14] And, of course, a further advance could be tacked if the intervening incumbrancer agreed.

2. After 1925. By the Law of Property Act 1925, s.94,[15] a legal *or equitable* mortgagee may tack further advances to rank in priority to intervening mortgages (whether legal or equitable) in the following cases.

(a) *Agreement of intervening mortgagee*: if an arrangement to this effect has been made with the intervening mortgagee.

(b) *Obligation to make further advances*: if the mortgage imposed an obligation on the mortgagee to make further advances. In this case it is immaterial if when the mortgagee made the further advance he had notice of the intervening mortgage or it was then registered. This extends the right to tack, for before 1926 notice prevented tacking even if the mortgagee was bound by contract to make the further advance.[16]

[11] *Marsh* v. *Lee* (1670) 2 Vent. 337; **2 W. & T.L.C. 103**; *Bailey* v. *Barnes* [1894] 1 Ch. 25. For a fuller treatment see the 28th edition of this work, pp. 429, 430.
[12] L.P.A. 1925, s.94(3).
[13] See generally R. G. Rowley (1958) 22 Conv.(N.S.) 44.
[14] *Goddard* v. *Complin* (1669) 1 Ch.Cas. 119; *Hopkinson* v. *Rolt* (1861) 9 H.L.C. 514; *Bradford Banking Co. Ltd.* v. *Henry Briggs, Son & Co. Ltd.* (1886) 12 App.Cas. 29.
[15] As amended by L.P.(Am.)A. 1926, Sched.
[16] *West* v. *Williams* [1899] 1 Ch. 132.

(c) *No notice of the intervening mortgage*: if the mortgagee had no notice of the intervening mortgage when the further advance was made. The normal rule that registration amounts to notice applies here, and a mortgagee cannot tack under this head as against an intervening mortgage which was registered at the time of the further advance. But this is subject to an important exception. If the prior mortgage was made expressly for securing a current account or other further advances, the mortgagee making the further advance will not be deemed to have notice of another mortgage merely by reason that it was registered as a land charge or in a local deeds registry (*i.e.* in Middlesex or Yorkshire[17]) if it was not so registered at the time when the original mortgage was created, or when the last search (if any) by or on behalf of the mortgagee was made, whichever last happened. Consequently in cases of a mortgage made expressly to secure further advances, such as an overdraft at a bank, the mortgagee need not search before making the further advance.

Section 94 applies to mortgages of land whenever made, but not to charges registered under the Land Registration Act 1925, or any enactment replaced by that Act.[18] The priority of further advances under registered charges is preserved by a provision in the Land Registration Act 1925 which produces substantially the same effect.[19]

---

[17] These registries are now closed: see *ante*, p. 59, n. 14.
[18] L.P.A. 1925, s.94(4).
[19] L.R.A. 1925, s.30, as amended by L.P.(Am.)A. 1926, s.5.

CHAPTER 6

LIMITATION OF MORTGAGES

Section 1. Barring the Mortgagor

1. Land. Where a mortgagee of land has, as such,[1] been in possession of any of the mortgaged land for 12 years, no action to redeem the mortgage of that land may be brought by the mortgagor or any person claiming through him.[2] Further, if the mortgagee sells the land under the statutory power of sale, neither the mortgagor nor subsequent incumbrancers whose right to redeem has been barred can claim any surplus proceeds of sale, which thus belong to the mortgagee.[3] But time starts runnng afresh if the mortgagee either receives any sum in respect of principal or interest of the mortgage debt or gives a written acknowledgment of the title of the mortgagor[4]; and there is the usual extension of time for disability, fraud or mistake.[5] An acknowledgment by one of several mortgagees will be effectual only as against himself and not against the other mortgagees, although an acknowledgment given to one of several co-mortgagors enures for the benefit of all.[6]

2. Pure personalty. No Statute of Limitation bars the mortgagor's right to redeem pure personalty,[7] although the equitable doctrine of laches applies and may bar the right to redeem.[8] But where pure personalty and land are included in one mortgage and the mortgagor's right to redeem the land is barred, it has been held that the mortgagor cannot redeem the personalty, on the ground that he must redeem the whole or none.[9]

---

[1] See *Hyde* v. *Dallaway* (1843) 2 Hare 528.
[2] Limitation Act 1980, s.16. See *ante*, p. 411, for the mortgagee's power of enlargement when the mortgagor's right to redeem becomes barred.
[3] *Re Moat House Farm, Thurlby* [1948] Ch. 191.
[4] Limitation Act 1980, ss.29(4), 30.
[5] *Ibid.* ss.28, 32.
[6] *Ibid.* s.31(3)–(5).
[7] *Weld* v. *Petre* [1929] 1 Ch. 33; and see Fifth Interim Report of Law Revision Committee (1936, Cmd. 5334), p. 15.
[8] See *Weld* v. *Petre, supra*; *ante*, pp. 34, 35.
[9] *Charter* v. *Watson* [1899] 1 Ch. 175; but see *Re Jauncey* [1926] Ch. 471 at 478.

Section 2. Barring the Mortgagee

1. Foreclosure. An action to foreclose a mortgage of land, like an action for possession, is treated as an action to recover land[10] and is therefore barred after 12 years from the time when the mortgage money became due.[11] Formerly, if the property mortgaged was pure personalty there was no period of limitation[12]; but now there is a similar 12 year period, save that if the mortgagee was in possession of the mortgaged property after the date on which the right to foreclose accrued, time does not start to run until he ceases to be in possession.[13] And if a mortgagee obtains judgment for foreclosure, a new right of possession arises in his favour and so entitles him to a further 12 years.[14]

2. The running of time

(a) *Estate in possession.* Where an estate in possession has been mortgaged, the mortgagee's right to foreclose will normally accrue on the date fixed for redemption, so that time will begin to run against him then.[15] This is so despite the land being subject to an occupation lease,[16] or to a prior mortgage, and even if the mortgagee takes possession before the statutory period has expired.[17] If the debt is repayable on demand,[18] time will begin to run from the date of the demand.[19] Moreover, if a mortgage is made by a person against whom time has started to run, time will continue to run even as against the mortgagee, who merely by the execution of the mortgage obtains no new right of entry which will start time running afresh.[20]

(b) *Future interests.* Time does not begin to run against a mortgagee of pure personalty as long as the property mortgaged comprises any future interest or life insurance policy which has not matured or been determined.[21] Similarly time does not run against a mortgagee of a future interest in land until it falls into possession.[22]

[10] Limitation Act 1980, s.20(4); and see *Harlock* v. *Ashberry* (1882) 19 Ch.D. 539; *Pugh* v. *Heath* (1882) 7 App.Cas. 235.
[11] Limitation Act 1980, s.15(1).
[12] See *London and Midland Bank* v. *Mitchell* [1899] 2 Ch. 161.
[13] Limitation Act 1980, s.20(2).
[14] *Pugh* v. *Heath, supra.*
[15] See *Kibble* v. *Fairthorne* [1895] 1 Ch. 219 at 225; *Samuel Johnson & Sons Ltd.* v. *Brock* [1907] 2 Ch. 533 at 536; *cf. Doe* d. *Roylance* v. *Lightfoot* (1841) 8 M. & W. 364.
[16] *Wakefield and Barnsley Union Bank Ltd.* v. *Yates* [1916] 1 Ch. 452.
[17] *Samuel Johnson & Sons Ltd.* v. *Brock* [1907] 2 Ch. 533.
[18] For special provisions relating to contracts of loan not fixing a date for repayment, nor making the loan payable on demand, see Limitation Act 1980, s.6: time runs from the date of a demand in writing.
[19] *Lloyds Bank Ltd.* v. *Margolis* [1954] 1 W.L.R. 644.
[20] *Thornton* v. *France* [1897] 2 Q.B. 143.
[21] Limitation Act 1980, s.20(3), repeating Limitation Act 1939, s.18(3); for the rule prior to the Limitation Act 1939 see *Re Witham* [1922] 2 Ch. 413; *Re Jauncey* [1926] Ch. 471.
[22] *Hugill* v. *Wilkinson* (1888) 38 Ch.D. 480.

(c) *Disabilities, fraud and mistake.*   There are the usual extensions of time to cover disabilities, fraud and mistake.[23]

(d) *Payment or acknowledgment.*   A payment in respect of principal or interest, or a written acknowledgment of the right thereto, will set time running again in favour of the mortgagee, provided it is made by the person in possession of the property or liable for the mortgage debt (or an agent on his behalf[24]) to the mortgagee or his agent.[25] Such payment or acknowledgment is binding on all other persons in possession of the mortgaged property during the ensuing period of limitation.[26] Payment of rent by the occupying tenant without the authority of the mortgagor is not enough, for there is no payment in respect of principal or interest,[27] nor will it suffice if the mortgagee receives the surrender value of a policy included in the mortgage[28] or the proceeds of sale of part of the mortgaged property sold by him.[29]

A payment by a tenant for life, however, operates to give the mortgagee further time against the remainderman.[30] Again, payment of interest by the specific devisee of real property subject to a mortgage made by the testator, the devisee being bound as between himself and the other beneficiaries to keep down the interest, keeps the mortgage debt alive as against the rest of the testator's estate[31]; payment by a receiver and manager appointed by another mortgagee will apparently suffice as being payments by the agent of the mortgagor.[32] Further, if and as long as the mortgagor and the mortgagee are for the time being one and the same person (as occasionally happens), time does not run, for no actual payment is needed where the hand to pay and the hand to receive are the same.[33]

3. Effect of lapse of time.   In relation to land and chattels, the Limitation Act bars and extinguishes the title, and not merely the action or remedy of the dispossessed person,[34] whereas in relation to pure personalty (other than chattels) its effect is merely to bar the remedy without extinguishing the right. Thus where the rights of a mortgagee of land are barred, his mortgage is extinguished. He can neither redeem prior mortgages (so as to get into a position to retain his own debt),[35]

---

[23] Limitation Act 1980, ss.28, 32; see, *e.g. Purnell* v. *Roche* [1927] 2 Ch. 142.
[24] See, *e.g. Wright* v. *Pepin* [1954] 1 W.L.R. 635.
[25] Limitation Act 1980, ss.29(1)–(3), 30; see *Bradshaw* v. *Widdrington* [1902] 2 Ch. 430; *Re Edwards' W.T.* [1937] Ch. 553.
[26] Limitation Act 1980, s.31(1), (2).
[27] *Harlock* v. *Ashberry* (1882) 19 Ch.D. 539.
[28] *Re Clifden* [1900] 1 Ch. 774.
[29] See *Re McHenry* [1894] 3 Ch. 290.
[30] *Roddam* v. *Morley* (1856) 1 De G. & J. 1.
[31] *Re Lacey* [1907] 1 Ch. 330.
[32] *Re Hale* [1899] 2 Ch. 107.
[33] *Topham* v. *Booth* (1887) 35 Ch.D. 607; *Re Dixon* [1899] 2 Ch. 561; affirmed [1900] 2 Ch. 561; and see *Hodgson* v. *Salt* [1936] 1 All E.R. 95. For another illustration of this principle, see *ante*, p. 356.
[34] Limitation Act 1980, ss.3(2), 7.
[35] *Cotterell* v. *Price* [1960] 1 W.L.R. 1097.

nor enforce his claim to the land against the mortgagor or persons claiming under the mortgagor (such as subsequent mortgagees); this is so even though the mortgagor has given a written acknowledgment of the mortgagee's right after the expiration of the statutory period.[36] He can also be compelled by the person entitled to the land to hand over the mortgage and other title deeds.[37]

4. Arrears of interest. No arrears of interest charged on any property are recoverable in any action more than six years after the same became due[38] even though there is a covenant for payment.[39] This rule, however, is subject to important qualifications.

(a) *Redemption.* A mortgagor who seeks to redeem, either in redemption proceedings[40] or in foreclosure proceedings by the mortgagee,[41] will be allowed to do so only on the equitable terms of paying all arrears of interest, however old.

(b) *Sale.* If the mortgagee sells the mortgaged property under his statutory power of sale, he may retain all arrears of interest before accounting to subsequent mortgagees or the mortgagor.[42] The same applies if the property is sold under an order of the court; unless the mortgage itself is barred,[43] the mortgagee is entitled to his arrears of interest in full before the balance is paid out of court to the mortgagor.[44] A second mortgagee may claim all his arrears of interest out of the surplus on a sale by the first mortgagee,[45] unless his right to redeem is itself statute-barred.[46]

(c) *Prior mortgagee in possession.* A mortgagee may recover all arrears accruing while a prior incumbrancer was in possession if the action is brought within one year of this possession ceasing.[47]

(d) *Interest part of capital.* Where there is a mortgage of a future interest or life insurance policy with a provision that arrears of interest shall be treated as part of the capital due, the interest is not deemed to become due until the right to receive the capital has accrued.[48]

---

[36] *Kibble* v. *Fairthorne* [1895] 1 Ch. 219.
[37] *Lewis* v. *Plunket* [1937] Ch. 306.
[38] Limitation Act 1980, s.20(5).
[39] *Ibid.* s.8(2).
[40] *Elvy* v. *Norwood* (1852) 5 De G. & Sm. 240; Limitation Act 1980, s.20(4).
[41] *Dingle* v. *Coppen* [1899] 1 Ch. 726.
[42] *Re Marshfield* (1887) 34 Ch.D. 721; *Holmes* v. *Cowcher* [1970] 1 W.L.R. 834.
[43] *Re Hazeldine's Trusts* [1908] 1 Ch. 34.
[44] *Re Lloyd, Lloyd* v. *Lloyd* [1903] 1 Ch. 385.
[45] *Re Thomson's Mortgage Trusts* [1920] 1 Ch. 508.
[46] *Re Moat House Farm, Thurlby* [1948] Ch. 191; and see *C. & M. Matthews Ltd.* v. *Marsden B.S.* [1951] Ch. 758.
[47] Limitation Act 1980, s.20(6).
[48] *Ibid.* s.20(7).

5. Action on the covenant. Formerly there were difficulties in a mortgagee's action on the covenant to repay the capital. These have been swept away by the provision that no action is to be brought to recover any principal sum of money secured by a mortgage or other charge on property, whether real or personal, or to recover proceeds of the sale of land, after the expiration of 12 years from the date when the right to receive the money accrued.[49] This is subject to the usual extensions for disability, fraud or mistake,[50] or by a written acknowledgment[51] of indebtedness,[52] or a payment in respect of principal or interest[53]; and the right is not deemed to accrue as long as the property mortgaged comprises any future interest or any life insurance policy which has not matured or been determined.[54]

---

[49] Limitation Act 1980, s.20(1).
[50] *Ibid.* ss.28, 32.
[51] See *Howard* v. *Hennessey* [1947] I.R. 336 (will); and see *Jones* v. *Bellgrove Properties Ltd.* [1949] 2 K.B. 700 and *Re Gee & Co. (Woolwich) Ltd.* [1975] Ch. 52 (balance-sheet).
[52] *Dungate* v. *Dungate* [1965] 1 W.L.R. 1477, explaining *Good* v. *Parry* [1963] 2 Q.B. 418: see (1966) 82 L.Q.R. 17. And see *Kamouh* v. *Associated Electrical Industries International Ltd.* [1980] Q.B. 199, applying *Good* v. *Parry*, especially at p. 209, *per* Parker J.: "an admission that something is due and that something must be ascertainable by extrinsic evidence."
[53] Limitation Act 1980, s.29(5).
[54] *Ibid.* s.20(3).

CHAPTER 7

EQUITABLE MORTGAGES AND CHARGES

1. Equitable mortgages. Where a mortgage is created but the mortgagee gets no legal estate, his mortgage is an equitable mortgage. This will occur either because the mortgagor has only an equitable interest or because the mortgage is not created with the formalities required for a legal mortgage; and the chief instance of the latter is the mortgage by deposit of title deeds. In general, the position of an equitable mortgagee is similar to that of a legal mortgagee, but there are a number of differences which must be mentioned. These are principally due to the mortgagee not obtaining a legal estate.

2. Equitable charges. Equitable mortgages must be distinguished from equitable charges; for "every charge is not an equitable mortgage, though every equitable mortgage is a charge."[1] An equitable charge is created when X devises Blackacre to A subject to a charge for £1,000 in favour of B, or where Y signs a document charging Whiteacre with the payment of £500 to C. Again, if Z is bound by contract to pay a debt due to D out of specified property, then D has an equitable charge on the property for the amount of the debt, whether or not Z and D knew or intended such a result.[2] In each case there is no mortgage, because no estate or interest in the land has been conveyed or agreed to be conveyed, either at law or in equity; but there is an equitable charge because the property stands charged with the payment of the stated sum, and the chargee is entitled to have this realised by judicial process.[3] The rights of an equitable chargee are for the most part similar to those of an equitable mortgagee.

Section 1. Creation of Equitable Mortgages

A. Mortgages of Equitable Interests

1. Before 1926. A mortgage may be equitable because the mortgagor has only an equitable interest and so, having an interest

---

[1] *Shea* v. *Moore* [1894] 1 I.R. 158 at 168, *per* Walker L.C.
[2] *Swiss Bank Corporation* v. *Lloyds Bank Limited* [1979] Ch. 548 at 569 (reversed on construction [1982] A.C. 584, C.A. and H.L., esp. (in H.L.) at 613, citing *Palmer* v. *Carey* [1926] Ch. 703 at 706, 707).
[3] See generally *Matthews* v. *Goodday* (1861) 31 L.J.Ch. 282; *London County and Westminster Bank Ltd.* v. *Tompkins* [1918] 1 K.B. 515; and see *ante*, p. 389.

which exists only in equity, cannot create more than an equitable mortgage of it. Thus if before 1926 A conveyed the legal estate in fee simple in Blackacre to B by way of mortgage, and subsequently, during the subsistence of B's mortgage, purported to convey Blackacre to C by way of mortgage, C's mortgage was equitable only; for the legal fee simple was in B and so could not pass under the mortgage to C.

2. After 1925. After 1925, legal mortgages of freehold property can be effected only by demise for a term of years, and legal mortgages of leaseholds only by subdemise for a term of years.[4] As it is possible to create a legal term to take effect in reversion expectant on a prior legal term (even though the prior term is longer than the second term[5]) it is now possible to create any number of legal mortgages on the same property to subsist at the same time.

3. Transitional provisions. Where at the commencement of 1926 there were successive mortgagees by conveyances of the fee simple or assignments of the leasehold interest, the Law of Property Act converted the interests of all the mortgagees into legal terms of years.[6] The details of conversion will be of importance today only in rare cases.[7]

B. Informal Mortgages

1. Informal agreement. An equitable mortgage may arise even if the mortgagor has a legal estate. If the mortgagor uses a form of conveyance ineffectual to transfer a legal estate, or the parties deliberately abstain from any attempt at conveying a legal estate and agree for a mortgage effectual in equity only, the resulting mortgage will be equitable.

2. Deposit of title deeds

(a) *Actual deposit*

(1) THE DEPOSIT. If the property to be dealt with is land, the agreement to give a charge thereon is required by statute to be made in writing.[8] Nevertheless it is settled that a mere deposit of title deeds as security for a loan constitutes an equitable charge on the land.[9] The

---

[4] See *ante*, pp. 391, 392.
[5] L.P.A. 1925, s.149(5).
[6] L.P.A. 1925, 1st Sched., Pts. VII and VIII.
[7] See Megarry and Wade's *Law of Real Property* (5th ed., 1984), pp. 921, 924.
[8] Law of Property (Miscellaneous Provisions) Act 1989, s.2, *post*, p. 601.
[9] *Matthews* v. *Goodday* (1861) 31 L.J.Ch. 282; but see *ante*, p. 401, and *post*, p. 448.

deposit of deeds with a creditor to secure a debt gives rise to a presumption that the land is to be charged in equity, even where the debt is owed not by the depositor of the deeds but by a third party.[10] If there was an express or implied agreement for a mortgage, the deposit constituted an equitable mortgage, on the ground that although the agreement was not evidenced by writing, it had been partly performed.[11] Although the doctrine of part performance has no application to agreements made after September 26, 1989,[12] the category of mortgages by deposit is one expressly recognised by statute[13] and must therefore survive the removal of its original foundation. Actual deposit as security for the advance remains necessary, for only this would be sufficient as an act of part performance. Thus there was no equitable mortgage where a creditor who had been promised security over certain property accidentally came into possession of the deeds relating to the property in question, and intimated to the debtor that the deeds were held as security.[14] And, where land is jointly owned, all the co-owners must consent to the deposit if it is to be effective.[15]

(2) DOCUMENTS DEPOSITED. In order to create an equitable mortgage by deposit, it is not necessary that all the title deeds (or even all the material title deeds) should be deposited. It suffices if the deeds deposited are material to the title, and are proved to have been deposited with the intention of thereby creating a mortgage.[16] However, there is naturally great danger in leaving any of the title deeds in the custody of the mortgagor, as this may cause the equitable mortgagee to be postponed as against subsequent incumbrancers who are thereby induced to make advances in ignorance of his previous charge. There may be a valid equitable mortgage by deposit of the mere receipt for the purchase-money of an estate containing the terms of the agreement for sale if at the time there are no title deeds or conveyance in the depositor's possession[17]; but a deposit of an attested copy of a deed is not enough.[18] A deposit of a legal mortgage may constitute an equitable sub-mortgage[19]; and if there is a deposit of title deeds for the purpose of preparing a legal mortgage, and the money has actually been advanced, there is a valid interim equitable mortgage.[20]

[10] *Re Wallis & Simmonds (Builders) Ltd.* [1974] 1 W.L.R. 391.
[11] *Russel* v. *Russel* (1783) 1 Bro.C.C. 269; **2 W. & T.L.C. 69**; *Parker* v. *Housefield* (1834) 2 My. & K. 419; *Carter* v. *Wake* (1877) 4 Ch.D. 605; and see *Bank of New South Wales* v. *O'Connor* (1889) 14 App.Cas. 273 at 282. This used to be regarded as anomalous in that, apart from the payment of the money (as to which, see *post,* p. 600) the only performance by the mortgagee was the receipt of the deeds: see the criticisms of Lord Eldon L.C. in *Ex p. Whitbread* (1812) 19 Ves. 209 at 211 and *Ex p. Wright* (1812) 19 Ves. 255 st 258.
[12] See *post,* p. 601.
[13] See, *e.g.* L.P.A. 1925, s.97.
[14] *Re Beetham* (1887) 18 Q.B.D. 766.
[15] *Thames Guaranty Ltd.* v. *Campbell* [1985] Q.B. 210.
[16] *Lacon* v. *Allen* (1856) 3 Drew. 579.
[17] *Goodwin* v. *Waghorn* (1835) 4 L.J.Ch. 172.
[18] *Re Barrow* (1834) 1 Mont. & A. 635.
[19] *Lacon* v. *Liffen* (1862) 4 Giff. 75.
[20] *Edge* v. *Worthington* (1786) 1 Cox Eq. 211.

(3) PURE PERSONALTY. It is not only in respect of land that an equitable mortgage by deposit is possible; an equitable mortgage of personalty may be created by a deposit of the evidence of title, as where a share certificate is deposited as security for a loan, without any transfer or memorandum.[21] And a deposit of a policy of insurance may constitute an equitable mortgage of the policy.[22]

(b) *Agreement to deposit.* A mere agreement to deposit a document, unaccompanied by any actual deposit, is ineffectual; but if the agreement is sufficiently evidenced in writing, it will be effectual to establish a charge.[23]

3. Registration

(a) *Unregistered land.* Where an equitable mortgage or charge affecting land is secured by a deposit of documents relating to the legal estate affected there is no need to register the mortgage as a land charge. But if it is not secured by such a deposit, it must be registered as a land charge if it was created after 1925 or acquired under a conveyance made after 1925, otherwise it will be void against a purchaser for value of any interest in the land, even if he knows of the charge.[24]

(b) *Registered land.* The proprietor of any registered land or charge may, subject to any overriding interests, to any entry to the contrary on the register, and to any interests registered or protected by entry on the register at the date of the deposit, create a lien on the land or charge by deposit of the land certificate or charge certificate; the result will be the same as if the title deeds or mortgage deed of unregistered land had been deposited by an owner or mortgagee entitled for his own benefit.[25] If the title is registered as possessory and not absolute, the mortgagee should also insist on the deposit of the title deeds prior to registration.

4. Further advances. A mortgage by deposit will cover future advances if this was agreed when the first advance was made, or if the subsequent advance was made on an express or implied agreement that the deeds were to remain a security for it as well. Parol evidence is admissible to show such an agreement.[26]

---

[21] *Harrold* v. *Plenty* [1901] 2 Ch. 314; *post*, p. 449.
[22] *Ferris* v. *Mullins* (1854) 2 Sm. & G. 378.
[23] *Lloyd* v. *Attwood* (1859) 3 De G. & J. 614.
[24] L.C.A. 1972, s.4(5); L.P.A. 1925, s.199; *ante*, p. 60.
[25] L.R.A. 1925, s.66, replacing L.T.A. 1897, s.8.
[26] *Ex p. Langston* (1810) 17 Ves. 227; *Ex p. Kensington* (1813) 2 V. & B. 79.

5. Interest. Subject to any contrary agreement, a mortgage by deposit traditionally carries interest at the rate of 4 per cent. It has been the settled rule of equity to give interest at this rate on all equitable charges, unless otherwise agreed and even if the charge is altogether silent as to any interest being payable.[27] It is, however, probable that a higher rate would be allowed today.[28]

Section 2. Remedies of Equitable Mortgagees and Chargees

The remedies of an equitable mortgagee or chargee are for the most part the same as those of a legal mortgagee, although there are some important qualifications.

1. Sale. There is nothing to prevent an equitable mortgagee or chargee[29] from exercising the powers given by the Law of Property Act 1925. Hence, if his mortgage is by deed, as where he takes a memorandum of deposit under seal, he can exercise the powers of selling and of appointing a receiver. But even if the memorandum of deposit is under seal, it has been held that a mere equitable mortgagee cannot transfer the legal estate by virtue of his statutory power.[30] The memorandum should therefore contain some conveyancing device for the purpose, such as an irrevocable power of attorney given by the mortgagor to the mortgagee to convey the legal estate.[31] If there is no such power of sale, as where there is a mere equitable mortgage by deposit of title deeds or a mere equitable charge created by will or under hand, the court may order a sale.[32]

2. Receiver. As mentioned above, if an equitable mortgage is under seal, the mortgagee can appoint a receiver by virtue of his statutory powers; and any mortgagee can apply for the appointment of a receiver by the court.[33] However, even if the court has appointed a receiver on the application of an equitable incumbrancer, a first legal mortgagee is entitled to possession, provided he comes to the court for an order to that effect[34]; but he will be entitled to the rents only as from the date when proceedings for possession are commenced.[35]

[27] *Saville* v. *Drax* [1903] 1 Ch. 781.
[28] See *ante*, p. 392.
[29] See L.P.A. 1925, s.205(1)(xvi).
[30] *Re Hodson and Howe's Contract* (1887) 35 Ch.D. 668. But see *Re White Rose Cottage* [1965] Ch. 940 at 951, suggesting, *obiter*, that differences in drafting between C.A. 1881, s.21(1), and L.P.A. 1925, s.104(1), have changed the law. Yet the phrase relied on in the latter case ("the subject of the mortgage") is common to both subsections.
[31] See *Re White Rose Cottage, supra,* at p. 955.
[32] *Matthews* v. *Goodday* (1861) 31 L.J.Ch. 282; *Tennant* v. *Trenchard* (1869) 4 Ch.App. 537 at 542; *Oldham* v. *Stringer* (1885) 51 L.T. 895; *Re Owen* [1894] 3 Ch. 220; and see *ante*, p. 420.
[33] For receivers, see *post*, pp. 689 *et seq.*
[34] *Re Metropolitan Amalgamated Estates Ltd.* [1912] 2 Ch. 497 at 502.
[35] *Ibid.* at 502, 503.

3. Possession.   An equitable mortgagee or chargee has no legal estate and so is usually said to be unable to take possession or receive the rents and profits, without an order of the court.[36] But if a tenant, knowing the position, pays rent to the equitable mortgagee, he cannot recover the rents so paid.[37]

4. Foreclosure.   If there is an equitable mortgage, as where there is an express agreement to create a legal mortgage[38] or a mortgage by deposit of title deeds,[39] the mortgagee may foreclose. This is so even if there is no memorandum of deposit and undertaking to execute a legal mortgage, for the deposit of title deeds in itself implies such an undertaking, and confers the right of foreclosure.[40] But a person who has a mere equitable charge, as distinct from a legal or equitable mortgage, cannot foreclose,[41] for there has been no transfer of property to him subject to a right of redemption on a specified date, and so there is nothing to foreclose.[42] His remedy is to seek an order for sale in lieu of foreclosure.[43]

---

[36] *Ex p. Bignold* (1834) 4 D. & C. 259; *Garfitt* v. *Allen* (1887) 37 Ch.D. 48 at 50; *Barclays Bank Ltd.* v. *Bird* [1954] Ch. 274 at 280. *Sed quaere*: see (1954) 70 L.Q.R. 162; H. W. R. Wade (1955) 71 L.Q.R. 204.
[37] *Finck* v. *Tranter* [1905] 1 K.B. 427; *Vacuum Oil Co. Ltd.* v. *Ellis* [1914] 1 K.B. 693 at 703, 708.
[38] *Underwood* v. *Joyce* (1861) 7 Jur.(N.S.) 566.
[39] *James* v. *James* (1873) L.R. 16 Eq. 153.
[40] *James* v. *James, supra*; *Backhouse* v. *Charlton* (1878) 8 Ch.D. 444; and see *Jones* v. *Davies* [1940] W.N. 174.
[41] *Tennant* v. *Trenchard* (1869) 4 Ch.App. 537 at 542.
[42] See *Sampson* v. *Pattison* (1842) 1 Hare 533 at 536.
[43] *Ante*, p. 447.

CHAPTER 8

MORTGAGES OF PURE PERSONALTY

1. Similarity to mortgages of land. In general, subject to making the necessary allowances for the different character of the property, the position of a mortgagee of pure personalty is the same as that of a mortgagee of land. Thus, if foreclosure could be claimed where the property were land, it is equally available as a remedy where the security is pure personalty. A deposit of a share certificate as security for a loan has been held to amount to an equitable mortgage by deposit, and not to a mere pledge, and is therefore properly the subject of foreclosure.[1]

2. Power of sale. The statutory power of sale which applies to mortgages by deed extends to mortgages of pure personalty. Apart from the statutory power, and even if the mortgage is not by deed (*e.g.* where shares are mortgaged by a deposit of the share certificate), it has been held that there is a power of sale at common law analogous to the power of sale of a pledgee.[2] Where a mortgage of pure personalty names no date for repayment, and the mortgagee gives notice requesting payment to be made, intimating that in default of payment he intends to sell at the expiration of his notice, a power of sale arises, even if he has requested payment of a wrong amount.[3]

3. Possession. There is, of course, no need for a mortgagee of pure personalty to take possession of his security forthwith, even if he is entitled to do so, any more than in the case of a mortgage of land. As regards mortgages of personal chattels as defined by the Bills of Sale Acts 1878 and 1882, restrictions are placed on the mortgagee's right to take possession.[4] The intricate provisions of these Acts as to registration and otherwise are outside the scope of this book.

4. Mortgages of a settled fund. Where the property comprised in the mortgage is an interest in a settled fund, notice should be given to the trustees in order to secure priority against subsequent incumbrancers.[5] If

[1] *Harrold* v. *Plenty* [1901] 2 Ch. 314.
[2] *Deverges* v. *Sandeman, Clark & Co.* [1902] 1 Ch. 579. See *post*, p. 454.
[3] *Stubbs* v. *Slater* [1910] 1 Ch. 632.
[4] Further restrictions are to be found in the Consumer Credit Act 1974, ss.105–113.
[5] *Dearle* v. *Hall* (1828) 3 Russ. 1. See *ante*, p. 65.

the interest mortgaged is a reversion which falls into possession, the trustees may, if they act in good faith, pay the whole fund to the mortgagee without going into the mortgage accounts to discover what money (if any) remains due under the mortgage.[6] But they are not bound to do this, and they may refuse to pay the mortgagee more of the fund than is due to him under his mortgage[7]; and if it is not clear how much is due to him or to subsequent incumbrancers and the mortgagor, they may pay the fund into court.[8]

5. Mortgages of ships. A registered British ship, or a share therein, may be mortgaged to secure repayment of a loan or the discharge of any other obligation; and on production of the mortgage document, the registrar of the ship's port of registry must record it in the register which is kept under the relevant statutory provisions.[9] As between themselves, successive mortgages of ships rank according to the dates of their respective registrations.[10] Even if it is unregistered, a mortgage of a ship is good as between the mortgagor and the mortgagee; and any equities may be enforced against the mortgagees and owners of ships just as in the case of other personal chattels.[11] A mortgagee of a ship has a statutory power of sale.[12]

6. Appropriation of securities

(a) *Effect of appropriation.* Sometimes a charge arises from an appropriation of securities. Where B borrows money from L, B may arrange with L that goods or other securities belonging to B shall be appropriated to meet the loan. In such a case, to the extent of these securities, B is entitled to be indemnified by L against personal payment of the loan. In general, L may deal with the securities, paying B the surplus, if any, after payment of the loan; and except by previous agreement with B, L may not so deal with the securities as to deprive B of the indemnity which they afford him, so that to the extent that L disposes of the securities, the loan is discharged. Where B borrows from L on successive loans and gives successive securities to L to provide for the payment of the loans, B is deemed to have appropriated the successive securities to the loans in the order in which they were made; and the loans are successively discharged by the realisation of the securities respectively appropriated to them.

[6] L.P.A. 1925, s.107(1); *Hockey* v. *Western* [1898] 1 Ch. 350.
[7] *Re Bell, Jeffery* v. *Sayles* [1896] 1 Ch. 1 (fund of £1,000, £380 due under mortgage).
[8] *Hockey* v. *Western, supra;* see, however, *Re Bell, Jeffery* v. *Sayles, supra*, at p. 5 ("their duty to settle the claims": *per* Rigby L.J.).
[9] Merchant Shipping Act 1894, s.31, as amended by Merchant Shipping Act 1988, s.10(1), Sched. 1, para. 21. Mortgages of fishing vessels are dealt with separately: see Merchant Shipping Act 1988, s.21, Sched. 3.
[10] Merchant Shipping Act 1894, s.33, as amended by Merchant Shipping Act 1988, s.10(1), Sched. 1. para. 22.
[11] Merchant Shipping Act 1894, s.57, as amended by Merchant Shipping Act 1988, s.10(1), Sched. 1, para. 33.
[12] Merchant Shipping Act 1894, s.35.

(b) *Bills of exchange.* Questions of appropriation of securities most usually arise in conection with bills of exchange. B, wishing to borrow money from L, draws a bill of exchange on L which L accepts on the terms (either express or, more often, implied from general mercantile usage or from the course of dealing between the parties) that B shall remit to L securities to indemnify him from liability on the bill. As between B and L, the securities are thus appropriated to meet the bill. B is entitled to have the securities applied in payment of the bill, and if L fails to pay the bill at maturity, so that B is compelled to do so, B is entitled to have the securities retransferred to him. But the appropriation is only as between B and L. If the bill is indorsed to X, who is a stranger to the contract between B and L, X has no right to the benefit of the appropriation of the securities unless either the benefit has been assigned to him,[13] or the rule in *Ex parte Waring*[14] applies.

(c) *Rule in Ex parte Waring.* Under the rule in *Ex parte Waring*,[14] if both B and L are bankrupt, or if both their estates are insolvent and under a forced administration,[15] X, as the holder of the bill, is entitled to the benefit of the securities in L's hands. This rule is not founded upon any equity belonging to X, for he was a stranger to the appropriation and has not had the benefit of it assigned to him: it is a rule of convenience springing out of the necessities connected with the administration of the estates of B and L. L's general creditors are not entitled to the benefit of the securities because in L's hands they were impressed with a trust; nor are B's general creditors entitled to them, because B cannot have them back without meeting the bill. They are therefore applied for the purpose for which they were sent, namely, towards payment of the bill which X holds.[16]

The rule in *Ex parte Waring* applies only where—

(i) there is a double insolvency[17];

(ii) the creditor has a right to claim payment from both estates; and

(iii) there has been a specific appropriation of property to meet the bill.

If in the above example L alone were insolvent, the securities would have to be restored to B[18]; and if B alone were insolvent, L would pay

---

[13] *Banner* v. *Johnston* (1871) L.R. 5 H.L. 157; *Brown, Shipley & Co.* v. *Kough* (1885) 29 Ch.D. 848; *cf. Re Walker, Sheffield Banking Co.* v. *Clayton* [1892] 1 Ch. 621.

[14] (1815) 19 Ves. 345.

[15] *Powles* v. *Hargreaves* (1853) 3 De G.M. & G. 430; *Re Barned's Banking Co.* (1874) L.R. 19 Eq. 1 at 10; affd. (1875) 10 Ch.App. 198.

[16] *Re Suse, ex p. Dever (No. 2)* (1885) 14 Q.B.D. 611 at 623. See also on the rule *Re New Zealand Banking Corporation* (1867) L.R. 4 Eq. 226 at 229; *Re Richardson, ex p. Smart* (1872) 8 Ch.App. 220; *Re Leggatt, ex p. Dewhurst* (1873) 8 Ch.App. 965. It is not applied in Scotland: *Royal Bank of Scotland* v. *Commercial Bank of Scotland* (1882) 7 App.Cas. 366.

[17] Contrast *Re Yglesias & Co., ex p . General South American Co.* (1875) 10 Ch.App. 635.

[18] *Ex p. Pease, Re Boldero & Co.* (1812) 19 Ves. 25.

the bill and realise the securities to indemnify himself, handing over any balance to B's estate.

CHAPTER 9

PLEDGES

Section 1. Creation of Pledges

1. Nature of pledges. As has been seen, a mortgage is essentially a transfer of ownership to the mortgagee by way of security; and the mortgagor usually retains possession of the property. A pledge, on the other hand, is essentially a transfer of the possession of personal chattels to the pledgee by way of security; the ownership remains in the pledgor, subject only to the "qualified property" in the goods which passes to the pledgee by virtue of the bailment to him, and which entitles the pledgee to sue third persons in conversion.[1] The pledge includes, but is not identical with, a common law lien: a lien merely confers a right of retainer by way of security, and, unlike a pledge, generally gives no power of sale.

2. Delivery. In order to complete a pledge it is essential that there should be delivery of possession to the pledgee. This, however, need not be contemporaneous with the advance,[2] and may be symbolical, as by delivery of the key of the room where the goods are,[3] or by delivery of the documents of title relating to the goods, such as bills of lading.[4] In general, too, possession may be changed in law without any change in the physical situation of the goods or any change of the person who has the actual custody of them,[5] as where a pledgor retains actual possession of the goods but undertakes to hold them to the pledgee's order.[6]

3. Redelivery. Where possession has once been given, the pledgee's rights are not necessarily determined by a redelivery of the goods to the pledgor for only a limited purpose. Thus, the pledgee's rights as against the pledgor or his creditors are not determined by a redelivery of the

[1] *The Winkfield* [1902] P. 43.
[2] *Hilton* v. *Tucker* (1888) 39 Ch.D. 669.
[3] *Ibid.*; *Wrightson* v. *McArthur and Hutchisons (1919) Ltd.* [1921] 2 K.B. 807.
[4] *Grigg* v. *National Guardian Assurance Co.* [1891] 3 Ch. 206.
[5] *Mills* v. *Charlesworth* (1890) 25 Q.B.D. 421; *French* v. *Gething* [1922] 1 K.B. 236.
[6] *Martin* v. *Reid* (1862) 11 C.B.(N.S.) 730.

goods to the pledgor upon trust to sell them on the pledgee's behalf.[7]
But where goods or the documents of title thereto are allowed to come
into the possession of another, many dealings with the goods by the
person in possession are made valid by statute in favour of third parties,
even though the person in possession had no authority for the purpose.[8]

4. Property capable of being pledged. From the fact that possession
is necessary to a pledge, it follows that while, in general, all property of
a freely alienable nature is capable of being mortgaged, property can be
pledged only if it is capable of being actually or constructively delivered
in possession. A negotiable instrument, or even a portion thereof, such
as half a banknote, may be pledged.[9]

Section 2. Rights of the Parties

1. General and qualified property. Since a pledgor retains the
general property in the goods and the pledgee's rights cease on a proper
tender of the amount due, after tender the pledgor can sue the pledgee
for the goods in an action for wrongful interference; but a tender by one
of several pledgors who is entitled only to a part interest in the goods is
insufficient for this purpose.[10] The pledgor's retention of the general
property enables him to sell the goods subject to the rights of the
pledgee, and give the purchaser a legal title[11]; and after a proper tender
to the pledgee, the purchaser is entitled to sue the pledgee in conversion
as the pledgor himself could have done. Further, if the pledgee
wrongfully deals with the pledge, this not only may be a breach of
contract, but also may determine the bailment and render the pledgee
liable for conversion.[12]

2. Sale but not foreclosure. A pledgee has no right to foreclose, but
he has a right to a judicial sale, and may apply to the court for an order
to have his charge realised.[13] Moreover, without any order of the court
the pledgee has a power of sale at common law on default being made
in payment. This power arises if the loan is not repaid on the date
agreed, or, where no date was originally agreed, on the expiry of
reasonable notice to repay.[14]

[7] *North Western Bank Ltd.* v. *Poynter* [1895] A.C. 56.
[8] See, *e.g.* Factors Act 1889; and see *Babcock* v. *Lawson* (1879) 4 Q.B.D. 394.
[9] *Taylor* v. *Chester* (1869) L.R. 4 Q.B. 309.
[10] *Harper* v. *Godsell* (1870) L.R. 5 Q.B. 422.
[11] *Franklin* v. *Neate* (1844) 13 M. & W. 481. See also *The Odessa* [1916] 1 A.C. 145.
[12] *Halliday* v. *Holgate* (1868) L.R. 3 Ex. 299; *Donald* v. *Suckling* (1866) L.R. 1 Q.B. 585 at 614; *Johnson* v. *Stear* (1863) 15 C.B.(N.S.) 330.
[13] *Carter* v. *Wake* (1877) 4 Ch.D. 605.
[14] *Ex p. Hubbard* (1886) 17 Q.B.D. 698; *Re Morritt* (1886) 18 Q.B.D. 222; *Deverges* v. *Sandeman, Clark & Co.* [1902] 1 Ch. 579; *Stubbs* v. *Slater* [1910] 1 Ch. 632.

3. Redemption. At any time before sale the pledgor has a right to redeem the pledge.[15] The whole security must be redeemed, so that where two or more chattels are pawned together, there is no power to redeem one on payment of a proportionate part of the debt.[16] After the pledgor's death this right to redeem probably continues in favour of his executors.[17]

4. Pawns. Where a pledge is given under an agreement whereby a debtor obtains credit not exceeding £15,000,[18] the position is usually regulated by the Consumer Credit Act 1974.[19] The pawn remains redeemable for six months after it was taken or the duration of the credit (if longer).[20] If the redemption period was the former and the credit does not exceed £25, at the end of the period the property passes to the pawnee.[21] In all other cases the pawn becomes realisable by the pawnee[22]: but he must notify the pawnor of the asking price,[23] the pawn remains redeemable until sale,[24] and the pawnor is entitled to any surplus left after discharge of the debt and the expenses of sale.[25] Except so far as the Act lays down special rules, the common law rules apply.

---

[15] *Kemp* v. *Westbrook* (1749) 1 Ves.Sen. 278.
[16] *Dobree* v. *Norcliffe* (1870) 23 L.T. 552.
[17] *Ratcliffe* v. *Davis* (1610) Yelv. 178; Bac.Abr. *tit.* Bailment.
[18] Consumer Credit Act 1974, ss.8, 114; S.I. 1983 No. 1878.
[19] ss.114–121.
[20] Consumer Credit Act 1974, s.116(1), (2).
[21] *Ibid.* s.120(1)(*a*); S.I. 1983 No. 1571.
[22] *Ibid.* s.120(1)(*b*).
[23] *Ibid.* s.121(1).
[24] *Ibid.* s.116(3).
[25] *Ibid.* s.121(3), (5).

CHAPTER 10

LIENS

Section 1. Types of Lien

A lien may be legal or equitable, and particular or general.

1. Legal lien. A common law lien is the right of one person to retain possession of the goods of another until his claims are satisfied.[1] It depends upon possession, and so lasts only as long as possession is retained; but while it exists it is good against the whole world. Formerly, such a lien gave no right to sell the property, although the court had a discretionary power to authorise a sale[2]; but certain bailees now have a statutory power to sell goods on which they have a lien if their charges are unpaid.[3]

2. Equitable lien. An equitable lien is very different. It confers a charge upon property until certain claims are satisfied, and differs from an equitable charge only in that it arises by operation of equity from the relationship between the parties rather than by any act of theirs. It exists independently of possession,[4] but will not avail against a purchaser for value of a legal estate without notice of it. It is enforceable by means of an order for sale.[5]

3. Particular and general liens. A common law lien may be particular or general. A particular lien is the right to retain goods until charges in respect of those particular goods have been paid. A general lien is the right to retain goods until the payment of all claims against

---

[1] See *Hammonds* v. *Barclay* (1802) 2 East 227 at 235.
[2] *Larner* v. *Fawcett* [1950] 2 All E.R. 727.
[3] Torts (Interference with Goods) Act 1977, s.12 and Sched. 1, replacing Disposal of Uncollected Goods Act 1952.
[4] But see *Stephenson* v. *Barclays Bank Trust Co. Ltd.* [1975] 1 W.L.R. 882 at 890, 891, as to the trustee's equitable lien: *ante*, p. 257, and consider *ante*, p. 346.
[5] See *post*, pp. 465, 466.

the owner, whether or not in relation to the particular goods. A particular lien will usually arise when work has been done on chattels or they have been accepted under an obligation to receive them. Thus artisans working on goods[6] lawfully delivered to them,[7] innkeepers,[8] packers,[9] and carriers[10] are all entitled to a particular lien. An auctioneer has a lien on goods sold,[11] and this entitles him to sue the highest bidder for the whole price even if the latter has paid the vendor direct.[12] An accountant has at least a particular lien on his client's papers: whether he has a general lien is undecided.[13] However, there is no lien if the claimant is not bound to receive the goods, and effects no improvement of them. Thus a farmer tending livestock has no lien.[14] A general lien is created by custom or agreement. By custom it has been recognised in favour of solicitors,[15] stockbrokers,[16] factors[17] and bankers.[18]

4. Types of equitable liens. The principal equitable liens are the solicitor's lien on property recovered, the vendor's lien for his purchase-money and the purchaser's lien for his deposit. Another, already mentioned, is the lien of trustees and personal representatives on the trust property for their expenses.[19] These various liens may exist concurrently, even if one of them is paramount to another.[20]

Section 2. Solicitors' Liens

A solicitor may have two kinds of lien for his costs. First, he may have a common law lien on the property of his client in his possession; this merely gives him the right to retain the property until he is paid.[21] Secondly, he may have an equitable lien on property recovered or preserved through his instrumentality; this gives him a charge upon the property which he can assert actively by taking steps to realise the property by sale.

---

[6] *Keene* v. *Thomas* [1905] 1 K.B. 136.
[7] *Tappenden* v. *Artus* [1964] 2 Q.B. 185 (delivery by hirer or bailee).
[8] *Robins* v. *Gray* [1895] 2 Q.B. 501.
[9] *Re Witt* (1876) 2 Ch.D. 489.
[10] *Skinner* v. *Upshaw* (1702) 2 Ld.Raym. 752; and see Kahn-Freund, *Law of Carriage by Inland Transport* (4th ed., 1965), pp. 402 *et seq.*
[11] *Webb* v. *Smith* (1885) 30 Ch.D. 192; but see *Skinner* v. *Trustee of the Property of Reed* [1967] Ch. 1194 (auctioneer holding deposit as stakeholder postponed to mortgagee).
[12] *Chelmsford Auctions Ltd.* v. *Poole* [1973] Q.B. 542.
[13] *Woodworth* v. *Conroy* [1976] Q.B. 884.
[14] *Re Southern Livestock Producers Ltd.* [1964] 1 W.L.R. 24.
[15] See *infra.*
[16] *Re London and Globe Finance Corporation* [1902] 2 Ch. 416.
[17] *Kruger* v. *Wilcox* (1755) Amb. 252; and see *Stevens* v. *Biller* (1883) 25 Ch.D. 31.
[18] *Brandao* v. *Barnett* (1846) 12 Cl. & F. 787; *Re Keever* [1967] Ch. 182.
[19] *Ante*, pp. 257, 320.
[20] *The Emilie Millon* [1905] 2 K.B. 817.
[21] See *Barratt* v. *Gough-Thomas (No. 2)* [1951] Ch. 242 at 250.

A. On Property in his Possession

1. General lien on property received qua solicitor

(a) *The lien.*   The solicitor's lien on his client's property originated by custom and was afterwards sanctioned by the decisions of the courts of law and equity; it is not dependent on contract. It is merely a right to withhold from the client, until the bill of costs is paid, any money,[22] deeds, books and papers (other than the client's will[23]) which are the property of the client and have been entrusted to the solicitor as such, and upon which he has bestowed his skill and labour. Moreover, the client is not entitled to see the documents or take copies of them.[24]

(b) *Extent of lien.*   The lien extends to money paid into a joint account in the names of solicitors for the parties to an action to abide the event of the action.[25] But it is confined to property which has come into the solicitor's hands in his character of solicitor and not otherwise[26]; and it is confined to the solicitor's costs, *i.e.* to items properly included in his bill of costs,[27] and does not include debts.[28] But the lien is a general lien which extends to all costs due from the client, and is not restricted merely to the costs incurred in connection with the property over which the lien is claimed. Further, a town agent has against the country solicitor a lien which extends to all documents and money coming to his hands in any particular transaction for all his costs and disbursements, whether incurred in the same transaction or in any other[29]; but as against the client, the town agent will have no larger lien than the country solicitor himself has.[29a]

2. Lien commensurate only with client's right.
A solicitor's lien is not defeated by his being discharged by the client.[30] But as the lien exists only as between solicitor and client, the solicitor cannot refuse to produce documents on the lawful demand of a third party if the rights of the third party (*e.g.* the client's mortgagee) were expressly reserved on delivery of the documents to the solicitor[31]; or if the result would be to embarrass proceedings in an action taken by the third party,[32] *e.g.* an administration action.[33] Nor can the lien be asserted against the administrative receivers of a client company since they are given the

---

[22] *Loescher* v. *Dean* [1950] Ch. 491.
[23] See *Balch* v. *Symes* (1823) T. & R. 87.
[24] *Re Biggs and Roche* (1897) 41 S.J. 277.
[25] *Halvanon Insurance Co. Ltd.* v. *Central Reinsurance Corpn.* [1988] 1 W.L.R. 1122.
[26] *Ex p. Fuller* (1881) 16 Ch.D. 617.
[27] *Re Taylor, Stileman & Underwood* [1891] 1 Ch. 590 at 599.
[28] *Re Galland* (1885) 31 Ch.D. 296.
[29] *Re Jones and Roberts* [1905] 2 Ch. 219.
[29a] *Waller* v. *Holmes* (1860) 1 J. & H. 239.
[30] *Re Rapid Road Transit Co.* [1909] 1 Ch. 96; *Hughes* v. *Hughes* [1958] P. 224 (divorce proceedings).
[31] *Re Golden Properties Ltd.* [1988] I.R. 213.
[32] *Ackerman* v. *Lockhart* [1898] 2 Ch. 1.
[33] *Belaney* v. *Ffrench* (1873) 8 Ch.App. 918.

status of third parties by the Insolvency Act 1986.[34] Where a solicitor expressly[35] or impliedly[36] discharges himself from the further conduct of an action, he is required to give up all the papers in the action to the new solicitor, but without prejudice to the lien.[37] The usual practice is to require the new solicitor to re-deliver the papers to the old at the conclusion of the case.[38]

3. Loss of lien

(a) *Parting with documents.* The lien is lost if the solicitor parts with possession of the documents without reservation. But a reservation of the lien expressed on sending the documents to another solicitor suffices to preserve the lien even if the other solicitor refuses to assent to it,[39] and even if the documents change their character, *e.g.* by engrossments being executed.[40]

(b) *Change of client.* Even if the solicitor retains possession of the documents, he will lose his lien if he ceases to hold them on behalf of his client. For instance, the solicitor will lose his lien if the client mortgages the property to which the documents relate to another client (or even to the solicitor himself[41]) and the solicitor retains the deeds on the mortgagee's behalf; and once lost, the lien will not revive on redemption.[42]

(c) *Waiver.* The lien may be discharged by waiver which will occur where the solicitor takes a security for costs inconsistent with the retention of his lien, unless he expressly reserves his lien.[43] The enforcement of a judgment for costs does not lead to the inference that the lien is waived.[44]

B. On Property Recovered or Preserved

1. Particular lien declared on property recovered or preserved

(a) *Equitable lien.* Even apart from statute a solicitor has a lien on a fund recovered by his exertions,[45] including any costs recovered[46]; but

---

[34] *Re Aveling Barford Ltd.* [1989] 1 W.L.R. 360.
[35] *Heslop* v. *Metcalfe* (1837) 3 My. & Cr. 183.
[36] *Griffiths* v. *Griffiths* (1843) 2 Hare 587.
[37] *Re Boughton* (1883) 23 Ch.D. 169; and see *Re Dee Estates* [1911] 2 Ch. 85.
[38] *Gamlen Chemical Co. (U.K.) Ltd.* v. *Rochem Ltd.* [1980] 1 W.L.R. 614.
[39] *Caldwell* v. *Sumpters* [1972] Ch. 478.
[40] *Watson* v. *Lyon* (1855) 7 De G.M. & G. 288.
[41] *Barratt* v. *Gough-Thomas (No. 2)* [1951] Ch. 242 at 256.
[42] *Barratt* v. *Gough-Thomas (No. 2)* [1951] Ch. 242.
[43] *Re John Morris* [1908] 1 K.B. 473.
[44] *A.* v. *B.* [1984] 1 All E.R. 265.
[45] *Re Born* [1900] 2 Ch. 433; *Haymes* v. *Cooper* (1864) 33 Beav. 431; *Re Meter Cabs Ltd.* [1911] 2 Ch. 557.
[46] *Campbell* v. *Campbell* [1941] 1 All E.R. 274.

this lien does not extend to real property.[47] Though sometimes called a common law lien,[48] it is more properly regarded as a right to apply to the court for a charge,[49] or as an equitable lien,[50] because it does not depend on the fund being in the possession of the solicitor.[51]

(b) *Statutory lien.* Statute has provided that "any court in which a solicitor has been employed to prosecute or defend any suit, matter or proceeding may at any time declare the solicitor entitled to a charge on the property recovered or preserved through his instrumentality for his taxed costs in reference to that suit, matter or proceeding."[52] This applies to every type of property, including realty.[53] An executor[54] or assignee[55] of the solicitor may also be declared entitled to this charge; and even where the solicitor has been discharged by the client, he may be given the charge, although this will be subject to a like charge in the new solicitor, whose charge will always have precedence.[56]

(c) *Extent of lien.* The charge will usually be subject to the prior right of an executor or trustee to his costs.[57] But where a receiver is appointed in a partnership action, the right of the plaintiff's solicitor to a charge on the assets recovered by the receiver has priority over the claims of the partnership creditors.[58] Moreover, it is expressly provided that all conveyances and acts done in defeasance of the charge are, except in favour of a bona fide purchaser for value without notice, void as against the solicitor.[59] "Notice" here means notice of the right to apply for a charging order, not notice of the existence of such an order.[60] Thus an assignment of the assets recovered or some part of them, even before they are quantified, will be postponed to the charge.[61] Although the charge may extend to the entire costs of the litigation,[62] it will usually be confined to the costs properly incurred in the recovery or preservation of the property.[63] The grant of the charge is discretionary and may be withheld where the client has already been deemed to have received the costs by way of set-off,[64] or, possibly, where the assets have been diminished by prolonging the litigation.[65]

[47] *Shaw* v. *Neale* (1858) 6 H.L.C. 581.
[48] *Re Born* [1900] 2 Ch. 433 at 435; *Re Meter Cabs Ltd.* [1911] 2 Ch. 557.
[49] *James Bibby Ltd.* v. *Woods and Howard* [1949] 2 K.B. 449.
[50] See *Re Sullivan* v. *Pearson, ex p. Morrison* (1868) L.R. 4 Q.B. 153 at 156, 158.
[51] See *Loescher* v. *Dean* [1950] Ch. 491.
[52] Solicitors Act 1974, s.73, replacing earlier provisions (Solicitors Acts 1860, s.28; 1932, s.69; 1957, s.72).
[53] *Foxon* v. *Gascoigne* (1874) 9 Ch.App. 654 at 660.
[54] *Baile* v. *Baile* (1872) L.R. 13 Eq. 497.
[55] *Briscoe* v. *Briscoe* [1892] 3 Ch. 543.
[56] *Rhodes* v. *Sugden* (1886) 34 Ch.D. 155; *Knight* v. *Gardner* [1892] 2 Ch. 368; *Hyde* v. *White* [1933] P. 105.
[57] *Re Turner, Wood* v. *Turner* [1907] 2 Ch. 126, 539.
[58] *Ridd* v. *Thorne* [1902] 2 Ch. 344; *Newport* v. *Pougher* [1937] Ch. 214.
[59] Solicitors Act 1974, s.73.
[60] *Dallow* v. *Garrold* (1884) 14 Q.B.D. 543.
[61] *The Paris* [1896] P.77.
[62] See *Kay* v. *Lovell* [1940] Ch. 650.
[63] *Re Clayton* [1940] Ch. 539.
[64] *Re Cockrell's Estate* [1911] 2 Ch. 318, affd.: [1912] 1 Ch. 23.
[65] *Re Cockrell's Estate* [1912] 1 Ch. 23 at 27, 28.

2. Property within the lien

(a) "Recovered or preserved"

(1) SUCCESS. It has been held that property is recovered or preserved within the meaning of the statute where an action brought for the purpose of setting aside a deed is successfully defended,[66] or an action to prove a will is successfully brought,[67] or costs alone are recovered,[68] or where in an administration action an application to approve a conditional contract for the sale of part of the assets is successfully opposed on the ground of under-value, and an order for sale obtained instead.[69] It is immaterial at what stage the property is recovered. Thus a solicitor who takes over the conduct of an action after money has been deposited as a result of interlocutory proceedings has a claim on the part of the money to which his client is entitled.[70]

(2) LACK OF SUCCESS. Even though the party is unsuccessful[71] or only partly successful[72] in the litigation, property may be recovered and preserved if it has been secured to the plaintiff through the instrumentality of the solicitors. Thus where a party unsuccessfully propounded a will, his solicitors were entitled to a charge on the part of the estate to which he was entitled under the resulting intestacy.[73] But where a vendor unsuccessfully defends a specific performance action, the money which the purchaser has to pay before he can insist on a conveyance is not so recovered and preserved, for the purchaser has not been ordered to pay it.[74] Where a claim and counterclaim both succeed and judgment is entered merely for the excess of the claim over the counterclaim, only this balance is deemed to have been "recovered" in the action.[75] And where a plaintiff claims certain property, obtains the appointment of a receiver and then abandons his claim, the costs payable to the plaintiff's solicitors for procuring the appointment of the receiver cannot be charged on the defendant's property.[76]

(b) Property bound.
The charge arising under the Solicitors Act is not dependent on contract, but is rather in the nature of salvage.[77] The court may accordingly give the solicitor a charge on the entire property, and not merely on the share of his client therein,[78] though it is not

[66] Bulley v. Bulley (1878) 8 Ch.D. 479.
[67] Ex p. Tweed [1899] 2 Q.B. 167.
[68] Re Blake, Clutterbuck v. Bradford [1945] Ch. 61.
[69] Re Cockrell's Estate [1911] 2 Ch. 318 (affirmed on other grounds [1912] 1 Ch. 23).
[70] Wimbourne v. Fine [1952] Ch. 869.
[71] Hyde v. White [1933] P. 105.
[72] Wimbourne v. Fine, supra.
[73] Hyde v. White, supra.
[74] Loescher v. Dean [1950] Ch. 491.
[75] Westacott v. Bevan [1891] 1 Q.B. 774.
[76] Wingfield v. Wingfield [1919] 1 Ch. 462, esp. at 473, where Eve J. described the order sought as "an absurdity and . . . a great injustice."
[77] Greer v. Young (1882) 24 Ch.D. 545; Bulley v. Bulley (1878) 8 Ch.D. 479 at 484, 485.
[78] Scholey v. Peck [1893] 1 Ch. 709.

bound to do so[79]; and it may even charge the shares of persons who were not represented in the proceedings or were under disability.[80]

(c) *London agent.* At common law the town agent of a country solicitor has a general lien upon a fund recovered, extending to all costs of agency business and disbursements, whether in connection with the particular proceeding or not.[81] But as against the client the town agent may exercise the lien only to the extent of the country solicitor's lien against such client.[82] The town agent is not entitled to be given any charge under the Solicitors Act 1974.[83]

(d) *Concurrent liens.* A solicitor may be entitled both to his lien on the papers of his client and to his charge on the property recovered.[84] But the making of the order is purely discretionary, and no order will be made under the Act if an order for payment of costs out of the same fund has already been made.[85]

3. Costs within the lien. The statutory charge is confined to the costs of litigation or arbitration,[86] and does not extend to any costs incurred otherwise, even if incurred in forestalling any proceedings in court.[87] The charge under the Act can be given only in respect of the costs of the particular proceedings, and will not be extended even to the costs incurred in an auxiliary action.[88] But even if no charge is possible under the Act, there may be a common law lien on a fund recovered by a solicitor.[89]

4. Limitation. There is no period of limitation applicable to the solicitor's common law lien, whether on papers[90] or a fund recovered.[91] But the court cannot declare a charge under the Act if the claim to recover the costs is statute-barred,[92] although it will not refuse to do so merely on the ground of delay, unless third parties have acquired rights in respect of the property in the meantime.[93] And although the client may allege the bar of time in every taxation of costs, including a taxation under the common order to tax, yet if the client seeks an order for delivery of papers, the order should direct a taxation extending to

[79] *Wimbourne* v. *Fine* [1952] Ch. 869.
[80] *Greer* v. *Young* (1882) 24 Ch.D. 545; *Wright* v. *Sanderson* [1901] 1 Ch. 317.
[81] *Farewell* v. *Coker* (1728) 2 P.Wms. 459; *Lawrence* v. *Fletcher* (1879) 12 Ch.D. 858.
[82] *Ex p. Edwards* (1881) 8 Q.B.D. 262.
[83] *Macfarlane* v. *Lister* (1887) 37 Ch.D. 88.
[84] *Pilcher* v. *Arden* (1877) 7 Ch.D. 318.
[85] *Re Cockrell's Estate* [1912] 1 Ch. 23.
[86] Arbitration Act 1950, s.18(5).
[87] *Ex p. Lloyd-George* [1898] 1 Q.B. 520; *Meguerditchian* v. *Lightbound* [1917] 2 K.B. 298.
[88] *Macfarlane* v. *Lister* (1887) 37 Ch.D. 88.
[89] *Re Meter Cabs Ltd.* [1911] 2 Ch. 557; *Campbell* v. *Campbell* [1941] 1 All E.R. 274.
[90] *Curwen* v. *Milburn* (1889) 42 Ch.D. 424.
[91] *Higgins* v. *Scott* (1831) 2 B. & Ad. 413.
[92] Solicitors Act 1974, s.73(2).
[93] *Re Born* [1900] 2 Ch. 433.

statute-barred items so as to ascertain the amount for which the solicitor has a lien.[94]

5. Equities and set-off. The solicitor's lien on papers will not prejudice any prior existing equity,[95] nor will it be prejudiced by an equity arising subsequently.[96] But the solicitor's lien on a fund due to his client is subject to the power of the court under its inherent jurisdiction to allow a set-off for damages and costs between the parties[97]; and this may be allowed even where the lien is for costs in the particular cause or matter in which the set-off is sought.[98] A set-off in prejudice of the solicitor's lien may be allowed as between the damages recovered in independent actions.[99] And although the court in its discretion may order that the set-off be allowed only subject to the lien,[1] yet it has been said that "the old views as to the sanctity of a solicitor's lien no longer obtain,"[2] and the set-off will usually be allowed to the prejudice of the lien.[3]

6. Compromises. A solicitor's lien may be defeated by a compromise of the action if it has been fairly entered into,[4] but not if it is purposely designed to defeat the lien, or is otherwise an attempted fraud on the solicitor[5] by persons who have been given express notice of his lien.[6]

Section 3. Vendor's Lien

1. Vendor's trusteeship. When a specifically enforceable contract for sale has been made, the beneficial ownership of the property passes at once to the purchaser. Thereafter the vendor, in whom the legal estate is still vested, is to some extent a trustee for the purchaser.[7] Thus he will be liable to the purchaser if he fails to take reasonable steps to prevent damage to the property by trespassers[8] or by the elements,[9] or if he damages it himself[10] or grants tenancies of it on unfavourable terms[11] or if he withdraws an application for planning permission to

---

[94] *Re Brockman* [1909] 2 Ch. 170.
[95] *Boden* v. *Hensby* [1892] 1 Ch. 101.
[96] *Cole* v. *Eley* [1894] 2 Q.B. 350; *Wimbourne* v. *Fine* [1952] Ch. 869; *cf. James Bibby Ltd.* v. *Woods and Howard* [1949] 2 K.B. 449.
[97] *Puddephatt* v. *Leith (No. 2)* [1916] 2 Ch. 168 at 173.
[98] See *Re a Debtor* [1951] Ch. 612 at 619–621.
[99] *Blakey* v. *Latham* (1889) 41 Ch.D. 518; *Goodfellow* v. *Gray* [1899] 2 Q.B. 498; *Reid* v. *Cupper* [1915] 2 K.B. 147.
[1] *Edwards* v. *Hope* (1885) 14 Q.B.D. 922; and see *Knight* v. *Knight* [1925] Ch. 835.
[2] *Puddephatt* v. *Leith (No. 2)* [1916] 2 Ch. 168 at 180, *per* Younger J.
[3] *Puddephatt* v. *Leith (No. 2)* [1916] 2 Ch. 168.
[4] *The Hope* (1883) 8 P.D. 144; *Re Sullivan* v. *Pearson, ex p. Morrison* (1868) L.R. 4 Q.B. 153.
[5] *Re Margetson and Jones* [1897] 2 Ch. 314; and see *Wimbourne* v. *Fine* [1952] Ch. 869.
[6] *Ross* v. *Buxton* (1889) 42 Ch.D. 190.
[7] See *ante*, p. 195; Megarry and Wade's *Law of Real Property* (5th ed., 1984), pp. 602, 603.
[8] *Clarke* v. *Ramuz* [1891] 2 Q.B. 456 (removal of soil).
[9] *Lucie-Smith* v. *Gorman* [1981] C.L.Y. 2866.
[10] See *Cumberland Consolidated Holdings Ltd.* v. *Ireland* [1946] K.B. 264 at 269.
[11] *Abdulla* v. *Shah* [1959] A.C. 124.

develop the land.[12] If, before completion, the vendor wrongfully sells the property to another purchaser, he is accountable *qua* trustee to the first purchaser in respect of the proceeds of sale.[13] On the other hand, subject to the terms of the contract, he is entitled to retain possession and the income of the property between contract and completion, and any statutory compensation payable before completion in respect of prior damage to the land.[14] The vendor's trusteeship is thus of a special nature; and this is emphasised by the vendor's lien.

2. Creation of lien. As soon as a binding contract of sale is made,[15] the vendor has a lien on the property for the purchase-money and a right to retain the property until the money is paid. The lien may also secure the performance of the other obligations of the purchaser, *e.g.* an obligation on the sale of a business to collect the outstanding debts and account for them to the vendor.[16] Even if the vendor executes an absolute conveyance and parts with possession both of the property and of the title deeds to the purchaser, he still has an equitable lien on the property in respect of any part of the purchase-money which may not have been paid; and the lien is not excluded by the fact that the purchase-deed contains a receipt for the purchase-money.[17] The lien arises independently of any implied agreement between the parties, and attaches on a sale not only of realty, but also of leaseholds[18] and personalty such as a reversionary interest in a trust fund,[19] but not ordinary commercial goods.[20] The lien also exists where land is compulsorily acquired, and extends to unpaid compensation as well as purchase-money unless such compensation has been made the subject of a separate agreement.[21]

3. Transfer of lien. A third party who, at the request of the purchaser, provides some or all of the purchase money on his behalf will be subrogated to the position of the vendor and so obtain the benefit of the vendor's lien.[22] This principle did not, however, enable a mortgagee whose mortgage was unenforceable under the Moneylenders Act 1927 to rely on the lien[23]; and it probably does not assist a mortgagee who has

---

[12] *Sinclair-Hill* v. *Sothcott* (1973) 226 E.G. 1399.
[13] *Lake* v. *Bayliss* [1974] 1 W.L.R. 1073.
[14] *Re Hamilton-Snowball's Conveyance* [1959] Ch. 308.
[15] *Re Birmingham* [1959] Ch. 523.
[16] *Uziell-Hamilton* v. *Keen* (1971) 22 P. & C.R. 655.
[17] On the vendor's lien generally, see *Mackreth* v. *Symmons* (1808) 15 Ves. 329; **2 W. & T.L.C. 848**; 2 Williams' *Vendor and Purchaser* (4th ed., 1936), pp. 983 *et seq.*
[18] *Davies* v. *Thomas* [1900] 2 Ch. 462.
[19] *Re Stucley* [1906] 1 Ch. 67. And see *Dansk* v. *Snell* [1908] 2 Ch. 127 (royalties under patents).
[20] *Transport and General Credit Corporation* v. *Morgan* [1939] Ch. 531. The lien under the Sale of Goods Act 1979, s.41, is a common law lien, not equitable.
[21] *Walker* v. *Ware, Hadham, and Buntingford Ry.* (1865) L.R. 1 Eq. 195.
[22] *Boodle Hatfield and Co.* v. *British Films Ltd.* [1986] P.C.C. 176.
[23] *Orakpo* v. *Manson Investments Ltd.* [1978] A.C. 95, overruling *Congresbury Motors Ltd.* v. *Anglo-Belge Finance Co. Ltd.* [1971] Ch. 81. The Act was repealed by the Consumer Credit Act 1974: see *post*, p. 561.

made an unenforceable contract of loan with a minor, unless the minor has adopted the purchase after attaining his majority.[24]

4. Exclusion of lien. Occasionally, however, the vendor will have no lien. If he receives all that he bargained for, *e.g.* if he sells the property in consideration of the purchaser giving him a promissory note or a bond to pay him an annuity, and the promissory note or bond is duly given, there will be no lien on the property sold, even though the note is not met at maturity or the annuity is not paid.[25] Similarly, the lien is lost where the vendor takes a mortgage for the money, even if the mortgage later becomes void against successors in title for want of registration.[26] Moreover, the nature of the contract may exclude the vendor's lien, as where the existence of a lien would prevent the purchaser from selling the property,[27] or where the intention of the parties is that the purchaser shall resell or mortgage the property and pay off the vendor out of the proceeds[28]; but a mere power of resale in the contract is not enough.[29]

5. Enforceability of lien

(a) *Extent of right.* The vendor's lien may be enforced not only against the purchaser himself and his representatives after his death, but also against all persons taking as volunteers under him or them; and it is also enforceable against the purchaser's trustee in bankruptcy, for he takes the bankrupt's property subject to all the equities affecting it in the hands of the bankrupt.[30] Subject to the question of registration if the property is land, a vendor's lien may be enforced even against a subsequent purchaser, unless he obtained a legal estate for value without actual or constructive notice of the lien, or unless, though his interest is only equitable, he has a better equity than the vendor[31]. After the vendor has parted with the title deeds, his lien on land appears to be a general equitable charge and hence is registrable as a land charge[32]; but it is not registrable as a charge under the Companies Act 1985.[33]

---

[24] See *Nottingham Permanent Benefit B.S.* v. *Thurstan* [1903] A.C. 6, as explained in *Orakpo* v. *Manson Investments Ltd., supra*, at pp. 106, 113, 120, 121.
[25] *Parrott* v. *Sweetland* (1835) 3 My. & K. 655; *Buckland* v. *Pocknell* (1843) 13 Sim. 406.
[26] *Capital Finance Co. Ltd.* v. *Stokes* [1969] 1 Ch. 261 where, at pp. 278, 279, passages from this and the preceding page were cited; *Burston Finance Ltd.* v. *Speirway Ltd.* [1974] 1 W.L.R. 1648; *contra, Coptic Ltd.* v. *Bailey* [1972] Ch. 446.
[27] *Dixon* v. *Gayfere* (1857) 1 De G. & J. 655, a sale in consideration of an annuity to be paid for three lives.
[28] *Re Brentwood Brick and Coal Co.* (1876) 4 Ch.D. 562.
[29] *Re Birmingham* [1959] Ch. 523.
[30] *Ex p. Hanson* (1806) 12 Ves. 346 at 349; affd. (1811) 18 Ves. 232.
[31] *Rice* v. *Rice* (1854) 2 Drew. 73; *ante*, p. 58.
[32] See *ante*, p. 60.
[33] *London and Cheshire Insurance Co. Ltd.* v. *Laplagrene Co. Ltd.* [1971] Ch. 499. For this type of registration, see *ante*, p. 62.

(b) *Procedure.* The vendor may enforce his lien by issuing a writ in the Chancery Division claiming a declaration that he is entitled to a lien. On such declaration being made, he is entitled to all such remedies for enforcing payment of his purchase-money and interest as he would have been entitled to under an express mortgage or charge,[34] *e.g.* sale, or restoration of possession, or the appointment of a receiver. Further, where the contract provides for deferred payment, the court will not compel the vendor to transfer the property without safeguarding his lien.[35]

6. Loss of lien

(a) *Waiver.* The vendor may waive his lien by taking a security for the purchase-money; but a mere personal obligation, such as a bond[36] or a bill of exchange or promissory note,[37] will not of itself be sufficient to discharge the lien. "It depends upon the circumstances of each case, whether the court is to infer, that the lien was intended to be reserved; or that credit was given, and exclusively given, to the person, from whom the other security was taken."[38]

(b) *Limitation.* The vendor may also lose his lien by the operation of the Limitation Act. An equitable lien on any property, real or personal, is barred at the expiration of 12 years.[39]

Section 4. Purchaser's Lien

1. The lien. A purchaser has a lien which is somewhat analogous to the vendor's lien. This is a lien upon the property in the hands of the vendor for any deposit or instalment of his purchase-money which the purchaser has paid to the vendor (and not merely to a stakeholder[40]) without obtaining a conveyance. The purchaser has this lien not only when the contract goes off for want of title, but also where he rescinds the contract under a condition enabling him to do so,[41] or the vendor repudiates the contract[42]; but if the contract goes off through the purchaser's default, the lien is gone.[43] The lien extends not only to the purchase-money actually paid, but also to interest thereon, and to money paid as interest on the unpaid purchase-money,[44] and to the

---

[34] *Rose* v. *Watson* (1864) 10 H.L.C. 672 (purchaser's lien); *Re Stucley* [1906] 1 Ch. 67 (vendor's lien).
[35] *Langen & Wind Ltd.* v. *Bell* [1972] Ch. 685.
[36] *Collins* v. *Collins (No. 2)* (1862) 31 Beav. 346.
[37] *Hughes* v. *Kearney* (1803) 1 Sch. & Lef. 132.
[38] *Mackreth* v. *Symmons* (1808) 15 Ves. 329 at 350, *per* Lord Eldon L.C.; **2 W. & T.L.C. 848 at 853**.
[39] Limitation Act 1980, s.20(1); and see *Toft* v. *Stephenson* (1848) 7 Hare 1 (on appeal, 1 De G.M. & G. 28); *Re Stucley* [1906] 1 Ch. 67.
[40] *Combe* v. *Swaythling* [1947] Ch. 625.
[41] *Whitbread & Co. Ltd.* v. *Watt* [1901] 1 Ch. 911 at 915; affirmed [1902] 1 Ch. 835.
[42] *Lee-Parker* v. *Izzet* [1971] 1 W.L.R. 1688.
[43] *Dinn* v. *Grant* (1852) 5 De G. & Sm. 451; *Ridout* v. *Fowler* [1904] 2 Ch. 93.
[44] *Rose* v. *Watson* (1864) 10 H.L.C. 672.

costs properly incurred by the purchaser.[45] The lien will prevail against
all persons against whom a vendor's lien would prevail, and, like the
vendor's lien, it must apparently now be registered as a land charge in
order to bind subsequent purchasers.[46]

2. Lessee's lien. A similar lien exists if an intended lessee enters on
the land under a contract to grant him a lease and expends money in
repairing the premises in accordance with his contract, but the lessor
fails to grant the lease.[47]

Section 5. Lien for Sums Spent on Property of Another

1. Normally no lien. "The general principle is, beyond all question,
that work and labour done or money expended by one man to preserve
or benefit the property of another do not according to English law
create any lien upon the property saved or benefited, nor, even if
standing alone, create any obligation to repay the expenditure.
Liabilities are not to be forced upon people behind their backs any more
than you can confer a benefit upon a man against his will."[48] Thus,
where a man pays premiums on a policy of insurance belonging to
another person to save that policy from lapsing, he will normally be
unable to claim a lien on the policy moneys.[49]

2. Exceptions. To this general rule there are a number of
exceptions. A lien will arise if the person making the payments made
them out of his own moneys[50]—

(i)   under contract with the beneficial owner, either express or
      implied;

(ii) as trustee[51];

(iii) as mortgagee;

(iv) in circumstances giving rise to a claim by subrogation[52];

(v)   where the property was in the hands of an official receiver or
      other officer of the court[53] who knew[54] that the payments were
      being made; or

---

[45] *Kitton* v. *Hewett* [1904] W.N. 21; *Re Furneaux and Aird's Contract* [1906] W.N. 215.
[46] See *ante,* pp. 60, 465.
[47] *Middleton* v. *Magnay* (1864) 2 H. & M. 233.
[48] *Falcke* v. *Scottish Imperial Insurance Co.* (1886) 34 Ch.D. 234 at 248, *per* Bowen L.J.; and see *ante,*
     pp. 187, 188, *post,* pp. 573, 574. Maritime salvage is an exception; *ibid.* pp. 248, 249.
[49] *Falcke* v. *Scottish Imperial Insurance Co.* (1886) 34 Ch.D. 234; *Re Jones' Settlement* [1915] 1 Ch. 373;
     Re Stokes, ex p. Mellish [1919] 2 K.B. 256; and see *Ramsden* v. *Dyson* (1866) L.R. 1 H.L. 129.
[50] See *Re Sims' Question* [1946] 2 All E.R. 138 (wife's army allowance).
[51] See *ante,* p. 257; and see p. 248.
[52] This and the preceding three exceptions were listed in *Re Leslie* (1883) 23 Ch.D. 552, but the list is
     not exhaustive; *Strutt* v. *Tippett* (1889) 62 L.T. 475; *Re Foster (No. 2)* [1938] 3 All E.R. 610.
[53] *Re Tyler, ex p. The Official Receiver* [1907] 1 K.B. 865.
[54] See *Re Hall, ex p. The Official Receiver* [1907] 1 K.B. 875.

(vi)   in the erroneous belief that the property was his, and the true
        owner, knowing that he was the owner and knowing of the
        other's belief, stood by and allowed him to make the payments,
        so creating a proprietary estoppel.[55]

3. Joint owners.   Where one of two joint owners improves or repairs
the common property, he normally has no lien in respect of his outlay.[56]
But upon a subsequent partition or sale of the property compensation
may be made to him for what he has properly expended.[57]

Section 6. Other Equitable Liens

The categories of liens discussed above are not exhaustive. For example,
as already mentioned, a mere deposit of title deeds may operate to
confer an equitable lien on the land to which they relate if that is the
intention.[58] Further, a covenant for value to bring after-acquired
property into settlement binds the property from the moment it becomes
receivable into the settlement funds. Accordingly, if the property is not
at once brought into settlement, it can subsequently be recovered even
from a third person, unless he is a purchaser for value of a legal estate
without notice of the covenant.[59]

---

[55] For this, see *post*, p. 573.
[56] *Leigh* v. *Dickeson* (1884) 15 Q.B.D. 60. Contrast *Lake* v. *Gibson* (1729) 1 Eq.Cas.Abr. 290 at 291; **2
    W. & T.L.C. 876 at 878n.**
[57] See *post*, p. 640.
[58] See *ante*, p. 444.
[59] *Pullan* v. *Koe* [1913] 1 Ch. 9; *ante*, p. 127.

CHAPTER 11

SURETYSHIP

1. Definition. Sometimes security for a loan or other obligation is provided not by a mortgage or charge on property but by a contract of suretyship. A surety is "one who contracts with an actual or possible creditor of another to be responsible to him by way of security, additional to that other, for the whole or part of the debt."[1] The contract is often called a contract of guarantee, and the surety the guarantor. The duty of a surety who guarantees payment of a debt is to see that the debtor performs his obligations, so that if the debtor's failure to pay an instalment due under the contract makes the whole debt payable, the surety is forthwith liable for the whole debt and not merely for the instalment.[2]

2. Intervention of equity. Such contracts fell within the concurrent jurisdiction of equity. From early times the Court of Chancery intervened to protect sureties in a variety of cases. The main instances of this intervention are—

(i)   setting aside the contract of suretyship if there is evidence of fraud or misrepresentation or improper concealment;

(ii) allowing the surety to proceed by way of *quia timet* to compel the debtor to pay;

(iii) giving a surety who pays the debt more complete remedies for the recovery of the amount paid (or a proportion of it) than the common law provided; and

(iv) holding the surety released from his liability in certain events.

Section 1. Nature of Suretyship

1. Principal debtor. The contract of suretyship necessarily implies the principal liability of another person. "There can be no suretyship unless there be a principal debtor. ... Nor can a man guarantee anybody else's debt unless there is a debt of some other person to be

[1] *Rowlatt's Law of Principal and Surety* (4th ed., 1982), p. 1.
[2] *Moschi* v. *Lep Air Services Ltd.* [1973] A.C. 331.

guaranteed."[3] Thus where a company makes a loan for the purchase of its own shares, which is unlawful under the Companies Act 1985,[4] no action lies against the guarantor of the loan.[5] But the guarantor of *ultra vires* borrowing by a company cannot repudiate liability.[6] The basis of the distinction is not clear.[7] It may be that the cases turn on whether the guarantee is of all debts or merely of all lawfully enforceable debts.[8] A true exception to the general requirement of a principal liability is made by the Minors' Contracts Act 1987: the unenforceability of contractual obligations on the ground that a party was a minor when the contract was made does not affect the liability of a guarantor of those obligations.[9]

2. Not uberrimae fidei

(a) *Non-disclosure.* Unlike insurance contracts, ordinary contracts of guarantee do not in their inception require *uberrima fides* on the part of the creditor towards the surety. Unless there is fraud or misrepresentation, the contract will not be vitiated by mere non-communication to the surety by the creditor of facts known to him affecting the risk to be undertaken by the surety. "In general, the creditor does not himself go to the surety, or represent, or explain to the surety, the risk to be run. The surety often takes the position from motives of friendship to the debtor, and generally not as the result of any direct bargaining between him and the creditor, or in consideration of any remuneration passing to him from the creditor. The risk undertaken is generally known to the surety, and the circumstances generally point to the view that as between the creditor and surety it was contemplated and intended that the surety should take upon himself to ascertain exactly what risk he was taking upon himself."[10]

(b) *Misrepresentation.* Silence, however, may amount to a misrepresentation which will justify the surety in repudiating the contract. Failure to mention a fact which he would not expect to exist may constitute a representation that the fact does not exist. "Very little said which ought not to have been said, and very little not said which ought

---

[3] *Lakeman* v. *Mountstephen* (1874) L.R. 7 H.L. 17 at 24, *per* Lord Selborne; and see *Swan* v. *Bank of Scotland* (1836) 10 Bli.(N.S.) 627. See J. Steyn on "Guarantees: the Co-extensiveness Principle" in (1974) 90 L.Q.R. 246.

[4] Sections 151–158, replacing earlier legislation.

[5] *Heald* v. *O'Connor* [1971] 1 W.L.R. 497.

[6] *Yorkshire Railway Waggon Co.* v. *Maclure* (1881) 19 Ch.D. 478 (on appeal: (1882) 21 Ch.D. 309, where the borrowing was held *intra vires*); *Garrard* v. *James* [1925] Ch. 616.

[7] See *Coutts & Co.* v. *Browne-Lecky* [1947] K.B. 104 at 111; and see R. Else-Mitchell (1947) 63 L.Q.R. 355 at 363.

[8] See *Heald* v. *O'Connor, supra,* at p. 506.

[9] s.2. For the position under the Infants Relief Act 1874 (repealed by Minors' Contracts Act 1987, s.4(2)), see *Coutts & Co.* v. *Brown-Lecky* [1947] K.B. 104.

[10] *Seaton* v. *Heath* [1899] 1 Q.B. 782 at 793, *per* Romer L.J. (reversed on the facts *sub nom. Seaton* v. *Burnand* [1900] A.C. 135).

to have been said" may suffice to invalidate the contract.[11] Thus, a surety who is induced by an employer to guarantee the fidelity of a servant can repudiate the contract if the employer does not disclose to the surety the fact, known to the employer but unknown to the surety, that the servant had previously been guilty of dishonesty in his employment; for the surety believes that he is making himself answerable for a presumably honest man and not for a known thief.[12] But a surety who is asked to guarantee a banking account is not entitled to assume that the customer of the bank has not been in the habit of overdrawing, and so mere non-disclosure of the fact that he has done so does not vitiate the contract[13]; and the same applies to a failure to disclose that the customer's spouse has authority to draw on the account and is an undischarged bankrupt.[14]

Section 2. Position of Creditor

1. Terms of guarantee

(a) *Construction of instrument.* The rights of the creditor against the surety are wholly regulated by the terms of the instrument of guarantee. Where an obligation arises only by virtue of a written agreement, the extent of the obligation can be measured by the words of that agreement alone.[15] Thus, where a surety is bound by a joint bond, the court will not rectify the bond so as to make it several upon a mere presumption of a mistake from the nature of the transaction, but will require positive proof of the mistake before doing so.[16] The construction of the written agreement in the light of the surrounding circumstances will also determine matters such as the precise identification of the liability being guaranteed,[17] or the duration of the suretyship (*e.g.* whether it is for goods supplied once only or for a continuing supply),[18] or whether it is determined by notice of the death of the surety,[19] or whether the suretyship is for a part only or for the whole of the debt.[20]

(b) *Death of surety.* The nature of the liability insured against sometimes shows that the obligation is to continue after the surety's death. For instance, where a bond for the integrity of a person is given by a surety in consideration of that person being appointed to an office

[11] *Davies v. London & Provincial Marine Insurance Co.* (1878) 8 Ch.D. 469 at 475, *per* Fry J.; and see *post*, p. 549.
[12] *London General Omnibus Co. Ltd. v. Holloway* [1912] 2 K.B. 72.
[13] *Hamilton v. Watson* (1845) 12 Cl. & F. 109; *Wythes v. Labouchere* (1859) 3 De G. & J. 593; *National Provincial Bank of England v. Glanusk* [1913] 3 K.B. 335.
[14] *Cooper v. National Provincial Bank Ltd.* [1946] K.B. 1.
[15] *Sumner v. Powell* (1816) 2 Mer. 30; *Hyundai Shipbuilding & Heavy Industries Co. Ltd. v. Pournaras* [1978] 2 Lloyd's Rep. 502.
[16] *Rawstone v. Parr* (1830) 3 Russ. 539; see *post*, pp. 632, 633.
[17] *Perrylease Ltd. v. Imecar A.G.* [1988] 1 W.L.R. 463.
[18] *Heffield v. Meadows* (1869) L.R. 4 C.P. 595.
[19] *Harriss v. Fawcett* (1873) L.R. 15 Eq. 311; *Lloyd's v. Harper* (1880) 16 Ch.D. 290.
[20] *Re Sass* [1896] 2 Q.B. 12.

by the obligee of the bond, the surety's liability does not determine on his death unless the bond expressly so provides.[21] And the surety's death will not determine a suretyship which is expressed to be a continuing one if the agreement contains a specific provision for its determination which is as applicable after the death as before it.[22]

2. Revocation of guarantee on change of firm. In the absence of agreement to the contrary, a continuing guarantee given either to a partnership or to a third person in respect of the transactions of a partnership is revoked as to future transactions "by any change in the constitution of the firm to which, or of the firm in respect of the transactions of which, the guaranty or obligation was given."[23]

Section 3. Position of Surety

1. Status dependent on creditor's knowledge. The rights of the surety against the creditor depend not upon the fact that, as between himself and the principal debtor, the surety is only collaterally liable, but upon the creditor's knowledge of the fact. Of course, if S expressly contracts with the creditor as surety for D's debt, the creditor knows the position from the start, and must respect S's equitable rights. But it sometimes happens that, on the face of the agreement, S and D both appear to be principal debtors although they have arranged between themselves that S shall be only a surety for D's debt. In such a case, the creditor is not affected by S's equitable rights until he has notice of the arrangement; but after he has notice he is bound by the arrangement, whether it was made at the time that the debt was contracted or subsequently, and even if he has not assented to the change of the relations between the parties.[24]

2. Creditor's duty not to prejudice surety. The chief right of the surety against the creditor is a negative one. The creditor must do nothing to prejudice the surety's right to obtain indemnity from the principal debtor or contribution from co-sureties; if he does so, the surety will be either wholly or partially discharged from his liability. But this right of the surety is subject to the creditor's right to choose to require payment either by the principal debtor or by any surety: the surety cannot dictate to the creditor which remedy he should pursue. Apparently, therefore, the surety cannot compel the creditor to proceed first against the principal debtor,[25] or require the creditor to exact payment from the co-sureties rateably.[26]

Section 4. Remedies of Surety

A. Before Payment

1. Quia timet relief

(a) *Principle.* The surety has an equitable right to compel the principal debtor to pay the debt and so relieve the surety from the necessity of paying it out of his own pocket. It is in the nature of *quia timet*,[27] and is based on the principle that it is "unreasonable that a man should always have such a cloud hang over him,"[28] so that he ought to be entitled to remove it.[29] It is therefore immaterial that the creditor has refused to sue,[30] or even that he has made no demand.[31] A *fortiori*, the action lies where the principal debtor threatens to commit a breach of the obligations which the surety has guaranteed[32]; and an order may be made even though the principal debtor is without funds.[33] But the action will not lie if the debt is not an actual accrued and definite debt,[34] or if on its true construction the guarantee precludes action before the creditor demands payment.[35]

(b) *Order.* Where the action lies, the court will grant the surety a declaration that he is entitled to be discharged and exonerated from liability, and will order the principal debtor to pay the debt, with liberty to apply as to the mode of enforcement if he does not.[36]

2. No debt. This equitable right to indemnity against liability before payment does not create any debt due from the principal debtor to the surety. A release by the surety's will of all debts due from the principal debtor accordingly does not prevent the surety's executor from claiming

---

[25] *Wright* v. *Simpson* (1802) 6 Ves. 714 at 733.
[26] See, however, *Wolmershausen* v. *Gullick* [1893] 2 Ch. 514 at 522. For a discussion, see *Rowlatt's Law of Principal and Surety* (4th ed., 1982), pp. 132–134.
[27] *Wooldridge* v. *Norris* (1868) L.R. 6 Eq. 410; *Felton* v. *Callis* [1969] 1 Q.B. 200 at 216.
[28] *Ranelagh* v. *Hayes* (1683) 1 Vern. 189 at 190, *per* Lord Guilford L.K. The actual decree in this case was disapproved of in *Lloyd* v. *Dimmack* (1877) 7 Ch.D. 398.
[29] *Thomas* v. *Nottingham Incorporated Football Club Ltd.* [1972] Ch. 596 at 606.
[30] *Ascherson* v. *Tredegar Dry Dock and Wharf Co. Ltd.* [1909] 2 Ch. 401.
[31] *Tate* v. *Crewdson* [1938] Ch. 869; *Thomas* v. *Nottingham Incorporated Football Club Ltd.* [1972] Ch. 596, explaining *Ascherson* v. *Tredegar Dry Dock and Wharf Co. Ltd., supra.*
[32] *Re Anderson-Berry* [1928] Ch. 290.
[33] *Watt* v. *Mortlock* [1964] Ch. 84.
[34] *Padwick* v. *Stanley* (1852) 9 Hare 627; *Morrison* v. *Barking Chemicals Co. Ltd.* [1919] 2 Ch. 325 (fluctuating overdraft).
[35] *Bradford* v. *Gammon* [1925] Ch. 132, as explained in *Tate* v. *Crewdson, supra,* at p. 880 and *Thomas* v. *Nottingham Incorporated Football Club Ltd., supra.*
[36] *Watt* v. *Mortlock, supra.*

indemnity from the principal debtor in respect of sums paid under the guarantee after the surety's death.[37]

B. After Payment

A surety who pays the debt in accordance with his guarantee has—

(i)   a right to be indemnified by the principal debtor;

(ii) a right to take over any securities held by the creditor;

(iii) a right of contribution from co-sureties; and

(iv) a right to share in any securities which a co-surety may have.

These rights will be considered in turn.

1. Indemnity by debtor.   A surety who pays the debt is acting under the implied authority of the debtor; the law therefore implies a contract by the debtor to repay the money.[38] This is so even if the creditor could not have compelled the surety to pay because, *e.g.* the debt was unenforceable by reason of the absence of the requisite memorandum in writing.[39] The right of indemnity extends not only to any sums properly paid to the creditor, but also to 4 per cent. interest on such sums (and probably nowadays to a higher rate of interest)[40] and to any costs reasonably incurred by the surety in resisting the creditor's claims.[41] But if the surety discharges the obligation for less than its full amount, he can claim only this lesser sum from the principal debtor.[42]

2. Delivery of securities held by creditor

(a) *The right.*   If a surety pays the debt, and the creditor has taken a security for it from the principal debtor himself (and not from a stranger[43]), the surety is entitled to the benefit of the security. This right of subrogation is independent of contract, and extends to securities of which the surety had no knowledge at the time when he guaranteed the debt, and even to securities which were taken by the creditor after the

---

[37] *Re Mitchell, Freelove* v. *Mitchell* [1913] 1 Ch. 201. Nor could the surety's executor exercise his rights of retainer (now abolished: *ante*, p. 331) until he had paid the debt: *Re Beavan* [1913] 2 Ch. 595.
[38] *Toussaint* v. *Martinnant* (1787) 2 T.R. 100; *Anson* v. *Anson* [1953] 1 W.L.R. 573 at 576–579.
[39] *Alexander* v. *Vane* (1836) 1 M. & W. 511 (Statute of Frauds 1677, s.4); *Re Chetwynd's Estate* [1938] Ch. 13 (Moneylenders Act 1927, s.6: see *post*, p. 560).
[40] *Re Watson, Turner* v. *Watson* [1896] 1 Ch. 925. See *ante*, pp. 392 and 447, as to interest on mortgages.
[41] *Hornby* v. *Cardwell* (1878) 8 Q.B.D. 329.
[42] *Reed* v. *Norris* (1837) 2 My. & Cr. 361 at 375.
[43] *Chatterton* v. *Maclean* [1951] 1 All E.R. 761 at 766, 767.

date of the guarantee.[44] A surety for a limited amount of a debt is
entitled to a rateable proportion of securities held for the whole debt.[45]

(b) *Assignment.*   Formerly this right did not apply to such securities
as were extinguished by payment of the debt, *e.g.* bonds.[46] But since the
Mercantile Law Amendment Act 1856[47] a surety who pays the debt has
been entitled to have assigned to him every judgment, specialty or other
security which is held by the creditor in respect of the debt, whether or
not at law it is deemed to have been satisfied by the payment; and he is
entitled to stand in the place of the creditor and to use all his remedies
in order to obtain indemnification from the principal debtor, or
contribution from any co-surety, for the advances made and loss
sustained by him. In fact, after payment of the debt, the Act operates as
an implied assignment of the securities,[48] and places the surety in the
position previously occupied by the creditor. Thus if the creditor is a
specialty creditor, the surety becomes a specialty creditor likewise, and
if the creditor is the Crown, the surety has the Crown's priority, if
any.[49] The indorser of a bill of exchange who pays the bill on its
dishonour by the acceptor is in the position of a surety for the acceptor
and so comes within the Act.[50]

3. Contribution by co-sureties.   Where there are two or more sureties
for the same debt, and one of them pays the whole debt or more than
his proportion of it, he has a right to contribution from his co-surety or
co-sureties if he cannot obtain indemnity from the principal debtor.

(a) *Right independent of contract.*   This right of contribution "is
bottomed and fixed on general principles of justice, and does not spring
from contract; though contract may qualify it."[51] As it is independent of
contract, the doctrine of contribution applies whether the parties are
bound in the same instrument or in different instruments, provided they
are both sureties for the same principal and for the same debt. It is
immaterial that they are ignorant of the mutual relation of suretyship,
nor does it matter whether they are bound in the same sum or in
different sums, except that if each is surety for an equal amount all must
contribute equally, whereas if they are responsible for unequal amounts,
each must contribute proportionately up to the amount for which he is
surety.[52] And the surety must pay his full share to a co-surety who has

---

[44] *Mayhew* v. *Crickett* (1818) 2 Swans. 185; *Newton* v. *Chorlton* (1853) 10 Hare 646; *Forbes* v. *Jackson*
(1882) 19 Ch.D. 615 at 621.
[45] *Goodwin* v. *Gray* (1874) 22 W.R. 312.
[46] *Copis* v. *Middleton* (1823) T. & R. 224 at 229.
[47] s.5.
[48] *Re M'Myn* (1886) 33 Ch.D. 575.
[49] *Re Lord Churchill, Manisty* v. *Churchill* (1888) 39 Ch.D. 174; and see *Re Lamplugh Iron Ore Co.
Ltd.* [1927] 1 Ch. 308.
[50] *Duncan, Fox & Co.* v. *North and South Wales Bank* (1880) 6 App.Cas. 1.
[51] *Dering* v. *Earl of Winchelsea* (1787) 1 Cox Eq. 318 at 321, *per* Eyre C.B.; **2. W. & T.L.C. 488 at
490**; and see *Craythorne* v. *Swinburne* (1807) 14 Ves. 160 at 169; *Whitham* v. *Bullock* [1939] 2 K.B.
81 at 87.
[52] *Dering* v. *Earl of Winchelsea, supra; Craythorne* v. *Swinburne, supra; Pendlebury* v. *Walker* (1841) 4
Y. & C.Ex. 424 at 441; *Ellesmere Brewery Co.* v. *Cooper* [1896] 1 Q.B. 75.

paid the whole debt even if there is a counterclaim which the debtor might set up against the creditor.[53]

(b) *Modification of right by contract.* Although the right of contribution does not arise out of contract, it may be modified by contract. For instance, three persons became sureties and agreed among themselves that if the principal debtor failed to pay the debt, they should pay only their respective parts. Afterwards one of the three went bankrupt, and when one of the other two paid the whole debt, he was held entitled to recover only one-third from the solvent co-surety.[54] At common law the result would have been the same even if there had been no express contract that each surety should be liable only for his third; but in equity, in the absence of any contrary agreement, the surety who paid the whole debt could have recovered half of it from the solvent co-surety. The rule in equity is that "those who *can* pay must not only contribute their own shares, but they must also make good the shares of those who are unable to furnish their own contribution"; and since the Judicature Acts the rule of equity has prevailed.[55]

(c) *When right arises.* No action for contribution could be brought at law until the surety had actually paid more than his proportion of the debt. In equity, however, even before payment it has always been possible for a surety to bring an action in the nature of *quia timet* against his co-sureties if judgment has been obtained against him by the creditor for more than his proportion, or perhaps if he is merely threatened by the creditor with an action for more than his proportion.[56] Where the debt is payable by instalments, a surety who pays the whole of one instalment is not entitled to contribution if the amount of the instalment is less than his proportion of the whole debt.[57]

(d) *Running of time.* The Limitation Act 1980 begins to run against the right of contribution from the time when the surety pays more than his proportion of the debt, or possibly from the time when his liability to do so is ascertained.[58]

(e) *Joining of debtor.* In an action for contribution brought by a surety against his co-sureties, the principal debtor must be joined as defendant unless there is good reason for not doing so, *e.g.* if he is insolvent. This insolvency need not be proved strictly but may be inferred by the court from the facts of the case.[59]

---

[53] *Wilson* v. *Mitchell* [1939] 2 K.B. 869.
[54] *Swain* v. *Wall* (1642) 1 Rep.Ch. 149.
[55] *Lowe & Sons* v. *Dixon & Sons* (1885) 16 Q.B.D. 455 at 458, *per* Lopes J.; see *ante*, p. 16.
[56] *Wolmershausen* v. *Gullick* [1893] 2 Ch. 514.
[57] *Stirling* v. *Burdett* [1911] 2 Ch. 418.
[58] *Wolmershausen* v. *Gullick, supra; Robinson* v. *Harkin* [1896] 2 Ch. 415. (Limitation Act 1980, s.10, applies only to claims for contribution in respect of *damage* under the Civil Liability (Contribution) Act 1978: see *ante*, p. 297).
[59] *Hay* v. *Carter* [1935] Ch. 397.

(f) *Other cases of contribution.* The doctrine of contribution is not confined to co-sureties. As already explained,[60] there is in most cases contribution between two trustees who are both liable for the same breach of trust, and also between two directors who are both guilty of a breach of their duty.[61] There is now a statutory right of contribution where two or more persons are liable in respect of the same *damage*, whatever the legal basis of the liability "whether tort, breach of contract, breach of trust or otherwise."[62] In such cases the court fixes the amount of the contribution at such figure as it considers just and equitable having regard to the extent of the contributor's liability for the damage in question.[63] Cases of *debt* differ, first, in that the amount of the contribution does not lie in the discretion of the court, but is fixed in accordance with long-established rules of equity; and, secondly, in that there can be no contribution if the parties are not liable to a common demand. Thus where A is the assignee of part of the land comprised in a lease, and B is an underlessee of the rest of the land at a proportionate rent, if A pays the whole of the rent to the lessor under a threat of distress, A is not entitled to contribution from B, for B is only an underlessee and so is not liable to pay the rent to the lessor.[64]

4. Hotchpot of securities. If a surety obtains from the principal debtor a counter-security for the liability he has undertaken, he is bound to bring whatever he receives from that source into hotchpot for the benefit of his co-sureties. This is so even if he consented to be a surety only upon the terms of having such counter-security, and even if the co-sureties were ignorant of the agreement for such counter-security when they entered into the contract of suretyship.[65] But the creditor is not entitled to the benefit of the counter-security.[66]

Section 5. Discharge of Surety

Although suretyship is not in its inception a contract *uberrimae fidei*,[67] yet once the contract has been entered into the creditor must observe the utmost good faith towards the surety. Any dealings behind the surety's back, either between the creditor and the principal debtor or between the creditor and a co-surety, which have the effect of varying the liability of a surety or of prejudicing the exercise of his rights, will not only discharge him personally from liability, either wholly or

---

[60] *Ante*, p. 296.
[61] *Ramskill* v. *Edwards* (1885) 31 Ch.D. 100.
[62] Civil Liability (Contribution) Act 1978, ss.1(1), 6(1).
[63] *Ibid.* s.2(1).
[64] *Johnson* v. *Wild* (1890) 44 Ch.D. 146; and see *Smith* v. *Cock* [1911] A.C. 317.
[65] *Steel* v. *Dixon* (1881) 17 Ch.D. 825; *Berridge* v. *Berridge* (1890) 44 Ch.D. 168.
[66] *Re Walker, Sheffield Banking Co.* v. *Clayton* [1892] 1 Ch. 621.
[67] See, *ante*, p. 470.

partly,[68] but also free any property which he has mortgaged or pledged as security for the debt.[69]

1. Unauthorised variation of terms.   It is a general principle that a surety will be released from liability if without his assent the creditor varies the contract between himself and the principal debtor, *e.g.* by increasing the rate of interest,[70] or interferes with the rights of the surety against the principal debtor.[71] Thus, where S as surety gave a promissory note to C upon an agreement that the amount should be advanced to D by draft at three months' date, and without S's concurrence C paid the amount at once, it was held that the agreement had been varied and S thereby discharged.[72] Again, where S guaranteed the overdraft on D's bank account up to a stated sum, he was held to have been released by the bank permitting D to open and operate other accounts into which D made payments.[73] And a surety for payment of calls on shares was held to be discharged by the company forfeiting the shares, because under the articles forfeiture gave rise to a new and more onerous liability in respect of the unpaid calls, and also because the forfeiture deprived the surety of the lien he would have had on the shares if the company had instead compelled him to pay the call.[74] But there is no unauthorised variation merely because the creditor accepts the debtor's repudiation of his contract, and so the surety remains liable for the consequential damage.[75]

2. Unauthorised extension of time to debtor.   If, without the consent of the surety, the creditor enters into a binding agreement with the principal debtor to allow him further time for payment, he thereby discharges the surety.[76] The reason given for the rule is that by giving time to the principal debtor the creditor temporarily puts it out of the power of the surety to call upon the debtor to pay off the debt, or to pay it off himself and recover the amount from the debtor, and so the surety's position is altered to his detriment without his consent.[77] But it seems that an agreement by a *surety* to give time to the principal debtor will not discharge a co-surety.[78]

---

[68] *Bolton* v. *Buckenham* [1891] 1 Q.B. 278; *Re Wolmershausen* (1890) 62 L.T. 541.
[69] *Bolton* v. *Salmon* [1891] 2 Ch. 48; *Smith* v. *Wood* [1929] 1 Ch. 14.
[70] *Burnes* v. *Trade Credits Ltd.* [1981] 1 W.L.R. 805.
[71] *Polak* v. *Everett* (1876) 1 Q.B.D. 669 at 677; *Holme* v. *Brunskill* (1878) 3 Q.B.D. 495; *Bolton* v. *Salmon* [1891] 2 Ch. 48; *Smith* v. *Wood* [1929] 1 Ch. 14.
[72] *Bonser* v. *Cox* (1844) 13 L.J.Ch. 260; and see *Re Darwen and Pearce* [1927] 1 Ch. 176.
[73] *National Bank of Nigeria Ltd.* v. *Awolesi* [1964] 1 W.L.R. 1311.
[74] *Re Darwen and Pearce, supra*; and see *Guy-Pell* v. *Foster* [1930] 2 Ch. 169.
[75] *Moschi* v. *Lep Air Services Ltd.* [1973] A.C. 331.
[76] *Rees* v. *Berrington* (1795) 2 Ves.Jun. 540; **2 W. & T.L.C. 521**.
[77] *Samuell* v. *Howarth* (1817) 3 Mer. 272; *Polak* v. *Everett* (1876) 1 Q.B.D. 669 at 673, 677; *Petty* v. *Cooke* (1871) L.R. 6 Q.B. 790 at 795; *Rouse* v. *Bradford Banking Co.* [1894] 2 Ch. 32 at 75; on appeal [1894] A.C. 586.
[78] *Greenwood* v. *Francis* [1899] 1 Q.B. 312.

(a) *Binding arrangement requisite.* Mere inactivity on the part of the creditor is not sufficient to discharge the surety, nor is a merely voluntary promise to give further time. There must be a binding contract made with the debtor and not a third person, *e.g.* a co-surety.[79]

(b) *Reservation of creditor's rights.* Even if there is a binding arrangement to give the debtor further time for payment, the surety will not be discharged if in giving further time to the debtor the creditor reserves his right to proceed against the surety; for then there is no interference with the surety's right of indemnity.[80] "The principal debtor cannot say it is inconsistent with giving him time that the creditor should be at liberty to proceed against the sureties, and that they should turn round upon the principal debtor, notwithstanding the time so given him; for he was a party to the agreement by which that right was reserved to the creditor, and the question whether or not the surety is informed of the arrangement is wholly immaterial."[81]

(c) *Exceptions from rule*

(1) AGREEMENT. If the creditor gives time to the principal debtor, this naturally does not discharge the surety if it is expressly or impliedly authorised by the original agreement.[82]

(2) AFTER JUDGMENT. If the creditor obtains judgment against the surety,[83] or against the surety and the principal debtor together,[84] he will not discharge the surety if he subsequently gives time to the principal debtor. For the surety's original liability as surety is merged in the judgment debt, and he is now liable as judgment debtor and not as surety.

(3) DISTINCT DEBTS. Where the surety is liable for several distinct debts, the giving of time in respect of one of them does not free him from liability with regard to the rest. Thus, where there was a contract for the sale of goods to be delivered and paid for monthly, and the surety bound himself in respect of each monthly payment, the act of the creditor in giving the debtor time for the first instalment without the surety's assent was held to discharge the surety as to that instalment only, for the contract was separable.[85] But where a surety bound himself in respect of monthly repayments due under a hire-purchase agreement, it was held that he was entirely discharged by the giving of time without

---

[79] *Clarke* v. *Birley* (1889) 41 Ch.D. 422.
[80] *Cole* v. *Lynn* [1942] 1 K.B. 142.
[81] *Webb* v. *Hewitt* (1857) 3 K. & J. 438 at 442, *per* Page Wood V.-C.; *Boultbee* v. *Stubbs* (1810) 18 Ves. 20 at 26.
[82] See *Midland Counties Motor Finance Co. Ltd.* v. *Slade* [1951] 1 K.B. 346, where, however, the terms of the agreement were not complied with. Contrast *Burnes* v. *Trade Credits Ltd.* [1981] 1 W.L.R. 805 (extension of time coupled with increased rate of interest: surety discharged).
[83] *Jenkins* v. *Robertson* (1854) 2 Drew. 351.
[84] *Re a Debtor* [1913] 3 K.B. 11.
[85] *Croydon Commercial Gas Co.* v. *Dickinson* (1876) 2 C.P.D. 46.

his assent for the payment of one instalment, for the hire-purchase agreement was one and indivisible.[86]

3. Release of debtor

(a) *Express release.* A surety will be discharged by the creditor absolutely releasing the principal debtor from his liability, even if the creditor at the same time reserves his rights against the surety; for the release puts an end to the debt, and no one can be surety for a debt which does not exist.[87] Moreover, if the surety were not released in such a case, the release of the principal debtor would not be effectual, for on being sued by the creditor the surety might obtain reimbursement from the principal debtor. If, however, the suretyship agreement provides for a continuance of the surety's liability after the debt has been released, he will still be liable.[88] The same is true if the creditor has merely covenanted not to sue the principal debtor and has reserved his rights against the surety; and what purports to be a release may be construed as a covenant not to sue,[89] unless on the face of the instrument it is obviously intended as an absolute release.[90]

(b) *Composition with creditors.* If a creditor accepts a composition by the principal debtor with his creditors made voluntarily outside the bankruptcy laws, this discharges the surety unless the composition deed reserves the creditor's remedies against the surety.[91] But if the debtor is made bankrupt and the composition is effected under the bankruptcy laws,[92] or the debtor obtains his discharge,[93] the surety is not discharged, for the release of the principal debtor is brought about by operation of law and not by the act of the creditor, and the debtor is protected by the statute from any liability to the surety.[94]

(c) *Disclaimer of lease.* Where a person has guaranteed the payment of rent during the term of a lease, he is discharged as to future rent by the lessee's trustee in bankruptcy disclaiming the lease; for the disclaimer puts an end to the term, and thereafter there is thus no more rent due from the lessee.[95] Careful wording of the contract of suretyship could, however, prevent the discharge of the surety; for the contract may continue the surety's liability even after the principal debtor has ceased to be liable. For instance, where S guaranteed the regular

---

[86] *Midland Motor Showrooms Ltd.* v. *Newman* [1929] 2 K.B. 256.
[87] *Commercial Bank of Tasmania* v. *Jones* [1893] A.C. 313; *ante*, pp. 469, 470.
[88] *Cowper* v. *Smith* (1838) 4 M. & W. 519; *Perry* v. *National Provincial Bank of England* [1910] 1 Ch. 464.
[89] *Green* v. *Wynn* (1869) 4 Ch.App. 204.
[90] *Mercantile Bank of Sydney* v. *Taylor* [1893] A.C. 317.
[91] *Ex p. Smith* (1789) 3 Bro.C.C. 1; *Bateson* v. *Gosling* (1871) L.R. 7 C.P. 9; *Cragoe* v. *Jones* (1873) L.R. 8 Ex. 81.
[92] Insolvency Act 1986, Pt. VIII.
[93] *Ibid.* s.281(7).
[94] See *Ex p. Jacobs* (1875) 10 Ch.App. 211 at 214.
[95] *Stacey* v. *Hill* [1901] 1 K.B. 660; *Morris & Sons Ltd.* v. *Jeffreys* (1932) 148 L.T. 56.

payment of interest on debentures issued by a company until the company should repay the principal sum secured by the debentures, it was held that S was liable to pay the interest even after the company's dissolution, for the principal sum had not been repaid[96]; but where the contract was to pay the interest so long as the principal remained due, the company's dissolution discharged the surety from liability for future interest, because the principal was no longer due.[97]

(d) *Effect of limitation.*   A surety is not discharged by reason of the creditor's remedy against the principal debtor becoming statute-barred, provided that the remedy against the surety himself is not also statute-barred.[98]

4. Release of co-surety by creditor

(a) *Release.*   If a creditor absolutely releases one of two sureties who are liable jointly, or jointly and severally, the other surety is discharged, even though the release was given under a mistake of law; for the release of one joint debtor discharges all.[99] This is a legal rule which has no application where the sureties are liable severally and not jointly; but even in that case, an absolute release of one surety will, on equitable principles, discharge the other to the extent of the contribution which he could have claimed if there had been no release, and of which he is deprived by the release.[1]

(b) *Covenant not to sue.*   A mere covenant not to sue one of the sureties does not, however, discharge the other either at law or in equity; and an instrument purporting to release one surety but to reserve the creditor's remedies against the other may be construed as a covenant not to sue.[2] Yet where there is an absolute written release of one surety, parol evidence will not be admitted to show that it was intended to reserve the remedies against another surety.[3]

5. Loss of securities

(a) *Complete discharge.*   A creditor is under no general obligation to a surety to enforce securities taken from the principal debtor at any particular time or at all.[4] But where the surety executes the guarantee on the footing that the creditor will take certain securities from the

---

[96] *Re FitzGeorge* [1905] 1 K.B. 462.
[97] *Re Moss, ex p. Hallet* [1905] 2 K.B. 307.
[98] *Carter* v. *White* (1883) 25 Ch.D. 666 at 672.
[99] *Nicholson* v. *Revill* (1836) 4 A. & E. 675.
[1] *Ward* v. *National Bank of New Zealand* (1883) 8 App.Cas. 755; and see *Smith* v. *Wood* [1929] 1 Ch. 14.
[2] *Price* v. *Barker* (1855) 4 E. & B. 760 at 777.
[3] *Mercantile Bank of Sydney* v. *Taylor* [1893] A.C. 317.
[4] *China and South Sea Bank Ltd.* v. *Tan Soon Gin* [1990] A.C. 536.

principal debtor, or that there will be other sureties, the surety will be completely released if the securities are not duly taken and retained,[5] or if the other sureties do not execute the guarantee,[6] or they limit their liability under it[7]; for the contract to which he agreed has been varied.[8]

(b) *Discharge pro tanto.*   Even where there is no such variation, the surety may be discharged by the creditor depriving him of the right which he has to all the securities when he pays the debt.[9] Thus he will be discharged if the creditor loses the securities, or suffers them to get back into the possession of the debtor, or applies them to another debt,[10] or fails to make them effectual by giving any necessary notice[11] or effecting any necessary registration[12]; but in this case the discharge is not complete but only *pro tanto, i.e.* to the extent of the securities lost but no further.[13]

---

[5] *Polak* v. *Everett* (1876) 1 Q.B.D. 669; *Smith* v. *Wood* [1929] 1 Ch. 14.
[6] *Evans* v. *Bemridge* (1856) 8 De G.M. & G. 100; *Graham (James) and Co. (Timber) Ltd.* v. *Southgate-Sands* [1986] Q.B. 80 (forgery of co-surety's signature).
[7] *Ellesmere Brewery Co.* v. *Cooper* [1896] 1 Q.B. 75.
[8] See *Taylor* v. *Bank of New South Wales* (1886) 11 App.Cas. 596 at 603.
[9] See *ante*, p. 474.
[10] *Pearl* v. *Deacon* (1857) 1 De G. & J. 461.
[11] *Strange* v. *Fooks* (1863) 4 Giff. 408 (an assignment of a thing in action).
[12] *Wulff* v. *Jay* (1872) L.R. 7 Q.B. 756 (a bill of sale).
[13] *Taylor* v. *Bank of New South Wales* (1886) 11 App.Cas. 596 at 602, 603.

Part V

THE EQUITABLE DOCTRINES

THERE are five ancient equitable doctrines: conversion, reconversion, election, performance, and satisfaction. These doctrines operate not so much by way of creating substantive rights of property as by way of modifying existing rights of property in the interests of justice and equity. They will be examined in turn.

CHAPTER 1

CONVERSION

PART 1

THE DOCTRINE

1. Definition

(a) *Actual and notional conversion.* If land is sold, there is forthwith an actual conversion of the land into money; and similarly if land is purchased, there is an actual conversion of money into land. However, the rights of those respectively entitled to realty and personalty ought not to depend upon the precise moment at which a duty to convert is carried out,[1] and so in equity, on the principle that "equity looks on that as done which ought to be done,"[2] there is a notional conversion as soon as there is a binding obligation to convert.[3] Subject to the context, the word "conversion" by itself usually means notional conversion.[4]

(b) *The rule.* As Sir Thomas Sewell M.R. said in the leading case of *Fletcher* v. *Ashburner*,[5] nothing is better established than that "money directed to be employed in the purchase of land, and land directed to be sold and turned into money, are to be considered as that species of property into which they are directed to be converted; and this in whatever manner the direction is given; whether by will, by way of contract, marriage articles, settlement, or otherwise, and whether the money is actually deposited, or only covenanted to be paid, whether the land is actually conveyed or only agreed to be conveyed. The owner of the fund or the contracting parties may make land money, or money land." The rule, observed Sir Joseph Jekyll M.R., is so powerful "as to alter the very nature of things; to make money land, and on the contrary, to turn land into money."[6] But, said Sir George Jessel M.R.,

---

[1] See, *e.g. Re Richerson* [1892] 1 Ch. 379 at 383.
[2] *Ante*, p. 40.
[3] See performance (*post*, p. 513) for a similar distinction between the actual and the notional.
[4] For an historical survey of the precise scope of the doctrine, see Stuart Anderson (1984) 100 L.Q.R. 86.
[5] (1779) 1 Bro.C.C. 497 at 499; **1 W. & T.L.C. 293 at 295.**
[6] *Lechmere* v. *Earl of Carlisle* (1733) 3 P.Wms. 211 at 215, affirmed *sub nom. Lechmere* v. *Lady Lechmere* (1735) Cas.*t.*Talb. 80.

485

"He does not mean to say that the rule turns sovereigns into acres, or *vice versa*. What he means is that it works a conversion for the purpose of devolution."[7]

2. Importance of conversion. On an intestacy before 1926, realty devolved on the heir and personalty on the statutory next-of-kin, whereas after 1925 both realty and personalty devolve together.[8] The doctrine of conversion has thus lost some of its importance; but testators still sometimes dispose differently of their realty and their personalty, and this is not affected by the legislation of 1925. Conversion is also of importance in determining the incidence of inheritance tax on the death of the owner of an undivided share in land.[9]

3. Statutory references to land. Notwithstanding the doctrine of conversion, the courts have sometimes held that references to interests in land[10] in certain statutes extended to interests in the proceeds of sale. These are mostly obsolete,[11] but a person interested in the proceeds of sale of land is sufficiently "interested in land"[12] to be entitled to protect his interest by a caution at the Land Registry.[13] A purported charge of land executed by one of two joint owners may operate as a charge of his share of the proceeds of sale, on the basis that such share is an "interest in land."[14] It has been suggested that a contract for sale of land includes a contract for the sale of an interest in the proceeds of sale of land and so required to be evidenced in writing.[15] The modern tendency, however, in drafting statutes is to deal expressly with interests in the proceeds of sale of land.[16] The power of the court to impose a charge on the land of a judgment debtor to secure payment of a judgment debt now extends to interests in the proceeds of sale of land[17]; and the

---

[7] *Chandler* v. *Pocock* (1880) 15 Ch.D. 491 at 496 (affirmed 16 Ch.D. 648).

[8] A.E.A. 1925, ss.33, 45 *et seq.*

[9] *Post*, p. 490.

[10] In *Re Thomas, Thomas* v. *Howell* (1886) 34 Ch.D. 166 at 171, 172, Kay J. distinguished between estates and interests in land, holding that the latter comprehended interests in the proceeds of sale of land.

[11] *e.g.* Charitable Uses Act 1735, s.3 (*Brook* v. *Badley* (1868) 3 Ch.App. 672); Real Property Limitation Act 1833, s.1 (*Re Fox, Brooks* v. *Marston* [1913] 2 Ch. 75; and see *Re Witham* [1922] 2 Ch. 413); Fines and Recoveries Act 1833, s.77 (*Tuer* v. *Turner* (1855) 20 Beav. 560); Dower Act 1833, s.9 (*Re Thomas, Thomas* v. *Howell* (1886) 34 Ch.D. 166); Intestates' Estates Act 1884, ss.4, 7 (*Re Wood, Att.-Gen.* v. *Anderson* [1896] 2 Ch. 596). Contrast Yorkshire Registries Act 1884, s.4 (*Gresham Life Assurance Society* v. *Crowther* [1915] 1 Ch. 214, affirming [1914] 2 Ch. 219).

[12] Within the L.R.A. 1925, s.54(1).

[13] *Elias* v. *Mitchell* [1972] Ch. 652.

[14] The decision to the contrary in *Cedar Holdings Ltd.* v. *Green* [1981] Ch. 129 (as to which see [1979] C.L.J. 251–254 (M. J. Prichard)) was overruled in *Williams & Glyn's Bank Ltd.* v. *Boland* [1981] A.C. 487 at 507. See *Thames Guaranty Ltd.* v. *Campbell* [1985] Q.B. 210 at 236–239.

[15] *Cooper* v. *Critchley* [1955] Ch. 431; see (1955) 71 L.Q.R. 178, 179. Contrast *Re Rayleigh Weir Stadium* [1954] 1 W.L.R. 786 (such a contract not registrable as a land charge).

[16] *e.g.* A.E.A. 1925, s.3(1)(ii); Limitation Act 1980, ss.20(1), 38(1).

[17] Charging Orders Act 1979, ss.1 and 2; *National Westminster Bank Ltd.* v. *Stockman* [1981] 1 W.L.R. 67. For decisions on earlier provisions see *Irani Finance Ltd.* v. *Singh* [1971] Ch. 59 (Administration of Justice Act 1956, s.35) and *Stevens* v. *Hutchinson* [1953] Ch. 299 (L.P.A. 1925, s.195). See also A.E.A. 1925, s.51(2); *Re Donkin* [1948] Ch. 74; and contrast *Re Bradshaw* [1950] Ch. 582. *Cf. Edwards* v. *Hall* [1949] 1 All E.R. 352.

person who has obtained a charging order on the beneficial interest of one co-owner is sufficiently "interested" to apply for an order for sale of the land,[18] and the other co-owner is likewise "interested" so as to have a *locus standi* to apply for a discharge or variation of the charging orders.[19] But the charging order itself is not registrable under the Land Charges Act 1972[20]; and a charge imposed on the purchase moneys of land cannot be registered as a general equitable charge on the land itself.[21]

PART 2

CASES OF CONVERSION

There are six cases in which realty is treated in equity as personalty, or *vice versa*.

Section 1. Under an Express Trust

The commonest cause of a conversion is a direction given by a testator or settlor. Whenever trustees are directed to sell or to purchase realty, and there is some person who can insist upon their doing what they are directed to do, the property is treated as converted from the moment when the instrument comes into force. No failure by the trustees to carry out their duty can alter the character of the property.

1. Imperative direction. In order to effect a conversion, the direction must be imperative; for if conversion be merely optional, the property will be considered as real or personal, according to the actual condition in which it is found. For instance, the mere insertion of a power of sale in a mortgage will not effect a conversion, for there is no intention to convert at once. Accordingly, if in such a case a sale takes place after the mortgagor's death, any surplus proceeds will be treated as realty,[22] whereas if the sale is made before the mortgagor's death, the proceeds will pass as part of his personal estate.[23] No conversion will occur until there is an actual conversion by the exercise of the power of sale.[24] Again, where a testator gave £5,000 to a trustee in trust to lay it out in the purchase of land or to put it out on good securities for the separate use of his daughter D, and D died after the testator but before the

---

[18] *Midland Bank plc* v. *Pike* [1988] 2 All E.R. 434 (L.P.A. 1925, s.30).
[19] *Harman* v. *Glencross* [1986] Fam. 81.
[20] *Perry* v. *Phoenix Assurance plc* [1988] 1 W.L.R. 940, not following *Harman* v. *Glencross* [1985] Fam. 49.
[21] *Georgiades* v. *Edward Wolfe & Co. Ltd.* [1965] Ch. 487. For general equitable charges, see *ante*, p. 60.
[22] *Bourne* v. *Bourne* (1842) 2 Hare 35; *Wright* v. *Rose* (1825) 2 Sim. & St. 323.
[23] *Re Grange* [1907] 2 Ch. 20.
[24] *Re Bird, Pitman* v. *Pitman* [1892] 1 Ch. 279; *Re Dyson* [1910] 1 Ch. 750.

trustee had actually bought land, it was held that D's administrator was entitled to the money as against D's heir.[25]

2. Uncertain directions. Statute and the courts have resolved a number of instances of uncertain or defective directions, in most cases holding that there is a conversion.

(i) By statute, a trust either to retain or sell land is now to be construed as "a trust to sell the land with power to postpone the sale,"[26] and so produces a conversion.

(ii) If the conversion is apparently optional but the limitations and trusts of the money directed to be laid out either in the purchase of land or in other securities are only adapted to real estate, thereby denoting the settlor's intention that land shall be purchased, the money will be considered as land; for equity looks to the intent rather than the form.[27]

(iii) A discretion given to the trustees merely as to the time at which a sale or purchase shall be made does not prevent a conversion if it is clear that the settlor intended the sale or purchase to be made at some time. In such a case the property is converted from the time when the instrument comes into operation.[28]

(iv) Where there is a direction to sell or purchase *on the request* or *with the consent* of some person, the addition of these words does not by itself prevent the property from being treated as converted immediately.[29] But a trust merely to sell at the request of a person who is empowered to direct the trustees never to sell probably works no conversion.[30]

(v) If for any reason the direction to convert is void, *e.g.* under the rule against perpetuities, there will be no conversion in equity even if there is a conversion in fact.[31]

3. Time of conversion. Subject to the terms of the instrument, conversion under a will takes place from the death of the testator, and conversion under a deed takes effect from the date of execution.[32] This is so even if the trust to sell or purchase is not to arise until some future

[25] *Curling* v. *May* (1734) 3 Atk. 255; and see *Re Newbould* (1913) 110 L.T. 6; *Re Twopeny's Settlement* [1924] 1 Ch. 522.
[26] L.P.A. 1925, s.25(4); as to such trusts in dispositions coming into operation before 1926, see *Re White's Settlement* [1930] 1 Ch. 179; *Re Johnson, Cowley* v. *Public Trustee* [1915] 1 Ch. 435.
[27] *Earlom* v. *Saunders* (1754) Amb. 241.
[28] *Re Raw* (1884) 26 Ch.D. 601.
[29] *Re Goswell's Trusts* [1915] 2 Ch. 106; *Re Ffennell's Settlement* [1918] 1 Ch. 91.
[30] See *Re Goodall's Settlement* [1909] 1 Ch. 440.
[31] *Re Appleby* [1903] 1 Ch. 565.
[32] *Griffith* v. *Ricketts* (1849) 7 Hare 299 at 311.

time, *e.g.* after the settlor's death.[33] But there is no conversion if neither at the date of the deed nor at any subsequent time is there any person who could enforce a sale,[34] and it makes no difference if during that period it was uncertain whether any such person could come into existence.[35]

For example, in a marriage settlement a husband may convey realty to trustees on trust for himself for life, and after his death upon trust to sell and hold the proceeds on certain trusts for his wife and children, with an ultimate trust for himself, his executors, administrators and assigns. On the death of the settlor, the property will be realty if his wife predeceased him without issue, for there is no one, and there never has been anyone, who could enforce the trust for sale.[36] In such cases it may remain unknown for some while whether or not there has been a conversion, though when it has been ascertained that there has been a conversion, the conversion is treated as having taken place when the deed was executed.[37]

Section 2. Under a Statutory Trust

1. Imposition of trust. As part of the reforms of conveyancing under the 1925 legislation, statute imposes a trust for sale in a number of cases where there is no express trust. Four examples may be given:

(i) where two or more persons are entitled to land as joint tenants or tenants in common[38];

(ii) where a person dies intestate[39];

(iii) where trustees lend money on mortgage and the property becomes vested in them free from the right of redemption[40]; and

(iv) where trustees of a settlement of personalty or trustees for sale of land invest the trust funds in the purchase of land.[41]

Such trusts have sometimes produced unexpected results by reason of the doctrine of conversion.

[33] *Clarke* v. *Franklin* (1858) 4 K. & J. 257.
[34] *Re Lord Grimthorpe* [1908] 2 Ch. 675.
[35] See *Re Hopkinson, Dyson* v. *Hopkinson* [1922] 1 Ch. 65.
[36] *Re Lord Grimthorpe, supra.*
[37] See *Re Hopkinson, Dyson* v. *Hopkinson* [1922] 1 Ch. 65 at 74, 75.
[38] L.P.A. 1925, ss.34–36. See Megarry and Wade's *Law of Real Property* (5th ed., 1984), pp. 436 *et seq.*
[39] *Ante,* p. 314.
[40] *Ante,* p. 261.
[41] *Ante,* pp. 260, 261.

2. Effect of statutory trusts. In *Re Kempthorne*,[42] the Court of Appeal held that the statutory trust for sale to which land held in undivided shares is subjected by the Law of Property Act 1925 converts all undivided shares in realty into personal property. In that case a testator made a will in 1911 giving all his "freehold and copyhold property" to R, and all his leasehold property and personal estate to P. He owned certain undivided shares in freehold land, and in 1928 he died. His undivided shares were held to have been converted into personalty on January 1, 1926, so that they passed under the gift to P. The effect would have been the same if the will had been made after the Act had come into force.

This decision was followed by Farwell J. in *Re Newman*.[43] By a will made in 1922, a testator who was entitled to an undivided share in Blackacre devised "all my moiety or equal half part or share and all other my share in" Blackacre to his brother. He died in 1929 without having altered or confirmed his will. The devise to the brother was held to be adeemed by the imposition of the statutory trust for sale; it was a devise of land, and after the statutory trust had converted the land into personalty there was nothing for the devise to operate on. But the devise would have been effective if the will had been made after 1925 or confirmed by a codicil made after that date,[44] even if the codicil merely mentioned the will without expressly confirming it,[45] or if the words of the will could have been construed as showing an intention to give to the devisee whatever interest the testator might have in the land.[46]

For the purpose of determining the incidence of inheritance tax on death, undivided shares in realty are treated as personal property whether the trust for sale is statutory or express.[47]

Section 3. Under a Partnership

Unless a contrary intention appears, land which has become partnership property is treated as personalty and not realty, both as between the partners themselves and their representatives after death, and also as between the persons entitled to the property of a deceased partner.[48] The reason is that upon a dissolution of the partnership, the land will have to be sold for the purpose of division among the partners. After 1925 there will usually be a trust for sale imposed by statute by reason of the beneficial tenancy in common between the partners[49]; but there

---

[42] [1930] 1 Ch. 268, following *Re Price* [1928] Ch. 579. *Cf. Edwards* v. *Hall* [1949] 1 All E.R. 352.
[43] [1930] 2 Ch. 409.
[44] *Re Warren* [1932] 1 Ch. 42; and see *Drant* v. *Vause* (1842) 1 Y. & C.C.C. 580, and *Emuss* v. *Smith* (1848) 2 De G. & Sm. 722; *post*, p. 493.
[45] *Re Harvey, Public Trustee* v. *Hosken* [1947] Ch. 285. But see *Re Galway's W.T.* [1950] Ch. 1.
[46] *Re Mellish* (1927) [1929] 2 K.B. 82n. ("all my share and interest in ... ").
[47] See Capital Transfer Tax Act 1984, s.237(3); *Dymond's Capital Taxes*, para. 28.905. The position under estate duty law was otherwise: see Dymond's *Death Duties* (15th ed., 1973), p. 964.
[48] Partnership Act 1890, s.22.
[49] *Ante*, p. 489.

may still be cases where there will be conversion under the present head, *e.g.* where partners contract to purchase land.

Section 4. Under an Order of Court

1. The order. Conversion may occur by reason of an order of the court. If the court, acting within its jurisdiction, orders a sale of realty in which two or more persons are interested, and one dies before the sale takes place, his interest is part of his personalty and not of his realty. The conversion here takes effect not from the date of the sale but from the date of the order[50]; and it is immaterial that the sale was ordered for some particular purpose which will not exhaust the whole of the proceeds, *e.g.* for the payment of costs.[51]

2. Conversion. Where the property has been sold in pursuance of the order, there is, of course, an actual conversion; but this is immaterial, for there is no difference whether the realty is sold or merely ordered to be sold. In each case the realty is treated as personalty, unless the person entitled to the realty has some equity to have the property converted back to its original character. Such an equity may arise from the order of the court itself, for when the court orders a sale or purchase of realty, it has power to provide that the change in the nature of the property shall not affect its devolution on death[52]; or it may arise from the provision of some statute.[53]

Section 5. Under a Contract

The fifth case of conversion arises under a contract for the sale or purchase of realty.[54]

1. Contract for sale or purchase. Whenever there is a specifically enforceable contract to sell realty (including a notional contract imposed by statute[55]) the realty is treated as part of the vendor's personalty from the moment when the contract is made (or, in the case of a conditional contract, when the condition is fulfilled, even if this occurs after the vendor's death[56]); the vendor's remaining rights in the land are all

---

[50] *Fauntleroy* v. *Beebe* [1911] 2 Ch. 257; *Hyett* v. *Mekin* (1884) 25 Ch.D. 735; *Re Dodson* [1908] 2 Ch. 638.
[51] *Burgess* v. *Booth* [1908] 2 Ch. 648; *Steed* v. *Preece* (1874) L.R. 18 Eq. 192.
[52] *Att.-Gen.* v. *Marquis of Ailesbury* (1887) 2 App.Cas. 672; *Re Searle, Ryder* v. *Bond* [1912] 2 Ch. 365.
[53] *e.g.* Mental Health Act 1983, s.101.
[54] See generally P. H. Pettit (1960) 24 Conv.(N.S.) 47.
[55] *Re Hatfeild* (1944) 88 S.J. 289; *Re Galway's W.T.* [1950] Ch. 1 (Coal Act 1938).
[56] *Re Sweeting* [1988] 1 All E.R. 1016.

referable to his right to recover and receive the purchase-money.[57] Conversely, if the purchaser dies before completion, his interest is treated as real property, though usually the person who takes it must pay the purchase-money.[58] But a contract does not operate to convert the property unless it is one of which specific performance would be ordered.[59]

2. Notice to treat. A mere notice to treat given by an authority acquiring land under the Compulsory Purchase Act 1965[60] accordingly does not convert the land into personalty, for such a notice does not by itself constitute a contract of which the court would order specific performance.[61] But if the price is afterwards ascertained, whether by agreement, or by determination by the Lands Tribunal,[62] as from that date there is a conversion in equity, for then there is an enforceable contract.[63]

3. Option to purchase. The doctrine of conversion by contract of sale has been extended to cases where there is an option to purchase land. If a testator has granted such an option and it is not exercised until after his death, on principle his interest ought to be treated as realty, for at the moment of his death there was no contract of which specific performance would be ordered. However, in *Lawes* v. *Bennett*[64] it was held that the exercise of the option even after the testator's death retrospectively converts the property into personalty.

(a) *The rule.* In *Lawes* v. *Bennett*[65] L granted a lease for seven years to T and in the lease gave T an option to purchase the reversion for £3,000. L then made a will giving all his realty to R, and all his personalty to P, and soon afterwards T assigned the lease and the benefit of the option to A. L then died, and subsequently A exercised the option. Sir Lloyd Kenyon M.R. held that the £3,000 formed part of L's personal estate and so belonged to P. The principle is that L in his lifetime had give T and his assignee the unilateral power[66] to decide at a future date whether the property should be realty or personalty, so that L and those claiming under his will must take subject to this power and any exercise of it.[67] The effect is much as if the exercise of the option related back to the date when the option was granted.[68]

---

[57] *Hillingdon Estates Co.* v. *Stonefield Estates Ltd.* [1952] Ch. 627 at 632. For the vendor's lien, see *ante*, p. 463.
[58] See *ante*, pp. 338, 339.
[59] *Re Thomas, Thomas* v. *Howell* (1886) 34 Ch.D. 166.
[60] Formerly the Lands Clauses Consolidation Act 1845.
[61] *Haynes* v. *Haynes* (1861) 1 Dr. & Sm. 426.
[62] Land Compensation Act 1961, s.1; Compulsory Purchase Act 1965, s.6.
[63] *Harding* v. *Metropolitan Ry.* (1872) 7 Ch.App. 154.
[64] (1785) 1 Cox Eq. 167.
[65] *Ibid.* The statement of facts has been simplified.
[66] See *Baker* v. *Merckel* [1960] 1 Q.B. 657.
[67] See *Weeding* v. *Weeding* (1861) 1 J. & H. 424 at 430.
[68] See *Re Adams and the Kensington Vestry* (1884) 27 Ch.D. 394 at 399.

(b) *Operation of the rule.* The operation of the rule depends on whether there is a general or residuary devise, or a specific devise.

(1) GENERAL OR RESIDUARY DEVISE. Where, as in *Lawes* v. *Bennett*[69] itself, there is a general or residuary devise, it is immaterial whether the will was made before or after the option was granted. In either case, the conversion relates back to before the testator's death, and so the devise cannot include the property.

(2) SPECIFIC DEVISE. Where, however, there is a specific devise, the operation of the rule depends on the relative dates of the will and the grant of the option. If the will was made before the option was granted, the devise is adeemed by the exercise of the option, just as if the testator had sold the land in his lifetime.[70] But if the will was made[71] or confirmed by codicil[72] after the grant of the option, or substantially contemporaneously with it,[73] the specific devisee is entitled to the proceeds of sale; for the testator will be taken to have been aware of the option and to have intended the devisee to take the property whether it was land or purchase-money.[74] By parity of reasoning, where a testator held land under a voidable conveyance which was avoided after his death, the specific devisee of the land was held entitled to any moneys repayable to the testator's estate when the conveyance was set aside.[75]

(c) *Ambit of the rule.* The doctrine applies equally on intestacy, and even if the option cannot be exercised until after the lessor's death.[76] Further, once the option has been exercised, the mere fact that the purchase is not carried through does not undo the conversion which has taken place.[77] However, the retrospective effect of the doctrine is in effect limited to capital. Until the option is exercised the property remains realty.[78] The intermediate income accordingly belongs to the person who was entitled to the property as realty before the option was exercised, whether as residuary or specific devisee or heir-at-law.[79]

(d) *Practical problems.* The rule creates obvious practical problems. Thus as it gives T the power to decide whether R or P shall benefit, they may find themselves competing for T's favour.[80] Further, L's personal representatives may find that R requires an assent to be made

[69] (1785) 1 Cox Eq. 167.
[70] *Weeding* v. *Weeding* (1861) 1 J. & H. 424.
[71] *Drant* v. *Vause* (1842) 1 Y. & C.C.C. 580; *Re Calow* [1928] Ch. 710; *cf. Re Warren* [1932] 1 Ch. 42, *ante*, p. 490.
[72] *Emuss* v. *Smith* (1848) 2 De G. & Sm. 722.
[73] *Re Pyle* [1895] 1 Ch. 724.
[74] *Re Pyle, supra.*
[75] *Re Sherman* [1954] Ch. 653.
[76] *Re Isaacs, Isaacs* v. *Reginall* [1894] 3 Ch. 506.
[77] *Re Blake, Gawthorne* v. *Blake* [1917] 1 Ch. 18.
[78] *Re Marlay* [1915] 2 Ch. 264.
[79] *Townley* v. *Bedwell* (1808) 14 Ves. 591.
[80] See, however, *Lawes* v. *Bennett* (1785) 1 Cox Eq. 167 at 171.

to him, so that they must then protect themselves against any possible claim by P if the option is later exercised and R does not account to P for the proceeds of the land; probably they should refuse to assent to R unless he provides security for paying P.[81] In any event, T should protect himself by having the option registered as an estate contract.[82]

(e) *Application of the rule.* Although the principle of *Lawes* v. *Bennett*[83] is anomalous, the case has been acted on too long for the Court of Appeal to overrule it. It was applied in *Re Carrington*,[84] where it was held that a specific bequest of shares was adeemed by the exercise after the testator's death of an option to purchase given by him to a third person after the date of his will. But as the principle is recognised as being anomalous, it will not be further extended.[85] Thus it applies only between the persons claiming under the testator, and not between the testator and the holder of the option. Hence if a lessor has insured the demised premises and they are destroyed by fire, a lessee who then exercises an option in the lease to purchase the freehold cannot claim the insurance money as part of his purchase.[86]

Section 6. Preservation of Original State

Occasionally by statute an actual conversion of property does not effect a conversion at law or in equity. Thus by the Settled Land Act 1925[87] capital money arising under the Act is still to be treated as realty for all purposes of disposition, transmission or devolution,[88] though not for fiscal purposes.[89] Again, under the Mental Health Act 1983, where the Court of Protection has disposed of the real property of a mental patient,[90] the property representing it is, so long as it remains part of his estate, to be treated as if it were real property.[91] Similarly, where the court directs a disposal of personal property and the acquisition of real property, the court may direct that the property representing the property disposed of is to be treated as if it were personal property.[92] But "the first thing to ascertain is what is for the benefit of the lunatic,"[93] and where it is for his benefit, the court will make a conversion, whereupon the property will devolve in its converted form;

---

[81] A.E.A. 1925, s.36(10) (*ante*, p. 346) might cover such a case, though its language is hardly appropriate.
[82] See *ante*, p. 59.
[83] (1785) 1 Cox Eq. 167.
[84] [1932] 1 Ch. 1, criticised by H. G. Hanbury at (1933) 49 L.Q.R. 173, but followed in *Re Rose, Midland Bank Executor and Trustee Co. Ltd.* v. *Rose* [1949] Ch. 78. And see *Re Sweeting* [1988] 1 All E.R. 1016 (*ante*, p. 491, n. 56).
[85] See *Edwards* v. *West* (1878) 7 Ch.D. 858 at 863.
[86] *Edwards* v. *West* (1878) 7 Ch.D. 858; and see *Re Adams and the Kensington Vestry* (1884) 27 Ch.D. 394 at 400. Contrast *Reynard* v. *Arnold* (1875) 10 Ch.App. 386.
[87] s.75(5).
[88] See *Re Cartwright* [1939] Ch. 90.
[89] *Earl of Midleton* v. *Baron Cottesloe* [1949] A.C. 418 (estate duty; semble also for inheritance tax).
[90] See *post*, pp. 536, 537.
[91] Mental Health Act 1983, s.101(1); and see *Re E.D.S.* [1914] 1 Ch. 618.
[92] Mental Health Act 1983, s.101(2).
[93] *Re Pink* (1883) 23 Ch.D. 577 at 581, *per* Lindley L.J.; and see Mental Health Act 1983, s.95(2).

for as between those claiming through the patient, there is no equity for a reconversion.[94] Usually, however, the court preserves the original character of the property so as not to interfere with the rights of other persons interested.[95]

PART 3

FAILURE OF CONVERSION

Even if there is an effective direction to convert, there may be a total or partial failure of the objects for which conversion was directed. Only if the failure is partial does it make any difference whether the direction to convert was contained in a deed or in a will.

Section 1. Total Failure

1. No conversion.   There is a *total* failure where the purposes for which the conversion was intended have totally failed before or at the time when the deed or will came into operation, or in the case of a trust to sell at a future time, before the time has arrived at which the duty to convert is to arise.[96] In this event no conversion will take place at all, but the property will remain as it was; for there is no one who can insist on its character being altered.[97]

2. Examples.   Thus, if T devises freehold land to trustees on trust to sell and divide the proceeds between A and B, and they both die in T's lifetime, there is a lapse of the gift to them and the land will belong to T's residuary devisee as realty. Again, there was no conversion where a trust for sale was made exercisable outside the perpetuity period, and so was void for remoteness; the persons entitled to the property (provided they were all ascertainable within the period) took it as realty.[98]

Section 2. Partial Failure

As mentioned above, in the case of partial failure, a distinction must be made between deeds and wills.

[94] *Hartley* v. *Pendarves* [1901] 2 Ch. 498; and see *Re Searle, Ryder* v. *Bond* [1912] 2 Ch. 365; *Re Silva* [1929] 2 Ch. 198.
[95] *Att.-Gen.* v. *Marquis of Ailesbury* (1887) 12 App.Cas. 672; and see *Re Alston* [1917] 2 Ch. 226; *Re Walker, Goodwin* v. *Scott* [1921] 2 Ch. 63; *Re Silva, supra; Re Harding, Westminster Bank Ltd.* v. *Laver* [1934] Ch. 271; *Re Stillwell* [1936] Ch. 637.
[96] *Re Lord Grimthorpe* [1908] 2 Ch. 675; see *ante*, p. 489.
[97] *Smith* v. *Claxton* (1819) 4 Madd. 492.
[98] *Goodier* v. *Edmunds* [1893] 3 Ch. 455; *Re Appleby* [1903] 1 Ch. 565. See now Perpetuities and Accumulations Act 1964, s.8.

A. Deeds

The position is relatively simple where a deed directs a conversion, whether of realty into personalty or *vice versa*, and there is a failure of part but not all of the purposes for which conversion was directed. Such partial failure has occurred where a settlor has established a trust for sale of his property for the payment of his debts, and a surplus is left after the debts have been discharged[99]; and where a trust for sale of real and personal estate was established for specified private and charitable objects, and the trust for sale of the realty for charitable purposes was void under the mortmain legislation.[1] In cases like this the conversion remains wholly effective, for the property must still be actually converted; the part of the property for which the purposes have failed will therefore revert to the settlor in its converted form.[2] Thus if the settlor is dead, his interest in land directed to be sold will go to his residuary legatee, and his interest in money directed to be laid out in purchasing land will go to his residuary devisee.

B. Wills

The position under wills is more complex.

1. Land into money

(a) *Devolution as if unconverted.* In *Ackroyd* v. *Smithson*,[3] a testator gave all his realty to trustees upon trust to sell it and divide the proceeds between A and B equally. A died in the testator's lifetime and so the gift to him lapsed, but B outlived the testator. It was held that A's share ranked as realty which passed to the testator's heir-at-law, and not as personalty devolving on his next-of-kin. The ground of the decision was that the testator had directed the realty to be sold only for the purpose of dividing the proceeds between A and B; he had not shown any intention that, if A could not take, his share should pass to the testator's next-of-kin. In the case of a death before 1926, the heir's right to take any property which was realty at the owner's death could be defeated only by a gift of the property to someone else. In the absence of such a gift, the heir's claim would not be defeated even by a declaration that he should not take the realty,[4] or that the realty should be treated for all purposes as if it were personalty.[5]

---

[99] *Griffith* v. *Ricketts* (1849) 7 Hare 299.
[1] *Clarke* v. *Franklin* (1858) 4 K. & J. 257. Mortmain has now been abolished: *ante*, p. 174.
[2] *Griffith* v. *Ricketts, supra; Clarke* v. *Franklin, supra.*
[3] (1780) 1 Bro.C.C. 503; **1 W. & T.L.C. 327**. This is the case that the future Lord Eldon argued and won on appeal on a one-guinea brief to consent. His argument occupies nine pages of the report.
[4] *Fitch* v. *Weber* (1848) 6 Hare 146.
[5] *Re Walker, Macintosh-Walker* v. *Walker* [1908] 2 Ch. 705; *Re Twopeny's Settlement* [1924] 1 Ch. 522.

The principle of *Ackroyd* v. *Smithson*[6] cannot apply on an intestacy after 1925, for the same persons are entitled to both realty and personalty.[7] But it seems to be applicable where a testator makes a *specific* devise of a freehold estate to trustees on trust to sell it and divide the proceeds between A and B, and the gift to A lapses by his death in the testator's lifetime. Here A's lapsed share passes to the testator's residuary devisee and not to his residuary legatee.[8]

(b) *Received in converted form.* Although in these cases of partial failure the property passes to the person entitled to the realty of the testator, that person takes it as personalty. Thus if he dies before he receives it, it will pass to the person entitled to his personalty, whether or not the trustees of the will have in fact sold the realty in his lifetime.[9] For the failure of the objects of conversion is partial only, and so the trustees are under an enforceable duty to sell; the property is therefore converted into personalty, and those claiming the realty cannot claim to have the property reconverted, since they are mere volunteers.

2. Money into land

(a) *Devolves as if unconverted.* Subject to some uncertainties, similar rules apply to money directed to be converted into land. Thus where a testator died before 1926 leaving all his personalty to trustees upon trust to lay it out to the purchase of realty for the benefit of A and B, and only B survived the testator, A's share of the property belonged to the testator's next-of-kin and not to his heir-at-law.[10] Similarly, if the bequest were of part only of the personalty, A's share would belong to the residuary legatee and not to the residuary devisee, whenever the death of the testator occurred. The case is analogous to *Ackroyd* v. *Smithson*,[11] and the same reasoning applies to it.

(b) *Probably received in converted form.* With regard to the subsequent devolution of the property where the residiary legatee (or one of the next-of-kin) dies before receiving his share of the property, it has been laid down in general terms that he would take the property in the form in which he found it[12]; but there the money had been actually converted into land when one of the next-of-kin died, and there was no need to decide how it would have passed had it actually been personalty. It is clear that the property must be treated as realty if in fact land is bought, and there is authority for saying that this is so

---

[6] *Supra*, note 3.
[7] *Ante*, p. 486.
[8] But it seems arguable that if the conversion is directed for the purposes of the will (see, *e.g. Curteis* v. *Wormald* (1878) 10 Ch.D. 172 at 175) and not merely for those of the specific devise, it binds the residuary devisee, who must claim under the will.
[9] *Smith* v. *Claxton* (1819) 4 Madd. 492; *Re Richerson* [1892] 1 Ch. 379.
[10] *Cogan* v. *Stephens* (1835) 1 Beav. 482n.
[11] (1780) 1 Bro.C.C. 503; **1 W. & T.L.C. 327**.
[12] *Curteis* v. *Wormald* (1878) 10 Ch.D. 172 (Jessel M.R. and C.A.).

whether land was bought or not.[13] This certainly seems more consonant with principle than the other opinion, for the representatives of the residuary legatee or next-of-kin are volunteers and so have no equity to alter the form into which the property has been equitably converted by the will.

C. Summary

Stated briefly, the rule in cases of partial failure is that—

(i) under a deed the conversion takes effect for all purposes, whereas

(ii) under a will the property passes to the person entitled to it in its unconverted state, although he takes it in its converted form.[14]

[13] *Re Richerson* [1892] 1 Ch. 379 (Chitty J.).
[14] See *Re Walpole* [1933] Ch. 431 at 437.

RECONVERSION

1. Relation to failure of conversion. Failure of conversion deals with cases where there never has been a fully effective direction to convert. Reconversion, on the other hand, is concerned with the discharge of a direction to convert which was once effective.

2. Definition. Reconversion is that imaginary process by which a prior notional conversion is reversed or discharged, and the notionally converted property restored in contemplation of equity to its original actual quality. Thus, if real estate is devised on trust to sell it and pay the proceeds to A, from the moment of the testator's death A becomes absolutely entitled to the property as personalty, whether or not a sale has actually taken place. But A has a right to choose in what form he will take the property. He has a right to tell the trustees, "I prefer the land instead of the purchase-money of the land"[1]; and according to his decision the property will vest in him as land or money.

3. Forms. Reconversion may take place either by act of the parties, or by operation of law.

Section 1. Act of Parties

1. Absolute owner

(a) *Right to reconvert.* It is clear that an absolute owner solely entitled in possession and under no disability may choose to take the property in whatever form he pleases. If he expresses a wish to take the property in its unconverted form, the court will not compel the trustees to convert it, for the owner might immediately annul the effect of the

---

[1] See, *e.g. Re Daveron* [1893] 3 Ch. 421 at 425.

conversion by buying back or reselling the land, as the case might be. "Equity, like nature, will do nothing in vain."[2]

(b) *Mode of reconversion.* A person who is competent to reconvert may do so by any express declaration of intention in that behalf; and the reconversion may be inferred from acts showing that the owner means to take the property in its actual condition. Where the trust is to sell land, slight circumstances are deemed sufficient to raise the inference of a reconversion, such as keeping the land unsold for a time.[3] But where money is directed to be laid out in the purchase of land, the mere receiving of the *income* of the money, even for a long time, is not sufficient,[4] though the actual receipt of the capital moneys from the trustees would, of course, show a reconversion. The burden of proving a reconversion is on those who allege it.[5]

2. Undivided shares. Where two persons are interested in property as co-tenants, the rule is that one of them may reconvert without the concurrence of the other in the case of money to be invested in land, but not in the case of land to be converted into money. Thus if £50,000 is to be invested in the purchase of land to be held on trust for A and B as tenants in common, A may choose to take £25,000 of the £50,000 in the form of money.[6] But where land is to be sold, and the proceeds divided between A and B, A cannot choose to take his share as land, for by so doing he would prejudice B; an undivided share in land is far less marketable than the land in its entirety.[7]

3. Remainderman. It does not seem to be clearly settled whether a person not entitled in possession can reconvert or not. Naturally he cannot reconvert so as to affect the interests of prior owners. If, for instance, realty is directed to be sold and the proceeds held on trust for A for life, and then for B, B cannot elect to take the property as realty so as to prevent A from insisting on a sale. However, it seems that if during A's lifetime B declares that he will take the land as realty, then even if B's interest is contingent this will effectively reconvert the land (if it is still unsold) when his interest vests.[8] But in the case of a contingent interest, B cannot effect a reconversion by his will if his interest is still contingent at his death.[9]

---

[2] *Seeley* v. *Jago* (1717) 1 P.Wms. 389, *per* Lord Cowper L.C.; and see *Benson* v. *Benson* (1710) 1 P.Wms. 130. *Cf. post*, p. 592.

[3] *Crabtree* v. *Bramble* (1747) 3 Atk. 680; *Mutlow* v. *Bigg* (1875) 1 Ch.D. 385; *Re Gordon, Roberts* v. *Gordon* (1877) 6 Ch.D. 531.

[4] *Re Pedder's Settlement* (1854) 5 De G.M. & G. 890.

[5] *Griesbach* v. *Fremantle* (1853) 17 Beav. 314 at 317.

[6] *Seeley* v. *Jago* (1717) 1 P.Wms. 389.

[7] *Holloway* v. *Radcliffe* (1856) 23 Beav. 163; and see L.P.A. 1925, s.28(3). See also *ante*, p. 234.

[8] *Meek* v. *Devenish* (1877) 6 Ch.D. 566; *Re Cleveland* [1893] 3 Ch. 244. But see *Sisson* v. *Giles* (1863) 3 De G.J. & S. 614; *Re Douglas and Powell's Contract* [1902] 2 Ch. 296 at 312.

[9] *Re Sturt* [1922] 1 Ch. 416; and see *Re Cartwright* [1939] Ch. 90 at 106.

4. Minors. A minor cannot ordinarily reconvert.[10] However, if the matter cannot wait until he attains majority, the court may direct an inquiry whether it will be for his benefit to reconvert, and decide for him or sanction his decision; and this choice is capable of affecting the devolution of the property unless the court otherwise orders.[11]

5. Mental patients. In the case of mental patients, the Court of Protection similarly has jurisdiction to reconvert on their behalf, but will only reconvert if it is for the patient's benefit; the reconversion is capable of affecting the devolution of the property unless the court otherwise orders.[12]

Section 2. Operation of Law

1. Property "at home." Occasionally property which has been converted in equity becomes reconverted without any declaration or act of the party entitled. This occurs when the property is "at home," *i.e.* in the possession of some person absolutely entitled who, as it has been quaintly put, "had in himself both the heirs and executors,"[13] and he dies without making any declaration as to it.[14] For instance, since 1925 land belonging to persons beneficially entitled as joint tenants is subject to a trust for sale.[15] If thereafter one of the joint tenants becomes entitled to the entire legal and equitable interest by survivorship, a reconversion takes place, and hence the property will not pass under a gift in the survivor's will of "all my personal estate."[16]

2. Failure of trusts of marriage settlement. Again, suppose that H on his marriage with W agrees to lay out £50,000 in the purchase of land to be settled on the usual trusts of a marriage settlement of realty, including interests for the children, a jointure for W and an ultimate remainder to H in fee simple. If H dies without issue before any land is purchased, the money is nevertheless converted into realty, and passes as such under H's will or intestacy; for W is entitled to her jointure, which is charged on land and not on money.[17] But if W had died without issue before H, and at H's death the money had neither been invested in the purchase of land nor handed over to trustees for that

---

[10] *Seeley* v. *Jago* (1717) 1 P.Wms. 389.
[11] *Robinson* v. *Robinson* (1854) 19 Beav. 494; *Dyer* v. *Dyer* (1865) 34 Beav. 504; *Burgess* v. *Booth* [1908] 2 Ch. 648.
[12] On the principles stated *ante*, pp. 494, 495.
[13] *Wheldale* v. *Partridge* (1803) 8 Ves. 227 at 235, *per* Lord Eldon L.C.
[14] See *Rich* v. *Whitfield* (1866) L.R. 2 Eq. 583.
[15] L.P.A. 1925, s.36.
[16] *Re Cook* [1948] Ch. 212.
[17] *Walrond* v. *Rosslyn* (1879) 11 Ch.D. 640. *Secus*, it seems, as to portions (see at p. 643), which, unlike a jointure, are capital payments and not a continuing charge.

purpose, then on H's death the property would have been treated as part of his personalty unless he had shown an intention that it should still be regarded as realty.[18] "Where a sum of money is in the hands of one, without any other use but for himself, it will be money, and the heir cannot claim."[19]

3. Basis of doctrine. THE reason for this distinction is that although equity regards that as done which has been agreed to be done, yet it does so only where there is some person who could compel the performance of the agreement; and in the case of an agreement made in consideration of marriage, the only persons who could compel performance are the parties to the marriage, the issue of the marriage and the trustees of the settlement, if any, as representing these persons.[20] So long as the wife or any issue of the marriage is in existence, there is an equity to compel the investment of the money in the purchase of land; and as between the persons claiming the husband's property it will therefore be treated as realty. But if the wife is dead without issue there is no one who can compel the purchase of land; the person who claims the husband's realty is a mere volunteer who cannot require the agreement to be carried out and so cannot claim the money.

---

[18] *Chichester* v. *Bickerstaffe* (1693) 2 Vern. 295; *Pulteney* v. *Earl of Darlington* (1783) 1 Bro.C.C. 223; affd. (1796) 7 Bro.P.C. 530; *Wheldale* v. *Partridge* (1803) 8 Ves. 227 at 235; and see *Bowes* v. *Earl of Shrewsbury* (1758) 5 Bro.P.C. 144.
[19] *Pulteney* v. *Earl of Darlington, supra*, at p. 238, *per* Lord Thurlow L.C.
[20] See *ante*, p. 126; and see *Chandler* v. *Pocock* (1880) 15 Ch.D. 491 at 499 (affirmed 16 Ch.D. 648).

CHAPTER 3

ELECTION

Section 1. The Doctrine of Election

1. The principle. Election in equity arises where there is a duality of gifts or of purported gifts in the same instrument, one gift being of the donor's own property to E, and the other being of E's property to X. In such cases an intention is implied that the gift to E shall take effect only if E elects to permit the gift to X also to take effect.[1] This presumed intention is the foundation or principle of the doctrine of election; and the characteristic of that doctrine is that, by an equitable arrangement, effect is given to the purported gift to X so far as is possible. "The principle on which the doctrine of election is based is that a man shall not be allowed to approbate and reprobate"[2]; indeed, in Scotland the doctrine is known as that of Approbate and Reprobate.[3]

"The principle is, that there is an implied condition that he who accepts a benefit under an instrument must adopt the whole of it, conforming to all its provisions and renouncing every right inconsistent with it."[4] "Equity fastens on the conscience of the person who is put to his election and refuses to allow him to take the benefit of a disposition contained in the will, the validity of which is not in question, except on certain conditions."[5] The doctrine applies both to deeds and to wills.[6]

2. Taking under the instrument and taking against it. For example, if D by will or deed gives to X property belonging to E, and by the *same* instrument gives other property belonging to himself to E, equity will hold E to be entitled to the gift made to him by D only if E renounces his own property in favour of X. E has two courses open to him; he may either:

(i) take under the instrument, in which case X will take E's property, and E will take the property given to him by D; or

---

[1] *Noys* v. *Mordaunt* (1706) 2 Vern. 581; **1 W. & T.L.C. 366**; *Streatfield* v. *Streatfield* (1735) Cas.*t.*Talb. 176; **1 W. & T.L.C. 368**. For a critique of the doctrine, see N. Crago (1990) 106 L.Q.R. 487.
[2] *Re Lord Chesham* (1886) 31 Ch.D. 466 at 473, *per* Chitty J.
[3] See, *e.g. Pitman* v. *Crum Ewing* [1911] A.C. 217; and see *Lissenden* v. *C.A.V. Bosch Ltd.* [1940] A.C. 412 at 417.
[4] *Codrington* v. *Codrington* (1875) L.R. 7 H.L. 854 at 866, *per* Lord Chelmsford.
[5] *Re Mengel's W.T.* [1962] Ch. 791 at 797, *per* Buckley J.
[6] See, *e.g. Birmingham* v. *Kirwan* (1805) 2 Sch. & Lef. 444 at 449.

    (ii)   take against the instrument, in which case E will lose the gift made to him by D to the extent *required to compensate* X for the disappointment which X suffers through E's election to keep his own property.

Thus, where by his will D gives X property belonging to E worth £20,000, and also by will gives E a legacy of £30,000 out of his (D's) own property, if E is unwilling to part with his property and elects against the instrument, he will retain his property and will also receive £10,000 out of his legacy of £30,000, leaving X £20,000 out of the legacy of £30,000 to compensate him for the value of the property of which he has been disappointed by E's election against the instrument. Where the donee elects to take under the instrument, no question of compensation arises.[7]

    3. Other doctrines. The equitable doctrine of election must be distinguished from certain other rules.

    (a) *Express conditions.* If a testator gives property subject to some condition (*e.g.* as to abandoning some claim against the testator), the donee must "elect" in the sense of choosing whether to comply with the condition or lose the gift.[8] Thus if a testator gives E £30,000 subject to an express condition that he should transfer his family estate to X, E can take nothing if he refuses to comply with the condition, or is unable to do so.[9] This is accordingly quite distinct from the equitable doctrine of election, under which the question is one not of forfeiture but of compensation[10]; if under the equitable doctrine E had elected to take against the instrument he would only have to give up enough of the £30,000 to compensate X.[11]

    (b) *Two distinct gifts.* The doctrine of election does not apply where a testator makes two or more separate devises or bequests of his own property in the same instrument.[12] In this case, if one gift is beneficial and the other onerous, the donee may take the gift which is beneficial and reject the gift which is onerous, unless it appears by the will that the testator's intention was to make the acceptance of the burden a condition of the benefit. If, however, two properties are included in a single gift, as where there is a gift of a leasehold house with its contents, and the lease is onerous,[13] the beneficiary must take both or neither, in the absence of any intention to allow him to take one without the other.[14]

---

[7] *Re Lord Chesham* (1886) 31 Ch.D. 466.
[8] *Wilkinson* v. *Dent* (1871) 6 Ch.App. 339; *Central Trust and Safe Deposit Co.* v. *Snider* [1916] 1 A.C. 266.
[9] *Robinson* v. *Wheelwright* (1856) 6 De G.M. & G. 535 (married woman restrained from anticipation).
[10] See *Brown* v. *Gregson* [1920] A.C. 860 at 869.
[11] *Gretton* v. *Haward* (1819) 1 Swans. 433.
[12] *Lissenden* v. *C.A.V. Bosch Ltd.* [1940] A.C. 412 at 419. But see *Re Macartney* [1918] 1 Ch. 300.
[13] *Re Joel* [1943] Ch. 311.
[14] *Guthrie* v. *Walrond* (1883) 22 Ch.D. 573; *Re Baron Kensington* [1902] 1 Ch. 203; *Re Holt* (1916) 85 L.J.Ch. 779.

(c) *Ratification of voidable conveyance.* The equitable doctrine of election is quite distinct from the right to elect whether or not to ratify a voidable conveyance; for instance, the right of a minor who settles her property on marriage, but whose husband does not bring any property into the settlement, to *elect* (or choose) to ratify or repudiate the settlement within a reasonable time after attaining full age.[15] This has nothing to do with the equitable doctrine of election.[16] If, however, her husband also settled property, a true case of election would arise; if she did take back her own property, her interest in the property settled by the husband would be used to compensate the parties disappointed by her repudiation of the settlement.[17]

Section 2. Conditions to be Satisfied

In applying the doctrine, six conditions have to be considered.

1. Gift of E's property to X; and

2. Gift by same instrument of donor's property to E

(a) *Same instrument.* In order to raise a true case of election, not only must the donor give some of E's property to X, but he must also, by the same instrument, make an effectual gift of his own property to E; for otherwise there is no property out of which X can be compensated if E elects to keep his own property. For this purpose a will and any codicils to it are treated as one instrument.[18]

(b) *Powers.* This point is brought out very clearly by contrasting the decisions in *Bristow* v. *Warde* and *Whistler* v. *Webster.* Like many which raise questions of election, these cases concern special powers of appointment. In *Bristow* v. *Warde*,[19] a father had a power to appoint certain stock to his children, to whom the property was to go in default of appointment. By his will he appointed part of the stock to his children, and the remainder to strangers; but he gave the children *no property of his own.* It was held that the children were not bound to elect, but might keep their appointed shares and also take, as in default of appointment, the stock appointed to the strangers. In *Whistler* v. *Webster*,[20] the facts were substantially the same, except that by his will the father gave the children *some property of his own.* It was held that the children were bound to elect between:

---

[15] *Edwards* v. *Carter* [1893] A.C. 360.
[16] *Wilder* v. *Pigott* (1882) 22 Ch.D. 263.
[17] See *Re Vardon's Trusts* (1885) 31 Ch.D. 275.
[18] See *Cooper* v. *Cooper* (1874) L.R. 7 H.L. 53.
[19] (1794) 2 Ves.Jun. 336.
[20] (1794) 2 Ves.Jun. 367.

(i) taking under the will, in which case they would keep the benefit given to them by the testator out of his property, and would give up all claim to the property improperly appointed to the strangers; and

(ii) taking against the will, in which case they would be able to claim as in default of appointment the property improperly appointed to the strangers, but would have to compensate the strangers for their disappointment out of the gift of the testator's own property made to them by the will.

In either event, the children would keep the property appointed to them, for it was not the testator's own property to dispose of as he pleased and so could not be used for the purposes of compensation.

(c) *Mere object of power.* Only the person who is entitled in default of appointment is ever called upon to elect; a mere object of the power who is not entitled to the property in default of appointment is never put to his election. This is because a mere object has no interest in the property subject to the power, but only a hope that it will be appointed to him, whereas the persons entitled in default of appointment have the property vested in them until it is divested by an appointment being made.[21]

For instance, if O is the object of the power and E the person entitled in default of appointment, an appointment made to X is clearly bad, and in default of any valid appointment the property will pass to E; accordingly E will be put to his election if by the appointing instrument the appointor has conferred on E any benefits out of the appointor's own property. But O does not have to elect in such a case, even if the appointor has appointed some of the property to him and has also given him some of the appointor's own property; for no property belonging to O has been given to X. O is only an object of the power and so has no claim to the property subject to the power unless it is appointed to him, which, *ex hypothesi*, it is not. Had O been also entitled in default of appointment, *e.g.* if in the example O and E had been the same individual, he would have had to elect between any benefits conferred upon him by the appointor out of the latter's own property and the property appointed to X.[22]

(d) *Void appointment.* No case for election arises if an appointment is made to an object of the power upon trust for persons outside the scope of the power, or on condition that he shall settle it on such persons. In such a case the trust or condition is simply void; the property appointed is taken free from the trust or condition, and the appointee does not have to elect even if he is also entitled in default of

[21] See, *e.g. Re Brooks' S.T.* [1939] Ch. 993 at 996, 997.
[22] See *Wollaston* v. *King* (1869) L.R. 8 Eq. 165 at 173.

appointment and has other benefits conferred upon him.[23] And there is no election if an appointment to an object of the power offends against some statute,[24] or some rule of law, such as the perpetuity rule.[25] In such a case the person entitled in default of appointment can claim the property as being ineffectually appointed and yet keep any benefit given to him by the appointor.

(e) *Statute-barred debt.* Since a legacy in satisfaction of a statute-barred debt is mere bounty, E must elect if a testator, owing him such a debt, gives him a legacy in satisfaction of the debt and also gives some property of E's to X.[26]

(f) *Ademption.* For the purposes of election, an adeemed gift is treated as being wholly inoperative. Thus if a testator devises land to X and gives a share of residue to E, but later conveys the land to E, E need not elect. For even though at the testator's death land then owned by E is given by the will to X, that devise has been adeemed and so in effect taken out of the will.[27]

3. E's own property alienable. The property which the donor has purported to alienate must be alienable by the owner; for if it is inalienable, the owner cannot comply with the wishes of the donor. For instance, if trustees hold chattels in trust to permit them to be enjoyed with certain settled land, of which E is tenant for life, and a testator bequeaths the chattels to X and his residue to E, E can take the residue without compensating X; as E has no interest in the chattels which he could transfer to X, he need not elect.[28] On the other hand, there is nothing to exempt the owner of an *assignable* life interest from having to elect in respect of it. E similarly need not elect if his property which the testator has purported to give to X is foreign land and the *lex situs* prohibits compliance with the will.[29] If, however, E has an alienable interest in the property, he will have to elect even though it is not the full interest which the testator has purported to give.[30] Thus if Blackacre is owned by A, B and C as joint tenants, and a testator who gives legacies to each of them devises Blackacre to X, each must elect separately, even though each can contribute only part of what the testator has given to X.[31]

[23] *Woolridge* v. *Woolridge* (1859) Johns. 63; *Re Neave* [1938] Ch. 793. See, however, *White* v. *White* (1882) 22 Ch.D. 555.
[24] *Re Mulliss* [1933] O.R. 638 (equivalent of Married Women's Property Act 1882, s.11 (*ante*, p. 95; *sed quaere*: see at p. 641, *per* Middleton J.A.).
[25] *Wollaston* v. *King* (1869) L.R. 8 Eq. 165; *Re Handcock's Trusts* (1889) 23 L.R.Ir. 34; *Re Nash* [1910] 1 Ch. 1. But see the critical discussion in Gray, *Perpetuities* (4th ed., 1942), §§ 541–561, and *Re Ogilvie* [1918] 1 Ch. 492 at 501.
[26] *Re Fletcher's S.T.* [1936] 2 All E.R. 236.
[27] *Re Edwards, Macadam* v. *Wright* [1958] Ch. 168.
[28] *Re Lord Chesham* (1886) 31 Ch.D. 466.
[29] *Brown* v. *Gregson* [1920] A.C. 860.
[30] *Re Dicey* [1957] Ch. 145.
[31] *Re Dicey* [1957] Ch. 145 at 158, 159.

4. Property given to E available. The gift of the donor's own property must be such that the property can be used to compensate X if E elects against the instrument. Thus, if the gift to E is on protective trusts,[32] so that an attempt by E to make the property available for compensation would fail by reason of the forfeiture of his life interest, he will not have to elect.[33] Similarly, when a testator imposed a valid restraint on anticipation on a gift to a married woman,[34] and purported to give some of her free property to X, she did not have to elect, but could both retain her own property and take the gift, which had been made inalienable.[35] By giving her an interest of such a character as would prevent her from compensating X, the testator manifested an intention to exclude the doctrine of election.[36] But if the woman was unmarried, so that the restraint was merely potential in its operation, she had to elect.[37]

5. Donor's intention

(a) *General and particular intentions.* The doctrine is "founded upon the highest principles of equity,"[38] and is based upon a general and presumed intention of the testator or settlor that effect should be given to every part of the instrument.[39] This will not be rebutted merely by showing that the testator had not contemplated the circumstances giving rise to the election, though "it may be repelled by the declaration in the instrument itself of a particular intention inconsistent with the presumed and general intention."[40] In short, the doctrine is raised and imposed by equity unless an intention to exclude it appears.

(b) *Intention to dispose*

(1) THE INTENTION. The doctrine cannot apply unless the instrument displays an intention by the testator or settlor to dispose of that which is not his own, though it is immaterial whether he knew the property not to be his own, or by mistake conceived it to be his own.[41] In fact, probably most cases of election arise from a mistake of law or fact.[42]

For example, a wife may attempt to bequeath to a third person property which really belongs to her husband, and give the husband

---

[32] See, *ante*, p. 137.
[33] *Re Gordon's Will Trusts* [1978] Ch. 145.
[34] See, *post*, p. 534.
[35] *Re Vardon's Trusts* (1885) 31 Ch.D. 275.
[36] See *Re Hargrove* [1915] 1 Ch. 398 at 406.
[37] *Re Tongue* [1915] 1 Ch. 390 (in C.A. [1915] 2 Ch. 283); *Re Hargrove* [1915] 1 Ch. 398, not following *Haynes* v. *Foster* [1901] 1 Ch. 361.
[38] *Cooper* v. *Cooper* (1874) L.R. 7 H.L. 53 at 67, *per* Lord Cairns L.C.
[39] *Re Vardon's Trusts, supra*, at p. 279.
[40] *Ibid. per* Fry L.J.
[41] *Welby* v. *Welby* (1813) 2 V. & B. 187 at 199.
[42] See *Re Mengel's W.T.* [1962] Ch. 791 at 796.

some of her own property; or a person who has property in England and land abroad may make a will giving the foreign land to X and the English property to E, who is his heir according to the foreign law, and the will may be valid as to the English property but invalid as to the foreign land. Here the husband in the one case,[43] and E in the other,[44] will have to elect. Similarly a husband who was domiciled abroad when he married but in England when he died may, by overlooking the doctrine of community of property, put his widow to her election.[45] But, somewhat anomalously, it was established that the heir-at-law to English freeholds never had to elect; thus where a testator who died before 1926 ineffectually attempted to dispose of English realty by a will which effectually conferred a benefit on the heir, the heir was not made to elect.[46] It is doubtful whether a similar tenderness would be shown to the persons substituted for the heir by the Administration of Estates Act 1925.

(2) LIMITED INTERESTS. Where a testator devises an estate in which he has no interest, the cases are clear; but an element of much greater complication is introduced where the testator has only a limited interest in the property, e.g. a lease of Blackacre but not the freehold. In such a case "the Court will lean as far as possible to a construction which would make him deal only with that to which he was entitled"[47]; for the presumption is that a testator intends to give only what he has power to give, whereas a case of election arises only where it is clear that he intended to give something which he had no right or power to give.[48] Parol evidence is not admissible to show that the testator intended to include property which he wrongly thought to be his own in a general devise or bequest.[49]

6. Election tested as at death. In the case of a will, the foregoing conditions must be applied solely to the state of affairs existing at the testator's death.[50] If no case for election exists then, subsequent events cannot raise one. Thus if T dies in 1965 leaving £10,000 to F and E's Elmacre estate to X, and E dies in 1966 leaving all his property

---

[43] *Leacroft* v. *Harris* [1909] 2 Ch. 206.

[44] *Dewar* v. *Maitland* (1866) L.R. 2 Eq. 834; *Re Ogilvie* [1918] 1 Ch. 492; *cf. Brown* v. *Gregson* [1920] A.C. 860.

[45] *Re Mengel's W.T.* [1962] Ch. 791.

[46] *Hearle* v. *Greenbank* (1749) 3 Atk. 695 at 715; *Re De Virte* [1915] 1 Ch. 920.

[47] *Howells* v. *Jenkins* (1862) 2 J. & H. 706 at 713, *per* Page Wood V.-C.; affirmed 1 De G.J. & S. 617; and see *Maddison* v. *Chapman* (1861) 1 J. & H. 470; *Re Sexsmith* (1925) 57 O.L.R. 283.

[48] *Wintour* v. *Clifton* (1856) 8 De. G.M. & G. 641; and see *Shuttleworth* v. *Greaves* (1838) 4 My. & Cr. 35; *Drummer* v. *Pitcher* (1833) 2 My. & K. 262; *cf. Re Allen, Prescott* v. *Allen* (1945) 114 L.J.Ch. 298, criticised by J. H. C. Morris at (1945) 10 Conv.(N.S.) 102, and distinguished in *Re Mengel's W.T., supra*, where there were two gifts, one of which invoked the doctrine and the other did not.

[49] *Clementson* v. *Gandy* (1836) 1 Keen 309; but Jessel M.R. thought otherwise: *Pickersgill* v. *Rodger* (1876) 5 Ch.D. 163. See, however, *Re Edwards, Macadam* v. *Wright* [1958] Ch. 168 at 179.

[50] *Lady Cavan* v. *Pulteney* (1795) 2 Ves.Jun. 544; *Earl of Darlington* v. *Pulteney* (1797) 3 Ves. 384; and see *Re Lord Chesham* (1886) 31 Ch.D. 466 at 476 (subsequent statute); *Re Coole* [1920] 2 Ch. 536 (title acquired by limitation).

(including Elmacre) to F, it might be thought that F would have to elect between Elmacre and the £10,000. But F need not elect, for at the date of T's death no property then belonging to F was given to X; and E, who then owned Elmacre, was given nothing by T. The rule is well illustrated in *Grissell* v. *Swinhoe*.[51] There a fund belonged half to T and half to E. T purported to bequeath the whole fund, giving half to E's husband and the other half to Z. E died after the testator and her husband became entitled to her personalty. It was held that he need not elect between the quarter of the fund which T had effectually bequeathed to him and E's half, for it was not his when T died. He accordingly took three-quarters of the fund and Z took the other quarter.

Section 3. Derivative Interests

Difficulty is sometimes caused by the death of the person who is under a duty to elect. For instance, if D by his will devises E's Elmacre estate to X and gives a legacy of £10,000 to E, E clearly has to elect. If E dies, three main heads have to be distinguished.

1. Election before death. If E had elected before dying, this binds all who claim under him.

2. Properties devolving together. If E dies without electing, but both Elmacre and the £10,000 pass to F, F steps into E's shoes and has the same right and duty of electing.[52] If instead the properties had passed to a class of persons, each would elect separately in respect of his share.[53]

3. Properties diverging. If E dies without electing, leaving his realty to R and his personalty to P, the position is as if E had elected against the will. R will be entitled to Elmacre as being part of E's realty, and P will take the legacy of £10,000 as being part of E's personalty, although he will take it subject to X's right to receive compensation out of it for his failure to get Elmacre; the right to compensation is a sort of equitable charge on the legacy.[54] But the compensation is limited to the value of the benefit received by E under D's will, so that if Elmacre was worth more than £10,000, P would not have to make up the excess out of the rest of E's personalty.[55]

[51] (1869) L.R. 7 Eq. 291.
[52] *Cooper* v. *Cooper* (1874) L.R. 7 H.L. 53.
[53] *Fytche* v. *Fytche* (1868) L.R. 7 Eq. 494.
[54] *Pickersgill* v. *Rodger* (1876) 5 Ch.D. 163 at 173; *Re Macartney* [1918] 1 Ch. 300.
[55] *Rogers* v. *Jones* (1876) 3 Ch.D. 688; and see *Re Booth* [1906] 2 Ch. 321.

Section 4. Mode of Election

1. Express and implied election. Election may be either *express*, or it may be *implied* from conduct. Considerable difficulty often arises in deciding what acts of acceptance or acquiescence amount to an implied election; and, like any other question of fact, this depends upon the circumstances of each particular case.

2. Full knowledge. For a binding election there must be a deliberate choice made with full knowledge of the rules relating to election and the relevant circumstances, including the relative values of the properties[56]; and the onus of proof lies on him who asserts that such knowledge existed.[57] Thus an election made under a mistake of fact will not be binding; for while the court enforces the rule of equity that the party shall not avail himself of both his claims, it is anxious to secure to him the option of either, and not to hold him concluded by equivocal acts performed, perhaps, in ignorance of the value of the properties.[58] When made, the election relates back to the date of the gift, so that he who elects against the instrument must account for the intermediate income.[59] And where the election is to take against the instrument, the amount of compensation is ascertained as at the testator's death, and not when the election is made.[60]

3. Delay. When a time is limited for the making of the election, a person who does not elect within the time will be considered to have elected against the instrument.[61] On the other hand, where no time is limited, the court will not readily hold a man to be concluded by the mere lapse of time, so that if he merely continues in his former enjoyment, he will not be taken to have elected unless he has allowed the property to be enjoyed so long by others that it would be inequitable to disturb their enjoyment.[62]

4. Disabilities

(a) Minors. The practice is not quite uniform, being adapted to the necessities of the case. In some cases the period of election is deferred until the minor comes of age; in others, an inquiry is directed as to what

[56] *Dillon* v. *Parker* (1833) 1 Cl. & F. 303; *Wilson* v. *Thornbury* (1875) 10 Ch.App. 239.
[57] *Spread* v. *Morgan* (1865) 11 H.L.C. 588; *Sweetman* v. *Sweetman* (1868) I.R. 2 Eq. 141.
[58] *Kidney* v. *Coussmaker* (1806) 12 Ves. 136.
[59] *Davis* v. *Davis* (1896) 27 O.R. 532; and see *Padbury* v. *Clark* (1850) 2 Mac. & G. 298 at 308.
[60] *Re Hancock* [1905] 1 Ch. 16.
[61] See order in *Streatfield* v. *Streatfield, infra,* noted at 1 Swans. 447.
[62] *Tibbits* v. *Tibbits* (1816) 19 Ves. 656.

is most beneficial to the minor, and the court elects for him upon the result of that inquiry.[63]

(b) Mental patients. The practice is to refer the matter to the Court of Protection to report upon what is best for the patient, and the court elects on the report[64]; but in a proper case the court may defer the matter.

---

[63] *Streatfield* v. *Streatfield* (1735) Cas.*t.*Talb. 176; **1 W. & T.L.C. 368**; *Seton* v. *Smith* (1840) 11 Sim. 59 at 66.
[64] *Wilder* v. *Pigott* (1882) 22 Ch.D. 263; *Re Sefton* [1898] 2 Ch. 378. See Mental Health Act 1983, Pt. VII.

CHAPTER 4

PERFORMANCE

1. The doctrine. If a man who has covenanted to purchase land and settle it on his wife and issue fully carries out his covenant, he has of course performed it. The equitable doctrine of performance, however, is concerned with notional rather than actual performance.[1] Under the doctrine, if the covenantor has not fully performed his covenant but has done some other act which may fairly be supposed to have been a step towards performance, that step will be treated as having been taken in performance of the covenant, and the property concerned will be treated as being bound by the obligations of the covenant. "Where a man covenants to do an act, and he does an act which may be converted to a completion of this covenant, it shall be supposed that he meant to complete it."[2]

2. Operation of the doctrine. Thus if the covenantor purchases land but does not settle it in accordance with his covenant, the land will nevertheless be held to be subject to the trusts of the settlement, and the covenant will be regarded as having been to that extent performed. For "equity imputes an intention to fulfil an obligation"[3]: "the whole doctrine [of performance] proceeds upon the ground that a person is to be presumed to do that which he is bound to do; and if he has done anything, that he has done it in pursuance of his obligation."[4] The beneficiaries are thus not dependent upon any claim by the trustees against the covenantor for damages for breach of covenant,[5] but instead have the security of equitable interests in the land itself; and this may be important, *e.g.* if the covenantor is insolvent or the land has increased in value.

---

[1] See conversion (*ante*, p. 485) for a similar distinction between the actual and the notional.
[2] *Sowden* v. *Sowden* (1785) 1 Bro.C.C. 582 at 583, n.(3), *per* Kenyon M.R.
[3] *Ante*, p. 40.
[4] *Tubbs* v. *Broadwood* (1831) 2 Russ. & M. 487 at 493, *per* Lord Brougham L.C.
[5] See, *e.g. ante*, p. 121.

3. Categories.   Questions of performance arise in two classes of case, namely,

(i) where there is a covenant or statutory obligation[6] to purchase and settle lands,[7] and a purchase is in fact made; and

(ii) where there is a covenant to *leave* personalty to A, and property in fact comes to A under the covenantor's will or intestacy.

4. Obligation to purchase land

(a) *Lechmere* v. *Lady Lechmere.*   In *Lechmere* v. *Lady Lechmere,*[8] Lord L., upon his marriage with Lady E., covenanted to lay out £30,000 in the purchase of *freehold lands in possession* in the south part of Great Britain. The purchase was to be made within one year after his marriage, and with the consent of the trustees; and the property was to be settled on himself for life, with remainder (for so much as would amount to £800 a year) to his wife for her jointure, with remainder to the first and other sons in tail male and with the ultimate remainder to himself in fee simple. Lord L. was seised of certain lands in fee at the date of the marriage; and after the marriage, but without the consent of the trustees, he purchased other estates in fee simple of about £500 per annum, together with certain estates for lives and reversionary estates in fee simple expectant on lives, and contracted for the purchase of other estates in fee simple in possession.

Lord L. then died intestate, survived by Lady E. but no issue, without having made a settlement of any of these estates. The plaintiff was his heir-at-law, and as such claimed to have the £30,000 laid out as agreed.[9] It was held that the freehold lands purchased and contracted to be purchased in fee simple in possession after the marriage (though with but part of the £30,000) should go in part performance of the covenant, but that the estate purchased before the marriage, the leaseholds for lives, and the reversions in fee expectant on the estates for lives should not go in part performance of the covenant.

(b) *Operation of the doctrine.*   It will be seen that this decision established the four following points.

(1) PERFORMANCE PRO TANTO: where the lands purchased are worth less than the lands covenanted to be purchased and settled, they will be considered as purchased in *part* performance of the covenant. Performance may be good *pro tanto.*

---

[6] *Tubbs* v. *Broadwood* (1831) 2 Russ. & M. 487.
[7] Or to convey and settle lands, where the covenantor had no lands: *Deacon* v. *Smith* (1746) 3 Atk. 323.
[8] (1735) Cas.*t.*Talb. 80; **2 W. & T.L.C. 349**. Contrast *Perry* v. *Phelips* (1798) 4 Ves. 108.
[9] It should be noted that at the end of the year after the marriage the £30,000 was converted into realty by reason of Lord Lechmere's covenant, which was enforceable by the wife. As his wife survived him, the existence of her jointure prevented a reconversion: see *ante*, p. 501. Had she died before him, the heir, being a stranger to the marriage consideration, would have had no claim to the money.

(2) LAND ALREADY OWNED: where the covenant points to a *future* purchase of lands, lands of which the covenantor is already seised at the time of the covenant are not to be taken in part performance of it.

(3) NATURE OF PROPERTY: property of a different nature from that covenanted to be purchased by the covenantor is not available for performance.

(4) TRUSTEES' CONSENT: performance is not excluded by the land being purchased without the requisite consent of the trustees, nor does it matter if the covenant is not for the direct purchase of the lands but for the payment of the money to the trustees for them to make the purchase.[10]

(c) *Effect of covenant.*   A covenant to purchase and settle lands constitutes a specialty debt. In addition, it may create a lien on land; but this depends on the nature of the covenant and the object of the purchase.

(1) GENERAL COVENANT.   If the covenant is a general covenant to purchase and settle land, *e.g.* of a particular nature and value, it will create a lien on any land afterwards purchased in performance of the covenant; and if no contrary intention is shown it will be presumed that any suitable land so purchased was purchased with this object. But if the covenantor sells or mortgages the land, this shows that he did not intend a performance, and so the purchaser or mortgagee will not be affected by the covenant, even if he had notice of it.[11]

(2) SPECIFIC COVENANT.   If, however, the covenant is a covenant for value to settle *specific* property already belonging to the covenantor or afterwards to be acquired by him, or to settle *all* property he may afterwards acquire, it will create an equitable lien on the land; for the court would order specific performance of the covenant.[12] This lien will bind all who take the land except any who are free from it under the doctrine of purchaser without notice or for want of registration.[13] For instance, if in a marriage settlement the wife covenants to settle all property she may acquire during marriage, any property she does acquire will be bound by the covenant. Any person within the marriage consideration may thus compel the wife to settle the property. This is so even if the right of the trustees of the settlement to sue for damages for breach of the covenant has become statute-barred by the lapse of 12

---

[10] *Sowden* v. *Sowden* (1785) 1 Bro.C.C. 582.
[11] *Deacon* v. *Smith* (1746) 3 Atk. 323 at 327; but see *Ex p. Poole* (1847) 11 Jur. 1005.
[12] *Collyer* v. *Isaacs* (1881) 19 Ch.D. 342 at 351; *Pullan* v. *Koe* [1913] 1 Ch. 9.
[13] A covenant to settle land already belonging to the covenantor requires registration as a land charge, if entered into after 1925 (S.L.A. 1925, s.11; L.C.A. 1972, ss.2(4), 4(6); *ante*, p. 59).

years from the acquisition of the property.[14] A settlement may also be compelled where the property is given to the wife with a direction that it is to be free from the covenant,[15] unless the covenant excepts such property,[16] as it often does. But beneficiaries under the settlement who are not within the marriage consideration cannot compel a settlement of the property, and are without remedy,[17] at all events if the debt created by the covenant is statute-barred.[18]

5. Will or intestacy as performance of covenant

(a) *Performance by intestacy.*   If T covenants that he will bequeath a specified sum to X, or that his executors will pay this sum to X, and T then dies intestate, anything that X receives out of T's estate under the intestacy will be treated as a performance of the covenant, either in full or *pro tanto*.[19]

(b) *Covenant to give legacy.*   This kind of performance sometimes occurs in the case of a covenant by a husband to leave money to his widow. Thus in *Blandy* v. *Widmore*,[20] H covenanted before his marriage to leave his intended wife £620. The marriage took place, and H died intestate. The wife became entitled under the Statutes of Distribution to a moiety amounting to more than £620 of H's property. It was held that the wife could not come in first as a creditor for the £620 under the covenant, and then for a moiety under the statute; for as the husband had in fact left her more than £620, he had not broken his covenant. And the rule in *Blandy* v. *Widmore* has been held to apply also where the husband in fact makes a will but the gifts under it fail, so that the property becomes divisible under the statute.[21]

(c) *Performance by will.*   A gift by will may perform a covenant, as where a husband covenanted to leave his wife an annuity after his death, and his will gave her a life interest in residue.[22] But a legacy payable later than the debt,[23] or a specific bequest (as distinct from a pecuniary legacy)[24] is bounty, and not a performance of a covenant to pay money.[25]

---

[14] *Pullan* v. *Koe* [1913] 1 Ch. 9; Limitation Act 1980, s.8(1); *ante*, p. 127.
[15] *Scholfield* v. *Spooner* (1884) 26 Ch.D. 94.
[16] *Re Thorne* [1917] 1 Ch. 360.
[17] See *ante*, p. 120.
[18] *Re D'Angibau* (1880) 15 Ch.D. 228; *Re Plumptre's Marriage Settlement* [1910] 1 Ch. 609, *ante*, p. 126.
[19] *Garthshore* v. *Chalie* (1804) 10 Ves. 1.
[20] (1716) 1 P.Wms. 323; **2 W. & T.L.C. 357.**
[21] *Goldsmid* v. *Goldsmid* (1818) 1 Swans. 211.
[22] *Re Hall, Hope* v. *Hall* [1918] 1 Ch. 562.
[23] *Haynes* v. *Mico* (1781) 1 Bro.C.C. 129; *Adams* v. *Lavender* (1824) M'Cl. & Y. 41.
[24] *Devese* v. *Pontet* (1785) 1 Cox Eq. 188.
[25] See the discussion of the cases in the two previous notes by M. Cullity in (1964) 38 Austr.L.J. 147 at 150.

(d) *No performance after breach.* Once a breach of covenant has occurred, the subsequent intestacy of the covenantor will bring about no performance. Thus if a husband covenants to pay money in his lifetime, the widow's distributive share is not a performance of the obligation. For example, in *Oliver* v. *Brickland*[26] the husband covenanted to pay his wife a sum within two years after marriage. He did not pay it, but died intestate after the two years, and a larger sum then passed to his widow under his intestacy. It was held that she was entitled both to the money under the covenant and to her share of his estate; for there was a breach of covenant before his death, and a debt accrued to her from the moment of this breach.

[26] (1732) cited 3 Atk. 420, 422; 1 Ves.Sen. 1, Supp. 2.

CHAPTER 5

SATISFACTION

1. Nature. Satisfaction closely resembles performance.[1] Each depends upon a presumed intention to carry out an obligation; yet they differ in important respects. In performance, the question is whether the act done can fairly be regarded as being in fact a step towards performance of the precise acts covenanted to be done. In satisfaction, on the other hand, the thing done is something different from the thing agreed to be done, and the question is whether it was intended as a substitute for the thing covenanted; this is entirely a question of intention.[2] Further, payment of a lesser sum is always effective *pro tanto* under the doctrine of performance but not always under the doctrine of satisfaction.[3]

2. Categories. The cases on satisfaction are usually grouped under four heads, namely,

(i)   satisfaction of debts by legacies;

(ii) satisfaction of legacies by legacies;

(iii) satisfaction (or ademption) of legacies by portions; and

(iv) satisfaction of portion-debts by legacies, or by portions.

Strictly, however, only the first and last of these heads are really cases of satisfaction; for satisfaction presupposes an obligation, which, of course, does not exist in the case of a legacy in the will of a living person. Further, the four heads differ considerably in subject-matter. The first is concerned with the payment of debts, the second with the construction of wills, and the third and fourth are both manifestations of the rule against double portions, under which a father is presumed to intend to produce equality of benefit amongst his children.

---

[1] For a critical survey of performance and the satisfaction of debts by legacies, see M. Cullity (1964) 38 Austr.L.J. 147.
[2] See *Goldsmid* v. *Goldsmid* (1818) 1 Swans. 211 at 219.
[3] See *Re Hall, Hope* v. *Hall* [1918] 1 Ch. 562 at 569; *ante*, p. 514, and *post*, p. 519.

Section 1. Satisfaction of Debts by Legacies

1. The rule. The general rule is "that if one, being indebted to another in a sum of money, does by his will give him as great, or greater sum of money than the debt amounts to, without taking any notice at all of the debt, that this shall nevertheless be in satisfaction of the debt, so as that he shall not have both the debt and the legacy."[4] The rule is founded on the maxim *Debitor non praesumitur donare.* However, the rule has been described as being "artificial,"[5] and it has been said that "no sooner was it established than learned Judges of great eminence expressed their disapproval of it, and invented ways to get out of it."[6] Nevertheless, in 1946 it was said that "the rule, whatever judges in the recent past may have thought of it, is still the rule and has to be observed. ... The rule is just as strong now as it always has been."[7]

2. Conditions. For a debt to be satisfied by a legacy, the following conditions must be fulfilled.

(a) *The legacy must equal or exceed the debt.* If the legacy is less than the debt, it is not a satisfaction, even *pro tanto*.[8] But a debt of £100 with interest at 5 per cent. may be satisfied by a legacy of £100 free of duty.[9]

(b) *The legacy must be as beneficial to the creditor as the debt.* There will be no satisfaction if in its nature the legacy is not in every way as beneficial as the debt, *e.g.* if it is contingent or uncertain,[10] such as a share of residue,[11] or if it is an annuity which is unsecured and made subject to the testator's debts, whereas the debt consists of an annuity which is neither,[12] or if it is determinable on attempted alienation.[13] Moreover, a debt is not satisfied by a gift of property of a different nature, as by a devise.[14] Further, it is doubtful whether a legacy for which no time of payment is specified in the will can satisfy a debt which is owing at the date of the testator's death. Stirling J.[15] held that there was no satisfaction in such a case as the legacy was not so beneficial as the debt; payment of a legacy cannot be insisted upon until the end of

---

[4] *Talbott v. Duke of Shrewsbury* (1714) Prec.Ch. 394 at 394, 395, *per* Trevor M.R.; **2 W. & T.L.C. 323**.
[5] *Horlock v. Wiggins* (1888) 39 Ch.D. 142 at 147, *per* Bowen L.J.
[6] *Re Horlock* [1895] 1 Ch. 516 at 518, *per* Stirling J.
[7] *Re Stibbe* (1946) 175 L.T. 198 at 201, *per* Romer J.
[8] *Eastwood v. Vinke* (1731) 2 P.Wms. 613.
[9] *Fitzgerald v. National Bank Ltd.* [1929] 1 K.B. 394, an unsatisfactory decision: and see *ante*, p. 371.
[10] *Crichton v. Crichton* [1895] 2 Ch. 853, reversed on another point [1896] 1 Ch. 870.
[11] *Barret v. Beckford* (1750) 1 Ves.Sen. 519; *Devese v. Pontet* (1785) 1 Cox Eq. 188.
[12] *Re Stibbe* (1946) 175 L.T. 198; contrast *Re Haves* [1951] 2 All E.R. 928.
[13] *Re Van den Bergh's W.T.* [1948] 1 All E.R. 935.
[14] *Eastwood v. Vinke* (1731) 2 P.Wms. 613; *Richardson v. Elphinstone* (1794) 2 Ves.Jun. 463.
[15] *Re Horlock* [1895] 1 Ch. 516.

the executor's year,[16] unless an earlier date is specified for payment, whereas payment of a debt can be demanded at once. But Swinfen Eady J. subsequently decided otherwise, on the ground that the legacy carried interest from the death, and was therefore as beneficial as the debt.[17]

(c) *The will must have been made after the debt was incurred.* No presumption of satisfaction will be raised where the debt of the testator was incurred subsequently to,[18] or contemporaneously with,[19] the making of the will, because in such a case the testator could have had no intention of satisfaction. But if a will containing a legacy of the exact amount of the debt is made after the debt was incurred, and then the testator pays the debt, the legatee cannot take the legacy; for it was given merely to satisfy the debt, and when that was paid off, the legacy was adeemed.[20]

(d) *No contrary intention must be shown.* Under the rule in *Chancey's* case,[21] if there is an express direction in the will for the payment of debts and legacies, prima facie both the debt and the legacy will be payable. The same applies even if there is a mere direction to pay the debts,[22] although the law was formerly thought to be otherwise. As most wills contain such a direction, the doctrine is usually excluded.

Section 2. Satisfaction of Legacies by Legacies

Where two legacies of a sum of money or of stock are given to the same person, it is a question of construction of the instrument or instruments whether the legacies were intended to be cumulative or substitutional. In the absence of any internal evidence to show the testator's intention, the following presumptions arise.[23]

1. Same instrument. Where legacies of equal amounts are contained in the same will or codicil, and either no motive is expressed for either legacy, or else the same motive is expressed for each, a presumption arises that only one legacy was intended. Small differences in the way in which the gifts are conferred are not treated as internal evidence that the testator intended them to be cumulative.[24] But if the legacies are of unequal amounts, even though they are in the same instrument, both will be payable.[25]

---

[16] See *ante*, p. 310.
[17] *Re Rattenberry* [1906] 1 Ch. 667; *ante*, p. 371; and see *Fitzgerald* v. *National Bank Ltd.* [1929] 1 K.B. 394; but *cf. Re Stibbe* (1946) 175 L.T. 198.
[18] *Cranmer's Case* (1702) 2 Salk. 508.
[19] *Horlock* v. *Wiggins* (1888) 39 Ch.D. 142.
[20] *Re Fletcher. Gillings* v. *Fletcher* (1888) 38 Ch.D. 373; and see *post*, p. 525. *Quaere* if the legacy had exceeded the debt.
[21] (1725) 1 P.Wms. 408; **2 W. & T.L.C. 324**; see *Re Hall, Hope* v. *Hall* [1918] 1 Ch. 562.
[22] *Bradshaw* v. *Huish* (1889) 43 Ch.D. 260; *Re Manners* [1949] Ch. 613.
[23] See, *e.g. Lee* v. *Pain* (1845) 4 Hare 201, where there is an elaborate consideration of an elaborate set of repetitive legacies contained in a will and five codicils, set out in tabular form in the report. For a similar doctrine, see *ante*, p. 192.
[24] *Greenwood* v. *Greenwood* (1778) 1 Bro.C.C. 31n.
[25] *Curry* v. *Pile* (1786) 2 Bro.C.C. 225; *Yockney* v. *Hansard* (1844) 3 Hare 620.

2. Different instruments. Where the legacies are contained in different instruments, *e.g.* one in the will and another in a codicil, both legacies are payable unless the legacies are of the same amount and the same motive is expressed for each.[26] The court raises the presumption that the later legacy is a repetition of the earlier only where there is the double coincidence of the same motive and the same sum. If the legacies are of different amounts (even though the same motive may be expressed for each), or if they are of the same amounts but a different motive is expressed for each, or if a motive is expressed for one and not for the other, they are cumulative[27] unless it appears from internal evidence[28] or from the circumstances surrounding the execution of the instruments[29] that the second was a mere copy or duplicate of the first.[30]

3. Extrinsic evidence. The admissibility of extrinsic evidence of the testator's intention in these cases depends upon two rules.[31]

(a) *Admitted by the presumption*: where the court itself raises the presumption against double legacies, extrinsic evidence is admissible to show that the testator intended the legatee to take both, and also to show that one legacy only was intended.

(b) *Excluded if no presumption*: where the court does not raise a presumption against the two legacies being payable, no extrinsic evidence is admissible to show that the testator in fact intended the legatee to take one only.

Section 3. The Presumption Against Double Portions

The ademption of legacies by portions and the satisfaction of portion-debts by legacies or portions may be considered together. They depend alike on the principle that equity leans against double portions, and that a father is presumed to intend equality amongst his children. Further, the rules governing them are much the same; in particular, in each case the presumption operates *pro tanto*. The general nature of the doctrine may be shown by considering a husband who in a marriage settlement covenants to provide each child of the marriage with a portion of £5,000. Such a covenant creates a portion-debt to each child; and if the covenantor then dies before paying any portions, leaving his residue to his three children, A, B and C, and legacies to A and B only, it will be

---

[26] See, *e.g. Wray* v. *Field* (1826) 2 Russ. 257, affirming (1822) 6 Madd. 300, where at p. 305 a note classifies over 30 cases of this kind.
[27] *Hooley* v. *Hatton* (1772) 1 Bro.C.C. 390n.; **1 W. & T.L.C. 731**; *Roch* v. *Callen* (1847) 6 Hare 531; *Ridges* v. *Morrison* (1783) 1 Bro.C.C. 388.
[28] As, *e.g.* in *Re Bagnall* [1949] L.J.R. 1.
[29] As, *e.g.* in *Re Silverston* [1949] Ch. 270.
[30] *Currie* v. *Pye* (1811) 17 Ves. 462; *Whyte* v. *Whyte* (1873) L.R. 17 Eq. 50; *Re Michell* [1929] 1 Ch. 552.
[31] *Hurst* v. *Beach* (1821) 5 Madd. 351; *Hall* v. *Hill* (1841) 1 Dr. & War. 94; *Re Shields* [1912] 1 Ch. 591; *Re Resch's W.T.* [1969] 1 A.C. 514.

presumed that a legacy of £10,000 to A wholly satisfies the portion due to him, and that a legacy of £2,000 to B leaves only £3,000 of the portion-debt due to him; C, who is left no legacy, can claim his full portion of £5,000.

The main features of the doctrine are as follows.

1. Father or in loco parentis. The presumption against double portions applies only to provisions made for a child by his father or by a person who stands *in loco parentis* to him.[32] It does not apply to provisions made by a mother unless she is proved to have stood *in loco parentis* to the child.[33] In order to establish for this purpose that a person (whether the mother or anyone else) stands *in loco parentis*, it is wrong to say that "nothing short of assuming the whole functions and duties of the father" will do.[34] The true question is whether that person meant to undertake "the office and duty of the parent to make provision for the child"[35]; and of the many duties of a father this alone is here in point. Thus by undertaking this "office and duty" an uncle may put himself *in loco parentis* to his nieces,[36] and a grandfather to his grandchildren, even though the children continue to live with their father.[37] The assumption of this duty is usually inferred from the person in question making some provision for the child. In such cases the question is "whether the facts proved fairly led to the conclusion that he intended to provide a portion for the child, and not merely to bestow a gift"[38]; for only if the provision is a portion will it be presumed that the donor intended to stand *in loco parentis*.[39]

2. Portions

(a) *Nature of portions.* The presumption of ademption or satisfaction applies only where the two provisions are both in the nature of portions.[40] Not every gift made by a father or a person *in loco parentis* will be treated as a portion. Gifts made by will, even though not specially described as portions,[41] and gifts by marriage settlement are usually treated as portions,[42] and so are substantial advances made with

---

[32] *Fowkes* v. *Pascoe* (1875) 10 Ch.App. 343 at 350; *Re Ashton* [1897] 2 Ch. 574, not considered on appeal [1898] 1 Ch. 142; *Re Eardley's Will* [1920] 1 Ch. 397.

[33] *Re Ashton, supra.*

[34] *Fowkes* v. *Pascoe* (1875) 10 Ch.App. 343 at 350, *per* James L.J.

[35] *Powys* v. *Mansfield* (1837) 3 My. & Cr. 359 at 367, *per* Lord Cottenham L.C.; and see *Pym* v. *Lockyer* (1841) 5 My. & Cr. 29.

[36] *Powys* v. *Mansfield* (1837) 3 My. & Cr. 359.

[37] *Pym* v. *Lockyer, supra.*

[38] *Pym* v. *Lockyer, supra*, at p. 35, *per* Lord Cottenham L.C.

[39] See *Suisse* v. *Lord Lowther* (1843) 2 Hare 424 at 434; and see *ante*, p. 180.

[40] See *Re Lacon* [1891] 2 Ch. 482 at 496.

[41] See *Re Furness, Furness* v. *Stalkartt* [1901] 2 Ch. 346 at 348; *Re Dawson* [1919] 1 Ch. 102 at 107, citing *Ex p. Pye* (1811) 18 Ves. 140, 151, 153, 154; **2 W. & T.L.C. 314**.

[42] As in *Re Furness, Furness* v. *Stalkartt* [1901] 2 Ch. 346.

the object of establishing the child in life, or making provision for him.[43] A provision is not "substantial" for this purpose merely because it is a substantial proportion of the father's estate; it must be sufficiently substantial in itself to constitute a permanent provision for the child.[44] The court will not add up small gifts so as to make a portion.[45] To pay a son's debts is regarded as merely making a gift by way of temporary assistance and not as providing a portion[46]; a portion provides for the future rather than giving relief from the past.

(b) *Appointments under powers.* Property may constitute a portion not only if it is provided by a father out of his own assets, but also if he appoints it under a power of appointment, either general or special. Thus if a father makes a will appointing property under a special power to his seven children equally, and afterwards appoints a seventh part of the fund to one child, the portion is presumed to adeem the legacy and the child can take nothing under the testamentary appointment.[47] It would be otherwise if the power had been exercised by the mother, unless she were proved to be *in loco parentis*,[48] or the documents and the circumstances of the case had shown that she intended to ensure equality between the children.[49]

3. Operation of the presumptions. The operation of the presumptions against double portions may now be considered in each of the three possible cases.

(a) *Ademption of legacies by portions.* The doctrine of the satisfaction of a legacy by a portion, or as it is more properly called, the ademption of a legacy by a portion, has been stated thus: "When a testator gives a legacy to a child, or to any other person towards whom he has taken on himself parental obligations, and afterwards makes a gift or enters into a binding contract in his lifetime in favour of the same legatee, then (unless there be distinctions between the nature and conditions of the two gifts ...) there is a presumption prima facie that both gifts were made to fulfil the same natural or moral obligation of providing for the legatee; and consequently that the gift *inter vivos* is either wholly or in part a substitution for, or an 'ademption' of the legacy."[50] It was at one time thought, indeed, that the legacy would be

---

[43] *Taylor* v. *Taylor* (1875) L.R. 20 Eq. 155. See *Re George's W.T.* [1949] Ch. 154; *Re Livesey* [1953] 1 W.L.R. 1114; *ante*, pp. 275, 280; and see generally H. I. Elbert (1953) 52 Mich.L.R. 231 at 252 *et seq.*

[44] See *Re Hayward, Kerrod* v. *Hayward* [1957] Ch. 528 (savings certificates as advancement under A.E.A. 1925, s.47: £500 out of some £2,300 no advancement: see (1957) 73 L.Q.R. 21, 302).

[45] *Suisse* v. *Lord Lowther* (1843) 2 Hare 424 at 434; *Schofield* v. *Heap* (1858) 27 Beav. 93; *Watson* v. *Watson* (1864) 33 Beav. 574.

[46] *Re Scott, Langton* v. *Scott* [1903] 1 Ch. 1.

[47] *Re Peel's Settlement* [1911] 2 Ch. 165.

[48] *Re Ashton* [1897] 2 Ch. 574; on appeal [1898] 1 Ch. 142.

[49] *Re Eardley's Will* [1920] 1 Ch. 397; *Re Ware* (1926) 70 S.J. 691.

[50] *Re Pollock, Pollock* v. *Worrall* (1885) 28 Ch.D. 552 at 555, *per* Lord Selborne L.C.; and see *Re Vaux* [1939] Ch. 465 at 481, 482.

wholly adeemed by a portion of less value than the legacy; but it is now settled that there is only ademption *pro tanto* in such a case.[51] The doctrine applies not only to a legacy but also to a share of residue,[52] though not, it has been held, to a devise of land.[53]

(b) *Satisfaction of portion-debts by legacies*

(c) *Satisfaction of portion-debts by portions* These two cases of satisfaction may conveniently be considered together.

(1) SATISFACTION BY LEGACIES. When a father or person standing *in loco parentis* has incurred an obligation to give a portion to a child, upon marriage or otherwise, and afterwards he gives the child a legacy or share of residue equal to or greater than the agreed portion, a presumption arises that the legacy or share of residue was intended as a satisfaction of the portion-debt, so that prima facie the child cannot take both provisions.[54] And if the legacy is of less value than the portion, it is presumed to be a satisfaction *pro tanto*.[55] Where the portion-debt is settled, all that will be satisfied is the child's interest in it. Thus if a father covenants to settle £10,000 in trust for his daughter for life, with other beneficial interests for her husband and issue, a subsequent legacy to the daughter will satisfy her life interest in the £10,000 but not the interests of her husband and issue.[56]

(2) SATISFACTION BY PORTIONS. If a father or person *in loco parentis* agrees to give a portion to a child and subsequently makes some other provision for the child in his lifetime, the second provision is presumed to be a complete or partial satisfaction of the agreed portion. For instance, where F executed a bond to give £10,000 on a certain date to S, his illegitimate son to whom he stood *in loco parentis*, the bond was held to be satisfied when F took S into partnership before the date arrived and credited his partnership account with £19,000 as his share of the capital.[57]

(3) ORDINARY DEBTS. Where the debt owed by a father to his child is an ordinary debt and not a portion-debt, the position is governed by the rules relating to satisfaction of a debt by a legacy, and not by those relating to satisfaction of a portion-debt by a legacy. There will accordingly be no satisfaction even *pro tanto*, if the legacy is less than the debt; and even if it is greater, the presumption will be rebutted by

---

[51] *Pym* v. *Lockyer* (1841) 5 My. & Cr. 29.
[52] *Montefiore* v. *Guedalla* (1859) 1 De G.F. & J. 93.
[53] *Davys* v. *Boucher* (1839) 3 Y. & C. Ex. 397. *Sed quaere*, in so far as it rests on the Statute of Frauds 1677, s.6; for by the Wills Act 1837, s.20, the same rule now applies to all property. But as to *ejusdem generis*, see *post*, p. 526.
[54] *Weall* v. *Rice* (1831) 2 Russ. & M. 251.
[55] *Warren* v. *Warren* (1783) 1 Bro.C.C. 305.
[56] *Re Blundell, Blundell* v. *Blundell* [1906] 2 Ch. 222. *Cf. McCarogher* v. *Whieldon* (1867) L.R. 3 Eq. 236, as explained in *Re Gordon's W.T., National Westminster Bank Ltd.* v. *Gordon* [1978] Ch. 145 at 156–158.
[57] *Lawes* v. *Lawes* (1881) 20 Ch.D. 81.

any of those slight circumstances which will take a bequest to a stranger out of the general rule.[58] The position is the same in the case of a legacy by a husband to his wife to whom he is indebted.[59] But when a father who is indebted to his child makes in his lifetime an advancement to the child of a portion equal to or exceeding the debt, it will prima facie be considered a satisfaction; this is so even if the debt arose out of a breach of trust committed by the father of which the child was ignorant.[60] "There are very few cases where a father will not be presumed to have paid the debt he owes to his daughter, when, in his life-time, he gives her in marriage a greater sum than he owed her; for it is very unnatural to suppose that he would chuse to leave himself a debtor to her, and subject to an account."[61]

(4) NO PORTION-DEBT. The doctrine of satisfaction of a portion-debt by a legacy or by another portion has no application where the father actually gives property to the child and afterwards makes some other provision for him; for where the portion has been given, there is no portion-debt to satisfy.[62] For instance, if the father actually handed over £10,000 to the trustees of the child's marriage settlement, and subsequently made a will giving £10,000 to the trustees to hold upon the same trusts, the child would take both provisions. In such a case the father cannot intend to give what he has already given; there is no obligation which he can intend to satisfy. But where the will precedes the provision made *inter vivos*, the doctrine of ademption comes into play, whether the father gives or merely agrees to give the portion.

4. Inapplicability to strangers

(a) *No ademption or satisfaction of gift to a stranger.* As has been seen, the presumptions of satisfaction and ademption apply only where the provisions are made by a father or person *in loco parentis*. If, therefore, a person gives a legacy to a "stranger" (*i.e.* a person who is not a child within this relationship) and then makes a settlement on him, or first agrees to make a settlement on the stranger and then bequeaths a legacy to him, the stranger is entitled to claim both provisions. For this purpose a grandchild is treated as a stranger,[63] and so is an illegitimate child unless the putative father has placed himself *in loco parentis*.[64] The presumptions thus produce the "whimsical"[65] result that a father is treated as having "less affection for his legitimate child than

---

[58] *Crichton* v. *Crichton* [1895] 2 Ch. 853; reversed on another point [1896] 1 Ch. 870; and see *ante*, p. 519.
[59] *Fowler* v. *Fowler* (1735) 3 P.Wms. 353; *Cole* v. *Willard* (1858) 25 Beav. 568; *Re Fletcher, Gillings* v. *Fletcher* (1888) 38 Ch.D. 373.
[60] *Plunkett* v. *Lewis* (1844) 3 Hare 316; and see *Crichton* v. *Crichton* [1896] 1 Ch. 870.
[61] *Wood* v. *Briant* (1742) 2 Atk. 521 at 522, *per* Lord Hardwicke L.C.
[62] See, *e.g. Re Marks* (1921) 50 O.L.R. 473, applying *Hudson* v. *Spencer* [1910] 2 Ch. 285 (*ante*, p. 385).
[63] *Re Dawson* [1919] 1 Ch. 102.
[64] *Ex p. Pye* (1811) 18 Ves. 140; **2 W. & T.L.C. 314**.
[65] *Wetherby* v. *Dixon* (1815) 19 Ves. 407 at 412, *per* Grant M.R.

even for a stranger," so that "by a sort of artificial rule" the child is "very harshly treated."[66]

Nevertheless, even in the case of a stranger, a legacy expressly given for a particular purpose, or in pursuance of a specific moral obligation, is prima facie adeemed by an advance of money or money's worth in the testator's lifetime for the same purpose, or in pursuance of the same moral obligation.[67]

(b) *Stranger cannot profit from the doctrines.* As the underlying idea of the doctrines is to produce equality among children, strangers cannot profit from their operation. Thus if a testator directs his residuary estate to be divided equally between his two children, A and B, and X, a stranger, and he afterwards gives A and X advances, X, who does not have to account for his advance, cannot benefit from the share of A being wholly or in part adeemed. In such a case X would take a third share of the residue actually left by the testator, and equality would be produced between A and B by giving B a share of the remaining two-thirds equal to the advance which A has had, and then dividing any balance equally between them.[68] The same principle applies as between a surviving spouse and the children on a partial intestacy. For instance, if a testator gives a legacy to one of his children, and the residue, being undisposed of, passes as on an intestacy to his widow and all his children, the widow's interest in the residue would not be increased if the legacy to the child was adeemed by a subsequent portion.[69]

5. Rebutting the presumption. The presumption of satisfaction may be rebutted by either intrinsic evidence or extrinsic evidence[70]; the question is always what the actual intention of the father was.[71]

(a) *Instrinsic evidence.* The presumption may be rebutted by intrinsic evidence, *i.e* the existence of substantial differences between the two provisions; for "where the two provisions are of a different nature, the two instruments afford intrinsic evidence in favour of a double provision."[72]

(1) EJUSDEM GENERIS. The presumption will accordingly be rebutted if the two provisions are not *ejusdem generis*.[73] For instance, "land is not to be taken in satisfaction for money, nor money for land,"[74] unless the

---

[66] *Ex p. Pye, supra,* at pp. 148, 151, *per* Lord Eldon L.C.
[67] *Re Pollock, Pollock* v. *Worrall* (1885) 28 Ch.D. 552; *Re Corbett* [1903] 2 Ch. 326; *Re Aynsley* [1915] 1 Ch. 172; *Re Eardley's Will* [1920] 1 Ch. 397; *Re Jupp* [1922] 2 Ch. 359.
[68] *Re Heather* [1906] 2 Ch. 230.
[69] *Re Vaux* [1938] Ch. 581. On appeal it was unnecessary to decide the point, the court holding that the legacy was not adeemed: [1939] Ch. 465.
[70] *Weall* v. *Rice* (1831) 2 Russ. & M. 251 at 267.
[71] *Hopwood* v. *Hopwood* (1859) 7 H.L.C. 728; *Re Lacon* [1891] 2 Ch. 482.
[72] *Weall* v. *Rice, supra,* at p. 268, *per* Leach M.R.
[73] *Re Jaques* [1903] 1 Ch. 267.
[74] *Bellasis* v. *Uthwatt* (1737) 1 Atk. 426 at 428, *per* Lord Hardwicke L.C.

father had placed a money value on the land.[75] A legacy will similarly not be adeemed by a gift of stock-in-trade[76] which has not been given a money value[77]; and a contingent legacy is no satisfaction of a vested portion.[78]

(2) NATURE OF LIMITATIONS. Substantial differences in the limitations of the two provisions may also rebut the presumption. This occurred where the covenant was to settle a fund on the husband of the covenantee's daughter for his life, with remainder to the children of the marriage, and an ultimate trust in default of children to the daughter or as she should appoint: but the will gave a life interest to the daughter, gave nothing to the children, and gave the property after her death to such persons *excluding the husband* as she should appoint.[79] But mere differences in the trusts affecting the child's children are not enough.[80] The presumption similarly stood unrebutted where a will containing an absolute gift to a daughter was followed by a settlement on her marriage in which she took a life interest; but, as the basis of the decision was that the father is "the dictator of all settlements"[81] and the daughter would probably have settled her portion in the same way herself,[82] the case might well not be followed today.

(b) *Extrinsic evidence*

(1) ADMISSION. As already stated, the rule against double portions is a presumption of equity which, like other presumptions of equity,[83] may be rebutted by parol evidence of circumstances showing the father's actual intention.[84] Both for deeds and wills,[85] such evidence is admissible even if it is merely of words uttered in casual conversation, and whether before, after or at the time of the transaction; but the weight of the evidence may be affected by the time and the circumstances.[86]

(2) EXTENT OF ADMISSION. Where evidence is admissible to rebut the presumption, counter-evidence is also admissible to support it. "In such cases the evidence is not admitted on either side for the purpose of proving in the first instance, with what intent either writing was made; but for the purposes only of ascertaining whether the presumption which the law has raised be well or ill founded."[87] But if the court comes to

---

[75] *Bengough* v. *Walker* (1808) 15 Ves. 507.
[76] *Holmes* v. *Holmes* (1783) 1 Bro.C.C. 555; *Re Jaques* [1903] 1 Ch. 267.
[77] See *Re George's W.T.* [1949] Ch. 154.
[78] *Bellasis* v. *Uthwatt* (1737) 1 Atk. 426.
[79] *Lord Chichester* v. *Coventry* (1867) L.R. 2 H.L. 71.
[80] *Re Furness, Furness* v. *Stalkartt* [1901] 2 Ch. 346.
[81] *Stevenson* v. *Masson* (1873) L.R. 17 Eq. 78 at 84, *per* Bacon V.-C.
[82] *Lord Chichester* v. *Coventry, supra,* at p. 88.
[83] See, *e.g. ante,* p. 521.
[84] *Re Tussaud's Estate* (1878) 9 Ch.D. 363.
[85] *Ibid.*
[86] *Trimmer* v. *Bayne (No. 1)* (1802) 7 Ves. 508.
[87] *Kirk* v. *Eddowes* (1844) 3 Hare 509 at 517, *per* Wigram V.-C.; and see *Re Shields* [1912] 1 Ch. 591.

the conclusion on the construction of the two instruments that no satisfaction was intended, parol evidence is not admissible to raise a case of satisfaction, for that would be to contradict the written instrument.[88]

6. Order of provisions.   Although the presumption applies both to the ademption of legacies by portions (where the will comes first) and to the satisfaction of portion-debts by legacies (where the will comes second), there are important differences between the two cases.

(a) *Rebutting the presumption.*   It is more difficult to rebut the presumption of the ademption of a legacy than the satisfaction of a portion-debt. In the former case, the father is under no obligation to the child when he makes the second provision, and may do as he pleases, whereas in the latter case the portion-debt has created an obligation binding upon the father. "When the will precedes the settlement it is only necessary to read the settlement as if the person making the provision had said, 'I mean this to be in lieu of what I have given by my will.' But if the settlement precedes the will, the testator must be understood as saying, 'I give this in lieu of what I am already bound to give, if those to whom I am so bound will accept it.' It requires much less to rebut the latter than the former presumption."[89]

(b) *Election.*   Where a legacy is adeemed by a portion, the child has no choice; for the father has an absolute power to substitute the portion for the legacy if he so chooses.[90] But where a portion-debt is satisfied by a legacy, the child has an enforceable right to the portion, and cannot be deprived of it without his consent.[91] Accordingly, he has the right to choose between the two provisions.

For example, in *Thynne* v. *Earl of Glengall*[92] a father, on the marriage of his daughter, agreed to give her a portion of £100,000 Consols. He made an actual transfer of one-third of the Consols to the trustees of the marriage settlement, and gave them his bond for the transfer of the remainder on his death. The stock was to be held in trust for the daughter's separate use for life, and after her death, for the children *of the marriage* as the *husband and wife* should jointly appoint. Afterwards by his will the father gave the trustees a moiety of the residue of his personal estate, in trust for the daughter's separate use for life, with remainder for *her* children generally as *she* should by deed or will appoint. The court held that the moiety of the residue given by the

---

[88] *Hall* v. *Hill* (1841) 1 Dr. & War. 94; *Re Shields, supra*; and see M. Cullity in (1964) 38 Austr.L.J. 147 at 156.

[89] *Lord Chichester* v. *Coventry* (1867) L.R. 2 H.L. 71 at 87, *per* Lord Cranworth; and see *Re Tussaud's Estate* (1878) 9 Ch.D. 363 at 390.

[90] *Lord Chichester* v. *Coventry* (1867) L.R. 2 H.L. 71; and see *Earl of Durham* v. *Wharton* (1836) 3 Cl. & F. 146.

[91] *Thynne* v. *Earl of Glengall* (1848) 2 H.L.C. 131; *Lord Chichester* v. *Coventry, supra*. *McCarogher* v. *Whieldon* (1867) L.R. 3 Eq. 236, as explained in *Re Gordon's W.T., National Westminster Bank Ltd.* v. *Gordon* [1978] Ch. 145 at 156–158.

[92] (1848) 2 H.L.C. 131.

will was a satisfaction of the sum of stock secured by the bond, notwithstanding the differences between the trusts, and that she was bound to choose between the two provisions.

Part VI

EQUITABLE PROTECTION

IN some cases, the intervention of equity has led to the creation of new rights of property; the beneficial interests under a trust are, of course, the outstanding example of this. But in other cases, the intervention of equity has merely modified or controlled existing rights of property. Sometimes equity has intervened to protect those in a relatively defenceless position by reason of their status, as in the case of minors and married women. In other cases, the need for protection sprang from a transaction which put one of the parties in a position of inferiority. The mortgagor's equity of redemption arose in this way; but so also did other cases in which, unlike the mortgage, equity granted relief without creating any new interest, as with penalties, forfeitures, and accident. Finally, there were cases where the conduct of one of the parties moved equity to intervene, *e.g.* fraud and estoppel. These heads will be considered in turn.

CHAPTER 1

MARRIED WOMEN, MINORS AND PERSONS OF UNSOUND MIND

Section 1. Married Women

1. Historical development.[1] The position of a married woman at common law was a harsh one. She and her husband were deemed to be one person in law, and that person was the husband.[2] She could neither acquire nor hold property independently of him,[3] and he had extensive rights over her property whether it belonged to her at the date of the marriage or came to her afterwards. Equity in general followed the law by protecting the husband's interests[4]; but there were three important exceptions.

(a) *Wife's equity to a settlement.*[5] If a husband took proceedings in equity to recover his wife's property, the court would compel him to settle on his wife and children part of the property that he otherwise would be free to dispose of absolutely. As the doctrine was later developed, the wife,[6] or after her death her children,[7] could initiate the claim.

(b) *Separate estate.* Wherever real or personal property was given or devised or settled upon a married woman *for her separate use,*[8] the property was protected against the rights and claims of her husband and of his creditors.[9] Without his consent, she could thus dispose of the property either *inter vivos* or by will,[10] whether the interest was in reversion or possession.[11]

---

[1] For a fuller account, see the 27th edition of this work (1973), pp. 513–517.
[2] See generally Glanville Williams (1947) 10 M.L.R. 16.
[3] *Murray* v. *Barlee* (1834) 3 My. & K. 209 at 220.
[4] See *Countess of Strathmore* v. *Bowes* (1789) 1 Ves.Jun. 22; **1 W. & T.L.C. 537.**
[5] Though the doctrine is obsolete, it may be hoped that the wit of Knight Bruce L.J. in *Barrow* v. *Barrow* (1854) 5 De G.M. & G. 782 (see Megarry, *Miscellany-at-Law* (1955), pp. 112–115) will long outlive the subject-matter which occasioned it.
[6] *Elibank* v. *Montolieu* (1801) 5 Ves. 737; **1 W. & T.L.C. 541.**
[7] *Murray* v. *Lord Elibank* (1804) 10 Ves. 84; **1 W. & T.L.C. 544.**
[8] See *Ashworth* v. *Outram* (1877) 5 Ch.D. 923 at 941, "that blessed word and thing," *per* James L.J.
[9] *Bennet* v. *Davis* (1725) 2 P.Wms. 316; *Parker* v. *Brooke* (1804) 9 Ves. 583; *Newlands* v. *Paynter* (1840) 4 My. & Cr. 408; *Wassell* v. *Leggatt* [1896] 1 Ch. 554.
[10] *Fettiplace* v. *Gorges* (1789) 1 Ves.Jun. 46.
[11] *Sturgis* v. *Corp* (1806) 13 Ves. 190. See also *Peacock* v. *Monk* (1751) 2 Ves.Sen. 190; *Hulme* v. *Tennant* (1778) 1 Bro.C.C. 16; **1 W. & T.L.C. 555;** *Taylor* v. *Meads* (1865) 4 De G.J. & S. 597.

(c) *Restraint on anticipation.* This doctrine was invented by Lord Thurlow[12] to protect the wife's separate estate from the husband, who might persuade or coerce her to alienate it. If property given for the separate use of a married woman was given "without power of anticipation," or words to that effect, she was disabled during the marriage from alienating the property or anticipating the future income, and could only receive each payment of income as it fell due.[13]

2. Intervention by statute. Over the past century, the work of protecting a married woman in her property has been taken over by the legislature, so that the equitable doctrines mentioned above are of historical importance only. The doctrine of the separate estate was adopted and extended by the Married Women's Property Act 1882.[14] This in effect provided that if property was either acquired after 1882 or belonged to a woman married after 1882, it should be her separate property.[15] The Act was amended by several later statutes of the same name,[16] until by the Law Reform (Married Women and Tortfeasors) Act 1935 a married woman was placed in the same position as a *feme sole* with regard to the acquisition, holding and disposal of any property.[17] The same Act prevented the creation of any new restraints on anticipation,[18] and finally a later statute abolished as from December 16, 1949 all restraints which could not be attached to the enjoyment of property by a man.[19]

3. The modern position. Section 17 of the Act of 1882 introduced a procedure for the determination of questions between husband and wife as to the title to or possession of property. Proceedings under section 17 were frequently brought in the Chancery Division, but since October 1, 1971 they have been assigned to the Family Division.[20] Apart from such express assignment, the Family Division will generally be the proper forum for property disputes between spouses in view of the wide powers which are available to the court under the matrimonial property legislation.[21] The married woman and her property have thus passed procedurally as well as substantively out of the sphere of equity, and the subject now falls outside the scope of this book.[22]

---

[12] See *Pybus* v. *Smith* (1791) 3 Bro.C.C. 340; *Brandon* v. *Robinson* (1811) 18 Ves. 429 at 434; W. G Hart (1924) 40 L.Q.R. 221.
[13] For a more detailed account of the doctrine, see the 24th edition (1954) of this book, pp. 457–462.
[14] There had been earlier Acts of limited scope: Matrimonial Causes Act 1857, s.25; Married Women's Property Acts 1870 and 1874.
[15] Married Women's Property Act 1882, ss.2, 5.
[16] Married Women's Property Acts 1884, 1893, 1907 and 1908.
[17] Law Reform (Married Women and Tortfeasors) Act 1935, ss.1, 2.
[18] *Ibid.* s.2.
[19] Married Women (Restraint upon Anticipation) Act 1949.
[20] Administration of Justice Act 1970, s.1, Sched, brought into force by S.I. 1971 No. 1244, repealed by S.C.A. 1981, s.151(4) and Sched. 7, and replaced by s.61(1) and Sched. 1 of the latter Act. Certain county courts have jurisdiction: see Matrimonial and Family Proceedings Act 1984, s.43.
[21] *Williams (J.W.)* v. *Williams (M.A.)* [1976] Ch. 278 at 286.
[22] See, however, *post*, pp. 554, 555 as to gifts and other transactions between spouses and engaged couples.

Section 2. Minors

1. Chancery jurisdiction. The origin of the jurisdiction of the Court of Chancery over infants, or minors as they are more often called today,[23] has been the subject of much discussion. The better opinion seems to be that it was founded on the prerogative of the Crown as *parens patriae*, the exercise of which was delegated to the Chancellor.[24] But whatever may have been the origin of the jurisdiction, it was firmly established at the time of the passing of the Judicature Act 1873. That Act included in the list of matters specially assigned to the Chancery Division "the wardship of infants and the care of infants' estates," and provided that in questions relating to the custody and education of infants, the rules of equity should prevail over the rules of common law.[25]

2. Transfer of jurisdiction. In modern times, the most important part of the jurisdiction of the Chancery Division over minors was in relation to wards of court. Formerly this jurisdiction depended in the main upon the minor being entitled to property, but when over thirty years ago statute[26] made it possible for any minor to be made a ward of court even though no property was involved, the jurisdiction became in form what it had long been in fact, namely, a jurisdiction concerned more with welfare than with property. In common with other courts, the Chancery Division also exercised a statutory jurisdiction in relation to the guardianship of infants, their custody and maintenance, and their adoption. With the constitution of the Family Division of the High Court, the Chancery jurisdiction over minors was transferred to that Division on October 1, 1971.[27] The subject accordingly now falls outside the scope of this book.

Section 3. Persons of Unsound Mind

1. Chancery jurisdiction

(a) *Basis.* "It is to be borne in mind that unsoundness of mind gives the Court of Chancery no jurisdiction whatever. It is not like infancy in that respect. The Court of Chancery is by law the guardian of infants, whom it makes its wards. The Court of Chancery is not the curator

---

[23] Family Law Reform Act 1969, ss.1(2), 12.
[24] *R.* v. *Gyngall* [1893] 2 Q.B. 232 at 240, 247; *Official Solicitor* v. *K.* [1965] A.C. 201.
[25] See J.A. 1925, s.44: the express reference to infants is not repeated in S.C.A. 1981, s.49(1). For a comparison of common law and equity, see *Thomasset* v. *Thomasset* [1894] P. 295 at 297–300.
[26] Law Reform (Miscellaneous Provisions) Act 1949, s.9, repealed by S.C.A. 1981, s.151(4) and Sched. 7. The child becomes a ward of court on the making of the application: see S.C.A. 1981, s.41(2).
[27] See the provisions cited in n. 20, *supra.*

either of the persons or the estate of a person *non compos mentis*, whom it does not and cannot make its ward. It is not by reason of the incompetency, but notwithstanding the incompetency, that the Court of Chancery entertains the proceedings. It can no more take upon itself the management or disposition of a lunatic's property than it can the management or disposition of the property of a person abroad, or confined to his bed by illness. The court can only exercise such equitable jurisdiction as it could under the same circumstances have exercised at the suit of the person himself, if of sound mind."[28]

(b) *Exercise.*   The jurisdiction of the Chancery Division in respect of the interest of such a person in trust property is accordingly circumscribed. In most instances it will not be exercised, and the matter will be left to the Court of Protection, considered below. However, the Chancery jurisdiction will be exercised if three conditions are satisfied. They are, first, that the income of the trust fund is so small that it will all be used in maintaining the patient, as the person of unsound mind is called; second, that no proceedings in the Court of Protection are contemplated; and third, that the Chancery Division is already seised of the matter, *e.g.* because the fund is in court, or Chancery proceedings are already pending. In such cases, the Chancery Division will usually exercise its jurisdiction in order to make it unnecessary to launch proceedings in the Court of Protection; and the court may direct payment of the income, or even the capital, to the patient's guardian on his undertaking to apply it for the patient's maintenance.[29]

2. Statutory jurisdiction

(a) *Basis.*   Although there is no inherent equitable jurisdiction over lunatics, there has long been a statutory jurisdiction. This was originally based on the so-called statute *De Praerogativa Regis* of some date between 1255 and 1290,[30] the ninth chapter of which related to idiots and the tenth chapter to lunatics. Under that statute the Crown in effect acquired the management of the estates of idiots and lunatics, subject to the duty of maintaining the idiot or lunatic during all the period of mental incapacity, and rendering up the estate to the representatives of the idiot upon his death, or to the lunatic himself upon his recovery, or to his representatives in like manner upon his death.

(b) *Mental Health Act 1983.*   The statute at present in force is the Mental Health Act 1983,[31] which confers jurisdiction on the Lord Chancellor and one or more of the judges of the Supreme Court

---

[28] *Beall* v. *Smith* (1873) 9 Ch.App. 85 at 92, *per* James L.J.
[29] *Re K.'s S.T.* [1969] 2 Ch. 1, reviewing earlier authorities.
[30] See 1 Holdsworth, *H.E.L.* 473, note 8.
[31] This consolidated the Mental Health Act 1959 and other statutes. For an authoritative summary of the position before and after this Act, see R. Jennings (1960) 23 M.L.R. 421.

nominated by the Lord Chancellor.[32] At present the jurisdiction is exercised by a judge of the Chancery Division. In practice, nearly all the work is done by "an office of the Supreme Court, called the Court of Protection" under a Master,[33] subject to appeal to the judge,[34] and thence to the Court of Appeal,[35] and the House of Lords.[36] Specified functions of the Court of Protection may be exercised by the Public Trustee.[37] The jurisdiction of the Court, the details of which lie outside the scope of this work,[38] is exercisable over any person "incapable, by reason of mental disorder, of managing and administering his property and affairs."[39] Such a person is now known as a "patient"[40] or "mental patient." The normal course of events is for the Court of Protection to appoint a receiver for the patient[41] (usually a near relation), and for the receiver to exercise wide powers under the supervision of the court, in effect functioning as a general manager of the patient's property.

(c) *Settlements.*   The Court of Protection has wide powers of directing a settlement of the property of a mental patient and of making consequential vesting orders.[42] If the interests of the patient[43] or of his family[44] so require, the settlement need contain no power of revocation in the event of the patient recovering his sanity.[45] There is also power to vary any such settlement at any time before the death of the patient if it appears that any material fact was not disclosed before the settlement was made or that there has been any substantial change in the circumstances.[46]

---

[32] Mental Health Act 1983, s.93(1).

[33] *Ibid.* s.93(2).

[34] *Ibid.* s.105(1).

[35] *Ibid.* s.105(2); see *Re Cathcart* [1893] 1 Ch. 466.

[36] See generally T.C.S. Keely (1943) 8 C.L.J. 195.

[37] Mental Health Act 1983, s.94(1A), inserted by Public Trustee and Administration of Funds Act 1986, s.2(2)(c).

[38] See *ante*, pp. 494 (conversion), 501 (reconversion), 512 (election); *infra* (settlements).

[39] Mental Health Act 1983, s.94(2).

[40] *Ibid.*

[41] *Ibid.* s.99. The receiver is in a special position, differing from that of an ordinary receiver: see *post*, p. 690.

[42] Mental Health Act 1983, ss.95, 96(1)(d), (2), replacing earlier provisions. See *Re Freeman* [1927] 1 Ch. 479 and *Re Greene* [1928] Ch. 528 (on L.P.A. 1925, s.171); *Re L. (W.J.G.)* [1966] Ch. 135 (on Mental Health Act 1959, ss.102, 103).

[43] *Re C.* [1960] 1 W.L.R. 92.

[44] *Re C.W.M.* [1951] 2 K.B. 714.

[45] The preceding two cases concerned settlements under L.P.A. 1925, s.171, but the discretion would no doubt be exercised similarly under the Act of 1983.

[46] Mental Health Act 1983, s.96(3); see *Re C.W.H.T.* [1978] Ch. 67.

CHAPTER 2

PENALTIES AND FORFEITURES

Section 1. Penalties

1. Nature of penalty. Where a contract provides that, on breach of a duty owed to one party, the other shall pay a sum of money, the sum may be an agreed sum for damages, known as liquidated damages, or it may be a penalty to be held over the other party *in terrorem*. A sum payable on breach may be a penalty even though a similar sum is payable on other events, *e.g.* death.[1] A provision requiring the transfer of property on breach may likewise be a penalty.[2] But there can be no penalty where there is no breach, as where a sum is payable in the event of a party going into liquidation,[3] or where a party exercises an option to terminate a contract on payment of certain sums.[4] Similarly, there can be no penalty where the sum is payable under an indemnity clause brought into operation by the breach of a duty owed by a third party.[5]

2. Relief in equity. Courts of equity intervened to relieve against penalties, cutting them down to the actual damage sustained.[6] This equitable jurisdiction can be traced back to Sir Thomas More's chancellorship.[7] In what was probably the earliest class of case for such intervention, the common money bond,[8] the Administration of Justice Acts 1696 and 1705 conferred upon common law courts similar powers of relief. Relief is a matter of substance and must be claimed before judgment is given: it cannot be used as a ground for a stay of execution after judgment.[9]

---

[1] *Cooden Engineering Co. Ltd.* v. *Stanford* [1953] 1 Q.B. 86.
[2] *Jobson* v. *Johnson* [1989] 1 W.L.R. 1026.
[3] *Re Apex Shipping Co. Ltd.* [1942] Ch. 108; and see *Alder* v. *Moore* [1961] 2 Q.B. 57; *Stirling Industrial Facilities Ltd.* v. *Lydiate Textiles Ltd.* (1962) 106 S.J. 669.
[4] *Associated Distributors Ltd.* v. *Hall* [1938] 2 K.B. 83; *Campbell Discount Co. Ltd.* v. *Bridge* [1961] 1 Q.B. 445, reversed on the ground that there was in fact a breach: *Bridge* v. *Campbell Discount Co. Ltd.* [1962] A.C. 600, where Viscount Simonds and Lord Morton thought *Associated Distributors Ltd.* v. *Hall, supra*, was rightly decided, and Lord Denning and Lord Devlin thought the contrary.
[5] *Export Credits Guarantee Department* v. *Universal Oil Products Co.* [1983] 1 W.L.R. 399.
[6] *Sloman* v. *Walter* (1784) 1 Bro.C.C. 418; **2 W. & T.L.C. 221.**
[7] See *Wyllie* v. *Wilkes* (1780) 2 Doug.K.B. 519 at 523, cited in *Jobson* v. *Johnson, supra*, at p. 1038.
[8] *i.e.* a bond to secure repayment of principal and interest with a stipulation for a greater sum, usually double, if repayment was not made on the due date. For the history, see A. W. B. Simpson (1966) 82 L.Q.R. 392.
[9] *T. C. Trustees Ltd.* v. *J. S. Darwen (Successors) Ltd.* [1969] 2 Q.B. 295.

3. Penalties distinguished from liquidated damages. "The true ground of relief against penalties is from the original intent of the case."[10] Looking at the substance of the matter rather than the form of words, the court has to determine what was the real intention of the parties. To assist in this process the following rules[11] have been laid down.

(a) *Substance not form.* Parties to a contract who use the words "penalty" or "liquidated damages" may prima facie be supposed to mean what they say; yet the expression used is not conclusive. The court must find out whether the payment stipulated is in truth a penalty or liquidated damages.[12]

(b) *Difference in essence.* The essence of a penalty is a payment of money stipulated as *in terrorem* of the offending party, while the essence of liquidated damages is a genuine covenanted pre-estimate of damage.[13]

(c) *Construction.* The question whether a sum stipulated is a penalty or liquidated damages is a question of construction to be decided upon the terms and inherent circumstances of each particular contract,[14] judged as at the time of the making of the contract and not as at the time of the breach.[15] "The court should not be astute to descry a 'penalty clause' in every provision of a contract which stipulates a sum to be payable by one party to the other in the event of a breach by the former."[16]

(d) *Relation to loss suffered.* The sum will be held to be a penalty if it is extravagant and unconscionable in amount in comparison with the greatest loss that could conceivably be proved to have followed from the breach.[17]

---

[10] *Peachy* v. *Duke of Somerset* (1721) 1 Stra. 447 at 453, *per* Lord Macclesfield L.C.; **2 W. & T.L.C. 212 at 218.**

[11] What follows is based on Lord Dunedin's speech in *Dunlop Pneumatic Tyre Co. Ltd.* v. *New Garage and Motor Co. Ltd.* [1915] A.C. 79 at 86–88.

[12] *Kemble* v. *Farren* (1829) 6 Bing. 141; *Pye* v. *British Automobile Commercial Syndicate* [1906] 1 Q.B. 425; *Diestal* v. *Stevenson* [1906] 2 K.B. 345; *Cellulose Acetate Silk Co. Ltd.* v. *Widnes Foundry (1925) Ltd.* [1933] A.C. 20; *Robert Stewart & Sons Ltd.* v. *Carapanayoti & Co. Ltd.* [1962] 1 W.L.R. 34 ("penalty" held liquidated damages); and see *Alder* v. *Moore* [1961] 2 Q.B. 57.

[13] *Clydebank Engineering and Shipbuilding Co. Ltd.* v. *Don José Ramos Yzquierdo y Castaneda* [1905] A.C. 6; see *Anglo Auto Finance Co. Ltd.* v. *James* [1963] 1 W.L.R. 1042.

[14] *Lombank Ltd.* v. *Excell* [1964] 1 Q.B. 415. Contrast *Bridge* v. *Campbell Discount Co. Ltd.* [1962] A.C. 600 and *E. P. Finance Co. Ltd.* v. *Dooley* [1963] 1 W.L.R. 1313, where a clause providing for payment of depreciation was held a penalty, with *Phonographic Equipment (1958) Ltd.* v. *Muslu* [1961] 1 W.L.R. 1379, where it was declared valid.

[15] *Public Works Commissioner* v. *Hills* [1906] A.C. 368; *Webster* v. *Bosanquet* [1912] A.C. 394; *Cooden Engineering Co. Ltd.* v. *Stanford* [1953] 1 Q.B. 86.

[16] *Robophone Facilities Ltd.* v. *Blank* [1966] 1 W.L.R. 1428 at 1447, *per* Diplock L.J.

[17] *Clydebank Engineering and Shipbuilding Co. Ltd.* v. *Don José Ramos Yzquierdo y Castaneda* [1905] A.C. 6 at 10; and see *Lamdon Trust Ltd.* v. *Hurrell* [1955] 1 W.L.R. 391; *Financings Ltd.* v. *Baldock* [1963] 2 Q.B. 104; contrast *Imperial Tobacco Co. Ltd.* v. *Parslay* [1936] 2 All E.R. 515.

(e) *Payment of smaller sum.*   Where the payment of a smaller sum is secured by a larger, the larger sum is a penalty.[18] This will be the case whether the larger sum becomes payable only on the failure to perform the stipulation for payment of the smaller sum or on breach of any of a number of stipulations of which the undertaking to pay the smaller sum is only one.[19] The court will not sever the stipulations. In cases of this kind the sum is clearly penal, for the breach of the contract to pay the smaller sum would give rise to nothing more than a right of action for that smaller amount, and if the parties have agreed that the breach shall give rise to a claim to a larger amount, there is clearly no genuine pre-estimate of damage.[20] But if on a loan repayable by instalments it is agreed that on default as to any one instalment the whole amount shall become payable forthwith, the agreement is not penal and no relief against it will be granted.[21]

(f) *Single sum for any breach.*   Where "a single lump sum is made payable by way of compensation, on the occurrence of one or more or all of several events, some of which may occasion serious and others but trifling damage," there is a presumption (but no more) that the lump sum is a penalty.[22] But if the damage is the same in kind for every possible breach and is incapable of being precisely ascertained, the sum will be regarded as liquidated damages if it is a fair pre-estimate of the probable damage and not unconscionable.[23]

(g) *Difficulty of estimation.*   Sometimes the consequences of a breach of contract are such as to make precise pre-estimation almost an impossibility. This is no obstacle to regarding the sum stipulated as being a genuine pre-estimate of damage; on the contrary, it is just the situation where it is probable that a pre-estimate of the damage was the true bargain between the parties.[24]

4. Damages exceeding penalty.   It is not yet settled whether a plaintiff can ignore a penalty clause and sue for damages if the damage occasioned by the breach exceeds the penalty. Probably he can,[25]

---

[18] *Kemble* v. *Farren* (1829) 6 Bing. 141.
[19] *Ibid.*
[20] But see *Wallis* v. *Smith* (1882) 21 Ch.D. 243 at 257.
[21] *The Protector Endowment Loan and Annuity Co.* v. *Grice* (1880) 5 Q.B.D. 592; *Wallingford* v. *Mutual Society* (1880) 5 App.Cas. 685; *Thompson* v. *Hudson* (1869) L.R. 4 H.L. 1.
[22] *Lord Elphinstone* v. *Monkland Iron and Coal Co. Ltd.* (1886) 11 App.Cas. 332 at 342, *per* Lord Watson; *Cooden Engineering Co. Ltd.* v. *Stanford* [1953] 1 Q.B. 86; *Capital Finance Co. Ltd.* v. *Donati* (1977) 121 S.J. 270. Contrast *Robophone Facilities Ltd.* v. *Blank* [1966] 1 W.L.R. 1428.
[23] *Dunlop Pneumatic Tyre Co.* v. *New Garage and Motor Co.* [1915] A.C. 79; and see *Re Apex Supply Co. Ltd.* [1942] Ch. 108.
[24] *Clydebank Engineering and Shipbuilding Co. Ltd.* v. *Don José Ramos Yzquierdo y Castaneda* [1905] A.C. 6 at 11; *Webster* v. *Bosanquet* [1912] A.C. 394 at 398; *English Hop Growers Ltd.* v. *Dering* [1928] 2 K.B. 174.
[25] See *Wall* v. *Rederiaktiebolaget Luggude* [1915] 3 K.B. 66; *Watts, Watts & Co. Ltd.* v. *Mitsui & Co. Ltd.* [1917] A.C. 227 at 245, 246. *Cf.* (1976) 92 L.Q.R. 20 (J. L. Barton).

although he clearly cannot do so where the contract shows that if there is a breach of the contract the right to recover the specified sum is to be his only right.[26]

5. Enforcement by injunction. Where a man covenants to perform or abstain from some act, and further agrees to pay a penalty if he fails to observe his contract, he cannot justify a breach of contract by electing to pay the sum, but may be compelled by injunction to the agreed performance or abstention.[27] As Sir Edward Sugden L.C. observed,[28] "if a thing be agreed upon to be done, though there is a penalty annexed to secure its performance, yet the very thing itself must be done."

6. Non-payment of instalments. Contracts for sale in which the purchase-money is payable by instalments sometimes contain a proviso that if an instalment is not duly paid, the vendor may rescind the contract and retain the instalments already paid. The courts will not normally relieve against the forfeiture of the instalments, as the proviso is an integral part of the contract and not a mere collateral penalty.[29] Relief may be granted, however, if the purchaser is ready and willing to carry out the contract at the time of the action.[30]

Section 2. Forfeitures

1. Principles of relief. The principle is that in appropriate and limited cases courts of equity will grant relief against forfeiture for breach of covenant or condition where the primary object of the bargain is to secure a stated result and the provision for forfeiture is added as security for the production of that result.[31] In determining whether a case is appropriate for relief, the court considers the conduct of the applicant for relief (and in particular whether his default was wilful),

---

[26] *Cellulose Acetate Silk Co. Ltd.* v. *Widnes Foundry (1925) Ltd.* [1933] A.C. 20.

[27] *Weston* v. *Managers of the Metropolitan Asylums District* (1882) 9 Q.B.D. 404; *Hardy* v. *Martin* (1783) 1 Cox Eq. 26. And see *Howard* v. *Hopkyns* (1742) 2 Atk. 371 (specific performance).

[28] *French* v. *Macale* (1842) 2 Dr. & War. 269 at 274. See also *ante*, p. 333, and *post*, p. 648.

[29] *Mussen* v. *Van Diemen's Land Co.* [1938] Ch. 253, explaining *Steedman* v. *Drinkle* [1916] 1 A.C. 275; and see *Cooden Engineering Co. Ltd.* v. *Stanford* [1953] 1 Q.B. 86 at 112, *per* Jenkins L.J., dissenting; *Stockloser* v. *Johnson* [1954] 1 Q.B. 476; *Galbraith* v. *Mitchenall Estates Ltd.* [1965] 2 Q.B. 473, criticised by K. Polack [1965] C.L.J. 17.

[30] *Kilmer* v. *British Columbia Orchard Lands Ltd.* [1913] A.C. 319; *Mussen* v. *Van Diemen's Land Co.* [1938] Ch. 253 at 263, 264. The proposition in the text above was denied by Somervell and Denning L.JJ. (*obiter*) in *Stockloser* v. *Johnson, supra*, at pp. 487, 488, 492, but was affirmed by Romer L.J., *ibid.* at p. 501. For Canadian cases, see W. F. Ryan (1954) 32 Can.B.R. 568 at 574–577.

[31] *Shiloh Spinners Ltd.* v. *Harding* [1973] A.C. 691. See generally C. Harpum [1984] C.L.J. 134; A.G. Lang (1984) 100 L.Q.R. 427.

how grave the breaches were, and what disparity there is between the value of the property forfeited and the damage caused by the breach.[32] In general, equity granted relief only where the forfeiture in substance was merely security for payment of a monetary sum[33] as where the contract for sale of land makes provision for payment of the price by instalments and confers on the vendor a right in the event of default to rescind the contract and retain the moneys already paid[34]; but the jurisdiction is not confined to such cases, and it applies, *e.g.* to a right of entry reserved on an assignment of leasehold premises in respect of the assignee's breaches of positive and restrictive covenants designed to protect the assignor's adjoining premises.[35] The doctrine of relief against forfeiture is, however, restricted to contracts concerning the transfer of proprietary or possessory rights,[36] whether in land or other assets[37]; it is thus inapplicable to the right of shipowners under a time charter to withdraw the vessel upon non-payment of hire,[38] or to a provision for termination of an exclusive licence granted to the buyer of goods to use the plaintiff's trade names and trade marks.[39]

2. Forfeiture of leases. The most important illustration of these principles was the proviso for re-entry contained in a lease. Equity would relieve against forfeiture of the lease for non-payment of rent, even after a peaceable re-entry by the landlord without the assistance of the court,[40] for such a proviso was regarded simply as a security for rent.[41] This jurisdiction would probably not be exercised while the forfeiture was merely threatened and the lessor had neither taken possession nor commenced proceedings for forfeiture[42]; but it may not be confined to land, and so might be exercisable in respect of a hiring or lease of chattels.[43] However, save in very exceptional circumstances,[44] no relief was granted against forfeiture for other breaches of covenant, *e.g.* to repair,[45] or to lay out a specific sum of money on repairs in a given time,[46] or not to underlet without consent.[47] Jurisdiction to grant relief against most of such breaches of covenant is now conferred by

---

[32] *Shiloh Spinners Ltd.* v. *Harding* [1973] A.C. 691 at 723, 724; *The "Vainqueur José"* [1979] 1 Lloyd's Rep. 557 at 579.

[33] See *Hill* v. *Barclay* (1811) 18 Ves. 56; *Scandinavian Trading Tanker Co. A.B.* v. *Flota Petrolera Ecuatoriana* [1983] 2 A.C. 694 at 702.

[34] *Starside Properties Ltd.* v. *Mustafa* [1974] 1 W.L.R. 816, citing much of this passage at p. 821 (court may extend time originally allowed for compliance with terms on which relief granted).

[35] *Shiloh Spinners Ltd.* v. *Harding* [1973] A.C. 691. And see *Legione* v. *Hartley* (1983) 152 C.L.R. 406, *post*, p. 609, n. 76.

[36] *B.I.C.C. Plc* v. *Burndy Corporation* [1985] Ch. 232 at 252.

[37] *B.I.C.C. Plc* v. *Burndy Corporation* [1985] Ch. 232 (joint interest in patents).

[38] *Scandinavian Trading Tanker Co. A.B.* v. *Flota Petrolera Ecuatoriana* [1983] 2 A.C. 694.

[39] *Sport International Bussum B.V.* v. *Inter-Footwear Ltd.* [1984] 1 W.L.R. 776.

[40] *Howard* v. *Fanshawe* [1895] 2 Ch. 581.

[41] *Howard* v. *Fanshawe*, *supra*, at p. 588.

[42] *Barton Thompson & Co. Ltd.* v. *Stapling Machines Co.* [1966] Ch. 499.

[43] *Ibid.*

[44] See *Hannam* v. *South London Waterworks Co.* (1816) 2 Mer. 61; *Re Edridge, ex p. Vaughan* (1823) T. & R. 434.

[45] *Hill* v. *Barclay* (1811) 18 Ves. 56.

[46] *Bracebridge* v. *Buckley* (1816) 2 Price 200.

[47] *Barrow* v. *Isaacs & Son* [1891] 1 Q.B. 417.

statute,[48] the details of which lie outside the scope of this book.[49] Nevertheless the equitable jurisdiction survives in cases not falling within the statutory provisions.[50]

---

[48] As to non-payment of rent, by the Common Law Procedure Act 1852, ss.210–212 (replacing the Landlord and Tenant Act 1730, ss.2–4), and County Courts Act 1984, ss.138, 139, as amended by Administration of Justice Act 1985, s.55; as to other breaches, by L.P.A. 1925, s.146, replacing C.A. 1881, s.14, and C.A. 1892, ss.2, 4, 5.
[49] See, e.g. Megarry & Wade's *Law of Real Property* (5th ed., 1984), pp. 676 *et seq.*; *Woodfall's Law of Landlord and Tenant* (1990), paras. 1–1924—1–1950, 1–1956—1–1964.
[50] *Abbey National B.S.* v. *Maybeech Ltd.* [1985] Ch. 190.

CHAPTER 3

ACCIDENT

Section 1. Jurisdiction of Equity

1. The jurisdiction. Courts of equity granted relief where some accident rendered unjust the rigid application of common law rules. For this purpose, an "accident" was any unforeseen event which occasioned loss where neither the event nor the loss was attributable to any misconduct, negligence or culpable inadvertence on the part of the person concerned. Thus executors were relieved where assets in the estate had been lost without their fault[1]; and he who had lost documents, such as bonds or title deeds, might be aided in equity in cases where the common law rules as to secondary evidence were an inadequate protection.[2] But an accident which prevented a party from fulfilling his contract was no ground for the interference of equity. A lessee must pay his rent even if the premises are destroyed by fire.[3] In addition to unforeseen events, the mistake of a party to a transaction was relievable in equity under this head. Thus, where a deed is wholly misconceived, as where an appointment under a power is made in complete forgetfulness of a previous appointment to the same person,[4] it may be rescinded[5] or cancelled.[6]

2. Extent of the jurisdiction today. Mistake is not now regarded as exclusively resting on equitable principles, but has been absorbed by the common law; and the remainder of the jurisdiction of equity to grant relief against accidents is of little importance. The defective execution of powers, however, requires separate consideration.

[1] *Ante*, p. 355.
[2] See, *e.g. Dalston* v. *Coatsworth* (1721) 1 P.Wms. 731; *Dormer* v. *Fortescue* (1744) 3 Atk. 124 at 132.
[3] *Pym* v. *Blackburn* (1796) 3 Ves. 34; *Leeds* v. *Cheetham* (1827) 1 Sim. 146. Similarly as between vendors and purchasers: *Paine* v. *Meller* (1801) 6 Ves. 349 (fire); *Cass* v. *Rudele* (1693) 2 Vern. 280 (earthquake).
[4] *Lady Hood of Avalon* v. *Mackinnon* [1909] 1 Ch. 476.
[5] *Ibid.*; and see *Ellis* v. *Ellis* (1909) 26 T.L.R. 166.
[6] *Re Walton's Settlement* [1922] 2 Ch. 509.

Section 2. Defective Execution of Powers

1. Compliance with requirements of power. A person entitled to exercise a power of appointment may either make no attempt to exercise it, or he may attempt to exercise it in a way not authorised by the instrument creating the power, as where that instrument requires the power to be exercised by deed and an appointment is made under hand only. In each case the power will prima facie be treated as unexercised, and the objects of the power will take nothing. But this rule has been qualified both by statute[7] and by equity.

2. Statutory relaxations

(a) *Inter vivos.* By the Law of Property Act 1925,[8] a power to appoint by deed or by any non-testamentary instrument in writing may be validly exercised by a deed executed in the presence of and attested by at least two witnesses, even if the instrument creating the power expressly requires further formalities.[9] But this provision does not defeat any requirement making the consent of any particular person a condition of appointment, nor does it enable any requirements for due execution to be dispensed with, other than those relating to the mode of execution and attestation.[10] The section does not render a deed essential where the terms of the power do not require a deed, nor are two witnesses necessary if the appointment complies with the terms of the power.[11]

(b) *Wills.* A power to appoint by will sometimes imposes certain formal requirements for the exercise of the power, as by requiring the observance of some additional or other form of execution or solemnity. By statute, however, an appointment by will is not to be treated as an improper execution of the power merely because such formalities have not been observed, provided the will was executed in accordance with the formalities required by the Wills Act 1837,[12] or the execution of the will was otherwise valid under English law,[13] *e.g.* because it conformed to the internal law of the territory where it was executed or where the testator (either when he made the will or at his death) was domiciled or habitually resident, or had his nationality.[14] Thus if the power is to appoint by "deed or will to be respectively signed, sealed and delivered"

---

[7] As to the exercise of a power of leasing, see also L.P.A. 1925, s.152 (replacing the Leases Acts 1849 and 1850), applied in *Pawson* v. *Revell* [1958] 2 Q.B. 360. See also D. W. Elliott (1971) 87 L.Q.R. 338 as to defective leases by tenants for life, discussing S.L.A. 1925, s.110, and L.P.A. 1925, s.152.
[8] Replacing L.P.Am.A. 1859, s.12.
[9] L.P.A. 1925, s.159(1).
[10] *Ibid.* s.159(2).
[11] *Ibid.* s.159(3).
[12] Wills Act 1837, s.10.
[13] Wills Act 1963, s.2(2).
[14] *Ibid.* s.1, replacing and extending Wills Act 1861, s.1.

in the presence of three witnesses, it can nevertheless be duly exercised by a will merely signed (and not sealed) in the presence of two witnesses in the usual way[14a]; but such a will cannot exercise a power to appoint by an "instrument" which is to be "signed, sealed and delivered" in the presence of two witnesses, for it is not such an instrument.[15]

3. Relief in equity. The equitable doctrine is that while the total non-execution of a mere power will not be aided in equity,[16] yet where by reason of accident or mistake there is a defective execution of the power, equity will grant relief against formal defects in favour of certain favoured persons who are regarded as having provided good consideration.[17]

(a) *Relief only to favoured persons.* Equity will grant relief only in favour of certain persons, namely, a purchaser[18] (including a mortgagee[19] or a lessee[20]), a creditor,[21] a wife,[22] a legitimate child,[23] and a charity.[24] A defective execution will not be aided in favour of a husband,[25] an illegitimate child,[26] a grandchild,[27] or remote relations generally, or a volunteer.[28] Moreover, defective execution, even in favour of children, will not be aided if the result is to take away property from others of equal degree and thus leave them wholly[29] unprovided for.[30]

(b) *No relief against substantial defects.* Secondly, relief will be granted against only those defects which are not of the very essence and substance of the power.[31] Thus the execution by will of a power which should have been executed by deed is relievable, for the defect here is purely one of form.[32] But no relief will be granted where a power exercisable by deed executed before X attains twenty-five is exercised by a will executed before, but coming into operation after, that time,[33] or where the power is exercised without the consent of the persons required to consent to its execution.[34] Again, if the power is to be

[14a] *Taylor* v. *Meads* (1865) 4 De G. J. & S. 587 at 601.
[15] *Taylor* v. *Meads* (1865) 4 De G.J. & S. 597.
[16] *Garth* v. *Townsend* (1869) L.R. 7 Eq. 220; *Re Huddleston* [1894] 3 Ch. 595.
[17] For good consideration, see *ante*, p. 125.
[18] *Fothergill* v. *Fothergill* (1702) 2 Free.Ch. 256; *Re Dykes' Estate* (1869) L.R. 7 Eq. 337.
[19] *Taylor* v. *Wheeler* (1706) 2 Vern. 564.
[20] *Campbell* v. *Leach* (1775) Amb. 740.
[21] *Pollard* v. *Greenvil* (1661) 1 Ch.Ca. 10.
[22] *Clifford* v. *Burlington* (1700) 2 Vern. 379.
[23] *Bruce* v. *Bruce* (1870) L.R. 11 Eq. 371.
[24] *Att.-Gen.* v. *Sibthorpe* (1830) 2 Russ. & M. 107; *Innes* v. *Sayer* (1851) 3 Mac. & G. 606.
[25] *Moodie* v. *Reid* (1816) 1 Madd. 516.
[26] *Blake* v. *Blake* (1817) Beat. 575.
[27] *Kettle* v. *Townsend* (c. 1700) 1 Salk. 187; *Perry* v. *Whitehead* (1801) 6 Ves. 544.
[28] *Re Anstis* (1886) 31 Ch.D. 596.
[29] See *Morse* v. *Martin* (1865) 34 Beav. 500; *Re Walker, MacColl* v. *Bruce* [1908] 1 Ch. 560.
[30] *Chapman* v. *Gibson* (1791) 3 Bro.C.C. 229 at 230.
[31] *Cockerell* v. *Cholmeley* (1830) 1 Russ. & M. 418.
[32] *Tollet* v. *Tollet* (1728) 2 P.Wms. 489; **2 W. & T.L.C. 249.**
[33] *Cooper* v. *Martin* (1867) 3 Ch.App. 47; and see *Re Hambro's Marriage Settlements* [1949] Ch. 484.
[34] *Mansell* v. *Mansell* (1757) Wilm. 36.

executed by will only and it is executed by irrevocable deed, no relief
will be granted; for here the difference in the method of execution is
one of substance, resulting in an irrevocable appointment, whereas the
power only contemplated an appointment revocable at any time during
the appointor's lifetime [35]

(c) *Covenants.* A covenant as to the exercise of a testamentary
special power is not necessarily inoperative. True, a covenant to appoint
in a particular manner under a testamentary special power, or not to
revoke an appointment already made under such a power, has no legal
effect,[36] for this would be practically allowing the power to be exercised
by deed. But the donee of the power can by deed negatively tie his
hands as to the way in which he shall exercise the power, whether as to
the amounts to be appointed or as to the persons to benefit. Thus if A is
one of the persons entitled in default of appointment, the donee may
covenant that A shall not have less than the amount to which he would
be entitled in default of appointment, or some smaller amount. In that
case the donee cannot appoint so that A takes less than that amount,
either under an appointment or in default of appointment, or in both
ways.[37] And if as regards B, who is one of the objects of the power, the
donee releases the power, or covenants not to exercise it, no valid
appointment can thereafter be made in B's favour.[38]

4. Powers in the nature of a trust. As regards relief in equity,
powers in the nature of a trust are in a different position from mere
powers. A power in the nature of a trust is as binding upon the
conscience as an actual trust. Accordingly, equity relieves even against
the non-execution of the power, and in the absence of a more suitable
basis of division[39] decrees the objects of the power to take equally, since
equity is equality.[40]

---

[35] *Adney* v. *Field* (1767) Amb. 654; *Reid* v. *Shergold* (1805) 10 Ves. 370. See also *post*, p. 597.
[36] *Re Cooke, Winckley* v. *Winterton* [1922] 1 Ch. 292.
[37] *Re Evered* [1910] 2 Ch. 147; and see L.P.A. 1925, ss.155, 156.
[38] *Re Brown's Settlement* [1939] Ch. 944.
[39] See *ante*, p. 236.
[40] See *ante*, pp. 97, 98.

CHAPTER 4

FRAUD

Three things are to be helpt in Conscience;
Fraud, Accident, and things of Confidence.

THIS couplet, attributed to Sir Thomas More L.C.,[1] indicates the
general jurisdiction of the Court of Chancery. "Things of Confidence"
have been discussed in the chapters on trusts,[2] and "Accident" in the
last chapter. "Fraud" remains for this chapter. Fraud is far-reaching: for
centuries the rule has been that fraud unravels all.[3] One species of
fraud, fraudulent misrepresentation, was also remedied by the common
law courts and gives rise to a claim for damages. Purely equitable fraud,
on the other hand, merely entitles the victim to rescind the transaction
procured by or tainted with it, and to regain the position in which he
was before the injury.[4]

PART 1

ACTUAL FRAUD

1. Fraudulent misrepresentation

(a) *Definition.* Fraud which courts of equity remedied concurrently
with courts of common law can be defined with some precision. It
consists of a false statement of fact[5] which is made by D[6] to P[7]
knowingly, or without belief in its truth, or recklessly, without caring
whether it is true or false,[8] with the intent that it should be acted upon[9]

[1] (1668) 1 Roll.Abr. 374.
[2] See also *post*, p. 682.
[3] See *Master* v. *Miller* (1791) 4 T.R. 320 at 337; *May* v. *Platt* [1900] 1 Ch. 616 at 623; *London General Omnibus Co. Ltd.* v. *Holloway* [1912] 2 K.B. 72 at 81; *Lazarus Estates Ltd.* v. *Beasley* [1956] 1 Q.B. 702 at 712.
[4] *Redgrave* v. *Hurd* (1881) 20 Ch.D. 1. For rescission, see *post*, p. 616.
[5] See *Anderson* v. *Pacific Fire and Marine Insurance Co.* (1872) L.R. 7 C.P. 65; *Bisset* v. *Wilkinson* [1927] A.C. 177.
[6] *Karberg's Case* [1892] 3 Ch. 1 at 13.
[7] *Andrews* v. *Mockford* [1896] 1 Q.B. 372.
[8] *Derry* v. *Peek* (1889) 14 App.Cas. 337.
[9] *Peek* v. *Gurney* (1873) L.R. 6 H.L. 377.

548

and which is in fact acted upon by P.[10] D will be liable in such a case even though the misrepresentation was made with no corrupt motive[11] and with no expectation of profit,[12] and even though the person defrauded had a full opportunity of discovering the fraud[13] or had an agent who knew the truth.[14] But where an agent innocently makes a statement which his principal knows to be false, neither agent nor principal is guilty of fraud[15] unless the principal intended the agent to make the false statement.[16]

(b) *Silence.* Although a mere failure to reveal a fact is no fraud in this sense,[17] sometimes the maxim *suppressio veri suggestio falsi* will apply; for even if a partial statement is verbally accurate, it may be as false in effect as if the fact had been misstated altogether.[18] "If by a number of statements you intentionally give a false impression and induce a person to act upon it, it is not the less false, although if one takes each statement by itself there may be a difficulty in showing that any specific statement is untrue."[19] A similar rule applies if D induces P not to make further inquiry as to facts which might affect his judgment in respect of the contract.[20]

(c) *Damage.* Although P may resist specific performance of a contract induced by fraud without showing that he has suffered damage,[21] or may rescind it,[22] he cannot bring an action for deceit without proving that he has acted upon the misrepresentation to his damage.

2. Minor representing himself as of full age

(a) *The rule.* A special case is that of a minor fraudulently misrepresenting his age. Speaking generally, a minor may acquire and dispose of property[23] but cannot bind himself by contract.[24] Thus, where

---

[10] *Horsfall* v. *Thomas* (1862) 1 H. & C. 90. See *Macleay* v. *Tait* [1906] A.C. 24. Though the plaintiff must prove reliance on the statement (*Derry* v. *Peek* itself nearly foundered on this account: see *Horwood* v. *Statesman Publishing Co. Ltd.* (1929) 141 L.T. 54 at 58), his acting raises a rebuttable presumption of fact that it was in reliance on the statement: *Smith* v. *Chadwick* (1884) 9 App.Cas. 187 at 196; *Reynell* v. *Sprye* (1852) 1 De G.M. & G. 600; *Redgrave* v. *Hurd* (1881) 20 Ch.D. 1 at 21.

[11] *Polhill* v. *Walter* (1832) 3 B. & Ad. 114.

[12] *Pasley* v. *Freeman* (1789) 3 T.R. 51.

[13] *Redgrave* v. *Hurd* (1881) 20 Ch.D. 1; *Central Ry. of Venezuela* v. *Kisch* (1867) L.R. 2 H.L. 99.

[14] *Wells* v. *Smith* [1914] 3 K.B. 722.

[15] *Armstrong* v. *Strain* [1952] 1 K.B. 232; see L. C. B. Gower (1952) 15 M.L.R. 232; J. Unger, *ibid.* p. 508.

[16] *Ludgater* v. *Love* (1881) 44 L.T. 694.

[17] *Keates* v. *Earl of Cadogan* (1851) 10 C.B. 591. See *Walters* v. *Morgan* (1861) 3 De G.F. & J. 718 at 723, 724.

[18] *Arkwright* v. *Newbould* (1881) 17 Ch.D. 301 at 318; *Peek* v. *Gurney* (1873) L.R. 6 H.L. 377; and see *Coles* v. *White City (Manchester) Greyhound Association* (1929) 45 T.L.R. 230; *ante*, pp. 470, 471.

[19] *Aaron's Reefs Ltd.* v. *Twiss* [1896] A.C. 273 at 281, *per* Lord Halsbury L.C.

[20] *Porter* v. *Moore* [1904] 2 Ch. 367.

[21] See *post*, p. 602.

[22] See *post*, p. 617.

[23] *Taylor* v. *Johnston* (1882) 19 Ch.D. 603.

[24] See generally *Chitty on Contracts* (26th ed., 1989), Vol. 1, paras. 552–612; Minors' Contracts Act 1987.

a minor induces persons to deal with him by misrepresenting himself as of full age, there is no remedy against him in contract,[25] for that would deprive many minors of their contractual immunity; nor can he be made liable in tort[26] by an action for deceit, for the tort is too intimately connected with the contract. But equity provided a remedy against a minor who sought to take advantage of his minority to support a fraud. This remedy has been summarised thus: "When an infant obtained an advantage by falsely stating himself to be of full age, equity required him to restore his ill-gotten gains, or to release the party deceived from obligations or acts in law induced by the fraud, but scrupulously stopped short of enforcing against him a contractual obligation, entered into while he was an infant, even by means of a fraud."[27]

(b) *Operation of rule.* A minor who thus induces trustees to pay over a fund cannot afterwards treat the payment as ineffectual and make the trustees pay over again[28]; and where a minor obtained a lease of a furnished dwelling-house, the court ordered the lease to be cancelled and the property given up, although the minor could not be made liable for use and occupation in the meantime.[29] A minor must restore goods obtained by fraudulently misstating his age, and has even been made to account for the proceeds of sale of goods so obtained,[30] possibly on the ground that the goods may be traced into the proceeds of sale.[31]

(c) *Statutory remedy.* Statute now provides that, where a contract is unenforceable against a defendant (or he repudiates it) because he was a minor when the contract was made, "the court may, if it is just and equitable to do so, require the defendant to transfer to the plaintiff any property acquired by the defendant under the contract, or any property representing it."[32]

This remedy, which is available in addition to the equitable jurisdiction,[33] is of wider scope than the latter in that it is not confined to cases in which a representation as to age was the means by which the minor obtained property.

PART 2

CONSTRUCTIVE FRAUD

In equity, the term "fraud" embraces not only actual fraud, in the sense just defined, but also certain other conduct which falls below the

---

[25] *Jennings* v. *Rundall* (1799) 8 T.R. 335; *Levene* v. *Brougham* (1909) 25 T.L.R. 265.
[26] *Burnard* v. *Haggis* (1863) C.B.(N.S.) 45; see also *Ballett* v. *Mingay* [1943] K.B. 281.
[27] *R. Leslie Ltd.* v. *Shiell* [1914] 3 K.B. 607 at 618, *per* Lord Sumner.
[28] See *ante*, p. 52.
[29] *Lemprière* v. *Lange* (1879) 12 Ch.D. 675. See also *Clarke* v. *Cobley* (1789) 2 Cox.Eq. 173.
[30] *Stocks* v. *Wilson* [1913] 2 K.B. 235.
[31] See *R. Leslie Ltd.* v. *Shiell* [1914] 3 K.B. 607 at 619.
[32] Minors' Contracts Act 1987, s.3(1), applying to contracts made after June 9, 1987: see s.5(2).
[33] See *ibid.* s.3(2).

standards demanded by equity. Courts of equity did not even stop at "moral fraud in the ordinary sense" but took account of any "breach of the sort of obligation which is enforced by a court that from the beginning regarded itself as a court of conscience."[34] The courts have refused to define this extended, or constructive, fraud; for, in the words of Lord Hardwicke,[35] "Fraud is infinite, and were a Court of Equity once to lay down rules, how far they would go, and no farther, in extending their relief against it, or to define strictly the species of evidence of it, the jurisdiction would be cramped, and perpetually eluded by new schemes which the fertility of man's invention would contrive." Nevertheless, in *Earl of Chesterfield* v. *Janssen*[36] the same judge had classified fraud in a manner which coloured subsequent development. In the light of this development, constructive fraud may be treated under the four headings of undue influence, abuse of confidence, unconscionable bargains, and frauds on powers.

Section 1. Undue Influence

1. The rule. Gifts and other transactions will be set aside if they have been procured by undue influence. As in other contexts,[37] equity intervenes as a result of some unconscionable conduct on the part of the defendant. It does not save people from the consequences of their own folly, but will save them from being victimised by other people.[38] "Extravagant liberality and immoderate folly do not of themselves provide a passport to equitable relief."[39] Nor will relief be forthcoming where all that is shown is inequality of bargaining power.[40] Cases where the doctrine operates may be divided into two classes, which may overlap[41]: "First, where the court has been satisfied that the gift was the result of influence expressly used by the donee for the purpose; second, where the relations between the donor and donee have at or shortly before the execution of the gift been such as to raise a presumption that the donee had influence over the donor."[42] Furthermore, the person influenced need not be the owner of the property; it is sufficient if he controls it on behalf of the owner.[43] And it is no defence that the gifts

---

[34] *Nocton* v. *Lord Ashburton* [1914] A.C. 932 at 954, *per* Viscount Haldane L.C.

[35] In a letter to Lord Kames dated June 30, 1759, printed in Parkes' *History of the Court of Chancery* (1828), p. 508. See also *Reddaway* v. *Banham* [1896] A.C. 199 at 221, *per* Lord Macnaghten: "Fraud is infinite in variety; sometimes it is audacious and unblushing; sometimes it pays a sort of homage to virtue, and then it is modest and retiring; it would be honesty itself if it could only afford it."

[36] (1751) 2 Ves. Sen. 125; **1 W. & T.L.C. 248.**

[37] See *ante*, pp. 186, 192, and *post*, p. 569.

[38] *Allcard* v. *Skinner* (1887) 36 Ch.D. 145 at 182, 183, approved in *National Westminster Bank plc* v. *Morgan* [1985] A.C. 686 at 705; and see *Huguenin* v. *Baseley* (1807) 14 Ves. 273 at 287; **1 W. & T.L.C. 203 at 210, 211,** approved in *Dent* v. *Bennett* (1839) 4 My & Cr. 269 at 277.

[39] *Tufton* v. *Sperni* [1952] 2 T.L.R. 516 at 519, *per* Sir Raymond Evershed M.R.

[40] *National Westminster Bank plc* v. *Morgan* [1985] A.C. 686 at 707, 708, disapproving the dictum of Lord Denning M.R. in *Lloyds Bank Ltd.* v. *Bundy* [1975] Q.B. 326 at 339 (repeated in *Avon Finance Co. Ltd.* v. *Bridger* (1979) [1985] 2 All E.R. 281 at 286).

[41] *Morley* v. *Loughnan* [1893] 1 Ch. 736; *Goldsworthy* v. *Brickell* [1987] Ch. 378 at 402.

[42] *Allcard* v. *Skinner* (1887) 36 Ch.D. 145 at 171, *per* Cotton L.J. (dissenting, though not on this point).

[43] *Chennells* v. *Bruce* (1939) 55 T.L.R. 422. See *Luddy's Trustee* v. *Peard* (1886) 33 Ch.D. 500.

have been received by third parties[44] provided that they were procured by undue influence.[45] But where the property has been applied to charitable purposes which both parties were anxious to promote, the person exercising the influence is not liable to repay personally money so spent.[46]

2. Express influence. Where there is no fiduciary relationship between the parties to the transaction, the onus is on the party alleging the use of undue influence to prove it. It is difficult to distinguish between permissible forms of coercion and persuasion on the one hand, and undue influence on the other. The line between them is regulated by considerations of public policy.[47] An example of express undue influence is *Williams* v. *Bayley*.[48] In that case a mortgage by a father in favour of his son's bankers was set aside because the father had been induced to enter into the mortgage in order to avert the prosecution of his son for forgery of bills held by the bank. The court interferes in this class of case on the simple principle that no one is allowed to retain any benefit arising from his own fraud or wrongful act.[49] If, however, there is no benefit, there will be no relief. A transaction not manifestly disadvantageous will not be set aside even if undue influence is expressly exercised.[50]

3. Presumed influence. In the second class of case, where influence is presumed from some relationship between the parties, the onus is on the party taking the benefit to prove that it was not procured by undue influence.[51] In such cases "the Court interferes not on the ground that any wrongful act has in fact been committed by the donee, but on the ground of public policy, and to prevent the relations which existed between the parties and the influence arising therefrom from being abused."[52] There are three matters to be considered: the type of benefit, the relationship which gives rise to the presumption, and the circumstances necessary to rebut it.

(a) *Type of benefit.* It is not only gifts which are liable to be set aside, but also transactions arising out of contracts.[53] What is required is a gift so large or a transaction so improvident "as not to be reasonably accounted for on the ground of friendship, relationship, charity or other

---

[44] *Huguenin* v. *Baseley* (1807) 14 Ves. 273; **1 W. & T.L.C. 203,** citing *Bridgeman* v. *Green* (1757) Wilm. 58 at 64, 65.
[45] *Wright* v. *Carter* [1903] 1 Ch. 27; *Bullock* v. *Lloyds Bank Ltd.* [1955] Ch. 317.
[46] *Allcard* v. *Skinner* (1887) 36 Ch.D. 145 at 171.
[47] *Mutual Finance Ltd.* v. *John Wetton & Sons Ltd.* [1937] 2 K.B. 389 at 394, 395; *Kaufman* v. *Gerson* [1904] 1 K.B. 591.
[48] (1866) L.R. 1 H.L. 200. For other examples, see *Bank of Montreal* v. *Stuart* [1911] A.C. 120; *Re Craig* [1971] Ch. 95.
[49] *Allcard* v. *Skinner* (1887) 36 Ch.D. 145 at 171.
[50] *Bank of Credit and Commerce International S.A.* v. *Aboody* [1990] Q.B. 923.
[51] *Allcard* v. *Skinner* (1887) 36 Ch.D. 145 at 171, 181.
[52] *Ibid.* at p. 171, *per* Cotton L.J.
[53] *Tufton* v. *Sperni* [1952] 2 T.L.R. 516 at 526.

ordinary motives on which ordinary men act."[54] Examples are purchases at an undervalue or sales at an excessive price,[55] or leases which damage the reversion,[56] or mortgages or guarantees to secure the debts of another.[57] A transaction not manifestly to the disadvantage of the person influenced will not be set aside.[58] Undue influence is never presumed in the case of testamentary gifts, but the court will not admit a will to probate if its execution is shown to have been procured by express influence.[59]

(b) *Fiduciary relationship.* "At least since the time of Lord Eldon, equity has steadfastly and wisely refused to put limits on the relationships to which the presumption can apply."[60] There has to be found a degree of trust and confidence such that "the party in whom it is reposed, either because he is or has become an adviser of the other or because he has become entrusted with the management of his affairs or everyday needs or for some other reason, is in a position to influence him into effecting the transaction of which complaint is later made."[61] The degree of trust or confidence need not amount to domination[62]; simple reliance is sufficient. But there has to be some degree of trust or confidence. The mere existence of a fiduciary relationship will not inevitably raise the presumption,[63] as fiduciary relationships cover a wide range.[64] In those where the fiduciary relationship is alleged to arise from the reposing of trust or confidence there is normally no substitute in this branch of the law for a "meticulous examination of the facts" to determine whether the relationship exists.[65] In some cases no such relationship was established as where an independent old autocrat thrust a lease on a man of lower social status on whom he had come to rely as a dependable friend but not a confidential adviser.[66] Similarly in commercial relationships advice may be given or recommendations made which do not give rise to a fiduciary relationship, *e.g.* banker and customer,[67] petrol company and garage proprietor,[68] landlord and tenant combined with that of employer and employee.[69] In other cases

---

[54] *Goldsworthy* v. *Brickell* [1987] Ch. 378 at 401, *per* Nourse L.J.
[55] *Tate* v. *Williamson* (1866) 2 Ch.App. 55.
[56] *Goldsworthy* v. *Brickell* [1987] Ch. 378.
[57] *Lloyds Bank Ltd.* v. *Bundy* [1975] Q.B. 326.
[58] *National Westminster Bank plc* v. *Morgan* [1985] A.C. 686, esp. at 704; *Midland Bank plc* v. *Shephard* [1988] 2 All E.R. 17 at 21.
[59] *Craig* v. *Lamoureux* [1920] A.C. 349 at 356, 357. The separate doctrine of righteousness covers some of the ground: see (1970) 86 L.Q.R. 447; W. H. D. Winder (1939) 3 M.L.R. 97 at 104 *et seq.*
[60] *Goldsworthy* v. *Brickell* [1987] Ch. 378 at 401, *per* Nourse L.J.
[61] *Ibid.*; and see *Billage* v. *Southee* (1852) 9 Hare 534 at 540.
[62] *Goldsworthy* v. *Brickell* [1987] Ch. 378, explaining *National Westminster Bank plc* v. *Morgan* [1985] A.C. 686.
[63] *Re Coomber* [1911] 1 Ch. 723; *Smith* v. *Kay* (1859) 7 H.L.C. 750 at 771; *Goldsworthy* v. *Brickell*, *supra*, at p. 401.
[64] See *Re Coomber*, *supra* (son managing business for mother); and other examples, *ante*, p. 252.
[65] *National Westminster Bank plc* v. *Morgan* [1985] A.C. 686 at 709, *per* Lord Scarman; see, *e.g. Tufton* v. *Sperni* [1952] 2 T.L.R. 516.
[66] *Re Brocklehurst's Estate* [1978] Ch. 14; and see *Antony* v. *Weerasekera* [1953] 1 W.L.R. 1007.
[67] *National Westminster Bank plc* v. *Morgan* [1985] A.C. 686.
[68] *Alec Lobb (Garages) Ltd.* v. *Total Oil (Great Britain) Ltd.* [1983] 1 W.L.R. 87 at 97, 98; affd. [1985] 1 W.L.R. 173.
[69] *Matthew* v. *Bobbins* (1980) 256 E.G. 603.

the boundary will be crossed as where a bank's customer, elderly and financially embarrassed, relied on his bank manager for advice,[70] or where an octogenarian with £40,000 gave £27,000 to a secretary-companion on whom he was heavily dependent,[71] or where an impecunious young man sold his estate to a relative who was advising him and who concealed its true valuation.[72] Though normally the facts have to be closely examined, there are certain well-defined relationships "to which the presumption is, as it were, presumed to apply unless the contrary is proved. In such relationships it would seem that you only have to look at the relative status of the parties in order to presume that the requisite degree of confidence is there."[73]

(1) PARENTS. All transactions whereby benefits are conferred on parents by their children are objects of the court's jealousy, especially where the parent has been guardian of the child's property.[74] For example, where a daughter made over property to her father without consideration shortly after attaining her majority, the father was required to show that the daughter was a free agent.[75] The presumption operates even after the marriage of the child,[76] but normally lasts only a short time after he or she attains full age.[77]

(2) GUARDIANS. Dealings between guardian and ward may be set aside even if entered into after the wardship has ceased,[78] provided that the guardian has retained his control over the ward's property[79] or his influence over his actions.[80] But equity will not set aside a reasonable gift made by the ward after the wardship and the influence of the guardian have ceased.[81]

(3) FIANCÉS. A young woman engaged to be married "reposes the greatest confidence in her future husband; otherwise she would not marry him. In many, if not most, cases she would sign almost anything he put before her."[82] Accordingly the presumption applies to substantial gifts or benefits provided by an intended wife for her intended husband[83]; and this is so even if she is no longer young.[84] Further, if

---

[70] *Lloyds Bank Ltd.* v. *Bundy* [1975] Q.B. 326; contrast *National Westminster Bank plc* v. *Morgan* [1985] A.C. 686.
[71] *Re Craig* [1971] Ch. 95.
[72] *Tate* v. *Williamson* (1866) 2 Ch.App. 55.
[73] *Goldsworthy* v. *Brickell* [1987] Ch. 378 at 401, *per* Nourse L.J.
[74] *Wright* v. *Vanderplank* (1855) 2 K. & J. 1.
[75] *Bainbrigge* v. *Browne* (1881) 18 Ch.D. 188.
[76] *Lancashire Loans Ltd.* v. *Black* [1934] 1 K.B. 380 (daughter).
[77] *Re Pauling's S.T. (No. 1)* [1964] Ch. 303 at 337. For the modified application of the rule to the formerly customary resettlement of family estates, see *Hoblyn* v. *Hoblyn* (1889) 41 Ch.D. 200.
[78] *Hylton* v. *Hylton* (1754) 2 Ves.Sen. 547.
[79] *Pierse* v. *Waring* (1745) 1 P.Wms. 121n.
[80] *Hatch* v. *Hatch* (1804) 9 Ves. 292.
[81] *Hatch* v. *Hatch, supra,* at p. 297.
[82] *Re Lloyds Bank Ltd.* [1931] 1 Ch. 289 at 302, *per* Maugham J.
[83] *Re Lloyds Bank Ltd.* [1931] 1 Ch. 289; but consider *Zamet* v. *Hyman, infra*; (1962) 78 L.Q.R. 24.
[84] *Zamet* v. *Hyman* [1961] 1 W.L.R. 1442 (couple over 70).

either one of an engaged couple makes a gift to the other on an express or implied condition that the gift is to be returned if the engagement is broken off, the donor is not prevented from recovering the gift merely because it was he or she who broke off the engagement[85]; but there is a rebuttable presumption that a gift of an engagement ring is absolute.[86] In the absence of any contrary intention[87] the normal inference to be drawn in respect of wedding presents is that they belong to the spouse by whose relatives or friends they were given.[88]

(4) HUSBANDS. A wife may give the income or capital of any of her property to the husband. In any case where the money of a wife comes to the husband, whether from income or capital, the question is whether the wife intended to make a gift of it or not[89]; and the onus of proving a gift is on the husband.[90] If he proves that the income was received by him with her consent while they were living together, that is evidence of a gift, and she cannot compel him to refund the property unless there is evidence to prove that no gift was intended.[91] Further, once a marriage has taken place, there is no presumption of undue influence.[92] "Upon principle, it is clear that business could not go on if in every transaction by way of gift by a wife to her husband the onus were on the husband to show that the wife had had independent advice; such a position would render married life intolerable."[93] Yet circumstances of illness or dependency may give rise to the presumption in a particular case.[94] Again, transactions between spouses may be avoided if affirmative proof of undue influence is adduced[95]; and the jurisdiction probably extends to consent orders in matrimonial proceedings.[96]

(5) RELIGIOUS, MEDICAL AND OTHER ADVISERS. The court has also regarded jealously gifts to persons exercising religious influence, e.g. ministers of religion,[97] spiritualists,[98] mothers superior of convents[99] and

[85] Law Reform (Miscellaneous Provisions) Act 1970, s.3(1).

[86] Ibid. s.3(2).

[87] Samson v. Samson [1960] 1 W.L.R. 190 at 195; and see Kelner v. Kelner [1939] P. 411 (Jewish dowry).

[88] Samson v. Samson [1960] 1 W.L.R. 190; Hichens v. Hichens [1945] P. 23 at 26; and see Ex p. Pannell, Re Jamieson (1889) 37 W.R. 464; Williams v. Mercier (1884) 10 App.Cas. 1 at 4, 5; Lee v. Lee [1952] 2 Q.B. 489n. at 491.

[89] Mercier v. Mercier [1903] 2 Ch. 98.

[90] Rich v. Cockell (1804) 9 Ves. 369; Re Flamank (1889) 40 Ch.D. 461.

[91] Caton v. Rideout (1849) 1 Mac. & G. 599; Dixon v. Dixon (1879) 9 Ch.D. 587; Edward v. Cheyne (No. 2) (1888) 13 App.Cas. 385; Re Young, Young v. Young (1913) 29 T.L.R. 391; a fortiori an "unmarried wife": Hargreave v. Everard (1856) 6 Ir.Ch.R. 278.

[92] Howes v. Bishop [1909] 2 K.B. 390; Bank of Africa v. Cohen [1909] 2 Ch. 129 at 135; Mackenzie v. Royal Bank of Canada [1934] A.C. 468; Gillman v. Gillman (1946) 174 L.T. 272 (separation agreement); Midland Bank plc v. Shephard [1988] 3 All E.R. 17.

[93] Howes v. Bishop, supra, at p. 402, per Farwell L.J.

[94] Simpson v. Simpson (1989) 19 Fam.Law 20.

[95] Bank of Montreal v. Stuart [1911] A.C. 120; Mundinger v. Mundinger (1968) 3 D.L.R. (3d) 338; ante, p. 552.

[96] See Jenkins v. Livesey [1985] A.C. 424 a 440, 441; contra, Tommey v. Tommey [1983] Fam. 15.

[97] Huguenin v. Baseley (1807) 14 Ves. 273; 1 W. & T.L.C. 203.

[98] Lyon v. Homer (1868) L.R. 6 Eq. 655; Chennells v. Bruce (1939) 55 T.L.R. 422.

[99] Allcard v. Skinner (1887) 36 Ch.D. 145.

the like.[1] "The influence of one mind over another is very subtle, and of all influences religious influence is the most dangerous and the most powerful, and to counteract it Courts of Equity have gone very far."[2] Medical advisers,[3] those in charge of mental hospitals,[4] managers of businesses[5] and others who assume control over the property of another[6] are also within the scope of the principle.

(6) SOLICITORS. A gift by a client to his solicitor raises the presumption that it was unduly influenced by the fiduciary relationship subsisting between them.[7] And in general neither directly nor indirectly (e.g. through his wife[8] or son[9]) may a solicitor make any gain for himself at the expense of his client,[10] apart from the just and fair remuneration for his services. However, a client may make a valid gift by will to his solicitor, and a gift inter vivos may be effectively confirmed by will.[11]

(c) *Rebutting the presumption.* The presumption may be rebutted by affirmative proof that "the gift was the spontaneous act of the donor acting under circumstances which enabled him to exercise an independent will and which justify[12] the court in holding that the gift was the result of a free exercise of the donor's will."[13] More shortly, the gift was made as a result of "full, free and informed thought about it."[14] This depends on all the circumstances of the case. The size of the gift is material[15] and it is important to be able to show that at the time of the gift[16] the donor had independent advice[17] from a lawyer fully acquainted with the facts[18]; but except perhaps in the case of gifts to parents made by their children shortly after attaining majority,[19] it is not essential to show that the donor had independent advice.[20] And where a solicitor

---

[1] *Morley* v. *Loughnan* [1893] 1 Ch. 736; *cf. Lough* v. *Ward* [1945] 2 All E.R. 338; *Roche* v. *Sherrington* [1982] 1 W.L.R. 599 (Opus Dei).
[2] *Allcard* v. *Skinner* (1887) 36 Ch.D. 145 at 183, *per* Lindley L.J.
[3] *Dent* v. *Bennett* (1838) 4 My. & Cr. 269; *Billage* v. *Southee* (1852) 9 Hare 534; *Mitchell* v. *Homfray* (1881) 8 Q.B.D. 587.
[4] *Re C.M.G.* [1970] Ch. 574.
[5] *Inche Noriah* v. *Shaik Allie Bin Omar* [1929] A.C. 127; *Goldsworthy* v. *Brickell* [1987] Ch. 378.
[6] *Huguenin* v. *Baseley* (1807) 14 Ves. 273; *Tufton* v. *Sperni* [1952] 2 T.L.R. 516.
[7] *Wright* v. *Carter* [1903] 1 Ch. 27; *Tomson* v. *Judge* (1855) 3 Drew. 306; *Re a Solicitor* [1975] Q.B. 475 (disciplinary proceedings).
[8] *Liles* v. *Terry* [1895] 2 Q.B. 679.
[9] *Willis* v. *Barron* [1902] A.C. 271.
[10] *Tyrrell* v. *Bank of London* (1862) 10 H.L.C. 26. See *ante*, p. 252, for sales between solicitor and client.
[11] *Hindson* v. *Weatherill* (1854) 5 De G.M. & G. 301; but consider *Wintle* v. *Nye* [1959] 1 W.L.R. 284.
[12] By a manifest error the report reads "justifies," see *Inche Noriah* v. *Shaik Allie Bin Omar* [1929] A.C. 127 at 133.
[13] *Allcard* v. *Skinner* (1887) 36 Ch.D. 145 at 171, *per* Cotton L.J.
[14] *Zamet* v. *Hyman* [1961] 1 W.L.R. 1442 at 1444, *per* Lord Evershed M.R.; followed in *Re Craig* [1971] Ch. 95 at 105.
[15] *Allcard* v. *Skinner, supra*, at p. 185.
[16] *Allcard* v. *Skinner, supra*, at p. 173.
[17] See *Re Coomber* [1911] 1 Ch. 723 at 725, 726, 729, 730.
[18] See *Wright* v. *Carter* [1903] 1 Ch. 27; *Inche Noriah* v. *Shaik Allie Bin Omar* [1929] A.C. 127.
[19] *Powell* v. *Powell* [1900] 1 Ch. 243; and see *ante*, p. 554.
[20] *Inche Noriah* v. *Shaik Allie Bin Omar, supra*, at p. 135; *Demerera Bauxite Co. Ltd.* v. *Hubbard* [1923] A.C. 673 at 681, 682; *McMaster* v. *Byrne* [1952] 1 All E.R. 1362 at 1369; *Re Brocklehurst's Estate* [1978] Ch. 14.

purchases property from his client, the purchase will be upheld if the client was fully informed, had competent and independent advice[21] and received a fair price.[22]

4. Defences

(a) *General.* The normal equitable defecnces of laches, acquiescence and confirmation are available to defeat a claim based on undue influence.[23] They are treated generally elsewhere.[24] The following comments apply specifically to undue influence.

(b) *Lapse of time.* Proceedings to avoid a transaction may be taken at any time while the influence still persists, however long after the transaction.[25] But after the influence has ceased the donor must commence the proceedings within a reasonable time[26] or he will be taken to abide by the transaction and confirm it.[27] And a gift cannot be set aside by the personal representatives of a deceased donor, or by beneficiaries claiming through him, unless the donor himself had commenced proceedings for this purpose in his lifetime or was still entitled to do so at the death.

(c) *Purchaser without notice.* The defence of purchaser without notice will be available to the purchaser[28] of any interest[29] who has no notice that the consent of the other party to the transaction has been procured by undue influence exercised by a third party.[30] The first party is under no obligation to ensure that the other party has received independent legal advice.[31] The first party will, however, be "infected with the conduct"[32] of the third party if he has notice of the exercise of undue influence,[33] or if he has been content to leave to the third party the task of procuring the consent of the other party.[34]

---

[21] But see *Demerara Bauxite Co. Ltd.* v. *Hubbard, supra,* at pp. 681, 682.

[22] *Wright* v. *Carter* [1903] 1 Ch. 27 at 60.

[23] *Goldsworthy* v. *Brickell* [1987] Ch. 378 at 410.

[24] See *ante,* p. 35 and *post,* p. 655.

[25] *Hatch* v. *Hatch* (1804) 9 Ves. 292 (20 years).

[26] See *Bullock* v. *Lloyds Bank Ltd.* [1955] Ch. 317 (four years after cesser of influence and discovery of remedy no bar).

[27] *Allcard* v. *Skinner* (1887) 36 Ch.D. 145; *Turner* v. *Collins* (1871) 7 Ch.App. 329.

[28] For innocent donees, see *ante,* pp. 551, 552.

[29] See *ante,* pp. 25, 50.

[30] *Coldunell Ltd.* v. *Gallon* [1986] Q.B. 1184; *Midland Bank plc* v. *Perry* [1988] 1 F.L.R. 161.

[31] *Bank of Baroda* v. *Shah* [1988] 3 All E.R. 24.

[32] *Bank of Baroda* v. *Shah, supra,* at p. 25, *per* Dillon L.J., citing *Coldunell Ltd.* v. *Gallon, supra,* at p. 1196.

[33] *Bank of Credit and Commerce International S.A.* v. *Aboody* [1990] Q.B. 923 at 972.

[34] *Chaplin & Co. Ltd.* v. *Brammall* [1908] 1 K.B. 233; *Avon Finance Co. Ltd.* v. *Bridger* (1979) [1985] 2 All E.R. 281; *Barclays Bank plc* v. *Kennedy* (1988) 21 H.L.R. 132; and see *Kings North Trust Ltd.* v. *Bell* [1986] 1 W.L.R. 119 (execution procured by fraud); contrast *Midland Bank plc* v. *Shephard* [1988] 3 All E.R. 17 (undue influence negatived). See also *Bank of Baroda* v. *Shah, supra,* at pp. 27, 28, for means of appointment of agent.

(d) *Causation.* It is a defence to show that the complainant would have entered into the transaction in any event.[35]

Section 2. Abuse of Confidence

1. Nature. Persons in fiduciary positions owe a duty to those who repose confidence in them to take care and skill in the management of their affairs.[36] Thus an action may lie against a solicitor for loss sustained by his client through a misrepresentation made to his client in breach of this duty without fraudulent intent.[37] *A fortiori*, all transactions whereby persons in fiduciary positions procure a benefit for themselves will be set aside, *e.g.* trustees trafficking with the trust property or purchasing from their *cestuis que trust*, solicitors purchasing from their clients, agents receiving secret commissions, and the like. These rules have already been discussed.[38]

2. Relation to undue influence.[39] The principles of undue influence and abuse of confidence overlap but do not coincide. Thus a trustee who purchases from his *cestui que trust* at an undervalue will perhaps bring himself within both principles.[40] But a gift from the *cestui que trust* raises questions of undue influence alone, while trafficking with the trust property can be attacked only as an abuse of confidence, for it is an act of the trustee and not an act of the beneficiary under the trustee's influence. Again, there may be undue influence in the absence of any fiduciary relationship,[41] and conversely not in every fiduciary relationship will it be presumed.[42] Finally, while a transaction procured by undue influence will not be set aside unless it is shown to be manifestly disadvantageous,[43] there is no such requirement in cases of abuse of confidence.[44]

Section 3. Unconscionable Bargains

1. Unfair dealings with the poor and ignorant. A gift will be set aside if it is shown that the donor lacked the requisite mental capacity, and the degree of understanding required varies from a low degree where the subject-matter of the gift is trivial to a high degree where the

---

[35] *Bank of Credit and Commerce International S.A.* v. *Aboody* [1990] Q.B. 923 at 970, 971. Consider *Re Brocklehurst's Estate* [1978] Ch. 14.
[36] See *ante*, p. 213.
[37] *Nocton* v. *Lord Ashburton* [1914] A.C. 932. *Cf. Woods* v. *Martins Bank Ltd.* [1959] 1 Q.B. 55 (bank's duty to inform customer about conflict of interests).
[38] *Ante*, p. 245.
[39] See W. H. D. Winder (1940) 4 Conv.(N.S.) 274.
[40] See *Tate* v. *Williamson* (1866) 2 Ch.App. 55; *ante*, pp. 250, 251.
[41] *Ante*, p. 552.
[42] *Re Coomber* [1911] 1 Ch. 723; *ante*, p. 553.
[43] See *ante*, pp. 552, 553.
[44] *Bank of Credit and Commerce International S.A.* v. *Aboody* [1990] Q.B. 923 at 962–964, referring to this section.

donor is disposing of his only asset of value.[45] A contract may be set aside in equity if one party lacks sufficient mental capacity, if that lack of capacity is unknown to the other party,[46] and there is in the conduct of the latter unfairness amounting to equitable fraud which would have entitled the former to rescind the contract even if he had been sane.[47] But, while a transaction will not be set aside merely because it is improvident,[48] the intervention of equity does not stop short at want of mental capacity. Under a well-established jurisdiction, equity will set aside a purchase from a poor and ignorant vendor at a considerable undervalue, where the vendor acts without independent advice,[49] unless the purchaser satisfies the court that the transaction was fair, just and reasonable.[50] It has been said that "poor and ignorant" may nowadays be understood as "member of the lower income group" and "less highly educated," the latter requirement being applied in particular to the person's understanding of property transactions.[51] A fortiori, the jurisdiction must extend to the setting aside of gifts; and it has also been applied in cases of mortgages[52] and of compromises of litigation.[53]

2. Bargains with expectants

(a) *Equitable jurisdiction.* Bargains with reversioners or persons who hope to take a benefit under the will or intestacy of a person still alive (persons who are often called "expectants") will be set aside unless the purchaser can show that he paid a fair price,[54] *i.e.* the market price.[55] The fact that the father or other relative on whose death the expectancy depends was aware of or took part in the transaction will not validate what is otherwise bad,[56] although such a circumstance, especially if coupled with the fact that the expectant acted under professional advice, is material as rebutting the presumption of oppression and extortion.[57] Where, however, the father or other relative is a party by reason of the transaction being in the nature of a family arrangement the court will be anxious to uphold the arrangement; a transaction which would be invalid if made between strangers may thus be held good, the court not

---

[45] *Re Beaney* [1978] 1 W.L.R. 770.
[46] If the want of capacity is apparent, the contract is voidable at law: *Manches* v. *Trimborn* (1946) 115 L.J.K.B. 305.
[47] *Hart* v. *O'Connor* [1985] A.C. 1000.
[48] *Mountford* v. *Scott* [1975] Ch. 259 (option granted in consideration of £1).
[49] See *Butlin-Sanders* v. *Butlin* (1985) 15 Fam. Law 126.
[50] *Fry* v. *Lane* (1888) 40 Ch.D. 312 at 322; *How* v. *Weldon* (1754) 2 Ves.Sen. 516; *Wood* v. *Abrey* (1818) 3 Madd. 417.
[51] *Cresswell* v. *Potter* (1968) [1978] 1 W.L.R. 255n. at 257, 258, *per* Megarry J. (Post Office telephonist). *Cf. Backhouse* v. *Backhouse* [1978] 1 W.L.R. 243.
[52] *Morrison* v. *Coast Finance Ltd.* (1966) 55 D.L.R. (2d) 710. For the Canadian law in general, see (1966) 44 Can. Bar Rev. 142 (B. E. Crawford) and (1972) 50 Can.Bar.Rev. 296 (I. Davis).
[53] *Arrale* v. *Costain Civil Engineering Ltd.* [1976] 1 Lloyd's Rep. 98 at 102, applying *Lloyds Bank Ltd.* v. *Bundy, ante,* p. 554.
[54] *Perfect* v. *Lane* (1861) 3 De G.F. & J. 369.
[55] *Shelly* v. *Nash* (1818) 3 Madd. 232.
[56] *Savery* v. *King* (1856) 5 H.L.C. 627.
[57] *O'Rorke* v. *Bolingbroke* (1877) 2 App.Cas. 814.

inquiring too closely as to the exercise of the father's influence.[58] These principles apply to loans as well as purchases.[59] Two particular examples of these principles must now be mentioned.

(b) *Examples.*

(1) POST OBIT BONDS.   Under such a bond a borrower agrees to pay a sum exceeding the amount advanced in the event of his becoming entitled to some property on the death of a certain person. Equity would grant relief to the borrower, unless he confirmed the transaction after inheriting the property.[60]

(2) SALES OF REVERSIONS. By statute[61] equity may no longer exercise its former jurisdiction[62] to relieve against a sale or other dealing with a remainder or reversion at an undervalue on that ground alone. But the statute expressly preserves "the jurisdiction of the Court to set aside or modify unconscionable bargains."[63] Thus no alteration has been made in the general equitable principle which throws the burden of justifying the righteousness of bargains of this nature upon the party who claims the benefit. The nature of the bargain may still in itself be a sign of fraud in the estimation of the court, and undervalue is still a material element in cases in which it is not the sole equitable ground of relief.[64] This relief is given on terms of repayment of what is due *ex aequo et bono*, which is normally the sum actually advanced with reasonable interest, traditionally at the rate of 5 per cent.[65]

3. Moneylending transactions

(a) *Former Acts.* The equitable doctrines as to bargains with expectants have lost part of their importance since the Money-lenders Act 1900. This Act and the Moneylenders Act 1927 regulated transactions with moneylenders, who were defined as including every person whose business was that of moneylending or who held himself out as carrying on that business.[66] Under the Acts, the court had jurisdiction (even if there had been a settled account[67]) to reopen a transaction with a moneylender if it was harsh and unconscionable, or

---

[58] *Stapilton* v. *Stapilton* (1739) 1 Atk. 2; **1 W. & T.L.C. 178**; *Bellamy* v. *Sabine* (1847) 2 Ph. 425; *Savery* v. *King, supra.* See *ante,* p. 554.
[59] *Nevill* v. *Snelling* (1880) 15 Ch.D. 679.
[60] *Earl of Chesterfield* v. *Janssen* (1751) 2 Ves.Sen. 125; **1 W. & T.L.C. 248**; and see also *Levin* v. *Roth* [1950] 1 All E.R. 698n.
[61] L.P.A. 1925, s.124(1), replacing Sales of Reversion Act 1867.
[62] See *Fry* v. *Lane* (1888) 40 Ch.D. 312 at 320.
[63] L.P.A. 1925, s.174(2), giving effect to the court's interpretation of the Act of 1867: see *Earl of Aylesford* v. *Morris* (1873) 8 Ch.App. 484 at 490, 491.
[64] *Earl of Aylesford* v. *Morris* (1873) 8 Ch.App. 484; *Tyler* v. *Yates* (1871) 6 Ch.App. 665; *O'Rorke* v. *Bolingbroke* (1877) 2 App.Cas. 814; *Brenchley* v. *Higgins* (1900) 83 L.T. 751.
[65] For the modern position with regard to interest rates, see, *ante,* pp. 392, 447, 474.
[66] See *Tuchmann* v. *Schmerler* (1944) 172 L.T. 43 (distinction between amateurs and professionals); *Khoon's Official Assignee* v. *Ek Liong Hin Ltd.* [1960] A.C. 178.
[67] See *B. S. Lyle Ltd.* v. *Pearson* [1941] 2 K.B. 391.

otherwise such that a court of equity would give relief.[68] The fact that excessive interest was charged might in itself be sufficient evidence of harshness and unconscionableness.[69]

(b) *Present Act*

(1) GENERAL.   The Moneylenders Acts have now been repealed,[70] and the Consumer Credit Act 1974 has introduced a new body of law concerned with the provision of credit. Much of the Act, and of the statutory instruments made under it, is regulatory in nature and is outside the scope of this book[71]: what is of importance for present purposes is the preservation of a jurisdiction to reopen what are now called extortionate credit bargains.[72]

(2) EXTORTIONATE CREDIT BARGAINS.   A credit bargain is extortionate if it requires the debtor or a relative of his to make payments (whether unconditionally or on certain contingencies) which are grossly exorbitant; or if it otherwise grossly contravenes ordinary principles of fair dealing.[73] In determining whether a credit bargain is extortionate, regard must be had to the evidence which is adduced concerning interest rates prevailing at the time it was made, certain factors relating to the debtor and the creditor, and any other relevant considerations.[74] Factors applicable in relation to the debtor include his age, experience, business capacity and state of health, and any financial pressure to which he was subject at the time of making the credit bargain.[75] Factors applicable in relation to the creditor include the degree of risk accepted by him, his relationship to the debtor, and whether or not a colourable cash price was quoted for any goods or services included in the bargain.[76]

(3) POWERS OF COURT.   A credit bargain may, if the court thinks just, be reopened on the ground that it is extortionate, either on an application made for the purpose by the debtor or any surety or at the instance of the debtor or a surety in the course of other proceedings.[77] In reopening the agreement the court may, "for the purpose of relieving the debtor or a surety from payment of any sum in excess of that fairly due and reasonable," make any of several orders. Thus it may direct accounts to be taken; set aside the whole or part of any obligation

---

[68] Act of 1900, s.1.
[69] *Samuel* v. *Newbold* [1906] A.C. 461.
[70] Consumer Credit Act 1974, s.192(3)(*b*) and Sched. 5. For a full account of the Moneylenders Acts see Meston's *Law Relating to Moneylenders* (5th ed., 1968).
[71] For provisions of the Act relating to security, see, *ante*, pp. 449, 455. For a full account of the Act, see Guest and Lomnicka, *Introduction to the Law of Credit and Security* (1978), esp. paras. 155–168.
[72] Consumer Credit Act 1974, s.137.
[73] *Ibid.* s.138(1). See *Coldunell Ltd.* v. *Gallon* [1986] Q.B. 1184 on the burden of proof.
[74] *Ibid.* s.138(2). See *Davies* v. *Directloans Ltd.* [1986] 1 W.L.R. 823.
[75] *Ibid.* s.138(3).
[76] *Ibid.* s.138(4).
[77] *Ibid.* s.139(1).

imposed on the debtor or surety by the agreement; require repayment by the creditor of the whole or part of any sum paid by the debtor or surety; direct the return to the surety of any property provided for the purposes of the security; or alter the terms of the credit agreement or any security instrument.[78] The Act thus gives the court a high degree of flexibility, both in determining whether a bargain is extortionate and in exercising its powers of relief; but there are insufficient reported cases to show how much use is being made of what is, in essence, a modern form of equitable intervention.[79]

4. Transactions contrary to the policy of the law. Courts of equity set aside as unconscionable not only transactions where one of the parties needed protection but also transactions which were a fraud on third parties or upon the public generally.[80] In this category fall marriage-brokage contracts,[81] payments to a parent to consent to the marriage of his child,[82] loans to a woman to swell her dowry and thus deceive her husband,[83] rewards for influencing a testator,[84] and contracts in restraint of trade,[85] such as a loan with such stringent restrictions on the borrower as to savour of serfdom.[86] Similarly, if a debtor executes a deed compounding with his creditors, it is a fraud for a creditor who is a party to the deed to stipulate for some clandestine advantage as a condition of his executing it; the money paid may be recovered back,[87] and the other creditors are not bound by their release of the debtor.[88]

Section 4. Frauds on a Power

1. Power must be exercised bona fide. The donee of a special power of appointment must exercise the power bona fide and for the end designed[89] and not for any purpose which is foreign to the power.[90] If the power is exercised not bona fide, but for a purpose beyond the scope of the instrument creating the power, or not justified by it, the

---

[78] Consumer Credit Act 1974, s.139(2).
[79] See *A. Ketley Ltd.* v. *Scott* [1981] I.C.R. 241 (48 per cent. p.a. interest on loan to facilitate immediate completion of house purchase: transaction upheld); *Davies* v. *Directloans Ltd.* [1986] 1 W.L.R. 823 (21.6 per cent. p.a. on balance outstanding under deferred house purchase agreement: upheld). For a full account of cases under these provisions, see Guest and Lloyd, *Encyclopaedia of Consumer Credit Law* (1975), paras. 2–138–2–140.
[80] See *Earl of Chesterfield* v. *Janssen* (1751) 2 Ves.Sen. 125 at 156; **1 W. & T.L.C. 248 at 261.** This type of transaction is now regarded at law as being void for illegality.
[81] *Hall* v. *Potter* (1695) Show.P.C. 76; *Hermann* v. *Charlesworth* [1905] 2 K.B. 123.
[82] *Keat* v. *Allen* (1707) 2 Vern. 588.
[83] *Gale* v. *Lindo* (1687) 1 Vern. 475.
[84] *Debenham* v. *Ox* (1749) 1 Ves.Sen. 276.
[85] *Nordenfelt* v. *Maxim Nordenfelt Guns and Ammunition Co. Ltd.* [1894] A.C. 535.
[86] *Horwood* v. *Millar's Timber and Trading Co. Ltd.* [1917] 1 K.B. 305.
[87] *Higgins* v. *Pitt* (1849) 4 Exch. 312.
[88] *Dauglish* v. *Tennant* (1866) L.R. 2 Q.B. 49.
[89] *Aleyn* v. *Belchier* (1758) 1 Eden 132; **2 W. & T.L.C. 263.**
[90] *Re Cohen, Brookes* v. *Cohen* [1911] 1 Ch. 37.

appointment is said to be a fraud on the power, and equity holds it bad.[91]

2. Types of fraud on a power. There are three main categories of fraud on a power.

(a) *Corrupt purpose*: where the appointment is made with a corrupt purpose, as where the donee appoints to one of his children who is seriously ill, expecting that the child will die and that he will then take the property as the child's next-of-kin.[92] But it is not enough merely to show that in the event the appointor has received a benefit; it must be shown that the appointment was made with this purpose.[93] Further, an appointment by a parent to his children as a preliminary to purchasing their interests in the appointed fund at their full value is valid if his only purpose is a proper one, *e.g.* to benefit the children by saving estate duty,[94] even if in the result he takes some benefit.[95]

(b) *Foreign purpose*: where the appointment is made for purposes foreign to the power, as where a mother appoints property to one of her children intending him to use it for the benefit of his father, who is not an object of the power,[96] or where the property is intended to pass to the appointor's children (who are expressly excluded from the power) under an assignment in their favour already executed by the appointee.[97] In such cases it is immaterial that there is no bargain with the appointee, or that he is ignorant of the true motive for the appointment[98]; what vitiates the appointment is the appointor's intention to benefit a non-object.[99] Thus pressure upon the appointee to settle the property on himself and his issue (who are non-objects) will not necessarily indicate fraud, for the appointor's object may well in substance be to benefit the appointee.[1]

(c) *Bargain to benefit non-objects*: where the appointment is made in pursuance of a previous bargain with the appointee whereby persons who are not objects of the power will obtain some benefit, as where the appointee agrees to give part of the property appointed to the

---

[91] *Vatcher* v. *Paull* [1915] A.C. 372 at 378. See generally 36 Halsbury's *Laws of England* (4th ed., 1981), paras. 962–969, the only modern text on the subject.
[92] *Lord Hinchinbroke* v. *Seymour* (1789) 1 Bro.C.C. 395, as explained in *Henty* v. *Wrey* (1882) 21 Ch.D. 332.
[93] *Henty* v. *Wrey, supra.*
[94] *Re Merton* [1953] 1 W.L.R. 1096; consider also the transaction in *Re Greaves* [1954] Ch. 434 (see at p. 440).
[95] *Re Robertson's W.T.* [1960] 1 W.L.R. 1050; *Re Wallace's Settlements* [1968] 1 W.L.R. 711; contrast *Re Brook's Settlement* [1968] 1 W.L.R. 1661.
[96] *Re Marsden's Trusts* (1859) 4 Drew. 594; and see *Re Dick* [1953] Ch. 343.
[97] *Re Crawshay, Hore-Ruthven* v. *Public Trustee* [1948] Ch. 123, doubting *Re Crawshay, Crawshay* v. *Crawshay* (1890) 43 Ch.D. 615.
[98] *Re Marsden's Trusts, supra; Re Perkins, Perkins* v. *Bagot* [1893] 1 Ch. 283; *cf. Re Nicholson's Settlement* [1939] Ch. 11, *infra*, n. 6.
[99] *Re Dick, supra,* explaining *Re Crawshay, Hore-Ruthven* v. *Public Trustee, supra.*
[1] *Re Burton's Settlements* [1955] Ch. 82; contrast *Re Simpson* [1952] Ch. 412.

appointor,[2] or to the appointor's creditors,[3] or to a stranger.[4] In such cases the benefit need not be pecuniary; if a wife agrees with her husband to apply for a decree absolute of divorce in order to enable him to remarry, on condition that he appoints property to a child of the marriage who is an object, the appointment will be fraudulent.[5] Where the power is to appoint to one person only, it may still be fraudulent under this head, though not under the previous head; for under such a power there is no power of selection among two or more objects which might be warped by the mere presence of a foreign purpose, as distinct from a bargain.[6] But a bargain or condition which leads to the property going to the person entitled in default of appointment is not fraudulent, for it does not defeat the intention of the donor of the power.[7]

3. Effect.   An appointment held to be fraudulent is not illegal but merely void. The appointor may make a fresh appointment, and even if it is to the same person, it will be valid if the appointee can show that it was not tainted with the fraud of the original appointment.[8]

4. Severance of good from bad.   In some cases an appointment which cannot stand as a whole may be severable and held good in part. Where there is a genuine appointment to an object of the power, coupled with an attempt to subject the appointment to conditions or trusts in favour of persons who are not objects, then the appointment stands, free from the conditions or trusts. If there is no genuine appointment to an object of the power, but the appointment in fact made to that object is for purposes foreign to the power, then the whole appointment fails.[9] In such cases it is a question of fact and inference rather than of law whether the appointment is genuine, *i.e.* is bona fide intended to benefit the appointee. Thus, where under a special power of appointment in favour of the appointor's wife, an appointment to her was made upon a condition for payment of the appointor's debts thereout, it was held that this condition was not severable and that the appointment was bad *in toto*.[10]

5. Appointment by donee to himself.   The donee of a power to appoint to a limited class of persons may appoint to himself if on the true construction of the instrument creating the power he is himself a member of the class and is not excluded from it.[11]

[2] *Daubeny* v. *Cockburn* (1816) 1 Mer. 626.
[3] *Re Cohen, Brookes* v. *Cohen* [1911] 1 Ch. 37.
[4] *Birley* v. *Birley* (1858) 25 Beav. 299.
[5] *Cochrane* v. *Cochrane* [1922] 2 Ch. 230.
[6] *Re Nicholson's Settlement* [1939] Ch. 11 (see at pp. 18, 19).
[7] *Vatcher* v. *Paull* [1915] A.C. 372.
[8] *Topham* v. *Duke of Portland* (1869) 5 Ch.App. 40; *Re Chadwick's Trusts* [1939] 1 All E.R. 850.
[9] *Re Holland, Holland* v. *Clapton* [1914] 2 Ch. 595; see also *Re Oliphant* (1917) 86 L.J.Ch. 452; *Re Witty* [1913] 2 Ch. 666.
[10] *Re Cohen, Brooks* v. *Cohen* [1911] 1 Ch. 37; *Re Perkins, Perkins* v. *Bagot* [1893] 1 Ch. 283.
[11] *Re Penrose* [1933] Ch. 793.

6. Void and voidable appointments. In the case of a common law power, or a power operating under the Statute of Uses 1535, a fraudulent appointment by which a legal estate passed was merely voidable; a purchaser for value of a legal estate in the appointed property without notice of the fraud was not affected by the fraudulent execution of the power. But in *Cloutte* v. *Storey*[12] it was held that in the case of an equitable power (*i.e.* a power under which an appointment would not operate to pass a legal estate) a fraudulent appointment is void, and even a purchaser for value without notice of the fraud will obtain no title to the appointed property. In view of the repeal of the Statute of Uses 1535, and the conversion after 1925 of legal powers of appointment over land into powers operating only in equity,[13] this decision gains an added importance.

7. Protection of purchasers. When there has been a fraud on the power, statute[14] now gives a very limited measure of protection to purchasers and those deriving title under them.[15] This applies whenever the appointment was made, provided the purchase was made after 1925.[16] The purchaser must show—[17]

(i) that he purchased for money or money's worth without notice of the fraud or circumstances from which it might have been discovered if reasonable inquiries had been made; and

(ii) that the appointee with whom he dealt was not less than 25 years of age.

Even if he proves this, the purchaser is protected only to the extent of the amount to which, at the time of the appointment, the appointee was presumptively entitled in default of appointment, having regard to any advances made in his favour and to any hotchpot provision.[18] For instance, suppose that a father has a power to appoint £50,000 to his children, and in default of appointment the fund is given to his children equally. He has five children, but appoints the whole fund fraudulently to the eldest son, who thereupon mortgages the fund to a bona fide mortgagee. If the son at the date of the mortgage is 25 years old, the mortgagee is protected to the extent of a fifth of the fund, that being the amount to which at the time of the appointment the son was presumptively entitled in default of appointment.

---

[12] [1911] 1 Ch. 18.
[13] L.P.A. 1925, s.1(7).
[14] *Ibid.* s.157.
[15] *Ibid.* s.157(3).
[16] *Ibid.* s.157(4).
[17] *Ibid.* s.157(2).
[18] *Ibid.* s.157(1).

8. Exceptions. The doctrines relating to a fraud upon the power do not apply to certain transactions.

(a) *Power to jointure.* The doctrines do not apply in their entirety to a power to jointure a wife. Such a power stands in a peculiar position, and an exercise of the power is not bad solely by reason of a bargain that in consideration of the jointure the husband is to acquire an interest in the wife's property.[19]

(b) *Release of power.*[20] The doctrines do not apply to the release of a power; for the fiduciary duty attached to the exercise of a power of appointment is owed to the persons who take in default and not to the objects.[21] Unless the power is coupled with a duty,[22] the person to whom it is given may by deed release or contract not to exercise the power[23] even if he thereby acquires some pecuniary advantage for himself which he could not have obtained upon any actual exercise of the power[24]; but his trustee in bankruptcy cannot do this.[25] For example, a father had a power of appointment in favour of a daughter or her issue, the daughter being absolutely entitled to the property in default of appointment. The father released the power and his daughter mortgaged the property to secure a sum of £10,000 which was paid to the father and applied by him for his own purposes; it was held that the release was valid, and, with it, the mortgage.[26]

(c) *Revocation of appointment.* On the same principle as governs releases of powers, the doctrines as to frauds on a power do not apply to the revocation of a revocable appointment, even though the appointor intends to obtain a benefit by the revocation.[27]

9. Illusory appointments. Formerly, unless the power showed a contrary intention, the appointor could not entirely exclude any object of the power; each object had to have some share.[28] If a merely nominal share was appointed to one or more of the objects, there was a somewhat uncertain equitable jurisdiction to set aside the appointment as being "illusory."[29] But statute[30] now provides that no appointment is to be invalid on the ground merely that (i) an unsubstantial, illusory or

---

[19] *Saunders* v. *Shafto* [1905] 1 Ch. 126.
[20] See generally A. J. Hawkins (1968) 84 L.Q.R. 64.
[21] See *Re Greaves* [1954] Ch. 434 at 445, 446.
[22] *Re Eyre, Eyre* v. *Eyre* (1883) 49 L.T. 259; *Re Mills* [1930] 1 Ch. 654. For these powers, see *ante*, p. 97.
[23] L.P.A. 1925, s.155, replacing C.A. 1881, s.52.
[24] *Re Radcliffe, Radcliffe* v. *Bewes* [1892] 1 Ch. 227.
[25] *Re Rose, Rose's Trustee* v. *Rose* [1904] 2 Ch. 348.
[26] *Re Somes* [1896] 1 Ch. 250.
[27] *Re Greaves* [1954] Ch. 434, overruling *Re Jones' Settlement* [1915] 1 Ch. 373.
[28] See Sugden, *Powers* (8th ed., 1861), pp. 444 *et seq.*
[29] See *Wilson* v. *Piggott* (1794) 2 Ves.Jun. 351.
[30] L.P.A. 1925, s.158, replacing Illusory Appointments Act 1830, and Powers of Appointment Act 1874.

nominal share only of the property is appointed to any object of the power, or (ii) any object of the power is thereby altogether excluded.[31] The result is that the appointor may now "cut off" any appointee "with a shilling" or even "without a shilling."[32] But the section does not affect any provision in the instrument creating the power which declares the amount of any share from which any object of the power is not to be excluded.[33]

10. Delegation of power. The donee of a special power of appointment must apply his own mind as to how it is to be exercised and not, *e.g.* merely follow the wishes of the donor of the power.[34] He may not delegate to others (or even to himself[35]) the authority reposed in him.[36] Accordingly, he cannot appoint on discretionary trusts.[37] And where there is a power to appoint property vested in trustees, the power of the appointor over the beneficial interest normally does not enable him to direct the trustees to transfer the trust property to other trustees.[38]

---

[31] L.P.A. 1925, s.158(1).

[32] "The Act of 1830 enabled an appointor to cut off any object of the power with a shilling: the Act of 1874 enables him to cut off the shilling also": Farwell, *Powers* (3rd ed., 1916), p. 427.

[33] L.P.A. 1925, s.158(2); see *Re Capon's Trusts* (1879) 10 Ch.D. 484.

[34] *Turner* v. *Turner* [1984] Ch. 100.

[35] *Re Hay's S.T.* [1982] 1 W.L.R. 202.

[36] *Re Joicey* [1915] 2 Ch. 115; *Re Morris's S.T.* [1951] 2 All E.R. 528. Distinguish *Re Mewburn's Settlement* [1934] Ch. 112 (power of advancement validly introduced by exercise of power of appointment).

[37] See *ante*, p. 136.

[38] *Re Mackenzie, Bain* v. *Mackenzie* [1916] 1 Ch. 125.

CHAPTER 5

EQUITABLE ESTOPPEL

Section 1. Estoppel at Common Law

1. The doctrine. Equity did not invent the doctrine of estoppel but has for long supplemented it. The basic idea of estoppel at common law is that of precluding a man from denying the existence of a state of affairs which he has previously asserted. At common law, estoppel was at first narrowly confined to various formal matters, and estoppel *in pais* (*i.e.* by informal words or conduct) was but a shadow of its modern self.[1] Equity greatly extended the doctrine, and in the eighteenth century the common law came to adopt and apply the equitable rules.[2] By the nineteenth century, both at law and in equity, the rule was that there would be an estoppel where by words or conduct there had been a representation of existing facts[3] (not of law[4]) which was intended to be acted upon and was in fact acted upon to his prejudice by the person to whom it was made.[5] The maker of the representation (even if a minor at the time of making it[6]) will not be allowed to allege in proceedings against the person so acting that the facts are other than he has represented them to be.

2. Operation of the doctrine. Thus where land[7] or goods[8] are being offered for sale, and by standing by and encouraging the sale, the true owner produces the false impression that the purporting seller is the owner, the sale will bind the true owner. Similarly, a company which has issued certificates indicating that shares are fully paid will be estopped from alleging against a purchaser without notice that the

---

[1] See Co.Litt. 352a.
[2] See, *e.g. Montefiori* v. *Montefiori* (1762) 1 Wm.Bl. 363, and note the sardonic comments of Bacon V.-C. in *Keate* v. *Phillips* (1881) 18 Ch.D. 560 at 577.
[3] *Jorden* v. *Money* (1854) 5 H.L.C. 185; *Maddison* v. *Alderson* (1883) 8 App.Cas. 467; *Neville* v. *Wilkinson* (1782) 1 Bro.C.C. 543.
[4] *Territorial and Auxiliary Forces Association of the County of London* v. *Nichols* [1949] 1 K.B. 35; *Kai Nam* v. *Ma Kam Chan* [1956] A.C. 358; *Tomlin* v. *Reid* [1963] E.G.D. 338.
[5] See *Canadian Pacific Ry.* v. *R.* [1931] A.C. 414 at 429; and compare *Pickard* v. *Sears* (1837) 6 Ad. & E. 469 at 474 (law) with *Citizens' Bank of Louisiana* v. *First National Bank of New Orleans* (1873) L.R. 6 H.L. 352 at 360 (equity). See also *Dean* v. *Bruce* [1952] 1 K.B. 11.
[6] *Mills* v. *Fox* (1887) 37 Ch.D. 153.
[7] *Price* v. *Neault* (1886) 12 App.Cas. 110; and see *Savage* v. *Foster* (1723) 9 Mod. 35; **1. W. & T.L.C. 396.**
[8] *Pickard* v. *Sears* (1837) 6 Ad. & E. 469.

shares are not fully paid.[9] Estoppel, however, is not a cause of action, but a rule of evidence[10]; no action can be founded upon an estoppel.[11]

Section 2. Equitable Estoppel

1. Basis of the doctrine. The system of estoppel developed by equity to supplement the rather narrow rules at common law is based on the unconscionable or inequitable conduct of a party. It may be that such a party was seeking to do no more than enforce his legal rights (*e.g.* as to payment of rent, or to possession of his land), and yet he had been guilty of such conduct that equity would intervene to deny him his remedy and thus protect the other party. In other cases equity would compel the legal owner to take some positive step such as transferring his property or an interest in it. For E to be estopped in equity as against C there is a double requirement. First, C must have acted to his detriment in some way. Secondly, E must have been responsible for E acting thus.

2. Inequitable conduct. The cases show that at least three types of conduct suffice to raise the estoppel. First acquiescence,[12] succinctly described as follows: "If a stranger build on my land, supposing it to be his own, and I, knowing it to be mine, do not interfere, but leave him to go on, equity considers it to be dishonest in me to remain passive and afterwards interfere and take the profit."[13] Secondly, encouragement which occurs where a party under an expectation created or encouraged by a landowner that he will have an interest in it goes into possession and lays out money upon the land. Equity may compel the owner to give effect to the expectation.[14] Thirdly, promises or representations as to future conduct which may occur where a party is led to suppose that the other will not insist on his legal rights either at all or for the time being.[15] But all these are aspects of a wider doctrine. Recent authorities "have supported a much wider jurisdiction to interfere in cases where the assertion of strict legal rights is found by the court to be unconscionable."[16] The doctrine is, indeed, very flexible.

[9] *Burkinshaw* v. *Nicolls* (1878) 3 App.Cas. 1004; *Re Concessions Trust* [1896] 2 Ch. 757; and see *Robinson* v. *Montgomeryshire Brewery Co.* [1896] 2 Ch. 841.
[10] See *Dawson's Bank Ltd.* v. *Nippon Menkwa Kabushiki Kaisha* (1935) L.R. 62 Ind.App. 100 at 108 (which, incidentally, explains the term "O.K."); but consider *Simmons* v. *Rose* (1862) 31 Beav. 1 at 7 (solicitor bound to make good assertion to court).
[11] *Low* v. *Bouverie* [1891] 3 Ch. 82.
[12] The classic statement is the judgment of Fry J. in *Willmott* v. *Barber* (1880) 15 Ch.D. 96 at 105, 106. See also *Ramsden* v. *Dyson* (1866) L.R. 1 H.L. 129 at 140, 141 (Lord Cranworth L.C.) and *De Bussche* v. *Alt* (1878) 8 Ch.D. 286 at 314. On the relationship of acquiescence with promissory estoppel, see *Goldsworthy* v. *Brickell* [1987] Ch. 378 at 410.
[13] *Ramsden* v. *Dyson, supra,* at p. 168, *per* Lord Wensleydale.
[14] *Ramsden* v. *Dyson, supra,* at p. 170 (Lord Kingsdown).
[15] *Hughes* v. *Metropolitan Ry.* (1877) 2 App.Cas. 439 at 448; see *post,* p. 571.
[16] *Amalgamated Investment & Property Co. Ltd.* v. *Texas Commerce International Bank Ltd.* [1982] Q.B. 84 at 104, *per* Robert Goff J. And see *Taylors Fashions Ltd.* v. *Liverpool Victoria Trustees Co. Ltd.* (1979) [1982] Q.B. 133n. at 151, 152, 155.

3. Main forms of the doctrine. The two main forms in which the doctrine of equitable estoppel exists may be called "promissory estoppel"[17] and "proprietary estoppel,[18] respectively; for in the first form E is precluded from resiling from his representation or promise, whereas in the second form E is precluded from denying C's supposed rights in E's property. "Proprietary estoppel" has been described as "difficult to accept as a separate category" and "an amalgam of doubtful utility," partly because it is derived from two separate lines of authority in which the conduct of E has been passive ("acquiescence") or active ("encouragement").[19] Yet the distinction between promissory and proprietary estoppel is a valid one.[20] Despite many similarities, the two forms differ in important respects.[21] Two may be mentioned here. First, the effect of promissory estoppel may be only temporary, whereas that of proprietary estoppel is permanent. Secondly, promissory estoppel merely provides a defence, whereas proprietary estoppel sometimes provides a cause of action. The two forms are considered in more detail below.

4. Other examples. In addition to the two main forms of the doctrine there are cases where one party has represented to the other that a document has a legal effect it does not have,[22] or where parties have proceeded upon a mistaken assumption as to the legal effect of a transaction into which they have entered.[23] It is not, however, sufficient merely to show that the parties have a common view about the legal effect of a transaction; there has to be a conventional basis on which they have regulated their dealings.[24] Further, it is not unconscionable for a tenant to rely on the statutory protection afforded to tenants even though he was willing to take a lease which was mistakenly believed to exclude the protection.[25]

A. Promissory Estoppel

During the nineteenth century equity extended the doctrine of estoppel to cases where instead of a representation of an existing fact there was a

---

[17] *Dean* v. *Bruce* [1952] 1 K.B. 11 at 14; *Ajayi* v. *R.T. Briscoe (Nigeria) Ltd.* [1964] 1 W.L.R. 1326 at 1330.

[18] See *E.R. Ives Investments Ltd.* v. *High* [1967] 2 Q.B. 379 at 399; *White* v. *Taylor (No. 2)* [1969] 1 Ch. 160 at 189.

[19] *Amalgamated Investment & Property Co. Ltd.* v. *Texas Commerce International Bank Ltd.* [1982] Q.B. 84 at 103, *per* Robert Goff J., in C.A. *ibid.* 109. For similar doubts, see *Crabb* v. *Arun D.C.* [1976] Ch. 179 at 193.

[20] Proprietary estoppel was treated as a separate category in *Att.-Gen. of Hong Kong* v. *Humphreys Estate (Queen's Gardens) Ltd.* [1987] A.C. 114 at 121.

[21] For a comparison between waiver and estoppel, see *Auckland Harbour Board* v. *Kaihe* [1962] N.Z.L.R. 68 at 88.

[22] *de Tchihatchef* v. *The Salerni Coupling Ltd.* [1932] 1 Ch. 330. See also *Spiro* v. *Lintern* [1973] 1 W.L.R. 1002.

[23] *Amalgamated Investment & Property Co. Ltd.* v. *Texas Commerce International Bank Ltd.* [1982] Q.B. 84; *Waltons Stores (Interstate) Ltd.* v. *Maher* (1988) 164 C.L.R. 387, noted A. Duthie (1988) 104 L.Q.R. 362.

[24] *Keen* v. *Holland* [1984] 1 W.L.R. 251 at 261.

[25] *Keen* v. *Holland* [1984] 1 W.L.R. 251.

representation of intention, or a promise. More recently, this extension became prominent in a sequence of cases following the *obiter*[26] statement by Denning J. in *Central London Property Trust Ltd. v. High Trees House Ltd.*,[27] though these cases "may need to be reviewed and reduced to a coherent body of doctrine by the courts."[28]

1. The doctrine

(a) *The rule.* Where by his words or conduct one party to a transaction freely[29] makes to the other an unambiguous[30] promise or assurance which is intended to affect the legal relations between them[31] (whether contractual or otherwise[32]), and, before it is withdrawn,[33] the other party acts upon it, altering his position[34] to his detriment,[35] the party making the promise or assurance will not be permitted to act inconsistently with it.[36] It is essential that the representor knows that the other party will act on his statement.[37] Yet the conduct of the other party need not derive its origin only from the encouragement or representation of the first: the question is whether it was *influenced* by such encouragement or representation.[38]

(b) *Operation of rule.* For example, if a landlord tells his tenant towards the end of the term that he proposes to demolish the premises after the term expires, he cannot claim damages from the tenant for leaving the premises unrepaired,[39] and if he agrees to accept a reduced

---

[26] See (1947) 63 L.Q.R. 278; (1948) 64 L.Q.R. 28, 29, 193; *post*, p. 572, n. 41.

[27] [1947] K.B. 130.

[28] *Woodhouse A.C. Israel Cocoa Ltd. S.A. v. Nigerian Produce Marketing Co. Ltd.* [1972] A.C. 741 at 758, *per* Lord Hailsham of St. Marylebone L.C. The modern text is Spencer Bower and Turner's *Estoppel by Representation* (3rd ed. 1977). See also D. Jackson (1965) 81 L.Q.R. 84, 223; M. P. Thompson [1983] C.L.J. 257; S. J. Burridge [1982] C.L.J. 290 (care of the elderly).

[29] See *D. & C. Builders Ltd. v. Rees* [1966] 2 Q.B. 617 (intimidation).

[30] *Woodhouse A.C. Israel Cocoa Ltd. S.A. v. Nigerian Produce Marketing Co. Ltd.* [1972] A.C. 741; *Spence v. Shell U.K. Ltd.* (1980) 256 E.G. 55. And see *Legione v. Hateley* (1983) 152 C.L.R. 406.

[31] *Foot Clinics (1943) Ltd. v. Cooper's Gowns Ltd.* [1947] K.B. 506; *Charles Rickards Ltd. v. Oppenheim* [1950] 1 K.B. 616; *Braithwaite v. Winwood* [1960] 1 W.L.R. 1257. But see *Amalgamated Investment & Property Co. Ltd. v. Texas Commerce International Bank Ltd.* [1982] Q.B. 84 at 107; in C.A. *ibid.* 109.

[32] *Durham Fancy Goods Ltd. v. Michael Jackson (Fancy Goods) Ltd.* [1968] 2 Q.B. 839.

[33] *Bhimji v. Salih* [1981] C.A.T. No. 30 (unreported).

[34] *Commissioner of Inland Revenue v. Morris* [1958] N.Z.L.R. 1126 at 1136; *Ajayi v. R.T. Briscoe (Nigeria) Ltd.* [1964] 1 W.L.R. 1326 at 1330. This is "the gist of the equity": *Tool Metal Manufacturing Co. Ltd. v. Tungsten Electric Co. Ltd.* [1955] 1 W.L.R. 761 at 764, *per* Lord Simonds; see also at pp. 781, 799.

[35] *Morrow v. Carty* [1957] N.I. 174; *Je Maintiendrai Pty. Ltd. v. Quaglia and Quaglia* (1980) 26 S.A.S.R. 101, where the evidence of detriment was tenuous. Contrast *W.J. Alan & Co. Ltd. v. El Nasr Export and Import Co.* [1972] 2 Q.B. 189 at 213, *per* Lord Denning M.R., denying the need for detriment, the other members of the court expressing no opinion (pp. 218, 221). Yet an equity could hardly be raised by a man altering his position to his *advantage*. See the full discussion (but not citing *Morrow v. Carty*) by M. Clarke [1974] C.L.J. 260 at 281–287.

[36] *Hughes v. Metropolitan Ry.* (1877) 2 App.Cas. 439; *Birmingham & District Land Co. v. L. & N.W. Ry.* (1888) 40 Ch.D. 286; *Central London Property Trust Ltd. v. High Trees House Ltd.* [1947] K.B. 130; *Combe v. Combe* [1951] 2 K.B. 215.

[37] *James v. Heim Gallery (London) Ltd.* (1980) 256 E.G. 819 at 823.

[38] *Amalgamated Investment & Property Co. Ltd. v. Texas Commerce International Bank Ltd.* [1982] Q.B. 84 at 104, 105.

[39] *Marquess of Salisbury v. Gilmore* [1942] 2 K.B. 38.

rent, and the tenant acts on this agreement to his detriment,[40] the landlord cannot thereafter demand the full rent.[41] Again, if a landlord gives his tenant notice to repair the premises within six months, and then there are negotiations for the landlord to purchase the tenant's interest, the six months will be calculated from the ending of the negotiations.[42] Where a lease was executed after the lessor gave the intending lessee certain assurances about liability for repairs, those assurances were binding on the lessor against an assignee of the term in a claim for a contribution towards the cost of repairs: though the majority view was that this was on the basis of waiver or collateral contract, rather than estoppel.[43] So, too, if after a divorce the husband is told, wrongly, on behalf of the wife that he is no longer liable for payments under a separation deed, and he accordingly refrains from exercising a statutory right to have the deed set aside, his wife cannot later sue him for subsequent payments in fact due under the deed.[44] And if an employer, in answer to a specific inquiry from his employee, assures the latter that his pay is correct, and the employee in reliance on this incurs expenditure and omits to claim social security benefits, the employer cannot recover overpayments of salary.[45] But mere acts of forbearance or indulgence, without more, do not create rights[46]; thus a bare promise to keep an offer open for a period is not by itself binding.[47] The doctrine does not seem to be "capable of extension so as to create rights in the promisee for which he has given no consideration."[48]

(c) *Promise.* In some cases a contract can be found.[49] Thus, if X makes some promise or gives some consent in order to induce Y to do some act, such as executing a document or refraining from discontinuing a business, and Y agrees, this constitutes a contract.[50] But in other cases there is no more than a bare representation or promise not to enforce a right, and it is here that a promissory estoppel may arise if the necessary conditions are satisfied. It may be that such an estoppel will apply even if the representations are of law[51]; but, like estoppel at common law,

---

[40] Perhaps spending the money would suffice: see, *e.g. Holt* v. *Markham* [1923] 1 K.B. 504, and contrast *Larner* v. *L. C. C.* [1949] 2 K.B. 683.

[41] *Central London Property Trust Ltd.* v. *High Trees House Ltd.* [1947] K.B. 130 (*obiter*: the actual decision on the facts was that the tenant must pay the full rent; nor was there any detriment: see (1952) 15 M.L.R. 6).

[42] *Hughes* v. *Metropolitan Ry.* (1877) 12 App.Cas. 439.

[43] *Brikom Investments Ltd.* v. *Carr* [1979] Q.B. 467.

[44] *P.* v. *P.* [1957] N.Z.L.R. 854. *Cf. Bojtar* v. *Parker* (1979) 99 D.L.R. (3d) 147 (promise not to require payments due under mortgage).

[45] *Avon C.C.* v. *Howlett* [1983] 1 W.L.R. 605.

[46] *Tool Metal Manufacturing Co. Ltd.* v. *Tungsten Electric Co. Ltd.* [1955] 1 W.L.R. 761 at 764; and see *Re Venning* (1947) 63 T.L.R. 394.

[47] *Morrow* v. *Carty* [1957] N.I. 174.

[48] *Ajayi* v. *R. T. Briscoe (Nigeria) Ltd.* [1964] 1 W.L.R. 1326 at 1330, *per* Lord Hodson.

[49] See *China-Pacific S.A.* v. *Food Corporation of India* [1981] Q.B. 403 at 430, reversed in H.L. on grounds not affecting this point: [1982] A.C. 939.

[50] *Re William Porter & Co. Ltd.* [1937] 2 All E.R. 361, as explained in *City & Westminster Properties (1934) Ltd.* v. *Mudd* [1959] Ch. 129 at 145; *Ledingham* v. *Bermejo Estancia Co. Ltd.* [1947] 1 All E.R. 749. *Buttery* v. *Pickard* (1945) 174 L.T. 144 seems explicable thus. See also *Lubovsky* v. *Snelling* [1944] K.B. 44 (implied agreement not to plead period of limitation).

[51] *Beesly* v. *Hallwood Estates Ltd.* [1960] 1 W.L.R. 549 at 561 (affirmed [1961] Ch. 105).

though it may bind the Crown,[52] it cannot negative the operation of a statute.[53]

2. Effect of estoppel. Like estoppel at common law, promissory estoppel may provide a defence, but it can create no cause of action.[54] Yet its effect may be to enable a party to enforce a cause of action which, without the estoppel, would not exist,[55] e.g. by giving rise to a binding obligation where none existed before.[56] However, unlike estoppel at common law, a promissory estoppel is usually not permanent in its effect. The promisor may resile from his position by giving the promisee notice (which need not be formal) so that he has a reasonable opportunity of resuming his former position; and only if that is impossible does the promise become final and irrevocable.[57] Thus if a patentee grants a licence to manufacture in return for certain periodical payments, and later agrees not to enforce the payments, he may nevertheless again enforce the making of future payments (as distinct from arrears[58]) when a reasonable time has elapsed after giving notice of his intention to do so.[59]

B. Proprietary Estoppel

Proprietary estoppel is one of the qualifications to the general rule that a person who spends money on improving the property of another has no claim to reimbursement or to any proprietary interest in the property.[60] Proprietary estoppel is older than promissory estoppel.[61] It is permanent in its effect,[62] and it is also capable of operating positively so as to confer a right of action.[63] The term "estoppel," though often used,[64] is thus not altogether appropriate.[65] Yet the equity is based on estoppel[66] in that one (A) is encouraged to act to his detriment by the

---

[52] *Robertson* v. *Minister of Pensions* [1949] 1 K.B. 227.

[53] See *Lyle-Meller* v. *A. Lewis & Co. (Westminster) Ltd.* [1956] 1 W.L.R. 29; *Rhyl U.D.C.* v. *Rhyl Amusements Ltd.* [1959] 1 W.L.R. 465; *Western Fish Products Ltd.* v. *Penwith D.C.* [1981] 2 All E.R. 204; and see *post*, p. 576.

[54] *Combe* v. *Combe* [1951] 2 K.B. 215.

[55] *Amalgamated Investment & Property Co. Ltd.* v. *Texas Commerce International Bank Ltd.* [1982] Q.B. 84 at 105; in C.A., *ibid.* at 131, 132.

[56] *Ibid.* at p. 107.

[57] *Ajayi* v. *R.T. Briscoe (Nigeria) Ltd.* [1964] 1 W.L.R. 1326 at 1330.

[58] See, *e.g. P.* v. *P.* [1957] N.Z.L.R. 854.

[59] *Tool Metal Manufacturing Co. Ltd.* v. *Tungsten Electric Co. Ltd.* [1955] 1 W.L.R. 761.

[60] *Ante*, p. 467, for the general rule. See, *e.g. Ahmad Yar Khan* v. *Secretary of State for India in Council* (1901) L.R. 28 Ind.App. 211 at 218, *per* Lord Macnaghten ("acquired a proprietary interest").

[61] See, *e.g. Huning* v. *Ferrers* (1711) Gilb.Eq. 85; *East India Co.* v. *Vincent* (1740) 2 Atk. 83; *Att.-Gen.* v. *Baliol College, Oxford* (1744) 9 Mod. 407 at 411; *Stiles* v. *Cowper* (1748) 3 Atk. 692 at 693.

[62] Contrast promissory estoppel, *supra*.

[63] This passage was cited in *Denny* v. *Jensen* [1977] 1 N.Z.L.R. 635 at 638, where the claim failed on the facts.

[64] See, *e.g. Inwards* v. *Baker* [1965] 2 Q.B. 29 at 38.

[65] See *Canadian Pacific Ry.* v. *R.* [1931] A.C. 414 at 429. This statement of principle referring to facts seems unduly restrictive.

[66] See *Att.-Gen. to the Prince of Wales* v. *Collom* [1916] 2 K.B. 193 at 204.

representations or encouragement of another (O) so that it would be unconscionable for O to insist on his strict legal rights.[67]

The subject will be considered under three main heads, the conditions giving rise to the equity, the extent of the equity, and the satisfaction of the equity.[68]

1. The equity. The doctrine has been concerned almost exclusively with the acquisition of rights in or over land.[69] But it can extend to other forms of property,[70] such as insurance policies,[71] and to future property such as O's residuary estate.[72] For the equity to arise in favour of A against O, the following four conditions must be satisfied.[73]

(a) *Detriment.* "There is no doubt that for proprietary estoppel to arise the person claiming must have incurred expenditure or otherwise have prejudiced himself or acted to his detriment."[74]

(1) EXPENDITURE. In many cases A has spent money on improving property which in fact belongs to O, as by building a house on O's land,[75] or by doing repairs to O's house and paying mortgage instalments and other outgoings,[76] or by contributing to a joint venture to be carried out on O's land,[77] or by paying premiums required to maintain O's life insurance policy.[78] Further, it suffices if A's expenditure has been made on his own property in reliance upon some right to be granted over O's land, as where A has built a mill on his land depending on a supposed right to take water for it from O's canal,[79] or where A has altered his ancient lights relying on having a right of light for his altered windows over O's land.[80] It also suffices where A has purchased and built on a new site where O has expressed an intention to acquire compulsorily A's old site.[81] But expenditure by

---

[67] *Griffiths* v. *Williams* (1977) 248 E.G. 947 at 949; *Taylors Fashions Ltd.* v. *Liverpool Victoria Trustees Co. Ltd.* (1979) [1982] Q.B. 133n. at 151, 152 (Oliver J.); *Habib Bank Ltd.* v. *Habib Bank A.G. Zurich* [1981] 1 W.L.R. 1265 at 1285 (Oliver L.J.); *Re Sharpe (A Bankrupt)* [1980] 1 W.L.R. 219 at 223; *Ward* v. *Kirkland* [1967] Ch. 194 at 235, 239.

[68] See the three questions posed by Scarman L.J. in *Crabb* v. *Arun D.C.* [1976] Ch. 179 at 192, 193 and applied in *Jones (A.E.)* v. *Jones (F.W.)* [1977] 1 W.L.R. 438 at 443; *Griffiths* v. *Williams* (1977) 251 E.G. 159.

[69] See *Western Fish Products Ltd.* v. *Penwith D.C.* [1981] 2 All E.R. 204.

[70] *Moorgate Mercantile Co. Ltd.* v. *Twitchings* [1976] Q.B. 225 at 242.

[71] *Re Foster, Hudson* v. *Foster (No. 2)* [1938] 3 All E.R. 610.

[72] *Re Basham* [1986] 1 W.L.R. 1498. Contrast *Layton* v. *Martin* [1986] 2 F.L.R. 227 (offer of "financial security" too vague).

[73] See generally *Ramsden* v. *Dyson* (1886) L.R. 1 H.L. 129 at 140, 168, 170; *Willmott* v. *Barber* (1880) 15 Ch.D. 96 at 105, as explained in *Shaw* v. *Applegate* [1977] 1 W.L.R. 970 at 977, 978, 980.

[74] *Greasley* v. *Cooke* [1980] 1 W.L.R. 1306 at 1313, 1314, *per* Dunn L.J. It is suggested that the dictum of Lord Denning M.R. in the same case at p. 1311 must be confined to disputing that *expenditure* is essential, not that no detriment of any kind is a necessary element. And see *ante*, p. 571, n. 35.

[75] *Dillwyn* v. *Llewelyn* (1862) 4 De G.F. & J. 517; *Inwards* v. *Baker* [1965] 2 Q.B. 29.

[76] *Dann* v. *Spurrier* (1802) 7 Ves. 231; *Thomas* v. *Thomas* [1956] N.Z.L.R. 785; *Pascoe* v. *Turner* [1979] 1 W.L.R. 431.

[77] *Holiday Inns Inc.* v. *Broadhead* (1974) 232 E.G. 951.

[78] *Re Foster, Hudson* v. *Foster (No. 2)* [1938] 3 All E.R. 610.

[79] *Rochdale Canal Co.* v. *King (No. 2)* (1853) 16 Beav. 630.

[80] *Cotching* v. *Bassett* (1862) 32 Beav. 101.

[81] *Salvation Army Trustee Co. Ltd.* v. *West Yorkshire Metropolitan C.C.* (1980) 41 P. & C.R. 179, discussed in *Att.-Gen. of Hong Kong* v. *Humphreys Estate (Queen's Gardens) Ltd.* [1987] A.C. 114 at 126, 127.

A on his own land in the expectation that he had or would obtain planning consent does not raise the equity, for that is concerned with the acquisition of rights in another's land.[82]

(2) OTHER DETRIMENT. The detriment may consist of A's giving up his job and going to live near O in a house owned by O,[83] or by A's acting as an unpaid housekeeper and later mistress,[84] or by A, a maid, cohabiting with O's son and nursing O's daughter,[85] or it may arise from A's disposing of part of his land without being able to gain access to his retained land otherwise than over O's land.[86]

(b) *Expectation or belief.* A must have acted in the belief either that he already owned a sufficient interest in the property to justify the expenditure or that he would obtain such an interest.[87] But if A has no such belief,[88] and improves land in which he knows he has no interest or merely the interest of a tenant, or licensee,[89] or occupier under an incomplete or revocable contract,[90] he has no equity in respect of his expenditure.[91] Similarly, if shortly before A incurred the expenditure O asserted his claim to the land, no equity will arise against him, even if he claims a greater interest than he in fact had, and gave no details of his title; nor need he reassert his title when the expenditure begins.[92]

(c) *Encouragement.* A's belief must have been encouraged by O[93] or his agent[94] or predecessor in title.[95] This may be done actively, as where a father persuades his son to build a bungalow on the father's land,[96] or a mother assures her daughter that she will have the family home for her life,[97] or a man assures his former mistress that the house in which they lived together is hers.[98] The equity will also arise where O merely encourages A's belief passively, as where a mortgagee stood silently by while a purchaser in ignorance of the mortgage built on the land.[99] "The circumstance of looking on is in many cases as strong as using terms of encouragement."[1] Before the equity can arise in such circumstances, O

---

[82] *Western Fish Products Ltd.* v. *Penwith D.C.* [1981] 2 All E.R. 204.
[83] *Jones (A.E.)* v. *Jones (F.W.)* [1977] 1 W.L.R. 438.
[84] *Pascoe* v. *Turner* [1979] 1 W.L.R. 431. Contrast *Coombes* v. *Smith* [1986] 1 W.L.R. 808.
[85] *Greasley* v. *Cooke* [1980] 1 W.L.R. 1306.
[86] *Crabb* v. *Arun D.C.* [1976] Ch. 179.
[87] See *Ramsden* v. *Dyson* (1866) L.R. 1 H.L. 129 at 140, 168, 170; *Inwards* v. *Baker* [1965] 2 Q.B. 29.
[88] As in *Coombes* v. *Smith* [1986] 1 W.L.R. 808.
[89] *E. & L. Berg Homes Ltd.* v. *Grey* (1979) 253 E.G. 473.
[90] *Att.-Gen. of Hong Kong* v. *Humphreys Estate (Queen's Gardens) Ltd.* [1987] A.C. 114; and see *Haslemere Estates Ltd.* v. *Baker* [1982] 1 W.L.R. 1109 at 1119.
[91] *Ramsden* v. *Dyson, supra,* at pp. 141, 168, 171; *Brand* v. *Chris Building Co. Pty. Ltd.* [1957] V.R. 625.
[92] *Master, etc., of Clare Hall* v. *Harding* (1848) 6 Hare 273.
[93] See *e.g. Michand* v. *City of Montreal* (1923) 129 L.T. 417.
[94] *Att.-Gen. to the Prince of Wales* v. *Collom* [1916] 2 K.B. 193. Contrast *Moorgate Mercantile Co. Ltd.* v. *Twitchings* [1977] A.C. 890 (limited agency only); *Swallow Securities Ltd.* v. *Isenberg* [1985] 1 E.G.L.R. 132; 274 E.G. 1028 (knowledge of agent insufficient).
[95] *Hopgood* v. *Brown* [1955] 1 W.L.R. 213; *Jones (A.E.)* v. *Jones (F.W.)* [1977] 1 W.L.R. 438.
[96] *Inwards* v. *Baker* [1965] 2 Q.B. 29.
[97] *Griffiths* v. *Williams* (1977) 248 E.G. 947.
[98] *Pascoe* v. *Turner* [1979] 1 W.L.R. 431.
[99] *Steed* v. *Whitaker* (1740) Barn. Ch. 220.
[1] *Dann* v. *Spurrier* (1802) 7 Ves. 231 at 236, *per* Lord Eldon L.C.

must have known of A's expenditure. Further, normally he must also have known that the property was his,[2] or that his property was being improved,[3] or that he was entitled to interfere,[4] for such knowledge makes it dishonest for him to remain wilfully passive and thereby afterwards profit by a mistake which he might have prevented.[5] But this knowledge is not essential, for even without it, O's encouraging conduct considered in conjunction with A's actions and belief, may be such that it would be dishonest and unconscionable for O to seek to stand on his legal rights.[6] Once it is shown that O gave assurances or other encouragement to A, and A suffers detriment, it will readily be inferred that the detriment was suffered as a result of the encouragement: the burden of proof is on O to show that A's conduct was not induced by the assurances.[7]

(d) *No bar to the equity.* No equity will arise if to enforce the right claimed would contravene some statute,[8] or prevent the exercise of a statutory discretion or prevent or excuse the performance of a statutory duty.[9] Nor will the equity arise if O was a minor when the improvements were made.[10] Yet it will arise if after O attains full age there is prolonged acquiescence by him in the use of the improvements by A, *e.g.* for 40 years[11]; and neither the Crown[12] nor limited companies[13] can claim exemption from the equity. Further A may disentitle himself by his own conduct from seeking equitable relief against the enforcement of O's legal rights,[14] for he must come with clean hands.[15]

2. Extent of the equity. The extent of the equity is to have made good, so far as may fairly be done between the parties, the expectations of A which O has encouraged.[16] A's expectation or belief is the maximum extent of the equity,[17] so that if, for example, A's expectation

---

[2] *Armstrong v. Sheppard & Short Ltd.* [1959] 2 Q.B. 384.
[3] *Brand v. Chris Building Co. Pty. Ltd.* [1957] V.R. 625 (builder builds on wrong land).
[4] *Svenson v. Payne* (1945) 71 C.L.R. 531.
[5] *Ramsden v. Dyson* (1866) L.R. 1 H.L. 129 at 141; contrast *Proctor v. Bennis* (1887) 36 Ch.D. 740 at 760.
[6] *Taylors Fashions Ltd. v. Liverpool Victoria Trustees Co. Ltd.* [1982] Q.B. 133n.; and see *Shaw v. Applegate* [1977] 1 W.L.R. 970 at 977, 978.
[7] *Greasley v. Cooke* [1980] 1 W.L.R. 1306, explained in *Coombes v. Smith* [1986] 1 W.L.R. 808 at 821; and see *Brikom Investments Ltd. v. Carr* [1979] Q.B. 467 at 482, 483. But see M. P. Thompson (1981) 125 S.J. 539.
[8] *Chalmers v. Pardoe* [1963] 1 W.L.R. 677, distinguished in *Maharaj v. Chand* [1986] A.C. 898; contrast *Ward v. Kirkland* [1967] Ch. 194 at 241, 242, as to which, *quaere.* And see *ante,* p. 573.
[9] *Western Fish Products Ltd. v. Penwith D.C.* [1981] 2 All E.R. 204.
[10] *Somersetshire Coal Canal Co. v. Harcourt* (1858) 2 De G. & J. 596.
[11] *Ibid.*
[12] *Att.-Gen. to the Prince of Wales v. Collom* [1916] 2 K.B. 193.
[13] *Laird v. Birkenhead Ry.* (1859) Johns. 500.
[14] See *Williams v. Staite* [1979] Ch. 291 at 299, 300; *J. Willis & Son v. Willis* [1986] 1 E.G.L.R. 62. See M. P. Thompson [1986] Conv. 406 distinguishing between pre- and post-judgment misconduct.
[15] For this maxim, see *ante,* p. 31.
[16] *Grffiths v. Williams* (1977) 248 E.G. 947 at 949; and see *Jones (A.E.) v. Jones (F.W.)* [1977] 1 W.L.R. 438 at 443.
[17] See *Dodsworth v. Dodsworth* (1973) 228 E.G. 1115 at 1115, 1117; *Griffiths v. Williams, supra,* at p. 949.

is that he could stay in a house for the rest of his life, this will not be given effect to in such a way as to confer on him the rights of a tenant for life under the Settled Land Act 1925, for that, with its concomitant right of sale, would give him a greater interest than he was entitled to expect.[18] Accordingly A may have to be content with something less than his expectations, *e.g.* some form of lease at a rent.[19] In other cases a full life interest operating under the Settled Land Act 1925 may be given.[20] Further the position of O has to be considered. Thus the courts are reluctant to compel two persons to live together when they have fallen out, and even after O has died, the due administration of his estate and the rights of those taking under it are factors to be considered.[21] In its search for "the minimum equity to do justice"[22] to A, and shaping it to the facts of the case, "equity is displayed at its most flexible."[23]

3. Satisfaction of the equity. If the equity is established, effect is given to it in whatever is the most appropriate way.[24] Often it suffices merely to dismiss an action brought by O to enforce his legal rights. Thus a claim for possession may be dismissed[25] or a claim to enforce a mortgage may be restrained.[26] Similarly, where O and A are trustees for sale, O's application to have the trust executed may be refused.[27] In such cases the equity is given effect as a defence like any other estoppel. Often, however, more positive action is required.[28]

(1) INJUNCTIONS. O may be restrained by injunction from interfering with possession of land,[29] or from exercising a right to cut down trees and so destroy the beauty of improvements made by A in which he has acquiesced,[30] or from obstructing ancient lights altered by A with O's acquiescence.[31] Further, the injunction may be granted subject to an undertaking by A, *e.g.* to exercise compulsory powers of acquisition.[32]

---

[18] *Dodsworth* v. *Dodsworth* (1973) 228 E.G. 1115, discussed in *Griffiths* v. *Williams, supra*, at pp. 949, 950. And see *Binions* v. *Evans* [1972] Ch. 359 for the effect of the S.L.A. 1925 on licences.
[19] *Griffiths* v. *Evans* (1977) 248 E.G. 947 (parties accepting judge's suggestion).
[20] See *Ungurian* v. *Lesnoff* [1990] Ch. 206.
[21] *Dodsworth* v. *Dodsworth* (1978) 228 E.G. 1115.
[22] *Crabb* v. *Arun D.C.* [1976] Ch. 179 at 198, *per* Scarman L.J.; and see *Pascoe* v. *Turner* [1979] 1 W.L.R. 431 at 438.
[23] *Crabb* v. *Arun D.C., supra*, at p. 189, *per* Lord Denning M.R., citing this book.
[24] See *Lord Cawdor* v. *Lewis* (1835) 1 Y. & C. Ex. 427 at 433; *Plimmer* v. *Mayor, etc., of Wellington* (1884) 9 App.Cas. 699 at 713, 714. The assumption of a general discretion is criticised in a closely reasoned article by S. Moriarty (1984) 100 L.Q.R. 376 but defended by M. P. Thompson [1986] Conv. 406.
[25] *Forbes* v.*Ralli* (1925) L.R. 52 Ind.App. 178; *Inwards* v. *Baker* [1965] 2 Q.B. 29; *Williams* v. *Staite* [1979] Ch. 291; and see *Powell* v. *Thomas* (1848) 6 Hare 300 (injunction restraining action for ejectment).
[26] *Steed* v. *Walker* (1740) Barn. Ch. 220.
[27] *Jones (A.E.)* v. *Jones (F.W.)* [1977] 1 W.L.R. 438.
[28] *Quaere* why in *Cullen* v. *Cullen* [1962] I.R. 268 the equity was held to give no more than a defence.
[29] *Duke of Devonshire* v. *Eglin* (1851) 14 Beav. 530 (obstruction of water course).
[30] *Jackson* v. *Cator* (1800) 5 Ves. 688.
[31] *Cotching* v. *Bassett* (1862) 32 Beav. 101.
[32] *Somersetshire Coal Canal Co.* v. *Harcourt* (1858) 2 De G. & J. 596.

(2) CHARGE FOR EXPENDITURE. A may be given an equitable lien on the property for his expenditure,[33] or for the value of his improvements[34]; and in such case he will be treated as a mortgagee in possession.[35] Alternatively, an order for possession against A may be made conditionally upon O repaying the cost of improvements effected by A.[36] Or it may appear that A has already had "sufficient satisfaction" for his expenditure, and so is entitled to no relief.[37]

(3) CONFERMENT OF TITLE. In many cases justice cannot be done by the mere use of the doctrine by way of defence, or by the recoupment of expenditure, even where this is small,[38] but A must be granted some right. Thus if O has made an imperfect gift of the land to A, as by merely signing an informal memorandum[39] or uttering words of abandonment,[40] the court will compel O to perfect the gift by conveying the land to A.[41] In such cases the court may act by analogy with the specific performance of contracts: A's expenditure with O's knowledge plays the part both of valuable consideration and of part performance.[42] If the circumstances do not suggest a gift, O may be compelled to convey the land on being paid its unimproved value,[43] or to hold the land on trust for sale, and to hold the proceeds after discharge of the respective expenditure of A and O to divide the residue between them.[44] Or the circumstances may indicate that A is to have a lease,[45] a perpetual easement,[46] a life interest,[47] a perpetual licence[48] or a licence as long as he desires to use the premises as his home[49] or a licence to remain until a loan is repaid,[50] and a lessor may be compelled to grant a licence to assign.[51] Again, if O has encouraged A to move to other

---

[33] *Unity Joint Stock Mutual Banking Association* v. *King* (1858) 25 Beav. 72 (land); *Re Foster, Hudson* v. *Foster (No. 2)* [1938] 3 All E.R. 610 (life insurance policy): and see *Veitch* v. *Caldicott* (1945) 173 L.T. 30; *Taylor* v. *Taylor* [1956] N.Z.L.R. 99; *Neesom* v. *Clarkson* (1845) 4 Hare 97 (form of account); *Hussey* v.*Palmer* [1972] 1 W.L.R. 1286 (trust interest proportionate to expenditure); *sed quaere*: see (1973) 89 L.Q.R. 2.
[34] *Raffaele* v. *Raffaele* [1962] W.A.R. 238, discussed by D. E. Allan (1963) 79 L.Q.R. 238.
[35] *Neesom* v. *Clarkson* (1845) 4 Hare 97.
[36] *Dodsworth* v. *Dodsworth* (1973) 228 E.G. 1115.
[37] *Att.-Gen.* v. *Baliol College, Oxford* (1744) 9 Mod. 407 at 412, *per* Lord Hardwicke L.C. (expenditure by lessee).
[38] See *Pascoe* v. *Turner* [1979] 1 W.L.R. 431 at 438.
[39] *Dillwyn* v. *Llewelyn* (1862) 4 De G.F. & J. 517.
[40] *Thomas* v. *Thomas* [1956] N.Z.L.R. 785 (husband and wife).
[41] *Pascoe* v. *Turner* [1979] 1 W.L.R. 431; contrast *ante*, p. 124.
[42] See *Dillwyn* v. *Llewelyn, supra*, at pp. 521, 522; and see Lord Russell of Killowen's restrictive interpretation of *Ramsden* v. *Dyson, infra*, in *Ariff* v. *Jadunath Majumdar* (1931) L.R. 58 Ind.App. 91 at 102, 103.
[43] *Duke of Beaufort* v. *Patrick* (1853) 17 Beav. 60.
[44] *Holiday Inns Inc.* v. *Broadhead* (1974) 232 E.G. 951 (proposed joint venture to build and operate hotel on O's land).
[45] *Stiles* v. *Cowper* (1748) 3 Atk. 692; *Siew Soon Wah* v. *Yong Tong Hong* [1973] A.C. 836; *Griffiths* v. *Williams* (1977) 248 E.G. 947 (see *ante*, pp. 576, 577); and see *Gregory* v. *Mighell* (1811) 18 Ves. 328; *Ramsden* v. *Dyson* (1866) L.R. 1 H.L. 129; *Taylors Fashions Ltd.* v. *Liverpool Victoria Trustees Co. Ltd.* [1982] Q.B. 133n.
[46] *Ward* v. *Kirkland* [1967] Ch. 194; *E.R. Ives Investment Ltd.* v. *High* [1967] 2 Q.B. 379; *Crabb* v. *Arun D.C.* [1976] Ch. 179 (where payment was considered but not imposed in the circumstances).
[47] *Ungurian* v. *Lesnoff* [1990] Ch. 206
[48] *Plimmer* v. *Mayor, etc., of Wellington* (1884) 9 App.Cas. 699.
[49] *Inwards* v. *Baker* [1965] 2 Q.B. 29 (son builds a bungalow on father's land); *Maharaj* v. *Chand* [1986] A.C. 898.
[50] *Re Sharpe* [1980] 1 W.L.R. 219.
[51] *Willmott* v. *Barber* (1880) 15 Ch.D. 96 (where the claim failed).

land, O may be compelled to purchase A's original land.[52] Interests created by the doctrine are not registrable as land charges.[53]

---

[52] *Salvation Army Trustee Co. Ltd.* v. *West Yorkshire Metropolitan C.C.* (1981) 41 P. & C.R. 179, *ante*, p. 574, n. 81.
[53] *E.R. Ives Investment Ltd.* v. *High* [1967] 2 Q.B. 379; and see J. F. Garner (1967) 31 Conv.(N.S.) 332.

PART VII

EQUITABLE REMEDIES

1. Legal remedies. One of the most striking characteristics of equity has been its inventiveness in providing a diversity of remedies. At law, the normal relief granted was an award of damages, and this was enforced by forms of execution primarily directed to realising the sum awarded. Thus under a writ of *fieri facias* the sheriff would seize and sell goods owned by the defendant, or under a writ of *elegit*[1] he would put the plaintiff into possession of the defendant's land, so that he might obtain satisfaction out of the income or use of the land. Also, when land or chattels were themselves in dispute, the sheriff could put the plaintiff in possession under a writ of possession or a writ of delivery. The remedies at law were thus both circumscribed and impersonal. The law acted *in personam* only to a limited extent, principally by imprisonment for debt under a writ of *capias ad satisfaciendum*; and the Debtors Act 1869 abolished this remedy save in certain somewhat special cases.

2. Equitable remedies. Equity supplemented the limited range of legal remedies by providing a wide range of new remedies. A remarkable feature over the centuries was "the ability and willingness of equity to grant elastic remedies ... which were not obtainable at law."[2] These remedies gradually evolved and became settled in their rules and principles. Certain common features in them may be discerned.

(a) *Equity acts in personam.* First, equity relied strongly on the doctrine of acting *in personam*. The defendant would be ordered to do what appeared to the Chancellor to be just and equitable, and if he disobeyed he would be committed or attached for contempt of court.

---

[1] Abolished by Administration of Justice Act 1956, s.34, and replaced by a power to impose a charge on the land: *ibid.* s.35. See now Charging Orders Act 1979. And see Drug Trafficking Offences Act 1986, ss.9, 10.

[2] *Gilligan* v. *National Bank Ltd.* [1901] 2 I.R. 513 at 542, *per* Barton J.

581

(b) *Remedies discretionary.* Secondly, equitable remedies are in general[3] discretionary. At law, a plaintiff who proved his case was entitled as of right not only to his judgment but also to enforce it by the forms of execution available at law, however little his conduct appealed to the court, however dilatory he had been, and however unfair the result. Equity, on the other hand, exercised a discretion in granting its remedies, looking to the conduct not merely of the defendant but also of the plaintiff. Thus it would usually refuse relief to those who had unclean hands, or who were not willing to do equity, or who slept on their rights, or whose claim would produce unfair results. Plaintiffs such as these would be left to whatever remedy they might have at law; and if a plaintiff had an adequate remedy at law, that of itself was a ground for refusing equitable relief.

3. Types of equitable remedy. The principal remedies that equity evolved are those of specific performance; rescission; delivery up and cancellation of documents; rectification; account; injunctions; and the appointment of receivers. Each of these must be considered in some detail. Before doing so, however, it must be made clear that they do not exhaust the field of equitable remedies, though in the main the other remedies are procedural in nature and since the Judicature Act 1873 have been assimilated with the general rules of practice. It must suffice merely to mention the following remedies.

(a) *Discovery.* The procedural remedy of discovery was invented by equity.[4] Although it is now part of the ordinary process of litigation[5] the independent action for discovery may still be brought against a person who has, without incurring any liability of his own, become involved in or facilitated the tortious acts of others.[6]

(b) *Suits for the perpetuation of testimony.* If there was a danger of evidence being lost (*e.g.* by the death of aged witnesses), a suit might be brought in Chancery to take and preserve the evidence.[7] This too is now part of the general process of litigation.[8]

(c) *Quia timet actions.* An action might be brought in Chancery to protect the plaintiff against an injury which was merely threatened, and was not present or existing[9]; and this is still the case.[10]

[3] See, *e.g. post*, p. 652.
[4] See *ante*, p. 28; 3rd edition of this book (1874) (cited as "Snell"), pp. 516–521.
[5] R.S.C., Ord. 24.
[6] *Norwich Pharmacal Co.* v. *Commissioners of Customs and Excise* [1974] A.C. 133.
[7] Snell, 522–525.
[8] R.S.C., Ord. 39, r. 15.
[9] Snell, 526.
[10] See, *e.g. ante*, pp. 473, 476, and *post*, pp. 651, 656, 659.

(d) *Bills of peace.* If there was a dispute as to some right involving a multiplicity of persons (*e.g.* as to a man's right to take tolls, or as to a right of way traversing many estates), a bill of peace could be brought in equity to establish (or quiet[11]) the right and so secure repose from the prospect of incessant or multifarious litigation.[12] Bills of peace have now in practice been superseded by modern procedural provisions for the joinder of parties and for representative actions.[13]

(e) *Ne exeat regno.*[14] A writ *ne exeat regno* could be used to prevent a person who was liable to some equitable claim for a liquidated sum from leaving the country without first giving security for the sum claimed.[15] Today, it is available only in cases where, if the debt was legal, the debtor would be liable to arrest and imprisonment under the Debtors Act 1869, s.6.[16] The writ will be issued only where the absence of the defendant abroad would materially prejudice the plaintiff in prosecuting his action, as when the defendant is a trustee in breach of trust who alone has all the information and documents relating to the trust property.[17] The writ cannot be obtained merely to prevent the defendant from taking his assets out of the jurisdiction so as to put them beyond the plaintiff's reach; and even where the writ can be issued, it is a discretionary remedy.[18] It has, however, enjoyed something of a revival in recent years. Thus, *ne exeat regno* has been issued in aid of a "*Mareva*" injunction,[19] and injunctions restraining a defendant from leaving the jurisdiction have been granted[20] to secure compliance with "*Mareva*" and "*Anton Piller*"[21] orders,[22] and to compel the attendance of the director of a company in liquidation for examination before the Companies Court.[23]

4. Declarations. One type of remedy requires special mention. This is the grant of a declaration by the court of a litigant's rights in the matter in question. Before the Judicature Acts 1873–75, the courts of law and equity had for long made declarations in claims brought against the Crown[24]; and the courts of equity had made declarations in other cases where consequential relief was also claimed.[25] But "an innovation

[11] See *Letton* v. *Goodden* (1866) L.R. 2 Eq. 123 at 130.
[12] Snell, 526–529.
[13] R.S.C. Ord. 15, rr. 4, 5, 12–15. See, *e.g. John* v. *Rees* [1970] Ch. 345.
[14] For a critical survey, see L. J. Anderson (1987) 103 L.Q.R. 246.
[15] Snell, 538, 539; and see *Felton* v. *Callis* [1969] 1 Q.B. 200, where the earlier authorities are fully reviewed.
[16] *Felton* v. *Callis, supra*; *Allied Arab Bank Ltd.* v. *Hajjar* [1988] Q.B. 787; *Drover* v. *Beyer* (1879) 13 Ch.D. 242 at 243.
[17] *Hands* v. *Hands* (1881) 43 L.T. 750.
[18] *Felton* v. *Callis, supra*, at pp. 211–214.
[19] *Al Nahkel for Contracting and Trading Ltd.* v. *Lowe* [1986] Q.B. 235. For the "*Mareva*" injunction see, *post*, pp. 670–673.
[20] Pursuant to S.C.A. 1981, s.37(1).
[21] For the "*Anton Piller*" order see, *post*, pp. 673, 674.
[22] *Beyer A.G.* v. *Winter* [1986] 1 W.L.R. 497.
[23] *Re Oriental Credit Ltd.* [1988] Ch. 204.
[24] See *Dyson* v. *Att.-Gen.* [1911] 1 K.B. 410 at 421.
[25] See *Guaranty Trust Co. of New York* v. *Hannay & Co.* [1915] 2 K.B. 536 at 538.

of a very important kind"[26] was made when in 1850 statute[27] empowered the Court of Chancery to make a declaration without granting any consequential relief; and the jurisdiction was extended further when under the Judicature Acts 1873–75 the Supreme Court was empowered to make declarations whether or not any consequential relief was or even could be claimed.[28] The remedy has always been discretionary,[29] and it is perhaps this, coupled with the fact that statute originally gave the extended jurisdiction to the Court of Chancery, which has led some to assert that declarations are a form of equitable relief.[30] However, the Court of Appeal has held that they are not[31]; they are "neither law nor equity"[32] but primarily statutory, and so they need not be considered further here.[33]

5. Spurious equitable remedies. Occasionally other processes of equity are described as equitable remedies. The constructive trust[34] is sometimes described thus, and so is the process of tracing in equity.[35] Yet these are not so much remedies as part of the process of establishing the substantive rights of the parties. By holding, for example, that there is a right to trace property and that the recipient is bound by a constructive trust, the court is able to decide what order to make; but the tracing and the constructive trust can hardly be said to be a "remedy," at all events in the sense that an injunction or a decree of specific performance is a remedy.

[26] *Ellis* v. *Duke of Bedford* [1899] 1 Ch. 494 at 515, *per* Lindley M.R. (affirmed, [1901] A.C. 1).
[27] Court of Chancery Act 1850, s.14, generalised by Chancery Procedure Act 1852, s.50.
[28] R.S.C., Ord. 15, r. 16, replacing Ord. 25, r. 5, made in 1883 and overcoming the limitation shown by *Rooke* v. *Lord Kensington* (1856) 2 K. & J. 753 (contrast *Cox* v. *Barker* (1876) 3 Ch.D. 359); and see J.A. 1873, ss.5, 6, 16.
[29] See *Russian Commercial and Industrial Bank* v. *British Bank for Foreign Trade Ltd.* [1921] 2 A.C. 438.
[30] See, *e.g. Barnard* v. *National Dock Labour Board* [1953] 2 Q.B. 18 at 31, *per* Denning L.J.
[31] *Chapman* v. *Michaelson* [1909] 1 Ch. 238; and see *ante*, p. 30, *post*, p. 625.
[32] *Gray* v. *Spyer* [1921] 2 Ch. 549 at 557, *per* Younger L.J. (reversed on other grounds [1923] 2 Ch. 22).
[33] See generally Zamir, *The Declaratory Judgment* (1962), esp. at pp. 187–191, accepting *Chapman* v. *Michaelson, supra.*
[34] See *ante*, pp. 196, 197.
[35] See *ante*, p. 299.

CHAPTER 1

SPECIFIC PERFORMANCE

Section 1. Jurisdiction

1. Relation to remedy at law

(a) *Law and equity.* The only remedy which the common law afforded for breach of contract was an award of damages. In equity, however, the due performance of the contract itself was in many cases enforced upon the ground of the inadequacy of the damages recoverable for the breach.

(b) *Damages.* Jurisdiction in specific performance is based on the inadequacy of the remedy at law,[1] and so it follows as a general principle that equity will not interfere where damages at law will give a party the full compensation to which he is entitled and will put him in a position as beneficial to him as if the agreement had been specifically performed.[2] For example, a normal[3] contract for the loan of money, whether or not on mortgage, will not be specifically enforced; for the borrower can obtain money elsewhere, and if he has to pay more for it, he may sue for damages.[4] But by a statute a contract to take up and pay for debentures in a company is specifically enforceable.[5]

(c) *No breach required.* Although in most cases no action for specific performance will be commenced until a breach of the contract has occurred, a breach is not an essential part of the cause of action in equity. Whereas the breach is of the essence of an action for damages at law, an action for specific performance is based on the mere existence of

[1] *Hutton* v. *Watling* [1948] Ch. 26 at 36 (affirmed [1948] Ch. 398).
[2] *Harnett* v. *Yielding* (1805) 2 Sch. & Lef. 549 at 552.
[3] For exceptional cases, see *post*, pp. 587, 588.
[4] *South African Territories Ltd.* v. *Wallington* [1898] A.C. 309.
[5] Companies Act 1985, s.195 (first introduced by the Companies Act 1907, s.16).

the contract, coupled with circumstances which make it equitable to grant a decree.[6] And an action properly commenced before breach of contract may be continued, notwithstanding performance by the defendant, for the purpose of obtaining damages for delay.[7] A plaintiff who needlessly sues for specific performance of an unbroken contract may obtain his decree but may have to pay the costs.[8]

2. Contracts relating to land. The commonest case in which the court specifically enforces a contract is where the contract is for the sale of land or for the granting of a lease. Contracts relating to land differ greatly from contracts respecting most goods, because the land may have a peculiar value to the purchaser or lessee. Where the necessary conditions are satisfied, the court will therefore almost invariably decree specific performance of a contract regarding land, even if the interest to be granted is no more than a licence of short duration[9]; and where the contracting parties are within the jurisdiction this willingness to decree specific performance extends even to land out of the jurisdiction.[10] Further, as the court will not interfere in favour of one party alone, the vendor or lessor can maintain an action for specific performance as well as the purchaser or lessee, although in most cases payment of damages would give the vendor or lessor a complete remedy.[11]

3. Contracts relating to other property. Where the court orders the specific performance of a contract, it proceeds not upon any mere distinction between land and other property, but simply upon the ground that the damages recoverable at law will not in the particular case afford a complete remedy.

(a) *Chattels*

(1) SPECIFIC PERFORMANCE. A contract for the sale of articles of unusual beauty or rarity may be specifically enforced.[12] And a contract to deliver "specific or ascertained goods" may be ordered to be

---

[6] *Hasham* v. *Zenab* [1960] A.C. 316; and see (1960) 76 L.Q.R. 200.
[7] *Oakacre Ltd.* v. *Claire Cleaners (Holdings) Ltd.* [1982] Ch. 197.
[8] See, *e.g. Bass* v. *Clivley* (1829) Taml. 80. Contrast *Marks* v. *Lilley* [1959] 1 W.L.R. 749 (costs awarded where writ was issued after contractual date for completion but before breach).
[9] *See post*, pp. 592, 593.
[10] *Penn* v. *Lord Baltimore* (1750) 1 Ves.Sen. 444; **1 W. & T.L.C. 638**; *ante*, p. 42.
[11] *Cogent* v. *Gibson* (1864) 33 Beav. 557.
[12] *Falcke* v. *Gray* (1859) 4 Drew. 651 (two china vases); *Thorn* v. *Commissioners of Public Works* (1863) 32 Beav. 490 (stone from old Westminster Bridge); *Phillips* v. *Lamdin* [1949] 2 K.B. 33 (Adam door in a house); and see *Pearne* v. *Lisle* (1749) Amb. 75 at 77, *per* Lord Hardwicke L.C. ("a cherry-stone, very finely engraved").

performed specifically without giving the seller the option of retaining the goods and paying damages.[13]

(2) SPECIFIC DELIVERY. Further there is an analogous jurisdiction to order the specific delivery of chattels wrongfully detained by the defendant. At common law, the defendant had the option of keeping the chattel and paying damages. But in equity an order for delivery of the chattel could be obtained if the thing was of peculiar value to the owner, *e.g.* if it was an heirloom[14]; and if the defendant stood in a fiduciary position to the plaintiff, whether as agent, trustee or broker, equity would order specific delivery of the chattel, even if the plaintiff would have been fully compensated by the payment of damages.[15] In 1854 the common law courts were given a corresponding power in actions of detinue[16]; and now, in any action for wrongful interference with goods against a defendant who is in possession or control of the goods, the court may make an order for delivery of the goods.[17]

(b) *Choses in action.* Although the court will not order the seller of Government stock actually to deliver the stock, because Government stock is always readily obtainable in the market,[18] it will order specific performance of an agreement for the sale and purchase of stock or shares which cannot always be bought in the market.[19] So, too, specific performance has been ordered of a contract for the sale of an annuity,[20] and for the sale of debts proved in a bankruptcy, for as the dividends were uncertain, the damages recoverable at law might not accurately represent their value.[21]

(c) *Timber.* The court will also enforce an agreement for the purchase of growing timber if damages would not be a complete remedy to the seller or buyer[22]; and the seller will be restrained by injunction from preventing the buyer from entering on the land to cut the timber.[23]

(d) *Money.* In exceptional cases a contract for the payment of money may be specifically enforced. This may occur where the contract is to pay a third party, so that the damages recoverable by the contracting party would be merely nominal,[24] or where the contract is to

---

[13] See Sale of Goods Act 1979, s.52(1) (jurisdiction), s.61(1) (meaning of "specific"); and see *Re Wait* [1927] 1 Ch. 606 (on "ascertained") and *Cohen* v. *Roche* [1927] 1 K.B. 169 (power to order specific performance is discretionary).

[14] *Pusey* v. *Pusey* (1684) 1 Vern. 273; **2 W. & T.L.C. 404**; *Duke of Somerset* v. *Cookson* (1735) 3 P.Wms. 390; **2 W. & T.L.C. 405.**

[15] *Wood* v. *Rowcliffe* (1847) 2 Ph. 383.

[16] Common Law Procedure Act 1854, s.78.

[17] Torts (Interference with Goods) Act 1977, s.3.

[18] *Cuddee* v. *Rutter* (1720) 5 Vin.Abr. 538, pl. 21; **2 W. & T.L.C. 368.**

[19] *Duncuft* v. *Albrecht* (1841) 12 Sim. 189. *Secus* if the company is being wound up: *Sullivan* v. *Henderson* [1973] 1 W.L.R. 333. See generally A. Neef (1953) 51 Mich.L.R. 408.

[20] *Kenney* v. *Wexham* (1822) 6 Madd. 355.

[21] *Adderley* v. *Dixon* (1824) 1 Sim. & St. 607.

[22] *Buxton* v. *Lister* (1746) 3 Atk. 383.

[23] *James Jones & Sons Ltd.* v. *Earl of Tankerville* [1909] 2 Ch. 440.

[24] *Beswick* v. *Beswick* [1968] A.C. 58.

make periodical payments, requiring a multiplicity of actions at law to enforce payment.[25] Although the third party cannot himself sue on the contract, he can enforce any order for specific performance which the contracting party obtains.[26]

4. Specific performance a discretionary remedy. Although the court will not order specific performance where damages would fully compensate the plaintiff, the converse of this proposition is not true. There are many cases in which the court will not grant specific performance even if the remedy in damages is insufficient; for specific performance is a discretionary remedy.[27] This does not mean that it will be granted or withheld arbitrarily; the discretion is a judicial discretion, and is exercised on well-settled principles. It means that in an action for the specific performance of a contract of the class usually enforced, the court may take into account, as a ground for refusing specific performance or granting it subject to conditions,[28] circumstances which could not be taken into account in an action for damages for breach of contract, such as the conduct of the plaintiff,[29] or the hardship which an order would inflict on the defendant.[30]

5. Damages in substitution for specific performance

(a) *Power to award damages.* Formerly, where the Court of Chancery refused specific performance of a contract, it had no power to award damages for the breach, and in order to recover damages the plaintiff had to start another action in a common law court. By Lord Cairns' Act 1858,[31] however, in all cases in which the Court of Chancery had jurisdiction to entertain an application for an injunction or specific performance, it was empowered, if it thought fit, to award damages "either in addition to or in substitution for" the injunction[32] or specific performance. Although the Act has been repealed, the repeal has not affected the jurisdiction of the court[33]; and by virtue of the fusion of the courts, complete relief, whether specific performance, damages in substitution, or damages at common law, can now be given.[34]

---

[25] *Beswick* v. *Beswick, supra*; compare *ante*, pp. 94, 95.
[26] See *Gurtner* v. *Circuit* [1968] 2 Q.B. 587 at 596, 598, 599, 602, 606.
[27] It is otherwise in Roman-Dutch law: see *Abdeen* v. *Thaheer* [1958] A.C. 116.
[28] See *Harvela Investments Ltd.* v. *Royal Trust Company of Canada (C.I.) Ltd.* [1986] A.C. 207 (plaintiff required to pay interest).
[29] See *ante*, pp. 30–32.
[30] See *post*, pp. 603, 612.
[31] Chancery Amendment Act 1858, s.2.
[32] For the corresponding jurisdiction for injunctions, see *post*, p. 656.
[33] *Sayers* v. *Collyer* (1884) 28 Ch.D. 103; *Leeds Industrial Co-operative Society Ltd.* v. *Slack* [1924] A.C. 851.
[34] *Elmore* v. *Pirrie* (1887) 57 L.T. 333. See *Soames* v. *Edge* (1860) Johns. 669 (specific performance of agreement to take lease, damages for failure to build). See generally A. J. Oakley [1980] C.L.J. 58; M. H. Ogilvie (1980) 58 Can.B.R. 394.

(b) *Contract specifically enforceable.* Damages in substitution for specific performance can be awarded only if the court could specifically enforce the contract.[35] Thus no such damages can be awarded if the contract is of a type which is not specifically enforceable (*e.g.* to borrow money),[36] or if the plaintiff has disabled himself from performing his part of the bargain (*e.g.* by selling the land in question to another),[37] or if the right in question was exercisable only for a limited time which has expired.[38] But damages may be awarded if there is jurisdiction to decree specific performance but it is refused (or subsequently rescinded[39]) on some discretionary ground[40] such as laches[41] or mistake,[42] or if the making of an order for specific performance would for some reason be inappropriate.[43] A plaintiff who enforces an award of damages may thereby estop himself from seeking his primary remedy of specific performance on appeal.[44]

(c) *Measure of damages.* A purchaser claiming damages for breach of a contract for the sale of land made before September 27, 1989, is confined by the rule in *Bain* v. *Fothergill*[45] to recovering no more than his conveyancing expenses if the breach of contract arises only from a defect in the vendor's title. The rule, which was much criticised,[46] has been abolished in relation to contracts made after September 26, 1989,[47] so as to permit the recovery of damages for loss of bargain by purchasers and vendors alike on the same basis as at common law.[48]

(d) *Time of assessment.* If damages awarded to a purchaser are to be truly compensatory, then when the market is rising the value of the property should be taken at the date of judgment,[49] although an earlier date may be substituted if the plaintiff has delayed unduly in making his claim.[50] Where a decree of specific performance is obtained and subsequently discharged by reason of the vendor's failure to comply with

---

[35] *Lavery* v. *Pursell* (1888) 39 Ch.D. 508; *J.C. Williamson Ltd.* v. *Lukey* (1931) 45 C.L.R. 282.

[36] *Rogers* v. *Challis* (1859) 27 Beav. 175.

[37] *Hipgrave* v. *Case* (1885) 28 Ch.D. 356.

[38] *Lavery* v. *Pursell, supra.*

[39] See *post*, pp. 591, 592.

[40] *Wroth* v. *Tyler* [1974] Ch. 30; *Price* v. *Strange* [1978] Ch. 337 at 358–360, 368–370.

[41] *McKenna* v. *Richey* [1950] V.L.R. 360; and see *Eastwood* v. *Lever* (1863) 4 De G.J. & S. 114; *Senior* v. *Pawson* (1866) L.R. 3 Eq. 330; *Sayers* v. *Collyer* (1884) 24 Ch.D. 103, all cases on refusal of injunctions.

[42] *Dell* v. *Beasley* [1959] N.Z.L.R. 89.

[43] *Tito* v. *Waddell (No. 2)* [1977] Ch. 106 at 321–323, 325–328 (damages instead of replanting of trees over a small number of isolated plots).

[44] *Meng Leong Development Pte. Ltd.* v. *Jip Hong Trading Co. Pte. Ltd.* [1985] A.C. 511.

[45] (1873) L.R. 7 H.L. 158. For more detail, see the 28th edition of this book, p. 573.

[46] See, *e.g. Sharneyford Supplies Ltd.* v. *Edge* [1987] Ch. 305 at 318, *per* Balcombe L.J.: counsel "submitted to us that the rule still serves a useful purpose in Yorkshire. ... It serves no useful purpose anywhere in England or Wales."

[47] Law of Property (Miscellaneous Provisions) Act 1989, ss.3, 5(3), (4)(a).

[48] As in *Johnson* v. *Agnew* [1980] A.C. 367; *Malhotra* v. *Choudhury* [1980] Ch. 52; *Sharneyford Supplies Ltd.* v. *Edge* [1987] Ch. 305 (all cases outside the rule in *Bain* v. *Fothergill*).

[49] *Wroth* v. *Tyler* [1974] Ch. 30 (contract to buy for £6,000 a bungalow worth £7,500 at date of breach and £11,500 at date of judgment); *Grant* v. *Dawkins* [1973] 1 W.L.R. 1406; *Suleman* v. *Shahsavari* [1988] 1 W.L.R. 1181 (damages for breach of warranty of authority).

[50] *Malhotra* v. *Choudhury, supra.*

the order, the proper date for valuation is that on which the remedy was aborted.[51] Where the market is falling, damages will be assessed as at the date of the breach.[52]

6. Parties to action for specific performance

(a) *Contracting parties.* Generally speaking it is only the parties to the contract or their representatives who should be made plaintiffs and defendants respectively in the action. Thus where a mortgagor has sold property, the mortgagee is not a necessary defendant to the purchaser's action for specific performance.[53] Again, where a mortgagee has sold property and no relief other than the specific performance of the contract is claimed, the mortgagor is not a necessary defendant.[54] Similarly, if L agrees to grant a lease to T, and before doing so he executes a mortgage to M, the action by T for specific performance of the agreement is properly against L only and not also against M, even though M may take subject to the agreement.[55] And if V has agreed to sell property to P, and V subsequently agrees to sell the same property to X, an action by P merely for specific performance should be brought against V alone, without making X a co-defendant.[56] But if V has actually conveyed the land to X, then unless X takes free from P's contract under the doctrine of purchaser without notice or for want of registration,[57] he should be joined as a defendant so that he may be ordered to convey the land to P.[58] Where a contract has been made by co-owners of land, all must be parties to the action in which specific performance is sought, for it may be that some would prefer damages or even not to sue at all.[59] A plaintiff who has entered into two contracts for the purchase of the same property from separate vendors, *e.g.* the owner and a mortgagee, can obtain a decree of specific performance in relation to only one of the contracts at a time.[60]

(b) *Agency.* Where an agent has bought property in his own name, the vendor properly sues the agent only.[61] But the undisclosed principal can usually sue the vendor for specific performance, joining the agent as co-defendant if he will not join as plaintiff; and this is so even though the contract is under seal.[62]

---

[51] *Johnson* v. *Agnew* [1980] A.C. 367.
[52] *Woodford Estates Ltd.* v. *Pollack* (1979) 93 D.L.R. (3d) 350.
[53] *Tasker* v. *Small* (1837) 3 My. & Cr. 63.
[54] *Corder* v. *Morgan* (1811) 18 Ves. 344.
[55] *Long* v. *Bowring* (1864) 33 Beav. 585.
[56] *Cutts* v. *Thodey* (1844) 1 Coll.C.C. 223.
[57] See *Greaves* v. *Tofield* (1880) 14 Ch.D. 563 at 572; *ante*, pp. 47 *et seq.*, 58 *et seq.*
[58] *Potter* v. *Sanders* (1846) 6 Hare 1; and see *Smith* v. *Phillips* (1837) 1 Keen 694.
[59] *Tito* v. *Waddell (No. 2)* [1977] Ch. 106 at 323–325.
[60] *Casey* v. *Irish Intercontinental Bank Ltd.* [1979] I.R. 364 at 371.
[61] *Chadwick* v. *Maden* (1851) 9 Hare 188.
[62] *Harmer* v. *Armstrong* [1934] Ch. 65.

(c) *Company in receivership.* A limited company may be sued for specific performance notwithstanding the appointment of a receiver by the holder of a debenture.[63]

7. Summary judgment. Under Order 86 of the Rules of the Supreme Court, an expeditious procedure is available for obtaining summary judgment in actions for specific performance. This resembles the procedure under Order 14 for money claims and for most other proceedings commenced by writ.[64] Mere complexity of law is no bar to a decree under this procedure[65] if in the end the court is satisfied that there is a clear case for granting the decree, as where the case turns on the construction of documents, and not on disputed issues of fact[66] which ought to be resolved on a trial with pleadings, discovery and oral evidence.[67] If the purchaser has gone into possession and accepted the title, the vendor may move for judgment that the purchaser lodge the purchase money in court, or give up possession, but the latter alternative may be withheld if he has done great and lasting damage to the land.[68]

8. Effect of order.[69] After specific performance has been decreed the contract continues to exist and is not merged in the order,[70] but the working out of the order (and hence the contract) is subject to the control of the court. In making a decree, the court usually directs the conveyance to be settled in chambers in case of difference between the parties; but the insertion of any particular clause will be decided at the trial of the action if the matter is sufficiently raised on the pleadings.[71] Damages payable in addition to specific performance may be secured by a "*Mareva*" order pending assessment.[72] Facts which occur or emerge after specific performance has been decreed may justify making a supplemental order, *e.g.* to direct an inquiry as to damages suffered by one party through the delay of the other in complying with the original decree,[73] or through his failure to discharge a mortgage to which the property is subject.[74] In the more extreme case of the order proving

---

[63] *Freevale Ltd.* v. *Metrostore (Holdings) Ltd.* [1984] Ch. 199.
[64] The difficulties revealed by cases such as *Young* v. *Markworth Properties Ltd.* [1965] Ch. 475 (see (1965) 81 L.Q.R. 178) have now been cured by amendment: see Ord. 14, r. 1(3); Ord. 86, r. 1(1)(*a*).
[65] See, *e.g. Richard West & Partners (Inverness) Ltd.* v. *Dick* [1969] 2 Ch. 424; *Brickwoods Ltd.* v. *Butler* (1969) 21 P. & C.R. 256; affirmed (1970) 23 P. & C.R. 317.
[66] See, *e.g. Bigg* v. *Boyd Gibbins Ltd.* [1971] 1 W.L.R. 913.
[67] See *Sullivan* v. *Henderson* [1973] 1 W.L.R. 333 (normally no cross-examination should be permitted under Ord. 86)
[68] *Maskell* v. *Ivory* [1970] Ch. 502.
[69] For the usual form of order, see *Palmer* v. *Lark* [1945] Ch. 182.
[70] *Singh (Sudagar)* v. *Nazeer* [1979] Ch. 474.
[71] *Hart* v. *Hart* (1881) 18 Ch.D. 670.
[72] *Seven Seas Properties Ltd.* v. *Al-Essa* [1988] 1 W.L.R. 1272; see *post,* p. 670.
[73] *Ford-Hunt* v. *Raghbir Singh* [1973] 1 W.L.R. 738; *Easton* v. *Brown* [1981] 3 All E.R. 278.
[74] *Grant* v. *Dawkins* [1973] 1 W.L.R. 1406.

useless (as where mortgages on the property cannot be discharged), the court may discharge the decree and substitute an award of damages[75] or, in a vendor's action, direct that the deposit be forfeited[76]: but the party not in default is not at liberty to exercise his contractual rights, *e.g.* to resell the land to a third party, without obtaining an order of the court.[77]

Section 2. Contracts not Specifically Enforceable

There are certain contracts which equity will not specifically enforce.

1. Illegal or immoral contracts. Equity will not compel the specific performance of a contract which is immoral or which is contrary to public policy,[78] or otherwise contrary to the law of England,[79] even though it may be legal in the country where it was made.[80]

2. Agreements without consideration. Equity will not specifically enforce an agreement which is merely voluntary, even if it is contained in a deed.[81] But the fact that the agreement results from the exercise of an option for which a token consideration was paid will not deprive the grantee of the remedy of specific performance at any rate if the option price is itself substantial.[82]

3. Contracts for transient interests. Equity will not specifically enforce agreements for transient interests, such as an agreement for a tenancy at will, or to enter into partnership for no fixed term[83]; for "equity, like nature, does nothing in vain."[84] The court would at one time refuse specific performance of agreements for short tenancies, such as one day[85] or even one year[86]; though specific performance would be granted of an agreement for a tenancy from year to year.[87] But now

---

[75] *Johnson* v. *Agnew* [1980] A.C. 367, overruling *Capital and Suburban Properties Ltd.* v. *Swycher* [1976] Ch. 319. And see *post*, p. 623.
[76] *Hall* v. *Burnell* [1911] 2 Ch. 551.
[77] *G.K.N. Distributors Ltd.* v. *Tyne Tees Fabrication Ltd.* (1985) 50 P. & C.R. 403.
[78] *Sutton* v. *Sutton* [1984] Ch. 184.
[79] *Ewing* v. *Osbaldiston* (1837) 2 My. & Cr. 53.
[80] *Hope* v. *Hope* (1857) 8 De G.M. & G. 731; *post*, p. 613.
[81] *Jefferys* v. *Jefferys* (1841) Cr. & Ph. 138.
[82] *Mountford* v. *Scott* [1975] Ch. 258 (option to purchase at £10,000 granted for £1).
[83] *Hercy* v. *Birch* (1804) 9 Ves. 357.
[84] *Cf. ante*, p. 500.
[85] *Glasse* v. *Woolgar* (1897) 41 S.J. 573.
[86] *Lavery* v. *Pursell* (1888) 39 Ch.D. 508 at 519.
[87] *Lever* v. *Koffler* [1901] 1 Ch. 543.

specific performance will be granted in such cases,[88] provided of course that the action is heard before the agreed term has expired.[89] Otherwise, the plaintiff will be left to such other remedies as may be appropriate, *e.g.* a declaration[90] or an order for payment of rent[91] or return of a deposit.[92] Where there is a contract for the sale of an annuity, the death of the annuitant before judgment is not a bar to specific performance of the contract.[93]

4. Partnership. A contract for partnership even for a fixed term will not be specifically enforced[94] unless the partners have begun to act upon the agreement.[95]

5. Contracts involving personal skill. The incapacity of the court to compel the complete performance of a contract sometimes limits its jurisdiction to order specific performance. This principle, which has been given statutory force in relation to contracts of employment,[95a] is most frequently illustrated in cases of agreements to do acts involving personal skill, knowledge or inclination. Thus, in *Lumley* v. *Wagner*,[96] a lady agreed with a theatrical manager to sing at his theatre for a definite period, but the court could not compel her to sing[97]; although the threat of committal might induce some sort of performance, the court could not control imperfections of performance or judge whether they were natural or self-induced.[98] For similar reasons a contract to report cases for a series of law reports will not be specifically enforced,[99] nor will a contract to publish an article not in its final agreed form.[1] But a contract to publish a completed musical work has been specifically enforced, notwithstanding that some supervision would be required.[2] The difficulty of controlling the work and the refusal of equity to decree specific performance against a minor[3] both prevented the enforcement of a minor's apprenticeship deed.[4] Yet after the apprenticeship has ended

---

[88] *Verrall* v. *Great Yarmouth B.C.* [1981] Q.B. 202 (licence to use meeting hall for two days).
[89] *Nesbitt* v. *Meyer* (1818) 1 Swans. 223.
[90] *De Brassac* v. *Martyn* (1863) 11 W.R. 1020.
[91] *Wilkinson* v. *Torkington* (1837) 2 Y. & C.Ex. 726; *Gilbey* v. *Cossey* (1912) 106 L.T. 607.
[92] *De Brassac* v. *Martyn, supra.*
[93] *Kenney* v. *Wexham* (1822) 6 Madd. 355.
[94] *Scott* v. *Rayment* (1868) L.R. 7 Eq. 112 (see *supra*, n. 83, for partnerships at will).
[95] As in *England* v. *Curling* (1844) 8 Beav. 129, explained in *Sichel* v. *Mosenthal* (1862) 30 Beav. 371 at 375, 376.
[95a] Trade Union and Labour Relations Act 1974, s.16.
[96] (1852) 1 De G.M. & G. 604. For the Lumley background, see (1973) 117 S.J. 160.
[97] But she was enjoined from singing elsewhere: see *post*, p. 678.
[98] See *C.H. Giles & Co. Ltd.* v. *Morris* [1972] 1 W.L.R. 307 at 318.
[99] *Clarke* v. *Price* (1819) 2 Wils.Ch. 157.
[1] *Joseph* v. *National Magazine Co. Ltd.* [1959] Ch. 14.
[2] *Barrow* v. *Chappell & Co. Ltd.* [1976] R.P.C. 355.
[3] See *post*, p. 596.
[4] See *De Francesco* v. *Barnum (No. 1)* (1889) 43 Ch.D. 165; *(No. 2)* (1890) 45 Ch.D. 430 (where in any case the deed was unreasonable).

the court may grant an injunction to prevent the breach of a reasonable restrictive covenant contained in it.[5]

6. Contracts requiring constant supervision

(a) *The rule.* It was at one time thought that a contract to do continuous successive acts (which would include a contract for personal services) would not be enforced specifically, as it would involve constant and possibly ineffective supervision by the court: thus the court refused to enforce a covenant in a lease by the landlord to employ a resident porter,[6] or by the tenant to repair the premises.[7] This is no longer the rule.[8] Contracts of this kind will often be unsuitable for specific performance, because of the difficulty of defining with precision what has to be done[9] or because the inconvenience which would be worked by the decree makes damages a more appropriate remedy.[10] But, in principle, the need for supervision is by itself no bar.[11] And if a contract as a whole[12] is suitable for specific performance, a decree will not be refused merely because the contract contains a provision which on its own would not be specifically enforced.[13] Further, in a proper case specific performance of an agreement to sign or otherwise execute an instrument will be ordered even if the obligations under that instrument would not themselves be specifically enforced (*e.g.* because they are obligations to perform personal services[14]) so that breaches of them would sound only in damages.[15]

(b) *Contract to build.* The requirement of supervision has sometimes been said to be the foundation of the rule that specific performance will not usually be ordered of a contract to build or repair.[16] This seems debatable; but, now that supervision by itself does not make specific performance unobtainable, the rationale of the rule need not be investigated.[17] In many building cases, specific performance will not be granted because damages will be adequate compensation for the breach of such a contract; for if the defendant will not build the plaintiff can find some other builder ready to do so, and can recover any loss from

---

[5] *Gadd* v. *Thompson* [1911] 1 K.B. 304.
[6] *Ryan* v. *Mutual Tontine Westminster Chambers Association* [1893] 1 Ch. 116. But see now *Posner* v. *Scott-Lewis* [1987] Ch. 25.
[7] *Hill* v. *Barclay* (1810) 16 Ves. 402 at 405.
[8] *Shiloh Spinners Ltd.* v. *Harding* [1973] A.C. 691 at 724; *Posner* v. *Scott-Lewis* [1987] Ch. 25.
[9] *Tito* v. *Waddell (No. 2)* [1977] Ch. 106 at 321, 322.
[10] *C.H. Giles & Co. Ltd.* v. *Morris* [1972] 1 W.L.R. 307 at 318, 319, approved in *Price* v. *Strange* [1978] Ch. 337 at 359, 360.
[11] *Shiloh Spinners Ltd.* v. *Harding, supra; Tito* v. *Waddell (No. 2), supra; C.H. Giles & Co. Ltd.* v. *Morris, supra.*
[12] For divisible contracts, see *post,* p. 595.
[13] *C.H. Giles & Co. Ltd.* v. *Morris* [1972] 1 W.L.R. 307; and see *McCarthy & Stone Ltd.* v. *Julian S. Hodge & Co. Ltd.* [1971] 1 W.L.R. 1547.
[14] *Ibid.*
[15] *Wilson* v. *West Hartlepool Ry.* (1865) 2 De G.J. & S. 475; *C.H. Giles & Co. Ltd.* v. *Morris, supra.*
[16] See, *e.g. Ryan* v. *Mutual Tontine Westminster Chambers Association* [1893] 1 Ch. 116 at 128.
[17] Contrast *Blackett* v. *Bates* (1865) 1 Ch.App. 117 at 124, 125 with *Grace* v. *Baynton* (1877) 25 W.R. 506.

the defendant as damages.[18] Nevertheless, in several cases the court has ordered the defendant to build[19] or repair[20] in accordance with his contract.

(c) *Conditions for specific performance.* The rule[21] has now become settled that the court will order specific performance of an agreement to build if:

(i)   the building work is sufficiently defined by the contract, *e.g.* by reference to detailed plans[22];

(ii)   the plaintiff has a substantial interest in the performance of the contract of such a nature that damages would not compensate him for the defendant's failure to build; and

(iii) the defendant[23] is in possession of the land so that the plaintiff cannot employ another person to build without committing a trespass.[24]

7. Contracts to transfer goodwill alone. An agreement for the sale of the goodwill of a business unconnected with the business premises will not be specifically enforced. The reason is the uncertainty of the subject-matter and the consequent incapacity of the court to give specific directions as to what is to be done to transfer it.[25] But specific performance will be decreed where the goodwill is annexed to the premises and the contract is to sell both.[26]

8. Divisible contracts. A contract may be divisible, containing what in substance are two or more contracts. If one or more of these cannot be specifically enforced, a decree may still be granted for the remainder unless they are dependent upon the others.[27] Thus where a building

---

[18] See *Flint* v. *Brandon* (1803) 8 Ves. 159 at 163.

[19] *Att.-Gen.* v. *Colchester Corporation* [1955] 2 Q.B. 207 at 216; see, *e.g. Storer* v. *Great Western Ry.* (1842) 2 Y. & C.C.C. 48; *Wilson* v. *Furness Ry.* (1869) L.R. 9 Eq. 28; *Greene* v. *West Cheshire Ry.* (1871) L.R. 13 Eq. 44; *Fortescue* v. *Lostwithiel and Fowey Ry.* [1894] 3 Ch. 621 (covenants by railway companies to build a station or siding).

[20] *Jeune* v. *Queen's Cross Properties Ltd.* [1974] Ch. 97 (landlord's repairing covenant). And see *post*, p. 597, for a statutory right.

[21] See *Wolverhampton Corporation* v. *Emmons* [1901] 1 K.B. 515; *Molyneux* v. *Richard* [1906] 1 Ch. 34; Fry, *Specific Performance* (6th ed., 1921), p. 48.

[22] Contrast *Mosely* v. *Virgin* (1796) 3 Ves. 184 (covenant "to lay out £1,000 in building": decree refused).

[23] In *Greene* v. *West Cheshire Ry.*, *supra*, a decree was made though the plaintiff was in possession: *sed quaere*.

[24] *Carpenters Estates Ltd.* v. *Davies* [1940] Ch. 160, explaining *Wolverhampton Corporation* v. *Emmons, supra*; and see *Hounslow L.B.C.* v. *Twickenham Garden Developments Ltd.* [1971] Ch. 233 at 251. This passage was cited and applied in *Jeune* v. *Queen's Cross Properties Ltd., supra*, at pp. 99, 100.

[25] *Baxter* v. *Connolly* (1820) 1 J. & W. 576; *Darbey* v. *Whitaker* (1857) 4 Drew. 134 at 139.

[26] *Darbey* v. *Whitaker, supra*, at p. 140.

[27] *Ogden* v. *Fossick* (1862) 4 De G.F. & J. 426; *Ryan* v. *Mutual Tontine Westminster Chambers Association* [1893] 1 Ch. 116; *Barnes* v. *City of London Real Property Co.* [1918] 2 Ch. 18.

agreement provided that the lessor should grant leases piecemeal to the builder upon the completion of the buildings on the several plots, and the conditions as to building on one plot had been fulfilled, the court enforced the agreement to grant a lease of that plot even though the court could not specifically enforce the agreement to build on the other and unbuilt-on plots.[28] Again, where some of the terms of an agreement are legal and the others are illegal, the court will sometimes specifically enforce the terms which are legal if the illegal terms are clearly severable.[29]

9. Contracts for arbitration. Equity will not directly enforce an agreement to appoint an arbitrator.[30] But the court may indirectly compel performance of the agreement by staying any action which is brought, if a party to the proceedings so applies[31]; and in certain cases the court has statutory powers to appoint arbitrators[32] or itself to act as arbitrator.[33]

10. Contracts wanting in mutuality

(a) *The rule.* It was until recently accepted that in order to be specifically enforceable, a contract must, at the time when it is made,[34] be mutually binding.[35] As a rule, the court would not grant specific performance at the suit of one party when it could not do so at the suit of the other.[36] Thus if a vendor had no title to the estate which he contracted to sell and no right to compel the real owner to convey it,[37] he could not force the purchaser to take a conveyance from the true owner, even if he was willing to convey the property, for the purchaser had no right to compel a conveyance by the true owner.[38] Again, a minor could not compel specific performance, for the court could not compel specific performance against him.[39] One apparent exception to the rule as to mutuality arose by reason of the Law of Property Act

---

[28] *Wilkinson* v. *Clements* (1872) 8 Ch.App. 96; *cf. Soames* v. *Edge* (1860) Johns. 669.
[29] *Odessa Tramways Co.* v. *Mendel* (1878) 8 Ch.D. 235.
[30] *Re Smith & Service and Nelson & Sons* (1890) 25 Q.B.D. 545.
[31] Arbitration Act 1950, s.4(1); Arbitration Act 1975, s.1(1).
[32] See Arbitration Act 1950, ss.10, 25.
[33] Administration of Justice 1970, s.4 (judge of Commercial Court).
[34] *Re Bayley and Shoesmith's Contract* (1918) 87 L.J.Ch. 626; contrast *Joseph* v. *National Magazine Co. Ltd.* [1959] Ch. 14 at 20.
[35] See Fry's *Specific Performance* (6th ed., 1921), pp. 219–228, and contrast J. B. Ames (1903) 3 Col.L.R. 1 (reprinted in *Lectures on Legal History* (1913), p. 370); W. W. Cook (1927) 36 Yale L.J. 897. The doctrine finds little favour in America: see *Epstein* v. *Gluckin*, 135 N.E. 861 at 862 (1922), *per* Cardozo J. (mutuality is important only to secure that the decree will operate without injustice to either party); and see generally 5A *Corbin on Contracts* (1964), cap. 65; Chafee and Re, *Cases and Materials on Equity* (5th ed., 1967), pp. 677–693. For a detailed account of the modern law, see Jones & Goodhart, *Specific Performance* (1986), pp. 22–27; and for mutuality in the law of contracts generally, see G. H. Treitel (1961) 77 L.Q.R. 83.
[36] See *Blackett* v. *Bates* (1865) 1 Ch.App. 117.
[37] See *Elliott and H. Elliott (Builders) Ltd.* v. *Pearson* [1948] Ch. 452.
[38] *Forrer* v. *Nash* (1865) 35 Beav. 167 at 171; and see *Re Bryant and Barningham's Contract* (1890) 44 Ch.D. 218. *Cf. Hoggart* v. *Scott* (1830) 1 Russ. & M. 293.
[39] *Flight* v. *Bolland* (1828) 4 Russ. 298; *Lumley* v. *Ravenscroft* [1895] 1 Q.B. 683 at 684.

1925, s.40. If one party had signed a written memorandum of a contract for the sale of land, and the other had not signed it, the latter might maintain an action for specific performance against the former, though not *vice versa*. Such cases were supported on the ground that the statute only required the agreement to be signed by the party to be charged, and that by bringing an action the plaintiff waived the want of mutuality and made the remedy mutual.[40]

(b) *The rule restated.*   The more recent approach is to regard a want of mutuality as a discretionary, not an absolute, bar to specific performance. The court considers the defence "on the facts and circumstances of the case as they exist at the hearing, albeit in the light of the whole conduct of the parties in relation to the subject-matter, and in the absence of any disqualifying circumstances the court will grant specific performance if it can be done without injustice or unfairness to the defendant."[41] In particular, if the plaintiff has performed all his obligations under the contract, specific performance can be decreed against the defendant[42]; and specific performance has even been ordered against the vendor of shares in a case where the price could not be ascertained for two years.[43] Further, if the defendant has stood by and allowed the plaintiff to carry out an appreciable part of the contract, he will have created an equity which disables him from asserting want of mutuality[44]; and if the defendant has himself performed part of the plaintiff's obligations (*e.g.* to do building work), the plaintiff may nonetheless obtain specific performance subject to a financial adjustment to compensate the defendant.[45]

(c) *Repairing covenants.*   By statute, a tenant may at the discretion of the court obtain specific performance of a landlord's repairing covenant in the lease of a dwelling "whether or not the breach relates to a part of the premises let to the tenant and notwithstanding any equitable rule restricting the scope of that remedy, whether on the basis of a lack of mutuality or otherwise."[46]

11. Contracts to exercise a testamentary power of appointment. Equity will not specifically enforce a contract by the donee of a testamentary power of appointment to appoint by will to any particular individual, even if the contract is for value; by making the power exercisable only by will the donor intended the donee to have power to

[40] *Flight* v. *Bolland, supra,* at p. 301. For the repeal of s.40, see *post,* p. 601.
[41] *Price* v. *Strange* [1978] Ch. 337 at 357, *per* Goff L.J. (agreement to grant underlease in consideration of execution of repairs).
[42] *Kirkland* v. *Bird* (1968) 112 S.J. 440 (option to buy land in return for personal services; services performed); *Price* v. *Strange, supra.*
[43] *Langen & Wind Ltd.* v. *Bell* [1972] Ch. 685.
[44] *Price* v. *Strange* [1978] Ch. 337; *Sutton* v. *Sutton* [1984] Ch. 184 at 193, citing this passage.
[45] *Price* v. *Strange, supra.*
[46] Landlord and Tenant Act 1985, s.17(1), replacing Housing Act 1974, s.125(1). And see *Jeune* v. *Queen's Cross Properties Ltd.* [1974] Ch. 97, *ante,* p. 595.

exercise it until his death, and the court will not help to defeat the donor's intention.[47]

Section 3. Defences to an Action for Specific Performance

Even where the contract is one which is specifically enforceable, a decree will not follow as of course. The remedy is discretionary. In addition to normal defences that are available to any defendant, including the right to set off sums due under the contract,[48] there are a number of special defences to the action for specific performance. Even if the defendant succeeds in establishing such a defence, it may leave the contract actionable at law, though not necessarily so.[48a]

1. No effective contract

(a) *Creation of contract.* There can be no specific performance unless there is a complete and definite contract.[49] The question whether or not there is a complete contract often arises where negotiations for the sale of property have been carried on by correspondence.[50]

(b) *Condition precedent.* If the contract is subject to a condition precedent, specific performance will not be decreed unless the condition has been fulfilled,[51] or, if it is solely for the benefit of the plaintiff, he has waived it.[52] A contract is nonetheless a contract although the parties have stipulated that a formal document shall be drawn up,[53] unless the drawing up of the document is made a condition precedent to the agreement becoming effective as a contract.[54] In the normal contract for sale of land, the payment of a deposit is not a condition precedent for the formation of the contract.[55]

(c) *Want of certainty.* Want of certainty in the contract is also a ground for resisting specific performance.[56] Where, for instance, the contract is for a lease, any uncertainty as to the date at which the term is to begin will be fatal,[57] unless the contract itself and the surrounding circumstances make it plain that the term is to begin from the date when

[47] *Re Parkin* [1892] 3 Ch. 510; *Re Cooke, Winckley* v. *Winterton* [1922] 1 Ch. 292; and see *Beyfus* v. *Lawley* [1903] A.C. 411. See also *ante*, pp. 546, 547.
[48] *B.I.C.C. plc* v. *Burndy Corpn.* [1985] Ch. 232; see 100 L.Q.R. 145.
[48a] See, *e.g. Re Banister* (1879) 12 Ch.D. 131 at 142, 146, 147, 149; *post*, pp. 602, 611.
[49] *Gibson* v. *Manchester City Council* [1979] 1 W.L.R. 294; and see *post*, p. 602.
[50] See *Hussey* v. *Horne-Payne* (1879) 4 App.Cas. 311; *Gibson* v. *Manchester City Council* [1979] 1 W.L.R. 294.
[51] See *Heron Garage Properties Ltd.* v. *Moss* [1974] 1 W.L.R. 148.
[52] *Hawksley* v. *Outram* [1892] 3 Ch. 359; *Morrell* v. *Studd & Millington* [1913] 2 Ch. 648.
[53] *Rossiter* v. *Miller* (1878) 3 App.Cas. 1124.
[54] As in *Von Hatzfelt-Wildenburg* v. *Alexander* [1912] 1 Ch. 57.
[55] *Damon Compania Naviera S.A.* v. *Hapag-Lloyd International S.A.* [1985] 1 W.L.R. 435 (sale of ship), approving *Millichamp* v. *Jones* [1982] 1 W.L.R. 1422 and overruling *Myton Ltd.* v. *Schwab-Morris* [1974] 1 W.L.R. 331.
[56] *Douglas* v. *Baynes* [1908] A.C. 477.
[57] *Marshall* v. *Berridge* (1881) 19 Ch.D. 233; and see *Harvey* v. *Pratt* [1965] 1 W.L.R 1025.

possession is given.[58] But in cases of fraud, the court strives to find sufficient certainty,[59] and even if it fails the plaintiff may not be left without relief.[60] Further, a trivial uncertainty which can be removed by inquiry will not make the contract void; specific performance has accordingly been decreed where the specific acreage to be sold[61] or the specific rent to be paid[62] has been left indefinite but ascertainable.

2. Absence of writing

(a) Contracts made before September 27, 1989

(1) WRITING REQUIRED.   The effect of s.40 of the Law of Property Act 1925, which replaced s.4 of the Statute of Frauds 1677, is that for an action for the specific performance of a contract for the sale of land or any interest in land to succeed, there must usually be a written memorandum of the contract signed by the defendant or by his duly authorised agent.[62a] The memorandum must contain all the terms of the contract,[63] although if it omits a term which is solely[64] for the benefit of one party, that party may specifically enforce the contract if he waives the omitted term[65]; and similarly for the other party if he agrees to perform it.[66] The rule is a rule of evidence; the contract is valid but no action may be brought until a memorandum is signed, and this may occur at any time after the contract is entered into.[67] The rule does not affect sales by the court.[68] Nor does it debar a plaintiff from obtaining specific performance if the defendant fails to rely on the absence of a written memorandum in his defence.[69] The rule is subject to two exceptions.

(2) FRAUD.   Despite the absence of writing, the court will enforce the contract where the plaintiff has been put into a situation which makes it unconscionable for the defendant to insist on the want of writing as a bar to the relief.[70] The Statute of Frauds 1677 was passed to prevent fraud, and cannot be used as an engine of fraud, or to cover fraud.[71]

---

[58] *Re Lander and Bagley's Contract* [1892] 3 Ch. 41; and see *Brilliant* v. *Michaels* [1945] 1 All E.R. 121.
[59] *Chattock* v. *Muller* (1878) 8 Ch.D. 177.
[60] *Pallant* v. *Morgan* [1953] Ch. 43 (resale ordered).
[61] *Chattock* v. *Muller, supra.*
[62] *Gregory* v. *Mighell* (1811) 18 Ves. 328.
[62a] See Megarry & Wade's *Law of Real Property* (5th ed., 1984), pp. 571–587, for a full treatment of this provision.
[63] *Tweddell* v. *Henderson* [1975] 2 All E.R. 1096; *Ram Narayan s/o Shankar* v. *Rishad Hussain Shah s/o Tasaduq Hussain Shah* [1979] 1 W.L.R. 1349.
[64] See *Hawkins* v. *Price* [1947] Ch. 645.
[65] *North* v. *Loomes* [1919] 1 Ch. 378 at 386; and see *ante*, p. 598, n. 52.
[66] *Martin* v. *Pycroft* (1852) 2 De G.M. & G. 785; *Scott* v. *Bradley* [1971] Ch. 850, adopting the criticism of *Burgess* v. *Cox* [1951] Ch. 383 at (1951) 67 L.Q.R. 299.
[67] *Re Holland, Gregg* v. *Holland* [1902] 2 Ch. 360.
[68] L.P.A. 1925, s.40(2), making statutory the decision in *Att.-Gen.* v. *Day* (1748) 1 Ves.Sen. 218.
[69] *Gunter* v. *Halsey* (1739) Amb. 586. On amendment to plead s.40, see *Re Gonin* [1979] Ch. 16.
[70] *Bond* v. *Hopkins* (1802) 1 Sch. & Lef. 413 at 433.
[71] *Lincoln* v. *Wright* (1859) 4 De G. & J. 16; *Re Duke of Marlborough* [1894] 2 Ch. 133; and see *ante*, p. 108.

Thus if an agreement which was intended to be put into writing is in fact not put into writing owing to the fraud of the defendant, he will not be allowed to set up the statute as a bar to the action.[72]

(3) PART PERFORMANCE. If the plaintiff has wholly or in part carried out his part of a parol agreement in the confidence that the defendant would do the same, the court often orders specific performance on the ground that it would be a fraud on the defendant's part not to carry out the contract.[73] This is the doctrine of part performance; it was expressly recognised by the Law of Property Act 1925, s.40.[74]

The doctrine of part performance is purely equitable, applicable only to actions for specific performance; if specific performance is not available, the doctrine does not open the door to an award of damages.[75] To bring the doctrine into play, it is necessary, first, that the acts be done by the plaintiff[76]; secondly, that they be referable to the contract[77]; thirdly, that they be referable to land[78] (thus, for a woman to act as unpaid housekeeper to a man is not in its nature referable to a promise by him to leave her a life interest in the house[79]); and, fourthly, that they be acts done "in furtherance of the contract and not merely a recognition of its existence or its contemplation."[80] This last requirement means that acts which are merely preparatory to performance, such as making applications for planning permission[81] or delivering a draft contract and a cheque for the deposit payable under that contract,[82] will not suffice.

Of these requirements it is the second, that the acts done be referable to the contract, which has given rise to most difficulty. Under the modern formulation of the rule[83] in *Steadman* v. *Steadman*[84] "you take the whole circumstances, leaving aside evidence about the oral contract, to see whether it is proved that the acts relied on were done in reliance on a contract: that will be proved if it is shown to be more probable than not." This broad approach has rendered obsolete many of the old decisions on sufficiency of acts alleged to constitute part performance. In particular, it is no longer the rule that payment of money cannot amount to part performance[85]; and in *Steadman* v. *Steadman*[86] itself the

---

[72] *Maxwell* v. *Montacute* (1719) Prec.Ch. 526; and see *Wakeham* v. *Mackenzie* [1968] 1 W.L.R. 1175 at 1182.
[73] *Lester* v. *Foxcroft* (1701) Coll.P.C. 108; **2 W. & T.L.C. 410.**
[74] For a fuller treatment of part performance, see the 28th edition of this work, pp. 583–585.
[75] *Re Northumberland Avenue Hotel Co.* (1886) 33 Ch.D. 16 at 18; *Lavery* v. *Pursell* (1888) 39 Ch.D. 508; *J.C. Williamson Ltd.* v. *Lukey* (1931) 45 C.L.R. 282.
[76] *Caton* v. *Caton* (1865) 1 Ch.App. 137.
[77] See *infra.*
[78] *Re Gonin* [1979] Ch. 16.
[79] *Maddison* v. *Alderson* (1883) 8 App.Cas. 467. And see *Re Gonin, supra.* But see *ante*, p. 573 (proprietary estoppel).
[80] *Elsden* v. *Pick* [1980] 1 W.L.R. 898 at 905, *per* Shaw L.J.
[81] *New Hart Builders Ltd.* v. *Brindley* [1975] Ch. 343.
[82] *Daulia Ltd.* v. *Four Millbank Nominees Ltd.* [1978] Ch. 231.
[83] The classic formulation is that of Lord Selborne L.C. in *Maddison* v. *Alderson* (1883) 8 App.Cas. 467 at 479. The doctrine is as old as *Gunter* v. *Halsey* (1739) Amb. 586. And see *Lester* v. *Foxcroft* (1701) Coll.P.C. 108; **2 W. & T.L.C. 410.**
[84] [1976] A.C. 536 at 541, 542, *per* Lord Reid. See (1974) 90 L.Q.R. 433 (H. W. R. Wade).
[85] See *Maddison* v. *Alderson* (1883) 8 App.Cas. 467 at 479.
[86] [1976] A.C. 536.

act relied upon and held to suffice was payment by a husband of arrears of maintenance under an oral contract the terms of which included the purchase by him of his wife's interest in the matrimonial home. Other examples are the taking,[87] or giving up,[88] of possession under the contract; or the execution of works on the land at the request of the other party[89]; or not bidding at an auction pursuant to an agreement made between prospective purchasers beforehand[89a]; or consenting to a divorce (where the terms orally agreed included a provision for vesting the matrimonial home in the sole name of one of the parties).[90]

(b) Contracts made after September 26, 1989

(1) REPEAL OF LAW OF PROPERTY ACT 1925, s.40. Under the Law of Property (Miscellaneous Provisions) Act 1989, the familiar s.40 ceased to have effect save in relation to contracts made before September 27, 1989.[91] The provisions of the 1989 Act which supersede s.40[92] are significantly different from it in two respects.

(2) THE NEW REQUIREMENTS. In the first place, a contract for the sale or other disposition of an interest in land can now only be made in writing: this goes beyond the old requirement that there be written evidence of a contract (which could have been made orally).[93] All the terms which the parties have expressly agreed must be incorporated in one document or, where contracts are exchanged, in each.[94] Secondly, the contract or, where exchange takes place, one copy (but not necessarily the same one) must be signed by or on behalf of each party: this goes further than s.40 which merely required signature by or on behalf of the party to be charged.[95]

(3) EXCEPTIONS. These requirements do not apply in relation to a contract to grant a lease which is to take effect in possession for a term not exceeding three years at the best rent reasonably obtainable[96]; nor to a contract made in the course of a public auction; nor to a contract regulated under the Financial Services Act 1986.[97] Nor do the new requirements affect the creation or operation of resulting, implied or constructive trusts.[98] But there are no exceptions for sales by the court,[99] nor for the doctrine of part performance, which thus disappears

---

[87] Brough v. Nettleton [1921] 2 Ch. 25.
[88] Liddell v. Hopkinson (1974) 233 E.G. 513.
[89] Dickinson v. Barrow [1904] 2 Ch. 339.
[89a] Du Boulay v. Raggett (1988) 58 P. & C.R. 138.
[90] Sutton v. Sutton [1984] Ch. 184.
[91] Law of Property (Miscellaneous Provisions) Act 1989, ss.2(7), (8), 5(3), (4)(b).
[92] Ibid. s.2(1)–(6).
[93] Ibid. s.2(1). See ante, p. 599.
[94] The terms "may be incorporated in a document either by being set out in it or by reference to some other document": ibid. s.2(2).
[95] Ibid. s.2(3). See ante, p. 599.
[96] See L.P.A. 1925, s.54(2).
[97] Law of Property (Miscellaneous Provisions) Act 1989, s.2(5).
[98] Ibid.
[99] See ante, p. 599.

from the field of equity after some two-and-a-half centuries.[1] Cases of
fraud will presumably fall outside the new statute as they fell outside the
old.[2]

3. Misrepresentation by the plaintiff.   Any misrepresentation, fraudulent or innocent, which justifies the rescission of the contract[3] affords a
defence to proceedings for specific performance against the party
misled,[4] even if it affects only a small part of the contract which the
party making the misrepresentation offers to waive.[5] Further, in some
cases specific performance may be refused even where there is no right
to rescind,[6] *e.g.* where, although it cannot be proved that the
misrepresentation actually induced the contract, it can be inferred that
the purchaser would not have entered into the contract but for the
misrepresentation.[7] The misrepresentation of an agent acting within the
scope of his authority is the misrepresentation of his principal.[8] And
there is a misrepresentation if a statement was true when made, but
before the signing of the contract became untrue to the knowledge of
the party who made it.[9]

On a sale of leaseholds, it is a misrepresentation to state that the
lease contains no unusual covenants, if in fact the lease contains a
covenant to build and thereafter maintain buildings of a value to
command double the rent reserved by the lease, or contains a covenant
to erect only one house on the land, or any other like restrictive
covenant; accordingly, the purchaser will be discharged from the
contract, because if he completed he would be bound by the covenants
in question.[10]

4. Mistake.   Mistake may also be a ground of defence. Parol
evidence is admissible to prove the mistake despite the statutory
requirement of writing, for the question is whether what appears to be a
written agreement is in truth an agreement.

(a) *Fundamental mistake in formation of contract.*   The mistake may
be of such a nature as to preclude that *assensus ad idem* which is
required in every contract, and so render the seeming contract no
contract at all. Such a mistake may be common or unilateral. The ambit

---

[1] See *ante*, p. 600, n. 83.
[2] See *ante*, pp. 599, 600.
[3] See *post*, p. 617.
[4] *Walker* v. *Boyle* [1982] 1 W.L.R. 495; *Smelter Corporation of Ireland Ltd.* v. *O'Driscoll* [1977] I.R.
305.
[5] *Viscount Clermont* v. *Tasburgh* (1819) 1 J. & W. 112.
[6] *Lamare* v. *Dixon* (1873) L.R. 6 H.L. 414 at 428; *Re Banister* (1879) 12 Ch.D. 131 at 142, 147, 149.
[7] *Holliday* v. *Lockwood* [1917] 2 Ch. 47 at 56, 57; *Hope* v. *Walter* [1900] 1 Ch. 257.
[8] *Mullens* v. *Miller* (1882) 22 Ch.D. 194.
[9] *With* v. *O'Flanagan* [1936] Ch. 575.
[10] *Andrew* v. *Aitken* (1882) 22 Ch.D. 218; and see *Charles Hunt Ltd.* v. *Palmer* [1931] 2 Ch. 287.

of common mistake is very circumscribed, being such as to make the subject-matter of the contract something essentially different from what it is supposed to be.[11] Unilateral mistake occurs where the mistake of one party is known to the other, thus precluding agreement.[12] Where either type of mistake exists there is no contract, and there can be no damages and no specific performance. Thus, to take an example of unilateral mistake, where a vendor by mistake offered to sell an estate for £1,100 instead of for £2,100 as he intended, and the purchaser knew that the figure was a mistake, the court refused specific performance.[13]

(b) *Other mistakes in formation of contract*

(1) HARDSHIP. Some mistakes, while not sufficiently grave to preclude the existence of a contract, have an effect in equity as a ground for either refusing specific performance or allowing rescission, with or without conditions.[14] This will occur if the parties to a contract are under a common misapprehension either as to the facts or their relative rights, provided that the misapprehension is fundamental and the party seeking to resist enforcement is not blameworthy.[15] Where the mistake is unilateral, specific performance may be refused if the plaintiff has contributed to the defendant's mistake, however unintentionally.[16] Even if the mistake is purely that of the defendant himself and is not in any way induced by the plaintiff, a decree may be refused if to grant it would be "highly unreasonable"[17] or would cause the defendant "a hardship amounting to injustice."[18] In these cases the court may simply refuse specific performance, leaving the plaintiff to his right to damages, or it may rescind the contract, possibly on terms that the defendant undertakes to enter into a fresh contract on the basis of the true facts.[19]

(2) EXAMPLES. For instance, specific performance was refused where a house had been sold at a very low price because both parties mistakenly thought it was occupied by a protected tenant.[20] Again, specific performance was refused where the purchaser bid for and bought one lot at an auction in the belief that he was buying a totally different lot, and it would have been a great hardship on him to compel him to take the property.[21] On the other hand there was no "hardship amounting to injustice" where a purchaser bought an inn and a shop at an auction in the mistaken belief that two plots of ground at the back formed part of

[11] *Bell* v. *Lever Bros. Ltd.* [1932] A.C. 161.
[12] *Hartog* v. *Colin & Shields* [1939] 3 All E.R. 566.
[13] *Webster* v. *Cecil* (1861) 30 Beav. 62.
[14] For rescission, see *post*, p. 616.
[15] *Solle* v. *Butcher* [1950] 1 K.B. 671; *Grist* v. *Bailey* [1967] Ch. 532; *Taylor* v. *Johnson* (1983) 151 C.L.R. 422 (vendor contracted to sell five acres for $15,000, believing she was getting $15,000 *per acre*).
[16] *Denny* v. *Hancock* (1870) 6 Ch.App. 1; *Wilding* v. *Sanderson* [1897] 2 Ch. 534.
[17] *Stewart* v. *Kennedy* (1890) 15 App.Cas. 75 at 105, *per* Lord Macnaghten.
[18] *Tamplin* v. *James* (1880) 15 Ch.D. 215 at 221, *per* James L.J. And see *post*, p. 612.
[19] See *Grist* v. *Bailey* [1967] Ch. 532 at pp. 542, 543.
[20] *Grist* v. *Bailey* [1967] Ch. 532.
[21] *Malins* v. *Freeman* (1837) 2 Keen 25; but see *Tamplin* v. *James* and *Van Praagh* v. *Everidge*, *infra*.

the property; the particulars of sale and the plan exhibited at the auction described the property correctly, and the purchaser was compelled to perform his contract.[22] The purchaser was similarly held to be unable to escape the contract where by his own mistake he bought an entirely different property from that which he had intended to buy.[23]

(c) *Mistake in recording contract.* Where the mistake occurs not in the formation of the contract but in its reduction into writing, the defendant can always set up the error as a defence; he must produce evidence to show that on account of an omission, mistake or fraud, the agreement as written does not represent the real agreement between himself and the plaintiff. Thus, where an action was brought for the specific performance of an agreement to grant a lease at a rent of £9 per annum, evidence was admitted to prove that it ought to have been a term of the agreement as recorded that the plaintiff should pay all taxes.[24] Where a mistake in the writing is proved, the court may either dismiss the plaintiff's action or grant specific performance, taking care that the real contract is carried into effect. Which course the court will adopt depends upon the particular circumstances of each case.[25]

(d) *Rectification.*[26] Before the Judicature Act 1873 it appears to have been settled that except in a few cases the plaintiff in an action for specific performance could not allege that the written memorandum of the contract did not represent the true agreement, and claim to have specific performance of the true agreement.[27] But the court is now required to grant to the parties in one action all the relief to which they are entitled,[28] and there is now jurisdiction to rectify a written agreement which by mistake does not represent the real contract and, where proper,[29] to order in the same action specific performance of the agreement as rectified.[30]

(e) *Subsequent parol variation.* Where the parol variation set up is a further term arrived at *after* the written contract was made, there is no question of mistake; and there is nothing to exclude parol evidence of the further term,[31] statute apart. If, however, the original contract was

---

[22] *Tamplin* v. *James* (1880) 15 Ch.D. 215.
[23] *Van Praagh* v. *Everidge* [1902] 2 Ch. 266, reversed on another ground (want of sufficient memorandum): [1903] 1 Ch. 434.
[24] *Joynes* v. *Statham* (1746) 3 Atk. 388; *cf. Clark* v. *Barnes* [1929] 2 Ch. 368.
[25] *London and Birmingham Ry.* v. *Winter* (1840) Cr. & Ph. 57; *Smith* v. *Wheatcroft* (1878) 9 Ch.D. 223.
[26] See *post*, p. 626, for rectification generally.
[27] See *Woollam* v. *Hearn* (1802) 7 Ves. 211; **2 W. & T.L.C. 464**; *Martin* v. *Pycroft* (1852) 2 De G.M. & G. 785; *Marquis Townshend* v. *Stangroom* (1801) 6 Ves. 328.
[28] S.C.A. 1981, s.49(2), replacing J.A. 1925, s.43, which replaced J.A. 1873, s.24(7).
[29] See *Nolan* v. *Graves* [1946] I.R. 376.
[30] *Craddock Bros.* v. *Hunt* [1923] 2 Ch. 136, and *U.S.A.* v. *Motor Trucks Ltd.* [1924] A.C. 196, following *Olley* v. *Fisher* (1886) 34 Ch.D. 367 in preference to *May* v. *Platt* [1900] 1 Ch. 616.
[31] *Price* v. *Dyer* (1810) 17 Ves. 356; *Van* v. *Corpe* (1834) 3 My. & K. 269 at 277; *Legal* v. *Miller* (1750) 2 Ves.Sen. 299.

required by statute to be made in writing, the same statutory requirement will exclude parol evidence of the variation save for the purpose of showing that the effect of the further agreement was to discharge the original contract.[32] Whether the further agreement had this effect depends on the intention of the parties. "If the new agreement reveals an intention to rescind the old, the old goes; and if it does not, the old remains in force and unamended."[33]

5. Misdescription. One not uncommon ground of defence is that, by a misdescription of the property, the defendant has purchased what he never intended to purchase. Misdescription consists of an error in the terms of the contract itself, as opposed to a misrepresentation which merely induces the contract. Under this defence, two classes of cases arise:

(a) Cases where a misdescription is of a substantial character which will not in justice admit of compensation.

(b) Cases where the misdescription is such as fairly to admit of compensation.

(a) *Substantial misdescription*

(1) PURCHASER'S RIGHT TO RESCIND. Where the misdescription is substantial, the purchaser is entitled to resist specific performance and, moreover, to rescind the contract. "This court," said Lord Eldon L.C.,[34] "is from time to time approaching nearer to the doctrine that a purchaser shall have that which he contracted for, or not be compelled to take that which he did not mean to have." In other words, if the effect of the misdescription is to prevent the purchaser from really getting the property which he bought, there is no enforceable contract.[35]

Thus a purchaser who has contracted to buy a lease will not be compelled to take an underlease, the differences between an original lease and an underlease being differences not of value but of tenure[36]; nor can a vendor who has purported to sell "registered freehold property" enforce the contract if he is registered with a title that is possessory and not absolute.[37] Again, where on the sale of a residence and four acres of land it appeared that there was no title to a slip of

[32] See *Morris* v. *Baron & Co.* [1918] A.C. 1 (rescission); *British and Beningtons Ltd.* v. *North Western Cachar Tea Co.* [1923] A.C. 48 (no rescission); and *United Dominions Corporation (Jamaica) Ltd.* v. *Shoucair* [1969] 1 A.C. 340 (no rescission).

[33] *United Dominions Corporation (Jamaica) Ltd.* v. *Shoucair, supra,* at p. 348, *per* Lord Devlin.

[34] *Knatchbull* v. *Grueber* (1817) 3 Mer. 124 at 146.

[35] *Flight* v. *Booth* (1834) 1 Bing.N.C. 370; *Charles Hunt Ltd.* v. *Palmer* [1931] 2 Ch. 287. Contrast *Shepherd* v. *Croft* [1911] 1 Ch. 521; *Re Belcham and Gawley's Contract* [1930] 1 Ch. 56.

[36] *Madeley* v. *Booth* (1845) 2 De G. & Sm. 718; *Re Beyfus and Masters' Contract* (1888) 39 Ch.D. 110; *Re Russ and Brown's Contract* [1934] Ch. 34; *cf. Cunningham* v. *Shackleton* [1935] L.J.N.C.C.A. 177.

[37] *Re Brine & Davies' Contract* [1935] Ch. 388.

ground of about a quarter of an acre between the house and the high-road, so that people in passing could look in at the windows, the court refused specific performance[38]; the same was done where on a sale of agricultural land there proved to be no right of cartway to it.[39] In these cases of substantial misdescription, the purchaser is not prevented from resisting specific performance and rescinding the contract by a condition of sale which provides that errors shall not annul the sale but shall be a matter for compensation only[40]; and the case is *a fortiori* if the condition provides that no compensation shall be allowed for a misdescription.[41]

(2) SPECIFIC PERFORMANCE WITH ABATEMENT.   Even if the misdescription is such as to entitle the purchaser to refuse to be bound by the contract, in many cases he may, if he wishes, insist on the vendor conveying what he has and abating the purchase-money as compensation. "If," said Lord Eldon L.C., "a man, having partial interests in an estate, chuses to enter into a contract, representing it, and agreeing to sell it, as his own, it is not competent to him afterwards to say, though he has valuable interests, he has not the entirety; and therefore the purchaser shall not have the benefit of his contract. For the purpose of this jurisdiction, the person contracting under those circumstances, is bound by the assertion in his contract; and, if the vendee chuses to take as much as he can have, he has a right to that, and to an abatement; and the court will not hear the objection by the vendor, that the purchaser cannot have the whole."[42]

This rule applies whether the misdescription is as to the acreage of the land,[43] or as to the vendor's interest in it.[44] But it does not apply if the purchaser knew at the date of the contract of the vendor's inability to make a title,[45] or if there are no data from which the amount of the compensation can be ascertained,[46] or if a partial performance of the contract would entail great hardship on the vendor or would be prejudicial to third parties interested in the property,[47] or where the misdescription was clearly and distinctly corrected by the auctioneer at the time of the sale, even though the purchaser did not hear the correction.[48] And the purchaser may be deprived of the right to claim compensation by a condition in the contract.[49] Nor does the principle

---

[38] *Perkins* v. *Ede* (1852) 16 Beav. 193; and see *Peers* v. *Lambert* (1844) 7 Beav. 546.
[39] *Denne* v. *Light* (1857) 8 De G.M. & G. 774.
[40] *Re Arnold, Arnold* v. *Arnold* (1880) 14 Ch.D. 270.
[41] *Jacobs* v. *Revell* [1900] 2 Ch. 858; *Lee* v. *Rayson* [1917] 1 Ch. 613.
[42] *Mortlock* v. *Buller* (1804) 10 Ves. 292 at 315, 316.
[43] *Hill* v. *Buckley* (1810) 17 Ves. 394.
[44] *Barnes* v. *Wood* (1869) L.R. 8 Eq. 424; *Horrocks* v. *Rigby* (1878) 9 Ch.D. 180; *Basma* v. *Weekes* [1950] A.C. 441.
[45] *Castle* v. *Wilkinson* (1870) 5 Ch.App. 534.
[46] *Durham* v. *Legard* (1865) 34 Beav. 611; *Rudd* v. *Lascelles* [1900] 1 Ch. 815.
[47] *Thomas* v. *Dering* (1837) 1 Keen 729 followed in *Cedar Holdings Ltd.* v. *Green* [1981] Ch. 129 at 147 and *Thames Guaranty Ltd.* v. *Campbell* [1985] Q.B. 210 at 239, 240. *Cedar Holdings Ltd.* v. *Green* was overruled in *Williams & Glyn's Bank Ltd.* v. *Boland* [1981] A.C. 487 at 507, but not affecting this point: *Thames Guaranty Ltd.* v. *Campbell, supra*, at p. 239.
[48] *Re Hare and O'More's Contract* [1901] 1 Ch. 93.
[49] *Cordingley* v. *Cheeseborough* (1862) 4 De G.F. & J. 379; *Re Terry and White's Contract* (1886) 32 Ch.D. 14.

apply where there is no misdescription in the actual contract but there has been a misrepresentation inducing the contract.[50] In such cases, since the purchaser cannot insist on specific performance with compensation, he must either rescind, or take without compensation what the vendor is able to convey.[51]

(b) *Slight misdescription*

(1) ENFORCING CONTRACT WITH COMPENSATION. Where the misdescription is insignificant, so that the purchaser gets substantially though not precisely what he bargained for, the court will enforce the contract even at the suit of the vendor, compelling him to make compensation to the purchaser. Thus where on the sale of a large estate there was an objection to the title to six acres which did not appear material to the enjoyment of the rest, specific performance was decreed,[52] as it was also where 14 acres of land were sold as watermeadow and only 12 answered that description.[53]

(2) EXCLUSION OF COMPENSATION. The principle of granting compensation in lieu of rescission is not one to be extended, and will never be applied in an action by the vendor to enforce the contract where he has been guilty of fraud or wilful[54] misrepresentation.[55] Nor will the 'court apply this principle at the suit of either party if the proper amount of compensation cannot be ascertained.[56] Further, a condition is commonly inserted in contracts for the sale of land to the effect that the lots are believed to be correctly described, but that errors shall not annul the sale and that no compensation shall be paid for or in respect of any misdescription. Notwithstanding such a condition, however, the purchaser may repudiate the contract if the misdescription is fraudulent or, though not fraudulent, is on a material and substantial point so that, but for the misdescription, the purchaser would not have entered into the contract.[57] But such a clause prevents the purchaser from enforcing specific performance with compensation.[58]

(c) *Compensation after completion.* After completion of the contract by the conveyance of the property, it is generally too late for the purchaser to claim compensation for a misdescription; for he is deemed to waive his right to compensation by taking a conveyance without

---

[50] *Rutherford* v. *Acton-Adams* [1915] A.C. 866; *Gilchester Properties Ltd.* v. *Gomm* [1948] 1 All E.R. 493.
[51] *Durham* v. *Legard* (1865) 34 Beav. 611.
[52] *M'Queen* v. *Farquhar* (1805) 11 Ves. 467.
[53] *Scott* v. *Hanson* (1829) 1 Russ. & M. 128; and see *Re Fawcett & Holmes' Contract* (1889) 42 Ch.D. 150.
[54] *Quaere* whether wilful misrepresentation here differs from fraud.
[55] See *Price* v. *Macaulay* (1852) 2 De G.M. & G. 339 at 344.
[56] *Lord Brooke* v. *Rounthwaite* (1846) 5 Hare 298 (vendor's action); *Rudd* v. *Lascelles* [1900] 1 Ch. 815 (purchaser's action).
[57] *Flight* v. *Booth* (1834) 1 Bing.N.C. 370; *Jacobs* v. *Revell* [1900] 2 Ch. 858; *Lee* v. *Rayson* [1917] 1 Ch. 613; *Walker* v. *Boyle* [1982] 1 W.L.R. 495.
[58] Williams' *Vendor and Purchaser* (4th ed., 1936), pp. 74, 727.

demanding compensation,[59] at any rate if the misdescription is on a point as to which he could have discovered the truth before completion.[60] After completion his remedy, if any, is under the covenants for title in the conveyance.[61] If, however, the contract contains an express provision for compensation which is not limited to errors discovered before completion (as it ought to be, and generally is), the purchaser can claim compensation even after he has taken a conveyance.[62]

6. Default by the plaintiff.[63]   A plaintiff who seeks to enforce a contract must show (i) that he has performed, or has been ready and willing to perform, all terms and conditions (apart from trivial ones[64]) then to be performed by him,[65] (ii) that he is ready and willing to perform all terms and conditions thereafter to be performed by him,[66] and (iii) that he has not acted in contravention of the essential terms of the contract.[67] But it is not incumbent on a plaintiff to show that he was in a position to complete (*e.g.* if he is the purchaser, by having the price available) during the period from repudiation by the defendant to the date of the order for specific performance.[68] And omission, by a mere oversight, to pay a deposit on time will not necessarily debar a purchaser from obtaining specific performance.[69]

7. Lapse of time.   The objection that a plaintiff has not performed his part of the contract within the proper time may furnish grounds of defence to an action for specific performance.

(a) *At law.*   At law, the plaintiff had to show that all those things which were on his part to be performed had been performed within a reasonable time, or, where a time was specified by the contract, within the time so specified. At law, time was always of the essence of the contract.

---

[59] *Jolliffe* v. *Baker* (1883) 11 Q.B.D. 255.
[60] *Clayton* v. *Leech* (1889) 41 Ch.D. 103.
[61] *Eastwood* v. *Ashton* [1915] A.C. 900.
[62] *Bos* v. *Helsham* (1866) L.R. 2 Ex. 72; *Palmer* v. *Johnson* (1884) 13 Q.B.D. 351. As to the measure of compensation, see *Royal Bristol Society* v. *Bomash* (1887) 35 Ch.D. 390; *Re Chifferiel* (1888) 40 Ch.D. 45.
[63] See further *post*, pp. 654, 655 (injunction).
[64] *Stanbridge* v. *Browning*, unrep., January 12, 1984 (C.A.T. No. 2): obligation to lay linoleum and repair fence.
[65] *Australian Hardwoods Pty. Ltd.* v. *Commissioner for Railways* [1961] 1 W.L.R. 425; and see *Cornish* v. *Brook Green Laundry Ltd.* [1959] 1 Q.B. 394.
[66] *Franklin* v. *Lord Brownlow* (1808) 14 Ves. 550; *Powell* v. *Marshall Parkes & Co.* [1899] 1 Q.B. 710 (supervening bankruptcy of plaintiff). Contrast *Dyster* v. *Randall and Sons* [1926] Ch. 932 (plaintiff bankrupt at time of contract).
[67] *Coatsworth* v. *Johnson* (1886) 54 L.T. 520; *Swain* v. *Ayres* (1888) 21 Q.B.D. 289.
[68] *Davis* v. *Spalding* (1974) 231 E.G. 373.
[69] *Millichamp* v. *Jones* [1982] 1 W.L.R. 1422.

(b) *In equity*. Equity, however, discriminated between (i) those terms of a contract which were formal, so that it would be inequitable for either party to insist on them as a bar to the other's rights, and (ii) those which were of the substance and essence of the agreement.[70] The principles which governed the interference of equity in relation to mortgages were applied to contracts,[71] and time was thus held to be prima facie non-essential.[72] Equity accordingly granted specific performance of agreements even after the plaintiff had suffered the time for their performance to pass. Conversely, if one party repudiates his obligations after the date fixed for completion but before the other party has become in unreasonable delay, the latter may accept the repudiation as a discharge of the contract even though he cannot show that he was himself ready and able to complete.[73]

(c) *After Judicature Acts.* The rule of equity is now also the rule of law, for by the Law of Property Act 1925, s.41,[74] "stipulations in a contract, as to time or otherwise, which according to rules of equity are not deemed to be or to have become of the essence of the contract, are also construed and have effect at law in accordance with the same rules." Nonetheless, failure to complete on the day fixed by the contract is a breach of contract and as such actionable in damages.[75]

(d) *When time is of the essence.*[76] There are, however, three cases in which time is of the essence of the contract:

(i) Where the contract expressly states that time shall be of the essence of the contract.[77]

(ii) Where time was not originally of the essence of the contract but has been made so by one party giving a notice to the other. Such notice, however, can only be given after the other party has been guilty of unreasonable delay, and the time mentioned in the notice must be reasonable.[78] Reasonableness is a question of fact, and the facts may justify as little as six days.[79] The existence of a contractual right to give a notice of particular

---

[70] *Parkin* v. *Thorold* (1852) 16 Beav. 59; *Harold Wood Brick Co. Ltd.* v. *Ferris* [1935] 2 K.B. 198.

[71] *Seton* v. *Slade* (1802) 7 Ves. 265 at 273; **2 W. & T.L.C. 425 at 430**.

[72] See generally *United Scientific Holdings Ltd.* v. *Burnley Borough Council* [1978] A.C. 904 (rent review clause).

[73] *Rightside Properties Ltd.* v. *Gray* [1975] Ch. 72.

[74] Repeating J.A. 1873, s.25(7).

[75] *Raineri* v. *Miles* [1981] A.C. 1050. See (1980) 96 L.Q.R. 481.

[76] See *Legione* v. *Hateley* (1983) 152 C.L.R. 406: court may allow relief from forfeiture (*sci.* of purchaser's equitable interest) by way of specific performance even where time has been made of the essence.

[77] *Steedman* v. *Drinkle* [1916] 1 A.C. 275; *Brickles* v. *Snell* [1916] 2 A.C. 599; *Mussen* v. *Van Diemen's Land Co.* [1938] Ch. 253; *Harold Wood Brick Co. Ltd.* v. *Ferris, supra.*

[78] *Green* v. *Sevin* (1879) 13 Ch.D. 589; *Compton* v. *Bagley* [1892] 1 Ch. 313; *Stickney* v. *Keeble* [1915] A.C. 386; *Re Bayley and Shoesmith's Contract* (1918) 87 L.J.Ch. 626; *Smith* v. *Hamilton* [1951] Ch. 174; *Re Barr's Contract* [1956] Ch. 551.

[79] *Ajit* v. *Sammy* [1967] 1 A.C. 255.

length does not exclude a party's right under the general law to give notice requiring completion within a shorter, reasonable period.[80] The party giving the notice is also bound by it, and so must be ready to complete on its expiry.[81] Once the time specified in the notice has expired, mere inactivity on his part will not amount to a waiver of his rights[82]; but if he allows the defaulting party to try to remedy the position (*e.g.* by negotiating a fresh completion date), he cannot then call the bargain off without first fixing a new time limit, reasonable in the circumstances.[83]

(iii)   Where from the nature of the property time may be considered to be of the essence of the contract, *e.g.* in the case of mercantile contracts,[84] or contracts for the sale of leaseholds,[85] reversionary interests,[86] a colliery business,[87] a public-house as a going concern,[88] a house required for immediate residence,[89] or an option to buy shares which fluctuate in value.[90] But if the terms of the contract demonstrate that time is not intended to be of the essence, they will prevail.[91]

(e) *Delay by plaintiff.*   Even where time is not of the essence of the contract, the plaintiff may have been guilty of such delay as to evidence an abandonment of the contract on his part, thereby precluding him from obtaining specific performance.[92] For a plaintiff to obtain specific performance, he must have shown himself "ready, desirous, prompt, and eager."[93] Where, however, the plaintiff has been let into possession under the contract and has obtained the equitable interest, so that all he requires is a mere conveyance of the legal estate, even many years' delay in enforcing his claim will not prejudice him.[94] Moreover, delay in proceeding to trial after the issue of the writ will not be fatal unless the defendant is led to believe that only damages are being sought.[95]

---

[80] *Dimsdale Developments (South East) Ltd.* v. *De Haan* (1983) 47 P. & C.R. 1, not following *Rightside Properties Ltd.* v. *Gray* [1985] Ch. 72 at 81.
[81] *Finkielkraut* v. *Monohan* [1949] 2 All E.R. 234; *Quadrangle Development and Construction Co. Ltd.* v. *Jenner* [1974] 1 W.L.R. 68.
[82] *Buckland* v. *Farmer & Moody* [1979] 1 W.L.R. 221.
[83] *Luck* v. *White* (1973) 26 P. & C.R. 89.
[84] *Reuter* v. *Sala* (1879) 4 C.P.D. 239 at 249. *Cf. Bunge Corpn., New York* v. *Tradax Export S.A., Panama* [1981] 1 W.L.R. 711.
[85] *Hudson* v. *Temple* (1860) 29 Beav. 536 at 543 (term with almost 24 years to run; *quaere* as to the position where a much longer term is sold).
[86] *Levy* v. *Stogdon* [1899] 1 Ch. 5.
[87] *Macbryde* v. *Weekes* (1856) 22 Beav. 533.
[88] *Tadcaster Tower Brewery Co.* v. *Wilson* [1897] 1 Ch. 705; *Lock* v. *Bell* [1931] 1 Ch. 35.
[89] *Tilley* v. *Thomas* (1867) 3 Ch.App. 61, not considered in *Smith* v. *Hamilton* [1951] Ch. 174.
[90] *Hare* v. *Nicoll* [1966] 2 Q.B. 130.
[91] See (1967) 86 L.N. 191; and consider *Smith* v. *Hamilton, supra.*
[92] *Mills* v. *Haywood* (1877) 6 Ch.D. 196; and see *Walker* v. *Jeffreys* (1842) 1 Hare 341; *Cornwell* v. *Henson* [1900] 2 Ch. 298; *ante*, pp. 35, 36.
[93] *Milward* v. *Earl Thanet* (1801) 5 Ves. 720n., *per* Arden M.R., repeated by Cotton L.J. in *Mills* v. *Haywood* (1877) 6 Ch.D. 196 at 202.
[94] *Crofton* v. *Ormsby* (1806) 2 Sch. & Lef. 583 at 603; *Shepheard* v. *Walker* (1875) L.R. 20 Eq. 659; *Williams* v. *Greatrex* [1957] 1 W.L.R. 31; *cf. Mills* v. *Haywood, supra.*
[95] *Du Sautoy* v. *Symes* [1967] Ch. 1146. See also *Easton* v. *Brown* [1981] 3 All E.R. 278 (eight years' delay after decree).

8. Trickiness

(a) *Refusal of specific performance.* Specific performance will be refused where the contract is tainted with fraud, even if it is not a fraud on the other party to the contract, but on the public,[96] or where the plaintiff has made some positive misrepresentation,[97] or has been guilty of fraudulent suppression,[98] or if the particulars or conditions of sale are misleading[99]; indeed, in such cases the contract will be rescinded, and cannot be enforced even at law.[99a] But even if there is no fraud or misrepresentation sufficient to justify the rescission of the contract, the court may still refuse the equitable remedy of specific performance if the conduct of the plaintiff has been tricky or unfair, for "he who comes into equity must come with clean hands," and the court is not bound to decree specific performance in every case in which it will not set aside the contract.[1] Thus the remedy has been refused to a plaintiff who was aware that the defendant did not appreciate the effect of the contract.[2] It was, however, granted to a plaintiff who obtained the property cheaply at auction following a bidding agreement.[3]

(b) *Mere silence not enough.* It seems that the mere silence of a vendor or purchaser on some material point which there is no legal duty to disclose does not prevent him from obtaining specific performance.[4] For instance, a purchaser could apparently enforce specific performance even if he did not disclose facts known to him but not to the vendor which materially increased the value of the property, unless he stood in a fiduciary position to the vendor and so was under a duty of disclosure.[5] And a purchaser who conceals his identity by buying through an agent can compel specific performance even if he knew that the vendor would not have sold the property to him if his identity had been disclosed, unless the possession by the purchaser of some personal quality is a material ingredient of the contract.[6] But a vendor of land is bound to disclose defects in his title,[7] and perhaps also any latent defects in the quality of the land known to him. Yet if there is a physical defect unknown to either party, the purchaser will be bound to complete the contract unless the defect is such as to prevent him from acquiring what he has contracted to buy.[8]

---

[96] *Post* v. *Marsh* (1880) 16 Ch.D. 395 (publishers' description of book written by A as being written by B, a well-known author, who in fact wrote none of it).
[97] *Higgins* v. *Samels* (1862) 2 J. & H. 460.
[98] *Shirley* v. *Stratton* (1785) 1 Bro.C.C. 440.
[99] *Re Banister* (1879) 12 Ch.D. 131.
[99a] *Ibid.*
[1] *Mortlock* v. *Buller* (1804) 10 Ves. 292; *Buckley* v. *Irwin* [1960] N.I. 98.
[2] *Pateman* v. *Pay* (1974) 232 E.G. 457.
[3] *Harrop* v. *Thompson* [1975] 1 W.L.R. 545.
[4] *Turner* v. *Green* [1895] 2 Ch. 205; *Greenhalgh* v. *Brindley* [1901] 2 Ch. 324.
[5] *Fox* v. *Mackreth* (1788) 2 Cox Eq. 320; affirmed (1791) 4 Bro.P.C. 258; **2 W. & T.L.C. 663**; *Percival* v. *Wright* [1902] 2 Ch. 421. And see *ante*, p. 558.
[6] *Dyster* v. *Randall & Sons* [1926] Ch. 932.
[7] *Re Haedicke and Lipski's Contract* [1901] 2 Ch. 666; *Becker* v. *Partridge* [1966] 2 Q.B. 155.
[8] *Re Puckett and Smith's Contract* [1902] 2 Ch. 258; *Shepherd* v. *Croft* [1911] 1 Ch. 521; *Re Belcham and Gawley's Contract* [1930] 1 Ch. 56. See also *Yandle & Sons* v. *Sutton* [1922] 2 Ch. 199; *Beyfus* v. *Lodge* [1925] Ch. 350.

9. Great hardship.[9]

(a) *The principle.*   As the remedy of specific performance is equitable and discretionary, the court will not grant it where it would inflict great hardship on the defendant.

(b) *Illustrations.*   Thus as has been already pointed out,[10] sometimes a purchaser who has made a mistake as to the property which he is buying has escaped specific performance on this ground, even though estopped from setting up his mistake as preventing the formation of a contract. On this ground, too, the court refused specific performance of a contract to purchase a lease where pending and threatened litigation made it impossible to ascertain to whom the ground-rent was payable, and the purchaser would have been involved in immediate litigation.[11] And where a vendor cannot perform his contract unless he litigates (*e.g.* in order to obtain vacant possession), then except in clear cases the court is slow to decree specific performance against him, particularly if the proceedings would be against his wife.[12] Intoxication of the defendant when the contract was made is also a ground for refusing specific performance even though the defendant "may not have been drawn in to drink" by the plaintiff[13]; so, too, ignorance and a mental state not amounting to incapacity may be a defence.[14]

(c) *Supervening hardship.*   The fact that one party has made a poor bargain,[15] or that he is financially unable to complete, is not hardship,[16] nor is inadequacy of price a ground for refusing specific performance, unless the purchaser stands in a fiduciary position to the vendor, or fraud enters into the contract.[17] The reason is that, save in exceptional circumstances, the hardship which will constitute a defence to a claim for specific performance must have existed at the date of the contract.[18] Nevertheless, in one case specific performance of an agreement to sell land to a railway company for the purposes of its undertaking was refused after the company had abandoned the project, for the decree would have worked more injustice than justice.[19] So also, the serious illness of the vendor, combined with the bankruptcy of her husband and long delay in completion which was not attributable to her, was a ground for confining the purchaser to his remedy in damages.[20]

---

[9] For an historical account of this subject, see (1987) 103 L.Q.R. 118 (J. L. Barton).
[10] *Ante*, p. 603.
[11] *Pegler* v. *White* (1864) 33 Beav. 403.
[12] *Wroth* v. *Tyler* [1974] Ch. 30. And see, *post*, p. 615.
[13] *Malins* v. *Freeman* (1837) 2 Keen 25 at 34, *per* Lord Langdale M.R.; Fry, *Specific Performance* (6th ed., 1921), p. 192.
[14] *Jacobs* v. *Bills* [1967] N.Z.L.R. 249.
[15] *Adams* v. *Weare* (1784) 1 Bro.C.C. 567; *Roberts* v. *O'Neill* [1983] I.R. 47 (great increase in value of land after contract).
[16] *Nicholas* v. *Ingram* [1958] N.Z.L.R. 972. And see *Francis* v. *Cowcliff* [1976] *The Times*, March 30 (landlord's financial inability to provide and maintain a lift).
[17] *Coles* v. *Trecothick* (1804) 9 Ves. 234 at 246: *Sullivan* v. *Jacob* (1828) 1 Moll. 472 at 477.
[18] *Nicholas* v. *Ingram, supra.*
[19] *Webb* v. *Direct London & Portsmouth Ry. Co.* (1852) 1 De G.M. & G. 521 at 529, 530.
[20] *Patel* v. *Ali* [1984] Ch. 283.

10. Illegality

(a) *The rule.* As already mentioned,[21] the court will not enforce a contract which involves any illegality. If a statutory corporation enters into a contract which is *ultra vires*, there can accordingly be neither specific performance nor an award of damages, for the contract is illegal and void.[22] Nor will the court grant specific performance of an agreement which involves the breach of a prior agreement,[23] such as a covenant in a lease which prohibits subletting,[24] or a breach of trust,[25] or a fraud on a third party (even though the intention to commit the fraud is abandoned before trial),[26] or the payment of an unlawful premium,[27] or of a higher rent than the law allows[28]; and an injunction may be granted to prevent the completion of such an agreement.[29]

(b) *Separation agreements.* The court will not enforce an agreement between husband and wife for *future* separation,[30] unless the parties were already living apart at the time of the agreement and the agreement relating to the future separation was part of a contract of reconciliation.[31] It was at one time thought that an agreement even for immediate separation was contrary to the policy of the law and therefore unenforceable,[32] and this may still be so in the absence of any actual or possible legal proceedings.[33] But such an agreement is not illegal, and will be enforced, if it is made by way of compromise of matrimonial or other proceedings which one party has taken or is in a position to take against the other.[34]

(c) *Depreciatory conditions.* Formerly, where trustees sold under unnecessarily depreciatory conditions of which the beneficiaries could complain, the court would not compel the purchaser to complete, nor could he obtain an order for specific performance; it was immaterial whether or not the conditions had in fact damped the sale.[35] Now, however, a purchaser cannot object to completing on the ground that the conditions are unnecessarily depreciatory, for after he has obtained a conveyance his title will be unimpeachable by the beneficiaries unless

[21] *Ante*, p. 592.

[22] *Corbett* v. *South Eastern and Chatham Ry.* [1906] 2 Ch. 12.

[23] *Willmott* v. *Barber* (1880) 15 Ch.D. 96.

[24] *Warmington* v. *Miller* [1973] Q.B. 877.

[25] *Sneesby* v. *Thorne* (1855) 7 De G.M. & G. 399; but see *Briggs* v. *Parsloe* [1937] 3 All E.R. 831.

[26] *Zimmerman* v. *Letkeman* (1977) 79 D.L.R. (3d) 508 (contract document showing price higher than agreed price in order to deceive prospective mortgagees).

[27] *Rees* v. *Marquis of Bute* [1916] 2 Ch. 64.

[28] See *Brilliant* v. *Michaels* [1945] 1 All E.R. 121 at 128; and consider *Mauray* v. *Durley Chine (Investments) Ltd.* [1953] 2 Q.B. 433.

[29] *Manchester Ship Canal Co.* v. *Manchester Racecourse Co.* [1900] 2 Ch. 352; affirmed [1901] 2 Ch. 37.

[30] *Cartwright* v. *Cartwright* (1853) 3 De G.M. & G. 982; *Re Hope Johnstone* [1904] 1 Ch. 470; *Brodie* v. *Brodie* [1917] P. 271.

[31] *Re Meyrick's Settlement* [1921] 1 Ch. 311. See also *Lurie* v. *Lurie* [1938] 3 All E.R. 156.

[32] *McGregor* v. *McGregor* (1888) 21 Q.B.D. 424 at 430.

[33] See *Hulse* v. *Hulse* (1913) 103 L.T. 804.

[34] *Wilson* v. *Wilson* (1848) 1 H.L.C. 538; **1 W. & T.L.C. 506**; *Cahill* v. *Cahill* (1883) 8 App.Cas. 420; *Hart* v. *Hart* (1881) 18 Ch.D. 670; *Besant* v. *Wood* (1879) 12 Ch.D. 605.

[35] *Dance* v. *Goldingham* (1873) 8 Ch.App. 902; *Dunn* v. *Flood* (1883) 28 Ch.D. 586.

he was acting in collusion with the trustees at the date of the contract; nor can the beneficiaries impeach the sale, even before conveyance, unless they can show that the consideration for the sale was rendered inadequate by the conditions.[36] It therefore seems that the court would order specific performance, unless it appeared that by reason of the conditions the price was an undervalue.

11. Defective title

(a) *Bad title.* When an action for specific performance is brought by a vendor, it is a defence for the purchaser to show that the vendor cannot make a title to the property in accordance with the contract. In such cases, the purchaser not only can resist specific performance, but also is entitled forthwith to be discharged from his contract altogether.[37] But a vendor whose title is bad at the date of the contract can nevertheless compel specific performance if the defect is cured before the purchaser has definitely repudiated the contract.[38] Conversely, where the vendor's title becomes bad before completion, specific performance will not be ordered.[38a]

(b) *Incumbrances.* A purchaser may repudiate a contract if there are undisclosed restrictive covenants which will be binding upon him when he completes.[39] Conditions of sale which, *e.g.* deem the purchaser to have knowledge of specified matters of title, cannot be relied upon by the vendor in respect of undisclosed incumbrances which were within his knowledge or that of his solicitor.[40] If on a sale of leaseholds it appears that the lease contains onerous and unusual covenants which were not disclosed by the vendor and that the purchaser was afforded no opportunity of inspecting the lease before he entered into the contract, the purchaser may repudiate[41] even though the contract stipulates that "the vendor's title is accepted by the purchaser."[42] He may also repudiate if the defect in the vendor's title cannot be removed without the concurrence of a third party whose concurrence the vendor has no power to require.[43] But if the defect is one not of title but of conveyance only (*i.e.* a defect removable by the vendor, such as an outstanding mortgage), the purchaser cannot repudiate at the time fixed

---

[36] T.A. 1925, s.13, replacing T.A. 1893, s.14.
[37] *Bellamy* v. *Debenham* [1891] 1 Ch. 412; *Pips (Leisure Productions) Ltd.* v. *Walton* (1980) 43 P. & C.R. 415.
[38] *Re Hailes and Hutchinson's Contract* [1920] 1 Ch. 233.
[38a] *Sullivan* v. *Henderson* [1973] 1 W.L.R. 333, where a good contract to sell shares became void as against the company. And see *post*, p. 617.
[39] *Nottingham Patent Brick Co.* v. *Butler* (1886) 16 Q.B.D. 778; *Re Nisbet and Potts' Contract* [1906] 1 Ch. 386.
[40] *Rignall Developments Ltd.* v. *Halil* [1988] Ch. 190.
[41] *Molyneux* v. *Hawtrey* [1903] 2 K.B. 487.
[42] *Re Haedicke and Lipski's Contract* [1901] 2 Ch. 666.
[43] *Re Bryant and Barningham's Contract* (1890) 44 Ch.D. 218; *Re Head's Trustees and Macdonald* (1890) 45 Ch.D. 310; *cf. Re Baker and Selmon's Contract* [1907] 1 Ch. 238; see *ante*, p. 596.

for completion unless time is of the essence of the contract; he must give the vendor a reasonable opportunity of removing the defect.[44]

(c) *Doubtful title.* If the vendor's title, without being clearly bad, nevertheless depends upon a doubtful question of fact, the court may refuse to force it on an unwilling purchaser and may relieve him from his contract,[45] *e.g.* if it depends upon proof that the vendor bought without notice of an adverse equitable interest.[46] The court will not compel a purchaser to buy a lawsuit,[47] a term which means not a bare possibility of proceedings but "a reasonable, decent probability of litigation."[48] Yet "it is the duty of the Court, unless in very exceptional circumstances, to decide the rights between the vendor and the purchaser, even though a third person not a party to the action will not be bound by the decision."[49] This principle applies both to questions of law which may arise on the title[50] and to cases in which the question whether a good title has been shown depends on a conclusion as to fact.[51] If the court concludes beyond reasonable doubt that the purchaser will not be at risk of a successful assertion of an incumbrance against him, the possibility that the claimant to the incumbrance might take proceedings against the purchaser will not deter the court from declaring that a good title has been shown.[52]

[44] *Hatten* v. *Russell* (1888) 38 Ch.D. 334; and see *Tadcaster Tower Brewery Co.* v. *Wilson* [1897] 1 Ch. 705.
[45] *Pyrke* v. *Waddingham* (1852) 10 Hare 1; *Mullings* v. *Trinder* (1870) L.R. 10 Eq. 449.
[46] *Re Handman and Wilcox's Contract* [1902] 1 Ch. 599.
[47] *Re Nichols' and Von Joel's Contract* [1910] 1 Ch. 43 at 46; and see *Re Marshall and Salt's Contract* [1900] 2 Ch. 202; *Wilson* v. *Thomas* [1958] 1 W.L.R. 422.
[48] *Cattell* v. *Corrall* (1840) 4 Y. & C.Ex. 228 at 237, *per* Alderson B.; and see *George* v. *Thomas* (1904) 90 L.T. 505 (action for specific performance stood over to see if lawsuit ensues). And see *ante*, p. 612.
[49] *Smith* v. *Colbourne* [1914] 2 Ch. 533 at 541, *per* Lord Cozens-Hardy M.R.
[50] *Smith* v. *Colbourne* [1914] 2 Ch. 533; *Johnson* v. *Clarke* [1928] Ch. 847; *Alexander* v. *Mills* (1870) 6 Ch.App. 124. But see *Re Thackwray and Young's Contract* (1888) 40 Ch.D. 34 and *Re Hollis* [1899] 2 Ch. 540 (where the titles were too doubtful to be forced upon a purchaser).
[51] *MEPC Ltd.* v. *Christian-Edwards* [1981] A.C. 205.
[52] *MEPC Ltd.* v. *Christian-Edwards, supra.*

CHAPTER 2

RESCISSION

1. Nature. The right to rescind is a right which a party to a transaction sometimes has to set that transaction aside and be restored to his former position. Rescission is thus not strictly a judicial remedy but the act of the party entitled to rescind.[1] Nevertheless it is best discussed as a remedy, for the assistance of the court is often required both to determine whether a person is entitled to rescind and also to obtain restitution of property which has been handed over pursuant to the transaction. Moreover, rescission was regarded as an equitable remedy, for only a court of equity could do what was necessary to make restitution, *e.g.* take accounts and make allowances for deterioration in the property dealt with by the contract.[2] A right to rescind is not assignable.[3]

2. Relation to other rules of contract

(a) *Discharge by breach.* A party to a contract may commit such a breach as goes to the root of the contract and releases the other party from his obligation to perform his part.[4] A party who has been discharged by breach may yet recover damages for the breach,[5] even though his acceptance of the other party's breach as a discharge may be expressed in terms of rescission.[6]

(b) *Mistake.* A contract void for mistake is void *ab initio*.[7] A contract which a party may rescind is valid unless and until it is rescinded. This is of importance where third parties have acquired rights under the contract, for this will bar the right to rescission and restitution of property.[8]

---

[1] *Abram Steamship Co. Ltd.* v. *Westville Shipping Co. Ltd.* [1923] A.C. 773 at 781; *Horsler* v. *Zorro* [1975] Ch. 302 at 310; *Johnson* v. *Agnew* [1980] A.C. 367 at 392, 393. For the different meanings of "rescission," see A. Bate (1955) 19 Conv.(N.S.) 116.
[2] *Erlanger* v. *New Sombrero Phosphate Co.* (1878) 3 App.Cas. 1218 at 1278; *cf. Leaf* v. *International Galleries* [1950] 2 K.B. 86 at 94.
[3] *Ante*, pp. 75, 85.
[4] *Harold Wood Brick Co. Ltd.* v. *Ferris* [1935] 2 K.B. 198; and see *Mersey Steel and Iron Co. Ltd.* v. *Naylor, Benzon & Co.* (1884) 9 App.Cas. 434; *Thorpe* v. *Fasey* [1949] Ch. 649.
[5] *Harold Wood Brick Co. Ltd.* v. *Ferris, supra.*
[6] See *post*, p. 623.
[7] *Cundy* v. *Lindsay* (1878) 3 App.Cas. 459.
[8] *Post*, p. 622.

(c) *Illegality.* A contract may be void for illegality. Where this occurs the maxims *in pari delicto potior est conditio defendentis* and *ex turpi causa non oritur actio* may operate to prevent any restitution of property.[9] On the other hand, a party who has rescinded a contract is entitled to recover and bound to restore property which has passed pursuant to the contract.

(d) *Repudiation.* A purchaser may repudiate a contract for the sale of land if the vendor's title is defective.[10] After repudiation the vendor will be unable to obtain specific performance, but he will be able to recover damages if he acquires a title before the date fixed for completion.[11]

3. Grounds for rescission. The following are the most important grounds upon which a party may rescind a transaction.

(a) *Fraudulent misrepresentation.* A party may rescind a contract which he has been induced to enter into by fraudulent misrepresentations.[12]

(b) *Innocent misrepresentation*

(1) RESCISSION. A contract procured by innocent misrepresentations may be rescinded by the party to whom the representations are made.[13] A misrepresentation is innocent if the defendant honestly believes in the truth of his assertion, even if he has no reasonable ground for his belief,[14] or if he once knew the true facts but has forgotten them.[15] Thus a contract for a lease may be rescinded if the intending lessor misstates to the lessee the length of the term which it is within his power to grant[16] or the position with regard to the availability of planning permission for the proposed user of the premises.[17]

(2) DAMAGES. Unlike fraudulent misrepresentations,[18] innocent misrepresentations were not recognised as a ground for relief by the common law unless they had become incorporated as terms in the contract.[19] Accordingly, although the party deceived might rescind or resist specific performance,[20] he could not recover damages, whether by

---

[9] *Gascoigne* v. *Gascoigne* [1918] 1 K.B. 223 (*ante,* p. 181); *Berg* v. *Sadler and Moore* [1937] 2 K.B. 158.
[10] *Ante,* p. 614.
[11] *Halkett* v. *Earl of Dudley* [1907] 1 Ch. 590 at 596, 597.
[12] See *ante,* p. 548.
[13] *Redgrave* v. *Hurd* (1881) 20 Ch.D. 1.
[14] *Derry* v. *Peek* (1889) 14 App.Cas. 337.
[15] *Low* v. *Bouverie* [1891] 3 Ch. 82.
[16] *Mapes* v. *Jones* (1974) 232 E.G. 717.
[17] *Laurence* v. *Lexcourt Holdings Ltd.* [1978] 1 W.L.R. 1128.
[18] *Ante,* p. 548.
[19] *Bannerman* v. *White* (1861) 10 C.B.(N.S.) 844. See *Heilbut Symons & Co.* v. *Buckleton* [1913] A.C. 30.
[20] See *ante,* p. 602.

an action for damages,[21] or by other means,[22] *e.g.* by claiming specific performance with an abatement of the purchase price.[23]

This rule was altered by the Misrepresentation Act 1967.[24] If a contract is made after one party has made a misrepresentation to the other which, if fraudulent, would make the misrepresentor liable for damages, then he is liable for damages even if the misrepresentation was innocent "unless he proves that he had reasonable ground to believe and did believe up to the time the contract was made that the facts represented were true."[25] If the misrepresentation is made by an agent, the liability for damages is that of his principal.[26] If a misrepresentation is made to a party and afterwards corrected by a statement to the party's agent, the agent's knowledge is imputed to the party even if the agent fails to inform his principal.[27] Damages for misrepresentation are limited to the expenses to which the plaintiff was put by entering into the contract, but do not extend to damages for loss of bargain.[28] They remain recoverable even though the right of rescission is lost.[29] Moreover, the court can declare the contract to be still subsisting and award damages in lieu of rescission if would be equitable to do so, having regard to the nature of the misrepresentation and the loss that would be caused by it if the contract were upheld, as well as to the loss that rescission would cause to the other party.[30] A term[31] in the contract which purports to exclude or restrict liability for misrepresentations is of no effect except to the extent to which the court allows reliance on it as being fair and reasonable in the circumstances.[32]

(c) *Constructive fraud.* Gifts and bargains procured by undue influence and unconscionable bargains may be set aside by the victim.[33]

(d) *Contracts uberrimae fidei.* Although there is normally no duty for one party to a contract to make disclosures to the other,[34] certain contracts are such that one party has the command of means of knowledge not available to the other who may therefore rescind the contract if he is not fully informed. These contracts are known as contracts *uberrimae fidei*, and comprise contracts of insurance of all types, and contracts for family settlements and arrangements.[35] Thus an

---

[21] *Derry* v. *Peek* (1889) 14 App.Cas. 337; *Newbigging* v. *Adam* (1886) 34 Ch.D. 582 at 592 (affirmed sub nom. *Adam* v. *Newbigging* (1888) 13 App.Cas. 308).

[22] *Heilbut Symons & Co.* v. *Buckleton* [1913] A.C. 30 at 48, 49, 51.

[23] *Gilchester Properties Ltd.* v. *Gomm* [1948] 1 All E.R. 493.

[24] Applying to misrepresentations made after April 21, 1967: see ss.5, 6(2).

[25] Misrepresentation Act 1967, s.2(1). See *Howard Marine & Dredging Co. Ltd.* v. *A. Ogden & Sons (Excavations) Ltd.* [1978] Q.B. 574.

[26] *Resolute Maritime Inc.* v. *Nippon Kaiji Kyokai* [1983] 1 W.L.R. 857.

[27] *Strover* v. *Harrington* [1988] Ch. 390.

[28] *Sharney Food Supplies Ltd.* v. *Edge* [1986] Ch. 128 (Mervyn Davies J.), not following *Watts* v. *Spence* [1976] Ch. 165. The decision of Mervyn Davies J. was reversed by C.A. (see *ante*, p. 589), but not affecting this point: [1987] Ch. 305 at 323. See also (1975) 91 L.Q.R. 307.

[29] *Production Technology Consultants Ltd.* v. *Bartlett* [1988] 1 E.G.L.R. 182.

[30] Misrepresentation Act 1967, s.2(2). For the effect of rescission, see *post*, p. 622.

[31] See *Cremdean Properties Ltd.* v. *Nash* (1977) 244 E.G. 547.

[32] Misrepresentation Act 1967, s.3; and see *Walker* v. *Boyle* [1982] 1 W.L.R. 495; *South Western General Property Co.* v. *Marton* (1982) 263 E.G. 1090.

[33] See *ante*, pp. 550 *et seq.* for constructive fraud.

[34] *Ante*, p. 549.

[35] Some would add other classes of contracts: see *ante*, p. 470 (suretyship), and generally *Chitty on Contracts* (26th ed., 1989), Vol. 1, paras. 481–483.

agreement of the latter type was set aside where the rights of the parties depended on a secret marriage known to one side and not disclosed to the other,[36] or where one party was not informed of a legal opinion which had been taken,[37] or was misinformed as to its contents.[38]

On the other hand, where a family arrangement is entered into with due deliberation and full disclosure, it cannot be set aside on the ground that the parties were under a mistake as to their rights,[39] even though they were misled by their legal advisers.[40] The whole object of such a contract is to obtain a settlement of admittedly doubtful rights, and the court is anxious to uphold and not disturb the quiet which is the consequence of such an agreement,[41] even though it rests "upon grounds, which would not have been considered satisfactory, if the transaction had occurred between mere strangers."[42]

(e) *Terms in contracts*

(1) RIGHT TO RESCIND. Contracts often contain terms entitling one or other party to rescind in certain events or for certain defaults. For instance, there is usually a condition in contracts for sale of land which provides that the vendor may rescind if the purchaser makes or persists in any objection or requisition which the vendor is unable or unwilling to remove or comply with.[43] A notice of rescission is valid which alleges an actual default even if it alleges another default which is not specified or which has not occurred.[44]

(2) UNREASONABLE USE OF RIGHT. The vendor cannot take advantage of such a condition if he has knowingly sold without having any title to the property,[45] or where he has a title to part only of the property[46]; the condition does not give him an arbitrary power to rescind the contract without showing some reasonable ground for so doing.[47] He can rescind only if he entered into the contract in ignorance of some material fact or document, or under some mistaken notion that he was entitled to sell and could make a title; there must be no failure of duty on his part, no element of shortcoming, and he must have omitted nothing which the ordinarily prudent man, having regard to his contractual relations with other persons, is bound to do.[48] The vendor must not "play fast and

---

[36] *Gordon* v. *Gordon* (1821) 3 Swans. 400.
[37] *Harvey* v. *Cooke* (1827) 4 Russ. 34.
[38] *Re Roberts, Roberts* v. *Roberts* [1905] 1 Ch. 704.
[39] *Stapilton* v. *Stapilton* (1739) 1 Atk. 2; **1 W. & T.L.C. 178**; *Stone* v. *Godfrey* (1854) 5 De G.M. & G. 76.
[40] *Rogers* v. *Ingham* (1876) 3 Ch.D. 351.
[41] *Gordon* v. *Gordon* (1821) 3 Swans. 400 at 463.
[42] *Westby* v. *Westby* (1842) 2 Dr. & War. 402 at 525, *per* Sugden L.C.
[43] See, *e.g.* The Law Society's Conditions of Sale (1984), cl. 16; The National Conditions of Sale (20th ed., 1981), cl. 10; Standard Conditions of Sale (1990), para. 4.5.2.
[44] *Green* v. *Sommerville* (1979) 141 C.L.R. 594 at 667; *Legione* v. *Hateley* (1983) 152 C.L.R. 406.
[45] *Re Des Reaux and Setchfield's Contract* [1926] Ch. 178.
[46] *Re Deighton and Harris's Contract* [1898] 1 Ch. 458; *Re Jackson and Haden's Contract* [1906] 1 Ch. 412.
[47] *Duddell* v. *Simpson* (1866) 2 Ch.App. 102; *Re Weston and Thomas's Contract* [1907] 1 Ch. 244.
[48] *Re Jackson and Haden's Contract, supra*; *Merrett* v. *Schuster* [1920] 2 Ch. 240; *Proctor* v. *Pugh* [1921] 2 Ch. 256; *Baines* v. *Tweddle* [1959] Ch. 679; *Selkirk* v. *Romar Investments Ltd.* [1963] 1 W.L.R. 1415.

loose," holding his right of rescission in suspense while negotiating with some third person for a resale.[49]

(3) PURPORTED EXERCISE OF RIGHT.   A party who in good faith relies, albeit erroneously, on a rescission clause in a contract and purports to exercise the right to rescind conferred by that clause will not be held to have repudiated the contract unless he has demonstrated an intention not to be bound by it in any event.[50]

(4) LEGAL PROCEEDINGS.   The vendor cannot rescind after a judicial decision has been given against him.[51] But the mere institution of proceedings does not destroy his right of rescission,[52] although the court may order him to pay the costs if he exercises this right after litigation has been started.[53] And there can be no rescission by a vendor as long as a writ in which he claims specific performance is on foot, for the two claims are inconsistent.[54] But if the vendor sues for specific perform-ance, and the purchaser fails to comply with the order for specific performance, the vendor is entitled to an order for rescission.[55]

(5) OTHER LIMITS TO RIGHT.   Apart from any special condition of sale, the vendor cannot rescind the contract for mere delay in the payment of instalments of the purchase-money, unless the delay shows that the purchaser has totally abandoned the contract.[56] Nor can the vendor rescind if the purchaser commits an act of bankruptcy before completion, for this would defeat the rights of the trustee in bankruptcy.[57]

(f) *Mistake.*   A party who enters into a contract under a fundamental mistake as to the facts or his rights may be able to rescind, possibly subject to conditions.[58]

(g) *Misdescription.*   The purchaser under a contract for the sale of land may rescind on account of substantial misdescription of the property.[59]

4. Loss of right of rescission

(a) *By acquiescence.*   Where a right of rescission exists, it will be lost if the person entitled to rescind has elected to waive rescission and affirm the contract after the facts conferring the right have come to his notice, *e.g.* where with full knowledge of a fraud upon him he

[49] *Smith* v. *Wallace* [1895] 1 Ch. 385.
[50] *Woodar Investment Development Ltd.* v. *Wimpey Construction U.K. Ltd.* [1980] 1 W.L.R. 277.
[51] *Re Arbib and Class's Contract* [1891] 1 Ch. 601.
[52] *Isaacs* v. *Towell* [1898] 2 Ch. 285.
[53] *Re Spindler and Mear's Contract* [1901] 1 Ch. 908.
[54] *Public Trustee* v. *Pearlberg* [1940] 2 K.B. 1.
[55] See *Olde* v. *Olde* [1904] 1 Ch. 35; *ante,* pp. 591, 592.
[56] *Cornwall* v. *Henson* [1900] 2 Ch. 298.
[57] *Jennings' Trustee* v. *King* [1952] Ch. 899.
[58] See *ante,* p. 602.
[59] See *ante,* p. 605.

nevertheless takes a benefit under the contract. Both the facts which give rise to the right of rescission and the existence of that right must be fully known to the party misled before he can be considered to have waived the right.[59a] And even after knowledge has been acquired, it seems that the mere lapse of time is in itself no bar to rescission, although in these circumstances a great lapse of time may be evidence of an acquiescence and waiver of the right to rescind.[60] These principles seem to be applied with special strictness to the repudiation of shares in a company. Where the shareholder is fully informed of the circumstances, he ought to lose no time in repudiating, for even so short a delay as a fortnight may be too long.[61]

(b) *By impossibility of restitutio in integrum.* In general, a contract that is liable to be rescinded remains valid until it is set aside. A contract may cease to be capable of being rescinded as where the parties cannot be restored to their original position.[62] Thus if an agent who has misled his principal has under his agency agreement acquired property for the principal from third parties, that agreement will not be rescinded, for that would make the agent the beneficial owner of the property which he has never previously owned.[63] But the rule is not applied very strictly; for equity will relieve wherever it can do what is practically just, even though it cannot restore the parties precisely to the state in which they were before the contract was made. Thus an agreement to become a partner in a business may be rescinded even though the business has in the meantime become worthless.[64] Further, rescission may be decreed at the suit of a party who has obtained incidental benefits from the contract on terms that he restores the value of those benefits, even though precise restitution is impossible.[65]

On the other hand, where A by fraud obtained the execution of a deed of dissolution of partnership whereby B released him from all liabilities of the partnership in consideration of A giving up all claim to the partnership assets, B was held to be unable to disaffirm the deed of dissolution and recover damages for breach of the original partnership agreement when he later discovered the fraud; for the release of A could not be severed from the rest of the deed of dissolution, and as B did not and could not disaffirm the deed under which he claimed all the partnership assets, he could not repudiate the release of A which formed part of that deed.[66]

[59a] *Peyman* v. *Lanjani* [1985] Ch. 457.

[60] *Life Association of Scotland* v. *Siddal* (1861) 3 De G.F. & J. 58; *Charter* v. *Trevelyan* (1844) 11 Cl. & F. 714; *Leaf* v. *International Galleries* [1950] 2 K.B. 86.

[61] *Re Scottish Petroleum Co.* (1883) 23 Ch.D. 434.

[62] *Erlanger* v. *New Sombrero Phosphate Co.* (1878) 3 App.Cas. 1218; *Clarke* v. *Dickson* (1859) E.B. & E. 148; *Lagunas Nitrate Co.* v. *Lagunas Syndicate* [1899] 2 Ch. 392; *Steedman* v. *Frigidaire Corporation* [1932] W.N. 248; *Thorpe* v. *Fasey* [1949] Ch. 649; *Butler* v. *Croft* (1973) 27 P. & C.R. 1 (party's own conduct making restitution impossible).

[63] *Northern Bank Finance Corporation Ltd.* v. *Charlton* [1979] I.R. 149 (a 3–2 decision of the Supreme Court).

[64] *Adam* v. *Newbigging* (1888) 13 App.Cas. 308.

[65] *Wandinger* v. *Lake* (1977) 78 D.L.R. (3d) 305 (purchaser of motel obtained rescission even though he had the benefit of occupation and had taken away chattels from premises).

[66] *Urquhart* v. *Macpherson* (1878) 3 App.Cas. 831.

(c) *After completion.* An innocent misrepresentation was considered to give no right to rescind a contract after completion. This rule applied whether the contract was for the sale of freeholds,[67] the grant of a lease[68] or the sale of a chattel[69] or chose in action.[70] The rule was strongly criticised,[71] and in 1967 it was abrogated by statute.[72] It is now no bar to the rescission of a contract for innocent misrepresentation that the contract has been performed.[73]

(d) *By intervention of third parties*

(1) PURCHASERS. Repudiation of a contract is impossible where third parties have intervened and acquired rights thereunder for value. An illustration of this is to be found in the rule that a shareholder who on account of fraud wishes to repudiate his contract to take the shares must do so before the commencement of the winding up of the company. For after the winding up commences, the rights of the company's creditors are fixed, and they stand in the position of purchasers for value.[74]

(2) VOLUNTEERS. The intervening rights of third parties will not affect the right of the person defrauded to disaffirm the transaction unless such parties are claimants for value. Thus where a surety for a debt is released by the creditor in consideration of the transfer to the creditor of a mortgage which the debtor fraudulently misrepresents as being valid and effectual, the release of the surety can be avoided even though the surety did not participate in the fraud, for in respect of the release he is a mere volunteer.[75] Similarly, where a contract is voidable against a party to it, it is equally voidable against his trustee in bankruptcy, who in this respect stands in no better position than the bankrupt.[76]

5. Effect of rescission. A person who rescinds a contract is entitled to be restored to the position he would have been in had the contract not been *made.* Hence, property must be returned, possession given up, and accounts taken of profits or deterioration.[77] But no damages are recoverable,[78] since the purpose of damages is to place the party

---

[67] *Wilde* v. *Gibson* (1848) 1 H.L.C. 605.
[68] *Angel* v. *Jay* [1911] 1 K.B. 666.
[69] See *Seddon* v. *North Eastern Salt Co. Ltd.* [1905] 1 Ch. 326; but see *Leaf* v. *International Galleries* [1950] 2 K.B. 86.
[70] *Seddon* v. *North Eastern Salt Co. Ltd., supra; Lecky* v. *Walter* [1914] 1 I.R. 378. The rule did not prevent a shareholder from rescinding a contract to take shares in a company even after his name had been placed on the register: see *First National Reinsurance Co. Ltd.* v. *Greenfield* [1921] 2 K.B. 260 at 272.
[71] *Solle* v. *Butcher* [1950] 1 K.B. 671 at 695, 696; but see *ibid* at p. 703; *Leaf* v. *International Galleries* [1950] 2 K.B. 86 at 95.
[72] Misrepresentation Act 1967, applying to misrepresentations made after April 21, 1967: see ss.5, 6(2).
[73] *Ibid.* s.1.
[74] *Oakes* v. *Turquand* (1867) L.R. 2 H.L. 325.
[75] *Scholefield* v. *Templer* (1859) Johns. 155.
[76] *Re Eastgate* [1905] 1 K.B. 465; *Tilley* v. *Bowman Ltd.* [1910] 1 K.B. 745.
[77] See *ante*, p. 616.
[78] *Redgrave* v. *Hurd* (1881) 20 Ch.D. 1.

recovering them in the same position (so far as money can do it) as he would have been in, had the contract been *carried out*. It is otherwise where a specific performance order is rescinded or discharged following non-compliance with the decree. The House of Lords has held, overruling many earlier authorities,[79] that the party who obtained the order is then entitled to recover damages on a common law basis for breach of contract.[80] This is not true rescission *ab initio*, but rather an acceptance of a repudiatory breach of contract, and there is thus no inconsistency between the termination of an existing contract and the award of damages for its breach.[81] The same principle would apply where, without seeking specific performance from the court, one party expresses his election to treat the other's breach as discharging the contract in terms of rescission.[82]

6. Forfeiture of deposit. A vendor who accepts the purchaser's default as a breach which discharges the contract may forfeit and retain any deposit already paid, and may recover by way of damages the amount of any deposit which has not been paid.[83] If the vendor rescinds under a condition which (as is usual) enables him to resell, and to charge the defaulting purchaser with any deficiency, any deposit must be taken into account when computing the deficiency, even though it has been forfeited.[84]

---

[79] *Henty* v. *Schröder* (1879) 12 Ch.D. 666; *Barber* v. *Wolfe* [1945] Ch. 187; *Capital and Suburban Properties Ltd.* v. *Swycher* [1976] Ch. 319; and *Horsler* v. *Zorro* [1975] Ch. 302.

[80] *Johnson* v. *Agnew* [1980] A.C. 367. See *ante*, pp. 589, 591, 592. The development had been anticipated in Australia: W. Gummow (1976) 92 L.Q.R. 5.

[81] *Heyman* v. *Darwins Ltd.* [1942] A.C. 356 at 399; *Johnson* v. *Agnew, supra*, at p. 393.

[82] *Buckland* v. *Farmer & Moody (a firm)* [1979] 1 W.L.R. 221.

[83] *Damon Compania Naviera S.A.* v. *Hapag-Lloyd International S.A.* [1985] 1 W.L.R. 435, following *Dewar* v. *Mintoft* [1912] 2 K.B. 373 and disapproving *Lowe* v. *Hope* [1970] Ch. 94.

[84] *Shuttleworth* v. *Clews* [1910] 1 Ch. 176, disapproving *Griffiths* v. *Vezey* [1906] 1 Ch. 796.

CHAPTER 3

DELIVERY UP AND CANCELLATION OF DOCUMENTS

1. The jurisdiction. If a document appears to be valid but is in fact void or voidable (*e.g.* for fraud), its mere existence may nevertheless be embarrassing, *e.g.* lest some claim be founded upon it, or some third party be deceived by it. In such cases equity accordingly assumed jurisdiction to order the document to be delivered up and cancelled.[1] This would be done even if the document was wholly void at law,[2] unless the defect appeared on the face of the document, so that it carried its own refutation and there was no need for equity to intervene.[3]

2. Exercise of jurisdiction. This jurisdiction may be exercised in a variety of cases, as where a defective negotiable instrument might be used for some improper purpose to the injury of a third party[4]; where a conveyance has been made for an immoral consideration[5]; where a guarantee has been procured by misrepresentation[6]; where a lease has been granted at what the lessee knew to be a mistakenly low rent[7]; and where there is a forged conveyance which may endanger a title,[8] though here the document will not be torn or defaced but will be preserved as evidence for a prosecution.[9] Even if the document is initially valid, an order for delivery up may be made if subsequently it becomes ineffective, *e.g.* by release,[10] or by the breaking off of the engagement for the marriage in contemplation of which it was executed.[11] But no such order will be made if the document is not wholly void, as where it is a settlement which is merely void as against creditors,[12] or where it is

---

[1] See generally *Story on Equity* (3rd English ed., 1920), pp. 293–301.
[2] See *Ryan* v. *Mackmath* (1789) 3 Bro.C.C. 15; *Davis* v. *Duke of Marlborough* (1819) 2 Swans. 108 at 157.
[3] *Simpson* v. *Lord Howden* (1837) 3 My. & Cr. 97.
[4] *Wynne* v. *Callender* (1826) 1 Russ. 293 (bills given for gambling transaction); and see *Earl of Milltown* v. *Stewart* (1837) 3 My. & Cr. 18; *Jervis* v. *White* (1802) 7 Ves. 413.
[5] *W.* v. *B.* (1863) 32 Beav. 574.
[6] *Cooper* v. *Joel* (1859) 1 De G.F. & J. 240.
[7] *Gun* v. *M'Carthy* (1884) 13 L.R.Ir. 304.
[8] *Peake* v. *Highfield* (1826) 1 Russ. 559; and see *Burton* v. *Gray* (1873) 8 Ch.App. 932.
[9] *Frankland* v. *Hampden* (1682) 1 Vern. 66.
[10] *Flower* v. *Marten* (1837) 2 My. & Cr. 459; and see *Wekett* v. *Raby* (1724) 2 Bro.P.C. 386, as explained in *Re Appelbee* [1891] 3 Ch. 422.
[11] *Bond* v. *Walford* (1886) 32 Ch.D. 238.
[12] *Ideal Bedding Co. Ltd.* v. *Holland* [1907] 2 Ch. 157; see *ante*, p. 130, as to the beneficiaries' right to any surplus.

624

a contract which is merely incapable of being performed.[13] Similarly a policy of insurance which is not vitiated by any fraud or misrepresentation will not be cancelled at the instance of the underwriters merely because they have a complete defence to any claim which may be brought under the policy.[14]

3. Terms of relief. As the relief is equitable, he who seeks it must be prepared to do equity. Thus where a loan was made on unconscionable terms, an order for delivery up of bills given as part of the transaction was ordered only on terms of repaying the money actually lent, with 5 per cent. interest.[15] This may in some degree account for the comparative infrequency today of claims for delivery up. The modern practice tends to be to claim a declaration that the document is void; and as the power to make a declaration is statutory and not equitable,[16] a plaintiff can obtain the declaration without being put on terms.[17]

[13] *Onions* v. *Cohen* (1865) 2 H. & M. 354.
[14] *Brooking* v. *Maudslay, Son & Field* (1888) 38 Ch.D. 636 (marine insurance: defence of deviation).
[15] *Earl of Aylesford* v. *Morris* (1873) 8 Ch.App. 484; and see *Bromley* v. *Holland* (1802) 7 Ves. 3; but see *Davis* v. *Duke of Marlborough* (1819) 2 Swans. 108 at 157 (adequate remedy at law).
[16] See *ante*, p. 584.
[17] *Chapman* v. *Michaelson* [1909] 1 Ch. 238; and see *ante*, p. 30.

CHAPTER 4

RECTIFICATION

Section 1. Nature of Rectification

1. The remedy. If by mistake a written instrument does not accord with the true agreement between the parties, equity has power to reform, or rectify, that instrument so as to make it accord with the true agreement.[1] What is rectified is not a mistake in the transaction itself, but a mistake in the way in which that transaction has been expressed in writing. "Courts of Equity do not rectify contracts; they may and do rectify instruments purporting to have been made in pursuance of the terms of contracts."[2]

2. Discretion. Rectification is a discretionary remedy "which must be cautiously watched and jealously guarded."[3] But unlike remedies such as specific performance, which are based on the inadequacy of the remedy at law, rectification "gives relief from the inflexibility of the common law, and from the nature of the case involves a contravention of its rules."[4]

3. Jurisdiction. Claims for rectification are expressly assigned to the Chancery Division.[5] But the other Divisions may grant any remedy or relief connected with matters before them,[6] and, further, any Division may give effect to a defence of rectification as regards past transactions without actually rectifying the instrument.[7] Normally claims for

---

[1] See *M'Cormack* v. *M'Cormack* (1877) 1 L.R.Ir. 119; *Frederick E. Rose (London) Ltd.* v. *William H. Pim Jnr. & Co. Ltd.* [1953] 2 Q.B. 450.
[2] *Mackenzie* v. *Coulson* (1869) L.R. 8 Eq. 368 at 375, *per* James V.-C.
[3] *Whiteside* v. *Whiteside* [1950] Ch. 65 at 71, *per* Evershed M.R.
[4] *Thompson* v. *Hickman* [1907] 1 Ch. 550 at 562, *per* Neville J.
[5] See *ante*, p. 18.
[6] See *ibid.* n. 5.
[7] J.A. 1925, s.40, replacing J.A. 1873, s.24(2), on equities "appearing incidentally" in the course of proceedings: s.40 was repealed by S.C.A. 1981, s.151(4) and Sched. 7 but was not replaced by that Act. See further *Breslauer* v. *Barwick* (1876) 36 L.T. 52; and see *Mostyn* v. *West Mostyn Coal & Iron Co. Ltd.* (1876) 1 C.P.D. 145.

rectification must be pleaded,[8] but in a clear case a court has rectified a document even without the claim having been pleaded.[9]

Section 2. Conditions to be Satisfied

A claim for rectification cannot succeed unless the following conditions are satisfied.

1. Absence of alternative remedy

(a) *Other remedies.* Rectification will not be decreed if the desired result can conveniently be achieved by other means. Thus the material which it is sought to insert in the written instrument may itself be enforceable as a collateral contract.[10] Again, if those concerned voluntarily rectify the instrument, the court will not decree rectification, even if such a decree would, by operating retrospectively,[11] have fiscal advantages which the voluntary rectification lacks.[12]

(b) *Construction.* Sometimes it is sufficient merely to construe the document; for if it contains some obvious clerical blunder or grammatical mistake, the courts will usually correct it as a matter of construction, without decreeing rectification. "Both courts of law and of equity may correct an obvious mistake on the face of an instrument without the slightest difficulty."[13] Many errors escape the rigours of rectification in this way. Thus, where the mistake is plain, an erroneous "not" may be ignored,[14] "male" may be excluded from "tail male,"[15] an omitted "shall appoint" may be treated as being included,[16] "£1,000" may be read as '£100,"[17] "7700" may be construed as "£7,700,"[18] an error in nomenclature may be corrected,[19] and a term of years to arise on a death may be declared to be an immediate term.[20] But where there is clearly some mistake, yet no certainty what the real intention was, the court will give effect to the instrument as it stands[21]; and the court will

---

[8] *Blay* v. *Pollard* [1930] 1 K.B. 628 at 634, 637.
[9] *Butler* v. *Mountview Estates Ltd.* [1951] 2 K.B. 563, where *Blay* v. *Pollard, supra,* does not appear to have been cited.
[10] See *Walker Property Investments (Brighton) Ltd.* v. *Walker* (1947) 177 L.T. 204.
[11] See *post,* p. 635.
[12] *Whiteside* v. *Whiteside* [1950] Ch. 65.
[13] *Wilson* v. *Wilson* (1854) 5 H.L.C. 40 at 66, *per* Lord St. Leonards.
[14] See *Bache* v. *Proctor* (1780) 1 Doug.K.B. 382 at 384.
[15] *Re Alexander's Settlement* [1910] 2 Ch. 225.
[16] *Kirk* v. *Unwin* (1851) 6 Exch. 908.
[17] *Elliott* v. *Freeman* (1863) 7 L.T. 715.
[18] *Coles* v. *Hulme* (1828) 8 B. & C. 568.
[19] *Nittan (U.K.) Ltd.* v. *Solent Steel Fabrication Ltd.* [1981] 1 Lloyd's Rep. 633.
[20] *Annesley* v. *Annesley* (1893) 31 L.R.Ir. 457.
[21] *Doe d. Spencer* v. *Godwin* (1815) 4 M. & S. 265.

do the same where there is not even an obvious mistake, notwithstanding that the parties have interpreted the instrument in some different way.[22] In these cases, rectification must be sought.

2. Mistake. There must be a mistake sufficient to invoke the doctrine. This will be considered under the two heads of common mistake and unilateral mistake.

(a) *Common mistake.* The general rule is that rectification will not be granted unless there has been a mistake in expression which is common to all parties.[23] In general, a claim will succeed only if it is established, first, that there was some prior agreement between the parties; second, that this was still effective when the instrument was executed; third, that by mistake the instrument fails to carry out that agreement; and fourth, that if rectified as claimed, the instrument would carry out the agreement.[24] These points will be taken in turn.

(1) PRIOR AGREEMENT. The prior agreement between the parties on which a claim for rectification is based need not amount to an enforceable contract; it suffices if there is a common intention in regard to the particular provisions of the agreement in question[25] continuing up to the date of the written instrument,[26] together with some outward expression of accord.[27] Thus a contract sealed by a corporation may be rectified even if the contract is one that the corporation can validly make only by deed, so that no antecedent enforceable contract was possible.[28] If in fact there is an antecedent enforceable agreement, extrinsic evidence is admissible in a proper case to rectify both the agreement and the deed.[29]

(2) CONTINUING INTENTION. Any difference between the instrument and the terms previously agreed may be due not to mistake but to a decision by the parties to depart from those terms. A claim for rectification must therefore establish that the parties intended the instrument merely to carry out those terms and not to vary them.[30] If one of the parties denies that the instrument was contrary to his

[22] *North Eastern Ry.* v. *Lord Hastings* [1900] A.C. 260.
[23] *Murray* v. *Parker* (1854) 19 Beav. 305; *Vaudeville Electric Cinema Ltd.* v. *Muriset* [1923] 2 Ch. 74; *W. Higgins Ltd.* v. *Northampton Corporation* [1927] 1 Ch. 128.
[24] See generally *Fowler* v. *Fowler* (1859) 4 De G. & J. 250 at 264, 265.
[25] *Joscelyne* v. *Nissen* [1970] 2 Q.B. 86, applying *Crane* v. *Hegeman-Harris Co. Inc.* [1939] 1 All E.R. 662; [1971] 3 All E.R. 245n.; [1971] 1 W.L.R. 1390n. (affd. [1939] 4 All E.R. 68), and not following dicta in *Lovell and Christmas Ltd.* v. *Wall* (1911) 104 L.T. 85 and *Frederick E. Rose (London) Ltd.* v. *William H. Pim Jnr. & Co. Ltd.* [1953] 2 Q.B. 450. See also *Monaghan County Council* v. *Vaughan* [1948] I.R. 306; *Slee* v. *Warke* (1952) 86 C.L.R. 271 at 280, 281.
[26] *Crane* v. *Hegeman-Harris Co. Inc., supra.*
[27] *Joscelyne* v. *Nissen, supra,* at p. 98, criticised by L. J. Bromley (1971) 87 L.Q.R. 532.
[28] *Shipley U.D.C.* v. *Bradford Corporation* [1936] Ch. 375. See now Corporate Bodies' Contracts Act 1960.
[29] *Craddock Bros.* v. *Hunt* [1923] 2 Ch. 136.
[30] *Marquess of Breadalbane* v. *Marquess of Chandos* (1837) 2 My. & Cr. 711 at 740; *George Cohen, Sons & Co. Ltd.* v. *Docks and Inland Waterways Executive* (1950) 84 Ll.L.R. 97 (see esp. at p. 113).

intention this accordingly has considerable weight[31]; but like other evidence in cases of rectification, this evidence must be directed to the intention existing when the instrument was executed, or earlier, and not at some later time.[32]

Further, what is relevant is "the intention of the parties at the time when the deed was executed, and not what would have been their intent if, when they executed it, the result of what they did had been present to their minds."[33] There can thus be no rectification if the omission of a term was deliberate,[34] even if this was due to an erroneous belief that the term was unnecessary[35] or that it was sufficiently dealt with in the antecedent oral agreement,[36] or that the term was illegal,[37] or a breach of covenant,[38] and similarly if the instrument intentionally contains a provision which in fact means something different from what the parties thought it meant.[39] Rectification ensures that the instrument contains the provisions which the parties actually intended it to contain, and not those which it would have contained had they been better informed.[40]

(3) FAILURE TO REPRESENT AGREEMENT. There must be clear and unambiguous evidence that the instrument either does not accurately represent the true agreement of the parties at the time when it was executed,[41] or at least that it is doubtful whether it does.[42] What is required is a literal disparity between the language of the agreement and that of the instrument, and not merely a misunderstanding of the meaning of that language; if the oral agreement is for "horsebeans" and the written contract is for "horsebeans," there can be no rectification merely because the parties mistakenly believed that horsebeans were the same as feveroles.[43] But the omission of a term not in the parties' minds may be cured by rectification if the term is one that is always taken for granted, e.g. a force majeure clause in a shipping contract.[44]

Usually the mistake is one of fact, but rectification may also be granted where the mistake is as to the legal effect of the language used.[45] Thus it could be decreed where a covenant to pay an annuity[46] or royalties[47] of £x used the formerly[48] ineffective phrase "free of tax"

---

[31] *Fowler* v. *Fowler* (1859) 4 De G. & J. 250 at 273.
[32] *Earl of Bradford* v. *Earl of Romney* (1862) 30 Beav. 431; and see *Stait* v. *Fenner* [1912] 2 Ch. 504 at 519.
[33] *Tucker* v. *Bennett* (1887) 38 Ch.D. 1 at 16, *per* Lopes L.J.
[34] See *Whiteside* v. *Whiteside* [1950] Ch. 65 (correct phrase struck out of draft).
[35] *Worrall* v. *Jacob* (1817) 3 Mer. 256 at 271.
[36] *Maralinga Pty. Ltd.* v. *Major Enterprises Pty. Ltd.* (1973) 128 C.L.R. 336.
[37] *Lord Irnham* v. *Child* (1781) 1 Bro.C.C. 92.
[38] *City and Westminster Properties (1934) Ltd.* v. *Mudd* [1959] Ch. 129; and see *Hazell, Watson & Viney Ltd.* v. *Malvermi* [1953] 2 All E.R. 58 (omitted from [1953] 1 W.L.R. 782).
[39] *Frederick E. Rose (London) Ltd.* v. *William H. Pim Jnr. & Co. Ltd.* [1953] 2 Q.B. 450.
[40] See *Marquis Townshend* v. *Stangroom* (1808) 6 Ves. 328 at 322.
[41] *Fowler* v. *Fowler* (1859) 4 De G. & J. 250 at 265; *Constantinidi* v. *Ralli* [1935] Ch. 427.
[42] *Walker* v. *Armstrong* (1856) 8 De G.M. & G. 531 (a happy example of judicial scorn appears at p. 538); and see *Re Walton's Settlement* [1922] 2 Ch. 509.
[43] *Frederick E. Rose (London) Ltd.* v. *William H. Pim Jnr. & Co. Ltd.*, *supra*.
[44] *Caraman Rowley & May* v. *Aperghis* (1923) 40 T.L.R. 124.
[45] See *Whiteside* v. *Whiteside* [1950] Ch. 65 at 74; contrast *Napier* v. *Williams* [1911] 1 Ch. 361 at 367.
[46] *Burroughes* v. *Abbott* [1922] 1 Ch. 86.
[47] *Jervis* v. *Howle & Talke Colliery Co. Ltd.* [1937] Ch. 67.
[48] Until *Ferguson* v. *I.R.C.* [1970] A.C. 442.

instead of the efficacious expression requiring payment of such a sum as after deduction of tax would leave £x.[49] So also rectification of a settlement was granted where the settlor had intended that a majority of trustees should have a general power to bind a minority,[50] but by an error in drafting the settlement gave a majority such a power only in specified circumstances.[51] Whether equity will relieve against mistakes of law in general is far from clear[52]; but it is no ground for rectification that subsequent legislation has frustrated the intention of the parties.[53]

(4) ACCURATE IF RECTIFIED.   It must appear that if rectified as claimed the instrument would accurately represent the true agreement of the parties at the time when it was executed.[54]

(b) *Unilateral mistake.*   The general rule is that there can be no rectification where the mistake is merely unilateral,[55] as where one party had never even heard of the term sought to be inserted because his agent had not told him of it.[56] But there are three cases where the foregoing conditions are modified and a unilateral mistake may be rectified.

(1) FRAUD.   "Fraud unravels all,"[57] and so rectification may be granted in cases where although only one party is mistaken the other is fraudulent.[58] Constructive fraud[59] suffices, and so rectification may be decreed where a father has failed in his duty of explaining to his son a provision for the father's benefit[60] or to the son's disadvantage[61] in a resettlement by the son, or where a retired solicitor has failed to explain to his fiancée provisions to his advantage in a marriage settlement drafted by him and made by her.[62]

(2) ESTOPPEL.   By what appears to be a species of equitable estoppel,[63] if one party to a transaction knows that the instrument contains a mistake in his favour but does nothing to correct it, he (and those claiming under him) will be precluded from resisting rectification on the

[49] Consider also *Cooper* v. *Phibbs* (1867) L.R. 2 H.L.149; *Earl Beauchamp* v. *Winn* (1873) L.R. 6 H.L. 223. But contrast *Jackson* v. *Stopford* [1923] 2 I.R. 1.
[50] See *ante,* p. 260.
[51] *Re Butlin's S.T.* [1976] Ch. 251; *post,* p. 634.
[52] Contrast, *e.g., Rogers* v. *Ingham* (1876) 3 Ch.D. 351 at 357 and *Watson* v. *Marston* (1853) 4 De G.M. & G. 230 at 236 (as reported 1 W.R. 362) with *Midland Great Western Ry. of Ireland* v. *Johnson* (1858) 6 H.L.C. 798 at 811 and *Jackson* v. *Stopford* [1923] 2 I.R. 1.
[53] *Pyke* v. *Peters* [1943] K.B. 242.
[54] *Fowler* v. *Fowler* (1859) 4 De G. & J. 250 at 265.
[55] *Sells* v. *Sells* (1860) 1 Dr. & Sm. 42; *Mortimer* v. *Shortall* (1852) 2 Dr. & War. 363 at 372.
[56] *Fowler* v. *Scottish Equitable Life Insurance Society* (1858) 28 L.J.Ch. 225.
[57] See *ante,* p. 548.
[58] See *Ball* v. *Storie* (1823) 1 Sim. & St. 210 at 219.
[59] See *ante,* p. 550.
[60] *Hoblyn* v. *Hoblyn* (1889) 41 Ch.D. 200.
[61] *McCausland* v. *Young* [1949] N.I. 49.
[62] *Lovesy* v. *Smith* (1880) 15 Ch.D. 655; and see *Clark* v. *Girdwood* (1877) 7 Ch.D. 9.
[63] See *ante,* p. 569.

ground that the mistake is unilateral and not common.[64] Under this head the evidence of the knowledge and intention of the defendant must be such as to involve him in a degree of sharp practice,[65] or at least "the conduct must be such as to affect the conscience of the party who has suppressed the fact that he has recognised the presence of a mistake."[66]

Fraud and estoppel apart, there is a line of cases in which there has been mere unilateral mistake by the plaintiff and yet the court has put the defendant to his election of either accepting a variation of the contract which will mend the plaintiff's mistake (*i.e.* rectification) or submitting to rescission of the contract.[67] As a result of the decision of the Court of Appeal in *Riverlate Properties Ltd.* v. *Paul*[68] these cases are of doubtful authority. For the most part they can be explained as having been decided when the fact that the defendant knew of the plaintiff's unilateral mistake was not recognised (as it now is) as a ground for rectification, but only for rescission: the court, by putting the defendant to his election, gave him the opportunity of preserving the transaction, but only upon terms that he did not take advantage of the plaintiff's mistake.[69] But now, if the defendant was ignorant of that mistake when the contract was made, he will not be compelled afterwards to choose between mending or abandoning his bargain. "If conscience is clear at the time of the transaction, why should equity disrupt the transaction?"[70]

(3) UNILATERAL TRANSACTIONS. Where the transaction is unilateral, unilateral mistake suffices.[71] Thus a deed poll may be rectified on sufficient proof of a mistake[72] in carrying out the intention of the grantor,[73] and so may provisions in favour of volunteers in an ante-nuptial[74] or post-nuptial[75] settlement. Nor is there anything to prevent a

---

[64] *Whiteley* v. *Delaney* [1914] A.C. 132; *Monaghan County Council* v. *Vaughan* [1948] I.R. 306; *George Cohen, Sons & Co. Ltd.* v. *Docks and Inland Waterways Executive* (1950) 84 Ll.L.R. 97 at 111; *A. Roberts & Co. Ltd.* v. *Leicestershire County Council* [1961] Ch. 555 where this passage was cited and applied at 570; *Thomas Bates and Son Ltd.* v. *Wyndham's (Lingerie) Ltd.* [1981] 1 W.L.R. 505 at 515, 516; and see (1961) 77 L.Q.R. 313.
[65] *Riverlate Properties Ltd.* v. *Paul* [1975] Ch. 133 at 140.
[66] *Thomas Bates and Son Ltd.* v. *Wyndham's (Lingerie) Ltd.* [1981] 1 W.L.R. 505 at 515, *per* Buckley L.J.; and see *ibid.* at 515, 516, setting out the conditions which must be satisfied to obtain rectification on this basis.
[67] *Garrard* v. *Frankel* (1862) 30 Beav. 445; *Harris* v. *Pepperell* (1867) L.R. 5 Eq. 1; *Bloomer* v. *Spittle* (1872) L.R. 13 Eq. 427; *Paget* v. *Marshall* (1884) 28 Ch.D. 255; and see *Gun* v. *M'Carthy* (1884) 13 L.R.Ir. 304; *Solle* v. *Butcher* [1950] 1 K.B. 671.
[68] [1975] Ch. 133. See (1974) 90 L.Q.R. 439; (1975) 53 Can.Bar.Rev. 339 (S. M. Waddams).
[69] *Bloomer* v. *Spittle*, *supra*, and *Solle* v. *Butcher*, *supra* were explained in *Riverlate Properties Ltd.* v. *Paul* [1975] Ch. 133 at 143, 144, as cases of common mistake.
[70] [1975] Ch. 133 at 141, *per* Russell L.J.
[71] See *Wright* v. *Goff* (1856) 22 Beav. 207 at 214.
[72] *Bonhote* v. *Henderson* [1895] 1 Ch. 742; [1895] 2 Ch. 202.
[73] *Wright* v. *Goff* (1856) 22 Beav. 207; *Killick* v. *Gray* (1882) 46 L.T. 583; but see *Phillipson* v. *Kerry* (1863) 32 Beav. 628, although this can hardly be read as a decision by Romilly M.R. denying the jurisdiction to rectify a deed poll that he had exercised in *Wright* v. *Goff, supra*. If the deed is wholly misconceived, it may be cancelled or rescinded: see *ante*, p. 544.
[74] *Maunsell* v. *Maunsell* (1877) 1 L.R.Ir. 529 (see at pp. 539, 540); and see *Van der Linde* v. *Van der Linde* [1947] Ch. 306 (deed of covenant).
[75] *Lackersteen* v. *Lackersteen* (1860) 30 L.J. Ch. 5.

volunteer claiming rectification,[76] at any rate after the settlor's death.[77] And there is now a statutory jurisdiction to rectify wills.[78]

3. "Strong irrefragable evidence"

(a) *Burden of proof.* He who seeks rectification must establish his case by "strong irrefragable evidence,"[79] which means "something more than the highest degree of probability."[80] There must be evidence "of the clearest and most satisfactory description"[81] that will establish the mistake with a "high degree of conviction,"[82] and "leave no fair and reasonable doubt upon the mind that the deed does not embody the final intention of the parties."[83] In the modern phrase, there must be "convincing proof"[84] of the mistake on the part of all parties.[85] This heavy burden of proof becomes even more difficult to discharge with the passage of the years.[86]

(b) *Settlor's evidence.* If it is explicit enough and is uncontradicted, the evidence of a settlor may suffice for the rectification of a settlement[87]; and even a mere perusal of the document itself may satisfy the court.[88] Nevertheless, in the case of a voluntary settlement the court is especially cautious in granting rectification merely on the settlor's evidence if it is unsupported by other evidence such as his contemporaneous written instructions. This is so even if on rectification the settlement would more nearly accord with recognised precedents and the probable intention,[89] and be more beneficial to the settlor.[90]

(c) *Evidence of intention.* Subject to any written evidence,[91] the true intention of the parties may be established both by evidence of their acts, as where for a long time they have observed the true agreement and not the words of the instrument,[92] and also by oral evidence of their

---

[76] *Thompson* v. *Whitmore* (1860) 1 J. & H. 268 at 273; *Weir* v. *Van Tromp* (1900) 16 T.L.R. 531.
[77] *Lister* v. *Hodgson* (1867) L.R. 4 Eq. 30 at 34; *M'Mechan* v. *Warburton* [1896] 1 I.R. 435 at 439.
[78] See *post*, p. 634.
[79] *Countess of Shelburne* v. *Earl of Inchiquin* (1784) 1 Bro.C.C. 338 at 341, *per* Lord Thurlow L.C.; and see *Marquis Townshend* v. *Stangroom* (1801) 6 Ves. 328 at 334.
[80] *Fowler* v. *Fowler* (1859) 4 De G. & J. 250 at 265, *per* Lord Chelmsford L.C.
[81] *Fowler* v. *Fowler, supra,* at p. 264, *per* Lord Chelmsford L.C.
[82] *Crane* v. *Hegeman-Harris Co. Inc.* [1939] 4 All E.R. 68 at 71, *per* Greene M.R.
[83] *Fowler* v. *Fowler, supra,* at p. 265, *per* Lord Chelmsford L.C.
[84] *Joscelyne* v. *Nissen* [1970] 2 Q.B. 86 at 98, *per curiam* (Russell L.J.).
[85] See *Lloyd* v. *Stanbury* [1971] 1 W.L.R. 535. But see *Thomas Bates and Son Ltd.* v. *Wyndham's (Lingerie) Ltd.* [1981] 1 W.L.R. 505 at 514 on this "variety of formulations" which "is not very helpful" and "may, indeed, be confusing" (Buckley L.J.)
[86] *Fredensen* v. *Rothschild* [1941] 1 All E.R. 430 (lapse of over 33 years).
[87] *Hanley* v. *Pearson* (1870) 13 Ch.D. 545; but see *Tucker* v. *Bennett* (1887) 38 Ch.D. 1.
[88] *Banks* v. *Ripley* [1940] Ch. 719.
[89] *Bonhote* v. *Henderson* [1895] 1 Ch. 742; affd. [1895] 2 Ch. 202.
[90] *Van der Linde* v. *Van der Linde* [1947] Ch. 306; and see *Whiteside* v. *Whiteside* [1950] Ch. 65.
[91] *Lackersteen* v. *Lackersteen* (1860) 30 L.J.Ch. 5.
[92] *M'Cormack* v. *M'Cormack* (1877) 1 L.R.Ir. 119; and see *Dormer* v. *Sherman* (1966) 110 S.J. 171.

intentions and states of mind.[93] This is so even if the instrument carries out a transaction which by statute must be made or evidenced by deed or in writing; for all that equity does is to make the writing record the true agreement instead of the untrue.[94] Thus a lease granted in pursuance of an oral agreement may be rectified so as to accord with that agreement.[95] It was at one time thought that where the plaintiff relied solely on parol evidence without any documentary corroboration, and that evidence was denied by the defendant, the plaintiff would be without a remedy.[96] Nowadays, in a proper case, the court may accept the evidence of the plaintiff in preference to that of the defendant.

Section 3. Instruments that will be Rectified

1. Contracts and other documents inter partes.   The jurisdiction to rectify is quite general, and may be exercised in respect of a wide range of instruments. These include mercantile documents such as a policy of marine insurance,[97] a bill of exchange,[98] a transfer of shares,[99] and a bill of quantities[1]; conveyancing documents such as a conveyance,[2] a marriage settlement,[3] and a disentailing deed (despite a statutory provision[4] which to some extent excludes equitable jurisdiction[5]); a lease[6]; and a consent order, which for this purpose stands on the same footing as an agreement *inter partes*,[7] even though the mistake on which it is founded is as to the effect of a particular instrument.[8] But the articles of a company will not be rectified[9]; for not only would rectification be inconsistent with the provisions of the Companies Acts, but also the articles are (*inter alia*) a contract between the company and its members,[10] and *ex hypothesi* the company cannot have had a different intention before incorporation.

---

[93] *Murray* v. *Parker* (1854) 19 Beav. 305 at 308.
[94] *Re Boulter* (1876) 4 Ch.D. 241; *Johnson* v. *Bragge* [1901] 1 Ch. 28; *Craddock Bros.* v. *Hunt* [1923] 2 Ch. 136 (for earlier conflicting authorities see at p. 151); *United States of America* v. *Motor Trucks Ltd.* [1924] A.C. 196.
[95] *Cowen* v. *Truefitt Ltd.* [1899] 2 Ch. 309.
[96] *Mortimer* v. *Shortall* (1842) 2 Dr. & War. 363 at 374.
[97] *Spalding* v. *Crocker* (1897) 2 Com.Cas. 189 at 193.
[98] *Druiff* v. *Lord Parker* (1868) L.R. 5 Eq. 131.
[99] See *Re International Contract Co.* (1872) 7 Ch.App. 485 (shares wrongly numbered in transfer).
[1] *Neill* v. *Midland Ry.* (1869) 17 W.R. 871.
[2] *Beale* v. *Kyte* [1907] 1 Ch. 564; *Wilson* v. *Wilson* [1969] 1 W.L.R. 1970; *Re Colebrook's Conveyances* [1972] 1 W.L.R. 1397.
[3] *Bold* v. *Hutchinson* (1856) 5 De G.M. & G. 558; *Maunsell* v. *Maunsell* (1877) 1 L.R.Ir. 529.
[4] Fines and Recoveries Act 1833, s.74.
[5] *Hall-Dare* v. *Hall-Dare* (1885) 31 Ch.D. 251; *Meeking* v. *Meeking* [1971] 1 Ch. 77.
[6] *Thomas Bates and Son Ltd.* v. *Wyndham's (Lingerie) Ltd.* [1981] 1 W.L.R. 505 (rent review clause).
[7] *Huddersfield Banking Co.* v. *Henry Lister & Son Ltd.* [1895] 2 Ch. 273; and see *Mullins* v. *Howell* (1879) 11 Ch.D. 763 (consent order rectified for unilateral mistake: but the order was made on an interlocutory application, where the rules are not so strict: see *Ainsworth* v. *Wilding* [1896] 1 Ch. 673 at 675, 679).
[8] *Allcard* v. *Walker* [1896] 2 Ch. 369 at 381.
[9] *Scott* v. *Frank F. Scott (London) Ltd.* [1940] Ch. 794.
[10] Companies Act 1985, s.14.

2. Voluntary settlements. Marriage settlements were early instances of instruments that were rectified.[11] Although a man who makes a voluntary settlement would not be compelled to alter his own grant,[12] he may himself obtain rectification by proving that the settlement does not represent his true intention: it is unnecessary for him to prove that it does not represent the true intention of the trustees, if there was no actual bargain between him and them.[13]

3. Wills. Formerly, short of fraud, there was no power to rectify a will[14]; the furthest the court could go was to omit spurious words.[15] Now, however, by statute, if a court is satisfied that a will is so expressed that it fails to carry out the intentions of the testator in consequence of a clerical error or failure to understand his instructions, the court may order that the will be rectified.[16] The action for rectification cannot, without the permission of the court, be commenced later than six months after the grant of probate.[17]

Section 4. Defences

1. Valid defences. Even if the foregoing requirements are satisfied, the court may still refuse to order rectification; for the remedy is equitable and discretionary.[18] Thus, it will not be granted to the prejudice of a bona fide purchaser for value without notice who takes an interest conferred by the instrument[19]; and laches or acquiescence will bar the claim.[20] Where rectification is sought of a voluntary settlement and one of the trustees objects, the court may in its discretion refuse rectification.[21] Further, it is too late to claim rectification of a contract if it is no longer capable of performance,[22] or if, after being construed by the court, it has been wholly performed under the judgment of the court.[23]

[11] See, *e.g. Thin* v. *Thin* (1650) 1 Rep.Ch. 162.
[12] On the evidence required where the settlement was preceded by marriage articles, see *Legg* v. *Goldwire* (1736) Cas.*t*.Talb. 20; **2 W. & T.L.C. 728**; *Bold* v. *Hutchinson* (1856) 5 De G.M. & G. 558; *Cogan* v. *Duffield* (1876) 2 Ch.D. 44.
[13] *Re Butlin's S.T.* [1976] Ch. 251.
[14] *Harter* v. *Harter* (1873) L.R. 3 P. & D. 11; *Collins* v. *Elstone* [1893] P. 1.
[15] *In b. Schott* [1901] P. 190; *Vaughan* v. *Clerk* (1902) 87 L.T. 144.
[16] Administration of Justice Act 1982, s.20(1), applying where the testator has died after 1982 (see ss.73(1), 76(11)).
[17] *Ibid.* s.20(2).
[18] See *ante*, p. 626.
[19] *Bell* v. *Cundall* (1750) Amb. 101; *Garrard* v. *Frankel* (1862) 30 Beav. 445; *Coates* v. *Kenna* (1873) 7 I.R.Eq 113; and see *Smith* v. *Jones* [1954] 1 W.L.R. 1089; *Thames Guaranty Ltd.* v. *Campbell* [1985] Q.B. 210 at 240, citing this passage.
[20] *Beale* v. *Kyte* [1907] 1 Ch. 564 (holding that time runs from discovery of the mistake); *McCausland* v. *Young* [1949] N.I. 49; *cf. Dormer* v. *Sherman* (1966) 110 S.J. 171 at 172.
[21] *Re Butlin's S.T.*, *supra* at p. 262 (rectification granted).
[22] *Borrowman* v. *Rossell* (1864) 16 C.B.(N.S.) 58.
[23] *Caird* v. *Moss* (1886) 33 Ch.D. 22.

2. Bad defences. It is no defence that the plaintiff[24] or his solicitor[25] was careless, or that the plaintiff, being a solicitor, drafted the instrument himself.[26] Similarly, the death of a party is no defence,[27] nor is the absence of any privity of contract between the parties[28] so that rectification may in appropriate cases be granted to[29] or ordered against[30] successors in title; nor is it a defence that a party to the transaction who will not be affected by the order is not before the court.[31] Further, rectification will not be refused merely because some fiscal advantage would accrue to one of the parties in consequence of the order[32]; and the decree may be obtained even where the sole purpose of seeking it is to secure to the parties a legitimate tax advantage which they intended to obtain at the time of execution of the document.[33] Further, the rule that equity will not grant relief against the non-execution of a power of appointment (as distinct from defective execution[34]) does not preclude rectification of a settlement so as to make it carry out an intended exercise of a power[35]; for rectification is an independent remedy.

Section 5. Effect of Order

1. Form of order. Where rectification is ordered, no new document need be executed; a copy of the order of the court may be indorsed on the instrument rectified, which will then operate accordingly.[36] The decree has retrospective force. The effect is not that the instrument continues to exist, though with a parol variation, but that "it is to be read as if it had been originally drawn in its rectified form,"[37] and will include any implied easements and other rights which its new form imports.[38] Thus, existing transactions which only the rectified instrument would have authorised become retrospectively valid.[39] But until rectification has been decreed, the instrument is binding as it stands; "so long as it remains uncorrected, it is no defence to say, that it does not truly ascertain the real contract of the parties."[40]

---

[24] *Monaghan County Council* v. *Vaughan* [1948] I.R. 306.
[25] *Weeds* v. *Blaney* (1977) 247 E.G. 211, where at p. 213 this sentence is cited with approval.
[26] *Ball* v. *Storie* (1823) 1 Sim. & St. 210.
[27] See *Johnson* v. *Bragge* [1901] 1 Ch. 28.
[28] *Shepheard* v. *Graham* [1947] N.Z.L.R. 654; and see *Van der Linde* v. *Van der Linde* [1947] Ch. 306 at 311.
[29] See *Boots the Chemist Ltd.* v. *Street* (1983) 268 E.G. 817.
[30] See *Equity & Law Life Assurance Society Ltd.* v. *Coltness Group Ltd.* (1983) 267 E.G. 949.
[31] *Wilson* v. *Wilson* [1969] 1 W.L.R. 1470 (declaration of trust by purchasers in transfer rectified in absence of vendor).
[32] *Re Colebrook's Conveyances* [1972] 1 W.L.R. 1397, distinguishing *Whiteside* v. *Whiteside* [1950] Ch. 65; *ante*, p. 627.
[33] *Re Slocock's W.T.* [1979] 1 All E.R. 358.
[34] *Ante*, p. 545.
[35] *Johnson* v. *Bragge, supra.*
[36] *White* v. *White* (1872) L.R. 15 Eq. 247; *Hanley* v. *Pearson* (1879) 13 Ch.D. 545.
[37] *Craddock Bros.* v. *Hunt* [1923] 2 Ch. 136 at 151, *per* Lord Sterndale M.R.; and see at p. 160.
[38] *Rice* v. *Dodds* (1969) 213 E.G. 759.
[39] *Earl of Malmesbury* v. *Countess of Malmesbury* (1862) 31 Beav. 407 at 418 (grant of leases).
[40] *Law* v. *Warren* (1843) Dr.t.Sugd. 31 at 41; *per* Sugden L.C.; but see *ante*, p. 626, as to past transactions.

Rectification of a contract and specific performance of the contract as rectified may be decreed together in the same action.[41]

2. Costs.   Although a plaintiff whose own carelessness gave rise to the mistake may be refused his costs of a successful action for rectification,[42] there is no rule of practice which requires the court to make no order as to costs in such a case.[43] Indeed, the court will only occasionally depart from the ordinary rule of practice whereby costs follow the outcome of the litigation. But where, for example, the defendant tries to take advantage of what he knew to be a mistake by resisting rectification, he may be ordered pay the costs notwithstanding the negligence of the plaintiff or his solicitor.[44]

---

[41] See *ante*, p. 604.
[42] As in *Harris* v. *Pepperell* (1875) L.R. 5 Eq. 1.
[43] *Weeds* v. *Blaney* (1977) 247 E.G. 211 at 213, treating *Harris* v. *Pepperell*, *supra*, at p. 5, as setting out "statements for the guidance of the court in its discretion."
[44] *Weeds* v. *Blaney*, *supra*.

CHAPTER 5

ACCOUNT

Section 1. Chancery Jurisdiction

1. Origin. At common law an action of account lay in certain cases[1]; but the procedure was very unsatisfactory, and when the Court of Chancery began to assume jurisdiction in matters of account, the remedy at law gradually fell into disuse.[2] The superiority of the equitable remedy arose mainly from the facts that the Court of Chancery could compel the defendant to make discovery on his oath, which the common law courts could not do, and that its machinery and administrative powers were better adapted for taking accounts than those of the common law courts. The jurisdiction of the Court of Chancery to order an account was of a twofold character.[3]

2. Account in aid of an equitable right. First, equity had an exclusive jurisdiction to order an account in aid of a purely equitable right. Thus a *cestui que trust* could obtain an account from his trustee, or a mortgagor from a mortgagee who had entered into possession[4]; and a remainderman could compel a tenant for life whose estate was granted to him without impeachment of waste to account for the proceeds of equitable waste committed by him.[5]

3. Account in aid of a legal right. Secondly, the Court of Chancery had a concurrent jurisdiction to order an account in certain cases in aid of a legal right. These cases appear to have been the following.

(a) *Principal and agent.* A principal could maintain a suit in equity for an account against his agent on the ground of the confidence reposed by the principal in the agent and the impossibility of discovering, except by the oath of the agent, how he had acted in the execution of his

[1] For the history of the action, see S. J. Stoljar (1964) 80 L.Q.R. 203.
[2] In *Godfrey* v. *Saunders* (1770) 3 Wils.K.B. 73, however, a plaintiff revived the common law action. He had waited fruitlessly for over 12 years for judgment in Chancery; in the King's Bench he obtained judgment within two years.
[3] See *London, Chatham & Dover Ry.* v. *South Eastern Ry.* [1892] 1 Ch. 120 at 140 (affirmed [1893] A.C. 429).
[4] For accounting on the footing of wilful default, see *ante*, pp. 284 (trustees), 409 (mortgagees).
[5] *Duke of Leeds* v. *Earl of Amherst* (1846) 2 Ph. 117; and see *post*, p. 680.

agency[6]; and the agent was also required to account for any secret profits he had made.[7] But normally an agent could not obtain an account against his principal, for an agent usually has all the knowledge requisite to support his rights and so requires no discovery, and he reposes no special confidence in his principal.[8] Equity would also decree an account against the infringer of a patent, copyright or trade mark, on the ground that the owner of the right might treat the infringer as his agent; but the owner could not claim both damages and an account of the profits, for "if you take an account of profits you condone the infringement."[9]

(b) *Mutual accounts.* Equity also assumed jurisdiction where there were mutual accounts between the plaintiff and the defendant, *i.e.* where it was not merely a case of the one party receiving money and paying it on account of the other, but where each of two parties had received and paid money on the other's account.[10]

(c) *Special complication.* Equity also entertained a suit for an account where there were circumstances of special complication rendering the taking of the account difficult at law.[11] But it was uncertain what measure of complication was necessary to give equity jurisdiction,[12] especially as the common law courts had a statutory power to refer matters of account to arbitration.[13]

(d) *Incidental to an injunction.* Equity had also jurisdiction to order an account in connection with its power of granting an injunction to prevent the violation of a legal right. Thus where the court granted an injunction to prevent legal waste, it might order the defendant to account for any profit derived from acts of waste already committed. But this jurisdiction existed only as incident to an injunction. If there was no power to grant an injunction, the Court of Chancery could not order an account of the profit made by the commission of a tort.[14]

4. Effect of Judicature Acts. Since the Judicature Act 1873, an action for an account can be brought in any case in which equity or the common law formerly had jurisdiction to order an account. The taking of partnership or other accounts is expressly assigned to the Chancery Division[15] and, except in simple cases,[16] if an account is claimed in the

---

[6] *Beaumont* v. *Boultbee* (1802) 7 Ves. 599; *Mackenzie* v. *Johnston* (1819) 4 Madd. 373.
[7] *Ante,* p. 251.
[8] *Padwick* v. *Stanley* (1852) 9 Hare 627.
[9] *Neilson* v. *Betts* (1871) L.R. 5 H.L. 1 at 22, *per* Lord Westbury; see Patents Act 1949, s.60; Patents Act 1977, s.61.
[10] *Phillips* v. *Phillips* (1852) 9 Hare 471.
[11] *O'Connor* v. *Spaight* (1804) 1 Sch. & Lef. 305.
[12] *Taff Vale Ry.* v. *Nixon* (1847) 1 H.L.C. 111; *South Eastern Ry.* v. *Martin* (1848) 2 Ph. 758; *Phillips* v. *Phillips* (1852) 9 Hare 471.
[13] Common Law Procedure Act 1854, s.3; see now S.C.A. 1981, s.68 (references to official and special referees and to masters); R.S.C., Ord. 36; and see *Re Taylor, Turpin* v. *Pain* (1890) 44 Ch.D. 128.
[14] *Jesus College* v. *Bloom* (1745) 3 Atk. 262; and see *Parrott* v. *Palmer* (1834) 3 My. & K. 632.
[15] See *ante,* p. 18.
[16] *York* v. *Stowers* [1883] W.N. 174.

Queen's Bench Division the case will be dealt with by an official referee[17] or transferred to the Chancery Division, which has suitable machinery for the purpose.[18] Accounts are often ordered on a claim by a *cestui que trust* against a trustee, by a beneficiary or creditor against an executor or administrator, by a mortgagor against a mortgagee, by a principal against an agent, and by one partner against another. But no account can be obtained by a customer against his banker, for the relation between them is in no sense fiduciary, and is merely that of debtor and creditor[19]; nor is the remedy available in respect of the performance of a public duty imposed by statute.[20]

5. Co-tenants

(a) *Background.*   Where land is held by several co-tenants they are all, as between themselves, entitled to possession of the whole. Hence there is no remedy in trespass against an occupying co-owner unless he has ousted or excluded the other or others.[21] There is no exclusion if one merely stays away, allowing the other to occupy a house[22] or take all the profits whether by way of rents, crops[23] or minerals.[24] Where one ousts the other or others, he will be liable for an occupation rent.[25] Where there is no ouster there is no such liability[26] in the absence of any contract to pay rent[27] or other assumption of liability.[28] If a co-tenant was dissatisfied with the situation, his remedy was to apply to the court for an order compelling partition. From 1868 the court was empowered, in the alternative, to order a sale of the jointly-owned land.[29]

(b) *Accounting.*   A statute of 1705[30] gave a joint tenant or tenant in common at law a right to an account against the other co-owners where they had taken more than their fair share of the rents and profits of the land.[31] Courts of equity would direct similar inquiries especially in the case of beneficiaries under trusts. More significantly, in partition actions in which courts of equity had exclusive jurisdiction, the court would

---

[17] R.S.C., Ord. 36, r. 1.
[18] *Leslie* v. *Clifford* (1884) 50 L.T. 590.
[19] *Foley* v. *Hill* (1848) 2 H.L.C. 28.
[20] *Swain* v. *The Law Society* [1983] 1 A.C. 598.
[21] *Jacobs* v. *Seward* (1872) L.R. 5 H.L.; *Glyn* v. *Howell* [1909] 1 Ch. 666 (where there was an exclusion from one part of a mine but not the coalface).
[22] *M'Mahon* v. *Burchell* (1846) 2 Ph. 127; 1 Coop.t.Cott. 457.
[23] *Jacobs* v. *Seward, supra.*
[24] *Job* v. *Potton* (1875) L.R. 20 Eq. 84; *Glyn* v. *Howell, supra.*
[25] See *Pascoe* v. *Swan* (1859) 27 Beav. 508.
[26] *M'Mahon* v. *Burchell, supra*; *Jones (A.E.)* v. *Jones (F.W.)* [1977] 1 W.L.R. 438 (where, additionally, the claim was defeated by equitable estoppel).
[27] See *Kennedy* v. *De Trafford* [1897] A.C. 180 at 191 (agency).
[28] See *M'Mahon* v. *Burchell, supra*, at p. 137.
[29] Partition Acts 1868 and 1876.
[30] Administration of Justice Act 1705, s.27, repealed by L.P.(Am) Act 1924, s.10 and 10th Sched.
[31] See *Sturton* v. *Richardson* (1844) 13 M. & W. 17; *Job* v. *Potton, supra.*

inquire into the position between the co-owners so as to adjust accounts between them consequent on making an order for partition or sale.[32] If it were found that one party was in occupation to the exclusion of the other, the court would direct an inquiry as to the occupation rent to be paid unless it were shown that the party not in occupation could have enjoyed the right to occupy but chose not to do so voluntarily.[33] Conversely, if the occupier has expended money in improvements or repairs, the court will inquire into the amount of the increased value as a result of such expenditure and give him credit for it.[34] The increased value is a charge on the land to be paid out of the proceeds before division, but liability for an occupation rent is personal to the occupying co-owner and is not chargeable on the purchaser or mortgagee of his share.[35] The 1925 legislation abolished partition actions and imposed a trust for sale on all forms of co-ownership.[36] A co-owner who wishes to terminate the joint tenancy may seek an order for sale[37] and as ancillary to the sale the court can direct the same type of accounts as formerly in a partition action.

(c) Joint occupation. The commonest case in modern times where questions between co-owners arise is where a house is bought with the aid of a mortgage as a home for two parties to live in together and later the relationship breaks up with one party leaving the other in the house. Save as mentioned below,[38] the rules are the same whether the parties are married or not.

(1) ISSUES.   The principal issue in most cases is to determine the size of the respective shares of the parties in the property.[39] Then comes the question whether and when the property is to be sold.[40] Finally there is the equitable accounting between the parties in relation to the period following the separation.

(2) EQUITABLE ACCOUNTING.   In the taking of accounts a party left in sole occupation may have to be debited with an occupation rent but credited with mortgage instalments which he has paid or with the increase in the sale price produced by money he has spent on repairs and decorations. "These are but examples of the way in which the balance is to be struck."[41] Such debits and credits do not alter the *shares* in the property, but operate to adjust the *sums* ultimately payable on sale.[42] The provision for occupation rent and mortgage

---

[32] See Daniell's Chancery Practice (8th ed., 1914, reprinted 1985), pp. 1170 *et seq.*
[33] See *Dennis* v. *McDonald* [1982] Fam. 63 at 70, 71; *M'Mahon* v. *Burchell* (1846) 1 Coop.*t.*Cott. 457 at 467–469.
[34] *Leigh* v. *Dickeson* (1884) 15 Q.B.D. 60 at 67; *Re Jones, Farrington* v. *Foster* [1893] 2 Ch. 461 (partition); *Re Cook's Mortgage* [1896] 1 Ch. 923 (sale).
[35] *Hill* v. *Hickin* [1897] 2 Ch. 579.
[36] See *ante*, pp. 263, 264.
[37] Under L.P.A. 1925, s.30.
[38] *Post*, p. 642.
[39] See *ante*, pp. 184 *et seq.*
[40] See *ante*, p. 237.
[41] *Bernard* v. *Josephs* [1982] Ch. 391 at 405, *per* Griffiths L.J.
[42] *Bernard* v. *Josephs, supra,* at p. 405.

payments and the relationship between them have been the subject of a number of decisions. From those one can say that there are no rigid rules, but rules of convenience aimed at producing a fair result and avoiding expensive and protracted inquiries.

(3) OCCUPATION RENT.   If one party ousts the other either directly or constructively as a result of violence or other intolerable behaviour, the party remaining will be liable for an occupation rent.[43] In a clear case of ouster it was said that this liability was "an exception from the general rule that each tenant in common has the right of occupation of the property... while if one of them occupies that property to the exclusion of the other that does not give rise to any right of compensation."[44] That dictum would appear to be too restrictive. In the first place, in the older cases on taking accounts, as distinct from actions for trespass, the test has been whether the house is open to the absent tenants rather than whether they have been ousted from it.[45] In most cases of break down of cohabitation it is unrealistic to say that the absent party is free to return.[46] Secondly, other cases have charged the party remaining without investigating the conduct which led to the departure of the other.[47] Thirdly, in any event, a rent[48] or payment of interest[49] may be charged as a term of postponing an order for sale.[50]

(4) ASSESSMENT OF RENT.   Where an occupation rent has to be assessed, the court has adopted that which would be fixed as a fair rent by the rent officer.[51] Although an annual assessment may be refused on grounds of cost and inconvenience,[52] there seems to be no objection in principle to the making (where appropriate) of different orders in respect of different periods of occupation. The purpose to which the occupying party is to put the property, e.g. to house the children of the family, is irrelevant to the assessment, for the payment is in the nature of compensation by a trustee to a beneficiary.[53]

(5) MORTGAGE REPAYMENTS.   Where the party who stays continues to pay mortgage instalments, he is entitled in the ultimate distribution of the proceeds of sale to credit for the appropriate proportion (according to the other party's interest) of the mortgage payments since the separation.[54] He is indubitably entitled to them so far as they consist of capital. In some cases he has been permitted to take credit for the

---

[43] *Dennis* v. *McDonald* [1982] Fam. 63.
[44] *Dennis* v. *McDonald, supra,* at p. 80, C.A., *per* Sir John Arnold P.
[45] *M'Mahon* v. *Burchell* (1846) 2 Ph. 127.
[46] See the inquiries directed in *Shinh* v. *Shinh* [1977] 1 All E.R. 97.
[47] *Leake* v. *Bruzzi* [1974] 1 W.L.R. 1528; *Suttill* v. *Graham* [1977] 1 W.L.R. 819. *Contra Cracknell* v. *Cracknell* [1971] P. 356 at 362, 363.
[48] See *Suttill* v. *Graham, supra,* at p. 823.
[49] *Re Gorman (a bankrupt)* [1990] 1 W.L.R. 616 at 629, 630.
[50] See J. Martin [1982] Conv. 305.
[51] *Dennis* v. *McDonald* [1982] Fam. 63.
[52] *Ibid.,* at p. 82.
[53] *Ibid.,* at pp. 80, 81.
[54] See *Re Gorman (a bankrupt), supra,* at p. 627.

interest element as well.[55] This can be justified on the principle that he who discharges another's secured obligation (which includes the interest) is entitled to be repaid out of the security the amount of the sum or sums paid by him.[56] In other cases he has been refused credit for the interest element unless he submitted to being charged an occupation rent over the relevant period.[57] This is a rule of convenience, not of law.[58] Further, where credit is to be given for interest and a debit made for rent, and the amounts of the credit and debit would be broadly the same, the court may do rough justice by refusing an account of either.[59]

(6) RENTS RECEIVED. If the party who stays in occupation receives rent from the house, *e.g.* by letting rooms, he must when claiming credit for the interest paid also give credit for a due proportion of the rents received by him[60]; alternatively, he may be regarded as having paid half the mortgage instalments out of the other party's resources by reason of his receipt of rent, which leads to the simple solution that he will neither be credited with the mortgage interest nor debited with the rents.[61]

(7) SPOUSES. As has been noted, in general the rules are the same for joint occupiers whether they are married or not. There are three points of difference. First, if a spouse remains in a house owned by the other, he cannot be charged with mesne profits or an occupation rent so long as the marriage subsists and there has been no order to remove him.[62] Thereafter he will be liable for mesne profits.[63] Secondly, property adjustment orders may be made under the Matrimonial Causes Act 1973 varying or abrogating the parties' rights of property.[64] Thirdly, applications may be made under section 17 of the Married Women's Property Act 1882, but this is merely procedural. Even though under that section no sale would necessarily be ordered, there would not be any different accounting than if the proceedings had been under section 30 of the Law of Property Act 1925.[65]

6. Minors A remedy of account is available against a person who takes possession of the land of a minor; the court treats him as a bailiff and not as a trespasser or adverse possessor.[66] He is thus accountable for a proper occupation rent less the cost of repairs and less a

---

[55] *Davis* v. *Vale* [1971] 1 W.L.R. 1022; *Cracknell* v. *Cracknell* [1971] P. 356.
[56] See *Cowcher* v. *Cowcher* [1972] 1 W.L.R. 425 at 432, 433; *Re Gorman (a bankrupt)* [1990] 1 W.L.R. 616 at 626, 627.
[57] *Leake* v. *Bruzzi* [1974] 1 W.L.R. 1528; *Suttill* v. *Graham* [1977] 1 W.L.R. 819; and see *Bernard* v. *Josephs* [1982] Ch. 391 at 401.
[58] *Re Gorman (a bankrupt)* [1990] 1 W.L.R. 616 at 626.
[59] *Dennis* v. *McDonald* [1982] Fam. 63 at 74, 75 (affd. *ibid.* 79 *et seq.*).
[60] *Davis* v. *Vale* [1971] 1 W.L.R. 1022.
[61] *Coley* v. *Coley* (1975) 5 Fam.Law 195, also holding that it would be inequitable to order accounts on the ground of delay.
[62] *Morris* v. *Tarrant* [1971] 2 Q.B. 143.
[63] *Ibid.*
[64] *Ante*, p. 245.
[65] *Dennis* v. *McDonald* [1982] Fam. 63 at 72 (affd. *ibid.*).
[66] *Howard* v. *Earl of Shrewsbury* (1874) L.R. 17 Eq. 378; *Re Hobbs* (1887) 36 Ch.D. 553.

reasonable allowance for maintaining the minor if residing with him.[67] These are exceptional cases. Normally the land of a minor will be in the control of personal representatives or express trustees accountable as such.

Section 2. Defences to an Action for an Account

1. Account stated

(a) *Defence.* It is ordinarily a good defence to an action for an account that the parties have already in writing stated and adjusted the items of the account and struck the balance; and the case is *a fortiori* if the account has been settled by payment.

(b) *Liberty to surcharge and falsify.* If there has been any mistake, accident or fraud by which the account stated is in truth vitiated and the balance incorrectly fixed, equity will not suffer the account to be conclusive upon the parties; in cases of fraud or of serious errors, equity will direct the account to be opened and taken afresh, and in other cases the plaintiff will be given liberty to "surcharge and falsify." The effect of the liberty to surcharge and falsify is to leave the account in full force as a stated or settled account, except so far as it can be impugned by the plaintiff, on whom lies the burden of proving errors and mistakes.[68] The showing of an omission for which credit ought to be given is a surcharge; proof that a purported payment is wrongly inserted is a falsification. In addition, the court has a statutory power to reopen extortionate credit bargains,[69] and this jurisdiction would not be affected by the existence of a settled account.

(c) *Setting up settled accounts.* Where an order directs an account without referring to settled accounts, the accounting party may set up any settled accounts even though the order does not direct that settled accounts shall not be disturbed, and the opposite party may impeach these accounts even though the order does not expressly give him liberty to do so.[70]

2. Lapse of time. Whether the Limitation Act 1939 applied to equitable, as well as common law, actions of account is uncertain[71]: if it did not, the six-year period for common law claims would probably have

---

[67] *Re Howlett* [1949] Ch. 767.
[68] *Pitt* v. *Cholmondeley* (1754) 2 Ves.Sen. 565.
[69] See *ante*, p. 561.
[70] *Holgate* v. *Shutt* (1884) 28 Ch.D. 111.
[71] See Limitation Act 1939, s.2(2), (7); *Poole Corporation* v. *Moody* [1945] K.B. 350; *Tito* v. *Waddell (No. 2)* [1977] Ch. 106 at 250, 251.

been applied by analogy to equitable claims.[72] The Limitation Act 1980 applies to all actions of account,[73] and an action for an account cannot now be brought after the expiration of any time limit under the Act which bars the claim which is the basis of the duty to account.[74]

---

[72] For the application of the Act by analogy see *ante*, p. 34.
[73] See Limitation Act 1980, ss.23 and 36(1) (which does not except claims to an account from the general operation of the Act): for a hesitant view to the contrary, see *Att.-Gen.* v. *Cocke* [1988] Ch. 414 at 420.
[74] Limitation Act 1980, s.23.

CHAPTER 6

INJUNCTION

Section 1. Nature and Jurisdiction

1. Nature. An injunction is an order of the court directing a party to the proceedings to do or refrain from doing a specified act. It is granted in cases in which monetary compensation affords an inadequate remedy to an injured party. Thus in one old case the plaintiffs had been annoyed by the daily ringing of a nearby church bell at 5 a.m. The parson, churchwardens and others on behalf of the parish agreed to stop the ringing of the five o'clock bell during the lives of the plaintiffs if they provided the church with a new cupola, clock and bell; and when the bell was rung in breach of this agreement, the court restrained it by injunction.[1]

2. Types of injunction

(a) *Prohibitory or mandatory.* An injunction restraining the doing or continuance of some wrongful act is called *prohibitory* or *restrictive*. An injunction to restrain the continuance of some wrongful omission is called *mandatory*. Prohibitory injunctions are far more common than mandatory. Indeed, owing to doubts as to the jurisdiction to grant mandatory injunctions, until late in the nineteenth century all injunctions were couched in prohibitive form.[2] Thus a court which wished to secure the removal of buildings wrongfully erected formerly used to order the defendant not to allow them to remain on the land, a form of order which seems strange in a jurisdiction which traditionally looks to the substance rather than the form. Now, however, a

---

[1] *Martin* v. *Nutkin* (1725) 2 P.Wms. 266 (probably the last injunction granted by Lord Macclesfield L.C. before his disgrace).
[2] See the convoluted order made by Lord Eldon L.C. in *Lane* v. *Newdigate* (1804) 10 Ves. 192 (on which see the astringent comments of Lord Brougham L.C. in *Blakemore* v. *The Glamorganshire Canal Navigation* (1832) 2 Myl. & K. 155 at 183, 186); and see generally *Smith* v. *Smith* (1875) L.R. 20 Eq. 500 at 504.

mandatory injunction is made in a positive form, ordering some act to be done.[3]

(b) *Perpetual or interlocutory.* A perpetual (or final) injunction is granted only after the plaintiff has established his right and the actual or threatened infringement of it by the defendant. An interlocutory (or interim) injunction, on the other hand, is granted before the trial of an action; its object is to keep matters *in statu quo* until the question at issue between the parties can be determined. Accordingly, the plaintiff may obtain it without making out a case which will necessarily entitle him to a perpetual injunction. A perpetual injunction is so called because it is granted at the final determination of the parties' rights and not because it will necessarily operate for ever. For instance, a perpetual injunction may be granted so as to continue only during the currency of a lease.[4]

(c) *Common or special.* Before 1875, the Court of Chancery might grant an injunction restraining a person from proceeding in the common law courts or from executing a judgment obtained there.[5] Such injunctions were known as *common* injunctions, and like all injunctions they were directed not to the court but to the parties to the proceedings,[6] in accordance with the principle that equity acts *in personam.*[7] An injunction granted to give effect to an equitable right, or to provide an additional remedy in aid of rights enforceable at common law, was known as a *special* injunction. With the fusion of the administration of law and equity, common injunctions were no longer required and were abolished.[8] As all injunctions are now technically "special," the terms have dropped out of use.

3. Jurisdiction. Despite early attempts,[9] the common law courts failed to add the injunction to their judicial armoury, so that the Chancellor had to come to the aid of those whose wrongs could not be adequately redressed by damages. This often necessitated concurrent proceedings, in the common law courts to establish the right, and in the Court of Chancery to obtain the remedy. The Common Law Procedure Act 1854[10] went some way towards meeting this defect by empowering the common law courts to grant injunctions in certain cases; but in 1875 the situation was radically altered when the courts were amalgamated and the power to grant injunctions was conferred on all Divisions of the

---

[3] *Jackson* v. *Normanby Brick Co.* [1899] 1 Ch. 438.
[4] See *Moore* v. *Ullcoats Mining Co. Ltd.* [1908] 1 Ch. 575 at 585; *Jones* v. *Chappell* (1875) L.R. 20 Eq. 539 at 544 (weekly tenant).
[5] See *ante*, p. 12, for the struggle between the Chancellor and the common law courts over common injunctions.
[6] See *Re Connolly Bros. Ltd.* [1911] 1 Ch. 731.
[7] See *ante*, p. 41.
[8] See J.A. 1925, s.41, replacing J.A. 1873, s.24(5). s.41 was repealed by S.C.A. 1981, s.151(4) and Sched. 7, but was not re-enacted in that statute.
[9] See 2 Pollock and Maitland's *History of English Law* (2nd ed., 1898), pp. 595, 596. And see *Goodeson* v. *Gallatin* (1771) 2 Dick. 455; *post*, p. 679.
[10] ss.79, 82.

High Court.[11] But although it has been expressly enacted that interlocutory injunctions may be granted "in all cases in which it appears to the court to be just or convenient so to do,"[12] and this rule extends to perpetual injunctions,[13] the principles on which the court acts have not been altered[14]; the plaintiff must still establish some legal or equitable right or interest before he can obtain an injunction.[15] This requirement has, however, been widely interpreted. Thus injunctions may be granted in aid of other orders of the court,[16] *e.g.* for discovery.[17] Further, a police officer has been granted an injunction to prevent the dissipation of identifiable money alleged to have been procured by fraud.[18] The basis is that the officer has a duty to recover stolen property.[19] There is, accordingly, no jurisdiction to grant an injunction to the police freezing an accused person's assets not shown to be the subject of a crime as security for a possible compensation order.[20] Similarly, where the right is one cognisable only by ecclesiastical law, the court cannot grant an injunction to restrain a breach of it.[21]

In actions within its jurisdiction a county court may also grant injunctions.[22]

Section 2. General Rules Relating to Injunctions

Perpetual and interlocutory injunctions must be considered separately.

A. Perpetual Injunctions

1. Damages an insufficient remedy. "The very first principle of injunction law is that prima facie you do not obtain injunctions to restrain actionable wrongs for which damages are the proper remedy."[23] Thus no injunction will be granted where an illegal act has been done in the past but there is no intention of repeating it,[24] or no scope for

---

[11] See J.A. 1925, ss.37, 38, replacing J.A. 1873, s.24(1),(2). ss.37 and 38 were repealed by S.C.A. 1981, s.151(4) and Sched. 7, but were not replaced by that Act.
[12] S.C.A. 1981, s.37(1), replacing J.A. 1925, s.45(1), which itself replaced J.A. 1873, s.25(8).
[13] *North London Ry.* v. *Great Northern Ry.* (1883) 11 Q.B.D. 30 at 32, 33; *Beddow* v. *Beddow* (1878) 9 Ch.D. 89 at 93.
[14] *Day* v. *Brownrigg* (1878) 10 Ch.D. 294 at 307.
[15] *Day* v. *Brownrigg* (1878) 10 Ch.D. 294, *post*, pp. 648, 649.
[16] *Bayer A.G.* v. *Winter* [1986] 1 W.L.R. 497; *Re Oriental Credit Ltd.* [1988] Ch. 204.
[17] *Bayer A.G.* v. *Winter, supra.*
[18] *Chief Constable of Kent* v. *V.* [1983] Q.B. 34; and see *West Mercia Constabulary* v. *Wagener* [1982] 1 W.L.R. 127.
[19] See *Chief Constable of Hampshire* v. *A. Ltd.* [1985] Q.B. 132 at 136, 137, 139.
[20] *Chief Constable of Hampshire* v. *A. Ltd.* [1985] Q.B. 132; *Chief Constable of Leicestershire* v. *M.* [1989] 1 W.L.R. 20.
[21] *Att.-Gen.* v. *Dean and Chapter of Ripon Cathedral* [1945] Ch. 239 (failure to hold "full choral services" in the cathedral).
[22] See *ante*, p. 21.
[23] *London and Blackwall Ry.* v. *Cross* (1886) 31 Ch.D. 354 at 369, *per* Lindley L.J. (a comma after "wrongs" in the original has been deleted as obscuring the sense).
[24] See *post*, pp. 653, 654.

repeating it,[25] or where the injury can be adequately compensated by money.[26] But an injunction may be granted if an award of damages would be useless, *e.g.* because the defendant is a pauper,[27] and many wrongs, such as continuing nuisances[28] or infringements of trade marks,[29] demand more adequate relief than money.[30] Moreover, a party to a contract has a right to its performance and not merely to compensation for breach,[31] and hence an injunction will be granted to restrain breaches of negative contracts.[32] If, however, the parties have specified a sum as liquidated damages[33] for breach of a negative contract, the plaintiff cannot both recover the sum and claim an injunction.[34]

2. Plaintiff must establish right

A perpetual injunction is granted only when the party who seeks it has a cause of action (which includes statutory as well as private rights of action[35]) justiciable before the court[36]; and, in order to obtain the injunction, he must show either that there is an actual or threatened injury to some legal or equitable right of his or that the other party has behaved, or threatened to behave, in an unconscionable[37] manner.[38] The jurisdiction to restrain foreign proceedings is wider.[38a]

(a) *No injunction to remedy mere inconvenience*

(1) SUFFICIENT INTEREST.   In order to obtain an injunction, and indeed any equitable relief, "the Plaintiff must show some property, right, or interest, in the subject-matter of his complaint."[39] Thus in *Day* v. *Brownrigg*[40] the court refused to grant an injunction to prevent the

---

[25] *Desk Advertising Co. Ltd.* v. *Société Civile De Participations Du Group S.T. Dupont* (1973) 117 S.J. 483.
[26] *Wood* v. *Sutcliffe* (1851) 2 Sim.(N.S.) 163; *Garden Cottage Foods Ltd.* v. *Milk Marketing Board* [1984] A.C. 130.
[27] *Hodgson* v. *Duce* (1856) 2 Jur.(N.S.) 1014.
[28] *Martin* v. *Nutkin* (1725) 2 P.Wms. 266; *ante*, p. 645. And see *Pride of Derby and Derbyshire Angling Association Ltd.* v. *British Celanese Ltd.* [1953] Ch. 149 at 181.
[29] See *post*, p. 680.
[30] See *Lumley* v. *Wagner* (1825) 1 De G.M. & G. 604 at 616.
[31] *Lumley* v. *Wagner, supra*, at p. 619; *National Provincial Bank of England* v. *Marshall* (1888) 40 Ch.D. 112. *Cf. Ahmed Angullia bin Hadjee Mohamed Salleh Angullia* v. *Estate and Trust Agencies (1927) Ltd.* [1938] A.C. 624; *ante*, p. 323. See also *ante*, p. 541.
[32] *Lumley* v. *Wagner* (1852) 1 De. G.M. & G. 604; *post*, p. 676.
[33] See *ante*, p. 538.
[34] *Sainter* v. *Ferguson* (1849) 1 Mac. & G. 286. *Cf. Aspden* v. *Seddon* (1875) 10 Ch.App. 394.
[35] *Securities and Investment Board* v. *Pantell S.A.* [1989] 3 W.L.R. 698.
[36] *Siskina (Owners of cargo lately laden on board)* v. *Distos Compania Naviera S.A.* [1979] A.C. 210; *ante*, p. 647. For an exception in the case of interim injunctions, see *post*, p. 670.
[37] See *British Airways Board* v. *Laker Airways Ltd.* [1985] A.C. 58 at 81.
[38] *South Carolina Insurance Co.* v. *Assurantie Maatschappij "De Zeven Provincien" N.V.* [1987] A.C. 24 at 40.
[38a] *Ibid.* at pp. 40, 44, 45. See *post*, p. 687.
[39] *Maxwell* v. *Hogg* (1867) 2 Ch.App. 307 at 311, *per* Turner L.J.; and see *Emperor of Austria* v. *Day* (1861) 3 De G.F. & J. 217 (*post*, p. 651).
[40] (1878) 10 Ch.D. 294. And see *Street* v. *Union Bank of Spain and England* (1885) 30 Ch.D. 156 (identical telegraphic addresses).

defendant from calling his house by the same name as the plaintiff's house, although the parties lived next door to each other and the name had been used by the plaintiff for 60 years; there is no legal or equitable right to the exclusive use of the name of a private residence. "You must have in our law injury as well as damage ... If a man erects a wall on his own property and thereby destroys the view from the house of the Plaintiff he may damage him to an enormous extent. He may destroy three-fourths of the value of the house, but still, if he has the right to erect the wall, the mere fact of thereby causing damage to the Plaintiff does not give the Plaintiff a right of action."[41] So also, a public authority will not be restrained at the suit of a foreign supplier from pursuing a "Buy British" policy[42]; and a woman will not be restrained from undergoing a lawful abortion at the suit of her husband[43] or the putative father of the child she is carrying.[44]

(2) SPECIAL DAMAGE. Where special damage is an essential ingredient of the cause of action, as in the tort of slander of title, no injunction will be granted in the absence of proof of special damage. Thus in *White* v. *Mellin*[45] the plaintiff was refused an injunction to restrain the defendant from affixing a label vaunting the superiority of his own goods when he retailed the plaintiff's goods. But where a plaintiff has established his right and its infringement, he may obtain an injunction even though he has suffered no damage.[46]

(b) *Breach of statutory duty*

(1) GENERAL. An injunction will not be granted merely[47] to compel the performance of positive statutory duties.[48] Further, where a statute imposes a new and particular negative duty and provides a remedy for its infringement, *e.g.* a fine, a person aggrieved by its breach is not entitled to enjoin the wrongdoer[49] unless property rights of his have been invaded.[50] There are, however, two ways in which breaches of

---

[41] *Day* v. *Brownrigg* (1878) 10 Ch.D. 294 at 304, *per* Jessel M.R. *Cf. Ingram* v. *Morecraft* (1863) 33 Beav. 49. The proprietors of the Albert Hall failed to enjoin Mr. Albert Edward Hall from using for his small orchestra in London the name "The Albert Hall Orchestra": *Corporation of the Hall of Arts and Sciences* v. *Hall* (1934) 50 T.L.R. 518.

[42] *Honeywell Information Systems Ltd.* v. *Anglian Water Authority, The Times*, June 30, 1976 (computer equipment).

[43] *Paton* v. *British Pregnancy Advisory Service Trustees* [1979] Q.B. 276.

[44] *C.* v. *S.* [1988] Q.B. 135 (held at first instance that foetus had no *locus standi*; no decision on *locus standi* of foetus or father in C.A.).

[45] [1895] A.C. 154.

[46] *Jones* v. *Llanrwst U.D.C.* [1911] 1 Ch. 393 at 402 (pollution of river); *Kemp* v. *Sober* (1851) 1 Sim.(N.S.) 517 at 520.

[47] See *Pride of Derby and Derbyshire Angling Association Ltd.* v. *British Celanese Ltd.* [1953] Ch. 149.

[48] *Glossop* v. *Heston and Isleworth Local Board* (1879) 12 Ch.D. 102; *Att.-Gen.* v. *Clerkenwell Vestry* [1891] 3 Ch. 527.

[49] *Institute of Patent Agents* v. *Lockwood* [1894] A.C. 347; *Devonport Corporation* v. *Tozer* [1903] 1 Ch. 759; *Thorne* v. *British Broadcasting Corporation* [1967] 1 W.L.R. 1104 (Race Relations Act 1965); *Gouriet* v. *Att.-Gen.* [1978] A.C. 628; *Ex p. Island Records Ltd.* [1978] Ch. 122; *Ashby* v. *Ebdon* [1985] Ch. 394; *C.B.S. Songs Ltd.* v. *Amstrad Consumer Electronics plc* [1988] Ch. 61, affd. [1988] A.C. 1013.

[50] *Cooper* v. *Whittingham* (1880) 15 Ch.D. 501; *Stevens* v. *Chown* [1901] 1 Ch. 894.

statutory duty may be restrained by injunction, one developed judicially and the other of statutory origin. These will now be considered.

(2) ATTORNEY-GENERAL. The Attorney-General,[51] as the upholder of public rights,[52] may sue for an injunction if the statutory penalty is shown to be inadequate,[53] if irremediable damage is threatened,[54] or if the enforcement of the penalty would otherwise be too dilatory for the gravity of the case.[55] Such actions are often brought as "relator" actions, whereby the Attorney-General sues "on the relation" (*i.e.* at the suggestion) of some person, who need not have any interest in the subject-matter of the action.[56] Thus in *Att.-Gen.* v. *Sharp*,[57] an injunction was granted against an omnibus proprietor who had been refused a licence but nevertheless found it profitable to run his omnibuses and pay the prescribed fines almost daily; and the same principle was applied where the somewhat cumbrous statutory machinery for enforcing town and country planning control proved ineffective.[58] Where, moreover, the statute merely re-enacts a liability existing at common law but provides a special form of remedy, the court may still restrain a breach by injunction unless the language of the statute necessarily excludes former remedies.[59] If the Attorney-General refuses or delays lending his name to the proceedings, the complainant has no residual right to bring the action himself.[60]

(3) LOCAL AUTHORITIES. Local authorities have by statute power to institute civil proceedings in their own name (*i.e.* without the intervention of the Attorney-General) where they consider it expedient for the promotion or protection of the interests of the inhabitants of their area.[61] Thus injunctions have been granted at the instance of local authorities to restrain breaches of the laws relating to Sunday trading,[62] nuisances by noise,[63] town and country planning[64] and preservation of trees,[65] and they will not be refused on the ground that proceedings in

---

[51] And see *post*, p. 681.
[52] See *Att.-Gen.* v. *Harris* [1961] 1 Q.B. 74 (two Manchester flower sellers with 237 convictions between them).
[53] *Att.-Gen.* v. *Ashborne Recreation Ground Co.* [1903] 1 Ch. 101; *Att.-Gen.* v. *Sharp* [1931] 1 Ch. 121. For binding over as an alternative remedy, see (1961) 77 L.Q.R. 26 (C.K.A.).
[54] *Att.-Gen.* v. *Melville Construction Co. Ltd.* (1968) 20 P. & C.R. 131 (felling protected trees: interlocutory injunction).
[55] *Att.-Gen.* v. *Chaudry* [1971] 1 W.L.R. 1614 (fire risk in hotel).
[56] *Att.-Gen.* v. *Crayford U.D.C.* [1962] Ch. 575 at 585, 596.
[57] [1931] 1 Ch. 121.
[58] *Att.-Gen.* v. *Bastow* [1957] 1 Q.B. 514; *Att.-Gen.* v. *Smith* [1958] 2 Q.B. 173; *Att.-Gen.* v. *Morris* (1973) 227 E.G. 991. And see *Att.-Gen.* v. *Wellingborough U.D.C.* (1974) 72 L.G.R. 507 (Rivers (Prevention of Pollution) Act 1951).
[59] *Stevens* v. *Chown* [1901] 1 Ch. 894 (not a relator action).
[60] *Gouriet* v. *Att.-Gen.* [1978] A.C. 628 disapproving *Att.-Gen. ex rel. McWhirter* v. *Independent Broadcasting Authority* [1973] Q.B. 629 at 649. See generally D. Feldman (1979) 42 M.L.R. 369.
[61] Local Government Act 1972, s.222.
[62] *Stafford B.C.* v. *Elkenford Ltd.* [1977] 1 W.L.R. 324; *Stoke-on-Trent City Council* v. *B. & Q. (Retail) Ltd.* [1984] A.C. 754.
[63] *Hammersmith L.B.C.* v. *Magnum Automated Forecourts Ltd.* [1978] 1 W.L.R. 50.
[64] *Westminster City Council* v. *Jones* (1981) 80 L.G.R. 241.
[65] *Kent County Council* v. *Batchelor (No. 2)* [1979] 1 W.L.R. 213 (motion to discharge injunction).

relation to the same matter are pending in other courts.[66] But, to obtain an injunction, the authority must show that the defendant is, not merely breaking the law, but deliberately and flagrantly flouting it.[67]

(c) *Quia timet*

(1) THE PRINCIPLE. Although the plaintiff must establish his right, he may be entitled to an injunction even though an infringement has not taken place but is merely feared or threatened[68]; for "preventing justice excelleth punishing justice."[69] This class of action, known as *quia timet*, has long been established,[70] but the plaintiff must establish a strong case; "no one can obtain a quia timet order by merely saying 'Timeo.' "[71] He must prove that there is an imminent[72] danger[73] of very substantial damage,[74] or further damage,[75] *e.g.* by showing that the threatened act "is attended with extreme Probability of irreparable Injury to the Property of the Plaintiffs, including also Danger to their existence."[76] A *quia timet* injunction may be granted to restrain an anticipated breach of statutory duty.[77]

(2) OPERATION OF THE PRINCIPLE. For example, in *Att.-Gen.* v. *Nottingham Corporation*[78] the court refused to grant an injunction against a corporation which wished to erect a smallpox hospital within 50 feet of dwelling-houses as there was no proof of "actual and real danger—a strong probability, almost amounting to moral certainty, that if the hospital be established, it will be an actionable nuisance."[79] Again, an injunction may be refused if the defendant is a responsible body which offers an assurance to make every effort to suppress the threatened nuisance.[80] But in *Emperor of Austria* v. *Day*,[81] the manufacture of a spurious issue of foreign banknotes was restrained, as likely to cause damage to the property of the foreign sovereign and his

---

[66] *Stafford B.C.* v. *Elkenford Ltd.*, *supra* (appeal pending against conviction); *Hammersmith L.B.C.* v. *Magnum Automated Forecourts Ltd.*, *supra* (appeal pending against abatement notice).

[67] *Stafford B.C.* v. *Elkenford Ltd.*, *supra*, at p. 330; *Stoke-on-Trent City Council* v. *B. & Q. (Retail) Ltd.*, *supra*, at pp. 767, 776.

[68] See *Lord Cowley* v. *Byas* (1877) 5 Ch.D. 944.

[69] 2 Co.Inst.299, cited in *Graigola Merthyr Co. Ltd.* v. *Swansea Corporation* [1928] Ch. 235 at 242 (affirmed [1929] A.C. 344).

[70] *Att.-Gen.* v. *Long Eaton U.D.C.* [1915] 1 Ch. 124 at 127. See Holdsworth, *H.E.L.*, Vol. 2, p. 344, note 6, for remedies *quia timet* at common law.

[71] *Att.-Gen. for the Dominion of Canada* v. *Ritchie Contracting and Supply Co. Ltd.* [1919] A.C. 999 at 1005, *per* Lord Dunedin.

[72] See *Hooper* v. *Rogers* [1975] Ch. 43 at 49, 50 (damages in lieu of *quia timet* mandatory injunction).

[73] See *Celsteel Ltd.* v. *Alton House Holdings Ltd.* [1986] 1 W.L.R. 512 (no threat established).

[74] *Fletcher* v. *Bealey* (1885) 28 Ch.D. 688.

[75] See *Redland Bricks Ltd.* v. *Morris* [1970] A.C. 652 at 665.

[76] *Crowder* v. *Tinkler* (1816) 19 Ves. 617 at 622, *per* Lord Eldon L.C. See also *Pattison* v. *Gilford* (1874) L.R. 18 Eq. 259; *Medcalf* v. *R. Strawbridge Ltd.* [1937] 2 K.B. 102 at 111.

[77] *Att.-Gen.* v. *Wellingborough U.D.C.* (1974) 72 L.G.R. 507.

[78] [1904] 1 Ch. 673.

[79] *Ibid.* at p. 677, citing Fitzgibbon L.J. in *Att.-Gen.* v. *Rathmines & Pembroke Joint Hospital Board* [1904] 1 I.R. 161 at 171. See also *Att.-Gen.* v. *Manchester Corporation* [1893] 2 Ch. 87; *Earl of Ripon* v. *Hobart* (1834) 3 My. & K. 169.

[80] *Bridlington Relay Ltd.* v. *Yorkshire Electricity Board* [1965] Ch. 436 (interference with television).

[81] (1861) 3 De G.F. & J. 217.

subjects.[82] Again, where a plaintiff was entitled to repair water-pipes of his which ran through land adjoining his estate, he obtained an injunction to restrain his neighbour from building a house over the pipes.[83] Similarly, the sureties to an administration bond are entitled to restrain the administrator from distributing the estate without providing for a contingent liability.[84]

3. Whether discretionary or obligatory

(a) *Obligatory.* Although the court has, in general, a discretion whether to grant or withhold an injunction, an order to restrain the breach of a negative contract may be obtained almost as of right.[85] In *Doherty* v. *Allman*[86] Lord Cairns L.C. said: "If parties, for valuable consideration, with their eyes open, contract that a particular thing shall not be done, all that a Court of Equity has to do is to say, by way of injunction, that which the parties have already said by way of covenant, that the thing shall not be done; and in such case the injunction does nothing more than give the sanction of the process of the Court to that which already is the contract between the parties. It is not then a question of the balance of convenience or inconvenience,[87] or of the amount of damage or of injury—it is the specific performance, by the Court, of that negative bargain which the parties have made, with their eyes open, between themselves." Thus a purchaser who covenants not to carry on any trade, business or calling in the premises can be restrained by the vendor from opening a school there, even though the vendor would sustain no damage.[88]

It is doubtful whether the court must grant an injunction where there is no privity of contract,[89] *e.g.* against successors in title of land burdened by restrictive covenants, who are bound only in equity. Further, if Lord Cairns' doctrine applies to interlocutory injunctions at all,[90] it does so only in clear cases,[91] and, where the injunction claimed is mandatory, only in a modified form.[92]

[82] See the explanation in *R.C.A. Corporation* v. *Pollard* [1983] Ch. 135 at 144, 151, 152; *Kingdom of Spain* v. *Christie, Manson & Woods Ltd.* [1986] 1 W.L.R. 1120; *Associated Newspapers Group plc* v. *Insert Media Ltd.* [1988] 1 W.L.R. 509 at 512, 513; and see *C.B.S. Songs Ltd.* v. *Amstrad Consumer Electronics plc* [1988] Ch. 61 at 71, 72, 83, 84 (affd. [1988] A.C. 1013).
[83] *Goodhart* v *Hyett* (1883) 25 Ch.D. 182. See also *Jackson* v. *Cator* (1800) 5 Ves. 688; *Hodges* v. *London Trams Omnibus Co.* (1883) 12 Q.B.D. 105; and for another example, see *ante*, pp. 283, 284.
[84] *Re Anderson-Berry* [1928] Ch. 290; and see *ante*, p. 473.
[85] *Quaere* whether the court is bound to grant an injunction to restrain the *ultra vires* acts of a local authority: *Att.-Gen.* v. *Crayford U.D.C.* [1962] Ch. 575 at 585.
[86] (1878) 3 App.Cas. 709 at 720; and see at pp. 729, 730. Yet specific performance is itself a discretionary remedy; see *ante*, p. 588. For negative contracts, see *post*, p. 676.
[87] See *Jenkins* v. *Jackson* (1888) 40 Ch.D. 71 at 77; *Texaco Ltd.* v. *Mulberry Filling Station Ltd.* [1972] 1 W.L.R. 814 at 830.
[88] *Kemp* v. *Sober* (1851) 1 Sim.(N.S.) 517; and see *Lord Manners* v. *Johnston* (1875) 1 Ch.D. 673.
[89] *Kelly* v. *Barrett* [1924] 2 Ch. 379 at 397 (left open by C.A.; *ibid.* pp. 404, 411, 412); *Osborne* v. *Bradley* [1903] 2 Ch. 446 at 451. Contrast *Achilli* v. *Tovell* [1927] 2 Ch. 243 at 247; *Richards* v. *Revitt* (1877) 7 Ch.D. 224.
[90] *Texaco Ltd.* v. *Mulberry Filling Station Ltd.* [1972] 1 W.L.R. 814.
[91] *Hampstead & Suburban Properties Ltd.* v. *Diomedous* [1969] 1 Ch. 248.
[92] *Shepherd Homes Ltd.* v. *Sandham (No. 1)* [1971] Ch. 340.

(b) *Discretionary.* Normally the jurisdiction of the court to grant an injunction is discretionary. Yet "the discretion is not one to be exercised according to the fancy of whoever is to exercise the jurisdiction of Equity"; it must be exercised judicially according to the rules which have been established by precedent.[93] As a general rule a party who establishes his right and its violation will be entitled to an injunction[94]; but the main circumstances which the court will consider in determining whether or not to withhold the remedy are as follows.

(1) SMALL DAMAGE. The fact that the plaintiff has suffered very small or merely nominal damage will not disentitle him to an injunction.[95] If the law were otherwise, the plaintiff might be left to bring action after action to recover damages,[96] and one man might be enabled to use the land of another (*e.g.* by laying pipes under it[97] or taking water from it[98] or placing scaffolding upon it[99]) without his consent and without making proper payments of rent or other sums.[1] Indeed, that the damage is trifling may be "the very reason why an injunction should be granted."[2] It is, however, a circumstance to be taken into account,[3] *e.g.* where the plaintiff has merely suffered trespasses by the public which do not injure him.[4] Furthermore, the court may award damages in lieu of an injunction[5] and, in deciding whether to do so, will weigh the private interest of the complainant in having the wrongful activity stopped against any public interest in its continuance.[6]

(2) ANNOYANCE CEASED. If the injury complained of has ceased before trial[7] or is merely temporary,[8] and there is no intention of renewing it,[9] the court may refuse an injunction.[10] But an injunction was granted where after the writ was issued the injury had ceased

---

[93] *Doherty* v. *Allman* (1878) 3 App.Cas. 709 at 728, 729, *per* Lord Blackburn.
[94] *Fullwood* v. *Fullwood* (1878) 9 Ch.D. 176; *Imperial Gas Light and Coke Co.* v. *Broadbent* (1859) 7 H.L.C. 600 at 612.
[95] *Rochdale Canal Co.* v. *King (No. 1)* (1851) 2 Sim.(N.S.) 78; *Wood* v. *Sutcliffe* (1851) 2 Sim.(N.S.) 163 (where, however, injunctions were refused on the ground of acquiescence; see *post*, p. 655); *Goodson* v. *Richardson* (1874) 9 Ch.App. 221; *Marriott* v. *East Grinstead Gas and Water Co.* [1909] 1 Ch. 70; *Woollerton & Wilson Ltd.* v. *Richard Costain Ltd.* [1970] 1 W.L.R. 411 (crane jib in airspace).
[96] See *Wood* v. *Sutcliffe, supra,* at p. 165.
[97] *Goodson* v. *Richardson, supra.*
[98] *Rochdale Canal Co.* v. *King, supra.*
[99] *John Trenberth Ltd.* v. *National Westminster Bank Ltd.* (1979) 39 P. & C.R. 104.
[1] See *Cooper* v. *Crabtree* (1882) 20 Ch.D. 589 at 592.
[2] *John Trenberth Ltd.* v. *National Westminster Bank Ltd., supra* at p. 107, *per* Walton J.
[3] See *Elmhirst* v. *Spencer* (1849) 2 Mac. & G. 45; *Doherty* v. *Allman* (1878) 3 App.Cas. 709 (ameliorating waste); *Armstrong* v. *Sheppard & Short Ltd.* [1959] 2 Q.B. 384.
[4] *Behrens* v. *Richards* [1905] 2 Ch. 614; and see *Llandudno U.D.C.* v. *Woods* [1899] 2 Ch. 705 (no injunction to restrain sermons on foreshore at Llandudno).
[5] See *post,* p. 656.
[6] Contrast *Miller* v. *Jackson* [1977] Q.B. 966 (cricket balls coming into house and garden: £400 damages) with *Kennaway* v. *Thompson* [1981] Q.B. 88 (noise from motor boat racing: injunction).
[7] *Barber* v. *Penley* [1893] 2 Ch. 447 (crowds waiting to see "Charley's Aunt," eventually regulated by police); *Proctor* v. *Bayley* (1889) 42 Ch.D. 390.
[8] *Leader* v. *Moody* (1875) L.R. 20 Eq. 145.
[9] *Fielden* v. *Cox* (1906) 22 T.L.R. 411; *Wilcox* v. *Steel* [1904] 1 Ch. 212.
[10] And see *ante,* pp. 647, 648.

because of the financial difficulties and resulting voluntary liquidation of the defendant company.[11]

(3) COMPLIANCE DIFFICULT. It is no defence to an action for an injunction that compliance will be inconvenient and expensive, as where a river is being polluted by the outfall from large sewers.[12] The severity of the rule that a defendant must find his own way out of the difficulty, whatever the cost, is frequently mitigated by not immediately imposing the injunction, or by suspending its operation.[13]

(4) ORDER INEFFECTIVE. The court will not make "an idle and ineffectual order. ... The simplest illustration of this is the case of cutting down timber. It would be idle when the trees have been cut down to make an order not to allow the trees to remain prostrate, and all that can be done in such a case is to leave the parties to their remedy for damages."[14]

(5) UNDERTAKING BY DEFENDANT. If the defendant gives an undertaking to the court to abstain from the acts of which the plaintiff complains,[15] or even to give sufficient notice before attempting to act,[16] an injunction may be refused. Such an undertaking is equivalent to an injunction, and a breach may be punished in the same way as a breach of an injunction.[17] A defendant will not, however, avoid an injunction merely by denying any intention of repeating wrongful acts.[18]

(6) ORDER UNNECESSARY. An injunction may also be refused where the plaintiff has a remedy available in his own hands, e.g. by refusing to supply goods to defendants who were dealing with them in breach of contract.[19]

4. Conduct of the plaintiff

(a) *Types of conduct.* He who comes into equity must come with clean hands.[20] Thus a trader whose trade mark makes untrue representations to the public cannot protect it by injunction,[21] though mere collateral misrepresentations, e.g. in advertisements, are no bar.[22]

---

[11] *Dean and Chapter of Chester* v. *Smelting Corporation Ltd.* (1901) 85 L.T. 67.
[12] *Att.-Gen.* v. *Colney Hatch Lunatic Asylum* (1868) 4 Ch.App. 146; and see *Pride of Derby and Derbyshire Angling Association Ltd.* v. *British Celanese Ltd.* [1953] Ch. 149. But see *Barber* v. *Penley* [1893] 2 Ch. 447 at 460, 461.
[13] See *post*, p. 674.
[14] *Att.-Gen.* v. *Colney Hatch Lunatic Asylum, supra,* at p. 154, *per* Lord Hatherley L.C.
[15] *Jenkins* v. *Hope* [1896] 1 Ch. 278.
[16] *Lord Cowley* v. *Byas* (1877) 5 Ch.D. 944; *Smith* v. *Baxter* [1900] 2 Ch. 138.
[17] See *Neath Canal Co.* v. *Ynisarwed Resolven Colliery Co.* (1875) 10 Ch.App. 450; *Biba Ltd.* v. *Stratford Investments Ltd.* [1973] Ch. 281.
[18] *Proctor* v. *Bayley* (1889) 42 Ch.D. 390 at 399, 400.
[19] *Elliman, Sons & Co.* v. *Carrington & Son Ltd.* [1901] 2 Ch. 275.
[20] See *ante*, pp. 31, 32.
[21] *Leather Cloth Co. Ltd.* v. *American Leather Cloth Co. Ltd.* (1863) 4 De G.J. & S. 137; affirmed, 11 H.L.C. 523.
[22] *Ford* v. *Foster* (1872) 7 Ch.App. 611; and see *J. H. Coles Proprietary Ltd.* v. *Need* [1934] A.C. 82.

Again, an injunction may be refused if the plaintiffs have misled the defendant and the court,[23] or if they are seeking to protect not their own rights, but a monopoly they have purported to confer on others,[24] or if they are seeking the return of property which they had been holding contrary to statute,[25] or if they have behaved in a petty-minded way,[26] or if they have treated the case as a matter for monetary compensation.[27] Further, an injunction will be refused to a contracting party who fails to perform his part of the contract[28] or refuses to give the court an assurance that he will do so in future.[29] On the other hand, an injunction will not be refused merely on the ground that the plaintiff could not be compelled specifically to perform his part of the contract,[30] or that he has committed breaches of covenant if they are only trifling.[31]

(b) *Laches and acquiescence.* A claim to an injunction may also be barred by the plaintiff's acquiescence[32] or laches.[33] Acquiescence primarily means conduct from which it can be inferred that a party has waived his rights.[34] Mere inactivity is insufficient, for "quiescence is not acquiescence."[35] Acquiescence is more easily established where the right to be protected is equitable only,[36] and in the case of a legal right it can only be established by showing that it has become dishonest or unconscionable on the part of the owner of the right to press for its enforcement.[37] On this ground an injunction to restrain the use of a house as a shop was refused on proof that the plaintiff had himself bought goods there[38]; but acquiescence in a small breach will not bar proceedings to restrain a wider breach.[39] Lapse of time is an important element in considering whether there has been acquiescence,[40] but there may be acquiescence even without any delay. Moreover, lapse of time or laches may exist as a defence even in circumstances not amounting to acquiescence, *e.g.* where the defendant's witnesses have died. The areas

---

[23] *Armstrong* v. *Sheppard & Short Ltd.* [1959] 2 Q.B. 384.
[24] *Corporation of London* v. *Lyons, Son & Co. (Fruit Brokers) Ltd.* [1936] Ch. 78.
[25] *Malone* v. *Metropolitan Police Commissioner* [1980] Q.B. 49 (exchange control).
[26] *Tollemache & Cobbold Breweries Ltd.* v. *Reynolds* (1983) 268 E.G. 52 at 56.
[27] *Wood* v. *Sutcliffe* (1851) 2 Sim.(N.S.) 163; *Ormerod* v. *Todmorden Joint Stock Mill Co. Ltd.* (1883) 11 Q.B.D. 155 at 162; *Aspden* v. *Seddon* (1875) 10 Ch.App. 394; *Blue Town Investments Ltd.* v. *Higgs and Hill plc* [1990] 1 W.L.R. 696 (claim to injunction struck out: see *post*, p. 688). *Aliter* if the compensation is a mere penalty: *ante*, pp. 539, 540.
[28] *Measures Bros. Ltd.* v. *Measures* [1910] 2 Ch. 248; *General Billposting Co. Ltd.* v. *Atkinson* [1909] A.C. 118; and see *ante*, p. 608 (specific performance).
[29] *Chappell* v. *Times Newspapers Ltd.* [1975] 1 W.L.R. 482.
[30] *James Jones & Sons Ltd.* v. *Earl of Tankerville* [1909] 2 Ch. 440; but see *Page One Records Ltd.* v. *Britton* [1968] 1 W.L.R. 157; *post*, p. 678.
[31] *Western* v. *MacDermott* (1866) 2 Ch.App. 72; *Besant* v. *Wood* (1879) 12 Ch.D. 605.
[32] *Parrott* v. *Palmer* (1834) 3 My. & K. 632 at 640; *Blue Town Investments Ltd.* v. *Higgs and Hill plc*, *supra*.
[33] See *ante*, p. 35.
[34] See *Duke of Leeds* v. *Earl of Amherst* (1846) 2 Ph. 117 at 123.
[35] *Lamare* v. *Dixon* (1873) L.R. 6 H.L. 414 at 422, *per* Lord Chelmsford.
[36] *Shaw* v. *Applegate* [1977] 1 W.L.R. 970 at 979.
[37] *Shaw* v. *Applegate* [1977] 1 W.L.R. 970.
[38] *Sayers* v. *Collyer* (1884) 28 Ch.D. 103.
[39] *Richards* v. *Revitt* (1877) 7 Ch.D. 224. Cf. *McKinnon Industries Ltd.* v. *Walker* [1951] W.N. 401 (acquiescence during war).
[40] See, *e.g. Rundell* v. *Murray* (1821) Jac. 311.

of acquiecence and laches thus overlap, yet neither is wholly included in the other.

5. Damages in substitution for injunction

(a) *Jurisdiction.* The Court of Chancery originally had no power to award damages, though where the defendant had made a profit out of his wrongful act, it might decree an account.[41] The Chancery Amendment Act 1858 (more commonly called Lord Cairns' Act), however, authorised the court, if it thought fit, in all cases in which it had jurisdiction to grant an injunction or to order specific performance,[42] to award damages to the injured party, "either in addition to or in substitution for" the other relief.[43] Although the Act has been repealed, the jurisdiction under it is still preserved.[44]

(b) *Extent of jurisdiction.* The court can accordingly give damages for an injury which is only threatened or apprehended[45] and, it seems, for an infringement of a purely equitable right, *e.g.* a breach by a subsequent purchaser of a restrictive covenant[46] by which he is bound only in equity.[47] In neither of these cases could damages have been recovered at common law. But the Act gives no power to award damages when the court is absolutely precluded from granting an injunction, *e.g.* because there is no threat to continue the wrong.[48] Yet damages may be awarded under the Act where equitable relief is refused merely on some discretionary ground.[49] Since the Judicature Act 1873, the Chancery Division has had power to award damages in any case in which a common law court could have done so before 1875,[50] and so the jurisdiction under Lord Cairns' Act is not often invoked where a claim for damages lies at law.

(c) *Exercise of jurisdiction.* Though the court may award damages in all cases where it can award an injunction, in exercising the jurisdiction it will apply well-settled principles, and will not "allow a wrong to continue simply because the wrongdoer is able and willing to pay for the injury he may inflict."[51] If the plaintiff establishes his legal right and the

---

[41] See *ante*, pp. 581. 637.

[42] For the corresponding jurisdiction in specific performance, see *ante*, p. 588.

[43] s.2. See J. A. Jolowicz [1975] C.L.J. 224 (general); P. H. Pettit [1977] C.L.J. 369 (county court).

[44] *Leeds Industrial Co-operative Society Ltd.* v. *Slack* [1924] A.C. 851; *Sayers* v. *Collyer* (1884) 28 Ch.D. 103; and see *Re R.* [1906] 1 Ch. 730 at 735, 739.

[45] *Leeds Industrial Co-operative Society Ltd.* v. *Slack, supra.*

[46] See *post*, p. 678.

[47] *Eastwood* v. *Lever* (1863) 4 De G.J. & S. 114 at 128; and see, *e.g. Baxter* v. *Four-Oaks Properties Ltd.* [1965] Ch. 816.

[48] *Proctor* v. *Bayley* (1889) 42 Ch.D. 390.

[49] See *ante*, p. 589.

[50] See *ante*, pp. 19, 20.

[51] *Shelfer* v. *City of London Electric Lighting Co.* [1895] 1 Ch. 287 at 315, 316, *per* Lindley L.J.; applied in *Kelsen* v. *Imperial Tobacco Co. (of Great Britain and Ireland) Ltd.* [1957] 2 Q.B. 334.

actual or threatened violation of it, he is entitled to an injunction as of course, unless there is something special in the case.[52] This applies forcibly where the wrong consists of a continuing nuisance, and where the defendant has given an undertaking to pull down any offending building if he loses.[53]

(d) *Relevant considerations.* In a case of nuisance by noise and vibration it was accordingly said in 1895 that "as a good working rule" an injunction would be refused and damages awarded only where there is a small injury which is capable of being estimated in money and adequately compensated by a small sum, and the grant of an injunction would be oppressive.[54] Some later cases, especially of interference with light,[55] show that an injunction may be refused even if one of these conditions is unfulfilled, *e.g.* where the damages suffered are substantial.[56] In 1980, however, the Court of Appeal reaffirmed the rule and held that in cases of continuing nuisance the jurisdiction to award damages should be exercised only under very exceptional circumstances.[57] Nevertheless the "working rule" is for guidance only in the circumstances of each case,[58] among which may be reckoned the conduct of the defendant in giving warning of what was going to be done,[59] the conduct of the plaintiff in showing that "he only wants money,"[60] delay on his part in moving for interlocutory relief,[61] the fact that the defendant's breach to some extent benefits the plaintiff,[62] and any public interest in permitting the continuance of the state of affairs of which complaint is made.[63]

(e) *Measure of damages.* "It is manifest that damages cannot be an adequate substitute for an injunction unless they cover the whole area which would have been covered by the injunction."[64] The damages must therefore include damage accruing after the issue of the writ[65]; indeed,

[52] *Imperial Gas Light and Coke Co.* v. *Broadbent* (1859) 7 H.L.C. 600 at 612; *Achilli* v. *Tovell* [1927] 2 Ch. 243; *Sefton* v. *Tophams Ltd.* [1965] Ch. 1140 at 1162, 1169 (not argued on appeal: see at pp. 1186, 1195; on further appeal, held no breach: [1967] 1 A.C. 50).
[53] *Greenwood* v. *Hornsey* (1886) 33 Ch.D. 471.
[54] *Shelfer's Case, supra,* at pp. 322, 323, *per* A. L. Smith L.J.
[55] *Fishenden* v. *Higgs and Hill Ltd.* (1935) 153 L.T. 128; and see *Colls* v. *Home and Colonial Stores Ltd.* [1904] A.C. 179 at 192, 193; *Slack* v. *Leeds Industrial Co-operative Society Ltd. (No. 2)* [1924] 2 Ch. 475.
[56] *Fishenden* v. *Higgs and Hill Ltd., supra.*
[57] *Kennaway* v. *Thompson* [1981] Q.B. 88 (limited injunction granted); and see *Tetley* v. *Chitty* [1986] 1 All E.R. 663 (damages insufficient remedy). On the choice of remedy in nuisance cases, see [1982] C.L.J. 87 (C.J. Tromans).
[58] *Fishenden* v. *Higgs and Hill Ltd., supra.* For circumstances other than those mentioned in the text of which the court will take account, see *Shelfer's Case, supra,* at p. 317; *Colls's Case, supra,* at p. 193.
[59] *Fishenden* v. *Higgs and Hill Ltd., supra.*
[60] *Fishenden* v. *Higgs and Hill Ltd., supra,* at p. 141, *per* Romer L.J. But see *Cowper* v. *Laidler* [1903] 2 Ch. 337; *Osborne* v. *Bradley* [1903] 2 Ch. 446 at 457.
[61] *Bracewell* v. *Appleby* [1975] Ch. 408.
[62] *National Provincial Plate Glass Insurance Co.* v. *Prudential Assurance Co.* (1877) 6 Ch.D. 757 at 769 (light).
[63] See *Wrotham Park Estate Co. Ltd.* v. *Parkside Homes Ltd.* [1974] 1 W.L.R. 798 (mandatory injunction to pull down houses erected in breach of covenant refused); and see the cases cited *ante,* p. 653, n. 6.
[64] *Fritz* v. *Hobson* (1880) 14 Ch.D. 542 at 566, *per* Fry J.; and see *ante,* p. 589.
[65] *Fritz* v. *Hobson* (1880) 14 Ch.D. 542.

in a *quia timet* action they can include only such damage.[66] Damages in
lieu of an injunction against breach of a restrictive covenant are assessed
by reference to what the covenantee might reasonably have demanded
as a licence fee for relaxing the covenant.[67]

6. Mandatory injunctions

(a) *Principles.* In general, the principles regulating the grant of
mandatory injunctions are the same as those regulating prohibitory
injunctions; for otherwise a defendant who had committed a breach of
his obligations would be better off than one who merely threatened to
commit a breach. The mere fact that the injury has been completed
before the action is commenced is no bar to the grant of a mandatory
injunction.[68] The grant of a mandatory injunction is nevertheless always
discretionary.[69] Important factors are the extent of the damage which
would accrue to the plaintiff if relief is withheld,[70] the cost to the
defendant if it is granted,[71] and the conduct of the defendant in rushing
on with building works after notice of the plaintiff's objections.[72]
Accordingly, if a restrictive covenant has been broken knowingly and
after notice from the plaintiff, the general rule is that a mandatory
injunction will be granted to restore the status quo.[73]

(b) *Examples.* A mandatory injunction will not be granted to compel
the execution of successive operations requiring the continuing
superintendence of the court,[74] *e.g.* repairs or building works,[75] or the
running of an airport[76] or a ferry,[77] especially if such an injunction
might force the defendant into bankruptcy.[78] Again, a mandatory
injunction was refused to compel the Post Office to deliver mail during
an industrial dispute with its staff.[79] Further, a mandatory injunction
was refused where, in breach of covenant, a frosted window was let into

---

[66] See *Leeds Industrial Co-operative Society Ltd.* v. *Slack* [1924] A.C. 851.
[67] *Wrotham Park Estate Co. Ltd.* v. *Parkside Homes Ltd.* [1974] 1 W.L.R. 798.
[68] *Durell* v. *Pritchard* (1865) 1 Ch.App. 244.
[69] *Sharp* v. *Harrison* [1922] 1 Ch. 502 at 512; *Shepherd Homes Ltd.* v. *Sandham (No. 1)* [1971] Ch. 340;
Wrotham Park Estate Co. Ltd. v. *Parkside Homes Ltd., supra.*; *Wakeham* v. *Wood* (1982) 43 P. &
C.R. 40 at 45, 46, disapproving dictum in *Achilli* v. *Tovell* [1927] 2 Ch. 243 at 247.
[70] *Durell* v. *Pritchard, supra,* at p. 250; *Price* v. *Hilditch* [1930] 1 Ch. 500.
[71] See *Shepherd Homes Ltd.* v. *Sandham (No. 1)* [1971] Ch. 340 at 351; but see *Charrington* v. *Simons
& Co. Ltd.* [1971] 1 W.L.R. 598 at 603.
[72] *Bickmore* v. *Dimmer* [1903] 1 Ch. 158 at 168; *Price* v. *Hilditch, supra,* at pp. 509, 510; *Mathias* v.
Davies [1970] E.G.D. 370; 114 S.J. 268; but see *Isenberg* v. *East India House Estate Trading Co.
Ltd.* (1863) 3 De G.J. & S. 263 at 273, 274.
[73] *Wakeham* v. *Wood* (1982) 43 P. & C.R. 40.
[74] See *Att.-Gen.* v. *Dean and Chapter of Ripon Cathedral* [1945] Ch. 239 at 249.
[75] *Att.-Gen.* v. *Staffordshire County Council* [1905] 1 Ch. 336; contrast *Kennard* v. *Cory Bros. & Co.
Ltd.* [1922] 2 Ch. 1 (the "moving mountain" case).
[76] *Dowty Boulton Paul Ltd.* v. *Wolverhampton Corporation* [1971] 1 W.L.R. 204.
[77] *Att.-Gen.* v. *Colchester Corporation* [1955] 2 Q.B. 207.
[78] *Ibid.* at p. 217.
[79] *Harold Stephen & Co. Ltd.* v. *Post Office* [1977] 1 W.L.R. 1172 (interlocutory application).

a wall overlooking the plaintiff's premises, the plaintiff suffering no damage,[80] or where a coal shed had been demolished between trial refusing an injunction and successful appeal.[81] But an injunction was granted where the defendant built a skylight obstructing the access of light to the plaintiff's skylight and on the facts the damage to the plaintiff was great but the inconvenience to the defendant insignificant.[82] Further, to avoid the risk of serious consequences for a number of people the court has ordered the removal of houses wrongfully built over water mains, despite the grave loss to the defendants.[83]

(c) *Quia timet.* There is a special application of the *quia timet* principle in relation to mandatory injunctions. This occurs where the plaintiff has been fully recompensed for the damage already suffered but alleges that there is a risk that further damage may occur, as where the defendant has carried on operations on his land which imperil the stability of his neighbour's land. In such cases the court may order preventive works. The general principles governing the grant of the remedy are as follows.[84]

(1) GRAVE DAMAGE.   The plaintiff must show a very strong probability that grave damage will accrue to him in the future. The jurisdiction is exercised sparingly and with caution, but in a proper case unhesitatingly.

(2) DAMAGES INADEQUATE.   It must be shown that if such grave damage happens an award of damages will not be a sufficient or adequate remedy.

(3) RELEVANCE OF COST.   Where a future apprehended wrong is in issue, the cost of the necessary works is an element to be taken into account as follows:

   (i)   Where the defendant has acted wantonly and quite un- reasonably, and against the plaintiff's objections, he may be ordered to restore the *status quo* even if the expense is out of all proportion to the advantage accruing to the plaintiff.

   (ii) Where the defendant has acted reasonably but wrongly, the heavy cost may be a reason for withholding an injunction; no legal wrong for which the plaintiff will be unrecompensed may occur, and if it does, he may then sue in respect of it.

---

[80] *Sharp* v. *Harrison* [1922] 1 Ch. 502.
[81] *Wright* v. *Macadam* [1949] 2 K.B. 744 at 755.
[82] *McManus* v. *Cooke* (1887) 35 Ch.D. 681; and see *Smith* v. *Smith* (1875) L.R. 20 Eq. 500; *Att.-Gen.* v. *Parish* [1913] 2 Ch. 444; *Allport* v. *The Securities Co. Ltd.* (1895) 72 L.T. 533; *Kelsen* v. *Imperial Tobacco Co. (of Great Britain and Ireland) Ltd.* [1957] 2 Q.B. 334.
[83] *Abingdon Corporation* v. *James* [1940] Ch. 287.
[84] *Redland Bricks Ltd.* v. *Morris* [1970] A.C. 652 at 665, 666.

(4) PRECISION OF ORDER. The order must define with precision, in fact and in law, what the defendant has to do.

B. Interlocutory Injunctions

1. General principles. Though the proverbial delays of Lord Eldon's chancellorship no longer exist, there is still an inevitable lapse of time between the commencement of an action and the trial. The injury being suffered by the plaintiff may be such that it would be unjust to make him wait until the trial for relief. In such cases the court may grant an injunction[85] operating until the trial or further order, thereby maintaining the *status quo*[86] and facilitating the administration of justice at the trial[87]; and a plaintiff who has been refused an injunction until trial may, if he wishes to appeal against the refusal, be granted an injunction pending the hearing of his appeal.[88] In a proper case an interlocutory injunction may be granted even though it gives the plaintiff the whole of the relief for which he would ask at the trial.[89]

(a) *Strength of plaintiff's case.* The application for an interlocutory injunction must normally be heard on the basis of affidavit evidence, without cross-examination.[90] This gives rise to a major difficulty in deciding whether or not the injunction ought to be granted, for at this stage disputed questions of fact cannot satisfactorily be resolved, which in turn leads to difficulties in determining how strong a case the plaintiff must establish in order to obtain an interlocutory injunction. Over the years a rule was evolved that the plaintiff would be granted an interlocutory order only if, on the material before the court, he could show a strong prima facie case that he was entitled to the right which he claimed and also that his allegation that this right had been infringed was reasonably capable of succeeding.[91] In time this test was rejected on the ground that the remedy of an interlocutory injunction must be kept flexible and discretionary, and that the case must be considered as a whole on the basis of fairness, justice and common sense[92]; but subject to this, the plaintiff would fail if he could not establish a prima facie case.[93]

[85] An order for possession cannot be granted as interlocutory relief: *Manchester Corporation* v. *Connolly* [1970] Ch. 470.
[86] *Jones* v. *Pacaya Rubber and Produce Co. Ltd.* [1911] 1 K.B. 455 at 457. See *post*, p. 662.
[87] *Smith* v. *Peters* (1875) L.R. 20 Eq. 511 at 513.
[88] *Erinford Properties Ltd.* v. *Cheshire C.C.* [1974] Ch. 261; *Orion Property Trust Ltd.* v. *Du Cane Court Ltd.* [1962] 1 W.L.R. 1085.
[89] See *Heywood* v. *B.D.C. Properties Ltd. (No. 1)* [1963] 1 W.L.R. 975 (order vacating entry of land charge), and the other authorities collected in *Woodford* v. *Smith* [1970] 1 W.L.R. 806 at 817, 818.
[90] See R.S.C., Ord. 38, r. 2(3).
[91] *Harman Pictures N.V.* v. *Osborne* [1967] 1 W.L.R. 723.
[92] *Hubbard* v. *Vosper* [1972] 2 Q.B. 84.
[93] See *American Cyanamid Co.* v. *Ethicon Ltd.* [1975] A.C. 396 at 407.

In 1975, in *American Cyanamid Co.* v. *Ethicon Ltd.*,[94] the House of Lords swept away this requirement, and held that, in the case of prohibitory injunctions,[95] the plaintiff need establish only a real possibility of success, and not a probability. This meant that the balance of convenience, which had always been an important factor, became decisive in many more cases, since the initial hurdle in the plaintiff's path had been lowered. But the case has not affected the rules which restrict the grant of interlocutory injunctions in cases of defamation.[96]

(b) *The principles after American Cyanamid.* The *American Cyanamid* case[97] established a series of questions which have to be considered in deciding whether or not an interlocutory injunction should be granted.

(1) SERIOUS QUESTION. At the outset the court must be satisfied that "there is a serious question to be tried." This means something more than the plaintiff can avoid having the action struck out as frivolous and vexatious in the sense of being one which no reasonable person could treat as bona fide.[98] He does not now have to show a prima facie case, but only an issue for which there is some supporting material and the outcome of which is uncertain.[99] An injunction will be refused to a plaintiff who has no "real prospect of succeeding in his claim for a permanent injunction at the trial." If the plaintiff fails to satisfy this requirement, there is an end of the matter.[1] If he does satisfy this requirement, the court must go on to consider the balance of convenience.[2]

(2) BALANCE OF CONVENIENCE. This may have to be dealt with in three stages.

(i) The "governing principle" is that if the plaintiff would be adequately compensated by an award of damages if he succeeds at the trial, and the defendant would be able to pay them, no injunction should be granted, however strong the plaintiff's case.[3] In appropriate cases the court may refuse interlocutory relief if the defendant undertakes to keep proper accounts of his receipts from the activity in respect of which the injunction was

---

[94] [1975] A.C. 396.
[95] See *Locabail International Finance Ltd.* v. *Agroexport* [1986] 1 W.L.R. 657 at 664. For interlocutory mandatory injunctions, see *post*, p. 669.
[96] *Herbage* v. *Pressdram Ltd.* [1984] 1 W.L.R. 1160 at 1162; *Khashoggi* v. *I.P.C. Magazines Ltd.* [1986] 1 W.L.R. 1412 at 1418. For the rules, see *post*, p. 681.
[97] *American Cyanamid Co.* v. *Ethicon Ltd.* [1975] A.C. 396, especially at 407–409.
[98] *Mothercare Ltd.* v. *Robson Brooks Ltd.* [1979] F.S.R. 466 not following *John Walker & Son Ltd.* v. *Rothmans International Ltd.* [1978] F.S.R. 357 at 361.
[99] *Cayne* v. *Global Natural Resources plc* [1984] 1 All E.R. 225.
[1] *Re Lord Cable* [1977] 1 W.L.R. 7; *Associated British Ports* v. *Transport and General Workers Union* [1989] 1 W.L.R. 939.
[2] " … an unfortunate expression. Our business is justice, not convenience": *Francome* v. *Mirror Group Newspapers Ltd.* [1984] 1 W.L.R. 892 at 898, *per* Sir John Donaldson M.R.
[3] *Garden Cottage Foods Ltd.* v. *Milk Marketing Board* [1984] A.C. 130.

sought and to pay a proportion of such receipts into court or a joint account.[4]

(ii)   If the claim survives the previous head, the court must consider whether, if an interlocutory injunction is granted but the defendant succeeds at the trial, the defendant would be adequately compensated in damages which then would have to be paid by the plaintiff,[5] and whether the plaintiff would be able to pay those damages. If such damages would be an adequate remedy and the plaintiff would be in a position to pay them, then the defendant's prospects of success at the trial would be no bar to the grant of the injunction.[6]

(iii) If there is doubt as to the adequacy of the respective remedies in damages available to either party or to both,[7] the court must consider the wide range of matters which go to make up the general balance of convenience. These will vary from case to case: three, which are dealt with below, were expressly mentioned in the *Cyanamid* case.[8]

(3) STATUS QUO.   "Where other factors appear to be evenly balanced it is a counsel of prudence to take such measures as are calculated to preserve the status quo."[9] Thus a new venture on the part of the defendant may be restrained by injunction where an established enterprise would not be restrained: there is a great difference in the effect of injunctions in such cases, for in the one the undertaking will merely be postponed, while in the other it may be destroyed. Further, it has been held that where both parties might suffer unquantifiable damages, the status quo should be maintained unless there are compelling reasons to the contrary: such a reason would be a risk of damage to the plaintiff, yet a certainty of damage to the defendant.[10] The status quo refers to the period immediately preceding the issue of the writ (or the notice of motion if substantially later), and not to the period before the conduct which led to the litigation.[11]

---

[4] *Warren* v. *Mendy* [1989] 1 W.L.R. 853 at 863, warning against the assumption that damages will not be an adequate remedy for breach of a covenant in restraint of trade.
[5] Under the undertaking in damages: *post*, p. 666.
[6] For an old illustration of the principle, see *Hilton* v. *Earl of Granville* (1841) Cr. & Ph. 283, especially at 297, 298. And see *Jennings* v. *Jennings* [1898] 1 Ch. 378, especially at 390, 391 (injunction to restrain breach of an agreement which would be rescinded if defence were to succeed at trial).
[7] As in *Foseco International Ltd.* v. *Fordath Ltd.* [1975] F.,S.R. 507; *Catmic Components Ltd.* v. *Hill & Smith Ltd.* [1975] F.S.R. 529. Contrast *Aljose Fashions Ltd. (trading as Fiona Dresses)* v. *Alfred Young & Co. Ltd.* [1978] F.S.R. 364, and *Monet of London Ltd.* v. *Sybil Richards Ltd.* [1978] F.S.R. 368, where both sides were adequately provided with money and the matter was left to be dealt with in damages; but these cases do not lay down a general rule: *The Quaker Oats Co.* v. *Alltrades Distributors Ltd.* [1981] F.S.R. 9 at 13, 14.
[8] [1975] A.C. 396 at 408, 409.
[9] *Ibid.* at p. 408, *per* Lord Diplock.
[10] *John Walker & Sons Ltd.* v. *Rothmans International Ltd.* [1978] F.S.R. 387 ("Red Label" cigarettes: injunction refused).
[11] *Garden Cottage Foods Ltd.* v. *Milk Marketing Board* [1984] A.C. 130 at 140, disapproving on this point *Texaco Ltd.* v. *Mulberry Filling Station Ltd.* [1972] 1 W.L.R. 814 at 831; *Hubbard* v. *Pitt* [1976] Q.B. 142 at 190.

(4) RELATIVE STRENGTH OF CASES. The court should not embark on anything resembling a trial of the action on conflicting affidavits. However, sometimes on undisputed facts (or facts as to which there is no credible dispute) the strength of one party's case is disproportionate to that of the other, and this may be taken into account in tipping the balance.[12] This may be done where, as often occurs, there are some disadvantages to both parties which could not be adequately compensated in damages, and there is no wide difference in the extent of these.

(5) SPECIAL FACTORS. "There may be many other special factors to be taken into consideration in the particular circumstances of individual cases."[13] This, however, refers to special factors affecting the balance of convenience, and does not give a general licence to disregard the *Cyanamid* principles.[14] There was a special factor in the *Cyanamid* case itself.[15] The plaintiff sought an injunction to restrain the defendant from marketing surgical products in alleged breach of the plaintiff's patent. Once doctors and patients had got used to the defendant's products in the period prior to the trial, it might well be commercially impracticable for the plaintiff to insist on a permanent injunction at the trial, owing to the damaging effect which this would have on its goodwill in the pharmaceutical market: and this told in favour of granting interlocutory relief. Further, at the interlocutory stage of the notorious "Spycatcher" litigation the public interest in maintaining the secrecy of the security services weighed heavily with the House of Lords when it decided to continue until trial injunctions restraining publication.[16] A special factor against the grant of an injunction would be the need to secure to the public the benefit of a life-saving drug.[17]

(c) *The limits of the Cyanamid guidelines.* The principles established in *Cyanamid* are of general application. Thus interlocutory injunctions which are sought to enforce a covenant in restraint of trade do not constitute a special category of case which is exempt from the principles.[18] Nevertheless, one must not forget "that words in a judgment ought not, however eminent the judge, to be construed as if they were an Act of Parliament," but "must be very careful to apply the relevant passages from Lord Diplock's familiar speech in the *Cyanamid* case not as rules but only as guidelines."[19] There remains the overall discretion to do what is "just and convenient."[19a] Indeed in a number of cases the guidelines are inappropriate.

[12] *The Quaker Oats Co.* v. *Alltrades Distributors Ltd.* [1981] F.S.R. 9 especially at 13, 14 (plaintiff "almost certain to succeed"; injunction granted notwithstanding some delay in applying).
[13] *American Cyanamid Co.* v. *Ethicon Ltd.* [1975] A.C. 396 at 409, *per* Lord Diplock.
[14] *Hubbard* v. *Pitt* [1976] Q.B. 142 at 185, 188.
[15] [1975] A.C. 396 at 410
[16] *Att.-Gen.* v. *Guardian Newspapers Ltd.* [1987] 1 W.L.R. 1248, esp. at 1298, 1305, 1306. Further proceedings: [1990] A.C. 109.
[17] See *Roussel Ucla* v. *G.D. Searle & Co. Ltd.* [1977] F.S.R. 125. Further proceedings: [1978] F.S.R. 95.
[18] *Dairy Crest Ltd.* v. *Pigott* [1989] I.C.R. 92; *Lawrence David Ltd.* v. *Ashton* [1989] I.C.R. 123, disapproving *Fellowes & Son* v. *Fisher* [1976] Q.B. 122 at 133, 134.
[19] *Cayne* v. *Global Natural Resources plc* [1984] 1 All E.R. 225 at 237, *per* May L.J.
[19a] S.C.A. 1981, s. 37.

(1) CLEAR CASE. It has already been shown that where there is no serious question to be tried, an injunction will be refused[20]; conversely if at the interlocutory stage it is plain that the plaintiff is in the right, the balance of convenience will play no part,[21] for example where the plaintiff's title is clear and the defendant's trespass indisputable,[22] or where the defendant is in clear breach of a covenant which binds him,[23] as distinct from cases where his liability is arguable.[24] Similarly, an injunction was granted without regard to balance of convenience against an education authority which had manifestly not complied with the statutory requirements in reorganising its schools.[25] "Even if chaos should result, still the law must be obeyed."[26]

(2) SIMPLE POINT OF CONSTRUCTION. Though it was said in *Cyanamid* that at the interlocutory stage it is no part of the court's function "to decide difficult questions of law which call for detailed argument and mature consideration,"[27] a court may grant or refuse interlocutory relief without applying the *Cyanamid* guidelines if the action is concerned only with a simple question of construction of a statute or document,[28] *e.g.* a lease or contract.

(3) NO PROSPECT OF TRIAL. It is a prerequisite for the application of the guidelines laid down in the *Cyanamid* case "that a trial is in fact likely to take place, in the sense that the plaintiffs' case shows that they are generally concerned to pursue their claim to trial, and that they are seeking the injunction as a means of a holding operation pending the trial."[29] Accordingly, where the grant or refusal of an interlocutory injunction will have the practical effect of putting an end to the action (as frequently occurs in labour disputes[30]) "the degree of likelihood that the plaintiff would have succeeded in establishing his right if the action had gone to trial is a factor to be brought into the balance by the judge in weighing the risks that injustice may result from his deciding the application one way rather than another."[31] Such cases have to be approached "on a broad principle: what can the court do in its best endeavours to avoid injustice?"[32] One very important element in such

[20] *Ante*, p. 661.
[21] *Official Custodian for Charities* v. *Mackey* [1985] Ch. 151.
[22] *Patel* v. *W.H. Smith (Eziot) Ltd.* [1987] 1 W.L.R. 853.
[23] *Hampstead & Suburban Properties Ltd.* v. *Diomedous* [1969] 1 Ch. 248.
[24] *Texaco Ltd.* v. *Mulberry Filling Station Ltd.* [1972] 1 W.L.R. 814.
[25] *Bradbury* v. *Enfield L.B.C.* [1967] 1 W.L.R. 1311; and see *Legg* v. *Inner London Education Authority* [1972] 1 W.L.R. 1245.
[26] *Bradbury* v. *Enfield L.B.C., supra*, at p. 1324, *per* Lord Denning M.R.; and see at p. 1325, *per* Danckwerts L.J.: "It is essential that bureaucracy should be kept in its place."
[27] *American Cyanamid Co.* v. *Ethicon Ltd.* [1975] A.C. 396 at 407, *per* Lord Diplock (amending the last word, "considerations").
[28] See *Fellowes & Son* v. *Fisher* [1976] Q.B. 122 at 141; *Associated British Ports* v. *Transport and General Workers' Union* [1989] 1 W.L.R. 939 at 979, 980.
[29] *Cayne* v. *Global Natural Resources plc* [1984] 1 All E.R. 225 at 234, *per* Kerr L.J.
[30] See *infra*.
[31] *NWL Ltd.* v. *Woods* [1979] 1 W.L.R. 1294 at 1307, *per* Lord Diplock.
[32] *Cayne* v. *Global Natural Resources plc* [1984] 1 All E.R. 225 at 232, *per* Eveleigh L.J.

circumstances is that the grant of an injunction denies the defendant the right to trial.[33] Hence a plaintiff in a passing-off case must show more than an arguable case as the injunction will often be final in effect.[34] Further, if the interlocutory injunction is sought for the purpose of restraining the commencement of litigation, the court will not grant the order unless there is sufficient prima facie evidence that the plaintiff will succeed in establishing subsequently that the intended litigation is an abuse of process: otherwise the court would be interfering with a legitimate approach to the seat of justice.[35]

(d) *Labour disputes.* An act done in contemplation or furtherance of a trade dispute is not actionable in tort on the ground only that it induces another person to break a contract or interferes, or induces another to interfere, with its performance.[36] If an employer who sought to obtain an injunction restraining workers or trade unions from disrupting his business were to have his application dealt with strictly on *American Cyanamid*[37] principles, he would almost always succeed for on a balance of convenience he would have little difficulty in showing that the status quo should be preserved until trial.[38] Whether the defendant would establish the statutory defence of contemplation or furtherance of a trade dispute would not fall to be considered at the interlocutory stage, and "the trade union's bargaining counter would disappear. Its power to bring instant and real pressure on the employer would be denied."[39] It has therefore been provided that where the party against whom an interlocutory injunction is sought claims that he acted in contemplation or furtherance of a trade dispute, the court shall, in exercising its discretion whether or not to grant the injunction, have regard to the likelihood of his establishing the statutory defence at the trial.[40] If, however, the consequences to the plaintiff of the injunction not being granted would be disastrous, the defendant will have to show a high degree of probability that the defence of statutory immunity would succeed if he is to defeat the claim for interlocutory relief.[41] Further, the likelihood of the defendant's establishing the statutory defence is only one of the factors to be considered by the court,[42] and as respects all other defences the *Cyanamid*[43] principles remain applicable.[44]

---

[33] *Ibid.* at p. 233.
[34] *Parnass Pelly Ltd.* v. *Hodges* [1982] F.S.R. 329.
[35] *Bryanston Finance Ltd.* v. *De Vries (No. 2)* [1976] Ch. 63 at 80, 81; and see at p. 78 where Buckley L.J. considered this "a special factor."
[36] Trade Union and Labour Relations Act 1974, s.13(1), as substituted by Trade Union and Labour Relations (Amendment) Act 1976, s.3(2).
[37] *American Cyanamid Co.* v. *Ethicon Ltd.* [1975] A.C. 396.
[38] *NWL Ltd.* v. *Woods* [1979] 1 W.L.R. 1294 at 1305.
[39] *Ibid.* at p. 1315, *per* Lord Scarman.
[40] Trade Union and Labour Relations Act 1974, s.17(2), inserted by Employment Protection Act 1975, s.125, Sched. 16, Pt. III, para. 6. This applies also to defences under ss.14(2) and 15 of the Act of 1974.
[41] *NWL Ltd.* v. *Woods* [1979] 1 W.L.R. 1294.
[42] *NWL Ltd.* v. *Woods, supra.*
[43] *American Cyanamid Co.* v. *Ethicon Ltd.* [1975] A.C. 396.
[44] *Dimbleby & Sons Ltd.* v. *National Union of Journalists* [1984] 1 W.L.R. 427.

(e) *Conduct of the parties.*   As with perpetual injunctions,[45] the court has always considered the conduct of the parties in deciding whether to grant an interlocutory injunction, and this appears to be unaffected by the *Cyanamid*[46] decision. Thus a plaintiff who complains of the defendant's breach of contract will not obtain an injunction if he, too, is substantially in breach.[47] Again, a lesser degree of acquiesence or laches suffices to debar a plaintiff from interlocutory relief than from obtaining a perpetual injunction; the refusal of an interlocutory injunction is merely a temporary rebuff, whereas the refusal of a perpetual injunction at the trial of the action "amounts to a decision that a right which has once existed is absolutely and for ever lost."[48] Moreover, interlocutory relief is granted only in matters of urgency, so that a plaintiff who delays thereby demonstrates the absence of any urgency requiring prompt relief. Even a month's delay between the assertion of a right and the issue of a writ may debar the plaintiff if in the meantime the defendant has contracted to let the subject-matter to third parties.[49] Delay is, however, of less significance where the case turns simply on the construction of documents.[50]

2. Conditions.   The court may impose terms as a condition of granting or withholding an interlocutory injunction.

(a) *Imposed on plaintiff.*

(1) GENERAL RULE   A plaintiff is almost invariably required to give an "undertaking in damages"; and an undertaking to this effect will be implied if the court grants an injunction or accepts an undertaking in lieu thereof.[51] If in the drawing up of the order for an interlocutory injunction, the undertaking is inadvertently omitted, it will be inserted by the court afterwards.[52] The undertaking is to pay damages for any loss to the defendant if at the trial it appears that the injunction was wrongly granted,[53] whether because the plaintiff is unable to prove at the trial the case he alleged at the granting of the injunction, or because the court granting the injunction took a wrong view of the law.[54] The undertaking is given to the court, and is not a contract between the plaintiff and defendant, although analogous principles apply in assessing

---

[45] See *ante,* p. 654.
[46] *American Cyanamid Co.* v. *Ethicon Ltd., supra.*
[47] *Jackson* v. *Hamlyn* [1953] 2 W.L.R. 709 at 713 (omitted from [1953] Ch. 577); *Litvinoff* v. *Kent* (1918) 34 T.L.R. 298; *ante,* p. 31.
[48] *Johnson* v. *Wyatt* (1863) 2 De G.J. & S. 18 at 25, *per* Turner L.J.; and see *Richards* v. *Revitt* (1877) 7 Ch.D. 224 at 226.
[49] *Selbit* v. *Goldwyn Ltd.* (1923) 58 L.J. News. 305 (film disclosing secret of sawing a woman in half).
[50] *Leigh* v. *National Union of Railwayman* [1970] Ch. 326.
[51] *Howard* v. *Press Printers Ltd.* (1904) 74 L.J.Ch. 100 at 104, 105.
[52] *Colledge* v. *Crossley, The Times,* March 18, 1975.
[53] For the origin of the practice, see *Chappell* v. *Davidson* (1856) 8 De G.M. & G. 1 at 2; *Smith* v. *Day* (1882) 21 Ch.D. 421 at 424; *Att.-Gen.* v. *Albany Hotel Co.* [1896] Ch. 696 at 703.
[54] *Griffith* v. *Blake* (1884) 27 Ch.D. 474, dissenting from a dictum of Jessel M.R. in *Smith* v. *Day, supra,* at pp. 424, 425.

whether the damages suffered by the defendant are too remote.[55] The plaintiff should adduce evidence as to his ability to meet the undertaking,[56] and if he gives misleading information as to means *ex parte*, the injunction may be discharged regardless of the merits.[57] The plaintiff may also be required to pay money into court,[58] or, if abroad, to give security for the damages.[58a] The undertaking cannot be enforced until it is established at or before trial that the injunction ought not to have been granted[59]; nor can it be enforced if the defendant admits liability and pays money into court which the plaintiff accepts without going on to claim a perpetual injunction.[60]

(2) NO UNDERTAKING. There are three categories of case in which the requirement that the plaintiff should give an undertaking in damages is modified.

(i) Where the Crown seeks to enforce the general law (as distinct from its proprietary rights[61]) the court will require the undertaking as a condition of granting the injunction only in exceptional cases, *e.g.* where the defendant shows a strong prima facie case that the statutory instrument under which the Crown is proceeding is invalid.[62] Where local authorities are seeking to enforce the general law, the court may in its discretion not require the undertaking.[63]

(ii) In matrimonial proceedings, an undertaking will not be incorporated in the order for an interlocutory injunction unless it has been specifically required by the court and expressly given by the plaintiff.[64]

(iii) Liquidators of a company, who are performing their statutory duties and have no personal interest in the outcome of the proceedings, may not be required to give an unlimited undertaking, but only one which is commensurate with the size of the assets of the company.[65]

(3) AVOIDING THE UNDERTAKING. Quite frequently a plaintiff who is claiming a perpetual injunction, *e.g.* to restrain the defendant from proceeding with a major construction project, chooses not to apply for

---

[55] *Smith* v. *Day, supra*, at p. 428. See *Graham* v. *Campbell* (1878) 7 Ch.D. 490.
[56] *Brigid Foley Ltd.* v. *Ellott* [1982] R.P.C. 433e.
[57] *Luck International plc* v. *Beswick* [1989] 1 W.L.R. 1268.
[58] *Jones* v. *Pacaya Rubber and Produce Co. Ltd.* [1911] 1 K.B. 455; *Baxter* v. *Claydon* [1952] W.N. 376.
[58a] *Harman Pictures N.V.* v. *Osborne* [1967] 1 W.L.R. 723 at 739.
[59] *Ushers Brewery Ltd.* v. *P. S. King & Co. (Finance) Ltd.* [1972] Ch. 148, approved in *Colledge* v. *Crossley, supra*.
[60] *Wiltshire Bacon Co.* v. *Associated Cinema Properties Ltd.* [1938] Ch. 268.
[61] *Att.-Gen.* v. *Wright* [1989] 1 W.L.R. 164.
[62] *F. Hoffman-La Roche & Co. A.G.* v. *Secretary of State for Trade and Industry* [1975] A.C. 295; *Director General of Fair Trading* v. *Tobyward Ltd.* [1989] 1 W.L.R. 517. For the former practice or rule, whereby it was "the inveterate practice" not to require an undertaking from the Crown, see *Att.-Gen.* v. *Albany Hotel Co.* [1896] 2 Ch. 696 at 704; *Secretary of State for War* v. *Cope* [1919] 2 Ch. 339 at 341.
[63] See *Rochdale B.C.* v. *Anders* [1988] 3 All E.R. 490; *Kirklees B.C.* v. *Wickes Building Supplies Ltd., The Independent*, May 15, 1990.
[64] Practice Direction (Injunction): Undertaking as to Damages [1974] 1 W.L.R. 576.
[65] *Re D.P.R. Futures Ltd.* [1989] 1 W.L.R. 778.

an interlocutory injunction because of the high cost of compensating the defendant for delay in completing the work in the event of the plaintiff not establishing his case at the trial. The defendant for his part cannot risk going on with the works in case the plaintiff succeeds at the trial but as no undertaking in damages has been given, he will obtain no recompense for his inevitable loss if the plaintiff's claim fails at the trial. Exceptionally, a plaintiff in such a case may be forced by the court to elect between applying for an interlocutory injunction on the usual terms or having his claim for a final injunction struck out.[65a]

(b) *Offered by defendant.* Upon the defendant giving suitable undertakings the court may withhold an injunction.[66] Thus in an action for interfering with a market by holding a rival market, an injunction was refused on the defendant's undertaking to keep an account of the animals received for sale and of the sums received for them and for stallage.[67] If an undertaking is given pending the hearing of the motion, and the plaintiff thereafter decides not to proceed for an injunction until trial, the defendant will have an unanswerable case for release from his undertaking.[68] If the motion for an injunction is stood over until trial upon the giving of undertakings, the defendant will only be able to obtain a discharge or modification of the undertaking upon good grounds, *e.g.* a significant change of circumstances[69]; but no such restriction applies where the motion has not been stood over until trial, but merely adjourned.[70]

3. Procedure

(a) *Chancery Division*

(1) ON NOTICE. In the Chancery Division, an application for interlocutory relief is made by motion in open court. The normal procedure is to serve two clear days' notice of motion, either with the writ or after service of it, whether or not the defendant has appeared.[71] In cases of urgency the court may give leave to serve short notice of motion, *i.e.* less than two clear days.[72] Motions are dealt with on every sitting day (except the last) in term.[73] Special arrangements are made for the hearing of motions in each vacation.

(2) EX PARTE. The court may also grant an injunction *ex parte, i.e.* without notice to the other side,[74] "if satisfied that the delay caused by

---

[65a] *Blue Town Investments Ltd.* v. *Higgs and Hill plc* [1990] 1 W.L.R. 696; but see *Oxy Electric Ltd.* v. *Zainuddin* [1990] 2 All E.R. 902.

[66] See *Cromford and High Peak Ry.* v. *Stockport, Disley and Whaley Bridge Ry.* (1857) 1 De G. & J. 326; *Mitchell* v. *Henry* (1880) 15 Ch.D. 181.

[67] *Elwes* v. *Payne* (1879) 12 Ch.D. 468; distinguished in *Birmingham Corporation* v. *Perry Barr Stadium Ltd.* [1972] 1 All E.R. 725; *Coco* v. *A.N. Clark (Engineers) Ltd.* [1969] R.P.C. 41 (undertaking to keep account of royalties).

[68] See *Woodcock* v. *Denton Tackle Co. Ltd.* [1978] F.S.R. 548.

[69] *Chanel Ltd.* v. *F.W. Woolworth & Co. Ltd.* [1981] 1 W.L.R. 485.

[70] *Butt* v. *Butt* [1987] 1 W.L.R. 1351.

[71] R.S.C., Ord. 8, rr. 2, 4.

[72] R.S.C., Ord. 8, r. 2(2).

[73] Practice Direction (Chancery Division: Motions Procedure) [1980] 1 W.L.R. 751.

[74] For "opposed *ex parte* motions" see *Pickwick International (G.B.) Ltd.* v. *Multiple Sound Distributors Ltd.* [1972] 1 W.L.R. 1213.

proceeding in the ordinary way would or might entail irreparable or serious mischief."[75] Such injunctions are thus for cases only of real urgency[76] but in such cases may be granted even before a writ has been issued.[77] They will usually be granted on an undertaking to issue the writ forthwith or as soon as practicable[78] and normally to operate for not more than seven days, and they may be varied or discharged on an application by the other party, even if made *ex parte*.[79] An *ex parte* injunction may also be granted if pressure of business in the courts prevents the prompt hearing of an opposed application.[80]

(b) *Queen's Bench Division.* In the Queen's Bench Division an application for interlocutory relief is made to a judge after service of a summons on the defendant. Again, two days' notice is required.[81] As the hearing takes place in chambers, a plaintiff who desires privacy should issue his writ in the Queen's Bench Division,[82] whereas if he seeks publicity he should sue in the Chancery Division.[83] *Ex parte* orders obtained in the Queen's Bench Division are usually granted for seven days, at the expiration of which the summons is returnable *inter partes.*

4. Mandatory interlocutory injunctions

The court has jurisdiction to grant a mandatory injunction on an interlocutory application,[84] but will very seldom do so[85]; the court usually requires a high degree of assurance that at the trial it will appear that the injunction was rightly granted.[86] Thus in a clear case a mandatory interlocutory injunction may be granted even though it amounts to decreeing specific performance of part of a contract.[87] Where a right of light is being infringed the court has compelled the defendant to pull down the building where he has endeavoured to steal a march by hurrying on the building after being served with notice of

---

[75] R.S.C., Ord. 8, r. 2(!).
[76] *Bates* v. *Lord Hailsham of St. Marylebone* [1972] 1 W.L.R. 1373 at 1380. And see *Bolivinter Oil S.A.* v. *Chase Manhattan Bank N.A. (Practice Note)* [1984] 1 W.L.R. 392 (*ex parte* injunction to restrain bank from payment under irrevocable letter of credit to be granted only in wholly exceptional circumstances).
[77] R.S.C., Ord. 29, r. 1(3): the applicant is normally required to undertake to issue a writ.
[78] *P.S. Refson & Co. Ltd.* v. *Saggers* [1984] 1 W.L.R. 1025.
[79] *London City Agency (J.C.D.) Ltd.* v. *Lee* [1970] Ch. 597.
[80] *Beese* v. *Woodhouse* [1970] 1 W.L.R. 586, disapproving *Graham* v. *Campbell* (1878) 7 Ch.D. 490 on this point.
[81] R.S.C., Ord. 32, r. 3.
[82] See *P. A. Thomas & Co.* v. *Mould* [1968] 2 Q.B. 913 (protection of confidential material).
[83] But "*Anton Piller*" applications in the Ch.D. (*post*, p. 673) are normally heard *in camera*. And see Practice Note (Court of Appeal: Anton Piller Orders) [1982] 1 W.L.R. 1420.
[84] *Strelley* v. *Pearson* (1880) 15 Ch.D. 113; *Bonner* v. *Great Western Ry.* (1883) 24 Ch.D. 1 at 10; *Hermann Loog* v. *Bean* (1884) 26 Ch.D. 306 at 314.
[85] *Blakemore* v. *The Glamorganshire Canal Navigation* (1832) 1 My. & K. 155.
[86] *Shepherd Homes Ltd.* v. *Sandham (No. 1)* [1971] Ch. 340; *Locabail International Finance Ltd.* v. *Agroexport* [1986] 1 W.L.R. 670. But see *Films Rover International Ltd.* v. *Cannon Film Sales Ltd.* [1987] 1 W.L.R. 670 at 679–682.
[87] *Smith* v. *Peters* (1875) L.R. 20 Eq. 511; *Astro Exito Navegacion S.A.* v. *Southland Enterprise Co. Ltd. (No. 2)* [1982] Q.B. 1248 (on appeal, not affecting this point, [1983] 2 A.C. 787). And see *Parker* v. *Camden L.B.C.* [1986] Ch. 162.

the proceedings,[88] or has evaded service of the writ[89] and continued the
building after due warning from the plaintiff. Again, the unlawful
eviction of a tenant will be met by a mandatory injunction for his
reinstatement.[90]

5. "Mareva"[91] injunctions

(a) *Origins.* It had been long established that the court would not
grant an injunction to restrain a defendant from parting with his assets
pending trial[92]: "the plaintiff, like other creditors of the defendant, must
obtain his judgment and then enforce it."[93] In 1975, the Court of
Appeal introduced an exception to this principle by granting *ex parte*
injunctions restraining defendants from disposing of or dealing with any
of their assets within the jurisdiction of the court,[94] or (in another case)
removing or disposing out of the jurisdiction moneys standing to the
credit of the defendants at a bank in London.[95] Injunctions of this kind
are now frequently granted, particularly in the Chancery Division and
the Commercial Court of the Queen's Bench Division. They are usually
obtained at an early stage of the proceedings, but may also be granted
after judgment so as to prevent the judgment being rendered
nugatory.[96]

(b) *Principles.* In order to found the jurisdiction to grant a *Mareva*
injunction, one of two conditions must be satisfied: that the plaintiff has
against the defendant some substantive cause of action justiciable in
England,[97] or that proceedings whose subject matter is within the scope
of the 1968 Brussels Convention on Jurisdiction and the Enforcement of
Judgments are or will be on foot in another country which is a signatory
to that Convention.[98] Since "the heart and core of the *Mareva*
injunction is the risk of the defendant removing his assets from the
jurisdiction and so stultifying any judgment given by the courts in the

---

[88] *Daniel* v. *Ferguson* [1891] 2 Ch. 27; *Mathias* v. *Davies* [1970] E.G.D. 370; 114 S.J. 268.
[89] *Von Joel* v. *Hornsey* [1895] 2 Ch. 774.
[90] *Luganda* v. *Service Hotels Ltd.* [1969] 2 Ch. 209; and see *Warder* v. *Cooper* [1970] Ch. 495. For
   further examples, see *Allport* v. *The Securities Co. Ltd.* (1895) 72 L.T. 533 (replacement of
   staircase); *Smith* v. *Peters* (1875) L.R. 20 Eq. 511 (order to admit valuer); *Thompson* v. *Park* [1944]
   K.B. 408 (forcible trespass); *Canadian Pacific Ry.* v. *Gaud* [1949] 2 K.B. 239 (refusal of discharged
   crew to leave ship); *Ghani* v. *Jones* [1970] 1 Q.B. 693 (police ordered to return passports); *Esso
   Petroleum Co. Ltd.* v. *Kingswood Motors (Addlestone) Ltd.* [1974] Q.B. 142 (land conveyed to avoid
   solus agreement: reconveyance ordered); *John Trenberth Ltd.* v. *National Westminster Bank Ltd.*
   (1979) 39 P. & C.R. 104 (flagrant trespass).
[91] *Mareva Compania Naviera S.A.* v. *International Bulk Carriers S.A.* [1975] 2 Lloyd's Rep. 509.
[92] *Lister & Co.* v. *Stubbs* (1890) 45 Ch.D. 1.
[93] *Barclay-Johnson* v. *Yuill* [1980] 1 W.L.R. 1259 at 1262, *per* Megarry V.-C.
[94] *Nippon Yusen Kaisha* v. *Karageorgis* [1975] 1 W.L.R. 1093.
[95] *Mareva Compania Naviera S.A.* v. *International Bulk Carriers S.A.* [1975] 2 Lloyd's Rep. 509.
[96] *Orwell Steel (Erection and Fabrication) Ltd.* v. *Asphalt and Tarmac (U.K.) Ltd.* [1984] 1 W.L.R.
   1097.
[97] *Siskina (Owners of cargo lately laden on board)* v. *Distos Compania Naviera S.A.* [1979] A.C. 210.
   In *A* v. *B* [1989] 2 Lloyd's Rep. 423 a conditional injunction was granted in anticipation of a cause
   of action arising.
[98] Civil Jurisdiction and Judgments Act 1982, s.25(1); *Republic of Haiti* v. *Duvalier* [1990] Q.B. 202;
   X v. *Y* [1990] Q.B. 220.

action,"[99] such injunctions are most often granted against defendants who are resident abroad. But the jurisdiction is not limited to foreign defendants.[1] It is exercisable when the defendant is domiciled, resident or present within the jurisdiction, as well as when he is not.[2] The injunctions may go, not merely to prevent the removal of assets from the jurisdiction, but to restrain the defendant from dissipating them within the jurisdiction.[3]

(c) *Guidelines.* The following guidelines have been laid down for determining whether a *Mareva* injunction should be granted[4]:

(1) DISCLOSURE. The plaintiff must make full and frank disclosure of all matters in his knowledge which are material for the judge to know.[5] He must also make proper inquiries for any relevant additional facts.[6] If there is non-disclosure of material facts, the injunction may be discharged irrespective of the merits of the case[7]; and the defendant may be entitled to damages without waiting for trial.[7a] Nevertheless the court has a discretion, upon consideration of the importance of the matters not disclosed and the culpability involved in the non-disclosure, to continue the injunction or to make a fresh order.[8]

(2) STATEMENT OF NATURE OF CASE. The plaintiff must state the ground of his claim against the defendant and its amount, and also state any points against it which the defendant has made. Further, he must show, on the evidence as a whole, that there is at least a good arguable case to be made on his behalf.[9]

(3) ASSETS IN ENGLAND OR ABROAD. Originally, the court would grant a *Mareva* injunction only if there was clear evidence that the defendant had movable assets in England,[10] and it became the established practice to limit the scope of the injunction to such assets.[11] The jurisdiction has, however, recently been extended.[11a] The existence of sufficient assets within the jurisdiction remains an excellent reason for confining the injunction to such assets.[12] But the court is now prepared, in

---

[99] *Barclay-Johnson* v. *Yuill* [1980] 1 W.L.R. 1259 at 1264, *per* Megarry V.-C., approved in *Rahman (Prince Abdul) bin Turki al Sudairy* v. *Abu-Taha* [1980] 1 W.L.R. 1268 at 1272.
[1] *Barclay-Johnson* v. *Yuill* [1980] 1 W.L.R. 1259 (defendant sold flat in London and was believed to be cruising in Mediterranean).
[2] S.C.A. 1981, s.37(3).
[3] *Z Ltd.* v. *A-Z* [1982] Q.B. 558, not following *A. J. Bekhor & Co. Ltd.* v. *Bilton* [1981] Q.B. 923 at 941, 942.
[4] *Third Chandris Shipping Corporation* v. *Unimarine S.A.* [1979] Q.B. 645 at 668, 669. And see *Z Ltd.* v. *A-Z* [1982] Q.B. 558 at 574, 578.
[5] See *Negocios Del Mar S.A.* v. *Doric Shipping Corporation S.A. (The Assios)* [1979] 1 Lloyd's Rep. 331.
[6] *Brink's Mat Ltd.* v. *Elcombe* [1988] 1 W.L.R. 1350.
[7] *Lloyd's Bowmaker Ltd.* v. *Britannia Arrow Holdings plc* [1988] 1 W.L.R. 1337.
[7a] *Ali and Fahd Shobokshi Group Ltd.* v. *Moneim* [1989] 1 W.L.R. 710 at 722.
[8] *Brink's Mat Ltd.* v. *Elcombe, supra; Behbehani* v. *Salem (Note)* [1989] 1 W.L.R. 723.
[9] *Ninemia Maritime Corpn.* v. *Trave Schiffahrtsgesellschaft m.b.H. und Co. K.G.* [1983] 1 W.L.R. 1412.
[10] *MBPXL Corporation* v. *International Banking Corporation Ltd.* (unreported) [1975] C.A.T. No. 411.
[11] *Ashtiani* v. *Kashi* [1987] Q.B. 888.
[11a] See *Derby & Co. Ltd.* v. *Weldon (No. 6)* [1990] 1 W.L.R. 1139.
[12] *Derby & Co.* v. *Weldon (Nos. 3 & 4)* [1990] Ch. 65 at 80.

exceptional circumstances and subject to appropriate safeguards designed to protect third parties,[13] to grant the injunction in "worldwide" form, before judgment[14] or afterwards,[15] and irrespective of the existence or otherwise of assets in England.[16]

(4) RISK OF REMOVAL OR DISSIPATION. The plaintiff should give some grounds for believing that there is a risk of the assets being removed before the judgment is satisfied. The existence of such a risk is essential: the injunction will not be granted merely to provide plaintiffs with security even where this could be done without causing hardship to the defendant.[17]

(5) UNDERTAKING IN DAMAGES. The usual undertaking in damages[18] must be given, and in suitable cases may have to be supported by a bond or security. However, the poverty of the plaintiff will not necessarily deprive him of his injunction if the balance of justice requires it.[19]

(d) *Form of order.* The form of order which is now customary restrains the defendant from removing from the jurisdiction, or otherwise disposing of or dealing with any of his assets within the jurisdiction, including a specified asset (*e.g.* money in a named bank account), save in so far as such assets exceed in value the amount (which is specified) of the plaintiff's claim.[20] An order originally made in this wide form may later be varied, *e.g.* if the defendant bona fide wishes to make payments in the ordinary course of his business or to provide for his living expenses[21] or for the costs of defending the action.[22] The application to vary may be made by a third party,[23] *e.g.* to obtain payment of a debt which would have been paid if the injunction had not been granted.[24]

(e) *Operation.* The *Mareva* injunction operates *in rem* on the assets of the defendant,[25] and the court is accordingly astute to protect the interests which third parties may have in these assets or otherwise.[26] If the injunction will interfere substantially with the business of an innocent third party, it should not be granted at all (or should be

---

[13] See *Babanaft International Co. S.A.* v. *Bassatne* [1990] Ch. 13 at 40, 41; *Republic of Haiti* v. *Duvalier* [1990] Q.B. 202 at 217–219.

[14] *Republic of Haiti* v. *Duvalier* [1990] Q.B. 202; *Derby & Co.* v. *Weldon* [1990] Ch. 48; *Derby & Co.* v. *Weldon (Nos. 3 & 4)* [1990] Ch. 65.

[15] *Babanaft International Co. S.A.* v. *Bassatne* [1990] Ch. 13.

[16] *Derby & Co.* v. *Weldon (Nos. 3 & 4), supra.*

[17] *Ninemia Maritime Corp.* v. *Trave Schiffahrtsgesellschaft m.b.H. und Co. K.G.* [1983] 1 W.L.R. 1412.

[18] See *ante,* p. 666.

[19] *Allen* v. *Jambo Holdings Ltd.* [1980] 1 W.L.R. 1252.

[20] *A.J. Bekhor & Co.* v. *Bilton* [1981] Q.B. 923 at 936; *Z Ltd.* v. *A-Z* [1982] Q.B. 558 at 576.

[21] *A.J. Bekhor & Co.* v. *Bilton* [1981] Q.B. 923; *PCW (Underwriting Agencies) Ltd.* v. *Dixon* [1983] 2 All E.R. 158, 697n; *Avant Petroleum Inc.* v. *Gatoil Overseas Inc.* [1986] 2 Lloyd's Rep. 236.

[22] *A* v. *C (No. 2)* [1981] Q.B. 961n.; *PCW (Underwriting Agencies) Ltd.* v. *Dixon, supra.*

[23] See *Iraqi Ministry of Defence* v. *Arcepey Shipping Co. S.A.* [1981] Q.B. 65.

[24] *A* v. *B (X Intervening)* [1983] 2 Lloyd's Rep. 532.

[25] *Z Ltd.* v. *A-Z* [1982] Q.B. 558 at 573.

[26] See *S.C.F. Finance Co. Ltd.* v. *Masri* [1985] 1 W.L.R. 876 at 883.

discharged[27]) or at least be made subject to adequate undertakings.[28] Frequently the assets caught by the injunction will be moneys held at the defendant's bank: in such a case the plaintiff will be required to give an undertaking to pay any expenses reasonably incurred by the bank in complying with the injunction,[29] and the injunction should be made expressly without prejudice to any right of set-off which the bank may have in respect of loans made to the defendant before the grant of the injunction.[30]

(f) *Ancillary orders.* In order that the *Mareva* injunction shall not be stultified by the defendant, the court may make ancillary orders, *e.g.* for discovery or interrogatories as to the defendant's assets.[31] This jurisdiction is to be exercised sparingly and not where the same object could be achieved by other means, such as directing the defendant to attend for cross-examination on affidavits sworn by him.[32] But, in an extreme case, the court may go so far as to order delivery up of assets to the plaintiff's solicitor[33]; and, where appropriate, the writ *ne exeat regno*[34] may be issued in conjunction with a *Mareva* order.[35]

6. Anton Piller orders

The *Anton Piller*[36] order is another modern development,[37] but is something of a hybrid between discovery[38] and injunction. It is designed for cases in which there is a serious risk that the defendant may destroy vital material so as to defeat the ends of justice before any application on notice to the defendant could be brought before the court. It enables the plaintiff, attended by his solicitor,[39] to go to the premises of the defendant and to inspect and take away the documents or articles specified in the order. The order is obtained on an *ex parte* application in chambers and has proved of particular use in cases of "pirated" sound recordings.[40] The order may be granted in aid of a *Mareva* injunction,[41] and sometimes extends to requiring the defendant to answer questions on oath or to disclose documents. The usual cross-undertaking in damages[42] must be given by the plaintiff and, if the order

---

[27] *Galaxia Maritime S.A.* v. *Mineralimportexport* [1982] 1 W.L.R. 539.
[28] *Clipper Maritime Co. Ltd. of Monrovia* v. *Mineralimportexport* [1981] 1 W.L.R. 1262.
[29] *Z Ltd.* v. *A-Z* [1982] Q.B. 558 at 577.
[30] *Oceanica Castelana Armadora S.A. of Panama* v. *Mineralimportexport* [1983] 1 W.L.R. 1294.
[31] *A* v. *C* [1981] Q.B. 956n.; *A.J. Bekhor & Co. Ltd.* v. *Bilton* [1981] Q.B. 923; *Z Ltd.* v. *A-Z* [1982] Q.B. 558.
[32] *A.J. Bekhor & Co. Ltd.* v. *Bilton, supra.*
[33] *C.B.S. United Kingdom Ltd.* v. *Lambert* [1983] Ch. 37 (alleged infringer of copyright buying Lotus Elite and Jaguar XJ–6 cars).
[34] See *ante*, p. 583.
[35] *Al Nahkel for Contracting and Trading Ltd.* v. *Lowe* [1986] Q.B. 235.
[36] *Anton Piller K.G.* v. *Manufacturing Process Ltd.* [1976] Ch. 55.
[37] The first reported case was *E.M.I. Ltd.* v. *Pandit* [1975] 1 W.L.R. 302.
[38] See *ante*, pp. 29, 582.
[39] *Anton Piller K.G.* v. *Manufacturing Process Ltd., supra*, at p. 61 (also discussing other safeguards).
[40] See *Ex p. Island Records Ltd.* [1978] Ch. 122.
[41] *Johnson* v. *L. & A. Philatelics Ltd.* [1981] F.S.R. 286.
[42] See *ante*, p. 666.

is executed in an excessive or oppressive manner, the defendant may be awarded aggravated damages.[43] He will also be awarded damages immediately on the cross-undertaking if the plaintiff fails to make a material disclosure as to means.[44] Like the *Mareva* injunction, the *Anton Piller* order may be made, not merely at an early stage of the action, but in aid of the final judgment.[45]

In relation to the requirement that the defendant should answer questions on oath or disclose documents, the usual privilege against self-incrimination is available[46] save in proceedings for infringement of rights in intellectual property or for passing-off, from which the privilege has been removed by statute.[47] Documents obtained under an *Anton Piller* order are subject to an implied undertaking not to use them for any collateral or ulterior purpose, but the court may in special circumstances release the plaintiff from the undertaking.[48]

C. Operation of Injunction

1. Suspension. "In cases where a good deal of time must necessarily elapse to enable the parties to comply with an injunction without being put to grievous annoyance and expense,"[49] the court may, in a proper case (and not, *e.g.* in order to allow the defendant to carry out ameliorative works on the plaintiff's land against the plaintiff's wishes[50]), grant an injunction but suspend its operation.[51] Alternatively, the court may delay imposing the injunction[52] until the defendant has had a reasonable opportunity of setting his house in order; and this may be done even if the Attorney-General is plaintiff.[53] The court will be the more ready to refrain from imposing an immediate injunction where the plaintiff has suffered no pecuniary damage,[54] where the injury is temporary and the defendant has offered compensation,[55] where the plaintiff has in the past permitted the conduct of which he complains,[56]

---

[43] *Columbia Picture Industries Inc.* v. *Robinson* [1987] Ch. 38: the judgment contains a comprehensive review of the *Anton Piller* jurisdiction.

[44] *Lock International plc* v. *Beswick* [1989] 1 W.L.R. 1268.

[45] *Distributori Automatici Italia SpA* v. *Holford General Trading Co. Ltd.* [1985] 1 W.L.R. 1066.

[46] *Rank Film Distributors Ltd.* v. *Video Information Centre (a firm)* [1982] A.C. 380.

[47] S.C.A. 1981, s.72; *Universal City Studios Inc.* v. *Hubbard* [1984] Ch. 225.

[48] *Crest Homes plc* v. *Marks* [1987] A.C. 829.

[49] *Att.-Gen.* v. *Bradford Canal Proprietors* (1866) L.R. 2 Eq. 71 at 83, 84, *per* Page Wood V.-C.

[50] *Charrington* v. *Simons & Co. Ltd.* [1971] 1 W.L.R. 598.

[51] *Att.-Gen.* v. *Colney Hatch Lunatic Asylum* (1868) 4 Ch.App. 146; *Stollmeyer* v. *Petroleum Development Co. Ltd.* [1918] S.C. 498n.; *Pride of Derby and Derbyshire Angling Association Ltd.* v. *British Celanese Ltd.* [1953] Ch. 149; *Harlow Development Corporation* v. *Cox Bros. (Butchers) Ltd.* [1975] J.P.L. 289; (1974) 233 E.G. 765.

[52] *Stollmeyer* v. *Trinidad Lake Petroleum Co. Ltd.* [1918] A.C. 485; *Vestry of St. Mary, Islington* v. *Hornsey U.D.C.* [1900] 1 Ch. 695.

[53] *Att.-Gen.* v. *Birmingham, Tame and Rea District Drainage Board* [1912] A.C. 788 at 812.

[54] *Stollmeyer* v. *Trinidad Lake Petroleum Co. Ltd.*, *supra.*

[55] *Woollerton & Wilson Ltd.* v. *Richard Costain Ltd.* [1970] 1 W.L.R. 411 (crane jib in airspace); but this particular application of the power to suspend was doubted in *Charrington* v. *Simons & Co. Ltd.*, *supra*, at p. 603, and not followed in *John Trenberth Ltd.* v. *National Westminster Bank Ltd.* (1979) 39 P. & C.R. 104 (immediate injunction to compel removal of scaffolding from plaintiff's land).

[56] *Vestry of St. Mary, Islington* v. *Hornsey U.D.C.*, *supra.*

where the injunction is mandatory and there is no immediate damage,[57] or where war conditions make this course desirable. Thus an injunction to restrain the use of a house as a hospital in breach of a covenant to use it only as a private dwelling-house was suspended during the war.[58]

2. Enforcement. Once an injunction has been granted, it may be enforced by committal, fine, or sequestration.[59]

(a) *Committal.* The court may commit to prison any person who disobeys an injunction; and the court (including a county court) may do this even if the injunction has subsequently ceased to be effective.[60] The act of disobedience need not be contumacious; provided the act is clearly a breach,[61] it suffices if it is intentional and not merely casual or accidental.[62] The contempt must be proved according to the standard appropriate in criminal proceedings, *i.e.* beyond reasonable doubt.[63] Acts done in defiance of the injunction are illegal and may be declared invalid.[64] The court may commit not only the parties enjoined but also directors and officers (though not, it seems, individual members[65]) of any corporate party enjoined,[66] and also any persons who knowingly abet the parties in their breach of the injunction, on the ground that they are obstructing the course of justice.[67] Thus new trustees are in contempt if they do an act which they know the former trustees had been restrained from doing.[68] This power normally makes it inappropriate to grant an injunction against a non-party abetting a breach,[69] and if one is desired an action against the abettors should be commenced.[70]

Despite these wide powers of enforcement, the correct wording of an injunction is not that "the defendant, his servants and agents" are restrained, but that "the defendant whether by himself or by his servants or his agents" is restrained; for it is wrong to suggest that a

---

[57] *Abingdon Corporation* v. *James* [1940] Ch. 287.
[58] *Frost* v. *The King Edward VII Welsh National Memorial Association for Prevention, Treatment and Abolition of Tuberculosis* [1918] 2 Ch. 180 (compromised on appeal: (1918) 35 T.L.R. 138).
[59] R.S.C., Ord. 45, r. 5; and see Ord. 46, r. 5 (sequestration) and Ord. 52 (committal).
[60] *Jennison* v. *Baker* [1972] 2 Q.B. 52.
[61] *P. A. Thomas & Co.* v. *Mould* [1968] 2 Q.B. 913.
[62] *Heatons Transport (St. Helens) Ltd.* v. *Transport & General Workers' Union* [1973] A.C. 15 at 108, 109.
[63] *Re Bramblevale Ltd.* [1970] Ch. 128; *Kent County Council* v. *Batchelor* (1976) 75 L.G.R. 151.
[64] *Clarke* v. *Chadburn* [1985] 1 W.L.R. 78 (change in union rules).
[65] See *Pride of Derby & Derbyshire Angling Association Ltd.* v. *British Celanese Ltd.* [1953] Ch. 149 at 192.
[66] See *Lewis* v. *Pontypridd, Caerphilly, and Newport Ry.* (1895) 11 T.L.R. 203; *Biba Ltd.* v. *Stratford Investments Ltd.* [1973] Ch. 281.
[67] *Seaward* v. *Paterson* [1897] 1 Ch. 545; *Malavez* v. *Knox* [1977] 1 N.Z.L.R. 467 (breach of undertaking).
[68] *Avery* v. *Andrews* (1882) 51 L.J.Ch. 414; and see *Smith-Barry* v. *Dawson* (1891) 27 L.R.Ir. 558 (copies of injunction conspicuously exhibited).
[69] *Elliot* v. *Klinger* [1967] 1 W.L.R. 1165.
[70] *Acrow (Automation) Ltd.* v. *Rex Chainbelt Inc.* [1971] 1 W.L.R. 1676 (injunction against obeying another company's instructions given in breach of injunction).

direct order has been made against servants or agents who are not parties to the proceedings.[71]

(b) *Sequestration.* An injunction may also be enforced by sequestrating the property of the disobedient parties and of directors and officers of corporate parties.[72] Hence an injunction may be effectively granted against a foreign corporation which has assets within the jurisdiction.[73]

(c) *Fine.* As an alternative to committal[74] or sequestration[75] the court may impose the lesser penalty of a fine.

Section 3. Exercise of Jurisdiction

It is impossible to enumerate all the cases in which the remedy by way of injunction is available. It may be used to give effect to a right recognisable only in equity, *e.g.* to restrain breaches of trust[76] or breaches of restrictive covenants enforceable only in equity[77] or acts of equitable waste.[78] More commonly it is used to aid a legal right, *e.g.* by restraining a tort or breach of contract. Sometimes it is used to restrain breaches of the criminal law.[79] Moreover, despite the abolition of the common injunction, it may still be used to restrain certain judicial proceedings. The following are the more important classes of case in which injunctions are granted.

1. Breach of contract

(a) *General.* The equitable jurisdiction to grant an injunction to restrain a breach of contract is closely allied to its jurisdiction to order specific performance of a contract; and often what is a defence to one type of remedy will also be a defence to the other.[80] The natural method of enforcing a contract in equity is by specific performance if the contract is positive[81] and by injunction if it is negative.[82] Thus an injunction is the remedy for a breach of a valid covenant not to carry on a certain trade,[83] unless the conduct of the covenantee has disentitled him to that relief.[84]

---

[71] See *Marengo* v. *Daily Sketch and Sunday Graphic Ltd.* [1948] 1 All E.R. 406.
[72] R.S.C., Ord. 45, r. 5.
[73] *Hospital for Sick Children (Board of Governors)* v. *Walt Disney Productions Inc.* [1968] Ch. 52.
[74] *Phonographic Performance Ltd.* v. *Amusement Caterers (Peckham) Ltd.* [1964] Ch. 195.
[75] *Steiner Products Ltd.* v. *Willy Steiner Ltd.* [1966] 1 W.L.R. 986; *Shoreham-by-Sea U.D.C.* v. *Dolphin Canadian Proteins Ltd.* (1972) 71 L.G.R. 261.
[76] *Ante*, p. 283.
[77] *Post*, p. 678.
[78] *Post*, p. 680.
[79] *Ante*, p. 650.
[80] See *Lumley* v. *Ravenscroft* [1895] 1 Q.B. 683 at 685.
[81] But see *ante*, pp. 658, 669, for mandatory injunctions to enforce contractual obligations.
[82] See *Doherty* v. *Allman* (1878) 3 App.Cas. 709 at 720; *ante*, p. 652.
[83] See *Nordenfelt* v. *Maxim Nordenfelt Guns and Ammunition Co. Ltd.* [1894] A.C. 535.
[84] *General Billposting Co. Ltd.* v. *Atkinson* [1909] A.C. 118; *Measures Bros. Ltd.* v. *Measures* [1910] 2 Ch. 248; *ante*, p. 654.

(b) *Negativity.* A covenant may be negative in substance, though not in form. Thus if A agrees to take from B the whole of the electric energy required for his premises, B may obtain an injunction to prevent A from taking any electric energy from C; for in substance the agreement does not oblige A to take any electricity but merely not to take it from anyone but B.[85] Similarly, an injunction may be granted to enforce a "tied-house" covenant, whereby a publican agrees that a certain brewer shall have the exclusive right of supplying beer to the public house.[86]

(c) *Negative and positive.* An agreement may be in part negative and in part positive. Here the court may grant an injunction restraining a breach of the negative part[87] even if it would not decree specific performance of the positive part (*e.g.* as being an agreement for personal services[88]), and even if the plaintiff does not show that the breach will cause him damage.[89] Mere inconsistency with positive obligations is not enough; there must be some express or implied prohibition against doing the particular acts in question.[90] Even if there is an express negative term, no injunction will be granted if that term merely repeats in a negative form the whole of the positive obligation, instead of prohibiting particular acts.[91]

(d) *Personal services.* Not every obligation in a contract for personal services (whether between employer and employee, manager and artiste, or otherwise) will be enforced by means of an injunction. Three kinds of case have to be considered.

First, no injunction will be granted if the contract is purely affirmative, as where a company's manager agrees to give the whole of his time to the company's business during a specified period.[92]

Secondly, no injunction will be granted to enforce a negative stipulation preventing the defendant from entering into *any* other employment during a specified period, for the effect would be to compel him either to carry out the contract or to remain idle.[93]

Thirdly, where the services involve some special skill or talent, the court will not enforce negative obligations (typically, not during a specified period to work in a *defined activity* otherwise than in association with the other party) if to do so would effectively compel the

---

[85] *Metropolitan Electric Supply Co. Ltd.* v. *Ginder* [1901] 2 Ch. 799.
[86] *Catt* v. *Tourle* (1869) 4 Ch.App. 654.
[87] *Lumley* v. *Wagner* (1852) 1 De G.M. & G. 604; *Warner Brothers Pictures Incorporated* v. *Nelson* [1937] 1 K.B. 209. See also *National Provincial Bank of England* v. *Marshall* (1888) 40 Ch.D. 112; *Grimston* v. *Cunningham* [1894] 1 Q.B. 125.
[88] See *ante*, p. 593.
[89] *Marco Productions Ltd.* v. *Pagola* [1945] K.B. 111.
[90] *Bower* v. *Bantam Investments Ltd.* [1972] 1 W.L.R. 1120; and see n. 92, *infra*. But see *Sky Petroleum Ltd.* v. *V.I.P. Ltd.* [1976] 1 W.L.R. 576 (injunction restraining seller from withholding supplies).
[91] *Chapman* v. *Westerby* [1913] W.N. 277.
[92] *Whitwood Chemical Co.* v. *Hardman* [1891] 2 Ch. 416; *Mortimer* v. *Beckett* [1920] 1 Ch. 571 (Joe Beckett, the boxer).
[93] *Rely-a-Bell Burglar and Fire Alarm Co. Ltd.* v. *Eisler* [1926] Ch. 609.

defendant to perform his positive obligations under the contract. Compulsion is a question to be decided on the facts of each case, with a realistic regard for the probable impact of an injunction on the need of the defendant to maintain the skill or talent.[94] The duration of the contract is a highly material consideration, for the longer the term for which the injunction is sought, the more readily will compulsion be inferred.[95] For this purpose, the courts appear to draw the line between long- and short-term engagements at two years or thereabouts.[96] Other factors which may weigh against the grant of an injunction are: that the plaintiff's own obligations could not be enforced against him[97] (although want of mutuality by itself is unlikely to be decisive[98]); or that the plaintiff will give no assurance of his intention to perform his own obligations[99]; or that the contract involves obligations of mutual trust and confidence, especially where the defendant's trust in the plaintiff may have been betrayed or his confidence in him has genuinely gone.[1] And an injunction was refused when the real object of seeking it was to gratify the pride of a football club by restraining one of its players from playing for a rival club.[2]

(e) *Covenants concerning land.* Normally no one except a party to a contract can sue or be sued on it.[3] But the burden or benefit of a covenant entered into between landlord and tenant may run with the land and with the reversion so that an assignee of the lease or of the reversion may sue or be sued on the covenant.[4] Moreover, negative or restrictive covenants concerning land may, in some circumstances, be enforced by and against persons who are neither the original contracting parties nor connected by the relationship of landlord and tenant.[5] Prohibitory injunctions are frequently obtained for the purpose of enforcing restrictive covenants, the details of which lie outside the scope of this work.[6]

(f) *Terms of partnership.* In many cases the court will enforce by injunction the due observance of the terms of a partnership and of the duties which under the general law the partners owe to each other. For instance, an injunction may be granted to prevent one partner from

---

[94] *Warren* v. *Mendy* [1989] 1 W.L.R. 853 at 867.
[95] *Ibid.*
[96] *Warren* v. *Mendy, supra,* at pp. 865, 866. See *Lumley* v. *Wagner* (1852) 1 De G.M. & G. 604 (three months: injunction granted); *Page One Records Ltd.* v. *Britton* [1968] 1 W.L.R. 157 ("The Troggs" pop group; five years: injunction refused); *Warren* v. *Mendy, supra* (two years: injunction refused). But see *Warner Brothers Pictures Inc.* v. *Nelson* [1937] 1 K.B. 309 (Bette Davis), doubted in *Warren* v. *Mendy, supra,* at p. 865.
[97] *Page One Records Limited* v. *Britton, supra.* See *ante*, p. 596, for mutuality in specific performance.
[98] *Warren* v. *Mendy, supra,* at p. 866.
[99] *Chappell* v. *Times Newspapers Ltd.* [1975] 1 W.L.R. 482.
[1] *Warren* v. *Mendy, supra,* at pp. 866, 867.
[2] *Radford* v. *Campbell* (1890) 6 T.L.R. 488 (Nottingham Forest v. Blackburn Rovers); and see *Detroit Football Co.* v. *Dublinski* [1956] O.R. 744; [1957] O.R. 58.
[3] See *ante*, pp. 93 *et seq.*, for the rule and some other exceptions.
[4] *Spencer's Case* (1583) 5 Co.Rep. 16a; L.P.A. 1925, ss.140–142.
[5] A relatively late development of equity: the *fons et origo* is generally considered to be *Tulk* v. *Moxhay* (1848) 2 Ph. 744. See *ante*, p. 11, n. 43.
[6] See Megarry and Wade's *Law of Real Property* (5th ed., 1984), pp. 760–793.

excluding another from taking part in the management of the partnership business,[7] a right to which he is entitled in the absence of any contrary agreement.[8] Such an injunction would, however, be refused to a partner who has been convicted of dishonesty.[9] Again, a partner who becomes insane,[10] or commits a breach of the terms of partnership,[11] may be restrained from interfering in the business pending an action for dissolution. Again, an injunction may be granted to enforce a partner's right to inspect the partnership books, either personally or by a proper agent,[12] or to restrain the improper exercise of a power of expulsion.[13] And an injunction may be granted to prevent a partner from engaging in another business contrary to a clause in the partnership articles, or, if the business is a rival business, even though there be no such clause.[14]

2. Other wrongs. An injunction is not restricted to remedying breaches of contract but will be granted to restrain other wrongs. Indeed, the origin of the jurisdiction seems to have been derived from the old common law writ of prohibition of waste.[15] The following are the more important cases remedied by the grant of an injunction.

(a) *Waste.* Waste consists of any act by a tenant for years or for life or *pur autre vie* which alters the nature of the land, whether for the better or the worse. An injunction will not be granted to restrain an alteration for the better, or *ameliorative* waste, as, for instance, the conversion of dilapidated barracks into dwelling-houses.[16] Nor will an injunction be granted to restrain merely *permissive* waste, that is, failure to do that which ought to be done, as by allowing buildings to fall into disrepair.[17]

(1) VOLUNTARY WASTE. The commission of *voluntary* waste, that is, acts of destruction in lands or buildings, as, for instance, the opening of mines or the cutting of timber, will be restrained[18] unless the instrument granting the tenant his interest exempts him from liability for waste.[19] The injunction may be obtained not only by the owner of the inheritance, but also by a remainderman with only a limited interest.[20]

---

[7] *Hall* v. *Hall* (1850) 12 Beav. 414.
[8] Partnership Act 1890, s.24(5).
[9] *Carmichael* v. *Evans* [1904] 1 Ch. 486 (interlocutory injunction). An appeal was compromised, the expelled partner acquiring the business: [1904] W.N. 47.
[10] *J.* v. *S.* [1894] 3 Ch. 72.
[11] See *Green* v. *Howell* [1910] 1 Ch. 495.
[12] *Bevan* v. *Webb* [1901] 2 Ch. 59; Partnership Act 1890, s.24(9); and see *post*, pp. 684, 685.
[13] *Hall* v. *Hall, supra* (injunction granted: further proceedings: (1850) 3 Mac. & G. 79 (see at p. 84); (1855) 20 Beav. 139); *Carmichael* v. *Evans, supra* (injunction refused); and see *Blisset* v. *Daniel* (1853) 10 Hare 493.
[14] *England* v. *Curling* (1844) 8 Beav. 129.
[15] *Goodeson* v. *Gallatin* (1771) 2 Dick. 455.
[16] *Doherty* v. *Allman* (1878) 3 App.Cas. 709. See also *Meux* v. *Cobley* [1892] 2 Ch. 253.
[17] *Powys* v. *Blagrave* (1854) 4 De G.M. & G. 448.
[18] See *Garth* v. *Cotton* (1753) 1 Dick. 183; **2 W. & T.L.C. 896.**
[19] See *Smythe* v. *Smythe* (1818) 2 Swans. 251.
[20] See *Garth* v. *Cotton, supra*, at p. 197.

(2) EQUITABLE WASTE. Even where the tenant is made unimpeachable for waste at law,[21] equity will by injunction restrain acts of malicious or wanton destruction known as *equitable* waste, such as dismantling the mansion house[22] or felling ornamental timber.[23] Further, although a tenant in tail after possibility of issue extinct is not liable for waste at law, he will be restrained from committing equitable waste,[24] and so will a tenant in fee simple defeasible.[25] But a tenant in tail absolute will not, even if he is restrained by statute from barring the entail.[26]

(b) *Trespass.* A landowner whose title is not disputed is prima facie entitled to an injunction to restrain a threatened or apprehended[27] trespass on his land even if the trespass will not harm him.[28] An injunction may also be granted against a defendant who disputes the plaintiff's title, *e.g.* where he entered and felled a tree and threatened to cut more.[29] But the court refused to enjoin some lepidopterists who committed a mere technical trespass without intending to infringe any rights of property and who desisted on request.[30] Moreover, the court is especially slow to grant an injunction which will exclude even an adult child from his parent's home,[31] but will do so in grave circumstances, as where the child has assaulted the parent.[31a] The person entitled in possession is normally the proper plaintiff[32]; a reversioner or remainder-man can sue only if he can show that the trespass causes damage to his reversionary interest.[33]

(c) *Nuisance*

(1) PRIVATE NUISANCE. Injunctions are often used in cases of nuisance, thus obviating a multiplicity of suits for damages. In contrast with its treatment of waste,[34] "equity will only interfere, in case of nuisance, where the thing complained of is a nuisance at law; there is no such thing as an equitable nuisance."[35] As with trespass,[36] an action to restrain a nuisance is usually brought by the person in occupation of the property affected; a reversioner can bring an action for damages or an

---

[21] See L.P.A. 1925, s.135, re-enacting J.A. 1873, s.25(3).
[22] *Vane* v. *Lord Barnard* (1716) 2 Vern. 738.
[23] *Micklethwait* v. *Micklethwait* (1857) 1 De G. & J. 504; *Baker* v. *Sebright* (1879) 13 Ch.D. 179; *Weld-Blundell* v. *Wolseley* [1903] 2 Ch. 664.
[24] *Abrahall* v. *Bubb* (1679) 2 Swans. 172.
[25] *Turner* v. *Wright* (1860) 2 De G.F. & J. 234; *Re Hanbury* [1913] 2 Ch. 357.
[26] *Att.-Gen.* v. *Duke of Marlborough* (1818) 3 Madd. 498.
[27] On *quia timet* injunctions generally see *ante*, pp. 651, 659.
[28] *Patel* v. *W.H. Smith (Eziot) Ltd.* [1987] 1 W.L.R. 853.
[29] *Stanford* v. *Hurlstone* (1873) 9 Ch.App. 116.
[30] *Fielden* v. *Cox* (1906) 22 T.L.R. 411 (one Rupert Brooke who with three other defendants "went to catch a butterfly and caught a writ"; plaintiff awarded the 1s. damages paid into court and made to pay defendants' costs).
[31] *Waterhouse* v. *Waterhouse* (1905) 94 L.T. 133.
[31a] *Stevens* v. *Stevens* (1907) 24 T.L.R. 20; *Egan* v. *Egan* [1975] Ch. 218.
[32] See *Cooper* v. *Crabtree* (1882) 20 Ch.D. 589.
[33] *Mayfair Property Co.* v. *Johnston* [1894] 1 Ch. 508; *Jones* v. *Llanrwst U.D.C.* [1911] 1 Ch. 393.
[34] *Supra.* For damages in lieu of injunction in cases of nuisance, see *ante*, p. 657.
[35] *Soltau* v. *De Held* (1851) 2 Sim.(N.S.) 133 at 151, *per* Kindersley V.-C.
[36] *Supra.*

injunction only if the nuisance causes a permanent injury to his reversion,[37] *e.g.* if it consists of a building obstructing an ancient light.[38]

(2) PUBLIC NUISANCE. If there is a public nuisance, *e.g.* the obstruction or excessive user of a highway,[39] the usual remedy is by criminal proceedings by way of indictment to punish the offender. But an action may be brought by the Attorney-General to redress the grievance by way of injunction[40]; and a private individual who suffers particular damage from the nuisance may maintain an action in his own name for an injunction.[41]

(d) *False statements.* Before the Judicature Act 1873, the Court of Chancery had no jurisdiction to restrain the publication of a libel,[42] although this power had been conferred on the common law courts in 1854.[43] Since 1875, all Divisions of the High Court have had jurisdiction to grant injunctions (even interlocutory injunctions) restraining the publication of a libel.[44] An interlocutory injunction, however, will be granted only in the clearest cases,[45] *i.e.* where the court would set aside the verdict as unreasonable if the jury did not find the matter complained of to be libellous,[46] and there is a danger of a repetition of the libel.[47] Such an injunction ought not to be granted if the defendant intends to plead justification, fair comment[48] or qualified privilege,[49] though where malice is in issue and the plaintiff adduces overwhelming evidence of it, an injunction may be granted.[50] The court may also restrain the making of untrue statements calculated to injure a man in his trade or business,[51] or false statements of fact as to the personal character or conduct of a candidate at a parliamentary or local election,[52] or groundless threats[53] of legal proceedings for an alleged infringement of a patent[54] or registered design.[55] But where a trade

[37] *White* v. *London General Omnibus Co.* [1914] W.N. 78.
[38] *Jones* v. *Llanrwst U.D.C.* [1911] 1 Ch. 393 at 404.
[39] *Att.-Gen.* v. *Brighton & Hove Co-operative Supply Association* [1900] 1 Ch. 276; *Att.-Gen.* v. *Scott* [1905] 2 K.B. 160.
[40] See *Att.-Gen.* v. *Logan* [1891] 2 Q.B. 100; *Att.-Gen.* v. *Cockermouth Local Board* (1874) L.R. 18 Eq. 172 at 176; *Att.-Gen.* v. *P.Y.A. Quarries Ltd.* [1957] 2 Q.B. 169.
[41] *Lyon* v. *Fishmongers' Co.* (1876) 1 App.Cas. 662; *Vanderpant* v. *Mayfair Hotel Co. Ltd.* [1930] 1 Ch. 138; *Boyce* v. *Paddington Borough Council* [1903] 1 Ch. 109 at 114 (reversed: [1903] 2 Ch. 556; restored: [1906] A.C. 1).
[42] *Prudential Assurance Co.* v. *Knott* (1875) 10 Ch.App. 142.
[43] Common Law Procedure Act 1854, ss.79, 82. See *Quartz Hill Consolidated Gold Mining Co.* v. *Beall* (1882) 20 Ch.D. 501 at 507, 509, 510.
[44] *Quartz Hill Consolidated Gold Mining Co.* v. *Beall* (1882) 20 Ch.D. 501.
[45] *Ibid.*
[46] *Bonnard* v. *Perryman* [1891] 2 Ch. 269; *Monson* v. *Tussauds Ltd.* [1894] 1 Q.B. 671.
[47] See *Quartz Hill Consolidated Gold Mining Co.* v. *Beall, supra*, at p. 509.
[48] *Bonnard* v. *Perryman, supra*; *Fraser* v. *Evans* [1969] 1 Q.B. 349 at 360, 361.
[49] *Harakas* v. *Baltic Mercantile and Shipping Exchange Ltd.* [1982] 1 W.L.R. 958.
[50] *Herbage* v. *Pressdram Ltd.* [1984] 1 W.L.R. 1160 (justification of "spent" conviction).
[51] *Thorley's Cattle Food Co.* v. *Massam* (1879) 14 Ch.D. 763; *Hermann Loog* v. *Bean* (1884) 26 Ch.D. 306 (oral statement). See *White* v. *Mellin* [1895] A.C. 154; *Hubbuck* v. *Wilkinson* [1899] 1 Q.B. 86 (mere puffs); *Gulf Oil (Great Britain) Ltd.* v. *Page* [1987] Ch. 327 (interlocutory injunction).
[52] Representation of the People Act 1983, s.106(1), (3).
[53] See *Willis & Bates Ltd.* v. *Tilley Lamp Co.* (1943) 61 R.P.C. 8.
[54] Patents Act 1949, s.65; Patents Act 1977, s.70.
[55] Registered Designs Act 1949, s.26, as amended by Copyright, Designs and Patents Act 1988, s.272, Sched. 3, para. 15.

testimonial was given to A and B, the court refused to restrain B from publishing a version which suppressed A's name.[56]

(e) *Passing-off and trade marks.* Where a plaintiff proves that in the mind of the public some title or mode of presentation has become attached to his product,[57] and that the defendant is passing off his product in a form which deceives the public into thinking it is the plaintiff's product,[58] the plaintiff may obtain an injunction to restrain the passing-off.[59] A particular instance of this class of action is where a manufacturer identifies his goods with a distinctive mark which acquires a public reputation. Here the Court of Chancery granted injunctions restraining an infringement on the ground that the manufacturer had acquired a right of property in the mark, recognisable in equity.[60] This remedy proved inadequate because of the difficulty in proving reputation, and accordingly in 1875 a register of trade marks was established.[61] The owner of a registered trade mark does not have to prove his title by reputation.[62] The old action for "passing-off" is still possible,[63] and retains considerable importance in cases where the mode of presentation is not registrable as a trade mark, or has not been registered.[64]

(f) *Patents, designs and copyright.* Injunctions are commonly granted against infringers of patents, registered designs and copyrights. These branches of the law are now statutory.[65]

(g) *Confidential information*

(1) BREACH OF CONFIDENCE.[66] Quite apart from enforcing any statutory or common law rights, equity has an original and independent jurisdiction to grant an injunction to restrain what the court considers to be wrong, whether arising from violation of a right or from breach of contract or confidence. Thus in *Prince Albert* v. *Strange*,[67] Prince Albert obtained an injunction to restrain the publication of a catalogue of

---

[56] *Warren* v. *D. W. Karn Co.* (1907) 15 O.L.R. 115.

[57] See *Licensed Victuallers' Newspaper Co.* v. *Bingham* (1888) 38 Ch.D. 139.

[58] See *Borthwick* v. *The Evening Post* (1888) 37 Ch.D. 449.

[59] The classic statement of principle is in the speech of Lord Parker of Waddington in *A. G. Spalding & Bros.* v. *A. W. Gamage Ltd.* (1915) 32 R.P.C. 273 at 283. The most authoritative modern statements are in the speeches of Lord Diplock and Lord Fraser of Tullybelton in *Warnink (Erven) B.V.* v. *J. Townend & Sons (Hull) Ltd.* [1979] A.C. 731 at 742 and 755, 756 respectively.

[60] *Leather Cloth Co. Ltd.* v. *American Leather Cloth Co. Ltd.* (1863) 4 De G.J. & S. 137 (affirmed 11 H.L.C. 523), where on the facts an injunction was refused.

[61] Trade Marks Registration Act 1875; see now Trade Marks Act 1938 and Trade Marks (Amendment) Act 1984.

[62] Trade Marks Act 1938, ss.4, 5.

[63] *Ibid.* s.2.

[64] The standard work on trade marks and passing off is Kerly's *Law of Trade Marks* (12th ed., 1986).

[65] Patents Act 1949; Patents Act 1977; Registered Designs Act 1949; Copyright, Designs and Patents Act 1988. The standard works are Terrell's *Law of Patents* (13th ed., 1982) and Copinger and Skone James' *Copyright* (12th ed., 1980).

[66] For a general survey, see G. Jones (1970) 86 L.Q.R. 463.

[67] (1849) 1 Mac. & G. 25; and see *Pollard* v. *Photographic Co.* (1888) 40 Ch.D. 345 at 354; *Duchess of Argyll* v. *Duke of Argyll* [1967] Ch. 302; and see D. L. Mathieson (1961) 39 Can.B.R. 409, arguing that the appropriation of another's personality can be restrained.

unpublished etchings which he and Queen Victoria had made, when the catalogue could have been compiled only by using copies of the etchings obtained in breach of some trust, confidence, or contract[68]; and the principle applies even to a stranger who is "quite innocently and properly" in possession of information to which he is not entitled.[69] Again, where the owner of a statesman's papers gave access to them to an author who was writing a book for a laudatory series of biographies, he was held entitled to restrain the author's use of the material in a critical book to be published elsewhere.[70] And in Australia the representatives of an aboriginal tribe have been granted an injunction to restrain an anthropologist from disclosing tribal secrets imparted to him in confidence.[71] One party to a marriage, too, may, even after divorce, restrain the other party, or other persons,[72] from publishing confidential communications made during the marriage between the spouses.[73] Again, a solicitor will be restrained from disclosing the secrets of his clients,[74] though there is no rule that, if he has acted for one person either before or after litigation has begun, he can in no case act instead for that person's adversary.[75]

Only the person to whom a duty of confidence is owed can restrain a breach of it, so that a person who contracts to prepare a confidential report for another cannot restrain its unauthorised publication.[76] Considerations of public interest may be important. Thus an injunction may be granted on the basis that there is a public interest in maintaining confidentiality which overrides any public interest in disclosure, as at the interlocutory stage of the "Spycatcher" litigation,[77] and, similarly, in a case in which the publication of the names of doctors suffering from AIDS was restrained.[78] Or there may, at the interlocutory stage, simply be no public interest to be served by pre-trial publication.[79] In other cases, the public interest in disclosure may override the duty of confidence,[80] as where a doctor engaged on behalf of a mental patient who had committed several offences of manslaughter made a report which was disclosed to the hospital where the patient was detained and to the Home Office.[81] In such cases, publication will be restrained at the interlocutory stage unless the defendant can show "a legitimate ground

---

[68] *Prince Albert v. Strange, supra.*
[69] *Rex Co.* v. *Muirhead* (1926) 136 L.T. 568 at 573, *per* Clauson J.; *Printers & Finishers Ltd.* v. *Holloway* [1965] 1 W.L.R. 1 at 7; and see *Mayall v. Higby* (1862) 10 W.R. 631.
[70] *Lindsey* v. *Le Sueur* (1913) 29 O.L.R. 648.
[71] *Foster* v. *Mountford* [1973] F.S.R. 582.
[72] *Lord Ashburton* v. *Pape* [1913] 2 Ch. 469; and see *Printers & Finishers Ltd.* v. *Holloway, supra,* at p. 7.
[73] *Duchess of Argyll* v. *Duke of Argyll* [1967] Ch. 302. And see *Stephens* v. *Avery* [1988] Ch. 449 as to a lesbian couple (not an injunction case).
[74] *Rakusen* v. *Ellis* [1912] 1 Ch. 831 at 835, 840, 842.
[75] *Rakusen* v. *Ellis* [1912] 1 Ch. 831.
[76] *Fraser* v. *Evans* [1969] 1 Q.B. 349.
[77] *Att.-Gen.* v. *Guardian Newspapers Ltd.* [1987] 1 W.L.R. 1248.
[78] *X v. Y* [1988] 2 All E.R. 648. And see *Distillers Co. (Biochemicals) Ltd.* v. *Times Newspapers Ltd.* [1975] Q.B. 613; *Schering Chemicals Ltd.* v. *Falkman Ltd.* [1982] Q.B. 1.
[79] *Francome* v. *Mirror Group Newspapers Ltd.* [1984] 1 W.L.R. 892.
[80] *Fraser* v. *Evans, supra,* at p. 362; *Hubbard* v. *Vosper* [1972] 2 Q.B. 84; *Lion Laboratories Ltd.* v. *Evans* [1985] Q.B. 526.
[81] *W.* v. *Edgell* [1990] 2 W.L.R. 471.

for supposing it is in the public interest for it to be disclosed"[82]; a mere plea of public interest is insufficient, and an arguable defence must be shown.[83] Where the Government is plaintiff, it is required to go further than a private individual and show, not merely a breach of the duty of confidence, but that publication would be harmful to the public interest.[84] Moreover, "there is no confidence as to the disclosure of inquity."[85] Thus a housekeeper will not be restrained from disclosing alleged criminal offences, and perhaps the sexual misconduct, of her employer.[86] An employee will not be restrained from disclosing his employer's affairs to a regulatory body or the Revenue.[87] Nor will the jurisdiction be exercised to restrain the disclosure of "tittle-tattle"[88] or "pernicious nonsense."[89] And the injunction may be refused on the ground of unfairness, as where the information had already been used by some (but not all) participants in a take-over bid[90]; or futility, where the information has become generally[91] or widely[92] known and has thus lost the quality of confidentiality. If the injunction is granted, it may contain provisions allowing disclosure to the police or some other authority.[93]

(2) TRADE CONFIDENCES.   One particular aspect of the doctrine is that of trade confidences: if one trader gives confidential trade information to another, he can restrain that other from using it in competition with him,[94] e.g. where an inventor protected by no patent gives a manufacturer information about his invention with a view to a joint venture.[95] At least in this form the doctrine has three essentials: (i) that the information imparted is of a confidential nature; (ii) that it was communicated in circumstances importing an obligation of confidence; and (iii) that there has been an unauthorised use of the information, normally (though perhaps not necessarily) to the detriment of the plaintiff.[96]

The doctrine operates independently of any contract,[97] but doubtless it influences the obligations that will be implied in a contract. Thus one

---

[82] *Khashoggi* v. *Smith* [1980] C.A.T. No. 58, p. 15, *per* Sir David Cairns, not in 124 S.J. 149.
[83] *Lion Laboratories Ltd.* v. *Evans* [1985] Q.B. 526 at 538.
[84] *Att.-Gen.* v. *Guardian Newspapers Ltd. (No. 2)* [1990] A.C. 109.
[85] *Gartside* v. *Outram* (1856) 26 L.J.Ch. 113 at 114, *per* Page Wood V.-C.
[86] *Khashoggi* v. *Smith* (1980) 124 S.J. 149. See also *Initial Services Ltd.* v. *Putterill* [1968] 1 Q.B. 396 (not an injunction case).
[87] *Re a Company's Application* [1989] Ch. 477.
[88] *Coco* v. *A. N. Clark (Engineers) Ltd.* [1969] R.P.C. 41 at 48.
[89] *Church of Scientology of California* v. *Kaufman* [1973] R.P.C. 627 at 658.
[90] *Dunford & Elliott Ltd.* v. *Johnson & Firth-Brown Ltd.* [1977] 1 Lloyd's Rep. 505 (the use had been proper).
[91] *Att.-Gen.* v. *Guardian Newspapers Ltd. (No. 2), supra.*
[92] *Lord Advocate* v. *The Scotsman Publications Ltd.* [1990] A.C. 812 (279 copies of book distributed).
[93] *Francome* v. *Mirror Group Newspapers Ltd.* [1984] 1 W.L.R. 892.
[94] *Saltman Engineering Co. Ltd.* v. *Campbell Engineering Co. Ltd.* (1948) 65 R.P.C. 203; [1963] 3 All E.R. 413n.; *Terrapin Ltd.* v. *Builders Supply Co. (Hayes) Ltd.* [1960] R.P.C 128; *Peter Pan Manufacturing Corporation* v. *Corsets Silhouette Ltd.* [1964] 1 W.L.R. 96; and see *Seager* v. *Copydex Ltd. (No. 1)* [1967] 1 W.L.R. 923; *(No. 2)* [1969] 1 W.L.R. 809 (damages). For difficulties in applying the doctrine, see *Coco* v. *A. N. Clark (Engineers) Ltd.* [1969] R.P.C. 41 at 48–50.
[95] *Coco* v. *A. N. Clark (Engineers) Ltd.* [1969] R.P.C. 41.
[96] *Ibid.* at p. 47.
[97] *Ibid.* at p. 46.

partner owes another a high duty of honesty and good faith, and so cannot use partnership papers and information for his own purposes without his partner's consent.[98] An ex-servant, too, may be required to deliver up lists of customers of his former master,[99] though he cannot be restrained from using memorised lists of customers or agents.[1] Yet he may be restrained from improperly using knowledge (even if merely memorised[2]) of any secret process acquired by him during the employment,[3] though this liability ends if the secret process is published, whether by the master, e.g. in a patent specification,[4] or by a third party.[5] Further, an ex-servant may be ordered to transfer to his master the benefit of his inventions if his master is contractually entitled to them.[6] A skilled worker may also be under an implied obligation not to work for a trade rival, so that even if there is no disclosure of confidential information, the rival may be restrained from procuring a breach of that obligation by offering him spare-time employment.[7]

3. Expulsion from clubs or societies

(a) *Clubs.* An injunction may be granted to restrain the wrongful expulsion or exclusion of a member from an ordinarily constituted members' club; the court interferes to protect the member's proprietary interest in the assets of the club.[8] But an injunction will not be granted to restrain an expulsion where the member has no right of property, as in the case of a proprietary club[9]: the member's contractual right to enter the club is too personal to be specifically enforced,[10] and the effect of the expulsion on his character and position in society,[11] or on his right to play some game,[12] is not a sufficient foundation for an injunction.

(b) *Trade or profession.* Wrongful expulsion from societies which regulate the members of a trade or profession will, however, be restrained by injunction, despite the absence of a proprietary interest in the member; the court here will specifically enforce the member's

---

[98] *Floydd* v. *Cheney* [1970] Ch. 602.
[99] *Robb* v. *Gren* [1895] 2 Q.B. 315; *Measures Bros.* v. *Measures* [1910] 1 Ch. 336 (affd. on another point [1910] 2 Ch. 248).
[1] *Baker* v. *Gibbons* [1972] 1 W.L.R. 693.
[2] See *Printers & Finishers Ltd.* v. *Holloway* [1965] 1 W.L.R. 1.
[3] *Amber Size & Chemical Co. Ltd.* v. *Menzel* [1913] 2 Ch. 239.
[4] *O. Mustad & Son* v. *S. Allcock & Co. Ltd.* (1928) [1963] 3 All E.R. 416.
[5] See *Att.-Gen.* v. *Guardian Newspapers Ltd. (No. 2)* [1990] A.C. 109 at 285, disapproving *Cranleigh Precision Engineering Ltd.* v. *Bryant* [1965] 1 W.L.R. 1293 and *Speed Seal Products Ltd.* v. *Paddington* [1985] 1 W.L.R. 1327.
[6] *Triplex Safety Glass Co.* v. *Scorah* [1938] Ch. 211; *British Celanese Ltd.* v. *Moncrieff* [1948] Ch. 564; and see *Sterling Engineering Co. Ltd.* v. *Patchett* [1955] A.C. 534.
[7] *Hivac Ltd.* v. *Park Royal Scientific Instruments Ltd.* [1946] Ch. 169; see O. Kahn-Freund (1946) 9 M.L.R. 145.
[8] *Baird* v. *Wells* (1890) 44 Ch.D. 661 at 675; *D'Arcy* v. *Adamson* (1913) 29 T.L.R. 367; but see *Woodford* v. *Smith* [1970] 1 W.L.R. 806 (ratepayers' association with small assets).
[9] *Baird* v. *Wells* (1890) 44 Ch.D. 661.
[10] *Lee* v. *The Showmen's Guild of Great Britain* [1952] 2 Q.B. 329 at 342.
[11] *Baird* v. *Wells, supra,* at p. 677.
[12] *Rowe* v. *Hewitt* (1906) 12 O.L.R. 13.

contract with his society.[13] Thus the courts may prevent expulsion from
a friendly society,[14] a trade union,[15] or a professional institute.[16] The
courts may also grant an injunction to prevent the removal of a
preacher[17] or schoolmaster[18] where a governing body has acted not
fairly and honestly but corruptly or from some improper motive.[19] The
jurisdiction of the court over societies and unions cannot be ousted by
their rules.[20]

4. Judicial proceedings. Although no proceedings pending in the
High Court or Court of Appeal can be restrained by injunction[21] (and
this includes garnishee proceedings[22]), it is still possible in certain cases
to restrain the institution of proceedings in the High Court.[23] Thus, an
injunction may be granted to restrain the presentation or advertisement
of a petition to wind up a company, if the petition would be an abuse of
the process of the court,[24] or if it is a creditor's petition based upon a
debt alleged to be presently due and there is a bona fide dispute as to
the debt[25] or as to its being presently due.[26] It may also be granted to
restrain a threatened action against a receiver appointed by the court in
respect of acts done by him in discharge of his office.[27] Further, the
High Court may restrain a person from prosecuting vexatious civil[28] or
criminal[29] proceedings in inferior courts, even if pending, as where it is
sought to litigate in magistrates' courts issues which are already being
litigated in the High Court.[30] Whether the High Court will restrain the
enforcement of a county court order which is said to be a nullity is
uncertain.[31]

---

[13] See *Lee* v. *The Showmen's Guild of Great Britain, supra*, at pp. 341, 343.
[14] *Andrews* v. *Mitchell* [1905] A.C. 78.
[15] *Osborne* v. *Amalgamated Society of Railway Servants* [1911] 1 Ch. 540; *Amalgamated Society of
Carpenters* v. *Braithwaite* [1922] 2 A.C. 440; *Lee* v. *The Showman's Guild of Great Britain* [1952] 2
Q.B. 329.
[16] *Law* v. *Chartered Institute of Patent Agents* [1919] 2 Ch. 276; *Thompson* v. *New South Wales Branch
of the British Medical Association* [1924] A.C. 764 at 778.
[17] *Daugars* v. *Rivaz* (1860) 28 Beav. 233.
[18] *Willis* v. *Childe* (1850) 13 Beav. 117.
[19] See *Hayman* v. *Governors of Rugby School* (1874) L.R. 18 Eq. 28 for a full review of the cases.
[20] *Leigh* v. *National Union of Railwaymen* [1970] Ch. 326.
[21] See J.A. 1873, s.24(5), replaced by 1925, s.41, which was itself repealed by S.C.A. 1981, s.151(4)
and Sched. 7 but was not re-enacted; *ante*, pp. 20, 646. For limited exceptions, see Insolvency Act
1986, ss.126(1) (proceedings against company after presentation of winding-up petition), 147
(winding-up proceedings), 132(1), (2) (proceedings and remedies against individual when bankruptcy
petition pending or after adjudication).
[22] *Llewellyn* v. *Carrickford* [1970] 1 W.L.R. 1124.
[23] *Besant* v. *Wood* (1879) 12 Ch.D. 605 at 630; *Hart* v. *Hart* (1881) 18 Ch.D. 670; but see *Re Alison's
Trusts* (1878) 8 Ch.D. 1.
[24] *Bryanston Finance Ltd.* v. *De Vries (No. 2)* [1976] Ch. 63 (injunction refused).
[25] *Cercle Restaurant Castiglione Co.* v. *Lavery* (1881) 18 Ch.D. 555.
[26] *Stonegate Securities Ltd.* v. *Gregory* [1980] Ch. 576.
[27] *Re Maidstone Palace of Varieties Ltd.* [1909] 2 Ch. 283.
[28] *Re Connolly Bros. Ltd.* [1911] 1 Ch. 731.
[29] *Thames Launches Ltd.* v. *Trinity House Corporation (Deptford Strond)* [1961] Ch. 197.
[30] *Hedley* v. *Bates* (1880) 13 Ch.D. 498; *Thames Launches Ltd.* v. *Trinity House Corporation (Deptford
Strond), supra*; and see *Stannard* v. *Vestry of St. Giles* (1882) 20 Ch.D. 190 (injunction refused); *Re
Connolly Brothers Ltd., supra* (Chancery of Lancaster, now abolished).
[31] *Johns* v. *Chatalos* [1973] 1 W.L.R. 1437.

The court may also restrain a person from prosecuting proceedings in a foreign court[32] or from enforcing a judgment obtained abroad.[33] But the court will do this only rarely and with great caution,[34] as where the foreign proceedings are vexatious and oppressive,[35] or where an order has been obtained in breach of contract or by fraud.[36] The approach of the court is different where the claim is justiciable only abroad and where it is justiciable abroad or in England. In the former case, the foreign proceedings will be restrained only if the party seeking the injunction can show either a legal or equitable right not to be sued in the foreign court or that the other party is acting unconscionably in bringing proceedings abroad.[37] In the latter case, the proceedings may be restrained simply on the ground that it is more appropriate, in the interests of justice, that the dispute should be tried in England.[38] There is a corresponding power to stay proceedings in England in favour of foreign proceedings.[39]

5. Arbitrations. An injunction may be granted to restrain a party to an arbitration agreement from proceeding with the arbitration, if it is alleged that the arbitration agreement was void or voidable *ab initio*,[40] or that the arbitrator is or has become disqualified by bias.[41] But an injunction will not be granted to restrain further proceedings in an arbitration on the ground that one party has been guilty of inordinate and inexcusable delay.[42]

6. Proceedings in Parliament. The courts may have jurisdiction to restrain a person from seeking a private Act of Parliament, or opposing the passage of such an Act, *e.g.* if he is bound by a contractual obligation not to do so. However, public policy appears to require that the courts should not prevent Parliament from determining the question for itself, so that even if the jurisdiction exists, it is unlikely to be exercised.[43] Further, a Minister of the Crown, acting as such, cannot be ordered to withdraw draft subordinate legislation which has been

---

[32] *Settlement Corporation* v. *Hochschild* [1966] Ch. 10.
[33] *Ellerman Lines Ltd.* v. *Read* [1928] 2 K.B. 144.
[34] *Settlement Corporation* v. *Hochschild, supra.*
[35] *McHenry* v. *Lewis* (1882) 22 Ch.D. 397; *Cohen* v. *Rothfield* [1919] 1 K.B. 410; *Orr-Lewis* v. *Orr-Lewis* [1949] P. 347.
[36] *Ellerman Lines Ltd.* v. *Read* [1928] 2 K.B. 144.
[37] *British Airways Board* v. *Laker Airways Ltd.* [1985] 1 A.C. 58; *Société Nationale Industrielle Aérospatiale* v. *Lee Kui Jak* [1987] A.C. 871.
[38] *South Carolina Insurance Co.* v. *Assurantie Maatschappij "De Zeven Provincien" N.V.* [1987] A.C. 24 at 40.
[39] *Ionian Bank Ltd.* v. *Couvreur* [1969] 1 W.L.R. 781; and see *McHenry* v. *Lewis* (1882) 22 Ch.D. 397.
[40] *Kitts* v. *Moore* [1895] 1 Q.B. 253.
[41] *Malmesbury Ry. Co.* v. *Budd* (1876) 2 Ch.D. 113; *Beddow* v. *Beddow* (1878) 9 Ch.D. 89.
[42] *Bremer Vulkan Schiffbau und Maschinenfabrik* v. *South India Shipping Corpn. Ltd.* [1981] A.C. 909.
[43] See *Bilston Corporation* v. *Wolverhampton Corporation* [1942] Ch. 391; *Ware* v. *Grand Junction Water Works Co.* (1831) 2 Russ. & M. 470; Holdsworth (1943) 59 L.Q.R. 2; G. Sawer (1944) 60 L.Q.R. 83; W. Pollak, *ibid.* 226; Z. Cowen (1955) 71 L.Q.R. 336. No reliance can be placed on the assertion in the headnote to *McHenry* v. *Lewis, supra,* of a jurisdiction to "restrain vexatious and oppressive legislation."

presented to each House of Parliament for approval,[44] nor, after such approval, will he be restrained from presenting such legislation to the Privy Council for enactment.[45] But in the absence of any such considerations, there seems to be nothing to prevent the courts from restraining an authority, however distinguished, from improperly exercising a power to make delegated legislation.[46]

[44] *Merricks* v. *Heathcote-Amory* [1955] Ch. 567.
[45] *Harper* v. *Home Secretary* [1955] Ch. 238.
[46] See *Bates* v. *Lord Hailsham of St. Marylebone* [1972] 1 W.L.R. 1373 (no impropriety: injunction refused).

CHAPTER 7

RECEIVERS

Section 1. Appointment and Functions

1. Nature of receivers

(a) *Origin and purpose.* By the time of Elizabeth I the jurisdiction of the Court of Chancery to appoint a receiver had become well established[1]; indeed, such an appointment "is one of the oldest remedies in this Court."[2] The remedy is purely equitable in its origin. The common law courts had no power to appoint receivers, but the Judicature Act 1873[3] enabled all Divisions of the High Court to make such an appointment, though this power is exercisable only in accordance with the settled practice of equity.[4] In broad terms, the main function of a receiver is to collect, preserve and apply the income of the property which is subject to his authority, and preserve the outstanding assets.[5] A receiver may be appointed either out of court or in court.

(b) *Appointment out of court.* In many cases receivers are appointed by a person acting under the authority of some statute or some contractual power. Thus a mortgagee by deed has wide statutory powers of appointing a receiver[6]; and when a company borrows on debenture, the debentures or the debenture trust deed almost invariably provide for the appointment of a receiver. In such cases the apppointment is a means of enforcing the lender's rights, and is usually authorised only when the borrower is in default. The appointment takes effect when the document of appointment is handed to the receiver by a person having authority to do so and the receiver accepts the proffered appointment.[7]

(c) *Appointment by court.* The court appoints receivers for two quite different purposes. First, the court may appoint a receiver as an interim means of preserving property until the rights of those interested in it can be determined. In the words of Lord Hardwicke L.C., the power to

---

[1] Spence, *Equitable Jurisdiction* (1846) Vol. 1, pp. 378, 673.
[2] *Hopkins* v. *Worcester & Birmingham Canal Proprietors* (1868) L.R. 6 Eq. 437 at 447, *per* Giffard V.-C.; and see *Rowley* v. *Ridley* (1784) 2 Dick. 622 at 630 (distinguishing receivers from sequestrators).
[3] J.A. 1873, s.25(8); J.A. 1925, s.45; S.C.A. 1981, s.37.
[4] *Harris* v. *Beauchamp Bros.* [1894] 1 Q.B. 801.
[5] See *Evans* v. *Coventry* (1854) 3 Drew. 75 at 80 (reversed on another point, 5 De G.M. & G. 911); *Wright* v. *Vernon* (1855) 3 Drew. 112 at 121; *Re Manchester & Milford Ry.* (1880) 14 Ch.D. 645 at 653.
[6] See *ante*, p. 416.
[7] *R.A. Cripps & Son Ltd.* v. *Wickenden* [1973] 1 W.L.R. 944, esp. at 953.

appoint a receiver "is a discretionary power exercised by this court with as great utility to the subject as any sort of authority that belongs to them, and is provisional only for the more speedy getting in of a party's estate, and securing it for the benefit of such person who shall appear to be intitled and does not at all affect the right."[8] Secondly, where a litigant has obtained judgment, the court will sometimes appoint a receiver as a form of execution.[9]

(d) *Mental patients.* A receiver appointed for a mental patient by the Court of Protection[10] or the Public Trustee[11] is in a special position, and his wide powers and duties give him the functions of a general manager of the patient's property rather than those of an ordinary receiver.[12]

2. Managers. Receivers must be distinguished from managers. A receiver as such has no authority to carry on a business; if he is appointed receiver of property which includes a business, he must stop the trading, collect the debts and realise the assets.[13] A manager, on the other hand, has power to continue a business, so that if it is desired that trading should not cease, a receiver and manager should be appointed[14]; and usually the same person is appointed both receiver and manager. A receiver's duty is to receive, a manager's to manage.

3. Status of receiver and manager

(a) *Appointed out of court.* A receiver and manager appointed out of court is *prima facie* merely an agent for the person appointing him, so that he incurs no personal liability for acts done within his authority.[15] However, by statute a receiver appointed by a mortgagee is expressly made the agent of the mortgagor.[16] Debenture trust deeds and debentures (which in any case may also be mortgages[17]) usually contain corresponding provisions making a receiver appointed by debenture holders an agent of the company[18]; the agency terminates when the company is put into liquidation at which time the receiver becomes the agent of the party who appointed him,[19] and loses his power to bind the company by acting as its agent.[20] The powers of a receiver appointed by

---

[8] *Skip* v. *Harwood* (1747) 3 Atk. 564.
[9] See *post*, p. 697.
[10] Mental Health Act 1983, s.99(1).
[11] Public Trustee and Administration of Funds Act 1986, s.3(2).
[12] Mental Health Act 1983, ss.95, 96, 99(2).
[13] *Re Manchester & Milford Ry.* (1880) 14 Ch.D. 645 at 653.
[14] See *Taylor* v. *Neate* (1888) 39 Ch.D. 538; *Re Newdigate Colliery Ltd.* [1912] 1 Ch. 468.
[15] *Owen & Co.* v. *Cronk* [1895] 1 Q.B. 265.
[16] See *ante*, p. 417.
[17] *Knightsbridge Estates Trust Ltd.* v. *Byrne* [1940] A.C. 613.
[18] See *Re B. Johnson & Co. (Builders) Ltd.* [1955] Ch. 634 at 644.
[19] *American Express International Banking Corp.* v. *Hurley* [1985] 3 All E.R. 564.
[20] *Gosling* v. *Gaskell* [1897] A.C. 575. On the interaction of winding-up and receivership, see (1979) 53 A.L.J. 264 (J. O'Donovan).

a debenture holder depend on the terms of the debenture,[21] but usually include a power to dispose of the assets of the company. Such a power survives the winding-up of the company,[22] and is accompanied by a duty (owed both to the company and to a guarantor for the company) to take reasonable care to obtain the best price that the circumstances permit.[23] Subject to his statutory duty[24] to pay preferential creditors in priority to the debenture holders,[25] the primary duty of a receiver and manager is to the debenture holders rather than to the company; he is manager not of the company but of the company's property, and so is not an officer of the company,[26] and is not bound by the company's contracts.[27] Further, if he is later also appointed receiver by the court, he thereupon ceases to be an agent for any of the parties.[28]

(b) Appointed by the court

(1) OFFICER OF COURT. A receiver and manager appointed by the court is not an agent for any of the parties,[29] but is an officer of the court,[30] so that the court "in effect assumes the management into its own hands."[31] He has no estate or interest in the property, but recovers the income from it as an officer of the court and upon the title of those who are parties to the action.[32] The mere appointment of a receiver operates as a general injunction restraining any interference with him in the performance of his duties[33]; and any such interference may be punished as a contempt[34] and further restrained by an injunction specifically addressed to the person interfering.[35]

(2) AUTHORITY. A receiver appointed by the court has no authority until he has given proper security (usually by means of a guarantee by himself and a guarantee company[36]) that he will duly account for what he receives.[37] He is personally liable for his acts, e.g. under any contracts made by him for goods for the business in his charge,[38] or under any existing contracts which he adopts as his own.[39] He is not

---

[21] Contrast *Gough's Garages Ltd.* v. *Pugsley* [1930] 1 K.B. 615 with *Newhart Developments Ltd.* v. *Co-operative Commercial Bank Ltd.* [1978] Q.B. 814.
[22] *Sowman* v. *David Samuel Trust Ltd.* [1978] 1 W.L.R. 22.
[23] *Standard Chartered Bank Ltd.* v. *Walker* [1982] 1 W.L.R. 1410, overruling *Latchford* v. *Beirne* [1981] 3 All E.R. 705; *American Express International Banking Corp.* v. *Hurley* [1985] 3 All E.R. 564.
[24] Under the Insolvency Act 1986, s.40.
[25] *I.R.C.* v. *Goldblatt* [1972] Ch. 498.
[26] *Re B. Johnson & Co. (Builders) Ltd.* [1955] Ch. 634; see especially at pp. 661, 664.
[27] *Airlines Airspares Ltd.* v. *Handley Page Ltd.* [1970] Ch. 193.
[28] See *Hand* v. *Blow* [1901] 2 Ch. 721.
[29] *Corporation of Bacup* v. *Smith* (1890) 44 Ch.D. 395.
[30] See *Aston* v. *Heron* (1834) 2 My. & K. 390.
[31] *Gardner* v. *London Chatham & Dover Ry.* (1867) 2 Ch.App. 201 at 211, *per* Cairns L.J.
[32] See *Vine* v. *Raleigh* (1883) 24 Ch.D. 238 at 243.
[33] See *Evans* v. *Coventry* (1854) 5 De G.M. & G. 911 at 916; *Tyrrell* v. *Painton* [1895] 1 Q.B. 202 at 206.
[34] *Helmore* v. *Smith (No. 2)* (1886) 35 Ch.D. 449.
[35] *Dixon* v. *Dixon* [1904] 1 Ch. 161.
[36] See R.S.C., Ord. 30, r. 2.
[37] *Edwards* v. *Edwards* (1876) 2 Ch.D. 291.
[38] *Burt, Boulton & Hayward* v. *Bull* [1895] 1 Q.B. 276.
[39] *Re Botibol* [1947] 1 All E.R. 26.

entitled to any personal indemnity by the persons interested in the property, or the parties to the action for his remuneration and expenses.[40] Yet, like a personal representative,[41] he is entitled to be indemnified out of the property concerned[42] in so far as he has acted not merely on his own account but for the benefit of the property.[43] Further, his creditors are entitled by subrogation to the same rights as he has against the property, and this may be valuable to them, *e.g.* if he becomes bankrupt.[44]

4. Remuneration

(a) *Appointed out of court.* A receiver appointed by a mortgagee is entitled to retain out of any money received by him, for his remuneration and in satisfaction of all costs, charges, and expenses incurred by him as receiver, a commission at such rate, not exceeding 5 per cent. on the gross amount of all money received, as is specified in his appointment. If no rate is so specified, he is entitled without any order of the court[45] to five per cent. of that gross amount, or such other rate as the court thinks fit to allow on an application made by him for that purpose.[46] This right is not excluded merely because the mortgagee, being a company, has appointed one of its directors as receiver.[47] A receiver for debenture holders is entitled to whatever remuneration the debentures or trust deed provide for; and if the company is in liquidation, the court may fix the remuneration.[48]

(b) *Appointed by the court.* Unless otherwise ordered, a receiver appointed by the court will be allowed proper remuneration.[49] The amount is usually fixed by the Master, or sometimes by the Taxing Master.[50] There is no fixed rule as to quantum, though five per cent. on the amount of income received is usual in straightforward cases.[51]

Section 2. Persons who may be Appointed

1. Out of court. Provided there is a proper exercise of the statutory or contractual power to appoint a receiver out of court, there is in general no restriction on the person who can be appointed. Thus a mortgagee's statutory power is to appoint "such person as he thinks

---

[40] *Boehm* v. *Goodall* [1911] 1 Ch. 155; *Evans* v. *Clayhope Properties Ltd.* [1988] 1 W.L.R. 358.
[41] See *ante*, p. 320.
[42] *Burt, Boulton & Hayward* v. *Bull* [1895] 1 Q.B. 276; *Strapp* v. *Bull, Sons & Co.* [1895] 2 Ch. 1.
[43] *Re Dunn* [1904] 1 Ch. 648 (defence against charge of personal fraud).
[44] *Re London United Breweries Ltd.* [1907] 2 Ch. 511; and see *ante*, p. 321 (personal representatives).
[45] *Marshall* v. *Cottingham* [1982] Ch. 82.
[46] L.P.A. 1925, s.109(6).
[47] See *Bath* v. *Standard Land Co. Ltd.* [1911] 1 Ch. 618.
[48] Insolvency Act 1986, s.36.
[49] R.S.C., Ord. 30, r. 3.
[50] *Silkstone & Haigh Moor Coal Co.* v. *Edey* [1901] 2 Ch. 652 at 655.
[51] See *Day* v. *Croft* (1840) 2 Beav. 488.

fit."[52] But the appointment of a body corporate as receiver of a company is a nullity[53]; and it is an offence for an undischarged bankrupt to act as a receiver of a company.[54]

2. In court

(a) *Impartiality.* When the court appoints a receiver, the general rule is that "some entirely indifferent person ought to be appointed."[55] Thus it is a valid ground of objection that the proposed receiver has displayed partisanship for one of the persons interested,[56] or is solicitor for one of them.[57] Nor will the court usually appoint a person who ought to examine and check the activities of the receiver.[58] Thus a trustee will normally not be appointed receiver of the trust property, for the court expects a trustee to see that the receiver does his duty,[59] so that the beneficiaries will secure the skill of both.[60]

(b) *Person interested.* However, this is merely a general principle, and if there is some good reason to the contrary, or the parties agree, it may well be departed from. Thus in partnership cases a solvent partner who has not behaved improperly[61] is usually appointed receiver and manager,[62] so avoiding an undue disruption of business. Again, where a company is in liquidation, trouble and expense is usually avoided by appointing the liquidator as receiver.[63]

Section 3. Appointment out of Court

Although most of the receivers appointed out of court are appointed under mortgages and debentures, there are some other cases in which such an appointment can be made. Thus a landowner may appoint a receiver of his estate in order to secure the payment of annuities which he has granted.[64] Again, partners who are dissolving partnership may agree on the appointment of a receiver in order to realise the assets of the business.[65]

[52] L.P.A. 1925, s.109(1).
[53] Insolvency Act 1986, s.30; *Portman B.S.* v. *Gallwey* [1955] 1 W.L.R. 96.
[54] Insolvency Act 1986, s.31.
[55] *Fripp* v. *Chard Ry.* (1853) 11 Hare 241 at 260, *per* Page Wood V.-C.; and see *Re Lloyd, Allen* v. *Lloyd* (1879) 12 Ch.D. 447.
[56] *Blakeway* v. *Blakeway* (1833) 2 L.J.Ch. 75 ("a partiality, which renders him unfit for the office of receiver"; *per* Shadwell V.-C.); *Wright* v. *Vernon* (1855) 3 Drew. 112.
[57] *Garland* v. *Garland* (1793) 2 Ves.Jun. 137.
[58] *Re Lloyd, Allen* v. *Lloyd* (1879) 12 Ch.D. 447.
[59] *Sykes* v. *Hastings* (1805) 11 Ves. 363.
[60] *Sutton* v. *Jones* (1809) 15 Ves. 584 at 586.
[61] *Young* v. *Buckett* (1882) 46 L.T. 266.
[62] *Sargant* v. *Read* (1876) 1 Ch.D. 600; *Collins* v. *Barker* [1893] 1 Ch. 578.
[63] *British Linen Co.* v. *South American & Mexican Co.* [1894] 1 Ch. 108.
[64] *Knight* v. *Bowyer* (1858) 2 De G. & J. 421.
[65] *Turner* v. *Major* (1862) 3 Giff. 442.

Section 4. Appointment by the Court

The Supreme Court Act 1981 gives to all Divisions of the High Court jurisdiction to appoint a receiver by final or interlocutory order "in all cases in which it appears to the court to be just and convenient to do so," but subject to any terms and conditions that the court thinks just.[66] The Court of Appeal[67] and county courts[68] have a similar power. The jurisdiction formerly exercised by the Court of Chancery thus extends to other courts. Yet although the courts will now appoint a receiver in many cases in which equity would not in practice have exercised its jurisdiction,[69] they still will not do so in cases where equity regarded itself as having no jurisdiction.[70] Thus a receiver will not be appointed to perform a duty which statute has imposed on a public authority.[71] The principles relating to the grant of injunctions[72] are relevant, for where an injunction would be granted, it follows on principle that in an appropriate case a receiver will be appointed.[73] Conversely, where the plaintiff has no cause of action justiciable in England (and so could not obtain an injunction[74]), a receiver will not be appointed.[75] In practice, most applications for the appointment of a receiver are made in the Chancery Division. The cases in which a receiver will be appointed by the court may be classified under the following heads.

1. Preservation of property

(a) *Disputed property.*   One of the most important grounds on which a receiver may be appointed is in order to preserve property that is in dispute until the rights of the parties can be determined.[76] The principle is to place the property "in a state of security pending litigation."[77] If nobody is in possession of the property, a receiver will be appointed almost as a matter of course; "it is the common interest of all parties that the Court should prevent a scramble."[78] On the other hand, where some person other than a bare trespasser is in possession, the former rule was that the court would not interfere with a legal title save in cases of fraud or other exceptional circumstances.[79] This rule has now been displaced by the Judicature Acts,[80] but the courts are still slow to

---

[66] s.37(1), (2), replacing J.A. 1925, s.45(1), (2), which itself replaced J.A. 1873, s.25(8).
[67] See *Hyde* v. *Warden* (1876) 1 Ex.D. 309 (appointment made on appeal though not sought below).
[68] See the general provisions of the County Courts Act 1984, ss.38, 39.
[69] *Cummins* v. *Perkins* [1899] 1 Ch. 16 at 20.
[70] *Harris* v. *Beauchamp Bros.* [1894] 1 Q.B. 801; and see *post*, pp. 698, 699.
[71] *Parker* v. *Camden London Borough Council* [1986] Ch. 162.
[72] See *ante*, pp. 660 *et seq.*
[73] *Cummins* v. *Perkins* [1899] 1 Ch. 16 at 20.
[74] See *ante*, pp. 648, 649.
[75] *Maclaine Watson & Co.Ltd.* v. *International Tin Council* [1989] Ch. 253.
[76] See, *e.g. Fripp* v. *Chard Ry.* (1853) 11 Hare 241; *White* v. *Smale* (1856) 22 Beav. 72.
[77] *Free* v. *Hinde* (1827) 2 Sim. 7 at 11, *per* Hart V.-C.; and see *Taylor* v. *Eckersley* (1876) 2 Ch.D. 302.
[78] *Owen* v. *Homan* (1853) 4 H.L.C. 997 at 1032, *per* Lord Cranworth L.C.
[79] *Earl Talbot* v. *Hope Scott* (1858) 4 K. & J. 96.
[80] *Berry* v. *Keen* (1882) 51 L.J. Ch. 912.

appoint a receiver in such cases[81]; they will do so only if circumstances such as the financial responsibility of the rival claimants and the relative strength of their titles to the property indicate that this is desirable.[82]

(b) *Precautionary.* A receiver may be appointed even if no actual litigation is pending. Thus in a proper case a beneficiary or creditor may protect the assets of a deceased person by obtaining the appointment of a receiver pending the grant of probate or letters of administration[83]; but usually,[84] though not always,[85] it is both possible and preferable in such cases to obtain a grant of administration *pendente lite.*

2. Mortgages. Under a mortgage, the mortgagee usually has power to appoint a receiver.[86] Even if such a power exists, however, the court can still in a proper case appoint a receiver,[87] whether the mortgage is legal[88] or equitable.[89] This jurisdiction is not excluded merely because the mortgagee is in possession and has appointed his own receiver,[90] though a sufficient case for intervention by the court must be made out.[91] Similarly, an appointment of a receiver by debenture holders does not preclude the court from appointing a receiver,[92] *e.g.* if the power to appoint the receiver has not been exercised in the proper fiduciary manner for the benefit of all debenture holders.[93]

3. Creditors. At the suit of a person who has a right to be paid out of some specific fund a receiver may be appointed in order to prevent the fund being dissipated. This is so even if the precise amount due to the creditor has not been ascertained, as where the claim is for costs not yet taxed[94]; and nowadays a "*Mareva*" injunction[95] may be granted for the purpose of preserving assets to meet such a claim.[96]

4. Vendor and purchaser. A receiver is sometimes appointed as between vendor and purchaser. Thus a receiver and manager may be appointed at the suit of a purchaser of a mine who is in possession of it but is seeking to rescind the contract, in order to keep the mine in

---

[81] *Foxwell* v. *Van Grutten (No. 2)* [1897] 1 Ch. 64.
[82] *John* v. *John* [1898] 2 Ch. 573.
[83] *Re Oakes* [1917] 1 Ch. 230.
[84] *Ibid.* at p. 232.
[85] *Re Sutcliffe* [1942] Ch. 453.
[86] See *ante,* p. 416.
[87] *Tillett* v. *Nixon* (1883) 25 Ch.D. 238.
[88] *Ibid.*
[89] *Re Crompton & Co. Ltd.* [1914] 1 Ch. 954.
[90] *County of Gloucester Bank* v. *Rudry Merthyr Steam & House Coal Colliery Co.* [1895] 1 Ch. 629.
[91] *Re Prytherch* (1889) 42 Ch.D. 590.
[92] *Re "Slogger" Automatic Feeder Co. Ltd.* [1915] 1 Ch. 478.
[93] *Re Maskelyne British Typewriter Ltd.* [1898] 1 Ch. 133.
[94] *Cummins* v. *Perkins* [1899] 1 Ch. 16.
[95] *Ante,* pp. 670–673.
[96] *Faith Panton Property Plan Ltd.* v. *Hodgetts* [1981] 1 W.L.R. 927, applying *Cummins* v. *Perkins, supra.*

operation[97]; and where the purchaser was in possession, the unpaid vendor of land for a railway obtained a receiver as against the railway company.[98]

5. Landlord and tenant. Where a landlord is failing to comply with his covenants to repair a building or provide services to his tenants, the court may, at the instance of a tenant, appoint a receiver to collect the rents and manage the building in accordance with the landlord's obligations.[99] This may be done even when the landlord has abandoned the premises.[1]

6. Executors and trustees. The court has power to displace executors or trustees by appointing a receiver, provided that a strong case is made out,[2] *e.g.* on establishing misconduct,[3] or where there is a breach of trust or improper management endangering the trust property.[4] But the modern practice in appropriate cases is to apply for the appointment of a judicial trustee[5] or substitute personal representative[5a] rather than a receiver.

7. Partnerships. In partnership cases a receiver and manager will be appointed almost as a matter of course if the partnership is clearly at an end,[6] *e.g.* so that the business may be sold as a going concern.[7] But if it is contended that the partnership is still in being, a receiver will not be appointed unless it is reasonably clear that at the trial a dissolution will be ordered,[8] for otherwise the appointment would take the conduct of the business out of the hands of partners who may well prove to be entitled to carry it on[9]; and in such cases "What right has the Court to appoint a receiver, and make itself the manager of every trade in the kingdom?"[10] An injunction, however, may be granted to restrain a partner from doing the acts complained of.[11] A receiver may be appointed even if the existence of any partnership is disputed, though the court is slow to do this if it would seriously injure the defendant, unless, *e.g.* the assets are in jeopardy.[12]

---

[97] *Gibbs* v. *David* (1875) L.R. 20 Eq. 373.
[98] *Munns* v. *Isle of Wight Ry.* (1870) 5 Ch.App. 414.
[99] *Hart* v. *Emelkirk Ltd.* [1983] 1 W.L.R. 1289.
[1] *Daiches* v. *Bluelake Investments Ltd.* (1985) 51 P. & C.R. 51.
[2] *Middleton* v. *Dodswell* (1806) 13 Ves. 266; and see *Barkley* v. *Lord Reay* (1843) 2 Hare 306.
[3] *Anon* (1806) 12 Ves. 4.
[4] *Evans* v. *Coventry* (1854) 5 De G.M. & G. 911; *Nothard* v. *Proctor* (1875) 1 Ch.D. 4. See also *Bainbridge* v. *Blair* (1835) 4 L.J.Ch. 207 (failure to provide satisfactory accounts); *Swale* v. *Swale* (1856) 22 Beav. 584 (absence of unanimity, as to which see *ante*, p. 237).
[5] See *ante*, p. 206.
[5a] See *ante*, p. 355.
[6] *Pini* v. *Roncoroni* [1892] 1 Ch. 633.
[7] *Taylor* v. *Neate* (1888) 39 Ch.D. 538.
[8] *Smith* v. *Jeyes* (1841) 4 Beav. 503.
[9] See *Madgwick* v. *Wimble* (1843) 6 Beav. 495 at 500.
[10] *Goodman* v. *Whitcomb* (1820) 1 Jac. & W. 589 at 592, *per* Lord Eldon L.C.
[11] See *Hall* v. *Hall* (1850) 3 Mac. & G. 79 at 87; and see *ante*, pp. 678, 679.
[12] *Floydd* v. *Cheney* [1970] Ch. 602.

8. Companies. Although in the case of companies receivers are usually appointed under debentures or a trust deed, the court will in a proper case appoint a receiver; and this is so even if no event has occurred to make the power under the debentures exercisable.[13] The mere insolvency of the company is not enough[14]; but a receiver and manager may be appointed if in addition the security is in jeopardy[15] (as where the prior claims[16] of the debenture holders are being defeated by ordinary creditors levying execution on the company's assets[17]), or if the company proposes to distribute nearly all its assets to its shareholders,[18] or it has ceased to be a going concern,[19] or there is an order or resolution for winding it up.[20] Further, on the application of any shareholder, if "there is no properly constituted governing body, or there are such dissensions in the governing body that it is impossible to carry on the business with advantage to the persons interested ... the Court will interfere, but only for a limited time, and to as small an extent as possible,"[21] in order to enable the management to be restored to a proper footing.[22]

9. Other cases. Receivers may also be appointed in a variety of other cases, as where the owner of a chattel sues a bailee for its return,[23] or where foreign litigation concerning the property is pending.[24]

Section 5. Receiver by way of Equitable Execution

1. Jurisdiction

(a) *General.* A judgment creditor normally obtains satisfaction of his judgment by execution at common law, using the writ of *fieri facias*, attachment of debts and, formerly, in the case of land, the writ of *elegit*. There were cases, however, where the creditor could not levy execution at law owing to the nature of the property, the principal case being where the property was merely equitable, such as an interest under a

[13] *McMahon* v. *North Kent Ironworks Co.* [1891] 2 Ch. 148.
[14] *Re New York Taxicab Co. Ltd.* [1913] 1 Ch. 1.
[15] *Re Victoria Steamboats Ltd.* [1897] 1 Ch. 158.
[16] *Re Panama, New Zealand and Australian Royal Mail Co.* (1870) 5 Ch.App. 318.
[17] *Edwards* v. *Standard Rolling Stock Syndicate* [1893] 1 Ch. 574.
[18] *Re Tilt Cove Copper Co. Ltd.* [1913] 2 Ch. 588.
[19] *Hubbuck* v. *Helms* (1887) 56 L.T. 232.
[20] *Hodson* v. *Tea Co.* (1880) 14 Ch.D. 859.
[21] *Trade Auxiliary Co.* v. *Vickers* (1873) L.R. 16 Eq. 298 at 305, *per* Malins V.-C.
[22] *Stanfield* v. *Gibbon* [1925] W.N. 11.
[23] *Hatton* v. *Car Maintenance Co. Ltd.* [1915] 1 Ch. 621.
[24] *Transatlantic Co.* v. *Pietroni* (1860) Johns. 604; and see *Kerr on Receivers* (17th ed., 1989), p. 85; and see generally pp. 12–86.

trust or an equity of redemption.[25] Another example was a covenant of indemnity or other chose in action of which the debtor has the benefit, but which could not be reached by attachment.[26] In order to meet this difficulty, the Court of Chancery evolved a process of execution by way of appointing a receiver of the equitable interest,[27] and if necessary supplemented this by an injunction restraining the judgment debtor from disposing of his interest in the property.[28] This process was not "execution" in the ordinary sense of the word,[29] but a form of equitable relief for cases where execution was not possible.[30] The effect of such an appointment "is that it does not create a charge on the property, but that it operates as an injunction against the judgment debtor receiving the income,"[31] or dealing with the property to the prejudice of the judgment creditor.[32] The jurisdiction is discretionary, and save in respect of interests in land, will not be exercised unless there is some hindrance or difficulty in using the normal processes of execution.[33] It is not sufficient that appointing a receiver would be more convenient.[34] Although the court's power to appoint receivers is now conferred by statute in general terms,[35] these principles continue to be applied.[36]

(b) *Land.* The writ of *elegit* was abolished in 1956[37] and replaced by a system of charging orders.[38] At the same time the High Court[39] was empowered to appoint a receiver by way of equitable execution in relation to legal estates and interests in land whether or not a charging order has been obtained.[40]

(c) *Property not available for execution.* A receiver will not be appointed if there is no property which can be reached either in law or equity for equity does nothing in vain.[41] Thus no receiver will be appointed to enforce rights not justiciable in England[42] or to seize a judgment debtor's future earnings,[43] or a patent which is not being

---

[25] *Anglo-Italian Bank* v. *Davies* (1878) 9 Ch.D. 275.
[26] *Bourne* v. *Colodense Ltd.* [1985] I.C.R. 291, applied in *Maclaine Watson & Co. Ltd.* v. *International Tin Council, infra.*
[27] *Re Shephard* (1889) 43 Ch.D. 131; *Anglo-Italian Bank* v. *Davies* (1878) 9 Ch.D. 275.
[28] See *Lloyd's Bank Ltd.* v. *Medway Upper Navigation Co.* [1905] 2 K.B. 359.
[29] *Norburn* v. *Norburn* [1894] 1 Q.B. 448.
[30] *Re Shepherd, supra;* but see *Re Pope* (1886) 17 Q.B.D. 743.
[31] *Stevens* v. *Hutchinson* [1953] Ch. 299 at 305, *per* Upjohn J.
[32] *Re Marquis of Anglesey* [1903] 2 Ch. 727.
[33] *Manchester & Liverpool District Banking Co. Ltd.* v. *Parkinson* (1888) 22 Q.B.D. 173; *Morgan* v. *Hart* [1914] 2 K.B. 183; *Maclaine Watson & Co. Ltd.* v. *International Tin Council* [1988] Ch. 1 (on appeal, see [1989] Ch. 253 at 271).
[34] *Harris* v. *Beauchamp Bros.* [1894] 1 Q.B. 801.
[35] S.C.A. 1981, s.37(1), (2), replacing J.A. 1925, s.45, which replaced J.A. 1873, s.25(8). See *ante,* p. 694.
[36] See *Harris* v. *Beauchamp Bros., supra,* at p. 810.
[37] Administration of Justice Act 1956, s.34(1).
[38] Now the Charging Orders Act 1979.
[39] The county courts also have jurisdiction: see *ante,* p. 694.
[40] S.C.A. 1981, s.37(4), replacing Administration of Justice Act 1956, s.36(1).
[41] See *Hall* v. *Vernon,* 34 S.E. 764 at 765 (1899), cited Megarry, *A Second Miscellany-at-law* (1973), p. 295.
[42] *Maclaine Watson & Co. Ltd.* v. *International Tin Council* [1989] Ch. 253.
[43] *Holmes* v. *Millage* [1893] 1 Q.B. 551. But see now Attachment of Earnings Act 1971.

worked in this country.[44] "The only cases of this kind in which Courts of equity ever interfered were cases in which the judgment debtor had an equitable interest in property which could have been reached at law, if he had had the legal interest in it, instead of an equitable interest only. ... It is an old mistake to suppose that, because there is no effectual remedy at law, there must be one in equity."[45] Further, if a person or a company is insolvent, no receiver by way of equitable execution[46] will be appointed to secure payment of a debt, for that would in effect be an irregular substitute for the normal processes of bankruptcy or liquidation.[47]

---

[44] *Edwards & Co.* v. *Picard* [1909] 2 K.B. 903.

[45] *Holmes* v. *Millage, supra,* at p. 555, *per* Lindley L.J.

[46] Contrast an interim receiver: *ante,* p. 697.

[47] *Harris* v. *Beauchamp Bros.* [1894] 1 Q.B. 801; *Re Swallow Footwear Ltd., The Times,* October 23, 1956, where Roxburgh J. held that six Queen's Bench judges had in turn acted without jurisdiction.

INDEX

701